W9-AKX-688

The Mass Media and the Law

JOHN J. WATKINS

Professor of Law
University of Arkansas,
Fayetteville

Prentice Hall
Englewood Cliffs, N.J. 07632

Library of Congress Cataloging in Publication Data
Watkins, John J., [date].
  The mass media and the law / John J. Watkins.
    p. cm.
  Includes index.
  ISBN 0-13-558818-9
  1. Mass media—Law and legislation—United States.   I. Title.
KF2750.W37   1989
343.7309′9—dc20   89-8762
[347.30399]   CIP

To my mother, Kathryn Day Watkins,
and in memory of my father,
John H. Watkins, Jr.

Editorial/production supervision and
    interior design: Fred Dahl and Rose Kernan
Cover design: Wanda Lubelska Designs
Manufacturing Buyer: Carol Bystrom

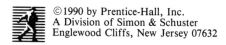 ©1990 by Prentice-Hall, Inc.
A Division of Simon & Schuster
Englewood Cliffs, New Jersey 07632

All rights reserved. No part of this book may be
reproduced, in any form or by any means,
without permission in writing from the publisher.

Printed in the United States of America

10 9 8 7 6 5 4 3 2 1

ISBN 0-13-558818-9

Prentice-Hall International (UK) Limited, *London*
Prentice-Hall of Australia Pty. Limited, *Sydney*
Prentice-Hall Canada Inc., *Toronto*
Prentice-Hall Hispanoamericana, S.A., *Mexico*
Prentice-Hall of India Private Limited, *New Delhi*
Prentice-Hall of Japan, Inc., *Tokyo*
Simon & Schuster Asia Pte. Ltd., *Singapore*
Editora Prentice-Hall do Brasil, Ltda., *Rio de Janeiro*

CONTENTS

PREFACE

This is not a a book for lawyers and law students, nor is it an historical look at the development of the extremely varied and complex body of law that affects the American mass media. Its purpose is not to teach its readers to "think like lawyers," something that generally takes three years of law school and may not be particularly desirable anyway. Instead, it is a book written for those who plan careers in the mass media, particularly the news business, and is intended to provide a practical overview of the legal principles they are likely to encounter in the working world. In an era in which the media are attractive targets for multimillion dollar lawsuits, such a basic understanding of the law is vital. Because media organizations obviously cannot—and, indeed, should not—involve lawyers at every stage of the process by which news is gathered and disseminated, journalists are the "front line" defense against potentially crippling litigation.

The book's organization is straightforward. Each chapter begins with a judicial opinion dealing with the chapter's subject matter. These cases, decided by state and federal appellate courts, are meant to give the reader some insight into the manner in which judges actually decide questions brought before them and to illustrate the kind of "real life" difficulties facing media organizations. Because a single court decision will not touch upon all facets of a particular area of the law, each case is followed by a textual discussion elaborating on various legal issues and offering other examples to flesh out the principles involved. Finally, each chapter contains a series of problems to test the reader's understanding of the concepts that have been explored and to suggest matters that might merit further examination or classroom discussion.

Hoping to assist readers who have not had "close encounters" with law and legal jargon, I have included in the appendix a brief overview of the American legal system and a glossary of common legal terms. Also reproduced there for reader convenience are excerpts from the Constitution of the United States, the Communications Act of 1934, the Cable Communications Policy Act of 1984, federal criminal statutes, and state "shield laws" protecting news sources.

Three comments on stylistic convention are in order here. First, I have omitted the legal citations to cases and statutes mentioned in the reproduced judicial opinions and in the text. These cumbersome references, which can easily disrupt a sentence, may be found in a table at the end of the book. (I have, however, used citations in the problems found at the end of each chapter, since their inclusion at that point is not disruptive and gives the reader a ready reference to cases and other materials that shed light on the problems.) While citations are often provided in footnotes, I have chosen to avoid this technique in an effort to keep the number of footnotes to a minimum. The use of footnotes has become something of a plague in legal writing; for example, the author of a recent law journal article saw fit to include 1,247 footnotes, and a federal district judge once wrote an opinion with more than 1,700. My aversion to footnotes is shared by others, including Noel Coward, who once said that encountering them "is like going downstairs to answer the doorbell while making love."

Second, in editing the opinions set out at the beginning of each chapter, I have used brackets to indicate my own additions to the material and ellipses (. . . or * * *) to mark deletions. However, I have not so indicated the points at which I have omitted footnotes and references to other decisions. The foonotes that are included have been renumbered, and any footnote within an opinion is that of the court unless enclosed in brackets.

Finally, I have for the most part succumbed to grammatical tradition and used nouns and pronouns of the masculine variety. Novelist Tom Robbins did the same thing in *Even Cowgirls Get the Blues*, and offered an explanation that captures my sentiments. "To readers who may be offended by this, I apologize sincerely," he wrote in an author's note. "Unfortunately, there are at this time no alternatives that do not either create confusion or impede the flow of language; which is to say, there are no acceptable alternatives." I, too, do not mean to seem insensitive, but my writing style—already strained by years of drafting various legal documents in the "language of the law"—needs as much "flow" as possible.

ACKNOWLEDGMENTS

This book has emerged from more than a decade of teaching and writing about media law, and I owe a great deal to my former students at the University of Arkansas School of Law, the Baylor University School of Law, and the journalism departments at the University of Arkansas and the University of Texas. I am also indebted to two former teachers, Professor David A. Anderson of the University of Texas School of Law and the late Norris G. Davis, former chair of the University of Texas journalism department. Dr. Davis sparked my interest in media law while I was an undergraduate and graduate student, while Professor Anderson has provided guidance, support, and friendship since my first year of law school. Moreover, as a practicing attorney I was fortunate to work with and learn from three colleagues at Arnold & Porter in Washington, D.C.: Reed Miller, Robert Alan Garrett, and the late David H. Lloyd.

Several people have had a hand in making this book a reality: my wife Joan, without whom I could never have completed the project; Steve Dalphin, my editor at Prentice-Hall, who provided encouragement and exhibited extraordinary patience; Dean J.W. Looney of the University of Arkansas School of Law, who made life easier for me during the three years I spent researching and writing; Louise Lindsey, associate law librarian at the University of Arkansas and master of computerized legal research; attorneys Mark Pelesh of Washington, D.C., and Margaret Boulware of Houston, who helped me keep up with developments in highly specialized areas of the law; Lisa Pruitt and Charlyn Jarrells, 1989 University of Arkansas law graduates whose research assistance was invaluable; and Terri Snavely, my secretary, who helped prepare the manuscript.

I am also grateful to several law, journalism, and communications professors
who reviewed portions of the manuscript prior to publication: the aforementioned
David Anderson; my colleagues Mark Killenbeck and Dick Richards; James Boylan,
University of Massachusetts; Juliet Dee, University of Delaware; Donna L. Dicker-
son, University of South Florida; Bruce L. Plopper, University of Central Arkansas;
Sam G. Riley, Virginia Polytechnic Institute; Gerald P. Smeyak, University of Florida; Jeffery A. Smith, University of Iowa; David L. Wagner, California State University; and Richard A. Wright, Wayne State University. Of course, I am solely
responsible for any errors that may have found their way into print.

Finally, I wish to thank the copyright owners who graciously permitted me to
quote from the following books and articles:

Cassell, Paul G., "Restrictions on Press Coverage of Military Operations: The
Right of Access, Grenada, and 'Off-the-Record Wars,' " 73 *Georgetown Law Journal* 931 (1985). Copyright 1985 by the Georgetown Law Journal Association. Reprinted by permission of the *Georgetown Law Journal.*

Kendrick, Walter, *The Secret Museum.* Copyright © by Walter Kendrick, 1987.
Reprinted by permission of Viking Penguin, Inc., a division of Penguin Books,
USA, Inc.

Restatement (Second) of Torts. Copyright 1977 by The American Law Institute.
Reprinted by permission of The American Law Institute.

Sanford, Bruce W., *Libel and Privacy: The Prevention and Defense of Litigation.* Copyright 1985, 1987 by Prentice Hall Law & Business. Reprinted by permission of Prentice Hall Law & Business.

Smolla, Rodney A., *Law of Defamation.* Copyright 1986 by Clark Boardman
Company, Ltd., New York, N.Y. Reprinted by permission of Clark Boardman
Company, Ltd.

Westenberg, David A., "What's in a Name? Establishing and Maintaining
Trademark and Service Mark Rights," 42 *Business Lawyer* 65 (1986). Copyright
1986 by the American Bar Association. Reprinted by permission of the American
Bar Association.

Special thanks go to the Arkansas Law Review and Bar Association Journal,
Inc., the Board of Trustees of the University of Arkansas, and the Arkansas Bar
Association, who allowed me to borrow liberally from my previously published
work. Some of the material in Chapter 5 originally appeared in "Access to Public
Records under the Arkansas Freedom of Information Act," 37 *Arkansas Law Re-
view* 741 (1984), and "Open Meetings under the Arkansas Freedom of Information
Act," 38 *Arkansas Law Review* 268 (1984), copyright 1984 by the Arkansas Law
Review and Bar Association Journal, Inc. Similarly, portions of Chapter 6 were
initally published in "Free Press vs. Fair Trial," a chapter in the *Arkansas Media
Law Handbook* (1987), copyright 1987 by the Arkansas Bar Association. Finally,
Chapter 7 is drawn heavily from "The Journalist's Privilege in Arkansas," 7
U.A.L.R. Law Journal 473 (1984), copyright 1984 by the Board of Trustees of the
University of Arkansas.

CHAPTER

1

FREEDOM OF EXPRESSION

United States Constitution, Amendment I (1791).

"Congress shall make no law respecting an establishment of religion, or prohibiting the free exercise thereof; or abridging the freedom of speech, or of the press; or the right of the people peaceably to assemble, and to petition the Government for a redress of grievances."

Whitney v. California, 274 U.S. 357 (1927).

[Responding to the patriotism fueled by the First World War and the fear of Communism that followed it, two-thirds of the states had, by 1925, passed statutes—often referred to as "criminal syndicalism" acts—aimed at quieting criticism of the government and thwarting political radicalism. The Congress had passed two such measures soon after the nation entered the war, the Espionage Act of 1917 and the Sedition Act of 1918, both of which provided criminal sanctions for speech that interfered with the war effort. The California Criminal Syndicalism Act made it a felony for any person to teach or advocate, or to be a member of a group that teaches or advocates, use of "unlawful acts of force and violence or unlawful methods of terrorism as a means of accomplishing a change in industrial ownership or control, or effecting any political change."

Anita Whitney, a sixty-year-old philanthropist and niece of former U.S. Supreme Court Justice Stephen Field, was convicted of violating this statute following a convention of the California branch of the Communist Labor Party in 1919. As a delegate to the convention, Miss Whitney took an active role in the proceedings and was elected a member of various committees. Although she did not support use of violence and signed a resolution calling for the party to seek change through the political process, the delegates approved a more radical

FACTS

1

platform urging a "revolutionary class struggle" to overthrow the government. Nonetheless, Miss Whitney continued to participate in the convention and subsequently attended meetings of the party's executive committee, having been chosen an alternate member. At the time of her trial, she was still a member of the party.

The U.S. Supreme Court unanimously affirmed Miss Whitney's conviction, although two Justices—Louis Brandeis and Oliver Wendell Holmes, Jr.—agreed with that result but hardly with the reasoning employed by Justice Edward Sanford, author of the Court's opinion. Relying upon the Court's decision two years earlier in *Gitlow v. New York*, Justice Sanford summarily dismissed the claim that the California statute impermissibly infringed Miss Whitney's first amendment rights. The state, he observed, "in the exercise of its police power may punish those who abuse this freedom [to speak] by utterances inimical to the public welfare, tending to incite to crime, disturb the public peace, or endanger the foundations of organized government and threaten its overthrow by unlawful means. . . ." In a separate concurring opinion joined by Justice Holmes, Justice Brandeis took the position that the first amendment question was not a proper issue on appeal because it had not been sufficiently presented to the trial court. Nevertheless, Justice Brandeis seized the opportunity to criticize Justice Sanford's use of the so-called "bad tendency" test for determining when speech can constitutionally be abridged.]

MR. JUSTICE BRANDEIS, concurring.

[A]ll fundamental rights comprised within the term liberty are protected by the Federal Constitution from invasion by the States. The right of free speech, the right to teach and the right of assembly are, of course, fundamental rights. * * * These may not be denied or abridged. But, although the rights of free speech and assembly are fundamental, they are not in their nature absolute. Their exercise is subject to restriction, if the particular restriction proposed is required in order to protect the State from destruction or from serious injury, political, economic or moral. That the necessity which is essential to a valid restriction does not exist unless speech would produce, or is intended to produce, a clear and imminent danger of some substantive evil which the State constitutionally may seek to prevent has been settled. * * *

This Court has not yet fixed the standard by which to determine when a danger shall be deemed clear; how remote the danger may be and yet be deemed present; and what degree of evil shall be deemed sufficiently substantial to justify resort to abridgement of free speech and assembly as the means of protection. To reach sound conclusions on these matters, we must bear in mind why a State is, ordinarily, denied the power to prohibit dissemination of social, economic and political doctrine which a vast majority of its citizens believes to be false and fraught with evil consequence.

Those who won our independence believed that the final end of the State was to make men free to develop their faculties; and that in its government the deliberative forces should prevail over the arbitrary. They valued liberty both as an end and as a means. They believed liberty to be the secret of happiness and courage to be the secret of liberty. They believed that freedom to think as you will and to speak as you think are means indispensable to the discovery and spread of political truth; that without free speech and assembly discussion would be futile; that with them, discussion affords ordinarily adequate protection against the dissemination of noxious doctrine; that the greatest menace to freedom is an inert people; that public discussion is a political duty; and that this should be a fundamental principle of the American government. They recognized the risks to which all human institutions are subject. But they knew that order cannot be secured merely through fear of punishment for its infraction; that it is hazardous to discourage thought, hope and imagination; that fear breeds repression; that repression breeds hate; that hate menaces stable government; that the path of safety lies in the opportunity to discuss freely supposed grievances and proposed remedies; and that the fitting remedy for evil counsels is good ones. Believing in the power of reason as applied through public discussion, they eschewed silence coerced by law—the argument of force in its worst form. Recognizing the occasional tyrannies of governing majorities, they amended the Constitution so that free speech and assembly should be guaranteed.

Fear of serious injury cannot alone justify suppression of free speech and assembly. Men feared witches and burnt women. It is the function of speech to free men from the bondage of irrational fears. To justify suppression of free speech there must be reasonable ground to fear that serious evil will result if free speech is practiced. There must be reasonable ground to believe that the danger apprehended is imminent. There must be reasonable ground to believe that the evil to be prevented is a serious one. Every denunciation of existing law tends in some measure to increase the probability that there will be violation of it. Condonation of a breach enhances the probability. Expressions of approval add to the probability. Propagation of the criminal state of mind by teaching syndicalism increases it. Advocacy of law-breaking heightens it still further. But even advocacy of violation, however reprehensible morally, is not a justification for denying free speech where the advocacy falls short of incitement and there is nothing to indicate that the advocacy would be immediately acted on. The wide difference between advocacy and incitement, between preparation and attempt, between assembling and conspiracy, must be borne in mind. In order to support a finding of clear and present danger it must be shown either that immediate serious violence was to be expected or was advocated, or that the past conduct furnished reason to believe that such advocacy was then contemplated.

Those who won our independence by revolution were not cowards. They did not fear political change. They did not exalt order at the cost of liberty. To courageous, self-reliant men, with confidence in the power of free and fearless reasoning applied through the processes of popular government, no danger flowing from speech can be deemed clear and present, unless the incidence of the evil apprehended is so imminent that it may befall before there is opportunity for full discussion. If there be time to expose through discussion the falsehood and fallacies, to avert the evil by the processes of education, the remedy to be applied is more speech, not enforced silence. Only an emergency can justify repression. Such must be the rule if authority is to be reconciled with freedom. Such, in my opinion, is the command of the Constitution. It is therefore always open to Americans to challenge a law abridging free speech and assembly by showing that there was no emergency justifying it.

Moreover, even imminent danger cannot justify resort to prohibition of these functions essential to effective democracy, unless the evil apprehended is relatively serious. Prohibition of free speech and assembly is a measure so stringent that it would be inappropriate as the means for averting a relatively trivial harm to society. A police measure may be unconstitutional merely because the remedy, although effective as a means of protection, is unduly harsh or oppressive. Thus, a State might, in the exercise of its police power, make any trespass upon the land of another a crime, regardless of the results or of the intent or purpose of the trespasser. It might, also, punish an attempt, a conspiracy, or an incitement to commit the trespass. But it is hardly conceivable that this Court would hold constitutional a statute which punished as a felony the mere voluntary assembly with a society formed to teach that pedestrians had the moral right to cross unenclosed, unposted, waste lands and to advocate their doing so, even if there was imminent danger that advocacy would lead to a trespass. The fact that speech is likely to result in some violence or in destruction of property is not enough to justify its suppression. There must be the probability of serious injury to the State. Among free men, the deterrents ordinarily to be applied to prevent crime are education and punishment for violations of the law, not abridgement of the rights of free speech and assembly. * * *

Whenever the fundamental rights of free speech and assembly are alleged to have been invaded, it must remain open to a defendant to present the issue whether there actually did exist at the time a clear danger; whether the danger, if any, was imminent; and whether the evil apprehended was one so substantial as to justify the stringent restriction interposed by the legislature. The legislative declaration, like the fact that the statute was passed and was sustained by the highest court of the State, creates merely a rebuttable presumption that these conditions have been satisfied. * * *

INTRODUCTION

Properly understood, the first amendment embraces multiple concerns: freedom of religion, freedom of speech, freedom of the press, and the right to petition government for redress of grievances. Of these, the principle focus of this book is what is broadly called "freedom of expression," particularly as applied to the mass media. Justice Brandeis' opinion in *Whitney* is important for a variety of reasons, not the least of which is its eloquent summary of the justifications for protecting freedom of expression. In addition, the opinion makes plain that although the first amendment literally places limits only upon the authority of Congress to regulate speech, its prohibitions are equally applicable to the states. And, despite the first amendment's seemingly absolute language, Justice Brandeis indicates that the fundamental rights it protects must yield to other societal interests under certain circumstances. Indeed, the debate between Justice Brandeis and Justice Sanford centers upon the measuring stick to be used in determining the propriety of a restraint on freedom of expression.

These issues, as well as others, are considered in the sections that follow. Before plunging into first amendment theory and jurisprudence, however, a word of caution is in order. Over the past sixty years, the period in which most of the key judicial developments in this area of the law have occurred, the U.S. Supreme Court—the ultimate arbiter of the Constitution—has been forced to apply the first amendment in wildly different settings. The Court has had to tackle free speech problems ranging from door-to-door solicitation to protests on military bases; from comedy skits featuring four-letter words to advertisements for prescription drugs; and from purloined government documents whose publication allegedly threatened the nation's security to regulations requiring "fairness" on the part of radio and television stations in their coverage of matters of public importance. As Justice Robert Jackson once noted, each method of communicating ideas is "a law unto itself" that must reflect the "differring natures, values, abuses and dangers" of the particular medium. Not surprisingly, principles that have emerged in one context may seem strangely out of place in another, and formulation of a "general" theory for application of the first amendment has proven difficult indeed.

Values Underlying Freedom of Expression

As originally adopted in 1787, the Constitution did not contain the provisions now known as the "Bill of Rights," and while all thirteen states ratified the document, five specifically noted their dissatisfaction with the omission. As a result, James Madison introduced a slate of amendments to the Constitution when the first Congress convened in 1789, and of the twelve that were submitted to the states for approval, ten were ratified by the requisite number of states by the end of 1791. Although some commentators over the years have pointed to the "position" of the amendment protecting freedom of expression as an indicator of its significance, what is now the first amendment was actually third on the original list. It became the first added to the Constitution only because proposed amendments one and two, which dealt with apportionment of seats in the House of Representatives and the ever-popular issue of congressional salaries, were rejected by the states.

That the "first amendment" was among those approved came as no surprise, for nine of the eleven states that at the time had included in their own constitutions some form of protection for freedom of expression. Although history affords few clues as to the intent of those who drafted and adopted what became the first amendment, those supporting free speech and press in 1791 clearly believed that government censorship in advance of publication was intolerable. Indeed, Sir William Blackstone's *Commentaries on the Laws of England*, a multi-volume work published in the decade preceding the American revolution which had a significant impact upon the development of law in the new nation, had defined freedom of expression as "laying no previous restraints upon publication." As discussed more fully later in this chapter, such "previous restraints" are presumptively invalid under the first amendment.

Beyond this restriction however, there is little agreement on the first amendment's intended scope. Professor Leonard Levy, whose book *Emergence of a Free Press* (1985) is a landmark work in the field, has adopted a rather narrow interpretation. While conceding that the first amendment was meant to do more than simply codify Blackstone, he concluded that its draftsmen did not intend to wipe out the crime of seditious libel, which punished those who dared criticize the government. Other scholars have taken a much broader view of the protection afforded by the first amendment. Professor Zechariah Chafee, for example, argued in *Free Speech in the United States* (1941) that "freedom of speech was conceived as giving a wide and genuine protection for all sorts of public matters," including criticism of the government. This view is supported by the experience of the American colonies under British rule and the role of the press in advancing the cause of revolution and freedom.

Even if the historical evidence were more conclusive, of what relevance today is the meaning of the first amendment at the time of its adoption? After all, the Framers simply could not have envisioned the new communication technologies that have helped create a "global village," or even imagined a newspaper environment in which chain ownership by media conglomerates is the norm and the disappearance of competing dailies in all but the largest of our cities is a sad fact of life. As is the case with the Constitution generally, the task of applying and interpreting the first amendment in light of such changing conditions rests with the U.S. Supreme Court. Although this power of "judicial review" has been settled since Chief Justice John Marshall wrote in *Marbury v. Madison* (1803) that "it is emphatically the province and duty of the judicial department to say what the law is," there has been considerable dispute as to the methods the Court should employ in going about that task.

Participants in the debate can be placed in three camps. The "interpretivists" believe that constitutional decision making should be based upon the words of the Constitution as understood by those who wrote or ratified them. At the other extreme are the supporters of a "value-oriented" approach based on the notion that the Supreme Court should promote the social good by requiring all branches of government to comply with moral and political principles evidenced by the history and provisions of the Constitution and societal consensus on fundamental values. Advocates of this approach often refer to the Constitution as a "living document" and criticize the "rigidity" of the interpretivists. Somewhere in between lie the proponents of "process-oriented" constitutional jurisprudence who argue that judges should limit their role to independent review of government action that appears to violate the specific wording of a particular constitutional provision, restrict the political process, or discriminate against minorities. The debate is obviously more complex than suggested by those (primarily politicians) who criticize judges as either "liberal" and "activist" or "conservative" and "strict constructionist."

Because the intent of those who led the fight for adoption of the first amendment is shrouded in history, the interpretivist approach is ill-suited for judicial decision making in cases involving freedom of expression. In this area of the law, the Supreme Court has leaned more toward the other schools of thought concerning judicial review, though it has fully embraced neither. It is clear, however, that as the Court encounters situations that the Framers could not possibly have foreseen, the values underlying protection for freedom of speech and press become extremely important in judicial analysis. As Professor Thomas I. Emerson observed in *The System of Freedom of Expression* (1970), the first amendment was "plainly intended to assure the new nation the basic elements of a system of free expression as then conceived" and today "has the same broad significance for our present, more complex times."

In his *Whitney* opinion, Justice Brandeis identified four values associated with freedom of expression that assist the courts in fashioning first amendment principles. In shorthand form, those values may be described as:

- self-fulfillment;
- enlightenment;
- self-governance; and
- safety-valve.

These four values—or premises, or justifications, or functions—associated with freedom of expression have been used by the Supreme Court in resolving a variety of first amendment questions and are thus worthy of closer examination here.

Self-Fulfillment. Justice Brandeis wrote that "[t]hose who won our independence believed that the final end of the state was to make men free to develop their faculties . . . [and] valued liberty both as an end and as a means." That end has been labeled in various ways, perhaps most usefully by Professor Melville Nimmer as "self-fulfillment" and Professor Emerson as "the achievement of self-realization." As Justice Thurgood Marshall observed in *Procunier v. Martinez* (1974):

> The First Amendment serves not only the needs of polity but also those of the human spirit—a spirit that demands self-expression. Such expression is an integral part of . . . a sense of identity. To suppress expression is to reject the basic human desire for recognition and affront the individual's worth and dignity.

Thus, it matters not whether a speaker has a receptive or hostile audience, or whether he has any audience at all, for there is a measure of inner satisfaction stemming from the speech itself. Professor Nimmer, in his 1984 treatise *Freedom of Speech*, noted that a speaker is likely to experience a sense of fulfillment "by the mere act of speaking out on an issue of importance to him," even if the message is without meaningful content or has no chance of persuading anyone who is listening. One may also experience such satisfaction even "by singing a song aloud although there is no one to hear."

Several commentators have asked whether the self-fulfillment value, standing alone, justifies protection of expression. For example, an enraged husband who hires a professional "hit man" to kill his wife's lover undoubtedly receives considerable satisfaction from making the arrangements and discussing the matter with the hired killer. But is there any reason to protect speech designed to solicit murder, even though the speech may have made the husband "feel good about himself"? To take the matter a step further, suppose the husband decided to eliminate the middleman and handle the murderous chore himself. Presumably he would achieve the same sense of perverted self-satisfaction from the act itself as from communicating his desire to a hit man. As is discussed in more detail below, the courts have attempted to distinguish between speech, which is presumably protected by the first amendment, and conduct, which is not. But if self-fulfillment can be realized through either speech or conduct, what justification exists for protecting only speech?

The foregoing suggests that the self-fulfillment value may in itself be insufficient to justify protection of expression. However, this inner satisfaction may become important when considered with other values associated with the first amendment. For example, the producer of an "obscene" film or author of an "obscene" novel undoubtedly receives the same sort of self-fulfillment as the creator of a film or book that does not fall into that category. Although the Supreme Court has had great difficulty defining obscenity, it has consistently held that such speech is wholly outside the first amendment and thus not worthy of protection. Accordingly, one might conclude that it is not only the self-fulfillment that stems from nonobscene speech but also other factors—perhaps the purpose or content of such speech—that warrant treating it differently from obscene speech.

Enlightenment. According to Justice Brandeis, "freedom to think as you will and to speak as you think are means indispensable to the discovery and spread of political truth." Of course, this concept is equally as applicable to "scientific" or "religious" truth as to the political variety; the need for knowledge and informed opinion is not restricted by subject matter. The notion that unrestricted debate will lead to the discovery of truth and the enhancement of knowledge came from John Milton's *Areopagitica* (1644), in which the poet argued that the Crown's licensing scheme for printers resulted in intellectual stagnation. In Milton's view, truth would ultimately emerge from a free exchange of ideas, even though some of those ideas were demonstrably and, perhaps, dangerously false. This justification for freedom of expression is popularly known as the "marketplace of ideas" theory.

Milton's philosophical approach has been refined over the centuries by a variety of thinkers, including John Locke, John Stuart Mill, and Justice Holmes, who, along with Justice Brandeis, wove the concept into first amendment jurisprudence. In the 1919 case of *Abrams v. United States*, which arose from the same combination of patriotism and fear of Communism as *Whitney*, the Supreme Court affirmed the conviction of five Russian citizens living in the United States for violating the Sedition Act of 1918. The men had circulated leaflets criticizing President Wilson for sending American troops to Russia and calling for a strike to stop production of arms for the war effort. Joined by Justice Brandeis, Justice Holmes filed a stinging dissent:

> Persecution for the expression of opinions seem to me perfectly logical. If you have no doubt of your premises or your power and want a certain result with all your heart you

naturally express your wishes in law and sweep away all opposition. To allow opposition by speech seems to indicate that you think the speech impotent, as when a man
says that he has squared the circle, or that you do not care whole-heartedly for the
result, or that you doubt either your power or your premises. But when men have
realized that time has upset many fighting faiths, they may come to believe even more
than they believe the very foundations of their own conduct that the ultimate good
desired is better reached by free trade in ideas—that the best test of truth is the power
of the thought to get itself accepted in the competition of the market; and that truth
is the only ground upon which their wishes safely can be carried out. That, at any rate,
is the theory of our Constitution. It is an experiment, as all life is an experiment. Every
year, if not every day, we have to wager our salvation upon some prophecy based upon
imperfect knowledge. While that experiment is part of our system, I think that we
should be eternally vigilant against attempts to check the expression of opinions that
we loathe and believe to be fraught with death, unless they so imminently threaten
immediate interference with the lawful and pressing purposes of the law that an immediate check is required to save the country. * * *

Only the emergency that makes it immediately dangerous to leave the correction of evil
counsels to time warrants making any exception to the sweeping command, "Congress
shall make no law abridging the freedom of speech." Of course, I am speaking only
of expressions of opinion and exhortations, which were all that were uttered here; but
I regret that I cannot put into more impressive words my belief that in their conviction
upon this indictment the defendants were deprived of their rights under the Constitution of the United States.

   While it offers an attractive metaphor, the "marketplace of ideas" concept is not
without its flaws. First, as Mill recognized in his famous essay "On Liberty" (1858),
there is no such thing as absolute certainty on any issue of fact or opinion and no
guarantee that "truth" will always emerge from the marketplace of competing
ideas. Is it not as likely that falsity will triumph when, in Milton's phrase, it "grap-
ples" with truth? As Professor Nimmer has pointed out, "[c]hildren of the age
which produced the Holocaust and the Gulag are not prepared easily to accept the
inevitable triumph of truth."
   These criticisms seem to miss the point of the marketplace concept, as Mill, Nimmer, and others have forcefully argued. Professor Emerson, for example, speaks not
of a search for absolute truth, but rather of a "rational social judgment." Similarly,
Professor Nimmer has written that the focus should be on the role of freedom of
expression as a "necessary condition of an enlightenment which will direct us as
close to an approximation of truth as nonomniscient humanity can reach." Elaborating on Justice Holmes' statement in *Abrams* that the marketplace is the "best test
of truth," Judge Learned Hand wrote in *United States v. Associated Press* (1943)
that the first amendment "presupposes that right conclusions are more likely to be
gathered out of a multitude of tongues, than through any kind of authoritarian
selection." Simply put, the risk that falsity will win the battle for acceptance in the
marketplace is one we as a society should be willing to take when the alternatives
are considered. And, even if falsity should prevail, how can it ever be dislodged
without the free exchange of ideas?
   The second major attack on the marketplace of ideas theory is aimed at the metaphor itself. Just as the economic marketplace is an imperfect one in which antitrust
laws are necessary to ensure free competition and protect against monopolization,

the idea marketplace, the argument goes, is subject to similar distortions that impair its function as a truth-seeking mechanism. Sounding this theme, Professor Jerome Barron contended in a provocative law review article that the first amendment should be interpreted to require a right of access to the mass media by those desiring to be heard in the marketplace. According to Professor Barron, new or unpopular ideas often never reach the idea marketplace because of the concentration of media ownership in relatively few hands and the extreme difficulties, both economic and technological, faced by those nonowners who in an earlier age could have established new media outlets to communicate their ideas. Under the Barron scheme, the mass media would be required under certain circumstances to grant "access" to persons who desire entry into the marketplace, thus ensuring that more diverse views will be heard. We will return to this argument in more detail in Chapter 10.

On a related point, some commentators have taken the position that the marketplace metaphor is inappropriate because people simply do not behave in a manner consistent with the model. Marxist philosopher Herbert Marcuse, whose works were widely read on college campuses during the volatile 1960s, criticized the marketplace concept as based on the flawed premises that citizens engage in the free exchange of ideas and information and possess the ability to separate truth from falsehood. Marcuse blamed the mass media for much of the problem, arguing that the media— as well as government—manipulate individuals and the marketplace to serve their own ends. Others have suggested that there is not so much reasoned debate leading to understanding but a cacophony of voices resulting in confusion. Because an individual is obviously partial to his own ideas, he resists contrary notions and becomes hardened in his own views. Responding to this contention, Professor Chafee noted that although neither Lincoln nor Douglas convinced the other in their famous debates, many of their listeners or readers "may have reshaped their half-formed views because of what Lincoln and Douglas said." And, he observed that even individuals with settled positions may be prompted to rethink those views as a result of ideas advanced by others, although they may ultimately reach the same conclusions.

Self-Governance. "Those who won our independence," Justice Brandeis wrote in *Whitney*, "believed that . . . public discussion is a political duty[,] and that this should be a fundamental principle of American government." On many occasions since that decision, the Supreme Court has emphasized the role of the first amendment in "protect[ing] the free discussion of governmental affairs" and has described freedom of expression as "the essence of self-government." That a democratic people cannot make essential choices without the ability to exchange freely ideas and information is a thesis traceable to the Founding Fathers. As James Madison wrote:

> A popular Government, without popular information, or the means of acquiring it, is but a Prologue to a Farce or a Tragedy; or perhaps both. Knowledge will forever govern ignorance: And a people who mean to be their own Governors must arm themselves with the power which knowledge gives.

Although it is possible to view self-governance as a type of enlightenment rather than an independent first amendment value, most commentators have treated it separately. The leading proponent of the notion that such political speech lies at the core of the first amendment is political scientist Alexander Meiklejohn. In his 1948 book, *Free Speech and Its Relation to Self-Government*, Dr. Meiklejohn drew a distinction between "private speech" on the one hand and "political speech"—that concerning the process of government—on the other. The latter, he said, should be absolutely protected under the first amendment, while all other speech should be subject to some regulation, though it, too, is afforded some protection by the "due process" clause of the fifth amendment. Later included in the fourteenth amendment and thus made applicable to the states, the due process clause prohibits improper governmental interference with "fundamental" rights that are not necessarily spelled out in the Constitution. Meiklejohn wrote:

> The First Amendment is not, primarily, a device for the winning of new truth, though that is very important. It is a device for the sharing of whatever truth has been won. Its purpose is to give every voting member of the body politic the fullest possible participation in the understanding of those problems with which the citizens of a self-governing society must deal. * * * The primary purpose of the First Amendment is . . . that all the citizens shall, so far as possible, understand the issues which bear upon our common life. That is why no idea, no opinion, no doubt, no belief, no counter-belief, no relevant information, may be kept from them. Under the compact upon which the Constitution rests, it is agreed that men shall not be governed by others, that they shall govern themselves. . . .

The Meiklejohn approach is not free of problems, as critics were quick to point out. In a review of Meiklejohn's book published in the *Harvard Law Review*, Professor Chafee noted that there was no indication that the Framers had intended to protect any form of speech via the due process clause. More importantly, he also expressed concern about Meiklejohn's definition of the "political speech" that was to be absolutely immune from abridgement under the first amendment. If the definition were too narrow, Chafee wrote, such "vital matters" as literature and scholarship would be considered only "private" speech worthy of lesser protection, a result he considered "shocking." On the other hand, he feared that a broad definition might result in protection of matters generally thought outside the first amendment, such as libel and obscenity. In a subsequent article, "The First Amendment Is An Absolute" (1961), Dr. Meiklejohn opted for a broad definition of political speech that includes matters touching on education, literature, the sciences, philosophy and the arts. He admitted that his inclusion of literature and art would eliminate criminal prosecution for obscenity and that libel involving criticism of government officials would require protection. As we shall see, his revised thesis has had a significant impact on the Supreme Court, particularly in the area of libel law.

Another difficulty with the Meiklejohn theory stems not from the line that must be drawn between political and nonpolitical speech, but from his basic premise that political speech requires protection because of its relation to self-government. After all, as Professor Vince Blasi has observed, voter turnout in American elections has traditionally been quite low, and political discussion seems less important to many citizens than commercial information and entertainment. Accordingly, Professor Blasi has emphasized the role of the news media in providing a "check" against abuses in government or serving as a "watchdog" against government corruption and other wrongdoing. In his view, the institutional press is the only private group sufficiently well-financed to perform this task, which he views as essential in light of the perceived failure of the electorate to participate in the process of self-government. Of course, it can be argued that in performing the "watchdog" function, the news media also contribute to effective self-government by providing critical information to the public. The Supreme Court made this point in *Mills v. Alabama* (1966), noting that the press functions as a "powerful antidote to any abuses of power by governmental officials" and, through communication, helps keep them "responsible to the people whom they were elected to serve."

Safety-Valve. Justice Brandeis wrote in *Whitney* that "repression breeds hate [which] menaces stable government" and that "the path of safety lies in the opportunity to discuss freely supposed grievances and proposed remedies. . . ." Put another way, free expression can serve as an alternative to violent conduct, as a safety-valve that makes people less likely to resort to mob or vigilante action to achieve their objectives. As Professor Emerson has written:

> [F]reedom of expression is a method of achieving a more adaptable and hence a more stable community, of maintaining the precarious balance between healthy cleavage and necessary consensus. This follows because suppression of discussion makes a rational judgment impossible, substituting force for reason. . . . Freedom of expression . . . provides a framework in which the conflict necessary to the progress of society can take place without destroying the society. It is an essential mechanism for maintaining the balance between stability and change.

Viewed in this light, the importance of the safety-valve function lies not only in the cathartic effect of speech, but also in its relationship to the self-fulfillment, enlightenment, and self-governance values.

The Press Clause

The draftsmen of the first amendment provided that Congress was to make no law "abridging the freedom of speech, or of the press." Although the generally accepted view has been that the Framers probably considered the speech and press clauses to be synonymous, Justice Potter Stewart challenged the conventional wisdom in a now-famous 1974 speech at the Yale Law School. "If the Free Press guarantee meant no more than freedom of speech," Justice Stewart told his audience, "it would be a constitutional redundancy. * * * By including both guarantees in the First Amendment, the [Framers] quite clearly recognized the distinction between the two." A recent historical study by Professor David A. Anderson supports Justice Stewart's thesis. After exhaustive research, Professor Anderson wrote in the *U.C.L.A. Law Review* that "freedom of the press was neither equated with nor viewed as a derivative of freedom of speech" by those who authored and supported the first amendment.

Justice Stewart viewed the press clause as a "structural provision" of the first amendment designed to safeguard the institutional press by mandating its independence from the government. Given the press' adversarial role as the "fourth estate" in monitoring the government (the "checking" value noted by Professor Blasi), the press clause, rather than working in tandem with the speech clause to guarantee freedom of expression for all, performs a wholly separate protective function for the news media. The press must not only be insulated from government interference, but also be free from governmental assistance because either would compromise its independence. Thus, in Justice Stewart's opinion, a journalist should not ordinarily be required to divulge the names of confidential sources who have provided him information, for such government interference would reduce press autonomy by turning reporters into investigators for law enforcement agencies. However, none of us, as individuals, would have a "free speech" right to refuse to tell a grand jury the identity of someone who has knowledge relevant to its investigation. On the other hand, Justice Stewart argued, the need for an autonomous press requires that there be no special right of the news media to obtain, under the first amendment, access to particular government information or ensure openness from the bureaucracy. Such assistance would place the press in the position of dependence upon the very government it must "check." While the press is "free to do battle against secrecy and deception in government," Justice Stewart said, "[it] cannot expect from the Constitution any guarantee that it will succeed."

The Stewart speech sparked considerable debate in legal and judicial circles. Although the Supreme Court has not directly addressed the question of whether the press clause confers upon the news media any freedom from government restraint not enjoyed by individual citizens, Chief Justice Warren Burger strongly disagreed with Justice Stewart. In a concurring opinion in *First National Bank of Boston v. Bellotti* (1978), the Chief Justice doubted that the framers intended to give the press special protection. "The Speech Clause standing alone may be viewed as a protection of the liberty to express ideas and beliefs, while the Press Clause focuses specifically on the liberty to disseminate expression broadly," he wrote. "[T]he press merited special attention because it had more often been the subject of official restraints" during the colonial period. The Chief Justice also doubted the wisdom of giving legislatures, courts, or administrative agencies power to decide what constitutes "the press." That reminded him of "the abhorred licensing system of Tudor and Stuart England—a system the First Amendment was intended to ban from this country."

It is possible, of course, that the speech and press clauses offer identical protection in most situations, for as the Supreme Court noted in the *Bellotti* decision, "the press does not have a monopoly on the ability to enlighten." Media attorney Floyd Abrams has taken this position, arguing that "when the government cannot stifle the press, more often than not it will, for identical reasons, be barred from stifling speech." Thus, a prior restraint is unconstitutional whether its subject is the *New York Times* or an individual mounting a soapbox in a public park. However, in some circumstances the press may need protection that others do not.

For example, Abrams contends that those who pander idle gossip hardly require first amendment protection for confidential sources who pass along juicy information, while journalists must be able to promise such confidentiality lest valuable sources of news dry up, cutting off the flow of important information to the public. Justice Lewis Powell made a similar argument in *Saxbe v. Washington Post Co.* (1974), a case involving the question of whether the news media should be granted greater access to correctional institutions than members of the general public. Responding to the Court's opinion answering that question in the negative, Justice Powell argued in dissent that the press should have greater ability to enter prisons and observe conditions because it "acts as an agent of the public at large" in gathering information about this type of governmental activity.

We will examine such issues as source confidentiality and access to government facilities in later chapters, and we shall see that the question of special treatment for the press has arisen in other contexts as well. For example, the Supreme Court has developed constitutional safeguards for the news media in libel suits, and it is not clear whether these complex rules also apply to nonmedia defendants. For the present, it is sufficient to note that the press has been unsuccessful in obtaining from the courts special first amendment protection for its activities. Nonetheless, the matter has not been definitively resolved by the Supreme Court, which has observed on more than one occasion that "without some protection for seeking out the news, freedom of the press could be eviscerated." Because the emphasis of this book is on the news media, the student should review the chapters that follow with the role of the institutional press in our society firmly in mind.

The First Amendment and Governmental Action

By its terms, the first amendment applies only to laws passed by the Congress of the United States; in fact, the Senate, while debating the proposed Bill of Rights, specifically rejected a freedom of expression provision directed at the states. That the first amendment is limited in such fashion is hardly surprising, for the Bill of Rights was a response to concerns that the newly ratified Constitution lacked some of the fundamental guarantees found in state constitutions. Although the latter would protect citizens from the actions of their own state governments, the federal government—endowed with considerably more power than under the old Articles of Confederation—would not be subject to similar constraints. And, because Madison and his fellow supporters of the Bill of Rights assumed that the powers of the federal government were lodged primarily in the Congress, they directed their attention to the legislative branch. Moreover, the colonial experience had taught them that legislative assemblies had been the principal culprits in punishing expression.

Under modern judicial interpretation, however, the first amendment has a much broader scope. First, it applies to all branches of the federal government—legislative, executive, and judicial. The first amendment limits not only the power of Congress to make laws, but also the authority of judges to enter orders and administrative agency officials to adopt regulations. Thus, the relevant inquiry is whether *governmental action* of some type has infringed upon rights protected by the first amendment. For example, in the famous "Pentagon Papers" case, *New York Times Co. v. United States* (1971), the U.S. Department of Justice asked federal trial courts in New York City and Washington, D.C. to issue orders prohibiting a classified report about the Vietnam War. The U.S. Supreme Court ruled that the requested court orders would contravene the first amendment. Similarly, in *Quincy Cable T.V., Inc. v. Federal Communications Commission* (1985), a federal appellate court ruled that administrative regulations requiring cable television systems to carry the signals of certain broadcast stations violated the first amendment rights of cable operators.

Second, the first amendment now reaches state and local governments, as well as the federal government. The extension of the first amendment beyond the federal level was a direct outgrowth of the Civil War. Prior to the war, the Supreme Court made plain that the Bill of Rights bound only the federal government. However, three postwar constitutional amendments—the thirteenth, fourteenth, and fifteenth—radically altered the relationship between the federal government and the states. The most important of these is the fourteenth amendment, ratified in 1868, which provides in part:

> No State shall make or enforce any law which shall abridge the privileges or immunities of citizens of the United States; nor shall any State deprive any person of life, liberty, or property, without due process of law; nor deny to any person within its jurisdiction the equal protection of the laws.

In light of this amendment, the argument was made that its "privileges and immunities" clause and "due process" clause made the guarantees of the Bill of Rights applicable to the states. Although the Supreme Court has consistently rejected such a theory of "total incorporation," it has nevertheless held that provisions of the Bill of Rights considered "fundamental" to the American system of law are applied to the states via the due process clause. The first amendment is such a fundamental right. Thus, if a state were to abridge freedom of speech or press, it would be violating the first amendment as incorporated and made applicable by the fourteenth. The same principle applies to local governments, which are political subdivisions of the states.

After adoption of the fourteenth amendment, more than half a century passed before the Court issued a ruling directly addressing its impact upon the states' power to abridge freedom of expression. Two decisions of the Court illustrate its indifference to first amendment issues during that period. Both came in opinions written by Justice Holmes. In *Patterson v. Colorado* (1907), the Court affirmed the contempt conviction of a Denver newspaper publisher who had printed articles and a cartoon criticizing the Colorado Supreme Court. Eight years later, in *Fox v. Washington*, the Court upheld a newspaper editor's conviction under a Washington statute making it a crime to publish writings "which tend to encourage or advocate disrespect for the law." The offensive publication was an editorial supporting "the nudes," members of the community who liked to swim in the buff—much to the chagrin of "the prudes," who objected to such behavior. Then, in *Prudential Insurance Co. v. Cheek* (1922) the Court flatly stated that "neither the 14th Amendment nor any other provision of the Constitution . . . imposes upon the states any restrictions about 'freedom of speech.' "

By 1925, however, the Court again considered the first amendment's application to the states via the fourteenth amendment to be an open question. Although in *Gitlow v. New York* the Justices upheld the conviction of a radical socialist for publishing an article urging mass strikes to bring about revolution, they assumed without deciding that the first amendment governed Benjamin Gitlow's case. By the time *Whitney* was decided in 1927, the matter appeared to be settled, although it was not until *Stromberg v. California* (1931) that the Court expressly ruled that the fourteenth amendment protected freedom of expression from abridgement by the states. In another 1931 decision, the landmark "prior restraint" case of *Near v. Minnesota*, Chief Justice Charles Evans Hughes wrote that "[i]t is no longer open to doubt that liberty of the press and of speech is within the liberty safeguarded by the due process clause of the 14th Amendment from invasion by state action."

Because the first amendment is now applicable to the states, it is tempting to cast all speech and press issues in terms of the federal constitution. However, virtually all state constitutions contain provisions protecting freedom of expression, and state conduct must also be evaluated in terms of these guarantees. Although state supreme courts have in the past tended to follow federal court interpretations of the U.S. Constitution in construing parallel state constitutional provisions, a new trend toward independent analysis is developing. Of course, the first amendment acts as a "floor" providing minimum guarantees for freedom of expression, but the state courts may apply their own constitutions in such a way as to provide greater protection for speech and press than exists under the first amendment. For example, prior to the U.S. Supreme Court's ruling in *Richmond Newspapers, Inc. v. Virginia* (1980) that the press and public have a first amendment right to attend criminal trials, some state courts had already reached the same result under their own constitutions.

Keep in mind that the first amendment affords protection only from governmental action. In a broad sense, this means that the first amendment does not provide redress against a private person or corporation who seeks to abridge the expression of others. Thus, the president of a private college does not offend the first amendment by ordering the campus newspaper not to publish a controversial story. However, the same act by the president of a state-supported institution could raise first amendment problems.

Unfortunately, the distinction between private and governmental action is not always easily drawn. If, for example, the local newspaper published a defamatory article about one of the town's citizens, a libel suit based on the story would seem to be a purely private dispute. In this situation, however, the requisite governmental action is present because the plaintiff has invoked the assistance of the court—a unit of government—in enforcing the state's defamation laws. The U.S. Supreme Court so ruled in *New York Times Co. v. Sullivan* (1964), pointing out that applying Alabama libel law to the plaintiff's case would infringe upon the defendants' first amendment rights. Without the enforcement mechanism provided by the courts, the state law of libel could not have had an adverse affect on freedom of expression. The same principle applies when a property owner attempts to use a state's criminal trespass law to prevent would-be speakers from using that property as a forum to present their views. Although private property is involved, as was the case in *Marsh v. Alabama* (1946), enforcement of the trespass law in the courts necessarily requires action by the government and thus brings into play the first amendment.

APPLYING THE FIRST AMENDMENT

Recall that in *Whitney* all members of the Court agreed that the first amendment did not provide absolute protection for Miss Whitney's expression and that the government, under appropriate circumstances, could restrict or punish her speech. What split the Court and prompted Justice Brandeis' famous concurring opinion was the test to be employed in determining whether the State of California's abridgement of her speech was constitutionally permissible. In such a case the court must *balance* competing societal interests—freedom of expression on the one hand and some other interest, such as preserving the security of the nation, on the other. In *Whitney*, Justices Sanford and Brandeis struck that balance in very different ways. Before examining this balancing approach to first amendment rights in more detail, let us turn to a preliminary question: whether particular speech is protected at all by the first amendment.

Protected vs. Unprotected Speech

Justice Hugo Black was known as a champion of first amendment rights primarily because of his well-publicized view that the first amendment means precisely what it says. As he wrote in dissent in *Beauharnais v. Illinois* (1952), the command that Congress "shall make no law" is absolute, "without any ifs, buts, or whereases." The Supreme Court, however, has never accepted this position, and even such staunch defenders of the first amendment as Justices William Brennan and William

O. Douglas never embraced it fully. Justice Black himself believed that action did not deserve absolute protection even though such conduct was combined with speech, and in *Adderly v. Florida* (1966) he clearly rejected the notion that "people who want to propagandize protests or views have a constitutional right to do so whenever and however and wherever they please." Recall that another advocate of an absolutist interpretation of the first amendment, Alexander Meiklejohn, was unwilling to extend such full protection to speech that could not be considered "political."

One result of the Supreme Court's refusal to adopt the absolutist position is that expression may be categorized as to the level of protection it will receive. Under such a scheme, it is possible that some speech will be deemed unworthy of any protection at all. In *Chaplinsky v. New Hampshire* (1942), the Court affirmed the defendant's conviction for cursing a police officer, concluding that protection for such "fighting words" was unwarranted. The Court said:

> There are certain well-defined and narrowly limited classes of speech, the prevention and punishment of which have never been thought to raise any constitutional problem. These include the lewd and obscene, the profane, the libelous, and the insulting or "fighting" words—those which by their very utterance inflict injury or tend to incite an immediate breach of the peace. It has been well observed that such utterances are no essential part of any exposition of ideas, and are of such slight social value as a step to truth that any benefit that may be derived from them is clearly outweighed by the social interest in order and morality.

This list is no longer complete or accurate. For example, in a case decided the same year as *Chaplinsky*, the Court held that commercial advertising was not entitled to first amendment protection. More than thirty years later, the Court reclassified truthful commercial speech as protected expression, although it left false and misleading advertising on the "unprotected" side of the line. Moreover, as we shall see in Chapter 11, commercial speech is afforded less first amendment protection than "political" speech. Similarly, the Court eventually moved libelous statements into the protected category, at least in part, by establishing a first amendment defense to defamation suits.

This "two-tier" method of classifying speech as protected or unprotected is the first step in analyzing any first amendment problem. If a movie is determined to be obscene, for example, its exhibition may be prohibited or its distributors criminally punished. Both sanctions are impermissible, however, if the film does not meet the legal test for obscenity. But the inquiry does not end at that point, for not all speech falling within the "protected" category is treated in the same fashion.

If a film, while not obscene as a matter of law, is nonetheless pornographic, it is subject to regulation that would be unconstitutional if applied to, say, a G-rated Disney feature. Thus, in *Young v. American Mini Theatres, Inc.* (1976), the Supreme Court upheld a Detroit zoning ordinance requiring dispersion of "adult" movie theaters throughout the city. Similarly, in the defamation area, the Court made clear in *Gertz v. Robert Welch, Inc.* (1974), that the states are free to treat libels against private citizens more severely than libels against public officials. Moreover, because broadcasters operate on public airwaves that will support a finite number of channels, the courts have approved regulations upon broadcast speech that would be unconstitutional if applied to print media. For example, in *Federal Communications Commission v. Pacifica Foundation* (1978), the Court upheld a statute forbidding broadcasters from airing "indecent" or "profane" language, even though the words are not legally obscene. Finally, so-called "pure speech" is given more protection than "speech-plus" consisting of expression accompanied by conduct, such as picketing or staging a sit-in.

The Balancing Approach

If particular expression falls within the category of protected speech, the next step is to ascertain the circumstances under which its regulation or abridgement is constitutionally acceptable. The most frequently used method of making this determination is the "balancing test," under which speech may be restricted or punished if there is a sufficiently compelling reason to do so. Obviously, the result reached in a given case can be colored by the "strength" of the speech involved; that is, expression lying close to the line separating protected and unprotected speech can be counterbalanced by a societal interest that might not be "heavy" enough to justify regulation of speech that is further away from the boundary. For example, because commercial speech such as advertising is not as close to the "core" of the first amendment as political expression, it is subject to government-imposed restrictions that would be unconstitutional if applied to political expression. However, it is not only the strength or value of the speech but also the interests of the speaker and his audience that must be weighed against a competing social concern when using the balancing approach.

Actually, there are two different methods of balancing first amendment rights against other interests considered worthy of protection. *Ad hoc balancing* calls upon the court to determine which of the conflicting interests demands greater protection under the particular facts of the case before it. This approach is often criticized because it provides no guidance as to how the balance might be struck in a different situation. The lack of such a standard might cause a speaker to forego his planned speech rather than risk punishment, thus depriving society of his views. Moreover, this case-by-case approach has all too often resulted in the balance being struck against the free speech interest, perhaps in part because the courts have been willing to defer to the judgment of the other branches of government in evaluating the competing interest said sufficient to justify regulation or punishment of speech. As Professor Nimmer has noted, "the mere fact that a popularly elected legislature passed a law repressing speech and a popularly elected executive brought the prosecution would automatically condemn the speech. . . ."

In using *definitional balancing*, a court engages in a more general type of analysis that goes beyond the facts of the case before it. While the decision necessarily determines which party is to prevail in the case at hand, it also establishes a standard— or a rule of law—that will be used in subsequent cases without further balancing. This approach thus brings a degree of certainty to first amendment law that arguably encourages future expression. Examples of definitional balancing can be found in the line of Supreme Court decisions involving libel and the first amendment.

In the landmark case of *New York Times Co. v. Sullivan*, the Court for the first time held libelous statements entitled to some protection under the first amendment. The Court balanced speech interests against reputational interests of defamed public officials and concluded that the former should prevail, unless the damaging information was published recklessly or with knowledge of its falsity. The Court thus established a general rule applicable to all libel suits brought by public officials. As we shall see in detail in Chapter 2, the Court gave greater weight to reputational interests in *Gertz v. Robert Welch, Inc.*, a case in which the injured party was not a public official but a private individual.

In using either type of balancing test, an important question is obviously the competing interests that will be placed on either side of the scale. One can easily imagine the result if, in the libel cases noted above, the interests to be balanced were described as the speaker's interest in communicating with others and the state's interest in protecting from harm the reputations of its citizens. In that balance, the state's interest plainly seems to dominate that of the individual speaker. As Professor Chafee warned, balancing requires identification of both individual *and* societal interests on opposite sides of the scale, and it "cannot be properly done unless all the interests involved are adequately ascertained." Thus, in the libel cases, the interests to be balanced should look like this:

Speech Interests	Reputational Interests
1. Individual speaker's interest in expression. 2. Audience's interest in receiving the communication. 3. Societal interest in protecting the speech.	1. Individual interest of the subject of the speech in protecting his "good name." 2. Societal interest in deterring defamatory speech and in compensating citizens for the harm caused them by libelous speech.

Unless the societal interest in protecting freedom of expression is factored into the equation in each case, the competing interests are likely to be deemed more significant so that the speech is suppressed or punished. That danger is one reason why Justice Black supported an absolutist interpretation of the first amendment: he feared that freedom of expression could too easily be "balanced away."

Another important question in balancing is whether one side or the other of the scale will be given any advantage in the process. In legal terms, this advantage is usually described as a "presumption." For example, in a criminal case, the accused is presumed innocent, and the jury is told that it must return a verdict of not guilty if there is any "reasonable doubt" as to guilt. A similar presumption comes into play in the balancing approach, and it can be traced to one of the most famous footnotes in Supreme Court history. In *United States v. Carolene Products Co.* (1938), the Court upheld the validity of a federal economic regulation, applying the generally accepted principle that the courts presume statutes passed by legislative bodies are constitutional. In a footnote to his opinion for the Court, however, Justice Harlan Fiske Stone (who later served as Chief Justice) suggested that this presumption should be reversed when the legislation in question threatens freedoms protected by the bill of rights.

Subsequent cases referred to the first amendment as occupying a "preferred position" in our constitutional scheme, and, although that terminology caused some controversy among members of the Court, the law is now clear that freedom of expression enjoys a presumption in the balancing process. That is, first amendment rights will not be abridged unless the interests on the other side of the scale are deemed sufficiently "compelling." Put another way, any significant restriction of freedom of expression carries a heavy burden of justification, and doubtful balancing questions are thus to be resolved in favor of the first amendment.

The "Clear and Present Danger" Test

Justice Brandeis' opinion in *Whitney v. California* reflects a particularized balancing approach known as "clear and present danger" analysis. Because it played a prominent role in the evolution of first amendment jurisprudence, the clear and present danger test is sometimes considered—mistakenly—a general theory of protection for freedom of expression. It is better viewed as a type of balancing applicable only in a narrow range of circumstances. As Professor Paul Freund has written, the clear and present danger test "is not a broad-spectrum sovereign remedy for such other complaints as defamation, obscenity, and invasions of privacy, where the complex of interests at stake requires closer diagnosis and more refined treatment." With that caveat in mind, we now turn briefly to a review of this special balancing approach.

The clear and present danger test made its initial appearance in *Schenck v. United States* (1919), in which the Court, in an opinion by Justice Holmes, affirmed the conviction of the general secretary of the Socialist Party and others for violating the Espionage Act of 1917. Among other things, the defendants had been charged with conspiracy to obstruct the draft by circulating a leaflet urging draft resistance. Writing for a unanimous Court, Justice Holmes used language that was to become widely quoted:

> The most stringent protection of free speech would not protect a man in falsely shouting fire in a theater and causing a panic. It does not even protect a man from an injunction against uttering words that may have all the effect of force. The question in every case is whether the words are used in such circumstances and are of such a nature as to create a clear and present danger that they will bring about the substantive evils that Congress has a right to prevent. It is a question of proximity and degree.

The result reached in this case demonstrates, however, that the Court did not apply the newly announced test very stringently, for it was indeed unrealistic to conclude that leaflets distributed by a minor socialist group created the requisite danger. Indeed, it was apparent from *Schenck* and two Espionage Act cases decided a week later, *Frohwerk v. United States* and *Debs v. United States*, that the Court was willing to permit punishment of expression that merely had the "tendency" to hinder the American war effort.

Later in the year, however, Justices Holmes and Brandeis dissented in *Abrams v. United States*, linking the clear and present danger test to the marketplace of ideas concept. In this case, discussed previously, and others such as *Whitney*, the two dissenting justices stated their view that only an imminent emergency can justify repression, for otherwise the idea marketplace should be allowed to function. "If there be time to expose through discussion the falsehood and fallacies, to avert the evil by the processes of education," Brandeis wrote in *Whitney*, "the remedy to be applied is more speech, not enforced silence." It was not until the 1937 case *Herndon v. Lowry* that this doctrine was used by a majority of the Court to reverse a speech-related conviction.

During the early 1950s, however, the Court reexamined the clear and present danger test and, in so doing, adopted a watered-down version that perhaps reflected McCarthyism and the "red scare" paranoia that harkened back to the environment of the World War I period. In *Dennis v. United States* (1951), the Court affirmed the conviction of several defendants for conspiring to organize the Communist

Party of the United States in violation of the Smith Act. Although there was no majority opinion, Chief Justice Fred Vinson, writing for himself and three other Justices, applied a quite different clear and present danger test: "whether the gravity of the 'evil,' discounted by its improbability, justifies such invasion of free speech as is necessary to avoid the danger." Under this formulation, the conspiracy of the defendants to advocate revolution, though only in the preparatory stage, was held to create a clear and present danger. In effect, *Dennis* marked a return to the "bad tendency" test that Holmes and Brandeis so eloquently attacked.

Although the Court gradually retreated from the *Dennis* position, it was not until the late 1960s that the Court returned to the clear and present danger test as originally conceived by Holmes and Brandeis. In *Brandenburg v. Ohio* (1969), for example, the Court expressly overruled *Whitney* and made clear that even advocacy of violence is protected by the first amendment so long as the advocacy does not incite people to imminent lawless action.

In *Brandenburg*, a Ku Klux Klan leader had been accused of advocating political reform through violence and assembling with a group formed to teach this doctrine in violation of the Ohio criminal syndicalism statute. The Court struck down the statute as unconstitutional, holding that it did not satisfy the clear and present danger test: the state may not "forbid or proscribe advocacy of the use of force or of law violation except where such advocacy is directed to inciting or producing imminent lawless action and is likely to incite or produce such action." Because the statute did not adequately distinguish between advocacy and incitement, it was an impermissible restraint on expression. After *Brandenburg,* then, the proper focus is on the inciting language of the speaker and the need to show not only that the speech is directed to produce imminent lawless action but also that such a result is likely to follow from the speech.

It should be obvious from the foregoing that the clear and present danger test is to be used in determining when speech advocating criminal conduct may constitutionally be punished. The test is also used, in somewhat different form, when speech is likely to cause interference with the administration of justice. For example, in *Craig v. Harney* (1947), the Court reversed the conviction of a journalist who had been held in contempt of court for criticizing in print procedures that a judge had used during a trial. Writing for the Court, Justice Black said that the contempt power may not be used unless the speech constitutes a clear and present danger to the administration of justice. More recently, in *Nebraska Press Association v. Stuart* (1976), the Court adopted a similar approach in striking down a "gag order" that prohibited reporters from publishing information they had learned at a preliminary hearing in a sensational murder case. We shall return to these issues in Chapter 6.

Prior Restraints

As we have seen, Blackstone's *Commentaries on the Laws of England* defined freedom of expression as prohibiting "previous restraints upon publication, [but not] censure for criminal matter when published." Although the first amendment has been interpreted as reaching subsequent punishment of speech, as well as prior restraints, the distinction between the two remains important. For example, in the *Nebraska Press* case noted above, Chief Justice Burger emphasized that "prior restraints on speech and publication are the most serious and least tolerable infringements on First Amendment rights." And, as the Court stated in the Pentagon Papers case, "[a]ny system of prior restraints of expression comes to this Court bearing a heavy presumption against its constitutionality."

What is so pernicious about prior restraints that they are given even more stringent judicial scrutiny than other limitations on expression? Put another way, why are the scales of the balancing test weighted more heavily toward freedom of speech and press when prior restraints are involved?

It is true, of course, that the threat of subsequent punishment may have a significant deterrent effect upon the exercise of one's freedom to speak and publish. In fact, legislatures would not enact statutes imposing criminal penalties for speech—such as the criminal syndicalism acts at issue in *Whitney* and *Brandenburg*—unless they intended to discourage expression on certain subjects. Moreover, fear of being sued for libel and ordered to pay a large sum of money to the injured plaintiff can obviously make a speaker or publisher "think twice" about whether to exercise his freedom of expression. But in each of these situations, the decision to speak or publish remains in the hands of the individual, while a system of prior restraint places that decision in the hands of the government. Viewed in terms of the marketplace theory, a prior restraint limits public debate and knowledge more severely than subsequent punishment because it ensures that the speech will never reach the marketplace.

In Blackstone's day, licensing boards or other government censors imposed prior restraints, and such administrative control in advance of publication was undoubtedly the sort of activity he considered impermissible. This type of regulation is rare in the United States today, although administrative censorship of motion pictures exists in some states and cities. In *Freedman v. Maryland* (1965), the Supreme Court upheld state requirements that all films be submitted for advance approval in order that obscene and, therefore, constitutionally unprotected movies could be prohibited. The Court also ruled that such screening procedures must include certain safeguards, including a prompt determination of whether a particular film will be barred on grounds that it is obscene.

Prior restraint problems remain in other areas as well, although in most situations the courts rather than administrative bodies impose the restrictions upon speech. For example, in the *Nebraska Press* case noted above, a state trial judge directed reporters not to publish what transpired in open court during a criminal proceeding, and in the Pentagon Papers case the *New York Times* was ordered not to publish a secret government study involving the Vietnam War.

It could be argued, of course, that such restraints are not prohibited by the first amendment because they differ dramatically from the administrative censorship condemned by Blackstone. The Supreme Court, however, rejected this narrow interpretation of the prior restraint doctrine in the landmark case of *Near v. Minnesota*. At issue there was a state court order prohibiting any future publication or distribution of a small weekly newspaper pursuant to a Minnesota statute allowing abatement, as a public nuisance, of a "malicious, scandalous and defamatory newspaper or other periodical." The newspaper, the *Saturday Press*, had published inflammatory and anti-Semitic articles charging that "Jewish gangsters" were controlling various illegal activities in Minneapolis while city officials looked the other way. The local prosecutor initiated an abatement action against the *Press* and convinced the trial judge to "perpetually enjoin" publication of the newspaper. The order would be lifted only if the publishers could convince the court that the paper would remain free of any "objectionable" material. The Minnesota Supreme Court affirmed, holding the statute a constitutional exercise of the state's police power.

In a 5 to 4 decision, the U.S. Supreme Court reversed. The four dissenters, in an opinion by Justice Pierce Butler (himself a former Minnesota county attorney), argued that the statute authorized a judicial decree "to prevent *further* publication of malicious, scandalous and defamatory articles," not a "*previous* restraint upon the press by licensers as referred to by Blackstone. . . ." Writing for the majority, Chief Justice Hughes made clear that he did not consider the statute a form of subsequent punishment but rather a prior restraint:

> If . . . the publisher has a constitutional right to publish, without previous restraint, an edition of his newspaper charging official derelictions, it cannot be denied that he may publish subsequent editions for the same purpose. He does not lose his right by exercising it.

The Chief Justice also indicated that the prohibition against prior restraints is not absolute, citing examples of speech that might under appropriate circumstances be enjoined. These included obscene materials, information that threatened the national security, and speech that incited acts of violence.

The type of judicial order at issue in the *Near* case suggests additional reasons why prior restraints are considered more serious abridgements of speech than subsequent punishments. Important differences in the procedures for obtaining such orders and for securing criminal convictions based on speech make the former a particularly attractive—and effective—vehicle for suppressing expression. For example, the government can obtain a court order prohibiting certain expression almost immediately. Such a "temporary restraining order" remains in effect for a brief period until the court holds a hearing on whether a "preliminary injunction" should be issued. An injunction of this type maintains the status quo until a full-blown trial on the merits of the case is held and, as a practical matter, often determines the outcome of the dispute.

In contrast, a prosecutor who seeks a criminal conviction must take several time-consuming steps before the accused is even brought to trial: obtain an indictment or information setting forth the charges, arraign the defendant, file various pretrial motions, and select a jury in cases where there is a right to jury trial. The right to trial by jury exists when there is the possibility of imprisonment for six months or more, but there is no right to jury trial at all in cases involving injunctions. And, if the government loses its bid for an injunction in the trial court, it can appeal that ruling. In criminal cases, however, the government is generally barred from appealing a favorable verdict for the defendant.

Given these procedural safeguards applicable in criminal cases, it is not surprising that this form of subsequent punishment is a far less attractive alternative to the injunction, which is a civil proceeding. For example, although the federal government moved quickly against the *New York Times* and *Washington Post* to prevent publication of the Pentagon Papers, it did not initiate criminal prosecutions against the newspapers even though some Supreme Court Justices suggested that such a prosecution might be constitutional even though the prior restraint was invalid.

As Professor Emerson succinctly put it, "suppression by a stroke of the pen is more likely to be applied than suppression through a criminal process." This statement also suggests that the courts, which must try to predict the future in determining the dangerous consequences which might flow from publication, are often inclined to exaggerate or overemphasize the potential damages and thus enter the orders restraining speech. Accordingly, most commentators agree that a prior restraint is a more potent weapon against freedom of expression than the threat of subsequent punishment.

The modern system of judicially imposed prior restraints also poses particular problems for the news media. Under the process for injunctive relief described previously, a judge who issues a temporary restraining order prohibiting publication may ultimately conclude, in a subsequent hearing, that his order had been improperly issued. By the time the restraint is lifted, however, the news value of the information in question may have passed and, accordingly, publication often will not occur. Moreover, the government may have achieved its purpose in merely postponing publication for a few days.

A related problem involves the consequences of violating an order restraining speech. In *United States v. Dickinson* (1972), the U.S. Court of Appeals for the Fifth Circuit concluded that a trial judge had impermissibly ordered journalists not to report testimony that had taken place in open court. Nonetheless, the appeals court upheld the contempt of court convictions of two reporters who had ignored the trial court's order and published the testimony. Even though the "gag order" was an unconstitutional prior restraint, the appeals court said, the journalists "may not now escape the inescapable legal consequence for their flagrant intentional disregard of the mandates of a court." This is known as the collateral bar rule: a party against whom an injunction is issued must obey that order until it is dissolved or reversed on appeal, and, if he does not, he may not claim in a contempt of court proceeding that the order he violated was invalid. In contrast, one may violate a statute that restricts freedom of expression without forfeiting his right to challenge the statute as unconstitutional.

The collateral bar rule appears to leave reporters facing an unconstitutional court order a Hobson's choice: they may either violate the order and risk contempt convictions even though the order is ultimately held invalid, or comply with its terms and seek reversal on appeal, a lengthy process during which the news value of the enjoined material may simply vanish. However, as the *Dickinson* court pointed out, special procedures for expediting appeals exist in the federal courts (and in most state courts as well) that offer "speedy and effective but orderly review . . . swiftly enough to protect the right to publish news while it [is] still 'news.' " Indeed, under a federal statute and the laws of most states, a single judge of an appeals court can temporarily "stay" a lower court order, thus postponing its effect pending an appeal.

The *Dickinson* case is not universally followed, however. In some states, including Arizona, California, Illinois, Massachusetts, and Washington, a person held in contempt may challenge an unconstitutional prior restraint on certain types of speech while appealing the contempt conviction. Moreover, the U.S. Court of Appeals for the First Circuit has parted company with its fellow federal judges on the Fifth Circuit by creating an exception to the *Dickinson* rule. In a 1987 case, *In re Providence Journal Co.*, the First Circuit ruled that a "transparently invalid" order is not subject to the collateral bar rule and can be challenged on appeal from a contempt conviction. The case arose when the son of a reputed organized crime figure obtained a court order prohibiting the *Providence Journal* from publishing information about his late father obtained under the federal Freedom of Information Act. The newspaper disregarded the order, published the information, and was held in contempt of court. The editor was sentenced to eighteen months in jail and 200 hours of public service, and the paper was fined $100,000.

Refusing to apply *Dickinson*, the First Circuit held that a "transparently invalid" order cannot support a contempt conviction. Because the lower court's order met that description, it could be attacked even though it had been disobeyed. Unfortunately, however, the court did not provide much guidance as to what makes an order transparently invalid. However, the court held that journalists should make an effort to appeal what they think is such an order rather than simply disregard it. Noting that expedited appellate review is typically available, the court said that such relief should be sought before the order is disobeyed. "If timely access to the appellate court is not available or if a timely decision is not forthcoming, the publisher may then proceed to publish and challenge the constitutionality of the order in the contempt proceedings," the court wrote.

Corporate Speech

For several decades it was unclear whether corporations (business entities organized in accordance with certain requirements established by state law) were to be treated in the same manner as "natural" persons for purposes of the first amendment. Although the Supreme Court seemed to assume that corporations operating newspapers and other media enjoyed the same rights as individual publishers and speakers, considerable doubt existed as to the status of nonmedia corporations. In large part, the problem stemmed from the fact that a corporation is a legal fiction, a creature of the law which, unlike a flesh-and-blood person, exists only on paper. Consequently, the courts often drew distinctions between corporations and individuals in applying various legal doctrines. As discussed in Chapter 3, for example, a corporation cannot sue for invasion of privacy, for this tort evolved primarily to redress emotional injury that can be suffered only by human beings.

Today, however, it is settled that so-called "corporate speech" is protected by the first amendment to the same extent as "individual speech." The constitutional question is not the status of the speaker, but the nature of the speech. Suppose, for instance, that a corporation engaged in an aggressive marketing campaign that featured false and misleading advertisements. As noted previously, commercial speech enjoys somewhat less first amendment protection than "political" speech, and false and misleading commercial messages are unprotected. Consequently, commercial speech is subject to greater government regulation than political speech, and the corporation in the above example could be ordered to stop the misleading advertisements. This result does not follow from the fact that the speaker is a corporation, for the restrictions on commercial speech apply to individual and corporate speakers alike.

By the same token, government restrictions on political speech are evaluated under more stringent first amendment standards, no matter whether the speaker is a corporation or an individual. This is the message of the Supreme Court's 1978 ruling in *First National Bank of Boston v. Bellotti,* mentioned previously in connection with the press clause. The case arose when five corporations—two banks and three businesses—planned to contribute to a campaign against a proposed constitutional amendment that would have authorized the Massachusetts legislature to impose a graduated tax on individual income. However, a state statute prohibited corporate contributions or expenditures to influence the vote on referendum questions which did not materially affect the business or property of the corporation. In addition, the statute specifically forbade such contributions with respect to referenda "solely concerning the taxation of the income, property or transactions of individuals." After being advised by the state attorney general that the statute would be enforced against them, the corporations filed a suit asking that the provision be declared unconstitutional.

The Massachusetts Supreme Court upheld the statute, reasoning that corporate speech is protected only as an incident of property rights guaranteed by the fourteenth amendment. Since the speech at issue did not touch on the business or property of the corporations, it was not protected. The U.S. Supreme reversed, 5 to 4. Writing for the majority, Justice Powell pointed out that speech in question was political in nature and thus at the core of the first amendment. "If the speakers here were not corporations," he wrote, "no one would suggest that the State could silence their proposed speech." Labeling the speech as the type that is "indispensable to decisionmaking in a democracy," he added the importance of the speech does not change because the corporation comes from a corporation rather than an individual. "The inherent worth of the speech in terms of its capacity for informing the public does not depend upon the identity of its source, whether corporation, association, union, or individual."

In pointing to the importance of corporate political speech in informing the public, as well as the right of the public to receive such information, Justice Powell was obviously relying on the enlightenment and self-governance values reflected in the first amendment. In dissent, however, Justice Byron White emphasized quite different values. Joined by two of his brethren, Justice White argued that corporate speech "is subject to restrictions which individual expression is not." The first amendment is intended to facilitate individual "self-expression, self-realization and self-fulfillment," he said, and corporate speech fails to serve these interests. In a separate dissent, Justice William Rehnquist (now Chief Justice) argued that corporate speech is wholly without first amendment protection. He argued that corporations, as creatures of the state, are entitled only those constitutional protections "incidental to [their] very existence" and thus implied by their creation. Freedom of expression, he said, is not "necessary to effectuate the purposes for which States permit commercial corporations to exist."

Justice White also expressed concern that corporations might use their vast wealth, amassed at least in part as a result of special privileges conferred by the state, to obtain an unfair advantage in the political process. This potential for imbalance in the marketplace of ideas, he said, justified the Massachusetts statute. The majority, however, rejected this argument, concluding that fears of corporate domination were not supported by the evidence. Moreover, Justice Powell took the position that it is safer to entrust the marketplace of ideas to diverse viewpoints—including those of corporate speakers—than to allow the state to control access to the marketplace and thus limit the number of speakers and the variety of messages. "[T]he people in our democracy are entrusted with the responsibility for judging and evaluating the relative merits of conflicting arguments," Justice Powell wrote. "They may consider, in making their judgment, the source and credibility of the advocate."

In subsequent cases, the Supreme Court has elaborated somewhat upon its holding in *Bellotti*. For example, in *Consolidated Edison Co. v. Public Service Commission* (1980), the Court struck down a New York regulation that prohibited an electric company from inserting material advocating nuclear power in the monthly bills sent to its customers. "The restriction on bill inserts cannot be upheld on the ground that Consolidated Edison is not entitled to freedom of speech," the Court said, citing *Bellotti*. "[W]e [have] rejected the contention that a State may confine corporate speech to specified issues."

Six years later, in *Pacific Gas & Electric Co. v. Public Utilities Commission*, the Court made plain that a corporate newsletter that addresses matters of public concern "receives the full protection of the First Amendment." At issue was a newsletter, prepared by a California electric company for its consumers, that contained everything from political editorials and feature stories to energy-saving tips and recipes. Describing the newsletter as similar to a "small newspaper," the Court noted that it "includes the kind of discussion of 'matters of public concern' that the First Amendment both fully protects and implicitly encourages."

There is one significant limit on corporate speech. In *Bellotti*, the Court noted that its ruling that a corporation has "a right to speak on issues of general public interest implies no comparable right in the quite different context of participation in a political campaign for election to public office." This passage suggests that federal and state statutes barring corporate campaign contributions to candidates and independent corporate expenditures on their behalf are constitutional.

The Court subsequently reaffirmed this position in *Federal Election Commission v. Massachusetts Citizens for Right to Life, Inc.* (1986), which involved a challenge by a nonprofit corporation to such a ban found in the Federal Election Campaign Act. Though the Court ruled the prohibition unconstitutional with regard to nonprofit corporations organized for "ideological" purposes, it was careful to point out that traditional business corporations present a different situation. "Direct corporate spending on political activity raises the prospect that resources amassed in the economic marketplace may be used to provide an unfair advantage in the political marketplace," the Court said with respect to profit-making corporations. "The availability of these resources may make a corporation a formidable political presence" and thus "pose a danger of corruption." This threat to the integrity of the electoral process is not presented by nonprofit "ideological" corporations, the Court said, since they are "formed to disseminate political ideas, not to amass capital."

Other Doctrines

As emphasized previously, the divergent situations in which first amendment problems arise make it difficult, if not impossible, to formulate a general, across-the-board approach to free speech issues. We will explore in the chapters that follow a variety of contexts in which the news media encounter first amendment problems, ranging from libel and privacy to newsgathering activities and protection of confidential news sources. Before turning to the particular problems of the institutional press, let us first briefly examine some first amendment problems that typically do not involve the news media.

Two closely related doctrines that are often important in free speech cases are the prohibitions against the "overbreadth" and "vagueness" of statutes. Although these concepts are distinct, the courts often speak of them together. An overbroad statute is one aimed at punishing or restricting activities that do not enjoy constitutional protection but also reaches activities falling under the first amendment. A vague statute is one that is drafted in such a way that it can be interpreted to allow restrictions or burdens on protected speech, or that fails to give an individual notice that his particular speech is subject to the statute.

The overbreadth doctrine is illustrated by *City of Houston v. Hill* (1987), which involved a first amendment attack on a city ordinance that made it unlawful to "interrupt any policeman in the execution of his duty." Raymond Hill was convicted of violating this ordinance after shouting "why don't you pick on somebody your own size" to an officer who was making an arrest. Although "fighting words that by their very utterance inflict injury or tend to incite an immediate breach of the peace" are not protected by the first amendment, the ordinance also prohibited protected speech that "interrupted" a police officer. "The Constitution does not allow such speech to be made a crime," the Supreme Court said.

A famous example of the vagueness doctrine is *Smith v. Goguen* (1974), in which the defendant had been convicted under a federal "flag-misuse" statute for sewing a small American flag to the seat of his pants. The statute, which made it a crime to "mutilate, trample upon, deface or treat contemptuously" the U.S. flag, was held unconstitutional because it did not provide sufficiently clear guidelines as to what type of conduct was prohibited.

The *Smith* case suggests another thorny first amendment problem: if the defendant in that case had sewn the flag to his pants in order to communicate his distaste for, say, American foreign policy, to what extent could the government regulate his symbolic gesture? The leading case involving symbolic speech is *United States v. O'Brien* (1968). David O'Brien burned his draft card on the steps of the South Boston courthouse to demonstrate his opposition to the Vietnam War and the selective service system. He was convicted for violating a federal statute punishing anyone who "forges, alters, knowingly destroys, [or] knowingly mutilates" a draft card. The Supreme Court assumed that O'Brien's action had a "communicative element" that implicated the first amendment but ruled that when "speech" and "nonspeech" elements are combined in the same course of conduct, "a sufficiently important governmental interest in regulating the nonspeech element can justify incidental limitations on First Amendment freedoms."

The Court explained that the statute at issue served substantial governmental interests, such as the speedy induction of men into the military during a national emergency and deterrence for the deceptive use of draft cards. Moreover, the statute's impact on expression was incidental, since these interests were unrelated to the suppression of speech. The result would have been different, the Court said, had the statute prohibited only the *public* destruction of draft cards, for such a provision would indicate that its purpose was to punish the expression of certain opinions.

In contrast to *O'Brien* stands *Texas v. Johnson* (1989), in which the Supreme Court reversed the conviction of a man who burned an American flag during a demonstration to protest policies of the Republican Party. The incident took place in downtown Dallas while the Republicans were holding their 1984 national convention in the city. Gregory Johnson was sentenced to a year in prison and fined $2,000 for violating a Texas statute that made it a crime to intentionally or knowingly desecrate a state or national flag. The term "desecrate" was defined to mean "deface, damage, or otherwise physically mistreat in a way the [person] knows will seriously offend one or more persons likely to observe or discover his action." The Supreme Court reversed Johnson's conviction in a controversial 5 to 4 decision that prompted calls for a constitutional amendment to protect the flag.

The State of Texas argued that in this case, as in *O'Brien,* the expressive conduct could be regulated because "significantly important governmental interests" unrelated to the suppression of speech justified regulation of the conduct. Those interests, the state said, were preventing breaches of the peace and preserving the flag as a symbol of nationhood and national unity. Writing for the majority, Justice Brennan disagreed. As for the first asserted interest, he pointed out that no breach of the peace had occurred at the time of or in response to the burning of the flag. Moreover, under the clear and present danger test, the mere possibility that a breach of the peace will occur is not sufficient to warrant restrictions on expression. In any event, he added, the state's interest in maintaining order was protected by another statute that specifically prohibited breaches of the peace.

Turning to the second justification, Justice Brennan concluded that a governmental interest in "preserving the flag's special symbolic value" is directly related to expression and thus fails to pass muster under *O'Brien*. "The State apparently is concerned that [burning the flag] will lead people to believe either that the flag does not stand for nationhood and national unity, but instead reflects other, less positive concepts, or that the concepts reflected in the flag do not in fact exist, that is, we do not enjoy unity as a Nation," he wrote. "These concerns blossom only when a person's treatment of the flag communicates some message, and are thus related to the suppression of free expression. . . ."

Having found *O'Brien* inapplicable, the Court then considered whether, under the balancing test described previously, preserving the flag as a national symbol was a "compelling state interest" that outweighed the defendant's freedom of expression. After first pointing out that Johnson had been prosecuted for political expression that lies at the core of the first amendment, Justice Brennan answered that question in the negative. "If there is a bedrock principle underlying the First Amendment, it is that the Government may not prohibit the expression of an idea simply because society finds the idea itself offensive or disagreeable," he wrote. "We have not recognized an exception to this principle even where our flag has been involved." The way to preserve the flag's special role is not to punish those who feel differently about the principles that it symbolizes, but to "persuade them that they are wrong."

Another important case involving symbolic speech is *Tinker v. Des Moines Independent School District* (1969), which arose from a "silent protest" by students who wore black armbands to class to express their opposition to the war in Vietnam. School officials suspended students who refused to remove the armbands, relying on a policy adopted a few days earlier in anticipation of the protest. Finding the policy unconstitutional, the Supreme Court stressed that school authorities had not banned all political symbols; in fact, students were permitted to wear the Nazi "Iron Cross."

Thus, unlike the draft card statute in *O'Brien*, the school board policy in *Tinker* was definitely related to expression of ideas rather than regulation of conduct. As the Court pointed out, the policy was based on "an urgent wish to avoid the controversy which might result from the expression, even by the silent symbol of armbands, of opposition to this Nation's part in the conflagration in Vietnam." Because the policy did not satisfy the *O'Brien* test, it was evaluated under traditional first amendment balancing principles. Striking that balance, the Court concluded that the interest in speech must prevail, for there was no showing that the protest had disrupted school activities or created discipline problems. By way of comparison, the Supreme Court in *Bethel School District v. Fraser* (1986) upheld the suspension of a high school student for delivering a vulgar—but not legally obscene—speech at an assembly held in connection with student government elections. Distinguishing *Tinker*, the Court concluded that the content of the speech was sexual rather than political and that it "undermine[d] the school's basic educational mission."

By banning armbands but not other political symbols, the school authorities in *Tinker* ran afoul of another basic first amendment principle: the government must be "content neutral" with respect to speech. This rule is aptly illustrated by *Boos v. Barry* (1988), a case involving a District of Columbia ordinance that prohibited the display of any sign within 500 feet of a foreign embassy if that sign tended to bring the foreign government into "public odium" or "public disrepute." Striking down the ordinance, the Supreme Court described its fatal flaw as distinguishing between permissible and impermissible signs on the basis of their content. "Whether individuals may picket in front of a foreign embassy depends entirely upon whether their picket signs are critical of the foreign government or not," Justice Sandra Day O'Connor wrote for the Court. "One category of speech has been completely prohibited within 500 feet of embassies. Other categories of speech, however, such as favorable speech about a foreign government or speech concerning a labor dispute with a foreign government, are permitted." As the Court observed in an earlier case, *Police Department of Chicago v. Mosley* (1972), "above all else, the First Amendment means that the government has no power to restrict expression because of its message, its ideas, its subject matter, or its content."

Also at issue in *Boos v. Barry* was the power of the state to restrict expression in certain *places*. Recall that this problem arose in *Adderly v. Florida*, in which civil rights demonstrators held a protest on the grounds of a county jail. In deciding cases of this type, the Supreme Court has developed the "public forum" doctrine, which can be traced to the plurality opinion of Justice Owen Roberts in *Hague v. CIO* (1939). It was not until 1983, however, in *Perry Education Association v. Perry Local Educators' Association* that the Supreme Court painted a comprehensive picture of the concept. According to *Perry*, there are three types of public fora:

- places traditionally open to the public for expressive activity, such as streets, sidewalks, and parks;
- areas that the state has specifically opened to speech, such as meeting facilities in public buildings; and
- public property that is not by tradition or designation a forum for public communication, such as the jail in *Adderly*.

The category into which the particular place falls determines the extent of permissible regulation. When a "traditional" public forum is involved, the government may impose content-neutral time, place, and manner restrictions if alternative means of communication remain open, but may not, absent compelling reasons, prohibit all communicative activity or deny access based on content. The same limitations on government regulation apply to a "limited" public forum, although the state is not required to keep the forum open to the public. If the property is a "nonpublic" forum, however, the government's powers are greater: the state may "reserve the forum for its intended purposes, communicative or otherwise, as long as the regulation on speech is reasonable and not an effort to suppress expression merely because public officials oppose the speaker's view."

The public forum cases have dealt with a wide variety of public facilities, including municipally-owned theaters, military bases, airports, university buildings, jails, mailboxes, school board meetings, state fairs, and even the sidewalks surrounding the U.S. Supreme Court building. Of this group, all except jails, mailboxes, and military bases have been placed in either the first or second of the *Perry* categories.

Even if a traditional or limited public forum is involved, keep in mind that the government is permitted to regulate the time, place, and manner of the speech in a content-neutral fashion. For example, a public street is a "traditional" public forum, but a demonstration on a busy thoroughfare during the morning rush hour would obviously snarl traffic and delay commuters on their way to work. Thus, the city could constitutionally refuse to grant a parade permit for that particular hour or that particular street. However, the city could not grant a parade permit to an anti-abortion group but deny such a permit to a pro-choice organization.

A 1981 case involving the Hare Krishna religious sect illustrates these principles. In *Heffron v. International Society for Krishna Consciousness*, the Supreme Court upheld Minnesota State Fair regulations requiring persons wanting to sell merchandise or distribute written material to do so from fairground booths that could be rented from fair officials for a small fee. The regulation applied to any group or individual, whether their activities were commercial, nonprofit, or charitable. The Krishna organization challenged the regulation, claiming that it unconstitutionally denied them the right to distribute and sell literature and solicit donations, as required by their religion. The Court concluded that although the state fair was a limited public forum, the regulation was a permissible time, place, and manner restriction. The state had a strong interest in maintaining order and smooth traffic flow at the heavily congested fair, and the regulation did not discriminate against certain groups or individuals but applied across-the-board to everyone. Moreover, alternative means of communication were available: members of the group could perform their ritualistic solicitation outside the entrance to the fairgrounds and, once inside, could engage in face-to-face discussions with others attending the fair.

More recently, the Supreme Court held in *Hazelwood School District v. Kuhlmeier* (1988) that a high school newspaper written and edited by a journalism class was not a public forum. The Court first pointed out that school facilities may, in certain circumstances, be deemed to be public forums: "if school authorities have by policy or by practice opened those facilities for indiscriminate use by the general public or by some segment of the public, such as student organizations." In this case, however, the student newspaper was "a supervised learning experience for journalism students." As a "laboratory" paper published in connection with "regular classroom activity," its pages were not open to "indiscriminate use by its student reporters and editors or by the student body generally." Because the newspaper was not a public forum, school officials were entitled to regulate its contents in any reasonable manner.

A problem related to the public forum doctrine deserves mention here, for it brings into sharp focus the often divergent interests of speaker and listener in first amendment analysis. Recall that the enlightenment rationale for the first amendment and the marketplace of ideas concept both demand recognition of the interest of the audience in receiving messages. What if some or all members of that audience do not want to hear what the speaker has to say? The Supreme Court has used the term "captive audience" in addressing this question.

In one of the earlier cases dealing with such unwilling listeners, the Court held in *Kovacs v. Cooper* (1949) that a city may, in a content-neutral fashion, prohibit "loud and raucous" sound trucks from roaming residential neighborhoods. In this situation, persons seeking to avoid the message would have a difficult time doing so, even in the privacy of their own homes. The city ordinance in *Kovacs* can be viewed as a type of time, place, and manner restriction designed to safeguard the privacy interests of the audience or to screen out messages that its members would be otherwise unable to avoid. More recently, in *Frisby v. Schultz* (1988), the Court upheld a city ordinance that prohibited picketing in residential neighborhoods. Citing the *Kovacs* case, the Court ruled that protection of that "privacy of the home" is a compelling governmental interest that justifies restrictions on speech. "One important aspect of residential privacy is protection of the unwilling listener," Justice

O'Connor wrote for the majority. "[I]ndividuals are not required to welcome unwanted speech into their own homes."

Outside the home, however, the Court has been reluctant to rely upon the captive audience concept. For example, in *Cohen v. California* (1971), the Court rejected the argument that a man wearing a jacket emblazoned with the slogan "Fuck the Draft" was, by appearing so clothed in a public place, thrusting his message upon an unwilling audience. The Court reasoned that those "briefly exposed" to the objectionable language could "effectively avoid further bombardment of their sensibilities simply by averting their eyes." Similarly, in *Erznoznik v. Jacksonville* (1975), the Court struck down a city ordinance that banned films showing nudity from drive-in theaters, pointing out that outdoor movie screens are "not so obtrusive as to make it impossible for an unwilling individual to avoid exposure to it."

The Court took a different approach in *Lehman v. City of Shaker Heights* (1974). There a political candidate had sought unsuccessfully to purchase advertising space inside city-owned buses. He was rebuffed by transit system officials because city policy permitted only commercial advertising on these "car cards." The Court, in a 5 to 4 decision, upheld the city's policy of prohibiting political advertising. Although there was no "opinion of the Court" with which at least five Justices could agree, the majority did conclude that the bus riders were a captive audience who could not avoid the message. Justice Brennan, joined in dissent by three other Justices, argued that the passengers could avert their eyes, as was the case in *Cohen*.

The foregoing cases raise as many questions as they answer about the captive audience concept. For example, are there other situations outside the home that create captive audiences? What about a cafeteria or restaurant? Must it be government owned? Are large billboards adjacent to major highways as intrusive and as difficult to escape as signs in the relatively small interior of a bus? Or are such billboards more like outdoor movie screens? Does the form of the message—written or aural—play an important role, since it is arguably easier to close one's eyes than one's ears? For present purposes, it is sufficient to note that the presence or absence of a captive audience may be a useful factor in the balancing process described previously. Moreover, the captive audience doctrine focuses on the interests of the recipient in the communications process and suggests that there might be other situations in which those audience's interests might be more important than those of the speaker. We will explore these issues in connection with the regulation of broadcasting in Chapter 10.

Although it is perhaps best described as a captive audience case, the *Kovacs* decision also points to a possible conflict between the first amendment and private property rights. Suppose that, instead of using the sound trucks, the speakers in that case decided to distribute leaflets to homeowners and solicit contributions for a political candidate or a charitable cause. Although a total ban on such door-to-door activities was held unconstitutional in *Martin v. Struthers* (1943), later cases, notably *Schaumburg v. Citizens for a Better Environment* (1980), suggest that a city may by ordinance require such a solicitor to depart immediately if the homeowner has posted a "no soliciting" sign. As Justice John Marshall Harlan observed in *Garner v. Louisiana* (1961), the right to freedom of speech "surely would not encompass . . . expression in a private home if the owner has not consented." Thus, trespass statutes or anti-solicitation ordinances that prohibit unwanted speech on private property are generally valid under the first amendment, even though official punishment of such speech, as we have seen, constitutes governmental action. As Professor Nimmer has aptly pointed out, such regulations "are valid because the interest in the homeowner's privacy outbalances whatever speech interest the stranger to the home may claim.''

The balance is not necessarily struck in the same manner when private property other than residences is the setting for the speech. In *Marsh v. Alabama*, for example, the Supreme Court reversed the criminal trespass conviction of a member of the Jehovah's Witnesses who had distributed religious literature in a "company town" owned by a shipbuilding company. In an opinion by Justice Black, the Court concluded that the defendant's first amendment rights outweighed the privacy interests of the property owner, for "the more an owner . . . opens up his property for use by the public in general, the more do his rights become circumscribed by the statutory and constitutional rights of those who use it."

In a series of cases beginning in 1968, the Court returned to this problem of "quasi-public" property in the context of privately-owned shopping centers. After two contradictory and confusing decisions, the Court ultimately held in *Hudgens v. National Labor Relations Board* (1976) that the *Marsh* rule is limited to the "company town" setting and does not extend to shopping centers. Thus, there is a first amendment right to engage on speech activities on private property, despite the owner's wishes, only if the property is the functional equivalent of a company town. Lower courts have ruled that migrant labor camps satisfy this standard but that nursing homes do not. Conflicts between first amendment rights and property rights can also arise when the mass media are involved, particularly with respect to distribution and newsgathering activities.

A Note on the "New Technology"

Charles Ferris, then chairman of the Federal Communications Commission, raised a few eyebrows in 1980 when he asked whether news delivered directly to subscribers via a teletext service would be treated as a printed newspaper or would be considered broadcasting and thus subject to more governmental controls. One could rephrase the question in more general terms: how do the first amendment principles that have developed over the past sixty years apply to newly emerging means of communication brought about by ever-expanding technology? The importance of this issue cannot be overstated. As Professor Ithiel de Sola Pool pointed out in his book *Technologies of Freedom*:

> Networked computers will be the printing presses of the twenty-first century. If they are not free of public control, the continued application of constitutional immunities to the [traditional print media] may become no more than a quaint archaism, a sort of Hyde Park Corner where a few eccentrics can gather while the major policy debates take place elsewhere.

The so-called "new technology" that has brought us into the information age will directly affect the application of the first amendment doctrines discussed in this chapter and considered in specific contexts throughout this book. For example, the emerging electronic publishing industry will pose difficult first amendment questions. The term itself is shorthand for a variety of systems, including: teletext, a one-way broadcast transmission of textual information using a portion of the "space" available in a television signal; videotext, a two-way service using telephone lines or cable linked to a personal computer; electronic mail, a videotext service by which messages are transmitted from one computer to another; and the electronic bulletin board, a publicly accessible videotext computer file. How do we categorize these services for first amendment purposes? Is electronic mail "media" speech or "individual" speech? What about videotext? Does the distinction matter in terms of permissible government regulation?

As Justice White observed in *Metromedia, Inc. v. City of San Diego* (1981), the Supreme Court "has often faced the problem of applying the broad principles of the First Amendment to unique forums of expression." In that case, he said, the Court was "deal[ing] with the law of billboards." The Court has recently been faced with questions involving the first amendment rights of cable operators, and similar problems are in store as electronic publishing matures. The principal difficulty is that electronic publishing does not fit neatly into the first amendment pigeonholes that presently exist. Consider Mr. Ferris' question about teletext, which is delivered via broadcast signals. As noted previously, the broadcast media have been afforded less first amendment protection than the print media. If teletext is to be considered broadcasting, the first amendment would allow certain government regulation that would not be permissible with respect to the print media. But what of videotext, which is delivered by telephone lines or cable? Should the delivery system determine the permissible amount of government regulation?

New forms of "publishing" may also force us to alter the way we have traditionally thought about "the press" or "the media." In a 1988 report to Congress entitled *Science, Technology, and the First Amendment*, the Office of Technology Assessment said:

> Taken together, current and anticipated advances in technology suggest a fundamental shift from the concept of "press" to the concept of "network." To some extent, the past mode of one organization *publishing* for many may give way to a *communications* mode in which many share knowledge among themselves. One-to-many publishing will no doubt continue, but will be joined by new and unfamiliar forms. Gathering, editing, and disseminating news and information, which today is commonly integrated in one organization, may eventually be fragmented between many specialized entities. The electronic publisher of the future may act more as a clearinghouse for the exchange of news and information than as a gatherer. * * * One-to-many publishing will also coexist with one-to-one publishing, such as electronic mail, and many-to-many publishing, such as computer conferencing.

These developments raise interesting questions with respect to editorial control and liability under the first amendment. Traditionally, we have concluded that while editors have discretion under the first amendment to print what they choose, they also have to face potential liability—for defamation and other injuries—as a result of their decisions. On the other hand, a common carrier such as a telegraph company must carry all messages on a nondiscriminatory basis. Because anyone who wants to use its services may do so, the carrier generally has no liability for the content of the messages it transmits. As the Office of Technology Assessment report points out, however, this "simple symmetry between control and liability may become hard to apply to electronic publishers."

In one sense, electronic publishers exert editorial control by choosing what information services to provide their subscribers. At the same time, however, they "are less often in control over what is said over the network." Since that control is absent, what is the extent of their liability for, say, defamation or copyright infringement? Should it matter that the electronic publisher may not, as a practical matter, be able to exercise the same type of control as a newspaper editor? On networks that provide bulletin board and news services, for example, there may be thousands of messages delivered so fast that no "editor" could possibly scan them. Does this mean that the "electronic" press should be given more latitude than the print media?

The new technology will also have a significant impact on newsgathering. Databases, for example, are powerful tools for an investigative reporter who wants to know more about a given person or issue. As the Office of Technology Assessment pointed out in its report, databases enable their users to create "whole new bodies of knowledge out of heretofore unconnected pieces of information." Similarly, communications satellites that have revolutionized the delivery of information may one day serve as newsgathering devices. The same technology that permits the Defense Department to operate high-powered "spy satellites" capable of providing detailed photographs of enemy military installations would allow the news media to obtain potentially sensitive information about people, businesses, and governments. Obviously, the media's use of databases and satellites for newsgathering purposes could cause a collision with the right to privacy and the need for national security. Because first amendment rights are typically balanced against such competing interests, do these technological developments require that the balance be struck in a different manner?

Keep in mind that the questions posed in this section barely scratch the surface. But they are not hypothetical; the courts, for example, are already grappling with various legal problems raised by the regulation of cable television at the federal, state, and local levels. As we return to various "new technology" issues from time to time, it is useful to recall that society and law have encountered similar difficulties before. Although Gutenberg's printing press led to widespread licensing and censorship, it also led to the first amendment. This time around, perhaps the path will not be as tortuous.

PROBLEMS

1. A nude dancer was one of several persons arrested during two police "sweeps" of topless bars in Little Rock, Arkansas. She was fined $700 and received a thirty-day suspended sentence under a state statute that makes it a misdemeanor for a person "to arouse or gratify the sexual desire of himself or of any other person [by exposing] his sex organs . . . in a public place or public view." The Arkansas Supreme Court affirmed her conviction, and the U.S. Supreme Court refused to hear the case. *See Young v. State,* 692 S.W.2d 752 (Ark. 1985), *cert. denied,* 474 U.S. 1070 (1986). The Court has indicated, however, that barroom-type nude dancing is a type of expression that is protected under the first amendment under some circumstances. *See, e.g., Schad v. Borough of Mount Ephraim,* 452 U.S. 61 (1981). Evaluate the speech interests present in the *Young* case, taking into account the values underlying freedom of expression discussed previously. If such expression is protected under the first amendment, under what circumstances can it be regulated or punished by the state? Put another way, what competing interests must be balanced against the speech interests?

2. In 1970, Congress passed a statute providing that "[a]fter January 1, 1971, it shall be unlawful to advertise cigarettes on any medium of electronic communication subject to the jurisdiction of the Federal Communications Commission." 15 U.S.C. §1335. The

statute was upheld as constitutional by a federal district court, and that ruling was affirmed without opinion by the U.S. Supreme Court. *See Capital Broadcasting Co. v. Mitchell*, 333 F. Supp. 582 (D.D.C. 1971), *aff'd*, 405 U.S. 1000 (1972). In 1986, Congress extended the law to so-called "smokeless tobacco" products. 15 U.S.C. §4402(f). The American Medical Association has recently proposed legislation to prohibit *all* cigarette advertising, including that appearing in newspapers and magazines or on billboards. Keeping in mind that broadcast media have been subject to greater regulation than print media, would such an extension of the ban be constitutional? What are the competing interests that must be balanced? Does it make any difference that commercial speech is involved? Should it?

3. In 1985, the wives of sixteen Congressmen and an influential cabinet member formed the Parents Music Resources Center to rally support for their contention that some rock-and-roll lyrics are sexually explicit and glorify drug abuse, violence, suicide, and disrespect for parents. After a hearing before a Senate committee at which such performers as Dee Snider of "Twisted Sister," Frank Zappa, and John Denver testified in support of the "free speech" rights of recording artists, the Center reached an agreement with the Recording Industry Association of America to place warning labels on records that may be offensive. Under the voluntary plan, records will carry a label ("Explicit Lyrics—Parental Advisory") or print the lyrics on album covers where they can be read by parents. *See* "Recording Group Tells of New Steps on Lyrics," *New York Times* (November 1, 1985), sec. 1, p. 14; "Rock is a Four-Letter Word," *Time* (September 30, 1985), p. 70.

   Suppose that the influential Washington wives had convinced the Congress to pass a statute requiring that record companies take these steps. Would the statute be constitutional? In engaging in the requisite balancing, should courts take into account the fact that most rock music seems to be aimed at teenagers and even younger children? That the records can be heard on the radio or MTV? Could the warning requirement constitutionally be applied to those outlets?

4. A news story in *Business Week* magazine reported attempts by Denny, a dissatisfied stockholder in a corporation, to oust its management. On the basis of that story, Denny brought a libel suit against the magazine and Mertz, a former company official and source of the allegedly libelous statements. As a private individual, Denny must as a matter of constitutional law establish that the magazine was negligent—that is, careless—in publishing the statements about him. It is unclear, however, whether the same requirement applies in cases brought against nonmedia defendants such as Mertz. Should Denny be allowed to recover against Mertz, the source of the story, without having to show carelessness, even though he must demonstrate such fault on the part of *Business Week* to recover against the magazine? Does Justice Stewart's view of the press clause help resolve the question? Does it make a difference that in this case the nonmedia defendant was the source of the news story? Does that make Mertz part of the "press" and entitle him to greater protection against libel suits? What if no media defendant were involved in the litigation, and Denny had simply sued on the basis of a statement Mertz made to a group of fellow workers? *See Denny v. Mertz*, 318 N.W.2d 141 (Wis.), *cert. denied*, 459 U.S. 883 (1982).

5. Apply the clear and present danger test in the following situations:
   a. A radical graduate student, obviously a holdover from another era, delivered a stirring speech to a meeting of the local League of Women Voters, concluding his remarks with the observation that "the world would be a lot better off without our President." *Cf. Watts v. United States*, 394 U.S. 705 (1969); *Rankin v. McPherson*, 483 U.S. 378 (1987).

b. The same graduate student gave the same speech to a secret meeting of Libyan terrorists who had illegally entered the country with machine guns, plastic explosives, and other instruments of destruction. Their mission as a "hit squad" was to "bring terrorism into the United States."

c. Following the assassination of Julius Caesar, Marc Antony spoke to the citizens of Rome, having been given permission to do so by the conspirators. In his funeral oration ("I come to bury Caesar, not to praise him"), Antony referred to the murderers as "honorable men" but made plain that he viewed them as traitors. He advocated violence through the use of language that did not literally advocate action, and the result was a riot. *See* William Shakespeare, *Julius Caesar*, Act III, scene ii.

6. A woman in her early twenties was forcibly abducted from her home early one morning, driven to a secluded area on the outskirts of town, and repeatedly raped by two men. The police, acting on the description of the assailants provided by the woman, were able to make arrests and file formal charges against the men later in the same day. Should the local media, as a matter of policy, identify the victim and her accused attackers? Would your answer be different if the victim were the daughter of the mayor? If the men were prominent businessmen or athletes at the local college? Suppose the state had passed a statute making it a crime to report the name of a rape victim. Would the statute be constitutional? What if it also punished publication of the name of the accused? *See Cox Broadcasting Corp. v. Cohn,* 420 U.S. 469 (1975); *Florida Star v. B.J.F.,* 109 S.Ct. 2603 (1989).

7. The Board of Airport Commissioners of the City of Los Angeles adopted a resolution banning all "first amendment activities" within the central terminal area at Los Angeles International Airport. About a year after the resolution was passed, a minister was stopped by an airport security officer while distributing free religious literature on a pedestrian walkway in the central terminal. After being informed that the city would take legal action against him if he refused to leave, the minister stopped distributing the leaflets and left the terminal. Is the airport a "public forum"? If so, what type? Even if the airport is not a public forum, can the resolution pass muster under the "overbreadth" doctrine? *See Airport Commissioners of Los Angeles v. Jews for Jesus, Inc.,* 482 U.S. 569 (1987).

8. The Foreign Agents Registration Act, a federal statute, requires that "political propaganda" entering the United States must be conspicuously marked with a statement that the materials have been issued by an agent of a foreign government or political party. 22 U.S.C. § 614(b). In 1983, the Justice Department designated three films produced by the National Film Board of Canada as "political propaganda" and required that they be so labeled. Two of the films dealt with the acid rain problem, while the third—which had won an Academy Award—examined nuclear war. A California state senator challenged the Justice Department decision and the statute, arguing that the labeling requirement infringed his first amendment rights by imposing a pejorative classification that deterred him from exhibiting the films. What result? *See Meese v. Keene,* 481 U.S. 465 (1987); Rodney A. Smolla and Stephen A. Smith, "Propaganda, Xenophobia, and the First Amendment," 67 *Oregon Law Review* 253 (1988).

9. In May 1988, nine Chicago aldermen seized and damaged a student painting satirizing the city's late mayor, Harold Washington. The painting, the work of a student at the School of the Art Institute of Chicago, was part of a juried critique for graduating seniors and was not open to the general public. Entitled "Mirth and Girth," the painting showed Mayor Washington, a large man, naked except for a bra, bikini underpants, a garter belt, and stockings. The late mayor, who was serving his second term when he died

suddenly in November 1987, was black, as are the aldermen who seized the painting. The student artist, David Nelson, is white. After the painting was seized, it was kept at police headquarters for two days before being returned to Nelson. Moreover, before it was taken into custody, the city council voted to cut off all funds to the Art Institute if the painting were not removed from display. Did the seizure and the threat to discontinue funding violate the first amendment? Another controversy arose in 1989 when legislation was introduced in Congress to prohibit federal funding of sexually explicit or blasphemous works of art. The proposed statute was aimed at the National Endowment for the Arts, which had provided federal funds for exhibits featuring photographs of homosexual and heterosexual acts and a crucifix in a jar of urine. Would such a statute be constitutional? *See* Michael Brenson, "A Savage Painting Raises Troubling Questions, *New York Times* (May 29, 1988), sec. 2, p. 29; Grace Glueck, "Art on the Firing Line," *New York Times* (July 9, 1989), sec. 2, p. 1.

10. As part of its statutory responsibility for counter-intelligence activities, the Federal Bureau of Investigation has instituted a "library awareness program" in an effort to find out what sort of books certain foreign nationals—particularly those from the Soviet Union and Eastern European countries—have been reading. Under the program, FBI agents have visited libraries and made inquiries of library staff members, tapped telephone lines to reference desks, and employed hidden cameras. According to FBI officials, these steps are necessary for two reasons. First, foreign intelligence agents use libraries, particularly those that specialize in scientific and technical information, to gather information that might prove valuable at home, even though the information is not "classified." Second, these agents routinely attempt to develop librarians as sources of information and recruit them for intelligence-gathering activities. Does the FBI's program violate the first amendment? *See* "FBI Defends Library Monitoring Program," *New York Times* (July 14, 1988), p. 17A; "FBI Search for Spies in Libraries is Assailed," *New York Times* (June 21, 1988), p. 16A.

CHAPTER

2

DEFAMATION

Liberty Lobby, Inc. v. Dow Jones & Co., 838 F.2d 1287 (D.C. Cir.), *cert. denied,* 109 S.Ct. 75 (1988).

Before EDWARDS, BORK, and WILLIAMS, Circuit Judges.

BORK, Circuit Judge:

This is a libel action in which Liberty Lobby, Inc., a citizens' group, seeks fifty million dollars in compensatory and punitive damages from the publisher of *The Wall Street Journal.* After more than a year of [pretrial] discovery, the district court granted defendants' motion for summary judgment on the first count, and judgment on the pleadings as to the remaining four counts of Liberty Lobby's complaint. We affirm the district court's disposition of the case in all respects, although we sometimes follow a different route to the same result.

I.

On September 28, 1984, *The Wall Street Journal* published a column entitled "Controversial Publisher—Racial Purist Uses Reagan Plug." The article, written by defendant Rich Jaroslovsky, a ten-year veteran of *The Journal*'s news staff, bore the logo "Politics 84," and was published as part of *The Journal*'s coverage of the 1984 presidential campaign. * * * The article states that one Roger Pearson, an advocate of racial betterment through genetic selection, had received a letter of commendation from President Reagan and that he had exploited the letter to promote his controversial publications. According to the story, the letter was composed by a Pearson associate on the White House staff, and President Reagan had never met Mr. Pearson. Jaroslovsky concluded that the incident demonstrated "how a highly ideological presidency—conservative or liberal—can be used by well-connected outside activities to gain respectability."

In the course of discussing Pearson's past activities and associations, the article asserted:

Other Pearson writings appeared in Western Destiny, a magazine published by the far right, anti-

Semitic Liberty Lobby. Mr. Pearson edited Western Destiny briefly in the mid–1960s and wrote several books on race and eugenics that were issued by Liberty Lobby's publishing arm. These pamphlets are still sold by the National Socialist White People's Party, the Arlington, Va. based American Nazi group; Mr. Pearson says he doesn't have any connection with that group.

On November 15, 1984, Liberty Lobby filed a complaint for libel in the United States District Court for the District of Columbia, basing jurisdiction on diversity of citizenship. . . . Named as defendants were Dow Jones & Co., Inc., the company that publishes *The Journal*, and Rich Jaroslovsky, the author of the Pearson article.

Liberty Lobby claims that the quoted passage is false and defamatory in two respects. First, although Liberty Lobby admits to being an anti-Zionist organization, it claims that *The Journal*'s characterization of it as "anti-Semitic" is false and injurious to its reputation. Second, Liberty Lobby contends that it never published the magazine, *Western Destiny*; nor did it issue any books by Mr. Pearson. It further contends that no books or pamphlets issued by Liberty Lobby are or were sold by the National Socialist White People's Party.

In November, 1985, after eleven months of voluminous discovery had been completed, Liberty Lobby sought and was granted leave to amend its complaint to add four additional causes of action for libel against Dow Jones. These claims were based upon a column entitled "There's Nothing Like a Libel Trial for an Education" which appeared in the editorial section of *The Wall Street Journal* on October 11, 1985. The column was written by Ms. Suzanne Garment, a member of *The Journal*'s editorial staff. . . .

Using as a vehicle the trial of another libel action, one between Liberty Lobby and *The National Review*, a magazine of opinion, the column gave the author's views "about libel suits in general and their place in democratic politics." In introducing its theme, the Garment column noted that Liberty Lobby's claim based on the Jaroslovsky article was at

that time pending before the district court, stating:

Over the years, Liberty Lobby and Mr. Carto have sued a number of publishers that called them racist and anti-Semitic. Still pending is a Liberty Lobby suit against The Wall Street Journal, which last year called Liberty Lobby "anti-Semitic" and reported that it had published various tracts by a promoter of racial betterment through genetic selection.

This republication of allegedly defamatory material from the Jaroslovsky story forms the basis for Liberty Lobby's second cause of action.

The body of the Garment column discussed Liberty Lobby's trial strategy in defending a counterclaim for libel brought against it by *The National Review*. The column described in detail the courtroom scene prior to the delivery of opening arguments to the jury. It noted the presence of "a good-looking black female lawyer" at Liberty Lobby's counsel table with Mr. Lane, the lead counsel, and went on to state, "[t]he moment the jury filed in— all black, as is not uncommon in the District— you began to suspect that Mr. Lane might have something in mind." The column then summarized Liberty Lobby's opening argument to the jury, at one point quoting Mr. Lane as saying:

If you read the words of Adolf Hitler regarding superior races and advanced races and inferior races, you will have difficulty separating the words of Mr. Buckley in his editorials in the National Review from the words of Adolf Hitler.

The column summed up its discussion of Liberty Lobby's trial strategy by stating:

So we see the Liberty Lobby standing up in court and calling Mr. Buckley racist, most likely calculating that black jurors will be too hypnotized by this possibility to consider other facts important. This is not just an ordinary lawyer's trick. This is breathtaking in its daring. Most of us would be embarrassed to appeal to a racial or religious minority audience so crudely. We know the Fair Play Patrol would at once swoop down and cart us away. But the Carto team is of sterner stuff, able to put its head down and go for broke.

The column questioned the utility of highly inflammatory libel suits in a democratic society, and compared "Louis Farrakhan wowing them at Madison Square Garden" to "Mark Lane in front of the jury." The statements in the Garment column concerning Liberty Lobby's conduct during *The National Review* trial form the basis for its third, fourth and fifth causes of action for libel against Dow Jones.

On December 16, 1985, appellees filed a motion for summary judgment on the first cause of action based on the Jaroslovsky article, and for judgment on the pleadings as to the four claims based on the Garment column.

On July 10, 1986, the district court issued its memorandum opinion and order, granting appellee's motions and dismissing Liberty Lobby's complaint with prejudice. The district court found that the truth or falsity of *The Journal*'s statements concerning Liberty Lobby's publishing activities was "immaterial," for, even if false, they were not "defamatory in the least of Liberty Lobby but for the . . . characterization of the entire conglomerate as 'anti-Semitic.' " On the latter score, the district court "suspect[ed] . . . that the term 'anti-Semitic,' as Jaroslovsky has used it, is probably constitutionally protected opinion." However, the district court went on to hold that, to the extent the charge of anti-Semitism had any objectively verifiable factual content, the statement was substantially true. Relying upon the contents of a multi-volume file Liberty Lobby kept on publications about Jews and upon the views expounded in Liberty Lobby's official organ, *The Spotlight,* the district court found that appellees' "evidence of Liberty Lobby's institutional anti-Semitism in its most malign sense" was "compelling." With only the bald denial of the affidavit of Willis Carto, Liberty Lobby's founder and chief executive officer, weighing against appellees' evidence, the district court concluded that no reasonable jury could find by a preponderance of the evidence that the ascription of anti-Semitism to Liberty Lobby was false.

The district court also found that dismissal of Liberty Lobby's claims based on the Jaroslovsky article was mandated by the complete lack of evidence that any of the allegedly defamatory statements were published with actual malice. The court noted that Jaroslovsky had spent three months on intermittent research, had reviewed a large number of Liberty Lobby documents, and had consulted various articles about Liberty Lobby. Jaroslovsky had shown these materials to his editor, who concurred in his judgment that Liberty Lobby was anti-Semitic. *The Journal*'s Washington bureau chief, who was familiar with Liberty Lobby's radio program and its official publication, *The Spotlight*, agreed. The district court concluded that no reasonable jury could find that *The Journal* had acted with knowledge of falsity or reckless disregard of the truth, "there being no evidence of [actual malice] at all, much less proof that is clear and convincing."

Turning to the Garment column's reference to the Jaroslovsky article, the district court found that this claim was "extinguished by the demise of Count I." In the alternative, the court held that the "republication" was shielded by the common law privilege accorded to fair and accurate accounts of official reports and records.

The remainder of the Garment column was, in the district court's view, "simply descriptions of Garment's personal reactions to Liberty Lobby's attorney's opening statement, nothing more." Even assuming Liberty Lobby's charges of bias or vindictiveness were true, Garment's comments on *The National Review* trial were, in the lower court's view, expressions of opinion entitled to absolute first amendment protection.

II.

* * *

Where a public figure, which Liberty Lobby concedes that it is, or a public official pursues a libel action, first amendment requirements supplant both the common law of defamation and the normal standards of appellate review in several respects. First, such a plaintiff must demonstrate by at least a fair preponderance of the evidence that the allegedly defamatory statement is false. *See Philadelphia Newspapers, Inc. v. Hepps* (1986). . . .

This requirement is fully applicable at the summary judgment stage. Thus, where a district court concludes upon motion or its own initiative (after proper notice) that no reasonable jury could find by a fair preponderance of the evidence that the statement complained of is false, summary judgment for the defendant should be granted. Where the question of truth or falsity is a close one, a court should err on the side of nonactionability.

Second, a public figure or official must demonstrate by clear and convincing evidence that the defendant published the defamatory falsehood with "actual malice," that is, with "knowledge that it was false or with reckless disregard of whether it was false or not." *New York Times v. Sullivan* (1964). To support a libel judgment, there must be evidence which establishes in convincing fashion "that the defendant in fact entertained serious doubts as to the truth of his publication." *St. Amant v. Thompson* (1968). Through the defendant's own actions or statements, the dubious nature of his sources, the inherent improbability of the story or other circumstantial evidence, the plaintiff must demonstrate that the defendant himself entertained a "high degree of awareness of . . . probable falsity." This requirement, too, is applicable when considering a motion for summary judgment. The question for the court is "whether the evidence presented is such that a reasonable jury might find that actual malice had been shown with convincing clarity." *Anderson v. Liberty Lobby* (1986).

Finally, statements of opinion or belief are nonactionable as a matter of law. *See Bose Corp. v. Consumers Union of United States* (1984) ("Under our Constitution 'there is no such thing as a false idea. However pernicious an opinion may seem, we depend for its correction not on the conscience of judges and juries but on the competition of other ideas.'") (quoting *Gertz v. Robert Welch, Inc.* (1974)). The absolute protection accorded statements of opinion stems, in part, from plaintiff's burden of proving falsity, a component of which is proving that a statement is amenable to disproof. But as the language of *Gertz* suggests, the rule has independent roots in the limitations which the first amendment places on the intrusion of any branch of government, including [the federal] courts, into the marketplace of ideas.

First amendment concerns also affect a court's posture in reviewing the evidence presented on summary judgment. Normally, the evidence presented upon a motion for summary judgment is construed in favor of the party opposing the motion. As to the nonconstitutional issues in a libel action, this standard still obtains. However, where the constitutional prerequisites of falsity and actual malice are at issue "an appellate court has an obligation to 'make an independent examination of the whole record' in order to make sure that 'the judgment does not constitute a forbidden intrusion on the field of free expression.'" While . . . prior cases involved appellate review of trial verdicts in libel actions, logic and considerations of judicial administration dictate that the same level of review apply to the granting of summary judgment.

We turn to an analysis of the statements at issue and the district court's rulings.

A.

Unlike the district court, we think Jaroslovsky's statements concerning Liberty Lobby's publishing activities have defamatory content independent of the charge of anti-Semitism. Under District of Columbia law, a statement is defamatory, "if it tends to injure plaintiff in his trade, profession or community standing, or lower him in the estimation of the community." *Howard Univ. v. Best* (1984). "It is only when the court can say that the publication is not reasonably capable of any defamatory meaning and cannot reasonably be understood in any defamatory sense that it can rule as a matter of law that it was not libelous." *Levy v. American Mut. Ins. Co.* (1964).

Here, *The Journal* article by Jaroslovsky

indicated that Liberty Lobby had published Pearson's theories of racial supremacy and genetic selection, and that these publications were sold by an American Nazi organization. A jury could find that such an allegation, standing alone, tended "to lower [Liberty Lobby] in the estimation of the community or to deter third persons from dealing or associating with [Liberty Lobby]." We have little doubt that a District of Columbia court would find that the allegation of this type of publishing activity has sufficient defamatory content to go to a jury.

We find, however, that these statements about Liberty Lobby's publishing activities are nonactionable as a matter of federal constitutional law for two reasons. First, we are convinced that no reasonable jury could find by a fair preponderance of the evidence that these statements are false. Second, even if a jury could find that the Jaroslovsky article falsely exaggerated the connection between Liberty Lobby and Pearson's writings, there is absolutely no evidence that the statements were made with "a high degree of awareness of . . . probable falsity."

1.

It is undisputed that both *Western Destiny* and the Pearson books mentioned in the Jaroslovsky article were published by an unincorporated entity located in Torrance, California, doing business as The Noontide Press. The record evidence that both Mr. Carto and Liberty Lobby exercise substantial financial and editorial control over the publishing activities of Noontide is, in our view, compelling.

In their first set of interrogatories, appellees asked Liberty Lobby to:

state whether plaintiff or any of its officers or directors or their spouses controls or ever has controlled, in whole or in part, directly of indirectly, formally or informally, any aspect of the business or publishing activities or operations or the editorial policy or decision-making of The Noontide Press.

In an answer sworn by Mr. Carto, the appellant responded in the affirmative and went on to indicate that Mr. Carto had acted in an "advisory capacity" to Noontide for the last twenty years. In deposition testimony, Mr. Carto admitted that he was the central figure in the establishment of Noontide Press and had chosen its name. Noontide's nominal director, Mr. Thomas Marcellus, testified that Mr. Carto exercises considerable control over the selection of the books that Noontide will publish. In support of their dispositive motion, appellees also introduced the sworn testimony of Mr. Robert M. Bartell, a member of Liberty Lobby's Board of Policy until 1984. In this testimony, given in an unrelated action involving Liberty Lobby, Mr. Bartell described Noontide's publishing activities as follows:

a pamphlet or a book of some kind was run through Liberty Lobby's executive staff for reading, for approval, for changes, for whatever. . . . And the finished copy is then given back to Mr. Carto and it goes back to California and is published by Noontide Press, and this has been going on for years and years and years, then [Mr. Carto] doesn't have to say that I am Noontide Press although we all know he is.

Until a fire in 1984, Liberty Lobby and The Noontide Press shared office space in Torrance, California. During the 1960s, when the Pearson books were published, Mr. Carto was a board member of The Legion, the incorporated entity behind Noontide Press. Mr. Bruce Hollman, a Liberty Lobby director, also sat on The Legion's board at the time of the publications at issue. At the same time, Mr. Robert Kuttner, listed as a contributing editor of *Western Destiny*, was also a member of Liberty Lobby's Board of Directors. During this time, Roger Pearson was the editor of *Western Destiny*, and Mr. Carto, under the pseudonym "E.L. Anderson," was its sole associate editor.

The Legion's application to do business as Noontide Press is signed by Mrs. Elizabeth Carto, Mr. Carto's wife, and a supervisor at Liberty Lobby. The application also lists Bruce Hollman as one of Noontide's principals, himself a Liberty Lobby director. Mr. Carto has personally chosen the only two directors of Noontide, and they received their positions by contacting Liberty Lobby through *The Spotlight*. The record also indicates that The Noontide Press advertises only in Liberty Lobby's official organ, *The Spotlight*. In return, Liberty Lobby purchases almost half of the books for its "Liberty Library" from Noontide. Appellees have also adduced evidence that Liberty Lobby provides substantial financial support to The Legion and Noontide.

Upon this record, we have little difficulty in concluding that both *The Journal*'s characterization of Noontide as Liberty Lobby's "publishing arm" and its statement that Liberty Lobby "published" *Western Destiny* are substantially true. Given the substantial ties between Mr. Carto, Liberty Lobby and Noontide, we are convinced that Liberty Lobby could not demonstrate by a fair preponderance of the evidence that these statements are false.

In *Tavoulareas v. Piro* (1987), *The Washington Post* ran a story charging that the President of Mobil Oil Corp., William Tavoulareas, had "set up" his son Peter in a shipping company which did substantial business with Mobil. Both father and son sued in libel, claiming that the "set-up" allegation was false and defamatory. In fact, Atlas Shipping, the company Peter Tavoulareas was associated with, dealt only with Samarco, a Saudi/Mobil joint venture. The Tavoulareases claimed that the article created the false and defamatory impression that there was a "direct link" between Mobil and Atlas.

Reviewing the record, this court found that Mobil's and the elder Tavoulareas' links with Atlas were substantial and palpable, although in no way formalized. Mobil had recruited the first head of Atlas Shipping, had provided it with ships and office space, and had even supplied it with an interim manager when its most senior executive departed. Under these circumstances, the court held that "even if *The Post* article failed to make clear the formal, corporate relationship between Mobil, Samarco, and Atlas . . . the defendants cannot in reason and in law be held liable for accurately reporting the direct link that undisputably did exist between Mobil and Atlas."

We think the logic of *Tavoulareas* is controlling here. Newspaper reporters should not be required to convert the results of investigative journalism into a Standard & Poor's report on the formalities of corporate structure. The sting of the charge that Liberty Lobby has approved of and assisted in the dissemination of Mr. Pearson's controversial views and the *Western Destiny* magazine, is substantially true. *See Restatement (Second) of Torts*, §581A comment f (1977). ("It is not necessary to establish the literal truth of the precise statement made. Slight inaccuracies of expression are immaterial provided that the defamatory charge is true in substance."). Moreover, there is evidence in this record that Mr. Carto specifically designed the Liberty Lobby/Legion/Noontide/IHR network so as to divorce Liberty Lobby's name from those of its less reputable affiliates. It is Mr. Carto's right to pour his political activities into whatever corporate shell he desires. What he may not do is silence those who see through the form to the reality.

2.

Even if a reasonable jury could find that Jaroslovsky and his editors falsely exaggerated Liberty Lobby's role in the dissemination of the Pearson books and *Western Destiny*, no jury could find that they did so with knowledge of falsity or reckless disregard for truth. After over a year of discovery, Liberty Lobby has not been able to adduce a scintilla of evidence indicating that anyone involved in the preparation of the Pearson article entertained any doubt about its veracity.

To the contrary, appellees' evidence reveals that Jaroslovsky thoroughly documented his story and relied upon wholly reputable sources in drawing the connection between Liberty Lobby and Noontide's publishing activities. Among Jaroslovsky's sources was a June 1980 issue of the *Facts* newsletter published by the Anti-Defamation League of B'nai B'rith ("ADL"). Under the subtitle "Front for Anti-Semitism," the article states:

For almost a quarter century, Liberty Lobby has served as a front for Carto's seamier operations and activities. Among these have been . . . *Western*

Destiny, a magazine that published racist, Nazi-tinged articles extolling the Nordic mystique; and Noontide Press, publisher of anti-Semitic, racist, and pro-Nazi books. . . .

Later, the article refers to Noontide as "a Carto-influenced front." Other ADL publications which Jaroslovsky reviewed in preparing the Pearson story referred to the "Carto Network" and described Noontide and *Western Destiny* as "Carto-run" and "official partners" in the Liberty Lobby conglomerate.

Jaroslovsky also relied upon an article by C.H. Simonds, entitled "The Strange Story of Willis Carto," which appeared in the September 10, 1971 issue of *The National Review*. The article flatly states that "[t]he sole owner and proprietor of Noontide is Willis Carto." The article chronicles Mr. Carto's attempts to distance himself and Liberty Lobby from The Legion/Noontide network but concludes that "[t]he most casual observer soon detects a tight relationship among the various components of Carto's empire. The same names keep popping up on this letterhead, that masthead or board; it's a closed group, and only very rarely will the name of an outsider appear."

During the composition of the story Jaroslovsky also possessed a copy of the masthead of *Western Destiny*, listing "E. L. Anderson," a known Carto pseudonym, as the sole associate editor. He also had obtained an advertisement published in *Western Destiny*, listing two Pearson books as available from Noontide Press. Finally, Jaroslovsky had a clipping from the Nazi publication, *White Power*, which advertised two of the Pearson works published by Noontide.

We think *The Wall Street Journal*'s good faith reliance on previously published reports in reputable sources of Liberty Lobby's connections with Noontide and *Western Destiny* precludes a finding of actual malice as a matter of law. *See Rosanova v. Playboy Enterprises, Inc.* (1978) ("The subjective awareness of probable falsity required by [*St. Amant*] cannot be found where, as here, the publisher's allegations are supported by a multitude of previous reports upon which the publisher reasonably relied.").

B.

We turn next to the charge of anti-Semitism, leveled against Liberty Lobby in the Jaroslovsky article and reported as the subject of a lawsuit in the Garment column. The district court suggested that the term "anti-Semitic" as used by Jaroslovsky is probably a constitutionally protected statement of opinion. The court went on to say that if "anti-Semitism" were regarded as an "objectively vertifiable fact," it was amply proved against Liberty Lobby in this case. We are unwilling to say that the term has no core meaning so that it is an expression of opinion in any context, and, as such, always constitutionally protected. Like many words, the term "anti-Semitic" has both descriptive and normative content. Compare, for example, the use of "fascist" as a generic epithet, with its use in such a statement as "He was a close companion of Mussolini and a Fascist." We tend to agree with the district court that if the term "anti-Semitic" has a core, factual meaning, then the truth of the description was proved here.

We rest our decision, however, on the fact that Liberty Lobby has adduced no evidence tending to show the charge of anti-Semitism was made with the requisite actual malice. In preparing his story, Jaroslovsky relied upon various ADL publications, the Simonds article in *The National Review*, as well as the statements of the former general counsel of Liberty Lobby which were published in *The Washington Star*.

The Journal's reliance on these and other reputable sources would preclude any finding of actual malice as a matter of law. In *Liberty Lobby v. Anderson (1984)*, Liberty Lobby and Mr. Carto sued the journalist Jack Anderson and others for referring to Mr. Carto as "the leading anti-Semite in the country" and characterizing Liberty Lobby as "anti-Semitic." In preparing their story, Mr. Anderson's reporters had relied upon various published accounts of Liberty Lobby's activities, including the ADL publications and *The National Review* article relied upon by Jaroslovsky here. Even applying the less stringent preponderance of the evidence test, this court held that reliance on these sources precluded a jury from finding actual malice. Liberty Lobby was well aware of its status as a public figure from the outset of this litigation. Moreover, this court's decision in the *Anderson* case was issued two weeks before Liberty Lobby filed its complaint in this action. Yet, after a year of discovery Liberty Lobby has produced *no evidence* to indicate that Jaroslovsky or his editors had any reason to doubt the same sources relied upon by *Anderson*. The district court's entry of summary judgment for appellees was clearly warranted on this ground alone.

C.

Count three of Liberty Lobby's amended complaint seeks to attach liability to the Garment column's repetition of the charge of anti-Semitism and the publishing statements in referring to this lawsuit. Our prior determination that the publishing statements are substantially true would seem to preclude liability for their repetition. It is conceivable that liability could attach to the Garment column's repetition of the charge of anti-Semitism if it could be shown that the statement was false and was repeated with knowledge of falsity or reckless disregard of truth. However, we think the Garment column's discussion of a pending lawsuit is privileged as a fair and accurate description of a judicial proceeding under both the common law of the District of Columbia and the Constitution.

The Garment column states, "[s]till pending is a Liberty Lobby suit against *The Wall Street Journal*, which last year called Liberty Lobby 'anti-Semitic' and reported that it had published various tracts by a promoter of racial betterment through genetic selection." The common law of libel has long held that one who republishes a defamatory statement "adopts" it as his own, and is liable in equal measure to the original defamer. * * *

To ameliorate the chilling effect that the republication rule would have on the reporting of controversial matters of public interest, common law courts, including those of the District of Columbia, recognize a privilege of fair and accurate accounts of governmental proceedings. *See Phillips v. Evening Star Newspaper Co.* (1980). Following the *Restatement*, the District of Columbia common law abandons the concept of "adoption" where a report of an official proceeding is "(a) accurate and complete, or a fair abridgement of what has occurred, and (b) published for the purpose of informing the public as to a matter of public concern." *Phillips* (quoting *Restatement (Second) of Torts* §611 (1977)).

Federal constitutional concerns are implicated as well when common law liability is asserted against a defendant for an accurate account of judicial proceedings. In *Cox Broadcasting Co. v. Cohn* (1975), the father of a deceased rape victim brought suit for common law invasion of privacy against a television station which mentioned his minor daughter's name in conjunction with its report on the trial of those charged with the crime. The station's reporter had obtained the victim's name by attending the trial and inspecting the indictments in the case. The Georgia Supreme Court rejected the television station's first amendment defense, holding that the father was entitled to take his claim to a jury.

The Supreme Court reversed, noting that, "[w]ith respect to judicial proceedings in particular, the function of the press serves to guarantee the fairness of trials and to bring to bear the beneficial effects of public scrutiny upon the administration of justice." *See also Craig v. Harney* (1947) ("A trial is a public event. What transpires in a courtroom is public property. . . . Those who see and hear what transpired can report it with impunity."). The Supreme Court held that Mr. Cohn's suit was barred as a matter of law, stating, "the First and Fourteenth Amendments command nothing less than that the states may not impose sanctions on the publication of truthful information contained in official court records open to public inspection.''

The Garment column's report on this lawsuit is privileged both under the common law and the Supreme Court's decision in *Cox*. It fairly and accurately describes the substance of this action, in the context of a broader discussion of libel suits in general, clearly a matter of public concern. Indeed, since libel suits are government proceedings which by definition involve material that is allegedly false and defamatory, no meaningful discussion of such suits would be possible unless such reports were privileged. The district court's dismissal of this count on the pleadings was clearly appropriate.

D.

The Garment column's discussion of *The National Review* trial is similarly protected. To the extent that it constitutes a factual report on Liberty Lobby's opening argument in *The National Review* trial, the Garment column is privileged as an accurate report of a government proceeding. It is undisputed that Ms. Garment attended the opening day of the trial and used the official transcript of that proceeding in the preparation of her column. Where the column quotes or summarizes Mr. Lane's opening argument, comparison with the official transcript reveals that it does so with complete accuracy. Mr. Lane did indeed ''explain[] how *The National Review* had tried to bring down great black men'' and he did compare the writings of Mr. Buckley to the words of Adolf Hitler.

No extended analysis is necessary to conclude that the remainder of the Garment column is constitutionally protected opinion under *Ollman v. Evans* (1984). The column appeared on the editorial page of *The Journal*, and is shot through with the language of personal opinion. The column characterizes Mr. Lane's argument as ''crude,'' ''ugly,'' ''pernicious'' and ''breathtaking in its daring.'' These are clearly statements of opinion dependent upon personal perspective: what is a crude and ugly appeal to some, may be forthright and vigorous advocacy to others.

* * * Statements of this type are simply not amenable to disproof. Whether or not Mr. Lane in front of a jury ''generates a distinct shiver'' is a subjective impression, and as such inherently unverifiable. * * *

On appeal, Liberty Lobby contends that several alleged factual errors in the Garment column strip it of the constitutional protection otherwise accorded to statements of opinion. Appellant argues that the ''black lawyer'' placed at its counsel table by the Garment column, although a law school graduate, was not a member of the bar. It further contends that *The National Review* exercised its preemptory challenges to assure an all black jury at trial because it intended to put on favorable testimony from black witnesses. Thus, the Garment column's ''implication'' that Liberty Lobby chose a black lawyer and a black jury to further its trial strategy is, in Liberty Lobby's view, false. * * * Liberty Lobby argues that the Garment column's failure to fully and accurately disclose the underlying facts of *The National Review* trial precludes it from claiming the status of protected opinion.

As both a legal and factual matter, Liberty Lobby's argument is utterly devoid of merit. First, * * * [w]hile the stated facts underlying an opinion may support a libel action if they are themselves false and defamatory, an opinion itself never can.

Second, the alleged inaccuracies here are either minor in the extreme or nonexistent. That the black woman at Liberty Lobby's counsel table was a law school graduate but not a member of the bar is immaterial. Referring to her as a lawyer is not of itself defamatory, and is, in any event, substantially true. Moreover, the Garment column does not state that Liberty Lobby selected on all black jury. The article stated that an all black jury ''is not uncommon in the District''; it did not implicitly or explicitly attribute the composition of the jury to either party. The district court was clearly correct in holding that the bulk of the Garment column is constitutionally protected under *Ollman*. Since opinions are nonactionable as a matter of law, dismissal on the pleadings of counts three, four, and five of Liberty Lobby's amended complaint was appropriate.

III.

On appeal, Liberty Lobby raises several issues collateral to the merits of its libel action. First, appellant asserts that the district court judge erred in failing to recuse himself after counsel for Liberty Lobby made two oral motions for his disqualification. These motions were based upon the district court's decision not to allow Liberty Lobby to further depose Ms. Garment. Second, Liberty Lobby asks us to pass on a third written motion for the recusal of the district court judge. This motion was filed after the district court granted appellees' dispositive motion, and has not been passed upon by the district court judge. Finally, Liberty Lobby claims that the district court's discovery rulings precluded it from developing evidence of actual malice on the part of Ms. Garment, and prevented it from discovering who actually authored the Garment column's reference to the Jaroslovsky article. These claims need detain us only briefly. * * *

IV.

This suit epitomizes one of the most troubling aspects of modern libel litigation: the use of the libel complaint as a weapon to harass.[1] Despite the patent insufficiency of a number of appellant's claims, it has managed to embroil a media defendant in over three years of costly and contentious litigation. The message to this defendant and the press at large is clear: discussion of Liberty Lobby is expensive. However well-documented a story, however unimpeachable a reporter's source, he or she will have to think twice about publishing where litigation, even to a successful motion for summary judgment, can be very expensive if not crippling.

We have conducted an independent review of the record in this case, and have found that each of appellant's claims is clearly barred on several common law and constitutional grounds. The district court's judgment dismissing all of Liberty Lobby's claims with prejudice is

Affirmed.

---

[1]Liberty Lobby has brought a number of libel suits against media defendants that have characterized it as racially prejudiced or anti-Semitic. * * * None of these suits has been successful and in *no instance* has Liberty Lobby been allowed to present its claims to a jury.

INTRODUCTION

Defamation law today is a jumble of constitutional and state law rules. Its status is largely the result of historical accident, and in the often-quoted words of the late Dean William Prosser, "[t]here is a great deal of the law of defamation which makes no sense." Prior to the landmark 1964 Supreme Court decision in *New York Times Co. v. Sullivan*, defamation—which includes the twin torts of libel and slander [2]—was considered wholly outside the purview of the first amendment. Since that decision, however, a variety of constitutional requirements have been superimposed over the already complex body of state law, which was largely adopted by state courts from the English common law and, in some cases, refined statutorily by state legisla-

---

[2]Historically, the law of libel applied to written defamation, while the law of slander dealt with oral defamation. Today, however, virtually all American jurisdictions treat defamation suits against the mass media—even broadcast stations—as libel rather than slander. Accordingly, the discussion in the text will use the terms "libel" and "defamation" synonymously, and the peculiar rules regarding slander will not be considered here.

tures. Although many of these concepts remain extremely important in defamation cases, the constitutional rules developed in *New York Times* and its progeny, which have rendered portions of state law obsolete, are central in virtually all such suits against the media. Nonetheless, some state courts have continued to cling to as much of the old common law as they can, thus adding to the confusion in many jurisdictions.

The *New York Times* case arose out of the civil rights movement of the late 1950s and early 1960s, and the facts of the case illustrate dramatically the potentially crippling impact of defamation suits. L. B. Sullivan, police commissioner of Montgomery, Alabama, sued the *Times* for $500,000 on the basis of a March 29, 1960, advertisement run in the newspaper by a civil rights group. Also named as defendants were four black ministers from Alabama who were connected with the group. Of the 650,000 copies of the *Times* containing the advertisement, only 394 were distributed in Alabama, and only 35 or so found their way into Montgomery County.

The full-page ad, headlined "Heed Their Rising Voices," claimed that nonviolent civil rights workers in the South were being met "by an unprecedented wave of terror" and described a variety of incidents in which peaceful protests had been answered by public officials with violence and harassment. It detailed the efforts of "Southern violators" to intimidate Dr. Martin Luther King, Jr., and explained that such tactics had included arrests on trumped-up charges and assaults on his person and family. While Sullivan was not mentioned by name, two of the incidents—a demonstration at the state capitol and a protest at Alabama State College—took place in Montgomery.

The commissioner argued that because he was in charge of the city's police, the advertisement imputed to him police misconduct in connection with these events and linked him to the harassment of Dr. King. He also pointed to various factual errors, all relatively minor, contained in the ad; for example, Montgomery police had not literally "ringed" the Alabama State campus, though they had appeared there in large numbers on various occasions, and Dr. King had been arrested only four times, not seven. But most importantly, Sullivan contended that the ad's statements were untrue because most of the incidents had taken place before he became commissioner; therefore, the statements were false because they erroneously suggested his involvement. Notice the twist of logic here: in order to demonstrate that the ad referred to him, Sullivan argued that it made him appear responsible for the police misconduct; but to show that the statements were untrue, he reversed field and claimed that he had not been responsible in any way.

Not surprisingly, an all-white Alabama jury wasted little time in awarding Sullivan the full $500,000 he had sought, an amount one thousand times the criminal penalty for libel then provided under state law. Meanwhile, a whole string of defamation suits against the *Times* had cropped up across Alabama, with the damages claimed exceeding $5 million. Sullivan's suit was obviously part of a Southern strategy: if officials could not stop the protest marches and demonstrations, they could at least stifle the media's coverage of the civil rights movement, coverage that was essential to the movement's success. Defamation suits offered a potent weapon, for few news organizations could afford to pay a succession of huge libel judgments. The *New York Times* was not the only target; by the time the Sullivan case reached the Supreme Court, suits totalling nearly $2 million had also been filed against CBS. Commissioner Sullivan's suit brought home in dramatic fashion the potentially "chilling effect" of the law of defamation upon the exercise of first amendment rights.

But the jury's award of $500,000 to Sullivan was completely consistent with the principles of libel law that existed in 1960, at which time defamation was considered completely outside any protection afforded by the constitution. The advertisement at issue in *New York Times Co. v. Sullivan* was not literally true, and the errors could easily have been discovered by the *Times* advertising department had staff members checked the newspaper's own files. But such carelessness on the part of one who published a falsehood that tarnished someone's reputation was irrelevant. Defamation was a "strict liability" tort, which meant that a plaintiff could recover even if there had been no carelessness—no "fault"—on the part of the defendant. The same principle applies today with respect to manufacturers who place defective and dangerous productions on the market.

Moreover, the law permitted the jury to assume that the plaintiff's reputation had been injured merely because a falsehood had been published, thus opening the door to huge verdicts against the defendant without actual proof that the plaintiff had suffered any harm. In other words, the law *presumed* that serious injury to reputation flowed from lies, even though the published material may have had the opposite effect. Justice Hugo Black, a native of Alabama who represented that state in the U.S. Senate before his appointment to the Supreme Court, observed that the *Times* ad probably made Mr. Sullivan something of a folk hero and thus actually enhanced his standing and prestige in the community. Yet the jury, consistent with the law, awarded the commissioner a half million dollars on the basis of an advertisement that appeared almost invisibly in Montgomery, referred to him only by a strained construction of its language, contained relatively minor misstatements of fact, and arguably boosted rather than harmed his reputation in the community. The Supreme Court of Alabama affirmed.

On appeal to the U.S. Supreme Court, the *Times'* lawyers drew an analogy between the Sedition Act of 1798 and the defamation law of Alabama which permitted Commissioner Sullivan's suit. The act, they pointed out, punished criticism of the government by making seditious libel a crime, and Alabama law accomplished the same result by authorizing government officials to recover damages for criticism directed at them. If, as was widely believed despite the lack of a Supreme Court ruling directly on the question, the Sedition Act was unconstitutional, Alabama's libel law also offended the first amendment. The Supreme Court agreed, and the seditious libel analogy was an important part of its rationale for reversing the judgment entered against the *New York Times*. " What a State may not constitutionally bring about by means of a criminal statute is likewise beyond the reach of its civil law of libel," Justice William Brennan wrote for the Court. "The fear of damage awards under a rule such as that invoked by the Alabama courts here may be markedly more inhibiting than the fear of prosecution under a criminal statute."

The Court observed that this inhibiting effect of defamation law—a sort of self-censorship arguably as offensive as censorship by the government in advance of publication—was inconsistent with the our "profound national commitment to the principle that debate on public issues should be uninhibited, robust and wide-open, and that it may well include vehement, caustic, and sometimes unpleasantly sharp attacks on government and public officials." Justice Brennan reasoned that such expression does not forfeit first amendment protection merely because it contains factual errors and defamatory statements. "[E]rroneous statement is inevitable in free debate, and . . . it must be protected if the freedoms of expression are to have the 'breathing space' that they need to survive. * * * Whatever is added to the field of libel is taken from the field of free debate."

Accordingly, the Court for the first time ruled that defamatory statements enjoy some first amendment protection, but it stopped well short of doing away with the law of libel. Instead, the Court balanced the reputational and speech interests at stake and fashioned a rule of constitutional law designed to restrict the ability of public officials to recover for libel in all but the most egregious circumstances. Under what is now popularly known as the *"New York Times* rule," a public official may not recover damages for a defamatory statement relating to his official conduct unless he proves with "convincing clarity" that the statement was made with knowledge of its falsity or with reckless disregard for whether it was true or not.

Mr. Sullivan, the Court concluded, did not meet this burden, for he failed to demonstrate that the *Times* had acted recklessly in publishing the advertisement. Although the newspaper may have been careless in failing to verify the information in the ad by checking material in its own files, such carelessness was an insufficient basis for recovery. Moreover, the advertisement bore the endorsements of several prominent Americans, including Eleanor Roosevelt, Jackie Robinson, Bayard Rustin, Mahalia Jackson and Marlon Brando, and the *Times* advertising department had reasonably relied upon the good reputations of these individuals.

As the *Liberty Lobby* case reproduced at the beginning of this chapter indicates, the *New York Times* rule has been extended to defamation suits brought by persons in the public eye—"public figures"—who do not hold any government office. In *Gertz v. Robert Welch, Inc.*, the Supreme Court applied a different principle in suits by private individuals, ruling that such plaintiffs may recover upon a lesser showing of fault, usually simple carelessness or, in legal parlance, "negligence." Whatever the status of a given plaintiff, it is now clear that the era of "strict liability" in defamation law is over, at least in cases brought against the news media.[3] Other troublesome features of the old system, such as the rule that allowed a jury to presume a plaintiff had been harmed, have also been eliminated or significantly modified. Before considering in detail the principles that govern modern defamation litigation, however, it is important to examine the environment in which these suits arise more than twenty years after *New York Times Co. v. Sullivan*.

As the nation has moved steadily into the "information age," defamation suits—particularly against the news media—have become a growth industry. A recent study conducted at the University of Iowa reveals that during the period 1974–1984, seventy percent of all libel cases were brought against the news media, with more than two-thirds of those directed towards newspapers (despite the fact that broadcast stations outnumber newspapers nationwide by about six to one). Moreover, in sixty percent of those suits against the press, the plaintiffs were politicians, nonelected public officials, entertainers, businessmen and other highly visible, prominent persons who routinely find themselves the subjects of news stories. As Professor Rodney Smolla has pointed out in his provocative book *Suing the Press* (1986), "the list of famous Americans who have taken to suing publishers, broadcasters, reporters, writers, and advertisers . . . reads as if it were randomly generated from *Who's Who*." That list includes Carol Burnett, General William Westmoreland, Johnny

---

[3] Although the *New York Times* case itself involved four clergymen as well as the newspaper, there has been considerable confusion as to whether the first amendment safeguards announced in that decision and in *Gertz* apply to nonmedia defendants. The Supreme Court suggested in *Dun & Bradstreet, Inc. v. Greenmoss Builders, Inc.* (1985) that the constitutional rules are the same no matter who the defendant happens to be. Subsequently, however, the Court indicated in *Philadelphia Newspapers, Inc. v. Hepps* (1986) that the question is still open.

Carson, Ralph Nader, Norman Mailer, Elizabeth Taylor, Wayne Newton, former Senator Paul Laxalt, Jerry Falwell, William Tavoulareas, and former Philadelphia Mayor William J. Green.

These "public" plaintiffs have not asked for paltry sums in compensation for the alleged harm to their reputations. Senator Laxalt, for example, sought $250 million in a suit against the *Sacramento Bee* for stories linking him to a grand jury investigation of Nevada gambling casinos. General Westmoreland sued CBS for $120 million after the network broadcast a documentary accusing him of participating in a conspiracy to falsify intelligence estimates of enemy troop strength in Vietnam. Tavoulareas, president of the Mobil Oil Corporation, claimed $100 million in a suit against the *Washington Post*, which had published a story stating that he had "set up" his son in a sweetheart business deal with Mobil and implying that this conduct violated business ethical standards and maybe even federal securities laws. Entertainer Burnett sought $10 million from the *National Enquirer* based on a four-sentence report in a gossip column implying that she had been drunk at a Washington restaurant. Mayor Green asked for $5.1 million from a CBS-owned television station that had reported he was under federal criminal investigation.

While a jury rarely awards the fully amount of damages claimed in any kind of case, jurors in many recent defamation suits against the media have not been at all stingy; in fact, the *average* award exceeds $1 million. Mr. Tavoulareas, for example, received a $2.2 million verdict, Miss Burnett a $1.6 million award. And these verdicts pale in comparison to the $9.2 million assessed against the small *Alton* (Illinois) *Telegraph*, which forced the paper into bankruptcy, the $19 million verdict returned in singer Wayne Newton's suit against NBC, and the $26.5 million awarded a former "Miss Wyoming" in a suit against *Penthouse* magazine.

Moreover, a jury in a defamation case is quite likely to find in favor of the plaintiff. A recent study shows that juries in defamation cases brought against media defendants return verdicts favorable to the plaintiffs a whopping ninety percent of the time. The same study, however, shows that about seventy-five percent of those cases are reversed on appeal, and "megaverdicts" of the type noted above are usually reduced significantly or eliminated altogether by the trial judge or the appellate court. For example, Miss Burnett's award was ultimately reduced to $200,000, Mr. Tavoulareas' jury verdict was overturned by the trial judge, and the Miss Wyoming's case reversed on appeal, which of course meant that she received nothing. The trial judge in Mr. Newton's case found the jury's verdict excessive and gave the entertainer a choice: accept a reduced award of $5.3 million or face a new trial. Mr. Newton chose the former.

Media defendants do not necessarily escape large verdicts simply by appealing, however. According to a study by the Libel Defense Resource Center, a media-funded organization, the average award being affirmed on appeal from 1984–1986 was approximately $150,000. Until recently, the highest figure approved by an appellate court was $850,000. But in late 1987, the U.S. Court of Appeals for the Seventh Circuit upheld a $3.05 million award in *Brown & Williamson Tobacco Corp. v. Jacobson*. The case arose from a broadcast report stating that the plaintiff tobacco company had employed an advertising strategy "for attracting young people . . . to smoking." A few months later, in *DiSalle v. P.G. Publishing Co.* (1988), a Pennsylvania appellate court affirmed a jury award of $2.2 million on the basis of a newspaper article reporting accusations that a state judge had committed fraud while a practicing lawyer.

The fact that juries are inclined to find liability in the first place and to return large verdicts is disturbing to the news media for several reasons, even if the decisions of those juries are later reversed. First, as Judge Robert Bork pointed out in the *Liberty Lobby* case, vindication is not without its price. Defending even the simplest libel suit through the trial stage can cost as much as $250,000, and the price tag is higher if an appeal is necessary. The defense costs (primarily lawyers' fees) can be much, much higher; CBS, for example, is said to have spent $6 million defending the Westmoreland suit, which the general dropped midway through the trial. Similarly, *Time* magazine reportedly spent $4 million in its successful defense, at trial, of a $50 million suit brought by former Israeli Defense Minister Ariel Sharon.

Second, these enormous defense costs, as well as the possibility of a large verdict being left intact upon appeal, have caused considerable chaos in the defamation insurance market. Many media companies are finding that they can afford such insurance only if the coverage is reduced to the point that the policies protect against only the most catastrophic cases. Third, there is concern that jurors simply cannot understand the complex legal rules that govern defamation suits and thus decide cases on the basis of what they think is "fair." As Professor Smolla has observed, "[v]ery few judges and lawyers can keep [the rules] straight, let alone hope to translate them into intelligible guides for a jury."

Finally, and perhaps most important, is the fear that journalism—particularly investigative reporting—has become more timid in light of this spate of million-dollar defamation suits brought by public persons, juries that seem prone to make enormous damage awards, and spiraling legal defense costs. It was precisely this "chilling effect" on first amendment rights that the Supreme Court hoped to alleviate in *New York Times* and subsequent cases, but the "chill" seems very real today in spite of the constitutional protection afforded by those decisions.

Not surprisingly, what Professor Smolla has called the "new national pasttime" of suing the press for defamation has led to various proposals for reform, including incentives for negotiated settlements without litigation, a requirement that the unsuccessful plaintiff pay the defendant's attorney fees, and abolition of punitive damages. It may well be that the constitutional safeguards developed to date are inadequate and that significant change in this complex corner of the law is inevitable. For the moment, however, we are left with the common law rules that have emerged over centuries, overlaid by first amendment doctrine that is a product of the past twenty-five years. We now turn to an examination of these principles.

THE PLAINTIFF'S CASE

A libel plaintiff must clear several hurdles in order to prevail in his lawsuit. He is required, either by state or constitutional law, to prove that: the communication in question was *defamatory*, that is, injurious to his reputation; the statement *identified* other otherwise referred to him; the defendant *published* the offending material; the defendant was at *fault* in publishing the statement; the information was indeed *false*; and the plaintiff suffered *damages* (harm or injury) as a result of the publication. Moreover, if the defendant asserts certain defenses on his own behalf, the plaintiff must show that the defendant is not entitled to the protection of those defenses in the particular case. This section will consider the six basic elements of the plaintiff's case, leaving until later the various defenses available and the plaintiff's obligation to overcome them.

Defamatory Statements

While definitions of libel are legion, the one found in *Liberty Lobby* is as good as any: "a statement is defamatory if it tends to injure plaintiff in his trade, profession, or community standing, or to lower him in the estimation of the community." As Dean Prosser explained in his treatise on the law of torts, the key inquiry is whether the statement lowers the esteem, respect, goodwill or confidence in which the subject of that statement is held or whether it produces adverse, derogatory or unpleasant feelings or opinions about him.

Although more flowery language detailing the ways that one's reputation can be harmed are found in some court decisions and state statutes, many courts have recognized that a comprehensive definition is impossible and that each case must be decided on its own facts. As the Hawaii Supreme Court has observed, whether a statement is defamatory depends on several factors, including "the temper of the times, the current of contemporary public opinion, with the result that words, harmless in one age, in one community, may be highly damaging . . . at another time or in a different place." But even if the words are injurious to reputation, they must also be false in order to be actionable.

"Red Flag" Words. In his book *Libel and Privacy: The Prevention and Defense of Litigation*, noted libel lawyer Bruce W. Sanford wrote that "[t]he types of libel are as infinite as humanity's inhumanity—as limitless as our ability to accuse, humiliate and disgrace others." Nonetheless, defamation suits tend to involve false charges that fall into one or more of the following categories:

- criminal conduct;
- sexual impropriety or other immoral behavior;
- loathsome disease;
- professional incompetence or misconduct in one's trade or business;
- poverty or financial irresponsibility; and
- disgraceful or unusual behavior.

Obviously, words that fall into these categories should serve as a "red flag" warning reporters and editors of the defamatory potential of a particular news story.

Statements that impute criminal conduct are probably the greatest single cause of libel suits. For example, in *Marcone v. Penthouse International* (1985), the court had little difficulty in concluding that a magazine article listing the plaintiff among a group of "attorney criminals" involved in drug trafficking was defamatory. Of course, the sale of marijuana is obviously a criminal offense; other conduct, however, may or may not rise to that level. For example, some states have decriminalized possession of small amounts of marijuana for personal use, and adultery and fornication are crimes in some states but not in others.

The seriousness of the offense is also important, for courts often take into account the nature of the crime in determining whether it is defamatory. While jaywalking is undoubtedly a crime under most city ordinances, it is hardly as serious as drunken driving, and an erroneous statement that a person was charged with driving while intoxicated plainly has a greater impact on reputation than a report that he had been arrested for jaywalking. The severity of a crime enters the picture in another way as well, for a journalist may get into trouble by erroneously reporting the charges filed against the accused. For example, to report that someone is being prosecuted for murder when the actual charge is negligent homicide can be defamatory. Murder is a much more serious crime that involves intent to kill on the part of the defendant, while negligent homicide charges are filed on the basis of carelessness that results in the death of another.

The reported cases are packed with examples of words that smack of criminal activity: bigamy, assault and battery, fraud, blackmail, extortion, bribery, bootlegging, conspiracy, embezzlement, murder, obstruction of justice, selling obscene publications, rape, arson, prostitution, "organized crime," gambling, attempted suicide, thief, burglary, larceny, treason, and spying. Simply put, an accusation is defamatory if it is understood as imputing a specific criminal or wrongful act. For example, in *Dairy Barn Stores, Inc. v. ABC* (1988), a television station owned by the network broadcast a news report of an indictment charging that eight wholesale milk dealers had conspired to fix prices. Dairy Barn was not implicated, but the company's trade name was briefly displayed in the videotape accompanying the report. A New York court concluded that the broadcast could leave the impression that Dairy Barn was involved in the conspiracy.

On the other hand, if a statement is merely rhetorical hyperbole, it may be deemed opinion and thus not libelous. In *Greenbelt Cooperative Publishing Association v. Bresler* (1970), the U.S. Supreme Court ruled that a statement characterizing a developer's land deal with the city as "blackmail" was only opinion that did not charge a crime. We will return to the fact versus opinion question later in this chapter.

In common law England, a statement falsely accusing a woman of unchastity was automatically libelous. Some states so provide today by statute, and, despite the "sexual revolution" in this country during the 1960s and 1970s, charges of sexual impropriety can easily lead to defamation suits. Indeed, if *Time* magazine and other popular journals are correct in pronouncing the end of the sexual revolution, statements of sexual misconduct may once again convey the same message of immorality they carried in an earlier era.

The impact of shifting societal values on the law of defamation cannot be ignored, for what is injurious to reputation at one time might not be ground for recovery in another. It was not long ago, for example, that white persons sued newspapers that had mistakenly identified them as being black. But changing mores probably have their greatest impact in connection with concepts of immorality and unethical behavior. A statement that a man and woman were "living together" without a marriage license would hardly raise an eyebrow today, though in 1950 it undoubtedly would have suggested immoral conduct.

Because attitudes are constantly changing, journalists should be cautious with regard to *any* story about sexual behavior. As a practical matter, accusations of sexual misconduct are more likely to be considered defamatory with respect to women, perhaps because of the still-prevalent "double standard" of sexual behavior. However, comments about unusual or generally unaccepted sexual practices—regardless of the sex of the individual—are particularly dangerous. Although the "gay rights" movement has made considerable headway in this country, most courts would still consider defamatory a false statement that a man or woman is homosexual. Reports of exhibitionism, sadomasochism, or other "kinky" behavior should be treated with kid gloves, but far more "routine" matters may also cause difficulty. For example, it would be defamatory to report falsely that a man is impotent, or that an unmarried woman has had an abortion or given birth to a child.

The category for "loathsome diseases" is closely related to that for sexual misconduct and probably was developed because of the manner in which victims of venereal disease were once shunned by society. Moreover, to charge one with having a venereal disease suggests some sort of sexual misconduct, since to some extent society has long associated such afflictions with irresponsible sexual behavior. Today, it would be defamatory to report falsely that one has syphilis, genital herpes, or acquired immune deficiency syndrome (AIDS).

It is clear, however, that this category is not limited to sexually transmitted diseases. AIDS, for example, can be spread in other ways, such as through intravenous drug injections; but the charge would have the same impact upon an individual's reputation regardless of the manner in which he may have been thought to have contracted it. Thus, diseases other than those that are transmitted sexually may be considered sufficiently "loathsome," such as leprosy, mental illness, infectious hepatitis, and alcohol or drug addiction.

Charges of criminal conduct or sexual impropriety can injure the reputation of anyone, but those accusations can have a particularly serious impact upon businessmen or professionals, since they can suffer loss of business as well as reputational harm. Other types of statements can have the same negative effect upon one's business or profession, and the law has long recognized that any comment that tends to impair an individual's means of earning a living or which discredits him in his business or profession can be defamatory.

Statements about honesty, business ethics, competence, and quality of work can easily result in litigation and liability. For example, charges that an attorney engages in unethical "ambulance chasing" to obtain clients are libelous, as is a comment that a corporate executive practiced nepotism by "setting up" his son in business. A teacher's reputation would undoubtedly be tarnished by an accusation that he could not read beyond the elementary school level, and a mechanic's business would obviously suffer if word spread that he regularly used rebuilt parts but charged his customers for new ones. A corporation or other business entity can be defamed in much the same manner; for example, a Texas court once held it defamatory to state that an engineering company had no engineers on its staff.[4]

Perhaps the most common type of statement falling into this category, however, deals with the financial condition of a business. Numerous cases have arisen from incorrect reports of a company's bankruptcy and similar statements reflecting adversely on solvency. Not surprisingly, comments about personal monetary woes can also lead to trouble, for Americans tend to be quite sensitive about their financial affairs. For instance, it would be defamatory to report erroneously that a family receives welfare, that a woman is unable to obtain a loan because of a poor credit rating, or that the mayor has a string of upaid bills all over town.

The remaining category—comments reflecting disgraceful or unusual behavior—is a bit of a catch-all and, by its terms, quite subjective. A statement that a man was unkind and verbally abusive to children and small animals could lead to litigation, as could a report that he was having "wife trouble" and was about to be divorced. In a recent case falling into this broad category, author Gore Vidal brought suit after another writer, Truman Capote, stated that Vidal had been thrown out of the Kennedy White House for being drunk and insulting members of the President's family.

---

[4]"Trade libel," a related but separate tort, involves the disparagement of a company's product. It is discussed in Chapter 11 in connection with advertising.

Moreover, a news story attributing odd or eccentric behavior to a person can be be dangerous if it makes an individual appear foolish or ridiculous. For example, in a famous Maine case, *Powers v. Durgin-Snow Publishing Co.* (1958), a small town newspaper columnist observed that a local resident was a "classic example of typical Yankee thrift," since he was building his own casket and planning to dig his own grave. Although the man had told others that prices were so high that a man might soon be forced to construct his own coffin, he did not go so far as to begin the task. The court held that the article was defamatory.

Deciding What is Defamatory. As *Liberty Lobby v. Dow Jones* indicates, a judge in a defamation suit must first determine if the article in question is reasonably susceptible of a defamatory connotation. In cases involving charges of criminal misconduct or other offensive behavior, the defamatory impact is so plain that the charge is automatically deemed libelous "as a matter of law." At the other extreme, the judge may conclude that the statement cannot reasonably be read as defamatory, and the lawsuit comes to a grinding halt. A ruling that the statement is capable of a defamatory meaning results in submission of the question to the jury, which must determine whether the defamatory meaning was in fact conveyed.

In making the threshold ruling on the defamatory capability of the statement, the judge must consider the allegedly libelous passages in the context of the entire article and evaluate the words as they are commonly understood. Put another way, he must put himself in the shoes of the "average" reader and decide whether such a reader would interpret the message as libelous. Similarly, the jury is instructed that, in considering whether a defamatory meaning was actually conveyed by the article, it must take the offending statements in context, give the words their usual meaning, and measure the impact of the article as a whole upon the ordinary reader. Of course, the jury uniquely qualifies as representative of that typical reader, since jurors are, at least in theory, a representative cross-section of the community.

In many cases the question of defamatory meaning is a close one, and the context is often determinative. For example, a statement that Mr. Jones is "queer" could mean either that he is odd, eccentric or unusual, or that he is homosexual. If the story in which the comment appeared was a light feature article describing colorful local "characters," the former meaning would probably have been conveyed. If, however, the statement had been included in an article about the Mayor of New York closing the city's notorious "gay bath houses," a different connotation would obviously be drawn. The word "murderer" would seem to be automatically defamatory, but assume that a newspaper carried a photograph of antiabortion protesters picketing a clinic where abortions are performed, and one of the placards clearly visible in the photo stated that "Dr. Jones is a murderer." Surely in that context the statement would be an opinion that doctors who perform abortion engage in an immoral act, not that Dr. Jones in fact committed the crime of murder.

Some courts, particularly those in Illinois, have fashioned the "innocent construction rule" which gives defendants the benefit of the doubt in cases where the words in question are ambiguous and thus capable of different interpretations. If there are two reasonable ways to interpret a statement, one defamatory and the other nondefamatory, the court will choose the "innocent" meaning. For example, in *Rasky v. CBS* (1981), a broadcaster charged a real estate owner with being a "slumlord" in a news report that focused on his poor treatment of tenants and record of housing code violations. The Illinois Court of Appeals ruled that the word "slumlord" could mean simply that the property owner was a "landlord in a slum" and was thus capable of an innocent intrepretation. The vast majority of states do not follow this rule, however, and even the Illinois Supreme Court has cast doubt on its continuing validity in that state. Some jurisdictions go so far as to take precisely the opposite approach by presuming that an ambiguous statement is defamatory.

A related problem arises when part of an article has a defamatory impact, but another part negates that impact or clarifies the meaning. While one might think that the rule noted above that requires an article to be taken "as a whole" would govern this situation, some courts take the position that the key factor is the article's impact on the average reader. For example, in *Kunst v. New York World Telegram Corp.* (1967), a story's opening paragraph and a caption under an accompanying photograph were capable of a defamatory interpretation, but a paragraph much lower in the story clarified the meaning of the earlier comments—that is, it would have provided that clarification had a persistent reader gotten that far. A New York appellate court concluded that the subsequent paragraph was irrelevant, stressing that the article must be construed "as it would be read and understood by an ordinary member of the public to whom it was directed." Obviously the court felt that the "average" reader would not have waded through all of the story and thus would have been left with the defamatory impression left by the lead paragraph and the photo caption. This case also illustrates that while photographs alone rarely cause any libel problems, the combination of the picture plus the caption can be defamatory.

A decision of the West Virginia Supreme Court demonstrates how headlines can cause similar difficulties. In *Sprouse v. Clay Communications, Inc.* (1975), the court upheld a $250,000 libel judgment against a newspaper that had published "misleading words in oversized headlines" accompanying a series of stories about lands deals involving an unsuccessful candidate for governor. The court ruled that the headlines could be considered separately for their defamatory impact, although the stories painted a different picture and fleshed out the "shorthand" account of the headlines. Courts in some jurisdictions, therefore, are sensitive to the fact that newspaper readers often skim the headlines without reading the stories. In other states, however, the defamatory meaning of an article is determined by the headline and the story taken together.

Errors of omission can also result in creation of a defamatory impression, even though all of the facts contained in the offending statement or news story are correct. For example, a Memphis newspaper published a routine police story reporting that a Mrs. Nichols had been shot in the arm at her home by another woman, who had "arrived at the Nichols home and found her husband there with Mrs. Nichols." While that was indeed what had happened, the story did not mention that Mr. Nichols and two neighbors were also in the house at the time of the shooting. In *Memphis Publishing Co. v. Nichols* (1978), the Tennessee Supreme Court concluded that the article falsely implied that Mrs. Nichols and the husband of the woman who shot her had been committing adultery. If the newspaper had published, in Paul Harvey's phrase, "the rest of the story," a reasonable reader would not have gotten the impression that Mrs. Nichols had been involved in an affair.

Along somewhat the same lines, a remark that is innocent on its face may become defamatory when other facts not contained in the story are known to those who read it. For example, there is nothing defamatory in reporting that Farmer Brown burned his own barn, since one is generally entitled to do as he pleases with his own possessions. However, a neighbor, aware that Brown carried insurance on the structure, could draw the conclusion that the farmer had defrauded the insurance company and was thus guilty of arson. When such extrinsic facts are necessary to give otherwise innocent words a defamatory meaning, the courts often use the term "libel per quod" in contrast to "libel per se," which refers to a statement defamatory on its face. The plaintiff must make the extrinsic facts known to the court, which must decide whether those facts and the published information, taken together, are capable of a defamatory meaning.

The terms libel per se and libel per quod have had a long confusing history within the law of defamation, but the primary difference between the two has been in the area of damages, discussed more fully later in this chapter. In contrast to a libel per se case in which damages were "presumed" from the mere fact of publication, the plaintiff in a libel per quod suit had to show that he had suffered actual, out-of-pocket loss as a result of the publication. In *Gertz v. Robert Welch, Inc.*, however, the U.S. Supreme Court held as a matter of constitutional law that libel plaintiffs must almost always establish such actual harm, thus rendering the distinction between libel per se and libel per quod largely obsolete.

The Court also suggested in *Gertz* that the degree of fault required to be established by a libel plaintiff is higher than simple carelessness if the statement in question did not warn a journalist of its defamatory potential. Because libel per quod involves precisely that situation, the *Gertz* decision arguably protects the press when the words at issue become defamatory only when extrinsic facts are added. This aspect of the *Gertz* case is considered in the section of this chapter dealing with fault.

Identification

Libel is considered a "personal" tort, which means that only the person who is defamed may bring a suit to recover for that injury. One consequence of such a rule is that a husband, for example, cannot sue for defamation on the basis of a statement about his wife, although the offending words may have caused him emotional distress or indirectly reflected adversely upon him. In addition, the rule makes it impossible to libel the dead, for when a person dies, his reputation dies with him. Similarly, the right to sue for libel does not pass to an individual's survivors at death, even if the defamatory statement had been published while he was still alive.[5] As we have seen previously, a corporation or other business entity is treated as a fictional "person" for purposes of defamation and may thus maintain a libel action. The same is true with respect to nonbusiness organizations, such as nonprofit corporations that perform charitable work.

Even though the plaintiff may be an appropriate person to bring a defamation suit, he cannot possibily establish any injury to his reputation unless he shows that the offending words referred to him. Under longstanding common law principles, a libel plaintiff must thus demonstrate that the statement was "of and concerning" him.

This requirement of identification may also have constitutional dimensions. As a federal district judge noted in *Barger v. Playboy Enterprises, Inc.* (1983), the courts, under the first amendment, "have chosen not to limit freedom of public

---

[5]There are cases to the contrary, particularly where the libel suit had already been filed at the time of the plaintiff's death. In that situation, the New Jersey courts, for example, permit the suit to be continued by the survivors.

discussion except to prevent harm occasioned by defamatory statements reasonably susceptible of special application to a given individual.'' The judge cited the landmark decision in *New York Times Co. v. Sullivan* in support of this proposition. Recall that the advertisement at issue in that case did not mention Police Commissioner Sullivan by name or refer to his official position and that many of the allegedly libelous statements had nothing to do with the police. After ruling that appellate courts must carefully scrutinize the facts in cases implicating the first amendment, the Supreme Court concluded that the evidence was insufficient to support the jury's finding that the defamatory statements were ''of and concerning'' plaintiff Sullivan.

The *New York Times* case does not mean, of course, that an allegedly libelious statement must refer to the plaintiff by name for the requisite identification to be present. The law books are filled with cases in which recovery has been allowed even though the plaintiff was not directly identified. In this situation, however, the plaintiff has a more difficult task than he would face if his name had actually been used in the offending material. He must first convince the trial judge that a reasonable reader could interpret the statement as referring to him. The intent of the defendant in publishing the material and the plaintiff's own interpretation of it are not important; instead, as one court has said, the key is the ''reasonable understanding of the recipient of the communication.'' If the judge believes that a statement could reasonably be understood as referring to the plaintiff, he then submits the question to the jury, which must decide whether it was so understood on the facts of the particular case. It is sufficient for purposes of showing identification that only a handful of those who read the statement interpreted it as referring to the plaintiff. However, a low number of such readers may suggest that the plaintiff was not damaged significantly by the comment.

Identification problems can arise in a variety of contexts. For example, in *Cosgrove Studio and Camera Shop, Inc. v. Pane* (1962), the Pennsylvania Supreme Court reversed the trial judge's dismissal of a suit brought by a camera shop against a competitor. At issue was an advertisement placed by defendant Pane in a local newspaper in response to an ad run by Cosgrove Studio promising a free roll of film for every roll brought in for developing and printing. Pane's ad stressed that he would not inflate the prices for processing in order to give away a ''free'' roll of film or print blurred negatives to increase the price charged for printing individual pictures. Cosgrove Studio sued for libel, claiming that Pane's ad implied that it engaged in shady business practices and that readers of the newspaper would link Pane's statements to Cosgrove's ''free film'' offer. The Pennsylvania court agreed that there had been sufficient identification although Cosgrove had not been specifically named in the competitor's ad.

In a 1978 Kentucky case, *E.W. Scripps Co. v. Cholmondelay*, a newspaper reported the death of a boy following a fight in which another child pounded his head repeatedly against the pavement. In reality, the victim had slipped into a coma and died as the result of a single punch thrown by the other boy, whose name was not mentioned in the article. The boy accused by the article of administering the ''savage beating'' filed suit, and the court found identification because ''his friends and acquaintances familiar with the incident were certain to recognize [him] as the unnamed perpetrator.''

Broadcast news reports can also cause problems even though names are not used. In *Duncan v. WJLA-TV, Inc.,* a 1984 case from the District of Columbia, a television station had used videotape of people walking down a crowded street as the backdrop for a story on genital herpes. At one point in the newscast, when the anchorman noted in a "voice-over" that there is no cure for the disease, the videotape quite clearly showed the face of a woman who had paused at a street corner. Because her face was recognizable from the videotape, she had been identified.

There are also numerous cases in which the press has used the wrong name in a news story or has printed a name without full identification. If, for instance, the local school board fired a teacher named "John Watkins" and a newspaper incorrectly identified the man as "John Watson," a teacher by that name in the same school system would have little trouble establishing identification. The practice of providing additional descriptive information such as age and street address can go a long way toward avoiding problems in this area. For example, in *Summerlin v. Washington Star Co.* (1981), the paper reported that District of Columbia police had arrested "Jerry Summerlin, 22, of the 5500 block of Dana Place, N.W." as a murder suspect. All of the information was correct except the man's name, and a Jerry Summerlin who lived in a nearby suburb filed a libel suit. The court dismissed the case because the plaintiff did not live at the address given in the story and was not twenty-two years old; accordingly, the story could not reasonably be taken to refer to him, even though his name had been used.

Recent cases demonstrate that a plaintiff can establish identification despite the fact that the allegedly defamatory article is fiction rather than fact. For example, in *Pring v. Penthouse International* (1982), the plaintiff sued the magazine because of an obviously fictional story about a "Miss Wyoming" named Charlene whose talent included baton twirling and performing oral sex upon beauty pageant judges. Kimerli Jayne Pring, a former Miss Wyoming who did in fact twirl batons, claimed the story would be understood by readers as referring to her. She won a $26.5 million judgment that was later reversed on appeal, although the appellate court's decision was based on grounds other than identification. In an earlier case, *Bindrim v. Mitchell* (1979), a California court awarded a psychologist $75,000 (which was affirmed on appeal) in a suit based on a novel that described nude "encounter group sessions" conducted by a fictional therapist. The only apparent resemblance between the plaintiff and the fictional character was that both used this type of therapy, but the court concluded that the plaintiff had proven identification.

Perhaps the most thorny question involving identification has arisen from defamatory statements directed at groups rather than particular individuals. In a well-known Oklahoma case, *Fawcett Publications v. Morris* (1962), a member of the 1956 University of Oklahoma football team sued *True* magazine on the basis of an article implying that the Sooners had used stimulative drugs. Although no players were named in the article and more than 60 were on the squad, the state supreme court held that the suit could be maintained, concluding that the article defamed every member of the team, including the plaintiff. It is also possible for a plaintiff to recover in the "group libel" setting if he can show that the defamatory matter specifically applies to him. Generally, however, the question turns on the size of the particular group.

In spite of the *Morris* case, most courts and commentators suggest that members of a group larger than 25 cannot bring suit even though the statement was inclusive. An influential case in this area, *Neiman-Marcus Co. v. Lait* (1952), stemmed from the book *U.S.A. Confidential*, which made general statements about the sexual activities of models, salesmen, and saleswomen employed at an exclusive Dallas department store. Although no names were mentioned, the court permitted suit by the models and salesmen, groups which numbered nine and twenty-five, respectively, but dismissed the suit filed by about thirty of the store's more than 350 saleswomen. Similarly, a California appeals court ruled in *Grimes v. Swank Magazine Corp.* (1988) that ten members of the Fairfax, California, police department could not maintain a suit based on an "adult" magazine's review of an X-rated film. The plaintiffs contended that an accompanying "still" photo, which showed two actors wearing uniforms with "Fairfax Police" shoulder patches, implied that Fairfax officers had participated in the movie. The court disagreed, noting that there were about 100 past and present members of the department and that only two actors appeared in the photo. Thus, there was no "blanket slur" reaching all members of the group.

Some states attempted at one point to deal with defamatory remarks directed at large groups—particularly religious, ethnic or political groups—via criminal libel statutes. These laws, which covered individual defamation as well, typically made defamation that exposed a person or group to hatred, contempt or ridicule a criminal offense punishable by fine, imprisonment, or both. In the group libel context, the Supreme Court upheld the consitutionality of such a statute in *Beauharnais v. Illinois*, a 1952 case decided well before defamation was deemed worthy of some first amendment protection. In *Garrison v. Louisiana* (1964), however, the Court ruled that the first amendment safeguards set forth in *New York Times Co. v. Sullivan* must also govern a criminal libel prosecution based upon the alleged defamation of a public official. Although the Court did not expressly address the continuing viability of *Beauharnais*, the reasoning of that case no longer seems valid, and some state courts—including those in Arkansas, California, and Pennsylvania—have declared criminal libel laws unconstitutional. While such statutes remain on the books in several states, only a handful specifically deal with group libel. In any event, prosecutions for any type of criminal libel are extremely rare, particularly with respect to the news media. It seems that prosecuting attorneys have more than enough to keep them busy without worrying about filing charges under criminal libel statutes that are of dubious constitutionality.

Publication

While questions as to whether an article defames and identifies a plaintiff can be sticky indeed, the publication requirement is relatively straightforward. Because libel law protects one's reputation, it is essential that the defamatory statement be communicated to someone other than its subject. Given the mass audience of newspapers, magazines, and broadcast stations, publication is hardly difficult for a plaintiff to establish in a case against the press.

Interesting problems have arisen in the nonmedia context, however. For example, a sealed letter from one person to another would not constitute publication. But if the writer showed a copy of that letter to his business associate, the requisite publication to a third party would have taken place. Publication in this sense is not limited to written or printed material. A gesture, drawing, or spoken word constitutes publication, so long as a third person receives and understands the communication. Thus, words spoken in a foreign language are not "published" unless a third party comprehends as well as hears them.

Despite the fact that many courts presume publication to have occurred in libel cases involving the news media, certain trouble spots exist. The law of libel has long recognized the principle that "tale bearers are as bad as tale makers," and anyone who repeats a defamatory statement is technically just as liable as its originator. Applied in the news media context, this "republication rule" means that a newspaper is not insulated from potential liability because it reprints a story from another publication, carries a news account furnished by a wire service, or attributes a defamatory remark to a police official or other source. Thus, the phrases "according to" or "it was alleged by" do not change the fact that the newspaper has republished the libel. As the *Liberty Lobby* case indicates, however, the paper might be able to escape liability in such situations for reasons unrelated to the republication concept.

Because a new libel occurs each time the statement is republished, plaintiffs can sue virtually everyone in the "chain" of a news operation, from the "source" of the information to the reporter who wrote the story, the editor who edited it, and the paper boy who delivered it. Technically, there has been a republication of the libel at each step of the process. As a practical matter, however, the newspaper or broadcast outlet is the likely target of a defamation suit, since media organizations have sufficiently "deep pockets" from which a plaintiff can extract a sizable damage award. Nevertheless, reporters and their sources are frequently named as defendants in defamation cases, just as advertisers and advertising agencies are often sued along with the medium that actually carried the finished ad.

The republication rule has in the past created some confusion for the mass media because of the multiple copies printed of newspapers, magazines, and books. Theoretically, each sale or delivery of a single copy of any of these publications could be considered a separate publication, thereby allowing a plaintiff to bring several lawsuits in various states on the basis of one defamatory statement. The English courts took this approach, as did the American courts in early decisions. Today, either by statute or court ruling, most states instead follow the so-called "single publication rule," under which an entire edition of a newspaper, magazine, or book is treated as only one publication, and all damages for the publication must be recovered in a single lawsuit. However, if a new edition is published—such as a later edition of a daily newspaper or an updated version of a book—a new publication is considered to have occurred and a separate libel suit may be brought.

Despite adoption of the single publication rule, complex problems often exist when the published material is circulated in several states, as is the case with books and such nationwide periodicals as *Time* and the *Wall Street Journal*. One such difficulty, a detailed discussion of which is obviously beyond the scope of this book, is known as the "choice of law" problem. That is, a court must decide which state law is to apply in a particular case, an inquiry that can be extremely important if the potentially applicable laws differ significantly. For example, assume that a New York plaintiff sued a Florida newspaper over a story that was circulated in Georgia. Even if the suit were filed in Florida, a court in that state would not necessarily follow Florida law but might instead choose the law of New York or Georgia. If one state made it more difficult to recover damages for emotional harm flowing from the libel, the defendant would have an obvious advantage if that state's law were applied.

Another question stemming from interstate circulation involves the power of a court to assert jurisdiction over an out-of-state publisher. Generally speaking, the due process clause of the U.S. Constitution places limits on the power of state and federal courts to force an out-of-state defendant to respond to a suit brought in the state where the court sits. If, for instance, an Illinois manufacturer produced a boiler that exploded at a factory in Nebraska, can it be required to defend a personal injury suit filed in Nebraska by a factory worker hurt in the explosion? The courts have answered the question affirmatively, so long as the defendant has sufficient connection with the state in which the suit is brought that it would not be unfair to demand that he litigate the question of his liability there.

The analysis used by the courts in libel cases is illustrated by *Edwards v. Associated Press* (1975), in which a Mississippi sheriff brought suit against the wire service for an erroneous report linking him to drug dealing. The story was prepared by an AP correspondent in New Orleans, where it was transmitted to the wire service's subscribers in Mississippi. A broadcaster in the sheriff's home county picked up the story, and he subsequently filed suit against the AP. It is generally settled that a court may hear a case against an out-of-state defendant who has committed a tort within the state. Thus, if a Connecticut motorist causes an accident while visiting New York, he is subject to suit there. Did the AP commit the tort of libel in Mississippi? Although the publication originated in New Orleans, the court emphasized that the injury to the sheriff occurred in Mississippi. Accordingly, it ruled that the libel occurred at least in part in Mississippi, thus subjecting the AP to a libel suit there. The court also stressed that it would hardly be unfair to require AP to defend the suit in Mississippi, since it had several contacts with the state. For example, AP maintained five news correspondents and an office in Mississippi, and it regularly transmitted news reports to its customers in the state. In fact, the report about the sheriff was specifically directed at Mississippi, given the interest in such a story among AP subscribers there.

A court would have no difficulty reaching the same result in a case involving a nationwide publication. In *Calder v. Jones* (1984), actress Shirley Jones and her husband, entertainment broker Marty Ingels, sued the Florida-based *National Enquirer* and an editor and writer employed by the paper. According to an *Enquirer* report, Ms. Jones was drinking heavily because of the "bizarre behavior" of her husband, who had "one of the most notorious casting couches in all of Hollywood." The central issue in the case, as it reached the U.S. Supreme Court, was jurisdiction of the California courts over the *Enquirer* writer and editor; the Court ruled that the journalists had sufficient contacts with California for that state's courts to try a suit against them. The case also makes clear that there would have been jurisdiction over the *Enquirer* itself (an issue the newspaper did not even bother to contest), since it circulated more than a half million copies of each edition in the state, carried on newsgathering activities there, and aimed many of its stories at its California audience.

Significantly, the Court also held in *Calder* that cases involving first amendment questions do not require any more substantial connection between the defendant and the state of trial than ordinary cases. Thus, an out-of-state media defendant's contacts with the state where the suit is filed are to be evaluated in the same fashion as those of the boiler manufacturer or a visiting motorist. The Court applied that principle in *Keeton v. Hustler Magazine, Inc.*, handed down shortly after *Calder*. The plaintiff, Kathy Keeton, lived in New York, while *Hustler* is published by a corporation chartered in Ohio but with headquarters in California. Yet the suit was brought in New Hampshire, a state that seemingly had little to do with the dispute, because the time period for filing libel suits—the "statute of limitations" period[6]— had expired in every state except New Hampshire.

---

[6]Statutes of limitations typically range from one to four years. With few exceptions, the time period in which the suit must be brought begins running on the day following the date of publication of the defamatory material. The single publication rule discussed previously also applies in this context. In some jurisdictions—Texas, for example—the time period runs from the date that the plaintiff learned

Unlike the Associated Press in the *Edwards* case, *Hustler* had no offices or employees in the New Hampshire, and its circulation there was small compared to that of the *National Enquirer* in California. New Hampshire sales accounted for less than one percent of the magazine's monthly circulation, and sales in the state ranged from a high of 15,000 copies to a low of ten. Thus, *Hustler*'s only connection with New Hampshire was the fact that its magazine was for sale there, and those sales were quite small indeed. Moreover, plaintiff Keeton had no contact with the state, since she lived in New York. Yet the Supreme Court upheld jurisdiction over the magazine in the New Hampshire courts, in part on the theory that the state had an interest in protecting not only the plaintiff's reputation, but also in preventing its citizen-readers from being exposed to falsehoods. Thus, Ms. Keeton was allowed to sue in New Hampshire for all of the damages she may have suffered from circulation of the article nationwide, although only a tiny fraction of that harm could possibly have occurred in the state because she lived elsewhere and only a comparative handful of magazines were sold there.

Does this case mean that a newspaper or magazine can be sued anywhere that it circulates copies? Probably not, although some media lawyers have predicted such dire consequences. Assume, for instance, that the *Arkansas Democrat*, a newspaper published in Little Rock, prints an article that defames a citizen of New Orleans, Louisiana. Assume further that the *Democrat* maintains no offices in Lousiana, employs no reporters or anyone else salesmen in the state, solicits no advertising there, and sells only ten or twenty papers each month south of the Arkansas state line. To make the case even more extreme, assume the same facts, except that the plaintiff is from New York City and only one or two copies of the paper each month find their way that far north. Courts have historically taken these factors into account in evaluating whether an out-of-state publication has sufficient contacts with the state where it is sued. The *Keeton* case arguably does not change that, at least where the publication does not have a truly national circulation. But if a nationwide journal such as *Time* or *Newsweek* is involved, *Keeton* indicates that it can be sued anywhere in the country.

Fault

At least where media defendants are involved, a defamation plaintiff must, as a matter of constitutional law, prove that the defendant was at fault in publishing the allegedly defamatory statement. Put another way, the plaintiff must demonstrate that the defendant acted carelessly or recklessly with regard to the truth or falsity of the particular information. Prior the *New York Times* case, defamation was a "strict liability" tort, meaning that a defendant could be held liable despite his most conscientious efforts to verify the truth of the matter. In that decision, however, the Supreme Court concluded that such a rule was inconsistent with the first amendment when the defamatory comment was aimed at a public official. After expanding this constitutional protection to include suits by public figures as well as public officials, the Court held in *Gertz* that the first amendment precludes holding a media defendant liable for defamation without some showing of fault, regardless of whether the plaintiff is a private or public person.

---

of the defamation or should have learned of it by the exercise of reasonable diligence. Under this approach, the clock does not necessarily begin ticking upon publication.

The public or private status of the plaintiff remains extremely important, however, for it is determinative of the precise level of fault that the plaintiff must establish in a given case. Generally speaking, a private person need only establish that the defendant acted negligently—that is, carelessly—in publishing the defamatory statement. The *Liberty Lobby* case makes plain that public officials and public figures have a more difficult task: they must prove that the defendant acted with reckless disregard for the truth or knowledge of falsity.[7] Thus, the first step in evaluating fault is to categorize the plaintiff's status as either public or private. This analysis, performed by the trial judge, determines whether the plaintiff must prove recklessness or mere carelessness on the part of the defendant. The next question, of course, is whether the defendant's conduct in the case rose the level of fault required. This decision is made by the jury.

Public Officials. Of the two types of public plaintiffs, the "public official" category is the most straightforward. Recall that the *New York Times* case involved an elected municipal official, the police commissioner of Montgomery, Alabama. In a subsequent case, *Ocala Star-Banner Co. v. Damron* (1971), the Court made clear that the definition also includes a candidate for elective office, even though that person is not at that point an elected official. Accordingly, any person holding or running for public office is considered a public official, and that list includes everyone from the President or a U.S. Senator to members of the local city council or school board. Even former public officials fall within the category if the subject matter of the allegedly libelous statement relates to their conduct in office or their suitability for other public service.

Of course, a significant number of government officials are appointed rather than elected, from members of the President's Cabinet and his White House staff to city managers, school superintendents, and fire chiefs. Not surprisingly, persons occupying such important positions are considered to be public officials for purposes of the *New York Times* rule. The harder question is whether virtually all government workers—such as policemen, teachers, sanitation workers, and secretaries—are to be deemed within the definition. The Supreme Court dealt with this problem in *Rosenblatt v. Baer* (1966), in which the plaintiff was the supervisor of a county-owned ski area. Because the suit had been tried before *New York Times* was decided, the Supreme Court sent the case back to the lower courts for a determination of the supervisor's status. Nonetheless, the Court announced a broad definition of the term "public official" that would include "those among the hierarchy of government employees who have, or appear to the public to have, substantial responsibility for or control over the conduct of public affairs."

This expansive approach focuses not only on the actual job of the particular employee but also on the public's perception of the importance of his work. In fleshing out the definition, the lower courts have looked to such factors as the conse-

---

[7]Many courts use the term "actual malice" as a shorthand expression of the "reckless disregard/ knowledge of falsity" level of fault. This is not surprising, for the Supreme Court itself so used the phrase in *New York Times Co. v. Sullivan*. The Court has come to regret its choice of words, however, because the lower courts have often mistakenly equated this "constitutional" malice with the meaning of the word at common law—ill will, spite, or hatred. It is clear, however, that this traditional notion of malice has nothing to do with the showing of fault required by *New York Times*. Accordingly, this text will not use "actual malice" but will instead refer to the *New York Times* standard in shorthand fashion as "reckless disregard" or "recklessness."

quences to the public of an employee's abuse of his position, his responsibilities for making important policy choices or control over expenditures of public funds, and the supervisory nature of his job. All of these factors need not be present in a single situation, however. For example, the courts have ruled that workers ranking at the lower end of the bureacratic totem pole—such as clerks or secretaries—may in appropriate cases be treated as public officials, even though they play no role in formulating policy. A clerk who meets the public on a daily basis might be perceived as playing an important governmental role, and a secretary may be in a position to "juggle the books" to hide questionable expenditures of public funds. Nonetheless, in *Hutchinson v. Proxmire* (1979) the Supreme Court cautioned that the public official category "cannot be thought to include all public employees."

Examples of government employees held to be public officials include:

- professors and administrators at a state university;
- teachers, principals, and coaches in a public school system;
- deputy sheriffs and police officers;
- court clerks, secretaries to high-ranking city officials;
- tax assessors;
- county and city attorneys;
- public defenders;
- county medical examiners;
- military officers;
- social workers;
- Internal Revenue Service agents;
- city building inspectors;
- federal drug enforcement agents; and
- grand jurors.

On the other hand, court reporters, police informers, lawyers appointed by courts to represent indigent defendants, part-time employees, a staff psychologist at a Veterans' Administration hospital, and the head of a state university's print shop have not been placed in the public official category. Courts in different jurisdictions have disagreed over the status of some employees, particularly classroom teachers. One should consult the law of each jurisdiction to see how far down the ladder the courts have extended the "public official" designation.

More helpful than a mere list are the factors that courts have taken into account in evaluating a particular libel plaintiff. For example, employees with substantial decision making or supervisory responsibilities—such as a city manager, department head, or personnel director—would plainly be public officials. Lower-ranking employees, such as the head mechanic at the county motor pool, may lack broad authority but may be authorized to direct expenditures of public funds and make purchasing decisions. The ability to control public spending, even to a limited extent, suggests that such an employee should be considered a public official. Although law enforcement officers, particularly those who "walk a beat," do not formulate public policy, they play an important role in its implementation. Moreover, policemen wield extraordinary power over the lives of ordinary citizens and can exercise tremendous discretion that is often subject to abuse. To most citizens, no one is more representative of "the government" than the policeman. Other employees lacking the raw power of law enforcement officials—such as tax assessors, court clerks, or building inspectors—are nonetheless representatives of the government who come into contact with the public on a daily basis. And, while teachers are not typically viewed as having great power, their unique responsibilities with respect to the children of a community place them in positions of public trust.

Even if the plaintiff is within the "public official" definition, the *New York Times* case also requires that the defamatory statement "relate to his official conduct." However, the Court made clear in *Garrison v. Louisiana* and *Monitor Patriot Co. v. Roy* (1971) that virtually anything is relevant to the fitness of an elected official for the office he holds or of a candidate for the position he seeks. For example, in the *Roy* case, a newspaper had described a candidate for the U.S. Senate as a "former small-time bootlegger." The Supreme Court rejected the plaintiff's argument that this information involved "long forgotten misconduct" that did not relate to the office for which he was a candidate.

It seems clear, however, that something does remain of the requirement that the libel relate to the official's conduct, even if an elective position is involved. First, the statement challenged as defamatory apparently must identify the plaintiff as an officeholder. In *Foster v. Laredo Newspapers, Inc.* (1976), the Texas Supreme Court refused to apply the *New York Times* rule when an article said to have libeled a county surveyor made no mention of his official position. Emphasizing that the news report failed to link the alleged misconduct and the plaintiff's elective office of surveyor, the court concluded that the article could not be said to relate to the plaintiff's fitness for that office.

Second, when appointed officials or other government employees bring libel suits, the courts are more likely to apply the relationship test more stringently if the plaintiff holds a comparatively minor government position. As the Washington Supreme Court observed in *Clawson v. Longview Publishing Co.* (1979), there are two pertinent variables: "the importance of the position held, and . . . the nexus between that position and the allegedly defamatory information—specifically, how closely the defamatory material bears upon fitness for office." Thus, while virtually anything about an official "wielding great power and exercising broad discretion" is relevant to his position, statements about lower-level workers must be "more closely connected to actual job performance." Media attorney Robert Sack has offered a useful example to illustrate this rule. A statement that a publicly employed stenographer had a nervous breakdown would seemingly have little bearing on his duties, but the same charge about the governor or a policeman would obviously be relevant to the performance of official responsibilities.

Public Figures. The second type of public plaintiff—the so-called "public figure"—is more difficult to describe. As one federal court has complained, the task of drawing the line between public and private figures "is much like trying to nail a jelly fish to the wall." There are, however, two basic categories of public figures: those who are so well-known or influential that they are public figures for all purposes and in all contexts, and those who become public figures only with regard to a particular controversy. In addition to these "all-purpose" and "limited" public figures, there is a very small third category known as "involuntary" public figures who have not purposefully taken action that results in notoriety.

Before turning to the three categories, it is important to examine why these persons are, for defamation purposes, treated the same as public officials. With respect to the latter, the Supreme Court in *New York Times* relied heavily on the analogy between "seditious libel" of the government and criticism of public officials. That analogy does not apply where the victim of the defamatory statement is merely a well-known person who holds no office, for the public figure is not in any sense "the government." Nonetheless, the Supreme Court recognized in the 1967 companion cases *Curtis Publishing Co. v. Butts* and *Associated Press v. Walker* that certain individuals, "by reason of their fame, shape events in areas of concern to society at large." In the landmark *Gertz* decision of 1974, the Court reaffirmed its view that the first amendment demands sufficient "breathing space" for errors about persons who have "assumed roles of especial prominence in the affairs of society," just as it demands protection for the inevitable erroneous statements about public officials.

The "all-purpose" public figure is, as a practical matter, someone whose name has become a household word. As the courts have pointed out, few persons have achieved the fame that would make them public figures for all purposes, regardless of the context in which the defamatory statement arose. Most often the courts have placed into this category "celebrities" from the entertainment world, such as Johnny Carson and Carol Burnett. However, author and political commentator William F. Buckley, Jr. has also been deemed to have achieved this status. Other persons who might so qualify include consumer advocate Ralph Nader, actress Jane Fonda, and former First Lady Jacqueline Kennedy Onassis.

Typically, such persons have actively sought the spotlight and have ready access to the news media to respond to defamatory charges leveled against them. Because they have achieved such pervasive fame and national recognition, defamatory remarks about them may be protected under the first amendment even if unrelated to the reason that the person became so widely known. For example, although Jane Fonda achieved notoriety as an actress and an activist in liberal politics, a statement impugning her fitness as a mother could not be the basis for liability unless she established that it was made with reckless disregard for the truth or knowledge of falsity.

Although the all-purpose public figures listed above are all nationally known individuals, the Supreme Court indicated in *Gertz* that the appropriate inquiry is whether an individual has achieved "general fame or notoriety *in the community*," thereby suggesting that there may also be local or regional all-purpose public figures. In *Steere v. Cupp* (1979), the Kansas Supreme Court ruled that the plaintiff, a prominent local attorney, was an all-purpose public figure. The court pointed out that he had practiced law for thirty-two years in the county, served for eight years as county attorney, participated extensively in civic, social and professional organizations, and capped his career by representing a woman in a sensational murder trial. In short, he was a household word in his home county and, therefore, a public figure for all purposes.

In stark contrast to those persons who vigorously seek out or welcome media attention and thus run the risk that erroneous comments about them will be made, some individuals are drawn into the public eye by circumstances completely beyond their control. This group of "involuntary" public figures is extremely small; examples include the children of convicted Ethel and Julius Rosenberg, who were executed after their convictions for passing atomic secrets to the Russians, and the wife of Johnny Carson. Some courts have placed notorious gangsters in this category, on the theory that they obviously do not want the media or the public to focus on their illegal activities. However, it is more useful to treat such persons as "limited" public figures because of their voluntary involvement in a controversial matter that will obviously attract the attention of the public and the press.

The "limited" public figure category is not only the largest of the three, but also the most difficult to define or describe. Under the principles set forth in *Gertz*, a court must employ a two-step process in evaluating a particular plaintiff's status. The court must initially determine whether there exists a "public controversy" and then decide whether the plaintiff is sufficiently involved in it. If the answer to both questions is affirmative, then the plaintiff is a public figure for purposes of allegedly defamatory statements growing out of the controversy.

The identification of the given controversy and determination of its "public" status often play crucial roles in a libel suit. Three Supreme Court decisions provide some guidance in this regard. In *Time, Inc. v. Firestone* (1976), the Court made plain that a "public controversy" is not necessarily something that the media consider newsworthy or that the public happens to be interested in. There *Time* had reported, incorrectly, that Russell Firestone, a member of "one of America's wealthier industrial families," had been granted a divorce because of his wife's adultery. Although the Florida judge who presided over the divorce proceedings had observed that certain testimony indicated that "the extra-marital escapades of [Mary Alice Firestone] were "bizarre and of an amatory nature which would have made Dr. Freud's hair curl," the technical grounds for divorce, while not particularly clear, did not include adultery. The Court rejected the magazine's argument that Mrs. Firestone was a public figure because the divorce suit was a matter of great public interest that had received considerable news coverage.

"Dissolution of a marriage through judicial proceedings is not the sort of 'public controversy' referred to in *Gertz*, even though the marital difficulties of extremely wealthy individuals may be of interest to some portion of the reading public," the Court said. This passage suggests that the appropriate inquiry is not what the public *is* interested in, but rather what it *should be* interested in. Thus, intense public interest in a particular matter does not elevate it to the status of a "public controversy" for purposes of deciding whether a plaintiff is a public figure. Sometimes, of course, the controversy is too inconsequential to be treated as "public." For example, the lower courts have held that a civil suit between two private parties and the dismissal of a tennis professional from his job at local country club were not "public controversies."

In two 1979 cases decided the same day, the Supreme Court demonstrated the narrow approach it considers appropriate in identifying a given controversy. In *Wolston v. Reader's Digest Association*, the defendant had published a book that identified the plaintiff as one of several Soviet agents convicted of espionage in the United States. Although the plaintiff had been convicted of contempt of court for failing to appear before a grand jury investigating espionage some fifteen years prior to the book's publication in 1974, he had never even been indicted for spying or similar offenses. Justice William Rehnquist, author of the *Firestone* opinion, observed that the controversy was not "espionage in the United States," since all "responsible" Americans were opposed to that sort of activity. Becasue there was no room for debate on the question, it could not be considered a controversy. While admitting that it was difficult to determine the precise nature of the controversy, Justice Rehnquist suggested that it should be defined narrowly: the propriety of law enforcement activities in pursuing alleged Russian spies.

Similarly, in *Hutchinson v. Proxmire* Chief Justice Warren Burger wrote for the

Court that "concern about general public expenditures" could not be considered a public controversy, since that concern is shared by most citizens. At issue in that case was the status of a psychologist whose government-sponsored research had been criticized as a waste of taxpayer dollars by former U.S. Senator William Proxmire, orignator of the infamous "Golden Fleece" award. If government spending were labeled a public controversy, the Chief Justice pointed out, "everyone who received or benefited from the myriad public grants for research could be classified as a public figure. . . ." Obviously, identification of a controversy in narrow terms makes it more difficult to demonstrate the plaintiff's involvement in that controversy and thus decreases the likelihood that he will be considered a public figure.

A 1987 Georgia Supreme Court decision illustrates this narrow approach. In *Georgia Society of Plastic Surgeons v. Anderson*, the journal of that state's medical association published an article with a title borrowed from Gilbert and Sullivan: "Things Are Never Quite What They Seem, Skim Milk Masquerades as Cream." The article had its genesis in a long-simmering dispute between two groups of doctors who perform reconstructive surgery, so-called "plastic surgeons" and otolarnygologists. According to the court, plastic surgeons have been concerned for years about the growing number of otolaryngologists, who perform surgery on the head and neck, and have sought ways to combat such competition. The "skim milk" article, written by plastic surgeons, was a critical piece written in response to a previous article by otolaryngologists explaining how their speciality had broadened to include reconstructive surgery of the head and neck. The trial court ruled that the plaintiffs, an otolaryngologist and two professional organizations of such physicians, were public figures. The Georgia Supreme Court disagreed: "[T]he controversy in which [plaintiffs] have become involved is primarily a private struggle within the confines of the medical profession [and] is chiefly of interest to plastic surgeons and other physicians who perform plastic surgery."

By way of comparison, the U.S. Court of Appeals for the District of Columbia Circuit had little difficulty concluding in *Tavoulareas v. Piro* (1987) that government policy toward the oil industry is a "public controversy." This highly-publicized case arose when the *Washington Post* published a story in 1979 stating that William Tavoulareas, president of Mobil Oil Corporation, had "set up" his son as a partner in a shipping firm that did millions of dollars in business with Mobil. In ruling that Tavoulareas was a limited purpose public figure, the court noted that throughout the 1970s there was extensive public debate "over whether the management and structure of the United States' private oil industry was in need of alteration or reform." Alternatively, the court ruled that there was a more narrowly defined public controversy involving the participation of Tavoulareas' son in a company that did substantial business with Mobil. The company disclosed to its stockholders the son's status as a principal in the shipping firm, and the Securities and Exchange Commission investigated the business relationship between the two companies. Congressional investigators also looked into the matter, and members of Mobil's board of directors expressed their concern. These developments took place prior to publication of the *Post* article.

After the controversy is identified and deemed sufficiently public, the next step is to determine the nature and extent of the plainitff's connection with it. In *Gertz*, the Court described "limited" public figures as those who "have thrust themselves to the forefront of particular public controversies in order to influence the resolution of the issues involved." Under this definitional approach, anyone who takes a public stand on important matters is a public figure for purposes of statements dealing with his activities as an advocate. As one court has put it, a person who "literally or figuratively mounts a rostrum to advocate a particular view" is a limited public figure. In the *Tavoulareas* case, for instance, the president of Mobil Oil achieved that status by playing an "influential public role" in mounting a "counterattack on the movement for reform of the oil industry."

Other limited public figures include:

- a scientist who wrote articles and gave speeches opposing flouridation of water;
- a high school student who assumed a leadership role in a dispute between students and faculty about drugs;
- an attorney who initiated a recall campaign against city council members;
- a Nobel Prize winner who had actively been involved in the movement to ban testing of nuclear weapons;
- an "animal rights" organization that had urged people not to buy fur coats; and
- a newspaper publisher who regularly took positions on controversial issues.

On the other hand, one does not become a public figure simply through association with a particular controversy. In the landmark *Gertz* decision, the Supreme Court ruled that prominent Chicago lawyer Elmer Gertz was not a limited public figure with regard to a right-wing magazine article about the murder trial of a Chicago policeman who had shot and killed a teenager. Gertz, a noted civil rights lawyer who had long been active in civic and professional affairs and who had written numerous books and articles, had been retained by the boy's family to bring a civil suit for damages against the policeman. The magazine, published by the John Birch Society, portrayed the criminal trial as part of a nationwide Communist conspiracy to descredit Chicago police and to "frame" the particular officer, identified Gertz as a leading figure in this conspiracy, and labeled him a "Communist-fronter" and a "Leninist."

The Supreme Court, in an opinion by Justice Lewis Powell, first ruled out the possibility that Gertz was an all-purpose public figure. Although he was undoubtedly well-known in certain circles, he had not achieved general fame in the community. For example, none of the prospective jurors called at his libel trial against the magazine had ever heard of him. The Court also rejected the argument that he was a limited public figure based on his "participation in the particular controversy giving rise to the defamation." While Gertz was involved to some extent with the controversy that stemmed from the shooting death of a youth at the hands of the police, his participation was insufficient to make him a public figure. Justice Powell stressed that he played no role in the criminal matter and merely represented his client's interest in connection with the civil suit.

Obviously, the Court was concerned that elevating a lawyer to public figure status simply because he represented someone in a controversial case could discourage lawyers from handling those cases. However, a lawyer's "grandstanding" in a case may make him a public figure for purposes of that litigation. The Michigan Court of Appeals so concluded in *Hayes v. Booth Newspapers* (1980), in which the criminal defense lawyer in a murder trial used controversial tactics and sought media attention by consenting to interviews during the course of the trial.

Just as an attorney is not automatically a limited public figure, a litigant in a civil or criminal case does not become one solely by becoming involved with the judicial process in some way. Mary Alice Firestone did not "voluntarily thrust herself to the forefront of a controversy" just by filing suit for divorce from her husband. Resort to the courts for this purpose was not really voluntary, Justice Rehnquist concluded for the Supreme Court, because the state compelled this procedure for those desiring to end a marriage. Along the same lines, the Court held in *Wolston* that the alleged Soviet agent did not become a limited public figure simply because the government had investigated him and demanded his appearance before a grand jury. Again writing for the Court, Justice Rehnquist noted that Ilya Wolston had been "dragged unwillingly into the controversy" and could hardly be labeled a voluntary participant. Although Wolston had been convicted of contempt of court for his failure to appear before the grand jury, the Court rejected the argument that "any person who engages in criminal conduct automatically becomes a public figure for purposes of comment on a limited range of issues relating to his conviction."

However, under appropriate circumstances one charged with criminal activity can be a limited purpose public figure. For example, in *Rosanova v. Playboy Enterprises, Inc.* (1978), the U.S. Court of Appeals for the Fifth Circuit held that a reputed underworld leader was a public figure for purposes of his connection with organized crime, since he had voluntarily engaged in a course of conduct bound to invite public attention.

Examples of persons held not to be limited public figures include:

- the psychologist in *Hutchinson* who had applied for government grants to fund his research;
- a stockholder in a corporation who initiated a campaign to replace the company's top management;
- a criminal defendant charged with murder;
- a doctor accused of aiding drug abuse by writing unnecessary prescriptions;
- a lawyer who was the subject of disciplinary proceedings as the result of his misconduct;
- the owner of a home mistakenly referred to in a news story as the headquarters of a gang;
- the defendant in a civil suit stemming from a house fire;
- a rancher accused in a news report of mistreating his livestock;
- a political consultant working for the reelection campaign of a U.S. Senator; and
- a police informant.

Two cases, however, illustrate the uncertainty that exists in this area. In *Lloyds v. UPI* (1970), a New York court treated a well-known trainer of thoroughbred horses as a public figure, while in *Wheeler v. Green* (1979), an Oregon court concluded that a well-known trainer of Apaloosa horses was not a public figure. The law is indeed an inexact science.

Thus far, our discussion of limited public figures has dealt with the question of whether one has voluntarily "thrust" himself into a public controversy in an attempt to influence its resolution. But what of the college football coach, the professional athlete, or the television actor, none of whom are sufficiently well-known to be all-purpose public figures, and none of whom are "advocates" of controversial positions? Long before the Supreme Court "constitutionalized" the law of libel, the common law recognized that protection was needed for "fair comment and criticism" of such persons in the public spotlight. This concept remains an important defense to defamation suits and is discussed below in connection with the defendant's case.

However, the Supreme Court has also treated such persons as limited public figures. For example, in *Curtis Publishing Co. v. Butts*, the *Saturday Evening Post* published a story accusing University of Georgia athletic director Wally Butts of conspiring with Alabama coach "Bear" Bryant to fix a football game between the two schools. Butts, the former football coach at Georgia, was not a state employee (and, therefore, a public official) but was paid by a private "booster" group. Although Butts was undoubtedly well-known in football circles, his name was hardly a household word. Yet the Supreme Court ruled that he was a public figure because the defamatory statements were obviously related to the reason for his fame—football. Unlike an all-purpose public figure such as Johnny Carson who is a "public personality for all aspects of his life," this type of libel plaintiff is a public figure only with respect to libelous statements about his position in the public eye.

Examples of persons falling into this category include professional athletes (and perhaps some amateurs as well), coaches, actresses and actors, singers and musicians, nude dancers, belly dancers, authors, Nobel Prize winners, a *Playboy* "Playmate of the Month," and the former "number one girlfriend" of Elvis Presley. Although these persons may never have become involved in public issues or injected themselves in a given controversy, they are nonetheless public figures for purposes of libelous statements related to their careers in the spotlight. Like the person who has played an activist role in a matter or public concern, these individuals have voluntarily put themselves in the public arena and must assume the risk that erroneous statements will be made about them.

Two types of libel plaintiffs have given the courts considerable difficulty in making the public figure determination: persons who have drifted into obscurity after once being in the public eye, and corporations and other business entities. The Supreme Court has addressed neither problem directly. Recall that in *Wolston*, some fifteen years had passed between the plaintiff's failure to appear before the grand jury and the book linking him to the Soviet espionage apparatus in the United States. Although the Supreme Court did not decide the case on the basis of this time lapse, Justices Harry Blackmun and Thurgood Marshall wrote in a concurring opinion that a person can, under some circumstances, lose his public figure status through the passage of time. Most lower courts, however, have held that so long as there is continuing public interest in the matter that gave rise to public figure status, the individual remains a public figure for purposes of later stories dealing with the reason for his prior fame or notoriety.

For example, in *Contemporary Mission, Inc. v. New York Times Co.* (1988), a group of priests were held limited public figures with respect to a religious controversy that had occurred ten years prior to publication of the allegedly defamatory article. Among other things, the priests had formed a folk-rock group that recorded eighteen albums and gave over 200 concerts, published books and articles, and issued press releases. Although this had occurred a decade earlier, the court ruled that "an individual who becomes a limited purpose public figure with respect to a particular controversy retains that status for the purpose of later commentary on that controversy."

Similarly, in *Brewer v. Memphis Publishing Co.* (1980), the U.S. Court of Appeals for the Fifth Circuit ruled that the plaintiff, who had once been romantically involved with Elvis Presley, was a public figure for purposes of a news report about that relationship even though she had since married and led a wholly private life. The U.S. Court of Appeals for the Sixth Circuit reached the same result in *Street v. NBC* (1981), a suit which grew out of a television "docudrama" based on the infamous 1931 rape trial of the "Scottsboro boys" in Alabama. Victoria Price Street had been the primary prosecution witness against the defendants, all black, accused of raping her. The Sixth Circuit held that she remained a public figure in connection with that controversy, despite the passage of time.

With respect to corporations and other business organizations, the lower courts have taken several approaches. For example, a federal district court in the District of Columbia ruled in *Martin Marietta Corp. v. Evening Star Newspaper Co.* (1976) that all corporations are to be treated as public figures, reasoning that such entities do not have the same interest in reputation as to individuals and that the first amendment should thus be given greater weight in the constitutional balance. Most courts, however, have declined to follow *Martin Marietta* and have instead attempted to use the same guidelines established for individuals. In *Reliance Insurance Co. v. Barron's* (1977), a federal district court in New York concluded that a company that has achieved general prominence, evidenced by the trading of its stock on national stock exchanges or by heavy government regulation of its activities, should be treated as a public figure.

Other courts have focused instead upon the question of whether the business has "voluntarily thrust itself" into a given controversy. Even here, however, the courts have differed. In *Steaks Unlimited, Inc. v. Deaner* (1980), the U.S. Court of Appeals for the Third Circuit held that the offering of goods or services in the marketplace through aggressive advertising or other promotional activities is a sufficient "thrust." Thus, a company that engages in this sort of "purposeful" conduct would be a limited public figure for purposes of news reports about its business activities. For example, a Kentucky appeals court ruled in *J&C, Inc. v. Combined Communications Corp.* (1987) that a company that voluntarily sought publicity with respect to its plan to use treated sewage to reclaim strip-mined lands was a public figure. The company had issued "press kits" to the media, and its officials had appeared at public meetings and on television to discuss the project.

On the other hand, the U.S. Court of Appeals for the Fourth Circuit held in *Blue Ridge Bank v. Veribanc, Inc.* (1989) that mere advertising did not make a bank a limited public figure for purposes of a false report about its financial health, since the bank's promotional activities had not dealt with that issue. Moreover, the court pointed out that there had been no public controversy involving the bank prior to publication of the defamatory information.

The Fault Requirement. As noted previously, a libel plaintiff's status as either public or private determines the level of fault he must establish in order to recover against the defendant. If the plaintiff is "public," he must, under *New York Times*, prove that the defendant acted with reckless disregard for the truth or knowledge that the information was false. Private plaintiffs, however, usually have an easier task. The Supreme Court in *Gertz* ruled that the states may determine for themselves the "appropriate standard of liability for a publisher or broadcaster of a defamatory falsehood injurious to a private individual," so long as they do not impose liability without fault.

Most states have adopted a simple negligence standard; that is, a private plaintiff must establish, by a preponderance of the evidence, that the defendant was careless with respect to the truth or falsity of the information he published. Under the "preponderance" standard of proof, the plaintiff must convince the jury that it is more likely than not that the defendant was indeed at fault. In a handful of states, such as California, Colorado, Indiana, and New York, the courts have concluded that the negligence standard offers insufficient protection for the news media and have required a private plaintiff (at least one involved in a public issue but not qualifying as a public figure) to establish a higher level of fault—reckless disregard for the truth in most of these states, "gross irresponsibility" in New York.

Negligence. Negligence has historically been defined in tort law as what a reasonably prudent person would have done under the same or similar circumstances. The courts have gone to great lengths to explain that this "reasonable person" does not really exist, but merely represents a community ideal of reasonable behavior against which a jury is to measure the conduct of a particular defendant. The best example of this individual might be Ward Cleaver, the fictional father on the old "Leave it to Beaver" television series, who never acted unreasonably and who was always up to standard. Because Ward Cleaver would never have dreamed of driving down an icy highway at breakneck speed, such conduct on the part of someone else would certainly be negligent. Indeed, in that situation the driver might have departed so greatly from the community ideal that his would be considered reckless.

While the basic negligence concept makes sense when the behavior of ordinary citizens is at issue, a problem arises when the conduct of a professional must be evaluated. Surely we would not want a jury to determine whether a surgeon had been negligent in the operating room based on the jury's view of what Ward Cleaver would have done with the scalpel. Thus, the courts developed a "professional negligence" test applicable in these situations: what a reasonable professional would have done under those circumstances.

As a result of the *Gertz* decision, the state courts have struggled to apply these principles to the law of defamation, and there has been considerable disagreement as to whether the "reasonable person" or "reasonable professional" standard should be used in evaluating negligence. The Tennessee Supreme Court, in *Memphis Publishing Co. v. Nichols*, refused to adopt what it called a "journalistic malpractice" test where liability is "based upon a departure from supposed standards of care set by publishers themselves." Instead, the court chose the "reasonable person" standard, thus allowing "the jury to rely on its own experience and instincts to determine whether an ordinarily prudent person would have behaved as the defendant did." Courts in Arkansas and Illinois have taken the same approach, reasoning that a "professional" negligence test would allow media defendants to establish their own standards of care.

In contrast, the Kansas Supreme Court applied the "reasonable professional" test in *Gobin v. Globe Publishing Co.* (1975), and that standard has also been adopted in the *Restatement (Second) of Torts*, an influential summation of the law published by the American Law Institute. Of course, use of the professional negligence analysis does not end the matter. For example, is the *Podunk Herald* to be held to the same standards as the *New York Times*? Is the conduct of a newspaper reporter to be compared with that of television or radio journalists? Are the various "codes of ethics" prepared by such groups as the Society of Professional Journalists relevant?

What about a news organization's own guidelines for handling particular stories, which may not have been followed in preparation of the article that gave rise to the libel suit?

According to *Gobin* and the *Restatement*, the conduct of the media defendant is to be measured against professional standards in the defendant's own community or similar communities. Moreover, the question is whether the defendant's conduct is reasonable in light of what other professionals in the community would have done under same or similar circumstances. This test recognizes that professional standards might vary from one type of media to another within the same community.

Other courts, as well as the *Restatement*, have indicated that deadline pressures and the "hot news" status of a story are relevant considerations, and it is obvious that those factors differ substantially depending upon the news organization involved. For example, a television journalist working on a breaking story just before air time faces pressures that a magazine reporter with six months to prepare a story generally does not encounter. Thus, customs and practices within a particular segment of the news media are important, as are such practices among all members of the press in a given community. Internal operating procedures prepared by a particular news organization may also be relevant, along with guidelines found in industry ethical codes.

Even in jurisdictions employing the "reasonable person" standard, the courts will typically allow both parties to introduce evidence of the sort described above to give the jury some guidance as to what a "reasonable" person would have done in a situation similar to the one that led to the lawsuit. Practicing journalists not involved in the case and journalism professors might serve as expert witnesses to describe how a story should or should not be handled.

The principal difference between the two negligence approaches lies in the instructions given the jury to guide its deliberations. As the *Nichols* case indicates, jurors working with the "reasonable person" standard are able to rely on their own instincts in evaluating media conduct, and because appellate courts are generally unwilling to overturn jury findings of negligence, the jury has considerable flexibility in reaching its decision. On the other hand, jurors in a case where the "professional person" test applies are specifically instructed that they are to base their decision not upon what they might have done or what they might consider reasonable, but instead on what a responsible professional journalist would have done in a similar setting. Theoretically, jurors in such a case rely on the evidence presented in court as to the "standard of care" rather than on their own experience or feelings. Many lawyers doubt that this is so in practice, however, and believe that jurors do pretty much what they want irrespective of the instructions given them by the court.

Professor Marc Franklin, in a 1984 study of cases applying the negligence standard, found that errors arose at four different stages of the publication process:

- *newsgathering,* where the reporter is given inaccurate information by a source;
- *recording the information,* where the reporter errs in taking notes or in interpreting what he was told;
- *writing the story,* where the journalist draws inaccurate conclusions based on his information; and
- *preparing the story* for publication or broadcast, where typographical or other technical errors occur.

Many courts, as well as the *Restatement*, have also recognized that the "hot news" nature of a story and the accompanying deadline pressure will often play a role in evaluating whether negligence has occurred in these situations.

Most cases fall into the first category, and the crucial question is whether the defendant had reasonable grounds to believe that the information he published was true. This inquiry generally turns on whether a reasonable journalist would have investigated the story further before printing or broadcasting it. The reliability of a reporter's source or sources for the story is the key, and the reporter is usually on safe ground if the source is a government official or a public document. For example, in *Wilson v. Capital City Press* (1975), the newspaper incorrectly reported that the plaintiff had been among several persons arrested in a drug raid. The paper had obtained the arrest list, which erroneously contained the plaintiff's name, from the state police, and a Louisiana court ruled that reliance on that source was not negligent. Similarly, in *LaMon v. Butler* (1988), the Washington Supreme Court ruled that a newspaper reporter was not negligent in relying on the city attorney's interpretation of an ambiguous municipal court order.

The reporter should more carefully evaluate source reliability when the information comes from someone who lacks such official status. If, for example, the source has an "axe to grind" against the person accused of misconduct, the journalist's failure to seek corroboration probably will be considered negligent. For example, in *Peagler v. Phoenix Newspapers* (1977), the reporter had written a story charging that the local Better Business Bureau had among its members companies that engaged in questionable sales methods. Two disgruntled former employees of the BBB were the sources for the article, and the reporter did not attempt to verify the information from more objective sources. The Arizona Supreme Court ruled that the reporter had been negligent.

Similarly, in *Richmond Newspapers, Inc. v. Lipscomb* (1987), the Virginia Supreme Court ruled that a jury could reasonably have found a reporter negligent in failing to contact additional sources for his story about a local teacher. The reporter confined his investigation to students and parents who had complained about the teacher's performance. Like the former employees in *Peagler*, they were not the most objective sources of information. At trial, a supervisor, fellow teacher, and student contradicted the information contained in the story, and none had been interviewed by the reporter. These cases suggest that the "two source" rule adopted by Watergate reporters Carl Bernstein and Bob Woodward does not always preclude a finding of negligence. It should also be noted that anonymous sources are likely to cause trouble, for as a Florida appellate court observed in *Holter v. WLCY-TV, Inc.* (1978), "anonymous [tips] are customarily relied upon for direction [in pursuing a story] but not for information."

Multiple sources who provide contradictory information also create problems for the journalist. Several courts have ruled that once a reporter has been put on notice that some of his information is incorrect, his duty is to make a reasonably thorough investigation. The precise nature or depth of that investigation might vary, of course, depending upon whether the story is "hot news" and whether a deadline is rapidly approaching. While this approach makes sense as a general rule, what if, upon looking into the matter in more detail, the reporter simply cannot determine which source is correct? Professor David Robertson, in an influential article in the *Texas Law Review*, has suggested that the journalist is not negligent if he prepares a "balanced" story making plain that the facts are uncertain and attributing the conflicting statements to their sources. In the interest of such balance, the reporter should also give the subject of accusations in the story an opportunity to respond to those charges, or at least to deny them, even though this person would hardly be an "objective" source. As *Lipscomb* indicates, failure to obtain "the other side" of the story has been considered negligent, although mitigating factors such as the subject's refusal to talk to the press or his unavailability as the deadline for a "hot news" item approaches, may come into play.

As noted previously in connection with the republication rule, a newspaper or broadcast station that uses a wire service report is potentially liable for any defamatory material that it contains. The fault requirement, however, makes it unlikely for a libel plaintiff to recover in this situation, since in most situations a newspaper or broadcast station would not be negligent in relying on the accuracy of the wire service account. In fact, many courts have recognized what is often called the "wire service defense": if a media organization republishes a story, without substantial change, from a reputable news service, it is not negligent as a matter of law unless the story is so inherently improbable or inconsistent that an editor would have some reason to doubt its accuracy.

One of the leading cases with respect to the "wire service defense" is *Appleby v. Daily Hampshire Gazette*, decided by the Massachusetts Supreme Court in 1985. After pointing out that newspapers, radio and television stations, and other media customarily publish wire service stories without independent corroboration of the information they contain, the court observed:

> [R]equiring verification of wire service stories prior to publication would impose a heavy burden on the media's ability to disseminate newsworthy material. * * * Because verification would be time-consuming and expensive, imposing such a burden would probably force smaller publishers to confine themselves to stories about purely local events. This, in turn, could make it extremely difficult for the smaller newspapers to compete with those publishers who "can afford to verify or to litigate." Moreover, . . . we recognize that society has an interest, embodied in the First Amendment, in avoiding "apprehensive self-censorship" by the news media. In light of all these factors, we conclude that a newspaper ordinarily has exercised "due care in gathering information" when it publishes material taken from a reputable wire service.

The *Firestone* case falls into the second category, although the Supreme Court did not squarely rule on the question of *Time*'s negligence in inaccurately reporting the grounds for Mrs. Firestone's divorce. Nonetheless, Justice Rehnquist's opinion for the Court suggested that the magazine was liable because its reporter misinterpreted the order of the Florida court granting the divorce. Although the meaning of the divorce decree was unclear, Justice Rehnquist emphasized that *Time* was not free to "choose from among several conceivable interpretations the one most damaging" to Mrs. Firestone (i.e., that her husband had been granted the divorce on grounds of her adultery). Although Justice Powell stressed in his concurring opinion that the magazine's interpretation of the ambiguous document had been confirmed by a wire service report, a newspaper article, and *Time*'s own staff, the majority opinion seems to suggest that *Time* did not take the most obvious step when faced with a confusing legal document—contacting a Florida lawyer familiar with that state's divorce laws.

The third category is illustrated by a 1983 Arkansas case, *KARK-TV v. Simon,* in which a reporter at the scene of an apparent robbery attempt did not know the circumstances surrounding what she had observed. There a television station's news staff learned from the police radio that a robbery was reportedly in progress at a store and relayed the information to a reporter who happened to be nearby. When she arrived, she observed the police handcuffing two men and placing them in a squad car. A film crew sent to meet the reporter recorded this activity and quickly returned to the station to begin editing the material for the rapidly approaching evening newscast. The reporter interviewed police officers on the spot but was told that no information would be available until later that evening. She also questioned a store clerk but received only vague responses. The reporter then returned to the station, and an attempt to obtain further details from police headquarters was unsuccessful. On its evening newscast, the station reported that police had foiled an attempted robbery at which a store clerk had been allegedly held hostage and that two suspects were in custody. A film clip showed the two men, handcuffed, being placed in a police car. Unfortunately, the men had not been arrested and had been released by police at the scene shortly after the reporter had left. The Arkansas Supreme Court ruled that these facts constituted sufficient evidence of negligence to send the question to the jury. Moreover, the court did not discuss the time pressures associated with the story as a mitigating factor.

In contrast, a Massachusetts court found that reporters had not acted negligently in *Dwyer v. Globe Newspaper Co.* (1980), a case which grew out of a tip that a bar owner was taking bets over the telephone. Two reporters followed up that information by observing activity at the bar for a week and by placing two phone calls themselves, posing as persons desiring to place bets. Satisfied that the owner was involved, the reporters prepared a story identifying him as the resident bookmaker. Although the court determined that this was erroneous, it ruled that the journalists' lengthy first-hand observation precluded a finding of negligence, although the reporters had failed to interview the owner himself. Thus, even though they drawn the wrong conclusion from what they had witnessed, the reporters' otherwise thorough investigation, which had produced nothing to warn them of their error, was deemed reasonable.

Production errors seem less likely to cause negligence problems because they do not involve any editorial judgment with respect to truth or falsity, the cornerstone of the *Gertz* approach. As the New York Court of Appeals observed in *Chapadeau v. Utica Observer-Dispatch, Inc.* (1975), typographical errors are inevitable in a newspaper and cannot be sufficient to satisfy the state's "gross irresponsibility" standard for private figure libel cases. Other courts have found that such errors do not constitute "reckless disregard" under the *New York Times* rule. In *Channel 4, KGBT v. Briggs* (1988), for example, a television station mistakenly aired a video tape of a political candidate in connection with a report on the Ku Klux Klan, a group with which he was not associated. The Texas Supreme Court ruled that the error, which was caused by the station's failure to completely erase the tape of the candidate before using it for the Klan story, did not constitute reckless disregard.

As Professor Franklin has pointed out, similar results should be reached when simple negligence analysis is employed because of the Supreme Court's statement in *Gertz* that the fault requirement applies when the information "makes substantial danger to reputation apparent." The Court noted that different considerations are involved when a state attempts to impose liability on the basis of "a factual misstatement whose content did not warn a reasonably prudent editor or broadcaster of its defamatory potential." As discussed earlier in connection with the concept of libel per quod, the Court's statement indicates that liability should not attach unless the story on its face reveals that it could cause reputational harm. An innocent story that becomes defamatory when extrinsic information is known—the libel per quod situation—apparently does not satisfy this requirement. Similarly, Professor Franklin has argued that a publisher should not be liable, even if negligent with respect to a typographical error or similar production mistake, if the error "turns an innocent story into a defamatory one."

Reckless Disregard. A public official or public figure must prove more than mere negligence in order to recover in his defamation suit. Under the *New York Times* rule, the "public" plaintiff must establish, by clear and convincing evidence, that the defendant published the information with reckless disregard for the truth or knowledge that it was false. The "clear and convincing" standard of proof is significantly greater than the "preponderance of the evidence" test used in the negligence cases, and it thus affords greater protection to libel defendants. Legal scholars describe the "clear and convincing" standard as falling between the "preponderance" test and the very stringent "beyond a reasonable doubt" requirement in criminal cases. Thus, even if the evidence tips slightly in favor of a finding of fault (thus justifying a verdict for a plaintiff under the preponderance test), the jury must find for the defendant because the evidence is not "clear and convincing."

Though the Supreme Court has emphasized several times that there is no first amendment value in a "knowing falsehood," the cases turning on publication with knowledge of falsity are few and far between. Most of the time, the central question is the defendant's recklessness, since proof that someone had deliberately lied is usually quite difficult. In *Goldwater v. Ginzburg* (1969), however, the U.S. Court of Appeals for the Second Circuit concluded that Senator Barry Goldwater had carried that heavy burden in his suit against Ralph Ginzburg, publisher of *Fact* magazine. Ginzburg had published an article, titled "The Unconscious of a Conservative," purporting to marshall psychiatric evidence that the Senator, then running for President, was mentally ill. Among other things, there was evidence that the magazine's staff had a preconceived plan to discredit Goldwater, ignored information contrary to the conclusion they wanted to reach in the article, and failed to heed warnings from experts as to the invalidity of certain data and techniques. The appellate court found that this evidence was sufficient to establish that the article contained deliberate falsehoods.

While the Supreme Court has left to the states the task of refining the negligence concept used in "private figure" libel suits, it has spelled out in some detail what does or does not constitute "reckless disregard" in cases brought by public officials and public figures. In *New York Times* itself, for example, the Court made clear that the newspaper's advertising department was not reckless simply because it failed to check material in the paper's own files that would have revealed inaccuracies in the civil rights advertisement. Thus, this type of failure to investigate, while possibly negligent, is not reckless. The Court began to elaborate on the meaning of the reckless disregard test in *Garrison v. Louisiana*, a decision handed down shortly after *New York Times*. There the Court defined a reckless statement as one made with a "high degree of awareness of [its] probable falsity."

The Court began to give more meaning to these concepts in the 1967 companion cases of *Curtis Publishing Co. v. Butts* and *Associated Press v. Walker.* In the *Butts* case, discussed previously, the Saturday Evening Post had published a story charging that a football game between Georgia and Alabama had been "fixed." The magazine's source for the article was George Burnett, an Atlanta salesman who claimed that, because of an electronic error, he had overheard a telephone conversation between Georgia athletic director Butts and Alabama coach Bryant.

Writing for a plurality of the Court, Justice John Marshall Harlan stressed that the story was not "hot news" (the game had long been played) and that the magazine's editors recognized the need for a thorough investigation of such serious charges. Instead, they relied only on Burnett, whom they knew had been placed on probation for passing bad checks, without any independent verification. The editors did not review Burnett's notes of the telephone conversation prior to publishing the story, made no attempt to interview another person present with Burnett when he overheard the conversation, and did not examine films of the game to ascertain whether Burnett's information had been accurate. Moreover, the writer who prepared the story knew relatively little about football, and no effort was made to check the story with someone knowledgeable about the sport. Not surprisingly, the Court affirmed a judgment of $460,000 against the magazine.

In *Walker*, however, the Court reached a different result. There the Associated Press had reported, erroneously, that retired General Edwin Walker, a segregationist, had taken command of a hostile crowd and "personally led a charge" against federal marshals enforcing a court order to admit black student James Meredith to the University of Mississippi. The AP account came from one of its own correspondents who was on the campus at the time of the incident and who gave every indication of being reliable. Further, the Court emphasized that this was "hot news" requiring immediate distribution and that the information in the story was not inherently improbable in light of Walker's widely publicized stand on segregation. Given such evidence that the wire service had acted reasonably under the circumstances, the Court reversed lower court decisions awarding Walker $500,000 in damages.

The *Butts* and *Walker* cases created some confusion, however, because of uncertainty among the Justices as to the standard of fault to be used in public figure cases. Of course, the Court subsequently made clear that they must show reckless disregard, just like public officials, and the *Butts* and *Walker* cases have since come to stand as good examples of what does and does not constitute recklessness.

The most important case in this area is *St. Amant v. Thompson* (1968), which arose from a political campaign. During a televised speech, St. Amant, a candidate for public office, repeated various statements by a local union leader implying that Thompson, a deputy sheriff, had taken bribes. The union leader's statements had been contained in an affidavit made under oath, and St. Amant made no independent verification of the charges, which turned out to be false. The state court found that St. Amant had been reckless, but the Supreme Court reversed. Writing for the Court, Justice Byron White said that there must be "sufficient evidence to permit the conclusion that the defendant entertained serious doubts as to the truth of his publication." However, a defendant cannot automatically ensure a favorable verdict simply by testifying that he believed the statements were true. Justice White said:

> The finder of fact must determine whether the publication was indeed made in good faith. Professions of good faith will be unlikely to prove persuasive, for example, where a story is fabricated by the defendant, is a product of his imagination, or is based wholly on an unverified anonymous telephone call. Nor will they be likely to prevail when the . . . allegations are so inherently improbable that only a reckless man would have put them in circulation. Likewise, recklessness may be found where there are

obvious reasons to doubt the veracity of the informant or the accuracy of his information.

The Court concluded that St. Amant lacked the requisite "awareness of probable falsity" of the defamatory statements because he had known the union leader for several years, the charges had been made in a sworn affidavit, and St. Amant had verified other information provided by the same individual. Accordingly, the fact that he failed to investigate the charges himself was not reckless.

Similarly, in *Rosenbloom v. Metromedia, Inc.* (1971), a plurality of the Justices found that the reckless disregard test had not been met where a radio station relied on a local police captain for its report on the arrest, on obscenity charges, of a distributor of nudist magazines. Although the *Rosenbloom* case was overruled by *Gertz* with respect to another issue (the level of fault that a private individual must prove in a libel suit), its discussion of the reckless disregard test remains "good law." Writing for the plurality, Justice Brennan emphasized that the radio station's half-hour deadlines made it necessary to rely on the wire services and oral reports from previously reliable sources. Because the station had obtained its information from a public official whose veracity was not subject to doubt, a jury could not find recklessness even though the station had failed to contact the magazine distributor for his side of the story. While this conduct might be considered negligent, Justice Brennan observed, it did not rise to the level of reckless disregard.

In contrast to *St. Amant* and *Rosenbloom* is *Harte-Hanks Communications, Inc. v. Connaughton* (1989), in which the Supreme Court upheld a jury's finding of reckless disregard in a suit brought by an unsuccessful candidate for municipal judge. A week before the election, the Hamilton (Ohio) *Journal News* published allegations that the candidate had promised to provide a job, an expenses-paid vacation, and other favors to a woman if she would testify before a grand jury investigating the court administrator, an appointee of the incumbent judge. Also included in the story was a charge that the candidate had planned not to publicly disclose the damaging information about the administrator but to use it covertly to force the judge to resign. The newspaper's source was the woman's sister, who claimed that the candidate had also offered her various favors.

The Supreme Court, in an opinion by Justice John Paul Stevens, likened the case to *Butts* and emphasized that the newspaper had several reasons to doubt the veracity of its source but nonetheless failed to investigate further. The source was at times equivocal and unresponsive in her tape-recorded interview with the newspaper, and one of her key charges was "highly improbable" in light of facts known to reporters prior to the story's publication. Though she had claimed that the candidate intended to keep the information secret and use it only to "scare" the judge into resigning, he had in fact taken the matter to the police and filed a written complaint against the administrator, who was ultimately indicted and convicted on charges of "fixing" various criminal cases.

Moreover, the candidate acknowledged in an interview with the *Journal News* that he had met with the two women about the administrator but categorically denied having offered them any sort of "deal." Five other persons who had been present at that meeting were also interviewed for the story, and all corroborated the candidate's account of what transpired there. No one at the newspaper bothered to listen of a tape recording of that meeting (which the candidate had provided), and no effort was made to interview the source's sister, who actually had the information that the candidate was said to have improperly solicited. "[I]t is likely that the newspaper's inaction was a product of a deliberate decision not to acquire knowledge of facts that might confirm the probable falsity of [the source's] charges," Justice Stevens wrote. "Although failure to investigate will not alone support a finding of [recklessness], the purposeful avoidance of the truth is in a different category."

As the foregoing cases indicate, the same situations that can give rise to a finding of negligence in cases brought by private plaintiffs can cause similar trouble when a public official or public figure who must prove reckless disregard is involved. Therefore, the same sort of inquiry must be employed. Was reliance upon a particular source reckless? Did the source "have an axe to grind"? Has the investigation been sufficiently thorough, particularly in light of deadline pressures and the "hot news" nature of the story? Is there contradictory information available? The bottom line, as libel specialist Bruce Sanford has noted, is that the law "seldom demands more from a journalist than do the ethics of his profession."

Keep firmly in mind, however, that a showing of substantially more than mere negligence is necessary, and the focus is upon whether the information is inherently improbable and whether the defendant entertained "serious doubts" about its truth. For example, in *Costello v. Capital Cities Communications, Inc.* (1988), the Illinois Supreme Court ruled that a newspaper had not acted recklessly in printing an editorial that accused the plaintiff of acting dishonestly. Although the editorial writer did not contact the plaintiff and offer him an opportunity to respond to the charges, the court concluded that the writer had no reason to doubt the veracity of four sources who provided him information for the editorial. As noted previously, the failure to seek out "the other side of the story" may constitute negligence, at least under certain circumstances.

Although there has from time to time been some confusion in the lower courts, it is now settled that a defendant's subjective feelings about a particular plaintiff—such as hostility will or spite—do not, standing alone, constitute reckless disregard. Moreover, as the U.S. Court of Appeals for the Second Circuit recently observed in the *Contemporary Mission* case, the mere fact that a newspaper may have been "somewhat aggressive and expressed a point of view in its presentation of the facts" is not sufficient. The rationale behind this rule is that no matter what the defendant's motive, speech that is honestly believed contributes to the free exchange of ideas and is thus worthy of first amendment protection. Under some circumstances, however, strained relations between plaintiff and defendant, an avowed policy of "muckraking," and similar factors can be circumstantial evidence of the defendant's recklessness when considered with other evidence more directly indicative of fault.

In the *Harte-Hanks* case, evidence suggested that the defendant had an improper motive in publishing the defamatory story: the newspaper supported the plaintiff's opponent in the municipal judge race and was involved in a bitter circulation battle with a competing daily. While emphasizing that a newspaper's motive is not, standing alone, sufficient to establish reckless disregard, the Supreme Court indicated that evidence of this type can help support a finding of recklessness when there is other proof of fault. Because "a plaintiff is entitled to prove the defendant's state of mind through circumstantial evidence," the Court observed, "it cannot be said that evidence concerning motive . . . never bears any relation to the [reckless disregard] inquiry." However, the Court did not rely on that evidence in upholding the jury's determination that the newspaper acted with reckless disregard.

Improper motive was a factor in *Herron v. KING Broadcasting Co.* (1987), in which the Washington Supreme Court reversed the trial court's grant of summary judgment for the defendant, ruling that there was sufficient evidence of reckless disregard to be submitted to the jury. There KING-TV broadcast a story suggesting an improper relationship between plaintiff, a prosecuting attorney, and bail bondsmen. The report also stated—erroneously—that bondsmen had contributed "approximately half" of all campaign funds raised by the prosecutor. Although the reporter claimed to have examined the campaign contribution records (which, under state law, were open to the public), he could apparently not explain why his story was incorrect on this point. While this alone would not amount to reckless disregard, the court also pointed out that the reporter relied on sources he knew or should have known to be unreliable, including the former prosecutor who had lost a bitter race to the plaintiff. Moreover, the evidence showed that the reporter had a hostile conversation with the prosecutor's deputy during which he threatened to "get" the prosecutor and his staff. These facts, coupled with the station's destruction of the tapes of the broadcast, were sufficient to raise a jury question on the issue of reckless disregard, the court said.

Vicarious Liability. In defamation as in other areas of tort law, an employer can be held liable based on the fault of an employee even though the employer himself was blameless. This doctrine, known as vicarious liability or *respondeat superior*, is based upon the notion that an employer should be responsible for the wrongs of employees committed during the course of their jobs. In *Cantrell v. Forest City Publishing Co.* (1974), the Supreme Court reaffirmed the applicability of this principle in media cases, stating that although there was no evidence that the newspaper had knowledge of the inaccuracies in the article prepared by its reporter, the company was liable because the story had been written by the journalist in the normal course of his work at the paper. Both negligence and reckless disregard on the part of such employees as reporters, editors, archorpersons, producers, and other "in house" personnel may be imputed to a publisher or broadcaster. Essentially, the doctrine applies to any employee in part responsible for the content of the offending story.

In contrast, an employer is not vicariously liable for the acts of an "independent contractor"—that is, someone who performs a given task but who is not a regular employee. In the media context, the fault of freelance writers, syndicated columnists, wire services, or persons who write letters to the editor would not be imputed to a publisher or broadcaster. This is not to say, however, that a news organization automatically escapes liability in such situations, for a publisher or broadcaster is always liabile for its *own* fault regarding information it prints or broadcasts.

The proper analysis is illustrated by *Marcone v. Penthouse International*, a case that involved an article written by a freelance writer. In determining whether the magazine was to be held liable for defamatory statements in the article, the court did not focus on the fault of the freelance writer, whose recklessness could not be attributed to *Penthouse*. Instead, the court inquired as to whether the magazine itself had been at fault in relying on this particular freelancer. Concluding that *Penthouse* not acted recklessly, the court pointed out that the freelancer had substantial professional experience in print and broadcast journalism, had written for several newspapers (including the *Los Angeles Times*), and had worked previously with the magazine's editorial director, who found his investigative reporting to be reliable. The same analysis would be used in a case based on a libelous letter to the editor. However, the courts typically hold that reliance upon a wire service or syndicated columnist is neither negligent nor reckless as a matter of law.

Strict Liability. Although the foregoing discussion has preceded upon the premise that at least some sort of fault must be shown before a libel plaintiff can recover against a media defendant, the Supreme Court's 1985 decision in *Dun & Bradstreet, Inc. v. Greenmoss Builders, Inc.* casts some doubt on that assumption. This case, discussed in more detail in the section on damages that follows, suggests that a private plaintiff might be able to establish liability without proving fault if the subject matter of the defamatory statement is not a matter of public concern. Accordingly, it could be possible for a public official or public figure to sue successfully a media defendant on a strict liability theory *if* the issue giving rise to the defamatory statement is deemed a private matter.

When the Supreme Court accepted the *Greenmoss* case for review, some commentators believed that the Court might seize the opportunity to draw a distinction between media and nonmedia defendants in libel cases and hold that only the former are entitled to the constitutional protection afforded by *New York Times* and *Gertz.* Although at least five members of the Court appear to have rejected such a distinction in *Greenmoss*, Justice Powell's plurality opinion indicates that purely private speech is not worthy of the first amendment safeguards. It seems clear that information published by the press is much more likely to be treated as a matter of public concern than purely private speech between two individuals. Accordingly, the status of the defendant—media or nonmedia—may still be significant, at least indirectly, in libel cases. Indications are, however, that the last word has not been written on the subject, for a footnote in a subsequent case suggests that the Court considers the media-nonmedia question unresolved.

More importantly, *Greenmoss* leaves open the possibility that, even where media defendants are involved, the fault requirements found in *Gertz* and *New York Times* may not be applicable if the speech is deemed "private." *Greenmoss* involved an erroneous report that a company had filed for bankruptcy, a matter that Justice Powell considered "private" and not a "matter of public concern." The meaning term "matter of public concern" is not altogether clear, though it sounds much like the "public controversy" concept used in determining whether a plaintiff is a limited public figure. Despite their superficial similarlity, the terms seem to address different problems. While the "public controversy" test looks primarily to the plaintiff's participation in the public arena, the "public concern" test focuses on the nature of the defamatory speech itself. This interpretation appears to be consistent with both *Greenmoss* and *Gertz*, for these cases recognize that even a "private" plaintiff who does not qualify as a public figure or public official will on occasion be required to establish negligence. If the two terms are equated, however, a "private" plaintiff would be able to claim that his status alone compels the conclusion that the speech is not of public concern and that he can, therefore, recover without a showing of fault.

Moreover, the *Greenmoss* decision could mean that a public figure or public official might, under certain circumstances, be able to recover under the old "strict liability" concept. If, as the Court ruled in that case, the financial condition of a business is not a matter of public concern, one could make the same argument with respect to the financial status of a public figure such as Johnny Carson. In a libel suit against a newspaper that published a story inaccurately portraying his finances, Mr. Carson would, under this interpretation, not be required to prove that the defendant had acted with reckless disregard for the truth. So read, *Greenmoss* has the potential for destroying a significant amount of the first amendment protection from defamation suits that has evolved over the past two decades. Moreover, if this interpretation of the case is accurate, the law of defamation has become more confusing than ever, with liability hinging not only on the public or private status of the plaintiff but also the public or private nature of the issue involved. The following chart shows the possible combinations.

Category	Standard of Liability
1. Public Plaintiff, Public Issue.	Reckless disregard for truth, knowledge of falsity.
2. Public Plaintiff, Private Issue.	Strict liability.
3. Private Plaintiff, Public Issue.	Fault, usually negligence.
4. Private Plaintiff, Private Issue.	Strict liability.

As the reader is undoubtedly aware after reaching this point in the chapter, the law of defamation is complicated enough without considering the possible impact of *Greenmoss* on the liability question. Things would get even worse if the courts were also to add to the equation the question of whether the defendant was or was not part of the news media, for in that event the four categories shown on chart would expand to eight. The growing complexity of the constitutional law of defamation and the considerable uncertainty that now exists suggest that the Court may reevaluate *New York Times* and its progeny, a course suggested by Chief Justice Burger and Justice White in their separate opinions in the *Greenmoss* case.

Falsity

Under the common law of libel, the plaintiff is required to allege that the assertedly defamatory statement made about him is false, and it is up to the defendant to prove that the statement is true. As in all other types of litigation, the assignment of the burden of proof in defamation cases is extremely important; simply put, the party with the burden of proof loses the case if he fails to carry that burden. In the typical automobile accident case, for example, neither the parties to the collision nor bystanders who witness the wreck might be able to explain with any degree of certainty what happened at the fateful intersection. Because the injured party in such a case has the burden of proving that the defendant caused the collision, the plaintiff loses if he cannot produce sufficient evidence as to the cause of the accident and how it occurred. If, however, the law placed on the defendant the burden of showing that the accident was not his fault, the plaintiff would win if the defendant were unable to demonstrate with sufficient evidence the cause of the wreck. Burden of proof is particularly important in defamation cases because truth is often an elusive concept that can never be established with certainty. And, even if a statement is true, a defendant with the burden of proof is nonetheless liable if he cannot convince a jury of its truth.

In light of the constitutional requirement that a libel plaintiff prove that the defendant negligently or recklessly made a defamatory statement, it seems logical to require—contrary to the common law—that he also prove that the statement is indeed false. After several years of conflicting lower court decisions, the U.S. Supreme Court so ruled in *Philadelphia Newspapers, Inc. v. Hepps* (1986), although the decision leaves open some important questions as to its scope. In that case, the *Philadelphia Inquirer* published a series of articles linking the plaintiffs to organized crime and claiming that the plaintiffs exploited those links to influence state government. Pennsylvania followed the common law rule assigning to the defendant the burden of proving truth. The Supreme Court, in an opinion by Justice Sandra Day O'Connor, concluded that the first amendment requires that the burden of proving falsity be placed on the plaintiff. She wrote:

> There will always be instances when the fact-finding process will be unable to resolve conclusively whether the speech is true or false; it is in those cases that the burden of proof is dispositive. * * * Because the evidence is ambiguous, we cannot know how much of the speech . . . is true and how much is false. In a case . . . where the scales are in such an uncertain balance, we believe that the Constitution requires us to tip them in favor of protecting true speech. * * * We recognize that requiring the plaintiff to show falsity will insulate from liability some speech that is false, but unprovably so. Nonetheless, . . . the First Amendment requires that we protect some falsehood in order to protect speech that matters.

Although this rationale could be applied in all types of defamation cases, the Court expressly limited its ruling in *Hepps* to cases in which the defamatory statement involves a matter of public concern and a media defendant is being sued. (The plaintiff's status—private person, public official, or public figure—is unimportant.) But what if a nonmedia defendant is the target of the suit, or the case does not involve a matter of public concern? The Court did not address these situations, thereby leaving some unanswered questions, much as it did in *Greenmoss*. However, most legal scholars believe that the *Hepps* principle should be extended to all defamation cases. Professor Smolla, for example, has argued that, irrespective of the type of libel case, the defendant should be "innocent until proven guilty." Moreover, tort law routinely places the burden of proof on plaintiffs when matters just as important as reputation are being litigated, and there is no logical reason to treat defamation cases any differently.

Regardless of who must bear the burden of proof with respect to truth or falsity, a statement is protected if it is "substantially true." That is, literal truth is not required, and slight inaccuracies are immaterial if the substance of the statement— its "gist" or "sting"—is true. For example, in *Fort Worth Press v. Davis*, a 1936 Texas case, the newspaper had charged that the mayor had wasted $85,000 on a useless water supply project. While evidence revealed that only $17,500 had been spent on the project, the court held that difference in amounts did not have any bearing on the imputation. Similarly, in a 1969 Texas case, *Dunn v. Newspapers, Inc.*, a congressional candidate sued on the basis of a news story stating that he was "once again" running against the incumbent and that in a race several years before had received only one write-in vote. Though he had actually received twenty-three such votes in the prior election, the court had little difficulty finding the statement substantially true.

At some point, however, a statement becomes substantially false. For example, in the *KING Broadcasting* case discussed previously, the defendant's report linked the plaintiff and bail bondsmen by stating, among other things, that bondsmen had "contributed approximately half of all campaign money" collected by the plaintiff in his race for prosecuting attorney. The trial court concluded that the story was substantially true, but the Washington Supreme Court reversed, pointing out that public records showed that only about two percent of the plaintiff's campaign contributions had been made by bondsmen. "[T]he statement that 'approximately half' of [the] contributions came from bail bondsmen carries significantly greater opprobrium than the more accurate figure," the court said. "The false statement affected the 'sting' of the story itself, *i.e.*, that the plaintiff had bargained away his ethics and integrity in exchange for campaign contributions."

The substantial truth doctrine often comes into play with respect to the reporting of legal terms. For example, in *Piracci v. Hearst Corp.* (1967), the newspaper reported that the plaintiff had been arrested for "possession of marijuana." In fact, he had been charged with "deliquency due to the act of possessing marijuana," a different offense. The U.S. Court of Appeals for the Fourth Circuit upheld the trial court's judgment that the news report was substantially true. Similarly, in *Joyce v. George W. Prescott Publishing Co.* (1965), the Massachusetts Supreme Court ruled that a newspaper story stating that plaintiff had been "committed" to a hospital when he had actually been "admitted" was substantially true, even though commitment is confinement by court order. Loose use of legal terms can result in liability, however. Recall that in the *Firestone* decision *Time* magazine's report of the divorce on grounds of adultery was not protected, since the use of that term had a different "sting" than the actual reason for the divorce, "lack of domestication."

Damages

Tort law generally recognizes two types of damages that can be awarded a plaintiff who prevails in litigation. Compensatory damages are designed to compensate him for his loss or injury, while punitive (or "exemplary") damages are meant to punish the defendant for his wrongdoing and to deter him and others from engaging in such conduct. Unfortunately, the law of defamation has been considerably more complex than this basic scheme. Although the Supreme Court's decision in the *Gertz* case radically altered the common law approach to damages in the defamation context, remants of that system still remain important today.

The type of compensatory damages that could be awarded a defamation plaintiff at common law hinged on the nature of the injuries he claimed. In certain types of slander cases and in all libel cases except the libel per quod category, injury to one's reputation was presumed to have occurred as a result of the publication. An award of *general damages* would theoretically compensate the plaintiff for the loss of esteem and standing in society stemming from the defamatory statement. Because this injury was presumed, no proof of actual impact on reputation was required, and the jury was free to arrive at a monetary figure it deemed adequate to repair the harm. The results could be staggering, as illustrated by the $500,000 awarded Police Commissioner Sullivan at trial in the *New York Times* case. However, the concept of *nominal damages* allowed the jury to make a token award, usually one dollar, to a plaintiff who had technically been defamed but had suffered no real reputational injury.

In suits involving libel per quod and certain types of slander, the law did not presume injury to reputation but instead demanded that the plaintiff establish *special damages*—that is, specific, measurable pecuniary harm that had been caused by the defamatory statement. For example, a businessman who could prove that particular customers no longer frequented his shop or that another company had refused to renew its contract with him would be entitled to damages based on the loss of such business. Similarly, an individual who could identify friends who no longer associated with him could recover if he could link their loss to some pecuniary harm. In some jurisdictions, special damages could be awarded if the plaintiff were able to show mental or physical illness requiring medical treatment as a result of the defamation. Once the plaintiff made out a case for special damages, he was then entitled to the presumption of injury applicable in other defamation suits and thus to an award of general damages as well.

Any of the three types of compensatory damages could serve as a predicate for an award of punitive damages if the jury found that the defendant had acted in bad faith or with ill will or spite in publishing the defamatory matter. In other words, the law recognized that such malicious conduct should be punished and the defendant be held out as an example of what might happen to others who chose to act in such a manner. The jury was given virtual carte blanche authority to assess a sum of money sufficient to achieve those purposes, although most jurisdictions gave either the trial or appellate court power to reduce or overturn "excessive" punitive damage awards. Some jurisdictions adopted other measures to control juries with respect to punitive damages. For example, in some states nominal damages cannot serve as the basis for an award of punitive damages, and in others the amount of punitive damages must be reasonably proportional to the amount of compensatory damages. And, a few states have eliminated punitive damages altogether.

In the landmark *Gertz* decision, the Supreme Court ruled that the first amendment limits the types and amounts of damages that can be awarded to libel plaintiffs. In accommodating the competing interests at stake—the first amendment on the one hand and an individual's interest in his "good name" on the other—the Court concluded that "the States may not permit recovery of presumed or punitive damages, at least when liability is not based on a showing of knowledge of falsity or reckless disregard for the truth." Justice Powell explained the reasoning behind this rule as follows:

> The common law of defamation is an oddity of tort law, for it allows recovery of purporedly compensatory damages without evidence of actual loss. Under the traditional rules pertaining to actions for libel, the existence of injury is presumed from the fact of publication. Juries may award substantial sums as compensation for supposed damage to reputation without any proof that such harm actually occurred. The largely uncontrolled discretion of juries to award damages where there is no loss unnecessarily compounds the potential of any system of liability for defamatory falsehood to inhibit the vigorous exercise of First Amendment freedoms. Additionally, the doctrine of presumed damages invites juries to punish unpopular opinion rather than compensate individuals for injury sustained by the publication of a false fact. More to the point, the States have no substantial interest in securing for plaintiffs . . . gratuitous awards of money damages far in excess of any actual injury. * * *

> We also find no justification for allowing awards of punitive damages against publishers and broadcasters held liable under state-defined standards of liability for defamation. In most jurisdictions jury discretion over the amounts awarded is limited only by the gentle rule that they not be excessive. Consequently, juries assess punitive damages in wholly unpredictable amounts bearing no necessary relation to the actual harm caused. And they remain free to use their discretion selectively to punish expressions of unpopular views. Like the doctrine of presumed damages, jury discretion to award punitive damages unnecessarily exacerbates the danger of media self-censorship, but, unlike the former rule, punitive damages are wholly irrelevant to the state interest that justifies a negligence standard for private defamation actions. They are not compensation for injury. Instead, they are private fines levied by civil juries to punish reprehensible conduct and to deter its future occurrence. In short, the private defamation plaintiff

who establishes liability under a less demanding standard than that stated by *New York Times* may recover only such damages as are sufficient to compensate him for actual injury.

The Court did not define precisely what it meant by "actual injury" (usually called "actual damages" by the lower courts) but explained that it is "not limited to out-of-pocket loss," meaning that the term is not to be equated with special damages under the common law. Moreover, the Court said that actual injury can include "impairment of reputation and standing in the community, personal humiliation, and mental anguish and suffering." Subsequently, in *Time, Inc. v. Firestone*, the Court made plain that emotional harm alone is sufficient to support an award of actual damages and that no injury to reputation need be shown. There Mrs. Firestone based her claim for damages on the emotional distress she suffered from the magazine's description of her as an adulteress. While damages based on such "mental anguish" are indeed speculative and could create problems similar to those caused by the doctrine of presumed damages, *Gertz* does require some type of proof that the injury has occurred, something that was not necessary with respect to presumed damages. Moreover, several courts have, as a matter of state law, adopted the requirement that a defamation plaintiff seeking to recover damages for emotional injury must first prove actual injury to his reputation.

It is important to keep in mind that *Gertz* has not completely eliminated the common law categories of damages. For example, the Court said that presumed and punitive damages are not permissible, "at least" where liability is based on a showing of something less than reckless disregard for the truth or knowledge of falsity. Although the Court's cautious language suggests that it may at some point abolish altogether presumed and punitive damages and that their constitutional validity is in doubt,[8] most lower courts have interpreted *Gertz* to mean that presumed and punitive damages are allowable so long as the plaintiff shows that the defendant was reckless. Because a public official or public figure must prove such recklessness in order to establish liability, this rule has the greatest impact in "private figure" suits. There, the defamation plaintiff must prove some degree of fault, usually negligence, in connection with liability, but must prove recklessness if he is to obtain presumed or punitive damages. If he cannot establish such reckless conduct, he is limited to a damage award for his "actual injury." Of course, the state courts are free in interpreting their own law to abolish presumed or punitive damages, and a handful have done so.

In *Dun & Bradstreet, Inc. v. Greenmoss Builders, Inc.*, a badly divided Supreme Court ruled that a "private" plaintiff in a libel suit need not establish recklessness in order to recover presumed or punitive damages if the defamatory statement did not relate to a matter of public concern. In *Greenmoss*, a Vermont high school student employed part time by the credit reporting agency Dun & Bradstreet to

---

[8]Apart from any first amendment restrictions, the due process clause of the fourteenth amendment, which ensures fairness in judicial proceedings, may impose some limits on the amount of punitive damages that may be awarded. The Supreme Court expressly left open this question in *Browning-Ferris Industries of Vermont, Inc. v. Kelco Disposal, Inc.* (1989) while deciding that the excessive fines clause of the eighth amendment applies only to penalties assessed by government and thus does not limit punitive damages in civil suits between private parties. With respect to the due process question, four Justices indicated that they were troubled by the virtually unbridled discretion of juries as to the amount of punitive damages.

review local bankruptcy petitions, told the firm that Greenmoss Builders, Inc., a contractor, had filed a voluntary petition in bankruptcy. Dun & Bradstreet circulated this unverified and inaccurate information to five subscribers, and Greenmoss brought suit. The jury returned a verdict of $50,000 actual damages and $300,000 punitive damages against Dun & Bradstreet, but the trial judge ordered a new trial. The Vermont Supreme Court reversed and reinstated the verdict.

The question on appeal to the U.S. Supreme Court was whether the *Gertz* rule barring presumed and punitive damages absent a showing of recklessness applied in this case. Writing for the plurality, Justice Powell—the author of *Gertz*—concluded that the rule was inapplicable where, as in *Greenmoss*, the plaintiff was a private figure and the defamatory information did not involve a matter of public concern. Reasoning that the false credit report was a nonpublic issue entitled to less first amendment protection than speech dealing with issues of public importance, he determined that the $300,000 punitive damage award was permissible even though the plaintiff had not established recklessness. Justice Powell's opinion was joined by two other members of the Court, and two more Justices concurred in the result reached but not the reasoning employed by Justice Powell.

Although the situation is indeed muddled, it apears that after *Greenmoss* a private plaintiff in a defamation suit based on a statement that is not a matter of public concern need not prove reckless disregard to recover presumed or punitive damages. All other private plaintiffs, as well as public officials and public figures, must satisfy *Gertz* and establish reckless disregard to obtain those damages. Because *Greenmoss* holds that this *Gertz* protection does not extend to private plaintiff/private issue defamation suits, it is arguable that none of the *Gertz* safeguards are applicable in that context. Accordingly, a private plaintiff in a case not involving a matter of public concern may be able to proceed under a strict liability theory without proving fault of any kind and also obtain presumed and punitive damages absent a showing of fault. In other words, this private plaintiff/private issues suits would be governed by the set of common law rules of liability and damages that existed prior to *Gertz* and *New York Times*.

Another area of the common law that remains intact after *Gertz* involves mitigation of damages, though this matter is now governed by statute in many states. The law has long allowed a defendant to plead and prove the existence of certain "mitigating" circumstances that justify a reduction in the amount of damages that might otherwise be awarded the plaintiff. For example, evidence of the defendant's good faith in publishing the information is often admissible in mitigation of compensatory damages and may serve to eliminate punitive damages. Moreover, a defendant may be able to show that the plaintiff had ample opporunity to rebut the defamatory charges, thereby reducing the harm that he suffered, or had such a tarnished reputation already that he was "libel-proof."

The most common form of mitigation is the retraction, which, though not a defense in a libel suit, can indicate good faith on the part of the publisher to reduce the harm to the plaintiff. The terms of the state statutes vary widely with respect to retractions. Some provide that punitive damages may not be awarded if a full and prompt retraction is published, while others go even further and limit recovery to special damages. Regardless of the particular statute, the retraction should be complete and with reservation and should be given similar treatment in terms of space or time afforded the original story. Keep in mind, however, that publication of a retraction is not a defense to a libel suit but merely serves as a way of reducing damages.

THE DEFENDANT'S CASE

The foregoing material, while technically part of the plaintiff's case, obviously suggests methods for a defendant to avoid liability in a defamation suit. For example,
he can introduce evidence showing that he was not at fault or that the statement in
question was true, thereby making it difficult for the plaintiff to prove the elements
necessary to win his case. Indeed, the Iowa libel research project found that the
constitutional principles of *New York Times* and *Gertz* are involved in virtually all
defamation suits against the news media. This section considers additional defenses,
with emphasis on those most useful to the news media:

- common law and constitutional protection for statements of opinion;
- the "fair report" privilege and the related constitutional doctrine of neutral
  reportage; and
- the concept of summary judgment.

Matters of Opinion

Although the common law technically imposed liability on a publisher irrespective
of his fault, it also recognized that at times this "strict liability" had to give way in
order to encourage free communication about important matters. Accordingly,
there developed various "privileges" in the law of libel that barred a plaintiff's
recovery despite the fact that he had been defamed. In some cases, the law creates
absolute immunity; for example, a person who consents to publication of defamatory information cannot recover, nor can one who has been defamed by a public
official in the performance of his official duties. Other privileges—known as "qualified" or "conditional"—do not offer such complete protection. Rather, the privilege will not apply if the plaintiff demonstrated that the defendant has "abused" it
in some fashion.

One of the most important types of qualified privilege is that of "fair comment,"
which originated in English cases holding that a critic describing a literary, musical,
or artistic endeavor was protected from a libel judgment if his opinions and conclusions were based on an accurate and fair protrayal of underlying facts. American
courts expanded the privilege to include comments about matters of public interest,
the conduct of public officials, or private citizens involved in matters of community
concern. In its most widely adopted form, the fair comment privilege protects statements of opinion but not misstatements of fact.

The rules pertaining to fair comment are easily stated but often difficult to apply.
The subject matter of the statement must be of public concern, given the purpose
of the privilege in protecting communications about public issues. The statement
must be one of opinion rather than fact, since an opinion cannot be "false" and is
likely to be understood as an individual viewpoint instead of a factual assertion that
might damage reputation. Moreover, the factual basis for the opinion must be set
forth in the statement or be readily available, thus enabling the reader to form his
own opinion and evaluate the views of the commentator. Finally, the statement must
not have been motivated by ill will, spite, or other improper motive, for such a showing by the plaintiff defeats or overcomes the privilege. The question is really one of
intent—did the defendant publish his comments to warn or enlighten the public, or

did he make known his views because he disliked the plaintiff and sought to cause him harm?

Examples of the fair comment doctrine in operation are legion. These statements have been held privileged: a sports article stating that the plaintiff, "who shouldn't be coaching anything, is coaching the Houston receivers"; William F. Buckley, Jr.'s description of Gore Vidal's novel *Myra Breckinridge* as "simply a pornographic potboiler done for money"; a restaurant review labeling two dishes as "trout a la green plague" and "yellow death on duck"; and a statement that Will Rogers, who never a man he didn't like, must have never met the plaintiff. The classic American fair comment case, however, is undoubtedly *Cherry v. Des Moines Leader* (1901), which stemmed from a newspaper critic's review of a performance by the "Cherry Sisters." That the critic did not find the performance particularly appealing is a considerable understatement. He described them as "strange creatures with painted faces" and "rancid features" whose voices were "like the wailing of damned souls." The Iowa Supreme Court held that the fair comment privilege applied, pointing out that one "who goes upon the stage to exhibit himself to the public . . . may be freely criticized."

The fair comment doctrine has been "constitutionalized" in the wake of *Gertz v. Robert Welch, Inc.* Although this landmark decision did not involve a statement of opinion, Justice Powell began his discussion of the constitutional issues at stake with these words: "Under the First Amendment there is no such thing as a false idea. However pernicious an opinion may seem, we depend for its correction not on the conscience of judges and juries but on the competition of other ideas. But there is no constitutional value in false statements of fact. . . ." As media lawyer Robert Sack has observed, the implications of these few words are profound: "If as a matter of constitutional law an opinion can be neither true nor false and the law of defamation permits recovery only for statements proved to be false, then a statement of opinion can *never* give rise to a successful action for libel. . . ."

This interpretation of *Gertz*, which has been adopted by most lower courts, was buttressed by the Supreme Court's 1988 decision in *Hustler Magazine v. Falwell*, discussed later in this chapter in connection with a related tort, intentional infliction of emotional distress. There the Court ruled that the Rev. Jerry Falwell could not recover damages on the basis of an offensive "ad parody" published in *Hustler* magazine. Although the case did not directly involve the law of defamation, the Court made plain that a libel plaintiff must prove publication of "a false statement of fact" and that a statement of opinion—such as an editorial cartoon or the *Hustler* parody—will not suffice. As a result, the fair comment privilege is largely irrelevant, since a statement not entitled to protection under that doctrine (because of improper motive, for instance) would nonetheless enjoy the broader first amendment shield.

The major difficulty under both the fair comment privilege and the corresponding first amendment doctrine is, of course, distinguishing fact from opinion. Recall that in *Liberty Lobby* the court suggested that the statement that the plaintiff organization is "anti-Semitic" constituted protected opinion but expressly refused to decide the case on that ground. As the court pointed out, "[l]ike many words, the term . . . has both descriptive and normative content." Take another example: a statement that "Smith is crazy." In one sense, the remark seems factual, for it suggests that the individual is mentally ill—something that surely could be true. However, if the comment had been made about a candidate planning to challenge an incumbent officeholder considered politically unbeatable, the impression created is very different—an opinion that the challenger has no chance of winning the election. Because no all-purpose test for separating fact from opinion has been devised, the distinction hinges in large part on the impact of the statement on a typical reader or listener; that is, would the recipient of the statement be likely to understand it as an expression of opinion or a statement of fact?

Although there is considerable disagreement among the courts as to the analytical method to be employed in answering this question, three factors have emerged as significant. These are:

- the nature of the language used (i.e., whether it is typically understood as stating an opinion, or whether it is ambiguous on that score);
- the verifiability of the statement (i.e., whether it is capable of being objectively characterized as true or false); and
- the context in which the statement was made, including both the factual setting (labor dispute, political campaign) and the type of writing or commentary involved (restaurant review, news story, editorial cartoon).

As one court observed, however, "ultimately the decision whether a statement is fact or opinion must be based on all the circumstances involved."

With respect to the language employed, some words are commonly understood as expressions of opinion: ugly, crude, beautiful, unfair, best, worst, inept. Moreover, some statements are so obviously rhetorical or hyperbolic that the average reader would not mistake them as factual assertions. For example, in *Blouin v. Anton* (1981) the Vermont Supreme Court dismissed as mere rhetoric the description of the plaintiff as a "paranoid jerk" and a "horse's ass." To the same effect is *Stepien v. Franklin* (1988), in which the Ohio Court of Appeals ruled that a radio talk show host's statements that the plaintiff was an "egomaniac" and a "pathological liar" were not actionable. This sort of name-calling is commonly understood as opinion. On the other hand, such words as "thief," "corrupt," and "blackmail" seem to have a factual basis or are at best ambiguous. When the language is susceptible of being interpreted as "fact," the other factors listed above come into play.

Before leaving the "language" issue, another point should be emphasized. Qualifying language, such as "I think" or "in my opinion" labels the statement and thus suggests to the reader that no factual allegation is being made. Similarly, if the language is "cautiously phrased in terms of apparency," the courts are more likely to conclude that the statement is one of opinion. In *Alfego v. CBS* (1981), a Massachusetts federal court noted that the offending words were consistently prefaced with the phrase "in my opinion" and ruled that the statements were protected. The California Supreme Court reached the same conclusion in *Gregory v. McDonnell Douglas Corp.* (1976), where the word "apparently" had been used as a qualifier. However, the use of such terminology is not dispositive. In *Cianci v. New Times Publishing Co.* (1980), the U.S. Court of Appeals for the Second Circuit rejected the argument that the phrase "I think he is a rapist" was mere opinion, since the thrust of the statement was to accuse the plaintiff of a criminal act.

The "verifiability" factor is well illustrated by *Ollman v. Evans* (1984), an influential decision of the U.S. Court of Appeals for the District of Columbia Circuit mentioned briefly in *Liberty Lobby*. The case grew out of a controversy that arose when Bertell Ollman, a Marxist professor at New York University, was nominated to head the political science department at the University of Maryland. Syndicated columnists Roland Evans and Robert Novak jumped into the fray, writing that Ollman was "widely viewed in his profession as a political activist" whose writings reflected a desire to use the classroom as an "instrument" for revolution. "What is the true measurement of Ollman's scholarship?" they asked. "Does he intend to use the classroom for indoctrination?" Shortly after the column appeared, the president of the University of Maryland rejected Ollman's appointment. Ollman then sued Evans and Novak for libel.

The trial court dismissed the suit, ruling that the column was protected opinion. The D.C. Circuit agreed. With respect to the charge that Ollman was a "political activist," the court rejected professor's argument that use of the term defamed him by implying that he was not a scholar. Noting that scholarship and activism are not incompatible, the court ruled that the term "political activist" is an unverifiable statement of opinion. "It is difficult to imagine . . . a means of deciding the quantum of political activity justifying the label," the court said. Similarly, the "indoctrination" comment was the columnists' interpretation of the professor's own writings and did not "admit of a method of proof or disproof."

The factual setting in which a statement is made can also suggest that it is opinion rather than fact. For example, in *Greenbelt Cooperative Publishing Association v. Bresler*, the U.S. Supreme Court concluded that use of the term "blackmail" at a politically charged city council meeting was merely "rhetorical hyperbole" that would not be understood by readers as accusing the plaintiff of a crime. To the same effect is *National Association of Letter Carriers v. Austin* (1974), in which the Supreme Court ruled that the words "scab" and "traitor" published in a union newspaper article were protected opinion. The statements came during the course of a heated labor dispute and were used in a "loose, figurative sense to demonstrate the union's strong views." The Court cautioned, however, that there could be other situations in which the words could be interpreted to convey false assertions of fact.

Finally, the very nature of a particular story often makes plain to the reader that opinions are being offered. In the column that gave rise to the *Ollman* case, for example, Evans and Novak had quoted an unnamed political science professor as saying that "Ollman has no status within the profession. . . . " Describing this comment as "the most troublesome statement in the column," the court nonetheless concluded that it, like the other statements described above, was protected opinion. Here the court emphasized that the remark came in a column "by well-known, nationally syndicated columnists on the Op-Ed page of a newspaper, the well-recognized home of opinion and comment."

To the same effect is *King v. Globe Newspaper Co.* (1987), in which the Massachusetts Supreme Court ruled that several editorial cartoons about then-Governor Edward J. King qualified as opinion. "Cartoons are seldom vehicles by which facts are reported. . . . ," the court said. "Reasonable readers are well aware that cartoonists employ hyperbole, exaggeration, and caricature to communicate their messages." By the same token, editorials, sports columns, and various types of reviews (restaurant and movie reviews, for example) almost always signal opinion.

It bears repeating that there is disagreement among the courts in this area and that many do not employ the foregoing analysis. Instead, several have adopted the position of the *Restatement (Second) of Torts* that a statement of opinion can serve as the basis for a libel suit "only if it implies the allegation of undisclosed defamatory facts as the basis for the opinion." According to the *Restatement*, there are two types of opinion—"pure" and "mixed." Pure opinion involves publication accompanied by the facts on which it is based (or those facts are known by or readily available to all parties to the communication), while mixed opinion implies defamatory facts because it is not supported by stated or assumed facts. As we have seen, the common law of fair comment drew a similar distinction, so there is no major change here. However, this newly recognized first amendment protection differs significantly from the common law in that "pure" opinion is safeguarded even if it is "unfair" or not sincerely held, is not about a matter of public interest or concern, or is motivated by spite, ill will, or bad faith. Instead, the protection is absolute. Mixed opinion remains actionable, as under the common law.

The following illustrations, drawn from the *Restatement*, highlight the difference between the two types of opinion. Suppose Smith and Jones are discussing the growing social problem of alcoholism, and Smith mentions his friend Johnson, whom Jones does not know. "I think Johnson is an alcoholic," Smith says. It would be reasonable for Jones to conclude that Smith knows underlying facts that justify his comment. Because those facts have not been disclosed and are not known to Jones, the opinion is "mixed" and, therefore, actionable. But suppose that Smith says instead that "Johnson has three martinis every day at lunch, and I think he is an alcoholic." Because the underlying facts have been supplied (assuming, of course, that they are correct), the opinion is "pure" and thus absolutely protected. The same result would follow if Smith and Jones saw a drunken stranger walking ahead of them on the sidewalk and Smith said "I think that man is an alcoholic." In this situation the underlying facts, while not stated by Smith, are plainly available to Jones.

Two cases also serve to emphasize the distinction. In *Rinaldi v. Holt, Rinehart & Winston, Inc.* (1977), an author had written that a judge was "incompetent." The New York Court of Appeals ruled that the statement was protected opinion, since the author had "set forth the basis for his belief that plaintiff is incompetent and should be removed." Based upon the facts stated and public debate provoked by the statements, "each reader may draw his own conclusions as to whether [the author's] views should be supported or challenged." In contrast, a New Mexico appellate court held in *Kutz v. Independent Publishing Co.* (1981) that statements describing the plaintiff as a "rabid environmentalist" who had written letters to the newspaper that were "so violent we turned them over to the police" were mixed opinions. Because no underlying facts were provided, the court said, a reader might reasonably infer that the plaintiff's letters had threatened such serious harm that police intervention was necessary. Thus, the statements could imply privately known defamatory facts about the plaintiff, and nothing in the article enabled the reader to draw an independent conclusion.

Fair Report

The common law has long recognized a qualified privilege to make fair and accurate reports of government proceedings and records, even if the information is false and defamatory. Today, as the *Liberty Lobby* case indicates, this privilege is also of constitutional dimension. The rationale for the privilege was succinctly stated in a 1886 English case, *MacDougall v. Knight & Son*, which involved an allegedly libelous statement made at a court proceeding and reported in the press. The newspaper article, the court said, "places those who were not present in Court in the same position as those who were." Put another way, the press in such circumstances acts as an agent or surrogate of those citizens who, while free to attend the proceeding, are unable to do so. Moreover, as Justice Holmes pointed out in *Cowley v. Pulsifer*

(1884), the privilege is also justified by "the security which publicity gives for the proper administration of justice."

These rationales obviously extend beyond the reporting of judicial proceedings. The fair report privilege has been applied not only to news accounts of trials, but also meetings of legislative and administrative bodies, public statements of executive branch officials, and law enforcement records. In many jurisdictions, the privilege applies to reports of any meeting open to the public at which important matters are discussed. Keep in mind, however, that the privilege is qualified rather than absolute. It is lost if the report is unfair or inaccurate.

The fair report privilege obviously represents an exception to the general rule that one who republishes a defamatory statement is just as liable as the person who initially made it—the notion that "tale bearers are as bad as tale makers." It remains quite important today, for it provides protection beyond that afforded by the constitutional principles of *New York Times Co. v. Sullivan* and its progency. For example, a journalist cannot invoke the *New York Times* rule if he knows a statement to be false or has serious doubts about its falsity. However, the fair report privilege offers protection even if a reporter knows something is false, so long as the statement was made in a setting in which the privilege applies and the journalist provides an accurate report of what was said.

It is this feature of the privilege that also distinguishes it from the defense of truth, although the courts sometimes confuse the two. For example, assume that during the embezzlement trial of a bank employee, a co-worker offered key testimony that the defendant had on various occasions stuffed large amounts of cash into a briefcase. After this testimony, the defendant admitted his guilt. A news report of the day's activity in court would be protected on two grounds: the information was true, since the defendant admitted having stolen money in the method described, and the article was also an accurate account of the trial testimony and, therefore, privileged as a fair report. Suppose, however, that the defendant denied any wrongdoing and testified that he did not even own a briefcase, and that the co-worker admitted several days later during the trial that he had lied about the briefcase incidents. In that situation, a news story reporting the co-worker's original testimony would not be protected by the truth defense, since the information was indeed false. However, the fair report privilege would be applicable so long as the article gave an accurate account of the co-worker's initial testimony.

The qualified fair report privilege is related to the absolute privilege afforded some speakers. As a general rule, if an individual has an absolute privilege to defame, the news media enjoy a qualified privilege to report accurately that libelous statement. For example, statements made at judicial proceedings are absolutely privileged because of the societal interest in encouraging every individual to come forward and give relevant testimony in court. Thus, in the situation described in the preceding paragraph, the witness has an absolute privilege even though he lied (of course, he could still be punished for perjury—a crime—despite the fact that he could not be sued for libel), and the press has a qualified privilege to report accurately his testimony. Similarly, legislators enjoy an absolute privilege for their speeches on the floor of their particular assemblies, and the news media thus possess a qualified privilege to report those statements in an accurate fashion. And, because a member of the executive branch of government usually has an absolute privilege in connection with the performance of his official duties, the press has a qualified privilege to report accurately a statement he makes in conducting the business of his office.

Most confusion surrounding the fair report privilege involves its scope; that is, what types of proceedings are covered by it? The privilege is most frequently used in cases involving reports of judicial proceedings. Anything said in open court during a trial or hearing is protected, whether the statement is made by a judge, witness, juror, attorney, or other participant. On the other hand, a remark made by a judge or attorney outside the context of the official proceeding—such as a statement by a lawyer to a reporter on the way out of the courtroom after the trial had recessed— might not be considered within the privilege. In civil cases, the states take differing views as to whether the pleadings in a lawsuit are privileged upon their filing, or whether the privilege does not attach until there has been some formal judicial action in the case. The plaintiff's complaint in a suit contains allegations of wrong-doing on the part of the defendant; otherwise, there would be no lawsuit. The question is whether the press may report freely those allegations merely because the complaint has been filed with the court, or whether it must wait until some later point to obtain benefit of the privilege. Although the *Restatement* clings to the position that some judicial action is necessary before the privilege attaches, the better view is to the contrary. Indeed, the first amendment may prohibit imposition of liability for accurate publication of a matter of public record, whether or not the court has acted in the case. The constitutional considerations are discussed below in connection with the "neutral reportage" doctrine.

In the criminal law context, the fair report privilege extends not only to trials and hearings, but also to official action taken at earlier stages of the criminal justice process. For example, virtually all jurisdictions agree that arrest reports prepared by police or other law enforcement officials are privileged. Courts have extended the privilege to a wide variety of pretrial action, including grand jury reports, arrest warrants, indictments and other forms of criminal charges, bond documents, affidavits, and papers filed by attorneys in the case. However, some states do not take such an expansive view with respect to some of these preliminary matters. In Texas and the District of Columbia, for example, the courts have ruled that a document or proceeding is privileged only if it is required by state law. Thus, in *Phillips v. Evening Star Newspaper Co.* (1980), a District of Columbia court held that a newspaper story based on a police "hot line" set up to provide the media with summaries of arrest reports was not an official record required by law to be kept and that the privilege did not attach.

There has also been a difference of opinion with respect to statements made in connection with a criminal investigation. The *Restatement*, for example, takes the position that the privilege does not cover statements "made by the police, or by the complainant or other witnesses, or by the prosecuting attorney as to the facts of the case or the evidence expected to be given." Following this rule, a Texas court refused to apply the privilege in *Hornby v. Hunter* (1964), which involved an erroneous account of a car theft provided by a deputy sheriff. In contrast, the U.S. Court of Appeals for the Second Circuit ruled in *Foster v. Turner Broadcasting System, Inc.* (1988) that the privilege was applicable, under New York law, to a broadcast interview with an FBI agent regarding a raid on what was incorrectly described as the "national headquarters" of a group plotting to overthrow the federal government. The court stressed that the agent was the head of the FBI's New York office and noted that the New York courts do not extend the privilege to statements by lower-level police officers.

Another problem area involves law enforcement reports that are not available to the public. Two cases from the same court involving *Time* magazine illustrate the divergent views. In *Medico v. Time, Inc.* (1981), *Time* magazine published a summary of confidential FBI documents identifying the plaintiff as a member of an organized crime "family." Interpreting Pennsylvania law, the U.S. Court of Appeals for the Third Circuit ruled that the privilege was applicable. Although the court recognized that the "press as surrogate" rationale described previously could not justify the privilege when proceedings or reports are not open to the public, it concluded that the privilege should apply because of the public interest in assuring the proper operation of law enforcement agencies. Seven years later, in *Schiavone Construction Co. v. Time, Inc.*, the court cast doubt on this analysis. The case, which arose under New Jersey law, involved a magazine article based on a confidential FBI memorandum concerning the disappearance of Teamster president Jimmy Hoffa. Noting that the "historical justification for the privilege . . . is that the report is already in the public domain," the court feared that extension of the privilege could allow confidential documents "leaked" to the media to become "powerful tools for injuring citizens with impunity." However, the court was able to dispose of the case on other grounds without actually deciding this question.

In addition to reports of judicial proceedings and records, the privilege is applicable to legislative proceedings at all levels of government, from the Congress and state legislatures to city councils and school boards. Meetings or records of committees of these groups would also be subject to the privilege. The fair report privilege attaches to statements made at such proceedings by members of the governmental body, witnesses, or others in attendance and also extends to formal reports issued by the entity, such as the "committee reports" regularly prepared by the various congressional committees. The privilege also applies to proceedings before and records of administrative agencies, which, although often located within the executive branch of government, perform quasi-legislative and quasi-judicial functions. For example, the Texas Supreme Court has applied the privilege to meetings of one of the nation's most powerful state agencies—the Texas Railroad Commission—which, despite its name, oversees the oil and gas industry in the state.

A 1961 Arkansas case, *Brandon v. Gazette Publishing Co.*, illustrates the utility of the fair report privilege in connection with the actions of executive branch officials. There the governor, after an investigation of conditions at nursing homes in the state, held a press conference and issued a statement describing conditions at many facilities as "sordid and shocking." A press release also identified a particular nursing home by name and stated that the plaintiff, its administrator, had been involved in certain irregularities. The Arkansas Supreme Court held that news stories reporting these statements by the governor were within the fair report privilege:

> The fact that the Governor's report was given to the press rather than filed with an agency of the state government (where reporters could have copied the contents), is of no moment. It was still an executive report, embracing the findings of a thorough investigation. The purpose of affording a conditional privilege to the publication of the report of an executive officer is based upon the fact that the general public has an interest in, and a right to be informed of, the official acts of such officers.

In many states, accurate accounts of the meetings of nongovernmental bodies, open to the general public, are also protected by the privilege. According to the *Restatement*, "a report of any meeting, assembly, or gathering that is open to the general public and is held for the purpose of discussing or otherwise dealing with matters of public concern" is privileged. The "public concern" test is rather loosely applied, and the crucial question seems to be whether the meeting was indeed open to the general public. Thus, courts have held privileged news stories about political rallies, church board meetings, disciplinary proceedings of a medical society, and meetings of citizens groups. However, a meeting of the shareholders of a private corporation would not be covered, since such a gathering is not open to the general public.

Once a defendant demonstrates that his report is one to which the privilege applies, the burden shifts to the plaintiff to demonstrate that the defendant has somehow "abused" it and is therefore not entitled to its protection. At common law, the same sort of ill will, spite, or improper motive that would defeat other privileges (including the privilege of fair comment) would also overcome the fair report privilege. However, the *Restatement* has abandoned this rule, and its draftsmen have pointed out that there are no reported decisions in which the fair report privilege was lost on the ground that the defendant was motivated solely by an improper purpose. Nonetheless, the "improper motive" ground remains technically available in some jurisdictions, either by virtue of statutory language or dicta in judicial opinions.

It is clear, however, that the privilege is lost if the defendant's report is inaccurate. Although a verbatim account of what transpired is not necessary, the reporter's abridgment must be a substantially accurate summary of the proceeding or report. As the New York Court of Appeals explained in *Holy Spirit Association v. New York Times Co.* (1979):

> [N]ewspaper accounts of [public] proceedings must be accorded some degree of liberality. When determining whether the article constitutes a fair and [accurate] report, the language used therein should not be dissected and analyzed with a lexicographer's precision. This is so because a newspaper article is, by its very nature, a condensed report of events which must, of necessity, reflect to some degree the subjective reporting of its author. Nor should a fair report which is misleading, composed and phrased in good faith under the exigencies of a publication deadline, be thereafter parsed and dissected on the precise denotative meanings which may literally, although not contextually, be ascribed to the words used.

Accordingly, an immaterial error will not destroy the privilege, just as such a mistake will not preclude a defendant from asserting the separate defense of truth. For example, in *Dudley v. Farmers Branch Daily Times* (1977), a Texas appellate court ruled that the privilege was not lost because a news report had stated that plaintiff had been charged with theft of $168,000 worth of materials when the actual amount was only $6,600. Similarly, in *Orr v. Argus-Press Co.* (1978), the U.S. Court of Appeals for the Sixth Circuit applied the privilege although the news story used the term "swindle" to describe the wrongdoing with which plaintiff was charged, although he had actually been accused of "fraud."

This is not to say, however, that every inaccuracy is considered insubstantial. For example, in *Liquori v. Republican Co.* (1979), a news story reported accurately that a man had pled guilty to a criminal offense but gave the address, obtained from a telephone book, of another man with the same name. The Massachusetts appeals court refused to apply the privilege, observing that the article was neither substantially accurate nor fair.

The Texas Supreme Court also rejected the privilege in *Denton Publishing Co. v. Boyd* (1970), in which a news report of a city council meeting included a sentence that a developer had "declared bankruptcy." The problem, the court said, was that the reporter had stated as a bald fact that the developer was bankrupt instead of indicating that one of the councilmen present at the meeting *said* he was bankrupt. Thus, the lack of attribution converted what would have been a privileged report into an unprivileged one. Similarly, in *Dameron v. Washington Magazine, Inc.* (1985), the District of Columbia Circuit ruled the privilege inapplicable where the story did not specifically identify its statement that the plaintiff was "partially to blame" for a serious plane crash as coming from a report prepared by the National Transportation Safety Board.

The news account must also be "fair" to be privileged. The courts are generally quite liberal in this area, holding that exaggeration and the use of vivid language will not render a report unfair. In *Binder v. Triangle Publications, Inc.* (1971), for example, the Pennsylvania Supreme Court found privileged the characterization of testimony at a murder trial as a "bizarre love triangle" when the evidence showed that the victim had at one time lived with the plaintiff and her husband.

However, there are limits placed upon the privilege. For example, in the *Schiavone Construction* case discussed previously, a *Time* magazine story based on a confidential FBI memo asserted that "the name of Schiavone appeared several times in the [FBI's] reports on the 1975 disappearance of former Teamster Boss Jimmy Hoffa." The article did not include this important statement from the memo: "none of these [references to Schiavone in the Hoffa files] suggested any criminality or organized crime associations." Observing that "even a report that is accurate so far as it goes may be so edited and deleted as to . . . be misleading," the court concluded that *Time*'s story had been unfair, since it omitted information that was "obviously exculpatory."

Several recent cases, including the *Liberty Lobby* decision, reflect the view that the fair report privilege is compelled by the first amendment, although the Supreme Court has not directly ruled on the question. As adopted by some lower courts, this first amendment privilege to report with substantial accuracy statements made by others is significantly broader than its common law counterpart, which in several jurisdictions is limited to accounts of governmental proceedings. Moreover, this developing doctrine of "neutral reportage" also affords more protection to the news media than *New York Times* and *Gertz*, for it, like the common law privilege of fair report, is applicable even if the journalist entertains doubts about the truth or falsity of the statement, so long as his report represents a substantially accurate report of that statement.

While there is no Supreme Court decision squarely dealing with this issue, several of the Court's cases provide some support for the neutral reportage doctrine recognized by the lower courts. For example, in *Greenbelt Cooperative Publishing Association v. Bresler*, the defendant newspaper accurately reported that members of the audience at a city council meeting had used the word "blackmail" to describe the plaintiff developer's dealings with the city. The Court concluded that, as a matter of constitutional law, the word could not have been understood in that context to imply commission of a crime, but also noted that the news story was an accurate report of what had been said at the public hearing. The newspaper "was performing its wholly legitimate function as a community newspaper when it published full reports of these public debates in its news columns," the Court said. This language suggests that there is an important first amendment interest in reporting what transpires at public meetings, even if the statements are made by participants who are not governmental officials. However, the Court did not base its decision on this rationale.

In *Time, Inc. v. Pape* (1971), *Time* magazine published a story about a report by the U.S. Civil Rights Commission, which included some unverified complaints of police brutality. The article quoted one of these complaints from the report, but did not indicate that it was unverified. The police officer named in the complaint brought a defamation suit against *Time,* and the Supreme Court ruled that under the *New York Times* rule there was no basis for finding reckless disregard or knowledge of falsity. As in *Greenbelt,* however, the Court also pointed out that the charges had been reported by the magazine in a substantially accurate fashion and recognized that "a vast amount of what is published in the . . . press purports to be descriptive of what somebody said rather than of what anybody did." Because there was no recklessness as required by *New York Times,* the Court did not consider the possibility of creating a new first amendment privilege.

Two other Supreme Court cases are also relevant here. In *Cox Broadcasting Corp. v. Cohn* (1975), the Court ruled that publication of the name of a rape victim obtained from public judicial records was protected by the first amendment and could not be the basis for an invasion of privacy suit. Although this case, discussed more fully in Chapter 3, involved invasion of privacy rather than libel, the Court's rationale—that the news media's role in a democratic society necessarily involves publication of governmental records and proceedings—is equally applicable in the defamation context. In *Landmark Communications, Inc. v. Virginia* (1978), the Court declared unconstitutional a state statute that made confidential all proceedings and records of a state's judicial conduct commission and imposed a criminal fine upon those who violated this confidentiality rule. A newspaper was convicted under the statute after it published an article that accurately described a pending commission inquiry into alleged judicial misconduct and named the judge who was the target of the investigation. In reversing the conviction, the Court again emphasized the role of the press in monitoring government activities and recognized the first amendment value of reports of governmental proceedings.

The leading case adopting a constitutional privilege of "neutral reportage" is *Edwards v. National Audubon Society, Inc.* (1977), decided by the U.S. Court of Appeals for the Second Circuit. There proponents of pesticides cited Audubon Society statistics showing a steady increase in the sightings of birds despite increased pesticide use to support their argument that the chemicals were not harming animal life. The editor of an Audubon Society publication felt that the group's statistics were being misused and wrote in *American Birds* that scientists who relied on the bird sighting data in that fashion were "being paid to lie." A reporter for the *New York Times* read the article and called the editor to find out more details. The editor revealed to the *Times* reporter the names of five scientists he thought misused the statistics, and the reporter wrote a story summarizing the charges made in the *American Birds* article—including the "paid to lie" allegation—and then listed the names of the five scientists. Three of them sued the *Times* for libel and won in the trial court.

In reversing that judgment, the Second Circuit, in an opinion by Judge Irving R. Kaufman, recognized a first amendment privilege of neutral reportage. Judge Kaufman wrote:

> At stake in this case is a fundamental principle. Succinctly stated, when a responsible, prominent organization like the Audubon Society makes serious charges against a public figure, the First Amendment protects the accurate and disinterested reporting of those charges, regardless of the reporter's private views regarding their validity. What

is newsworthy about such accusations is that they were made. We do not believe that the press may be required under the First Amendment to suppress newsworthy statements merely because it has serious doubts regarding their truth. Nor must the press take up cudgels against dubious charges in order to publish them without fear of liability for defamation. The public interest in being fully informed about controversies that often rage around sensitive issues demands that the press be afforded the freedom to report such charges without assuming responsibility for them.

Despite *Edwards*, the contours of this privilege are unclear. For example, that case involved charges against a public figure leveled by a responsible organization, and the *Times* reporter had attempted to contact all five scientists to obtain their responses and had reached three, all of whom denied the charges. What if none of these factors are present? In *Dixson v. Newsweek, Inc.* (1977), the Tenth Circuit refused to apply *Edwards* in a case brought by a "private figure," and in *Fogus v. Capital Cities Media, Inc.* (1982), an Illinois appellate court ruled the privilege inapplicable where charges of police brutality had been made by five arrested youths, whom the court did not consider "responsible." Other courts, including the Third Circuit in *Dickey v. CBS, Inc.* (1978) and the New York Court of Appeals in *Hogan v. The Herald Co.* (1982), have rejected the neutral reportage doctrine altogether.

Summary Judgment

While not actually a defense to a defamation suit, summary judgment is an important procedural device for implementing the constitutional and common law protections for the news media discussed in this chapter. In essence, summary judgment is a decision rendered by the court without a full-blown trial. Because, as noted previously, libel litigation can be very costly, summary judgment enables a defendant to terminate the lawsuit at an early stage in the proceedings and thus avoid the substantial legal fees necessary to take a case to trial. Obviously, the fear of the high costs of litigation can have just as significant a "chilling effect" on the exercise of first amendment freedoms as the fear of a large damage award made by jury. The courts have been willing to employ liberally the summary judgment device in disposing of libel suits. According to a recent study, media defendants have a seventy-five percent success rate in obtaining summary judgments.

Under the procedural rules found in most jurisdictions, summary judgment is available if "there is no genuine issue as to any material fact" and the defendant "is entitled to a judgment as a matter of law." Put another way, the judge is not to resolve disputed factual issues, but to consider whether, on the basis of those facts agreed upon by the parties, the law would permit the plaintiff to recover. If it would not, there is no purpose in allowing the suit to proceed further, and summary judgment would be appropriate. However, if key facts necessary to resolution of the suit are hotly contested, a trial must be held to enable a jury to determine the question.

Summary judgment has been most useful in cases involving public officials and public figures, who must under *New York Times* prove with convincing clarity that the defendant acted recklessly in publishing the defamatory material. In *Anderson v. Liberty Lobby* (1986), the U.S. Supreme Court ruled that a trial judge must take this requirement into account when considering a defense motion for summary judgment. If the evidence of reckless disregard gathered by the plaintiff is "of insufficient caliber or quantity to allow a rational [jury] to find [reckless disregard] by clear and convincing evidence," summary judgment must be granted.

This principle is illustrated by *Silvester v. ABC*, a 1988 decision of the U.S. Court of Appeals for the Eleventh Circuit. The case grew out of a "20/20" segment on corruption in the jai alai industry. The program dealt with gambling and conspiracies among bettors, management, and players, as well as a suspicious fire that destroyed a jai alai fronton. The plaintiffs, who were deemed public figures, argued that ABC had relied too heavily on a former employee who had cooperated with law enforcement officials. According to affidavits obtained by the plaintiffs from two police officers, the source was not reliable. ABC, on the other hand, presented evidence showing that it had not relied exclusively on the former employee, but had interviewed numerous law enforcement officials, attorneys, and journalists in putting together its story. The trial judge granted ABC's motion for summary judgment, and the courts of appeals affirmed, ruling that the plaintiffs had not produced "clear and convincing" evidence of reckless disregard.

On the other hand, most courts have been reluctant to grant summary judgment in "private figure" cases where the question is whether the defendant was negligent. In other areas of tort law where the "reasonable person" analysis is employed, the traditional approach has been to let the jury decide whether the defendant's conduct met that test. This is so, as one court has observed, because a determination of negligence "requires experience with the mainsprings of human conduct and reference to the data of practical human experience." Because courts do not often grant summary judgment for defendants in ordinary tort cases involving negligence (such as personal injury suits), they tend to treat "private figure" defamation cases in the same manner.

This is not to say, however, that summary judgment is impossible in cases where the negligence standard applies. The question is whether the plaintiff has put forward sufficient facts to enable a reasonable jury to find, by a preponderance of the evidence, that the defendant was negligent. For example, in *LaMon v. Butler*, discussed earlier in connection with the negligence standard, the Washington Supreme Court affirmed the trial judge's grant of summary judgment for the defendant, ruling that the facts did not show negligence where the reporter relied on a city attorney's interpretation of an ambiguous court order.

More typical is *KARK-TV v. Simon*, the Arkansas case mentioned previously. There the court gave short shrift to the television station's argument that summary judgment should have been granted because the plaintiff's evidence was insufficient to establish negligence. That question was for the jury, the court said, despite the fact that the station had reported a fast-breaking news story "on deadline," had based its report on eyewitness observations of an experienced journalist, and had attempted without success to obtain further details from police. As one commentator observed, if summary judgment were inappropriate in this case, then "virtually all libel cases . . . where negligence is the applicable standard will go to the jury."

The summary judgment procedure is not limited to the fault issue and is often used when a common law privilege is asserted. For example, if a media defendant claimed that its news report was a fair and accurate account of a public meeting, the critical question might be whether, under the particular state's law, that type of meeting was covered by the privilege. The judge could decide the case on that basis without need for trial, and if he concluded that the privilege did apply, he would enter summary judgment for the defendant.

INFLICTION OF EMOTIONAL DISTRESS: AN ALTERNATIVE TO LIBEL

Because the law is evolutionary, lawyers must frequently attempt to "stretch" existing legal principles to cover the facts of particular cases. There is nothing unethical or unsavory about this; in fact, it is the creative aspect of practicing law. In many cases, an attorney is confronted with problems on the cutting edge of legal developments, and he must convince a court that existing law must be expanded or modified in order for his client to prevail. If the judge agrees, the law grows a bit as a result of his ruling. Numerous examples of this process at work can be found in this chapter; for instance, recall how the *New York Times* rule—which first applied to public officials—was enlarged to include public figures as well.

It should come as no surprise, therefore, that the safeguards spawned by the constitutionalization of defamation law have prompted lawyers to seek other means of obtaining relief for libel plaintiffs. As we shall see in Chapter 3, the law of invasion of privacy may, in some situations, provide an alternative remedy for a plaintiff who may not be able to win a libel suit. By and large, however, the same type of first amendment considerations that have dramatically altered the law of libel have also shaped the development of the law of privacy. Thus, lawyers zealously representing the interests of their clients have turned to other theories, most notably a fairly new tort known as intentional infliction of emotional distress.

Unlike defamation, which involves injury to reputation, this tort is meant to remedy injury to one's mental state. Its hallmark is outrageous conduct that causes severe emotional harm to the plaintiff. For conduct to be sufficiently "outrageous," it must, in the words of one court, "transcend all bounds of decency tolerated by society." The tort is not meant to encompass all of the many forms of "run of the mill" mental distress brought about by the friction of modern life, but rather is reserved for conduct that is truly atrocious. Thus, while insulting language or profanity would be insufficient to trigger liability, offensive bullying tactics on the part of landlords, employers, or bill collectors could qualify. The problem, of course, is that there is no objective way to measure outrageous behavior; consequently, juries might be persuaded to award substantial damages for conduct that most of us would not consider atrocious.

In defamation cases, intentional infliction of emotional distress quickly became an alternative theory for plaintiffs who, of one reason or another, could not win under the law of libel. Fortunately, however, the U.S. Supreme Court has imposed first amendment safeguards in this area of the law much like those found in defamation. In *Hustler Magazine v. Falwell*, the Court held that public figures and public officials "may not recover for the tort of intentional infliction of emotional distress . . . without showing in addition that the publication contains a false statement of fact which was made with . . . knowledge that the statement was false or with reckless disregard to whether or not it was true."

The case arose when *Hustler* published an "ad parody" based on an advertising campaign for Campari Liqueur that included interviews with various celebrities about the "first time" they had sampled Campari. The *Hustler* "ad," which was labeled as a parody, contained a purported interview with Moral Majority founder Jerry Falwell in which he talked about his "first time," meaning his first sexual experience. According to the "interview," that encounter was a drunken incestuous rendezvous with his mother in an outhouse. Reverend Falwell brought suit for defamation, invasion of privacy, and intentional infliction of emotional distress. The trial court ruled in *Hustler*'s favor on the privacy claim, but sent the other two issues to the jury. Although the jury found for the magazine on the libel claim because the parody could not have been understood by a reasonable reader as stating actual facts about Falwell, it returned a $200,000 verdict in his favor on the emotional distress claim. The U.S. Court of Appeals for the Fourth Circuit affirmed, but the Supreme Court reversed.

Writing for the Court, Chief Justice Rehnquist observed that the "robust political debate" encouraged by the first amendment is bound to produce sharp and caustic comments, vehement attacks, and immoderate and poorly reasoned criticism about public people. Although falsehoods have "little value in and of themselves," he said, the safeguards developed in *New York Times* and subsequent cases recognize that "they are nevertheless inevitable in free debate." The requirement that a public plaintiff prove falsity and reckless disregard in order to prevail in a defamation case provides necessary "breathing space" for errors and prevents a "chilling effect" speech that it does have constitutional value.

In contrast, the standard by which liability is imposed in intentional infliction of emotional distress cases (i.e., whether the conduct is outrageous) is not sufficient to provide such protection. The "outrageousness" requirement, the Chief Justice said, possesses "an inherent subjectiveness about it which would allow a jury to impose liability on the basis of the jurors' tastes or views, or perhaps on the basis of their dislike of a particular expression." The Justices obviously feared that, under such a subjective standard, plaintiffs could use the tort of intentional infliction of emotional distress to circumvent the safeguards developed over the past twenty-five years in the libel area. Accordingly, the Court ruled that public officials and public figures who bring suit for intentional infliction of emotional distress must prove falsity and reckless disregard for the truth, just as in defamation cases.

Of particular concern to the Court was the impact of the tort on satire and parody, both staples of editorial cartoons. "Despite their sometimes caustic nature," Chief Justice Rehnquist wrote, "from the early cartoon portraying George Washington as an ass down to the present day, graphic depictions and satirical cartoons have played a prominent role in public and political debate. * * * From the viewpoint of history it is clear that our political discourse would have been considerably poorer without them." The Court rejected Rev. Falwell's efforts to distinguish the *Hustler* parody from editorial cartoons. Although the magazine's ad parody may "at best [be] a distant cousin of the political cartoons" of Thomas Nast and others, the Court doubted that anyone could establish a "principled standard to separate one from the other." In the Court's view, the "outrageousness" test certainly did not qualify.

A POSTSCRIPT: AVOIDING LIBEL LITIGATION

A journalist who understands the legal principles discussed in this chapter is obviously in a better position to avoid a defamation suit than one who does not. For example, an awareness of "red flag" words and an appreciation for the hazards of relying on an embittered source can go a long way toward preventing litigation. Because defending a lawsuit is an expensive proposition even if the plaintiff is ultimately unsuccessful, the maxim that "an ounce of prevention is worth a pound of cure" certainly rings true in this context.

In addition to acquiring a working knowledge of the law, journalists should pay heed to a 1985 study by Professors Randall Bezanson, Gilbert Cranberg, and John Soloski of the University of Iowa, who concluded that common courtesy on the part of reporters and editors might well convince potential plaintiffs not to sue. According to the study, a summary of which was published in the *Iowa Law Review*, most libel plaintiffs bring suit not to recover damages but to restore the harm to their reputations or to punish the news media. In fact, winning the suit may not be particularly important, since plaintiffs typically feel vindicated by the very act of suing. And, because about half of these plaintiffs tend to contact the media about the offending statement before consulting with an attorney, the potential media defendant often has a chance to head off a lawsuit before a lawyer enters the picture.

Unfortunately, the Iowa professors also reported that most news organizations make little of this opportunity and often act in a manner that encourages rather than discourages litigation. "Instead of diverting complainants from court, the media contact propels them to court," wrote Professor Cranberg, formerly editorial page editor of the *Des Moines Register.* "An overwhelming number of plaintiffs told us that their postpublication experiences with the press influenced their decisions to bring suit." For example, the study revealed that newsroom personnel are often rude and abusive to these potential plaintiffs. Indeed, Professor Cranberg cited instances in which reporters cursed complainants who dared question the accuracy of allegedly false and defamatory stories. Such behavior is plainly inexcusable, and it certainly can be costly.

Apart from rudeness, however, many reporters and editors simply become overly defensive in the face of criticism by a potential plaintiff. Although such a reaction can be attributed to human nature, the Iowa study indicates that journalists are more likely to respond in this fashion because media personnel are "conditioned to resist pressure." Demands for corrections or retractions from persons who believe they have been defamed are perceived as a form of "outside" pressure, and a "seige mentality" among journalists often develops as a result. A reporter or editor who receives a complaint about a story "immediately think[s] that the complainant is a nut or a kook or self-serving," one editor told Professor Cranberg.

The study recommends several steps that a media organization can take to deal with complaints in a manner that can reduce the likelihood of a lawsuit:

- impress on reporters, editors, and other employees the power of the media to hurt people;
- insist that journalists deal with complaints courteously, and provide in-house training in human relations;
- place responsibility for handling complaints in a person who is not involved in day-to-day news coverage and who is therefore less likely to be defensive about stories;
- establish written policies for dealing with complaints; and
- make plain that employees who "sit" on complaints rather than inform their superiors are subject to termination.

Beyond these recommendations, news organizations can sometimes avoid litigation by simply agreeing to print a retraction. Unfortunately, the defensive attitude identified in the Iowa study sometimes stands as a barrier to this course of action, for reporters and editors—and virtually anyone else, for that matter—usually do not like to admit mistakes. A willingness to correct the error, however, may convince the potential plaintiff not to sue, and an agreement to publish a retraction or correction may be embodied in a negotiated settlement under which the plaintiff in return promises not to bring suit. Even if litigation ensues, a retraction generally serves to reduce actual damages or to bar recovery of punitive damages.

PROBLEMS

1. The freeway that encircles the Washington, D.C., area is lined with the offices of consultants—known popularly as the "beltway bandits"—who make their living from federal contracts. The practice is hardly limited to the nation's capital; for example, major accounting firms routinely perform management studies for cities and counties across the country. Even though many governmental agencies employ their own staff attorneys, architects, accountants, or engineers, professionals from the private sector are often retained to work on particular agency projects. If these consultants were indeed full-time employees on the government payroll, their jobs would seem to qualify them for "public official" status under the *New York Times* rule. In an era in which the government more frequently "farms out" important decisions to private entities (and then routinely rubber stamps the recommendations it receives), is it logical to treat these consultants, these members of a "shadow government," as public officials? *Compare Adey v. United Action for Animals, Inc.*, 361 F. Supp. 457 (S.D.N.Y. 1973), *aff'd*, 493 F.2d 1397 (2d Cir.), *cert. denied*, 419 U.S. 842 (1974), and *Turley v. WTAX, Inc.*, 236 N.E.2d 778 (Ill. App. 1968), with *Arctic Co. v. Loudoun Times Mirror,* 624 F.2d 518 (4th Cir. 1980), *cert. denied*, 449 U.S. 1102 (1981), and *Forrest v. Lynch,* 347 So.2d 1255 (La. App. 1977), *cert. denied*, 435 U.S. 971 (1978).

2. Radio station WBOX's afternoon call-in "talk" show is one of the most popular programs in town. On a day when the topic was the "drug problem," a caller, without identifying himself, said on the air that prescription drugs were readily available at a local pizza parlor. He added that a "Dr. Newman" wrote the prescriptions, which were filled by a pharmacist named Snowden, who made them available to the owner of the restaurant. The doctor, pharmacist, and owner of the pizza parlor all filed suit for defamation against the radio station, which did not have a delay device allowing the monitoring of callers before their comments went "on the air." What result? *Compare Snowden v. Pearl River Broadcasting Corp.*, 251 So.2d 405 (La. App. 1971), with *Adams v. Frontier Broadcasting Co.*, 555 P.2d 556 (Wyo. 1976). Suppose a television reporter conducted a live interview with a local civic leader, who made the same charges noted above. Does your analysis change because a news broadcast is involved? Does it make any difference that the statements were made by a community leader rather than an anonymous caller?

3. A newspaper published a letter to the editor implying that a kennel licensed to supply animals for medical research sold dogs to persons who used them for dog fighting. The letter was written by the vice president of the local Humane Society. Under both state and federal law, it is a crime to sell dogs for that purpose, and the owners of the kennel brought a libel suit against the newspaper. A jury found that the letter was defamatory. With regard to the fault question, the editor of the newspaper admitted that he normally verified accusations of criminal activity contained in letters but did not do so in this case. He also testified that he knew of no criminal charges pending against the kennel owners and that he had no reason to believe that they sold dogs for use in dog fights. Moreover, there was evidence that the newspaper's publisher was a strong supporter of the Humane Society, which was competing with the kennel for a county contract to dispose of unwanted animals in the area. In addition, the newspaper published editorials favoring an

award of the contract to the Humane Society. Is this evidence sufficient to show that the letter was published negligently? Recklessly? Are the kennel owners public figures? *See Hodgins v. Times Herald Co.*, 425 N.W.2d 522 (Mich. App. 1988).

4. The staff of the *Yale Daily News* complies and publishes *The Insider's Guide to the Colleges*, a book containing descriptive information about 230 colleges and universities throughout the country. The 1978–79 edition of the book contained this material about Ithaca College, a private liberal arts school in New York with an undergraduate enrollment of about 2,000:

> Life at Ithaca is anything but harsh. (Watch out, though. The weather stinks, except in the summer when you're home.) The Pub, located in the middle of the campus, provides the center of social life for many students. Sex, drugs, and booze are the staples of life. If Ithaca has a reputation as a party school, it is well deserved. The predominant attitude among the upper-middle class student body is that "we're here to party." Sex is casual, and formal dating is unheard of; the pickup scene thrives in Ithaca. The women are reportedly attractive, and the guys weight-trained. The use of pot is a foregone conclusion, and cocaine occasionally manages to wend its way into the hands of those who can afford it.

The *Yale* journalists base their evaluations of the colleges in the survey on reports filed by "correspondents," usually members of student newspaper staffs at the various colleges. The Ithaca College correspondents, all students at the school, were picked for the task by the editor of the student newspaper there.

   Discuss the defamation problems associated with the above excerpt from the book. Who could sue? Students at the college? Ithaca College itself? What phrases are potentially defamatory? Is there sufficient evidence of fault? What defenses might be available? Would your analysis be any different if the book's preface stated that "we would be the last to say that all of what you read here is gospel . . . [since] our correspondents are rarely unanimous," and that the reader should "take our words with more than just a polite grain of salt"? *See Ithaca College v. Yale Daily News Publishing Co.*, 433 N.Y.S.2d 530 (Sup.Ct. 1980), *aff'd*; 445 N.Y.S.2d 621 (App. Div. 1981).

5. Randall Wood is president of the local Taxpayers' Association, a citizens group formed to monitor and work against wasteful government spending. Al Jackson is vice president of the organization, which has about 150 members. Wood is manager of a shoe store at the local shopping mall, and Jackson owns and operates a machine shop. The two men, on behalf of the Association, spearheaded a drive against a new city fire station by circulating petitions. They eventually submitted to the city council petitions opposing the new station signed by more than 5,000 citizens. Shortly thereafter, a reporter for the local paper learned from the city manager, who had been on the job for only two weeks, that the city attorney was planning to file charges against Wood and Jackson because of "irregularities" concerning the petitions. The reporter prepared a story, and, as city editor, you are reviewing it. The headline says: "City Attorney Rules Association Petitions Improper; Forgery Charges May Loom for Wood, Jackson." The story itself states that the city attorney is preparing to charge the two men with "false swearing," a misdemeanor, because some of the signatures were apparently phony. The story also stated that the city attorney was out of town and unavailable for comment, and that Wood and Jackson had denied any wrongdoing. As city editor, what goes through your mind with respect to any libel problems suggested by the story and headline? *See Lawrence v. Bauer Publishing & Printing Ltd.*, 446 A.2d 469 (N.J.), *cert. denied*, 459 U.S. 999 (1982).

6. A father who had kidnapped his son from his ex-wife, who had custody of the child, appeared twice on the "Donahue" television program to discuss his views on the custody

rights of fathers. Although he appeared in disguise, his ex-wife apparently recognized him, and he was subsequently located and arrested. A newspaper published a story about the incident, and the father sued for libel. Is he a limited purpose public figure? What is the "controversy"? Is it relevant that he appeared on the nationally syndicated television program in a disguise designed to conceal his identity? *See Anderson v. Rocky Mountain News*, 15 Media L. Rptr. 2058 (10th Cir. 1988).

7. Jack Martin is a state senator. A newspaper published a story linking him to a shady land development deal engineered by his brother, Jim, who was widely known as a con artist. The story also suggested that the senator had received illegal campaign contributions from the corporation formed by his brother to handle the development project. The principal source for the story was Jim Martin's ex-wife, who told the reporter that "Jack will do pretty much as Jim tells him" and described her ex-husband as "an incredible con man and manipulator." The reporter mentioned to his editor that "I've got something really juicy on Senator Martin" and told a friend that "I never liked those Martin brothers anyway." Another writer for the paper, who had once worked as a press aide to the senator, told the reporter that Jack Martin was completely above board in all his business dealings and campaign financing matters. Nonetheless, the reporter wrote the story without further investigation, and the paper printed it. The senator sued for libel. What are his chances for success? *See Stevens v. Sun Publishing Co.*, 240 S.E.2d 812 (S.C.), *cert. denied*, 436 U.S. 945 (1978).

8. In April 1982, *TV Guide* magazine and the *Atlanta Constitution* printed an advertisement for an upcoming television documentary series on the topic of teenage pregnancies. The advertisement was prepared and submitted for publication by WXIA-TV of Atlanta as a promotion for a special feature it was planning to run on its local news. The ad, headlined "Guess What Lori Found Out Today," included two photographs. One was a close-up of a diary, lying open on a desk, which contained this handwritten entry: "Dear Diary, I found out today that I'm pregnant. What will I do now?" The second photograph showed a teenage girl embracing a young man. Claiming that she was the girl in the photograph and that the ad clearly implied that she was pregnant, the plaintiff brought a libel suit against the newspaper, *TV Guide,* and the television station. An employee of the newspaper stated that although its advertising department "screened" certain ads prior to publication, this advertisement was not scrutinized because the advertising staff felt that was not a "suspect" ad that needed checking. A *TV Guide* employee said that the magazine does not as a matter of policy use such a screening procedure but instead relies on the reputation of those who submit advertisements, such as WXIA-TV in this case. Is the plaintiff likely to prevail in her suit? Against which defendant does she have the strongest case? Would it make any difference if the ad had been prepared by an advertising agency retained by WXIA rather than by the station's own staff? *See Triangle Publications, Inc. v. Chumley*, 317 S.E.2d 534 (Ga. 1984).

9. A college professor owned various rental properties near the campus. When he learned that the editor of the college's student newspaper was preparing a story about the poor conditions at some of the residences, he filed suit in the local state court seeking to enjoin publication of the article until he had an opportunity to review it and prepare a response. A short hearing on the suit was held, and the trial judge granted the professor's request to withdraw his petition for an injunction as moot because the student newspaper had published the article three days earlier. A reporter for a television station and a camera crew were present at the hearing. At its conclusion they videotaped interviews with the professor, the editor of the student newspaper, and the president of the college. They then went to a house owned by the professor and, after receiving permission from the

tenants there, filmed the interior of the house. That evening, the station broadcast a report about the incident that included videotape of the house's interior revealing a water-stained ceiling, an unshaded light bulb suspended from the ceiling, and exposed insulation on the back porch. A "voice over" accompanying that footage attributed to the tenants complaints of "leaking roofs, faulty wiring, and other eyesores." The professor sued the station for libel, and the station raised the defense of "fair report," claiming that the broadcast was a fair and accurate account of the injunction hearing. What result? *See Lal v. CBS*, 726 F.2d 97 (3d Cir. 1984). *Compare Roehsler v. ABC*, 11 Media L. Rptr. 2444 (D.N.J. 1985).

10. Jeannie Braun was employed at an amusement park in San Marcos, Texas, where she worked in a novelty act with "Ralph, the Diving Pig." In the act, Ms. Braun, treading water in a pool, would hold out a bottle of milk with a nipple on it. Ralph would then dive into the pool and feed from the bottle. Pictures and postcards were made of the act, showing Ralph, in good form, legs fully extended, diving toward Ms. Braun, shown in profile holding the bottle. This photograph found its way into *Chic* magazine, published by Larry Flynt. It is safe to say that *Chic*, like Flynt's *Hustler* magazine, is largely devoted to photographs of nude women. Ms. Braun found out about the publication one day when she stopped at a convenience store near her home. A stranger walked up to her and said, "Hey, I know you," explaining that he had seen the picture in *Chic*. Ms. Braun then looked at a copy of the issue on the store's magazine rack, and was "terrified" to find her picture included with those of nude women. "My legs were like jelly," she said. "I felt like crawling in a hole." Ms. Braun brought suit against *Chic* for defamation (among other things). Is she a public figure? What sort of damages do you think she can prove? *See Braun v. Flynt*, 726 F.2d 245 (5th Cir.), *cert. denied*, 469 U.S. 883 (1984).

11. Which of the following, if any, are defamatory?

    a. A magazine feature on the "best" and "worst" in Boston: the "worst" local sportscaster is "enrolled in a course for remedial speaking." *See Myers v. Boston Magazine Co.*, 403 N.E.2d 376 (Mass. 1980).

    b. A television advertisement for Budweiser beer that featured an excerpt from the actual radio broadcast of the seventh game of the 1960 World Series, including the announcer's erroneous statement that the plaintiff was pitching for the New York Yankees when Bill Mazeroski hit a tie-breaking home run in the bottom of the ninth inning to win the Series for the Pittsburgh Pirates. *See Ditmar v. Needham, Harper, Worldwide, Inc.*, 14 Media L. Rptr. 1281 (N.D. Ohio 1987), *aff'd*, 848 F.2d 189 (6th Cir.), *cert. denied*, 109 S.Ct. 210 (1988).

    c. Comedian David Letterman, during NBC's "Late Night" program: "I saw the most terrifying commercial on television last night, featuring Martha Raye, actress, condom user." *See Raye v. Letterman,* 14 Media L. Rptr. 2047 (Cal. Super. 1987).

    d. The headline of a newspaper story about state employees using publicly owned cars for commuting: "Abuse of State Vehicles Affirmed." *See Stevens v. Independent Newspapers, Inc.*, 15 Media L. Rptr. 1097 (Del. Super. 1988).

    e. *Hustler* magazine's naming plaintiff, who was active in the anti-pornography movement, its "Asshole of the Month." *See Ault v. Hustler Magazine, Inc.*, 860 F.2d 877 (9th Cir. 1988), *cert. denied*, 109 S.Ct. 1532 (1989).

    f. An article by a *Boston Globe* political columnist criticizing then-Governor Edward J. King for treating other elected officials as his subordinates: "That condescending attitude was never more in evidence than in October when King called a judge and demanded that he change a decision he had rendered in a gang-rape case." *See King*

v. *Globe Newspaper Co.*, 512 N.E.2d 241 (Mass. 1987), *cert. denied*, 108 S.Ct. 1121 (1988).

12. A California statute provides that a retraction, in order to be effective, must be published within three weeks in as "substantially conspicuous a manner . . . as were the statements claimed to be libelous." On November 18, 1979, the *San Francisco Examiner* published a story identifying Willie Lee Beasley as being sought for questioning in connection with a fatal shooting. The story was headlined "Manhunt in Killer's Death." In fact, the suspect in the shooting was one Willie *Ray* Beasley. The day after the story appeared, Willie Lee Beasley hand delivered to the *Examiner* a letter demanding a retraction. The newspaper published a retraction on Wednesday, November 21. Although the original story appeared on page one, the retraction was carried in a "correction box" on page three. Also, the original article, carried in a Sunday edition, reached more than 460,000 subscribers, while the net paid circulation of the Wednesday edition carrying the retraction was just under 150,000. Did the retraction satisfy the statute's "substantially conspicuous" requirement? *See Beasley v. Hearst Corp.*, 11 Media L. Rptr. 2067 (Cal. Super. 1985).

13. William Peter Blatty is the author of a number of novels, including *The Exorcist*. When his hardcover novel *Legion* was published, the *New York Times* did not include the book on its list that ranks best-selling books on the basis of sales. Believing that the *Times* knew or had reason to know that sales of *Legion* were sufficient to make the best-seller list, Blatty sued the newspaper and claimed that the omission resulted in decreased sales and adversely affected the value of paperback and film rights. Is this a complaint for defamation? Would he be able to sue under another legal theory? *See Blatty v. New York Times Co.*, 728 P.2d 1177 (Cal. 1986), *cert. denied*, 108 S.Ct. 1107 (1988).

14. Given the complexities of libel law, it should come as no surprise that various reforms have been urged. Consider, for example, a model statute proposed by the Libel Reform Project of Northwestern University's Annenberg Washington Program in Communications Policy Studies. Operating under the premise that the ultimate purpose of libel law is the "timely dissemination of truth," the statute sets up a process by which both sides are encouraged to assess their own positions and settle their differences without resorting to a suit for damages. Here are the model statute's key provisions:

- *Retraction or reply.* Every plaintiff must seek a retraction or an opportunity to reply from the defendant before filing suit. If the defendant honors the request within thirty days, there can be no suit. The statute establishes specific requirements governing the timing, placement, and format of retraction and replies, and in some cases the plaintiff may file suit to argue that the retraction was inadequate.

- *Declaratory judgment.* A plaintiff who fails to get a retraction or opportunity to reply may file suit. If, however, either plaintiff or defendant request a declaratory judgment trial, the plaintiff will not be able to obtain damages, while the defendant will not enjoy the protection of the first amendment doctrines discussed throughout this chapter. In a declaratory judgment suit, the only question litigated is the truth or falsity of the defamatory statement, and the only money paid by the loser is the winner's attorney fees. Declaratory judgment trials are likely to be less expensive than damages trials and usually must begin within 120 days after the suit is filed.

- *Damages.* A suit for damages will be possible only if both parties agree, since either may choose the declaratory judgment option. In a damages action, each side must bear its own attorney fees, and the plaintiff is limited to actual damages. Presumed and punitive damages are not available.

Evaluate this statute, taking into account how it would change existing law and the impact that it would likely have on the behavior of libel plaintiffs and defendants. *See* Libel Reform Project of the Annenberg Washington Program in Communications Policy Studies, *Proposal for the Reform of Libel Law* (1988).

CHAPTER

3

PRIVACY

Dietemann v. Time, Inc., 449 F.2d 245 (9th Cir. 1971).

Before CARTER and HUFSTEDLER, Circuit Judges, and VON DER HEYDT, District Judge.

HUFSTEDLER, Circuit Judge.

This is an appeal from a judgment for plaintiff in an action for invasion of privacy. Jurisdiction was grounded in diversity. The parties agreed that California law governed. After a court trial plaintiff was awarded $1000 general damages. On appeal we are asked to consider significant questions involving the relationship between personal privacy and the freedom of the press.

* * * The facts, as narrated by the district court, are these:

"Plaintiff, a disabled veteran with little education, was engaged in the practice of healing with clay, minerals, and herbs—as practiced, simple quackery.

"Defendant, Time, Incorporated, a New York corporation, publishes Life Magazine. Its November 1, 1963, edition carried an article entitled 'Crackdown on Quackery.' The article depicted plaintiff as a quack and included two pictures of him. One picture was taken at plaintiff's home on September 20, 1963, previous to his arrest on a charge of practicing medicine without a license, and the other taken at the time of his arrest.

"Life Magazine entered into an arrangement with the District Attorney's Office of Los Angeles County whereby Life's employees would visit plaintiff and obtain facts and pictures concerning his activities. Two employees of Life, Mrs. Jackie Metcalf and Mr. William Ray, went to plaintiff's home on September 20, 1963. When they arrived at a locked gate, they rang a bell and plaintiff came out of his house and was told by Mrs. Metcalf and Ray that they had been sent there by a friend, a Mr. Johnson. The use of Johnson's name was a ruse to gain entrance. Plaintiff admitted them and all three went into the house and into plaintiff's den.

"The plaintiff had some equipment which could at best be described as gadgets, not equipment which had anything to do with the practice of medicine. Plaintiff, while examining Mrs. Metcalf, was photographed by Ray with a hidden camera without the consent of plaintiff. One of the pictures taken by him appeared in Life Magazine showing plaintiff with his hand on the upper portion of Mrs. Metcalf's breast while he was looking at some gadgets and holding what appeared to be a wand in his right hand. Mrs. Metcalf had told plaintiff that she had a lump in her breast. Plaintiff concluded that she had eaten some rancid butter 11 years, 9 months, and 7 days prior to that time. Other persons were seated in the room during this time.

"The conversation between Mrs. Metcalf and plaintiff was transmitted by radio transmitter hidden in Mrs. Metcalf's purse to a tape recorder in a parked automobile occupied by Joseph Bride, Life employee, John Miner of the District Attorney's Office, and Grant Leake, an investigator of the State Department of Public Health. While the recorded conversation was not quoted in the article in Life, it was mentioned that Life correspondent Bride was making notes of what was being received via the radio transmitter, and such information was at least referred to in the article.

"The foregoing events were photographed and recorded by an arrangement among Miner of the District Attorney's Office, Leake of the State Department of Public Health, and Bride, a representative of Life. It had been agreed that Life would obtain pictures and information for use as evidence, and later could be used by Life for publication.

"Prior to the occurrences of September 20, 1963, on two occasions the officials had obtained recordings of conversations in plaintiff's home; however, no pictures had been secured. Life employees had not participated in obtaining the recordings on these occasions.

"On October 15, 1963, plaintiff was arrested at his home on a charge of practicing medicine without a license in violation of Section 26280, California Health and Safety Code. At the time of his arrest, many pictures were made by Life of plaintiff at his home. Plaintiff testified that he did not agree to pose for the pictures but allowed pictures because he thought the officers could require it. Also present were newspaper men who had also been invited by the officials to be present at the time of arrest. * * *

"Plaintiff, although a journeyman plumber, claims to be a scientist. Plaintiff had no listings and his home had no sign of any kind. He did not advertise, nor did he have a telephone. He made no charges when he attempted to diagnose or to prescribe herbs and minerals. He did accept contributions. * * *"

The appeal presents three ultimate issues: (1) Under California law, is a cause of action for invasion of privacy established upon proof that defendant's employees, by subterfuge, gained entrance to the office portion of plaintiff's home wherein they photographed him and electronically recorded and transmitted to third persons his conversation without his consent as a result of which he suffered emotional distress? (2) Does the First Amendment insulate defendant from liability for invasion of privacy because defendant's employees did those acts for the purpose of gathering material for a magazine story and a story was thereafter published utilizing some of the material thus gathered? (3) Were the defendant's employees acting as special agents of the police and, if so, did their acts violate the First, Fourth, and Fourteenth Amendments of the Federal Constitution, thereby subjecting defendant to liability under the Civil Rights Act (42 U.S.C. § 1983)? Because we hold that plaintiff proved a cause of action under California law and that the First Amendment does not insulate the defendant from liability, we do not reach the third issue.

Were it necessary to reach the Civil Rights Act questions, we would be obliged to explore the relationship between the defendant's employees and the police for the purpose of ascertaining the existence of the "color of law" element of the Act. Because we do not reach the issue, we can and do accept the defendant's disclaimer that its employees were acting for or on behalf of the police.

In jurisdictions other than California in which a common law tort for invasion of privacy is recognized, it has been consistently held that surreptitious electronic recording of a plaintiff's conversation causing him emotional distress is actionable. Despite some variations in the description and the labels applied to the tort, there is agreement that publication is not a necessary element of the tort, that the existence of a technical trespass is immaterial, and that proof of special damages is not required. * * *

Although the issue has not been squarely decided in California, we have little difficulty in concluding that clandestine photography of the plaintiff in his den and the recordation and transmission of his conversation without his consent resulting in his emotional distress warrants recovery for invasion of privacy in California. California began developing a common law privacy tort in 1931 with the decision of *Melvin v. Reid*. Since then, the California Supreme Court has decided a number of privacy cases in some of which there are indications that California would recognize the plaintiff's claim.

The most recent expression is found in *Briscoe v. Reader's Digest Ass'n* (1971), a privacy action based upon . . . of an article disclosing plaintiff's conviction of a felony 11 years earlier. The court equated the growing acceptance of the right of privacy with

"the increasing capability of * * * electronic devices with their capacity to destroy an individual's anonymity, intrude upon his most intimate activities, and expose his most personal characteristics to public gaze. * * *

"Men fear exposure not only to those closest to them; much of the outrage underlying the asserted right to privacy is a reaction to exposure to persons known only through business or other secondary relationships. The claim is not so much one of total secrecy as it is of the right to define one's circle of intimacy—to choose who shall see beneath the quotidian mask. Loss of control over which 'face' one puts on may result in literal loss of self-identity

and is humiliating beneath the gaze of those whose curiosity treats a human being as an object."

In *Gill v. Hearst Publishing Co.* (1953), which denied recovery . . . to plaintiffs whose picture was taken in a public market and later published without their consent, the court stressed that the picture had not been "surreptitiously snapped on private grounds, but rather was taken of plaintiffs in a pose voluntarily assumed in a public market place."
* * *

We are convinced that California will "approve the extension of the tort of invasion of privacy to instances of intrusion, whether by physical trespass or not, into spheres from which an ordinary man in plaintiff's position could reasonably expect that the particular defendant should be excluded."

Plaintiff's den was a sphere from which he could reasonably expect to exclude eavesdropping newsmen. He invited two of defendant's employees to the den. One who invites another to his home or office takes a risk that the visitor may not be what he seems, and that the visitor may repeat all he hears and observes when he leaves. But he does not and should not be required to take the risk that what is heard and seen will be transmitted by photograph or recording, or in our modern world, in full living color and hi-fi to the public at large or to any segment of it that the visitor may select. A different rule could have a most pernicious effect upon the dignity of man and it would surely lead to guarded conversations and conduct where candor is most valued. . . .

The defendant claims that the First Amendment immunizes it from liability for invading plaintiff's den with a hidden camera and its concealed electronic instruments because its employees were gathering news and its instrumentalities "are indispensable tools of investigative reporting." We agree that newsgathering is an integral part of news dissemination. We strongly disagree, however, that the hidden mechanical contrivances are "indispensable tools" of newsgathering. Investigative reporting is an ancient art; its successful practice long antecedes the invention of miniature cameras and electronic devices. The First

Amendment has never been construed to accord newsmen immunity from torts or crimes committed during the course of newsgathering. The First Amendment is not a license to trespass, to steal, or to intrude by electronic means into the precincts of another's home or office. It does not become such a license simply because the person subjected to the intrusion is reasonably suspected of committing a crime.

Defendant relies upon the line of cases commencing with *New York Times Co. v. Sullivan* (1964) . . . to sustain its contentions that (1) publication of news, however tortiously gathered, insulates defendant from liability for the antecedent tort, and (2) even of it is not thus shielded from liability, those cases prevent consideration of publication as an element in computing damages.

As we previously observed, publication is not an essential element of plaintiff's cause of action. Moreover, it is not the foundation for the invocation of a privilege. Privilege concepts developed in defamation cases and to some extent in privacy actions in which publication is an essential component are not relevant in determining liability for intrusive conduct antedating publication. * * * Nothing in *New York Times* or its progeny suggests anything to the contrary. Indeed, the Court strongly indicates that there is no First Amendment interest in protecting news media from calculated misdeeds. * * *

No interest protected by the First Amendment is adversely affected by permitting damages for intrusion to be enhanced by the fact of later publication of the information that the publisher improperly acquired. Assessing damages for the additional emotional distress suffered by a plaintiff when the wrongfully acquired data are purveyed to the multitude chills intrusive acts. It does not chill freedom of expression guaranteed by the First Amendment. A rule forbidding the use of publication as an ingredient of damages would deny to the injured plaintiff recovery for real harm done to him without any countervailing benefit to the legitimate interest of the public in being informed. The same rule would encourage conduct by news media that grossly offends ordinary men.

The judgment is affirmed.

[The separate opinion of Judge Carter is omitted.]

INTRODUCTION

The *Dietemann* case involved intrusion of the news media into the plaintiff's solitude; as the court noted in its opinion, Mr. Dietemann's den "was a sphere from which he could reasonably expect to exclude eavsdropping newsmen." Intrusion is one branch of the tort known as invasion of privacy. The three others are: public disclosure of private or embarassing facts, placing a person in a false light in the public eye, and appropriation of one's name or likeness for commercial purposes. The four branches overlap to some extent, and a particular plaintiff may well be able to squeeze his case into more than one category. The principles that govern the various types of invasion of privacy have little in common, other than the fact that they represent an effort to protect what has been called "the right to be let alone."

The privacy tort is largely a creature of the twentieth century, and its origin can be traced to one of the most influential law journal articles in history. Boston lawyer Samuel D. Warren—along with his law partner, future Supreme Court Justice Louis Brandeis—published an article in the 1890 *Harvard Law Review* arguing for judicial recognition of a remedy for invasion of one's privacy. Warren and Brandeis wrote:

> The press is overstepping in every direction the obvious bounds of propriety and of decency. * * * To satisfy a prurient taste the details of sexual relations are spread broadcast in the columns of the daily papers. To occupy the indolent, column upon

column is filled with idle gossip, which can only be procured by intrusion upon the domestic circle. The itensity and complexity of life, attendant upon advancing civilization, have rendered necessary some retreat from the world, and man, under the refining influence of culture, has become more sensitive to publicity, so that solitude and privacy have become more essential to the individual; but modern enterprise and invention have, through invasions upon his privacy, subjected him to mental pain and distress, far greater than could be inflicted by mere bodily injury.

The Warren and Brandeis proposal was initially met with judicial hostility. In the first major case to consider it, the New York Court of Appeals ruled in *Roberson v. Rochester Folding-Box Co.* (1902) that no such right of privacy existed under the common law. There the defendant had used the picture of an attractive young lady—without her consent—to advertise its flour, and the plaintiff claimed in her suit that, as a result, she had suffered great distress and humiliation. In a 4 to 3 decision, the court concluded that the purely mental nature of the alleged harm, the "vast amount" of litigation that would likely ensue, and the potential threat to a free press counseled against recognition of a right to privacy.

The *Roberson* case had little long-lasting effect, however, for the New York legislature quickly passed a statute—still on the books—making it a misdemeanor and a tort to use the name or likeness of any person for "advertising purposes or for the purposes of trade." Moreover, courts in other states flatly refused to follow *Roberson*, choosing instead to adopt the tort of invasion of privacy as part of the common law. Today, the "right to be let alone" is protected in virtually all jurisdictions, though New York and a handful of other states do not recognize all of the "branches" of the tort.

Privacy also has a constitutional dimension, and here again the views of Justice Brandeis have been influential. In *Olmstead v. United States* (1928), defendants were convicted in federal court of selling liquor in violation of the Prohibition Act. Federal officers had obtained key evidence by wiretapping the defendants' telephone lines, and the district court allowed this evidence to be used at trial despite objections that it was obtained in violation of the fourth and fifth amendments, which, respectively, prohibit unreasonable searches and seizures and compulsory self-incrimination. The Supreme Court rejected these arguments and affirmed the convictions. Justice Brandeis, dissenting, took issue with the majority's conclusion that the fourth amendment applied only to physical invasions, such as the search of a home or the seizure of documents. He wrote:

> The protection guaranteed by the [fourth and fifth] amendments is much broader in scope. The makers of our Constitution undertook to secure conditions favorable to the pursuit of happiness. They recognized the significance of man's spiritual nature, of his feelings and of his intellect. They knew that only a part of the pain, pleasure and satisfactions of life are to be found in material things. They sought to protect Americans in their beliefs, their thoughts, their emotions and their sensations. They conferred, as against the government, the right to be let alone—the most comprehensive of rights and the right most valued by civilized men. To protect that right, every unjustifiable intrusion by the government upon the privacy of the individual, whatever the means employed, must be deemed a violation of the Fourth Amendment. And the use, as evidence in a criminal proceeding, of facts ascertained by such intrusion must be deemed a violation of the Fifth.

Though it took nearly forty years, Brandeis' views ultimately prevailed. In *Katz v. United States* (1967), the Court rejected the notion that some sort of physical invasion is necessary for a fourth amendment violation, ruling that wiretapping or other electronic eavesdropping by the government can be unconstitutional. And, under the so-called "exclusionary rule," any evidence obtained in violation of the fourth or fifth amendments cannot be used in a criminal prosecution. This rule, while often criticized, gives teeth to these constitutional safeguards, since it excludes from the trial evidence secured in a fashion that violates an individual's privacy.

Although the right to privacy is not expressly mentioned in the Constitution, the Supreme Court has recognized that various provisions of that document—including the fourth and fifth amendments—create "zones" of privacy. As Justice William O. Douglas once wrote, "specific guarantees in the Bill of Rights have penumbras, formed by emanations from those guarantees that help give them life and substance."

Among these "penumbral rights" is the right to "privacy and repose." For example, the first amendment's protection for freedom of expression includes the right to associate freely with others to advance common beliefs. Accordingly, in *NAACP v. Alabama* (1958), the Court ruled unconstitutional the State of Alabama's attempt to force the NAACP to disclose the organization's membership lists, pointing out the "vital relationship between freedom to associate and privacy in one's associations." Similarly, in *Stanley v. Georgia* (1969), the Court concluded that the first amendment prohibits a state's making the mere private possession of obscene material a crime. "If the First Amendment means anything," Justice Thurgood Marshall wrote for the Court, "it means that a State has no business telling a man, sitting alone in his own house, what books he may read or what films he may watch."

Another line of cases involving what might be called "sexual privacy" is based in part on the ninth amendment, which provides that the enumeration of rights in the Constitution "shall not be construed to deny or disparage others retained by the people," and the fourteenth amendment, which protects against deprivations of "liberty . . . without due process of law." For example, in *Griswold v. Connecticut* (1965), the Supreme Court struck down a state statute making it a crime for even married couples to use contraceptives and for anyone to give information or instruction in their use. Writing for the Court, Justice Douglas noted that the "very idea" that police could "search the sacred precincts of marital bedrooms for telltale signs of the use of contraceptives . . . is repulsive to the notions of privacy surrounding the marriage relationship." In *Roe v. Wade* (1973), the Court found that its prior cases protecting privacy with respect to "marriage, procreation, contraception, family relationships, and child rearing" were broad enough "to encompass a woman's decision whether or not to terminate her pregnancy." However, the Court recently upheld the constitutionality of a Georgia sodomy statute, refusing in *Bowers v. Hardwick* (1986) to extend the concept of constitutional privacy to embrace homosexual conduct in one's own home.

For present purposes, our concern is not with these constitutional principles, but rather with the law of torts. As we shall see, however, first amendment limitations—similar to those examined in Chapter 2 with respect to defamation—will also come into play in some privacy cases. These constitutional doctrines will be explored in connection with each of the "branches" of the privacy tort. Before examining those categories, however, a brief look at some basic principles concerning the law of privacy is warranted.

GENERAL CONSIDERATIONS

The "right to be let alone" is frequently said to be "personal," a description which has important legal consequences. As a general rule, the right to privacy may be asserted only by the individual whose privacy has been invaded. For example, the public disclosure of private facts about Joe Smith does not enable his wife and children to bring suit, unless the offending material invades their privacy as well. Moreover, under the common law view, an action for invasion of privacy cannot be maintained after the death of the individual whose privacy interests are at stake. A few states have modified this rule by statute, however. In some jurisdictions, the right to sue "survives" if the invasion of privacy occurred before the person's death, and his estate or surviving relatives may bring a privacy suit based on the harm he suffered when alive. A less common type of statute permits relatives to sue even if the invasion took place after death.

The "survivability" question is particularly important in connection with invasion of privacy by appropriation of one's likeness for commercial purposes, since substantial sums of money may be at stake. Also significant in the appropriation area is the question of whether privacy rights may be assigned—that is, given or sold to third persons. Although the general rule is that no such assignment can be made in light of the "personal" nature of the privacy interest, an exception is made in the appropriation context. As discussed more fully below, a different approach is taken in this area because the ability to exploit commercially one's own likeness or identity is similar to a property right.

These general rules about privacy are similar to those found in the law of defamation. The two torts differ markedly, however, in their treatment of suits by corporations, partnerships, other business organizations, and unincoroprated associations such as labor unions and charitable groups. While such entities can sue for libel in most states (wholly apart from such suits that can be brought by individual members who claim to have been defamed), they cannot ordinarily maintain an action for invasion of privacy. This result should not be particularly surprising, since the privacy tort provides a remedy for mental or emotional harm—injuries that only human beings can suffer. However, business organizations have some protection under the law of unfair competition for exclusive use of their names or identities.

Libel and privacy also differ considerably with respect to the remedies available to an injured plaintiff. We have already seen one such difference: the theoretical basis for awarding damages in defamation suits is injury to reputation, while the rationale in privacy cases is emotional distress. Moreover, the complex set of common law and constitutional rules that govern damage awards in libel cases are for the most part inapplicable in privacy suits. An exception is the "false light" category, which overlaps to some extent with defamation. Because of similarities between the two legal actions, some of the constitutional requirements fashioned in the defamation context are used in false light cases. Finally, it should be noted that injunctive relief, quite rare in defamation suits, is much more frequently employed in privacy litigation. While courts ordinarily will not enter an order forbidding publication of a defamatory article (on the theory that the injured party can be adequately compensated by a damage award after publication), they are much more willing to issue such an injunction to protect a plaintiff from an imminent invasion of his privacy.

A court's enjoining publication to prevent an invasion of privacy raises serious questions under the first amendment, which generally prohibits such "prior restraints.'' The U.S. Supreme Court, however, has yet to rule definitively on the use of injunctions in this context, despite having had the opportunity to do so on at least three occasions over the past twenty years. For example, in *Doe v. Roe* (1973), the New York courts halted distribution of a book by a psychiatrist that described his treatment of the plaintiff, who claimed that she was easily identifiable even though her name had not been used. The trial court entered a temporary injunction that prohibited, pending trial, distribution of the book beyond the ''scientific community.'' On appeal, a state court modified the order and enjoined all distribution until the litigation was completed. The U.S. Supreme Court refused to hear the case. Subsequently, the trial court awarded the plaintiff $20,000 damages based on distribution of about 200 copies of the book before the temporary injunction was granted, entered a permanent injunction preventing distribution of the book, and ordered all remaining copies destroyed.

Defenses to privacy suits are discussed in connection with each of the four branches of the tort, but one—consent—should be briefly mentioned here. Technically part of the plaintiff's case rather than a defense, consent is often asserted by defendants seeking to avoid liability. The thrust of this concept, which runs throughout the law of torts, is well captured by the Latin phrase *volenti non fit injuria* (''to one who is willing, no wrong is done''). Thus, if the plaintiff consents to an invasion of his privacy, there has been no tort and there can be no recovery. Accordingly, the plaintiff is required to prove lack of consent in order to establish that an actionable invasion has occurred.

Consent may be either express or implied. The most common form of express consent is the so-called ''model release'' agreement typically signed by models in connection with photographic sessions. In some states, such prior written consent is required before a person's name or likeness can be used for commercial purposes. Since professional models are compensated (often quite well) for their services, the model release agreement is a binding contract that cannot be revoked. As in any case involving a contract, the terms of the agreement are most important and must be examined to determine the scope of the consent. For example, a photograph might ultimately be used for purposes other than those specified in the agreement or might be used for commercial purposes after the period of time authorized for such use had expired. In such circumstances, the consent is said to have been ''exceeded,'' and recovery is allowed. Hoping to avoid these problems, photographers rely on very broad release forms whereby the model consents to virtually unrestricted use of the photographs.

In the newsgathering context, express consent to publish particular information is usually not based on compensation, although such ''checkbook journalism'' is not uncommon. If there is merely gratuitous consent rather than a binding contract, revocation can occur at any time before the invasion of privacy actually occurs. For example, a person who provides a reporter with sensitive information and specifically permits its use in a story has consented to any invasion of his privacy that might result from publication of the material. However, the individual may withdraw that consent in advance of publication, provided that he does so in a timely manner, and any subsequent disclosure of the information is without consent.

Consent may also be implied from the circumstances. If an interview subject freely talks to a journalist who has identified himself as a reporter working on a story, he undoubtedly anticipates that the information he provides will be made public. Accordingly, his communication with the reporter will be construed as consent to publish the information even though the reporter and his subject never mentioned the consent issue. On the other hand, a different result would be reached if the reporter concealed the fact that he was a journalist. Consent must be knowing and voluntary, and in this situation it cannot be said that the subject spoke "freely" with the news media. Consent may also be implied from custom and practice. As discussed more fully below in connection with intrusion, it is customary for journalists to accompany law enforcement officials on to private property where newsworthy events such as crimes and fires have occurred. Courts have often ruled that this well-known and widespread practice constitutes implied consent on the part of the property owner, provided that he has not specifically objected to the presence of the reporters.

THE FOUR "BRANCHES" OF PRIVACY

Intrusion

Because this type of invasion of privacy requires judicial analysis of the media's newsgathering activities, it has a potentially greater impact on the press than the other privacy categories, which focus primarily upon the publication of information. For example, the *Dietemann* court allowed recovery because of the reporters' newsgathering methods—their using hidden cameras and microphones, their posing as patients in need of "treatment"—rather than *Life*'s publication of their story revealing Dietemann's quackery. Under this approach, which separates newsgathering from publication, a journalist can be liable for intrusion even if his story is never published or broadcast.

Unlike the familiar tort of trespass, intrusion does not require a physical entry upon one's property without permission. Thus, a peeping tom armed with high-powered binoculars or a news photographer with a telephoto lens could be liable for intrusion when he peers into the window of a house across the street, though he has technically not committed a trespass. Intrusion and trespass are closed linked, however, and several of the cases discussed below involve trespass allegations. Because intrusion is broader, it will be our focus here. The *Restatement (Second) of Torts* defines this type of invasion of privacy as follows:

> One who intentionally intrudes, physically or otherwise, upon the solitude or seclusion of another or his private affairs or concerns, is subject to liability to the other for invasion of his privacy, if the intrusion would be highly offensive to a reasonable person.

The obvious difficulty with this definition is that it offers precious little guidance to the working journalist. What, for example, is meant by "solitude"? By "private affairs or concerns?" And, what of the requirement that the intrusion be "highly offensive"? Generally speaking, some sort of balancing of interests is necessary, just as it is in the first amendment setting discussed in Chapter 1. The key judicial decisions in this area indicate that the following considerations are significant in the balancing process: whether a public or private location is involved; whether electronic devices or hidden cameras are utilized; and, to some extent, whether the story is newsworthy.

Public or Private Setting? The *Restatement* test speaks in terms of an intrusion upon one's solitude, seclusion, or private affairs, thereby suggesting that some legitimate expectation of privacy must be present. Such an expectation is at its greatest when a person is in a nonpublic setting, such as his living room or a fenced backyard, and at its lowest when he is in an area plainly open to the public, such as a shopping center, park, or government building. As a general rule, there is no invasion of privacy when a journalist records, photographs, or writes about something that occurs in a public place. The theory behind this rule is simple: in such circumstances, the press simply stands in the shoes of anyone who could have observed the same event.

For example, in *Gill v. Hearst Corp.* (1953), the plaintiff and his wife were photographed at the Farmer's Market in Los Angeles. The picture, taken by noted photographer Henri Cartier-Bresson, was used to illustrate an article in *Harper's Bazaar.* Rejecting the invasion of privacy claim, the California Supreme Court noted that the photo "was not surreptitiously snapped on private grounds, but rather was taken of plaintiffs in a pose voluntarily assumed in a public market place." Thus, the court explained, the picture "only extended knowledge of the particular incident to a somewhat larger public than had actually witnessed it at the time of occurrence." Similarly, in *Fogel v. Forbes, Inc.* (1980), a federal court found no intrusion where the plaintiff had been photographed at an airline counter in the Miami airport. A Kentucky court reached the same result in *Livingston v. Kentucky Post* (1987), in which a newspaper photograph showed the plaintiff emerging from a portable toilet set up at a college that had temporarily lost its water supply.

In unusual cases, however, even an event occurring in a public place can give rise to liability. In *Daily Times Democrat v. Graham* (1964), a newspaper published a photo of a woman whose dress was blown above her waist as she emerged from a carnival "fun house." Upholding her claim for invasion of privacy, the Alabama Supreme Court concluded that a person does not forfeit "his right to be protected from an indecent and vulgar intrusion of his right of privacy merely because misfortune overtakes him in a public place." And, in *Galella v. Onassis* (1973) a federal court ruled that a photographer's incessant hounding of Jacqueline Kennedy Onassis was an invasion of her privacy, although the photos were taken in public. In that case, the court concluded that the photographer's activities "went far beyond the reasonable bounds of newsgathering" and amounted to harassment of the former First Lady.

Although matters transpiring in public generally pose little risk of liability for intrusion, the journalist is on shakier ground when the event takes place on private property. Even in this situation, however, the courts have ruled that there is no intrusion if the journalist photographs or records what any other person could have seen or heard. For example, in *Mark v. Seattle Times, Inc.* (1981), a pharmacist brought a defamation suit against the newspaper and a television station for their coverage of his prosecution for Medicaid fraud. He also claimed that the television station invaded his privacy by airing a film clip showing him talking on the telephone inside the pharmacy. The pharmacy was closed at the time, but the cameraman was able to film the scene through a window. Dismissing the intrusion claim, the Washington Supreme Court pointed out that "the place from which the film was shot was open to the public and thus any passerby could have viewed the scene recorded by the camera."

As the *Dietemann* case makes plain, however, the courts are sensitive to the privacy interests of persons in their own homes or in other areas where they have a legitimate expectation of privacy. In a famous case, *Barber v. Time, Inc.* (1942), *Time* magazine published a photo of a woman in her hospital bed. Suffering from a disease that caused her to lose weight despite constant eating, the plaintiff had protested when a photographer came into her hospital room and snapped a picture. "[W]hatever may be the right of the press . . . to take and use pictures of persons in public places," the Missouri court said, "certainly any right of privacy ought to protect a person . . . in bed for treatment and recuperation."

Several "private property" cases have involved allegations of trespass, which, unlike intrusion, requires a physical invasion of the plaintiff's property. Because most jurisdictions have determined that only individuals possess privacy rights, corporations or other business entities cannot rely on intrusion principles and must instead resort to the law of trespass. For example, in *Le Mistral, Inc. v. CBS* (1978), a reporter and camera crew from CBS' wholly-owned New York City affiliate entered a fashionable Manhattan restaurant "with cameras rolling" to film a story on violations of the city's health code. After a verbal exchange with a member of the restaurant staff, as well as a little shoving, the crew left; a film of the encounter was broadcast on the evening news, along with more pleasant interviews with personnel of two other establishments charged with violations. The corporation that owned Le Mistral sued the network for defamation and trespass and ultimately recovered $1,200 on the latter theory after the libel claim was dismissed.

Even though a restaurant is generally considered a public place, the New York court concluded in *Le Mistral* that the reporter and camera crew did not enter to avail themselves of the food or drink served there. Accordingly, the court treated the restaurant as private property insofar as the newsmen were concerned and imposed liability because they were present without the consent of the corporate owner. In contrast, a Kansas court ruled in *Belluomo v. KAKE-TV* (1979) that a restaurant owner who permitted a television camera crew to accompany a health inspector's tour of the kitchen and basement—obviously nonpublic areas—could not recover for trespass.

The Role of Consent. Consent is an important defense in intrusion and trespass cases, as well as in other types of privacy suits. Consent may be either express, as in the *KAKE-TV* case, or implied from the circumstances. If the former, it must be validly obtained. Recall that in *Dietemann*, the quack "doctor" permitted the reporters to enter his home and thus arguably consented to the intrusion. However, the journalists had posed as potential patients in order to gain entry, and this subterfuge vitiated the consent. There was also a question in *KAKE-TV* whether the restaurant owner's consent had been fraudulently obtained, but the court left this issue to the jury.

Consent can be implied from "custom and practice." In *Florida Publishing Co. v. Fletcher* (1976), a fire damaged the home of the plaintiff and killed her teenaged daughter. Mrs. Fletcher was out of the city at the time of the incident; police and firemen arrived on the scene after neighbors had discovered the fire, but they were too late to save the child. When police and fire officials entered the home to make their official investigation, they followed their standard practice and invited newsmen to accompany them. At the fire marshal's request, a news photographer took a picture of the "silhouette" left on the floor after the removal of the dead girl's body. This photo, which police and fire officials described as necessary to show that the body was already on the floor before the fire did any damage to the room, became a part of the official investigation file for the fire and police departments. However, it also appeared with several others in the newspaper, and Mrs. Fletcher apparently first learned of the facts surrounding her daughter's death by reading the newspaper account.

Mrs. Fletcher brought suit for, among other things, invasion of privacy and trespass. The Florida Supreme Court ruled that the entry on to the premises by the news media was not actionable because it has been established that the prevailing custom and practice was for the press to enter private property upon the express invitation of law enforcement officials conducting an investigation. This practice, the court said, was sufficiently long-standing and widespread to constitute implied consent, and there had been no objection by the property owner to overcome that implication.

In a similar case, *Prahl v. Brosamle* (1980), a television reporter filmed police officers confiscating guns and interviewing the plaintiff in the man's home. Monitoring a police radio, the reporter had heard the call summoning officers to the scene and, upon his arrival, had received permission from them to enter the residence when the situation was under control. The Wisconsin Court of Appeals refused to imply consent as a matter of law, observing that while it is well-known that media representatives attempt to cover newsworthy events on private property, "[f]ew private persons anticipate . . . that an unplanned newsworthy event will occur on their property." The court also pointed out that, unlike the situation in *Fletcher,* there was no evidence demonstrating the existence of a custom or practice.

When the case was sent back to the lower court, however, the trial judge dismissed the trespass claim. He found that it was "a common and accepted custom in the State of Wisconsin and nationally for reporters and photographers to accompany public officers . . . onto private premises where newsworthy events of general public interest such as crime, shootings, fires or storms have [occurred] or are occurring. . . ." The judge noted, however, that entry on to the private property must be made peacefully for purposes of newsgathering, without objection from the property owner.

At some point, however, consent will not be implied. As the *Fletcher* and *Prahl* cases indicate, a specific objection from the property owner overcomes any implication of consent. Other cases suggest that the courts are unlikely to apply the doctrine when something other than a "routine" police or fire matter is involved and sensitive personal privacy concerns are evident. Another Florida case, decided about the same time as *Fletcher,* provides some indication of the outer limits of the implied consent doctrine. In *Green Valley School, Inc. v. Cowles Florida Broadcasting, Inc.* (1976), a private school sued for trespass after WESH-TV broadcast details of a midnight police raid at the school, which housed delinquent children and children with medical problems. The raiding party included some fifty policemen and several special investigators from the state attorney's office, as well as news media personnel who had received special invitations from the chief investigator. The search warrant recited the belief that the school was being used "as a means to commit the felony offense of false imprisonment, child abuse and lewd and lascivious behavior." A news story broadcast by WESH-TV told of filthy living conditions, detention cells, drug usage, sexual abuse, and the use of electric cattle prods on the children.

However, school personnel and students stated in affidavits and depositions that the news story grossly distorted conditions at the school and charged that newsmen had cooperated with the police in staging certain situations that were filmed and photographed by the media. The trial judge granted summary judgment for the television station on the trespass claim, but the Florida Court of Appeals reversed, rejecting the station's argument that the trespass was sanctioned by the police and was thus within the custom and practice doctrine. The court said:

To uphold [the stations's] assertion . . . could well bring to the citizenry of this state the hobnail boots of a Nazi stormtrooper equipped with glaring lights invading a couple's bedroom at midnight with the wife hovering in her nightgown in an attempt to shield herself from the scanning television camera. In this jurisdiction, a law enforcement officer is not as a matter of law endowed with the right or authority to invite people of his choosing to invade private property and participate in a midnight raid of the premises.

A 1986 California case reflects similar concerns. In *Miller v. NBC*, a network television crew working on a mini-documentary accompanied a team of paramedics as they responded to calls. On one such call, the journalists followed the paramedics into the apartment of a man suffering a heart attack and filmed them as they attempted, unsuccessfully, to save his life. Although the man's wife was present, the journalists did not seek her permission to enter the premises. The trial court dismissed the wife's suit against NBC for trespass and intrusion, but the California Court of Appeals reversed and ordered a trial.

Apparently rejecting the network's argument of implied consent, the court concluded that "the obligation not to make unauthorized entry into the private premises of individuals . . . does not place an impermissible burden on newsgathers." To hold otherwise, the court said, "might have extraordinarily chilling implications for all of us; instead of a zone of privacy protecting our secluded moments, a climate of fear might surround us instead."

Concealed Equipment in Newsgathering. In the *Dietemann* decision, the court placed considerable emphasis on the reporters' use of "miniature cameras and electronic devices" in the course of their newsgathering activities:

> One who invites another to his home or office takes a risk that the visitor may not be what he seems, and that the visitor may repeat all he hears and observes when he leaves. But he does not and should not take the risk that what is heard and seen will be transmitted by photograph or recording . . . to the public at large. . . .

This passage indicates that the court might have been more receptive to the defendant's arguments had the *Life* reporters simply posed as patients, received the "treatment," and prepared a story based on their recollections of what transpired in Mr. Dietemann's den. Even in the *Le Mistral* case, which did not involve concealed equipment, the court seemed to emphasize the fact that television cameras had been used. Surely there would have been no liability if, for instance, a journalist had visited the restaurant, ordered a drink or a meal, and written a story or review.

These cases, as well as others, suggest that reliance upon concealed or electronic devices in newsgathering is more likely to lead to a successful intrusion lawsuit than use of more traditional techniques. This result is troubling, since it can certainly be argued that mechanical devices enable journalists to be more accurate in doing their jobs. On the other hand, the tort of intrusion is not concerned with the publication of information, but rather the gathering of it, and the law tends to recognize that certain newsgathering methods are more intrusive than others. Accordingly, reporters should be cautious in using wiretaps, hidden tape recorders and cameras, "boom" microphones that can record conversations across a football field, infrared cameras, and similar "high-tech" devices.

Moreover, the interception of oral communications by wiretapping or secret tape or video recording can have other consequences. The Omnibus Crime Control and Safe Streets Act, a federal statute passed in 1968 and amended in 1986, prohibits the interception of any conversation carried over a wire or a nonwire conversation in a setting where one expects privacy. The statute specifically authorizes a civil damage action for persons harmed by a violation of these provisions. Therefore, a journalist who uses a wiretap to record a phone conversation between two persons or "bugs" a room in which a meeting is held would face potential liability under the statute.

There is an important exception, however. The statute expressly permits a party to the conversation to record it without the knowledge of the other parties, so long as the recording is not for the purpose of "committing [a] criminal or tortious act." Thus, in the examples given above, the recording would be permissible so long as one of the participants had consented. Similarly, the exception allows a reporter to tape record his telephone conversations with a person he is interviewing, since the consent of only one party to the conversation—in this case, the reporter himself—is necessary. Keep in mind that the exception is inapplicable if the recording is made for the purpose of committing a crime or a tort, such as defamation. The question of motivation in cases arising under the statute has generally been left to the jury.

A 1980 case involving ABC News illustrates the statute in operation. In *Benford v. ABC*, congressional investigators invited a network television crew to secretly tape a meeting at a private home between an insurance salesman and two investigators posing as potential purchasers of cancer insurance. Excerpts from the meeting, at which the salesman made his standard pitch, were broadcast on the ABC Nightly News. The salesman brought suit in a Maryland federal court, claiming, among other things, invasion of privacy and violation of the federal wiretapping statute. Noting that the statute protects "oral communication[s] uttered by a person exhibiting an expectation that such communication is not subject to interception under circumstances justifying such expectation," the court concluded that the salesman had a reasonable expectation that his conversation with the "prospects" would not be taped or overheard. The court then rejected ABC's argument that the television crew's conduct fell within the statutory provision permitting such secret recording so long as one party consents. The provision applies, the court said, only if the party intercepting the communication is not acting for the purpose of committing a crime or a tort. Since ABC's purpose in taping the meeting was for the jury to decide, the court denied the network's motion to dismiss the case. If ABC had invaded the salesman's privacy, for example, a jury might find that it made the recording for the purpose of committing a tort and thus violated the wiretap statute.

At the time *Benford* was decided, the wiretap statute provided that one-party recording of a conversation was permissible unless that interception was for criminal or tortious purposes or "for the purpose of committing any other injurious act." The quoted phrase was broadly interpreted by some courts, and, fearing that a chilling effect on newsgathering would result, Congress decided to delete the language from the statute in 1986. The most troubling case was *Boddie v. ABC,* decided by the U.S. Court of Appeals for the Sixth Circuit in 1984. There the plaintiff agreed to be interviewed "off camera" for an ABC investigative report about an Ohio judge who allegedly granted leniency to criminal defendants in return for sex. Unbeknown to the plaintiff, the journalists secretly recorded the interview by using a hidden video camera and concealed microphones. A segment of the interview was included in the broadcast report, entitled "Injustice for All," on ABC's "20/20" program. The plaintiff sued the network for defamation, false light invasion of privacy, and violation of the wiretap statute. A jury found for ABC on the tort claims, and the trial judge dismissed the statutory count. The Sixth Circuit disagreed on the wiretap question, ruling that the network may have recorded the interview for the purpose of committing an "injurious act" even though it had not libeled her or placed her in a false light. Thus, the network could be liable for damages under the statute, and the court sent the case back to the trial judge for further proceedings on this question.

In the Electronic Communications Privacy Act of 1986, Congress eliminated the "injurious act" language. According to a Senate report accompanying the legislation, the Sixth Circuit's opinion in *Boddie* "suggests that if the network intended to cause 'insult and injury' to plaintiff Boddie, she might be entitled to recover." This interpretation "places a stumbling block in the path of even the most scrupulous journalist," the report noted, since "[m]any news stories are embarrassing to someone." The threat of damages in a civil suit—or even criminal sanctions—under the wiretap statute was considered by Congress to be "inconsistent with the guarantees of the first amendment." As amended, the wiretap statute continues to prohibit recordings made for the purpose of committing a tort or a crime, thus affording the public "ample protection against improper or unscrupulous interception."

After this legislation was enacted, the trial court in *Boddie* again dismissed the plaintiff's wiretap claim against the network. Because the conduct that spawned the plaintiff's lawsuit occurred before the 1986 legislation, the initial version of the statute—rather than the amended version—applied in the case. However, the court concluded that the 1986 amendment simply clarified the meaning of the original statute; accordingly, the court refused to interpret the "injurious act" language to permit recovery where there had been no tortious or criminal conduct. On appeal, the Sixth Circuit rejected this reasoning but agreed that the case had been properly dismissed. Finding that Congress deleted the "injurious act" language "to eliminate [that] basis of liability altogether," the appellate court said that the term must have meant something other than tortious or criminal conduct. Just what it meant, however, was far from clear. Because journalists "could only guess" as to the conduct that might subject them to liability, the court held that the term "injurious act" was unconstitutionally vague.

Some states go even further than the federal statute in proscribing secret recording. A Florida statute, for example, makes it a crime for any person "not acting under color of law" to intercept a wire or oral communication unless all parties to the conversation had given prior consent. In *Shevin v. Sunbeam Television Corp.* (1977), the Florida Supreme Court rejected arguments by journalists that the statute unconstitutionally impaired investigative reporting. First amendment rights "do not include a constitutional right to corroborate newsgathering activities when the legislature has statutorily recognized the private rights of individuals," the court said. About a dozen other states—including California, where *Dietemann* arose—prohibit such "participant recording" absent consent of all parties to the communication.

Even in states without such stringent statutes, secret recording of telephone conversations in which a reporter participates may violate telephone company tariffs that require a person recording his conversation with someone else to advise the other party of the recording or provide a warning "beep." Theoretically, a violation of this regulation could result in termination of telephone service, but that possibility is rather remote. Broadcasters face a more serious restriction, however. Under a regulation adopted by the Federal Communications Commission, radio and television journalists must notify the other party to a telephone conversation that the discussion is being broadcast "live" or being recorded for subsequent broadcast. Such notice is not necessary where the other party is aware or may be presumed to be aware that the conversation is likely to be broadcast. Awareness is presumed to exist only when the other party is associated with the station or when he makes a call in connection with a "talk show" or similar program in which telephone conversations are customarily broadcast. The FCC reaffirmed this rule in late 1988, concluding that "there is a legitimate expectation of privacy that telephone calls will not be broadcast without the consent of the parties involved."

Newsworthiness. Although the *Dietemann* court flatly stated that the first amendment "is not a license to trespass . . . or intrude," the newsgathering process does not fall entirely outside the Constitution. As the U.S. Supreme Court has noted, "without some protection for seeking out the news, freedom of the press could be eviscerated." Obviously, the right to publish and disseminate news and information is meaningless without a correlative right to gather news. Equally obvious is the fact that a lawsuit for intrusion or trespass can have a chilling effect on the newsgathering process. Some accommodation must thus be made between the right of privacy and the right of the press to seek out the news.

With respect to the "private facts" branch of privacy law, the courts have long recognized a so-called "newsworthiness defense" that protects the news media when publication of private information about an individual is of legitimate interest to the public. This defense, discussed in more detail below in connection with public disclosure of private facts, also has some application in intrusion or trespass cases, though decisions such as *Dietemann* indicate that the courts have been less receptive toward it in this context. However, the test for intrusion set out in the *Restatement (Second) of Torts*—whether the intrusion is "highly offensive to a reasonable person"—leaves from for consideration of the newsworthiness of a story obtained by intrusive methods or trespassing.

The public interest in given story does not insulate the press from liability in all intrusion or trespass cases. Many of the cases previously discussed arguably involved subject matter of legitimate public concern. The plaintiff in *Dietemann* was practicing quackery; *Le Mistral* grew out of violations of the city sanitation code; *Fletcher* arose from the death of a young girl in a fire; and *Green Valley* involved allegations of wrongdoing at a private school for problem children. Even *Galella* presumably would satisfy the requirement, since the activities of former First Lady Jacqueline Kennedy Onassis are newsworthy. But the newsworthiness inquiry is only the first step; if the story concerns a matter of public interest, the question then becomes whether its newsworthiness outweighs the privacy interests of the individual plaintiff. Even if legitimate public interest in the subject matter does exist, liability will neverless be imposed if the media has "gone too far" in gathering the information.

In *Galella*, for example, the photographer's actions went beyond mere news coverage and become harassment, while in *Green Valley* the news media allegedly cooperated with police in the "staging" of photos and participated in the harassment of students and staff members during the midnight raid. The newsworthiness of any story obtained through such methods will not excuse the "highly offensive" intrusion. In contrast, the press acted responsibly in *Fletcher*, entering the home at the invitation of law enforcement officials. In that situation, the balance should be struck in favor of the media's right to gather news, and the Florida court quite properly ruled in favor of the press, though it did not use the newsworthiness rationale.

Cases such as *Dietemann* and *Le Mistral* make plain that some courts, perhaps most, will not give newsworthiness great weight. In *Le Mistral*, the court did not consider the fact that the public has an obvious interest in learning that a given restaurant is charged with violating city health standards. Similarly, the court in *Dietemann* expressly stated that the defendant magazine could not claim first amendment protection "simply because the person subjected to the intrusion is reasonably suspected of committing a crime." The court was thus unpersuaded that the public interest in the reporting of such illegal and potentially dangerous activities outweighed the privacy interests of the plaintiff. Significantly, both *Le Mistral* and *Dietemann* also involved newsgathering tactics that might be considered offensive—"ambush journalism" in the former, subterfuge and hidden microphones and cameras in the latter.

Under appropriate facts, the legitimate public interest in a story might be great enough to convince a court to reject an intrusion claim. That was arguably not the case in *Dietemman*, since the plaintiff did not advertise and did not charge for his services. However, if he had been a member of a "ring" of individuals engaged in the practice of quackery for the purpose of bilking the poor and ignorant, the court might have concluded that the newsgathering methods were justified. In any event, a claim of newsworthiness might tip the scales in a close case and help persuade a court that the intrusion was not "highly offensive."

Criminal Consequences. The court in *Dietemann* stated that the first amendment "has never been construed to accord newsmen immunity from torts or crimes committed during the course of newsgathering." Thus far, we have examined potential tort liability for intrusion and trespass; however, the activities that can lead to such actions can also result in criminal action against the reporter. Tort law and criminal law have common origins, and the same act may be both a tort against an individual and a crime against the state. Accordingly, a brief look at the criminal consequences of newsgathering is in order, and two recent cases are illustrative.

Stahl v. State (1983) stemmed from news coverage of a demonstration at the construction site of a nuclear power plant owned by the Public Service Company of Oklahoma, a private corporation. The property was closed to the public and press, though the utility company had set up a special "public viewing area" near the center of the site. Anyone desiring to go elsewhere in the construction area was required to obtain permission from utility officials. On the day of the demonstration, more than 300 members of the Sunbelt Alliance, a group opposed to nuclear power, crossed fences and occupied the construction site. Reporters followed them, ignoring warnings from utility officials that anyone who entered any portion of the grounds other than the viewing area would be arrested for trespass. The journalists were convicted in a nonjury trial and fined $25 each.

The Oklahoma Court of Criminal Appeals affirmed the convictions. After first determining that the requirements under the state's criminal trespass statute had been met, the court rejected the reporters' argument that their convictions violated the first amendment. Citing *Dietemann* and several of the other cases discussed previously in this section, the court said simply that the first amendment "does not shield newspersons from liability for torts or crimes committed in the course of newsgathering." Similar difficulties may arise when reporters attempt to cover news events taking place on public property. We shall examine those issues in Chapter 5 along with the broader question of access to information.

More recently, a New Jersey appellate court upheld the conviction of a newspaper reporter for impersonating a public official. In *State v. Cantor* (1987), a reporter had identified herself as a county official—"a lady from the morgue"—to obtain an interview with the mother of a homicide victim. The reporter's "status as a newsperson cannot protect her from the application of the criminal laws forbidding the false impersonation of a public official," the court said. "This is so especially where [the] alleged deceit was practiced upon an individual who was particularly vulnerable by virtue of her daughter's death." Recall that in *Dietemann* the journalists had posed as patients of the "doctor," conduct that presumably does not constitute a criminal offense.

Public Disclosure of Private Facts

While intrusion cases focus on the activities of the press in gathering the news, decisions involving "public disclosure of private facts" inquire into the dissemination of what reporters have learned. The gravamen of this type of invasion of privacy is the publication of embarrassing—but true—information that the plaintiff would rather not have circulated to the general public. It was this type of journalistic "prying" into private matters that Warren and Brandeis criticized in their historic *Harvard Law Review* article, arguing that all persons have the right to be free from publicity about certain parts of their lives.

Some journalists may be surprised—and disturbed—to learn that the publication of factually correct information can result in liability. Although truth is a defense in a defamation suit, it offers no protection in an invasion of privacy action of this type. The reason lies in the nature of the injury suffered by the plaintiff. With respect to defamation, the law of torts seeks to protect a person's interest in his reputation, in his "good name." At least in theory, defamation is not concerned with the individual's humiliation or embarrassment. On the other hand, the tort of invasion of privacy is concerned with precisely this type of "internal" injury, which exists irrespective of whether the published material is true or false.

Although truth is unavailable as a defense in a "private facts" case, successful suits of this nature against the news media are relatively unusual, certainly when compared to defamation actions. The reason lies in the requirements of the tort itself, defined by the *Restatement (Second) of Torts* as follows:

> One who gives publicity to a matter concerning the private life of another is subject to liability to the other for invasion of his privacy, if the matter published is of a kind that (a) would be highly offensive to a reasonable person, and (b) is not of legitimate public interest.

The requirements that the information be "highly offensive" and lacking in "legitimate public interest" (that is to say, not "newsworthy") are the common law's principal safeguards for the news media. Moreover, several decisions of the U.S. Supreme Court afford protection under the first amendment as well. We now turn to the elements of the tort and the constitutional considerations.

Public Disclosure. Recall that the law of defamation requires "publication" of the defamatory material—that is, the offending information must be communicated to someone other than the plaintiff. Broader circulation is necessary, however, for the plaintiff to prevail in a "private facts" case. As the name of the tort itself suggests, there must be "public disclosure," generally defined as sufficient publicity so as to make the matter one of public knowledge. As a practical matter, any publication by the news media will satisfy this requirement.

Private or Embarrassing Facts. There is considerable information that the average person considers "private" and would not want discussed in public: sexual matters, details of one's physical or mental health, idiosyncratic or eccentric behavior, involvement in criminal activities, and poverty. Material falling into these categories should alert reporters and editors to the possibility of privacy problems, but identifying the warning signals is only the first step in the analysis. Even if such matters are involved, the information may have already been made public or become part of the "public domain." In such circumstances, there is no liability when the defendant merely gives further publicity to a matter that is no longer private.

Two California cases illustrate the distinction between private facts and sensitive information that has become public. In *Diaz v. Oakland Tribune, Inc.* (1983), a newspaper columnist revealed that the student body president at a local community college had undergone sex-change surgery. The column said:

> The students at the College of Alameda will be surprised to learn that their student body president, Toni Diaz, is no lady, but is in fact a man whose real name is Antonio. Now I realize, that in these times, such a matter is no big deal, but I suspect his female classmates in P.E. 97 may wish to make other showering arrangements.

A jury awarded the plaintiff $775,000. Although a California court of appeals reversed because of errors in the trial judge's instructions to the jury, the court ruled that the plaintiff's "sexual identity is a private matter," pointing out that she had take affirmative steps to conceal the gender-corrective surgery (e.g., changing her name, driver's license, social security records, and school transcripts) and had informed only her family and closest friends of the operation.

In contrast is *Sipple v. Chronicle Publishing Co.* (1984), which grew out of Sara Jane Moore's attempted assassination of President Gerald Ford during a 1975 visit to San Francisco. Oliver Sipple, an ex-Marine well-known in San Francisco and elsewhere as a gay leader, grabbed Moore's arm as she attempted to shoot the President. Considered a hero for his selfless action, Sipple was the subject of substantial media attention. Several news stories mentioned the fact that he was a prominent member of the San Francisco gay community. In a lawsuit against the *San Francisco Chronicle*, which first identified him as a homosexual, and several other newspapers, Sipple argued that his sexual orientation was a private matter, the public disclosure of which was highly offensive. The California appellate court disagreed, noting that Sipple "did not make a secret of being a homosexual" and that his "sexual orientation was already in the public domain," having previously been reported in gay publications.

As a general rule, information gleaned from public records cannot be the basis for a "private facts" suit, since the material is already available to the public. As discussed more fully below, the U.S. Supreme Court has ruled in a series of cases that, in at least some circumstances, the first amendment prohibits the imposition of liability for the publication of facts obtained from public records. But this principle was also firmly established at common law. As the drafters of the *Restatement (Second) of Torts* have noted:

> There is no liability when the defendant merely gives further publicity to information about the plaintiff that is already public. Thus there is no liability for giving publicity to facts about the plaintiff's life that are matters of public record, such as the date of his birth, the fact of his marriage, his military record, the fact that he is admitted to the practice of medicine or is licensed to drive a taxicab, or the pleadings he has filed in a lawsuit. On the other hand, if the record is one not open to public inspection, as is the case if income tax returns, it is not public, and there is an invasion of privacy when it is made so.

State and federal "freedom of information" statutes, examined in Chapter 5, can come into play here, for they typically specify those records that are available for public inspection. For example, in *Howard v. Des Moines Register & Tribune Co.* (1979), the Iowa Supreme Court ruled that records of the plaintiff's involuntary sterilization while a resident of a county home were open to the public under the state's FOI statute. "Because the documents were public, the information which they contained was in the public domain," the court said. "The fact of plaintiff's sterilization was thus a public as opposed to a private fact. . . ." Accordingly, the newspaper's publication of the information was not actionable.

Difficulties have arisen where the news media has discovered and subsequently published information from old public records. Perhaps the classic case raising the question of the effect of a lapse of time upon the "public" nature of the information is *Melvin v. Reid*, a 1931 California decision. The plaintiff, a former prostitute, had been tried and acquitted in a famous murder case. She later changed her ways, got married, and "lived an exemplary, virtuous, honorable, and righteous life." Seven years after the murder trial, the defendants produced a movie based on her story. The film, entitled "The Red Kimono," was billed as a "true story" and used the plaintiff's real name. The court ruled that while the facts of the plaintiff's life were public, the use of her name—in light of the passage of time—was actionable. In another California case, *Briscoe v. Reader's Digest Association, Inc.* (1971), the court ruled that the plaintiff could sue for disclosure of private facts based on the defendant magazine's story about his conviction, eleven years earlier, for attempted hijacking. Relying primarily on *Melvin v. Reid*, the court noted the lapse of time and the plaintiff's subsequent rehabilitation.

These decisions have been limited by other California cases, are inconsistent with rulings in other states, and are of dubious validity in light of the constitutional developments discussed below. The general view is that once a matter is recorded in a public document, it can never again be considered private. For example, in *McCormack v. Oklahoma Publishing Co.* (1980), the defendant newspaper had reported that plaintiff had been "listed by the Justice Department as an organized crime principal subject, a listing usually reserved for Mafia members" and stated that he had been arrested eighteen times between 1934 and 1957, some twenty years prior to publication of the news story. The Oklahoma Supreme Court found no invasion of privacy. Similarly, in *Rawlins v. Hutchinson Publishing Co.* (1975), the Kansas Supreme Court rejected a privacy claim based on a newspaper's "Looking Backward" feature, a regular column noting news items on the corresponding date ten, twenty-five and fifty years previously. One such column stated that, ten years ago, the plaintiff had been indefinitely suspended for conduct unbecoming a police officer. The matter was of public record, the court said, and "we do not see how public facts, once fully exposed to public view, can ever become private again."

It should be noted that these principles regarding the effect of a lapse of time are not limited to cases involving public records maintained by the police, courts, or other branches of government. Once a matter is made public in any way—such as by news coverage at an earlier point in time—the genie is out of the bottle and the matter is in the "public domain" for purposes of a future invasion of privacy action. For example, in *Sidis v. F-R Publishing Co.* (1940), the plaintiff lived in obscurity, working at a routine clerical job. However, as an eleven-year-old he had attracted considerable media attention as a math whiz who lectured university professors. More publicity followed upon his graduation from Harvard at age sixteen. Some twenty years later, the *New Yorker* magazine published a brief biographical sketch of the plaintiff under the headline "Where Are They Now?" The article pictured him as something of an eccentric, living in a rooming house in a run-down area of Boston, studying an American Indian tribe, and collecting streetcar transfers. Although the U.S. Court of Appeals for the Second Circuit recognized that the plaintiff had shunned the spotlight over the past two decades, it denied recovery in his invasion of privacy action.

Highly Offensive Disclosure. The *Sidis* case also illustrates the principle that the disclosure of private facts must be highly offensive to a reasonable person in order to be actionable. Although the plaintiff was apparently an unusually sensitive man (in fact, there has been some speculation that the *New Yorker* article was in part responsible for his early death), the published information would have hardly ruffled an "average" person of "ordinary" sensibilities. Thus, the court ruled that the magazine was not liable, concluding that the revelations were not "so intimate and so unwarranted in view of the victim's position as to outrage the community's notions of decency."

Simply put, the "private facts" doctrine is not for protection of the hypersensitive. As the drafters of the *Restatement (Second) of Torts* have noted:

> The protection afforded to the plaintiff's interest in his privacy must be relative to the customs of the time and place, to the occupation of the plaintiff and to the habits of his neighbors and fellow citizens. Complete privacy does not exist in this world except in a desert, and anyone who is not a hermit must expect and endure the ordinary incidents of the community life of which he is a part. Thus he must expect the more or less casual observation of his neighbors as to what he does, and that his comings and goings and his ordinary daily activities, will be described in the press as a matter of casual interest to others. The ordinary reasonable man does not take offense at a report in a newspaper that he has returned from a visit, gone camping in the woods, or given a party at his house for friends. Even minor and moderate annoyance, as for example through public disclosure that the plaintiff has clumsily fallen downstairs and broken his ankle, is not sufficient to give him a cause of action. . . . It is only when the publicity given to him is such that a reasonable person would feel justified in feeling seriously aggrieved by it, that the cause of action arises.

The late Dean William Prosser suggested that something of a "mores" test will be employed by the courts, under which there will be liability only for disclosure of information which members of the community would regard as highly objectionable. Thus, the publication of a person's past sexual activities—as in *Melvin v. Reid,* where the plaintiff was a former prostitute—would be considered "highly offensive." Similarly, a Pennsylvania court concluded in *Harris v. Easton Publishing Co.* (1984) that the question of offensiveness should be left to the jury in a case where a newspaper column indicated that a woman and her pregnant daughter received food stamps and other welfare benefits. In contrast, a federal district court ruled in *International Union v. Garner* (1985) that a reasonable person would not be offended by the revelation that someone was engaged in union organizing activities.

Legitimate Public Concern. In order to prevail in a "private facts" suit, the plaintiff must prove that the published material is not "of legitimate public concern"— that is, he must show that it is not "newsworthy." Though technically part of the plaintiff's case, this requirement is extensively relied upon by media defendants to avoid liability. Because "newsworthiness" is given a broad and expansive interpretation, the plaintiff's burden is extremely difficult to carry; in fact, it is so difficult that some courts and commentators have observed that it is virtually impossible for a plaintiff to prevail against a media defendant in this type of invasion of privacy suit.

As a practical matter, the question of whether a matter is of "legitimate public concern" turns on media coverage, and the fact that a story has appeared in print or on a television newscast indicates that it is of interest to the public and, therefore, newsworthy. Wary of intruding upon constitutionally protected editorial discretion, the courts have been unwilling to second-guess the "news judgment" of professional journalists, and, as Dean Prosser observed, "the press, with its experience or instinct as to what its readers will want, has succeeded in making its own definition of news. . . ."[1] Consequently, the newsworthiness defense has swallowed up much of the "private facts" branch of the invasion of privacy tort, since a plaintiff generally cannot recover from a media defendant that has published the offending information even though all of the other requirements for liability are present.

In applying the newsworthiness doctrine, the courts must balance competing interests: the societal interest in receiving information about issues or events of public concern and the privacy interests of individuals who, one way or another, are involved in or connected with such matters. As we saw in Chapter 2, similar balancing takes place in defamation cases, and in that area of the law the courts have ruled that reputational interests must often give way to broader societal needs, particularly where public officials and public figures are concerned. In the privacy context, the courts are even more willing to strike the balance in favor of the news media, probably because in such cases—unlike defamation suits—the published material is concededly true. Moreover, a contrary approach would dissuade the press from tackling significant news stories that necessarily reveal some aspects of a person's life that he would prefer to keep off the front pages or the six o'clock news.

The press has an excellent track record in convincing the courts of the newsworthiness of particular stories that have given rise to "private facts" suits; in fact, over the past two decades only a handful of reported decisions have reached the conclusion that a given issue is not of legitimate public concern. However, the

---

[1]Recall that this is not so in the defamation context. As noted in Chapter 2, the Supreme Court has made plain that media coverage is not determinative of whether a matter is a "public controversy" for purposes of evaluating the plaintiff's status as a public figure under *Gertz v. Robert Welch, Inc.* For example, in *Time, Inc. v. Firestone* the Court found that the divorce of a wealthy socialite was not a public controversy despite the fact that it had received extensive media coverage.

newsworthiness defense is not, in gambler's parlance, a "lock," and, in any event, reporters should be aware of the type of story that is likely to give rise to litigation and other factors that might influence judicial decision making. Generally speaking, a court is more likely to rule that a matter is not newsworthy if the news organization has sensationalized the story by prominently featuring embarrassing matters or has used questionable newsgathering techniques in obtaining the information. In addition, a court might be a bit more reluctant to find the matter newsworthy if the plaintiff is an innocent victim of events beyond his control or if the information has been "dredged up" from the plaintiff's past.

As noted previously, the courts have generally accepted media coverage as the best indicator of whether the event or issue is indeed "newsworthy." For better or for worse, news consists of what the public *is* interested in, as opposed to what it *should be* interested in, and the newsworthiness concept embraces what the *Restatement* calls "matters of genuine, even if more or less deplorable, popular appeal." A glance at a typical daily newspaper or television newscast—not to mention *People* magazine or such supermarket tabloids as the *National Inquirer*—should make plain that Americans are more interested in the exploits of celebrities, the suffering caused by natural and man-made disasters, and unusual or even bizarre occurrences than in, say, the problem of Third World debt or the role of the Secretary of State in fashioning foreign policy. As one court has observed, "news" includes all events and items of information that have "that indefinable quality . . . which arouses public attention."

Not surprisingly, the courts have found a wide variety of matters to be newsworthy and thus not actionable invasions of privacy: a death from a drug overdose, affliction with a rare disease, the birth of a child to a twelve-year-old girl, the reappearance of a person thought to be dead, marriages and divorces, traffic accidents, the exploits of war heroes, the involuntary sterilization of a teenager at a county juvenile home, the suffocation of two children in a refrigerator, suicide attempts, the activities of entertainers and athletes, kidnappings and other crimes, police raids, the competence of physicians and other professionals, union organizing activities, the escape of dangerous animals, nude beaches, fad diets, and the antics of fans at professional football games.

Nonetheless, the possibility remains that a court (or a jury) will second-guess the news media's treatment of a story and conclude that it is not newsworthy. Although most courts accept media coverage as the "best evidence" of newsworthiness, a few have taken the position that "community standards" must be employed in evaluating the newsworthiness issue. In *Virgil v. Time, Inc.* (1975), the U.S. Court of Appeals for the Ninth Circuit wrote:

> [I]n the last analysis what is proper becomes a matter of the community mores. The line is to be drawn when the publicity ceases to be the giving of information of which the public is entitled and becomes a morbid and sensational prying into private lives for its own sake, with which a reasonable member of the public, with decent standards, would say that he had no concern.

Under this approach, the jury would obviously play an important role, since jurors theoretically represent a cross-section of the community. As in all civil cases, however, the court would make the initial determination of whether the case should go to the jury. After the appellate court's decision in *Virgil*, for example, the trial judge granted summary judgment for the defendant, ruling that the subject matter of a

Sports Illustrated story—the eccentric behavior of a bodysurfer—was newsworthy "as a matter of law." In other words, the judge was satisfied that a reasonable jury could not have reached the opposite conclusion under the "community standards" test set out above.

However, in *Bimbo v. Viking Press, Inc.* (1981), a federal judge in Massachusetts refused to find that incestuous relationships among gypsies are newsworthy as a matter of law, thus leaving the issue to the jury. The case involved the book *King of the Gypsies*, an outline of the life of the alleged gypsy "king" and an account of the gypsy lifestyle. In one passage, the gypsy leader recalled being ordered by his father to have sex with his mother. "It was crazy, sick," he was quoted as saying. "My mother was standing there saying nothing, like she was going to go along with it." The defendants argued that the mother's "private facts" claim was meritless because the episode itself and the broader issue of incest were matters of legitimate public concern. The court disagreed: "The incident depicted does not represent some significant societal pattern, but a private aberration regarded as such by the participants."

A 1986 South Carolina case reached a similar result. *Hawkins v. Multimedia, Inc.* stemmed from the defendant newspaper's publication of a feature on teenage pregnancies. In an accompanying "sidebar" focusing on a teenage mother who had an illegitimate child, the newspaper identified the plaintiff, also a teenager, as the child's father. Although the newspaper argued that the issue of teenage pregnancies is newsworthy, the court ruled that the trial judge properly submitted the issue to the jury. "Public or general interest does not mean mere curiosity, and newsworthiness is not necessarily the test," the South Carolina Supreme Court said. "Ordinarily, . . . whether a fact is a matter of public interest is a question of fact to be decided by the jury." The court affirmed the jury's award of $1,500 actual and $25,000 punitive damages.

Along the same lines *Buller v. Pulitzer Publishing Co.* (1984), in which a Missouri appellate court concluded that a story on the plaintiff's psychic ability was not newsworthy as a matter of law. The case arose when the *St. Louis Post-Dispatch* published an article about psychics who foretold future events. The plaintiff, one of five psychics discussed in the story, was identified by name, and her practice was described in considerable detail. Finding that the matter was not one in which the public had a legitimate interest, the court said that the plaintiff's practice "involves the highly personal business of attempting to predict future events in the lives of individual clients," something "far removed from the traumas and disasters . . . or . . . crimes and law enforcement with which the public is validly concerned."

Fortunately for the news media, decisions such as these are rare. It seems almost beyond argument, particularly to journalists, that incestuous relationships, the lifestyle of gypsies, teen pregnancies, and the activities of fortunetellers are of legitimate interest the the reading public, particularly when compared to the coverage of the bodysurfer found newsworthy in *Virgil*. Accordingly, one suspects that the courts in *Bimbo*, *Hawkins*, and *Buller* were influenced by other factors, such as the manner in which the information was presented or the newsgathering techniques employed in obtaining it. In *Bimbo*, for instance, there was some question as to whether the defendants had fraudulently induced the mother to consent to the use of facts about her life. Similarly, in *Hawkins* the court noted that the reporter, who had learned the name of the illegitimate child's father from its mother, twice talked with the boy by phone to obtain comments. "In neither call did the reporter request permission to identify or quote [him]," the court said, adding that the boy was "very shy." The *Buller* court pointed out that the reporter, like the journalists in *Dietemann*, had posed as a client to get the story and had concealed the fact that she was a reporter. Moreover, the story and an accompanying cartoon arguably cast the plaintiff in a less than flattering light by focusing on the "hokey" nature of psychic practice.

As these cases suggest, a court's newsworthiness analysis may turn on a story's sensationalized treatment or the activities of the press during the newsgathering phase. Perhaps no case makes this point as clearly—and as dramatically—as *Commonwealth v. Wiseman*, a 1969 decision of the Massachusetts Supreme Court. At issue was a documentary film, "Titticut Follies," which depicted patients and conditions at a state mental institution. The film showed identifiable mentally ill patients in a variety of embarrassing situations: naked, being force-fed, masturbating, and attempting to hide from the cameras. The court concluded that the film was of educational value and could be shown to special audiences (such as mental health professionals) but took the rare step of upholding an injunction that prevented the film's commercial distribution. Although the court found that the privacy interest of the patients was outweighed by the interest of specialized audiences in the conditions at the institutional and mental health treatment in general, it reached the opposite conclusion in balancing the patients' privacy interest against wider exhibition of the film "merely to satisfy general public curiosity."

Conceding that there was legitimate public concern about the mental health facility, the court was of the opinion that "an adequate presentation to the public of conditions at [the hospital] would not necessitate the inclusion of some episodes shown in the film. . . ." Put another way, the court believed that the filmmaker could have made his point without using the disturbing footage that the trial judge had described as "sensationalistic." Even more important to the court, however, was the fact that the filmmaker had not complied with conditions imposed upon him by state officials before granting their permission to make the film. For example, the filmmaker stated early in the negotiations with the state that only pictures of patients legally competent to sign releases would be used in the film. However, of the sixty-two patients shown in the film, only a dozen had signed the consent forms. Like the reporter in *Buller* who concealed the fact that she was a journalist, the filmmaker made a misrepresentation in order to "get the story."

The relationship between the plaintiff and the matter that has attracted media attention can, at least theoretically, also play a role in a court's newsworthiness analysis. As in the law of defamation, it is possible to draw a line between "voluntary public figures" who have purposefully sought the limelight and "involuntary participants" in events that give rise to news coverage. In the privacy context, however, the consequences of such line-drawing between types of plaintiffs is not nearly as severe, and it is clear that a matter may be of legitimate public concern irrespective of the plaintiff's status.

Nonetheless, it seems clear that persons who voluntarily place themselves before the public eye—such as public officials, actors and other entertainers, and anyone else who would qualify as a "public figure" under the law of defamation—necessarily relinquish a substantial portion of their right to avoid disclosure of "private facts." These individuals have in effect invited news coverage, and their exploits are undoubtedly of interest to the public. For example, the bodysurfer in *Virgil v. Time, Inc.* voluntarily brought himself into the spotlight by participating with great success in a dangerous sport and by adopting a daring and unique style. Despite having a significantly reduced "zone of privacy," however, such public figures obviously cannot be considered "fair game" with respect to *all* details of their lives. As the trial judge noted in *Virgil*, there was logical relationship between the facts revealed in the article concerning the plaintiff's rather bizarre behavior and his daring and aggressive surfing style.

Although some matters, such as financial information and sexual relationships, may be within a public person's "zone of privacy," even those issues may be newsworthy if linked to the individual's public life. For example, in *Alim v. Superior Court* (1986), a high-ranking official in the California Department of Veterans Affairs brought an invasion of privacy action after a *Sacramento Bee* article revealed that for more than twenty years he had received overpayments of his veteran's disability stipend from the U.S. Veteran's Administration. Rejecting the plaintiff's "private facts" claim, a California appellate court observed that "[a]lmost any truthful commentary on public officials or public affairs, no matter how serious the invasion of privacy, will be privileged," since an individual "who volunteer[s] his services for public office . . . waives much of his right to privacy." Moreover, the court described the published material in this case as "information bearing on the fitness for office of a public official. . . ."

In contrast, the court ruled in the *Diaz* case discussed previously that the fact of the plaintiff's sex change operation was not newsworthy as a matter of law, even though she was first woman president of the student body at a state-supported community college and had been embroiled in a controversy with the school's administration over misuse of student funds. Despite her voluntary action in seeking the elective position, the court concluded that there was "little if any relationship" between the sex change operation and her fitness for office. Moreover, the court pointed out that the office of student body president is a "concededly small . . . public arena," thus suggesting that the plaintiff had not relinquished much of her "zone of privacy." Accordingly, it would be for the jury to determine whether the gender-corrective surgery was a matter of legitimate public concern. Although the jury, in awarding the plaintiff substantial damages, had obviously concluded that the story was not newsworthy, the court of appeals reversed and ordered a new trial because of other errors. Shortly thereafter, the parties settled the case.

Although broad application of the newsworthiness standard is plainly justified in cases involving public officials and public figures, this important defense does not vanish merely because persons not falling into these categories are the subjects of news stories. Ordinary citizens unwillingly dragged into newsworthy events generally cannot recover for public disclosure of private facts even though their participation was wholly involuntary.

A 1982 Florida case, *Cape Publications, Inc. v. Bridges*, is illustrative. There the plaintiff, Hilda Bridges, was abducted by her estranged husband at gunpoint, taken to their former apartment, and forced to disrobe. Faced with a potentially explosive hostage situation, the police surrounded the apartment and began efforts to free the plaintiff. Meanwhile, members of the press had gathered at the scene. Upon hearing a gunshot, police stormed the apartment and rushed the plaintiff outside to safety. Clutching a dish towel to her body in an effort to conceal her nudity, she was quickly escorted to a police car. A photographer snapped several pictures of her, and the defendant newspaper used one to accompany its story about the incident. In reversing a $10,000 jury award to the plaintiff, the Florida appellate court found the matter to be of legitimate public concern.

"Just because the story and the photograph may be embarrassing or distressful to the plaintiff does not mean the newspaper cannot publish what is otherwise newsworthy," the court said, adding that it was "reluctant to interfere" with the paper's news judgment. Few would disagree with the court's conclusion that the story was newsworthy, even though the plaintiff was the innocent victim of a crime, an involuntary participant in what the court described as an "emotion-packed drama." *Bridges* reflects the approach taken by most courts in cases of this type. As the drafters of the *Restatement* have noted:

> These persons are regarded as properly subject to the public interest, and publishers are permitted to satisfy the curiosity of the public as to its heroes, leaders, villains and victims, and to those who are closely associated with them. As in the case of the voluntary public figure, the authorized publicity is not limited to the event that itself arouses the public interest, and to some extent includes publicity given to the facts about the individual that would otherwise be purely private.

Thus, there has been no liability for invasion of privacy when the media printed the name and address of a murder suspect's father, published a photograph showing the bloody body of a person injured in an automobile accident, ran a story identifying a teenager who had been involuntarily sterilized, and reported the arrest of man who was later released when police realized they had made an error.

The plaintiffs in the above examples had not wanted public attention but were instead drawn into the spotlight by events over which they had no control. In other cases, the plaintiffs may have acted in a voluntary fashion—as did Oliver Sipple in averting the assassination of President Ford—without deliberately seeking publicity. The courts have treated such persons as involuntary public figures but have typically denied recovery on newsworthiness grounds. For example, in *Samuel v. Curtis Publishing Co.* (1954), the plaintiff was photographed as he attempted to dissuade a woman from jumping off a bridge, while in *Johnson v. Harcourt, Brace, Jovanovich, Inc.* (1975), a janitor received a $10,000 reward for returning $240,000 in cash that had been lost by an armored courier service. Not surprisingly, the courts found these events newsworthy.

Difficulties involving stories based on events that occurred in the past—discussed previously in connection with the question of whether material gleaned from old public records can be considered "private"—also arise in the newsworthiness context. It seems obvious that an event once newsworthy does not "fade" merely because of the passage of time. Thus, as in the *Rawlins* case mentioned earlier, a matter that attracted news coverage when it initially arose will be protected when republished years later. Recall that in *Rawlins*, a newspaper's regular column, entitled "Looking Backward," revealed that on the same date a decade ago, the plaintiff, then a police officer, had been suspended for misconduct. Similarly, the now-familiar "where are they now" story, which focuses on the present activities of persons who had been the subject of news coverage in the past, are generally treated as newsworthy. The *Sidis* case, in which a magazine article described the adult life of a former child prodigy, is an example.

First Amendment Considerations. As noted in Chapter 2, the "constitutionalization" of the law of defamation has resulted in two different bodies of legal rules that affect libel: traditional common law principles and first amendment requirements. In many situations, the courts have in effect converted the common law rules into constitutional doctrine. For example, the *New York Times* rule and the constitutional protection for statements of opinion have their roots in the common law privilege for fair comment, and the emerging "neutral reportage" doctrine is a constitutional form of the fair report privilege. Parallel developments have taken place in the privacy area, though at a somewhat slower pace. We now turn to first amendment considerations that affect the "private facts" branch of the privacy tort.

We saw previously that, under the common law, recovery is not allowed in a private facts case if the information has been obtained from public records. The U.S. Supreme Court has elevated this rule to constitutional status. In *Cox Broadcasting Corp. v. Cohn* (1975), the Court held that the first amendment protects "publication of truthful information contained in official court records open to public inspection." Though the case involved only judicial records, the principle is not so limited. Other language in the *Cox Broadcasting* opinion suggests that there can be no tort liability if the information is obtained from any "public record" that is "open to public inspection," and lower courts have interpreted the decision in this fashion.

Cox Broadcasting grew out of criminal charges brought against six youths accused of raping and murdering a seventeen-year-old girl. The murder charges were subsequently dropped, and at a hearing some eight months after the incident, five of the defendants pleaded guilty to rape or attempted rape. The young woman's name had not been disclosed, probably because a Georgia statute made publishing or broadcasting the name of a rape victim a misdemeanor. However, a broadcast reporter covering the guilty plea hearing learned the victim's name by examining copies of the indictments against the defendants made available to him by the court clerk during a recess in the proceedings. Later that day, WSB-TV in Atlanta broadcast the reporter's account of the guilty pleas, an account that included the name of the girl. Relying on the criminal statute mentioned above and the common law protection against public disclosure of private facts, her father brought a civil action against the television station, arguing that identification of his daughter as a rape victim invaded his own privacy.

The Georgia Supreme Court agreed with the trial judge that the first amendment did not bar the privacy action, ruling that there was "no public interest or general concern about the identity of the victim of such a crime as will make the right to disclose the identity of the victim rise to the level of First Amendment protection." The U.S. Supreme Court reversed:

> We are reluctant to embark on a course that would make public records generally available to the media but forbid their publication if offensive to the sensibilities of the supposed reasonable man. Such a rule would make it very difficult for the media to inform citizens about the public business and yet stay within the law. The rule would invite timidity and self-censorship and very likely lead to the suppression of many items that would otherwise be published and that should be made available to the public. At the very least, the First and Fourteenth Amendments will not allow exposing the press to liability for truthfully publishing information released to the public in official court records. * * * Once true information is disclosed in public court documents open to public inspection, the press cannot be sanctioned for publishing it. In this instance as in others reliance must rest upon the judgment of those who decide what to publish or broadcast.

The Supreme Court also stated, however, that "[i]f there are privacy interests to be protected in judicial proceedings, the States must respond by means which avoid public documentation or other exposure of private information.'' This passage suggests that state could, for example, close a rape trial or pass a statute providing that any court records containing the names of rape victims are not open to the public. As we shall see in Chapter 6, the former course of action has been foreclosed to some extent by a series of subsequent Supreme Court decisions recognizing a qualified first amendment right of the press and public to attend criminal proceedings. As for the latter alternative, many state "freedom of information" statutes specify that records that would invade an individual's privacy are not open to the public. Under such statutes, or under a specific statute making confidential records that identify a rape victim, the courts would be faced with a question not resolved in *Cox Broadcasting*: does the first amendment protect the press from privacy actions based on publication of truthful information irrespective of whether it is obtained from public records?

The Supreme Court was faced with this question in *Florida Star v. B.J.F.* (1989) but managed to decide the case without providing a definitive answer. There a weekly newspaper in Jacksonville, Florida, published the name of a woman who had been raped, thereby violating a state statute making it unlawful to "print, publish, or broadcast . . . in any instrument of mass communication" the name of the victim of a sexual offense. A reporter-trainee for the *Florida Star* obtained the woman's name from an incident report available to journalists in the police department's press room. Ordinarily, such reports did not contain the names of rape victims, and the inclusion of the woman's name in this report was apparently inadvertent. After copying the report verbatim, the trainee prepared a one-paragraph story about the crime. The brief article, which noted that police had no leads, identified the woman by name, despite the newspaper's internal policy against publishing the names of rape victims.

Relying on the Florida statute, the woman filed a civil suit against the police department and the newspaper. She settled with the department for $2,500, and the case went to trial with the *Star* as the only defendant. At trial, the plaintiff testified that she had suffered emotional distress from the publication of her name. She stated that co-workers and acquaintances told her about the newspaper article; that her mother had received threatening phone calls from a man who stated that he would rape the woman again; and that she had been compelled to move to a new residence, change her phone number, seek police protection, and obtain mental health counseling. After the trial judge denied the newspaper's motion to dismiss the case on the ground that the statute was unconstitutional, a jury awarded the plaintiff $75,000 conpensatory and $25,000 punitive damages. A Florida appellate court affirmed, and the state supreme court refused to review the case.

The U.S. Supreme Court reversed in a 6 to 3 decision. Writing for the majority, Justice Thurgood Marshall first determined the *Cox Broadcasting* was not directly controlling, since that case involved judicial records open to the public under state law and obtained by the press during the course of a trial. In *Florida Star,* however, state law precluded public disclosure of the information, which police had inadvertently made available to the media. Moreover, Justice Marshall expressly declined the newspaper's invitation to broadly interpret *Cox Broadcasting* to mean that the first amendment prohibits civil or criminal actions against the press for publishing truthful information.

Instead, the Court decided the case on more limited grounds, holding that a newspaper that "lawfully obtains truthful information about a matter of public significance" cannot be held civilly or criminally liable "absent a need to further a state interest of the highest order.'' For this proposition, the Court relied on its 1979 decision in *Smith v. Daily Mail Publishing Co.* holding unconstitutional a West Virginia statute made it a crime to publish the names of juvenile offenders without a written order of the court. In that case, a newspaper violated the statute by identifying a suspect in a killing at a junior high school, its reporter having obtained the name by interviewing witnesses, the police, and a prosecuting attorney. The Court concluded that the state's interest in protecting the anonymity of juvenile offenders to further their rehabilitation was not sufficiently compelling to justify the criminal statute banning publication.

Like the name of the juvenile in the *Daily Mail* case, the name of the rape victim in *Florida Star,* though ordinarily not available to the public, was obtained lawfully by the newspaper. Moreover, Justice Marshall pointed out, the commission and investigation of violent crime is ''a matter of paramount public import.'' Accordingly, the newspaper could not constitutionally be held liable for publication of the rape victim's name unless the statute in question furthered ''a state interest of the highest order.'' The State of Florida claimed that three interests justified the statutory punishment for publication: the privacy of victims of sexual offenses, their physical safety, and the need to encourage victims to report such crimes.

While not ruling out the possibility that these asserted interests might be sufficient in an appropriate case to outweigh the competing first amendment considerations, the Court concluded that they did not provide adequate support for the Florida statute. Justice Marshall emphasized that the plaintiff's identity ''would never have come to light were it not for the erroneous, if inadvertent, inclusion by the [police] of her full name in an incident report made available in a press room open to the public.'' Thus, the government ''had, but failed to utilize, far more limited means of guarding against dissemination than the extreme step of punishing truthful speech.''

The Court was also concerned that the statute swept too broadly by not taking into account the circumstances of each particular case. Because the statute imposed liability from the mere fact of publication, a newspaper could be punished even though the victim of a sexual offense had invited media attention by voluntarily calling attention to the crime. In another sense, however, the Court found the statute too narrow to serve the interests asserted by the state. By prohibiting the publication of victims' names only by the mass media, the statute did not address the dissemination of such information by other means. ''An individual who maliciously spreads word of the identity of a rape victim is thus not covered,'' Justice Marshall wrote, ''despite the fact that the communication of such information to persons who live near, or work with, the victim may have consequences equally devastating as the exposure of her name to large numbers of strangers.''

The effect of the *Florida Star* decision on ''private facts'' cases brought under the common law is not clear. Writing for the three dissenters, Justice Byron White—the author of the Court's opinion in the *Cox Broadcasting* case—complained that the ruling ''obliterates'' this branch of the privacy tort, ''[e]ven if the Court's opinion does not say as much. . . .'' If the first amendment prohibits a ''wholly private'' person from recovering for ''the publication of the fact that she was raped,'' he argued, ''I doubt that there remain any 'private facts' which persons may assume will not be published in the newspapers or broadcast on television.''

As noted above, however, the majority expressly rested its decision on narrow grounds and refused to announce a general principle that the publication of truthful information can never serve as the basis for a ''private facts'' lawsuit. ''Our holding today is limited,'' Justice Marshall wrote. ''We do not hold that truthful publication is automatically constitutionally protected, or that there is no zone of personal privacy within which the State may protect the individual from intrusion by the press, or even that a State may never punish publication of the name of a victim of a sexual offense.'' Moreover, Justice Marshall drew a distinction between the Florida statute and the common law ''private facts'' tort, pointing out that the former imposed liability simply on the basis of publication, while the latter requires a showing that disclosure of the information is highly offensive to a reasonable person.

Prior to the *Florida Star* case, some lower courts recognized a constitutional privilege to publish truthful information of legitimate public concern. In effect, such cases supplant the common law rules discussed previously—including the ''newsworthiness'' requirement—with similiar restrictions grounded in the first amendment.

Perhaps the leading case in this area is *Campbell v. Seabury Press, Inc.*, a 1980 decision of the U.S. Court of Appeals for the Fifth Circuit that stemmed from a book about the life of a religious and civil rights leader. The plaintiff, who was at one time married to the subject of the book, argued that disclosures about her marriage and home life invaded her privacy. There was no indication that this information was obtained from public records, and, indeed, the nature of the information itself suggests that it did not. It is likely that the source of the material was the book's author, the younger brother of the civil rights leader and the plaintiff's former brother-in-law.

The trial court granted summary judgment for the defendant publisher, and the court of appeals affirmed, ruling that the first amendment ''mandates a constitutional privilege applicable to . . . the public disclosure of private facts.'' This privilege, the court said, protects publication of true information about public figures and matters of public interest. Moreover, the court took an expansive view of the latter term, making clear that it is not ''limited to the dissemination of news either in the sense of current events or commentary upon public affairs.'' The first amendment also protects ''information concerning interesting phases of human activity and embraces all issues about which information is needed or appropriate so that individuals may cope with the exigencies of their period.'' In effect, the court adopted a very broad definition of what is to be considered ''newsworthy'' under this first amendment privilege. Because the information about the plaintiff in the book was logically related to the life of the civil rights leader—obviously matter of public interest—the court ruled that publication of the material was constitutionally protected.

The North Carolina Supreme Court has taken a different approach, refusing as a matter of state law to recognize the ''private facts'' branch of the privacy tort because of first amendment considerations. In *Hall v. Post* (1988), the defendant newspaper published a story stating, correctly, that the plaintiff had been abandoned seventeen years earlier by her biological mother and adopted by another family. The trial court's grant of summary judgment for the defendants was upheld by the state supreme court, which ruled that the disclosure of such private facts does not constitute a legal wrong under North Carolina tort law. Although the court expressly declined to decide the case on constitutional grounds, it concluded that ''adoption of the tort . . . would add to the existing tensions between the First Amendment and the law of torts. . . . '' Relying heavily on the *Cox Broadcasting* and *Smith* decisions, the court pointed out that imposing liability for the disclosure of truthful information would ''directly confront the constitutional freedoms of speech and press.''

Placing a Person in a "False Light"

Unlike the "private facts" cause of action, which is premised upon publication of embarassing but true information about a person, this branch of the privacy tort subjects a defendant to liability if he makes public a matter that places the plaintiff in a "false light." According to the *Restatement (Second) of Torts*, this legal concept protects "the interest of an individual in not being made to appear before the public in an objectionable false light or false position, or in other words, otherwise than he is." The relationship of this type of invasion of privacy to the tort of defamation is obvious, and in many cases plaintiffs have alleged both libel and false light privacy claims. Given the similarities between the two, it is not surprising that courts in at least two states, Missouri and North Carolina, have refused to recognize a separate cause of action for false light invasion of privacy. Moreover, where the false light theory is available, many common law principles developed in defamation cases are employed, as is the constitutional "fault" requirement initially recognized in *New York Times Co. v. Sullivan*.

As noted previously, privacy law is concerned with providing redress for mental or "internal" injuries suffered when a person's "right to be let alone" is violated, while the law of defamation seeks to protect a person's interest in his reputation or "good name." This theoretical distinction is less than satisfactory, however, for the law of defamation has, at least as a secondary matter, also compensated a plaintiff's injured feelings. Indeed, in some libel cases the principal element of damages is not harm to reputation, but injury to one's psyche, and in *Time, Inc. v. Firestone* the U.S. Supreme Court ruled that such emotional harm alone is sufficient as a matter of constitutional law to support an award of actual damages in a libel case even though no injury to reputation is demonstrated.

A more meaningful distinction lies in the nature of the published material that gives rise to liability. In order to win a defamation case, the plaintiff must show that the falsehood published by the defendant lowers the esteem in which he is held. On the other hand, a false light claim can succeed even though the statements, while false, say something good about the plaintiff or actually enhance his reputation. For example, in *Spahn v. Julian Messner, Inc.* (1967), baseball star Warren Spahn successfully sued the publisher of an unauthorized biography which exaggerated his feats on the diamond and falsely portrayed him as a war hero. Thus, the gravamen of a false light privacy claim is not reputational harm, but rather the embarrassment of a person in being made out to be something he is not. The vast majority of courts accept this rationale for distinguishing false light privacy from defamation and, therefore, recognize the existence of both torts.

The *Restatement (Second) of Torts* defines "publicity placing person in a false light" as follows:

> One who gives publicity to a matter concerning another that places the other before the public in a false light is subject to liability to the other for invasion of his privacy, if
>
> (a) the false light in which the other was placed would be highly offensive to a reasonable person, and
>
> (b) the actor had knowledge of or acted in reckless disregard as to the falsity of the publicized matter and the false light in which the other would be placed.

As in private facts cases, disclosure to the public at large is necessary to satisfy the "publicity" requirement. Other than this obvious departure from the rule for defamation cases (in which publication to a third party is sufficient), the plaintiff in a false light case must generally clear the same hurdles as his counterpart in a libel suit. Paragraph (b) of the *Restatement* formulation incorporates the *New York Times* rule, for example, and the privacy plaintiff must also prove falsity, identification, and damages. Other familiar rules also apply: the entire article must be read as a whole, and the jury must determine whether the ordinary reader would perceive the information as placing the plaintiff in a false light.

Highly Offensive Matters. The notion that publication of highly offensive information can give rise to a false light privacy claim should not be surprising, since the same basic standard is employed with respect to intrusion and private facts cases. In the false light context, the question is whether a reasonable person would be justified in feeling seriously aggrieved by the false publicity. Thus, the hypersensitive nature of a particular plaintiff is not to be taken into account, and there is no tort if only minor inaccuracies are involved. According to the *Restatement:*

> Complete and perfect accuracy in published reports concerning any individual is seldom attainable by any reasonable effort, and most minor errors, such as a wrong address for his home, or a mistake in the date when he entered his employment or similar unimportant details of his career, would not in the absence of special circumstances give any serious offense to a reasonable person. The plaintiff's privacy is not invaded when unimportant false statements are made, even when they are made deliberately. It is only when there is such a major misrepresentation of his character, history, activities or beliefs that serious offense may reasonably be expected to be taken by a reasonable man in his position, that there is a cause of action for [false light] invasion of privacy.

Recent cases involving photographs in sexually explicit magazines make plain that false suggestions of sexual impropriety satisfy the "highly offensive" test. For example, in *Wood v. Hustler Magazine, Inc.* (1984), the U.S. Court of Appeals for the Fifth Circuit affirmed a $150,000 judgment against *Hustler* magazine based on publication of a stolen photograph of the plaintiff, in the nude, that had been submitted with a forged consent form. The plaintiff's theory was that publication of the photo falsely suggested that the plaintiff was willing to be associated with what the court described as a "coarse and sex-centered" magazine.

In an earlier case, *Braun v. Flynt* (the facts of which are briefly set out in Problem 10 of Chapter 2), the same court upheld a jury's determination that the use of a photograph of the plaintiff, dressed in a bathing suit, in another magazine of *Hustler* publisher Larry Flynt placed her in a false light. The jury could reasonably have found that the publication of the photograph "implied [plaintiff's] approval of the opinions expressed in *Chic* or that . . . [she] had consented to having her picture in *Chic*," the court said, pointing out that the magazine is "devoted exclusively to sexual exploitation and to disparagement of women." In *Douglass v. Hustler Magazine, Inc.* (1985), the U.S. Court of Appeals for the Seventh Circuit reached the same result in a case brought by actress Robyn Douglass, even though nude photographs of her had previously been published in *Playboy* magazine. Pointing to considerable differences in the content of the two magazines, the court concluded that "[t]o be depicted as voluntarily associated with [*Hustler*] is unquestionably degrading to the normal person. . . ."

In contrast is a 1988 Louisiana case, *Easter Seal Society v. Playboy Enterprises, Inc.*, in which a portion of a videotape of a Mardi Gras parade was used in an "adult" film. The plaintiffs, parade participants who were recognizable in this stock footage, claimed that the unauthorized use of their likenesses in a movie that included nudity, apparent sexual intercourse, and drug use placed them in a false light. Ruling in favor of the defendants, a Louisiana appellate court noted that the brief parade footage "was only a part of the New Orleans backdrop" for the film and that the plaintiffs were not connected in any significant way with the film's characters or subject matter." Rather, the movie simply "portrayed the plaintiffs as nothing more than what they were, parade participants." The court also found the case distinguishable from *Braun* in that the film could not be "categorized as being as socially unacceptable and offensive" as the magazine at issue in that case. In light of these considerations, the court concluded that an ordinary viewer would not "form an unfavorable opinion about the character of the parade participants or presume . . . [their] approval of the opinions advanced by the movie."

Information as to an individual's family and business can also cause difficulties. For example, in *Varnish v. Best Medium Publishing Co.* (1968), the husband of a woman who had killed herself and her three children claimed that he had been placed in a false light by a *National Enquirer* story about the incident. The U.S. Court of Appeals for the Second Circuit ruled that the question was properly submitted to the jury, which returned a judgment for the plaintiff. The husband's theory was that the story misrepresented his relationship with his wife, suggested that he was insensitive to her needs, and implied that he did not understand her.

In a 1982 Georgia federal court decision, the judge left to the jury the question of whether a news story made the plaintiff, a military officer, appear "weak." *Pierson v. News Group Publications, Inc.* stemmed from a report on an Army prisoner of war training program in which soldiers were subjected to simulated conditions that could be expected by a POW. The plaintiff contended that the story pictured him as someone who "broke down easily" under interrogation, and the court denied the newspaper's motion for summary judgment. Similarly, the West Virginia Supreme Court ruled that summary judgment was improper in *Crump v. Beckley Newspapers, Inc.* (1984), in which the photograph of a woman coal miner accompanied a story about some of the problems faced by women in that industry. The article related incidents in which women were "stripped, greased and sent out of the mine" as part of an initiation rite, attacked physically by male miners while underground, and threatened with harm unless they quit their jobs. The plaintiff, who was not named in the article, contended that the story and photo implied that she had been a victim of such harassment and discrimination, when in fact she had not.

Of course, not all errors will be considered "highly offensive to a reasonable person." For example, in the *Fogel* case mentioned previously, plaintiff and his wife were photographed while standing at an airline counter in the Miami airport, where they had gone to obtain flight information. Next to them were several boxes that belonged to someone else. The photo was used to illustrate a magazine article about the beneficial impact of purchases by Latin Americans upon the Miami economy. According to the story, Latin Americans purchased large quantities of consumer goods in Miami, shipped them home, and made huge profits by reselling them at three or for times the purchase price. In granting summary judgment for the magazine, the federal district court rejected plaintiff's argument that the implication of his involvement in such activity was highly offensive.

To the same effect is the New York Court of Appeals' decision in *Arrington v. New York Times Co.* (1982), in which the plaintiff alleged that use of his picture in connection with a story entitled "The Black Middle Class: Making It" painted him as materialistic and status-conscious. Assuming, without deciding, that New York would recognize the "false light" type of privacy suit, the court ruled that the "highly offensive" standard had not been satisfied.

Moreover, a false publication will not be considered highly offensive if the inaccuracies are only minor in nature. This principle, which is similar to the "substantial truth" rule in defamation, is illustrated by *Rinsley v. Brandt*, decided by the U.S. Court of Appeals for the Tenth Circuit in 1983. There the defendant's book, which was extremely critical of mental health care in the United States, cited as an example the plaintiff's treatment of a young girl who later died. The author stated that the girl's parents had "instituted a suit" against the plaintiff, a psychiatrist, but "later abandoned" it. However, the parents had only gone so far as to consult an attorney and had not brought legal action. The court found this error insubstantial, pointing out that the thrust of the statement (i.e., the parents were so upset that they pursued legal action) was true.

The Iowa Supreme Court took the same approach in *Winegard v. Larsen* (1978), ruling that erroneous statements concerning events relevant to the dissolution of plaintiff's common law marriage were too minor to be actionable. In that case, news stories reported that the plaintiff and his wife had "exchanged rings" (thus reflecting their intent to hold themselves out to the public as husband and wife) and had changed the last name of the wife's daughter by a prior marriage. According to the plaintiff, he had given his wife a ring but had not received one, and though the daughter had used plaintiff's last name, there had been no formal name change.

The most difficult cases in which the test must be applied are those in which the false assertion actually seems favorable to the plaintiff. The *Spahn* case mentioned previously falls into this category, and *Arrington* might also be considered an example. It may be difficult to imagine how a false but positive statement might be highly offensive to a reasonable person. In his treatise on defamation, Professor Rodney Smolla offers the following example to illustrate the point that "the lie alone causes injury, even if the lie is laudatory."

> Imagine . . . a Vietnam veteran who experienced many episodes of violent combat during the war, saw many comrades die, and witnessed many acts of valor on the part of others. The particular soldier did his duty, served his country well, yet was neither uncommonly brave nor cowardly. Imagine that on the anniversary of the war the local newspaper publishes a story on the veteran . . . making him out as almost a wild-eyed John Wayne hero, when in fact he was just a good soldier. These exaggerated acts of courage might well enhance the veteran's reputation, but he would still have a valid action for false light invasion of privacy. To the reasonable person in the veteran's circumstances, it would very probably be deeply offensive to endure these manufactured stories—the veteran would have seen real valor and real death, and would be profoundly disturbed and embarrassed at being made out as something he is not.

Two U.S. Supreme Court decisions, discussed in the following section with respect to the constitutional fault requirement, demonstrate this point. In *Time, Inc.*

v. Hill (1967), a family had been held hostage by escaped convicts. *Life* magazine published a story about a Broadway play produced several years later that was based loosely on the incident. According to the *Life* article, however, the play would enable the public to see the Hill episode "re-enacted." In addition, the article (and the play) portrayed the Hills as having courageously defied their violent and abusive captors, while in fact the convicts had treated the family rather decently. The lower courts upheld the false light claim, although the Supreme Court reversed on other grounds. Seven years later, in *Cantrell v. Forest City Publishing Co.*, the Court upheld a judgment for the plaintiff, whose husband had been killed when a bridge collapsed. A newspaper "follow-up" story some five months later pictured the plaintiff as stoically dealing with the tragedy and gamely coping with poverty. The reporter had not even interviewed the woman, however, and his portrait—while perhaps favorable—put her in a false light.

The Fault Requirement. In the *Hill* case, the Supreme Court held that the first amendment precluded recovery for false light invasion of privacy in cases involving matters of public interest "in the absence of proof that the defendant published the report with knowledge of falsity or in reckless disregard of the truth." That language should have a familiar ring to it, for it is the same test employed in *New York Times Co. v. Sullivan*. As in the libel setting, the false light plaintiff must prove that the defendant acted with the requisite level of fault in publishing the offending material. It goes without saying that this constitutional protection in false light cases is of crucial importance to the news media, particularly because two doctrines most useful in defending other types of privacy suits—newsworthiness and consent—are generally unavailable in false light cases.[2]

Borrowing heavily from *New York Times*, the Supreme Court said in *Hill* that inaccurate statements are "inevitable" in discussions of matters of public concern and that protection for such errors is essential if freedom of expression is to have the "breathing space" necessary to avoid self-censorship. Justice William Brennan, author of the opinion of the Court in *New York Times*, also spoke for the majority in *Hill*. He wrote:

> We create a grave risk of serious impairment of the indispensable service of a free press in a free society if we saddle the press with the impossible burden of verifying to a certainty the facts associated in news articles with a person's name, picture or portrait, particularly as related to nondefamatory matter. Even negligence would be a most elusive standard, especially when the content of the speech itself affords no warning of prospective harm to another through falsity. * * * [S]anctions against either innocent or negligent misstatement would present a grave hazard of discouraging the press from exercising the constitutional guarantees [of the first amendment].

---

[2]The common law newsworthiness rule, developed in the private facts cases, hinges on publication of *true* information about matters of legitimate public interest. It has no applicability where the published information is false. However, in a sense the *Hill* case—as a matter of constitutional law—"extended" this principle to false publications, much as the *New York Times* case went beyond the common law to provide additional first amendment protection in defamation cases. The consent defense is rarely invoked in false light cases, though it technically is available. A person is not likely to have consented to being portrayed in false light, just as he is not likely to have consented to being defamed. However, if a female model consented to publication of a nude photograph in *Hustler* magazine, for example, it would be difficult for her to argue that she had been placed in a false light.

Although the Hills were neither public officials nor public figures, the Court concluded that the reckless disregard test was applicable because of their involvement, albeit involuntarily, in a matter of public interest.

The continuing viability of the *Hill* case is a matter of some dispute, primarily because of developments in the constitutional law of defamation. In that area, the "reckless disregard" test applies only if the plaintiff is a public official or public figure, and, under *Gertz v. Robert Welch, Inc.*, a private plaintiff can recover on a showing of mere negligence. *Hill*, however, focuses not on the status of the plaintiff, but on whether the subject matter is of public interest. This approach was briefly applied in libel cases after *Rosenbloom v. Metromedia, Inc.* (1971), but that case was overruled by *Gertz* three years later. The question has thus become whether the public/private dichotomy of *Gertz* will apply in false light cases as well as in defamation, or whether the reckless disregard standard of *Hill* will govern all false light cases involving matters of public interest.

The Supreme Court had an opportunity to shed some light on this issue in the *Cantrell* case, which was decided shortly after *Gertz*, but was able to avoid the problem because it found that reckless disregard had been established on the facts of that case. Thus, the Court said, *Cantrell* presented "no occasion to consider whether a state may constitutionally impose a more severe standard of liability for a publisher or broadcaster of false statements injurious to a private individual under a false light theory of invasion of privacy, or whether the [reckless disregard] standard announced in *Time, Inc. v. Hill* applies to all false light cases." The lower courts have split on the issue, and the drafters of the *Restatement* declined to take a position on "whether there are any circumstances under which recovery can be obtained . . . if the actor did not know or act with reckless disregard as to the falsity of the matter publicized and the false light in which the other would be placed but was negligent as to these matters."

Lower courts ruling that a private plaintiff in a false light case need prove negligence rather than reckless disregard have emphasized the similarities between defamation and false light invasion of privacy discussed previously. In their view, the question should be not whether a matter of public interest is involved, but whether the plaintiff is a public official/figure or a private person. On the other hand, several courts have ruled that all false light plaintiffs must prove reckless disregard so long as the matter at issue is of public interest. These courts continue to adhere to *Hill* because they perceive the state interest in false light claims as less substantial than in defamation cases, since the former involve only injured feelings or mental distress rather than reputational harm. Thus, while the state interest in protecting reputation may justify a lower fault standard—such as negligence—for private plaintiffs in libel suits, that justification evaporates when the published material, though false, falls short of being defamatory. Moreover, in *Hill* Justice Brennan noted that the potential of information to cause harm will be much more difficult for editors to recognize in advance of publication when it is false but not defamatory.

Similar uncertainty exists as to whether other constitutional rules fashioned in the defamation context are applicable in false light cases, primarily because of the paucity of reported judicial decisions on these issues. It seems fairly clear, however, that false light plaintiffs have the burden of proving that the published material is false, as is constitutionally required of defamation plaintiffs. Moreover, at least some of the restrictions on damage awards imposed in *Gertz* are also being applied in false light cases. For instance, some courts have ruled that compensatory damages must be supported by evidence of actual harm, including proof of mental anguish. Further, if a court is of the view that a private figure can recover in a false light case upon a showing of negligence, another question arises: must the plaintiff establish reckless disregard in order to recover punitive damages? The few cases on point take the position that here, as in defamation cases, reckless disregard is a prerequisite for an award of punitive damages.

In determining whether the defendant has adhered to the applicable standard of care (whether it be reckless disregard or negligence), courts will use the same basic approach as in the defamation area. Thus, there is no need to repeat here the discussion of reckless disregard and negligence found in Chapter 2. However, a handful of examples drawn from false light cases might be useful.

In *Cantrell*, the Supreme Court had little difficulty finding that reckless disregard had been shown with respect to what it called "calculated falsehoods" in the article. Since the reporter had not interviewed the plaintiff but had purported to describe in his story her expression and emotional state, the Court concluded that he "must have known that a number of the statements . . . were untrue." Likewise, a federal appellate court ruled in the *Varnish* case that the *National Enquirer* was reckless in portraying the plaintiff's wife as a "happy mother" whose suicide was totally unexpected. The court pointed out that the reporter had information showing that the woman was depressed prior to the incident, as well as a copy of a suicide note that stated her reasons for taking her life.

By way of comparison is *Colbert v. World Publishing Co.*, a 1987 decision of the Oklahoma Supreme Court. There the newspaper published a story reporting the death of a former teacher who had been convicted of a gruesome murder and who was thought to have been mentally ill. Accompanying the story was a photograph of the plaintiff, who was alive and well and living in Arizona. The photo mixup apparently occurred when the plaintiff's photograph, which his family had sent to the paper along with information about his graduation from law school, was mishandled and erroneously included with the paper's files on the teacher. The jury found that the paper had been negligent and awarded the plaintiff $65,000. The supreme court reversed, ruling that a private plaintiff must establish reckless disregard and concluding that the newspaper's error had not risen to that level.

Along the same lines is *Cefalu v. Globe Newspaper Co.*, a 1979 Massachusetts case in which the defendant newspaper published a photograph of several people standing in line at the state unemployment office. The plaintiff, who was clearly visible in the photo, was not there to obtain unemployment benefits, but to serve as a translator for a friend who could not speak English. Applying a negligence standard, the court found that the newspaper acted reasonably, since there was no reason for an editor to believe that persons in line were not there to receive benefits.

Types of False Light Claims. Having considered the basic elements of the tort, we now turn to typical situations in which false light claims tend to arise:

- *embellishment,* where false material is added to news stories;
- *distortion,* where omitted information or the context in which the material is used creates an erroneous impression; and
- *fictionalization,* where a novel or other work of fiction (including the now-popular "docudrama" genre that blends fact and fiction) contains references to actual individuals, perhaps in a "disguised" manner.

Litigation involving the news media generally falls into the first two categories, since news and feature stories purport to be fact rather than fiction. However, a reporter who yields to the temptation to "dress up" a few quotes or throw in some choice adjectives might find himself or his employer in court. The juxtaposition of photographs and printed material—as well as their broadcast counterparts, videotape and "voice-overs"—also causes false light problems.

Embellishment. The *Cantrell* case discussed previously is an example of a false light claim based on embellishment. There the reporter described the plaintiff as wearing "the same mask of nonexpression" that she wore at her husband's funeral and as being a "proud woman" who refused financial assistance from neighbors despite her family's "abject poverty." Though the Supreme Court labeled these statements as "significant misrepresentations," it is certainly debatable whether they rise to the level of substantiality necessary for liability on a false light theory. That is particularly so with respect to the description of the family as being extremely poor, since accompanying photographs—which the Court found insufficient to support a claim against the photographer—depicted a dilapidated home and poorly-clothed children. Thus, the real problem in *Cantrell* appears to have been the impression created by the reporter that he had interviewed the plaintiff, when in fact he had not. The phrase "mask of non-expression," while nicely turned, was not based on the author's own observations but apparently was invented out of whole cloth in attempt to describe the woman's emotional state.

The *Spahn* case should also serve as a warning to journalists who seek to add a little spice to a story. As noted earlier, that case arose from a biography of Warren Spahn, the legendary lefthander who is a member of baseball's hall of fame. The author, who did not interview Spahn, his friends, or other players, invented page after page of dialogue and exaggerated various aspects of Spahn's life, including his military service in World War II. For example, the book, which was aimed at juvenile readers, said that Spahn had received the Bronze Star and had been wounded and "rolled on to a stretcher" after having "raced into the teeth of the enemy barrage." Though Spahn had indeed been wounded, the other information was incorrect and apparently the product of the author's imagination.

Another case mentioned previously, *Pierson v. News Group Publications, Inc.*, involved alleged exaggeration of an Army training exercise that simulated experiences a POW might face. The reporter described the exercise as "savage" and the tactics employed as "brutal and terrifying." The plaintiff was described as "near death" after having been "hosed down" with water for three hours and "dragged" behind a pickup truck. The court denied the defendant newspaper's motion for summary judgment.

On the other hand, descriptive writing that falls short of embellishment is not actionable simply because it is colorful. In *Goodrich v. Waterbury Republican-American, Inc.* (1982), a newspaper articles about a shopping center's financial problems gave rise to a suit alleging defamation and false light invasion of privacy. The reporter who wrote the stories described the shopping center as a "ghost town" that was "up to its rooftop in troubles." Moreover, the facility was said to be "a mere shell of a shopping center" that had been "plagued" by a "host of traffic, conservation and financial worries." The Connecticut Supreme Court affirmed the trial court's denial of relief on both the libel and false light counts, pointing out that these "colloquial and figurative expressions" would not have a significant impact on the typical reader's interpretation of the facts surrounding the shopping center controversy, which was concededly a newsworthy matter. Nonetheless, the fact remains that the newspaper had to defend the lawsuit not only at trial, but also in the state supreme court. Modern litigation is anything but cheap, and a journalist who uses flowery language might well be inviting a false light claim.

Distortion. While embellishment can be described as a sin of commission, distortion often results from an omission. That is, information that would give the reader or viewer a different impression of the plaintiff is not included in the final product, and the resulting "half-truth" places the plaintiff in a false light. Errors of omission are hardly the only source of distortion problems, however. More typically, the context in which material is presented gives rise to false light litigation, with photographs causing the lion's share of the headaches. Though a photograph, standing alone, may be entirely innocent, an accompanying caption or story may combine with the visual image to produce a quite different effect.

The *Varnish* case noted above demonstrates how omission of facts can distort a story. Apparently looking for a "good angle" for the suicide story, the reporter played up comments by neighbors about how the suicide victim seemed to be the "happiest mother" in the neighborhood but omitted information—including the reasons for her actions stated in a suicide note—that revealed her as despondent and depressed. So-called "selective editing" of film or videotape can cause similar problems for television journalists. In *Uhl v. CBS, Inc.* (1979), a federal district court in Pennsylvania refused to set aside a jury award of nominal damages in a suit based on a CBS documentary entitled "The Guns of Autumn." A sequence in that broadcast opened with wild geese walking in a field, followed by an immediate cut to plaintiff and other hunters firing from a "blind." The plaintiff was then shown walking into the field and picking up a dead goose. By editing the film in this manner, the court said, CBS erroneously suggested that the plaintiff shot the goose on the ground—an unsportsmanlike act—rather than in flight.[3]

We have already seen several examples of how context can give rise to false light suits based on distortion: the *Hustler* cases in which the plaintiffs convinced the courts that unauthorized publication of their photographs implied their approval of the magazine's content; *Crump v. Beckley Newspapers, Inc.*, where a photo of the plaintff used with a story about harassment of and discrimination against women coal miners arguably suggested that she had been a victim of such tactics; and the *Arrington* case, in which a black male complained, unsuccessfully, that use of his picture to illustrate a story on the black middle class falsely portrayed him as status-conscious. In each of these cases, the photographs may well have been innocuous, but their use in a particular context spawned litigation. The message to the journalist is clear: be extremely careful in selecting photographs to accompany news stories and in writing captions for those pictures.

No judicial decision makes this point any better than *Gill v. Curtis Publishing Co.*, a 1952 California case that grew out of the same Henri Cartier-Bresson photograph at issue in *Gill v. Hearst Corp.*, a case considered previously in connection with intrusion. There was nothing uncomplimentary about the picture (which showed Mr. Gill with his arm around his wife), and it was taken in a public place. However, the *Ladies Home Journal*, published by Curtis, used the photograph to

---

[3]Such distortion by the broadcast media can also have consequences beyond the "false light" area. In Chapter 10 we consider policies of the Federal Communications Commission on distortion in news coverage.

illustrate a story about love and included this caption: "Publicized as glamourous, desirable, 'love at first sight' is a bad risk." Moreover, the story said that this type of "love" is nothing more than "100% sex attraction." In reversing the trial court's dismissal of the case, the California Supreme Court said that the article, photograph, and caption arguably portrayed the Gills as having only a sexual interest in each other. Whether readers could reasonably interpret the material in that fashion was for a jury to decide.

Television broadcasters must exercise similar care in selecting film or videotape to illustrate news stories. Because television is a visual medium, news directors seek to avoid, whenever possible, the "talking head" shot in which an anchor person simply reads a news story while looking into the camera. One obvious solution is to use a street scene, the exterior of a building, or other stock footage along with the "voice-over" of the anchor or a reporter. This technique can cause the same type of problem present in *Gill*. For example, in *Duncan v. WJLA-TV* (1984), a television station in the District of Columbia broadcast a story about a new treatment for genital herpes. As the anchorman read the copy, the station aired film of pedestrians walking down a busy Washington street. The camera zoomed in on the plaintiff, who was waiting at an intersection, as the anchorman said: "For the twenty million Americans who have herpes, [the new treatment] is not a cure." The court said the question of whether the report placed the plaintiff in a false light by implying that she had the disease should go the jury.

The use of so-called "ambush" interview techniques can also lead to false light litigation. In essence, the argument is that the reporter's questions are really accusations which, by prompting an angry or evasive response, create the impression that the subject of the interview is guilty of criminal activity or other misconduct. Context is important here, too, for the "ambush" interview typically appears at a point in the television broadcast after which the reporter has documented in some detail the "guilt" of the interviewee. Viewers see the subject for the first time when confronted by the reporter and asked point blank if he is guilty, and virtually any response to those charges—a "no comment," an explanation marked by obvious nervousness, or a curse directed at the reporter—serves to underscore the "fact" that he has done something wrong. As *Washington Post* media critic Tom Shales once observed, "in the visual vocabulary of 'investigative' TV sleuthing, slamming a door [in response to a reporter's question] is tantamount to an admission of guilt."

The theory has been tested in only a few cases, and plaintiffs have been met with mixed results. In *Cantrell v. ABC, Inc.* (1981), a federal district court in Illinois denied the network's motion to dismiss a false light and defamation suit based on a "20/20" segment entitled "Arson for Profit." The story described an alleged conspiracy among a group of real estate owners and their associates in a Chicago neighborhood. The plaintiff, who was employed by a real estate brokerage firm, had managed an apartment building at the time of a fire that killed seven tenants. After a "20/20" producer posing as a real estate developer talked with the plaintiff in a conversation that was surreptitiously recorded, the producer and an ABC reporter confronted the plaintiff with incriminating accusations posed as questions. The plaintiff appeared "somewhat perplexed" by the interrogation, which, along with the secretly recorded interview and other information presented in the broadcast, arguably created the impression that he was part of the "arson for profit" scheme.

In *Machleder v. Diaz* (1986), a jury awarded the plaintiff $250,000 compensatory and $1 million punitive damages in an ambush interview case, but the U.S. Court of Appeals for the Second Circuit reversed. The basis for the suit was an investigative report by WCBS-TV in New York City concerning the dumping of toxic chemicals at a site across the river in Newark, New Jersey. The story included film of a large area overgrown with weeds and strewn with rusting metal drums labeled "hazardous" and "flammable." The reporter and camera crew approached the plaintiff, the seventy-one-year-old owner of a company adjacent the site that used hazardous chemicals in its operations, outside his office. The following exchange took place:

> Owner: Get that damn camera out of here.
> Reporter: Sir . . . Sir. . . .
> Owner: I don't want to be involved with you people. . . .
> Reporter: Just tell me why—why those chemicals are dumped in the back. . . .
> Owner: I don't want . . . I don't need . . . I don't need any publicity. . . .
> Reporter: Why are the chemicals dumped in the back?
> Owner: We don't . . . we didn't dump 'em.
> Reporter: Who did?
> Owner: You call the Housing Department. They have all the information.

This segment was followed by a clip of the reporter, who stated that the Newark Housing Authority did indeed own the property in question, that the company had previously complained about the illegal dumping to state and local authorities, and that nothing had been done.

The plaintiff's theory was that the broadcast placed him in a false light by making him appear to be responsible for the illegal dumping and by portraying him as intemperate and evasive. He also contended that he had been defamed by the accusation that his company was responsible for the dumping. In a rather confusing set of findings, the jury concluded that the story was not substantially false as to the dumping charge, a determination that precluded recovery on the first theory, but awarded damages based on the second theory. The court of appeals reversed, pointing out that "[a]ny portrayal of plaintiff as intemperate and evasive could not be false since it was based on his own conduct which was accurately captured by the cameras." Moreover, the court ruled that the portrayal, even if false, was not highly offensive. Though this decision seems to make recovery under a false light theory quite difficult in ambush interview cases, courts outside the Second Circuit are not bound by the decision and could choose to follow the approach suggested in *Cantrell v. ABC.*

Fictionalization. Unlike embellishment, in which a news story or historical account presented as being factual contains some information that has been exaggerated— or even invented—by the writer, fictionalization involves a work that is understood to be fiction rather than fact. Although this line may have been blurred somewhat by the so-called "docudrama," this genre is typically understood as a fictionalized account of actual events or, as the advertisements are fond of pointing out, a work of fiction "based on a true story." Whether the book, short story, film or television program is "pure" fiction or one that blends fact and fiction, the danger is that "real people" may see themselves in the work and claim that they have been defamed or placed in a false light. Judicial decisions in this area are inconsistent, but publishers and broadcasters have by and large been successful in defending these suits. Nonetheless, the uncertainty that exists has spawned considerable caution; for example, a suit brought by Elizabeth Taylor in 1982 prompted ABC to cancel a proposed docudrama on the actress' life.

An obvious problem for a plaintiff in this type of lawsuit is identification; whether the action is based on defamation or false light invasion of privacy, the plaintiff must show that the offending statements were "of and concerning" him. As a general rule, an author is on safer ground if he avoids the use of real names, particularly in stories based, however loosely, on actual people and events. Moreover, the author should attempt to disguise the individuals upon whom the characters are modeled as fully as possible. This safeguard is not always effective, however.

In *Bindrim v. Mitchell* (1979), a libel case that could just as easily have been brought under a false light theory, a California appeals court affirmed a $75,000 damage award to a psychologist who used "nude encounter-group therapy." The defendant author had attended one of the plaintiff's "nude marathon" sessions and used it as the basis for an episode in her novel, *Touching*. Though she made the therapist in the novel a psychiatrist rather than a psychologist and gave him a different name and physical description, the court of appeals found the similarities between the plaintiff and the fictional character sufficient to support the jury's finding of identification. The court also noted that the novel was based on the author's own experience at one of the plaintiff's sessions and that she had signed an agreement not to write about it.

The New York courts take a different approach, primarily because of the language of the state's privacy statute, which allows recovery based on the use of a person's "name or likeness." For instance, in *Wojtowicz v. Delacorte Press* (1978), the New York Court of Appeals affirmed dismissal of a privacy suit brought by the wife and children of a bank robber whose actual activities were portrayed in a novel, *Dog Day Afternoon*, which was also made into a film. Though the plaintiffs may have been readily identifiable despite the fact that their real names were not used, the court said there could be no recovery under the statute.

Writers may also get into trouble by simply selecting the name of a living person for a fictional character, even though the work is not based on actual events or the activities of the individual whose name is used. However, the mere fact that the names are the same is not enough to trigger liability; rather, there must be sufficient similarities between an individual and his literary namesake so that reasonable readers would link the two. For example, *Geisler v. Petrocelli* (1980) grew out of the novel *Match Set*, described by the U.S. Court of Appeals for the Second Circuit as a "potboiler concerning the odyssey of a female transsexual athlete through the allegedly corrupt and corrupting world of the women's professional tennis circuit." For his central character, the author used the name of the plaintiff, a casual acquaintance with whom he had once worked. The character's physicial description also matched that of the plaintiff. Although the trial court dismissed the case, the court of appeals reversed and ordered further proceedings.

Even if the plaintiff has been identified, there remains the question of whether a reasonable reader or viewer could consider the information to be true. Several courts have ruled that the first amendment precludes recovery if it is clear that the work is fiction and should not be taken as true. This principle applies not only where the story is so fantastic that no reader could possibly believe it to be true, but also where a dramatic work grounded in reality would not be understood as a true account.

The first situation is illustrated by the now-famous case of *Pring v. Penthouse International, Ltd.*, decided by the U.S. Court of Appeals for the Tenth Circuit in 1982. At issue was a plainly fictional story in *Penthouse* magazine describing how a Miss America contestant named Charlene performed oral sex on a man at the nationally televised pageant, causing him to levitate. Like the plaintiff, Charlene was "Miss Wyoming" and twirled batons for the talent portion of the competition. Determining that the plaintiff had been identified, defamed and placed in a false light, the jury awarded her $26.5 million in damages, though the trial judge reduced that amount to approximately $14 million. The court of appeals reversed. Leaving undisturbed the jury's finding of identification, the court ruled that the article was "complete fantasy" that could not have been interpreted in any other fashion. "It is impossible to believe that anyone could understand that levitation could be accomplished by oral sex before a national television audience or anywhere else," the court said. "The incidents charged were impossible. The setting was impossible."

Hicks v. Casablanca Records (1978) involved a novel with a plausible storyline: the actual disappearance of mystery writer Agatha Christie for eleven days in 1928. Emphasizing that there was no "attempt by [the] defendant to present the disputed events as true" and that a reader would know "by the presence of the word 'novel' . . . that the work was fictitious," a federal court in New York held that the first amendment precluded recovery.

The constitutional "fault" requirement also governs fictionalization cases, though its application is difficult because of the very nature of fiction. As media attorney Bruce Sanford has noted, the docudrama poses particular problems, presenting publishers and broadcasters with "a built-in quandary: since the dialogue of the work is by definition fictionalized, the work is known to be something less than the truth." Of course, the *New York Times* standard focuses on whether the publisher knew the material to be false or acted with reckless disregard of whether it was true or not. Sanford suggests that the standard of care issue in fiction cases should turn on the defendant's attempt to avoid identification of actual individuals, since it is "virtually impossible for a publisher, or for that matter, an author to ensure that no character in a work of fiction resembles someone in real life."

Bindrim illustrates the problem from the publisher's perspective. There the author did not inform Doubleday, her publisher, of her agreement not to write about her nude encounter-group experience. Moreover, the evidence indicated that the Doubleday had specifically told her that her characters had to be ficitious, and that she had assured her editors that her characters were not capable of being identified as real persons. The California courts thus found that the publisher had not acted recklessly, since it had no reason to doubt the veracity of the author. However, after the hardcover edition of *Touching* was published, the plaintiff psychologist complained to Doubleday that the novel disparaged him and his practice. The publisher sought and obtained assurances from the author that the therapist in the book was not based on an actual individual. The court said that under these circumstances Doubleday was at fault for not investigating further.

But what can—or must—a publisher do? Attorney Bruce Sanford, in his book on libel and privacy, suggests that the following steps can mitigate the possibility of a successful suit:

- inquire about the basis or inspiration for the book and the author's experiences or acquaintances;
- if the work is based on a real person, attempt to ensure that he is accurately described;
- have an expert in the subject matter of the book review it to determine if any characters or events have real-life counterparts;

- if a character seems to resemble an actual person, ask the author to change or disguise him by altering his race, sex, employment, geographical area, and similar identifying characteristics; and
- use disclaimers (e.g., "the characters in this book are wholly fictitious and not intended to bear any resemblance to any person, living or dead").

This brief list is not meant to be exhaustive, but merely illustrative. And, there is always another option: cancel the project, as was done in the Elizabeth Taylor case. That alternative is obviously not palatable under the first amendment, but it unfortunately will remain a viable choice until the courts further clarify this area of the law.

Appropriation for Commercial Purposes

The final of the four branches of invasion of privacy was at the forefront in the development of privacy law in the United States. Recall that the 1902 *Roberson* case rejected the Warren and Brandeis argument for a right of privacy and denied recovery to a young lady whose likeness had been used without her consent for advertising purposes. The New York legislature quickly passed a statute that in effect overturned that decision, and courts in other states refused to follow its reasoning. Today, the rules concerning commercial appropriation and a related concept known as "the right to publicity" are relatively well-developed and straightforward. Typically, lawsuits based on this theory involve the advertising and entertainment sides of the media "business" rather than the news operations, though news coverage can also give rise to litigation.

Appropriation differs in an important way from other types of invasion of privacy. As we have seen previously, the three other branches of the privacy tort focus on injury to one's dignity. In appropriation cases, however, economic injury is more frequently the basis for damage awards, though the mental distress component may also be present. Thus, the interest at stake is not so much one's right "to be let alone," but rather his right to exploit commercially his name, likeness or identity—his "persona." This difference caused considerable confusion among courts as the law of privacy developed and was largely responsible for the creation of a separate tort known as the "right to publicity."

The *Roberson* case helps illustrate the conceptual difficulties that surrounded appropriation in the earlier stages of its evolution. The young lady in that case was essentially claiming emotional harm flowing from knowing that her picture had been used, against her will, to help someone else sell a product. Seeing her photograph on posters advertising the defendant's flour and knowing that others would see the posters was, simply put, embarrassing. In this context, considering appropriation as part of the privacy tort makes a great deal of sense, because the plaintiff is complaining of the same sort of injury found in private facts, false light, and intrusion cases. But what if the young lady had been a professional model, an early-day Christie Brinkley or Cheryl Tiegs who received substantial compensation for endorsing products? In that situation, the unauthorized use of her likeness by the flour mill would undoubtedly cause her economic injury, since she ordinarily would receive a hefty fee in exchange for allowing her photograph to be associated with a given product. While she might also suffer some emotional distress (particularly if the advertising campaign or the product itself were offensive), the gravamen of her complaint would be that the defendant took her likeness—her "property"—and exploited it without compensating her.

Because such economic harm seemed far removed from the mental injury found in the typical privacy case, some courts were reluctant to allow recovery in suits brought by celebrities. For example, in *O'Brien v. Pabst Sales Co.* (1941), a nationally known football player who had won the coveted Heisman Trophy as a collegian sued the Pabst beer company for using his photograph on a calendar advertising its beer. Pabst had obtained the photograph from the publicity department of the college for whom the plaintiff had played. The plaintiff himself undoubtedly would not have consented to the use of his photo on the calendar, since he was active in a temperance organization and had previously turned down opportunities to endorse beer and other alcoholic beverages. The U.S. Court of Appeals for the Fifth Circuit denied recovery, however, reasoning that the plaintiff, a celebrity who had sought and received considerable public attention via his football exploits, could not suffer emotional harm from mere publicity. The court did not seriously consider whether the plaintiff suffered economic harm from the unpermitted use of his identity to bolster Pabst's beer sales.

Other courts did not take such a narrow view of the right to privacy and allowed celebrity plaintiffs to recover damages based on the commercial use of their names or identities. Hoping to avoid the conceptual difficulties inherent in this approach, the U.S. Court of Appeals for the Second Circuit ruled in a landmark 1953 case that recovery for such economic injury was permissible under a new tort wholly independent of the right to privacy. In *Haelan Laboratories, Inc. v. Topps Chewing Gum, Inc.*, plaintiff and defendant were rival chewing gum sellers seeking to obtain from professional baseball players the right to use their photographs on the popular trading cards. Though the plaintiff had obtained exclusive rights from ballplayers for the use of their pictures, defendant produced its own cards of those players without obtaining permission of the plaintiff or the athletes. Defendant argued that the plaintiff could not bring suit for any invasion of the players' right to privacy, since the right to be free from the mental distress caused by an invasion of privacy belonged only to the individual players and could not be assigned or sold to third parties—an argument that was obviously based on cases such as *O'Brien*. Rather than squarely rejecting this approach and opting for an expanded right to privacy, the court recognized a separate tort, the "right to publicity." Writing for the court, Judge Jerome Frank said:

> We think that in addition to and independent of [the] right of privacy . . . , a man has a right in the publicity value of his photograph, i.e., the right to grant the exclusive privilege of publishing his picture. . . . This right might be called a "right of publicity." For it is common knowledge that many prominent persons (especially actors and ball-players), far from having their feelings bruised through public exposure of their likenesses, would feel sorely deprived if they no longer received money for authorizing advertisements, popularizing their countenances, displayed in newspapers, magazines, buses, trains and subways.

As a result of *Haelan* and an influential law journal article by Professor Melville Nimmer the following year, some courts adopted a separate common law right of publicity. Most courts, however, simply took a broader view of the right to privacy, ruling that the plaintiff in an appropriation suit can recover for economic as well as emotional harm. The *Restatement (Second) of Torts* takes the latter approach, defining appropriation as a type of invasion of privacy but making plain that although the plaintiff's "personal feelings" are important, the protected interest is primarily "in the nature of a property right" that can be commercially exploited. Regardless of the label employed, the right to benefit economically from one's own name or identity is now firmly entrenched in American law.

Unfortunately, the question of whether appropriation is considered part of the law of privacy or as a separate "publicity" tort is still of some significance. While it is generally agreed that, no matter what label is used, the right to exploit one's likeness may be sold or licensed to third persons, the courts have disagreed as to whether the right survives the death of the person to whom it initially belongs. This question is of considerable importance, affecting not only the value of an assignment or license granted prior to the death of a celebrity, but also the ability of a famous person to pass on to his heirs the right to exploit his fame. Elvis Presley is a case in point. Although his estate was valued at only $5 million at his death, his heirs are estimated to take in as much as $15 million a year from merchandise and tourist exhibits associated with his name. Courts recognizing survivability generally employ the "publicity" terminology and describe the right at issue as a type of property, while courts taking the opposite view tend to treat the right as a type of privacy interest that is personal to the individual.

Given the confusion in this area, it is not surprising that the states have begun to address the problem statutorily. The legislatures in California and Tennessee, for example, both recently enacted statutes creating a post mortem duration for the right of publicity. Under the 1985 California statute, the right of publicity lasts of fifty years after the death of the individual, regardless of whether he exploited the right during his life. The 1984 Tennessee statute defines the right of publicity as transferrable property which lasts during one's life and for ten years after his death, irrespective of commercial exploitation during life. However, the statute also provides that the statutory right terminates if the person's heirs or estate do not exploit it for more than two years during the ten-year period following death.

First Amendment Considerations. There may be circumstances in which the right of publicity, whether or not it survives death, collides with the first amendment. Although the U.S. Supreme Court has done little to provide ground rules in this area, one can safely say that the first amendment protection from suits based on publicity or appropriation theories is not absolute. The landmark case is *Zacchini v. Scripps-Howard Broadcasting Co.* (1977), which arose from a television station's coverage of a "human cannonball" at an Ohio county fair. Hugo Zacchini's act consisted of his being fired from a cannon into a net about 200 feet away. Each performance took some fifteen seconds, and a television reporter filmed Zacchini—despite the entertainer's objections—at the fair. The film clip was shown on the evening news with favorable commentary: "[T]he great Zacchini is about the only human cannonball around these days. . . . [A]lthough it's not a long act, it's a thriller . . . and you really need to see it in person . . . to appreciate it." Zacchini brought suit against the station for damages, claiming that it had "showed and commercialized the film of his act without his consent" and thereby "appropriat[ed] plaintiff's professional property."

The trial court granted summary judgment for the station, and the Ohio Supreme Court affirmed, ruling that the first amendment barred recovery since the station's coverage was a news report of a matter of legitimate public interest. The U.S. Supreme Court reversed in a 5 to 4 decision: the first amendment does not "immunize the media when they broadcast a performer's entire act without his consent." As this passage suggests, the majority of the Court confined its opinion to the narrow facts of the case and did not provide any guidelines for resolution of other disputes involving newsgathering and the right of publicity or appropriation.

Writing for the majority, Justice White stressed that the law of publicity and appropriation protects the "proprietary interest of the individual in his act" and serves "in part to encourage such entertainment." In this sense, the interest is "closely analogous to the goals of patent and copyright law, focusing on the right of the individual to reap the reward of his endeavors. . . ." In contrast, he said, the interest protected in permitting recovery for placing the plaintiff in a false light is largely emotional, and reputational. Moreover, the torts differ "in the degree to which they intrude on dissemination of information to the public." That is, in false light cases the plaintiff might attempt to minimize publication of the damaging matter, while in publicity cases "the only question is who gets to do the publishing." An entertainer such as Mr. Zacchini "usually has no objection to the widespread publication of his act as long as he gets the commercial benefit of such publication." Accordingly, the majority concluded that cases such as *Time, Inc. v. Hill*—relied on by the Ohio Supreme Court—do not "mandate a media privilege to televise a performer's entire act without his consent," even if the act is newsworthy.

However, the Court left open the possibility that some sort of newsworthiness privilege might apply when the media uses something less than the performer's "entire act." In fact, the Court noted that the plaintiff's "right of publicity would not serve to prevent respondent from reporting the newsworthy facts about [Zacchini's] act." Justice White added:

> Wherever the line in particular situations is to be drawn between media reports that are protected and those that are not, we are quite sure that the First and Fourteenth Amendments do not immunize the media when they broadcast a performer's entire act without his consent. The Constitution no more prevents a State from requiring [the defendant] to compensate [the plaintiff] for broadcasting his act on television than it would privilege [the defendant] to film and broadcast a copyrighted dramatic work without liability to the copyright owner, or to film and broadcast a prize fight, or a baseball game, where the promoters or the participants had other plans for publicizing the event.

The Court also pointed out that broadcasting Mr. Zacchini's entire act "poses a substantial threat to the economic value of that performance." Much of that value lies in the right of exclusive control over the publicity given that performance, since members of the viewing public might be less willing to pay an admission fee to see an event available free on television. In this case, the economic harm is much greater than in other publicity/appropriation cases where someone has made unauthorized use of one's name or likeness, since the broadcasting of the "entire performance . . . goes to the heart of [the plaintiff's] ability to earn a living as an entertainer." In other words, the defendant has not merely used the entertainer's name or identity "to enhance the attractiveness of a commercial product," but has "appropriated the very activity by which the entertainer acquired his reputation in the first place."

The principal dissenting opinion was filed by Justice Lewis Powell. After expressing doubt as to whether Mr. Zacchini's entire act had been broadcast (since one can expect a certain amount of fanfare at this sort of event) and criticizing the majority for failing to provide any clear guidelines, Justice Powell argued that the focus should not be on whether the media used the performer's entire act, but rather on the use that the station made of the film footage. "When a film is used, as here, for a routine portion of a regular news program, I would hold that the First Amendment protects the station from a 'right of publicity' or 'appropriation' suit, absent a strong showing by the plaintiff that the news broadcast was a subterfuge or cover for private or commercial exploitation." Thus, he saw the case as easily distinguishable from those in which a broadcaster televises sports events or theatrical performances without authorization, since in those situations the station keeps the profits. Moreover, Justice Powell pointed out that Mr. Zacchini, like any other entertainer, undoubtedly welcomes publicity but complained in this case of the timing and manner of the exposure he received. "But having made the matter public—having chosen, in essence, to make it newsworthy—he cannot, consistent with the First Amendment, complain of routine news coverage."

As is true in other contexts, the first amendment problem here calls for balancing of competing interests: the "property" interest of the performer or celebrity and the public interest in the free flow of information. Nothing in *Zacchini* is to the contrary, for while the Court struck that balance in favor of the human cannonball's right of publicity where his entire act had been appropriated, it specifically indicated that in some circumstances the right of publicity will not be infringed when it would unreasonably interfere with the legitimate exercise of first amendment rights. The question then becomes: how do we identify those situations where the first amendment outweighs the individual's right to exploit his own identity, his own fame? Though *Zacchini* offers precious little help, several lower court decisions provide some clues. Moreover, these decisions suggest that Justice Powell's approach in his *Zacchini* dissent—focusing upon the manner in which the media used the individual's name or likeness—is the appropriate mode of analysis.

Perhaps the most obvious situation in which the balance must be struck in favor of the first amendment is the press conference. In *Current Audio, Inc. v. RCA Corp.* (1972), a New York court held that a report of a rare Elvis Presley press conference was not an infringement of his right of publicity. In mid-1972, Presley held a press conference prior to a series of concerts at Madison Square Garden in New York City. The conference was arranged by RCA, with whom Presley had an exclusive recording contract. In addition, that agreement gave RCA the exclusive right to use Presley's name and likeness for advertising and promotional purposes in connection with his records. Among those in attendance at the press conference was a reporter for Current Audio Magazine, a short-lived "mixed media" publication billed as "the magazine you listen to." Its format combined the sort of written material found in magazines with a stereo record that included interviews, commentaries and other material which supplemented and expanded upon the written and photographic content. Its first "issue" prominently featured the Presley press conference and included a photo of the rock star facing a barrage of microphones, printed material about Elvis, and a two-and-a-half minute audio excerpt from the press conference. RCA claimed that this partial reproduction of the interview session, plus the accompanying story and photo, constituted an infringement upon its exclusive agreement with Presley.

The court gave short shrift to RCA's contention, pointing out that "a press conference of a popular and prominent singing star" is plainly newsworthy. The court said:

Elvis Presley is concededly a singer of note whose unique style is manifested in the course of his musical performances. Such, however, was not the nature of the appearance here at issue. On that occasion, Mr. Presley was in no way "performing". . . . The spontaneous "give and take" of an unrehearsed public press conference is of a wholly different character than the . . . performance of a musical or artistic work. Indeed in many ways a press conference stands as the very symbol of a free and open press, using that term in its broadest sense to encompass all the media, in providing public access to . . . the notable and newsworthy. To hold, as [RCA] urges, that one who has freely and willingly participated in a press conference has some property right which supersedes the right of its free dissemination . . . would constitute an impermissible restraint upon the free dissemination of thoughts, ideas, newsworthy events, and matters of public interest.

Similarly, the publication of an unauthorized biography of a famous person is protected by the first amendment. In *Rosemont Enterprises, Inc. v. Random House, Inc.* (1968), the plaintiff, Rosemont, had allegedly acquired from billionaire Howard Hughes the exclusive right to "exploit commercially in any manner the name, personality, likeness or the life story" of the famed recluse. Rosemont brought suit against Random House, publisher of an unauthorized biography of Hughes, seeking a temporary injunction to prevent dissemination of the book. In dismissing the case, a New York court noted that "a public figure can have no exclusive rights to his own life story, and others need no consent or permission of the subject to write a biography of a celebrity." While the right of publicity recognizes "the pecuniary value" of a celebrity's name or likeness, "[i]t is not . . . every public use of a prominent person's name that he has a right to exploit financially." The publication of a biography, the court said, "is clearly outside the ambit of the 'commercial use' contemplated by the 'right to publicity,' and such right can have no application to the publication of factual material which is constitutionally protected." This right to publicity must yield when it "conflicts with the free dissemination of thoughts, ideas, newsworthy events, and matters of public interest."

The balancing process becomes more difficult when entertainment rather than news is involved, but, as noted earlier in this chapter, news is broadly defined to include what the public *is* interested in, not as what it *should be* interested in. Recall that in *Time, Inc. v. Hill*, the famous false light case, the Supreme Court observed that the subject of *Life* magazine's article—the opening of a new play based on an actual hostage incident—was a matter of public interest. In today's society, entertainment news is of great interest to the public (witness the rise of *People* magazine and television programs such as "Entertainment Tonight"), and celebrities must simply face the fact that they are newsworthy and thus may not be able to control publicity about their exploits. For example, in *Ann-Margret v. High Society Magazine, Inc.* (1980), actress Ann-Margret brought a publicity/appropriation action against a "skin" magazine that had published a photograph of her taken from a film in which she had appeared partially nude. Ruling in favor of the magazine, a federal court in New York concluded that coverage (or uncoverage) of the actress' topless movie appearance was protected by the first amendment. Pointing out that the "scope of what constitutes a newsworthy event has been given a broad definition and held to include even matters of entertainment and amusement," the court observed that the fact that Ann-Margret "chose to perform unclad in one of her films is a matter of great interest to many people."

As is the case with respect to false light invasion of privacy actions, fictionalized works—including the "docudrama"—have caused difficulties in the publicity/appropriation area. However, the majority view seems to be that such works are protected by the first amendment as informative or entertaining speech and, although factual errors may give rise to false light or defamation claims, the celebrity plaintiff will be unable to prevail on a publicity or appropriation theory.

Perhaps the leading case in this area is the California Supreme Court's 1979 decision in *Guglielmi v. Spelling-Goldberg Productions*, which involved a fictionalized television version of the life of Rudolph Valentino. The court rejected a claim by Valentino's nephew that the program violated the deceased actor's right of publicity, though some judges reached the same result on the ground that Valentino's right of publicity did not survive his death. Addressing the first amendment question, Chief Justice Rose Bird first emphasized that fictional works are constitutionally protected and that "no distinction may be drawn in this context between fictional and factual accounts of Valentino's life." She then rejected the plaintiff's argument that the producers of the television program had used Valentino's name solely to increase the film's marketability and value:

> Contemporary events, symbols and people are regularly used in fictional works. Fictional writers may be able to more persuasively, more accurately express themselves by weaving into the tale persons or events familiar to their readers. The choice is theirs. No author should be forced into creating mythological worlds or characters wholly divorced from reality. The right of publicity derived from public prominence does not confer a shield to ward off caricature, parody and satire. Rather, prominence invites creative comment. Surely, the range of free expression would be meaningfully reduced if prominent persons in the present and recent past were forbidden topics for the imagination of authors of fiction.

At some point, however, the use of a celebrity's likeness crosses over the line and becomes unworthy of first amendment protection. The clearest examples are commercial uses such as advertising, though drawing the line between such commercialization and protected uses may not be as easy as it may seem at first blush.

Commercialization. As was briefly mentioned in Chapter 1 and as is more thoroughly discussed in Chapter 11, commercial speech is not wholly without first amendment protection. However, it is given less constitutional protection than other forms of expression, and, when compared to the "property" right of an individual to exploit his own name or likeness, comes in a poor second. Accordingly, the courts have quickly brushed aside contentions that the first amendment insulates such commercialization from lawsuits based on publicity or appropriation theories. Indeed, the argument is so lacking in merit that it is rarely raised in cases of this type. The fallacy of the argument is obvious, for the rationale for affording some first amendment protection for commercial speech is to enable sellers to inform prospective buyers about their products. The free flow of such commercial information as price, quality, and product availability is hardly impaired if a seller is unable to use, without authorization, the identity of a famous person to help market a given product.

The fact that newspapers, television stations, and other media are generally designed as profit-making ventures does not convert what would otherwise be considered "news" into commercial speech or result in the loss of full-blown first amendment protection. As one court has observed, it is the content of the article and not a media defendant's motive to increase circulation or viewership—and, therefore, increase profits—that determines whether an item is newsworthy and thus protected by the first amendment. By way of comparison, sellers who seek to trade on the fame of a celebrity do not disseminate any newsworthy information, but merely use the individual's name or likeness to link that person with a product.

Two cases illustrate the distinction. In *Factors Etc., Inc. v. Pro Arts, Inc.* (1978), the defendant contended that its poster of Elvis Presley was a commentary on a newsworthy event (the singer's death) and, therefore, constitutionally protected. The U.S. Court of Appeals for the Second Circuit dismissed this argument in a single paragraph, leaving the distinct impression that the poster was, in the court's view, little more than a crass attempt to cash in on the death of a celebrity. Yet there is obviously no doubt that a photograph of Presley published in a newspaper the day after his death would be entitled to first amendment protection.

Though the court did not make this point, an earlier New Jersey case clearly distinguished between news and commercialization. In *Palmer v. Schonhorn Enterprises, Inc.* (1967), Arnold Palmer, Jack Nicklaus, and other professional golfers sought to enjoin the defendant from using their names in a board game about golf. The game included playing cards with information about the careers of two dozen touring pros. The defendant argued that because such information could not be the basis for legal action if published in the sports pages of a newspaper, then an injunction should not be granted against its use in the board game. A New Jersey court disagreed, pointing out that the defendant was not using the golfers' names and biographical data for news or informational purposes, but rather to capitalize upon their fame and stature in their sport in connection with the marketing of a commercial product.

The California Supreme Court has taken a somewhat different approach, distinguishing between traditional vehicles of expression such as books and films on the one hand and commercial products on the other. In the *Guglielmi* case considered previously, the court pointed out that the television movie about Rudolph Valentino "involves the use of a celebrity's identity in a constitutionally protected medium of expression, a work of fiction on film." In contrast, *Lugosi v. Universal Pictures* (1979) involved the use of the late Bela Lugosi's likeness, in his role as Count Dracula, in connection with the sale of such commercial products as plastic toy pencil sharpeners, soap products, target games, candy dispensers, and beverage stirring rods. The court noted in its *Guglielmi* opinion that these objects "are not vehicles through which ideas and opinions are regularly disseminated." Thus, at least as a legal matter, Marshall McLuhan was wrong—the medium is not the message.

The use of a celebrity's name or likeness for advertising purposes presents what is perhaps the clearest case of commercialization. The reported judicial decisions have involved advertising for a wide range of products, from automobiles and artificial Christmas trees to pharmaceuticals and wearing apparel. Some interesting recent cases have involved the use of celebrity "look-alikes" in advertising. In *Onassis v. Christian Dior-New York, Inc.* (1984), Jacqueline Kennedy Onassis obtained an injunction preventing further publication of an advertisement for Christian Dior clothing. The ad featured a photograph that included several real celebrities such as "Today" show film critic Gene Shalit and actress Ruth Gordon. Also in the photo was Barbara Reynolds, a model made up and dressed to resemble Mrs. Onassis as she appeared in the early 1960s as First Lady. A New York court, concluding that the advertiser intentionally sought someone who could pass for Mrs. Onassis, had little trouble finding an infringement upon her right of publicity. "If a person is unwilling to give his or her endorsement to help sell a product, either at an offered price or at any price, no matter—hire a double and the same effect is achieved," the court said. "No one is free to trade on another's name or appearance and claim immunity because what he is using is similar to but not identical with the original."

The use of celebrity "look-alikes" in advertising may also run afoul of federal law. Under Section 43(a) of the Lanham Act, as amended in 1988, anyone who falsely suggests that a person approves or is affiliated with particular products, services, or commercial activities is liable if that conduct is likely to confuse consumers or the general public. As discussed more fully in Chapter 11, the 1988 amendment in large part incorporated court decisions interpreting the original, less specific version of the statute. One such case was *Allen v. National Video, Inc.* (1985), in which filmmaker Woody Allen brought suit against a video store franchising company that had used an Allen "look-alike" in a magazine advertisement. The ad showed a model resembling Allen as a customer in a National Video store and pictured videotape cassettes of two of the director's well-known films, "Annie Hall" and "Bananas." A federal court in New York ruled that the ad violated the Lanham Act, since it falsely implied that Allen endorsed the video stores. The judge ordered a trial to determine the amount of damages, but the parties settled the case when National Video agreed to pay Allen $425,000.

Drawing the line between advertising and editorial matter may not always be as easy as one might think, however. As Justice Powell noted in his *Zacchini* dissent, there may be circumstances where a news story is "a subterfuge or cover for private or commercial exploitation." Most of these "advertisement in disguise" cases have arisen in New York, and several have involved photographs accompanying fashion stories in magazines. In *Grant v. Esquire, Inc.* (1973), *Esquire* magazine published an article on clothing trends. A photograph of Cary Grant's face was superimposed over that of a model wearing stylish clothes, and the altered photo accompanied the story. The text read in part:

> To give a proper good riddance to the excesses of the Peacock Revolution we have tried a little trickery. And what better way to show the longevity of tradition than by taking the pictures of six modish men that appeared in Esquire in 1946 and garbing the ageless enchantment of these performers in the styles of the seventies. Above, Cary Grant in a descendant of the classic cardigan, an Orlon double-knit navy, rust and buff sweater coat (Forum, $22.50).

Ruling in favor of Grant, a federal district court in New York observed that the article conveyed no information about the famous actor or his tastes in clothing and that the use of his photo served no function "but to attract attention to the article." Though the fashion feature may have been newsworthy, there was nothing newsworthy about the use of Grant's likeness. "The First Amendment does not absolve . . . publishers . . . from the obligation of paying their help," the court said. "They are entitled to photograph newsworthy events, but they are not entitled to convert unsuspecting citizens into unpaid [models]." Though the magazine could have reported, via photograph, any newsworthy activity in which Grant had been involved, it could not "appropriate his services as a professional model."

A similar problem arises when a news story is reprinted as an advertisement. As a general rule, a reprint of a constitutionally protected news story as part of an advertisement is treated as advertising rather than news and can result in liability under a publicity or appropriation theory. However, a special exception has been recognized when the news item is reprinted in an advertisement for the news medium itself.

Professor James Treece has provided a hypothetical situation that illustrates the general rule far better than any of the reported decisions. Several years ago, *Time* magazine published a story on Senator Edward Kennedy stating that on working days, Kennedy "slips behind the wheel of his 1971 Pontiac GTO convertible and drives rapidly to the Capitol, one foot on the accelerator, the other lightly on the brake." This news story is obviously protected by the first amendment and cannot serve as the basis for a publicity or appropriation suit. But suppose, Professor Treece says, that General Motors reprinted this portion of the story in an advertisement for its Pontiac automobiles. The advertisement would be actionable even though the news story is not, since GM's use of the information in an advertising context would plainly have been designed to link its product to a famous politician. As Professor Treece noted, the hypothetical ad "contains little useful information about Pontiacs [but] suggests that Kennedy endorses Pontiacs."

In contrast, consider the case of *Namath v. Sports Illustrated* (1975). After the New York Jets won the 1969 Super Bowl, *Sports Illustrated* published a story about the game, along with a photograph of Jets quarterback Joe Namath, who, prior to the contest, had "guaranteed" a victory for his underdog team. Subsequently, *Sports Illustrated* used the photograph in advertisements for the magazine. These ads, which appeared in *Sports Illustrated* itself as well as in other publications, told readers that they could "get close to Joe Namath" by subscribing to the magazine. Although this was plainly a commercial use, there was no recovery because the picture was merely "incidental" to advertising about a publication in which the football star had initially been depicted in connection with a news story. "[S]o long as the reproduction was used to illustrate the quality and content of the periodical in which it originally appeared," a New York appellate court said, "the law accords an exempt status to incidental advertising of the news medium itself."

A dissenting judge contended that the advertisement did more than indicate the nature of the content of the magazine by implying that Namath endorsed *Sports Illustrated*. Though rejected by the majority of the New York court in *Namath*, this type of argument was successfully advanced in a 1982 decision of the U.S. Court of Appeals for the Ninth Circuit, *Cher v. Forum International, Ltd.* In that case, singer-actress Cher was interviewed by a freelance journalist, who sold the resulting story to *Forum* magazine, a sex-oriented publication. The magazine published the story and used it, along with Cher's picture, as part of a promotional campaign to sell subscriptions. One such advertisement, which appeared in *Penthouse* magazine, also contained the following sentence: "So take a tip from Cher and hundreds of thousands of other adventurous people and subscribe to *Forum*." While the magazine would have been entitled to use Cher's photo and information about the story in its advertising, the court ruled that the advertisement fell outside the "incidental use" exception by suggesting that Cher endorsed the publication.

Consent. If a person agrees to the use of his likeness for commercial purposes, he effectively waives his right to sue for appropriation or infringement of his right to publicity. As noted in the introduction to this chapter, a general principle throughout the law of torts is that there can be no wrong done to one who consents to the activity that would otherwise be tortious. Since the appropriation branch of the law of invasion of privacy is a tort law concept, it is not surprising that the courts generally speak in terms of "consent" when faced with this issue in appropriation cases. However, the term "license" is also regularly used to express this concept, particularly in connection with the property-based right of publicity. But there is only a difference in terminology, not in meaning. Viewed from the licensing perspective, there is no right to sue for commercial exploitation where one has authorized the use of his identity for a particular purpose. For convenience sake, we will use the term "consent" in this discussion.

Whatever it is called, an agreement of this type is a contract and will be interpreted in accordance with principles established in that body of law. One cardinal rule of interpretation is that an unambiguous contract will not be modified by the court; that is, a party to the agreement will not be allowed to say, after the fact, that "this wasn't what we meant." Accordingly, photographers, advertising agencies, manufacturers, and others involved in such commercialization seek to avoid potential problems by using extremely broad consent forms. Here is an example of such a "model release" from *Sharman v. C. Schmidt & Sons, Inc.* (1963):

> I hereby grant to [the advertising agency] . . . the absolute right and permission to copyright, and/or use and/or publish photographic portraits of me, still, single, multiple or moving pictures, or in which I may be included in whole or in part, or composite, or distorted in character or form, in conjunction with my own or any other name, or reproductions thereof, in color or otherwise, made through any media at its studios or elsewhere, for art, advertising, trade or any other lawful purpose whatsoever. I hereby waive any right that I may have to inspect or approve the finished product or the advertising copy that may be used in connection therewith, or the use to which it may be applied.

In this case, Bill Sharman, a professional basketball player with the Boston Celtics, had retained an agent to help him find modeling jobs and endorsements as a means of supplementing his basketball income. He posed for several pictures, one of which was ultimately chosen for a beer advertisement (though his name was not used). After the ad appeared, Sharman filed suit for invasion of his rights of privacy and publicity, arguing that the use of his picture in a beer commercial jeopardized other possible endorsements, injured his standing as a professional athlete, and threatened his plans to become a coach. A federal district court in Pennsylvania ruled in favor of the defendant beer company, concluding that the model release was unambiguous and that Sharman "did not restrict the commercial use of his picture. . . ."

While a photographer or advertiser would undoubtedly prefer a broad agreement providing for virtually unrestricted use of a person's name or likeness, a model, actor, athlete, or other celebrity would, in many cases, desire to enter into a contract that imposed various restrictions on the use of his identity. Model release forms and similar consent agreements typically include restrictions on the period of time during which the consent is operative, the context in which the individual's name or likeness may be used. and the products with which the individual is willing to be associated. Beyond these limitations, an agreement might grant exclusive rights to the use of the person's identity or specify that his name may only be used in a given geographical area. Simply put, the parties are generally free to agree upon any conditions they may wish. This should not be surprising, for central to the concept of a right to exploit commercially one's identity is the notion that the individual should be able to control the use of his persona.

If the use is inconsistent with any limitations found in the consent agreement, the scope of the consent is exceeded and recovery is possible. Consider, for instance, the rather common limitation on the duration of a given use. In *Welch v. Mr. Christmas, Inc.*, a 1982 New York case, an actor consented to the use of his picture in advertising by the defendant, a manufacturer of artificial Christmas trees, for one year. When the defendant used the picture beyond that period, the actor successfully sued on an appropriation theory. "The right to withhold consent to a use includes the right to limit the period within which the consent remains in effect," the New York Court of Appeals said. "Use after expiration of the effective period of consent is no less an invasion of privacy than is use without consent."

Sometimes the courts are willing to imply a "reasonable" time period in an agreement that contains no express durational limitation. In a well-known Louisiana case, *McAndrews v. Roy* (1961), a twenty-four-year-old man who worked out in a gym gave the owner permission to use his photo in "before and after" advertisements. Ten years later, the owner used the picture in a newspaper ad. The court concluded there had been an invasion of privacy, pointing out that "people change" over a decade and that the plaintiff, at age thirty-four, might not have been as agreeable to this use of his photo as he had been at age twenty-four.

Consent agreements also commonly place limits on the context in which a person's name or likeness may be used. For example, in *Douglass v. Hustler Magazine, Inc.*, considered previously with respect to "false light" invasion of privacy, the court ruled that an actress' consent to the publication of nude photos in *Playboy* magazine did not constitute consent to *Hustler*'s use of the pictures. Similarly, in a dispute related to the Woody Allen case discussed above, a federal court allowed the "look-alike" model to proceed with a suit against a firm that used his photograph in a poster advertisement, since the consent agreement stipulated that it could be used only in magazine advertising. The problem can also arise in the news setting. A New Jersey court ruled in *Canessa v. J.I. Kislak, Inc.* (1967) that the plaintiff's consent to having his picture taken for purposes of illustrating a news story was not consent to the use of that photo in an advertisement.

A similar restriction is aimed at limiting the type of product with which a person's name or photo is to be associated. Had Bill Sharman specified that his photograph could not be used in advertisements for alcoholic beverages, for example, he would have been able to recover on the basis of the beer ad that included his picture. Another famous athlete, baseball player Orlando Cepeda, found himself in essentially the same predicament as Sharman. Though he had granted to Wilson Sporting Goods the exclusive right to the use of his name to sell baseballs and other equipment, he brought suit after Wilson had entered into a promotional campaign with the Swift meat company. Under the arrangement, Wilson provided "Orlando Cepeda baseballs" to Swift, which offered its consumers the opportunity to purchase such a ball for a dollar if they mailed in a hot dog wrapper. Apparently finding this marketing ploy distasteful, Cepeda argued that this use of his name exceeded the scope of the consent. In *Cepeda v. Swift & Co.* (1969), the U.S. Court of Appeals for the Eighth Circuit denied relief, pointing out that the contract contained no limitations on Wilson's use of baseballs bearing the player's name.

Even if, as in the *Cepeda* and *Sharman* cases, the consent is extremely broad, there may arise circumstances in which the use may be actionable. The most famous case of this type is *Russell v. Marboro Books*, a 1959 New York case, in which the plaintiff, a female model, posed for a photograph to be used by Marboro bookstores in promotional material. The photo showed her in bed, reading a book; a male model, also with a book, was in an adjoining bed. A caption—"For People Who Take Their Reading Seriously"—was added to complete the advertisement. Subsequently, Marboro sold the photo to Spring Mills, Inc., a company that manufactured bed linens, which used it in its own advertisement. The photo was retouched to make it appear as though the plaintiff were reading a book considered to be pornographic while in the company of an "elderly" man. A caption containing the phrases "Lost Weekend" and "Lost Between the Covers" helped convey a rather sexual message quite different from that in the bookstore advertisement. Because the photo had been substantially altered, the court ruled that the plaintiff's consent, which contained no limitations on the use of the photo, did not bar her recovery.

Like any contract, consent agreements must meet certain requirements to be effective. For example, statutes in six states—Massachusetts, New York, Rhode Island, Utah, Virginia, and Wisconsin—require that consent to use one's identity for commercial purposes must be in writing. Other states, such as Florida, expressly permit either written or oral consent, and most others, at least by implication, allow oral agreements. Moreover, consent obtained under false pretenses or by fraud is ineffective, as is permission secured when the subject is under duress. And, there are reported decisions involving forged consent agreements. In *Wood v. Hustler*, discussed in the "false light" section of this chapter, a neighbor broke into the plaintiff's home, stole nude photographs of her, and sent them to the magazine along with a forged consent form. Affirming a $150,000 judgment for the plaintiff, the court observed that the magazine was negligent in failing to guard against potential forgery.

The law of contracts also requires that the parties have the "legal capacity" to enter into the agreement. We have seen one example of persons who lack such capacity—the mentally disabled. Recall that in the "Titticut Follies" case the producer of a documentary film agreed not to photograph patients at a mental hospital who were not competent to provide consent. The rationale for providing such protection for the mentally disabled is obvious: meaningful consent requires that the person giving it understand fully the rights that he is relinquishing. Similarly, the law has long presumed that minor children are unable to consent and thus do not possess the requisite capacity. However, a child's parents may consent on his or her behalf. For example, in *Shields v. Gross* (1983), actress and model Brooke Shields sued a photographer to prevent his use of nude photos of her taken as a ten-year-old. The New York Court of Appeals upheld the consent agreement, which had been signed by Shields' mother, and ruled in favor of the photographer. However, had the model herself entered into the agreement as a ten-year-old, it would have been unenforceable.

As the *Shields* case makes plain, in some cases it is possible for one person to consent on behalf of another. In addition to consent by a parent or guardian as in that case, it is commonplace for an agent to enter into such agreements on behalf of his clients, which might include athletes or entertainers. For this type of consent to be valid, the agent must possess authority to contractually bind his client, and the consent is ineffective if such authority is lacking. This problem is illustrated by *National Bank of Commerce v. Shaklee Corp.*, a 1980 case decided by a federal district court in Texas. The defendant Shaklee, a direct sales organization that manufactured and sold household cleaners and similar products, obtained from King Features Syndicate the right to use the name of Heloise Bowles, author of the popular "Hints from Heloise" column, in connection with its marketing. However, King Features did not have authority to enter into this arrangement without first consulting Ms. Bowles, and the columnist was able to recover damages from Shaklee for appropriation.

PROBLEMS

1. Former Senator Gary Hart of Colorado was the frontrunner for the 1988 Democratic nomination for President until the *Miami Herald* published a page one story reporting that he had spent the weekend at his Washington, D.C., townhouse with Donna Rice, a young model from Miami. The *Herald's* story developed from an anonymous tip that Hart, a married man, was "involved" with the woman, who was on her way to Washington to visit him. The newspaper then sent reporters to keep Hart's home under surveillance. On the basis of this stakeout, the *Herald* reported the weekend tryst. Hart subsequently withdrew from the race, though he later re-entered the campaign for a brief period. Assume that Hart had sued the newspaper for invasion of privacy. Did the *Herald's* newsgathering techniques amount to intrusion? Did the published information constitute embarrassing "private facts"? Are the sexual exploits of a presidential candidate newsworthy? Would your evaluation of the case be any different if Ms. Rice were the plaintiff?

2. David and Patricia Hagler owned twenty-three acres of land and a cabin in rural Missouri. They placed a sign, "Hagler's El Rancho Rock," at the intersection of a county road and a private road leading to several tracts of land, including their own. The sheriff's department, having arrested two suspects on drug charges, conducted a raid on a "suspicious" cabin in the area and seized marijuana on the premises. A news photographer accompanied the law enforcement officials, and his pictures were included in a newspaper's account of the incident. One of the photos showed the Hagler's sign. It was apparently used to identify the area where the raid occurred, since there were few other landmarks. Do the Hagler's have a case against the paper for invasion of privacy? *See Hagler v. Democrat-News, Inc.* 699 S.W.2d 96 (Mo. App. 1985).

3. Former employees of U.S. Senator Thomas Dodd removed documents from his office, made copies for columnist Drew Pearson and his associate, Jack Anderson, and returned the originals to the files. The interlopers had entered Dodd's office and taken the papers without authority, a fact known to Anderson. The documents became the basis for six stories in Pearson's "Washington Merry-Go-Round" column detailing the senator's relationship with lobbyists and revealing that he had used campaign funds for personal purposes. Dodd brought an invasion of privacy action against the journalists. What result? *See Pearson v. Dodd*, 410 F.2d 701 (D.C. Cir.), *cert. denied*, 395 U.S. 947 (1969). Would the senator have had any luck in a privacy suit against his former employees? How does this case differ from *Dietemann*?

4. A man who had tested positive for HIV, the virus believed to cause AIDS, was participating in a research project at a hospital. He was not at that point suffering from the disease. Upon entering an examination room, he was asked if he would permit his photograph to be taken. Though he initially refused, the man agreed after assurances from the photographer and a physician that he would not be recognizable because the photo would be taken from a back angle and in silhouette. Believing the photographer to be connected with the hospital, the man thought that the photo would be used for internal or research

purposes. However, the photographer was employed by a local newspaper, which published a photo of the man, being examined by a doctor, to illustrate a story on the hospital's AIDS research. The caption named the physician and described his chief responsibility as "caring for AIDS patients." Although the photo had been shot from the rear and in silhouette, the man said that he was identifiable. Evaluate his chances of success in an invasion of privacy suit against the newspaper. *See Anderson v. Strong Memorial Hospital,* 531 N.Y.S.2d 735 (Sup. Ct. 1988), *aff'd,* 542 N.Y.S.2d 96 (App. Div. 1989).

5. Joe Jones is a handsome, athletic young man. From a building across the street, and using a powerful telephoto camera lens, a photographer took Jones' picture through the window of his tenth floor apartment. He was sitting in an easy chair, reading a book, and drinking a glass of apple cider over ice. The photographer sold the picture to the Highland Mist Scotch Company, which used it, without Jones' permission, in a magazine advertisement for the company's scotch whiskey. It appeared from the photo that Jones was serenely enjoying a glass of Highland Mist, while he was, of course, simply sipping cider. The ad said: "I like good books. I like good women. I like good scotch. I drink Highland Mist." Jones' name was not mentioned, but he was extremely upset by the use of his picture in the advertisement. He does not drink alcohol and, because of deeply held religious beliefs, abstains from sex because he is not married. What theories would support a privacy action by Jones against the photographer and/or Highland Mist?

6. A television cameraman photographed the scene of an automobile accident in which the plaintiff was injured. The plaintiff was recognizable and was shown bleeding and in pain while receiving emergency medical treatment. The defendant television station did not use the videotape or report the accident on its regular news program. Some time later, without seeking the plaintiff's consent, the station used a brief excerpt of the videotape showing the plaintiff to illustrate promotional spots advertising a special news report about a new system for dispatching emergency medical help. The plaintiff brought an action for invasion of privacy. What result? Why? Would your analysis be any different if the station had shown the videotape on its regular news program prior to using it for advertising purposes? *See Anderson v. Fisher Broadcasting Companies, Inc.,* 712 P.2d 803 (Or. 1986).

7. Jane Doe returned home one night to find the body of her roommate, who had been raped and murdered. The assailant was still in the apartment, and Ms. Doe fled when she saw him. Later, she was able to provide a description to the police. While the murderer was at large, the *Los Angeles Times* published a story identifying Ms. Doe by name and stating that she was the victim's roommate. The police had issued a statement that the dead woman's roommate had found the body but did not use Ms. Doe's name. Moreover, the coroner's report contained her name, though it was not available to the public until a month or so after the murder. On these facts, would Ms. Doe have a valid claim against the newspaper for publication of private facts? Would your analysis be different if the reporter who prepared the story had obtained Ms. Doe's name from an employee in the police department or coroner's office? *See Times Mirror Corp v. Superior Court,* 244 Cal. Rptr. 556 (Ct. App. 1988), *cert. dism'd,* 109 S.Ct. 1565 (1989).

8. On August 14, 1945—V-J Day—Alfred Eisenstadt took his famous photograph of a sailor kissing a nurse in Times Square moments after the announcement of Japan's surrender. The photo was initially published in *Life* magazine two weeks later, and it has been republished numerous times in *Life* and other publications. In August 1980, *Life* again published the photograph and asked individuals who claimed to be the sailor and the nurse to contact the magazine. George Mendonsa did so, identifying himself as the

sailor. Seven years later, *Life* ran an advertisement offering to sell "limited edition" copies of the photo for $1,600 each. Shortly thereafter, Mendonsa brought suit on an appropriation theory. What result? *See Mendonsa v. Time, Inc.*, 678 F. Supp. 967 (D.R.I. 1988).

9. So-called "spy satellites" are currently capable of providing detailed photographs of relatively small objects on earth, such as buildings, and can spot certain crimes, such as violations of the environmental laws. Eventually, these satellites may be able to monitor the activities of individuals. Assume that such an advanced satellite photographed Joe and Sue Smith sunbathing in the nude in their backyard, which is surrounded by a ten-foot privacy fence. The local newspaper purchased the photograph from a private firm that operated the satellite and used it to illustrate a story about suburban lifestyles. What branches of invasion of privacy are implicated here? Who would be possible defendants? Would the fact that Joe and Sue were not recognizable from the photo make any difference? Would you analysis change if the photo had been taken from a helicopter or hot air balloon rather than a satellite? *Cf. Florida v. Riley*, 109 S.Ct. 693 (1989); *California v. Ciraolo*, 476 U.S. 207 (1986).

10. Two prominent "corporate raiders" were competing to buy a major company. A journalist working on a story about the economic battle ran a check on both of their names in a computer database provided to libraries, universities, and other subscribers. He learned that one of the men was married to the sister of the lawyer who represented the target company. Moreover, he also discovered that the man and his wife had just returned from a weekend trip to visit the lawyer in Los Angeles. The journalist reported this information in his story and suggested that a conflict of interest might exist. Assuming that the underlying facts are correct, are there any invasion of privacy problems? Is your analysis affected by the fact that, absent the computer database, the reporter would not have been able to pull together the background information? *See* Office of Technology Assessment, *Science, Technology, and the First Amendment* 13–14 (U.S. Government Printing Office 1988); *cf. U.S. Department of Justice v. Reporters Committee for Freedom of the Press*, 109 S.Ct. 1468 (1989).

11. A Michigan company marketed a portable toilet under the brand name "Here's Johnny," a phrase that has long been used to introduce comedian and talk show host Johnny Carson. The toilet was also described in advertising and other promotional materials as "the world's foremost commodian." Carson brought suit, arguing that the toilet manufacturer had appropriated his identity. What result? Does it matter that toilets have long been popularly known as "johns"? That another company called its portable toilet "Johnny on the Job"? That Carson's name was not used in connection with the toilet? *See Carson v. Here's Johnny Portable Toilets, Inc.*, 698 F.2d 831 (6th Cir. 1983). *See also Ali v. Playgirl, Inc.*, 447 F. Supp. 723 (S.D.N.Y. 1978).

12. While investigating an arson-for-profit story in Chicago, ABC reporter Peter Lance interviewed Albert J. LaBunski at the offices of his real estate company. Unknown to LaBunski, Lance was equipped with a microphone and transmitter that relayed their conversation to a nearby ABC sound van, where it was recorded by a technician. Except for the technician, no one overheard the conversation. Under the Illinois Eavesdropping Act, Ill. Rev. Stat. ch. 38, ¶14–2, a person commits eavesdropping when he "[u]ses an eavesdropping device to hear or record all or part of any conversation unless he does so . . . with the consent of all of the parties to such conversation" or "[u]ses or divulges . . . any information which he knows or reasonably would know was obtained through the use of an eavesdropping device." The statute contains an exception, not relevant here,

that permits eavesdropping by law enforcement officers in certain situations. Has the ABC reporter violated the eavesdropping statute? Would there have been a violation if the conversation had been recorded by automatic equipment in the van rather than by a technician? If the reporter had secretly recorded the conversation on a hidden tape recorder and later played it for a third person? *See LaBunski v. American Broadcasting Companies*, 1988 U.S. Dist. Lexis 8852, 1988 Westlaw 96276 (N.D. Ill. 1988).

CHAPTER

4

COPYRIGHT

Harper & Row, Publishers, Inc. v.
Nation Enterprises, **471 U.S. 539**
(1985).

JUSTICE O'CONNOR delivered the opinion of the Court.

This case requires us to consider to what extent the "fair use" provision of the Copyright Revision Act of 1976 . . . sanctions the use of quotations from a public figure's unpublished manuscript. * * *

I

In February 1977, shortly after leaving the White House, former President Gerald R. Ford contracted with petitioners Harper & Row and The Reader's Digest to publish his as yet unwritten memoirs. The memoirs were to contain "significant hitherto unpublished material" concerning the Watergate crisis, Mr. Ford's pardon of former President Nixon and "Mr. Ford's reflections on this period of history, and the morality and personalities involved." In addition to the right to publish the Ford memoirs in book form, the agreement gave petitioners the exclusive right to license prepublication excerpts, known in the trade as "first serial rights." Two years later, as the memoirs were nearing completion, petitioners negotiated a prepublication licensing agreement with Time, a weekly news magazine. Time agreed to pay $25,000, $12,500 in advance and an additional $12,500 at publication, in exchange for the right to excerpt 7,500 words from Mr. Ford's account of the Nixon pardon. The issue featuring the excerpts was timed to appear approximately one week before shipment of the full length book ["A Time to Heal: The Autobiography of Gerald R. Ford"] to bookstores. Exclusivity was an important consideration; Harper & Row instituted procedures designed to maintain the confidentiality of the manuscript, and Time retained the right to renegotiate the second payment should the material appear in print prior to its release of the excerpts.

Two to three weeks before the Time article's scheduled release, an unidentified person secretly brought a copy of the Ford manuscript to Victor Navasky, editor of The Nation, a political commentary magazine. Mr. Navasky knew that his possession of the manuscript was not authorized and that the manuscript must be returned quickly to his "source" to avoid discovery. He hastily put together what he believed was "a real hot news story" composed of quotes, paraphrases and facts drawn exclusively from the manuscript. Mr. Navasky attempted no independent commentary, research or criticism, in part because of the need for speed if he was to "make news" by "publish[ing] in advance of publication of the Ford book." The 2,250 word article ["The Ford Memoirs—Behind the Nixon Pardon"] . . . appeared on April 3, 1979. As a result of The Nation's article, Time canceled its piece and refused to pay the remaining $12,500. * * *

[Alleging copyright infringement, Harper & Row and Reader's Digest brought suit against The Nation in a federal district court in New York City. After a nonjury trial, the court found infringement and awarded the plaintiffs $12,500 in actual damages. The U.S. Court of Appeals for the Second Circuit reversed, holding that The Nation article was a "fair use" of the copyrighted material.]

II

* * * The rights conferred by copyright are designed to assure contributors to the store of knowledge a fair return for their labors.

Article I, § 8, of the Constitution provides that:

"The Congress shall have Power . . . to Promote the Progress of Science and useful Arts, by securing for limited Times to Authors and Inventors the exclusive Right to their respective Writings and Discoveries."

As we noted last Term, "[this] limited grant is a means by which an important public purpose may be achieved. It is intended to motivate the creative activity of authors and inventors by the provision of a special reward, and to allow the public access to the products of their genius after the limited period of exclusive control has expired." *Sony Corp. v. Universal City Studios, Inc.* (1984). "The monopoly created by copyright thus rewards the individual author in order to benefit the public." This principle applies equally to works of fiction and nonfiction. The book at issue here, for example, was two years in the making, and began with a contract giving the author's copyright to the publishers in exchange for their services in producing and marketing the work. In preparing the book, Mr. Ford drafted essays and word portraits of public figures and participated in hundreds of taped interviews that were later distilled to chronicle his personal viewpoint. It is evident that the monopoly granted by copyright actively served its intended purpose of inducing the creation of new material of potential historical value.

Section 106 of the Copyright Act confers a bundle of exclusive rights to the owner of the copyright. Under the Copyright Act, these rights—to publish, copy, and distribute the author's work—vest in the author of an original work from the time of its creation. In practice, the author commonly sells his rights to publishers who offer royalties in exchange for their services in producing and marketing the author's work. The copyright owner's rights, however, are subject to certain statutory exceptions. Among these is § 107 which codifies the traditional privilege of other authors to make "fair use" of an earlier writer's work. In addition, no author may copyright facts or ideas. The copyright is limited to those aspects of the work—termed "expression"—that display the stamp of the author's originality.

Creation of a nonfiction work, even a compilation of pure fact, entails originality. The copyright holders of "A Time to Heal" complied with the relevant statutory notice and registration procedures. Thus there is no dispute that the unpublished manuscript of "A Time to Heal," as a whole, was protected by

§106 from unauthorized reproduction. Nor do respondents dispute that verbatim copying of excerpts of the manuscript's original form of expression would constitute infringement unless excused as fair use. Yet copyright does not prevent subsequent users from copying from a prior author's work those constituent elements that are not original—for example, quotations borrowed under the rubric of fair use from other copyrighted works, facts, or materials in the public domain—as long as such use does not unfairly appropriate the author's original contributions. Perhaps the controversy between the lower courts in this case over copyrightability is more aptly styled a dispute over whether The Nation's appropriation of unoriginal and uncopyrightable elements encroached on the originality embodied in the work as a whole. Especially in the realm of factual narrative, the law is currently unsettled regarding the ways in which uncopyrightable elements combine with the author's original contributions to form protected expression.

We need not reach these issues, however, as The Nation has admitted to lifting verbatim quotes of the author's original language totaling between 300 and 400 words and constituting some 13% of The Nation article. In using generous and verbatim excerpts of Mr. Ford's unpublished manuscript to lend authenticity to its account of the forthcoming memoirs, The Nation effectively arrogated to itself the right of first publication, an important marketable subsidiary right. For the reasons set forth below, we find that this use of the copyright manuscript, even stripped to the verbatim quotes conceded by The Nation to be copyrightable expression, was not a fair use within the meaning of the Copyright Act.

III

A

Fair use was traditionally defined as "a privilege in others than the owner of the copyright to use the copyrighted material in a reasonable manner without his consent." The statutory formulation of the defense of fair use in the Copyright Act of 1976 reflects the intent of Congress to codify the common-law doctrine. Section 107 requires a case-by-case determination whether a particular use is fair, and the statute notes four nonexclusive factors to be considered. * * * "The author's consent to a reasonable use of his copyrighted works ha[d] always been implied by the courts as a necessary incident of the constitutional policy of promoting the progress of science and the useful arts, since a prohibition of such use would inhibit subsequent writers from attempting to improve upon prior works and thus . . . frustrate the very ends sought to be attained." * * *

Perhaps because the fair use doctrine was predicated on the author's implied consent to "reasonable and customary" use when he released his work for public consumption, fair use traditionally was not recognized as a defense to charges of copying from an author's yet unpublished works. Under common-law copyright, "the property of the author . . . in his intellectual creation [was] absolute until he voluntarily part[ed] with the same." This absolute rule, however, was tempered in practice by the equitable nature of the fair use doctrine. In a given case, factors such as implied consent through *de facto* publication or performance or dissemination of a work may tip the balance of equities in favor of prepublication use. But it has never been seriously disputed that "the fact that the plaintiff's work is unpublished . . . is a factor tending to negate the defense of fair use." Publication of an author's expression before he has authorized its dissemination seriously infringes the author's right to decide when and whether it will be made public, a factor not present in fair use of published works. * * *

The Copyright Revision Act of 1976 represents the culmination of a major legislative reexamination of copyright doctrine. Among its other innovations, it eliminated publication "as a dividing line between common law and statutory protection," extending statutory protection to all works from the time of their creation. It also recognized for the first time a distinct statutory right of first publication, which had previously been an element of the common-law protections afforded unpublished works. * * *

Though the right of first publication, like the other rights enumerated in § 106, is expressly made subject to the fair use provision of § 107, fair use analysis must always be tailored to the individual case. The nature of the interest at stake is highly relevant to whether a given use is fair. * * * First publication is inherently different from other § 106 rights in that only one person can be the first publisher; as the contract with Time illustrates, the commercial value of the right lies primarily in exclusivity. Because the potential damage to the author from judicially enforced "sharing" of the first publication right with unauthorized users of his manuscript is substantial, the balance of equities in evaluating such a claim of fair use inevitably shifts. * * *

The author's control of first public distribution implicates not only his personal interest in creative control but his property interest in exploitation of prepublication rights, which are valuable in themselves and serve as a valuable adjunct to publicity and marketing. Under ordinary circumstances, the author's right to control the first public appearance of his undisseminated expression will outweigh a claim of fair use.

B

Respondents, however, contend that First Amendment values require a different rule under the circumstances of this case. The thrust of the decision below is that "[t]he scope of [fair use] is undoubtedly wider when the information conveyed relates to matters of high public concern." Respondents advance the substantial public import of the subject matter of the Ford memoirs as grounds for excusing a use that would ordinarily not pass muster as fair use—the piracy of verbatim quotations for the purpose of "scooping" the authorized first serialization. Respondents explain their copying of Mr. Ford's expression as essential to reporting the news story it claims the book itself represents. In respondents' view, not only the facts contained in Mr. Ford's memoirs, but "the precise manner in which [he] expressed himself was as newsworthy as what he had to say." Respondents argue that the public's interest in learning this news as fast as possible outweighs the right of the author to control its first publication.

The Second Circuit noted, correctly, that copyright's idea/expression dichotomy "strike[s] a definitional balance between the First Amendment and the Copyright Act by permitting free communication of facts while still protecting an author's expression." No author may copyright his ideas or the facts he narrates. As this Court long ago observed: "[T]he news element—the information respecting current events contained in the literary production—is not the creation of the writer, but is a report of matters that ordinarily are *publici juris*; it is the history of the day." *International News Service v. Associated Press* (1918). But copyright assures those who write and publish factual narratives such as "A Time to Heal" that they may at least enjoy the right to market the original expression contained therein as just compensation for their investment.

Respondents' theory, however, would expand fair use to effectively destroy any expectation of copyright protection in the work of a public figure. Absent such protection, there would be little incentive to create or profit in financing such memoirs, and the public would be denied an important source of significant historical information. The promise of copyright would be an empty one if it could be avoided merely by dubbing the infringement a fair use "news report" of the book.

Nor do respondents assert any actual necessity for circumventing the copyright scheme with respect to the types of works and users at issue here. Where an author and publisher have invested extensive resources in creating an original work and are poised to release it to the public, no legitimate aim is served by preempting the right of first publication. The fact that the words the author has chosen to clothe his narrative may of themselves be "newsworthy" is not an independent justification for unauthorized copying of the author's expression prior to publication.

In our haste to disseminate news, it should not be forgotten that the Framers intended copyright itself to be the engine of free expression. By establishing a marketable right to the use of one's expression, copyright supplies the economic incentive to create and disseminate ideas. * * * It is fundamentally at odds with the scheme of copyright to accord lesser rights in those works that are of greatest importance to the public. Such a notion ignores the major premise of copyright and injures author and public alike. "[T]o propose that fair use be imposed whenever the 'social value [of dissemination] . . . outweighs any detriment to the artist,' would be to propose depriving copyright owners of their right in the property precisely when they encounter those users who could afford to pay for it." * * *

In view of the First Amendment protections already embodied in the Copyright Act's distinction between copyrightable expression and uncopyrightable facts and ideas, and the latitude for scholarship and comment traditionally afforded by fair use, we see no warrant for expanding the doctrine of fair use to create what amounts to a public figure exception to copyright. Whether verbatim copying from a public figure's manuscript in a given case is or is not fair use must be judged according to the traditional equities of fair use.

IV

* * * The four factors identified by Congress [in §107 of the Copyright Act] as especially relevant in determining whether the use was fair are: (1) the purpose and character of the use; (2) the nature of the copyrighted work; (3) the substantiality of the portion used in relation to the copyrighted work as a whole; (4) the effect on the potential market for or value of the copyrighted work. We address each one separately.

Purpose of the Use. The Second Circuit correctly identified news reporting as the general purpose of The Nation's use. News reporting is one of the examples enumerated in §107 to "give some idea of the sort of activities the courts might regard as fair use under the circumstances." This listing was not intended to be exhaustive or to single out any particular use as presumptively a "fair" use. The drafters resisted pressures from special interest groups to create presumptive categories of fair use, but structured the provision as an affirmative defense requiring a case-by-case analysis. * * * The fact that an article arguably is "news" and therefore a productive use is simply one factor in a fair use analysis.

* * * The Nation has every right to seek to be the first to publish information. But The Nation went beyond simply reporting uncopyrightable information and actively sought to exploit the headline value of its infringement, making a "news event" out of its unauthorized first publication of a noted figure's copyrighted expression.

The fact that a publication was commercial as opposed to nonprofit is a separate factor that tends to weigh against a finding of fair use. "[E]very commercial use of copyrighted material is presumptively an unfair exploitation of the monopoly privilege that belongs to the owner of the copyright." In arguing that the purpose of news reporting is not purely commercial, The Nation misses the point entirely. The crux of the profit/nonprofit distinction is not whether the sole motive of the use is monetary gain but whether the user stands to profit from exploitation of the copyrighted material without paying the customary price.

In evaluating character and purpose we cannot ignore The Nation's stated purpose of scooping the forthcoming hardcover and Time abstracts. The Nation's use had not merely the incidental effect but the *intended purpose* of supplanting the copyright holder's commercially valuable right of first publication. Also relevant to the "character" of the use is "the propriety of the defendant's conduct." "Fair use presupposes 'good faith' and 'fair dealing.' " The trial court found that The Nation knowingly exploited a purloined manuscript. Unlike the typical claim of fair use The Nation cannot offer up even the fiction of consent as justification. Like its competitor newsweekly it was free to bid for the right of abstracting excerpts from "A Time to Heal." Fair use "distinguishes between 'a true scholar and a chiseler who infringes a work for personal profit.' ''

Nature of the Copyrighted Work. Second, the Act directs attention to the nature of the copyrighted work. ''A Time to Heal'' may be characterized as an unpublished historical narrative or autobiography. The law generally recognizes a greater need to disseminate factual works than works of fiction or fantasy. * * * Some of the briefer quotes from the memoirs are arguably necessary adequately to convey the facts; for example, Mr. Ford's characterization of the White House tapes as the ''smoking gun'' is perhaps so integral to the idea expressed as to be inseparable from it. But The Nation did not stop at isolated phrases and instead excerpted subjective descriptions and portraits of public figures whose power lies in the author's individualized expression. Such use, focusing on the most expressive elements of the work, exceeds that necessary to disseminate the facts.

The fact that a work is unpublished is a critical element of its ''nature.'' Our prior discussion establishes that the scope of fair use is narrower with respect to unpublished works. While even substantial quotations might qualify as fair use in a review of a published work or in a news account of a speech that had been delivered to the public or disseminated to the press, the author's right to control the first public appearance of his expression weighs against such use of the work before its release. The right of first publication encompasses not only the choice whether to publish at all, but also the choices when, where, and in what form first to publish a work.

In the case of Mr. Ford's manuscript, the copyright holders' interest in confidentiality is irrefutable; the copyright holders had entered into a contractual undertaking to ''keep the manuscript confidential'' and required that all those to whom the manuscript was shown also ''sign an agreement to keep the manuscript confidential.'' While the copyright holders' contract with Time required Time to submit its proposed article seven days before publication, The Nation's clandestine publication afforded no such opportunity for creative or quality control. It was hastily patched together and contained ''a number of inaccuracies.'' A use that so clearly infringes the copyright holder's interests in confidentiality and creative control is difficult to characterize as ''fair.''

Amount and Substantiality of the Portion Used. Next, the Act directs us to examine the amount and substantiality of the portion used in relation to the copyrighted work as a whole. In absolute terms, the words actually quoted were an insubstantial portion of ''A Time to Heal.'' The District Court, however, found that ''[T]he Nation took what was essentially the heart of the book.'' We believe the Court of Appeals erred in overruling the District Judge's evaluation of the qualitative nature of the taking. A Time editor described the chapters on the pardon as ''the most interesting and moving parts of the entire manuscript.'' The portions actually quoted were selected by Mr. Navasky as among the most powerful passages in those chapters. He testified that he used verbatim excerpts because simply reciting the information could not adequately convey the ''absolute certainty with which [Ford] expressed himself,'' or show that ''this comes from President Ford,'' or carry the ''definitive quality'' of the original. In short, he quoted these passages precisely because they qualitatively embodied Ford's distinctive expression.

As the statutory language indicates, a taking may not be excused merely because it is insubstantial with respect to the *infringing* work. As Judge Learned Hand cogently remarked, ''[N]o plagiarist can excuse the wrong by showing how much of his work he did not pirate.'' Conversely, the fact that a substantial portion of the infringing work was copied verbatim is evidence of the qualitative value of the copied material, both to the originator and to the plagiarist who seeks to profit from marketing someone else's copyrighted expression.

Stripped to the verbatim quotes, the direct takings from the unpublished manuscript constitute at least 13% of the infringing article. The Nation article is structured around the quoted excerpts which serve as its dramatic focal points. In view of the expressive value of the excerpts and their key role in the infringing work, we cannot agree with the Second Circuit that the "magazine took a meager, indeed an infinitesimal amount of Ford's original language."

Effect on the Market. Finally, the Act focuses on "the effect of the use upon the potential market for or value of the copyrighted work." This last factor is undoubtedly the single most important element of fair use. "Fair use, when properly applied, is limited to copying by others which does not materially impair the marketability of the work which is copied." The trial court found not merely a potential but an actual effect on the market. Time's cancellation of its projected serialization and its refusal to pay the $12,500 were the direct effect of the infringement. * * * Rarely will a case of copyright infringement present such clear cut evidence of actual damage. * * * Time cited The Nation's article, which contained verbatim quotes from the unpublished manuscript, as a reason for its non-performance. * * *

V

* * * The Nation conceded that its verbatim copying of some 300 words of direct quotation from the Ford manuscript would constitute an infringement unless excused as a fair use. Because we find that The Nation's use of these verbatim excerpts from the unpublished manuscript was not a fair use, the judgment of the Court of Appeals is reversed and remanded for further proceedings consistent with this opinion.

It is so ordered.

JUSTICE BRENNAN, with whom JUSTICE WHITE and JUSTICE MARHSALL join, dissenting.

* * * Although the Court pursues the laudable goal of protecting "the economic incentive to create and disseminate ideas," this zealous defense of the copyright owner's prerogative will, I fear, stifle the broad dissemination of ideas and information copyright is intended to nurture. Protection of the copyright owner's economic interest is achieved in

this case through an exceedingly narrow definition of the scope of fair use. * * *

I

This case presents two issues. First, did The Nation's use of material from the Ford manuscript in forms other than direct quotation from that manuscript infringe Harper & Row's copyright. Second, did the quotation of approximately 300 words from the manuscript infringe the copyright because this quotation did not constitute "fair use" within the meaning of §107 of the Copyright Act. The Court finds no need to resolve the threshold copyrightability issue. The use of 300 words of quotation was, the Court finds, beyond the scope of fair use and thus a copyright infringement. Because I disagree with the Court's fair use holding, it is necessary for me to decide the threshold copyrightability question.

* * * [The Copyright Act] extends copyright protection to an author's literary form but permits free use by others of the ideas and information the author communiticates. This limitation of protection to literary form precludes any claim of copyright of facts, including historical narration. * * *

The "promotion of science and the useful arts" requires this limit on the scope of an author's control. Were an author able to prevent subsequent authors from using concepts, ideas, or facts contained in his or her work, the creative process would wither and scholars would be forced into unproductive replication of the research of their predecessors. This limitation on copyright also ensures consonance with our most important First Amendment values. * * *

It follows that infringement of copyright must be based on a taking of literary form, as opposed to the ideas or information contained in a copyrighted work. Deciding whether an infringing appropriation of literary form has occurred is difficult for at least two reasons. First, the distinction between literary form and information or ideas is often elusive in practice. Second, infringement must be based on a *substantial* appropriation of literary form. This determination is equally challenging. Not surprisingly, the test for infringement has defied precise formulation. In general, though, the inquiry proceeds along two axes: *how closely* has the second author tracked the first author's particular language and structure of presentation; and *how much* of the first author's language and structure has the second author appropriated.

* * * Apart from the quotations, virtually all of the material in The Nation's article indirectly recounted Mr. Ford's factual narrative of the Nixon resignation and pardon, his latter-day reflections on some events of his Presidency, and his perceptions of the personalities at the center of those events. No copyright can be claimed in this information *qua* information. Infringement would thus have to be based on too close and substantial a tracking of Mr. Ford's expression.

[Justice Brennan then concluded that although The Nation had occasionally used sentences that "closely resembled language in the original manuscript," these similarities were not sufficient to constitute an appropriation of literary form. He pointed out that Harper & Row could not claim copyright on much of the paraphrased material, such as quotations of other persons, and that The Nation had paraphrased only "disparate isolated sentences" from the manuscript. "A finding of infringement based on paraphrase generally requires far more close and substantial a tracking of the original language than occurred in this case," he said. Justice Brennan also emphasized that 2,000-word article did not "mimic" Mr. Ford's structure and contained information drawn from "scattered sections" of the 200,000-word manuscript.]

II

The Nation is thus liable in copyright only if the quotation of 300 words infringed any of Harper & Row's exclusive rights under . . . the Act. * * * The question here is whether

The Nation's quotation was a noninfringing fair use within the meaning of § 107. * * *

With respect to a work of history, particularly the memoirs of a public official, the statutorily prescribed analysis cannot properly be conducted without constant attention to copyright's crucial distinction between protected literary form and unprotected information or ideas. The question must always be: Was the subsequent author's use of *literary form* a fair use . . . , in light of the purpose for the use, the nature of the copyright work, the amount of literary form used, and the effect of this use of literary form on the value of or market for the original?

* * * In my judgment, the Court's fair use analysis has fallen to the temptation to find copyright violation based on a minimal use of literary form in order to provide compensation for the appropriation of information from a work of history. The failure to distinguish between information and literary form permeates every aspect of the Court's fair use analysis and leads the Court to the wrong result in this case. * * *

The Purpose of the Use. The Nation's purpose in quoting 300 words of the Ford manuscript was, as the Court acknowledges, news reporting. * * * Section 107 lists news reporting as a prime example of fair use of another's expression. Like criticism and all other purposes Congress explicitly approved in § 107, news reporting informs the public; the language of § 107 makes clear that Congress saw the spread of knowledge and information as the strongest justification for a properly limited appropriation of expression. * * *

The Court's reliance on the commercial nature of The Nation's use . . . is inappropriate in the present context. Many uses § 107 lists as paradigmatic examples of fair use, including criticism, comment, and *news reporting*, are generally conducted for profit in this country, a fact of which Congress was obviously aware. . . . To negate any argument favoring fair use based on news reporting or criticism because that reporting or criticism was published for profit is to render meaningless the congressional imprimatur placed on such uses.

Nor should The Nation's intent to create a "news event" weigh against a finding of fair use. Such a rule, like the Court's automatic presumption against news reporting for profit, would undermine the congressional validation of the news reporting purpose. * * * Because Harper & Row had no legitimate copyright interest in the information and ideas in the Ford manuscript, The Nation had every right to seek to be the first to disclose these facts and ideas to the public. * * * The Nation's stated purpose of scooping the competition should under those circumstances have no negative bearing on the claim of fair use. Indeed the Court's reliance on this factor would seem to amount to little more than distaste for the standard journalistic practice of seeking to be the first to publish news.

The Court's reliance on The Nation's putative bad faith is equally unwarranted. No court has found that The Nation possessed the Ford manuscript illegally or in violation of any common-law interest of Harper & Row. . . . Even if the manuscript had been "purloined" by someone, nothing in this record imputes culpability to The Nation. On the basis of the record in this case, the most that can be said is that The Nation made use of the contents of the manuscript knowing the copyright owner would not sanction the use. * * * With respect to the appropriation of information and ideas other than the quoted words, The Nation's use was perfectly legitimate despite the copyright owner's objection because no copyright can be claimed in ideas or information. Whether the quotation of 300 words was infringement or a fair use . . . is a close question that has produced sharp division in both this Court and the Court of Appeals. The Nation's awareness of an objection that has a sigificant chance of being adjudged unfounded cannot amount to bad faith. * * *

The Nature of the Copyrighted Work. * * * The scope of fair use is generally broader when the source of borrowed expression is a factual or historical work. * * * Thus, the second statutory factor also favors a finding of fair use in this case.

* * * [T]he Court discounts the force of this consideration, primarily on the ground that "[t]he fact that a work is unpublished is a cru-

cial element of its 'nature.' " * * * This categorical presumption [against prepublication fair use] is unwarranted on its own terms and unfaithful to congressional intent. Whether a particular prepublication use will impair any interest the Court identifies as encompassed within the right of first publication will depend on the nature of the copyrighted work, the timing of prepublication use, the amount of expression used, and the medium in which the second author communicates. Also, certain uses might to tolerable for some purposes but not for others. * * *

To the extent the Court purports to evaluate the facts of this case, it relies on sheer speculation. * * * [Mr. Ford] intended the words in the manuscript to be a public statement about his Presidency. Lacking, therefore, is the "deliberate choice on the part of the copyright owner" to keep expression confidential, a consideration that [the Congress] . . . recognized as the impetus behind narrowing fair use for unpublished works. What the Court depicts as the copyright owner's "confidentiality" interest is . . . no more than an economic interest in capturing the full value of initial release of information to the public. * * * [T]he question of economic harm is properly considered under the fourth statutory factor—the effect on the value of or mark for the copyrighted work—and not as a presumed element of the "nature" of the copyright.

The Amount and Substantiality of the Portion Used. * * * [T]he Court purports to rely on the District Court factual findings that The Nation had taken "the heart of the book." This reliance is misplaced. . . . When the District Court made this finding, it was evaluating not the quoted words at issue here but the "totality" of the information and reflective commentary in the Ford work. The vast majority of what the District Court considered the heart of the Ford work, therefore, consisted of ideas and information The Nation was free to use. * * *

At least with respect to the six particular quotes of Mr. Ford's observations and reflections about President Nixon, I agree with the Court's conclusion that The Nation appropriated some literary form of substantial quality. I do not agree, however, that the substantiality of the epxression taken was clearly excessive or inappropriate to The Nation's news reporting purpose.

Had these quotations been used in the context of a critical book review of the Ford work, there is little question that such a use would be fair. . . . The amount and substantiality of the use—in both quantitative and qualitative terms—would have certainly been appropriate to the purpose of such a use. It is difficult to see how the use of these quoted words in a news report is less appropriate. * * *

The Effect on the Market. * * * In essence, the Court finds that by using some quotes in a story about the Nixon pardon, The Nation "competed for a share of the market of prepublication excerpts" because Time planned to excerpt from the chapters about the pardon.

The Nation's publication indisputably precipitated Time's eventual cancellation. But that does not mean that The Nation's use of the 300 quoted words caused this injury to Harper & Row. Wholly apart from these quoted words, The Nation published significant information and ideas from the Ford manuscript. If it was this publication of information, and not the publication of the few quotations, that caused Time to abrogate its serialization agreement, then whatever the negative effect on the serialization market, that effect was the product of wholly legitimate activity.

The Court of Appeals specifically held that "the evidence does not support a finding that it was the very limited use of expression per se which led to Time's decision not to print excerpts." I fully agree with this holding. * * * That the information, and not the literary form, represents most of the real value of the work in this case is perhaps best revealed by . . . the contract between Harper & Row and Mr. Ford[,] . . . which makes clear that Harper & Row sought to benefit substantially from monopolizing the initial revelation of information known only to Ford. * * * Harper & Row had every right to seek to monopolize revenue from that potential market through contractual arrangements but it has no right to set up copyright as a shield from competition in that market because copyright does not protect information. The Nation had every right to seek to be the first to publish that information.
* * *

INTRODUCTION

Copyright is part of what is known as "intellectual property" law, which also includes patent and trademark law. Although these three legal doctrines are obviously related, they are quite different, and it is important to understand the basic distinctions. Patent law can be traced to the efforts of medieval craftsmen to prevent others from making and selling similar items. Under the Patent Act of 1952, which governs patents in the United States, someone who has developed a new, useful, and "nonobvious" process or product is given the right to exclude others from making and selling the same item. The act thus offers an economic incentive for those who advance the boundaries of scientific and technological knowledge.

Trademark law grew out of the practice of medieval craftsmen to affix the mark of their guild on the goods they sold, thus distinguishing their products from those sold by other guilds. Today, the federal Lanham Act, as well as state law, seeks to avoid confusion among purchasers by granting a manufacturer or seller the exclusive use of the symbol he uses for marketing goods and services. We shall return to trademark law in our discussion of advertising in Chapter 11.

Just as the guildsmen played a major role in shaping patent and trademark law, English publishers were instrumental in the development of copyright law. Like their counterparts in manufacturing, the publishers sought to protect their financial positions within the industry, but the desire to control the content of what was being published was also important. In 1566, the English Crown concentrated the entire printing business in the hands of the Stationers' Company, whose members were the leading publishers in London. By royal decree, all published works had to be entered in the register of the Company in the name of one of its members. Upon registering the publication, the publisher claimed the sole right to print and publish the work for himself and his heirs forever; the author was completely disregarded. Moreover, because nothing could be published without registration, the government was also able to prevent the publication of seditious materials and "anti-clerical" works spawned by the Protestant Reformation. Violators were punished in the infamous Star Chamber.

This system of licensing was ultimately embodied in a series of statutes, the last of which expired in 1694. When the ban against unlicensed printing was lifted, a number of independent printers emerged to threaten the monopoly position of the Stationers' Company. Not surprisingly, the Company's members asked Parliament for protection from these "pirates," who were not recognizing the members' claim of an exclusive right to publish their works in perpetuity. Parliament, however, responded with something quite different: the Statute of Anne, enacted in 1710.

This statute, which is the foundation of modern copyright law, expressly recognized the right of authors to benefit economically from their work and limited the exclusive right of publication to a specific period. Under the statute, the author had the sole right of publication for fourteen years, subject to renewal for another fourteen years if he was living at the expiration of the initial period. Of course, that right could be sold to a commercial publisher, thus allowing the author to profit from his work. The statute also required the work to be registered with the government, but this registration was not for licensing purposes but rather to enable an author to prove ownership of his work.

This basic statutory scheme was exported to the United States. In the period immediately after the revolution, all states except Delaware had adopted some form of copyright law. These statutes had no force beyond the boundaries of the individual state, and the Articles of Confederation prevented enactment of a law at the federal level. The Framers of the Constitution, however, saw the need for a national statute. As the *Harper & Row* case indicates, Article I, Section 8 of the Constitution empowers the Congress "to Promote the Progress of Science and useful Arts, by securing for limited Times to Authors and Inventors the exclusive Right to their respective Writings and Discoveries." This provision specifically authorizes the Congress to adopt national patent and copyright legislation, and it has done so. (The trademark statute was enacted pursuant to another portion of Article I, Section 8, the interstate commerce clause.)

The first federal copyright statute was passed in 1790 and amended several times over the next century. After the 1886 Berne Convention for the Protection of Literary and Artistics Works, a multilateral treaty that established an international law of copyright, a movement began for reform of the American copyright statute. This effort culminated in the Copyright Act of 1909, which nonetheless fell far short of meeting the fundamental requirements of the Berne Convention. The act was not amended significantly until 1954, again in response to international developments. Following formation of the United Nations, another international agreement on copyright, the Universal Copyright Convention of 1952, was drafted in an effort to stabilize copyright law among nations. The United States was one of the first countries to ratify this treaty, and Congress amended the Copyright Act to reflect its requirements rather than those of the Berne Convention.

These relatively modest changes did not alter the basic structure of the 1909 act, and various technological developments—radio and television, cable, jukeboxes, records, photocopiers, and computers, for example—continued to place great strain on American copyright law. After years of study, Congress passed the Copyright Revision Act of 1976, a comprehensive overhaul of the statutory scheme. It was not until 1988, however, that Congress approved modifications that enabled the United States to become a party to the Berne Convention and thus join seventy-seven other nations, including most of the free market countries. About the same number belong to the Universal Copyright Convention, and more than fifty nations adhere to both. We will explore the key provisions of the 1976 act and the 1988 amendments later in this chapter.

COPYRIGHT AND THE FIRST AMENDMENT

A certain tension has always existed between copyright law and the first amendment. Although the copyright statute is expressly authorized by Article I, Section 8 of the Constitution, that grant of power is necessarily limited by the first amendment, which was subsequently added to the Constitution. How can the Copyright Act, which grants to authors the right to restrict use of their work, be squared with the first amendment, which is designed to ensure the widest possible circulation of ideas? After all, the first amendment tells us that "Congress shall make no law . . . abridging the freedom of speech, or of the press." Isn't the Copyright Act just that, a law that abridges freedom of expression by one who seeks to disseminate copyrighted materials?

The First Congress obviously did not think so, having enacted the first copyright statute in 1790, the year after it approved the first amendment. As the *Harper & Row* decision indicates, the Supreme Court has also had little difficulty reconciling copyright protection and freedom of expression. Justice Sandra Day O'Connor pointed out in that case that the copyright statute actually serves as "the engine of free expression" by supplying "the economic incentive to create and disseminate ideas." Without this incentive, the argument goes, the number of works available to the public would decrease and the marketplace of ideas would have little to offer. As one commentator has observed, "[i]f every volume that was in the public interest could be pirated away by a competing publisher, . . . the public [soon] would have nothing worth reading."

In addition, the copyright statute takes into account first amendment values in two ways: by recognizing the "fair use" defense at issue in *Harper & Row* and by placing limits on the type of material that can be copyrighted. We will consider fair use in some detail below. With respect to copyrightability, Section 102 of the Copyright Act makes clear that only the form of the author's expression may be copyrighted: "[i]n no case does copyright protection for an original work of authorship extend to any idea, procedure, process, system, method or operation, concept, principle, or discovery . . . explained, illustrated or embodied in such work." Consequently, facts, ideas, and theories set out in a copyrighted work may be freely used by anyone. This notion of "copyrightability," which is briefly noted by the majority in *Harper & Row* and discussed at some length in Justice William Brennan's dissent, assures a free flow of information to the public while protecting the means of expression utilized by a particular author.

The dichotomy between idea and expression was at issue in *Hoehling v. Universal City Studios, Inc.*, decided by the U.S. Court of Appeals for the Second Circuit in 1980. The plaintiff, A.A. Hoehling, wrote a book about the destruction of the German dirigible Hindenberg, which exploded in 1937 on a visit to the United States. After exhaustive research, he concluded that the zeppelin had been sabotaged and pointed the finger at one Eric Spehl, a crew member who was killed in the explosion. Ten years later, Michael Mooney published another book on the Hindenberg tragedy, and he, too, described Spehl as the saboteur. Universal Studios bought movie rights to Mooney's book and later made a film that, in fictionalized fashion, attributed the explosion to a crew member named Boerth. Hoehling brought a copyright infringement suit against Universal and Mooney, alleging that they had appropriated his sabotage theory. The trial court granted the defendants' motion for summary judgment, and the Second Circuit affirmed.

In rejecting Hoehling's claim, the appellate court concluded that neither the theory itself nor the supporting facts used to support it was copyrightable. "The hypothesis that Eric Spehl destroyed the Hindenburg is based entirely on the interpretation of historical facts," the court said. "Such an historical interpretation . . . is not protected by [Mr. Hoehling's] copyright and can be freely used by subsequent authors." Were this not the case, there could be "a chilling effect on authors who contemplate tackling an historical issue or event. . . ." Employing the same reasoning, the court also ruled that the plaintiff could not claim copyright protection for "the fruits of original research," that is, specific facts ascertained through his personal research efforts. Otherwise, the court said, an author would be "absolutely precluded from saving time and effort by referring to and relying upon prior published material." Knowledge is expanded "by granting new authors of historical works a relatively free hand to build upon the work of their predecessors."

Unfortunately, the task of separating an idea or fact from the form in which it has been expressed is not always a simple task. As Judge Learned Hand once observed, copyright "cannot be limited literally to the text, else a plagiarist would escape by immaterial variations." With that in mind, Professor Melville Nimmer, the nation's foremost authority on copyright law, posed the problem this way: "If the reach of copyright is thus not limited to verbatim repetition, yet does not extend to ideas per se, how does one draw the line that separates non-protectible ideas from the protectible 'expression of ideas'?"

The problem arose in the celebrated case of *Salinger v. Random House, Inc.* (1987). J.D. Salinger, the highly regarded American novelist best known for *The Catcher in the Rye*, was the subject of a literary biography to be published by Random House. The author of that work, Ian Hamilton, relied on several unpublished letters Salinger had written various people from 1939 to 1961. These letters had been donated to university libraries, where Hamilton was able to view them. In his manuscript, Hamilton quoted directly from the letters but dropped the quotations in favor of paraphrasing after Salinger (who had been sent a copy of the initial version) registered the letters for copyright protection. Salinger then sued Hamilton and Random House for infringement, seeking damages and an injunction against publication of the book. The federal district court in New York City refused a preliminary injunction barring publication, but the U.S. Court of Appeals for the Second Circuit reversed and ordered the district judge to enter the injunction.

After pointing out that letters, like other writings, may be copyrighted, the court of appeals started with the proposition that "the copyright owner secures protection only for the expressive content of the work, not the ideas or facts contained therein." However, that protected expression includes material that has "been quoted verbatim or only paraphrased." Consequently, one may not escape copyright liability by paraphrasing that captures an author's "manner of expression" and the "vividness of description," including the way the writer structures the material, chooses words, and places emphasis. Here the court had little trouble concluding that Hamilton's paraphrasing "track[ed] the original so closely as to constitute infringement." For example, in one letter Salinger said that Wendell Willkie "looks to me like a guy who makes his wife keep a scrapbook for him." Rather than stating simply that Salinger thought Willkie to be vain, Hamilton reported that "Salinger had fingered [Willkie] as the sort of fellow who makes his wife keep an album of his press cuttings."

The type of line-drawing evident in *Salinger* is also necessary in the context of news reporting. As the Supreme Court mentioned in the *Harper & Row* case, news itself—that is, the raw facts—is not copyrightable. Like the historical facts at issue in *Hoehling*, news is in the public domain and may be freely used by anyone. As a result, a newspaper's copyrighting a major story that it has developed does not prevent other media organizations from reporting the same story. Under the rationale of the *Salinger* decision, however, the form of a news story, including the reporter's choice of words, selection of facts, and manner of organization, is "expression" that may be protected under copyright law. How, then, does one distinguish between "news" and the "expression" of news for copyright purposes?

Justice Brennan's dissenting opinion in *Harper & Row* provides some guidance in this regard, as does a 1977 decision of the U.S. Court of Appeals for the Second Circuit, *Wainwright Securities, Inc. v. Wall Street Transcript Corp.* In that case, the plaintiff prepared and published in-depth analytical reports on various companies that examined financial characteristics, industry trends, growth prospects and profit potential, and corporate strengths and weaknesses. These reports were provided, for a fee, to over 900 of the plaintiff's clients. The defendant published the *Wall Street Transcript*, a weekly newspaper devoted to economic, business, and financial news. Among its regular features was "Wall Street Roundup," a column consisting of abstracts of research reports. When the *Transcript* began including the plaintiff's reports in the column, the plaintiff began copyrighting its work and subsequently sued for infringement. The Second Circuit upheld the trial judge's grant of a preliminary injunction preventing the *Transcript* from publishing abstracts of the plaintiff's reports.

"It is, of course, axiomatic that 'news events' may not be copyrighted," the court said. What is protected, however, "is the manner of expression, the author's analysis or interpretation of events, the way he structures his material and marshals facts, his choice of words, and the emphasis he gives to particular developments." In applying this test, the court concluded that the *Transcript* had taken in almost verbatim fashion "the most creative and original aspects" of the plaintiff's reports, the financial analyses. Moreover, the court stressed that the *Transcript* did not conduct its own independent analysis or research, solicit comments on the same topics from other financial analysts, or include reaction from industry officials or investors. In other words, the newspaper did not do any of its own "leg work" in preparing the abstracts but relied exclusively on the plaintiff's reports. Thus, a journalist may use a copyrighted news story as the starting point for his own article but may not simply rewrite the story and call it his own.

Journalists who "pirate" stories from other news organizations may also run afoul of state law. Recall from Chapter 3 that Hugo Zacchini, the human cannonball, alleged that a television station's film clip of his act violated his right to publicity under state common law. A newspaper or broadcast station that has been the victim of wholesale copying by a competitor can proceed under a similar theory, usually labeled misappropriation or unfair competition. The leading case is the U.S. Supreme Court's 1918 decision in *International News Service v. Associated Press*. There the AP claimed that INS, a rival wire service, picked up AP stories from early editions of newspapers, rewrote them, and put them on the INS wire. Ruling that the AP had a "quasi-property right" in the research, labor, and economic resources that went into its newsgathering activities, the Court concluded that INS had engaged in unfair competition by its appropriation of the AP material. Subsequently, newspaper publishers successfully invoked this doctrine against radio stations that had "lifted" stories from newspapers and simply read them over the air.

Before leaving the first amendment issue, a comment on the use of the injunction in copyright cases, as well as in unfair competition suits, is in order. In the *Hoehling*, *Salinger*, and *Wainwright* cases, the plaintiffs all asked the courts to halt publication of the works that allegedly infringed their copyrights. In the latter two cases, the courts did just that. Similarly, the *International News* case resulted in an injunction prohibiting INS from using AP wire stories. Is such judicial action a prior restraint on publication? Technically, the answer is "yes," for the injunction prevents the defendant from publishing material that he ordinarily would have published. If, however, one accepts the Supreme Court's proposition in *Harper & Row* that the first amendment and the Copyright Act may peacefully co-exist, a publication that infringes someone's copyright does not enjoy first amendment protection and the prior restraint problem disappears. The same result necessarily follows in unfair competition cases, since that state law doctrine protects the same sort of interests as does copyright law.

BASIC COPYRIGHT PRINCIPLES

Originality

At the heart of copyright law is the notion of originality. Even if one is seeking protection for expression rather than for facts or ideas, that expression must be original and involve a minimal amount of creativity in order to be copyrightable. This does not mean, however, that the author must have been the first to create the expression embodied in his work or that the expression be "novel." Consider, for example, a musician who writes a hit song based on an old folk tune. Although the music itself is hardly novel, the songwriter may copyright his arrangement of the song. By the same token, an engraver who painstakingly reproduces the paintings of the "old masters" can copyright his reproductions, on the theory that he has originated the copies. In contrast, patent law requires a substantial advance over the prior state of the art, and the invention cannot have previously been developed by another.

The issue of originality has recently arisen with respect to the "colorization" of motion pictures. This tedious process allows artists working with computers to change black-and-white films into color videotapes. The typical colorized film is the result of the selection of as many as 4,000 colors drawn from a pool of sixteen million colors. Not surprisingly, the cost is rather high: about $2,000 per minute of film. In June 1987, the U.S. Copyright Office announced that it would allow copyright registration for colorized versions of black-and-white movies, concluding that the requisite originality is present "where the [colorized version] consists of original selection, arrangement, or combinations of a large number of colors." However, the Copyright Office emphasized that the color selection must be made by human beings and stated that it "may reconsider the [originality] issue if the role of the computer in selecting the colors becomes more dominant."

The original expression must also be in a form recognized by the Copyright Act. Under Section 102 of the act, copyright protection is available for "original works of authorship fixed in any tangible medium of expression, now known or later developed. . . ." The statute also lists, by way of illustration, seven categories of works that qualify:

- literary works;
- musical works, including any accompanying words;
- dramatic works, including any accompanying music;
- pantomimes and choreographic works;
- pictorial, graphic, and sculptural works, including photographs, maps, and architectural plans;
- motion pictures and other audiovisual works; and
- sound recordings.

A variety of works fall under the broad terms of Section 102, ranging from advertisements and computer programs to greeting greeting cards and video games. Keep in mind that there must be a "tangible medium of expression." Choreography for a Broadway play, for example, is not protected unless it is reduced to film or diagrams, for otherwise it is not "fixed" in a "tangible medium." Similarly, a sports event is not copyrightable unless recorded in some manner.

The "Bundle of Rights"

If a work is copyrightable, the author (or the person to whom he has transferred ownership) has what Justice O'Connor described in the *Harper & Row* case as a "bundle of exclusive rights." Section 106 of the Copyright Act provides that the author has "the exclusive right to do and to authorize" any of the following: reproduce copies of the work; prepare derivative works based on the copyrighted material; distribute copies to the public by sale, rental, or lease; and perform or display the work publicly. These rights, which vest in the author at the time of the work's creation, extend throughout the author's lifetime, plus fifty years.

The most important of the rights enumerated in Section 106 is probably the right of reproduction, since it allows the copyright owner to prevent anyone else from reproducing the work. Thus, the owner may profit from his work by selling to others the right to make copies. The right to prepare derivative works is also quite significant, for it enables the owner to control the adaptation of the work. For example, a publisher who owns the copyright to a novel can sell the rights to make a movie based on the book. Because the rights for reproduction and derivative works enable the owner to benefit from any public distribution of the copyrighted material, the right of distribution adds relatively little by way of protection.

Moreover, there is also an important limitation: although the copyright owner has the right to sell copies of the work, once he has done so he cannot control or profit from subsequent sales and rentals of those copies. This "first sale doctrine" means that a copyright owner who sells copies of a movie on videotape cassettes cannot prevent a video store from renting those cassettes. This rule does not apply to sound recordings, however, which under a 1984 amendment to the Copyright Act may not be rented without the consent of the copyright owner.[1]

In light of today's communications and entertainment industries, the right of performance in Section 106 is also extremely valuable. Generally speaking, any time that a work is publicly performed—on television or in a movie, for example—the permission of the copyright owner must be obtained. The right of performance does not apply to visual works such as photographs or sculpture, since it is difficult to imagine the "performance" of a visual object. (The owner, however, has the right to publicly display these works.) More significantly, sound recordings are excluded from the performance right. This means that radio stations do not have to pay royalties to record companies and recording artists that own the copyright in the recordings themselves. However, the composer or owner of the copyright in the underlying musical composition has a right of performance and is entitled to royalties.

There are a variety of other exceptions to the performance right, including educational activities, religious services, and, under certain circumstances, nonprofit performances by charitable organizations. Special rules applicable to broadcasting, cable television, and jukeboxes are discussed below.

Infringement

Violation of one of the exclusive rights set forth in Section 106 constitutes copyright infringement. To prove infringement, the plaintiff must show that he owns the copyright and that the defendant copied the work without permission. Because such copying rarely occurs in front of eyewitnesses, the plaintiff must prove his case by what is known as circumstantial evidence. Typically, the plaintiff will attempt to demonstrate that his work was available to the defendant, who then produced a work strikingly similar to that of the plaintiff. Proof of these two facts—access and similarity—permits the conclusion that the defendant indeed copied the plaintiff's work.

A famous case involving musician George Harrison is illustrative. In *Bright Tunes Music Corp. v. Harrisongs Music, Ltd.* (1976), the copyright owner of "He's So Fine," a hit pop song recorded by the Chiffons in 1962, brought suit against the former Beatle, author of the hit "My Sweet Lord." Recorded in 1970, the song earned Harrison over $2 million in royalties. "My Sweet Lord" employed virtually the same melody as "He's So Fine," and Harrison was well aware of the earlier song, which had reached number one on the American charts and was also in the top twenty in England. Finding the requisite access and similarity present, the court ruled that Harrison was liable for copyright infringement. This was so although Harrison had not consciously employed the melody of "He's So Fine" in his own work. As he "sought musical materials to clothe his thoughts," the court said,

---

[1]As enacted, the Record Rental Amendment of 1984 included a so-called "sunset" clause under which the statute was to expire in 1989. In November 1988, however, President Reagan signed into law a bill extending the amendment for an additional eight years.

"there came to the surface of his mind a particular combination that pleased him . . . ." Harrison felt that "this combination of sounds would work . . . [b]ecause his subconscious knew it already had worked in a song his conscious mind did not remember."

The same analysis is used with respect to literary works. For example, in *Trust Company Bank v. Putnam Publishing Group* (1988), the copyright owner of the novel *Gone With the Wind* brought an infringement action against the American publishers of a 1981 French novel called *The Blue Bicycle*, seeking a temporary injunction to halt its publication in this country. The plaintiff alleged that *The Blue Bicycle* was little more than a remake of *Gone With the Wind* set in France during World War II. Published in the mid-1930s, *Gone With the Wind* achieved world-wide acclaim. There is little doubt that the author of *The Blue Bicycle* had access to the earlier book, though the court did not discuss this point. As to similarity, the court used a two-step process, first focusing on the "general ideas" of the books (plot, dialogue, setting, sequence of events, and characters) and then asking whether the alleged infringer had captured the "total concept and feel" of *Gone With the Wind*. Finding the evidence of infringement insufficient to warrant an injunction, the court said:

> The time and setting of *The Blue Bicycle* and *Gone With the Wind* are different. *The Blue Bicycle* takes place in occupied France during World War II. *Gone With the Wind* occurs in Civil War Georgia. In addition, while there are similarities and parallels be-tween the major characters . . . and the interrelationships among those characters, there are also significant differences. . . . Likewise, although there arc similarities in scenes and the sequence of events in the two works, the expression of the scenes . . . differs. Therefore, the court concludes that the "total concept and feel" of the works is not substantially similar. . . .

As the *Bright Tunes* and *Trust Company* cases indicate, damages and injunctive relief are available in copyright infringement cases. With respect to the latter, the court will issue an injunction prohibiting the defendant from violating the plaintiff's rights. Had the court in the *Trust Company* case found infringement, it would have entered an order temporarily preventing publication of *The Blue Bicycle* in the United States until a full trial on the infringement question could be held. After trial, the order would be made permanent if infringement were found. As noted previously, injunctions against publication do not violate the first amendment, de-spite the "prior restraint" overtones.

Damages are also common in infringement cases. In the Harrison lawsuit, the court ultimately determined that the copyright owner of "He's So Fine" was dam-aged to the tune of $1.5 million but reduced that award substantially because of certain irregularities involving the purchase of the copyright during the course of the litigation. Also, recall that *The Nation* magazine was ordered to pay $12,500 in damages in the *Harper & Row* case for publishing excerpts from President Ford's memoirs. The Copyright Act provides for two types of damages. First, a copyright owner can recover any losses stemming from the infringement, as well as any profits made by the infringer. Calculation of damages can be a complex process, and a clear-cut case such as *Harper & Row* is rare. In the *Bright Tunes* case, for example, the trial judge had to deal with the fact that "My Sweet Lord" appeared on a single record and two different albums and had to determine the extent to which profits from the song were attributable to Harrison's own status as an internationally known musician rather than to the plagiarized melody.

Second, the copyright owner may choose to receive damages in the amount set by statute. Under Section 504 of the Copyright Act, as amended in 1988, a plaintiff who proves infringement has the right to a minimum of $500 and a maximum of $20,000. If the court finds the infringement to be willful, the ceiling is raised to $100,000. Obviously, a copyright owner will resort to Section 504 only if his losses and the defendant's profits are difficult to prove or if these actual damages are lower than the amounts recoverable under the statute. The plaintiff may elect to receive statutory damages at any time before a final judgment is entered in his case.

In addition to damages and injunctive relief, the Copyright Act provides that a successful plaintiff may be able to recover his litigation costs, including attorney's fees, from the defendant. By the same token, a prevailing defendant may apply for such an award, which is discretionary with the court. Violation of the Copyright Act is also a criminal offense, though prosecutions have been infrequent except for "piracy" cases involving counterfeit records and tapes. Generally speaking, willful infringement for commercial gain is a misdemeanor punishable by a fine of up to $10,000 and/or a jail term not to exceed one year. However, a person found guilty of large-scale piracy of records and tapes can be fined up to $250,000 and imprisoned for five years.

Fair Use

The principal defense in a copyright suit is "fair use," a doctrine that can be compared to a qualified privilege in the law of defamation. As we saw in Chapter 2, a defendant in a libel action may escape liability for a defamatory publication if there is a social policy that recognizes the need for unfettered speech. For example, a newspaper that carries a fair and accurate story about a city council meeting is not liable for its report of defamatory statements made at the meeting, for there is a strong public interest in conveying information about such proceedings. Similarly, the Copyright Act recognizes that, in certain cases, the copyright owner's right to recover for infringement is outweighed by other policy considerations, including the first amendment interest in the widespread dissemination of information to the public.

In essence, the fair use doctrine allows someone to publish copyrighted material without the owner's permission, an act that would ordinarily constitute infringement. By way of illustration, Section 107 of the Copyright Act expressly states that the fair use doctrine covers "criticism, comment, news reporting, teaching . . . , scholarship, [and] research. . . ." That does not mean, however, that these uses are always fair, as the *Harper & Row* decision makes clear, or that other uses will not qualify. Instead, the fair use doctrine requires a balancing of competing interests, and Section 107 directs the courts to evaluate the facts of each case in light of the following factors:

- the purpose and character of the use, including whether the use is of a commercial nature or is for nonprofit educational purposes;
- the nature of the copyrighted work;
- the amount and substantiality of the portion used in relation to the copyrighted work as a whole; and

- the effect of the use upon the potential market for or value of the copyrighted work.

Moreover, keep in mind that the first amendment does not offer any additional protection for the news media, since the fair use doctrine itself is deemed sufficient to protect first amendment interests.

Although the four "fair use" factors are discussed at some length in *Harper & Row*, further elaboration here might be useful. Turning first to the "purpose and character" of the use, the fact that the infringer stands to benefit commercially from the use of the copyright owner's work militates strongly against a finding of fair use. In many cases, the fact that the copyrighted material is used for commercial purposes—in advertising campaigns, for instance—is the decisive factor in a court's ruling that the fair use doctrine does not apply.

Conversely, noncommercial uses are more likely to be considered "fair." For example, in the famous 1984 "Betamax" case, *Sony Corp. v. Universal City Studios, Inc.*, the U.S. Supreme Court ruled that the home taping of television programs on videocassette recorders was fair use. Writing for the majority, Justice John Paul Stevens emphasized that most VCR owners tape programs for their own viewing at a later time. This "time-shifting" is a "private, noncommercial activity [that] merely enables a viewer to see such a work which he had been invited to witness free of charge," Justice Stevens said. On the other hand, he noted that there would be a presumption of unfairness if VCR's were used "to make copies for a commercial or profit-making purpose."

The presence of a profit motive will not always vitiate a fair use claim, however. For example, in *Rosemont Enterprises, Inc. v. Random House, Inc.* (1966), the U.S. Court of Appeals for the Second Circuit concluded that the fair use doctrine applied in a case involving Random House's publication of a mass-market biography of billionare recluse Howard Hughes. Observing that "all publications are presumably operated for profit," the court focused on the public benefit that could be derived from the book rather than its profit potential. "[W]hile the Hughes biography may not be a profound work," the court said, "it may well provide valuable source material for future biographers (if any) of Hughes or for historians or social scientists." Therefore, the defendant's commercial motive in publishing a book designed for a mass audience rather than for scholars was "irrelevant to a determination of . . . fair use." Under this reasoning, the fact that newspapers, magazines, television stations, and even freelancers are in "the news business" to make money does not mean that they will be unable to rely on the fair use defense.

On the other hand, the *Harper & Row* decision makes plain that the fair use defense will not automatically be successful simply because a defendant is considered part of the "press." Recall that in that case, *The Nation* "knowingly exploited a purloined manuscript" in order to "scoop" a competitor that had purchased the right to publish excerpts from President Ford's memoirs. Under such circumstances, the Supreme Court had little difficulty concluding that the use was essentially commercial. The magazine "actively sought to exploit the headline value of its infringement, making a 'news event' out of its unauthorized first publication of a noted figure's copyrighted expression." Similarly, the court in the *Wainwright Securities* case discussed above rejected a fair use argument where the defendant newspaper had copied almost verbatim the plaintiff's financial reports. "This was not legitimate coverage of a news event," the court said. "[I]t was, and there is no other way to describe it, chiseling for personal profit."

The second factor—the nature of the copyrighted work—is based to some extent on the notion that the author impliedly consented to the use of his work without his permission. For example, a lawyer who publishes a book of legal forms to be used by practicing attorneys obviously intends that the forms be freely copied, for otherwise the book would have no value. On the other hand, it is safe to say that the author of a best-selling novel would not be pleased if a Hollywood studio made an unauthorized film version of the book. Although most situations are not as clear-cut as these, some guidelines do exist. For example, the fact that a work is unpublished will almost always preclude a finding of fair use, as the Supreme Court's decision in *Harper & Row* indicates. Relying on that case, the Second Circuit ruled in *Salinger* that the defendant could not claim fair use with respect to its paraphrasing of the plaintiff's unpublished letters.

The author's creativity and originality are also important in applying the "nature of the work" test. Thus, the fair use doctrine is more likely to be applied to a factual work than to a novel. For example, in *New York Times Co. v. Roxbury Data Interface, Inc.* (1977), a federal district court in New Jersey refused to halt publication of the defendants' directory listing all personal names that had appeared in the *New York Times Index.* "Since [the index] is a work more of diligence than of originality or inventiveness," the court said, "defendants have greater license to use portions . . . than if a creative work had been involved."

This is not to say, however, that one may freely copy from any factual work; indeed, the presidential memoirs at issue in *Harper & Row* case are best described as factual, yet the Supreme Court rejected the fair use doctrine. The courts have recognized that there are "gradations" among various types of factual works, some of which are more "expressive" than others. Although President Ford's book was factual in nature, the Supreme Court pointed out that *The Nation*'s excerpt contained "the most expressive elements" of the work, including the former president's "subjective descriptions and portraits of public figures whose power lies in the author's individualized expression."

The "substantiality" factor focuses on the extent of the defendant's copying. As a general rule, one could say that the likelihood of a successful fair use defense decreases as the amount of copying increases. The guidelines of major book publishers provide a hint as to how much copying is "fair." One publisher warns authors to credit all sources and to obtain permission if more than 200 words of a work are used. Another publisher sets the maximum at 400 words. Both, however, emphasize that these limits are cumulative; that is, six selections of eighty words each would be 480 words. But what if one uses 200 or 400 words of a 500 word poem? Since that would plainly be excessive, the publishers also state that authors should not use more than five percent of someone else's work without obtaining permission. Further, permission should be secured for reproducing any portion of a work of fewer than 200 words, such as a song or poem.

In the *Rosemont Enterprises* case, the 300-page Random House book had quoted two passages from a *Look* magazine article about Howard Hughes and had paraphrased another, attributing the material to the magazine on each occasion. The court concluded that the copying was minimal. Sheer numbers tell only part of the story, however, for quality can be just as important as quantity. In *Harper & Row*, for example, the material taken verbatim from the Ford memoirs amounted to about thirteen percent of *The Nation*'s article and constituted only a tiny percentage of the book. However, the court emphasized that the quoted portions were "among the most powerful passages" that could be described as "the heart of the book."

Employing the same approach, the Second Circuit found that the copying in *Salinger* was substantial because the material from the unpublished letters formed "an important ingredient" of the book and "[t]o a large extent [made it] worth reading." There the defendant had used about one-third of seventeen letters and at least ten percent of forty-two others. Material quoted or paraphrased from the letters appeared on about forty percent of the book's 192 pages.

According to the Supreme Court, the fourth factor, impact on the market, is "the single most important element of fair use." In *Harper & Row*, that impact was obvious, for *The Nation*'s "scoop" led to *Time*'s cancellation of its plans to publish excerpts from the Ford book. In most cases, however, a copyright owner will not be able to establish market impairment with that degree of certainty. Recognizing this problem, the courts have ruled that the plaintiff must show only that some meaningful likelihood of harm exists. For example, the court in the *Wainwright* case found that the defendant's use of the plaintiff's financial reports "was blatantly self-serving, with the obvious intent, if not the effect, of fulfilling the demand for the original work." In fact, the defendant's own advertising promised readers "a fast-reading, pinpointed account of heavy-weight reports from the top institutional research firms." In the court's view, the plaintiff's clients would probably be unwilling to pay for analyses that were printed almost verbatim in the defendant's newspaper.

Moreover, the copyright owner need demonstrate only that the defendant's unauthorized use would adversely affect the *potential* market for the copyrighted work. There is no better example of this principle than the *Salinger* case, in which the court found such an impact even though Salinger had disavowed any intention of publishing the letters in his lifetime. Because the novelist is always free to change his mind, the Copyright Act protects his opportunity to sell those letters, which, according to expert testimony, could fetch as much as $500,000. Although publication of a book relying heavily on Salinger's letters would not "displace the market for the letters," the court said, "some impairment of the market seems likely."

In contrast, the Supreme Court ruled in the *Sony* case that the copyright owners had not established the likelihood of potential future harm from home recording of television programs for noncommercial "time-shifting" purposes. The plaintiffs had put together a parade of horribles that would presumably follow from unrestricted home taping, including a distortion of the television "ratings" system for measuring audience, a decreasing audience for "live" television and movies and a corresponding decline in revenues, and a drop in the demand for television re-runs. The trial court had rejected these arguments, observing that "[h]arm from time-shifting is speculative and, at best, minimal." For example, the court pointed out that the ratings system takes time-shifting into account and that home recording should actually increase rather than decrease the viewing audience. The Supreme Court agreed, concluding that the plaintiffs had "failed to demonstrate that time-shifting would cause any likelihood of non-minimal harm to the potential market for, or the value of, their copyrighted works."

Even though *Sony* involved noncommercial use, a plaintiff may be unable to show potential market impact when the infringing use is commercial. For example, in *Triangle Publications, Inc. v. Knight-Ridder Newspapers, Inc.* (1980), the *Miami Herald* reproduced covers from *TV Guide* magazine in advertisements for the newspaper's own television publication. Not surprisingly, *TV Guide* was less than pleased with this tactic and brought an infringement action based on the *Herald*'s use of the copyrighted covers. Although the U.S. Court of Appeals for the Fifth Circuit agreed with *TV Guide* that the *Herald*'s purpose was commercial, it concluded that the use of the covers had no impact on the market or potential market for the copyrighted material. "To be sure, the *Herald*'s advertisements may have had the effect of drawing customers away from *TV Guide*," the court said. "But this results from the nature of advertising itself and in no way stems from the fact that *TV Guide* covers were used." The court also noted that the covers themselves, the only part of *TV Guide* used in the advertisements, were not substitutes for the entire magazine. "It is difficult to believe that anyone purchases the magazine simply to ponder the cover," the court said.

Mechanics: Notice and Registration

The 1988 amendments to the Copyright Act of 1976 necessary to enable the United States to join the Berne Convention made significant changes in the manner in which copyright protection is secured. Prior to these amendments, a published work in which a copyright was claimed had to carry a copyright notice—such as the familiar "C in a circle" symbol—in order to be protected. Moreover, registration of one's work with the U.S. Copyright Office was a prerequisite to a lawsuit for copyright infringement. These notice and registration requirements were inconsistent with the Berne Convention, which states that "the enjoyment and the exercise [of copyright] shall not be subject to any formality." Under the amended statute, notice is no longer mandatory and the registration provisions are inapplicable to works whose country of origin is a foreign nation adhering to the Berne Convention.

Notice. As amended, Section 401 of the Copyright Act provides that a notice of copyright "may be placed on publicly distributed copies from which the work can be visually perceived. . . ." If such a notice is utilized, it must contain: the symbol ©, the word "Copyright," or the abbreviation "Copr."; the year of the first publication of the work (unnecessary for some items, such as greeting cards, postcards and stationery); and the name of the copyright owner. Section 401 also provides that the notice is to be "affixed to the copies in such manner and location as to give reasonable notice of the claim of copyright." Copyright Office regulations offer examples of suitable placement, though other methods may suffice. For instance, the notice may be placed below the nameplate of a periodical, on the title page of a book, or on the back of a photograph or its mounting. Special rules govern sound recordings. Under Section 402 of the act, a different symbol—the letter "P" in a circle—may be placed on the record itself, its label, or its container, along with the year of first publication and the name of the copyright owner. If, however, no name appears other than that of the producer, the producer's name is considered a part of the notice.

Although notice is no longer mandatory, it is recommended. As the Senate Report accompanying the 1988 amendments pointed out, the placement of notice on publicly distributed copies of works "alerts users to the fact that copyright is claimed in the work in question, and may prevent many instances of unintentional infringement." Accordingly, Congress amended Sections 401 and 402 to provide an incentive for use of the notice: a copyright owner who places a proper notice on published copies of the work can prevent a defendant in an infringement suit who had access to such copies from attempting to mitigate damages on the ground that the infringement was innocent. If there is no such notice, a court has discretion under Section 504 of the act to reduce statutory damages to a sum of not less than $200 if it believes the infringement was innocent. As noted previously, a court may award statutory damages of up to $100,000 even though the plaintiff's actual losses are not that great or cannot be proved with certainty. Thus, the ability to preclude mitigation of such damages is a strong incentive for a copyright owner to employ the appropriate notice.

The elimination of mandatory notice marks a significant change in American copyright law. Prior to the Copyright Act of 1976, omission of the notice had rather dire consequences. Publication without notice, one court said, "amounts to a dedication of the work to the public sufficient to defeat all subsequent efforts at copyright protection." The 1976 statute took a less harsh approach by providing that the omission of the notice could be "cured" if registration were obtained within five years of publication and good faith efforts were made to affix the notice to all remaining copies of the work. Even if these steps were taken, however, the owner could not recover damages from the innocent infringer who relied in good faith on the lack of notice. These provisions of the 1976 act, as well as a similar section allowing one to cure errors in the name and date of a notice, continue to apply with respect to copies publicly distributed prior to March 1, 1989, the effective date of the 1988 amendments.

Registration. Under Section 102 of the Copyright Act, an author is automatically protected from the time that he has "fixed [the work] in any tangible medium of expression"—that is, from the moment that it is created. Registration of a claim of copyright with the Copyright Office is not technically a condition of copyright protection unless it is made to cure the omission of or an error in the notice as described above. However, the failure to register has a profound consequence: under Section 411(a) of the act, a suit for copyright infringement cannot be brought "until the registration of the copyright claim has been made," unless the Copyright Office has refused registration. As a result, compliance with the act's registration procedures is ordinarily a prerequisite to the right of the author or other copyright owner to seek redress for infringement of the work.

Section 411(a) is subject to an important exception: as amended in 1988, it does not apply to works whose country of origin is a foreign nation adhering to the Berne Convention. As a result of the amendment, infringement suits may be brought with respect to such works even if they have never been submitted for registration with the Copyright Office. All other works—including those of U.S. origin—are covered by Section 411(a). Creation of this two-tier system was necessary to eliminate a barrier to the United States' participation in the Berne Convention, since the registration prerequisite for foreign works was considered a "formality" of the type prohibited by the treaty.

Even if a work falls within the exception to Section 411(a), registration is advisable for two reasons. First, the issuance of a certificate of registration by the Copyright Office within five years of the first publication of the work is *prima facie* evidence of copyright validity and ownership. Accordingly, registration works to the advantage of the copyright owner in the event of litigation. Second, only the owners of registered works are entitled to statutory damages and an award of attorney's fees in infringement suits. Thus, a copyright owner who has not registered is limited to a recovery of actual damages stemming from the infringement. Because such losses may be difficult to prove, the availability of statutory damages can be quite important in infringement litigation. It is therefore anticipated that a substantial number of copyright owners who are not required to register as a result of the 1988 amendments will nonetheless do so voluntarily.

Registration is secured by sending $10 and the appropriate form to the Copyright Office at the Library of Congress in Washington, D.C. Two copies of the "best edition" of a published work and one copy of an unpublished work must also be "deposited" with the office. An individual author may take advantage of "group registration," a system that allows a writer to register up to a year's worth of articles published in various newspapers or magazines for only $10. This procedure is not available to publishers; accordingly, a news organization wishing to copyright each issue of its daily newspaper must pay $3,650 each year in registration fees. Periodical publishers can obtain relief from the deposit requirement, however. Instead of sending two copies of each issue, the publisher can arrange with the Copyright Office to deposit microfilm or microfiche on a quarterly basis. There are also special rules for other situations; for example, only one copy of a motion picture or television program is required, and photographs of three-dimensional works such as sculpture are to be submitted.

Duration

One of the major changes brought about by the Copyright Act of 1976 was the increase in the duration of copyright protection. Under the 1909 statute, such protection began on the date of publication and lasted twenty-eight years. The copyright could then be renewed for another twenty-eight year period, after which the work passed into the public domain. The 1976 act created a very different scheme. Generally speaking, copyright protection for works created on or after January 1, 1978, begins upon the work's creation and extends for fifty years past the death of the author. Works created prior to that date, however, are governed by the old method. The change brought U.S. law into conformity with international practice, since most nations use the "life-plus-fifty" formula.

As one might expect, there are exceptions to the duration rule. For example, works by joint authors are protected for fifty years past the death of the last surviving author. There is also special treatment for works "made for hire," those created "on the job" or with the express understanding that the person who commissions the work will own the copyright. (This doctrine, which has significant implications for freelancers, is discussed below.) The copyright for such a work expires seventy-five years from the year of first publication or one hundred years from the year of creation, whichever comes first. The same rule applies to anonymous or pseudonymous works; if, however, the author's identity is revealed before expiration of the copyright term, the "life-plus-fifty" rule comes into play.

SPECIAL ISSUES

The 1976 Copyright Act was the culmination of twenty years of study and work by the Copyright Office and the Congress. In tackling the outdated 1909 statute, reformers had to come to grips not only with various problems that had arisen under the old law, but also with the amazing technological developments of the past few decades. Because many of the changes embodied in the 1976 statute have a direct impact on the mass media, they are worth brief examination here. Specifically, we will focus on the "work-for-hire" doctrine and its implications for freelance writers and photographers; the "compulsory license" rules that affect broadcasters, cable television, and "superstations"; and various requirements that have had an important impact in the music business.

The Work-for-Hire Doctrine

The question of copyright ownership is of critical importance to the freelance writer or photographer. Under the 1976 Copyright Act, ownership rests with the author of the work from the point of its creation, unless he sells his rights to someone else. There is an important exception to this principle, however. In certain circumstances the act treats the author's employer or the person who commissions the work as the author for copyright purposes. This is known as the "work-for-hire" doctrine, a concept based on the notion that the work would not have come into existence without the economic support made available to the creator.

Section 101 of the Copyright Act defines a "work made for hire" as a work "prepared by an employee within the scope of his or her employment" or a work "specially ordered or commissioned for use as a contribution to a collective work . . . if the parties expressly agree in a written instrument signed by them that the work shall be considered a work made for hire." The first part of the statute clearly covers regular employees and the works they create "on the job." If, for example, a newspaper staff photographer assigned to cover a fire takes an award-winning photo, the newspaper—not the photographer—owns the copyright and may thus "sell" the picture to a national news magazine. By the same token, the photographer could not publish the photo elsewhere without the newspaper's permission. It is possible to vary these rules by contract; for instance, the newspaper and the photographer might agree that the photographer may sell to other publications any photos he produces on company time after initial publication in the newspaper.

Although the term "employee" is not defined in the act, it plainly covers salaried workers. Under certain circumstances, however, persons who do not work on a salaried basis—such as freelance writers and photographers—can be considered employees for copyright purposes. In *Community for Creative Non-Violence v. Reid* (1989), the U.S. Supreme Court ruled that the common law of agency must be consulted in determining whether such an individual is an employee.

Relevant factors include the hiring party's right to control the manner and means by which the work is done; the extent of the worker's discretion over when and how long to work; the duration of the relationship between the parties; the skill required to do the work; the source of any necessary instruments and tools; the location of the work; the method of payment; the provision of employee benefits; the tax treatment of the worker by the hiring party; and whether the work is part of the hiring party's regular business. This list is not exhaustive, and no single factor is determinative.

The *Reid* case arose when an organization dedicated to eliminating homelessness hired a sculptor to produce a statue depicting the plight of the homeless. Applying the agency principles noted above, the Supreme Court concluded that the sculptor was not an employee but an independent contractor. Although the organization had exercised some control over the sculptor to ensure that the finished product met its specifications, the other circumstances weighed against a finding that the sculptor was an employee. The Court pointed out that the sculptor was a skilled craftsman who furnished his own tools, worked in his own studio, and had complete freedom to decide when and how long to work. In addition, the organization paid the sculptor in a lump sum upon completion of the two-month project (as is typical with respect to independent contractors), did not withhold social security or payroll taxes, and provided no employee benefits. Obviously, sculpting was not part of the organization's regular business.

If a worker is not an employee, the work-for-hire doctrine applies only if two statutory conditions are met. First, the work must be "specially ordered or commissioned" as a "contribution to a collective work" (such as a newspaper or magazine), as part of a motion picture or other audiovisual work, or for certain other purposes. Second, there must be a written agreement, signed by the parties, that the work is "for hire." This part of the statute was not applicable in *Reid*, since the sculpture was not a "collective work" and did not fall within any of the other statutory categories. Moreover, there was no written agreement between the sculptor and the organization that commissioned the statue.

This aspect of the work-for-hire doctrine is of great importance to freelance writers and photographers whose work typically appears in newspapers and magazines. A freelancer who is not considered an employee retains the copyright in the work unless there is a specific "work-for-hire" provision in a contract between the freelancer and a publisher. Absent such an agreement, the freelancer is selling to the publisher only the right to publish the material one time. All other rights, including ownership of the copyright, remain with the freelancer. For example, suppose that a freelance writer sells a feature story to a magazine and that there is no "work-for-hire" agreement. The story attracts considerable attention in Hollywood, and a major studio wants to use it as the basis for a major film. Who owns the copyright and is thus in a position to benefit from the sale of movie rights? The writer, not the magazine.

Keep in mind, however, that the freelancer and the publisher may agree contractually to other arrangements. For example, a publisher may attempt to require a freelancer to sign a contract expressly relinquishing copyright ownership to the publisher. Writers or photographers without a "track record" may have little choice but to accept these conditions in order to get their material published, since the publisher has the upper hand in terms of bargaining power. But experienced freelancers whose work is in demand are in a position to resist such provisions and can thus retain copyright ownership and most rights for their own benefit. It is imperative, therefore, that the freelancer understand the terms of the contract.

A common arrangement gives the publisher "first North American serial rights." This means that the publisher purchases the right to use the article or photograph before anyone else in North America. The freelancer owns all other rights and, after publication, may sell the material to someone else. If the contract specifies "first serial rights," the publisher has the right of first publication anywhere in the world. Some publishers add other conditions that place time limits on the freelancer's subsequent sale of the material. For instance, a contract might give the publisher "first North American serial rights" but also provide that the freelancer may not sell the same story or photograph for one year after publication.

Broadcasting and Cable

The "Betamax" case discussed previously is a perfect example of how advancing technology has outstripped the law of copyright. In adopting the revised Copyright Act in 1976, Congress simply did not anticipate the widespread availability of video cassette equipment that would allow "home taping." Copyright problems stemming from technological developments are nothing new; broadcasters and cable operators, for example, have been at each other's throats since the inception of cable in the early 1950s.

Cable originated because many communities could not receive over-the-air broadcast signals, either because they were too far away from the major cities that had television stations or were located in mountainous areas where reception was poor. The cable systems simply retransmitted the programming carried by television stations, thus providing subscribers with higher quality television pictures or stations they would have not otherwise been able to watch at all. Although broadcasters had to pay royalties to copyright owners for programs they telecast, such as movies or game shows, cable operators paid nothing for retransmitting those programs. Moreover, the cable operators did not compensate broadcasters who produced their own copyrighted programming.

Litigation ensued, with the broadcasters and copyright owners taking the position that cable operators were guilty of copyright infringement. The Supreme Court rejected this argument, ruling in *Fortnightly Corp. v. United Artists Television, Inc.* (1968) that a cable system's retransmission of local television signals was not a "performance" and thus was not protected under the 1909 Copyright Act. Six years later, the Court reached the same result in *Teleprompter Corp. v. Columbia Broadcasting System* with respect to so-called "distant signals" (i.e., those that cannot be received locally without cable). Though the Court recognized the economic implications of its decisions, it concluded that "any ultimate resolution of the many sensitive and important problems in this field . . . must be left to Congress."

In enacting Section 111 of the Copyright Act of 1976, Congress determined that copyright owners should share in the substantial revenues generated by cable operators. At the same time, however, Congress realized that negotiations between the copyright owners and the individual cable systems would be an administrative nightmare. The response was a new scheme under which a cable operator has a "compulsory license" to retransmit to its customers any programs carried by a broadcast station without the consent of the copyright owners. In return, however, the cable operator must pay a fee that serves as a substitute for the copyright royalties which might have been negotiated by a copyright owner and a cable system on an individual basis. The fees are paid into a "royalty fund" and are distributed to the copyright owners under a complex formula developed by the Copyright Royalty Tribunal, a federal administrative agency. For example, seventy-five percent of the fees generated is distributed among program syndicators and movie producers, twelve percent goes to sports leagues, and only three and a half percent is allocated to television broadcasters.

Section 111 draws an important distinction between the signals of local and distant television stations. Cable operators need not pay fees for copyrighted programs on stations that are considered "local" under rules adopted by the Federal Communications Commission. However, fees are required if a station from a distant community is carried by the system, with the amount determined by the number of "distant signals" that are retransmitted and the status of those stations as network affiliates or "independent" stations. As a result, many cable systems are reluctant to carry more than two distant independent stations, since the addition of other nonlocal stations can increase significantly a cable operator's copyright liability. For example, several systems dropped one or more of the "superstations" from their lineups in 1983 when the Copyright Royalty Tribunal raised the rates that must be paid for distant signals. Thus, the Copyright Act has a direct impact on the choice of programming available to cable subscribers.

The superstations have presented other copyright difficulties. One such problem is illustrated by *Eastern Microwave, Inc. v. Doubleday Sports, Inc.* (1982), which arose from a dispute between the owners of the New York Mets baseball team and a common carrier that made available to cable systems the superstation that carried the Mets' games. Doubleday Sports, owner of the Mets, had sold the broadcast rights to about 100 Mets' games per season to WOR-TV, whose signal Eastern Microwave delivered to cable systems across the country via satellite and microwave links. Doubleday earned royalties from its broadcast contract with WOR and from the cable systems under the fee system described above. However, neither Doubleday nor WOR received anything from Eastern Microwave, which "sold" the station—and thus the Mets' games—to cable operators.

Doubleday obviously thought that Eastern Microwave was getting a free ride, much like cable operators prior to 1976. But, just as Section 111 of the Copyright Act deals with retransmission of broadcast signals by cable systems, it contains a provision covering retransmission by common carriers. Under Section 111, such a retransmission is not copyright infringement if the carrier "has no direct or indirect control over the content or selection of the [broadcast signal] or over the recipients of the . . . transmission." Doubleday, however, argued that Eastern Microwave did not meet these criteria because it exercised "control" by choosing WOR's signal for retransmission. In support of this argument, Doubleday pointed out that Eastern Microwave could have transmitted the signals of other stations but chose WOR in large part because the Mets' games made the station more "marketable" to cable systems. A federal court in New York ruled in the Mets' favor, but the U.S. Court of Appeals for the Second Circuit reversed. Even though Eastern Microwave selected WOR for retransmission, the court said, it did not pick and choose among WOR's programs but passively retransmitted everything that WOR aired. Thus, Eastern Microwave did not exercise impermissible "control" over the signal that it was retransmitting.

Moreover, the Second Circuit concluded that Doubleday's interpretation of Section 111 would upset the "compulsory license" scheme established by Congress. "That scheme is predicated on and presupposes a continuing ability of [cable] systems to receive signals for distribution to their subscribers," the court said. Eastern Microwave's position as a link in that chain would be jeopardized if the company were forced to negotiate individually with all of the copyright owners whose programs were carried on WOR. Imposing this burden on these intermediate carriers "would strangle [cable] systems by choking off their life line to their supply of programs . . . and would frustrate the . . . compulsory licensing program."

Another copyright problem involving superstations, recently addressed by legislation, stemmed from home satellite "dishes." Virtually unknown when the Copyright Act of 1976 was passed, these devices now number approximately two million. The Cable Communications Policy Act of 1984 permitted common carriers to "scramble" the signals of superstations—network affiliates as well as independents such as WGN and WTBS—and market them to individual dish owners. However, the carriers' copyright liability in that situation remained unclear. Specifically, the carriers were concerned that they would not be allowed to claim the protection of the "passive carrier" exemption involved in *Eastern Microwave* if they actively marketed superstation signals by making available descrambling devices and then charging dish owners a monthly fee.

Congress dealt with this issue in the Satellite Home Viewer Act of 1988, which automatically "sunsets" after six years. The act creates a temporary compulsory licensing system under which carriers that market scrambled superstation signals pay copyright royalty fees based on the number of subscribers who receive those signals. The fees are set by statute for the first four years and are then to be determined by negotiation and binding arbitration. Although the signals of independent superstations such as WTBS and WGN can be marketed to any dish owner, those of network affiliates can be delivered only to households in "white areas" where viewers cannot pick up network signals with a conventional rooftop antenna. This restriction on the marketing of network superstations was considered necessary to protect local network affiliates.

The Music Business

Prior to the growth of the recording industry fueled by the rock and roll explosion of the 1950s, music publishers made most of their money selling sheet music, deriving other revenues from live performances and, later, from radio play. Today, however, music publishing revenues come primarily from so-called "mechanical royalties" based on use of songs on phonograph records, tape cassettes, and compact discs. Fees paid for the playing of recorded music on radio and television are also important, as are royalties for the use of music in movies and commercials.

The copyright system has also changed with the times; prior to 1972, for example, phonograph records were not protected at all by copyright law, which meant that record piracy was a major problem. A record company could simply copy the records of a competitor and market them under its own label, since the law required only that a small statutory fee be paid to the composer. The performers who recorded the material and the company that originally produced the record had no copyright interest, and they received nothing from the "pirates."

Under the present law, one must distinguish among the underlying musical composition, the sound recording, and the record itself (i.e., the physical object). All are copyrightable, but different rules apply to each. With respect to the composition, a songwriter is treated the same as any other author for copyright purposes, with one major exception. Once the songwriter (or the copyright owner, usually a music publishing company) authorizes someone to record a composition, he cannot deny the same privilege to others. Under this compulsory license scheme, a record company must pay the copyright owner "mechanical royalties" under a formula established by the Copyright Royalty Tribunal. For records made and distributed after January 1, 1988, for example, the royalty is either 5.25 cents or 1 cent per minute of playing time, whichever is larger, for each record sold. The royalty is subject to adjustment every two years, based on the Consumer Price Index, but in no event will it fall below 5 cents or .95 cent per minute of playing time, whichever is larger.

The copyright owner of a musicial composition is also entitled to royalties for any public performance of the work, including its broadcast by television or radio.

These royalties are collected for the copyright owners by so-called "performing rights" organizations, the best known of which are the American Society of Composers, Authors and Publishers (ASCAP), and Broadcast Music, Inc. (BMI). In 1983, for example, ASCAP collected approximately $200 million in performance fees, while BMI collected about $125 million. Though the percentages for each organization vary slightly, more than forty percent of the fees are generated by television and more than a third by radio. Other sources of income include concerts and the playing of recorded "background" music in restaurants and bars.

The royalties are distributed to the copyright owners in accordance with extremely complex formulae developed by the organizations. In the case of radio, for example, BMI charges radio stations an annual fee based on the stations' gross receipts. It then pays songwriters and publishers for each time a song is played on the air. The amount of that payment is determined by multiplying the number of times the song is played by a "base rate" that varies according the annual fee paid by the station. In addition, a bonus is paid when certain levels of cumulative performances are attained; for example, in 1984 BMI paid four times the base rate for songs that had been played more than a million times. There are more than 350 songs in this category.

Prior to the 1988 amendments to the Copyright Act, a compulsory license governed performance rights and jukebox operators. Under a system adopted in 1976, jukebox owners—who paid no royalties under the 1909 statute—were required to pay an annual fee per jukebox into a fund administered by the Copyright Royalty Tribunal, which also set the amount of the fee. The Tribunal then distributed the proceeds to copyright owners of the songs, either directly or through one of the performing rights organizations. This scheme was jettisoned in 1988 because it conflicted with the Berne Convention. Under the new law, copyright owners and jukebox operators are free to negotiate their own royalty and licensing agreements and, if necessary, to settle their differences by arbitration. Until the parties reach an agreement, the annual fee in place on March 1, 1989—$63 per jukebox—remains effective. If the parties cannot agree, the Tribunal is authorized to institute a compulsory arrangement.

Copyright in a sound recording is not the same as copyright in the underlying musical composition that is recorded. A sound recording is defined by the Copyright Act as a work "that result[s] from the fixation of a series of musical, spoken, or other sounds, but not including the sounds accompanying a motion picture or other audiovisual work." Generally, copyright protection extends to two elements in a sound recording: the contribution of the person whose performance is captured on the recording, and the contribution of the record producer who processes the sounds and fixes them in the final recording. The performer and producer, who are considered the "authors" for copyright purposes, are protected against the unauthorized reproduction and distribution of the sounds by "pirates." However, the owner of the copyright in a sound recording cannot prevent others from recording the same music or from making records that imitate the copyrighted version.

In stark contrast to the owner of the copyright of the underlying composition, one who copyrights a sound recording does not have any performance rights that entitle him to receive royalties when it is played on a broadcast station or a jukebox. This means that record producers and musicians do not share in the economic pie produced by performances that is now divided between music publishers and songwriters. In the hearings that led to the Copyright Act of 1976, Congress considered the arguments in favor of establishing a limited performance right, in the form of a compulsory license, for copyrighted sound recordings but concluded that the problem required additional study.

Finally, the tangible record itself is copyrightable. In contrast to a sound recording, a "phonorecord" is the physical object in which the sound recording has become fixed. The term includes audio cassettes and compact discs as well as the traditional phonograph record. Here the "author" for copyright purposes is the manufacturer of the record, who has the right to prevent others from duplicating it.

PROBLEMS

1. The dichotomy between facts or ideas and the form in which they are expressed is central to copyright law. Is it always possible to separate the two? Consider the famous "Zapruder film" of the assassination of President John F. Kennedy. Abraham Zapruder, a businessman, happened to record the tragic events of November 22, 1963, with a home movie camera. Time, Inc. paid him $150,000 for exclusive rights to the film and published several blown-up frames in *Life* magazine. Subsequently, a publisher sought permission to use still photos from the film in a book about the assassination. When Time, Inc. refused, the publisher used drawings said to be "exact copies" of frames from the film. A suit for copyright infringement followed. What result? *See Time, Inc. v. Bernard Geis Associates*, 293 F. Supp. 130 (S.D.N.Y. 1968).

2. Recall that the *Eastern Microwave* case involved a dispute over royalties for broadcasts of major league baseball games. Is a baseball game copyrightable? If so, who owns the copyright? The ball clubs? The players? Apart from the game iself, is the telecast copyrightable? Does the fact that the efforts of a director, several camera operators, and others arc necessary have any bearing on your analysis? *See Baltimore Orioles, Inc. v. Major League Baseball Players Association*, 805 F.2d 663 (7th Cir. 1986), *cert. denied*, 480 U.S. 941 (1987).

3. The widespread use of the photocopying machine has caused copyright headaches. For example, in *Williams & Wilkins Co. v. United States*, 487 F.2d 1345 (Ct. Cl. 1973), *aff'd by an equally divided court*, 420 U.S. 376 (1975), the U.S. Court of Claims ruled that the National Institutes of Health had not infringed on the plaintiffs' copyrights by making thousands of copies of articles from medical journals, reasoning that the public interest in medical research outweighed the rights of the publishers. To what extent can such copying be "fair use" under Section 107 of the Copyright Act? What about photocopies made by teachers for research or for classroom use? *See* House Report No. 94–1476, 94th Cong., 2d Sess., pp. 66–74 (September 3, 1976). May a library make a photocopy of a book or periodical, or must it purchase a copy from the publisher? Does a library contribute to infringement by making a photocopying machine available for library patrons? *See* Section 108 of the Copyright Act.

4. Evaluate the following cases under the fair use doctrine:
   a. The day after Charlie Chaplin's death in 1977, CBS broadcast a documentary about the actor that included clips from several of his greatest films. This footage was taken from a videotape of NBC's broadcast of the 1973 Academy Awards, which featured a special tribute to Chaplin and scenes from several copyrighted movies. NBC had secured one-time rights to use this material. CBS, however, did not obtain permission from the copyright owner to use the footage and had in the past been denied such permission. Some of Chaplin's movies were in the public domain, and prior to his

death CBS had put together some of this material for possible use in a documentary. *See Roy Export Co. v. CBS*, 672 F.2d 1095 (2d Cir.), *cert. denied*, 459 U.S. 826 (1982).

  b. On July 19, 1988, Presidential candidate Jesse Jackson delivered a dramatic address at the Democratic National Convention in Atlanta. The speech was carried live by ABC, CBS, NBC, and CNN. A few days after the convention, MPI Home Video obtained a license to use the ABC news tape of the speech and began marketing a video casette containing the network's coverage. The packaging of the casette featured a photograph of Jackson, his name, two quotations from the address, and a reference to his "stirring Democratic National Committee speech, uncut and unedited." Jackson was not consulted about the project. *See Jackson v. MPI Home Video*, 694 F. Supp. 483 (N.D. Ill. 1988).

  c. Carolyn Duncan started a business called "TV News Clips." Her idea was to videotape the news programs of local television stations and sell copies to people and groups who had been subjects of news stories. Ms. Duncan sold a junior college a tape of a news feature about the school's physical fitness and jogging trail. The story had appeared on WXIA-TV in Atlanta, which copyrighted its news broadcasts. However, the station did not market its own clips and in fact erased its videotapes of the newscasts after seven days. *See Pacific & Southern Co. v. Duncan*, 744 F.2d 1490 (11th Cir. 1984), *cert. denied*, 471 U.S. 1004 (1985).

5. In a "Saturday Night Live" skit, the town leaders of Sodom discussed plans to improve their city's image. At the end of the skit, the actors sang "I Love Sodom" to the tune of "I Love New York," the theme song of a New York City promotional campaign. The copyright owner of "I Love New York" brought an infringement action. To what extent is parody and satire a good defense? *See Elsmere Music, Inc. v. NBC*, 482 F. Supp. 741 (S.D.N.Y.), *aff'd*, 623 F.2d 252 (2d Cir. 1980). *See also Walt Disney Productions v. Air Pirates*, 581 F.2d 751 (9th Cir. 1978), *cert. denied*, 439 U.S. 1132 (1979).

6. In 1985, Ford Motor Company aired a series of television advertisements using popular songs of the 1970s in an attempt to appeal to "yuppies." When Ford's advertising agency was unable to obtain permission to use the hit versions of the songs by the "original artists," it paid "sound-alikes" to record new versions. Bette Midler refused to allow use of her recording of "Do You Want To Dance," and the ad agency hired one of her former backup singers to record the song for the commercial and to "sound as much as possible like the Bette Midler record." Neither Midler's name nor picture was used in the commercial. Midler brought suit, claiming that Ford impermissibly imitated her voice. Can she succeed on a theory of copyright infringement? On some other theory? *See Midler v. Ford Motor Co.*, 849 F.2d 460 (9th Cir. 1988).

7. A process called "digital sampling" allows one to record a sound and encode it in the memory of a computer. A synthesizer can then be used to reproduce the sound. Suppose a record producer "samples" a few choice guitar licks from Eric Clapton during a recording session, without his knowledge, and uses them in music created for a television program or movie soundtrack. Is Clapton's "sound" copyrightable? If so, has the producer actually copied the sound, or has he simply imitated it through computer technology? Does this case differ from *Midler v. Ford Motor Co.*? Would the work for hire doctrine have any relevance in this situation? *See* Jessica D. Litman, "Performers' Rights and Digital Sampling under U.S. and Japanese Law," *Law Quadrangle Notes* (University of Michigan, Winter 1988), p. 37.

8. Newspaper A and Newspaper B are competitors. Newspaper A published an advertisement for a customer, the ad copy and layout having been prepared by employees in the

newspaper's advertising department and approved by the customer. Shortly thereafter, the customer decided to advertise in Newspaper B, which lacked the staff and equipment to compose advertisements. With the permission of the customer, Newspaper B simply reproduced the ad that had run in Newspaper A. Each edition of Newspaper A is copyrighted, with the appropriate notice appearing under the paper's nameplate on page one. Newspaper A brought a copyright infringement action against Newspaper B. What result? Why? *See Brunswick Beacon, Inc. v. Schock-Hopchas Publishing Co.*, 810 F.2d 410 (4th Cir. 1987).

9. An important feature of the Berne Convention is its recognition of the doctrine of "moral rights." Under this concept, the author of a work has the right to claim authorship (the "right of paternity") and the right to object to any distortion, mutilation, or other modification of the work that would prejudice his reputation (the "right of integrity"). Although the 1988 amendments to the Copyright Act do not specifically address moral rights, congressional reports accompanying the legislation take the position that other American legal doctrines—including the law of defamation, the right to publicity, state statutes, and Section 43(a) of the Lanham Act—satisfy the requirements of the Berne Convention in this regard. *See, e.g., Gilliam v. American Broadcasting Companies, Inc.*, 538 F.2d 14 (2d Cir. 1976)(recognizing remedy under Section 43(a) where ABC heavily edited three "Monty Python" programs originally broadcast in Great Britain by the BBC); California Art Preservation Act, Cal. Civil Code § 987 (prohibiting intentional destruction or alteration of work of fine art by anyone other than the creating artist who owns and possesses the work). Moreover, the reports specifically state that the 1988 amendments are not meant to "change, reduce, or expand existing U.S. law" in this area.

It is safe to say, however, that "existing U.S. law" is not particularly clear and that various questions are unresolved. Indeed, some provisions of the Copyright Act itself seem to conflict with a broad notion of "moral rights." For example, is the first sale doctrine, which extinguishes the copyright owner's ability to control subsequent sales or alteration of the work, at odds with the right to integrity? To what extent does the work-for-hire doctrine, under which a copyright is owned by the author's employer, conflict with the right to paternity? Is the right of integrity offended if a magazine editor heavily edits an employee's article? If the executive producer of a motion picture deletes various scenes that the director considers essential to the film? Could the doctrine of fair use be employed to limit moral rights? *See* Roberta R. Kwall, "Copyright and the Moral Right: Is an American Marriage Possible?" 38 *Vanderbilt Law Review* 1 (1985).

Controversy over the scope of the moral rights doctrine is particularly acute in the film industry. If, for example, a writer authorizes a motion picture company to produce a movie based on his play (a "derivative work"), can he complain if the final product is a film that departs substantially from the play? Should the director of a black-and-white film be able to prevent its subsequent colorization? *See,* Note, "An Author's Artistic Reputation Under the Copyright Act of 1976," 79 *Harvard Law Review* 1490 (1979); Note, "The Colorization of Black and White Films: An Example of the Lack of Substantive Protection for Art in the United States," 63 *Notre Dame Law Review* 309 (1988).

CHAPTER

5

NEWSGATHERING AND ACCESS TO INFORMATION

Pell v. Procunier,
417 U.S. 817 (1974).

MR. JUSTICE STEWART delivered the opinion of the Court.

These cases are here on cross-appeals from the judgment of a three-judge District Court in the Northern District of California. * * * The plaintiffs brought suit to challenge the constitutionality, under the First and Fourteenth Amendments, of §415.071 of the California Department of Corrections Manual, which provides that "[p]ress and other media interviews with specific individual inmates will not be permitted." * * * Section 415.071 . . . is applied throughout the State's penal system to prohibit face-to-face interviews between press representatives and individual inmates whom they specifically name and request to interview.

* * * The inmate plaintiffs contended that §415.071 violates their rights of free speech under the First and Fourteenth Amendments.

Similarly, the media plaintiffs asserted that the limitation that this regulation places on their newsgathering activity unconstitutionally infringes the freedom of the press guaranteed by the First and Fourteenth Amendments.

The District Court granted the inmate plaintiffs' motion for summary judgment, holding that §415.071, insofar as it prohibited inmates from having face-to-face communication with journalists, unconstitutionally infringed their First and Fourteenth Amendment freedoms. With respect to the claims of the media plaintiffs, the court granted the defendants' motion to dismiss. * * *

I

[In reversing the district court's ruling on the inmates' claim, the Court concluded that security and penological considerations were sufficient to justify the prohibition against face-to-face interviews. After noting that lawful incarceration "brings about the necessary withdrawal of many privileges and rights," Justice Stewart emphasized that "a prison inmate retains those First Amendment rights that are not inconsistent with his status as a prisoner or with the legitimate penological objectives of the corrections system." He also pointed out that prisoners had alternative means to communicate with the press and others outside the prison, including the mail, and that personal visits with family members, friends, attorneys, and clergy were permitted. Given these alternative channels of communication and the legitimate needs of the prison system, Justice Stewart found that the interview ban was a reasonable "time, place and manner" restriction on speech that was justified by a significant governmental interest.]

II

. . . [T]he media plaintiffs ask us to hold that the limitation on press interviews . . . violates the freedom of the press guaranteed by the First and Fourteenth Amendments. They contend that, irrespective of what First Amendment liberties may or may not be retained by prison inmates, members of the press have a constitutional right to interview any inmate who is willing to speak with them, in the absence of an individualized determination that the particular interview might create a clear and present danger to prison security or to some other substantial interest served by the corrections system. In this regard, the media plaintiffs do not claim any impairment of their freedom to publish, for California imposes no restrictions on what may be published about its prisons, the prison inmates, or the officers who administer the prisons. Instead, they rely on their right to gather news without government interference, which the media plaintiffs assert includes a right of access to the sources of what is regarded as newsworthy information.

We note at the outset that this regulation is not part of an attempt by the State to conceal the conditions in its prisons or to frustrate the press' investigation and reporting of those conditions. Indeed, the record demonstrates that, under current corrections policy, both the press and the general public are accorded full opportunities to observe prison conditions. The Department of Corrections regularly conducts public tours through the prisons for the benefit of interested citizens. In addition, newsmen are permitted to visit both the maximum security and minimum security sections of the institutions and to stop and speak about any subject to any inmates whom they might encounter. If security considerations permit, corrections personnel will step aside to permit such interviews to be confidential. Apart from general access to all parts of the institutions, newsmen are also permitted to enter the prisons to interview inmates selected at random by the corrections officials. By the same token, if a newsman wishes to write a story on a particular prison program, he is permitted to sit in on group meetings and to interview the inmate participants. In short, members of the press enjoy access to California prisons that is not available to other members of the public.

The sole limitation on newsgathering in California prisons is the prohibition in §415.071 of interviews with individual inmates specifically designated by representatives of the press. This restriction is of recent vintage, having been imposed in 1971 in response to a violent episode that the Department of Corrections felt was at least partially attributable to the former policy with respect to face-to-face prisoner-press interviews. Prior to the promulgation of §415.071, every journalist had virtually free access to interview any individual inmate whom he might wish. Only members of the press were accorded this privilege; other members of the general public did not have the benefit of such an unrestricted visitation policy. Thus, the promulgation of §415.071 did not impose a discrimination against press access, but merely eliminated a special privilege formerly given to representatives of the press vís-à-vís members of the public generally.

In practice, it was found that the policy in effect prior to the promulgation of §415.071

had resulted in press attention being concentrated on a relatively small number of inmates who, as a result, became virtual "public figures" within the prison society and gained a disproportionate degree of notoriety and influence among their fellow inmates. Because of this notoriety and influence, these inmates often became the source of severe disciplinary problems. For example, extensive press attention to an inmate who espoused a practice of noncooperation with prison regulations encouraged other inmates to follow suit, thus eroding the institutions' ability to deal effectively with the inmates generally. Finally, in the words of the District Court, on August 21, 1971, "[d]uring an escape attempt at San Quentin three staff members and two inmates were killed. This was viewed by the officials as the climax of mounting disciplinary problems caused, in part, by its liberal posture with regard to press interviews, and on August 23 §415.071 was adopted to mitigate the problem." It is against this background that we consider the media plaintiffs' claims under the First and Fourteenth Amendments. * * *

In *Branzburg v. Hayes* (1972), the Court . . . acknowledged that "news gathering is not without its First Amendment protections," for "without some protection for seeking out the news, freedom of the press could be eviscerated." In *Branzburg* the Court held that the First and Fourteenth Amendments were not abridged by requiring reporters to disclose the identity of their confidential sources to a grand jury when that information was needed in the course of a good-faith criminal investigation. The Court there could "perceive no basis for holding that the public interest in law enforcement and in ensuring effective grand jury proceedings [was] insufficient to override the consequential, but uncertain, burden on news gathering that is said to result from insisting that reporters, like other citizens, respond to relevant questions put to them in the course of a valid grand jury investigation or criminal trial."

In this case, the media plaintiffs contend that §415.071 constitutes governmental interference with their newsgathering activities that is neither consequential nor uncertain, and

that no substantial governmental interest can be shown to justify the denial of press access to specifically designated prison inmates. More particularly, the media plaintiffs assert that, despite the substantial access to California prisons and their inmates accorded representatives of the press—access broader than is accorded members of the public generally—face-to-face interviews with specifically designated inmates is such an effective and superior method of newsgathering that its curtailment amounts to unconstitutional state interference with a free press. We do not agree.

"It has generally been held that the First Amendment does not guarantee the press a constitutional right of special access to information not available to the public generally. . . . Despite the fact that news gathering may be hampered, the press is regularly excluded from grand jury proceedings, our own conferences, the meetings of other official bodies gathering in executive session, and the meetings of private organizations. Newsmen have no constitutional right of access to the scenes of crime or disaster when the general public is excluded." *Branzburg v. Hayes, supra*. Similarly, newsmen have no constitutional right of access to prisons or their inmates beyond that afforded the general public.

The First and Fourteenth Amendments bar government from interfering in any way with a free press. The Constitution does not, however, require government to accord the press special access to information not shared by members of the public generally. It is one thing to say that a journalist is free to seek out sources of information not available to members of the general public, that he is entitled to some constitutional protection of the confidentiality of such sources, and that government cannot restrain the publication of news emanating from such sources. It is quite another thing to suggest that the Constitution imposes upon government the affirmative duty to make available to journalists sources of information not available to members of the public generally. That proposition finds no support in the words of the Constitution or in any decision of this Court. Accordingly, since §415.071 does not deny the press access to sources of information available to members of the general public, we hold that it does not abridge the protections that the First and Fourteenth Amendments guarantee.

For the reasons stated, we reverse the District Court's judgment that §415.071 infringes the freedom of speech of the prison inmates and affirm its judgment that that regulation does not abridge the constitutional right of a free press. Accordingly, the judgment is vacated, and the cases are remanded to the District Court for further proceedings consistent with this opinion.

It is so ordered.

Judgment vacated and case remanded.

[Four Justices dissented on the access question posed by the media plaintiffs in *Pell*. A companion case, *Saxbe v. Washington Post Co.*, involved a similar interview ban promulgated by the federal Bureau of Prisons. A portion of Justice Powell's dissent in that case, also applicable to *Pell*, is reproduced below. Justice Douglas also filed a dissenting opinion.]

MR. JUSTICE POWELL, with whom MR. JUSTICE BRENNAN and MR. JUSTICE MARSHALL join, dissenting:

* * * From all that appears in the Court's opinion, one would think that any governmental restriction on access to information, no matter how severe, would be constitutionally acceptable to the majority so long as it does not single out the media for special disabilities not applicable to the public at large.

I agree, of course, that neither any news organization nor reporters as individuals have constitutional rights superior to those enjoyed by ordinary citizens. The guarantees of the First Amendment broadly secure the rights of every citizen; they do not create special privileges for particular groups or individuals. For me, at least, it is clear that persons who become journalists acquire thereby no special immunity from government regulation. To this extent I agree with the majority. But I cannot follow the Court in concluding that

any governmental restriction on press access to information, so long as it is nondiscriminatory, falls outside the purview of First Amendment concern. * * * At some point official restraints on news sources, even though not directly solely at the press, may so undermine the function of the First Amendment that it is both appropriate and necessary to require the government to justify such regulations in terms more compelling than discretionary authority and administrative convenience. It is worth repeating our adminition in [*Branzburg v. Hayes*] that "without some protection for seeking out the news, freedom of the press could be eviscerated."

* * * An informed public depends on accurate and effective reporting by the news media. No individual can obtain for himself the information needed for the intelligent discharge of his political responsibilities. For most citizens the prospect of personal familiarity with newsworthy events is hopelessly unrealistic. In seeking out the news the press therefore acts as an agent of the public at large. It is the means by which the people receive that free flow of information and ideas essential to intelligent self-government. By enabling the public to assert meaningful control over the political process, the press performs a crucial function in effecting the societal purpose of the First Amendment. That function is recognized by specific reference to the press in the text of the Amendment and by the precedents of this Court:

"The Constitution specifically selected the press . . . to play an important role in the discussion of public affairs. Thus the press serves and was designed to serve as a powerful antidote to any abuses of power by governmental officials and as a constitutionally chosen means for keeping officials elected by the people responsible to all the people whom they were elected to serve."

This constitutionally established role of the news media is directly implicated here. For good reasons, unrestrained public access [to prisons] is not permitted. The people must therefore depend on the press for information concerning public institutions. The Bureau's absolute prohibition of prisoner-press inter-views negates the ability of the press to dis-charge that function and thereby substantially impairs the right of the people to a free flow of information and ideas on the conduct of their Government. The underlying right is the right of the public generally. The press is the necessary representative of the public's inter-est in this context and the instrumentality which effects the public's right. I therefore conclude that the . . . ban against personal in-terviews must be put to the test of First Amendment review.

[Justice Powell then examined the asserted justifications for the interview ban and found them insufficient to warrant restrictions on constitutionally protected activity. Though he did not dispute the claim of prison officials that media interviews could create discipline problems by making celebrities of those in-mates chosen for press attention, Justice Po-well argued that "the remedy of no interview of any inmate is broader than is necessary to avoid the concededly real problems of the 'big wheel' phenomenon." In his view, prison offi-cials could "limit the number of interviews of any given inmate within a specified time per-iod" or "refuse to allow any interviews of a prisoner under temporary disciplinary sanc-tion such as solitary confinement." And, if prison administrators are concerned about po-tential difficulties in defining "the press" for purposes of establishing interview guidelines, that worry could be met by adopting the def-inition that the federal Bureau of Prisons used for other purposes: "a newspaper entitled to second class mailing privileges; a magazine or periodical of general distribution; a national or international news service; a radio or televi-sion network or station." If problems per-sisted, a pooling arrangement could be devel-oped.]

The Court's resolution of this case has the virtue of simplicity. Because the Bureau's in-terview ban does not restrict speech or pro-hibit publication or impose on the press any special disability, it is not susceptible to consti-tutional attack. This analysis delineates the outer boundaries of First Amendment con-cerns with unambiguous clarity. It obviates any need to enter the thicket of a particular factual context in order to determine the ef-fect on First Amendment values of a nondis-criminatory restraint on press access to infor-mation. As attractive as this approach may appear, I cannot join it. I believe that we must look behind bright-line generalities, however sound they may seem in the abstract, and seek the meaning of First Amendment guarantees in light of the underlying realities of a particu-lar environment. Indeed, if we are to preserve First Amendment values and the complexities of a changing society, we can do no less.

INTRODUCTION

Underlying the notion of a right of public access to government information and a special right of the press to "gather news" is the principle that a democratic govern-ment should conduct its affairs in public. As James Madison wrote:

> A Popular Government, without popular information, or the means of acquiring it is but a Prologue to a Farce or a tragedy; or perhaps both. Knowledge will forever govern ignorance; and the people who mean to be their own Governors must arm themselves with the power which knowledge gives.

The press obviously plays a key role in this scheme of self-governance, as Justice Lewis Powell argued in *Pell*. The news media vindicate this "right to know" by making available information by which citizens can form intelligent opinions about complex political, social, and economic issues at all levels of government. This relationship between the press and the democratic process should be self-evident to a nation that in Vietnam and Watergate witnessed aborted attempts by government to conceal its transgressions from the people.

Despite this interplay between press and government, the Supreme Court in *Pell* refused to construe the first amendment to encompass a right of access for the news media or the general public. As Justice Potter Stewart, the author of *Pell*, once observed in a speech, the press is "free to do battle against secrecy and deception in government," but "the Constitution [does not provide] any guarantee that it will succeed." Although the Court has subsequently recognized a limited first amendment right on the part of the press and public to attend criminal proceedings, the task has fallen to Congress and state legislatures to provide for access to government information and to require openness from the bureaucracy. We will consider both the constitutional and statutory access issues in this chapter but will reserve for Chapter 6 the special problems associated with the first amendment right of access to the courts.

At common law, there was no right to attend the meetings of governmental bodies and only a limited right to inspect public records. Parlimentary debates in England were routinely held behind closed doors until the late nineteenth century, initially on the theory that such secrecy protected against interference by the Crown and later because members desired to conceal their statements and votes from curious constituents. Not surprisingly, such secrecy was exported to colonial America, where legislatures excluded the press and public from and prohibited publication of their proceedings. These restrictions, as well as others placed on the press, played a role in fanning the revolutionary flames that swept the colonies.

However, the Continental Congress and the Constitutional Convention conducted their proceedings in secret, a practice followed by both the Senate and the House for several years under the present Constitution. The Senate has met in public on a regular basis since 1794, the House since the War of 1812. Today, proceedings of both chambers are televised via C-SPAN, a cable television network, and committee sessions—where the bulk of the Congress' work is done—have been routinely open to the public since the mid-1970s. The proceedings of federal administrative agencies, whose powers and numbers have increased dramatically since the New Deal, were not required to be held in public until 1976, when the federal Government in the Sunshine Act was passed. Although this statute, discussed more fully below, reaches only about fifty federal agencies, that number includes most of the major regulatory bodies.

The federal government obviously did not lead the way in open meetings legislation, for all states but New York had enacted such statutes by the time Congress finally took the step in 1976. This legislative activity has been a phenomenon of the past thirty-five years, with the news media having played a pivotal role in securing passage of such statutes. By 1950, members of the press had become disgruntled by the increasing frequency with which public officials were denying them admittance to meetings of governmental bodies. At that point, only one state—Alabama—had a meaningful open meetings statute on the books, and various journalism organizations—notably the American Society of Newspaper Editors and Sigma Delta Chi, the professional journalists' fraternity—began to press for openness from the bureaucracy. Today, all fifty states, the District of Columbia, and the federal government have in force so-called "government in the sunshine" laws reflecting Woodrow Wilson's comment that "light is the only thing that can sweeten our political atmosphere [and] open to view the innermost chambers of government.[1]

The push for open meetings also included a demand for a right to inspect government records and documents. Although the common law did not recognize a general right of this type, the English courts developed a limited right of access on behalf of those who sought to obtain evidence or information for use in litigation. This "litigation interest" rule found its way to the United States and was gradually broadened by the courts to permit inspection of government records by those seeking to vindicate the public interest. Inspection was typically allowed when a citizen or taxpayer sought to explore the financial condition of a governmental entity or expose irregularities in official conduct.

There were, however, some important barriers to public access. Inspection of public records was not permitted if the requester's purpose was an improper one such as idle curiosity, maliciousness, or commercial gain, and a governmental body could withhold records if disclosure would be detrimental to the "public interest." Moreover, the definition of "public record" was narrow; if, for example, a record was on file at a government agency but was not required by law to be kept there, it was not considered a public record. Finally, enforcement of the common law right of access proved troublesome in some cases, for the remedy employed by most courts—the writ of mandamus—was considered discretionary and could be denied by the judge even if the plaintiff established a clear right to the records. The court could properly refuse to grant the writ if its issuance would adversely affect the public interest or the rights of particular individuals.

These deficiencies in the common law prompted the news media to seek legislative relief, and today all states, the District of Columbia, and the federal government have some form of "freedom of information" or "open records" statute. In contrast to the situation regarding open meetings, the federal government's action with respect to inspection of records significantly influenced state laws. Though the same battle that had ensued over open meetings led to enactment of state laws allowing public inspection of government records, many were weak and ineffective. The federal Freedom of Information Act, signed into law by President Lyndon Johnson in 1966 and effective in 1967, has served as a model for many subsequent state statutes. Moreover, federal court decisions interpreting the FOIA have proven influential as state courts grapple with various questions concerning their own statutes. We will examine various issues stemming from the statutory right of access to records and meetings after a brief look at the constitutional question raised in *Pell v. Procunier.*

THE RIGHT TO GATHER NEWS

Until recently, the Supreme Court's first amendment decisions have concentrated on the right to publish and distribute information to ensure freedom of speech and

---

[1]The terms "government in the sunshine" and "sunshine laws" seem to stem from Justice Brandeis' famous statement that "publicity is justly commended as a remedy for social and industrial diseases" and that "sunlight is said to be the best of disinfectants." Florida apparently was the first state to label its statute a "government in the sunshine" measure, and it has been suggested that the phrase was derived in part from the notion of "out in the open" and from Florida's public relations slogan, "the sunshine state."

discussion. For example, in *New York Times Co. v. Sullivan* (1964), the Court spoke of the nation's commitment to "the principle that debate on public issues should be uninhibited, robust, and wide-open. . . ." However, scant judicial attention had been paid to the necessarily correlative right of the press to gather the information that will be published and distributed. The fact that this issue remained in the shadows is somewhat ironic, since without a right to gather information, the rights to publish and disseminate information are largely meaningless.

The Supreme Court spoke tangentially to the newsgathering question in *Zemel v. Rusk* (1965). There the Court rejected a United States citizen's contention that he had a first amendment right to visit Cuba in order to inform himself of conditions there. Ruling that governmental restriction on trips to Cuba was an inhibition of "action" rather than a restraint on "speech," the Court added that "the right to speak and publish does not carry with it the unrestrained right to gather information." Although this *dictum* could be read as rejecting first amendment protection for newsgathering, it was subsequently interpreted as implicit acknowledging that a right to gather information does exist.

For example, in *Branzburg v. Hayes*, the Court cited *Zemel* in coming to grips with at least one aspect of the newsgathering problem, the so-called "newsman's privilege" regarding protection for confidential sources discussed at length in Chapter 7. Writing for the Court, Justice Byron White stated in *Branzburg* that "without some protection for seeking out the news, freedom of the press could be eviscerated." However, he also made plain that such a right is limited: "It has generally been held that the First Amendment does not guarantee the press a constitutional right of access to information not available to the public generally." By way of illustration, Justice White listed several situations where the press is regularly excluded, despite the fact that newsgathering may be hampered: grand jury proceedings, conferences of the Supreme Court itself, and meetings of government bodies held in "executive session." Further, he added that newsmen have no constitutional right of access to scenes of crime or disaster when the general public is excluded and that the press may be prohibited in some situations from reporting information about criminal proceedings in order to assure that the defendant receives a fair trial.

This language unquestionably cast a cloud over the existence of a right of "special" access for the news media, thus setting the stage for the rejection of such a right in *Pell v. Procunier* and *Saxbe v. Washington Post Co.* As Justice Stewart noted in *Pell*, "newsmen have no constitutional right of access to prisons or their inmates beyond that afforded to the general public." One obvious difficulty with this holding is that the Court has done little more than define one unknown in terms of another, since judicial decisions shed virtually no light on the public's right of access under the first amendment. Moreover, as Justice Powell pointed out in his dissenting opinion, the logical extension of the Court's reasoning is that nondiscriminatory denial of access to both the public and the press would be constitutionally permissible.

The Court returned to the question of access to prisons in *Houchins v. KQED, Inc.* (1978). After a prisoner at the Alameda County Jail in Santa Rita, California, committed suicide, television station KQED from nearby San Francisco sent a camera crew to the jail to film conditions at the facility. The county sheriff denied them admittance, and at that time public tours of the jail were not allowed. KQED filed suit challenging the sheriff's exclusion of the station's personnel, and the sheriff subsequently announced that monthly public tours would be held. Several journalists, including a reporter from KQED, went on the first tour. However, the station continued to press its lawsuit, contending that the tours were unsatisfactory because timely access was not possible, cameras and tape recorders were barred, and interviews with inmates were not permitted. Moreover, the tours did not include a controversial portion of the jail facility known as "Little Greystone," where conditions were such that a federal judge had previously ruled that confinement there constituted cruel and unusual punishment in violation of the eighth amendment. The federal district court agreed with KQED and granted a preliminary injunction against the sheriff, ordering him to allow the media "reasonable access" to the jail. The U.S. Court of Appeals for the Ninth Circuit affirmed, rejecting the sheriff's argument that the district court's order was inconsistent with *Pell* and *Saxbe*.

A badly split Supreme Court reversed, 4 to 3, with two Justices not participating. Chief Justice Warren Burger's opinion, joined by only two other Justices, made plain that he considered KQED's arguments to be an attack on the reasoning of *Pell*: "The question presented is whether the news media have a constitutional right of access to a county jail, over and above that of other persons, to interview inmates and make sound recordings, films, and photographs for publication and broadcasting. . . ." Having posed the question in such terms, he then proceeded to answer it negatively: "[U]ntil the political branches decree otherwise, the media have no special right of access to the Alameda County Jail different from or greater than that accorded the public generally." Justice Stewart, the author of *Pell* and *Saxbe*, provided the crucial fourth vote for reversal, but wrote a separate opinion explaining his position. Though he agreed with Chief Justice Burger that "[t]he Constitution does no more than assure the public and the press equal access once government has opened its doors," Justice Stewart took the position that "equal access" does not in all cases mean "identical access."

In a passage that sounds as if it could have come from Justice Powell's dissenting opinion in *Pell* and *Saxbe,* Justice Stewart wrote:

> That the First Amendment speaks separately of freedom of speech and freedom of the press is no constitutional accident, but an acknowledgment of the critical role played by the press in American society. The Constitution requires sensitivity to that role, and to the special needs of the press in performing it effectively. A person touring Santa Rita jail can grasp the reality with his own eyes and ears. But if a television reporter is to convey the jail's sights and sounds to those who cannot personally visit the place, he must use cameras and sound equipment. In short, terms of access that are reasonably imposed on individual members of the public may, if they impede effective reporting without sufficient justification, be unreasonable as applied to journalists who are there to convey to the general public what the visitors see.

Because the press functions as a surrogate or stand-in for members of the general public, Justice Stewart concluded that the first amendment required the sheriff "to give . . . the press *effective* access to the same areas" that members of the public could observe on a regular tour. However, Justice Stewart agreed that the district court's order should be reversed because it required the sheriff to permit reporters to interview inmates and to view an area of the jail closed to the public. The district court erred, Justice Stewart said, in concluding that the first amendment "compelled this broader access for the press."

Justice John Paul Stevens, joined by Justice Powell and Justice William Brennan, dissented, arguing that the case did not involve any right of "special" access for the news media but rather the public's right of access to information concerning conditions at the jail. First, Justice Stevens criticized the notion that *Pell* and *Saxbe* could be interpreted as approving "a nondiscriminatory policy of excluding entirely both the public and the press from access to information about prison conditions. . . ." Second, he argued that because the public has a first amendment right to be informed about "conditions within those public institutions where some of its members are confined because they have been charged with or found guilty of criminal offenses," the sheriff's refusal to permit either the press or the public to view certain parts of the jail facility was unconstitutional. Justices Harry Blackmun and Thurgood Marshall did not participate in the case.

The *Pell*, *Saxbe*, and *Houchins* cases stand for two related propositions:

- the press has no constitutional right of access beyond that afforded the general public—in other words, there is no "special" right of access for the news media; and

- the general public does not have a constitutional right of access to information held by the government.

Without overturning these general rules, however, the Supreme Court in 1980 began to recognize a limited first amendment right of the public and the press to attend criminal proceedings in the courts. Although we will consider this line of cases in some detail in Chapter 6, brief treatment of the watershed case, *Richmond Newspapers, Inc. v. Virginia* (1980), is appropriate here.

The case began with the murder of a hotel manager. Defendant John Stevenson was tried four times in the circuit court of Hanover County, Virginia. His conviction in the first trial was overturned by the Virginia Supreme Court because a bloodstained shirt was improperly admitted into evidence, and the second and third trials ended in mistrials. When the case was called for trial a fourth time, Stevenson's lawyer moved that the proceedings be closed to the public. When the prosecutor stated that he had no objection to clearing the courtroom, the trial judge—who had presided over two of the three previous trials—entered an order to that effect. Under a Virginia statute, the trial judge in a criminal case could, in his discretion, "exclude from the trial any person whose presence would impair the conduct of a fair trial. . . ." Among the persons ordered to leave the courtroom were reporters from the *Richmond Times-Dispatch* and *Richmond News-Leader*, neither of whom objected at the time. Later, however, the reporters asked the trial judge to vacate the closure order, but he refused. After the judge dismissed the murder charges because of insufficient evidence on the second day of trial, the reporters appealed the closure order to the Virginia Supreme Court, which refused to hear the case.

The U.S. Supreme Court reversed, recognizing for the first time a right of access under the first amendment. Although there was no single opinion in which at least five Justices joined, a clear majority of the Court concluded that the public and the press have a first amendment right to attend criminal trials, absent a clear showing that such an open proceeding would deprive the accused of his constitutional right to a fair trial. In separate opinions, Chief Justice Burger (joined by Justices White and Stevens), Justice Brennan (joined by Justice Marshall) and Justice Stewart all stressed that criminal trials in this country and in England have long been open to the public. "This is no quirk of history," Chief Justice Burger wrote. "[R]ather, [openness] has long been recognized as an indispensable element of an Anglo-American trial." Because the Bill of Rights was enacted against this backdrop, the Justices agreed that the first amendment prohibits government from summarily closing courtroom doors which had long been open. But this first amendment right, like all others, is not absolute; indeed, the Court made plain that overriding interests—such as the need to protect the defendant's right to a fair trial—may in some cases compel closing the courtroom.

We will return to openness in judicial proceedings in the next chapter. For now, our concern is the impact of *Richmond Newspapers* upon earlier access cases such as *Pell v. Procunier*. At first blush, Chief Justice Burger's opinion seems to accept the premise, rejected in *Pell* and *Houchins*, that the press serves as a "stand-in" for members of the general public. The Chief Justice wrote:

> Instead of acquiring information about trials by firsthand observation or by word of mouth from those who attended, people now acquire it chiefly through the print and electronic media. In a sense, this validates the media claim of functioning as surrogates for the public. While media representatives enjoy the same right of access as the public, they often are provided special seating and priority of entry to that they may report what people in attendance have seen and heard. This contributes to the public understanding of the rule of law and to comprehension of the functioning of the entire criminal justice system.

The Chief Justice was also quick to point out, however, that he did not consider the ruling in *Richmond Newspapers* to affect the continuing vitality of *Pell* and other cases refusing to recognize a general right of access under the first amendment. He noted that *Pell* and *Saxbe* "are distinguishable in the sense that they were concerned with penal institutions which, by definition, are not 'open' or public places." And, because "prisons do not share the long tradition of openness" associated with criminal trials, the Chief Justice suggested that the first amendment right of access does not extend beyond criminal trials. Similarly, Justice Stewart—the author of *Pell*—emphasized in his concurring opinion that "[i]n conspicuous contrast to a military base, a jail, or a prison, a trial courtroom is a public place," thus intimating that *Pell*, *Saxbe*, and *Houchins* remain "good law" and that the *Richmond Newspapers* holding is to be limited to the judicial context.

In another separate opinion, Justice Brennan noted that the first amendment "has not been viewed by the Court in all settings as providing an equally categorical assurance of . . . freedom of access to information," but added that the Court has not completely "ruled out" a right of access. In his view, cases such as *Pell* "neither comprehensively nor absolutely deny that public access to information may at times be implied by the First Amendment. . . ." However, he pointed out that "the case for a right of access has special force when drawn from an enduring and vital tradition of public entree to particular proceedings or information." In light of the foregoing, Justice Brennan apparently did not perceive *Richmond Newspapers* as overruling *Pell, Saxbe,* and *Houchins,* but at the same time expressed a willingness not found in the opinions of Chief Justice Burger and Justice Stewart to apply the principles of *Richmond Newspapers* beyond the trial setting.

Justice Stevens took an even broader position, arguing in a concurring opinion that the Court's ruling in *Richmond Newspapers* represented recognition of a general right of access to government information. Citing the prison access cases, he observed that the Court had in those decisions "implied that any governmental restriction on access to information, no matter how severe and no matter how unjustified, would be constitutionally acceptable so long as it did not single out the press for special disabilities not applicable to the public at large." The *Richmond Newspa-*

pers ruling, he said, firmly rejects that notion: "for the first time, the Court unequivocally holds that an arbitrary interference with access to important information is an abridgment of the freedoms . . . protected by the First Amendment." In a later passage, Justice Stevens stated even more clearly his view that *Richmond Newspapers* adopts a general rule of access, not a principle restricted to criminal trials. "I agree that the First Amendment protects the public and the press for abridgment of their rights of access to information about the operation of the government, including the Judicial Branch. . . ."

In subsequent rulings, the Supreme Court has declined to interpret *Richmond Newspapers* in the expansive fashion urged by Justice Stevens. For example, as discussed in the following chapter, the Court has indicated that there is no right of access to information generated at the pretrial discovery stage of a lawsuit, since that material has traditionally been closed to the public. The lower courts have also been cautious, with most having refused to recognize a broad first amendment right of access. In an important 1986 case, *Capital Cities Media, Inc. v. Chester*, the U.S. Court of Appeals for the Third Circuit rejected a newspaper's argument that, under the first amendment, it had the right to inspect records of a state environmental protection agency concerning the pollution of public water supplies. In an exhaustive treatment of Supreme Court decisions from *Pell* through *Richmond Newspapers*, the court concluded that "the First Amendment guarantees no general access to government information." If the law were otherwise, the court said, the judiciary "would be required to fashion a constitutional freedom of information act," a task it considered unmanageable.

For the moment, therefore, the safest course is to assume that the principle of access established in *Richmond Newspapers* is limited to judicial proceedings and that the Supreme Court's decisions in the "prison access" cases retain their validity. To be sure, there are lower court decisions taking a broad view of the right of access. For example, in *Westinghouse Broadcasting Co. v. National Transportation Safety Board* (1982), a federal judge in Boston ruled unconstitutional a National Transportation Safety Board order limiting access to the site of a plane crash at a publicly owned airport. Similarly, a federal court in Utah ruled in *Society of Professional Journalists v. Secretary of Labor* (1985) that the public and press had a first amendment right to attend administrative hearings of a federal administrative agency investigating a coal mine fire that killed twenty-seven miners. These decisions, however, are of dubious precedential value. The court in *Westinghouse* also based its decision on the ground that the National Transportation Safety Board order violated the agency's own regulations regarding media access to crash sites, and the U.S. Court of Appeals for the Tenth Circuit subsequently vacated the *Society of Professional Journalists* case as moot.

Access to Crime or Disaster Scenes

Recall that in *Branzburg v. Hayes* the Supreme Court stated that "[n]ewsmen have no constitutional right of access to the scenes of crime or disaster when the general public is excluded." Although this comment was *dictum*, it represents the current state of the law, since the rule of *Richmond Newspapers* is limited to judicial proceedings. Even if the Court ultimately recognizes a general first amendment right of access to government information or proceedings, that right would not guarantee press access to all crime or disaster scenes. First, the right of access developed in *Richmond Newspapers* and later cases stems, at least in part, from the fact that a criminal trial is a "public event" held in a courtroom located on public property. Different considerations obviously apply if private property is involved; for example, we saw in Chapter 3 that trespass upon private property in the course of newsgathering activities can give rise to civil and criminal liability. If a newsworthy event such as a crime or disaster occurred on private property, there would be no first amendment right of access.

Second, even if the incident took place on public property, any first amendment right of access would not be absolute. As the Supreme Court made clear in *Richmond Newspapers*, a criminal trial may be closed to the press and public if necessary to protect other important interests, such as the right of the accused to a fair trial. Similarly, any constitutional right of access to the scene of a crime or other newsworthy event that takes place on public property may be restricted by law enforcement officials seeking to save lives, protect property, or preserve evidence.

Most states have enacted criminal statutes prohibiting citizens from obstructing governmental operations and requiring that they follow lawful orders issued by the police. Under such provisions, typically applicable whether the underlying incident is on public or private property, police officers have authority to exclude bystanders and reporters alike from the scene in order to assure that there is no interference with rescue attempts, the gathering of evidence, and other legitimate law enforcement activities. Failure to comply with police instructions could result in prosecution under the statutes.

An illustrative case is *State v. Lashinsky* (1979), in which the New Jersey Supreme Court affirmed the conviction of a news photographer for refusing to leave the scene of a fatal highway accident after a policeman had ordered him to do so. The photographer had been part of a crowd of about fifty persons who had gathered around a car that had run off the Garden State Parkway, crashed down an embankment, and overturned. A seriously injured girl was trapped inside the car under the body of her mother, who had been killed. Gasoline and oil were leaking from the vehicle, the car's battery had cracked open, and personal property was strewn about the area. Although the court recognized that newsgathering is entitled to constitutional protection, it ruled that the officer's order that all persons not involved in first aid efforts leave the scene was reasonable in light of the potential fire danger, the rescue attempt, and the need to preserve the area for investigation. Moreover, the court rejected the photographer's argument that the statute did not apply to him because he was a member of the press. The court noted that police officers should attempt to accommodate the legitimate interests of journalists in reporting the news, but held that those needs must yield in some circumstances so that the police can discharge their "paramount responsibilities for the safety and welfare of those who [are their] immediate concern."

Similarly, in *City of Oak Creek v. Ah King* (1989), the Wisconsin Supreme Court upheld the disorderly conduct conviction of a television cameraman who had entered the site of a plane crash after being told by a police officer that the area was closed. The case arose when a plane operated by a commuter airline crashed shortly after takeoff in a nonpublic area owned by the county and administered by the airport. A four-member crew from a Milwaukee television station went to the scene, where they went through a police roadblock without stopping. Upon locating the journalists near the crash site, a detective advised them that they would have to leave the restricted area. They did so, but the detective later encountered one of the crew members photographing the crash site and again told him to leave. When the cameraman refused, he was arrested and charged with disorderly conduct. In affirming his conviction, the court ruled that the defendant "does not have a first amendment right of access, solely because he is a newsgatherer, to the scene of this airplane crash when the general public has been reasonably excluded." The court also observed that the "injured and dying are entitled to receive the immediate and full attention of rescue workers" and that law enforcement personnel "should not be required to needlessly occupy themselves with persons who have a personal interest not related to restoration of order or with rescue attempts."

In addition to statutes of the type at issue in these cases, journalists should also be aware of state laws or regulations dealing specifically with media access to crime and disaster scenes. For example, a California statute that permits law enforcement officials to close disaster scenes to the public contains an exception for the press: "nothing in this section shall prevent a duly authorized representative of any news service . . . from entering the areas closed. . . ." Many law enforcement agencies have adopted regulations governing press access. Regulations of the Arkansas State Police provide that officers "should permit properly identified news media representatives free access to any disaster or emergency scene unless their presence would constitute a violation of the law or would substantially interfere with the officer's duty to protect life, collect and preserve evidence, protect property, or identify dead or injured persons." The regulations also call for the police to explain to journalists why they are being barred from an accident or crime scene when such action is taken. In such situations, the journalists also "should be permitted to remain as near as possible" to the area.

Selective Access

Although there is no general first amendment right of access for newsgathering purposes, the government is not free to discriminate among journalists or to grant access on a selective basis, absent legitimate government interests in restricting access. If space at a news conference is limited, for example, "pooling" arrangements are permissible. Similarly, no one seriously doubts that the White House may deny press credentials to persons considered security risks. As a general rule, however, once a government agency or official opens the door to the news media, access must be granted to all journalists. This is not to say that the reporters will be allowed the kind of access they desire. The courts have upheld restrictions that discriminate among types of media by forbidding the use of reportorial aids such as cameras and recording equipment. Thus, a broadcast journalist may not be denied access if print reporters are allowed to cover the event, but he may be required to "check his video camera at the door."

The leading "selective access" case is perhaps *Sherrill v. Knight*, decided by the U.S. Court of Appeals for the District of Columbia Circuit in 1977. The dispute arose when the White House denied press credentials to Robert Sherrill, Washington correspondent for *The Nation* magazine. Under White House press office procedures, a reporter seeking such credentials must show that he has similar press passes issued by the House and Senate, that he lives in Washington, and that his job demands that he report regularly from the White House. If these requirements are satisfied, the White House press pass is issued unless the Secret Service objects. Mr. Sherrill was denied credentials because the Secret Service thought he posed a security risk. In Mr. Sherrill's subsequent suit to compel issuance of the credentials, the federal district court concluded that the White House procedures for evaluating press pass requests were invalid because they left room for arbitrary action and did not give the applicant an adequate opportunity for input into the decision making process. The court of appeals affirmed that decision, with some modifications.

The appellate court pointed out that Mr. Sherrill was not arguing that, under the first amendment, the White House must "open its doors to the press, conduct press conferences, or operate press facilities." Instead, the reporter claimed that once access had been granted to the press, it could not be denied to individual reporters without good reason. The court agreed: because the White House had "voluntarily decided to establish press facilities . . . open to all bona fide Washington-based journalists," such access cannot "be denied arbitrarily or for less than compelling reasons." The court also ruled that while protection of the President is undoubtedly such a "compelling" reason, the standard applied by the White House in denying an application on this ground must be clearly articulated to ensure that it is not employed arbitrarily or in a discriminatory manner. Because no such standards or guidelines existed, denial of Sherrill's application was improper.

In addition, the court held that the application procedure for press credentials must include notice to the reporter of the factual bases for a decision denying access and an opportunity for him to respond to that decision before a final determination is made. These procedural safeguards, the court said, are necessary to make certain that the denial "is indeed in furtherance of Presidential protection, rather than based on arbitrary or less than compelling reasons."

In other cases, journalists have been denied access because government officials took issue with their reporting or the editorial position taken by their employers. Obviously, any discrimination based on the content of news stories or editorials cannot be justified. For example, in *Borreca v. Fasi* (1974), the mayor of Honolulu, Hawaii, refused to allow Richard Borreca, city hall reporter for the *Honolulu Star-Bulletin*, to attend mayoral press conferences. The mayor was upset over Borreca's reporting, having concluded that the reporter was "irresponsbile, inaccurate, biased and malicious" in covering the mayor and the city administration. The court enjoined the mayor from "preventing Borreca from attending any press conference on the same basis and to the same extent that other news reporters attend press conferences."

Similarly, in *Southwestern Newspapers Corp. v. Curtis* (1979), the prosecuting attorney in Amarillo, Texas, refused to meet with or answer questions from reporters for the *Amarillo Daily News* and *Amarillo Globe-Times* unless they made an appointment, a requirement that he did not impose on other journalists. The prosecutor took this action after he was the subject of news stories and critical editorials in the newspapers. "[I]n the absence of some compelling government interest . . . ," the Texas appeals court said, "all representatives of news organizations must not only be given equal access, but within reasonable limits, access with equal convenience to official news sources." Finding no such interest where the limitation on access was based on the prosecutor's disapproval of the news stories and editorials, the court ordered that he accord the reporters the same privileges given other journalists.

Other bases for discrimination among members of the news media may also be impermissible. For example, in a decision that rocked major league baseball, a New York federal judge ruled in *Ludtke v. Kuhn* (1978) that the New York Yankees could not bar Melissa Ludtke, a reporter for *Sports Illustrated*, from the team's locker room while continuing to permit male reporters to interview players there. Critical to the court's ruling that such sex discrimination is unlawful was the fact that Yankee Stadium is leased by the ball club from the City of New York. Accordingly, the ban on female reporters was considered governmental action for purposes of the fourteenth amendment. Since major league baseball teams are private concerns, the ruling would not apply to a team that plays in a privately owned stadium.

Labor disputes have also led to selective access problems. In *Westinghouse Broadcasting Co. v. Dukakis* (1976), a Boston television station, WBZ-TV, was engaged in a labor dispute, and, as a result, nonunion management personnel were serving on camera crews and performing other tasks normally handled by union members. The Boston City Council, acting solely out of sympathy for the union, barred the station's nonunion camera crews from an area of the city council chamber specifically set aside for television coverage. Although WBZ personnel were apparently free to sit in the spectator section, a federal district court issued a temporary restraining order requiring that the council provide WBZ camera crews equal access. After ruling that sympathy for the union's position was not a compelling governmental interest that could justify the council's action, the court observed that "WBZ is entitled to share the special facilities provided for other stations, even though they are provided as a convenience."

Despite the general rule that access must be nondiscriminatory, two types of selective access are quite common: "pooling" arrangements by which a limited number of print and broadcast reporters are allowed access to an event, with the understanding that they will share pictures and information with other media organizations; and governmental policies allowing access by reporters but prohibiting the use of tape recorders and cameras.

The pooling issue has arisen in a few cases, but there are no definitive rulings. In *Cable News Network v. ABC* (1981), CNN challenged White House pooling practices as unconstitutional. Under Reagan Administration policies then in effect, pooling was required if space limitations or other considerations required limiting the number of media representatives as a given event. No matter whether the pool was "tight" or "expanded"—a determination based on the number of media representatives who could attend—the pool included representatives of both print and television media. In its lawsuit, CNN contended that the White House had acted unconstitutionally in excluding CNN from the pools while rotating responsibilities for pool coverage among ABC, CBS, and NBC. After the suit was filed, the White House immediately changed its practice of selecting pool representatives, leaving to the television organizations themselves the task of determining who would provide the pool coverage. When the television groups could not agree on the representatives for a particular pool, the White House declined to permit any television participation in the pool for that event. Though the court ultimately found that action unconstitutional, it did not rule on the merits of CNN's initial complaint regarding the pool system. That aspect of the case was eventually settled, with the White House agreeing to include CNN in the pool rotation.

In other cases, however, the courts have either expressly approved pooling arrangements or refused to enjoin their operation. For example, in *Society of Professional Journalists v. Secretary of Labor*, the district court's order mandating access to the administrative hearings concerning the mine disaster specifically stated that "[s]uch a right of access includes, at a minimum, the right of access to such hearings by means of a pool reporter from the print media and a pool camera." Similarly, state courts that allow television cameras in the courtroom often require some sort of pooling, as discussed more fully in Chapter 6. Moreover, in *WPIX v. League of Women Voters* (1984), a federal court in New York refused to grant a preliminary injunction that would have required the League of Women Voters to allow the producer of a syndicated broadcast news program access to the 1984 presidential and vice-presidential debates beyond the pool coverage plan in effect for that event. However, the court left open the possibility—as did the court in *Cable News Network*—that under some circumstances the pooling arrangement may be impermissible. For example, pooling may not be justified if there is additional camera space available, if broadcasters with low budgets cannot afford to participate in the pool, or if the interests of all broadcasters are not adequately served by the pooling arrangement.

Although some issues with respect to pooling may be unresolved, there is general agreement among the courts that public entities may prohibit the use of certain equipment in the reporting of an event. The effect of these rulings is that while government cannot discriminate among print and broadcast reporters in terms of access, it can limit the nature of media coverage by banning television cameras, tape recorders, and still photographs. In one of the leading cases, *Garrett v. Estelle* (1977), the U.S. Court of Appeals for the Fifth Circuit upheld a Texas prison regulation forbidding the recording of an inmate's execution by any mechanical means, including still and video photography and audio recording.

Tony Garrett, a reporter for a Dallas television station, challenged the regulation, pointing out that the state Department of Corrections allowed two wire services reporters—one from AP, one from UPI—to witness executions and act as pool reporters, while permitting other journalists to view the events via simultaneous closed circuit telecast. He argued in part that the prohibition was invalid because "other members of the press are allowed free use of their usual reporting tools." The Fifth Circuit disagreed: the regulation "denies Garrett use of his camera, and it also denies the print reporter use of his camera, and the radio reporter use of his tape recorder." Moreover, the court said, "Garrett is free to make his report by means of anchor desk or stand-up delivery on the TV screen, or even by simulation."

Along the same lines is *Sigma Delta Chi v. Speaker, Maryland House of Delegates* (1973), which involved the state legislature's ban on the use tape recorders by journalists working in the house and senate chambers. The reporters contended that the prohibition discriminated against the broadcast media, since print journalists were permitted the use of the tools of their trade—pen and paper. The court rejected this argument, pointing out that unlike a ban on pen and paper, which "might frustrate *all* effective communication," the prohibition against tape recorders was a "mere inconvenience." Moreover, although the use of recorders might help ensure accuracy, as the reporters claimed, that interest was outweighed by the legitimate concern for "preservation of order and decorum in the legislative chambers. . . ." Similarly, in *CBS, Inc. v. Lieberman* (1976), a federal court in Illinois ruled that there is no first amendment right to film or record proceedings of a state regulatory agency. As we shall see in the next chapter, the federal courts have consistently upheld the constitutionality of regulations forbidding the use of cameras and audio recorders in federal courthouses.

Although a few courts have struck down prohibitions against the use of recording equipment and cameras, these decisions either turn on state law rather than the first amendment or are based on peculiar facts that limit their precedential reach. In a 1965 case, *Nevens v. City of Chino*, a California appeals court ruled that a city council ban on tape recorders was invalid because the recorders were unobtrusive and enabled journalists to report accurately what took place at council sessions. However, the case was based primarily on state law and was decided long before development of the access principles discussed earlier in this chapter. More recently, in the *Cable News Network* case, a federal judge in Atlanta ruled unconstitutional a White House policy that closed media pools to television journalists but allowed access to print reporters. Despite some rather sweeping language in the opinion, the case is best understood as a response to the reason for the White House policy, not the policy itself: television representatives had been barred because they could not agree among themselves on the question of who should provide pool coverage.

STATUTORY ACCESS

Even though a journalist may not have a first amendment right of access to government information, he may be able to inspect public records pursuant to freedom of information statutes. Similarly, a broadcast reporter who does not enjoy a first amendment right to use the tools of his trade in covering the proceedings of governmental bodies may be able to record or videotape those proceedings under open meetings laws. As noted in the introduction to this chapter, all fifty states, the District of Columbia, and the federal government have enacted such statutes. Because these provisions vary widely, our focus here will be the federal access statutes: the Freedom of Information Act, which covers public records, and the Government in the Sunshine Act, which deals with open meetings.

Public Records

Enacted in 1966 over the opposition of virtually all federal administrative agencies, the Freedom of Information Act ("FOIA") established for the first time an effective statutory right of access to records held by the federal government. As the U.S. Supreme Court noted in *National Labor Relations Board v. Robbins Tire & Rubber Co.* (1978), the purpose of the act is "to ensure an informed citizenry, vital to the functioning of a democratic society, needed to check against corruption and to hold the governors accountable to the governed." However, the FOIA also recognizes that certain societal interests—including the national security, personal privacy, and law enforcement—can outweigh the public interest in an open government. In seeking to accommodate these competing concerns, the FOIA establishes a general rule that any person has a right of access to federal agency records but exempts from disclosure records that fall into nine specific categories.

In this sense, the FOIA is an "open records" statute that creates a right to inspect documents in the government's possession that do not fit within one of the exemptions. The act also contains various "publication" requirements, the violation of which can lead to the invalidation of action taken by an administrative agency. For example, an agency must publish in the *Federal Register* such information as substantive regulations, general statements of policy, and procedural rules. Decisions in administrative hearings, staff manuals, and other material not published in the *Federal Register* must be indexed and made available for public inspection. While these provisions are obviously significant, they primarily involve "official" government action—the end product, if you will, of the vast federal bureaucracy. Of more concern to the news media are what one might call "supporting" documents that underlie official government action (or inaction), reflect the dealings of individuals and corporations with the government, or reveal government abuses and misdeeds. The federal government is an enormous repository for such documents, which often go unnoticed by the public. Accordingly, our focus in this section is on the "open records" provisions of the FOIA, which require the government to make records available for public inspection in response to a proper request.

It should be stressed that the FOIA is of considerable importance to persons outside the news media; for example, lawyers frequently utilize the act to gain access to records that directly affect their corporate clients. But the value of the act to the working journalist, and thus to the public at large, cannot be understated. Reporters, scholars, and public interest groups such as Common Cause have used the FOIA to reveal all kinds of information about the activities of the federal government and those who come into contact with it: details of the My Lai massacre during the Vietnam War, lobbying expenses of defense contractors and huge cost overruns on military projects by those same companies, FBI harassment of civil rights leaders, CIA spying on domestic political organizations, health dangers in the workplace, and environmental impact studies. Thus, the FOIA—as well as its state-law counterparts—can be a valuable newsgathering tool for the journalist who knows how to use it.

Agencies Subject to the FOIA. The Freedom of Information Act specifically defines those entities within the federal government subject to its provisions:

> [A]ny executive department, military department, Government corporation, Government controlled corporation, or other establishment in the executive branch of the Government (including the Executive Office of the President), or any independent regulatory agency.

This definition is quite broad, including, for example, Cabinet-level departments such as the Department of Defense and the Department of Justice; agencies with the Executive Office of the President, such as the Office of Management and Budget; independent regulatory agencies such as the Federal Communications Commission and the Federal Trade Commission; and government-controlled corporations, such as the U.S. Postal Service and the Legal Services Corporation.

Some important federal entities are not covered, however. The FOIA does not apply to the President or his staff, including, for example, the Council of Economic Advisers; the Congress and its support organizations, such as the General Accounting Office and the Library of Congress; and the federal court system. Moreover, in contrast to some state FOI statutes that reach private corporations that receive public funds, the federal act does not apply to entities merely because they receive federal money. For example, the Supreme Court ruled in *Forsham v. Harris* (1980) that a private corporation carrying on research under contracts with the federal government is not subject to the FOIA. Similarly, the act does not apply to federally funded state agencies (though the records of these bodies may well be obtainable under a state FOI statute), and it probably does not cover the Corporation for Public Broadcasting, an entity which receives federal funds but is not "controlled" by the federal government.

However, the Supreme Court in *Forsham* left open the possibility that a private organization might be subject to the FOIA under appropriate circumstances. The Court suggested that a private entity can fall within the FOIA definition if a federal agency is pervasively involved in the operation of the private body. Though the extent of this involvement necessary to trigger the FOIA is unclear, it seems that the federal agency must amount to virtual "day-to-day supervision" of the private entity's operations. Such government control was found missing in *Irwin Memorial*

Blood Bank v. Red Cross (1981), a case in which the U.S. Court of Appeals for the Ninth Circuit ruled that the American Red Cross was not an "agency" for FOIA purposes. To the same effect is *Public Citizen Health Research Group v. Department of Health, Education & Welfare* (1981), in which the U.S. Court of Appeals for the District of Columbia Circuit determined that Professional Standards Review Organizations that review doctors' decisions concerning the necessity of medical treatment for Medicare patients are not within the FOIA definition.

At the state level, questions have arisen as to whether advisory committees established to make recommendations to government bodies are covered by FOI statutes. Although such committees are not within the definition of "agency" found in the federal FOIA, another statute—the Federal Advisory Committee Act ("FACA")—requires that the records of these committees be made available to the public, subject to the exemptions found in the FOIA. The FACA defines an advisory committee as:

> [A]ny committee, board, commission, council, conference, panel, task force, or other similar group, or any subcommittee or other subgroup thereof . . . which is (A) established by statute or reorganization plan, or (B) established or utilized by the President, or (C) established or utilized by one or more agencies . . . in the interest of obtaining advice or recommendations. . . .

However, the statute expressly excludes from the definition the Advisory Commission on Intergovernmental Relations, the Commission on Government Procurement, any committee composed entirely of fulltime federal employees, an advisory committee excluded by Congress in another statute, advisory committees of the CIA and Federal Reserve System, local civic groups who render advice as a public service to federal programs, and state or local committees that advise state or local officials and agencies.

What is a "Record"? Despite its name, the FOIA applies to "records," not to "information." This distinction is important, for the act cannot be used to force an agency to answer specific questions that a person might have, or to compile data or create records in response to a request. Instead, an agency must produce for public inspection nonexempt "records," a term not specifically defined in the FOIA. The courts, however, have taken a broad view of the term, holding that it includes computer tapes, photos and recordings (both audio and video), and more traditional documents such as memoranda and letters. Moreover, the Computer Security Act of 1987 expressly prohibits agencies from withholding computerized records when they would be available under the FOIA if kept in another form.

To be subject ot the FOIA, a record need not have been generated internally by an agency. In *U.S. Department of Justice v. Tax Analysts* (1989), the Supreme Court emphasized that the act applies not only to records that an agency has created, but also to those that it has obtained from third parties. Limiting the reach of the FOIA to records produced by an agency, the Court said, "would frustrate Congress' desire to put within public reach the information available to an agency in its decisionmaking process." Moreover, it does not matter whether the entity from whom the agency obtained the records is covered by the FOIA. In the *Tax Analysts* case, for instance, the records in question were tax decisions issued by federal courts, which are expressly excluded form the FOIA's definition of "agency." By the same token, documents submitted to an agency by a private corporation are potentially available from the agency under the FOIA, even though the corporation is not within the act's scope.

A record must also be in the control of the agency at the time an FOIA request is made. As the Supreme Court explained in *Tax Analysts,* the term "control" means that the record "has come into the agency's possession in the legitimate conduct of its official duties." In that case, the Court had little difficulty finding that the requisite control was present, since the Justice Department acquired the records in the course of its representation of the federal government in tax cases.

The mere fact that records are physically located at an agency is not sufficient to trigger the FOIA, however. If that were so, a federal employee's personal records kept at his office would be available for public inspection. The Supreme Court rejected such a broad reading of the FOIA in *Kissinger v. Reporters Committee for Freedom of the Press* (1980), a case that arose when journalists sought access to records of telephone conversations that Henry Kissinger had made during his tenure as national security adviser to President Richard Nixon.

At the time of the request, the records were located at the State Department, where Kissinger had taken them when he left his White House position to become Secretary of State. Because the State Department is an "agency" for FOIA purposes, its records ordinarily would be open to the public, unless exempt. However, the Supreme Court ruled that the State Department did not have control over the records, pointing out that they had not been used by the agency for any purpose and had never entered its files. "If the mere physical location of papers and materials could confer status as an 'agency record,'" Justice William Rehnquist wrote for the majority, "Kissinger's personal books, speeches, and all other memorabilia stored in his office would have been agency records subject to disclosure under the FOIA."[2]

To the same effect is *Wolfe v. Department of Health and Human Services*, a 1983 decision of the U.S. Court of Appeals for the District of Columbia Circuit. There the director of a public interest organization filed an FOIA request with the Department of Health and Human Services seeking a copy of a report about the department prepared by President Reagan's "transition team" after the November 1980 election but before the President actually assumed office. Two copies of the report were in the office of a high-ranking department official but had never been used or relied on by the department and had not been assimilated into its system of records. The court of appeals ruled that the reports were in the personal possession of the official and not under the department's control. The physical location of the reports in the official's HHS office was not sufficient to make them agency records, the court said, since the department had not actually obtained them from him.

On the other side of the coin, nothing in the FOIA requires an agency to attempt to obtain records no longer in its possession, even if those records may have wrongfully been removed from the agency. This issue was also raised in the *Kissinger* case, since the plaintiff journalists had also sought records of Mr. Kissinger's telephone conversations while he had served as Secretary of State. By the time these FOIA requests were filed, however, the records were no longer at the State Department. Mr. Kissinger had given them to the Library of Congress, an entity not covered by

---

[2]The Court also ruled that these documents were not "agency records" at the time they were made, since the President and his immediate advisers are not included within the FOIA's definition of "agency."

the FOIA, under an agreement by which he retained authority to decide the terms of their release. Reversing lower court rulings in favor of the plaintiffs, the Supreme Court concluded that the FOIA does not give the federal courts jurisdiction to order an agency to retrieve or attempt to retrieve documents that have escaped its possession. The Court's decision was based on the language of the FOIA, which confers jurisdiction on the federal courts in cases where an agency has improperly "withheld" agency records. Since the State Department no longer had the records, it had not withheld them from the plaintiffs in violation of the FOIA. Thus, even assuming that the Kissinger records had been wrongfully removed from the State Department (an issue the Court did not decide), the FOIA could not be used to force the State Department to try to get them back.

The fact that a particular record within an agency's possession and control is available from another source does not affect its status under the FOIA. In the *Tax Analysts* case, for example, the Justice Department argued that it was not required to disclose the federal court opinions because those records were available under other federal statutes from the clerks of those courts, as well as from other sources. Rejecting this argument, the Supreme Court pointed out that Congress had not seen fit to exempt from disclosure any record that is publicly available elsewhere. "Congress surely did not envision agencies satisfying their disclosure obligations under the FOIA simply by handing requesters a map and sending them on scavenger expeditions throughout the Nation," the Court said. "Without some express indication in the Act's text or legislative history that Congress intended such a result, we decline to adopt this reading of the statute."

Exemptions. The basic premise of the Freedom of Information Act is that all agency records are open to public inspection unless they fall within one of nine exemptions. These exemptions cover:

- "classified" records, the release of which would damage the national security;
- internal agency records, such as documents involving personnel rules;
- records exempted from disclosure by other federal statutes;
- trade secrets and confidential commercial information;
- internal agency memoranda and material that would not be available to an opposing party in a lawsuit against the agency;
- medical files and similar records which, if disclosed, would cause a clearly unwarranted invasion of personal privacy;
- certain law enforcement records;
- reports prepared by federal regulatory agencies about the conditions of federally regulated banks and savings institutions; and
- geological records concerning oil and gas wells.

Before turning to the most important of these exemptions, three preliminary points should be made. First, in light of the FOIA's basic presumption favoring disclosure, the courts have consistently ruled that the exemptions are to be "narrowly construed." Put another way, any doubt as to whether a particular exemption applies is to be resolved in favor of disclosure. Second, the FOIA specifically states that an agency, upon locating a record covered by the request that includes exempt and nonexempt material, must delete the exempt information and make available to the requester the remainder of the record. Therefore, an agency cannot refuse to disclose an entire document merely because some of the material contained in it falls within an exemption. Third, the U.S. Supreme Court ruled in *Chrysler Corp. v. Brown* (1979) that the exemptions (except for exemption three, which covers records exempted by other statutes) are "permissive" rather than "mandatory." This means that an agency may, in its discretion, release to the public records that fall within an exemption. Accordingly, a requester might be able to convince an agency to disclose records that would seem to be exempt, particularly if release of the information would be in the public interest.

Exemption One: National Security. The spy novel has in recent years popularized the trenchcoat, romanticized the clandestine operations of governments, and made virtually everyone familiar with the terms "top secret," "classified information," and "eyes only." The so-called "national security" exemption recognizes that the United States government has a legitimate interest in protecting the confidentiality of records falling within these categories. As mentioned briefly in Chapter 1 and discussed more fully in Chapter 8, the U.S. Supreme Court has ruled that, under appropriate circumstances, even rights protected by the first amendment must yield when vital national security interests are at stake. If constitutional rights may be restricted in the name of national security, it should come as no surprise that the statutory right of access granted by the FOIA includes an exemption for sensitive documents which, if released, could harm the nation's security.

At the same time, however, experience has taught that the federal bureaucracy has used the "top secret" designation and similar labels to conceal embarrassing mistakes or actual dishonesty rather than to protect our national interests. The trick, of course, is to distinguish between documents that are properly classified and those that are classified merely to cover up wrongdoing on the part of the government or its agents. As initially enacted, the FOIA did not do a particularly good job of drawing this line, at least in the opinion of the Supreme Court. In an important 1973 case, *Environmental Protection Agency v. Mink*, the Court ruled that the national security exemption covered all records bearing a "top secret" stamp or some other label, regardless of whether the records actually fell within that category. The plaintiffs in *Mink* were members of Congress who had sought access to an environmental impact statement prepared by the Department of Defense in connection with an underground nuclear weapons test. Like other records associated with the project, the environmental analysis has been classified as "top secret," and the Court was unwilling to question whether that designation was proper.

That interpretation meant that the national security exemption was a virtually impenetrable barrier, even as to records sought by members of Congress. Not surprisingly, Congress acted quickly to change the exemption. Under an amendment to the FOIA adopted in 1974 and still in effect today, the exemption applies only to records that are:

> (A) specifically authorized under criteria established by an Executive order to be kept secret in the interest of national defense or foreign policy and (B) are in fact properly classified pursuant to such Executive order.

To satisfy these requirements, the government must convince a court that an executive order of the President allows classification of the records in question and that the standards for classification set out in that order were properly applied to those records. The court may review the agency's decision to classify the records and, at least theoretically, may reverse that determination. As a practical matter, however, the courts give agency decisions great deference, and an FOIA plaintiff in an Exemption One case faces an uphill battle.

The current executive order on classified information—No. 12356, adopted by President Reagan in April 1982—establishes procedural steps that must be followed in the classification of documents and sets forth substantive standards that must be used in deciding whether particular records are to be classified. The procedural regulations, for example, specify who within the federal government can make classification decisions and provide for the periodic review of classified records with an eye toward declassification. More important for FOIA purposes are the substantive standards for classification, which establish three categories of classified information (top secret, secret, and confidential) and general rules applicable to each category. A record will be classified as "confidential" if its unauthorized disclosure "reasonably could be expected to cause damage to the national security." Similarly, if "serious damage" could be reasonably anticipated, the record will be classified as "secret," and if "exceptionally grave damage" might result, it will be labeled "top secret."

In addition, the executive order lists various types of information that may be considered for classification, including military plans, weapons or operations; the vulnerabilities or capabilities of nonmilitary plans, projects or installations relating to the national security; information furnished by foreign governments; intelligence-gathering activities or methods; intelligence sources; foreign relations activities; scientific, technological or economic matters relating to the national security; programs for safeguarding nuclear materials or facilties; and cryptology. Obviously, this list is rather broad; however, the executive order specifically provides that certain information may not be classified. For example, "basic scientific research information not clearly related to the national security" may not be classified, nor may information that the federal government does not own or control. More importantly, the order expressly states that:

> In no case shall information be classified in order to conceal violations of law, inefficiency, or administrative error; to prevent embarrassment to a person, organization, or agency; to restrain competition; or to prevent or delay the release of information that does not require protection in the interests of national security.

The courts typically focus on two questions in FOIA cases involving the national security exemption: whether the records are of a type listed in the executive order and whether their disclosure could reasonably be expected to cause damage to the national security. By way of illustration, the courts have upheld agency classification of, and thus denied access under the FOIA to, records concerning FBI methods of infiltrating subversive organizations, State Department discussions with foreign governments, treaty negotiations, security at military installations, commercial information provided by a foreign government, the murder of a U.S. diplomat in Mexico, an accident involving an aircraft carrier, methods used by the CIA in gathering intelligence information, deposits in American banks by Arab countries, and foreign government communications intercepted by the CIA.

Cases in which the courts have reversed an agency's classification decision and ruled that the records were open to inspection under the FOIA are rare. Although the 1974 amendment that rewrote the national security exemption makes clear that the courts will not automatically accept the agency's determination that records have been properly classified, judges typically give the agency's decision great deference. The reason is simple: as a federal appeals court candidly observed in *Military Audit Project v. Casey* (1981), judges "lack the expertise to second-guess agency opinions in the typical national security FOIA case."

Nonetheless, the courts do have the power to review the disputed documents for themselves *in camera* (i.e., privately, without participation of counsel) and there are a few decisions on the books where they have overturned agency decisions that were patently erroneous. For example, in *Fitzgibbon v. Central Intelligence Agency* (1983), a federal judge in the District of Columbia concluded that the release of documents showing that the CIA had maintained a "station" in the Dominican Republic some twenty-five years ago would not damage the national security. The court also ruled that the CIA had improperly withheld records revealing such well-known intelligence-gathering techniques as interviewing people thought to have relevant information and staking out a house or apartment to observe who enters or leaves.

Although the courts generally refuse to second-guess agency decisions regarding classification of records, they have been rather strict in requiring that the procedural steps set out in the executive order be followed and in demanding that agencies explain in considerable detail the rationale for classifying documents and the perceived harm to the national security that would result from disclosure. (These explanations are usually in the form of affidavits, which themselves may be so sensitive that the judge will examine them *in camera*). Still, critics have charged that the courts have largely abdicated their responsibilities under the 1974 amendment and have created in the national security area a presumption that records are *not* available for public inspection, a presumption that runs counter to the basic premise of the FOIA. Moreover, as we shall see below, national security records are also often covered by Exemption Three, the so-called "catchall" exemption that applies when specific federal statutes require confidentiality.

Exemption Two: Internal Agency Rules. This exemption covers records "related solely to the internal personnel rules and practices of an agency." It has been interpreted by the courts as encompassing two distinct categories of records: those involving routine "housekeeping" matters of little interest to the public and those reflecting more important administrative policies and procedures which, if disclosed to the public, would allow the circumvention of statutes or agency regulations. The second category is by far the most controversial.

Regarding the first type of records, Congress clearly intended that Exemption Two reach records dealing with such mundane administrative matters as employee lunch breaks, sick leave policy, and assignment of parking spaces. Interpreting the exemption in *Department of the Air Force v. Rose* (1976), the Supreme Court said that it was meant to exempt routine or trivial agency policies, thus relieving agencies of the burden of providing access to records "in which the public could not reasonably be expected to have an interest." However, the Court indicated that records which could be viewed as the subject of legitimate public concern—such as personnel evaluation forms—cannot be withheld under the exemption. Applying the *Rose* guidelines, the lower courts have ruled that Exemption Two applies to records concerning agency policy on travel expenses, employee awards, transfers, and leave practices, but that it does not cover records involving evaluations of agency effectiveness, standards of employee conduct, and employee grievance procedures. Moreover, despite the language of the exemption, the courts have ruled that it applies to trivial housekeeping matters in general, not just those involving personnel.

Records of the second type raise a different problem. Although the public may have a legitimate interest in some agency records that could fairly be described as "internal" in nature, disclosure might give individuals or corporations insight as to how the agency carries out its responsibilities and enable them to circumvent the law. For example, it would not be a particularly wise idea to make available to federal prisoners an operations manual written for prison guards and other personnel, since that information might reveal a weak spot in jail procedures and suggest a strategy for escape. In the *Rose* case, the Supreme Court implied—without squarely deciding—that Exemption Two permits agencies to withhold records of this type when necessary to prevent potential circumvention of federal law. Most lower courts have adopted this approach, ruling that the exemption applies to records whose release to the public would significantly impede the law enforcement process or create the potential for circumvention of statutes or agency regulations.

At issue in many judicial decisions have been manuals developed by law enforcement agencies such as the Drug Enforcement Agency, the Bureau of Alcohol, Tobacco and Firearms, and the FBI. As a general matter, "administrative staff manuals and instructions to staff" must be made available for public inspection under the FOIA's "publication" requirement discussed previously. However, this provision does not apply to law enforcement manuals and instructional material, which fall under Exemption Two if the standard set out in the preceding paragraph is satisfied. Thus, the cases typically turn on two questions: whether a law enforcement manual is involved, and whether disclosure of the manual would adversely affect law enforcement. In a sense, the issues in these cases are similar to those raised in some cases involving the national security exemption. Just as the CIA would object to the disclosure of records revealing sensitive intelligence-gathering techniques, the FBI would would fight the release of documents detailing the agency's telephone surveillance methods. Not surprisingly, such records have been ruled exempt.

Other materials for which withholding has been allowed under Exemption Two include the Secret Service's operations manual, a State Department manual on protective services for the President, training materials developed for agents of the Bureau of Alcohol, Tobacco and Firearms, and a report concerning the FBI's undercover agent program. The exemption, however, is not limited to manuals of "traditional" law enforcement agencies such as the FBI. For example, the courts have ruled exempt a computer program used by the Department of Commerce to determine whether foreign steel producers have violated federal statutes prohibiting unfair pricing practices and documents revealing methods employed by the Internal Revenue Service in identifying tax protesters who seek to evade the tax laws by falsely claiming to be churches.

Exemption Three: The "Catchall" Provision. The third exemption includes records "specifically exempted from disclosure" by another federal statute, if that statute either "requires that the matters be withheld from the public" or "establishes particular criteria for [discretionary] withholding or refers to particular types of matters to be withheld." The effect of this exemption is to incorporate into the FOIA the nondisclosure provisions of dozens of federal statutes. Most state FOI statutes have similar "catchall" provisions, and their practical political importance should not go unnoticed. While a proposed amendment to an FOI statute might well stir substantial opposition, a legislative body can often avoid or minimize controversy by simply enacting a separate statute providing for confidentiality of records. By virtue of the "catchall" provision, the statute in effect becomes part of the FOI law.

Relatively few cases have arisen under the first portion of Exemption Three, under which a statute must expressly require confidentiality in such a way as to leave no administrative discretion on the matter. As one court has said, this provision "embraces only those statutes incorporating a congressional mandate of confidentiality that, however general, is absolute and without exception." Thus, the Export Administration Act, which requires agency officials to withhold confidential export administration *except* when withholding is "contrary to the national interest," does not qualify under the first category of Exemption Three. On the other hand, statutes that establish a complete bar to disclosure clearly satisfy the test. For example, in *Baldridge v. Shapiro* (1982), the Supreme Court ruled that the Census Act is such a statute, for it prohibits the Census Bureau, part of the Department of Commerce, from using census data for other than statistical purposes or publishing data that would identify individual citizens. The statute "explicitly provide[s] for the nondisclosure of certain census data," the Court said, and "[n]o discretion is provided to the Census Bureau on whether or not to disclose the information."

A comparative handful of federal statutes contain absolute prohibitions against disclosure. In addition to the census statute at issue in *Baldridge*, such statutes include those barring release of income tax returns, the personnel and organization of the CIA, grand jury records, information gained by law enforcement agencies through wiretaps, and applications for visas. Moreover, the CIA Information Act, passed in 1984, completely exempts from the FOIA the CIA's "operational files," which contain information concerning the conduct of foreign intelligence and counterintelligence operations, background investigations of informants, intelligence arrangements with foreign governments, and scientific and technical methods for gathering intelligence. Although most of this information had been withheld under the national security exemption prior to the act's passage, the CIA was required to review each document and justify its decision to deny access, a very time-consuming process that created a huge backlog of FOIA requests at the agency.

Statutes that do not satisfy the first provision of Exemption Three might nonetheless qualify under the second category, which covers statutes allowing for some agency discretion concerning disclosure of records. However, this discretion must be limited to certain defined areas or restricted by definite statutory criteria. Accordingly, statutes that give unbridled discretion to agency officials regarding disclosure or provide only that officials may release the records if they determine that such action is "in the public interest" does not satisfy the test and thus cannot serve as a basis for withholding records sought under the FOIA.

The Supreme Court dealt with the question of whether a "discretionary" disclosure statute qualifies under the second prong of Exemption Three in a 1980 case, *Consumer Product Safety Commission v. GTE Sylvania, Inc.* At issue was a statute providing that the CPSC could not release information reflecting unfavorably on a product until the manufacturer had been notified and given an opportunity to defend the product. Moreover, the statute stated that the agency could not release its evaluation of the product until satisfied that its information was accurate and that disclosure would be "fair in the circumstances" and "reasonably related to effectuating the purposes" of the Consumer Product Safety Act. The case arose when *Consumer Reports* magazine sought to obtain from the CPSC the results of its investigation into injuries caused when the picture tubes of televison sets had exploded. The magazine argued that the data collected by the agency was available under the FOIA, but the Supreme Court disagreed, ruling that the statute described above fell within Exemption Three because it provided sufficiently "particular criteria" for the agency's discretion in disclosing information.

Similarly, the Court ruled in *Central Intelligence Agency v. Sims* (1985) that a provision of the National Security Act of 1947 qualifies under Exemption Three. Under that statute, the director of the CIA is "responsible for protecting intelligence sources and methods from unauthorized disclosure." The CIA had invoked this statute in denying access to the names of various institutions and individuals who had been involved in a CIA-financed research project established to counter Soviet and Chinese advances in brainwashing and interrogation techniques. Because the statute "refers to particular types of matters to be withheld," the Court said, it satisfies Exemption Three. The Court also concluded that the names of the researchers and the institutions with which they were affiliated constituted "intelligence sources and methods" within the meaning of the statute because they provided "information the Agency needs to fulfill its statutory obligations with respect to foreign intelligence." This rather broad interpretation of the statute was in stark contrast to the ruling of the lower court, which had construed it to permit the CIA to withhold only those sources who had supplied the agency with information unattainable without a promise of confidentiality.

The Reporters Committee for Freedom of the Press has identified twenty federal statutes most frequently cited by administrative agencies as grounds for refusing to disclose records under the provisions of Exemption Three. These statutes affect many important federal agencies, including, in addition to agencies previously mentioned, the Department of Agriculture (records submitted by farmers under various federal programs), the Federal Trade Commission (investigative records obtained by the agency under laws governing false advertising and unfair business practices), the Department of Energy (records about public utilities), the Patent Office (information about inventions prior to the time an application is processed), the Veterans' Administration (VA benefits), the Postal Service (identities and addresses of "postal patrons," mailing lists and investigation files), and the Defense Department (information regarding weapons, equipment, and defense contractors).

There has been considerable confusion surrounding the relationship between the FOIA and the federal Privacy Act, which places restrictions upon the government's use of personal information that it has obtained about citizens. As a general rule, the Privacy Act prohibits the federal government from disclosing "private" information about individuals to any person or agency without the consent of the person about whom the records are maintained. There are various exceptions to this general rule, one of which covers records that are required to be disclosed under the FOIA. This means that an individual's records may be released to a third party if the FOIA so requires, that is, if the records do not fall within one of the FOIA's nine exemptions. Remember, however, that the FOIA exemptions are permissive rather than mandatory, and that an agency may in its discretion release records that would otherwise be exempt. Should an agency decide to disclose such records, it must do so only if permissible under the Privacy Act. These rules governing the effect of the Privacy Act on FOIA disclosures to third parties have always been relatively clear.

Confusion has arisen because the Privacy Act allows the person about whom records are kept a right of access to those records. In that sense, it works much like the FOIA; however, the Privacy Act contains various limitations on the individual's right of access to his own records. Thus, the courts were faced with a question: do the Privacy Act exemptions limiting individual access qualify under Exemption Three of the FOIA, thereby restricting access under the FOIA as well? The lower federal courts divided on the issue, and the Supreme Court agreed to hear a case and resolve the conflict. Before the Court could act, however, Congress amended the Privacy Act in 1984 to provide that agencies may not rely on a Privacy Act exemption to withhold from an individual any record which is otherwise available to that person under the FOIA. This amendment makes plain that the Privacy Act does not fall within Exemption Three.

Exemption Four: Trade Secrets. In the course of their regulatory activities, federal administrative agencies obtain a tremendous amount of information about private businesses. Some of that material, if disclosed under the FOIA, could cause harm to a company or give an advantage to its competitors. Accordingly, the FOIA—like most state "public records" statutes—exempts "trade secrets and commercial or financial information obtained from a person and privileged or confidential." The term "person" is defined to include business organizations such as corporation and partnerships, as well as individuals.

The exemption covers two distinct types of records: "trade secrets," a term that has been defined rather narrowly by the courts, and other sensitive "commercial or financial" data. Generally speaking, a trade secret is a "secret, commercially valuable plan, formula, process or device that is used for the making, preparing, compounding, or processing of trade commodities and that can be said to be the end product of either innovation or substantial effort." This definition, adopted by the U.S. Court of Appeals for the District of Columbia Circuit in *Public Citizen Health Research Group v. Food and Drug Administration* (1983), requires that there be a "direct relationship" between the trade secret and the productive process. There are only a handful of FOIA cases involving trade secrets, but it is clear that product designs and formulae are included. Probably the most famous example of a trade secret is the formula of Coca-Cola, undoubtedly one of the most carefully guarded recipes in the world.

Most Exemption Four cases are not concerned with trade secrets, but with "confidential" commercial information that has been submitted to the government. Virtually any information relating to a business or trade qualifies as "commercial," such as profit and loss statements, sales data, customer lists, or overhead and operating costs. The question, then, is whether this material is "confidential," and the courts have developed the following test: records are confidential if disclosure would either impair the government's ability to obtain such information in the future or cause substantial competitive harm to the submitter of the information.

The first part of the test is obviously no problem if the government can compel a business to furnish the information, and difficulties arise only when the data is provided voluntarily. Thus, most cases involve the second part of the test, which requires determination on a case-by-case basis of whether release of the records would cause competitive harm. Since the facts of each case and the particular business climate are critical, the courts have reached different results regarding similar information. For example, in some cases the courts have approved agency withholding of customer lists, while in others the courts have ordered the disclosure of such information. Generally speaking, however, the courts have found that competitive harm would result from disclosure of records showing assets, profits and losses, market shares, labor costs, freight charges, types of equipment, names of consultants and suppliers, bidding information, and descriptions of the company's work force.

The case of *National Parks & Conservation Association v. Kleppe*, decided by the U.S. Court of Appeals for the District of Columbia Circuit in 1976, is illustrative. The case involved information submitted to the National Park Service by concessioners providing food, lodging, and other goods and services in the national parks. The plaintiff, an association undertaking a study of the Park Service's oversight of these concessioners, sought access under the FOIA to records that the concessioners were required to file with the Service. The information was detailed and voluminous, including complete financial statements showing the concessioner's operating condition, descriptions of all projects then underway or planned for the future, a list of all facilities, and such related data as occupancy rates during peak tourist months. Since most of the concessioners faced competition from businesses set up immediately adjacent to the parks, this information would provide competitors with "valuable insights into the operational strengths and weaknesses of a concessioner." Meanwhile, the court said, competitors "could continue in their customary manner of playing their cards close to their chest." Accordingly, the court ruled that the potential for competitive harm justified withholding of the records under Exemption Four.

Exemption Four has been largely responsible for the development of the so-called "reverse-FOIA" lawsuit, in which a submitter of information seeks a court order prohibiting an agency from releasing records in response to a request from a third party. The terminology is somewhat misleading, for the Supreme Court ruled in *Chrysler Corp. v. Brown* that the FOIA creates a remedy for an agency's refusal to disclose records, not for its decision to make those records available to the public. The Court reasoned that the nine FOIA exemptions are permissive rather than mandatory and that an agency may, in its discretion, decide to disclose records that could be withheld under a particular exemption. Since the exemptions are permissve, the FOIA itself affords no basis for a lawsuit brought by a submitter desirous of preventing disclosure. However, the Court was careful to point out that other federal statutes may forbid release of particular records and that a submitter may be able to obtain judicial relief under these statutes. Such lawsuits are still generally known as "reverse-FOIA" suits, since their goal is to preclude release of records under the FOIA.

In *Brown*, for example, Chrysler Corporation brought suit to enjoin the release of information about its hiring of women and minorities that it had to file with the Defense Department in order to obtain a government contract for the manufacture of weapons. The dispute arose when a labor union filed an FOIA request for the records. Learning of the request, Chrysler asked a federal court to bar release of the data, arguing that its release would violate Exemption Four. Though the Supreme Court ruled that the Defense Department could release the information even if it were covered by the exemption, it left open the possibility that Chrysler might be able to bring suit under another law forbidding the release of the records.

In order to protect the interests of the businesses that submit sensitive commercial information to the government, President Ronald Reagan issued a 1987 executive order directing executive branch agencies to adopt "submitter notice" regulations under which businesses must be promptly notified of FOIA requests covering such records. These regulations must also give the submitter the opportunity to object to the disclosure of any portion of the requested records; provide notice of a decision to disclose the records and a statement of the reasons why the submitter's objections to disclosure were not sustained; and state the specific date on which the records are to be released. These requirements are obviously designed to give the submitter sufficient time to file a "reverse-FOIA" lawsuit to block disclosure of the records. If the agency decides not to release the records and the requester brings suit to compel their disclosure, the agency must notify the submitter that a lawsuit has been filed.

Exemption Five: Agency Memoranda. This exemption covers "inter-agency or intra-agency memorand[a] or letters which would not be available by law to a party other than an agency in litigation with the agency." Put another way, the exemption excludes from the FOIA records that would be unavailable during the pretrial phase of a civil lawsuit—known as "discovery"—involving the agency. During the discovery process, lawyers exchange information about the case; however, various legal doctrines allow a lawyer to withhold certain information from his adversary. Exemption Five was designed to incorporate into the FOIA these legal doctrines, the most important of which are executive privilege, the work-product doctrine, and the attorney-client privilege.

The most commonly invoked of the three doctrines in the FOIA context is executive privilege, which protects advice, recommendations, and opinions which are part of the decision making process within an agency. In *National Labor Relations Board v. Sears, Roebuck & Co.* (1975), the Supreme Court explained that this privilege is based on three policy considerations:

- encouraging open, frank discussions on matters of policy between subordinates and superiors;
- protecting against premature disclosure of proposed policies before they are finally adopted; and
- avoiding public confusion that might result from disclosure of reasons and rationales that were not in fact the ultimate basis for agency decisions.

The *Sears* case involved an FOIA request for memoranda prepared by the staff of the National Labor Relations Board in the course of deciding whether to file unfair labor practice charges. In a rather complex opinion, the Court concluded that decisions not to file such charges are "final" and thus available under the FOIA. However, memoranda directing the filing of charges are covered by Exemption Five, reasoning that this action constituted only the first step in an unfair labor practices complaint.

In a companion case, *Renegotiation Board v. Grumman Aircraft Engineering Corp.*, the records at issue were memoranda prepared as part of the process under which the Renegotiation Board, a federal agency, determines whether government contractors have received excessive profits. The memoranda, prepared by regional branches of the board, recommended how cases involving individual contractors should be decided. Because they had no binding effect on the board and were designed only to assist it in reaching a final decision, the Court ruled that the memoranda fell within Exemption Five. As the Court pointed out, the memoranda contained nothing more than recommendations similar to those made by employees at all federal agencies to their superiors who possessed the final authority to make a decision. Applying *Sears* and *Grumman*, the lower federal courts have ruled that "drafts" of suggested agency action are exempt because they are part of the deliberative process by which an agency reaches a final decision.

The U.S. Court of Appeals for the District of Columbia Circuit has recently taken an expansive view of this exemption. In *Wolfe v. Department of Health & Human Services* (1988), the court concluded that the Food and Drug Administration properly withheld "logs" showing how long it took for two other federal agencies—the Department of Health and Human Services and the Office of Management and Budget—to review proposed FDA regulations. In an opinion by Judge Robert Bork, the court ruled that this information would reveal approval or disapproval by HHS and OMB and that this disclosure would interfere with the deliberative process. A strong dissenting opinion took the position that release of the logs would not show either the reasoning of the agency decision makers or their tentative conclusions regarding the FDA proposals.

Many state FOI statutes do not contain a "deliberative process" exemption, and a powerful argument can be made that the public should have access to this type of agency raw material. If the public is to understand fully why an agency made a particular decision, the argument goes, it must be able to examine not only the stated rationale or justification ultimately chosen, but also the factors that were rejected during the decision making process. But the Congress struck the balance differently in the FOIA, having concluded that the need for robust debate and a free exchange of ideas within the agency outweighs the public's right to know in this instance.

The work-product doctrine protects the legal theories and litigation strategy of an attorney involved in a lawsuit or administrative proceeding. Accordingly, it is an exception to the general rule of "discovery" that requires opposing counsel to exchange information about the case. It is grounded largely in the adversarial nature of the American legal system, as well as in the notion that a lawyer must "do his own work" rather than mooch from his opponent. Lawyers working for the government need this protection just as much as their private sector counterparts, and the rules applicable in the courts and in quasi-judicial administrative hearings make no distinction between government lawyers and other attorneys. If Exemption Five did not encompass this information, however, the FOIA could be used to circumvent these rules, and government lawyers would find themselves at a considerable disadvantage. That is indeed the case in those states that do not have a version of Exemption Five in their FOI laws.

A 1983 Supreme Court case, *Federal Trade Commission v. Grolier, Inc.*, illustrates how the work-product doctrine operates. The case stemmed from an FTC suit charging that Grolier's salesmen used misleading tactics in selling encyclopedias. The suit was dismissed prior to trial, and Grolier filed an FOIA request asking for documents that FTC lawyers had prepared in connection with the case. The company admitted that it sought the records to find out exactly how much the agency had learned about its sales techniques. After the FTC refused to disclose the records, Grolier brought suit under the FOIA to obtain their release. The Supreme Court ultimately agreed with the trial judge that Exemption Five was applicable, reasoning that the documents constituted attorney work product even though the particular case for which they were prepared had ended. A contrary result, Justice Brennan pointed out in a concurring opinion, would enable an opposing party "to obtain work product generated by the agency in connection with earlier, similar litigation" and thus "get the benefit of the agency's legal and factual research and reasoning. . . ."

The attorney-client privilege is related to but conceptually distinct from the work-product doctrine. While both are based in part on the adversarial nature of our legal system, the attorney-client privilege focuses not on the working papers of the lawyer but on his confidential relationship with his clients. If a client is unable to speak freely with his lawyer, the attorney will be unable to render the most effective legal representation. When the attorney-client privilege is claimed by a government agency, it protects the agency's interest in obtaining legal advice based on full and frank discussions with agency lawyers. Some states, however, have established a "weaker" version of the privilege when government lawyers are involved, and others have provided no protection whatsoever in their FOI statutes for confidential attorney-client communications. Both of these approaches represent policy decisions by the states that, at least to some extent, the need to protect the relationship between the government lawyer and his agency client is counterbalanced by the public's need to know what the government is doing.

For purposes of Exemption Five, it is important to note one very significant way in which the attorney-client privilege differs from executive privilege and the work-product doctrine. Because these two concepts apply to the thought processes of agency employees and attorneys, respectively, they do not include factual information. Therefore, a memorandum that contains both facts and exempt information must be disclosed to the public with the exempt material deleted, provided that it is possible to separate the two. In contrast, the attorney-client privilege applies not only to legal advice rendered by an attorney, but also to factual material—furnished by the client—on which that advice is based.

On occasion, the courts have interpreted Exemption Five to protect records that would not be exempt under any of the three doctrines just discussed. The basic question, however, is the same: would the records be available during the pretrial discovery phase in litigation involving the agency? If not, they are covered by Exemption Five and may thus be withheld under the FOIA.

An illustrative decision is the Supreme Court's 1979 ruling in *Federal Open Market Committee v. Merrill*, which involved monthly decisions of the committee, a component of the Federal Reserve Board, regarding domestic monetary policy. These decisions, embodied in a document known as the "domestic policy directive," have a significant impact on the economy, for they indicate whether the committee plans to follow an expansionary, deflationary, or unchanged monetary policy in the month ahead. Believing that immediate release of this information would hamper its efforts to stabilize the economy, the committee made the directive available to the public only after it had been in effect for a month—that is, about the time when a new directive would be implemented. In *Merrill*, the Supreme Court rejected the plaintiff's argument that this one-month delay violated the FOIA. Because the committee could, in typical civil litigation, obtain a court order preventing an opposing party from "discovering" such sensitive commercial information, the directive was also covered by Exemption Five.

Exemption Six: Personal Privacy. The federal government is a vast depository for records concerning individual citizens, and the Privacy Act of 1974—discussed above in connection with Exemption Three—was a response to concerns about the government's collection, maintenance, and use of personal information. As we have seen, however, the Privacy Act does not serve as a basis for withholding records requested under the FOIA. Accordingly, the question becomes whether another FOIA exemption precludes the release of such personal information, and the answer is found in Exemption Six, which covers "personnel and medical files and similar files the disclosure of which would constitute a clearly unwarranted invasion of personal privacy." Without this exemption, the FOIA would transform the federal government into what one commentator has described as "an information clearinghouse [for] the curious, the envious, and the creditor." Similar "personal privacy" exemptions appear in the FOI statutes of most states.

As noted previously, the FOIA represents a legislative attempt to balance the need for confidentiality on the one hand and the public's "right to know" on the other. Exemption Six is perhaps the clearest example of this balancing in the FOIA, but the Congress has not specifically struck the balance. Instead, it has merely provided vague guidelines and has left to federal agencies and the courts the task of balancing the competing interests. Although the scales are generally tipped in favor of disclosure, the resolution of any "personal privacy" question obviously depends heavily on the particular facts and circumstances of each case.

The initial inquiry is whether the information is found in a medical file, personnel file, or "similar" file. The first two categories are largely self-explanatory, and the third has been broadly interpreted by the Supreme Court to include any information "which pertains to a particular individual." Thus, the label that an agency has placed on a particular file is irrelevant. The next step is more complicated. Because the FOIA creates an exemption only when disclosure would cause a "clearly unwarranted" invasion of personal privacy, it is obvious that certain "warranted" invasions will be tolerated. Accordingly, an agency must evaluate the impact that release of the information would have on the individual and then determine whether the public's interest in disclosure would outweigh those privacy concerns.

The privacy analysis is much the same as that employed in cases involving the "public disclosure of private facts" branch of the invasion of privacy tort. As the U.S. Court of Appeals for the Second Circuit observed in *Brown v. FBI* (1981), a person's privacy is invaded by the release of the "intimate details" of his or her life, including any information that might "subject the person . . . to embarrassment, harassment, disgrace [or] loss of employment or friends." Other types of harm may also suffice. For example, in *U.S. Department of State v. Washington Post Co.* (1982), the Supreme Court suggested, without directly deciding, that records showing whether two Iranian officials held American passports might qualify, since release of that information could place them in danger of physical harm given the anti-American sentiment in Iran. Because the statute uses the term "personal" privacy, it does not protect corporations, partnerships, associations, or governmental entities.

In one of the leading cases interpreting Exemption Six, *Rural Housing Alliance v. Department of Agriculture* (1974), the U.S. Court of Appeals for the District of Columbia Circuit found a substantial privacy interest in a government study reflecting marital status, legitimacy of children, health information, welfare payments, alcohol consumption, and family fights. Other information recognized to implicate privacy interests includes personal and family history, religious affiliation, employee disciplinary records, social security numbers, and personal financial data. By way of comparison, the courts have found relatively little privacy interest in records revealing names, addresses, telephone numbers (unless unlisted), date and place of birth, salaries of government employees, training or educational background, and job experience. Keep in mind, however, that the "strength" of the privacy interest does not necessarily mean that the information will be exempt. Even substantial privacy concerns can be overcome by a compelling public interest in obtaining access to the information.

The "public interest" to be considered in this balancing process, the Supreme Court has said, is "the citizens' right to be informed about what their government is up to." Accordingly, the public interest is more likely to outweigh individual privacy concerns when the records in question shed light on an agency's performance of its official duties, particularly if apparent violations of the public trust are involved. For example, in *Washington Post Co. v. Department of Health & Human Services* (1982), the U.S. Court of Appeals for the District of Columbia Circuit ruled that the need for oversight of the process for awarding government grants outweighed the privacy interests of an individual applicant who had submitted personal financial information. Similarly, in *Columbia Packing Co. v. Department of Agriculture* (1977), the U.S. Court of Appeals for the First Circuit ordered disclosure of the names of federal meat inspectors involved in a bribery scheme, pointing out that there is significant public interest in misconduct of public officials and employees.

On the other hand, privacy interests will ordinarily be paramount when the records at issue reveal little or nothing about the conduct or operations of a government agency. In *Department of the Air Force v. Rose*, for example, the Supreme Court indicated that summaries of disciplinary hearings at the U.S. Air Force Academy were subject to disclosure under the FOIA, so long as these records did not reveal the names of individual cadets or include other identifying details. Because these summaries contained information that would reveal how the academy's honor code and disciplinary system actually functioned, disclosure was appropriate. However, information that would identify individual cadets who had been involved in the proceedings fell within Exemption Six, for it was not relevant to the administration of the honor code. Similarly, in *Minnis v. Department of Agriculture* (1984), the U.S. Court of Appeals for the Ninth Circuit recognized a valid public interest in a government lottery system for awarding permits to raft on a scenic river. However, the court concluded that release of the requested records—lists containing the names and addresses of persons who had received permits—would not further a determination of agency fairness, since other information would be necessary for such an evaluation.

It should be emphasized that the public interest in disclosure is distinct from the interest of the person requesting information in a specific case. Because "any person" may obtain records under the FOIA, an inquiry into the requester's purpose or motive in seeking access is impermissible. As the Supreme Court observed in *U.S. Department of Justice v. Reporters Committee for Freedom of the Press* (1989), "whether disclosure . . . is warranted must turn on the nature of the requested document and its relationship to the basic purpose of the [FOI] Act to open agency action to the light of public scrutiny, rather than on the particular purpose for which the document is being requested." Thus, the news media do not enjoy special status under the FOIA, and a request by an investigative reporter is to be evaluated in the same fashion as one by an attorney or business owner. As a practical matter, however, a requester motivated solely by commercial considerations may have a more difficult time convincing a court that the public interest outweighs concerns over individual privacy. In the *Minnis* case noted above, for example, the requester owned a lodge on the scenic river and sought the names of permit holders for commercial reasons.

Exemption Seven: Law Enforcement. Like open records statutes in most jurisdictions, the FOIA contains a so-called "law enforcement" exemption designed to prevent disclosure of records that would jeopardize the work of law enforcement officials. The need for the exemption is obvious; for example, disclosure of certain records could hamper police in investigating a crime, reveal the identities of confidential informants, or pose a threat to the right of the accused to receive a fair trial. However, there has been considerable disagreement over the years regarding the scope of the exemption, with law enforcement officials arguing in favor of a broad exemption and journalists pressing for a provision restricted to specific types of records. In its original form, the exemption was interpreted to exempt virtually all records found in investigatory files, regardless of the status of the underlying investigation or the content of the records. Congress amended the statute in 1974 to exempt only records that fell within one of six categories. In 1986, however, the pendulum swung the other way as Congress expanded those particular categories in response to complaints from law enforcement officials.

Exemption Seven now allows agencies to withhold records "compiled for law enforcement purposes," but only to the extent that their release:

(A) could reasonably be expected to interfere with enforcement proceedings;

(B) would deprive a person of a right to a fair trial or an impartial adjudication;

(C) could reasonably be expected to constitute an unwarranted invasion of personal privacy;

(D) could reasonably be expected to disclose the identity of a confidential source, including a State, local, or foreign agency or authority or any private institution which furnished information on a confidential basis, and, in the case of a record or information compiled by criminal law enforcement authority in the course of criminal investigation or by an agency conducting a lawful national security intelligence investigation, information furnished by a confidential source;

(E) would disclose techniques and procedures for law enforcement investigations or prosecutions if such disclosure could reasonably be expected to risk circumvention of the law; and

(F) could reasonably be expected to endanger the life or physical safety of any individual. . . .

Two steps are necessary in applying this exemption. First, the records must be "compiled for law enforcement purposes." The records need not be investigatory in nature, as was the case prior to the 1986 amendment, but materials collected merely for administrative reasons (e.g., monitoring public employees to determine if internal disciplinary proceedings are necessary) are not covered. Moreover, the Supreme Court ruled in *Federal Bureau of Investigation v. Abramson* (1982) that information originally compiled for law enforcement purposes does not lose its protection under Exemption Seven when it is subsequently summarized in a new document created for purposes other than law enforcement. The exemption applies not only to agencies that deal with violations of the criminal law, such as the FBI or the Drug Enforcement Agency, but also to agencies with civil enforcement responsibilities, such as the National Labor Relations Board and the Federal Trade Commission.

Second, the agency must demonstrate that the records fit within one of the six categories set out above. Notice that the wording differs from category to category with respect to the government's burden. With respect to subsection (B), for example, the agency must show that disclosure of the records "would deprive" an individual of his right to a fair trial. Subsection (A), however, requires only a showing that disclosure "could reasonably be expected" to interfere with enforcement proceedings. Obviously, the government's burden is much heavier in the former situation than in the latter. The 1986 amendment added the "could reasonably be expected" language, thus making it easier for law enforcement agencies to claim the exemption. With that in mind, we now turn to the six categories.

As the U.S. Supreme Court observed in *National Labor Relations Board v. Robbins Tire & Rubber Co.,* subsection (A) is intended to apply when "the government's case in court [is likely to be] harmed by the premature release of evidence or information." In other words, we do not want to let the cat out of the bag too quickly. The subsection also applies where disclosure can be expected to impede an ongoing investigation that could lead to enforcement proceedings. When the proceeding is completed, however, the records are no longer exempt, unless the agency can demonstrate that subsequent proceedings are likely. If, for example, a criminal conviction has been obtained and all appeals exhausted, the agency's investigatory records pertaining to the case will ordinarily be available for public inspection unless one of the other subsections applies. On the other hand, the fact that an investigation remains "open" will usually enable the agency to claim the exemption. In *National Public Radio v. Bell* (1977), a federal district court upheld the FBI's decision not to release its records involving the death of antinuclear activist Karen Silkwood even though the investigation was dormant and all available leads had been explored.

In some situations, an agency is not even required to acknowledge the existence of records falling within subsection (A). Under the 1986 amendment, an agency may simply respond to an FOIA request by saying that there are no records subject to the act if there is reason to believe that the target of a criminal investigation or proceeding is unaware of it and that disclosure of the existence of records (not simply their contents) could reasonably be expected to interfere with the enforcement process. A similar provision allows the FBI to use the "no records exist" response with respect to FOIA requests for records pertaining to foreign intelligence or counterintelligence and international terrorism, provided that the records are properly classified under the national security exemption.

There are few cases under subsection (B), which is aimed at avoiding prejudicial pretrial publicity in criminal and civil cases and in administrative proceedings. In *Washington Post Co. v. U.S. Department of Justice* (1988), the U.S. Court of Appeals for the District of Columbia Circuit ruled that the government, in order to claim the exemption, must show that a trial or adjudication "is pending or truly imminent" and that it is "more probable than not" that disclosure of the requested material "would seriously interfere with the fairness of those proceedings." At issue in this case was a report filed with the Justice Department by a drug manufacturer against whom several civil lawsuits were pending. Although the court of appeals sent the case back to the trial court for further consideration of the subsection (B) question, it indicated that the report could properly be withheld if disclosure would spawn publicity sufficient to compromise the fairness of the pending trials or would provide an unfair litigation advantage to the persons suing the drug company.

Subsection (C) is much more frequently litigated. Like Exemption Six, it is designed to protect personal privacy interests, and a similar balancing process is employed. Despite some overlap between the two, subsection (C) affords more protection to privacy interests. First, while Exemption Six requires that the invasion of privacy be "clearly unwarranted," subsection (C) does not contain the adverb "clearly." Second, while Exemption Six refers to the release of records that "would constitute'' an invasion of privacy, subsection (C) encompasses any disclosure that "could reasonably be expected to constitute" such an invasion. As a result, the government's task of justifying its refusal to disclose records is a bit easier under subsection (C).

For example, the courts have ruled that an agency need not disclose records about persons who were targets of police investigations but who were not charged with any crime. This result makes sense, for the target of such an investigation is often unable to overcome the implication of wrongdoing. Privacy considerations also prevail when records would reveal the identity of a person who had supplied information to a law enforcement agency, even though that person did not qualify as a "confidential source" for purposes of subsection (D). Various concerns come into play here: the individual might be harmed or stigmatized for cooperating with the agency, and sources of information might "dry up" if names of informants were routinely revealed. Similarly, the courts have ruled that records containing the names of law enforcement officers are not subject to public inspection if there is a potential for harassment. If an officer's life or physical safety would be jeopardized, subsection (F) would permit withholding the records.

A recent controversy has arisen with respect to FBI "rap sheets" listing an individual's arrest, convictions, and imprisonment history. The FBI collects this information from federal, state, and local law enforcement agencies and stores it in a computer database. In most jurisdictions, the records from which these summaries are compiled are typically contained in police or court files that are open to public inspection. Nonetheless, all but three states (Florida, Oklahoma, and Wisconsin) place substantial restrictions on the availability of criminal history summaries. Relying on subsection (C), the FBI has also denied access to its rap sheets, and the U.S. Supreme Court upheld the agency in the 1989 *Reporters Committee* case mentioned above in connection with Exemption Six.

The case arose when a CBS news correspondent and the Reporters Committee made FOIA requests for FBI rap sheets concerning four members of the Medico family who had been linked to organized crime. Moreover, their company, Medico Industries, had allegedly obtained a number of defense contracts as a result of an improper arrangement with a corrupt congressman. Although the FBI initially refused the requests, it provided the records on three of the Medicos after their deaths. However, the agency declined to make available records concerning the fourth family member, Charles Medico. A federal district court in Washington, D.C., ruled that the records fell within subsection (C) of Exemption Seven, but the court of appeals reversed. Reasoning that there can be no privacy interest when information is already public, the court rejected the FBI's argument that access to the agency's database posed a significant threat to individual privacy.

On further appeal, the Supreme Court agreed with the FBI that the records fell within subsection (C). First, the Court found a significant privacy interest in the information contained in the rap sheets, pointing out that members of the general public could not, as a practical matter, piece together this material. "Plainly there is a vast difference between the public records that might be found after a diligent search of courthouse files, county archives, and police stations throughout the country and a computerized summary located in a single clearinghouse of information," the Court said. Second, in weighing this privacy interest against the public interest in disclosure, the Court determined that the balance tipped in favor of privacy. "The FOIA's central purpose is to ensure that the Government's activities be opened to the sharp eye of public scrutiny," the Court said, "not that information about private citizens that happens to be in the warehouse of the Government be so disclosed." Concluding that rap sheets do not shed any light on government activities or operations, the Court ruled that they are exempt under subsection (C).

In this balancing process, the Court focused on the category or type of records involved rather than on the particular records pertaining to Mr. Medico, thereby establishing a blanket exemption for *all* FBI rap sheets.[3] Of necessity, however, the Court discussed in some detail the asserted public interest in access to his rap sheet. First, the Court said, release was not warranted simply because it contained information about a person who allegedly had improper dealings with a congressman and who served as an officer of a corporation with defense contracts. Although the rap sheet would provide details about Mr. Medico's criminal record, it would not reveal anything about "the character of the congressman's behavior" or "the conduct of the Department of Defense in awarding one or more contracts to the Medico company." Second, the fact that the records were requested by journalists engaged in newsgathering activities was not a factor in evaluating the public interest, the Court noted, since the purpose or motive of a person requesting records under the FOIA is immaterial.

As mentioned previously, subsection (D) protects the identities of confidential sources. The term is broadly defined to include not only individuals, but also state, local, or foreign agencies. A promise of confidentiality, either express or reasonably implied, is necessary here, and protection is not limited to paid informants. With respect to criminal law enforcement agencies or those involved in national security matters, "information furnished by a confidential source" is also exempt. The courts have interpreted subsection (D) rather broadly. In fact, the U.S. Court of Appeals for the Sixth Circuit ruled in *Kiraly v. FBI* (1984) that this provision allowed the FBI to withhold the identity of a dead person who had served as an informant and whose status as an informant was known.

Subsection (E), which was substantially modified in 1986, enables agencies to withhold from disclosure records that reflect law enforcement operating procedures, techniques, and guidelines. Such information is often found in agency "manuals" that might also fall within Exemption Two. The purpose of subsection (E) is to prevent disclosure of records that would enable criminals to anticipate methods to be used in their apprehension, as well as records that reflect agency guidelines for investigating and prosecuting crimes. For example, guidelines that determine the types of cases that will receive priority in prosecution or list the criteria to be used in deciding whether charges are to be dropped or reduced are exempt. However, the courts have consistently ruled that the exemption does not apply to widely known law enforcement techniques, such as fingerprinting and ballistics tests.

Finally, subsection (F) protects records which, if released, could reasonably be expected to endanger the life of any person. It obviously includes the names of undercover law enforcement officers, but it is not so limited. For example, there may be a risk of harm to any officer, undercover or not, who worked on a particular case. Thus, in *Nunez v. Drug Enforcement Agency* (1980) the court denied a convicted drug dealer's FOIA request for the names of all officers who had been involved in the investigation of his case. There might also be a risk of harm to families of police officers, informants who have cooperated with an agency, and witnesses

---

[3]It is not clear whether this so-called "categorial balancing" approach will also be used in Exemption Six cases. In applying that exemption, the courts have in the past struck the appropriate balance on a case-by-case basis depending on the particular records involved.

given protection under the Justice Department's witness relocation program. Moreover, this provision could be used to justify nondisclosure of law enforcement techniques and procedures.

Making an FOIA Request. A request for records under the FOIA can be made by "any person," a term defined in the statute to include individuals, partnerships, corporations, associations, and state and local governments. American citizenship is not required, and foreign nationals can thus obtain access to records. In contrast, many state FOI statutes require that the person requesting records be a citizen of the state. No showing of "proper purpose" is necessary, and the requester need not indicate why he is seeking particular records. However, as we shall see below, the requester's purpose or motive may play a role in determining various procedural matters, such as whether fees charged for copying and search time will be waived or reduced. Moreover, the requester's purpose may convince an agency to exercise its discretion to release records that fall within one of the nine exemptions.

The request must be in writing, but in some cases an informal oral request will be sufficient to obtain the desired records. If that course proves unsuccessful, a formal written request must be made in accordance with the agency's procedural regulations implementing the FOIA. These regulations must inform the public of where and how to address FOIA requests, of what types of records are maintained by the agency, of its fee schedule for copying and search time, and of its administrative appeal procedures. Obviously, the FOIA regulations of a given agency serve as the starting point for anyone seeking records from that agency. Careful compliance with these requirements is extremely important, for absent compliance an agency is under no obligation to search for records or to release them. Of particular note are the rules designating the appropriate official to whom FOIA requests are to be made. All agencies require that the request must be sent, in writing, to a particular official at the agency, often called the "FOIA officer."

Large agencies with several administrative units can pose some difficulties for the requester, for the FOIA request must be submitted to the appropriate unit. For example, a person requesting records from the Secretary of Agriculture must send his request, in an envelope marked "FOIA Request," to the Director of Information, Office of Governmental and Public Affairs, U.S. Department of Agriculture. But a request involving the USDA's Animal and Plant Health Inspection Service must be directed to that division's freedom of information coordinator, and a request to the USDA's Soil Conservation Service may be made either to the Deputy Administrator for Administration of the SCS in Washington or to a regional SCS office. Fortunately, the USDA, like many large agencies, will refer misaddressed requests to the appropriate department or division for processing and will so advise the requester. That is not always the case, however. The FBI, for example, requires that requests for records at various FBI field offices around the country be sent to the particular field office. If a request is erroneously sent to the FBI in Washington, the agency will search only its central files.

The FOIA itself requires that a request must "reasonably describe" the records sought. According to the courts, a request passess muster if it enables a professional agency employee familiar with the subject matter to locate the record with a reasonable amount of effort. From a practical standpoint, agency employees are likely to be more helpful in responding to an FOIA request that is somewhat specific than one that requires them to look for the proverbial needle in a haystack. Not surprisingly, the FOIA regulations of some agencies advise that, whenever possible, a requester should supply specific information—such as dates and titles—that may help identify the records. Some agency rules also provide that if the request is not sufficiently specific, the agency must notify the requester of the deficiency and give him an opportunity to provide clarification or to confer with agency personnel for assistance in formulating a more specific request. Of course, there is a certain danger in being too specific, for a precisely framed request might not cover records that could be of significance to the requester.

Obtaining records under the FOIA is not without cost. Pursuant to the Freedom of Information Reform Act passed by Congress in late 1986, agencies may charge for the direct costs of providing FOIA services, including search, duplication, and, in some cases, review of records to determine what should be released. The 1986 amendments also directed the Office of Management and Budget to promulgate uniform guidelines for fees to be charged for these items. Office of Management and Budget regulations adopted under the statute do not establish across-the-board fees that agencies can charge, but rather set standards for calculating those fees.

The charge for "manual searches" for records is to be based on the salary rate of the employee performing the search, while the charge for "computer searches" can include computer time and operator salary. Copying charges are to be determined by "an average agency-wide per-page charge for paper and copy reproduction" that includes the salaries of operators and the costs of copying equipment. Thus, costs may vary considerably from agency to agency. According to the Reporters Committee for Freedom of the Press, a Washington-based organization that publishes a useful guide to the FOIA, manual search fees typically range from $11 to $28 per hour, and computer searches can be as high as $270 per hour. Copying costs are generally about 15 cents per page. Fees for a particular agency can be found in the *Federal Register* or *Code of Federal Regulations* and may be obtained from the agency's FOIA officer.

More significantly for the news media, the 1986 amendments specifically exempted the press from fee charges for searches and review of documents, as well as from the copying charges for the first 100 pages copied. A similar exemption applies to noncommercial requesters from educational or scientific institutions, and all other noncommercial requesters receive two hours of search time and 100 pages of copying at no charge. Thus, full fees for document search, duplication, and review may be charged only to requesters who seek the material for a commercial use. The OMB has issued guidelines defining each of these categories; for example, a representative of the news media qualifies for the exemption if he is actively gathering "news" for an organization that publishes or broadcasts news to the public. A freelance journalist may qualify under the definition if he can establish a firm basis for expecting publication, such as a contract or a commitment letter from an editor. Obviously, an FOIA request letter should point out that the records are being sought by representatives of the press (or other exempt organizations) and that the fee exemption is applicable.

Even with the exemption, FOI requests can be expensive for the news media, since records might well run into the thousands of pages—well beyond the 100 free copies provided under the exemption. Accordingly, requesters should take advantage of another provision in the FOIA requiring agencies to waive fees if "disclosure of the information is in the public interest because it is likely to contribute significantly to public understanding of the operations or activities of the government and is not primarily in the commercial interest of the requester." This provision, added in 1986, replaced an earlier version under which agencies were reluctant to waive fees and was plainly intended to increase the availability of such waivers.

The Department of Justice, however, has promulgated interpretive guidelines indicating that the "public interest" test may be more difficult to meet than Congress had intended. For example, the Justice Department guidelines—which have been adopted by several agencies—require requesters to show that the records they want are about the government itself, not about private firms regulated by the government. Moreover, journalists testifying before a Senate subcommittee hearing in late 1988 complained that agencies have refused to waive fees in connection with FOIA requests for records involving several matters of obvious public interest, including CIA recruiting activities on college campuses, the testing of biological weapons, and Justice Department files on such former public officials as Vice President Hubert Humphrey and FBI Director J. Edgar Hoover. In any event, a journalist's FOIA request should seek a waiver or reduction of fees and should include a brief explanation of how the public will benefit from disclosure of the records. For instance, a reporter might wish to describe the nature of the story he is developing and how the particular records relate to that story.

If copying and search costs are a concern, the requester should obtain from the agency an estimate of the costs. The agency's FOI officer is the best source of this information, but the estimate is only that—an estimate. For additional protection, the requester should state in his FOIA letter that he is willing to pay fees up to a specified amount and ask that the agency contact him in the event that the fees are likely to exceed that figure. Moreover, if copying fees are the major obstacle, the requester can ask to inspect the records in person at the agency's office. This approach obviously eliminates the need for copying and the associated expense. Further, a reporter may be able to avoid the delay that often comes with copying large numbers of documents, a factor that may be important when working against a deadline.

Generally, an agency must respond to a written FOIA request within ten working days; that is, the agency must inform the requester of its decision to grant or deny access within that period. Actual release of the records need not take place within that time frame, but access must be provided promptly, and the agency must advise the requester of the approximate date on which the records will be available. Moreover, the ten-day deadline may be extended up to an additional ten working days if there is a need to search for and collect records from separate offices, examine a voluminous amount of records, consult with other agencies, or deal with a heavy backlog of requests. The agency must give the requester notice of the extension and state the reasons for the delay. If the agency does not meet the ten-day or extended deadline, the requester may treat the agency's failure to respond as a denial of the request and turn immediately to the courts for relief. However, the court may allow the agency additional time to respond if it can show that its failure to meet the deadline resulted from exceptional circumstances and that it is exercising "due diligence" in processing the request. Accordingly, the better course is to negotiate with the agency regarding the delay and attempt to agree on a date by which the agency is to respond to the request.

If the agency refuses to disclose all or part of the records sought, determines that the requester is not entitled to an exemption from the payment of fees, refuses to grant a fee waiver, or fails to respond within the appropriate time frame, the requester may take an administrative appeal within the agency. All agencies have published regulations governing the appeal procedure. These include rules stating the time in which an appeal must be filed (usually thirty days from the date of the agency's initial denial), specifying the person to whom the appeal is to be directed, and requiring that the appeal be in writing and mailed in an envelope marked "FOIA Appeal."

Before taking such action, however, it is often a good idea to consult informally with the agency's FOIA officer and attempt to negotiate for disclosure of at least some of the records. If this fails, the administrative appeal is necessary before one can file suit under the FOIA in federal court. The appeal letter should ask for review of the initial decision regarding the request and should state the requester's views as to why denial or access or other agency action (such as the refusal to waive fees) was improper. After an appeal is filed, an agency has twenty working days to rule upon the matter, though the same rules for extensions of time governing initial FOIA requests also apply here.

The statutory "response times" discussed above were added to the FOIA in 1974, after journalists complained that the disclosure process was too slow to meet their needs and deadlines. These complaints were confirmed by a Senate report indicating that major government agencies had been taking an average of thirty-three days to respond to FOIA requests. Despite the 1974 amendments, lengthy delays remain common, since the FOIA expressly allows agencies extra time in certain situations. In addition, a recalcitrant agency can simply withhold the information and force the requester to file an administrative appeal and then pursue the matter in court, thus further delaying release of the records.[4] Even if an agency responds in accordance with the statutory provisions, the ephemeral nature of news often means that the story is "cold" by the time the records are released. Moreover, a successful FOIA request may not always result in an "exclusive" story, since the disclosed documents are also available to anyone else who requests them.

Judicial Relief. A requester who has not obtained the full relief he seeks via the administrative appeal may file suit in federal court against the agency under the FOIA. The requester may choose among several federal courts and should file suit in the court most convenient to him. That will usually be the court where he resides or has his principal place of business, but the suit may also be brought in the court where the agency records are located or in the District of Columbia. Although anyone can file a suit—including an FOIA suit—without an attorney, the assistance of a lawyer is advisable because body of judicial decisions interpreting the FOIA is rather complex. After the complaint is filed, the agency has the burden of justifying its refusal to disclose the requested records. The courts have been quite demanding in requiring that the agency offer detailed reasons for its actions, and sometimes the mere filing of a lawsuit will be enough to convince the agency to change its mind. Moreover, the FOIA requires that the government pay the requester's attorney fees if he is successful in the lawsuit, and this provision also encourages settlement.

---

[4] The performance of federal agencies in processing FOIA requests is mixed. For example, a General Accounting Office study released in March 1989 found that the typical response time at the State Department was more than six months, even though the agency's FOIA caseload—about 2,700 requests annually—is among the lightest in the government. At the other end of the spectrum is the Department of Health and Human Services, which, according to the *Washington Post*, responds to all but about forty of the 140,000 requests it receives each year within the ten-day statutory deadline.

Public Meetings

Paralleling the Freedom of Information Act at the federal level is a more recent "open meetings" statute, the Government in the Sunshine Act. There has been relatively little litigation under this statute, which was passed in 1976. In general, the act requires about fifty federal agencies—including major regulatory bodies such as the Federal Communications Commission, the National Labor Relations Board, and the Securities and Exchange Commission—to hold their meetings in public. However, the act allows closed sessions if the subject matter falls within one of ten exemptions. These provisions roughly correspond to the exemptions found in the FOIA, though there are some important differences. The act also prescribes in detail the procedures that an agency must follow to hold a closed meeting. Another statute, the Federal Advisory Committee Act, imposes similar requirements on advisory committees established by Congress, the President, or federal agencies.

As noted previously, all fifty states and the District of Columbia have also enacted open meetings statutes. Though these statutes vary tremendously in scope, they have much in common with each other and the federal sunshine act. In attempting to make use of any such statute, a reporter or other citizen must determine whether:

- the particular body is subject to sunshine requirements;
- the gathering is within the statute's definition of "meeting";
- an exemption allows a closed session;
- proper notice has been given and other procedural requirements followed; and
- meaningful judicial relief is available.

Though we examine these issues in connection with the federal act, much of the discussion is also relevant to state statutes.

Agencies Covered by the Sunshine Act. The Government in the Sunshine Act applies only to an agency that fits the definition found in the FOIA and is "headed by a collegial body composed of two or more individual members, a majority of whom are appointed by the President with the advice and consent of the Senate." This definition reaches many important regulatory agencies but excludes those headed by one person, such as the Environmental Protection Agency and the Department of Agriculture. The act also expressly applies to any subdivision of the body authorized to act on its behalf. The subdivision must be made up of members of the body, and, consequently, meetings of agency staff or employees are not covered, however. For example, in *Hunt v. Nuclear Regulatory Commission* (1979), the U.S. Court of Appeals for the Tenth Circuit held that the act did not apply to a hearing conducted by the Atomic Safety and Licensing Board, a body composed entirely of Nuclear Regulatory Commission employees.

The requirement that a majority of the body's members be appointed by the President and confirmed by the Senate was at issue in *Symons v. Chrysler Loan Guarantee Board* (1981). Established to oversee the federal "bailout" of Chrysler Motors, the board was composed of the Secretary of the Treasury, the Chairman of the Board of Governors of the Federal Reserve System, the Secretary of Labor, and the Secretary of Transportation. All of these individuals were appointed to their positions by the President, with the advice and consent of the Senate. However, they served on the board not as the result of direct presidential appointment, but rather by virtue of a statute that named the holders of those offices to the board. Concluding that the board members had not been appointed by the President, the U.S. Court of Appeals for the District of Columbia Circuit ruled that the board's meetings were not subject to the sunshine act.

What is a "Meeting"? Assuming that the statute does apply to a particular agency, the question arises as to what constitutes a meeting. For purposes of the act, a meeting is "the deliberations of at least the number of individual agency members required to take action on behalf of the agency where such deliberations determine or result in joint conduct or disposition of official agency business. . . ." This provision is an attempt to deal with a variety of questions that typically arise under open meetings statutes. First, it makes clear that there must be a quorum; accordingly, a gathering of members insufficient to constitute a quorum is not covered. The quorum rule also applies to subdivisions of the body, which means that in some cases a meeting of only two members would qualify.

Second, the definition seems to require some action or decision on the part of the body, thus suggesting that an informal discussion session would not be considered a meeting. However, the legislative history of the act indicates that final action is not necessary, so long as the discussion is "sufficiently focused" on particular issues so as to cause the members "to form reasonably firm positions regarding matters pending or likely to arise before the agency." For example, the act is violated if members of the body met in secret to discuss a particular issue and then held a public meeting simply to vote formally on the matter. In that situation, the public portion of the meeting would be a sham, for the result would have been preordained. Moreover, an agency can run into trouble by discussing official business in a conference telephone call involving at least a quorum of the members. Social gatherings and other "chance encounters" may cause similar problems if official business is discussed.

The leading case on the act's definition of "meeting" is *Federal Communications Commission v. ITT World Communications, Inc.*, decided by the U.S. Supreme Court in 1984. There three members of the FCC met with representatives of foreign governments to discuss the possibility of increased international competition in the area of overseas communications services. Because the three commissioners constituted a quorum of the Telecommunications Committee, the plaintiffs argued that the meeting was subject to the sunshine act. The Supreme Court disagreed. The FCC had already adopted a policy of increased competition, the Court said, and the meetings simply provided general background information and permitted the commissioners "to engage with their foreign counterparts in an exchange of views by which [those] decisions . . . could be implemented."

Third, there must be "joint conduct." For example, in the *ITT* case, the Supreme Court ruled that even if something more had been involved at the meeting, the sunshine act was inapplicable because the Telecommunications Committee lacked decision making authority with respect to the issues under discussion. Moreover, three members did not at the time constitute a quorum of the full FCC, which then had seven members. Accordingly, the meeting did not result in the "joint conduct or disposition of official agency business." By the same token, the act would not have applied had a single commissioner, acting with delegated authority from the commission, participated in that meeting, since there would have been no joint action. This "joint conduct" requirement has also permitted federal agencies to dispose of matters "by notation" without the need for a meeting. Under this practice, a staff memorandum advising action on a given matter is circulated, in sequence, to all members of the body for their approval, and no meeting is held. The courts have ruled that the sunshine act does not preclude this method of decision making, which shields important agency action from public view.

If a meeting is subject to the act, all portions of that meeting must be "open to public observation" unless an exemption applies. Though the public is entitled to attend the meeting, subject to reasonable seating limitations, there is no right to actively participate in the meeting. Moreover, the act does not address the question of whether audio and video recording or still photography is allowed, thus leaving this matter to the discretion of the individual agencies. In contrast, many state open meetings statutes expressly permit recording and photography.

Exemptions. An agency may close a meeting or portion of a meeting when it determines that an open session would likely reveal information falling into one of the act's ten exemptions. Even if an exemption is applicable, an agency must decide whether the public interest requires that the meeting remain open. As is the case with the FOIA, the exemptions are narrowly interpreted in light of Congress' intent that agencies conduct their business in public to the fullest extent possible. In large part, the exemptions mirror those found in the FOIA; for example, the sunshine act contains exemptions for national security information, internal personnel practices, matters exempted by other statutes, confidential business information, material which would cause a clearly unwarranted invasion of personal privacy, law enforcement information, and information relating to financial institutions. Obviously, the scope of these exemptions will hinge to some degree on judicial interpretation of the corresponding FOIA exemptions.

Conspicuously absent from the list of exemptions in the preceding paragraph is the "deliberative process" exemption found in the FOIA. That the sunshine act does not have such an exemption should come as no surprise, since the purpose of the statute is to open agency decision making to public scrutiny. However, the sunshine act recognizes that the deliberative process must be protected in certain circumstances. For example, agencies may hold closed sessions to consider whether to censure a person or bring criminal charges against him; to decide quasi-judicial cases pending before the agency; and to discuss litigation strategy with respect to pending or anticipated lawsuits. In addition, an agency may meet in private if public disclosure of information would likely frustrate action that the agency plans to take. Thus, a closed meeting would be permissible to decide whether to place an embargo on foreign shipments of particular goods, to discuss approval of a merger, to consider purchasing particular real estate, or to develop a strategy for collective bargaining with its employees. Similarly, agencies that regulate securities, commodities, or financial institutions may meet privately to protect information which, if disclosed, would lead to speculation or endanger the stability of financial institutions.

Procedural Requirements. An agency may invoke one of the exemptions only by a recorded vote of a majority of the members of the collegial body. Moreover, the agency's chief legal officer must certify that the meeting may be lawfully closed. Within one day of the vote, the agency must make public a written statement showing how each member voted and explaining, if necessary, why a meeting or portion of a meeting is to be closed. A list of persons expected to attend the closed session must also be provided. Regardless of whether a meeting is to be open or closed, an agency must publicly announce the time, place, and subject matter of the meeting at least one week in advance, unless circumstances require shorter notice. Moreover, the agency must submit the announcement for publication in the *Federal Register* and must use other "reasonable means" to assure that the public is informed of the meeting. For example, the agency might post notices on bulletin boards, publish them in special interest journals, or distribute them via a mailing list.

One of the most important provisions in the sunshine act requires an agency to keep records regarding all closed meetings or portions of meetings. Among other things, an agency must maintain a complete verbatim transcript or electronic recording of all closed meetings, although it may in some cases keep detailed minutes reflecting all actions taken and the vote of each member. After a closed meeting, an agency must "promptly" make available for public inspection those portions of the transcript, recording, or minutes that do not contain exempt information. If exempt matters are an integral part of the discussion, however, an agency may withhold the entire record of the meeting. The transcript, recording, or minutes must be maintained by the agency for at least two years.

Judicial Relief. The recording requirement is significant in terms of judicial enforcement of the sunshine act. If a court rules that an agency held a closed meeting in violation of the statute, it may order that the transcript, recording, or minutes be made available to the public. Accordingly, members of the public who were prevented from attending a meeting that should have been held "in the sunshine" may learn what transpired at the secret session. The court may also issue an injunction prohibiting future violations of the act, a remedy that may be particularly effective if the meeting has not yet taken place. In egregious cases, the court may invalidate agency action taken at an illegally closed meeting. Unfortunately, however, the sunshine act makes it difficult for courts to employ this extremely potent remedy, which is more frequently available at the state level. As a result, the fact that a court may order an agency to release the transcript, recording, or minutes of the closed session takes on increased importance.

A sunshine act suit may be brought in the federal district court located where the meeting was held, where the agency has its headquarters, or in the District of Columbia. Generally speaking, such a suit must be brought within sixty days of the meeting, unless the agency has failed to provide a public announcement of the meeting. As is the case under the FOIA, the burden of proof is on the agency to justify its conduct, and a successful plaintiff may recover his attorney fees and litigation costs from the government.

PROBLEMS

1. The Arizona Lottery Commission, a state agency which administers the Arizona lottery, contracted with two television stations—one in Phoenix, one in Tucson—for the live broadcast of weekly drawings in the Commission's "pick" game. The drawings were open to the public, including any media representatives, but the contracts awarded the two stations the exclusive right to film and televise the proceedings. Another Phoenix television station filed suit against the Commission, seeking an injunction that would allow any television broadcaster, without the necessity of a contract, to televise the weekly drawings. Its argument was that the contract unconstitutionally limited media access to the drawing, a newsworthy event. What result? *See KTSP-Taft Television v. Arizona*

State Lottery, 646 F. Supp. 300 (D. Ariz. 1986), *appeal dism'd*, 827 F.2d 772 (9th Cir. 1987).

2. As a result of the 1980 census, the number of members of the House of Representatives from Colorado increased from five to six. Redistricting plans to create a sixth congressional district were passed by the state legislature but vetoed by the governor. When a suit was brought against the governor and other state officials in federal court, the judge ordered that the governor and members of the legislature attempt to work out a compromise plan. The negotiators were directed to report their progress to the court. A meeting for that purpose was held in a courtroom at the federal courthouse. Though it was open to the public and press, the judge refused to allow television cameras, citing a local court rule prohibiting cameras in the courthouse. A television station challenged that rule as unconstitutional. What result? *See Combined Communications Corp. v. Finesilver,* 672 F.2d 818 (10th Cir. 1982).

3. A freelance photographer planned to attend concerts by several rock stars—including John Cougar Mellencamp, Sheena Easton, Pat Benatar, and Diana Ross—at the Providence, Rhode Island, Civic Center, a city-owned facility. The city had leased the center to a promoter, who entered into contracts with the various performers. Each contract contained a "no camera" clause forbidding photography during the concert. The photographer gained access to one concert, took photos, and was ejected from the center. Subsequently, he was refused admittance because he insisted on bringing his photographic equipment. He later filed suit, arguing that the camera ban violated the first amendment. Does he have a valid claim? *See D'Amario v. Providence Civic Center*, 639 F. Supp. 1538 (D.R.I. 1986), *aff'd*, 815 F.2d 692 (1st Cir.), *cert. denied*, 108 S.Ct. 172 (1987).

4. After the space shuttle Challenger exploded in January 1986, the *New York Times* filed an FOIA request for transcripts of all voice communications recorded aboard the shuttle, as well as copies of the tapes. NASA provided the *Times* with a transcript of the only voice recording that was made but, relying on Exemption Six, refused to supply a copy of the tape itself. The space agency claimed that release of the tape would encroach upon the personal privacy of the families of the seven astronauts killed in the disaster by subjecting them to replay of the voices of their loved ones. What result? Why? Does it matter that a transcript of tape had been made available to the newspaper? *See New York Times Co. v. NASA,* 852 F.2d 602, *rehearing granted,* 860 F.2d 1093 (D.C. Cir. 1988). Other FOIA litigation has also arisen as a result of the Challenger tragedy. For example, several news organizations filed suit to force the release of information about the settlement of claims brought by the families of the astronauts against the federal government and the manufacturer of the shuttle's booster rocket. In a separate case, the *Orlando Sentinel* filed an FOIA action against NASA after the agency refused access to autopsy reports on the seven astronauts prepared by the Armed Forces Institute of Pathology. Should the settlement documents and autopsy reports be disclosed? Which FOIA exemptions might come into play? Both cases were ultimately settled. *See* "Some Shuttle Settlement Terms Released," *The News Media & The Law* (Spring 1988), p. 39.

5. When a legislative body enacts a freedom of information act or a sunshine statute, it must balance competing interests: the public's right to know on the one hand, the government's legitimate need for confidentiality on the other. Assume that you are a member of a state legislature considering various bills to amend the state's access statutes. How would you vote on the following proposals?

   a. City councils, school boards, and similar bodies may hold closed sessions to confer with legal counsel.

    b. Death certificates, autopsy reports, and other records revealing a person's cause of death are open to the public.

    c. An agency may meet in executive session for purposes of collective bargaining with public employees or to discuss negotiating strategy.

    d. Annual evaluations and other job performance records of public employees, including school teachers, are open for public inspection.

    e. The names of persons who make gifts to public bodies are not available to the public if the donor requests that his name be kept confidential.

    f. A state or local industrial development board may go into executive session to discuss specific companies that could possibly be persuaded to locate manufacturing plants or other facilities in the area.

    g. Applications of businesses seeking government loans or grants are exempt from disclosure, as are the job applications of persons seeking public employment.

    h. The names of doctors, lawyers, and other professionals who fail state licensing examinations are open to the public.

    i. A city council or similar body may meet in executive session to receive staff briefings so long as members of the body do not discuss official business.

    j. A school board must meet in public to consider suspending, expelling, or otherwise disciplining any student.

    k. Probation and parole records are available for public inspection unless they involve juvenile offenders.

    l. The records of the State Judicial Ethics Commission are exempt from disclosure, and the commission may, in its discretion, hold closed meetings.

6. Under a Washington statute, "any exit poll or public opinion poll with voters" conducted within 300 feet of a polling place was a misdemeanor. Various news organizations, including the three television networks, challenged the statute as an unconstitutional infringement on their newsgathering activities. According to the media, the statute was designed to prevent the reporting of election results before the polls closed. Is the statute valid? Does it pose first amendment problems in terms of "access" by the media? Of what relevance, if any, is the public forum doctrine? See *Daily Herald Co. v. Munro*, 838 F.2d 380 (9th Cir. 1988).

7. For many years, reporters were allowed full access to the floor of the state house of representatives, from which the general public was excluded. Recently, however, the house adopted a resolution denying members of the press floor privileges while the house is in session. The resolution restricts the press to a portion of the gallery, though a pooling arrangement permits a handful of reporters and a single television camera operator to remain in a designated area on the floor itself. The official reason for the resolution, which also bans lobbyists and former legislators from the floor, was to ensure "decorum" in the crowded house chambers, but journalists suspect that it was passed because house members were upset with media coverage. Is the resolution constitutional? See *Lewis v. Baxley*, 368 F. Supp. 768 (M.D. Ala. 1973); *Consumers Union v. Periodical Correspondents' Association*, 365 F. Supp. 18 (D.D.C. 1973), *rev'd*, 515 F.2d 1341 (D.C. Cir. 1975), *cert. denied*, 423 U.S. 1051 (1976).

8. Between 1979 and 1981, the Federal Bureau of Investigation assisted the Atlanta police department in investigating a series of child murders that had shocked the city. The FBI also provided the local police with various documents relating to the investigation, with the understanding that the records remained the property of the FBI and would not be distributed outside the police department. In 1987, long after the case was closed and the suspect convicted, various news media successfully sued the City of Atlanta under the Georgia Open Records Act to obtain access to some of the files generated during the investigation. *See Napper v. Georgia Television Co.*, 356 S.E.2d 640 (Ga. 1987). Among the records released to the press and public were documents that the FBI had developed and furnished to the Atlanta police. Upon learning of the disclosure of these records, the FBI formally requested their return from the city and from the media organizations that had obtained them. After these requests were refused, the federal government brought suit against city officials in federal court to compel return of the records, arguing that they had merely been loaned to the Atlanta police and were exempt from disclosure under the federal FOIA. What result? *See United States v. Napper*, 694 F. Supp. 897 (N.D. Ga. 1988).

9. In selecting individuals to nominate for federal judgeships, the President considers numerous sources of information and advice, including that of private citizens, public officials, and government agencies. One particularly important source is the American Bar Association's Standing Committee on the Federal Judiciary, which evaluates the qualifications of potential nominees. (The ABA is a private organization with a membership of 328,000 lawyers.) The committee rates each candidate on a scale ranging from "exceptionally well qualified" to "not qualified" and makes a report for the Attorney General, who considers the information in making a recommendation to the President. These ratings and reports have been kept confidential, and the meetings of the committee have not been open to the public. Is the committee subject to the Federal Advisory Committee Act and, as a result, to the FOIA and the Government in the Sunshine Act? *See Public Citizen v. U.S. Department of Justice,* 109 S.Ct. 2558 (1989).

10. As noted previously, it is settled that computer tapes and disks are "records" under the federal Freedom of Information Act. *See, e.g., Long v. Internal Revenue Service*, 596 F.2d 362 (9th Cir. 1979), *cert. denied*, 446 U.S. 917 (1980). But must an agency program a computer in a particular way in order to retrieve information in the form requested, when it is technologically possible to do so? Would this process be the computer equivalent of searching paper records, or would it amount to "creation" of a record, something that the FOI Act does not require? *See Yeager v. Drug Enforcement Administration*, 678 F.2d 315 (D.C. Cir. 1982). If information on a computer tape is also available on paper or microfilm, may an agency make the material available in one of these other formats even though the requester has specifically asked for the computer version? *See Dismukes v. Department of Interior*, 603 F. Supp. 760 (D.D.C. 1984); *Blaylock v. Staley*, 732 S.W.2d 152 (Ark. 1987) (interpreting state FOI law). *See generally* "Computer Data Access is a Problem," *The News Media & the Law* (Winter 1989), p. 3.

CHAPTER
6
COVERING THE COURTS

Nebraska Press Association v. Stuart,
427 U.S. 539 (1976).

MR. CHIEF JUSTICE BURGER delivered the opinion of the Court.

The respondent State District Judge entered an order restraining the petitioners from publishing or broadcasting accounts of confessions or admissions made by the accused or facts "strongly implicative" of the accused in a widely reported murder of six persons. We [must] decide whether the entry of such an order on the showing made before the state court violated the constitutional guarantee of freedom of the press.

I

On the evening of October 18, 1975, local police found the six members of the Henry Kellie family murdered in their home in Sutherland, Neb., a town of about 850 people. Police released the description of a suspect, Erwin Charles Simants, to the reporters who had hastened to the scene of the crime. Simants was arrested and arraigned in Lincoln County Court the following morning, ending a tense night for this small rural community.

The crime immediately attracted widespread news coverage, by local, regional, and national newspapers, radio and television stations. Three days after the crime, the County Attorney and Simants' attorney joined in asking the County Court to enter a restrictive order relating to "matters that may or may not be publicly reported or disclosed to the public," because of the "mass coverage by news media" and the "reasonable likelihood of prejudicial news which would make difficult, if not impossible, the impaneling of an impartial jury and tend to prevent a fair trial." The County Court heard oral argument but took no evidence; no attorney for members of the press appeared at this stage. The County Court granted the prosecutor's motion for a restrictive order and entered it the next day, October 22. The order prohibited everyone in attendance from "releas[ing] or authoriz[ing] the release for public dissemination in any form or manner whatsoever any testimony given or evidence adduced"; the order also required members of the press to observe the Nebraska Bar-Press Guidelines.[1]

Simants' preliminary hearing was held the same day, open to the public but subject to the order. The County Court bound over the defendant for trial to the State District Court. The charges, as amended to reflect the autopsy findings, were that Simants had committed the murders in the course of a sexual assault.

Petitioners—several press and broadcast associations, publishers, and individual reporters—moved on October 23 for leave to intervene in the District Court, asking that the restrictive order imposed by the County Court be vacated. The District Court conducted a hearing, at which the County Judge testified and newspaper articles about the Simants case were admitted in evidence. The District Judge granted petitioners' motion to intervene and, on October 27, entered his own restrictive order. The judge found "because of the nature of the crimes charged in the complaint that there is a clear and present danger that pretrial publicity could impinge upon the defendant's right to a fair trial." The order applied only until the jury was impaneled, and specifi-

cally prohibited [the press] from reporting five subjects: (1) the existence or contents of a confession Simants had made to law enforcement officers, which had been introduced in open court at arraignment; (2) the fact or nature of statements Simants had made to other persons; (3) the contents of a note he had written the night of the crime; (4) certain aspects of the medical testimony at the preliminary hearing; and (5) the identity of the victims of the alleged sexual assault and the nature of the assault. It also prohibited reporting the exact nature of the restrictive order itself. Like the County Court's order, this order incorporated the Nebraska Bar-Press Guidelines. Finally, the order set out a plan for attendance, seating, and courthouse traffic control during the trial.

Four days later, on October 31, petitioners asked the District Court to stay its order. At the same time, they applied to the Nebraska Supreme Court for a writ of mandamus, a stay, and an expedited appeal from the order. The State of Nebraska and the defendant Simants intervened in these actions. The Nebraska Supreme Court heard oral argument on November 25, and issued its *per curiam* opinion December 1.

The Nebraska Supreme Court balanced the "heavy presumption against . . . constitutional validity" that an order restraining publication bears against the importance of the defendant's right to trial by an impartial jury. Both society and the individual defendant, the court held, had a vital interest in assuring that Simants be tried by an impartial jury. Because of the publicity surrounding the crime, the court determined that this right was in jeopardy. The court noted that Nebraska statutes required the District Court to try Simants within six months of his arrest, and that a change of venue could move the trial only to adjoining counties, which had been subject to essentially the same publicity as Lincoln County. The Nebraska Supreme Court held that "[u]nless the absolutist position of the [press] was constitutionally correct, it would appear that the District Court acted properly."

---

[1] These Guidelines are voluntary standards adopted by members of the state bar and news media to deal with the reporting of crimes and criminal trials. They outline the matters of fact that may appropriately be reported, and also list what items are not generally appropriate for reporting, including confessions, opinions on guilt or innocence, statements that would influence the outcome of a trial, the results of tests or examinations, comments on the credibility of witnesses, and evidence presented in the jury's absence. The publication of an accused's criminal record should, under the Guidelines, be "considered very carefully." The Guidelines also set out standards for taking and publishing photographs, and set up a joint bar-press committee to foster cooperation in resolving particular problems that emerge.

The Nebraska Supreme Court rejected that "absolutist position," but modified the District Court's order to accommodate the defendant's right to a fair trial and the [media's] interest in reporting pretrial events. The order as modified prohibited reporting of only three matters: (a) the existence and nature of any confessions or admissions made by the defendant to law enforcement officers, (b) any confessions or admissions made to any third parties, except members of the press, and (c) other facts "strongly implicative" of the accused. The Nebraska Supreme Court did not rely on the Nebraska Bar-Press Guidelines. After construing Nebraska law to permit closure [of the courtroom] in certain circumstances, the court remanded the case to the District Judge for reconsideration of the issue whether pretrial hearings should be closed to the press and public.

We granted certiorari to address the important issues raised by the District court order as modified by the Nebraska Supreme Court, but we denied the motion to expedite review or to stay entirely the order of the State District Court pending Simants' trial. We are informed by the parties that since we granted certiorari, Simants has been convicted of murder and sentenced to death. His appeal is pending in the Nebraska Supreme Court.

II

[Before turning to the merits, the Court considered whether the case was moot because the trial had already been held. The Court concluded that the dispute was not moot, noting that the issue was likely to arise again and that the "short-lived" nature of such restrictive orders would otherwise make appellate review almost impossible.]

III

The problems presented by this case are almost as old as the Republic. Neither in the Constitution nor in the contemporaneous writings do we find that the conflict between these two important rights was anticipated, yet is is inconceivable that the authors of the Constitution were unaware of the potential conflicts between the right to an unbiased jury and the guarantee of freedom of the press. The unusually able lawyers who helped write the Constitution and later drafted the Bill of Rights were familiar with the historic episode in which John Adams defended British soldiers charged with homicide for firing into a crowd of Boston demonstrators; they were intimately familiar with the clash of the adversary system and the part that passions of the populace sometimes play in influencing potential jurors. They did not addressed themselves directly to the situation presented by this case; their chief concern was the need for freedom of expression in the political arena and the dialogue in ideas. But they recognized that there were risks to private rights from an unfettered press. * * *

The trial of Aaron Burr in 1807 presented Mr. Chief Justice Marshall, presiding as a trial judge, with acute problems in selecting an unbiased jury. Few people in the area of Virginia from which jurors were drawn had not formed some opinions concerning Mr. Burr or the case, from newspaper accounts and heightened discussion both private and public. The Chief Justice conducted a searching *voir dire* of two panels eventually called, and rendered a substantial opinion on the purposes of *voir dire* and the standards to be applied. Burr was acquitted, so there was no occasion for appellate review to examine the problem of prejudicial pretrial publicity. Mr. Chief Justice Marshall's careful *voir dire* inquiry into the matter of possible bias makes clear that the problem is not a new one.

The speed of communication and the pervasiveness of the modern news media have exacerbated these problems, however, as numerous appeals demonstrate. The trial of Bruno Hauptmann in a small New Jersey community for the abduction and murder of the Charles Lindberghs' infant child probably was the most widely covered trial up to that time, and the nature of the coverage produced widespread public reaction. Criticism was directed at the "carnival" atmosphere that pervaded the community and the courtroom itself. Responsible leaders of press and the legal profession—including other judges—pointed out that much of this sorry performance could have been controlled by a vigilant trial judge and by other public officers subject to the control of the court.

The excesses of press and radio and lack of responsibility of those in authority in the Hauptmann case and others of that era led to efforts to develop voluntary guidelines for courts, lawyers, press, and broadcasters. The effort was renewed in 1965 when the American Bar Association embarked on a project to develop standards for all aspects of criminal justice, including guidelines to accommodate the right to a fair trial and the rights of a free press. The resulting standards, approved by the Association in 1968, received support from most of the legal profession. Other groups have undertaken similar studies. In the wake of these efforts, the cooperation between bar associations and members of the press led to the adoption of voluntary guidelines like Nebraska's.

In practice, of course, even the most ideal guidelines are subjected to powerful strains when a case such as Simants' arises, with reporters from many parts of the country on the scene. Reporters from distant places are unlikely to consider themselves bound by local standards. They report to editors outside the area covered by the guidelines, and their editors are likely to be guided only by their own standards. To contemplate how a state court can control acts of a newspaper or broadcaster outside its jurisdiction, even though the newspapers and broadcasts reach the very community from which jurors are to be selected, suggests something of the practical difficulties of managing such guidelines.

The problems presented in this case have a substantial history outside the reported decisions of the courts, in the efforts of many responsible people to accommodate the competing interests. We cannot resolve all of them, for it is not the function of this Court to write a code. We look instead to this particular case and the legal context in which it arises.

IV

The Sixth Amendment in terms guarantees "trial, by an impartial jury . . ." in federal criminal prosecutions. Because "trial by jury in criminal cases is fundamental to the American scheme of justice," the Due Process clause of the Fourteenth Amendment guarantees the same right in state criminal prosecutions. "In essence, the right to jury trial guarantees to the criminally accused a fair trial by a panel of impartial, indifferent jurors. * * * In the language of Lord Coke, a juror must be as 'indifferent as he stands unsworne.' His verdict must be based upon the evidence developed at the trial."

In the overwhelming majority of criminal trials, pretrial publicity presents few unmanageable threats to this important right. But when the case is a "sensational" one tensions develop between the right of the accused to trial by an impartial jury and the rights guaranteed others by the First Amendment. * * * [P]retrial publicity—even pervasive, adverse publicity—does not invariably lead to an unfair trial. The capacity of the jury eventually impaneled to decide the case fairly is influenced by the tone and extent of the publicity, which is in part, and often in large part, shaped by what attorneys, police, and other officials do to precipitate news coverage. The trial judge has a major responsibility. What the judge says about a case, in or out of the courtroom, is likely to appear in newspapers and broadcasts. More important, the measures a judge takes or fails to take to mitigate the effects of pretrial publicity . . . may well determine whether the defendant receives a trial consistent with the requirements of due process. * * *

The state trial judge in the case before us acted responsibly, out of a legitimate concern, in an effort to protect the defendant's right to a fair trial. What we must decide is not simply whether the Nebraska courts erred in seeing the possibility of real danger to the defendant's rights, but whether in the circumstances of this case the means employed were foreclosed by another provision of the Constitution.

V

The First Amendment provides that "Congress shall make no law . . . abridging the freedom . . . of the press," and it is "no longer open to doubt that the liberty of the press and of speech, is within the liberty safeguarded by the due process clause of the Fourteenth Amendment from invasion by state action." The Court has interpreted these guarantees to afford special protection against orders that prohibit the publication or broadcast of particular information or commentary—orders that impose a "previous" or "prior" restraint on speech. None of our decided cases on prior restraint involved restrictive orders entered to protect a defendant's right to a fair and impartial jury, but the opinions have a common thread relevant to this case. * * * "Any prior restraint on expression comes to this Court with a 'heavy presumption' against its constitutional validity." * * *

The damage can be particularly great when the prior restraint falls upon the communication of news and commentary on current events. Truthful reports of public judicial proceedings have been afforded special protection against subsequent punishment. For the same reasons the protection against prior restraint should have particular force as applied to the reporting of criminal proceedings, whether the crime in question is a single isolated act or a pattern of criminal conduct.

"A responsible press has always been regarded as the handmaiden of effective judicial administration, particularly in the criminal field. * * * The press does not simply publish information about trials but guards against the miscarriage of justice by subjecting the police, prosecutors, and judicial processes to extensive public scrutiny and criticism."

The extraordinary protections afforded by the First Amendment carry with them something in the nature of a fiduciary duty to exercise the protected rights responsibly—a duty widely acknowledged but not always observed by editors and publishers. It is not asking too much to suggest that those who exercise First Amendment rights in newspapers or broadcasting enterprises direct some effort to protect the rights of an accused to a fair trial by unbiased jurors.

Of course, the order at issue . . . does not prohibit but only postpones publication. Some news can be delayed and most commentary can even more readily be delayed without serious injury, and there often is a self-imposed delay when responsible editors call for verification of information. But such delays are normally slight and they are self-imposed. Delays imposed by governmental authority are a different matter. * * * "[W]e . . . remain intensely skeptical about those measures that would allow government to insinuate itself into the editorial rooms of this Nation's press." As a practical matter, moreover, the element of time is not unimportant if press coverage is to fulfill its traditional function of bringing news to the public promptly.

The authors of the Bill of Rights did not undertake to assign priorities as between First Amendment and Sixth Amendment rights, ranking one as superior to the other. In this case, the petitioners would have us declare the right of an accused subordinate to their right to publish in all circumstances. But if the authors of these guarantees, fully aware of the potential conflicts between them, were unwilling or unable to resolve the issue by assigning to one priority over the other, it is not for us to rewrite the Constitution by undertaking what they declined to do. It is unnecessary, after nearly two centuries, to establish a priority applicable in all circumstances. Yet it is nonetheless clear that the barriers to prior restraint remain high unless we are to abandon what the Court has said for nearly a quarter of our national existence and implied throughout all of it. * * *

VI

We turn now to the record in this case to determine whether . . . "the gravity of the 'evil,' discounted by its improbability, justifies such invasion of free speech as is necessary to avoid the danger." To do so, we must examine the evidence before the trial judge when the order was entered to determine (a) the nature and extent of pretrial news coverage; (b) whether other measures would be likely to mitigate the effects of unrestrained pretrial publicity; and (c) how effectively a restraining order would operate to prevent the threatened danger. The precise terms of the restraining order are also important. We must then consider whether the record supports the entry of a prior restraint on publication, one of the most extraordinary remedies known to our jurisprudence.

A

In assessing the probable extent of publicity, the trial judge had before him newspapers demonstrating that the crime had already drawn intensive news coverage, and the testimony of the County Judge, who had entered the initial restraining order based on the local and national attention the case had attracted. The District Judge was required to assess the probable publicity that would be given these shocking crimes prior to the time a jury was selected and sequestered. He then had to examine the probable nature of the publicity and determine how it would affect prospective jurors.

Our review of the pretrial record persuades us that the trial judge was justified in concluding that there would be intense and pervasive pretrial publicity concerning this case. He could also reasonably conclude, based on common human experience, that publicity might impair the defendant's right to a fair trial. He did not purport to say more, for he found only "a clear and present danger that pre-trial publicity *could* impinge upon the defendant's right to a fair trial." (Emphasis added.) His conclusion as to the impact of such publicity on prospective jurors was of necessity speculative, dealing as he was with factors unknown and unknowable.

B

We find little in the record that goes to another aspect of our task, determining whether measures short of an order restraining all publication would have insured the defendant a fair trial. Although the entry of the order might be read as a judicial determination that other measures would not suffice, the trial court made no express findings to that effect; the Nebraska Supreme Court referred to the issue only by implication.

Most of the alternatives to prior restraint of publication in these circumstances were discussed with obvious approval in *Sheppard v. Maxwell* (1966): (a) change of trial venue to a place less exposed to the intense publicity that seemed imminent in Lincoln County;[2] (b) postponement of the trial to allow public attention to subside; (c) searching questioning of prospective jurors, as Mr. Chief Justice Marshall used in [*United States v. Burr* (1807)], to screen out those with fixed opinions as to guilt or innocence; (d) the use of emphatic and clear instructions on the sworn duty of each juror to decide the issues only on the evidence presented in open court. Sequestration of jurors is, of course, always available. Although that measure insulates jurors only after they are sworn, it also enhances the likelihood of dissipating the impact of pretrial publicity and emphasizes the elements of the jurors' oaths. * * *

We have noted earlier that pretrial public-

---

[2]The respondent and intervenors argue here that a change of venue would not have helped, since Nebraska law permits a change of venue only to adjacent counties, which had been as exposed to pretrial publicity in this case as Lincoln County. We have held that state laws restricting venue must on occasion yield to the constitutional requirement that the State afford a fair trial. We also note that the combined population of Lincoln County and the adjacent counties is over 80,000, providing a substantial pool of prospective jurors.

ity, even if pervasive and concentrated, cannot be regarded as leading automatically and in every kind of criminal case to an unfair trial. * * * Appellate evaluations as to the impact of publicity take into account what other measures were used to mitigate the adverse effects of publicity. The more difficult prospective or predictive assessment that a trial judge must make also calls for a judgment as to whether other precautionary steps will suffice.

We have therefore examined this record to determine the probable efficacy of the measures short of prior restraint on the press and speech. There is no finding that alternative measures would not have protected Simants' rights, and the Nebraska Supreme Court did no more than imply that such measures might not be adequate. Moreover, the record is lacking in evidence to support such a finding.

C

We must also assess the probable efficacy of prior restraint on publication as a workable method of protecting Simants' right to a fair trial, and we cannot ignore the reality of the problems of managing and enforcing pretrial restraining orders. The territorial jurisdiction of the issuing court is limited by concepts of sovereignty. The need for . . . jurisdiction also presents an obstacle that applies to publication at large as distinguished from restraining publication within a jurisdiction.

The Nebraska Supreme Court narrowed the scope of the restrictive order, and its opinion reflects awareness of the tensions between the need to protect the accused as fully as possible and the need to restrict publication as little as possible. The dilemma posed underscores how difficult it is for trial judges to predict what information will in fact undermine the impartiality of jurors, and the difficulty of drafting an order that will effectively keep prejudicial information from prospective jurors. When a restrictive order is sought, a court can anticipate only part of what will develop that may injure the accused. But information not so obviously prejudicial may emerge, and what may properly be published in these "gray zone" circumstances may not

violate the restrictive order and yet be prejudicial.

Finally, we note that the events disclosed by the record took place in a community of 850 people. It is reasonable to assume that, without any news accounts being printed or broadcast, rumors would travel swiftly by word of mouth. One can only speculate on the accuracy of such reports, given the generative propensities of rumors; they could well be more damaging than reasonably accurate news accounts. But plainly a whole community cannot be restrained from discussing a subject intimately affecting life within it.

Given these practical problems, it is far from clear that prior restraint on publication would have protected Simants' rights.

D

Finally, another feature of this case leads us to conclude that the restrictive order entered here is not supportable. At the outset the County Court entered a very broad restrictive order, the terms of which are not before us; it then held a preliminary hearing open to the public and the press. There was testimony concerning at least two incriminating statements made by Simants to private persons; the statement—evidently a confession—that he gave to law enforcement officials was also introduced. The State District Court's later order was entered after this public hearing and, as modified by the Nebraska Supreme Court, enjoined reporting of (1) "[c]onfessions or admissions against interests made by the accused to law enforcement officials"; (2) "[c]onfessions or admissions against interest, oral or written, if any, made by the accused to third parties, excepting any statements, if any, made by the accused to representatives of the news media; and (3) all "[o]ther information strongly implicative of the accused as the perpetrator of the slayings."

To the extent that this order prohibited the reporting of evidence adduced at the open preliminary hearing, it plainly violated settled principles: "[T]here is nothing that proscribes the press from reporting events that transpire in the courtroom." The County Court could not know that closure of the preliminary hearing was an alternative open to it until the Nebraska Supreme court so construed state law; but once a public hearing had been held, what transpired there could not be subject to prior restraint.

The third prohibition of the order was defective in another respect as well. As part of a final order, entered after plenary review, this prohibition regarding "implicative" information is too vague and too broad to survive the scrutiny we have given to restraints on First Amendment rights. * * *

E

The record demonstrates, as the Nebraska courts held, that there was indeed a risk that pretrial news accounts, true or false, would have some adverse impact on the attitudes of those who might be called as jurors. But on the record now before us it is not clear that further publicity, unchecked, would so distort the views of potential jurors that 12 could not be found who would, under proper instructions, fulfill their sworn duty to render a just verdict exclusively on the evidence presented in open court. We cannot say on this record that alternatives to a prior restraint on petitioners would not have sufficiently mitigated the adverse effects of pretrial publicity so as to make prior restraint unnecessary. Nor can we conclude that the restraining order actually entered would serve its intended purpose. Reasonable minds can have few doubts about the gravity of the evil pretrial publicity can work, but the probability that it would do so here was not demonstrated with the degree of certainty our cases on prior restraint require.

Of necessity, our holding is confined to the record before us. But our conclusion is not simply a result of assessing the adequacy of the showing made in this case; it results in part from the problems inherent in meeting the heavy burden of demonstrating, in advance of trial, that without prior restraint a fair trial will be denied. * * * However difficult it may be, we need not rule out the possibility of showing the kind of threat to fair trial rights that would possess the requisite degree of cer-

tainty to justify restraint. This Court has frequently denied that First Amendment rights are absolute and has consistently rejected the proposition that a prior restraint can never be employed.

Our analysis ends, as it began, with a confrontation between prior restraint imposed to protect one vital constitutional guarantee and the explicit command of another that the freedom to speak and publish shall not be abridged. We reaffirm that the guarantees of freedom of expression are not an absolute prohibition under all circumstances, but the barriers to prior restraint remain high and the presumption against its use continues intact. We hold that, with respect to the order entered in this case prohibiting reporting or commentary on judicial proceedings held in public, the barriers have not been overcome; to the extent that this order restrained publication of such material, it is clearly invalid. To the extent that it prohibited publication based on information gained from other sources, we conclude that the heavy burden imposed as a condition to securing a prior restraint was not met and the judgment of the Nebraska Supreme court is therefore

Reversed.

MR. JUSTICE BRENNAN, with whom MR. JUSTICE STEWART and MR. JUSTICE MARSHALL join, concurring in the judgment.

* * * The right to a fair trial by a jury of one's peers is unquestionably one of the most precious and sacred safeguards enshrined in the Bill of Rights. I would hold, however, that resort to prior restraints on the freedom of the press is a constitutionally impermissible method for enforcing that right; judges have at their disposal a broad spectrum of devices for ensuring that fundamental fairness is accorded to the accused without necessitating so drastic an incursion on the equally fundamental and salutary constitutional madate that discussion of public affairs in a free society cannot depend on the preliminary grace of judicial censors. * * *

[Justices Powell and White also wrote concurring opinions, though each joined in the opinion of the Court. Justice Stevens concurred in the judgment. Justice Powell emphasized his view that a prior restraint is permissible "only when it is shown to be necessary to prevent the dissemination of prejudicial publicity that otherwise poses a high likelihood of preventing, directly and irreparably, the impaneling of a jury meeting the Sixth Amendment requirement of impartiality." This, he said, requires a showing that there is "a clear threat to the fairness of trial," the threat "is posed by the actual publicity to be restrained," and "no less restrictive alternatives are available." Even if such a showing is made, however, "a restraint may not issue unless it also is shown that previous publicity or publicity from unrestrained sources will not render the restraint inefficacious." Justice White noted that he had "grave doubt . . . whether orders with respect to the press such as were entered in this case would ever be justifiable." Justice Stevens wrote that he "subscribe[d] to most of what Mr. Justice Brennan says and, if ever required to face the issue squarely, may well accept his ultimate conclusion."]

INTRODUCTION

One of the fundamental principles of Anglo-American law is that the government has the burden of establishing the guilt of a criminal defendant solely on the basis of competent evidence produced in the courtroom before an impartial jury. As Justice Oliver Wendell Holmes, Jr. eloquently observed in *Patterson v. Colorado* (1907), "[t]he theory of our system is that the conclusions to be reached in a case will be induced only by evidence and argument in open court, and not by any outside influence, whether of private talk or public print." Obviously, jurors who have made up their minds as to a defendant's guilt on the basis of news reports can hardly be considered "impartial," and a trial that turns on press coverage rather than facts developed under the legal rules regarding admission of evidence cannot be considered "fair" under the sixth amendment.

At the same time, however, news coverage of the courts serves an important public interest, for the Anglo-American legal system has long distrusted secret trials. By subjecting the police, prosecutors, judges, and the judicial process itself to public scrutiny, the press helps ensure that justice is administered in an even-handed manner and that criminal defendants are treated fairly. In many instances, therefore, the first and sixth amendments act in a complementary fashion. When press coverage becomes so intense that publicity threatens the defendant's right to a fair trial, a conflict between the two constitutional provisions emerges. The difficulty, as *Nebraska Press* indicates, lies in finding a way to protect the sixth amendment rights of the criminal defendant without runnning afoul of the first amendment.

This problem arises in civil cases as well, for fairness—a vital element in any trial—is reflected in the seventh amendment right to a jury trial in civil cases and in the due process clause of the fifth and fourteenth amendments. But the "free press-fair trial" controversy has primarily involved criminal cases, due largely to the news media's penchant for sensationalistic crime reporting. In 1907, for example, the press had a field day with the trial of Harry Thaw, accused of the murder of noted architect Stanford White. Apparently convinced that White was seducing his wife, "glamour girl" Evelyn Nesbit, Thaw shot White to death in Madison Square Garden, a building that the architect had designed. Journalist Irwin S. Cobb alone wrote 600,000 words about the trial.

Perhaps the best—or worst—example, however, is the 1935 trial of Bruno Hauptmann, described briefly in *Nebraska Press*. Hauptmann, who was convicted of kidnapping and murdering the nineteen-month-old son of aviator Charles Lindbergh, was once described in the press as a "thing lacking in human characteristics." Seven hundred reporters flocked to his trial, which an American Bar Association report later called "the most spectacular and depressing example of improper publicity and professional misconduct" in American history.

Cases such as these prompted H.L. Mencken's famous remark that newspapers have "debauched the courts, and connived at crime, and made justice in America a joke." The media's infatuation with criminal cases is hardly a thing of the past. One need not stretch his memory very far to recall news accounts of the Chicago Seven; cult leader Charles Manson and his followers, including Lynette "Squeaky" Fromme; the Watergate conspirators; Patricia Hearst and the "Symbionese Liberation Army"; David Berkowitz, the "Son of Sam" killer; subway vigilante Bernhard Goetz; and socialite Claus von Bulow. Television has played a prominent role; for example, network news programs repeatedly showed a videotape of John Hinckley shooting President Ronald Reagan. Viewers also got to watch law enforcement surveillance tapes showing the "Abscam" defendants stuffing their pockets with money and undercover FBI agents arresting automaker John DeLorean on drug charges. Cable News Network broadcast the entire trial of four men accused of gang raping a woman in a Boston bar as patrons looked on.

The result of such saturation coverage has been two broad classes of prejudicial publicity cases which occasionally overlap. Most appellate decisions have involved prejudicial publicity prior to the trial. *Nebraska Press* falls into this category, and two earlier Supreme Court decisions also illustrate how pervasive pretrial publicity can be. In a 1961 case, *Irvin v. Dowd*, the Court reversed the murder conviction of an Indiana man described in the press as a "mad dog" killer. The pretrial publicity was so extensive that more than four hundred potential jurors were examined before a jury could be picked, and most of the jurors who were ultimately seated believed that Irvin was guilty before the trial began. Two years later, in *Rideau v. Louisiana*, the Court again reversed a murder conviction after a television station had broadcast the defendant's filmed confession three times over a period of two days. The sheriff had permitted a camera crew to record his questioning of the suspect in a jail cell, and during that conversation the man admitted that he had killed a person taken hostage in a bank robbery.

In the second category of cases, the prejudicial publicity occurs during the trial itself, after the jurors have been selected. For example, jurors may learn from news reports about the trial certain facts that could not be introduced into evidence. This occurred in *United States v. Williams* (1978), in which four law enforcement officers were on trial for beating an illiterate maintenance worker. After the first day of the trial, jurors saw a television news report stating that the defendants had previously been convicted of the offense but that a new trial had been ordered because of "erroneous testimony." In reversing the defendants' conviction at the second trial, the U.S. Court of Appeals for the Fifth Circuit said that it was "hard pressed to think of anything more damning to an accused than information that a jury had previously convicted him for the crime charged." Studies indicate that cases of this type occur less frequently than those involving pretrial publicity, but the potential for prejudice may be greater. As the court noted in *Williams*, information reported during the course of the trial may remain more firmly in the mind of the jurors exposed to it, given their personal involvement in the case.

The overlap between the two categories has resulted in the so-called "media circus" cases in which there was both pretrial publicity and extensive coverage of the trial itself. The most famous example is *Sheppard v. Maxwell*, a 1966 case mentioned in the *Nebraska Press* decision. Dr. Sam Sheppard, a surgeon, was convicted of murdering his pregnant wife, Marilyn, by bludgeoning her to death in their home in a Cleveland suburb. Though the investigation focused on Sheppard from the outset, the doctor steadfastly maintained his innocence. He told police that his wife had been killed by an intruder with whom Sheppard had "grappled" as the man tried to escape. Not satisfied with this explanation, the Cleveland newspapers, which published numerous stories about the crime, called for Sheppard's arrest in front-page editorials with headlines such as "Why Isn't Sam Sheppard in Jail?" News stories emphasized discrepancies in Sheppard's statements to police, reported the results of "scientific tests" that contradicted his account of the crime, and accused the doctor of having had several extramarital affairs.

Matters quickly got out of hand. A coroner's inquest at which Sheppard testified was held in a high school gym and broadcast live over television and radio. It ended in a brawl. When Sheppard was arrested and taken to the police station, hundreds of people, reporters, and photographers were awaiting his arrival. The publicity grew in intensity until his indictment by the grand jury two weeks later. News stories announced "new evidence" in the case, editorial cartoons appeared, and reports surfaced that Marilyn had "lived in fear" of her husband. As the trial date approached, the names of the potential jurors were published in the newspapers, and those individuals were bombarded with letters and telephone calls about the case. All but one of the potential jurors had read newspaper accounts of the crime or listened to television reports.

The trial itself was held only two weeks before the general election at which the presiding judge was a candidate for reelection and the prosecuting attorney was running for a judgeship. During the jury selection process, a radio station conducted a live "debate" on Sheppard's guilt, and a newspaper headline asked "But Who Will Speak for Marilyn?" Another story announced that the prosecution would produce testimony from a "bombshell witness" as to Sheppard's "fiery temper." The small courtroom was packed with reporters, who occupied almost all of the seats as well as a special table that the judge had set up immediately adjacent to the table at which Sheppard and his lawyers sat. The media also "took over" the courthouse. Reporters and photographers used all available rooms on the floor on which the courtroom was located, and a television station set up broadcasting facilities on the third floor, next to the jury room. Photographers roamed the corridors and were permitted to take pictures during the courtroom during breaks in the testimony. A court rule prohibited photography during the trial itself.

Despite the intense media coverage, the jury was not sequestered until it began its deliberations. When the trial was in its seventh week, two jurors admitted having heard radio and television broadcasts during which Walter Winchell reported that a woman arrested for robbery in New York had said she had borne Sheppard's child. When Sheppard himself testified that he had been mistreated by Cleveland detectives after his arrest, a police captain—who did not testify at trial—issued a press release denying the allegations. A newspaper story based on the press release carried a headline labeling Sheppard a "bare-faced liar." The news media also focused on the jurors themselves, turning them into celebrities. More than forty pictures of the jurors appeared in Cleveland newspapers during the trial; in fact, the jury even took time out from its deliberations to pose for pictures. Like other participants in the trial, jurors had to "run a gauntlet" of reporters and photographers as they entered and left the courthouse.

To no one's surprise, Sheppard was convicted and sentenced to life in prison. The Ohio Supreme Court affirmed the conviction, and the U.S. Supreme Court refused to review the case. After he had spent ten years in prison, Sheppard's family hired nationally known criminal lawyer F. Lee Bailey to bring a *habeas corpus* action in federal court to again challenge the conviction. The case ultimately reached the U.S. Supreme Court, which had little trouble concluding, in light of its recent decisions in *Irvin* and *Rideau*, that Dr. Sheppard had been denied a fair trial. In a strongly worded opinion, Justice Tom Clark described in detail the sensationalistic news coverage that contributed to the "carnival atmosphere" but saved his harshest criticism for the trial judge. "Given the pervasiveness of modern communications and the difficulty of effacing prejudicial publicity from the minds of the jurors, the trial courts must take strong measures to ensure that the balance is never weighed against the accused," he wrote. "We conclude that [adequate judicial supervision] would have been sufficient to guarantee Sheppard a fair trial. . . ." He received a new trial as a result of the Supreme Court's decision and was acquitted.

Before turning to the various techniques that the courts may use to combat prejudicial publicity, a point that Chief Justice Warren Burger made in *Nebraska Press* should be emphasized: extensive news coverage does not automatically result in an unfair trial. The sixth amendment does not require a perfect trial, but rather one that is fair. Although the cornerstone of fairness is an impartial jury, the mere fact that a juror has been exposed to media coverage of the crime does not mean that he cannot be impartial. "It is not required . . . that the jurors be totally ignorant of the facts," the Supreme Court said in *Irvin v. Dowd*. "It is sufficient if the juror can lay aside his impression or opinion and render a verdict based on the evidence presented in court." Under this test of impartiality, which dates to the 1807 trial of Aaron Burr, the question is not simply exposure to news coverage, but whether the juror has made up his mind as to the defendant's guilt prior to the trial. Obviously, someone with an unalterably closed mind cannot evaluate the case impartially on the basis of evidence presented trial.

A criminal case growing out of the Watergate episode makes the point that extensive publicity does not inevitably lead to an unfair trial. White House aides John Ehrlichman and H.R. "Bob" Haldeman were convicted of obstruction of justice for their role in the coverup of the Watergate break-in. Prior to their trial, media coverage of the Watergate affair had reached the saturation point. Investigative reporters Bob Woodward and Carl Bernstein of the *Washington Post* broke the story, which became a staple on the front page of the nation's newspapers and on network television news programs. Congressional hearings, including House impeachment proceedings against President Richard Nixon, were broadcast live by the networks, and the U.S. Supreme Court's decision on the "Watergate tapes" was widely covered. Nonetheless, the U.S. Court of Appeals for the District of Columbia Circuit ruled in *United States v. Haldeman* (1976) that the criminal trials had not been tainted by the massive pretrial publicity. The court found "no reason" for concluding that the jury was "aroused" against the defendants and unable "objectively to judge their guilt or innocence on the basis of the evidence presented at trial."

It should also be noted that the conditions necessary for media coverage to prejudice jurors and cause an unfair trial occur in an extremely small percentage of cases. According to a recent study by Ralph Frasca at the University of Iowa, the estimated frequency of press-induced bias in criminal cases is .0001 percent, or once in every 10,000 cases. This is so, he concluded, because several conditions must be present before prejudice is likely to occur. First, there must be a jury trial, which occurs in about ten percent of the felony arrests in metropolitan areas. Second, the case must attract sufficient media attention to result in the type of extensive coverage that can lead to prejudice. This happens in connection with about five percent of felony arrests. Finally, citizens who become jurors must actually be prejudiced by press coverage and retain that mindset until the moment they enter a jury room to decide the case, which occurs about two percent of the time.

"If . . . all crimes are equally likely to be covered prejudicially, if all crimes are equally likely to go to trial, and if all jurors will acquire and retain a bias at the same rate in all cases," Mr. Frasca concluded, "then an estimate of the frequency of press-induced juror bias can be determined by multiplying the estimates from each of the necessary conditions listed above (.10x.05x.02)." Thus, if one assumes random distribution of the three variables, press-induced bias would occur .0001 percent of the time. As Mr. Frasca points out, however, these variables are not randomly distributed in the real world. For example, homicides are more likely to be covered by the press and result in jury trials than other crimes. Nonetheless, the same technique can be used to estimate the frequency of juror prejudice stemming from media coverage of murders, and one would expect the percentage to be higher in those cases.

Of course, the fact that only a small percentage of criminal defendants face the prospect of prejudicial publicity does not diminish the right of those defendants to a fair trial. Given the empirical data, however, judges should not act on the assumption that media coverage will always result in an unfair trial. In deciding how to deal with potential prejudicial publicity problems, they should avoid prescribing a cure that could well be worse than the disease. This notion of taking action that has the least impact on the media's newsgathering activities should be kept in mind as we explore the techniques available to the courts.

JUDICIAL RESPONSES TO THE PROBLEM

As Chief Justice Burger pointed out in the *Nebraska Press* case, the *Sheppard* decision considered at some length the various tools for combating prejudicial publicity that a trial judge has at his disposal. These procedural devices—such as carefully examining potential jurors during the selection process, moving the trial to a different county, and sequestering the jury during the trial—have long been used, though some doubt exists as to their effectiveness. As *Nebraska Press* indicates, trial judges have also used more controversial techniques with significant first amendment consequences, including "gag orders" of the type at issue in that case and similar orders directing trial participants not to talk to the news media. Courts have also prohibited members of the press and general public from attending trials and related pretrial proceedings and have banned cameras from the courtroom. Each of these methods has its own difficulties, some of which are of constitutional dimension.

Procedural Devices

In *Nebraska Press* and subsequent cases, the U.S. Supreme Court has told trial judges that "traditional" techniques such as change of venue and jury sequestration must be tried and found wanting before more drastic alternatives that impinge on first amendment rights may be utilized. Accordingly, we will first examine four procedural devices available to the courts: change of venue, continuance, *voir dire* examination of potential jurors, and jury sequestration.[3] The first three are used in connection with pretrial publicity, while sequestering the jury helps deal with publicity occurring during the course of the trial.

One of the most common methods used to protect the defendant's right to a fair trial is the change of venue. The theory is simple: by moving the trial to another community, the court will be able to empanel jurors who have not been exposed to the prejudicial publicity surrounding the case. A defendant may perceive certain disadvantages with this approach, however. Moved away from home, the accused may lose the support of family and friends who cannot make the trip. Moreover, the composition of the pool from which prospective jurors are drawn may change dramatically, particularly if the trial is moved from an urban area to a rural community, or vice-versa. The prosecution might oppose a change of venue if the jury's makeup might be significantly affected, and increased costs of trying the case might also be a deterrent. In any event, the device might not be particularly effective in small states such as Arkansas, where two daily newspapers enjoy statewide circulation and broadcast stations in the state capital reach about seventy-five percent of the state's population.

A trial judge faced with pervasive pretrial publicity may also grant a continuance—that is, delay the trial—until news coverage has subsided. Of course, there is no guarantee that the publicity will die down, and past experience teaches that extensive coverage often begins again as the new trial date approaches. Moreover, because most of the criminal offenses that attract media attention are extremely serious, in many cases bail is not available or the amount is so high that the accused cannot obtain bail. In such situations, any continuance means that the defendant stays in jail for an extended period of time while he awaits trial. Also, federal and state law both provide the right to a speedy trial. Because a continuance granted at the defendant's request is typically excluded in computing the time in which the trial must take place, the defendant may be forced to choose between a speedy trial on the one hand and a later trial, hopefully unaffected by adverse publicity, on the other.

Careful questioning of prospective jurors during the jury selection phase of a criminal proceeding—known as *voir dire*—can reveal the extent to which pretrial publicity may have influenced persons in the jury pool. If sufficient prejudice or bias is demonstrated, the affected individual may be dismissed "for cause" and disqualified from serving on the jury. In addition, lawyers for the defense and prosecution have a limited number of "peremptory challenges" that they may use to strike from the jury an individual who, though not deemed sufficiently prejudiced to be eliminated "for cause," may appear to favor the other side. The number of peremptory challenges varies from jurisdiction to jurisdiction, with the number typically increasing along with the severity of the crime. There is no limit on the number of potential jurors who may be dismissed "for cause."

Keep in mind, however, that jurors need not be completely ignorant of facts surrounding the case; rather, the test is whether they can lay aside their impressions or opinions of the case formed from news accounts or other sources and render a

---

[3]Other techniques may also be permitted in some jurisdictions, although they are not as frequently used. A "change of venire," for example, brings to the place of trial potential jurors from another area where the pretrial publicity has not been as intense. Another device, the "blue ribbon jury," entails the selection of "special" jurors of above-average intelligence who are in theory more likely to be impartial.

verdict based on the evidence presented at trial. Prospective jurors are usually asked during *voir dire* whether they can do so, and human nature suggests that the typical answer will be "yes." These assurances will not necessarily prevent disqualification of the juror, however. The courts have recognized that the effect of exposure to publicity about a case may be substantial even though it is not perceived by the juror himself, and that a juror's good faith statement that he can decide the case based on the evidence cannot always counter this effect. In the final analysis, it is for the trial judge, not the jurors themselves, to determine whether they are qualified to serve. As one court has observed, "protestations of impartiality from prospective jurors are best met with a healthy skepticism," particularly if pretrial publicity has been heavy.

Once the jury has been selected and the trial has begun, the judge's concern shifts to the possibility that prejudicial news accounts will reach the jury while the case is being tried. This "during trial" publicity may be more damaging than news coverage prior to trial, though the reported cases suggest that this problem is not as widespread as pretrial publicity. As noted previously, information obtained from out-of-court sources during the trial seems more likely to remain in the minds of jurors exposed to it, and they may be more inclined to seek out such information when personally involved in the case. Moreover, though a judge might be able to "cure" the effects of pretrial news coverage, a fair trial may no longer be possible if the prejudicial information reaches a jury in the course of the proceeding. In that situation, the judge has no choice but to declare a mistrial and start over with a new jury.

One method of avoiding damage from "during trial" publicity is sequestering the jury—that is, insulating the jurors from news coverage by placing them under the court's control throughout the trial. This usually means housing jurors in hotels under the watchful eyes of bailiffs or other officials who monitor their conduct, shield them from reporters, family members, and the general public, and insulate them from any news reports that may be published or broadcast during the trial. Some judges are reluctant to "lock up" the jury, particularly in lengthy trials, because sequestration may affect the dynamics of the jury's deliberations by throwing together complete strangers for several weeks and denying them the opportunity to see family and friends. Moreover, this procedure may eliminate some groups from jury service, such as parents with young children or older people who need regular medical attention, and therefore affect the composition of the jury. Providing room and board for the jurors throughout the trial can also be expensive.

As an alternative to sequestration, courts routinely instruct jurors at the outset of the trial not to dsicuss the case with anyone other than fellow members of the jury and not to read any newspapers, watch television, or listen to the radio during the trial. If the judge is made aware that jurors ignored these instructions, he or she will further admonish them to disregard any information they have obtained in such impermissible fashion. The sufficiency of such an admonition usually depends on the type of material to which a juror is exposed and the timing of the exposure. For example, in *Wright v. State* (1979), the Arkansas Supreme Court ruled that the trial judge's admonition prevented any unfairness where jurors had read a news story on the first day of trial that briefly mentioned additional charges pending against the defendant. In contrast, the U.S. Court of Appeals for the First Circuit ruled in *United States v. Concepcion Cueto* (1975) that a new trial was necessary because a newspaper story seen by the jury on the day it began deliberations described the defendant as "one of the most dangerous drug traffickers" in the region.

Judges also have considerable authority to control decorum in the courtroom and its environs. Justice Clark made this point quite emphatically in the *Sheppard* case, noting that the trial judge could have limited the number of reporters in the courtroom itself and required that they conduct themselves in a nondisruptive manner. Although such restrictions do not insulate the jury from prejudicial information during the course of the trial, they help ensure the "judicial serenity and calm" to which a criminal defendant is entitled and avoid a carnival atmosphere.

Gagging the Media

A court order directing the news media not to publish information that it has learned about a case is an example of the harshest form of government control of the press, the prior restraint upon publication. The *Nebraska Press* case makes clear that such orders are presumptively unconstitutional. Though the Supreme Court did not in that case prohibit such "gag orders" in all circumstances, it ruled that they are permissible only where publication would constitute a clear and present danger to the defendant's right to a fair trial. Those situations are rare; in fact, it is hard to imagine a more compelling case for a gag order than *Nebraska Press*. The murders took place in a tiny Nebraska farm town, and the material covered by the trial court's order—including the accused's confession—was strongly implicative of guilt. Yet the Supreme Court ruled that the gag order violated the first amendment.

The Court's message is clear: gag orders directed against the news media may be used only as a last resort when all other means of protecting a defendant's sixth amendment rights would be ineffective. Recall that in *Nebraska Press* Chief Justice Burger outlined a three-part test for evaluating the propriety of such an order:

- the existence or likelihood of extensive prejudicial publicity;
- the gag order will mitigate that publicity; and
- other methods of ensuring a fair trial, such as a change of venue or continuance, will not work satisfactorily.

Moreover, each prong of the test must be established by convincing evidence, and the trial judge must make specific factual findings in support of his order. As one might expect from these requirements, the *Nebraska Press* hurdle is quite high, and few trial judges attempt to clear it.

A reporter faced with a gag order should seek immediate appellate court review, as was done in *CBS v. U.S. District Court* (1984). There the U.S. Court of Appeals for the Ninth Circuit reversed the trial judge's order that prohibited CBS from broadcasting FBI surveillance tapes showing automaker John DeLorean in what appeared to be a drug transaction with undercover officers. The gag order was issued on Saturday and overturned by the court of appeals on Sunday. Although the case had spawned enormous news coverage, the appellate court ruled that the "pool of potential jurors [in the Los Angeles area] is so large that even in cases attracting extensive and inflammatory publicity, it is usually possible to find an adequate number of untainted jurors." Moreover, the court of appeals determined that the trial judge had not properly considered the importance of alternative methods of ensuring a fair trial, notably careful *voir dire* examination of potential jurors.

Even if the gag order is unconstitutional, the reporter should not simply disregard it. Under the collateral bar rule discussed in Chapter 1, a journalist who publishes information in defiance of a gag order may be punished for contempt of court even though the order is ultimately found unconstitutional. Underlying the collateral bar rule is the notion that no one has the right to disobey a court order with impunity. As Justice Potter Stewart once wrote, "respect for the judicial process is a small price to pay for the civilizing hand of the law." The rule is not followed by all courts; for example, at least five state courts reject the doctrine, and one federal court has created an exception that would permit journalists to challenge a contempt citation based on a "transparently invalid" order that had been violated. Nonetheless, the *CBS* case reflects the safest approach: file an immediate appeal and ask for expedited review of the gag order.

Gagging Trial Participants

After the Supreme Court handed down the *Nebraska Press* decision in 1976, some trial judges sought to do indirectly what they could not do directly by issuing gag orders against those persons connected with the trial who might supply prejudicial information to the news media. This approach was not surprising; in fact, it had been suggested by Justice Clark in *Sheppard*. "[T]he [trial] court should have made some effort to control the release of leads, information, and gossip to the press by police officers, witnesses, and the counsel for both sides," he wrote. "Effective control of these sources—concededly within the court's power—might well have prevented the divulgence of inaccurate information, rumors, and accusations that made up much of the inflammatory publicity. . . ." Such orders are typically aimed at lawyers, defendants, witnesses, court officials, and jurors.

Because these gag orders are clearly prior restraints on the speech of the individuals against whom they are directed, they must be evaluated under the same first amendment standards announced in *Nebraska Press*. Though the courts have been hostile to orders that "gag" the media, they have given such restraints on trial participants a much warmer reception. For example, in *In re Dow Jones & Co.* (1988), a federal district judge in New York City entered an order prohibiting the U.S. Attorney and his assistants, defense counsel, and the defendants themselves from making "any extrajudicial statements concerning this case (1) to any person associated with a public communications media, or (2) that a reasonable person would expect to be communicated to a public communications media." The order came in a highly publicized criminal case involving Wedtech Corporation, a military contractor charged with fraudulently qualifying for "no-bid" federal contracts set aside for minority-owned companies. Among the individual defendants were a U.S. Congressman, a former Bronx Borough president, and the former regional director of the Small Business Administration.

Several news organizations, including Dow Jones & Co. (publisher of the *Wall Street Journal*), the *New York Times*, and NBC, appealed the order to the U.S. Court of Appeals for the Second Circuit. Though it admitted that the order "prohibits virtually all . . . extrajudicial speech relating to the pending Wedtech case," the Second Circuit upheld the trial judge. The question in such cases, the court said, is whether there is a reasonable likelihood that pretrial publicity will prejudice a fair trial. Extensive news coverage of the investigation had predated the initial indictment, which was followed by "massive publicity concerning the targets of the ongoing grand jury investigation." Given this background, the court of appeals agreed with the trial judge that the failure to restrain the trial participants would "add fuel to an already voracious fire of publicity" and create a "real and substantial likelihood that some, if not all, defendants might be deprived of a fair trial." The appellate court also accepted the trial judge's determination that the procedural devices discussed previously would be insufficient to protect the defendants' sixth amendment rights.

Similarly, in *Levine v. U.S. District Court* (1985), the trial judge ordered all attorneys and their representatives in the case of an FBI agent charged with espionage "not to make any statements to members of the news media concerning any aspect of this case that bears upon the merits to be resolved by the jury." The order came after defense lawyers were quoted at length in a newspaper article setting forth their contentions and theories of the case. Employing the test set out in *Nebraska Press*, the U.S. Court of Appeals for the Ninth Circuit upheld the trial judge's decision to impose the gag order, but sent the case back for further consideration because the language of the order was too broad.

The appellate court suggested, however, that the trial judge could appropriately order government attorneys to observe the limitations on dissemination of information adopted voluntarily by the U.S. Department of Justice and could direct defense counsel to follow limitations found in the Model Rules of Professional Conduct, a code of ethics for attorneys promulgated by the American Bar Association that has the force of law in most states. Both of these sources state that lawyers should not, for example, make available information about confessions or other statements of a defendant; the identity of prospective witnesses and their expected testimony; observations about the character of the defendant or other parties; and information about evidence gathered in the case.

Under Rule 3.6 of the Model Rules of Professional Conduct, a lawyer "shall not make an extrajudicial statement that a reasonable person would expect to be disseminated by means of public communication if the lawyer knows or reasonably should not that it will have a substantial likelihood of materially prejudicing an adjudicative proceeding." The rule, which has been upheld as constitutional by federal appellate courts, states that the following information is likely to have the requisite prejudicial effect:

- the character, credibility, reputation or criminal record of a party, suspect in a criminal investigation or witness, the identity of a witness, or the expected testimony of a party or witness;
- in a criminal case, the possibility of a plea of guilty to the offense or the existence or contents of any confession, admission, or statement given by a defendant or suspect or that person's refusal or failure to make a statement;
- the performance or results of any examination or test or the refusal or failure of a person to submit to an examination or test, or the identity or nature of physical evidence expected to be presented;
- any opinion as to the guilt or innocence of a defendant or suspect in a criminal case;
- information that the lawyer knows or reasonably should know is likely to be inadmissible as evidence at trial and would if disclosed create a substantial risk of prejudicing an impartial trial; or
- the fact that a defendant has been charged with a crime, unless there is included therein a statement explaining that the charge is merely an accusation and that the defendant is presumed innocent until and unless proven guilty.

On the other hand, Rule 3.6 expressly provides that a lawyer may state, "without elaboration," the general nature of the claim or defense, information contained in a public record, the existence of an investigation, the identity of the persons involved in the investigation (unless prohibited by law), the scheduling or result of any step in the litigation, a request for assistance in obtaining evidence, a warning of danger concerning the behavior of the person involved, background information about the accused (such as family status and occupation), information that could aid in the apprehension of a suspect who is at large, the circumstances surrounding an arrest, and the identity of investigating and arresting officers or law enforcement agencies and the length of the investigation. As noted previously, the U.S. Department of Justice has adopted similar rules regarding release of information by its personnel, including FBI officials. Many state and local law enforcement agencies have followed the Justice Department rules in establishing their own guidelines.

Gag orders can also be imposed on witnesses who are subpoenaed to testify at the trial. For example, in *In re Russell* (1984), several members of the Ku Klux Klan and Nazi party were charged with killing five persons in an incident that had racial and political overtones. The trial judge directed seventeen potential witnesses not to make "any extrajudicial statement that relates to, concerns, or discusses the testimony that [they] may give in this case . . . if such statement is intended for dissemination by means of public communication." The order also prohibited the witnesses from discussing the parties or issues involved in the case and the events leading up to and culminating in the killings. The U.S. Court of Appeals for the Fourth Circuit upheld the order, observing that such a "strong measure" was necessary in light of the "tremendous publicity attending this trial" and the "potentially inflammatory statements that could reasonably be expected" from the witnesses, many of whom were relatives of the victims.

Restrictions on jurors present somewhat different problems. It is common for trial judges to instruct members of the jury to refrain from discussing any aspect of the case with anyone during the course of the trial. No one doubts the validity of such orders, which are obviously necessary to protect the integrity of the jury's deliberative process and to ensure that jurors are not subjected to outside influences as they weigh the evidence presented at trial and attempt to reach a verdict.

But what if the trial judge goes further and prohibits post-trial communications as well? Because the trial has ended, there can obviously be no concern about interference with the defendant's right to a fair trial, and, not surprisingly, the courts have ruled that such broad orders are unconstitutional. For example, in *United States v. Sherman* (1978), the U.S. Court of Appeals for the Ninth Circuit struck down a trial judge's order instructing jurors not to discuss the case with anyone and directing everyone, including the news media, to "stay away" from the jurors. The U.S. Court of Appeals for the Fifth Circuit reached the same result in *In re Express-News Corp.* (1982), invalidating a trial judge's standing rule that prohibited anyone from interviewing a juror without his permission.

More narrowly drawn orders will withstand constitutional scrutiny, however. In *United States v. Harrelson* (1983), the Fifth Circuit approved a trial judge's order stating that no juror has any obligation to speak to any person about the case, that no one may make "repeated requests" for interviews with jurors, and that an interviewer cannot inquire into the vote of any juror other than the one being interviewed. This order, which was entered by the trial court during a highly publicized case growing out of the murder of a federal judge in San Antonio, Texas, did not prohibit jurors from talking to the press and did not forbid the news media from seeking such interviews. The appellate court also noted that the order served the legitimate purpose of protecting jurors from harassment and securing their privacy.

Closing the Courtroom

Trial judges also responded to the *Nebraska Press* case in another way: recognizing that gag orders against the news media would almost always be unconstitutional, they instead barred the press and the public from trials and pretrial hearings. In fact, language in Chief Justice Burger's opinion in that case suggested that this tactic was permissible: "[t]he County Court could not know that closure of the preliminary hearing was an alternative open to it until the Nebraska Supreme Court so construed state law. . . . " Subsequently, in the controversial case of *Gannett Co. v. DePasquale* (1979), the Court ruled that the press and public may not rely on the sixth amendment's "public trial" guarantee to gain access to criminal proceedings, since that provision protects only the defendant. However, a series of cases beginning in 1980 makes clear that the press and public enjoy a first amendment right of access to criminal proceedings. While this right, like all others emanating from the first amendment, is not absolute, the unmistakable message from these decisions is that closed courtrooms are to be extremely rare.

As noted in Chapter 5, the landmark case in this area is *Richmond Newspapers, Inc. v. Virginia* (1980), in which the Supreme Court ruled that the press and public cannot be excluded from a criminal trial absent a clear showing that a public proceeding would deprive the defendant of his sixth amendment rights. Central to the Court's holding was the long history of open trials in this county and in England, a tradition that was well known to the Framers of the Constitution. Openness "gave assurance that the proceedings were conducted fairly to all concerned," Chief Justice Burger wrote, "and it discouraged perjury, the misconduct of participants, and decisions based on secret bias or partiality." Moreover, he pointed out that public trials have considerable therapeutic value for the community. "When a shocking crime occurs, a community reaction of outrage and public protest often follows. Thereafter the open processes of justice . . . provid[e] an outlet for community concern, hostility, and emotion." Finally, the Chief Justice noted that open trials contribute "to public understanding of the rule of law and to comprehension of the functioning of the entire criminal justice system."

Because the only issue in *Richmond Newspapers* was closure of a criminal trial, the Court did not pass on the question of whether this qualified right of access also applied to pretrial proceedings in criminal cases. In subsequent decisions, however, the Court extended the constitutional presumption of openness to the *voir dire* process by which jurors are chosen and to preliminary hearings at which a judge determines whether there is sufficient evidence to charge the defendant with a criminal offense. Finding a tradition of openness with respect to both, the Court also emphasized that access plays "a significant positive role" in the functioning of these proceedings. Similarly, the lower courts have ruled that there is a qualified right of access to bail hearings, postconviction proceedings, sentencing hearings, parole revocation hearings, hearings on the release of convicted prisoners, contempt proceedings, and trials and hearings in civil cases. On the other hand, the courts have rejected a right of access to grand jury sessions, which have historically been closed to the public.

The most controversial type of proceeding to which the right of access has been deemed applicable is the pretrial suppression hearing. The purpose of these hearings is to screen out, in advance of trial, evidence that the jury will not, for one reason or another, be allowed to consider. For example, if a criminal defendant has been the victim of an illegal search, evidence obtained as a result of that search may not be used against him. Similarly, a confession that is the product of police coercion may not be admitted into evidence. Assuming that the judge rules that particular evidence cannot be used at the upcoming trial, prospective jurors may nonetheless learn of the evidence from news reports of the suppression hearing. Despite "special risks of unfairness" posed by suppression hearings that are open to the public and press, the Supreme Court made plain in *Press Enterprise Co. v. Superior Court* (1986) that these difficulties do not "automatically justify refusing public access to hearings on every motion to suppress." Like other criminal proceedings, pretrial suppression hearings are therefore presumptively open to the press and public.

Once it is determinated that there is a qualified first amendment right of access to a particular proceeding, the question becomes whether there are countervailing interests that would justify closing the courtroom. In the *Press Enterprise* case, the Court set forth the following standard for trial judges to use in attempting to strike the appropriate balance between the public's right to know and the defendant's right to a fair trial: "the . . . hearing may be closed only if specific findings are made demonstrating that first, there is a substantial probability that the defendant's right to a fair trial will be prejudiced by publicity that closure would prevent and, second, reasonable alternatives to closure cannot adequately protect the defendant's fair trial rights." Under the Court's 1984 decision in *Waller v. Georgia*, this test also applies when there is an attempt to close a criminal proceeding over the objection of the defendant, who has a qualified right to a public trial under the sixth amendment.

Obviously, the "substantial probability" of prejudice to the defendant will vary from case to case and from one type of proceeding to another. For example, the jury selection phase of a trial, a criminal arraignment at which the accused is formally charged and enters a plea, or a hearing at which the amount of bail is determined would ordinarily reveal little or nothing about the defendant's possible guilt and would have little impact on his right to a fair trial. Moreover, access to the trial itself should rarely be denied, since by that point the judge has ample means to protect the defendant's sixth amendment rights. On the other hand, it seems likely that a trial judge would be more willing to close a pretrial suppression hearing than any other type of proceeding, given the "special risks of unfairness" discussed previously.

Other interests can outweigh the first amendment right of access. For example, in *Globe Newspaper Co. v. Superior Court* (1982), the Court suggested that a judge may exclude the press and public from the testimony of minor victims of sex crimes, since closure could protect the children "from further trauma and embarrassment" and encourage them "to come forward and testify in a truthful and credible manner." In that case, however, the Court struck down a Massachusetts statute that required exclusion when such testimony was given. This mandatory closure rule swept too broadly, the Court said, since the "trial court can determine on a case-by-case basis whether [a closed proceeding] is necessary to protect the welfare of a minor victim." Among the relevant factors to be weighed are "the victim's age, psychological maturity and understanding, the nature of the crime, the desires of the victim, and the interests of parents and relatives."

In 1984, the Court ruled that privacy interests may also justify closure in certain circumstances. In *Press Enterprise v. Superior Court* (not to be confused with the 1986 case of the same name discussed above), the trial judge closed the jury selection phase of a rape-murder case. In light of the extensive news coverage of the crime, the judge believed that a searching *voir dire* was necessary and feared that that an open proceeding might discourage the potential jurors from being completely candid about their exposure to news coverage and their feelings about the case. The judge also denied the news media's requests for copies of the transcript of the closed proceeding, taking the position that disclosure would violate the jurors' right to privacy. On appeal, the U.S. Supreme Court reversed, pointing out that the trial court had not made specific findings of fact in support of its conclusions and had not adequately considered whether alternative methods to protect the fair trial and privacy interests were available. However, the Court also observed that juror privacy may warrant closed proceedings "when interrogation touches on deeply personal matters." Chief Justice Burger wrote:

> The trial involved testimony concerning an alleged rape of a teenage girl. Some questions may have been appropriate to prospective jurors that would give rise to legitimate privacy interests of those persons. For example, a prospective juror might privately inform the judge that she, or a member of her family, had been raped but had declined to seek prosecution because of the embarrassment and emotional trauma from the very disclosure of the episode. The privacy interests of such a prospective juror must be balanced against the . . . need for openness of the [jury selection] process.

To this point, we have considered cases involving the first amendment right to attend criminal trials and related proceedings. Although the Supreme Court has left open the question of whether there is a corresponding right of access in civil cases, the lower courts have extended the reasoning of *Richmond Newspapers* to the civil side of the docket. Perhaps the leading case is *Publicker Industries v. Cohen,* decided by the U.S. Court of Appeals for the Third Circuit in 1984. After a lengthy examination of British and American legal history, the court concluded that civil trials, like criminal proceedings, have long been open to the public. Moreover, the court observed that "[p]ublic access to civil trials, no less than criminal trials, plays an important role in the participation and the free discussion of government affairs." Such openness, the court said, increases the quality of judicial administration, enhances and protects the quality of the fact-finding process, helps ensure fairness, and fosters public trust in the judicial system. As is true in the criminal setting, however, the first amendment right of access is not absolute, and countervailing interests—such as the need to protect personal privacy or trade secrets, for example—may justify closure of civil proceedings.

Wholly apart from the first amendment right of access, state law may require public judicial proceedings, at least to the extent that openness does not interfere with the right to a fair trial. Under an 1839 Arkansas statute, for example, the "sittings of every court shall be public, and every person may freely attend same." Well before the *Richmond Newspapers* decision, the Arkansas Supreme Court had ruled that this statute guarantees the press and public the opportunity to attend a variety of judicial proceedings, including jury selection and suppression hearings. The statute is also broad enough to cover civil cases. However, other Arkansas statutes provide for closed hearings in a variety of situations, including juvenile matters, adoption and domestic relations cases, and proceeedings that involve trade secrets.

In other states, the right of access is constitutional rather than statutory. The

Oregon constitution states that "[n]o court shall be secret, but justice shall be administered openly and without purchase." Applying this provision, the Oregon Supreme Court has held invalid a statute that barred the public from juvenile proceedings absent permission of the trial judge.

When faced with the threatened closure of a judicial proceeding, a journalist in attendance should immediately notify the trial judge that he objects to any order closing the courtroom. If the judge issues the order in open court, the reporter, after being recognized by the judge, should identify himself and his news organization and object on the ground that a closed proceeding is contrary to the first amendment and/or state law. He should also ask the court for a hearing on the closure question at which counsel for the news organization may present legal arguments. Finally, the journalist should ask that the objection be placed in the official trial record by the court reporter in the event that an appeal is necessary.

ACCESS TO EVIDENCE AND COURT RECORDS

Court-related information sought by the news media typically falls into two categories: material introduced into evidence at trial, and material generated during the pretrial phase of the trial. The first category includes documents—such as letters and business records—used as evidence, as well as audio and video recordings played for the jury in open court. Pretrial records include those of grand jury proceedings, indictments in criminal cases, pleadings in civil cases, motions and supporting documents filed by the parties with the court, and material obtained by the parties during "discovery," a pretrial process by which litigants attempt to learn as much as they can about the case from each other. Generally speaking, the press and public have a right of access under either the first amendment or the common law to judicial records other than grand jury documents and most discovery materials, though this right is not absolute.

Whether there is a first amendment right of access to judicial records is not altogether clear. The leading Supreme Court case on the issue, *Nixon v. Warner Communications, Inc.* (1978), rejects such a right, but it was decided two years before *Richmond Newspapers*. In *Warner Communications*, broadcasters wanted to copy the White House tapes that had been played to the jury during the Watergate trial, as well as portions of the tapes that had not been admitted into evidence. The trial court denied access, and the Supreme Court ultimately affirmed. Though observing that there is a common law right "to inspect and copy public records and documents, including judicial records and documents," the Court found this common law rule inapplicable in light of a specific congressional statute governing access to the tapes. In addition, the Court declined an invitation to interpret the first amendment as embracing a constitutional right "to copy and publish . . . exhibits and materials displayed in open court." Pointing out that the public and press had "the opportunity . . . to attend the trial and to report what they ha[d] observed" and that reporters had been furnished transcripts of the tapes, the Court concluded that "there were simply no restrictions upon press access to, or publication of, any information in the public domain."

Some lower courts have taken the position that the subsequent *Richmond Newspapers* case did not affect the continuing validity of the *Warner Communications* decision and, accordingly, that there is no first amendment right of access to judicial records. For example, in *Belo Broadcasting Corp. v. Clark* (1981), the U.S. Court of Appeals for the Fifth Circuit rejected arguments by television stations that they had a first amendment right to copy FBI videotapes admitted into evidence at the trial of Texas officials who had been indicted in a bribery scheme. "[T]here is no such first amendment right," the court said. "Our reading of *Richmond Newspapers* convinces us that the holding of *Warner Communications* that the press enjoys no constitutional right of physical access to courtroom exhibits remains undisturbed." In the Fifth Circuit's view, the Supreme Court's decision in *Richmond Newspapers* was a "narrow one" limited to the "right of the press and public to attend criminal trials."

Most federal appellate courts, however, have recognized a first amendment right of access to court records, at least to those in criminal proceedings. The rationale for this view is that without access to these documents, the public often would not have a full understanding of the proceeding and would therefore not always be in a position to serve as an effective check on the judicial system. One of the leading cases adopting this position is *Associated Press v. U.S. District Court*, decided by the U.S. Court of Appeals for the Ninth Circuit in 1983. The case arose when the federal judge presiding over the drug trial of automaker John DeLorean entered an order directing that all documents filed in the pretrial stages of the case be "under seal," thus making them unavailable for public inspection. The Associated Press and the Los Angeles *Herald Examiner*, joined by other news organizations, asked the Ninth Circuit to vacate the order on the ground that it violated the first amendment. The appellate court agreed and reversed the trial judge.

Addressing the threshold question of whether the first amendment applied at all in these circumstances, the court said:

> [T]he first amendment right of access to criminal trials also applies to pretrial proceedings such as suppression hearings. There is no reason to distinguish between pretrial proceedings and the documents filed in regard to them. Indeed, the two principal justifications for the first amendment right of access to criminal proceedings apply, in general, to pretrial documents. * * * There can be little dispute that the press and public have historically had a common law right of access to most pretrial documents. . . . Moreover, pretrial documents, such as those dealing with the question of whether DeLorean should be incarcerated prior to trial and those containing allegations by DeLorean of government misconduct, are often important to a full understanding of the way in which "the judicial process and the government as a whole" are functioning. We thus find that the public and press have a first amendment right of access to pretrial documents in general.

The court emphasized that this right of access—like the right to attend criminal trials and pretrial proceedings—is not absolute and that documents can be sealed if necessary to protect the defendant's right to a fair trial. In this case, however, the court concluded that there had been no showing that "access to pretrial documents will create a substantial probability of irreparable damage to defendant's fair trial rights."

There is also a dispute among the lower courts as to the common law right of access. Although the Supreme Court recognized such a common law right in *Warner Communications*, its contours remain unclear. Some courts have interpreted the common law right expansively, ruling that there is a "strong presumption" in favor of access to judicial records that can be overcome only by "the most compelling of circumstances." Applying this standard, the U.S. Court of Appeals for the Second

Circuit ruled in *In re Application of NBC* (1980), that the broadcast media were entitled to copy FBI videotapes played during the trial of "Abscam" defendants who were caught in an FBI "sting" operation. On the other hand, the Fifth Circuit rejected such "an overpowering presumption" in the *Belo Broadcasting* case, fearing that this approach was tantamount to an absolute right of access. Instead, the court said that the need for access is simply one factor to be considered by the trial court in weighing the competing interests and that its decision will not be ordinarily be reversed on appeal.

It is settled, however, that there is neither a common law nor first amendment right of access to grand jury records. This should not be surprising, for, as noted previously, the courts have held that there is no right to attend grand jury proceedings, which historically have been closed to the press and public. "Although many governmental processes operate best under public scrutiny, it takes little imagination to recognize that there are some kinds of government operations that would be totally frustrated if conducted openly," the U.S. Supreme Court observed in the 1986 *Press Enterprise* case. "A classic example is that the proper functioning of our grand jury system depends upon the secrecy of grand jury proceedings."[4] Because there is no right to attend sessions of a grand jury, the lower courts have held that there is no right of access to grand jury records. Moreover, grand jury materials are typically exempt from disclosure under freedom of information statutes.

No matter whether one seeks access under the first amendment or the common law, the outcome usually turns on the strength of the competing interests that must be balanced against the right of access. With respect to evidence actually used at trial, the courts have uniformly held that these documents and other exhibits are presumptively available to the press and public. In some cases, however, this presumption in favor of access may be outweighed by the potential effect of the release of these materials—particularly video and audio recordings—on subsequent proceedings. For example, in *United States v. Webbe* (1986), the U.S. Court of Appeals for the Eighth Circuit affirmed the trial judge's refusal to allow the broadcast media to copy audio recordings used as evidence in the vote fraud trial of four defendants, including a St. Louis city councilman. The court noted that there were additional charges pending against one of the defendants and that the tapes admitted into evidence in the vote fraud trial might also be used in the other cases. Similarly, the defendants in *Belo Broadcasting* were being tried separately for related offenses, and the court expressed concern that permitting the broadcast media to copy videotapes used as evidence in the trial of the first defendant would cause prejudicial pretrial publicity problems with record to the trial of the second defendant.

Other considerations might also come into play in such cases. For example, in *In re Application of KSTP* (1980), a federal district court in Minnesota was faced with a television station's request to copy videotapes used as evidence in a rape trial. The defendant had made a color videotape while he raped the victim. Although the actual rape scene was not shown to the jury, portions of the tape picturing the victim, blindfolded and lying on the floor with her hands and feet bound, were played in open court. The judge denied the station's application to copy the tapes, pointing

---

[4]As the U.S. Court of Appeals for the Eleventh Circuit pointed out in *In re Subpoena* (1989), grand jury secrecy prevents the escape of persons against whom indictment may be sought; ensures freedom of deliberation among grand jurors; prevents subornation of perjury or tampering with witnesses who may later appear at trial; encourages full disclosure by witnesses; and protects an innocent person from publication of the fact that he has been under investigation.

out that the victim would be exposed to "public humiliation and degradation" if the tapes were disseminated. Any public interest in the tapes would be outweighed by the victim's right to privacy, the court said, and the information about the incident recorded on the tapes had already been made public.

Similarly, the federal judge who presided at the trial of presidential assailant John Hinckley refused to permit copying of the trial testimony of actress Jodie Foster, which had been presented to the jury on videotape. In that case, *In re ABC* (1982), the judge determined that Ms. Foster's safety and privacy interests outweighed any right of access to the videotapes.

After a trial is over, documents and other materials introduced into evidence are often returned to the litigants. At this point, they lose their status as court records and are not available to the press or public under either a common law or first amendment right of access. This issue arose in *Littlejohn v. BIC Corp.*, decided by the U.S. Court of Appeals for the Third Circuit in 1988. There the plaintiff alleged that she had been seriously injured by a defectively designed cigarette lighter. The suit was settled after a jury found for the plaintiff during the liability phase of the trial, and the documents introduced into evidence were subsequently returned to the parties pursuant to a court rule. Had the parties not claimed the trial exhibits within a specified period, the court clerk would have destroyed them under the same rule. Five months after the litigants had obtained their exhibits from the clerk, the *Philadelphia Inquirer* sought access to certain documents in connection with a story about lawsuits stemming from the defendant's lighters.

Although the documents had become judicial records when introduced into evidence at the trial and were at that point available for public inspection, the Third Circuit concluded that their status changed upon their return to the litigants. Emphasizing that the documents would have been destroyed by the clerk had the litigants not claimed them, the court ruled that trial exhibits subject to destruction by the clerk but instead restored to their owners after a case has been completely terminated are no longer judicial records to which a right of access applies. "Neither the first amendment nor the common law right of public access empowers the district court to require that litigants return such exhibits to the court for the purposes of copy and inspection by third parties," the court said. Although recognizing that public access helps ensure the integrity of the judicial process, the court found that this purpose was adequately served by access to the exhibits during the trial itself. "The public and the press had the opportunity then to observe the judicial process and to copy and inspect the testimony and exhibits that comprised the judicial record," the court said.

Because about seventy-five percent of all criminal cases are resolved through guilty pleas rather than by trial, it is is not surprising that the courts have recognized a first amendment right of access to plea bargaining hearings and records. Occasionally, however, there may be a compelling interest in withholding the details of the plea bargain agreement. An illustrative case is *United States v. Haller*, a 1988 decision of the U.S. Court of Appeals for the Second Circuit. There the business agent for a plumber's union pled guilty to embezzlement of union funds, and a portion of the three-page plea agreement was sealed at the request of the prosecutor. Affirming the trial judge's order, the appellate court pointed out that sealing part of the record was necessary to protect an ongoing criminal investigation. Public knowledge of the defendant's agreement, in his plea bargain, to cooperate with law enforcement officials could have alerted potential targets of the investigation.

With respect to pretrial materials in criminal cases, the courts have generally allowed access absent a clear showing that disclosure would interfere with the defendant's sixth amendment rights or with other important interests. For example, in *Seattle Times Co. v. U.S. District Court* (1988), the trial judge sealed pretrial documents filed in connection with a bail hearing for a woman charged with murdering her husband by placing cyanide in headache-pain capsules. The U.S. Court of Appeals for the Ninth Circuit reversed, ruling that the public and press had a qualified first amendment right of access to these records and that the documents "are not either so inflammatory or so prejudicial as to irreparably damage [the defendant's] right to a fair trial."

By way of comparison, the trial judge in *In re New York Times Co.* (1988) ordered the withholding of certain information from documents that accompanied a pretrial motion to suppress evidence obtained by electronic surveillance in the criminal prosecution of a New York congressman. On appeal, the Second Circuit recognized that the privacy interests of persons named in the documents could outweigh the first amendment right of access and directed the trial judge to employ a balancing approach. After further proceedings, the appellate court upheld the judge's order that the records be disclosed with certain material deleted.

Controversy has arisen with respect to search warrants and accompanying documents. The lower federal courts are divided on the question of whether there is a first amendment right of access to these materials. Two recent cases, both arising from a nationwide FBI investigation into alleged corruption in the defense industry, reflect the divergent judicial approaches.

In *In re Search Warrant for Secretarial Area* (1988), the U.S. Court of Appeals for the Eighth Circuit ruled that there is a qualified first amendment right of access to search warrants and related materials that can be overcome by a showing that disclosure of the documents would jeopardize an ongoing criminal investigation. At issue was a search warrant, issued in connection with the "Operation Ill-Wind" investigation, covering an office at McDonnell Douglas Corporation in St. Louis, a major defense contractor. Upon motion by the government, a federal district court placed under seal the search warrant, affidavits filed with the application for the warrant, and the description of property to be seized.

Concluding that the first amendment provides a right of access to these materials, the Eighth Circuit emphasized that a search warrant is an "integral part" of a criminal prosuection. "[P]ublic access to documents filed in support of search warrants is important to the public's understanding of the function and operation of the . . . criminal justice system and may operate as a curb on prosecutorial or judicial misconduct," the court said. Moreover, search warrants are "at the center of pretrial suppression hearings [that] often determine the outcome of criminal prosecutions." Such hearings are presumptively open to the press and public, and the court saw no reason to treat search warrant materials any differently for first amendment purposes.

Because any first amendment right of access is qualified rather than absolute, the court then considered whether there was a compelling government interest that would justify nondisclosure. In this case, the court concluded that such an interest was present—the need to protect the pending criminal investigation. "These documents describe in considerable detail the nature, scope and direction of the government's investigation and the individuals and specific projects involved," the court said, also pointing out that the documents contained information from electronic surveillance and confidential informants. "There is a subtantial probability that the government's ongoing investigation would be severely compromised if the sealed documents were released."

In *Times Mirror Co. v. United States* (1989), the U.S. Court of Appeals for the Ninth Circuit also denied access to search warrants and related documents stemming from Operation Ill-Wind, but on quite different grounds. The court held that there is no right of access to these materials under the first amendment, at least when the criminal investigation is ongoing and no indictments have been returned. The court also concluded that there is no common law right of access to search warrant records "in the midst of a preindictment investigation into suspected criminal activity."

Rejecting the Eighth Circuit's first amendment analysis, the court emphasized that there is "no history of openness" with respect to these records and that their disclosure "would hinder, rather than facilitate, the [search] warrant process and the government's ability to conduct criminal investigations." If search warrant records were open to the public, the court said, "persons identified as being under suspicion of criminal activity might destroy evidence, coordinate their stories before testifying, or even flee the jurisdiction." The court also likened search warrant records to grand jury proceedings (which are closed to the public and press), pointing out that the search warrant process develops evidence to be presented to a grand jury. Finally, the court noted that disclosure of the records before indictments are returned would infringe on the "significant privacy interests" of persons identified in the warrants and supporting materials. As is the case in the grand jury context, secrecy is necessary to "assure that persons who are accused but exonerated . . . will not be held up to public ridicule."

Discovery materials present somewhat different considerations, for most of this information is never admitted into evidence at trial or otherwise used in the judicial proceeding. In fact, much of the information that surfaces during this pretrial process is unrelated or only marginally related to the lawsuit. Absent some sort of controversy, the judge does not participate in the discovery process, which, as a practical matter, takes place in private. Depositions, for example, are usually conducted in lawyers' offices at times most convenient to those involved. Moreover, discovery records—such as transcripts of depositions and copies of documents—are not even filed with the clerk of the court in most jurisdictions unless the judge specifically so orders.

The leading case regarding access to discovery materials is the U.S. Supreme Court's 1984 decision in *Seattle Times Co. v. Rhinehart*. There the Court ruled that judicial orders restricting the release of discovery information do not offend the first amendment. At issue in that case was a so-called "protective order" that prohibited the *Seattle Times* from publishing information that it had learned from the plaintiff in the discovery phase of his libel suit against the newspaper. In rejecting the first amendment argument, the Court ruled that a right to disseminate such materials would impose an unwarranted restriction on the duty and discretion of a trial judge to oversee the discovery process, which is an essential part of modern litigation. The Court also pointed out that discovery materials "are not public components of a civil trial" and are not open to the public under the common law. In light of this decision, the news media will have a more difficult time gaining access to discovery materials than to evidence introduced at trial.

The Florida Supreme Court, for example, has ruled that there is no right under either state law or the first amendment to attend depositions or obtain copies of the transcripts of depositions that had not been filed with the trial court. In *Palm Beach Newspapers, Inc. v. Burk* (1987), a criminal case, the court emphasized that the purpose of depositions is "to develop evidence by discovering what potential witnesses may know about the subject of the trial." Because information obtained at a deposition is often irrelevant to the case and inadmissible into evidence at trial, public access to such material "has the substantial potential of hazarding the right to a fair trial, the privacy rights of both parties and non-parties, and the right to a trial in the venue of the alleged crime." In a subsequent decision, *Miami Herald Publishing Co. v. Gridley* (1987), the court extended the *Burk* rationale to discovery materials in civil cases.

The Florida decisions suggest, however, that discovery records are available to the public once they have been filed with the trial court. To the same effect is a recent federal case, *In re Agent Orange Litigation*, decided by the U.S. Court of Appeals for the Second Circuit in 1987. There the court concluded that the rules that govern procedure in federal civil cases provide for the public scrutiny of discovery materials filed with the court absent a judicial order to the contrary. Under the procedural rules, a trial judge may grant a protective order denying access to discovery information if there is a valid reason for doing so. In legal jargon, these orders may be entered if "good cause" is shown. However, a judge will not issue such an order simply because the parties to the case believe that the information should be kept secret.

This point is illustrated by *Public Citizen v. Liggett Group, Inc.*, a 1988 decision of the U.S. Court of Appeals for the First Circuit upholding a trial judge's modification of a protective order to permit public access to discovery materials in a lawsuit against a tobacco company by the survivors of a smoker. The trial judge had imposed the protective order during the discovery stage of the suit, which was later dismissed prior to trial when the judge ruled in the defendant's favor on certain legal issues. At that point, a public interest group and the *Wall Street Journal* sought access to the discovery documents that had been subject to the protective order. Ruling that the tobacco company had failed to demonstrate that the documents contained commercially sensitive information such as trade secrets or to establish any other compelling need for continued secrecy, the judge concluded that the public should be allowed to inspect the materials.

The court of appeals affirmed. Agreeing with the Second Circuit's decision in *Agent Orange* that federal procedural rules establish a right of access to discovery records filed with the court unless a protective order has been entered for "good cause," the First Circuit emphasized that the purpose of the order in this case had been to help minimize pretrial publicity. Because the suit had been resolved without a trial, the court said, there was no longer any reason to keep the documents secret.

Even if discovery materials do not become available to the public when they are filed with the court, they should be open to inspection when they form the basis for judicial action. For example, in *Rushford v. The New Yorker Magazine, Inc.* (1988), the U.S. Court of Appeals for the Fourth Circuit held that discovery documents attached to a motion for summary judgment in a libel case were presumptively available to the press and public under the first amendment. At this point, the court said, the documents had lost their status as "raw fruits of discovery" and had become part of the judicial proceeding itself. Other courts have reached the same result under the common law right of access to judicial records.

CAMERAS IN THE COURTROOM

Although the trial judge in *Sheppard v. Maxwell* allowed newspaper photographers and television camera crews almost free rein, he did not allow any photography or broadcasting during the trial itself. This bit of restraint can be traced to the notorious trial of Bruno Hauptmann in 1935, for shortly after that case the American Bar Association drafted a model rule of judicial ethics stating that a judge should prohibit the broadcasting, recording, or photographing of proceedings in the courtroom. The federal courts and those in all but two states, Colorado and Texas, adopted similar provisions, and for more than four decades television equipment, tape recorders, and still cameras were not permitted in the vast majority of the nation's courtrooms. Today, however, more than forty states allow the use of these devices, at least on a limited basis, though the federal courts continue to ban them.[5]

As the federal court prohibition suggests, there is no first amendment right to televise, photograph, or record a judicial proceeding. We shall return to this issue in a moment. What, then, accounts for the change in attitude among the states about the presence of cameras and tape recorders in the courtroom? The answer can be found in two U.S. Supreme Court decisions, *Estes v. Texas* (1965) and *Chandler v. Florida* (1981).

In the *Estes* case, the Court reversed the conviction of Texas financier Billie Sol Estes, who had been charged with theft by swindling in a massive scheme involving the "sale" of nonexistent fertilizer tanks to unsuspecting farmers. Because Texas was one of two states that allowed photography during trial, Estes' lawyers asked the trial judge court to exclude all cameras on the ground that such coverage would make it difficult for them to consult with their client, distract the jurors and witnesses, and make a fair trial impossible. The hearing on that request drew a standing room only crowd of media representatives and was televised live by stations in Tyler, where the trial was to be held, and in nearby Dallas. Though the judge denied the defense motion, he did impose certain restrictions on the use of cameras at the trial itself. The three major networks and one Tyler station could each have one camera in the courtroom, and they would make available film to other stations on a "pooled" basis. Sound recording was not permitted. Still cameramen from the local newspapers, the Associated Press, and United Press International were allowed in the courtroom as "pool" photographers.

The local television station constructed a crude booth at the rear of the small courtroom to house the four television cameras allowed under the judge's order. The cameras were clearly visible to all in attendance, however. Still photographers roamed the courtroom, though they could not enter the "bar" of the court reserved for trial participants and separated from the rest of the courtroom by a railing. Live television and radio coverage was not permitted until the trial's end, when the judge allowed such coverage of the prosecution's closing argument and the return of the jury's verdict. Because Estes' lawyers had objected to being photographed during their argument to the jury, the judge prohibited television cameramen and still photographers from aiming their lenses at the attorneys. Live television coverage continued during the defense summation, however, as the cameras focused on the judge and television reporters relayed the gist of the defense summation to the viewing audience.

---

[5]Only five states—Indiana, Missouri, Mississippi, South Carolina, and South Dakota—prohibit the use of all electronic recording devices. Texas allows the sound to be recorded but bars all cameras.

A divided Supreme Court ruled that Estes had been denied a fair trial, with Justice John Marshall Harlan casting the key vote in the 5 to 4 decision. In the principal opinion, Justice Clark focused on the presence of the television cameras and concluded that the televising of trials is "inherently prejudicial" to the rights of the defendant. Justice Clark listed virtually all of the concerns typically voiced about the impact of television on a trial, particularly its effect on members of the jury:

- jurors may feel pressured by the knowledge that "their friends and neighbors have their eyes on them";
- the physical presence of television cameras distracts jurors, who may feel self-conscious and uneasy about being televised and, more importantly, may ignore important testimony because of their preoccupation with the cameras;
- jurors who are not sequestered could be influenced by television news coverage of the trial, since the reports could emphasize certain testimony to the exclusion of contrary evidence; and
- prejudicial publicity problems could result if the initial conviction is reversed and a new trial is necessary, since the potential jurors would have been able to watch the first trial on television.

Further, Justice Clark argued that television would have a negative effect on other participants in the trial. Witnesses, for example, could be expected to "grandstand" in front of the cameras or to react self-consciously to their presence. In either situation, the "quality of the testimony" would be impaired, since the jury would be presented with a distorted view of the witness. A witness who thinks of himself as a "star" might be prone to exaggerate, while a shy witness embarrassed by the cameras might appear to lack credibility. The television camera's "telltale red light" can evoke similar responses from lawyers and judges, and television makes the judge's task of controlling the trial much more difficult. Judges are elected in almost all states, and a televised trial could become a potent "political weapon." Finally, courtroom television is "a form of mental—if not physical—harassment" for the defendant, whose every statement, move, and gesture is captured by the camera. The presence of cameras might also interfere with the confidential relationship between the defendant and his attorneys.

Justice Harlan, however, was not prepared to accept the conclusion that televising a trial is always prejudicial to a defendant. In his crucial concurring opinion, he wrote that "there is no constitutional requirement that television be allowed in the courtroom, and, at least as to a notorious criminal trial such as this one, the considerations against allowing television in the courtroom so far outweigh the countervailing factors advanced in its support as to require a holding that what was done in this case infringed the fundamental right to a fair trial. . . ." In addition to limiting his opinion to the "notorious" case, Justice Harlan left open the possibility that advancements in technology could alleviate the distortions that he perceived to flow from the presence of cameras. "[T]he day may come when television will have become so commonplace an affair in the daily life of the average person as to dissipate all reasonable likelihood that its use in courtrooms may disparage the judicial process," he wrote. "At the present juncture, I can only conclude that televised trials, at least in cases like this one, possess such capabilities for interfering with the even course of the judicial process that they are constitutionally banned."

Estes was decided in 1965, when television was in relative infancy. Sixteen years later, the Supreme Court returned to the "cameras in the courtroom" question in *Chandler v. Florida*. The first question was the scope of the *Estes* decision. Relying on Justice Harlan's concurring opinion, the Court rejected the argument that *Estes* "announc[ed] a constitutional rule barring still photographic, radio, and television coverage in all cases and under all circumstances." Writing for a unanimous Court, Chief Justice Burger then reevaluated the issue and concluded that an absolute ban on broadcast coverage of trials cannot be justified simply because there is a danger that, in some cases, the presence of cameras and audio recording devices may have an adverse impact on the jury or trial participants. Rather, the "appropriate safeguard against such prejudice" is the defendant's right to demonstrate that media coverage actually caused unfairness in his particular trial.

The *Chandler* case had its origins in an experimental plan for television, radio, and photographic coverage of civil and criminal trials adopted by the Florida Supreme Court in 1976. Similar pilot programs were underway in a few other states. Under Florida's experimental rules (which were later made permanent), coverage was permitted subject to certain safeguards. For example, a pool arrangement using only a single television camera from a fixed location was required, artificial lighting was not permitted, and recording of conversations between lawyers and their clients, other lawyers, and the trial judge was forbidden. Photographing the jury was not allowed, and the trial judge had discretionary authority to prevent coverage of certain witnesses. Moreover, the judge could also exclude cameras and microphones altogether when satisfied that such coverage would interfere with the right of the defendant to a fair trial.

The experimental rules were in effect at the burglary trial of two Miami policemen, Noel Chandler and Robert Granger, who had been "caught in the act" when a ham radio operator overheard them talking over police walkie-talkies as they broke into a restaurant. As one might expect, the case attracted considerable media attention, and, despite defense objections, cameras were present for part of the trial. Following a guilty verdict, the defendants appealed on the ground that television coverage had denied them a fair trial. In rejecting this argument, Chief Justice Burger pointed out that new technology had made television coverage less cumbersome and intrusive, no empirical evidence suggested that the mere presence of cameras has adverse psychological effects on trial participants, and the Florida regulations contained built-in safeguards designed to avoid the egregious problems envisioned in *Estes*. Thus, any claim of prejudice must be evaluated on a case-by-case basis, and defendants who contend that their sixth amendment rights have been violated must offer specific evidence "to demonstrate that their trial was subtly tainted by broadcast coverage." No such evidence was presented in *Chandler*.

This decision served as the impetus for other states to adopt rules permitting the use of cameras and tape recorders at trial. As noted previously, more than forty states now allow some type of coverage, though the guidelines—which are generally quite detailed—vary widely from state to state. In several states, for example, consent of the defendant is necessary, while in others the defendant's wishes are irrelevant. Pooling requirements are common, as are restrictions on photographing certain trial participants, including jurors, victims in sexual offense cases, minors, and undercover police officers or informants. Most importantly, trial judges are given broad discretion to prohibit television cameras, still photography, and audio recording in order to protect the defendant's right to a fair trial.

The Court's ruling in *Chandler* that the states are free to allow cameras and tape recorders in the courtroom is a far cry from recognition that the use of such devices is guaranteed by the first amendment. Indeed, the federal courts continue to ban broadcasting, video and audio recording, and still photography, as do courts in a handful of states. Although *Richmond Newspapers* makes clear that broadcast journalists and news photographers may attend a criminal trial, *Chandler* does not mean that they can take the "tools of their trade" with them. In short, *Chandler* is not an "access" case, and Justice Harlan's comment in his *Estes* concurrence that "there is no constitutional requirement that television be allowed in the courtroom" remains an accurate statement of the law.

The federal prohibition against cameras and tape recorders has consistently been upheld by the federal appellate courts. In *United States v. Hastings* (1983), various news organizations applied to the trial court for an order permitting them to use electronic audio-visual equipment during the trial of a federal judge accused of bribery. That motion was denied, and the U.S. Court of Appeals for the Eleventh Circuit affirmed. Rejecting the media's argument that *Chandler* and *Richmond Newspapers* rendered the camera ban unconstitutional, the court explained the relationship between those decisions as follows:

> First, [*Chandler* holds that] television coverage of a criminal trial is not inherently unconstitutional. * * * But just because television coverage is not constitutionally prohibited does not mean that television coverage is constitutionally mandated. Second, the press has a right of access [under *Richmond Newspapers*] to observe criminal trials, just as members of the public have the right to attend criminal trials. To conclude . . . that the right of access extends to the right to televise, record, and broadcast trials, misconceives the meaning of the right of access. . . . The right of access . . . [is] the right to attend. In the upcoming trial here, journalists will be able to attend, listen, and report on the proceedings as they always have. No part of the trial has been closed from public scrutiny.

The U.S. Court of Appeals for the Second Circuit was faced with a slightly different argument in *Westmoreland v. CBS* (1984) but reached the same result. There Cable News Network wanted to broadcast the trial of the highly publicized libel case brought by the commander of U.S. troops in Vietnam on the basis of a "60 Minutes" segment. CNN challenged the constitutionality of the federal rule that forbids broadcasting, arguing that the prohibition denies the public's right of access to the trial. Because the size of the courtroom prevents those who wish to attend from being physically present, CNN claimed, television is the only effective means of public access to the trial. The court rejected this argument. After first concluding that the right of access under *Richmond Newspapers* applies in civil cases, the court observed that "[t]here is a long leap . . . between a public right under the First Amendment to attend trials and a public right under the First Amendment to see a given trial televised. * * * It is a leap that we are not yet prepared to take."

PROBLEMS

1. The free press-fair trial controversy has been largely the product of criminal cases, where the defendant's right to a fair trial is guaranteed by the sixth amendment. Does the absence of such an express provision governing civil cases mean that criminal trials are subject to greater fair trial concerns than civil proceedings and, consequently, that restric-

tions on first amendment rights are harder to justify in the civil context? For example, should it be more difficult for a judge to issue a "gag order" directed at the litigants in a civil case than one aimed at the participants in a criminal trial? *Compare Bailey v. Systems Innovation, Inc.*, 852 F.2d 93 (3d Cir. 1988), with *Hirschkop v. Snead*, 594 F.2d 356 (4th Cir. 1979), and *Chicago Council of Lawyers v. Bauer*, 522 F.2d 242 (7th Cir. 1975), *cert. denied*, 427 U.S. 912 (1976).

2. The broad authority of judges to regulate judicial proceedings is enforced via the contempt power. There are two basic types of contempt. If used to force someone to do something (e.g., divulge a confidential source), the contempt is civil in nature, and the contempt citation remains in effect until it is obeyed. If, however, its purpose is to punish disrespect for the court or interference with judicial proceedings, the contempt is criminal and is punishable by a fixed jail term and/or fine. Violations of gag orders would fall into this category. Criminal contempt is considered "direct" if the offending conduct occurs in the judge's presence; otherwise, it is said to be "indirect" or "constructive."

   During jury selection for the "Iran-Contra" trial of Col. Oliver North, ABC reporter Tim O'Brien prepared a story on the difficulty of choosing jurors who had not yet formed an opinion about North's role in the episode. "The problem has been compounded by television," O'Brien said at the end of his report. "If you paid close attention to this report, you too are ineligible to serve as a juror." The next day, the presiding judge threatened to hold O'Brien in contempt. What is the nature of the alleged contempt? Would a contempt citation in this situation run afoul of the first amendment? *See Craig v. Harney*, 331 U.S. 367 (1947); *In re Stone*, 703 P.2d 1319 (Colo. App. 1985). Apart from the contempt issue, was O'Brien correct in stating that anyone who had carefully watched his report could not serve as a juror?

3. As the *Nebraska Press* case indicates, voluntary "bar-press guidelines" have been adopted in several states to deal with the problem of prejudicial publicity. These guidelines, developed by lawyers and journalists, were adopted in response to an American Bar Association report that examined the "free press-fair trial" problem in light of the *Sheppard* case and the criticism directed at the media by the Warren Commission report on the assassination of President John F. Kennedy. Generally speaking, the guidelines state that the press will not report information that could jeopardize a defendant's right to a fair trial, such as evidence that cannot be used at trial and the contents or existence of a confession. *See* footnote 1 in the *Nebraska Press* opinion. If a trial judge concludes that he could order a closed proceeding under *Richmond Newspapers* and its progeny, could he instead enter an order conditioning media attendance on a pledge to follow such guidelines? *See Federated Publications, Inc. v. Swedberg*, 633 P.2d 74 (Wash. 1981), *cert. denied*, 456 U.S. 984 (1982).

4. Many states have statutes that bar the press and public from attending juvenile trials or give trial judges broad discretion to restrict attendance. Are these statutes constitutional under *Richmond Newspapers*? Does it matter that proceedings involving juveniles have historically taken place in secret? Are closed proceedings justified on the theory that publicity will undermine efforts to rehabilitate juvenile offenders? Is a statute that prohibits access in all juvenile cases valid under *Globe Newspaper*? Should the severity of the offense make any difference? May a judge condition access on an agreement by the media not to publish the name of a juvenile defendant? May a state make it a crime for a media organization to publish the name of a juvenile offender? *See Smith v. Daily Mail Publishing Co.*, 443 U.S. 97 (1979); *State ex rel. Oregonian Publishing Co. v. Deiz*, 613 P.2d 23 (Or. 1980); *In re J.S.*, 438 A.2d 1125 (Vt. 1981); *Florida Publishing Co. v. Morgan*, 322 S.E.2d 233 (Ga. 1984); *Tribune Newspapers West, Inc. v. Superior Court*, 218

Cal. Rptr. 505 (Ct. App. 1985); *Associated Press v. Bradshaw,* 410 N.W.2d 577 (S.D. 1987); *Matter of N.H.B.,* 769 P.2d 844 (Utah App. 1989).

5. The Uniform Code of Military Justice, 10 U.S.C. §§801 *et seq.,* establishes rules of conduct for members of the armed forces and proscribes penalties for the violation of those rules. Specialized courts, ranging from courts martial in each military service to the U.S. Court of Military Appeals, hear cases arising under the code. This separate military justice system exists because of the unique needs of the military to maintain discipline and adherence to the chain of command. *See generally Parker v. Levy*, 417 U.S. 733 (1974). In light of these considerations, should the rule of *Richmond Newspapers* apply in the military courts? Is it relevant that these courts routinely hear criminal cases quite similar to those tried in civilian courts (e.g., murder, burglary, possession of illegal drugs)? *See United States v. Travers,* 25 M.J. 61 (C.M.A. 1987); *United States v. Hershey,* 20 M.J. 433 (C.M.A. 1985), *cert. denied,* 474 U.S. 1062 (1986).

6. The work of "courtroom artists" frequently appears on television, not only on network broadcasts but also on the news programs of local stations. To what extent, if any, can a judge prohibit these artists from sketching the action at a trial? *See United States v. CBS,* 497 F.2d 102 (5th Cir. 1974); *KPNX Broadcasting Co. v. Superior Court,* 678 P.2d 431 (Ariz. 1984).

7. In their 1974 book *All the President's Men,* Carl Bernstein and Bob Woodward described the process by which they pieced together the story of the Watergate episode. During the course of their investigation, they learned the names of persons serving on the Watergate grand jury and contacted several of them. This effort to learn about the grand jury's activities proved fruitless; in fact, only one person even admitted he was a member of the grand jury. However, at least one of the grand jurors told federal prosecutors that he had been approached by *Washington Post* reporters, and Judge John Sirica subsequently lectured the news media—without specifically identifying Bernstein and Woodward as the culprits—about the secrecy of the grand jury process and the oath taken by jurors not to reveal anything about their deliberations. Similar requirements are placed on grand jurors at the state level.

  Could Judge Sirica have held the two reporters in contempt of court for seeking to induce the grand jurors to disclose confidential information? Would your answer be different if the grand jury had already completed its work? How does the first amendment come into play, if at all, in this context? *See State v. Heltzel,* 533 N.E.2d 159, *rehearing denied,* 535 N.E.2d 1221 (Ind. App. 1989). Some states (but not the federal government) also impose a secrecy requirement on all witnesses who appear before a grand jury. Suppose that a witness wishes to discuss his testimony with reporters. Does the secrecy rule offend the witness' first amendment rights? The first amendment rights of the journalists? Does it matter whether the investigation is ongoing or completed? *See Smith v. Butterworth,* 866 F.2d 1318 (11th Cir. 1989); *Beacon Journal Publishing Co. v. Unger,* 532 F. Supp. 55 (N.D. Ohio 1982).

8. In its 1984 decision in *Press-Enterprise Co. v. Superior Court,* the U.S. Supreme Court indicated that privacy concerns might warrant closing jury selection proceedings to the press and public. May a court order a newspaper not to print the names and addresses of jurors? Deny access to court records containing the names of and information about jurors? Does your privacy analysis change if prospective jurors are involved? If the jury has already been seated? Is the possibility of intimidation of or retaliation against jurors a significant consideration? *See In re Baltimore Sun Co.,* 841 F.2d 74 (4th Cir. 1988); *Newsday, Inc. v. Sise,* 518 N.E.2d 930 (N.Y. 1987), *cert. denied,* 108 S.Ct. 2823 (1988); *Des Moines Register & Tribune Co. v. Osmundson,* 248 N.W.2d 493 (Iowa 1976).

9. The wife of a state senator filed for divorce. On the senator's motion, the trial court sealed the case file and ordered that all proceedings be conducted in private. Is this order valid? Suppose that the senator had been linked romatically with another woman and that the basis for the divorce action was an affair between the two. Assume further that the "other woman" was a long-time member of the senator's staff. Does this information affect your analysis of the trial judge's closure order? Is it important that one of the parties to the divorce action is a public official? *See Barron v. Florida Freedom Newspapers, Inc.*, 531 So.2d 113 (Fla. 1988). Can a state constitutionally enact a statute requiring that proceedings in domestic relations cases be closed to the general public and the press? *See In re Adoption of H.Y.T.*, 458 So.2d 1127 (Fla. 1984)(adoption); *Mayer v. State*, 523 So.2d 1171 (Fla. App.), *review dism'd*, 529 So.2d 694 (Fla. 1988)(child custody).

10. Litigants in civil cases who "settle" a dispute prior to trial frequently agree that the terms of the settlement are to remain confidential. Does the settlement agreement itself become a public document when filed with the court? Does it matter whether the parties bargained for confidentiality as part of settlement negotiations? Is the nature of the lawsuit relevant? For example, is a case involving allegations of wrongdoing by public officials different from a "routine" personal injury suit? Apart from the question of constitutional or common law access, might the agreement be available under a freedom of information statute? *See Wilson v. American Motors Corp.*, 759 F.2d 1568 (11th Cir. 1985); *Society of Professional Journalists v. Briggs*, 675 F. Supp. 1308 (D. Utah 1987); *Daily Gazette v. Withrow*, 350 S.E.2d 738 (W. Va. 1986); *Register Division of Freedom Newspapers, Inc. v. Orange County,* 205 Cal. Rptr. 92 (Ct. App. 1984).

11. In a suit stemming from the design and construction of a nuclear power plant, a federal district judge ordered the parties to participate in a "summary jury trial," a proceeding in which the litigants present their case before mock jurors in order to facilitate a settlement. After hearing abbreviated testimony and arguments, the jurors rendered an informal, nonbinding verdict that led to settlement of the case. Is there a first amendment right of access to such a proceeding? Does a summary jury trial differ significantly from an actual trial, or is it functionally part of the settlement process? Is it important that settlement negotiations have historically taken place in private? That the courts have long recognized a strong public policy in favor of encouraging settlement? *See Cincinnati Gas & Electric Co. v. General Electric Co.*, 854 F.2d 900 (6th Cir. 1988), *cert. denied*, 109 S.Ct. 1171 (1989).

12. In one of the most famous cases in Mississippi history, Marion Pruett, a self-described "mad-dog killer," was convicted of capital murder in 1982 for the death of a savings and loan officer. The conviction was subsequently overturned because of juror bias caused by massive pretrial publicity. Prior to Pruett's second trial, the trial judge entered an order sealing all court records in the case and excluding the public and the press from pretrial suppression hearings and juror selection. More than 350 newspaper stories about the crime had appeared in Mississipi, the "mad-dog killer" label was used in press accounts, and it was widely reported that Pruett had been convicted of murder in three other states following his first trial in Mississippi. Is the trial judge's order valid? Why or why not? *See Mississippi Publishers Corp. v. Coleman*, 515 So.2d 1163 (Miss. 1987).

13. Prior to the sentencing of a criminal defendant in federal court, the court's probation service prepares a "presentence investigation report" which includes information about the defendant's history, prior criminal record, financial condition, and circumstances affecting his behavior. The report also contains a classification of the offense charged and of the defendant under Federal Sentencing Commission guidelines, as well as a statement about the impact of the crime on the victim. *See* Rule 32(c), Federal Rules of Crimi-

nal Procedure. Should the press and public have access to the report? *See United States v. Schlette,* 842 F.2d 1574, *as amended,* 854 F.2d 359 (9th Cir. 1988). Does it matter that these reports are available under the Freedom of Information Act after sentencing, when they are used by the Bureau of Prisons and the Parole Commission in assessing the prisoner for purposes of incarceration, treatment, and release? *See U.S. Department of Justice v. Julian,* 486 U.S. 1 (1988).

14. A Massachusetts statute requires that court records be automatically sealed when the defendant is acquitted, when a grand jury refuses to indict the person, or when a judge decides that there is not probable cause to believe that the person has committed the crime. What is the rationale behind the statute? Is it constitutional? Would closure of these records on a case-by-case basis be permissible? *See Globe Newspaper Co. v. Pokaski,* 868 F.2d 497 (1st Cir. 1989).

CHAPTER
7
CONFIDENTIAL SOURCES

Zerilli v. Smith, **656 F.2d 705 (D.C. Cir. 1981).**

Before WRIGHT and ROBB, Circuit Judges, and PENN, District Judge.

J. SKELLY WRIGHT, Circuit Judge:

* * *Appellants Anthony T. Zerilli and Michael Polizzi brought an action under the Privacy Act and the Fourth Amendment against the Attorney General of the United States, the Director of the Federal Bureau of Investigation, and the Department of Justice. They contended that employees of the Department of Justice violated their constitutional and statutory rights by leaking to the *Detroit News* transcripts of conversations in which appellants discussed various illegal activities. These transcripts had originally been obtained by the Justice Department as the result of electronic surveillance conducted by the Federal Bureau of Investigation. According to appellants, a series of articles on organized crime written by reporter Seth Kantor and other members of

the *Detroit News* staff were based on information obtained from the transcripts. When appellants deposed Kantor he refused to reveal his sources, relying on a qualified reporter's privilege under the First Amendment. * * * Because we believe that in this case the First Amendment interest in protecting a news reporter's sources outweighs the interest in compelled disclosure, we affirm the District Court's decision to deny the motion to compel discovery [of those sources]. * * *

Appellants argue that the District Court erred when it denied their motion to compel Kantor to disclose his confidential sources. They claim that the First Amendment reporter's privilege should not prevail, since their interest in disclosure outweighs any public interest in protecting the sources. * * *

Compelling a reporter to disclose the identity of a confidential source raises obvious First Amendment problems. The First Amendment guarantees a free press primarily because of the important role it can play as "a vital source of public information." "The press was protected so that it could bare the secrets of government and inform the people." Without an unfettered press, citizens would be far less able to make informed political, social, and economic choices. But the press' function as a vital source of information is weakened whenever the ability of journalists to gather news is impaired. Compelling a reporter to disclose the identity of a source may significantly interfere with this news gathering ability; journalists frequently depend on informants to gather news, and confidentiality is often essential to establishing a relationship with an informant.

In *Branzburg v. Hayes* (1972), the Supreme Court held that a journalist does not have an absolute privilege under the First Amendment to refuse to disclose confidential sources to a grand jury conducting a criminal investigation, despite the potential interference with news gathering. The Court justified this decision by pointing to the traditional importance of grand juries and the strong public interest in effective criminal investigation. It recognized, however, that because news gathering is essential to a free press, it deserves some First Amendment protection. Thus the Court indicated that a qualified privilege would be available in some circumstances even where a reporter is called before a grand jury to testify. Moreover, Justice Powell, who cast the deciding vote in *Branzburg*, wrote a concurring opinion in which he stated that courts can determine whether a privilege applies by using a balancing test:

The asserted claim to privilege should be judged on its facts by the striking of a proper balance between freedom of the press and the obligation of all citizens to give relevant testimony with respect to criminal conduct. The balance of these vital constitutional and societal interests on case-by-case basis accords with the tried and traditional way of adjudicating such questions.

Although *Branzburg* may limit the scope of the reporter's First Amendment privilege in criminal proceedings, this circuit has previously held that in civil cases, where the public interest in effective criminal law enforcement

is absent, that case is not controlling. *Carey v. Hume* (1974). In *Carey* we considered the question whether a reporter being sued for libel could refuse to reveal the identity of confidential sources who provided the information on which the allegedly libelous news story was based. We decided that the circumstances of that case did not warrant application of a First Amendment privilege. We indicated, however, that a qualified reporter's privilege under the First Amendment should be readily available in civil cases. An approach similar to that described by Justice Powell in *Branzburg* was adopted. We held that to determine whether the privilege applies courts should look to the facts of each case, weighing the public interest in protecting the reporter's sources against the private interest in compelling disclosure. Every other circuit that has considered the question has also ruled that a privilege should be readily available in civil cases, and that a balancing approach should be applied.

In general, when striking the balance between the civil litigant's interest in compelled disclosure and the public interest in protecting a newspaper's confidential sources, we will be mindful of the preferred position of the First Amendment and the importance of a vigorous press. Efforts will be taken to minimize impingement upon the reporter's ability to gather news. Thus in the ordinary case the civil litigant's interest in disclosure should yield to the journalist's privilege. Indeed, if the privilege does not prevail in all but the most exceptional cases, its value will be substantially diminished. Unless potential sources are confident that compelled disclosure is unlikely, they will be reluctant to disclose any confidential information to reporters.

A number of more precise guidelines can be applied to determine how the balance should be struck in a particular case. The civil litigant's need for the information he seeks is of central importance. If the information sought goes to "the heart of the matter," that is, if it is crucial to his case, then the argument in favor of compelled disclosure may be relatively strong. In *Carey v. Hume*, for example, the privilege was not recognized in part because the identity of the reporter's source was central to the plaintiff's proof in his libel action. On the other hand, if the information sought is only marginally relevant, disclosure may be very difficult to justify.

The efforts made by the litigants to obtain the information from alternative sources is also of central importance. Even when the information is crucial to a litigant's case, reporters should be compelled to disclose their sources only after the litigant has shown that he has exhausted every reasonable alternative source of information. As we stated in *Carey v. Hume*, "The values resident in the protection of the confidential sources of newsmen certainly point towards compelled disclosure from the newsman himself as normally the end, and not the beginning, of the inquiry." To be sure, there are some limits to the obligation to pursue alternative sources. In *Carey*, for example, the reporter being sued had stated that his source was an employee of the national headquarters of the United Mine Workers of America. We decided that the litigant need not have deposed every one of the UMWA's employees. Nonetheless, the obligation is clearly very substantial. In *Carey* we suggested that an alternative requiring the taking of as many as 60 depositions might be a reasonable prerequisite to compelled disclosure.

A distinction can also be drawn between civil cases in which the reporter is a party, as in a libel action, and cases in which the reporter is not a party. When the journalist is a party, and successful assertion of the privilege will effectively shield him from liability, the equities weigh somewhat more heavily in favor of disclosure. As we suggested in *Carey v. Hume*, this will be particularly true in libel cases involving public officials or public figures where the rule of *New York Times Co. v. Sullivan* (1964) applies. Plaintiffs in those cases must prove both that the allegedly defamatory publication was false, and that it was made with "actual malice." Proof of actual malice will frequently depend on knowing the identity of the newspaper's informant, since a plaintiff will have to demonstrate that

the informant was unreliable and that the journalist failed to take adequate steps to verify his story. Protecting the identity of the source would effectively prevent recovery in many *Times*-type libel cases. We take care to point out, however, that disclosure should by no means be automatic in libel cases. Where other relevant factors suggest disclosure is inappropriate, the privilege should prevail.

Applying these guidelines to the facts of the case before us, we readily find that the District Court did not abuse its discretion when it concluded that a qualified First Amendment privilege should apply. It is true that appellants' suit is not frivolous. Moreover, the information they seek is crucial to their case. The success of their Privacy Act and Fourth Amendment claims may depend on the identities of the individuals who leaked the wiretap logs to Kantor. But appellants clearly have not fulfilled their obligation to exhaust possible alternative sources of information. In response to appellants' interrogatories the Department of Justice provided a list of the names of four employees who knew most about the wiretap logs. During the 1971 criminal trial the Government also provided a list of employees who had been given access to the transcripts. Yet appellants made no attempt to depose any of these individuals. Appellants cannot escape their obligation to exhaust alternative sources simply because they feared that deposing Justice Department employees would be time-consuming, costly, and unproductive. At the very least, they could have deposed the four employees who had the greatest knowledge about the logs. It is quite possible that interviewing these four individuals could have shed further light on the question whether the Justice Department was responsible for the leaks. Nor can appellants escape their obligation to exhaust alternatives because they were willing to accept the Justice Department's statement that an internal investigation had not revealed any wrongdoing by employees. Permitting this kind of gamesmanship would poorly serve the First Amendment values at stake here. Finally, we note that this is not a case like *Carey v. Hume, supra,* in which a reporter is being sued for libel under the rule of *New York Times Co. v. Sullivan, supra.* Nor is Kantor a party to these Privacy Act and Fourth Amendment claims. He is not asserting the privilege in order to protect himself from liability. * * *

[The concurring opinion of Judge Robb is omitted.]

INTRODUCTION

Ever since the days of John Peter Zenger, American journalists have felt obliged as a matter of conscience to protect the identities of their confidential sources, even at the cost of a stiff fine or jail term. In one of the more celebrated recent cases, for example, *New York Times* reporter Myron Farber spent forty days in jail and was fined $2,000 after refusing to honor a defense subpoena in a sensational murder case, and his newspaper was fined $285,000. Not surprisingly, journalists have long attempted to secure protection for their sources (as well as for unpublished notes and photographs), arguing in court for a "reporter's privilege" under the common law and the first amendment and lobbying in state legislatures and the Congress for passage of so-called "shield laws." That effort has been partially successful. Although American courts have refused to recognize protection for sources and "outtakes" under the common law, they have adopted, as *Zerilli* indicates, a limited privilege under the first amendment. Moreover, twenty-six states have enacted some form of "shield law" for journalists. We will examine both the constitutional and statutory privileges in this chapter.

In this context, the term "privilege" refers to an exception to a long-established principle in the law of evidence: that every individual with information relevant to a lawsuit can be compelled to tell what he knows. Although such privileges may interfere with the search for truth in judicial proceedings, they are created to foster relationships which society believes worthy of protection. For example, most states recognize the so-called "doctor-patient" privilege, which protects confidential communications between an individual and his physician on the theory that a person must be able to freely confide in his doctor in order to receive the best possible medical care. A similar privilege is recognized for communications between lawyers and their clients. As *Zerilli* indicates, the so-called "journalist's privilege" is grounded in the notion that the free flow of information to the public via the news media is enhanced by confidential relationships between reporters and their sources. Without such protection, the argument goes, there is a substantial possibility that many sources will be reluctant to provide information to reporters and, as a result, many stories of significant public interest would never be published.

Although John Peter Zenger refused to reveal the authors of allegedly libelous stories published in his newspaper in 1734, he faced no penalty for that refusal; indeed, he was already in jail awaiting a trial on criminal libel charges.[1] It was not

---

[1]Zenger, the printer, publisher, and editor of the *New York Weekly Journal*, was jailed and charged with criminal libel on the basis of articles critical of William Cosby, the colonial governor. Imprisoned for nine months because of his inability to post bond prior to his trial, Zenger steadfastly refused to reveal the names of individuals who wrote for the *Journal*, even though Cosby had offered a reward of fifty pounds for the identity of the author of the allegedly libelous articles. Zenger was ultimately acquitted, thanks largely to an emotional appeal to the jury by noted lawyer Andrew Hamilton, and his refusal to "name names" was not an issue at the trial.

until 1848 that a reporter was jailed for protecting his confidential sources. John Nugent of the *New York Herald* secured and sent to his editor a copy of the confidential draft of a proposed treaty to end the Mexican-American War. The U.S. Senate, which had been debating the treaty in secret session, subpoenaed Nugent and demanded that he reveal his source. The reporter refused and was jailed. Denying Nugent's petition for a writ of *habeas corpus,* a federal court concluded in *Ex parte Nugent* (1848) that it lacked jurisdiction to review the Senate's order holding the journalist in contempt and did not reach the privilege issue. More than a dozen similar incidents took place over the next thirty years, and legislative subpoenas directed at journalists have been fairly common during this century. For example, in 1951 a Senate subcommittee subpoenaed a *Povidence Journal* reporter who had written articles concerning the subcommittee's investigation of Senator Joseph McCarthy. Twenty years later, a House subcommittee subpoenaed Frank Stanton, then president of CBS, and demanded that he turn over all materials the network had used in producing a controversial television documentary, "The Selling of the Pentagon."

Most of the battles over source confidentiality, however, have been fought in the courts, which uniformly ruled that no protection for reporter's sources existed at common law. The earliest reported case apparently is *People ex rel. Phelps v. Fancher,* decided by a New York court in 1874. There the city editor of the *New York Tribune* was subpoenaed by a county grand jury in connection with an allegedly libelous article published by his newspaper. The grand jury sought the name of the article's author, having in mind an indictment against him for criminal libel, but the editor refused to answer on the ground that the newspaper's regulations prohibited such disclosure. The trial court held the editor in contempt and ordered him jailed until he answered the question. The appeals court affirmed, sustaining the contempt citation with the comment that "[a]s the law now is, and has for ages existed, no court could possibly hold that a witness could legally refuse to give the name of the author of an alleged libel, for the reason that the rules of a public journal forbade it."

Journalists asserted a variety of additional arguments in other cases but met with the same lack of success. Probably the most frequent defense was based on a "canon of journalistic ethics" prohibiting a newsman from revealing a confidential source. In a 1914 case, *In re Wayne,* a Hawaii court gave short shrift to this contention:

> Though there is a canon of journalistic ethics forbidding the disclosure of a newspaper's source of information,—a canon worthy of respect and undoubtedly well-founded, it is subject to a qualification: It must yield when in conflict with the interests involved of justice,—the private interests involved must yield to the interests of the public.

With the courts steadfastly declining to recognize a common law privilege for journalists to refuse to reveal confidential sources, it was left to the legislatures to provide such protection. Maryland became the first state to enact a "shield law," passing such a statute in 1896 after a journalist was jailed for refusing to divulge a source before a grand jury investigating his allegations that certain elected officials and policemen were being paid by illegal gambling establishments. Though the reporter was released five days later when the grand jury's term expired, an organization of journalists became alarmed at the prospect of reporters having to choose between imprisonment and protection of their sources. The group persuaded the Maryland legislature to enact protective legislation, which provided:

> No person engaged in, connected with or employed on a newspaper or journal shall be compelled to disclose, in any legal proceeding or trial or before any committee of the legislature or elsewhere, the source of any news or information procured or obtained by him for and published in the newspaper on and in which he is engaged, connected with or employed.

To note that the statute was not well received in legal circles would be a considerable understatement. Professor John Henry Wigmore of Northwestern University, author of a treatise on the law of evidence, wrote that the Maryland statute was "as detestable in substance as it is crude in form," pointing out that "for more than three centuries, it has been recognized as a fundamental maxim that the public is entitled to every man's evidence." He also predicted that the statute would "probably remain unique," a forecast that initially proved accurate: Maryland's law stood alone for more than thirty years.

During the period 1929–1935, however, there arose five highly publicized cases in which newsmen were jailed after refusing to reveal confidential sources, and these decisions provided the impetus for legislative action. The most significant of these cases was *People ex rel. Mooney v. Sheriff*, decided by the influential New York Court of Appeals in January of 1936. There a reporter for the *New York American* had written a series of articles revealing that illegal gambling was flourishing despite clean-up attempts. Called before a grand jury investigating the numbers racket, the journalist refused to provide the names of his sources for the stories. Affirming a fine of $250 and a jail term of thirty days, the court squarely rejected the reporter's arguments that he was entitled by law to protect his sources:

> The policy of the law is to require the disclosure of all information by witnesses in order that justice may prevail. The granting of a privilege from such disclosure constitutes an exception to that general rule. In the administration of justice, the existence of the privilege from disclosure as it now exists often, in particular cases, works a hardship. The tendency is not to extend the classes to whom the privilege from disclosure is granted, but to restrict that privilege. On reason and authority, it seems clear that this court should not now depart from the general rule . . . and create a privilege in favor of [journalists]. If that is to be done, it should be done by the Legislature. . . .

Following this flurry of judicial hostility to the privilege, seven states enacted shield laws during the period 1933–1937, and three more passed such statutes by 1943. By 1950, only one other state had enacted legislation, bringing the total to twelve, and the privilege issue was relatively dormant until the 1960s, when the number of subpoenas issued against reporters increased dramatically. During the first two and one-half years of the Nixon Administration, for example, 124 subpoenas were served on CBS and NBC, thirty on the *Chicago Sun-Times* and the *Chicago Daily News*, and thirty on the *Los Angeles Times*. The first major use of subpoenas came in connection with the 1969 trial of the so-called "Chicago Seven," the anti-war activists charged with inciting a riot at the 1968 Democratic National Convention in Chicago. The federal government served subpoenas on all four major Chicago daily newspapers, the three commercial television networks, and *Newsweek*, *Time* and *Life* magazines, demanding all of their notes, film footage, stories, rough drafts, and any other materials in their possession relating to the incident.

Not surprisingly, seven more states passed shield statutes in the period 1964–1971. At the same time, journalists were turning toward a first amendment argument in support of privilege to protect confidential sources. The question arose in *Garland v. Torre* (1958), a defamation suit brought by singer Judy Garland against a columnist for the *New York Herald Tribune* who had attributed to an unnamed CBS executive certain statements that the entertainer considered libelous. The journalist, Marie Torre, refused to reveal her source and was sentenced to ten days in jail for contempt of court. The U.S. Court of Appeals for the Second Circuit upheld the trial judge but recognized a qualified first amendment privilege for journalists. Justice Potter Stewart, then a circuit judge, wrote for a unanimous court that "compulsory disclosure of a journalist's confidential sources . . . may entail an abridgment of press freedom by imposing some limitation upon the availability of news." He added, however, that the privilege is qualified rather than absolute and must be balanced against "the interest to be served by compelling the testimony of the witness. . . ." Because the identity of the columnist's source "went to the heart" of Ms. Garland's libel claim, Justice Stewart concluded that the trial judge had properly struck the balance in ordering the journalist to reveal her informant.

Other courts took a dim view of *Garland*'s first amendment analysis, however, ruling that the Constitution offered no "shield," absolute or qualified, to a reporter who sought to protect the identity of a confidential source. This conflict among the lower courts led to the U.S. Supreme Court's 1972 decision in *Branzburg v. Hayes*, discussed briefly in the *Zerilli* case.

THE *BRANZBURG* CASE AND ITS AFTERMATH

The U.S. Supreme Court's 5 to 4 decision in *Branzburg* actually involved four separate cases consolidated on appeal. All arose when journalists asserted a first amendment privilege to refuse to respond to grand jury questions concerning suspected criminal activity. Two of the cases were from Kentucky, where a *Louisville Courier-Journal* reporter had personally observed the making of hashish and had watched drug users smoke marijuana in preparing a story about drugs in the Louisville area. In the third case, a Massachusetts television newsman had recorded and photographed Black Panther officials preparing for an anticipated police raid on their headquarters, though no news story was broadcast. In all three cases, the state courts rejected the journalists' first amendment claims. The fourth case, which attracted the most attention, involved a *New York Times* reporter who had covered the Black Panthers and other militant groups on the West Coast. He was subpoenaed to appear before a federal grand jury and to bring with him notes and recording of interviews with Black Panther leaders. The U.S. Court of Appeals for the Ninth Circuit, recognizing a qualified first amendment privilege, ruled that absent a compelling showing of need by the government, the reporter need not even appear before the grand jury, much less answer its questions.

The Supreme Court, in an opinion by Justice Byron White, ruled that the reporters had no first amendment privilege to refuse to respond to the grand juries' inquiries or to refuse to attend their sessions. Although the White opinion squarely rejected an absolute privilege, it acknowledged in principle that newsgathering is a protected first amendment activity and left room for development of a qualified privilege for protection of confidential sources. Justice White wrote that "without some protection for seeking out the news, freedom of the press could be eviscerated" and that "[o]fficial harassment of the press undertaken not for purposes of law enforcement but to disrupt a reporter's relationship with his news sources would have no justification." Moreover, he restricted the Court's opinion to the grand jury context, stating that the "sole issue before us is the obligation of reporters to respond to grand jury subpoenas . . . and to answer questions relevant to an investigation into the commission of a crime." The concurring opinion of Justice Lewis Powell, who provided the crucial fifth vote, offered even more hope for the press, as he took pains to emphasize the limited nature of the Court's holding and his view that an "asserted claim to privilege should be judged on its facts by the striking of a proper balance between freedom of the press and the obligation of all citizens to give relevant testimony with respect to criminal conduct."

While the Powell opinion is somewhat opaque, at least five members of the Court—Powell plus the four dissenters—recognized a qualified first amendment privilege in *Branzburg*. Some courts and commentators thus described Justice White's opinion as one for the "plurality" of the Court and focused instead upon Justice Powell's concurrence and Justice Stewart's dissent for guidance as to the nature and scope of the first amendment protection for confidential sources. Although Justice Powell was noncommital in this regard, Justice Stewart—the author of *Garland*—was quite specific. He wrote:

> [T]he government must (1) show that there is probable cause to believe that the news-man has information that is clearly relevant to a specific probable violation of the law; (2) demonstrate that the information sought cannot be obtained by alternative means less destructive of First Amendment rights; and (3) demonstrate a compelling and over-riding interest in the information.

Most lower federal courts and many state courts have interpreted *Branzburg* as creating a qualified first amendment privilege and have adopted the Stewart test or a variation thereof in applying that privilege. A notable exception is the U.S. Court of Appeals for the Sixth Circuit, which has construed *Branzburg* as wholly rejecting any sort of first amendment privilege. In that decision, *In re Grand Jury Proceedings* (1987), the court refused to interpret Justice Powell's concurring opinion in *Branzburg* in the fashion described above. To do so, the court said, "would be tantamount to our substituting, as the holding of *Branzburg*, the dissent written by Justice Stewart . . . for the majority opinion." The Sixth Circuit is a minority of one among the federal appellate courts, although a few state courts—including those in Colorado, Idaho, and New Jersey—have also taken such a narrow view of *Branzburg*. In contrast, nine federal appellate courts have recognized a qualified first amendment privilege.

Although confidential sources were the focus of *Branzburg*, some of the cases resolved in that opinion involved attempts to gain access to unpublished material, such as reporter's notes or "outtakes," a term generally used to refer to parts of film or videotape that were not broadcast. As Professor Marc Franklin has observed, this information is sought for two disparate reasons. First, outtakes may provide others with evidence of what occurred at a particular event. For example, in 1985 the U.S. Department of Justice subpoenaed photographs and videotapes from major news organizations that covered the hijacking of a Trans World Airlines jet and the ensuing hostage crisis at Beirut International Airport. The department claimed that it needed this material, which included outtakes, for a grand jury investigation of the incident. Second, outtakes or reporter's notes could reveal what was not included in the final news story, thereby helping demonstrate that the story was slanted or recklessly false because of the omissions. Such material could prove useful to a defamation plaintiff seeking to show that a news story or broadcast was distorted.

The Supreme Court was faced with the latter situation in *Herbert v. Lando* (1979). There the plaintiff, a retired army officer and admitted public figure, sued CBS and a "60 Minutes" producer and reporter for allegedly defamatory remarks aired on a segment about the Vietnam War. During a deposition, the producer refused to answer questions about why he had made certain investigations and not others, what he thought about the honesty and credibility of persons he had interviewed for the program, and what he had discussed with the reporter in preparing the program. The producer contended that these "thought processes" and internal editorial decisions were protected from disclosure by the first amendment, but the Supreme Court disagreed, ruling that the producer had no constitutional grounds for refusing to answer the questions. Writing for a 6 to 3 majority, Justice White conceded that the editorial process is entitled to some first amendment protection and asserted that it could not be subjected to "private or official examination merely to satisfy curiosity or to serve some general end such as the public interest." However, no constitutional barrier exists to probing that process when there is a "specific claim of injury arising from a publication that is alleged to have been knowingly or recklessly false." To hold otherwise, Justice White concluded, would "erect an impenetrable barrier" to a libel plaintiff's use of the direct evidence most relevant in establishing the requisite fault on the part of the defendant.

It seems clear that the *Lando* decision has no bearing on the confidential source issue, for the privilege for protecting such sources and that asserted in *Lando* for editorial and thought processes are not analogous. As the U.S. Court of Appeals for the Fifth Circuit observed in *Miller v. Transamerican Press, Inc.* (1980):

> In [*Lando*] the Supreme Court reasoned that requiring disclosure of journalists' thought processes would have no chilling effect on the editorial process; the only effect would be to deter recklessness. However, forced disclosure of journalists' sources might deter informants from giving their stories to newsmen. . . .

Most courts have not read *Lando* as affecting the qualified privilege established in *Branzburg* and have continued to apply the three-part test formulated by Justice Stewart in cases involving confidential sources.

The impact on *Lando* on attempts to obtain unpublished information is a bit more clouded, however. As noted previously, a libel plaintiff may desire to review such unpublished material in hope that information omitted from the published version would suggest fault on the part of the defendant news organization. These outtakes are plainly part of the editorial process, and their disclosure could reveal to a defamation plaintiff much the same information as an inquiry of the sort in *Lando* calling for the journalist's "intentions manifested by his decision to include or exclude certain material." However, most lower courts have continued to use the three-part Stewart test in cases involving outtakes and other unpublished information, as well as in cases in which confidential sources are implicated. As one court pointed out, compelled production of materials developed in preparation of a news story "is equally invidious as the compelled disclosure . . . of confidential informants." Moreover, it is important to note that *Lando* was uniquely based upon the constitutionalized law of defamation, and its effect—if any—upon *Branzburg* should be limited to the libel area.

At least two other developments should be noted here. First, in *Branzburg* itself Justice White issued a clear invitation to the states to adopt shield statutes protecting confidential sources, and seven states have responded since that decision, bringing the total to twenty-six. Second, while the Congress has not enacted a federal shield statute, Rule 501 of the Federal Rules of Evidence provides that in federal court cases involving questions of federal law, all privileges "shall be governed by the principles of the common law as they may be interpreted by the Courts of the United States in the light of reason and experience." Some federal courts have under this rule fashioned a journalist's privilege as a matter of federal common law. Because the analysis used by these courts parallels that employed in first amendment cases, our focus in this chapter will be on the constitutional basis for the privilege. Moreover, because shield statutes vary widely from state to state, we will examine the statutory issues in only a general fashion.

The First Amendment Privilege in Operation

As noted previously, the lower federal courts and most state courts have recognized a qualified first amendment privilege enabling journalists to protect their confidential sources and unpublished information. Obvious questions come to mind about the scope of that privilege; for instance, who may claim it? Though the courts most frequently deal with the privilege in cases involving journalists, it is not limited to "traditional" journalists.

For example, in *Silkwood v. Kerr-McGee Corp.* (1977), the U.S. Court of Appeals for the Tenth Circuit ruled that the privilege applied to a freelance documentary filmmaker who was making a movie about the suspicious death of antinuclear activist Karen Silkwood. Taking a broad view of what constitutes "reporting," the court noted that for first amendment purposes the press "comprehends different kinds of [media] which communicate to the public information and opinion." Under this approach, freelance writers and photographers would also be entitled to claim the privilege.

Historians and other scholars may also be protected. In a 1984 case, *In re Grand Jury Subpoena*, a federal district court in New York allowed a doctoral student to assert the privilege in connection with materials prepared for his dissertation. "Policies underlying a journalist's . . . privilege also support a limited privilege for a researcher in preparing a scholarly work," the court said. The U.S. Court of Appeals for the Second Circuit reversed, however, finding the facts too sketchy to support the recognition of such a privilege in this particular case.

Of course, the line has to be drawn somewhere. In *von Bulow v. von Bulow* (1987), the Second Circuit ruled that the first amendment privilege does not protect individuals who gather information for personal use and subsequently decide to disseminate it to the public. The issue arose in civil litigation involving Claus von Bulow, who, in a highly publicized case, had been acquitted of attempting to murder his wife by injecting her with drugs. During the criminal proceedings, a woman named Andrea Reynolds was von Bulow's steady companion. She was subpoenaed in a civil case brought against von Bulow by his wife's children and asked to turn over notes she had taken during the criminal trial, investigative reports she had commissioned on the children, and the unpublished manuscript of a book she had written about the case. She refused and was held in contempt of court. On appeal, the Second Circuit ruled the first amendment privilege inapplicable because she had "gathered information initially for purposes other than to disseminate information to the public."

Another important consideration is the setting in which the privilege is to be applied. As discussed more fully in the next section, the courts generally follow a three-part test based on Justice Stewart's dissent in *Branzburg*. Although the test remains essentially the same no matter what the context, it provides more protection in some situations than in others, as *Zerilli v. Smith* indicates. It is useful to envision a sort of "sliding scale" under which first amendment protection against compelled disclosure of sources and unpublished information is greater in civil cases than in criminal matters. By the same token, such protection will be greater in some civil actions than in others, depending upon whether the journalist or his employer is a defendant. Similarly, there may also be a difference in criminal cases, depending on whether the prosecution or defense seeks the information. The "sliding scale" might look like this:

Least Protection		Greatest Protection	
Criminal Case: Grand Jury or Prosecutor Wants Information	Criminal Case: Defendant Wants Information	Civil Case: Reporter Is Defendant	Civil Case: Reporter Is Not a Party

In *Branzburg*, Justice White stressed the special role of the grand jury in our criminal justice system, where its task is "to inquire into the existence of possible criminal conduct and to return only well-founded indictments. . . ." Accordingly, the grand jury's investigative powers must be "necessarily broad" to ensure "fair and effective law enforcement. . . ." This language suggests, of course, that first amendment protection is at its lowest ebb when journalists are called before grand juries and asked to reveal confidential sources or other information. But Justice White did not limit his analysis to the grand jury context, pointing out that "reporters, like other citizens, [must] respond to relevant questions put to them in the course of a valid grand jury investigation or criminal trial." Thus, it seems the first amendment privilege operates in the same fashion whether the grand jury is conducting an investigation or the prosecutor is preparing his case for trial.

The courts will almost invariably reject a privilege claim when the reporter observed his sources or other persons engaging in criminal activity or when his unpublished notes and background materials might lead law enforcement officials to the suspected criminals. In *Branzburg*, for example, one of the journalists had witnessed the manufacture and use of illegal drugs, while another had interviewed members of a militant group suspected of illegal activity. Along the same lines is *In re Ridenhour*, a 1988 Louisiana case, in which a reporter who had written a series of articles about the law enforcement of tax laws by the New Orleans Department of Finance was subpoenaed by a grand jury investigating the matter. Although the Louisiana Supreme Court recognized a qualified first amendment privilege for journalists, it ruled that the privilege is unavailable if the reporter has witnessed criminal activity or has physical evidence of a crime.

When a criminal defendant seeks to learn of a reporter's sources, somewhat different considerations come into play. Unlike the situation in which the grand jury or prosecutor attempts to force disclosure, the journalist cannot argue that he is being turned into an "agent of the police" whose information, gathered for news purposes, is being used to build a case against a suspected criminal. But the information in the reporter's possession may be critical to the suspect's right to a fair trial—a right of constitutional dimensions, as we saw in Chapter 6. A 1978 California case makes this point dramatically. In *CBS, Inc. v. Superior Court*, a sheriff's department had allowed CBS News to film meetings between undercover agents and two men suspected of selling drugs. These meetings led to the arrest of the men, and prior to trial, the attorney for one defendant subpoenaed CBS "outtakes." The trial judge ordered disclosure. On appeal, the court concluded that a criminal defendant should be able to obtain such material upon demonstrating that there is a reasonable possibility that the information could result in his exoneration. The outtakes were ultimately made available to the parties, and, as a result, the prosecutor dropped the charges against the defendant who had sought the tapes. Though this man had been present at the drug transaction, the film showed that he had not participated in it, contrary to testimony of the undercover officers.

Perhaps the most celebrated case of this type is *In re Farber*, decided by the New Jersey Supreme Court in 1978. There Myron Farber, a reporter for the *New York Times*, had written articles about some mysterious deaths at a New Jersey hospital. His series led to murder indictments against a physician, who subpoenaed Farber and the *Times* in an effort to force them to produce records of interviews with several witnesses who were to testify at trial. The trial court ordered the material handed over to the defendant, but the reporter and newspaper refused to comply and were held in contempt of court and fined. Farber also spent forty days in jail. On appeal, the New Jersey Supreme Court affirmed, concluding that *Branzburg* "squarely held" that there is no first amendment privilege for journalists. In addition to taking this extreme position (which is the minority view about the manner in which *Branzburg* should be interpreted), the court observed that, in any event, "the obligation to appear at a criminal trial on behalf of a defendant who is enforcing his Sixth Amendment rights [to a fair trial] is at least as compelling as the duty to appear before a grand jury." Thus, it is arguable that there is only one category for criminal cases on our sliding scale, and that for first amendment purposes it does not matter whether the grand jury, a prosecutor, or the defense is seeking the information from a reporter.

In civil cases, however, the societal interest present in criminal matters is absent, since no one's life or liberty is at stake in essentially private disputes between litigants. As the U.S. Court of Appeals for the Second Circuit observed in *Baker v. F & F Investment* (1972), "surely in civil cases, courts must recognize that the public interest in non-disclosure of journalists' confidential sources will often be weightier than the private interest in compelled disclosure." Accordingly, the court said, cases of this type in which the first amendment privilege must yield are "few in number," and the interests sufficiently compelling to force disclosure are "rare." However, as *Zerilli* makes plain, there is a substantial difference between a civil case where the reporter or his employer is a defendant—as in a libel case, for example—and one in which the reporter is a "stranger" to the litigation. In the former, successful assertion of a first amendment privilege to protect sources could effectively shield the journalist or his employer from liability, while in the latter, the equities that might favor disclosure of sources when the press is a defendant are not present.

The District of Columbia Circuit made this point in *Zerilli*, distinguishing that case—where the reporter was not a party—from one in which the reporter was sued for libel. The latter situation is illustrated by *Miller v. Transamerican Press, Inc.*, a defamation case in which the U.S. Court of Appeals for the Fifth Circuit ordered disclosure of a confidential source. The plaintiff, an official of the Teamsters union, sued the publisher of *Overdrive* magazine, contending that he had been libeled by an article charging misuse of the union's pension fund. During pretrial discovery, he learned that the author of the story had obtained the information from a confidential source. The author refused to name the source, and the trial judge ordered disclosure. In affirming that decision, the appellate court observed:

> . . . Transamerican's only source for the allegedly libelous comments is the informant. The only way that [plaintiff, a public figure] can establish malice and prove his case is to show that Transamerican knew the story was false or that it was reckless to rely on the informant. In order to do that, he must know the informant's identity.

This problem generally does not exist in cases in which the reporter is not a party, since in such circumstances refusal to disclose the source's identity would not protect the journalist or his employer from liability. Moreover, in cases of this type the litigants are often seeking to use the reporter and his sources to further their own private interests, with the net result being a negative impact on first amendment values. Not surprisingly, in such cases the courts have ruled that the burden upon the person seeking discovery of confidential information from journalists is significantly heavier than in cases where the reporter is a defendant.

A leading example, in addition to *Zerilli*, is *Baker v. F & F Investment*, mentioned briefly above. In that case, black plaintiffs alleged that real estate agents in Chicago had engaged in "blockbusting," a practice by which homes were purchased from whites at low prices and resold to blacks at higher prices. A reporter who had written a magazine article about the tactic was subpoenaed by the plaintiffs to help them prove their case. The court refused to require the reporter to reveal a source, despite the fact that the plaintiffs' purposes may have been laudable. This was not a case where the journalist was potentially liable, but a lawsuit involving private interests that were insufficient to overcome the free flow of news to the public that the first amendment privilege is designed to protect.

In rare cases, a reporter or news organization may be a plaintiff in a case in which the defendant wants to obtain confidential information. Having chosen to become a litigant, the reporter is in a particularly poor position to complain when the party he has sued seeks to learn more about the case. For example, in *Anderson v. Nixon* (1978), columnist Jack Anderson sued several Nixon Administration officials for harassing him. Asserting that the statute of limitations had run, the defendants sought to learn how and when Anderson learned of the alleged conspiracy. Anderson refused to provide this information, contending that it would require revealing the names of confidential informants. The federal district court ordered disclosure:

> Plaintiff is attempting to use the First Amendment simultaneously as a sword and a shield. He believes he was wronged by a conspiracy that sought to retaliate against his sources and to undermine his reliability and professional standing before the public because what he said was unpopular with the conspirators. But when those he accuses seek to defend by attempting to discover who his sources were, so that they may find out what the sources knew. . . , plaintiff says this is off limits. . . . He cannot have it both ways. Plaintiff is not a bystander in the process but a principal. He cannot ask for justice and then deny it to those he accuses.

The Three-Part Test

No matter what the underlying circumstances, the courts will generally employ a three-part test derived from Justice Stewart's *Branzburg* dissent. As the preceding section suggests, however, the courts apply the test more stringently in some cases than in others, fine-tuning it to the particular situation. The precise formulation of the test varies from court to court, but the most widely used version provides that a reporter will not be required to reveal a confidential source or unpublished material unless the person or governmental body seeking the information demonstrates that:

- there is probable cause to believe that the journalist has the information;
- the information is of critical relevance to the matter at hand, whether it be a grand jury investigation, civil or criminal trial, or other proceeding; and
- the information cannot be obtained elsewhere.

The first requirement—that there is good cause to believe that the reporter has information related to the underlying proceeding—is designed to protect the journalist from a "fishing expedition." Obviously, the reporter is likely to have the information if he has published a story quoting unnamed sources, but otherwise those seeking disclosure of sources or unpublished information must show "probable cause" to believe that the journalist in fact possesses the information.

Of more importance is the relevance requirement. In the criminal setting, for example, a defendant might want to learn the identity of a source who told a reporter that he had been threatened by the person whom the defendant allegedly killed. Such information might be relevant to such questions as motive and self-defense. However, if the defendant had asserted only the defense of insanity, the source's identity would plainly be irrelevant to the case and disclosure would not be required. Generally speaking, the courts are more willing to compel disclosure when the information sought would prove a necessary element of the government's case or provide a key part of the accused's defense.

For example, in *Waterman Broadcasting of Florida, Inc. v. Reese* (1988), a doctor told a television reporter that he had given his terminally ill wife a lethal dose of drugs to hasten her death. The doctor was indicted for murder, and the prosecuting attorney subpoenaed the reporter to testify. Finding the first amendment privilege inapplicable, a Florida appellate court had no difficulty deciding that the information went to the heart of the case. "In the context of a criminal case, it is obvious that a confession is relevant," the court said. "Each confession to a crime is unique." Along the same lines is *State v. Sandstrom* (1978), although there the defense rather than the prosecution sought the information. Testifying at the trial of a woman accused of killing her husband, a reporter stated that one of the prosecution witnesses was said to have threatened to kill the man. He refused, however, to identify his source of that information. The Kansas Supreme Court ordered disclosure, pointing out that the source's identity was critical to the woman's defense and that there was no other way to obtain the information.

The same approach is used in civil cases. As Justice Stewart wrote in the *Garland* case, the information sought must "go to the heart" of the claim or defense. For example, in a defamation case such as *Miller v. Transamerican Press*, the plaintiff might find it impossible to prove the requisite fault on the part of the defendant without learning the identity of the reporter's source, since a key question is often whether reliance on that source is reckless or negligent. If the reporter is not a party, however, the litigants may have more difficulty in establishing that the source or information is critical to their legal positions. Another Fifth Circuit decision, *In re Selcraig* (1983), is a good counterpoint to that court's decision in *Miller.*

Selcraig arose when two "high-placed administrators" in the Dallas school system told a *Dallas Morning News* reporter that an assistant superintendent was under investigation for allegedly attempting to bribe a custodian in order to gain access to another administrator's office. This information was later confirmed by the superintendent of schools, whose comments appeared in both Dallas papers. The assistant superintendent, who was ultimately discharged, brought a federal civil rights suit against the school district and various school officials for disseminating the information without giving him an opportunity to clear his name. During the course of pretrial discovery, he subpoenaed the reporter, who, after refusing to reveal his sources, was held in contempt of court. The Fifth Circuit reversed, ruling that the plaintiff did not need the names of the sources to prove his case against the defendants. While the plaintiff was required to show "public disclosure" of the damaging information by the defendants, he could do so by pointing to the subsequent confirmation of the facts reported in the initial story. Because it was not necessary for the plaintiff to establish a prior "secret" disclosure of the information to the reporter in order to prevail in his lawsuit, the names of the two confidential sources were irrelevant and thus protected by the first amendment.

It is important to keep in mind that the journalist's information must be of critical importance to the case before disclosure will be ordered. A 1987 federal district court case from Alabama is illustrative. In *Pinkard v. Johnson,* a newspaper reporter was subpoenaed by both plaintiff and defendant in a civil case brought by one member of a county board against another. The court ordered that the reporter testify at a deposition on behalf of the plaintiff, concluding that the information at issue was critical to the plaintiff's claim that the defendant had conspired with others to manufacture charges of impropriety against him. In contrast, the court ruled that the reporter was not required to provide information sought by the defendant, since that information related only to the credibility of a witness and was not central to the defendant's case. Although the courts have divided on the question of whether there is a compelling need for information that can be used to attack a witness' credibility, the *Pinkard* case reflects the better approach.

The third prong of the test—that the information be unavailable from other sources—is necessary to ensure that confidential sources are not routinely disclosed. As the District of Columbia Circuit pointed out in *Zerilli v. Smith,* "[t]he values resident in the protection of the confidential sources of newsmen certainly point toward compelled disclosure from the newsman himself as normally the end, and not the beginning, of the inquiry." Therefore, those seeking disclosure must demonstrate that they have exhausted available sources and that their only access to the information is through the journalist. In *Zerilli,* for example, the court rejected the plaintiff's argument that alternative sources had been exhausted because an internal investigation conducted by the defendant Justice Department indicated that its employees were not the reporter's sources. Instead, the court ruled that the plaintiffs had to conduct their own investigation via depositions before turning to the reporter as a "last resort," even though the process would be time-consuming, costly, and perhaps even unproductive. The court suggested that it would not be unreasonable to require the plaintiffs to take as many as sixty depositions in an attempt to learn the information from someone other than the journalist.

The "exhaustion" question also arose in *In re Special Grand Jury Investigation*, a 1984 Illinois case in which a reporter had obtained and published information from a judicial inquiry board that was investigating a juvenile court judge. Investigating the leak, a grand jury called three board members, who invoked their constitutional right not to testify. The prosecutor then sought to force the reporter to reveal his source, and the trial judge ordered disclosure. The Illinois Supreme Court reversed, concluding that alternative sources had not been sufficiently explored. The court noted that three other board members had access to the information, as did various staff members and other government officials. Even though there was obvious public interest in obtaining the information, the court said, the record revealed that other potential sources of that information had not been exhausted.

SHIELD STATUTES

When journalists discuss protection for confidential sources and outtakes, the talk frequently focuses upon the first amendment principles outlined above. While this body of constitutional law is obviously of great importance, so-called "shield laws" now on the statute books in twenty-six states[2] should not be overlooked. Some state courts, though a distinct minority, continue to interpret *Branzburg* as rejecting any sort of first amendment privilege for journalists, thus leaving a shield law—if one exists in the particular jurisdiction—as the only source of protection. Moreover, courts often prefer, for a variety of institutional reasons, to rest their decisions on statutory rather than constitutional grounds if at all possible. Thus, even if courts in a given state have adopted the three-part first amendment test examined in the preceding section, they may choose to avoid reaching the constitutional question in a case if it can be decided under the state shield statute.

The nation's twenty-six shield statutes vary widely, in part because there is considerable disagreement over the desirability of such legislation. Many lawyers and judges, for example, believe that privileges restricting the ability of litigants to obtain information helpful to their lawsuits should be few and far between. And, some journalists take the position that the news media should not be required to rely upon legislatures for protection, since these bodies can easily take away any statutory privilege that they have granted. Moreover, it is feared that a state legislature—or the Congress—might use such a shield law as justification for "meddling" in other press matters, a thought most journalists find abhorrent. This lack of consensus in both the legal and journalism communities is one reason that Congress has failed to pass a federal shield law despite Justice White's invitation in *Branzburg*.

Before turning to the questions posed by shield statutes, it is important to note that legislation of this type has received a rather hostile reception in the courts of some states, which have construed their statutes quite narrowly. Pointing out that the common law afforded no such privilege for journalists, courts in New York,

---

[2]The states are Alabama, Alaska, Arizona, Arkansas, California, Delaware, Illinois, Indiana, Kentucky, Louisiana, Maryland, Michigan, Minnesota, Montana, Nebraska, Nevada, New Jersey, New Mexico, New York, North Dakota, Ohio, Oklahoma, Oregon, Pennsylvania, Rhode Island, and Tennessee. In California, the privilege is also embodied in the state constitution.

Maryland, and New Jersey have ruled that shield statutes are to be strictly construed because they are contrary to the common law. In contrast, courts in other jurisdictions have held that the statutes must be liberally construed because of the public policy they reflect. For example, the Pennsylvania Supreme Court adopted a rule of liberal interpretation in *In re Taylor* (1963) because "independent newspapers are today the principal watch-dogs and protectors of honest, as well as good, Government." As we shall see below, shield statutes often leave unanswered a variety of important questions, and the rule of statutory interpretation followed by a particular court will often determine whether these questions are to be resolved favorably or unfavorably to the press.

A related difficulty is determining which state's law will apply in a given case. Though this "choice of law" problem is obviously beyond the scope of this book, it frequently arises in shield law settings. For example, in *Williams v. ABC* (1983), a federal district court in Arkansas had before it a defamation and invasion of privacy suit based on an ABC "20/20" segment. When the plaintiffs sought to obtain outtakes that were not broadcast, the network argued that it was protected by the New York shield statute, since its reporters resided in the state, all editorial decisions were made there, and the broadcast originated there. Moreover, the network contended that it would be unfair to subject its reporters to the varying shield laws or absence of such in the fifty states. The court, however, concluded that Arkansas law should apply under the general principle that questions involving evidence are to be determined by the law of the state in which the suit is filed.

While it is impossible to examine in detail each of the twenty-six shield laws, we can explore problems that arise under virtually all of them and, at the same time, consider the different statutory approaches to those problems. In evaluating a shield statute, one should determine:

- those persons covered by the statute;
- the circumstances in which the privilege applies;
- the type of material to which protection is extended; and
- whether the privilege is absolute or qualified, and, if the latter, the manner in which the privilege may be overcome.

Persons Covered

Because shield statutes are usually quite specific in identifying those persons entitled to claim the privilege, there is a danger that journalists who do not fall within those categories are without protection. For example, in *Deltec, Inc. v. Dun & Bradstreet, Inc.* (1960), a federal court ruled that the Ohio statute, which covered journalists employed by "any newspaper or press association," did not extend to the publisher of a bi-monthly report. Four years later, in *Application of Cepeda*, a federal court refused to apply the California statute to a magazine journalist, since the shield law did not mention magazines or periodicals. The California statute was subsequently amended to include magazine reporters; under Ohio statute, broadcast journalists now enjoy protection, but writers for periodicals are still out in the cold.

Some state statutes attempt to avoid this potential problem by providing "laundry lists" of news media whose employees enjoy the privilege. The Oklahoma statute, for instance, lists newspapers, magazines, other periodicals, books, pamphlets, news services, wire services, news or feature syndicates, broadcast stations or networks, and cable television systems. But there is always the danger that someone will fall between the definitional cracks in a statute, and in such cirsumstances courts need not follow the restrictive approach illustrated by the *Cepeda* and *Deltec* cases. For example, in *Williams v. ABC,* the Arkansas case noted previously, a federal court ruled that the state statute applied to television reporters, even though it expressly mentioned only newspapers, periodicals, and radio stations.

There may be other definitional problems as well. What is meant, for example, by the term "newspaper"? Is a weekly "shopper" within the definition? A student newspaper at the local high school or college? In one rather bizarre decision, a Montana court ruled that the state's shield law applied only to reporters, not to their employers. In that case, *In re Investigative File* (1978), the state subpoenaed a tape recording in which a gunman holding two hostages told an Associated Press reporter over the phone that he had shot a policeman. Relying on the shield law, the wire service refused to turn over the tape. However, the court ordered disclosure, ruling that the statute protected only persons "employed by" a news organization, not the organization itself.

Another question is whether a shield statute will apply to freelance writers or photographers. Some statutes speak directly to the question. For example, the New York law defines the term "journalist" to include "regular employees" of the news media and persons "otherwise professionally affiliated for gain or livelihood with a media organization." Similarly, the Tennessee statute covers persons "independently engaged in gathering information for publication or broadcast." Several states specify that a journalist must be "connected with or employed by" a news organization to invoke the privilege. Since it would be redundant to interpret the former term to mean the same as the latter, one could argue that "connected with" is broad enough to apply to freelancers. That does not necessarily mean that all freelance journalists are protected, however. For example, in *In re Van Ness* (1982), a freelance writer called before a grand jury investigating the death of comedian John Belushi relied on the California shield statute, which uses the "connected with or employed by" terminology. While concluding that the statute could cover freelancers, the court declined to apply it because the writer did not have a formal agreement with a news organization to write the story. If a statute is ambiguous on the point, the resolution of the issue will probably turn on whether the courts of the state follow a strict or liberal rule of statutory interpretation in privilege cases.

It seems clear that, under virtually all shield statutes, a journalist is entitled to the privilege only to the extent that he receives information from sources within the course of newsgathering activities. Thus, sources who provide material to a reporter in some capacity other than his role as a journalist would be subject to disclosure. This "scope of employment" limitation, expressly stated in some statutes, is a reasonable one, for one purpose of shield statutes—to encourage informants to confide in journalists—is not served when the privilege is applied to communications outside the scope of employment. By the same token, however, shield statutes should be construed to cover former journalists who, during their tenure as members of the working press, were supplied information by confidential sources. Some statutes expressly so provide. The privilege is of little value in encouraging the flow of information from source to reporter if it vanishes for purposes of past communications when the journalist enters a new line of work.

Though the "scope of employment" limitation makes sense, it has been interpreted too rigidly by some courts. For example, in a 1971 New York case, *In re WBAI-FM,* a radio station received an anonymous phone call advising that a bomb had been planted. The caller added that a letter containing more details had been placed in a nearby telephone booth. A newscaster picked up the letter, called the police, and read the letter over the air. The court ruled that the state shield statute did not protect the letter because the station did not obtain it in the course of news-gathering activities. The mere "passive" receipt of unsolicited information did not, in the court's view, constitute "newsgathering." The New York legislature subsequently amended the statute to include unsolicited as well as solicited material, thus effectively overturning the court's decision.

Because shield statutes are primarily aimed at journalists and the newsgathering process, they may be inapplicable to historians, researchers, educators, or others who disseminate information as opposed to "news." In *People v. LeGrand* (1979), for example, a New York court ruled that the state's shield law did not cover the author of a book on organized crime who had been subpoenaed in a murder case. As mentioned previously, however, the first amendment privilege has been extended to scholars and others who do cannot be squeezed into the traditional definition of "reporter" or "journalist."

It should also be noted at this point that shield statutes typically grant a privilege to the journalist, not to his source. Not surprisingly, the courts have uniformly held that the statutory privilege can be invoked only by journalists or others covered by the statute. For example, in *Lipps v. State* (1970), the Indiana Supreme Court rejected a criminal defendant's contention that the trial court had erred in allowing a newspaper reporter to testify, over the defendant's objection, to a conversation with the reporter while the defendant was in jail awaiting trial. The court ruled that the Indiana shield statute created a right personal to the reporter, a right that only he could seek to enforce. Since the journalist was willing to testify at trial about the conversation, there was no problem under the shield statute.

Where the Privilege Applies

As we saw in our discussion of the first amendment privilege, the courts have recognized protection for news sources in a variety judicial proceedings, both civil and criminal. And, although cases are scarce, there is no doubt that the constitutional privilege would apply if a reporter were subpoenaed by a legislative body. The vast majority of shield statutes also take a broad view of the circumstances in which the privilege may be asserted. The Arkansas statute, for example, may be invoked by a reporter asked to disclose a source "to any Grand Jury or to any other authority" of government, state or local. Thus, in that state the privilege should be available in grand jury proceedings, in a criminal case in which the reporter is subpoenaed by either the prosecution or defense, in a civil action regardless of whether the reporter is a defendant, plaintiff, or nonparty, or in hearings conducted by a legislative committee or an administrative agency.

In contrast, the Michigan statute applies only in grand jury proceedings, and statutes in Oklahoma, Rhode Island, and Tennessee contain exceptions for defamation cases. A journalist confronted with a confidential source problem in states with statutes of such limited scope must necessarily rely on the first amendment for protection in situations not covered by the shield law.

Even if a state shield statute appears quite broad, a court may interpret it narrowly and thereby cut back the protection it affords. Perhaps the best—or worst—example of this technique is *Farr v. Superior Court,* a 1971 California case. There Bill Farr, who covered the Charles Manson trial for the *Los Angeles Herald-*

Examiner, reported that a member of the Manson "family" had confessed to certain crimes for which the group had been charged. Fearing a problem with prejudicial publicity in the case, the trial judge had entered a gag order directing attorneys and others connected with the proceedings not to talk to the media about certain aspects of the case. After Farr's story about the confession was published, the court ordered that he reveal his source. Farr indicated that the information had come from two attorneys, but refused to disclose their names. All six attorneys involved in the case denied having been a source, and the judge again ordered Farr to "name names." He refused and was held in contempt of court.

The court of appeals affirmed. Even though the California shield law stated that a reporter could not be held in contempt court for refusing to disclose "the source of any information procured for publication and published in a newspaper," the court ruled that the law was an unconstitutional infringement upon the "inherent power" of the courts to control their own proceedings. In attempting the immunize persons from punishment for violating court orders, the legislature ran afoul of the "separation of powers" provision of the state constitution, the court said. Farr spent forty-six days in jail before Justice William O. Douglas of the U.S. Supreme Court ordered his release while a federal court considered the case. The contempt order was ultimately allowed to stand, but a state trial judge concluded some two years later that returning the reporter to jail would not induce him to reveal his sources. The *Farr* ruling on the separation of powers question led to a constitutional amendment making the shield law part of the California Constitution.

Protected Material

State shield laws vary tremendously with respect to the type of material they protect from disclosure. Some reach only the identity of confidential sources of information, while others seem to protect all sources, regardless of whether an express promise of confidentiality has been made. Moreover, some statutes apply to a reporter's notes, outtakes, and unpublished information—that is, virtually any material acquired or developed in the course of his newsgathering activities.

If the statutory protection is limited to sources of information, the courts generally will not expand it via interpretation to include outtakes and similar material. For example, in *Williams v. ABC*, a federal judge refused to bring unpublished material within the scope of the Arkansas shield law, pointing out that "the statute, by its own terms, applies only so as to protect 'the source,'" and that the plaintiffs sought outtakes, not "any information as to sources." This approach has been taken by most courts, though some have held that unpublished material is protected if its disclosure would reveal the identity of a source. However, the Pennsylvania Supreme Court has ruled that outtakes and similar material are protected under that state's shield law, even though it expressly applies to "sources of information." Reasoning that this term "includes documents as well as personal informants," the court held in *In re Taylor* that the statute covered a reporter's tape recordings, memoranda of interviews, and notes developed in connection with a news story. The court subsequently created a "defamation exception" to this principle, announcing in *Hatchard v. Westinghouse Broadcasting Co.* (1987) that unpublished material must be revealed in libel cases unless it contains the name of a personal source.

Because the majority of courts construe "source" to mean only the identities of persons who furnish information to journalists, it is important to understand enactly what is meant by the term in this context. One of the Kentucky cases that led to the U.S. Supreme Court's landmark decision in *Branzburg v. Hayes* offers perhaps the best illustration of the problem. In *Branzburg v. Pound* (1970), a reporter for the *Louisville Courier-Journal* refused to reveal his sources for a story about drug use, including the names of two individuals that he had observed synthesizing hashish from marijuana. Although the Kentucky shield law protects a reporter's "source of information," the state court of appeals concluded that the "source" of this article was the reporter's own personal observation and that the identities of the two persons making hashish were part of the "information" that he had obtained. Since the statute covered only the source and not the information itself, the reporter was compelled to name the drug manufacturers. Although this view has been criticized as an exercise in "verbal gymnastics," most courts have held that shield statutes do not protect a reporter's own observations.

It is reasonably clear, however, that the term "source" includes virtually anyone who furnishes information to a news organization. In a 1982 Louisiana case, *Becnel v. Lucia,* an appellate court ruled that the writer of a "letter to the editor" is a source within the meaning of the state shield law. The court reasoned that a letter writer, like any other source, "might hesitate to disclose matters of public import for fear of unfavorable publicity or the possibility of retribution resulting from [his] being revealed as the source of a particular news item."

As noted above, some shield statutes are not limited to confidential sources of information. Interpreting these provisions, courts have generally held that an express promise of confidentially is not required and that the privilege reaches the names of all sources, not just "confidential" informants. In *Lightman v. State* (1972), a Maryland court took this approach, reasoning that shield statutes that do not specifically restrict the privilege to confidential sources are "broad enough to encompass any source of news or information, without regard to whether the source gave his information in confidence or not." Although the primary purpose of shield laws may be to protect confidential reporter-source relationships, most courts have been reluctant to impose a confidentiality requirement when the legislature has not done so. A notable exception is the New York Court of Appeals, which ruled in *Knight-Ridder Broadcasting Co. v. Greenberg* (1987) that the state's shield law does not protect nonconfidential sources and information, even though the statute itself does not contain a confidentiality requirement. The North Dakota Supreme Court has taken a different approach, ruling in *Grand Forks Herald v. Grand Forks County District Court* (1982) that while the privilege is not by statute limited to confidential sources, confidentiality is a factor that a court may consider in determining whether the privilege has been overcome in a given situation.

A handful of statutes, including those in Alabama, Arkansas, and Kentucky, provide that the privilege may be invoked only if the source has supplied information for a story that is published or broadcast. Most shield laws do not contain this requirement, which appreciably weakens the privilege. For example, a reporter who has spent considerable time and effort developing a complex story may have to reveal the identity of his sources simply because the story has yet to be published or broadcast. An informant who provides material to a reporter is not concerned with the ultimate publication of the story, but rather with the assurance of confidentiality. Moreover, a reporter seeking to take advantage of the privilege may rush his story into print without further investigation, perhaps resulting in an incomplete or inaccurate account.

An unreported Arkansas case illustrates the shortcomings of statutes with such a "publication" requirement. In early 1967, two reporters were called before a grand jury investigating alleged bribe attempts to gain legislative support for a bill to legalize casino gambling in the resort town of Hot Springs. The investigation began after a state representative revealed that he had been offered $1,000 to vote for the gambling bill. News reports about the legislator had not indicated that any of his colleagues had been approached in this fashion, but the two newsmen intimated before the grand jury that other members of the legislature had been offered money in exchange for their votes. When the reporters refused to reveal the names of legislators who had told them of the bribery attempts, a trial judge held them in contempt and ordered them to jail. He concluded that the Arkansas shield statute was inapplicable because the questions asked of the reporters did not involve sources for stories that had been published. After the state supreme court dismissed their appeal, the journalists agreed to respond to the grand jury's questions, explaining that their sources had relieved them of their confidentiality obligations.

Nature of the Privilege: Absolute or Qualified?

About half of the state shield statutes appear "absolute" in nature; that is, they provide that a reporter need not reveal his sources in certain situations and say nothing about any exceptions. The other half, like the first amendment privilege, are "qualified" and make plain that in some circumstances the statutory protection must yield to other societal interests. Even those statutes that seem to be absolute may not, in practice, operate in such a fashion. For example, in the *Farber* case discussed previously, the New Jersey Supreme Court noted that the state's shield law, acknowledged to be "as strongly worded as any in the country," must give way to a criminal defendant's constitutional right to a fair trial.

Those statutes affording a qualified privilege employ different language in describing the circumstances under which the privilege may be overcome and the reporter required to reveal sources or other information. Minnesota and Tennessee, for example, have expressly adopted the three-part test developed by the courts in applying the first amendment privilege. This approach is particularly valuable because it eliminates the necessity for a separate inquiry under the shield law when both statutory and first amendment privileges are asserted. Other states, however, have employed vague terminology. The Arkansas statute states that the privilege may be overcome if a news story was written or broadcast "in bad faith, with malice, and not in the interest of the public welfare." Similarly, the North Dakota statute provides that the privilege must yield upon a judicial finding that "the failure of disclosure of such evidence will cause a miscarriage of justice." Obviously, opaque language such as this offers little assistance to the journalist in determining when the privilege may be inapplicable.

However, courts in both Arkansas and North Dakota have interpreted these provisions to require use of the three-part test that has evolved in the first amendment area. The Ohio Supreme Court has also taken this approach in dealing with that state's shield law, and other courts can be expected to follow suit, primarily because there already exists a substantial number of judicial decisions applying the first amendment privilege. These cases will provide considerable guidance to state courts struggling with vague language in their own shield laws.

The North Dakota Supreme Court has also adopted a version of the "sliding scale" analysis found in the first amendment cases. In the *Grand Forks Herald* case cited previously, the court pointed out that the North Dakota statute applies to "any proceeding or hearing" and "makes no distinction between civil and criminal actions or actions in which the news gatherer is or is not a party." Nonetheless, the court ruled that a trial judge may consider the nature of the underlying proceeding in determining whether the failure to disclose a source will cause a "miscarriage of justice." Accordingly, a court is free to balance the interests in each case, and it may well be that the balance may tip more easily in favor of disclosure in criminal matters than in civil cases. This same approach could be used in a state such as Arkansas, where the shield statute expressly provides that a court may consider the "public welfare" in determining whether the qualified privilege must yield to other interests.

RELATED ISSUES: NEWSROOM SEARCHES
AND TELEPHONE RECORDS

In the course of litigation, either civil or criminal, most parties to the dispute attempt to learn the identity of confidential news sources or to obtain outtakes and notes through a subpoena commanding the reporter to testify at trial or deposition and to bring with him specified documents. The reporter may seek to quash the subpoena prior to his testimony and is entitled to a hearing before a judge on the matter. However, law enforcement officials have other tools at their disposal that pose difficult problems for the reporter.

One such device is a search warrant directed to the newspaper office or broadcast station authorizing a search of the premises. The important distinction between a search warrant and a subpoena is that there is no opportunity to petition a court to quash a search warrant. Although such a warrant is issued by a judge, the proceeding is *ex parte*—that is, only one side of the case is presented—and the journalist or news organization does not participate. Thus, a law enforcement official executing a search warrant may discover notes or documents, including those that reveal the names of confidential sources, and seize them without any prior judicial ruling on the propriety of this procedure. The usual remedy is to exclude from evidence at trial the fruits of illegal searches, but this remedy is meaningless to a newspaper or anyone else who has been the subject of an unlawful search but who is not suspected or accused of a crime.

Despite these problems, the U.S. Supreme Court upheld the propriety of newsroom search warrants in *Zurcher v. Stanford Daily* (1978). The case grew out of a campus demonstration at Stanford University in 1971 that resulted in injuries to several police officers attempting to remove protesters from a campus building. The *Stanford Daily* published photographs of the incident, and county law enforcement officials thought they might be able to learn the identities of the students who injured the police officers by examining unpublished photos and other materials in the student newspaper's possession. The officials obtained a search warrant and searched the newsroom but found no evidence. The newspaper challenged the use of such "third-party" search warrants directed at persons not suspected of crimes, arguing that their use in the newsgathering context was inconsistent with the first amendment. The Supreme Court disagreed, upholding such newsroom searches in a 5 to 3 decision.

Writing for the majority, Justice White said that the press is adequately protected by the fourth amendment's prohibition against "unreasonable searches and seizures," as are all other citizens. The first amendment does not afford any additional protection to the press under these circumstances and certainly does not prohibit altogether searches of this type. There is no indication, Justice White said, that the Framers of the Constitution—who were obviously aware of government attempts to muzzle the press—believed that first amendment would supplement the guarantees of the fourth. Further, he noted that widespread abuse of the warrant procedure had not occurred, and that any abuse could be dealt with under the fourth amendment's bar against "unreasonable" searches. If materials sought to be seized may be implicate first amendment rights, he wrote, the fourth amendment must be applied with "scrupulous exactitude" to ensure that newsgathering efforts are not frustrated. But the newspaper's contention that newsroom searches would impede timely publication, cause confidential sources to dry up, discourage coverage of controversial matters, and deter reporters from preserving their notes was not sufficient to justify a constitutional rule prohibiting these searches.

After the *Stanford Daily* decision, nine states—California, Connecticut, Illinois, Nebraska, New Jersey, Oregon, Texas, Washington, and Wisconsin—enacted statutory bans on the issuance of search warrants against the news media. Individual state statutes, of course, apply only within state boundaries and have no effect on federal officials. Congress, which has been unwilling to enact a federal shield law, moved rather quickly to pass the Privacy Protection Act of 1980, a search statute applicable to federal, state and local law enforcement officials. The statute makes it unlawful for an official of any government to search or seize "any work product material possessed by a person reasonably believed to have a purpose to disseminate to the public a newspaper, book, broadcast or other similar form of public communication, in or affecting interstate or foreign commerce."

Like the state statutes, the federal privacy act is not an absolute prohibition. It does not apply where there is probable cause to believe that the person possessing the materials has committed or is committing a criminal offense to which the materials relate. (However, a search is not permissible under this exception when the suspected criminal offense involves receipt, possession, or communication of information related to the national defense, classified information, or restricted data under espionage, atomic energy, and subversive activities legislation.) A second exception allows newsroom searches when there is "reason to believe that the immediate seizure of such materials is necessary to prevent the death of, or serious bodily injury to, a human being."

The statute defines "work product" as materials prepared in anticipation of communication to the public, no matter who authored them, and may include the mental impressions, conclusions, opinions, or theories of the person who authored or created the material. Another portion of the statute deals with "documentary materials," defined as those "upon which information is recorded," including written or printed matter, photographs, films, and tapes. The same two exceptions to the ban on searches applicable to work product also apply to documentary materials. However, government officials may search for documentary materials where there is reason to believe that giving notice of a subpoena would lead to destruction or concealment and where the material has not been delivered in response to an earlier subpoena. Governments or officials who violate the statute are subject to civil penalties.

Despite the federal statute and several state laws restricting newsroom searches, police seizure of editorial material in this fashion is not a thing of the past. According to the Reporters Committee for Freedom of the Press, six such searches—three in California, three in Minnesota—occurred during the two-year period ending in August 1988. In one of the California cases, for example, sheriff's deputies in San Bernadino County, California, seized videotape from KCSB-TV in Los Angeles, which had aired a story about animal rights activists who ransacked a university research laboratory. In obtaining the newsroom search warrant, the sheriff's department stated that it was seeking evidence in connection with its investigation of the incident. Similarly, FBI agents in Minnesota confiscated film from *Minneapolis Star & Tribune* and WCCO-TV personnel who had photographed an undercover drug raid. The FBI apparently feared that undercover agents would be identified if the pictures were published or broadcast.

In the San Bernadino case, the state court judge who issued the search warrant subsequently ordered that the tapes be returned to the television station, concluding that the California newsroom search statute prohibited search warrants from being used to obtain unpublished information. The Minneapolis searches led a lawsuit by the media under the federal Privacy Protection Act. In *Minneapolis Star & Tribune Co. v. United States* (1989), a federal district court ruled that the FBI had violated the statute and awarded the four plaintiffs $750 each in damages, plus attorney's fees totaling more than $80,000. Short of this after-the-fact litigation, however, there is relatively little that a media organization can do when faced with a search warrant. Keep in mind that officers armed with a warrant can execute it on the spot, leaving journalists no time to seek to quash it in court.

Nonetheless, the Reporters Committee for Freedom of the Press suggests that newsroom personnel should contact an attorney immediately and attempt to delay the search until the lawyer has examined the warrant. Also, the Committee advises that employees photograph the police as they conduct the search. And, although staff members may not impede the search in any way, they need not assist the officers. If, however, the warrant specifies particular items to be seized (as is usually the case), it may be preferable for employees to provide these materials rather than have the police turn the newsroom upside down looking for them. Finally, the Committee recommends seeking judicial relief on an expedited basis, since a judge who has reason to believe that the search was unlawful may order the police to turn over the seized information to the court pending resolution of the legal issue.

In addition to subpoenas and search warrants, law enforcement officials have been able to uncover information about journalists' newsgathering activities by examining their telephone records. This method was upheld against a constitutional challenge in *Reporters Committee for Freedom of the Press v. American Telephone and Telegraph Co.* (1978). In that case, a group of reporters had demanded assurances from AT&T that their billing records—which showed toll calls charged to particular telephone numbers—would not be released to federal investigators without prior notice to the journalists concerned. Federal prosecutors and other law enforcement officials subpoena such billing records from the phone company, though evidence in this case indicated that reporters' records had been sought in only a handful of investigations. When AT&T refused the request, the journalists brought suit, arguing that prior notification was constitutionally required.

The U.S. Court of Appeals for the District of Columbia Circuit affirmed the trial judge's decision in favor of the phone company. Relying on the *Branzburg* and *Stanford Daily* decisions, the court rejected the journalists' argument that because billing records could reveal the identity of a confidential source, prior notice of a government subpoena of those records is required by the first amendment so that the reporters could attempt to quash the subpoena. The court said:

> In our view, plaintiffs' position is based on erroneous propositions. First, the so-called right of journalists to gather information from secret sources does not include a right to maintain the secrecy of those sources in the face of good faith felony investigations. Second, Government access to third-party evidence in the course of a good faith felony investigation in no sense "abridges" plaintiffs' information-gathering activities. * * * [T]he First Amendment does not guarantee a journalist, or any other citizen, the freedom to collect information immune from good faith criminal investigation by means which accord with Fourth and Fifth Amendment protections.

The court left open the possibility that, in theory, subpoenas issued in bad faith may in some cases abridge first amendment rights, but added that journalists attempting to make such a showing would have a "heavy burden."

In 1980, the U.S. Department of Justice adopted guidelines governing subpoenas for telephone records of journalists. If the investigation would not be jeopardized, the Attorney General's office will first negotiate with the journalist about release of the records prior to issuing a subpoena. If these discussions are not fruitful, express authorization of the Attorney General is required before a subpoena will be issued. Such permission should not be sought by law enforcement officials unless there are reasonable grounds to believe that a crime has been committed, that the information sought is essential to the investigation, and that all reasonable alternative means of obtaining the information have proven unsuccessful. If a subpoena is issued, it should be as limited in scope as possible and the reporter must be given timely notice. Moreover, any information obtained via a subpoena is to be closely guarded to prevent access by unauthorized persons. Keep in mind that these guidelines apply only to federal investigations, although some state and local law enforcement agencies have adopted similar regulations.

The Justice Department regulations do not specifically address the use of the "pen register," a mechanical device that records the numbers dialed on a telephone by monitoring electrical impulses caused during the dialing process. Neither a pen register nor a dialed number recorder, a similar device that also records the duration of calls, monitors telephone conversations. In *Smith v. Maryland* (1979), the U.S. Supreme Court ruled that police installation and use of a pen register is not a "search" within the meaning of the fourth amendment and, accordingly, that no search warrant is required. Writing for the majority, Justice Harry Blackmun pointed out that telephone customers "typically know" that phone companies record the numbers they dial for "a variety of legitimate business purposes." Consequently, although persons who use the phone can legitimately anticipate privacy regarding the content of their conversations, they do not "harbor any general expectation that the numbers they dial will remain secret." Without such a "reasonable expectation of privacy," the fourth amendment is inapplicable.

In a strong dissent joined by Justice William Brennan, Justice Thurgood Marshall argued that although individuals may be aware of internal telephone company monitoring (an assumption he was unwilling to accept), "it does not follow that they expect this information to be made available to the public in general or to the government in particular." Labeling the use of pen registers "an extensive intrusion," Justice Marshall wrote:

> Privacy in placing calls is of value not only to those engaged in criminal activity. The prospect of unregulated governmental monitoring will undoubtedly prove disturbing even to those with nothing to hide. Many individuals, including members of unpopular

political organizations or journalists with confidential sources, may legitimately wish to avoid disclosure of their personal contacts. Permitting governmental access to telephone records on less than probable cause may thus impede certain forms of political affiliation and journalistic endeavor that are the hallmark of a truly free society.

Justice Stewart also dissented, arguing that "broadcast[ing] to the world a list of the local or long distance numbers [a person has] called . . . could easily reveal the identities of persons and places called, and thus reveal the most intimate details of a person's life."

Some state courts have interpreted their own constitutions to require law enforcement officials to obtain search warrants prior to using pen registers. For example, in *State v. Thompson* (1988), the Idaho Supreme Court concluded that "in Idaho there is a legitimate and reasonable expectation of privacy in the phone numbers that are dialed." Quoting extensively from the dissenting opinions in *Smith*, the court construed a state constitutional provision prohibiting "unreasonable searches and seizures" as applicable to pen registers. "Perhaps the day will come when a majority of the United States Supreme Court will decide to overrule *Smith* and establish for the nation the protection to which we believe those who use telephones in Idaho are entitled," the court said. "Until then, [the state constitution] will stand as a bulwark against the intrusions of pen registers into our daily life in Idaho."

PROBLEMS

1. In 1984, NBC broadcast two news stories about extremist presidential candidate Lyndon LaRouche, reporting that he had stated, among other things, that NBC is supported by the KGB and that the Queen of England is a drug dealer. The second broadcast said that LaRouche had proposed the assassination of President Jimmy Carter and that an IRS investigation of the LaRouche organization would lead to a criminal indictment. LaRouche filed a libel suit against the network in a Virginia federal court, and, during the course of pretrial discovery, sought a court order requiring NBC to disclose the names of confidential sources used in preparing the stories. LaRouche claimed that he had deposed eleven individuals in an effort to learn the identities of the NBC sources, and argued that NBC's report on the IRS investigation came exclusively from confidential sources. Analyze and evaluate the arguments that LaRouche and NBC would likely make before the judge faced with the source question. *See LaRouche v. NBC,* 780 F.2d 1134 (4th Cir.), *cert. denied,* 479 U.S. 818 (1986). Would your analysis be any different if LaRouche had been prosecuted for a criminal offense and had sought this information from the network? *See United States v. LaRouche Campaign,* 841 F.2d 1176 (1st Cir. 1988).

2. A reporter in Illinois wrote a series of articles disclosing alleged wrongdoing at a museum. Thereafter, he provided an assistant attorney general with names of persons he had contacted in preparing the stories. When the state brought criminal charges based on the museum incident against the defendant, he subpoenaed the reporter and sought to learn the names of the sources. Has the reporter waived his privilege under the Illinois shield law by revealing this information to the assistant attorney general? Is it relevant that the Illinois statute protects sources and information irrespective of a promise of confidentiality? If the reporter's action in this case does not constitute a waiver of the privilege, what does? *See People ex rel. Scott v. Silverstein,* 412 N.E.2d 692 (Ill. App. 1980), *rev'd on*

other grounds, 429 N.E.2d 483 (Ill. 1981). *See also Altemose Construction Co. v. Building & Construction Trades Council*, 443 F. Supp. 489 (E.D. Pa. 1977) (applying Pennsylvania shield statute); *Saxton v. Arkansas Gazette Co.*, 569 S.W.2d 115 (Ark. 1978) (arising under Arkansas shield law).

3. An IRS official leaked information about the plaintiff's tax return to a reporter, who published it. Various federal statutes prohibit such disclosure of tax information and allow a taxpayer to sue the responsible government official. The reporter said that an IRS official had made the information available but declined to identify him. The plaintiff then sought to force the journalist to reveal his source. What result? *See United Liquor Co. v. Gard*, 88 F.R.D. 123 (D. Ariz. 1980), *appeal dism'd*, 685 F.2d 447 (9th Cir. 1982). Would your answer be any different if the plaintiff were also suing the reporter or his newspaper for invasion of privacy?

4. A newspaper photographer covered an anti-nuclear weapons rally during which several persons were arrested. Some of her photographs were published in the newspaper. Subsequently, three of the demonstrators, who were facing trial on charges of harassing police officers and resisting arrest, subpoenaed the unpublished photos from the newspaper. According to defense counsel, the pictures were necessary to test witness' recollections of what had happened at the rally. Defense attorneys had already obtained statements from several witnesses who were scheduled to testify at trial on behalf of the defendants. How does the first amendment privilege work in this situation? Would your answer change if defense lawyers had not been able to locate witnesses who had seen the events leading to the arrest of the three protestors? Does the nature of the evidence that the prosecution plans to present at trial have any bearing on your analysis? How does your evaluation of the case change if the state had a shield law appearing to create an absolute privilege for persons "connected with any medium of communication" with respect to "unpublished information obtained or prepared in the course of newsgathering"? *See State ex rel. Meyers v. Howell*, 740 P.2d 792 (Or. App. 1987).

5. A woman driving through a highway construction area lost control of her car, had an accident, and was injured. Shortly thereafter, an off-duty reporter for a local newspaper drove through the area and spotted the overturned vehicle. The reporter took several photographs of the scene, one of which appeared in the newspaper with a caption describing the accident. The injured woman subsequently sued the highway department and the contractor, alleging that their negligence in failing to mark the area under construction caused the mishap. In preparing its defense, the contractor subpoenaed the reporter and the newspaper and demanded that they turn over the published and unpublished photographs and the negatives. What result? Why? Assume that there is no shield law applicable in this situation. *See Carroll Contracting, Inc. v. Edwards*, 528 So.2d 951 (Fla. App.), *review denied*, 536 So.2d 243 (Fla. 1988).

6. If a journalist breaks a promise of confidentiality and reveals a source's identity, should the informant be able to sue him for damages? What would be the legal basis of liability? Does the first amendment come into play? Would the journalist have a defense if he was compelled by court order to disclose the information and did so rather than face a jail term? *See Cohen v. Cowles Media Co.*, 16 Media L. Rptr. 2209 (Minn. App. 1989).

7. In *Branzburg v. Hayes*, Justice White made the point that "we remain unclear how often and to what extent informers are actually deterred from furnishing information when newsmen are forced to testify before a grand jury." Justice Stewart, in dissent, criticized the majority for apparently demanding proof of "impairment of the flow of news . . . with scientific precision." How does one go about collecting such evidence? Recall that

about half the states have shield laws on the books today. Can we somehow determine whether journalists in states without shield laws suffer in comparison to their counterparts in the other jurisdictions? Does it really matter whether there is empirical data to support the argument that protection for confidential sources and information is necessary? *See generally* Vince Blasi, ''The Newsman's Privilege: An Empirical Study,'' 70 *Michigan Law Review* 229 (1971).

8. A federal statute makes it a crime to steal government property—''any record, voucher, money, or thing of value of the United States''—or to sell or dispose of it without authority. *See* 18 U.S.C. § 641. In August 1989 the U.S. Department of Justice stated its intention to use this statute to prosecute government employees who ''leak'' information about federal criminal investigations to the media. The announcement came shortly after a leak that led to an erroneous news report that the FBI was investigating a congressman's financial dealings. In explaining the decision to invoke the theft statute in such situations, Attorney General Richard Thornburgh said that the disclosure of such inaccurate material to the press can damage the reputations of innocent individuals, while the release of accurate information can compromise ongoing criminal investigations. Can information leaked to reporters be considered government property? Is the use of the statute to cut off the flow of information to the press consistent with the first amendment? Are journalists likely to be subpoenaed by grand juries attempting to identify employees to be prosecuted under the statute? *See* Thomas B. Rosentiel, ''Rule May Curb Press's Use of Secret Sources.'' *Los Angeles Times* (August 4, 1989), p. 1; Eleanor Randolph, ''Thornburgh and Leaks: Pressing the Issue,'' *Washington Post* (September 13, 1989), p. A23. Consider these questions in light of *United States v. Morison,* which begins on the next page.

CHAPTER

8

NATIONAL SECURITY

United States v. Morison, 844 F.2d
1057 (4th Cir.), *cert. denied,* 109
S.Ct. 259 (1988).

[Defendant Samuel Loring Morison was a civilian employee of the Naval Intelligence Support Center (NISC) in Suitland, Maryland, a
suburb of Washington, D.C. The holder of a
"top secret" security clearance, he was assigned as an amphibious and hospital ship and
mine warfare analyst. In addition, Morison
"moonlighted" as a contributor to *Jane's
Fighting Ships* and *Jane's Defence Weekly,*
two British publications that provide information on international naval operations. The
Navy had approved Morison's relationship
with *Jane's* subject to his agreement not to
provide any classified information on American naval forces or to extract unclassified data
on any subject for the publications. By 1984,
however, this arrangement had created some
friction between Morison and the Navy, and

he began to explore the possibility of full-time
employment with *Jane's.*

In July 1984, Morison discovered on the
desk of an NISC colleague three classified
photographs of a Soviet aircraft carrier taken
by a U.S. spy satellite. He took the photos,
cut off their "secret" labels, and mailed them
to *Jane's Defence Weekly,* which paid him
$300. *Jane's* published the photos a few weeks
later and also made copies available to other
news organizations. When one of the pictures
was published in the *Washington Post,* NISC
began an investigation that ultimately led to
Morison. That investigation also revealed that
he had provided *Jane's* intelligence information concerning an explosion at a Soviet naval
base. Morison was charged with theft of government property under 18 U.S.C. §641 and
with violating two provisions of the Espionage
Act of 1917, 18 U.S.C. §793.

Under subsection (d) of section 793, a person who lawfully has possession of "informa-

tion relating to the national defense" commits an offense if he "willfully communicates, delivers, [or] transmits" that information "to any person not entitled to receive it, or willfully retains the same and fails to deliver it on demand. . . ." Subsection (e) proscribes the same conduct by a person who lacks authority to possess national defense information. A federal court jury in Baltimore returned a verdict of guilty on all counts, and this appeal followed. Various news organizations, including CBS and the *Washington Post*, filed *amici curiae* ("friends of the court") briefs urging reversal of Morison's conviction.]

Before RUSSELL, PHILLIPS, and WILKINSON, Circuit Judges.

DONALD RUSSELL, Circuit Judge:
* * * The initial defense of the defendant to his prosecution . . . rests on what he conceives to be the meaning and scope of the two espionage statutes he is charged with violating. * * * [I]t is his view that the prohibitions of these two subsections [of section 793 of the Espionage Act] are to be narrowly and strictly confined to conduct represented "in classic spying and espionage activity" by persons who, in the course of that activity, had transmitted "national security secrets to agents of foreign governments with intent to injure the United States." He argues that the conduct of which he is charged simply does not fit within the mold of "classical spying" as that term was defined, since he transmitted the national security secret materials . . . to a recognized international naval news organization . . . and not to an agent of a foreign power. In short, he leaked to the press; he did not transmit to a foreign government. It therefore follows, under his construction of the statutes, that he was not guilty of their violation. . . .

The defendant does not predicate his argument relating to the scope of the statutory meaning on the actual facial language of the statutes themselves. It is fair to say he concedes that the statutes, in their literal phrasing, are not ambiguous on their face and provide no warrant for his contention. Both statutes plainly apply to "whoever" having access to national defense information has under section 793(d) "willfully communicate[d], deliver[ed] or transmit[ted] . . . to a person not entitled to receive it," or has retained it in violation of section 793(e). The language of the two statutes includes no limitation to spies or to "an agent of a foreign government," either as to the transmitter or the transmittee of the information, and they declare no exemption in favor of one who leaks to the press. It covers "anyone." It is difficult to conceive of any language more definite and clear.

Admitting, however, that the statutes construed literally . . . did apply to his conduct, the defendant posits that the legislative history demonstrates conclusively that these statutes, whatever their facial language, were to be applied only to "classic spying" and that they should be limited in their application to this clear legislative intent. The threshold difficulty [with this argument] is the rule that when the terms of a statute are clear, its language is conclusive and . . . there is no need to consult legislative history. * * * We are convinced, though, that the legislative history will not support the defendant's construction of sections 793(d) and (e). * * *

But, though he cannot point to anything in the legislative record which intimates that Congress intended to exempt "leaks to the press," as defendant describes it, he argues that, unless such an exemption is read into these sections they will run afoul of the First Amendment. Actually, we do not perceive any First Amendment rights to be implicated here. This certainly is no prior restraint case such as *New York Times v. United States* (1971) and *United States v. Progressive, Inc.* (1979). It is a prosecution under a statute, of which the defendant, who, as an employee in the intelligence service of the military establishment, had been expressly noticed of his obligations by the terms of his letter of agreement with the Navy, is being prosecuted for purloining from the intelligence files of the Navy national defense materials clearly marked as "Intelligence Information" and "Secret" and for transmitting that material to "one not entitled to receive it." And the [government] premises its prosecution on establishing that he did this knowingly and "willfully". . . . We do not think that the First Amendment offers asylum . . . merely because the transmittal was to a representative of the press. This conclusion in our view follows from the decision in *Branzburg v. Hayes* (1972).

* * * The [Supreme] Court, in Justice White's opinion in that case, said: "It would be frivolous to assert . . . that the First Amendment, in the interest of securing news or otherwise, confers a license on either the reporter or his news sources to violate valid criminal laws. Although stealing documents or private wiretapping could provide newsworthy information, neither reporter nor source is immune from conviction for such conduct." * * *

United States v. Marchetti (1972), though not as directly on point as *Branzburg*, is instructive in this regard. In that case, the United States sought an injunction to prevent a former Central Intelligence Agency (CIA) employee, who had signed a confidentiality agreement not to divulge naval classified information to which he had access, from publishing classified CIA information after he left the CIA. The employee contended such a restraint violated his First Amendment rights. We affirmed the granting of the restraint. * * * Subsequently, in *Snepp v. United States* (1980), . . . the Supreme Court reviewed the right of the United States to enforce an agreement by a former CIA employee that he would not "publish . . . any information or material relating to the Agency, its activities . . . without specific prior approval by the Agency." The defendant had violated the agreement by publishing a book with some material relating to the CIA in it without securing CIA prior approval for such publication. The Supreme Court assumed the propriety of the restraint on publication in this agreement.

If *Branzburg*, *Marchetti*, and *Snepp* are to be followed, it seems beyond controversy that a recreant intelligence department employee who had abstracted from the government files secret intelligence information and had willfully transmitted or given it to one "not entitled to receive it," as did the defendant, is not entitled to invoke the First Amendment as a

shield to immunize his act of thievery. To permit the thief thus to misuse the Amendment would be to prostitute the salutary purposes of the First Amendment. Sections 793(d) and (e) unquestionably criminalize such conduct by a delinquent governmental employee and, when applied to a defendant in the position of the defendant here, there is no First Amendment right implicated. And it is not necessary to read into sections 793(d) and (e) an exception for national defense secret materials given the press in order to sustain the constitutionality of such statutes. It is clear, as we have said, that Congress did not indicate anywhere in its legislative history that it intended to exempt from the coverage of section 793(d) and (e) one who, after stealing national defense secret material, "willfully" delivered it to a representative of the press.

In summary, we conclude that there is no basis in the legislative record for finding that Congress intended to limit the applicability of sections 793(d) and (e) to "classic spying" or to exempt transmittal by a governmental employee who, entrusted with secret national defense material, had . . . leaked to the press. Nor do we find any authority for the proposition that Congress could not validly prohibit a government employee having possession of secret military intelligence material from transmitting that material to "one not entitled to receive it," whether that recipient was the press or not, without infringing the employee's rights under the First Amendment. *Branzburg* is definitely to the contrary.

Even though the statutes are not to be confined strictly to "classic" spying and even though they contain no implicit exception in favor of transmittal of secret defense material to the press, the defendant argues that the statutes themselves are constitutionally infirm for vagueness and overbreadth and that the prosecution under them should be stricken. We, therefore, proceed to address these attacks on the constitutionality of the statutes.

While admittedly vagueness and overbreadth are related constitutional concepts, they are separate and distinct doctrines subject in application to different standards and intended to achieve different purposes. The vagueness doctrine is rooted in due process principles and is basically directed at lack of sufficient clarity and precision in the statute; overbreadth, on the other hand, would invalidate a statute when it "infringe[s] on expression to a degree greater than justified by the legitimate governmental need" which is the valid purpose of the statute. * * *

[The court then rejected Morison's argument that the statutory phrases "relating to the national defense" and "person entitled to receive" were impermissibly vague. With respect to the former, the court noted that Morison "was an experienced intelligence officer" who had been "instructed on all the regulations concerning the security of secret national defense materials." As for the latter, the court concluded that any question as to whether a particular person is "entitled to receive" information is answered by the federal government's scheme for classifying national security information, a system with which Morison was familiar. Turning to overbreadth challenges to the same phrases, the court noted that the provisions could be considered invalid under this doctrine only if "the substantial governmental interest reflected in the statutes could be achieved by means less invasive of free speech interests." Given the importance of national security, the court concluded that the statutes, as limited by the trial judge's instructions to the jury, were not unnecessarily broad.]

The defendant has also appealed his conviction under 18 U.S.C. §641. That statute . . . imposes criminal penalties on anyone who "embezzles, steals, purloins or knowingly converts to his use or the use of another, or without authority, sells, conveys or disposes of any record, voucher, money, or thing of value of the United States or of any department or agency thereof. . . ." [The indictment charged the defendant with stealing and selling the three secret photographs and portions of two intelligence reports concerning the Soviet naval base.] * * * It will be noted at the outset that section 641 . . . is not a disclosure statute such as section 793(d) and (e); it is a criminal statute covering the theft of

government property. It is written in broad terms with the clear intent to sweep broadly. . . . [T]he statute was not intended simply to cover "larceny" and "embezzlement" as those terms were understood at common law but was also to apply to "acts which shade into those crimes but which, most strictly considered, might not be found to fit their fixed definitions." * * *

The amicus *Washington Post*, though, argues that the statute has "as an essential element a permanent or substantial deprivation of an identifiable property interest," and since the property right asserted by the government relates to "a possessory right to information or intellectual property," . . . section 641 is without application. Whether pure "information" constitutes property which may be the subject of statutory protection under section 641 . . . is not, however, involved here. We are dealing with specific, identifiable tangible property, which will qualify as such for larceny or embezzlement under any possible definition of the crime of theft. The photographs and the reports were clearly taken illegally and by stealth and disposed of by the defendant to a third party for personal gain, both monetary and in request for a job. That would seem to represent a textbook application of the crime set forth in section 641.

The defendant would deny the application of the statute to his theft because he says that he did not steal the material "for private, covert use in illegal enterprises" but in order to give it to the press for public dissemination and information. He claims that to criminalize this conduct under section 641 would be to invade his First Amendment rights. The mere fact that one has stolen a document in order that he may deliver it to the press, whether for money or for other personal gain, will not immunize him from responsibility for his criminal act. To use the First Amendment for such a purpose would be to convert [it] into a warrant for thievery. As the Supreme Court made clear in *Branzburg*, the First Amendment may not be used for such a sordid purpose, either to enable the governmental employee to excuse his act of theft or to excuse him, as in

Snepp and *Marchetti*, from his contractual obligation.

Actually, it may be noted parenthetically that the government contends, and the record affords substantial evidence in support of such contention, that the defendant in this case was not fired by zeal for public debate into his acts of larceny of government property; he was using the fruits of his theft to ingratiate himself with one from whom he was seeking employment. It can be said that he was motivated not by patriotism and the public interest but by self-interest. * * * We find no error in the conviction of the defendant under section 641.

[The court also rejected defendant's argument that the trial court had erroneously allowed certain evidence to be considered by the jury.]

Having reviewed all of the defendant's claims of error herein and found them without merit, we affirm the judgment of conviction of the defendant herein.

AFFIRMED.

WILKINSON, Circuit Judge, concurring:

I concur in Judge Russell's opinion. I believe his analysis of the relevant statutes, instructions, and evidentiary rulings is both careful and correct.

Morison's constitutional challenge is specifically phrased in terms of notice, statutory vagueness, and overbreadth. Yet much of the argument in this case has been cast in broader terms. Amici, the *Washington Post*, et al., warn that this case "will affect, and perhaps dramatically alter, the way in which government officials deal with the press, the way in which the press gathers and reports the news, and the way in which the public learns about its government." The news organizations are necessasrily raising their concerns as amici, not as parties. No member of the press is being searched, subpoenaed, or excluded, as in a typical right of access case. Morison as a source would raise newsgathering rights on behalf of press organizations that are not being, and probably could not be, prosecuted under the espionage statute.

Perhaps because these press rights of access are not personal to Morison, we have thus been asked to import a weighty assortment of First Amendment values into Morison's notice, vagueness, and overbreadth claims. Although this is more freight than the Supreme Court has lately allowed these doctrines to carry, I would assume for purposes of this discussion that Morison is entitled to raise the serious claims urged by the press amici. Indeed, I cannot fully express my own view of this case without addressing these claims, not as unspoken aspects of a vagueness and overbreadth analysis, but directly and on their own terms.

I.

I do not think the First Amendment interests here are insignificant. Criminal restraints on the disclosure of information threaten the ability of the press to scrutinize and report on government activity. There exists the tendency, even in a constitutional democracy, for government to withhold reports of disquieting developments and to manage news in a fashion most favorable to itself. Public debate, however, is diminished without access to unfiltered facts. * * * We have placed our faith in knowledge, not in ignorance, and for most, this means reliance on the press. Few Americans are acquainted with those who make policy, fewer still participate in making it. For this reason, the press provides the "means by which the people receive that free flow of information and ideas essential to effective self-government."

The First Amendment interest in informed popular debate does not simply vanish at the invocation of the words "national security. National security is public security, not government security from informed criticism. No decisions are more serious than those touching on peace and war; none are more certain to affect every member of society. Elections turn on the conduct of foreign affairs and strategies of national defense, and the dangers of secretive government have been well documented. Morison claims he released satellite photographs revealing construction of the first Soviet nuclear carrier in order to alert the public to the dimensions of a Soviet naval buildup. Although this claim is open to serious question, the undeniable effect of the disclosure was to enhance public knowledge and interest in the projection of Soviet sea power such as that revealed in the satellite photos.

The way in which those photographs were released, however, threatens a public interest that is no less important—the security of sensitive government operations. In an ideal world, governments would not need to keep secrets from their own people, but in this world much hinges on events that take place outside public view. Intelligence gathering is critical to the formation of sound policy, and becomes more so every year with the refinement of technology and the growing threat of terrorism. Electronic surveillance prevents surprise attacks by hostile force and facilitates international peacekeeping and arms control efforts. Confidential diplomatic exchanges are the essence of international relations.

None of these activities can go forward without secrecy. When the identities of our intelligence agents are known, they may be killed. When our electronic surveillance capabilities are revealed, countermeasures can be taken to circumvent them. When other nations fear that confidences exchanged at the bargaining table will only become embarrassments in the press, our diplomats are left helpless. When terrorists are advised of our intelligence, they can avoid apprehension and escape retribution. * * * The type of information leaked by Morison may cause widespread damage by hampering the effectiveness of expensive surveillance systems which would otherwise be expected to provide years of reliable information not obtainable by other means.

Public security can thus be compromised in two ways: by attempts to choke off the information needed for democracy to function, and by leaks that imperil the environment of physical security which a functioning democracy requires. The tension between these two interests is not going to abate, and the question is how a responsible balance may be achieved.

II.

Courts have long performed the balancing task where First Amendment rights are implicated. The Supreme Court has often had to balance the value of unrestricted newsgathering against other public interests. * * * In these cases the courts have taken an "aggressive" balancing role, directly comparing the interests served by restraints on the press with the interest in unhindered newsgathering.

Although aggressive balancing may have characterized the judicial role in other contexts, I am not persuaded that it should do so here. In the national security field, the judiciary has performed its traditional balancing role with deference to the decisions of the political branches of government. Presented with First Amendment, Fourth Amendment, and other constitutional claims, the [Supreme] Court has held that government restrictions that would otherwise be impermissible may be sustained where national security and foreign policy are implicated. In the terminology associated with a balancing analysis, "the Government has a compelling interest in protecting . . . the secrecy of information important to the national security." Recognition of such a compelling state interest reflects an understanding of the institutional limitations of the judiciary and a regard for the separation of powers.

The aggressive balancing that courts have undertaken in other contexts is different from what would be required here. The government's interest in the security of judicial proceedings, searches by law enforcement officers, and grand jury operations . . . are readily scrutinized by courts. Indeed, they pertain to the judiciary's own systems of evidence. Evaluation of the government's interest here, on the other hand, would require the judiciary to draw conclusions about the operation of the most sophisticated electronic systems and the potential effects of their disclosure. An intelligent inquiry of this sort would require access to the most sensitive technical information, and background knowledge of the range of intelligence operations that cannot easily be presented in the single "case or controversy" to which courts are confined. Even with sufficient information, courts obviously lack the expertise needed for its evaluation. Judges can understand the operation of a subpoena more readily than that of a satellite. In short, questions of national security and foreign affairs are "of a kind for which the judiciary has neither aptitude, facilities nor responsibility and which has long been held to belong in the domain of political power not subject to judicial intrusion or inquiry."

The balancing process must thus accord Congress latitude to control access to national security secrets by statute and the executive some latitude to do so through the classification scheme. I do not come to this conclusion solely because the enumerated powers for the conduct of foreign affairs are lodged in the executive and legislative branches. The First Amendment presupposes that the enumerated powers—the raising of armies no less than the raising of revenue—will be executed in an atmosphere of public debate. I also recognize that the democratic accountability of the legislature and executive is not a wholly satisfactory explanation for deference in the area of national security secrets. Years may pass before the basis of portentous decisions becomes known. The public cannot call officials to account on the basis of material of whose existence and content it is unaware. What is more, classification decisions may well have been made by bureaucrats far down the line, whose public accountability may be quite indirect.

Rather, the judicial role must be a deferential one because the alternative would be grave. To reverse Morison's conviction on the general ground that it chills press access would be tantamount to a judicial declaration that the government may never use criminal penalties to secure the confidentiality of intelligence information. Rather than enhancing the operation of democracy, as Morison suggests, this course would install every government worker with access to classified information as a veritable satrap. Vital decisions and expensive programs set into motion by elected representatives would be subject to summary derailment at the pleasure of one disgruntled employee. The question, however, is not one of motives as much as who, finally, must decide. The answer has to be the Congress and those accountable to the Chief Executive. While periods of profound disillusionment with government have brought intense demands for increased scrutiny, those elected still remain the repositories of a public trust. Where matters of exquisite sensitivity are in question, we cannot invariably install, as the ultimate arbiter of disclosure, even the conscience of the well-meaning employee.

III.

The remaining question, then, is whether the application of this particular law to this particular defendant took place in accordance with constitutional requirements. For the reasons so carefully analyzed in Judge Russell's opinion, I am persuaded that it did. * * *

Morison's claim that he was not on notice that his conduct might lead to prosecution is unpersuasive. Morison was a trained national intelligence officer with a Top Secret security clearance. He signed a disclosure agreement specifically stating that criminal prosecution could result from mishandling of secret information, and he clipped explicit classification warnings from the borders of the satellite photographs before sending them to *Jane's*. Morison cannot use the fact that prosecutions under the statute have not been frequent to shield himself from the notice provided by these facts and the clear language of the statute. * * *

Morison's contention that potential future applications of the espionage statute to other sources render it invalid as to him is not, ultimately, persuasive. Amici, the *Washington Post*, et al., describe various press reports of illegal domestic surveillance by the CIA, design defects of the Abrams M-1 tank, Soviet arms control violations, and military procurement cost overruns. Amici contend that if the sources of such reports face prosecution under hypothetical applications of the statute, then "corruption, scandal, and incompetence in the defense establishment would be protected from scrutiny."

As the above examples indicate, investigative reporting is a critical component of the First Amendment's goal of accountability in government. To stifle it might leave the public interest prey to the manifold abuses of unexamined power. It is far from clear, however, that an affirmance here would ever lead to that result. The Supreme Court has cautioned that to reverse a conviction on the basis of other purely hypothetical applications of a statute, the overbreadth must "not only be real, but substantial as well." I question whether the spectre presented by the above examples is in any sense real or whether they have much in common with Morison's conduct. Even if juries could ever be found that would convict those who truly expose governmental waste and misconduct, the political firestorm that would follow prosecution of one who exposed an administration's own ineptitude would make such prosecutions a rare and unrealistic prospect. * * *

IV.

It may well be, as the government contends, that Morison released the satellite photos and weekly wires in order to receive cash and ingratiate himself with *Jane's* to gain future employment. But I do not think that Morison's motives are what is crucial here. Morison's

conduct has raised questions of considerable importance. At the same time, it is important to emphasize what is *not* before us today. This prosecution was not an attempt to apply the espionage statute to the press for either the receipt or publication of classified material. Neither does this case involve any prior restraint on publication. Such questions are not presented in this case, and I do not read Judge Russell's opinion to express any view on them.

The parties and amici have presented to us the broader implications of this case. We have been told that even high officials routinely divulge classified public secrets, that alternative sanctions may be imposed on such behavior, and that an affirmance here presents a vital threat to newsgathering and the democratic process. On the other side of the argument lies the commonsense observation that those in government have their own motives, political and otherwise, that ensure the continuing availability of press sources. * * * Problems of source identification and the increased security risks involved in discovery and trial make proceeding against press sources difficult. Moreover, the espionage statute has no applicability to the multitude of leaks that pose no conceivable threat to national security, but threaten only to embarrass one or another high government official. * * *

What is at issue in this case is the constitutionality of a particular conviction. As to that, I am prepared to concur with Judge Russell that the First Amendment imposes no blanket prohibition on prosecutions for unauthorized leaks of damaging national security information, and that this particular prosecution comported with constitutional guarantees.

[The concurring opinion of Judge Phillips is omitted.]

INTRODUCTION

In the landmark case of *Near v. Minnesota* (1931), the Supreme Court ruled that a prior restraint on speech and press is unconstitutional. But the Court also recognized in that case that this first amendment protection is not unlimited. By way of illustration, Chief Justice Charles Evans Hughes wrote that "[n]o one would question but that a government might prevent . . . the publication of the sailing dates of transports or the number and location of troops." This language, which was unnecessary to the Court's decision in *Near*, marked the beginning of what has become a broad "national security exception" to the guarantees of the first amendment. As Judge J. Harvie Wilkinson's concurring opiunion in the *Morison* case indicates, the balancing process employed in first amendment cases operates differently when matters of national security are involved, with the scales being weighted in favor of government restrictions on expression. In fact, some cases suggest that certain speech implicating the nation's security lacks first amendment protection altogether.

That the law has developed in this fashion is not particularly surprising, given the obsession with national security that has enveloped this country since the onset of the "cold war" with the Soviet Union in the late 1940s. In fact, secrecy in the conduct of foreign affairs is as old as the nation itself. "The nature of foreign negotiations requires caution and their success must often depend on secrecy," George Washington once said. He also observed that "[t]he necessity of procuring good intelligence is apparent," and that the "whole matter [should be kept] as secret as possible. . . ." John Jay, who later became the first Chief Justice of the United States, expressed similar sentiments in the *Federalist Papers*: "It seldom happens in the negotiation of treaties, of whatever nature, but that perfect secrecy and immediate dispatch are sometimes requisite. There are cases where the most useful intelligence may be obtained, if the persons possessing it can be relieved from apprehensions of discovery."

It was not until the beginning of the twentieth century, however, that Congress began to deal with sensitive military and national security information in a comprehensive fashion. By 1909, various statutes punished treason, unlawful entry on to military bases, and the theft of government property. Moreover, the Defense Secrets Act of 1911 proscribed various information-gathering activities around military installations and prohibited the communication of defense information to persons "not entitled to receive it." The 1911 statute was the precursor of the Espionage Act of 1917, which, as one might expect, grew out of the frenzy surrounding the United States' entry into World War I. Key provisions of the act remain on the books today, as the *Morison* case makes plain.

American involvement in the war also had an impact upon first amendment jurisprudence. In *Schenck v. United States* (1919), Socialist Party leader Charles Schenck, who had prepared and distributed 15,000 pamphlets calling for men to resist the draft, was convicted of violating an amendment to the Espionage Act making it a crime to obstruct military recruiting. The Supreme Court, in an opinion by Justice Oliver Wendell Holmes, upheld the conviction under the now-famous "clear and present danger" test discussed in Chapter 1. In applying that test, Justice Holmes emphasized the potential threat to the nation's war effort: "When a nation is at war many things that might be said in time of peace are such a hindrance to its effort that their utterance will not be endured so long as men fight and that no Court could regard them as protected by any constitutional right." Though one can certainly take issue with the Court's conclusion that a comparative handful of leaflets represented a "clear and present danger," Justice Holmes' statement as to the effect of national security concerns on the first amendment proved to be accurate.

Another war, the conflict in Vietnam, led to the Supreme Court's most famous national security decision, *New York Times Co. v. United States*—the "Pentagon Papers" case. In mid-June of 1971, the *New York Times* published summaries of a "top secret" Department of Defense study detailing American involvement in the war in Vietnam from 1945 to 1967. The 7,000 page history, which contained some embarassing information about the role of the United States in the war, had been made available to the *Times* (and later to other newspapers) by Daniel Ellsberg, a former defense department analyst who had access to the study through the Rand Corporation, a private "think tank" with which he was connected as a consultant.

On June 15, two days after the first *Times* article appeared, the Justice Department obtained a temporary restraining order from a federal judge in New York barring the *Times* from printing further stories based on the Vietnam study. This order was the first in American history prohibiting a newspaper from publishing specific information. After a full hearing, however, Judge Murray Gurfein concluded that such drastic relief was unwarranted. The ban on publication continued, however, while the government appealed. On June 23, the U.S. Court of Appeals for the Second Circuit ruled that the *Times* could not publish any material that the government decided was a threat to the national security, pending further review by Judge Gurfein. The next day, the newspaper asked the U.S. Supreme Court to review the case.

As the *Times* case was working its way through the courts, the *Washington Post* began publishing its own articles based on the Pentagon Papers. The government again went to court, this time in the District of Columbia. In the early evening of June 18, Judge Gerhard Gesell declined to stop publication, but the U.S. Court of Appeals for the District of Columbia Circuit reversed him a few hours later, entering a temporary order that literally "stopped the presses" at the *Post*. On June 23, however, the appellate court concluded that the government had not presented evidence of harm to the national security sufficient to justify an injunction against publication. Nonetheless, the judges granted an extension of the restraining order to allow the government to appeal to the Supreme Court, which it did the following day. Meanwhile, several other newspapers—including the *Boston Globe*, *Los Angeles Times*, and *St. Louis Post-Dispatch*—were publishing stories based on the leaked report.

The cases involving the *New York Times* and *Washington Post* moved through the clogged federal judicial system with extraordinary speed, a clear indication of the significance of the issues involved. Even more extraordinary was the Supreme Court's handling of the cases, which were consolidated for purposes of appeal. Argument was scheduled for an unusual Saturday session on June 26, and the Court handed down its decision four days later. Ruling 6 to 3 in favor of the newspapers, the Court issued an unsigned three-paragraph opinion noting simply that prior restraints are presumptively invalid and that the government had "not met" its "heavy burden of showing justification for the imposition of such a restraint." However, each of the nine Justices wrote an opinion expressing his own views, and a careful examination of those opinions reveals a three-way split among the members of the Court, with a majority willing to recognize, under certain conditions, the validity of a prior restraint on the press to protect the nation's security.

Justices Hugo Black and William O. Douglas took the position that the first amendment completely forbids orders restraining publication in the name of national security. "[W]e are asked to hold that despite the First Amendment's emphatic command, the Executive Branch, the Congress, and the Judiciary can make laws enjoining publication of current news and abridging freedom of the press in the name of 'national security,'" Justice Black wrote. "To find that the President has inherent power to halt the publication of news by resort to the courts would wipe out the First Amendment. . . ."

Justice William Brennan did not go so far; rather, he stressed that the government had offered no concrete evidence that publication of the Pentagon Papers would cause the type of grievous harm necessary to justify a prior restraint on publication. The first amendment "tolerates absolutely no prior judicial restraints on the press predicated upon surmise or conjecture that untoward circumstances may result," he wrote. Moreover, Justice Brennan was of the opinion that, under *Schenck* and *Near*, prior restraints are permissible only in exceptional circumstances when the nation is at war. "Even if the present world situation were assumed to be tantamount to a time of war, or if the power of presently available armaments would justify even in peacetime the suppression of information that would set in motion a nuclear holocaust, in neither of these [cases] has the Government presented or even alleged that publication of items from or based upon the [Pentagon Papers] would cause the happening of an event of that nature. . . ."

The second group of Justices—Potter Stewart, Byron White, and Thurgood Marshall—took a far different approach. All three emphasized the absence of a statute authorizing the federal government to seek a prior restraint against the press on national security grounds, thus suggesting that the result might have been different had Congress provided for this extraordinary remedy. "I do not say that in no circumstances would the First Amendment permit an injunction against publishing information about government plans or operations," Justice White wrote. "But I nevertheless agree that the United States has not satisfied the very heavy burden that it must meet to warrant an injunction against publication in these cases, at least in the absence of express and appropriately limited congressional authority for prior restraints in circumstances such as these." Although the Espionage Act and other federal statutes make unauthorized possession and dissemination of national security information a crime, Justice White continued, they do not authorize restraining orders of the type issued in these cases. By mentioning these criminal provisions, the Justices seemed to be suggesting that the newspapers could have been prosecuted for what they had published.

Finally, Chief Justice Warren Burger and Justices John Marshall Harlan and Harry Blackmun dissented, in large part because of the haste with which the cases were decided. Quoting Justice Holmes' famous remark that "great cases like hard cases make bad law," Justice Harlan complained that the Court "has been almost irresponsibly feverish in dealing with these cases." Joined by Justice Blackmun, he also argued that because the executive branch has broad discretion concerning foreign affairs, the courts should generally yield to the judgment of that branch with respect to matters of national security. "Even if there is some room for the judiciary to override the executive determination, it is plain that the scope of review must be exceedingly narrow," he wrote. "I can see no indication in [these cases] that the conclusions of the Executive were given [that] deference. . . ." Chief Justice Burger stated his general agreement with the remarks of Justice Harlan but specifically stated that he was "not prepared to reach the merits."

As this synopsis of the nine opinions indicates, the Pentagon Papers case cannot be described as a victory for the press, although the effect of the Court's ruling was to lift the lower court orders barring publication. Except for Justices Black and Douglas, all of the Justices concluded that prior restraints can be justified on national security grounds. While an act of Congress authorizing such a restraint may be necessary, such a statute would not offend the first amendment. Moreover, several of the opinions indicate that criminal prosecution of the media, not to mention those who "leak" sensitive information, is permissible. Indeed, Daniel Ellsberg and a colleague, Anthony Russo, were indicted, under the statutes later used in *Morison*, for making the Pentagon Papers available to the press, but the charges were dropped because of government misconduct. Finally, the Harlan position—that the courts should for the most part yield to the national security determinations of the executive branch—has since become a settled legal principle. In short, the Pentagon Papers case laid the groundwork for further expansion of the national security "exception" to the first amendment.

Perhaps the most significant of the Supreme Court's more recent decisions in this area is *Haig v. Agee* (1981). The case arose when Philip Agee, a former Central Intelligence Agency employee then living in West Germany, announced a campaign "to expose CIA officers and agents and to take the measures necessary to drive them out of the countries where they are operating." Between 1974 and 1978 he identified "hundreds of persons" as CIA operatives and traveled extensively in foreign countries to carry out his objective. In 1979, the Secretary of State revoked Agee's passport on the ground that his activities abroad were causing "serious damage to the national security or the foreign policy of the United States." Agee immediately filed suit against the Secretary, arguing, among other things, that this administrative action violated his first amendment rights. The Supreme Court, in an opinion by Chief Justice Burger, disagreed.

Pointing out that "no governmental interest is more compelling than the security of the Nation," the Chief Justice emphasized that the term "national security" extends beyond information about military operations in time of war and other defense matters. "History eloquently attests that grave problems of national security and foreign policy are by no means limited to times of formally declared war." Further, he said, measures to protect the secrecy of foreign intelligence operations plainly serve important national security interests. Because Agee's activities "jeopardized the security of the United States" and "creat[ed] serious problems for American foreign relations and foreign policy," the government could legitimately restrict his foreign travel in an effort to limit these activities. Citing *Near v. Minnesota*, the Court found no first amendment violation despite the fact that the revocation of Agee's passport rested in part on the content of his speech. "Agee's disclosures . . . have the declared purpose of obstructing intelligence operations and the recruiting of intelligence personnel," the Chief Justice wrote. "They are clearly not protected by the Constitution."

The *Agee* case seems to create a category of speech which, like obscenity, is completely without first amendment protection. That is, when certain "national security" speech is involved, there is no need to employ the balancing process usually employed in first amendment cases; rather, the speech may be proscribed or punished because it falls outside the scope of the first amendment. *Agee* itself, however, suggests that this category of unprotected speech is rather narrow and that one must look beyond the "national security" label in defining its parameters. Mr. Agee had a "declared purpose" of obstructing intelligence operations, had "insider" knowledge based on his service with the CIA, and conceded that his campaign was causing or was likely to cause serious damage to national security. If any of these three ingredients is missing from a given case, the speech is presumably protected and the courts must utilize the familiar balancing process in evaluating restrictions on the speech. As Judge Wilkinson suggested in *Morison*, however, the balance does not favor freedom of expression when national security concerns are implicated.

With this analytical framework in mind, let us now turn to the manner in which the government has attempted to protect national security information. We have already seen some examples, including prior restraint (*New York Times Co. v. United States*), prosecution of employees who "leak" sensitive material to the press

(*United States v. Morison*); and restrictions on travel (*Haig v. Agee*). Moreover, as discussed in Chapter 5, "classified" information is exempt from disclosure under the federal Freedom of Information Act. After another look at the prior restraint problem, we will examine three other weapons at the government's disposal: criminal prosecution on the basis of publication, contractual arrangements with employees having access to national security information, and restrictions on news coverage of military operations.

PRIOR RESTRAINTS

Some of the questions at issue in the 1971 Pentagon Papers case resurfaced eight years later in *United States v. The Progressive, Inc.* when a small Wisconsin-based magazine prepared to publish an article entitled "The H Bomb Secret: How We Got It, Why We're Telling It." Written by Howard Morland, a freelance journalist who specialized in energy and nuclear weapons issues, the article described in some detail the workings of the hydrogen bomb, a thermonuclear weapon whose secrets were known to only five nations, including the United States. Morland, whose goal was to enable "ordinary citizens [to] have informed opinions about nuclear weapons," said he based the article on information in the public domain and readily available to any diligent researcher.

Prior to the scheduled publication date, *The Progressive*'s editors sent a copy of the Morland article to the U.S. Department of Energy and asked that it verify technical information concerning the design and manufacture of hydrogen weapons. DOE officials determined that a significant portion of the article contained classified information and advised the magazine that publication of the article would violate the Atomic Energy Act and would give an advantage to foreign nations in the development of thermonuclear technology. When *The Progressive* declined DOE's request to delete the classified information from the article, the federal government filed suit in a Milwaukee federal court to enjoin publication.

Federal Judge Robert W. Warren granted a preliminary injunction. Although the article was not a "do-it-yourself guide for the hydrogen bomb," he concluded that it "could possibly provide sufficient information to allow a medium size nation to move faster in developing a nuclear weapon." After reviewing evidence submitted by the parties, Judge Warren also determined that the story contained information "vital to the operation of the bomb" not available "in the public realm." The classified information used in the article, he said, provided "a more comprehensive, accurate, and detailed analysis of the overall construction and operation of a thermonuclear weapon than any publication to date in the public literature."

Turning to the legal issues, Judge Warren pointed out that the Atomic Energy Act prohibits anyone from communicating, transmitting, or disclosing any "restricted data" to any person "with reason to believe such data will be utilized to injure the United States or to secure an advantage to any foreign nation." Publishing information in a magazine fell within the statute, he said, and there was no doubt that some of the material in the Morland article was "restricted data," a term defined by statute to include information concerning the "design, manufacture or utilization of atomic weapons." And, in addition to making the communication of such information a crime, the act expressly provides that the federal government may seek a court order enjoining "any acts or practices" which constitute or will constitute a violation of the statute. Given this statutory authorization for a prior restraint, the judge was not faced with the problem that troubled several of the Justices in the Pentagon Papers case.

At the heart of Judge Warren's decision, however, was his conclusion that the potential harm to the national security was much more substantial in this case than in *New York Times Co. v. United States*, which involved historical data about the Vietnam war. In this case, he said, the information was much more sensitive and the stakes were much higher: "A mistake in ruling against *The Progressive* will seriously infringe cherished First Amendment rights," he said. "A mistake in ruling against the United States could pave the way for thermonuclear annilhilation for us all. In that even, our right to life is extinguished and the right to publish becomes moot." Because publication of the classified information contained in the Morland article would cause "direct, immediate and irreparable injury to the United States by accelerating the capacity of certain nonthermonuclear nations to manufacture thermonuclear weapons," Judge Warren issued a preliminary injunction barring *The Progressive* from publishing the article in a form that included the "restricted data."

Two days after the U.S. Court of Appeals for the Seventh Circuit heard oral argument in the magazine's appeal, the *Madison Press Connection* published a letter containing the technical information that Judge Warren had forbidden *The Progressive* from printing. The *Chicago Tribune* also ran the letter. Because the disputed information had been made public, the order restraining *The Progressive* was obviously without justification. Accordingly, the government dropped its suit, the Seventh Circuit dismissed the appeal, and, in November 1979, *The Progressive* published the Morland article. A case that seemed destined for the Supreme Court thus ended with something of a whimper, at least in the sense that it did not "make law." Nonetheless, Judge Warren's decision seems entirely consistent with the principles announced in the *New York Times* decision.

The dispute between the Department of Energy and *The Progressive* magazine raised a question that goes to the heart of the problem surrounding national security matters: who is to decide whether the disclosure of certain information would harm the nation—the government or the press? Taken together, the Supreme Court's fragmented ruling in *New York Times* and Judge Warren's opinion in *The Progressive* case make plain that, legally speaking, the decision belongs to the government, with each of the three branches playing a role. Though the ultimate determination with respect to a prior restraint on the publication of such information rests with the courts, the judiciary gives great weight to the judgment of the legislative and executive branches as to the need for confidentiality in national security matters. As a practical matter, however, the press will often make the initial decision, since the government can obtain court order barring publication only when it has some advance warning of the impending disclosure. Had *The Progressive* simply published the Morland article without first alerting the government, for example, the prior restraint issue would never have arisen.

CRIMINAL PROSECUTION

When its case against *The Progressive* was frustrated by the action of the Madison newspaper, the federal government hinted at the possibility of criminal prosecutions under the Atomic Energy Act. No such charges were brought, but the message was clear: those who publish national security information in violation of the law face the imposition of criminal penalties. Obviously, the threat of a fine and/or jail term—up to $10,000 and ten years in jail under the Atomic Energy Act, for example—can have a significant impact on the exercise of first amendment rights. If, however, the more extreme prior restraint remedy may be employed to prevent the dissemination of such information, then "after-the-fact" criminal sanctions would seem to be constitutionally permissible in the national security setting.

The federal government has been reluctant to use criminal statutes against journalists and news organizations, preferring instead to prosecute their sources—Daniel Ellsberg and Samuel Morison, for example. As a result, the Supreme Court has not directly addressed the constitutionality of criminal statutes applied against the news media for publishing classified national security information. Recall, however, that several Justices warned in the Pentagon Papers case that various provisions of the Espionage Act could be used to punish reporters and publishers, with Justice White's opinion containing the most detailed analysis. "If any of the material here at issue is [covered by the act], the newspapers are presumably now in full notice of the position of the United States and must face the consequences if they publish," he wrote. "I would have no difficulty in sustaining convictions under these sections on facts that would not justify . . . the imposition of a prior restraint."

To explore this issue further, we must consider four Supreme Court decisions that did not involve national security. In *Landmark Communications, Inc. v. Virginia* (1978), the Court reversed the conviction of a newspaper under a Virginia statute providing that information about proceedings before the state judicial ethics commission "shall not be divulged by any person. . . ." Violation of this provision was a misdemeanor. A newspaper was convicted under the statute and fined $500 after it reported—accurately—that the commission was investigating a particular judge. Chief Justice Burger stated the issue as "whether the First Amendment permits the criminal punishment of third persons who are strangers to the inquiry, including the news media, for divulging or publishing truthful information regarding [the] confidential proceedings. . . ." In answering this question, the Chief Justice balanced the state's interest in confidentiality against the first amendment rights of the press. Although the state had a legitimate interest in protecting the reputation of judges and maintaining the integrity of its judiciary, that interest did not justify the "actual and potential encroachments on freedom of speech and of the press" flowing from the criminal penalty. Chief Justice Burger was careful to emphasize, however, that the newspaper had acquired the information in a lawful manner. Had a reporter broken into the commission's office to obtain the material, the result might well have been different.

In the second case, *Smith v. Daily Mail Publishing Co.* (1979), the Court struck down a West Virginia statute that made it a crime for a newspaper to publish the identity of a juvenile offender without court permission. There a newspaper had learned from witnesses and law enforcement sources the name of a juvenile suspected of murder. After it was indicted for violating the statute, the newspaper obtained a state court ruling that the provision was unconstitutional. The Supreme Court affirmed, with Chief Justice Burger again writing the opinion. "[I]f a newspaper lawfully obtains truthful information about a matter of public significance," he said, "then state officials may not constitutionally punish publication of the information, absent a need to further a state interest of the highest order." Finding the state's asserted interest in rehabilitating juvenile offenders to be insufficient, the Court ruled that the criminal provision was unconstitutional. The Chief Justice also noted that the juvenile's name was already known to the public, since three radio stations had previously identified the boy. The stations had not risked criminal punishment in broadcasting his name, since the statute applied only to newspapers.

The *Daily Mail* case differs from *Landmark* in one important respect: there the information covered by the statute was already in the public domain, having been revealed by law enforcement personnel who spoke with newspaper and broadcast reporters. Since the juvenile's name was made public as the result of government action, it can be argued that a criminal prosecution based on publication of that information should be precluded. This approach, though not used in *Daily Mail*, is supported by the Court's landmark privacy case, *Cox Broadcasting Corp. v. Cohn* (1975). As discussed in Chapter 3, the Court ruled in that case that an invasion of privacy suit could not be based on information obtained from public court records, since the state had "plac[ed] the information in the public domain. . . ." The *Daily Mail* case is distinguishable in that the information was not a matter of public record, but disclosure of confidential information by government employees is arguably sufficient to bring the rule of *Cox Broadcasting* into play. As noted in Chapter 3, however, the Court declined to so extend *Cox* in *Florida Star v. B.J.F.* (1989). In some cases, therefore, the government may be able to punish criminally the publication of information already in the public domain.

Transported into the national security arena, these four Supreme Court decisions suggest the following guidelines. First, the government may criminally punish the publication of confidential national security information that has been unlawfully obtained by the news media. Recall that the Court emphasized in both *Landmark* and *Daily Mail* that the media in those cases had not acted illegally in securing the information. Second, the government may likewise punish the publication of such information that has been lawfully acquired, so long as protection of the national security is an "interest of the highest order" warranting the imposition of criminal penalties for publication. In light of the cases discussed previously in this chapter, it seems clear that national security qualifies under this test. Third, the government may even be able to punish the publication of national security information that is in the public domain, although this power should be limited to extreme cases. As Judge Learned Hand once observed, espionage statutes should not be stretched to include the publication of information gathered from "sources that were lawfully accessible to anyone who was willing to take the pains to find, sift and collate it."

Several federal statutes contain criminal penalties for the disclosure of national security information. In addition to the Espionage Act and Atomic Energy Act discussed previously in connection with the *New York Times* and *Progressive* cases, a notable statute of this type is the Intelligence Identities Protection Act of 1982. Passed on the heels of the Supreme Court's decision in *Haig v. Agee*, the statute is directly aimed at the activities of persons determined to expose the identities of American intelligence agents and to otherwise frustrate covert national security operations. Foremost among them has been former CIA employee Philip Agee, whose books *Dirty Work: The CIA in Western Europe* and *Dirty Work 2: The CIA in Africa* revealed the names of over 1,000 alleged CIA officers. Another target of the legislation was Louis Wolf, co-editor of the *Covert Action Information Bulletin*, a periodical with a special section devoted to identifying CIA operatives. According to the congressional report accompanying the act, this practice of "naming names" led directly to the 1975 assassination of CIA Station Chief Richard Welch in Athens, Greece, and to other violent attacks on persons labled as CIA officers.

The Intelligence Identities Protection Act makes it a crime to intentionally disclose the identities of covert intelligence agents and establishes different penalties based on the defendant's degree of access to classified information. The harshest penalties are reserved for "insiders" who have had authorized access to classified information. If an individual who has had such access to information that identifies a covert agent intentionally discloses the agent's identity, he may be jailed for up to ten years and fined as much as $50,000. A person who intentionally reveals the identity of a covert agent after having had access to classified information in general faces a maximum five-year jail term and $25,000 fine. These penalties apply primarily to employees and former employees of the government. "Outsiders" who have not had authorized access to classified information are treated differently. If such persons intentionally disclose an agent's identy "in the course of a pattern of activities intended to identify and expose covert agents and with reason to believe that such activities would impair or impede the foreign intelligence activities of the United States," he may be imprisoned for up to three years and fined up to $15,000.

There is little dispute, particularly in light of the *Morison* case, that the "insider" provisions are constitutional. The portion of the act aimed at "outsiders" is more troublesome, for it appears to punish the publication of lawfully acquired information without proof that disclosure has harmed the national security. Moreover, the statute apparently applies when the information is in the public domain, for there is no requirement that the covert agent's identity be obtained from classified information. For these reasons, some commentators have suggested that the act's "outsider" provision violates the first amendment, relying on the *Landmark Communications*, *Daily Mail*, and *Cox Broadcasting* cases discussed above. There has been no litigation to date, however.

When the act was being considered in Congress, there was some concern among journalists that the "outsider" provision could be employed against reporters and news organizations. For example, a *Columbia Journalism Review* article listed eighty major books and news stories that identified CIA agents—including press reports that former CIA operatives had been involved in the Watergate episode—that arguably could have resulted in criminal charges. However, the act's requirement that there be a "pattern of activities intended to identify and expose covert agents" makes proseuction of conventional journalists and news organizations extremely unlikely. The legislative history of the statute confirms this view, making clear that the Congress did not intend that it reach traditional newsgathering activities. According to the conference committee report accompanying the legislation:

> A journalist writing stories about the CIA would not be engaged in the requisite "pattern of activities," even if the stories he wrote included the names of one or more covert agents, unless the government proved that there was an intent to identify and expose agents. To meet this standard . . . , a discloser must be engaged in a purposeful enterprise of revealing identities—he must, in short, be in the business of "naming names."

The report then listed several examples of activities that would not be covered by the act, including "[a]n investigation by a newspaper of possible CIA connections with the Watergate burglaries," a news story detailing "the activities of . . . former CIA employees who allegedly supplied explosives and terrorist training to Libya," and a biography of Martin Luther King, Jr., that "purported to give the identity of covert [FBI] agents" who wiretapped Dr. King's telephone. In each of these cases, the report said, the purpose of the newsgathering activities would be to "investigate illegal or controversial activities, and not to identify covert agents." The report also states that "the fact that a journalist had written articles critical of the CIA . . . could not be used as evidence that the intent standard was met."

CONTRACTUAL ARRANGEMENTS

For many years, the CIA and other federal agencies involved in intelligence, defense, and foreign policy matters have required their employees to sign secrecy agreements promising not to divulge classified information and not to publish any information about their work, classified or unclassified, without prior government approval. These provisions, which bind the employees after they have left the government, are legally enforceable in the courts like any other contract. In a series of cases beginning in 1972, the courts have ruled that these secrecy provisions do not offend the first amendment. The government may thus use them to seek restraining orders against publication of classified information and to seize the profits generated by works published without prepublication review by the government, regardless of whether classified information is involved.

The watershed case with respect to these contractual arrangements is *United States v. Marchetti*. Victor Marchetti worked for the CIA for fourteen years before resigning in 1969. He then embarked on a career as a writer, and his published work reflected his dissatisfaction with some CIA policies. In March 1972 he submitted an article about his CIA experiences to *Esquire* magazine and six other publications. Learning about the article, the CIA filed suit against Marchetti to halt its publication, claiming that he intended to violate his agreement not to disclose classified information. A federal judge in Virginia granted an injunction barring publication, and the U.S. Court of Appeals for the Fourth Circuit—the same court that later decided *Morison*—affirmed. In brushing aside Marchetti's contention that the trial judge's order enforcing this agreement was an unconstitutional prior restraint, the Fourth Circuit concluded that the former agent had given up his right to publish any classified information. The U.S. Supreme Court refused to review the decision.

Marchetti was subsequently involved in another case dealing with security agreements, *Alfred A. Knopf, Inc. v. Colby* (1975). The dispute arose when Marchetti and John Marks, a former state department employee who had also signed a secrecy agreement, submitted to the CIA their manuscript for a book entitled *The CIA and the Cult of Intelligence*. When the agency demanded that about twenty percent of the manuscript be cut because it contained classified information, the two authors and their publisher, Alfred A. Knopf, brought suit. Negotiations prior to trial reduced the number of deletions substantially, and the judge—who had also tried the *Marchetti* case—ruled that only twenty-six items could be censored. Though the Fourth Circuit sent the case back to the trial court for further proceedings, it reaffirmed the basic principle of *Marchetti*: by signing a secrecy agreement, a government employee "effectively relinquishe[s] his First Amendment rights" with respect to "classified information . . . acquired during the course of his employment."

Elaborating on the earlier case, the court also ruled that a former employee may not divulge classified information that is in the public domain "unless there has been official disclosure of it." The court reasoned that even though the information had previously turned up in print through "leaks" or otherwise, its republication by former employees who had access to sensitive data would lend it a particular credence. In addition, the court gave the government an almost completely free hand in determining whether the information had been properly classified. According to the court, "any significant intelligence operations" are classifiable, and the "presumption of regularity in the performance by a public official of his public duty" requires the courts to presume that information properly classifiable was in fact classified. In short, the courts will not second-guess an agency's determination that the information in question is classified. Again, the U.S. Supreme Court denied review. The Marchetti–Marks book was ultimately published with only a handful of deletions, the CIA having dropped its objections to most of the remaining twenty-six items.

A case involving employee secrecy agreements finally reached the Supreme Court in 1980. Frank Snepp, a former CIA agent who had signed such a contract, published a book, *Decent Interval*, without obtaining prior CIA approval. Though the book was highly critical of CIA activities in Vietnam, it contained no classified information. Because Snepp surreptitiously arranged to have the book published without the agency's knowledge, the CIA was unable to obtain a court order barring publication, as it had done in the *Marchetti* case. Instead, the agency sued Snepp for breach of contract and sought, as damages, the profits that the author had made from the book. The trial court agreed with the CIA and ordered that the author's profits—which exceeded $100,000—be turned over to the government and that he be enjoined from future publications without CIA approval. The U.S. Court of Appeals for the Fourth Circuit, however, concluded that Snepp's obligations extended only to classified information. In *Snepp v. United States* the Supreme Court reinstated the trial court's order, ruling that Snepp had violated his agreement to obtain prepublication review of *all* information about the CIA, whether classified or not. The decision was financially disastrous for Snepp.

The Supreme Court's brief opinion in the case, which was decided without full briefing and oral argument, discussed the first amendment only in a short footnote:

> [T]his Court's cases make clear that—even in the absense of an express agreement—the CIA could have acted to protect substantial government interests by imposing reasonable restrictions on employee activities that in other contexts might be protected by the First Amendment. Government has a compelling interest in protecting both the secrecy of information important to our national security and the appearance of confidentiality so essential to the effective operation of our foreign intelligence service. The agreement that Snepp signed is a reasonable means for protecting this vital interest.

Justice John Paul Stevens, joined by Justices Brennan and Marshall, filed a strong dissenting opinion criticizing the majority for creating a "drastic new remedy . . . to enforce a species of prior restraint on a citizen's right to criticize government." Justice Stevens emphasized that Snepp had not breached his contractual duty to protect classified information, but only his obligation to obtain prepublication review. Under those circumstances, Justice Stevens said, an order allowing the government to seize Snepp's profits was unwarranted. "[I]t is difficult to believe that the publication of a book like Snepp's, which does not reveal classified information, has significantly weakened the [CIA's] position."

RESTRICTIONS ON MILITARY COVERAGE

In the early morning hours of October 25, 1985, United States military forces invaded Grenada, a tiny island nation in the Caribbean. At 9 A.M. that morning,

President Ronald Reagan announced the invasion at a press conference, describing it as a measure to protect American citizens in Grenada and to assist in stabilizing the situation in that Marxist country. News media representatives had not been not permitted to accompany the invasion forces and were denied all access to the island for forty-eight hours. Reporters who managed to reach Grenada through their own devices were not permitted to transmit stories back to the United States. In short, the Reagan Administration imposed a total news blackout, and the only information available to the public about the invasion came from official government sources. Press pools were allowed on the island on October 27, but unlimited access was not permitted until November 7.

These restrictions breached a long tradition of media access to U.S. military operations; in fact, the press has reported from war zones since the American revolution, covering such important events as the blockade of Cuba during the Spanish-American War, the D-Day invasion in World War II, and the fall of Saigon during the war in Vietnam. However, press access has never been unlimited. During the Civil War, for example, generals on both sides of the conflict banished correspondents from time to time, and some completely excluded the press from their camps. Moreover, telegraph lines were under military control, and journalists thus had limited ability to transmit stories without government censorship. In World Wars I and II, "accredited" reporters were allowed to accompany troops into battle, but rigorous censorship was imposed. Without accreditation, journalists were not permitted in war zones, and one of the conditions of accreditation was a requirement to submit all stories to military censors. In Vietnam, however, reporters were given almost free rein, and censorship was virtually nonexistent.

To what extent are restrictions on the reporting of military operations constitutional? Larry Flynt, publisher of *Hustler* magazine, filed suit the day after the Grenada invasion, arguing that the initial ban on press coverage violated the first amendment. In *Flynt v. Weinberger* (1984), Federal Judge Oliver Gasch dismissed the case as moot, pointing out that the Grenada campaign had ended and that Flynt's complaint was directed only at the military's action in connection with that particular operation. However, he expressed "doubts" that Flynt's constitutional rights had been violated and stated that he was not prepared to enter an injunction barring the government from imposing news blackouts. Such an order, Judge Gasch noted, "would limit the range of options available to the commanders in the field in the future, possibly jeopardizing the success of military operations and the lives of military personnel and thereby gravely damaging the national interest." The U.S. Court of Appeals for the District of Columbia Circuit agreed that the case was moot but vacated Judge Gasch's opinion because of his comments as to the merits of the dispute.

No other cases directly deal with censorship imposed on reporters who cover military activities or with access to those operations. However, the principles discussed previously in this chapter suggest that restrictions of both types are constitutionally permissible. With respect to censorship, one need only recall Chief Justice Hughes' comment in *Near v. Minnesota* that "no one would question but that a government might prevent . . . the publication of sailing dates of transports or the number and location of troops." Moreover, the accreditation arrangements employed during the First and Second World Wars would also withstand constitutional scrutiny. As noted above, accreditation that would permit access to the front lines and other combat areas could be obtained only if correspondents agreed to submit their stories to military censors for prepublication review. These agreements are analogous to the CIA employment contracts upheld against first amendment challenges in *Marchetti* and *Snepp*.

With respect to the access question raised but not resolved in *Flynt*, it is doubtful that the first amendment right of access to criminal proceedings recognized in *Richmond Newspapers, Inc. v. Virginia* (1980) and subsequent decisions can be stretched to cover military operations. Unlike criminal trials, military campaigns have not traditionally been open to the public. Although members of the news media have been allowed to accompany the troops, their reports were subject to review by military commanders. Moreover, the Supreme Court has also ruled that a military base is not a "public forum" for first amendment purposes, pointing out in *Greer v. Spock* (1976) that a commanding officer at such a facility has the power "to exclude civilians from his area of command." If, as the Supreme Court held in *Pell v. Procunier* (1974) and *Houchins v. KQED, Inc.* (1978), there is no first amendment right of access to prisons and jails, there is probably no right of access to battlefields and other military operations.

Even if a first amendment right of access is recognized, that right is not absolute and may be restricted if there is a compelling governmental interest that outweighs access. As the cases surveyed throughout this chapter demonstrate, national security has long been considered such a countervailing interest. If a prior restraint can be justified in the name of national security, surely a restriction on press access also passes muster. As Paul Cassell observed in an important article in the *Georgetown Law Journal*:

> Even the strongest partisans of a right of access concede that the right is limited by national security concerns. And there is general agreement that there is no constitutional right of access to "lightning fast in-and-out military engagements such as the Iranian rescue mission, or access to extended covert action which is not publicly known." The invasion of Grenada may well have been such an operation, as several defenders of the press exclusion argued later. Also, the Pentagon pointed to the possibility of security breaches in support of its decision not to inform the press before the operation. Once the invasion began, the Pentagon argued, difficulties in conducting the operation made it impossible to bring the press to the island. While some of these arguments may have amounted to post hoc rationalizations, together they may well have reached the level of compelling interest.

Mr. Cassell also noted that a court deciding a case in which the media had been denied access would most likely give great deference to the reasons offered by the military for excluding the press. "In sum," he concluded, "a right of access to military operations is not required by the current right of access cases, and extension of those cases to cover military operations is improbable."

Following vigorous press objections to the news blackout imposed during the Grenada invasion, the Department of Defense appointed a panel headed by retired Major General Winant Sidle to recommend guidelines for media access to military operations. Taking the position that "it is essential that the U.S. news media cover U.S. military operations to the maximum degree possible consistent with mission security and the safety of U.S. forces," the panel recommended that "pool" reporters be afforded access to operations such as the Grenada invasion when unlimited access by journalists would not be feasible. The panel recognized, however, that pool reporters would not necessarily be allowed to accompany the "first wave" of troops in all situations. In response to the recommendations, the Defense Department issued regulations in late 1984 providing for pool coverage when operational considerations would prevent unlimited press access. The pool consists of two wire service reporters, four television reporters, a television camerman and a sound technician, a newspaper reporter, a magazine writer, and a still photographer. The Pentagon determines which news organizations are to be represented in the pool, and the organizations themselves select the particular journalists who will participate. In addition, the guidelines provide that the military may withhold any pool dispatches that contain "sensitive" information that might jeopardize the mission or human lives.

The pool arrangement has been used several times; for example, reporters aboard a Navy aircraft carrier covered the 1986 U.S. air attack on Libya, and journalists have accompanied American ships escorting oil tankers in the Persian Gulf. The arrangement has not always been satisfactory to the news media, however. During the summer of 1987, pool reporters on a Navy escort mission complained that the Pentagon withheld their stories for thirty-six to forty-eight hours, apparently fearing that earlier release would threaten the operation. Journalists who participated in another pool in the Persian Gulf criticized Navy officials for censoring information that, while potentially embarrassing, would not have endangered the mission. In another incident, reporters were frustrated because the Navy refused to permit the photographing of two Iranian boats disabled by U.S. helicopters. Despite these problems, some access is probably better than none at all, and for that reason most news organizations have accepted the restrictions.

PROBLEMS

1. On March 11, 1983, President Ronald Reagan issued National Security Decision Directive 84, an order aimed at "safeguard[ing] against unlawful disclosures of classified information." *See* 9 Media L. Rptr. 1759 (1983). This order directed all executive branch agencies to adopt policies requiring that federal employees with authorized access to classified information sign a nondisclosure agreement as a condition of access and that federal employees with access to "sensitive compartmentalized information"—a category of classified information regarding intelligence sources and methods—sign a similar nondisclosure agreement that also included a provision for prepublication review. Opposition in Congress led to a delay in implementation of the order, but the Information Security Oversight Office, the Director of the Central Intelligence Agency, and the Department of Defense eventually prepared various forms carrying out the directive.

   One such form embodied a nondisclosure agreement obligating employees not to reveal, without authorization, information that had been classified or was "classifiable" under the standards set forth in Executive Order No. 12356, discussed in Chapter 5 in connection with Freedom of Information Act's national security exemption. A second form contained a prepublication review agreement requiring employees who had access to "sensitive compartmentalized information" to submit for such review any manuscript (including works of fiction) containing, purporting to contain, or relating to such information. Are these requirements consistent with the first amendment? Does it matter that they reach not only classified information, but also any material that is "classifiable"? Is it relevant that they cover more than 100,000 federal workers and thus sweep more broadly than the agreements in *Snepp* and *Marchetti*, which applied only to CIA employees? *See*

National Federation of Federal Employees v. United States, 695 F. Supp. 1196 (D.D.C. 1988).

Congress subsequently included in appropriations bills for fiscal years 1988 and 1989 provisions proscribing the use of any nondisclosure form that reached "classifiable" information. The statutory language also prohibited any prepublication review requirement that obstructed "the rights of any individual to petition or communicate with Members of Congress in a secure manner as provided by the rules and procedures of the Congress." *See* Pub. L. No. 100-202, 101 Stat. 1329, 1329-432 (December 22, 1987); Pub. L. No. 100-440, 102 Stat. 1721, 1756 (September 2, 1988). The nondisclosure forms no longer use the term "classifiable" but state that the agreement covers both classified material and unclassified information "in the process of a classification determination." *See generally American Foreign Service Association v. Garfinkel,* 109 S.Ct. 1693 (1989). Does this change make any difference with respect to your first amendment analysis?

2. In September 1986, two National Guard fighter planes collided and crashed in New York, killing one of the pilots and injuring the other. Before the Air Force could seal off the crash site, a newspaper reporter hiked into the wooded area and shot two rolls of film of the wreckage. As he left the area, a state law enforcement officer stopped him and confiscated his film, later turning it over to the Air Force officials. After developing the film and concluding that "no compromise of security is evident in any of the pictures," the Air Force returned the negatives to the reporter's newspaper. Did seizure of the film violate the first amendment? Can the Air Force constitutionally ban media access to the site of the crash of one of its planes? Would your answer be different if a secret experimental aircraft, such as the Stealth bomber, were involved? *See* "Air Crash Coverage Hampered," *The News Media and the Law* (Winter 1987), p. 2.

3. One of the photographs leaked by Samuel Morison to *Jane's Defence Weekly* was published by the *Washington Post*. Could the federal government have prosecuted the *Post* under the same statutes that it used to convict Morison? Section 793(e) of the Espionage Act makes it a crime for one not authorized to possess national security information to willfully communicate, deliver, or transmit it. Was this statute designed to reach publication of such information by the news media? Recall that Judge Warren in *The Progressive* case concluded that similar language in the Atomic Energy Act covered the magazine's publication of the H-bomb story. *But see New York Times Co. v. United States*, 403 U.S. 713, 721-23 (1971)(Douglas, J., concurring)(arguing that the word "communicates" in Section 793(e) does not extend to publication). The press has been threatened with prosecution under other espionage statutes. *See* "Questions of National Security," *Time* (June 2, 1986), p. 67.

4. In 1986, Colombian journalist Patricia Lara came to the United States under a visa to attend an awards ceremony at Columbia University in New York City. The State Department detained her for five days at a federal prison, announced that her visa had been issued erroneously, and deported her to Colombia without giving an explanation. Later, a State Department spokesman claimed that Ms. Lara was a member of a violent leftist organization dedicated to overthrowing the Colombian government and an "active liaison" between that group and the Cuban secret police. *See* "INS Detains Latin Writers, Expels One; Confiscates Belgian's Papers at Airport," *The News Media and the Law* (Winter 1987), p. 4. Is such action against foreign journalists constitutional? *See Kleindienst v. Mandel*, 408 U.S. 753 (1972).

5. As discussed in Chapter 6, the press and public have a qualified first amendment right to attend criminal trials and related proceedings. To what extent do national security con-

cerns outweigh this right of access? For example, may a trial judge close a hearing at which an accused spy is to plead guilty and be sentenced? May the judge order that various documents relating to the case be sealed? *See In re Washington Post Co.*, 807 F.2d 383 (4th Cir. 1986); *United States v. Grunden*, 2 M.J. 116 (C.M.A. 1977).

Under the Classified Information Procedures Act, 18 U.S.C. app. §§ 1–16, a federal court may hold a closed pretrial hearing to determine whether classified information is to be admitted into evidence at trial. Employed in connection with the "Iran-Contra" trial of Col. Oliver North and in several recent espionage cases, the act enables a trial judge to rule on questions of admissibility of classified information before the introduction of that material in open court. Upon a determination that the material is admissible, the prosecution may request the use of a stipulation of facts or a summary of information as a substitute for the specific classified materials. If the substitute is inadequate to provide the accused a fair opportunity to mount a defense and the prosecution objects to disclosure of the classified information, the trial court shall dismiss the charges or "order such action . . . as the court determines is appropriate." *See generally* Note, "Government Secrets, Fair Trials, and the Classified Information Procedures Act," 98 *Yale Law Journal* 427 (1988).

May a judge hold a closed pretrial hearing under the act without first making the specific findings required by *Richmond Newspapers* and its progeny? Instead of dismissing the charges, could a judge, pursuant to the "appropriate order" provision, require that the trial itself, or a portion thereof, be closed? That classified documents introduced into evidence be sealed? *See In re Washington Post Co., supra.*

6. Under the so-called "Landsat Act," 15 U.S.C. §§ 4201 *et seq.*, a commercial operator of a land remote-sensing satellite must obtain a license from the Department of Transportation to launch the satellite and another from the Commerce Department to operate it. The Commerce Department has delegated licensing authority to the National Oceanographic and Atmospheric Administration (NOAA). Two such commercial satellite systems are in operation, and the three television networks have used their "photographs" in covering such events as the Iran–Iraq war and the nuclear accident at Chernobyl. To what extent may NOAA restrict the use of images from these satellites in the name of national security? *See* 15 C.F.R. § 960 (1988)(NOAA licensing regulations); "Satellite Image Rules Offered by Agencies," *The News Media and the Law* (Fall 1987), p. 16.

CHAPTER
9
MORALITY AND PUBLIC SAFETY

Herceg v. Hustler Magazine, Inc.,
814 F.2d 1017 (5th Cir. 1987).

Before RUBIN, JOHNSON, and JONES, Circuit Judges.

ALVIN B. RUBIN, Circuit Judge:

An adolescent read a magazine article that prompted him to commit an act that proved fatal. The issue is whether the publisher of the magazine may be held liable for civil damages.

I.

In its August 1981 issue, as part of a series about the pleasures—and dangers—of unusual and taboo sexual practices, *Hustler Magazine* printed "Orgasm of Death," an article discussing the practice of autoerotic asphyxia. This practice entails masturbation while "hanging" oneself in order to temporarily cut off the blood supply to the brain at the moment of orgasm. The article included

details about how the act is performed and the kind of physical pleasure those who engage in it seek to achieve. The heading identified "Orgasm of Death" as part of a series on "Sexplay," discussions of "sexual pleasures [that] have remained hidden for too long behind the doors of fear, ignorance, inexperience and hypocrisy" and are presented "to increase [readers'] sexual knowledge, to lessen [their] inhibitions and—ultimately—to make [them] better lover[s]."

An editor's note, positioned on the page so that it is likely to be the first text the reader will read, states: "Hustler emphasizes the often-fatal dangers of the practice of 'autoerotic asphyxia,' and recommends that readers seeking unique forms of sexual release DO NOT ATTEMPT this method. The facts are presented here solely for an educational purpose."

The article begins by presenting a vivid description of the tragic results the practice may create. It describes the death of one victim and discusses research indicating that such deaths are alarmingly common: as many as 1,000 United States teenagers die in this manner each year. Although it describes the sexual "high" and "thrill" those who engage in the practice seek to achieve, the article repeatedly warns that the procedure is "neither healthy nor harmless," "it is a serious—and often-fatal—mistake to believe that asphyxia can be controlled," and "beyond a doubt . . . auto-asphyxiation is one form of sex play you can try only if you're anxious to wind up in cold storage, with a coroner's tag on your big toe." The two-page article warns readers at least ten different times that the practice is dangerous, self-destructive and deadly. It states that persons who successfully perform the technique can achieve intense physical pleasure, but the attendant risk is that a person may lose consciousness and die of strangulation.

Tragically, a copy of this issue of *Hustler* came into the possession of Troy D., a fourteen-year-old adolescent, who read the article and attempted the practice. The next morning, Troy's nude body was found, hanging by its neck in the closet, by one of Troy's closest friends, Andy V. A copy of *Hustler Magazine*, opened to the article about the "Orgasm of Death," was found near his feet.

* * * Troy's mother, Diane Herceg, and Andy V. sued *Hustler* to recover damages for emotional and psychological harms they suffered as a result of Troy's death and for [punitive] damages. [Although the plaintiffs alleged that *Hustler* was responsible for Troy's death on various theories, including negligence, products liability, dangerous instrumentality, and attractive nuisance, the case was tried on an "incitement" theory (i.e., that Troy had read the article and was incited by it to perform the act that resulted in his death). The trial judge dismissed the claims based on the other theories.]

* * * Expert witnesses testified on behalf of both the plaintiffs and the defendant about the psychological implications of Troy's behavior and whether the magazine article implicitly advocated the practice it described or was likely to incite readers to attempt the procedure. The jury returned a verdict in favor of the plaintiffs, awarding Diane Herceg $69,000 in actual damages and $100,000 [punitive] damages and awarding Andy V. $3,000 for the pain and mental suffering he endured as the bystander who discovered Troy's body and $10,000 [punitive] damages. * * * *Hustler* appeals, but the plaintiffs do not cross-appeal or raise any issue concerning the correctness of the district court order dismissing their other claims.

II.

* * * The Supreme Court has recognized that some types of speech are excluded from, or entitled only to narrowed constitutional protection. Freedom of speech does not protect obscene materials, child pornography, fighting words, incitement to imminent lawless activity, and purposefully made or recklessly-made false statements of fact such as libel, defamation, or fraud. Whatever the problems created in attempting to categorize speech in such fashion, the *Hustler* article fits none of them.

Even types of speech protected generally by the first amendment may be subject to government regulation. Freedom of speech is not an absolute. If the state interest is compelling and the means of regulation narrowly tailored to accomplish a proper state purpose, regulation of expression is not forbidden by the first amendment. The extent of the danger created by a publication therefore is not immaterial in determining the state's power to penalize that publication for harm that ensues, but first amendment protection is not eliminated simply because publication of an idea creates a potential hazard. Whether the *Hustler* article, therefore, placed a dangerous idea into Troy's head is but one factor in determining whether the state may impose damages for that consequence. Against the important social goal of protecting the lives of adolescents like Troy, the Constitution requires us to balance more than *Hustler*'s right to publish the particular article, subject to the possibility of civil liability should harm ensue, but also the danger than unclear or diminished standards of first amendment protection may both inhibit the expression of protected ideas by other speakers and constrict the right of the public to receive those ideas.

While the plaintiffs alleged several different bases of liability . . . , the issue tried was the imposition of liability on the basis of incitement, and that is the sole basis for the verdict. The question before us therefore is whether, as a matter of law, the language of "Orgasm of Death" may be defined as incitement for purposes of removing that speech from the purview of first amendment protection. If not, the judgment entered on the jury verdict cannot be affirmed even if it is conceivable that, had the case been tried on some other ground, the jury might have reached the same verdict.

III.

* * * Although we are doubtful that a magazine article that is no more direct than "Orgasm of Death" can ever constitute an incitement in the sense in which the Supreme Court—in cases we discuss below—has employed that term to identify unprotected speech the states may punish without violating the first amendment, we first analyze the evidence on the theory that it might satisfy doctrinal tests relating to incitement, for that was the theory under which the case was tried and submitted. Substituting our judgment for the jury's, as we must, we hold that liability cannot be imposed on *Hustler* on the basis that the article was an incitement to attempt a potentially fatal act without impermissibly infringing upon freedom of speech.

The word incitement, like many of the words in our complex language, can carry different meanings. It is properly used to refer to encouragement of conduct that might harm the public such as the violation of law or the use of force. But when the word is used in that context, the state may not punish such an inducement unless the speech involved is, as the Supreme Court held in *Brandenburg v. Ohio* [1969], "directed to inciting or producing *imminent* lawless action and . . . *likely* to incite or produce such action."

Brandenburg, a Ku Klux Klan leader garbed in Klan regalia, had delivered a speech threatening that, "if our President, our Congress, our Supreme Court, continues to suppress the white, caucasian race, it is possible that there might have to be some revengence [sic] taken." He challenged his conviction under an Ohio statute that punished "advocacy of the duty, necessity, or propriety of crime, sabotage, violence, or unlawful methods of terrorism as a means of accomplishing industrial or political reform." The Supreme Court reversed his conviction because neither the statute nor the state court's jury instruction distinguished between advocacy and incitement to imminent lawless action, and only the latter might constitutionally be forbidden.

Hustler argues that *Brandenburg* provides the controlling principle, and the plaintiffs assume that it may. If that were so, it would be necessary for the plaintiffs to have proved that:

1. Autoerotic asphyxiation is a lawless act.
2. *Hustler* advocated this act.
3. *Hustler's* publication went even beyond "mere advocacy" and amounted to incitement.
4. The incitement was directed to imminent action.

The *Brandenburg* focus is repeated in subsequent Supreme Court decisions. * * * The crucial element to lowering the first amendment shield is the imminence of the threatened evil. In [*Hess v. Indiana* (1973)], the Court was faced with the question of whether an antiwar demonstrator could be punished under Indiana's disorderly conduct statute for loudly shouting, "We'll take the fucking street later," as police attempted to move the crowd of demonstrators off the street so that vehicles could pass. The Court noted that, viewed most favorably to the speaker, "the statement could be taken as counsel for moderation" and, at worst, as "advocacy of illegal action at some indefinite future time.'' The Court reasoned that, ''[s]ince the uncontroverted evidence showed that Hess' statement was not directed to any person or group of persons, it cannot be said that he was advocating, in the normal sense, any action. And since there was no evidence or rational inference from the import of the language that his words were intended to produce, and likely would produce, *imminent* disorder, those words could not be punished . . . on the ground that they had a 'tendency to lead to violence.' ''

We need not decide whether Texas law made autoerotic asphyxiation illegal or whether *Brandenburg* is restricted to the advocacy of criminal conduct. Even if the article paints in glowing terms the pleasures supposedly achieved by the practice it describes, as the plaintiffs contend, no reading of it can make its content advocacy, let alone incitement to engage in the practice.

Herceg and Andy V. complain that the article provides unnecessary detail about how autoerotic asphyxiation is accomplished. The detail is adapted from an article published by a psychiatrist in the *Journal of Child Psychiatry*. Although it is conceivable that, in some instances, the amount of detail contained in challenged speech may be relevant in determining whether incitement exists, the detail in ''Orgasm of Death'' is not enough to permit breach of the first amendment. The manner of engaging in autoerotic asphyxiation apparently is not complicated. To understand what the terms means is to know roughly how to accomplish it. Furthermore, the article is laden with detail about all facets of the practice, including the physiology of how it produces a threat to life and the seriousness of the danger of harm. * * *

IV.

Herceg and Andy V. contend that, while the first amendment might prevent the state from punishing publication of such articles as criminal, it does not foreclose imposing civil liability. In *New York Times Co. v. Sullivan* [1964], the Supreme Court held, ''what a State may not constitutionally bring about by means of a criminal statute is likewise beyond the reach of its civil law of libel,'' because the fear of civil liability might be ''markedly more inhibiting than the fear of prosecution under a criminal statute.'' The same rationale forbids the state to impose damages for publication of ''Orgasm of Death'' if it could not constitutionally make the publication of that article a crime.

One state supreme court decision, however, may be read to imply that the state may impose liability in such a situation. In *Weirum v. RKO General, Inc.* [1975], the Supreme Court of California held that a radio station catering primarily to teenagers could be held liable for wrongful death damages arising from an accident caused when two youths who listened to a promotional broadcast engaged in a street race in order to be the first to reach the site at which the station had announced prize money would be given away. Most of the opinion dealt with whether the radio station owed a duty of care to the killed non-listener, and the first amendment defense was summarily rejected because ''[t]he First Amendment does not sanction the infliction of physical injury merely because achieved by word, rather than act.''

* * * Because the speech challenged was merely a promotional device to encourage listeners to continue listening to the radio station, it may have been entitled only to limited first amendment protection. The broadcast announcements included light-hearted warnings that listeners should ''get your kids out of the street'' because of the reckless driving that the annoucement might incite, and no warning of any kind was given to urge listeners who sought to win the prizes to use discretion in driving. In contrast, the *Hustler* article, while published in a magazine published for profit, was not an effort to achieve a commercial result and, at least in the explicit meaning of the words employed, attempts to dissuade its readers from conducting the dangerous activity it describes.

V.

In the alternative, Herceg and Andy suggest that a less stringent standard than the *Brandenburg* test be applied in cases involving non-political speech that has actually produced harm. Although political speech is at "the core of the First Amendment," the Supreme Court generally has not attempted to differentiate between different categories of protected speech for the purposes of deciding how much constitutional protection is required. Such an endeavor would not only be hopelessly complicated but would raise substantial concern that the worthiness of speech might be judged by majoritarian notions of political and social propriety and morality. If the shield of the first amendment can be eliminated by proving after publication that an article discussing a dangerous idea negligently helped bring about a real injury simply because the idea can be identified as "bad," all free speech becomes threatened. An article discussing the nature and danger of "crack" usage—or of hanggliding—might lead to liability just as easily. As is made clear in the Supreme Court's decision in *Hess*, the "tendency to lead to violence" is not enough. Mere negligence, therefore, cannot form the basis of liability under the incitement doctrine any more than it can under libel doctrine.

VI.

Finally, even if this court were to determine that the plaintiffs may establish a cause of action under a theory of negligence, that theory could not form the basis of affirming the decision below. * * * This case . . . was not tried on a negligence theory. There are, therefore, no jury findings on the issue of negligence, and this court may not infer what those findings would have been had the issue been presented. The trial was conducted on an incitement theory after the plaintiffs' various other claims were dismissed. [*Hustler*] had prepared its defense accordingly. Had a negligence claim remained, *Hustler* may have settled out of court or purused alternative defense strategies. To allow *Hustler*'s victory at the summary judgment phase of trial to become a trap precluding it from preparing a negligence defense would be a miscarriage of justice.

VII.

Hustler's final challenge to the judgment below is to the award granted Andy V. as compensation for suffering he endured as a bystander. . . . Because we have held that no liability can attach to *Hustler*'s publication of "Orgasm of Death" under [the] incitement theory, we need not decide whether Andy V. would have been entitled to recover damages under Texas tort law.

For the reasons stated above, the judgment of the district court is REVERSED.

EDITH H. JONES, Circuit Judge, concurring and dissenting:

I concur in the result in this case only because I am persuaded that plaintiffs had an obligation to cross-appeal the court's dismissal of their claims based on negligence, attractive nuisance, and strict liability or dangerous instrumentality. The majority correctly reason that *Hustler* should have had an opportunity to prepare a defense specifically tailored against any of these theories. Although I believe a tort claim is here defensible, the undeniable novelty of plaintiff's "incitement" theory does not permit us fairly to support the judgment below.

What disturbs me to the point of despair is the majority's broad reasoning which appears to foreclose the possibility that any state might choose to temper the excesses of the pornography business by imposing civil liability for harms it directly causes. Consonant with the first amendment, the state can protect its citizens against the moral evil of obscenity, the threat of civil disorder or injury posed by lawless mobs and fighting words, and the damage to reputation from libel or defamation, to say nothing of the myriad dangers lurking in "commercial speech." Why cannot the state fashion a remedy to protect its children's lives when they are endangered by suicidal pornography? To deny this possibility, I believe, is to degrade the free market of ideas to a level with the black market for heroin. Despite the grand flourishes of rhetoric in many first amendment decisions concerning the sancity of "dangerous" ideas, no federal court has held that death is a legitimate price to pay for freedom of speech.

In less emotional terms, I believe the majority has critically erred in its analysis of this case under existing first amendment law. The majority decide at the outset that *Hustler*'s "Orgasm of Death" does not embody child pornography, fighting words, incitement to lawless conduct, libel, defamation or fraud, or obscenity, all of which categories of speech are entirely unprotected by the first amendment. Nor do they find in the article "an effort to achieve a commercial result," which would afford it modified first amendment protection. Comforted by the inapplicability of these labels, they then accord this article full first amendment protection, holding that in the balance struck between society's interest in Troy's life and the chilling effect on the "right of the public to receive . . . ideas," Troy loses. Any effort to find a happier medium, they conclude, would not only be hopelessly complicated but would raise substantial concerns that the worthiness of speech might be judged by "majoritarian notions of political and social propriety and morality." I agree that "Orgasm of Death" does not conveniently match the current categories of speech defined for first amendment purposes. Limiting its constitutional protection does not, however, disserve any of these categories and is more appropriate to furthering the "majoritarian" notion of protecting the sancity of human life. Finally, the "slippery slope" argument that if *Hustler* is held liable here, *Ladies Home Journal* or the publisher of an article on hang-gliding will next be a casualty of philistine justice simply proves too much: *This* case is not a difficult one in which to vindicate Troy's loss of life.

I

Proper analysis must begin with an examination of *Hustler* generally and this article in particular. *Hustler* is not a bona fide competitor in the "marketplace of ideas." It is largely pornographic, whether or not technically obscene. One need not be male to recognize that the principal function of this magazine is to create sexual arousal. Consumers of this material so partake for its physical effects much as they would use tobacco, alcohol or drugs for their effects. By definition, pornography's appeal is therefore noncognitive and unrelated to, in fact exactly the opposite of, the transmission of ideas.

Not only is *Hustler*'s appeal noncognitive, but the magazine derives its profit from that fact. If *Hustler* stopped being pornographic, its readership would vanish.

According to the trial court record, pornography appeals to pubescent males. Moreover, although sold in the "adults only" section of newsstands, a significant portion of its readers are adolescent. *Hustler* knows this. Such readers are particularly vulnerable to thrillseeking, recklessness, and mimickry. *Hustler* should know this. *Hustler* should understand that to such a mentality the warnings "no" or "caution" may be treated as invitations rather than taboos.

"Orgasm of Death" provides a detailed description of how to accomplish autoerotic asphyxiation. * * * The warnings and cautionary comments in the article could be seen by a jury to conflict with both the explicit and subliminal message of *Hustler*, which is to tear down custom, explode myths and banish taboos about sexual matters. The article trades on the symbiotic connection between sex and violence. In sum, as *Hustler* knew, the article is dangerously explicit, lethal, and likely to be distributed to those members of society who are most vulnerable to its message. "Orgasm of Death," in the circumstances of its publication and dissemination, is not unlike a dangerous nuisance or a stick of dynamite in the hands of a child. *Hustler*'s publication of this particular article bears the seeds of tort liability although, as I shall explain, the theory on which the case was tried is incorrect.

II.

First amendment analysis is an exercise in line-drawing between the legitimate interests of society to regulate itself and the paramount necessity of encouraging the robust and uninhibited flow of debate which is the life-blood of government by the people. That some of the lines are blurred or irregular does not, however, prove the majority's proposition that it would be hopelessly complicated to delineate between protected and unprotected speech in this case. * * * [I]n novel cases like this one, the reasons for protecting speech under the first amendment must be closely examined to properly evaluate *Hustler*'s claim to unlimited constitutional protection.

The Supreme Court recently engaged in the balancing appropriate to a novel first amendment case in *Dun & Bradstreet, Inc. v. Greenmoss Builders, Inc.* (1985). The Court concluded that the victim of a negligently erroneous credit report might recover presumed and punitive damages from the publisher, in the absence of actual damages. In so doing, it evaluated the interest sought to be protected by the state against the level of first amendment interest embodied in the communication at issue.

The state's "strong and legitimate" interest in protecting one's reputation was at issue in *Gertz v. Robert Welch, Inc.* [1974]: "the individual's right to the protection of his own good name 'reflects no more than our basic concept of the essential dignity and worth of every human being—a concept at the root of any decent system of ordered liberty. The protection of private personality, *like the protection of life itself*, is left primarily to the individual States under the Ninth and Tenth Amendments. . . .'" (emphasis added). The interest in protecting life is recognized specifically for first amendment purposes and, an-

alytically, can be no less important that the interest in reputation. The state's interest in this case is to protect the lives of adolescents who might be encouraged by pornographic publications and specifically instructed how to attempt life-threatening activities. * * *

Permitting recovery of damages in defamation cases offers an analogous framework. Balanced against the state interest, the Court held in *Dun & Bradstreet* that the first amendment interest at stake was less important than the one weighed in *Gertz*. While *Gertz* involved a libelous publication on a matter of public concern, the false information in *Dun & Bradstreet* was contained in a credit report distributed to merchants. The Court employed the test of content, form and context . . . to analyze whether the credit report was a matter of "public concern." Speech on matters of "private concern," the Court found, while not wholly unprotected, is not as substantial relative to important state interests. Thus, the credit report was prepared solely for the individual interest of the speaker and a specific business, it was false and clearly damaging, and, like advertising, it represents a form of speech unlikely to be deterred by incidental state regulation: The credit report involved a matter of "private concern."

Measured by this standard, both *Hustler* in general and "Orgasm of Death" in particular deserve only limited first amendment protection. *Hustler* is a profitable commercial enterprise trading on its prurient appeal to a small portion of the population. It deliberately borders on technical obscenity, which would be wholly unprotected, to achieve its purposes, and its appeal is not based on cognitive or intellectual appreciation. Because of the solely commercial and pandering nature of the magazine, neither *Hustler* nor any other pornographic publication is likely to be deterred by incidental state regulation. No sensitive first amendment genius is required to see that, as the Court concluded in *Dun & Bradstreet*, "[t]here is simply no credible argument that this type of [speech] requires special protection to insure that 'debate on public issues

[will] be uninhibited, robust, and wide-open.' ''

To place *Hustler* effectively on a par with *Dun & Bradstreet*'s ''private speech'' or with commercial speech, for purposes of permitting tort lawsuits against it hardly portends the end of participatory democracy, as some might contend. First, any given issue of *Hustler* may be found legally obscene and therefore entitled to no first amendment protection. Second, tort liability would result after-the-fact, not as a prior restraint, and would be based on harm directly caused by the publication at issue. Third, to the extent any chilling effect existed from the exposure to tort liability, this would, in my view, protect society from loss of life and limb, a legitimate, indeed compelling, state interest. Fourth, obscenity has been widely regulated by prior restraints for over a century. * * * [I]ncreasing leniency on pornography in the past three decades has allowed pornography to flourish, but it does not seem to have corresponded with an increased quality of debate on ''public'' issues. These observations imply that pornography bears little connection to the core values of the first amendment and that political democracy has endured previously in the face of ''majoritarian notions of social propriety.''

Rendering accountable the more vicious excesses of pornography by allowing damage recovery for tort victims imposes on its purveyors a responsibility which is insurable, much like a manufacturer's responsibility to warn against careless use of its products. A tort remedy which compensates death or abuse of youthful victims clearly caused by a specific pornographic publication would be unlikely to ''chill'' the pornography industry any more than unfavorable zoning ordinances or the threat of obscenity prosecution has done. The reasonableness of allowing a tort remedy in cases like this is reinforced by the fact that only one lawsuit was filed in regard to ''Orgasm of Death.'' The analogy with regulations on commercial speech is not inappropriate: pornography should assume a lower value on the scale of constitutional protection; and the state regulation by means of tort recovery for

injury directly caused by pornography is appropriate when tailored to specific harm and not broader than necessary to accomplish its purpose.

The foregoing analysis immediately differentiates this case from *Brandenburg v. Ohio*, which addressed prior restraints on public advocacy of controversial political ideas. Placing *Hustler* on the same analytical plane with *Brandenburg* represents an unwarranted extension of that holding, which, unlike *Dun & Bradstreet* and the commercial speech cases, rests in the core values protected by the first amendment. Even *Brandenburg*, however, recognized that the state's regulatory interest legitimately extends to protecting the lives of its citizens from violence induced by speech. Moreover, *Brandenburg* is intertwined with the context of the speech as well as its content—advocacy of inciteful ideas would thus be differently regarded in a collection of speeches by Tom Paine than it is among a crowd of armed vigilantes who proceed to riot. The *Brandenburg* test, implicitly rejected by the majority, is simply inappropriate to define the limits of constitutional protection afforded in this case. Viewed in the overall context of first amendment jurisprudence, moreover, *Brandenburg* does not exclude the possibility of state regulation.

III.

Texas courts have never been called upon to assess a claim like this one. Since there is no cross-appeal, we should not speculate on the precise nature of the theory of liability a Texas court might accept, although negligence and attractive nuisance seem theoretically appropriate. Texas law supplies no reason to conclude, as the district court did, that *Brandenburg v. Ohio,* representing a federal constitutional limitation on a state's restraints on speech, could be turned into an affirmative theory of tort law. I believe this use of *Brandenburg* is wrong, insofar as it suggests that federal constitutional law rather than state law governs the first issue in this case, which is the nature of the tort committed by *Hustler*.

Eliminating the *Brandenburg* incitement theory as a basis for recovery would have been sufficient to reverse the jury award here. The majority go much further, however, and afford *Hustler* virtually complete protection from tort liability under the first amendment. I vigorously oppose their unnecessary elaboration on first amendment law, which, I believe, will undercut the ability of the states to protect their youth against a reckless and sometimes dangerous business which masquerades as a beneficiary of the first amendment.

INTRODUCTION

The *Herceg* case lies at the intersection of two controversial areas of communications law. At the heart of the case is the question of media liability for personal injuries that seem to stem from a publication or broadcast. Cases of this type have emerged over the past decade or so, and the legal standards are not yet clear. Like the law of libel, these cases involve difficult issues of state tort law and first amendment doctrine. Further complicating *Herceg* is the nature of the defendant's magazine, an "adult" publication that can fairly be described as pornographic. While "obscene" speech is considered outside the first amendment altogether and thus subject to state regulation that would be unconstitutional with respect to protected speech, "pornographic" speech that does not qualify as "obscene" is entitled to first amendment protection. Just as courts have struggled for years to draw the line between the two, they are now grappling with the issue raised by Judge Edith Jones in *Herceg* (i.e., the scope of constitutional protection for pornographic speech that is not legally obscene).

In this chapter, we shall examine the collision between the first amendment and efforts to protect public morals and the public safety. First, we shall explore the law of obscenity, including the difficulties in separating protected from unprotected speech and the techniques utilized to combat obscenity. Then, we shall turn our attention to personal injury cases such as *Herceg* and the theory that the media may be liable for such injuries that can be traced to a publication or broadcast.

OBSCENITY

In his book *The Secret Museum*, Professor Walter Kendrick described in some detail the archeological "digs" at Pompeii in the mid-1700s. Some of the unearthed objects, he noted, presented a "special problem" for the authorities:

> [I]n 1758, for example, rumors circulated that "lascivious" frescoes had been found; not long thereafter, a particularly outrageous artifact turned up—a small marble statue, highly naturalistic in style, representing a satyr in sexual congress with an apparently undaunted goat. This distressing artwork, under special orders from King Charles, was entrusted to the royal sculptor, Joseph Canart, with the "strict injunction that no one should be allowed access to it." Evidently, the order was not strictly obeyed, because in 1786, in his *Discourse on the Worship of Priapus*, Richard Payne Knight referred to the statue, "kept concealed in the Royal Museum of Portici," as "well known." No doubt the procedure was already in operation, as it remained two centuries later, that a gentleman with appropriate demeanor (and ready cash for the custodian) would

be admitted to the locked chamber where controversial items lurked; women, children, and the poor of both sexes and all ages were excluded.

This passage makes two important points. First, sexually explicit materials have been with us a long time. As the Attorney General's Commission on Pornography noted in its 1986 report, "[d]escriptions of sex are as old as sex itself." Second, the Anglo-American response to these materials has been suppression, a tactic which, in Professor Kendrick's view, was designed primarily to protect most of society from the supposedly corrupting influence of sexually oriented writings, paintings, and other forms of expression.

Such information, however, was readily available to the social and political elite—that is, wealthy and educated "gentlemen"—who were apparently considered capable of withstanding its harmful effects. When the circulation of pornographic materials was so restricted, due in part to the scarcity and expense of books and rampant illiteracy, the law reflected little concern with them. But as advances in printing, the development of photography, and the extension of educational opportunities beyond the upper classes made sexually explicit materials more widely available to a more diverse audience, that attitude began to change.

Despite the recognition of "obscene libel" as a common law crime as early as 1727, the English legal system seemed concerned with bawdiness and depictions of sexuality primarily in connection with attacks on government or the church. There was relatively little interest in indecency for its own sake; for example, the publication of John Cleland's 1748 novel *Memoirs of a Woman of Pleasure*—better known as *Fanny Hill*—caused little stir and did not result in prosecution. By the early part of the nineteeth century, however, the alarms had sounded. As sexually explicit materials previously available only to the social elite became more widely circulated, private groups such as the Society for the Supression of Vice pressed for legislation. Parliament responded with the Vagrancy Act of 1824, which established criminal penalties for the publication of indecent pictures, and Lord Campbell's Act of 1857, which gave magistrates authority to issue warrants for the seizure and destruction of obscene materials.

In addition, criminal prosecutions for "obscene libel" became more common, particularly since English law at the time permitted private persons—such as members of the Society for the Suppression of Vice—to initiate criminal proceedings. It was not until the landmark decision in *Regina v. Hicklin* (1868), however, that the courts attempted to define precisely what material was obscene and thus illegal. The case involved an anti-religious pamphlet, "The Confession Unmasked," which accused Catholic priests of asking women "filthy and disgusting" questions during confession. The trial judge found the publication obscene, but an appellate court reversed. The Queen's Bench, on further appeal, reinstated the initial decision and in the process fashioned a "test" for obscenity that would last for a century in England and have a significant impact on American law.

Lord Chief Justice Alexander Cockburn stated the test this way: "whether the tendency of the matter charged as obscenity is to deprave and corrupt those whose minds are open to such immoral influences, and into whose hands a publication of this sort may fall." He added that this determination was to be based on the impact of certain parts of the offending material—rather than the work as a whole—on these susceptible individuals. Moreover, the author's intent was irrelevant, and an improper motive would be implied if the work itself was obscene. "[W]here a man publishes a work manifestly obscene," the Chief Justice wrote, "he must be taken to have had the intention which is implied from that act."

The *Hicklin* test was adopted by courts in this country, where the development of obscenity law paralleled that in England. Prior to 1800, governmental concern with immorality was largely limited to blasphemous and other anti-religious materials, and it was not until 1815 that an American court upheld a conviction on specific charges of obscenity. In that case, *Commonwealth v. Sharpless*, the Pennsylvania Supreme Court ruled that "[a]ny offence which in its nature and by its example, tends to the corruption of morals, as the exhibition of an obscene picture, is indictable at common law."

Shortly thereafter, Vermont became the first state to enact a statute criminalizing the publication and distribution of obscene materials, and by the mid-1800s legislation of this type was on the books across the country. At the federal level, the Customs Act of 1842 was the first statute dealing with obscene materials. It prohibited the importation of "all indecent and obscene prints, paintings, litographs, engravings and transparencies." In 1865, Congress passed the first statute prohibiting the shipment of obscene books and pictures through the mails.

Generally speaking, enforcement of these laws was rather lax, and, as was the case in England, private organizations sprang up to urge tougher laws and more vigorous government action. Probably the best known of these groups was the New York Committee for the Suppression of Vice, whose membership included anti-pornography crusader Anthony Comstock. An ardent opponent of abortion, contraceptives, gambling, saloons, and patent medicines as well as obscenity, he was instrumental in the passage of an 1873 statute popularly known as the "Comstock Act." Signed into law by President Grant, the act was much more specific than its predecessors. It provided in part that:

> [N]o obscene, lewd, or lascivious book, pamphlet, picture, paper, print, or other publication of an indecent character, or any article or thing designed or intended for the prevention of contraception or procuring of abortion, nor any article or thing intended or adapted for any indecent or immoral use or nature, nor any written or printed card, circular, book, pamphlet, advertisement or notice of any kind giving information, directly or indirectly, where, or how, or of whom, or by what means either of the things before mentioned may be obtained or made, nor any letter upon the envelope of which, or postal-card upon which indecent or scurrilous epithets may be written or printed, shall be carried in the mail. . . .

Congress also appropriated funds for a "special agent" to help enforce the new law, and the Postmaster General gave Comstock the job. Holding this position until his death in 1915, Comstock went about his task zealously; near the end of his career, he claimed that he had destroyed 160 tons of "obscene literature" and convicted enough people "to fill a passenger train of sixty-one coaches, sixty coaches containing sixty passengers each and the sixty-first almost full." As Professor Kendrick has observed, "[i]t is one of the most striking oddities of American history that for more than forty years . . . problems of public morality were entrusted almost wholly to the discretion of one man, an agent of the Post Office Department."

As noted previously, American courts looked to the *Hicklin* test in determining whether particular materials were obscene. During the first half of the twentieth century, a variety of critically acclaimed literary works were deemed obscene under the test, including Theodore Dreiser's *An American Tragedy*, Erskine Caldwell's *God's Little Acre*, and two novels by Henry Miller, *Tropic of Cancer* and *Tropic of Capricorn*. But the influence of *Hicklin* began to crumble as early as 1933, when a federal court rejected the test in a case involving James Joyce's novel *Ulysses*. The book had been controversial for more than a decade, and editions published in France and Germany were not permitted in England and the United States. After Bennett Cerf of Random House signed a contract with Joyce for an American edition, the noted publisher arranged for someone to bring—quite openly—a copy of *Ulysses* into the United States, where it was seized at customs under the Tariff Act of 1930. In the subsequent legal proceeding, *United States v. One Book Called "Ulysses,"* Judge John M. Woolsey of the U.S. District Court in Manhattan ruled that the book was not obscene and could thus be admitted into the country.

Judge Woolsey, whose decision was upheld by the U.S. Court of Appeals for the Second Circuit, rejected *Hicklin* in favor of a test asking whether the work "tends to stir the sex impulses or to lead to sexually impure and lustful thoughts." Evaluation of a particular book under this test, he added, must involve "its effect (when judged as a whole) on a person with average sex instincts." Moreover, the work's literary or artistic merit was to be considered, as well as the author's purpose: "it must . . . be determined whether the intent with which [the book] was written was . . . for the purpose of exploiting obscenity." Failing to find in *Ulysses* "the leer of the sensualist" or anything that he considered "to be dirt for dirt's sake," Judge Woolsey concluded that the novel was not obscene. Although other American courts continued to cling to the *Hicklin* test for several years, Judge Woolsey's opinion had a pronounced effect on the U.S. Supreme Court's landmark decision in *Roth v. United States* some twenty-five years later.

Obscenity and the Supreme Court

Recall from Chapter 1 the Supreme Court's 1942 decision in *Chaplinsky v. New Hampshire*, in which Justice Frank Murphy wrote that "certain well-defined and narrowly limited classes of speech," including "the lewd and obscene," are considered outside the protective scope of the first amendment. It was not until the *Roth* case in 1957, however, that the Court specifically upheld the constitutionality of obscenity statutes, attempted to define obscenity, and began to draw the line between protected and unprotected speech of a sexual nature. *Roth* involved a conviction under federal obscenity laws for sending circulars and a book, *American Aphrodite*, through the mails. In a companion case, *Alberts v. California*, the defendant challenged his conviction under a state obscenity statute for distributing a variety of books and pictures. Though the Court did not decide whether these particular materials were obscene, it affirmed Justice Murphy's *dictum* in *Chaplinsky* that obscenity is not protected by the first amendment. In so ruling, the Court made its first stab at defining obscene expression and, in the process, buried the *Hicklin* rule.

"[S]ex and obscenity are not synonomous," Justice William Brennan wrote for the Court. "The portrayal of sex, e.g., in art, literature, and scientific works, is not itself reason to deny material the constitutional protection of freedom of speech and press." Thus, the question is not whether the material depicts or describes sexual conduct, but "whether to the average person, applying contemporary community standards, the dominent theme of the material taken as a whole appeals to prurient interest," that is, "a shameful or morbid interest in nudity, sex, or excretion." For purposes of this definition, the term "community standards" did not refer to those of particular cities or towns, but to the attitude of society at large. In other words, the Court was attempting to establish a national definition of obscenity.

Over the next decade, the Court struggled to apply and refine this definition, which obviously owes a great deal to Judge Woolsey's formulation in the *Ulysses* case. Though the *Roth* decision commanded a majority of the Court, the Justices began to take divergent views on the definitional issue. These difficulties in reaching a consensus, which some commentators likened to a "judicial quagmire," prompted Justice Potter Stewart's famous remark in *Jacobellis v. Ohio* (1964), in which he equated obscenity with "hard-core" pornography: "I know it when I see it, and the motion picture involved in this case is not that."

In the most significant case of this era, *Memoirs v. Massachusetts* (1966), Justice Brennan added two additional elements to the standard he had developed in *Roth*: "patent offensiveness" and a complete lack of "redeeming social value." At issue was *Fanny Hill*, which by that point had been in print more than two centuries. The Court reversed the Massachusetts Supreme Court's decision that the novel was obscene, but a majority of the Justices could not agree on a legal test. Writing for the plurality, Justice Brennan concluded that a work is obscene only if:

> (a) the dominant theme of the material taken as a whole appeals to a prurient interest in sex; (b) the material is patently offensive because it affronts contemporary community standards relating to the description or representation of sexual matters; and (c) the material is utterly without redeeming social value.

The major problem with this formulation should be obvious, for it makes clear that only material that is totally devoid of social value is obscene and, conversely, that material with *some* social value—however slight—is protected by the first amendment.

Shortly after the decision in *Memoirs*, the Court gave up trying to define obscenity. In *Redrup v. New York* (1967), the Court issued a brief opinion setting forth the various standards espoused by the individual Justices and ruled that the material at issue was not obscene no matter which definition was employed. The Court then stopped writing opinions in obscenity cases altogether and instead simply issued orders reversing criminal convictions for obscenity law violations when at least five Justices—each using his own personal test—agreed that the material in question was not obscene. More than two dozen convictions were overturned in this manner, much to the frustration of local prosecuting attorneys who had received no guidance from the Court. Justice Hugo Black, whose absolutist views led him to the conclusion that obscene materials should be protected by the first amendment, complained that the Court was becoming a "Supreme Board of Censors," and other commentators found it somewhat amusing that the Court, made up of men in their sixties and seventies, was the nation's arbiter in sexual matters.[1]

---

[1] During this period, the Court regularly viewed movies involved in obscenity cases, and these private screenings were often rather humorous affairs. According to Bob Woodward and Scott Armstrong in *The Brethren* (1979), the Justices and their law clerks gathered for "movie day" in basement storeroom or one of the Court's conference rooms. Law clerks "frequently mocked [Justice] Stewart's approach to obscenity," Woodward and Armstrong wrote, "calling out in the darkened room: 'That's it, that's it. I know it when I see it.' " Though some Justices preferred not to attend the screenings, Justice John Marshall Harlan apparently decided that it was his duty to do so, despite the fact that he was nearly blind. "Harlan watched the films from the first row, a few feet from the screen, able only to make out

It was not until 1973, after President Richard Nixon had reshaped the Court by appointing four new Justices, that a majority could agree on a legal test for obscenity. The breakthrough came in *Miller v. California*, a case which, with a few subsequent refinements, continues to provide the underpinning for the regulation of obscenity. Writing for the five-member majority, Chief Justice Warren Burger sharply criticized the "utterly without redeeming social value" requirement of *Memoirs* as requiring proof of a negative, which is "a burden virtually impossible to discharge under our criminal standards of proof." He then announced a new three-part test:

> (a) whether "the average person, applying contemporary community standards" would find that the work, taken as a whole, appeals to the prurient interest . . . ; (b) whether the work depicts or describes, in a patently offensive way, sexual conduct specifically defined by the applicable state law; and (c) whether the work, taken as a whole, lacks serious literary, artistic, political, or scientific value.

In addition, the Chief Justice made plain that the "contemporary community standards" would be local rather than national, concluding that the nation is simply too diverse to permit articulation of a standard suitable for all fifty states. "It is neither realistic nor constitutionally sound," he wrote, "to read the First Amendment as requiring that the people of Maine or Mississippi accept public depiction of conduct found tolerable in Las Vegas or New York City." Local standards were thus to be utilized in determining whether material appealed to the "prurient interest" under part (a) of the test and was "patently offensive" under part (b). The Chief Justice also provided examples of the types of sexual conduct that the states could regulate by statute under part (b) of the new standard: "[p]atently offensive representations or descriptions of ultimate sexual acts, normal or perverted, actual or simulated" and "[p]atently offensive representations or descriptions of masturbation, excretory functions, and lewd exhibition of the genitals." After the *Miller* decision, virtually all states revised their obscenity statutes in accordance with the blueprint drawn by the Court, and local prosecutors began to enforce those statutes aggressively.

The *Miller* rule remains the law today, though the Court has from time to time clarified certain points and answered questions left unresolved in the 1973 ruling. We now turn to a more detailed examination of each part of the test. First, the "average person" means just that. The impact of the allegedly obscene material on a particularly prudish person—the test under *Hicklin*—or on one who is extremely tolerant does not matter. Moreover, children are not be to considered within the group of "average" persons unless they are part of the intended audience. Special considerations involving children and child pornography are discussed in the following section.

Second, the definition of "prurient interest" from *Roth* has retained its vitality: "a shameful or morbid interest in nudity, sex or excretion." Generally, the question is whether the material as a whole—not merely isolated parts—"excites lustful thoughts" in the average person. However, in *Mishkin v. New York* (1966), the

---

the general outlines," Woodward and Armstrong reported. "His clerk or another Justice would describe the action. 'By Jove,' Harlan would exclaim. 'How extraordinary.' "

Supreme Court ruled that when the material is aimed at a clearly defined deviate sexual group, the issue is whether the material appeals to the prurient interest of members of that particular group. In *Mishkin*, for example, some of the publications found obscene dealt with sadomasochism, a practice would no doubt disgust the average person rather than appeal to his prurient interest.

Third, the term "patently offensive" refers to "hard-core pornography," a term that the Court itself has used on numerous occasions. In *Hamling v. United States* (1974), for example, the Court upheld the convictions of two defendants under a federal statute that prohibited the mailing of obscene materials. At issue were advertising brochures that included explicit photographs of heterosexual and homosexual intercourse, fellatio, cunnilingus, masturbation, bestiality, and group sex. This sort of "hard-core pornography," as the Court described it, was obscene under *Miller*. In contrast, mere nudity is not considered patently offensive and cannot, without more, be legally obscene. Though the majority of obscenity cases today involve pictorial depictions in magazines, films, and videotapes, written materials with no photographs or drawings can also be obscene. "When the Court declared that obscenity is not a form of expression protected by the First Amendment, no distinction was made as to the medium of expression," Chief Justice Burger wrote in *Kaplan v. California* (1973).

Fourth, the standards of the local community govern the determination of whether the work is patently offensive and appeals to the prurient interest, and national standards are immaterial. Generally speaking, the "community" will be the particular city or county in which the allegedly obscene material had been distributed. In some cases, however, a statewide standard has been deemed appropriate. Cases arising under federal obscenity statutes—such as those governing the mails—are also tried under local standards rather than a uniform, nationwide yardstick. In such cases, the relevant "community" is the geographic area from which the jurors are selected for the particular federal court. Although there may be (and often is) expert testimony at trial as to community standards, prurient interest, and patent offensiveness, the jurors themselves are considered to be in the best position to evaluate these matters and are free to disregard the opinions of any experts.

The jury's discretion in this regard is not unbridled, however. In *Miller* itself, the Supreme Court made plain that appellate courts must independently review the jury's factual determination to ensure that a defendant is not punished for publishing materials that are in fact protected under the first amendment. The Court's 1974 decision in *Jenkins v. Georgia* is illustrative. There the Georgia courts had affirmed a jury's finding that a critically acclaimed film—Mike Nichols' *Carnal Knowledge*—was obscene. The Supreme Court reversed, ruling that the movie "could not, as a matter of constitutional law, be found to depict sexual conduct in a patently offensive way and that it is therefore not outside the protection of the First and Fourteenth Amendments because it is obscene." Although the film contained nudity and scenes in which sexual conduct was understood to be taking place, there was "no exhibition of the actors' genitals, lewd or otherwise, during these scenes." Simply put, the film "was not the public portrayal of hard-core sexual conduct for its own sake, and for the ensuing commercial gain."

Fifth, evaluation of the material's "serious literary, artistic, political, or scientific value" is not based on local community standards. Rather, as the Supreme Court held in *Pope v. Illinois* (1987), the test is an objective one that does not vary from community to community: whether a "reasonable person" would conclude that the work lacks serious value. In applying this standard, the jury must review the material as a whole, and a publisher's inclusion of "serious" information as window-dressing will not preclude a finding that the work is obscene. As the Supreme Court has noted, "a quotation from Voltaire on the flyleaf of a book will not constitutionally redeem an otherwise obscene publication."

Conversely, the fact that a work contains a sexually explicit photograph which, standing alone, might be deemed obscene does not justify the conclusion that the work as a whole is obscene. For example, in *Kois v. Wisconsin* (1972), the Supreme Court reversed the obscenity conviction of the publisher of an underground newspaper that had published two photographs of the type seized by police in arresting a photographer on obscenity charges. Pointing out that the photographs were rationally related to the news story about the photographer, the Court concluded that the newspaper was not a "mere vehicle for the publication of the pictures" and was thus not obscene.

In determining whether the allegedly obscene material lacks serious value, the jury may go beyond content and consider whether the defendant was "pandering" to prurient interests in the creation, promotion, or dissemination of the material. This is so, the Court explained in *Splawn v. California* (1977), because the deliberate marketing of materials as "erotically arousing" stimulates the reader to accept them as prurient and indicates that the target audience is seeking "titillation, not . . . saving intellectual content." In other words, the fact that the defendant commercially exploited the sexually provocative nature of the material suggests that it lacked the necessary "serious value." This principle was first adopted in the pre-*Miller* case of *Ginzburg v. United States* (1966), in which the defendant had titled his magazine "Eros," advertised it as "frankly and avowedly concerned with erotica," and attempted to obtain mailing permits from towns with such names as Intercourse, Blue Ball, and Middlesex.[2]

Finally, despite the Supreme Court's reaffirmation in *Miller* and other cases of the basic principle that obscenity is not entitled to first amendment protection, private possession of obscene materials cannot be made a crime. In *Stanley v. Georgia* (1969), Court ruled that the Constitution protects the right to receive information and ideas and to be generally free from government intrusion into one's privacy. "If the First Amendment means anything, it means that a State has no business telling a man, sitting alone in his own house, what books he may read or what films he may watch," Justice Thurgood Marshall wrote for the Court. "Our whole constitutional heritage rebels at the thought of giving government the power to control men's minds." However, the constitutional right to privacy does not encompass the right of an individual to watch obscene movies in a public theater or purchase obscene magazines at a newstand. In *Paris Adult Theatre I v. Slaton* (1973), another Georgia case, the Court made plain that the states have a legitimate interest in "stemming the tide of commercial obscenity" and may regulate the use of obscene material "in local commerce and in all places of public accommodation."

---

[2]Shortly after *Ginzburg*, the Congress passed an "anti-pandering" statute under which persons can choose not to receive "sexually provocative" advertisements by mail, regardless of whether the material is legally obscene. To invoke the protection of the statute, a person simply informs the post office that he has been sent unwelcome advertising, and the post office then directs the advertiser to remove the individual from its mailing list. Whether a particular advertisement is "sexually provocative" is within the sole discretion of the recipient. The Supreme Court upheld the statute in *Rowan v. U.S. Post Office* (1970).

It is tempting to suggest that the principles and cases summarized above give some content to the three-part test announced in *Miller*; for example, a would-be publisher can at least draw a rough comparison between his planned work and the materials at issue in such decisions as *Jenkins* and *Hamling*. The fact remains, however, that the imprecision of our language and the limited descriptive powers of lawyers and judges make it virtually impossible to define obsenity with sufficient specificity to provide a clear indication of the line between protected and unprotected speech. This problem is compounded by the fact that *Miller* gives considerable discretion to juries, which are called upon to apply standards that vary from community to community in evaluating particular materials. Because there is no way of knowing that something is obscene until it is distributed to the public and tested in a judicial proceeding, publishers may well decide to forego publication of works that, while controversial, are not legally obscene and thus protected by the first amendment. Perhaps Justice Stewart was right after all, for no matter how many times jurors and courts are called upon to apply the *Miller* test, the bottom line may well be that we all "know it when we see it." We simply may not "see it" the same way.

Special Problems in Regulating Obscenity

According to the 1986 report of the Attorney General's Commission on Pornography (the so-called "Meese Commission"), pornography is a multi-billion dollar industry in this country, with more than $500 million being generated from retail sales in the Los Angeles area alone. Moreover, the Commission pointed out that technological developments—including home videocassette recorders, cable television, and "dial-a-porn"—have significantly increased the availability of pornographic materials. And, in a finding that has sparked considerable controversy, the Commission concluded that there is a causal link between some forms of pornography and aggressive behavior toward women. Especially harmful, the Commission said, is sexually explicit material that either depicts sexual violence or degrades women by portraying them as subservient sex objects. Although members of the Commission disagreed as to the effect of "non-violent" and "non-degrading" pornography on adults, they concluded that such material is harmful in the hands of children. Much less controversial was the Commission's conclusion that so-called "child pornography" that visually depicts sexual conduct by children is nothing more than a form of child abuse.

It is hardly within the scope of this book to dissect the Commission's findings or enter the thicket of behaviorial research. Nonetheless, much of the material that the Commission identified as harmful is without a doubt legally obscene under the *Miller* test. Our concern, therefore, is the manner in which the government may regulate material of this type without interfering impermissibly with the flow of information that enjoys first amendment protection. As the Supreme Court has observed, the "separation of legitimate from illegitimate speech calls for . . . sensitive tools." We will focus on several of these tools here but will postpone until Chapter 10 consideration of problems stemming from the regulation of broadcasting and cable television.

Criminal Statutes. Most of the cases discussed in the preceding section involved convictions under state statutes or city ordinances that made the production and distribution of obscenity a crime. Others arose from federal statutes that bar the mailing of obscene materials and the importing of such materials into the United States. Such statutes have been frequently challenged as being unconstitutionally vague because they lack specific definitions of obscenity and thus do not give "fair warning" of the type of material that is unlawful. That such arguments have been made should surprise no one, given the centuries-old struggle to define obscenity. If Justice Stewart simply knew it when he saw it, how can we expect legislators to draft a statute that advises defendants that their magazines or films are illegal?

The short answer is that we cannot. Thus, the Supreme Court has ruled that obscenity statutes need not list every forbidden sexual act or practice in order to be valid. Rather, a statute gives fair notice if it refers to the type of material that is barred, much as Chief Justice Burger gave examples in *Miller* of "patently offensive" depictions or descriptions that may be proscribed. For example, in *Ward v. Illinois* (1977), a person who had sold sadomasochistic magazines was convicted under an Illinois obscenity statute that defined obscenity along the lines of *Miller*: "A thing is obscene if, considered as a whole, its predominant appeal is to prurient interest . . . and if it goes substantially beyond customary limits of candor in description or representation of such matters." The defendant argued that the statute was unconstitutionally vague, since it did not not by its terms mention sadomasochism. The Supreme Court disagreed, ruling that an "exhaustive list" of material deemed obscene is not required. Because most state statutes follow closely the language of *Miller*, they have survived similar vagueness challenges.

Even a statute that is not sufficiently specific can be made so by judicial rulings. In *Hamling v. United States*, for example, the defendants were convicted for violating a federal statute that prohibited sending "obscene, lewd, lascivious, indecent, filthy or vile" materials through the mail. The Supreme Court interpreted this provision as being limited to materials falling within the definition of obscenity set forth in the *Miller* case. In other words, the Court concluded that the "generic" terms used in the statute referred to materials that depict or describe the type of "hard-core sexual conduct" mentioned in *Miller*.[3]

Obscenity statutes have occasionally run afoul of the overbreadth doctrine, which focuses on whether a legislative enactment proscribes both protected and unprotected speech. The Supreme Court's 1975 decision in *Erznoznik v. City of Jacksonville* illustrates the application of this doctrine in the obscenity setting. There the manager of a drive-in theater was prosecuted under a city ordinance that prohibited the outdoor exhibition of films "in which the human male or female bare buttocks, human female bare breasts, or human bare pubic areas are shown." The Supreme Court ruled that the ordinance swept too broadly, for it barred not only hard-core films that would be obscene under *Miller*, but also movies "containing a picture of a baby's buttocks, the nude body of a war victim, or scenes from a culture in which nudity is indigenous." Since nudity alone is not obscene, the ordinance impermissibly prohibited the display of films protected by the first amendment, as well as those that are not.

Obscenity statutes must contain a requirement of "scienter," that is, guilty knowledge on the part of the person charged with illegal conduct. In *Smith v. California* (1959), the Supreme Court overturned the conviction of a bookseller under a Los Angeles ordinance that made him criminally liable even though he did not know the

---

[3]Problems might also arise if a statute is too specific. For example, the Fort Lauderdale city council once passed an obscenity ordinance which, according to news accounts, was so specific that the ordinance itself was obscene and could not be made public.

contents of an allegedly obscene book. "[I]f the bookseller is criminally liable without knowledge of the contents, he will tend to restrict the books he sells to those he has inspected," the Court said, "and thus the State will have imposed a restriction upon the distribution of constitutionally protected as well as obscene literature." However, it is not necessary that the defendant have actual knowledge that the material is legally obscene; rather, it is sufficient that he be aware or have reason to be aware of its general nature or character. Moreover, scienter may be proved by circumstantial evidence. For example, in *Volkland v. State* (1974), a Texas court inferred scienter from evidence that the manager of an "adult" bookstore, in the course of wrapping magazines in cellophane before placing them on the shelves, had looked through some of them and found photos of the type published in the magazines on which the obscenity charges were based.

A recent development in the enforcement of obscenity laws is the use of federal and state "anti-racketeering" statutes to prosecute persons who deal in obscene books, magazines, and films. Under these statutes, any person found to have committed a certain number of "predicate offenses"—often as few as two—within a specified period is deemed to have engaged in a "pattern" of criminal activity. Dealing in obscene materials is a "predicate offense" that will trigger the federal act and the statutes of more than a dozen states. Penalties for violating the anti-racketeering statutes are typically much stiffer than those for convictions under "ordinary" criminal obscenity laws.

In *Fort Wayne Books, Inc. v. Indiana* (1989), the U.S. Supreme Court upheld the constitutionality of a state anti-racketeering law in the obscenity context. There an adult bookstore was charged with selling six obscene magazines in violation of the Indiana criminal obscenity statute. In addition, prosecutors used these alleged predicate offenses to charge the defendant under the state's anti-racketeering act. Under Indiana law, an obscenity violation is a misdemeanor offense, while an anti-racketeering charge is a felony with a maximum jail term of eight years. The Court rejected the defendant's argument that the heavier penalties under the anti-racketeering statute would have an impermissible chilling effect on first amendment rights. "It may be true that the stiffer [anti-racketeering] penalties will provide an additional deterrent to those who might otherwise sell obscene materials . . . [and] that some cautious booksellers will practice self-censorship and remove . . . [nonobscene] materials from their shelves," the Court said. "But deterrence of the sale of obscene materials is a legitimate end of state anti-obscenity laws."

Forfeiture and "Padlocking" Statutes. The Supreme Court did not consider in the *Fort Wayne* case the constitutionality of a more controversial feature of anti-racketeering statutes that authorize law enforcement officials to confiscate, in either criminal or civil proceedings, property used in or derived from racketeering activities. These so-called "forfeiture" provisions, which are also found in obscenity statutes not limited to racketeering,[4] permit the seizure of all books, magazines, and

---

[4]For example, a statute passed by Congress in 1988 contains a criminal forfeiture provision applicable to anyone convicted of violating federal obscenity statutes, including those that prohibit mailing, broadcasting, and cablecasting obscene material, importing such material into the United States or transporting it in interstate commerce, and possessing or receiving it with intent to distribute. Other statutes provide for criminal and civil forfeiture proceedings in connection with violations of federal child pornography laws.

films at a bookstore or theater found to have sold obscene materials, even though the rest of the inventory is not legally obscene. Similar statutes enable state law enforcement officials to shut down businesses that deal in obscene materials on the ground that they are public nuisances.

Nuisance statutes, which have been on the books for years, typically define certain activities—prostitution, gambling, and obscenity, for example—as "public nuisances" that can be banned or shut down for the good of the community. Upon concluding that a business has engaged in such activities, a judge may "abate" the nuisance by entering an order closing the business for a specified period, usually one year. The business might be allowed to remain open if the owner posts a bond covering the full value of his property and convincing the judge that no further violations will occur during that time. Of course, the bond is forfeited and the owner held in contempt of court if he subsequently engages in the activity. Some appellate courts have ruled that these so-called "padlocking" statutes are unconstitutional in the obscenity context, though other courts have reached the opposite conclusion. The U.S. Supreme Court has not yet directly addressed the question.

Courts that have struck down nuisance statutes have generally labeled them impermissible prior restraints, reasoning that a court order closing a bookstore or theater for a year necessarily prohibits the owner from selling or displaying any material—whether obscene or constitutionally protected—during the relevant period. "Evidence of obscene conduct in the past does not justify enjoining future conduct which is protected by the First Amendment," the Alabama Supreme Court ruled in *General Corp. v. State ex rel. Sweeton* (1975). "The padlocking of [the defendant's] operation for one year constitutes prior restraint at its worst and is patently unconstitutional." Even the threat of a closure order may deter theater operators and bookstore owners from handling films, books, or magazines that are not legally obscene. As U.S. Court of Appeals for the Fifth Circuit observed in *Universal Amusement Co. v. Vance* (1978), a nuisance statute with a padlock provision "encourages a theater operator to steer wide of the danger zone by avoiding borderline films that are nonetheless protected under the First Amendment." The U.S. Supreme Court subsequently affirmed the Fifth Circuit's decision in *Vance* but did not settle the validity of using nuisance statutes to control obscenity.

Seeking to avoid these constitutional difficulties, other courts have interpreted nuisance statutes narrowly. For example, in *State ex rel. Ewing v. "Without a Stitch"* (1974), the Ohio Supreme Court ruled that a padlocking statute without a bond provision would be impermissible, but that the posting of a bond would enable the owner to sell material protected by the first amendment. In addition, the court said that only the particular book or film found obscene was to be abated as a nuisance, thus freeing the owner from the threat of forfeiture if he sold a different book or film later determined to be obscene. While this approach certainly reduces the harshness of the nuisance statute, it has no effect on padlocking orders directed at an owner unable to post a bond. Moreover, most nuisance statutes probably cannot be interpreted in this manner, since they specify abatement of the entire business—not a given book or film—as a nuisance.

In contrast, some courts have simply concluded that nuisance statutes do not violate the first amendment and are thus valid and fully enforceable. Perhaps the leading case is *State ex rel. Kidwell v. U.S. Marketing, Inc.*, decided by the Idaho Supreme Court in 1981. Like a fine or jail term, the nuisance statute "is intended to penalize past distributions of illegal and unprotected obscenity" rather than to restrict future conduct, the court said. Because the legislature could have imposed a fine or other property-related penalty for selling or displaying obscene materials, the court reasoned, it should be able "to punish the violator by temporarily depriving him of the property which was used in committing the violation." Moreover, if a bookseller is convicted under a criminal obscenity statute, "he may be imprisoned, and yet he will not be heard to complain that his incarceration constitutes a prior restraint upon his ability to disseminate protected speech, even though it is quite clear that it has that effect."

The forfeiture provisions found in anti-racketeering laws and other obscenity statutes pose similar constitutional problems, since the government's seizure of assets—including nonobscene books, magazines or films protected by the first amendment—would effectively put out of business a person found guilty of violating such a statute by selling some obscene materials. As noted previously, the U.S. Supreme Court in the *Fort Wayne* case specifically left open the question of whether this obviously harsh remedy is constitutionally permissible. The lower courts have divided on the issue.

For example, in *State v. Feld* (1987), the Arizona Court of Appeals took the position that the forfeiture provision in that state's anti-racketeering statute was an unconstitutional prior restraint. Because the act permitted the forfeiture of books and other materials not found to be legally obscene, the court said that it "act[ed] as a prior restraint on the sale of privileged matter" by effectively closing bookstores and theaters. "The sanctions restrict future, presumptively protected speech, rather than punishing the distribution of unprotected speech in the past," the court reasoned, pointing out that the entire inventory of a bookstore operator could be forfeited on a judicial determination that only a handful of books or magazines were obscene. Accordingly, the court invalidated the portion of the statute permitting forfeiture of materials that had not been judicially found to be obscene.

In contrast, a federal district court in Virginia upheld the forfeiture provisions of the federal anti-racketeering statute in *United States v. Pryba* (1987). The court reasoned that the forfeiture was punishment for disseminating obscene materials unprotected by the first amendment, not a prior restraint. "The Constitution does not forbid punishment for a crime simply because that punishment might affect [future] free expression," the court said, dismissing the argument that the threat of forfeiture would impermissibly deter the sale of nonobscene materials. "[A] dealer need only self-censor obscene matter to avoid [the] forfeiture penalties," the court pointed out. "This type of chilling or self-censorship is constitutionally permissible and Congress manifestly intended that it occur." After a jury found the defendant guilty of distributing $105 worth of obscene material, it decided that three bookstores and eight videotape clubs valued at $1 million were to be forfeited under the federal anti-racketeering statute.

Although the U.S. Supreme Court specifically declined to address this issue in the *Fort Wayne* case, its resolution of a related question in that decision lends support to the argument that forfeiture provisions, as well as public nuisance statutes, are invalid as applied to obscenity. In *Fort Wayne*, the Court ruled that allegedly obscene materials cannot be confiscated or a business "padlocked" pending a trial simply because law enforcement officials believe them to be obscene. Rather, such pretrial seizures are permissible only after a judicial determination, in an adversary hearing, that the materials are obscene. Acting under the Indiana anti-racketeering statute, prosecutors had filed a civil action for forfeiture and obtained a court order closing an adult bookstore and seizing thousands of books and films pending a trial. Although the trial judge who issued the order had found "probable cause" to believe that the materials were obscene, the Supreme Court said that this was not enough. "[O]ur cases firmly hold that mere probable cause to believe a legal violation has transpired is not adequate to remove books or films from circulation," Justice Byron White wrote. "Here there was not . . . any determination that the seized items were obscene. . . ."

Under this rationale, forfeiture statutes of the type at issue in *Feld* and *Pryba* seem unconstitutional, for they permit the confiscation of materials that have not been declared obscene in an adversarial judicial proceeding. As noted above, the statutes allow forfeiture of *all* assets, whether or not protected by the first amendment, on the basis of a finding in a criminal or civil case that a defendant has sold *some* unprotected obscene materials. Put another way, there is a judicial ruling as to the status of the materials that gave rise to the obscenity prosecution, but not the other materials seized under the forfeiture provision. The fact that anti-racketeering statutes and other laws allow permanent forfeiture of books, films, and magazines without a judicial determination of actual obscenity could mean that the use of this potent remedy contravenes the first amendment. The same reasoning could be employed to invalidate the public nuisance statutes discussed previously.

It is settled, however, that nuisance statutes may be invoked against "adult" theaters and bookstores at which illegal conduct unrelated to expression has taken place. For example, in *Arcara v. Cloud Books, Inc.* (1986), officials brought suit under a New York nuisance statute to close an "adult" bookstore after an undercover investigation revealed that prostitution and other illicit sexual activities had occurred on the premises. The bookstore argued that this application of the statute, which provided for closure of a business being used as a place for prostitution, was unconstitutional, but the U.S. Supreme Court disagreed. The statute "was directed at unlawful conduct having nothing to do with books or other expressive activity," Chief Justice Burger wrote for the majority. "Bookselling in an establishment used for prostitution does not confer First Amendment coverage to defeat a valid statute aimed at penalizing and terminating illegal uses of the premises."

Zoning Laws. Another technique for regulating obscenity—one whose constitutionality is beyond doubt—is the use of municipal zoning ordinances to limit the areas in which "adult" bookstores and theaters may operate. In *Young v. American Mini Theatres, Inc.* (1976), the U.S. Supreme Court upheld a Detroit ordinance that prohibited "adult" theaters and bookstores within 1,000 feet of other such businesses and a variety of other establishments, including hotels, motels, bars, pool halls, and pawn shops. A theater or bookstore was classified as "adult" even if it did not show movies or sell books and magazines that were legally obscene under *Miller*; instead, the question was whether the establishment presented "material distinguished or characterized by an emphasis on matter depicting, describing, or relating to" specified sexual activities and anatomical areas.

Writing for a plurality of the Court, Justice John Paul Stevens concluded that the ordinance did not operate as a prior restraint, but merely regulated the location of theaters without reducing their owners' access to the market or the viewing public's access to sexually explicit movies. Even though the ordinance applied only to "adult" theaters and bookstores and thus singled them out for special treatment on the basis of the content of the films exhibited or the books and magazines sold, Justice Stevens found that the city had a legitimate interest "in attempting to preserve the quality of urban life" that justified the disparate treatment. In the opinion of urban planners and real estate experts who supported the ordinance, the concentration of "adult" establishments tended to attract transients, criminals, and prostitutes, adversely affect property values, and encourage residents and businesses to move elsewhere.

Ten years later, the Court returned to the zoning issue in *Renton v. Playtime Theaters, Inc.*, and this time a majority of the Justices agreed that a zoning ordinance may restrict the location of "adult" theaters. In that case, the Court upheld a Renton, Washington, ordinance that prohibited such theaters within 1,000 feet of any residential zone, single or multiple family dwelling, church, park, or school. The definition of "adult" theater was virtually identical to that used in the Detroit ordinance at issue in *Young*. In an opinion by Justice William Rehnquist, the Court ruled that the ordinance was not aimed at the content of the speech but rather at the secondary effects of "adult" theaters on the surrounding community. The purpose of the ordinance, the Court noted, was to "prevent crime, protect the city's retail trade, maintain property values, and generally protect and preserve the quality of [the city's] neighborhoods [and] commercial districts. . . ." Justice Rehnquist also pointed out that the ordinance did not completely ban "adult" theaters from the city, since more than 500 acres of land was available for them under the zoning plan.

Under these decisions, a city may use zoning controls to regulate "adult" theaters and bookstores by dispersing them, as in Detroit, or by effectively concentrating them, as in Renton. "It is not our function to appraise the wisdom of [a city's] decision to require adult theaters to be separated rather than concentrated in the same areas," Justice Stevens observed in the *American Mini Theatres* case. "[T]he city must be allowed a reasonable opportunity to experiment with solutions to admittedly serious problems." A total ban, however, is not permissible. For example, in *Schad v. Borough of Mount Ephraim* (1981), the Court struck down a zoning ordinance that completely prohibited nude dancing within the city. Dancing is a form of expressive activity protected by the first amendment, the Court said, and nudity does not mean that the expression is obscene. Under this approach, a city may not ban "adult" theaters and bookstores altogether, for these outlets exhibit material which, though perhaps pornographic, is not legally obscene. Moreover, a city may not enact a zoning ordinance that has the effect of a total ban, even though it would appear to permit such theaters and bookstores in certain areas.

Censorship of Motion Pictures. The relationship between film and the first amendment has long been an uneasy one. It was not until 1952, for example, that the Supreme Court ruled that movies are "a significant medium for the communication of ideas" and thus worthy of first amendment protection. In a 1959 case, however, the Court specifically left open the question whether "the controls which a State may impose on [films] are precisely co-extensive with those allowable for newspapers, books, or individual speech." In other words, the Court intimated that movies could be second-class citizens for first amendment purposes. Subsequent decisions have made that point quite clearly, and it is now settled that state and local governments may establish administrative bodies to license films and bar the showing of movies deemed obscene. These bodies may also declare films "unsuitable for minors" and assign other ratings similar to those voluntarily adopted by the motion picture industry. Only a handful of these censorship boards remain in operation today, however.

In *Times Film Corp. v. City of Chicago* (1961), the Court upheld a city ordinance that forbade the exhibition of motion pictures "without having first secured a permit therefor from the superintendent of police.'' Despite the fact that this system of licensing is a classic prior restraint, the Court ruled that the censorship scheme was constitutionally permissible. The ordinance was designed to "protect [Chicago citizens] against the dangers of obscenity in the public exhibition of motion pictures," the Court observed, adding that obscenity falls into one of the long recognized exceptions to the general rule that prior restraints offend the first amendment. The Court also made plain, however, that city officials do not have unbridled power "to prevent the showing of any motion picture they deem unworthy of a license." In this case, however, the issue was the validity of the licensing ordinance on its face, not the action of city officials in censoring nonobscene films protected by the first amendment.

Four years later, the Court was faced with a constitutional challenge to a Maryland statute that required advance approval of films by a state censorship board. In *Freedman v. Maryland*, the plaintiff conceded that such a licensing arrangement is generally permissible under the *Times Film* decision but argued that the Maryland statute violated the first amendment because it allowed the board to prevent the showing of any film until the exhibitor undertook a time-consuming appeal to the state courts and succeeded in obtaining a reversal of the board's decision. Meanwhile, a movie would be banned—for as much as a year in some cases—without a prior judicial determine that it was legally obscene. The Supreme Court agreed, ruling that the Maryland statute lacked sufficient procedural safeguards to "obviate the dangers of a censorship system" with respect to constitutionally protected expression. At the same time, however, the Court reaffirmed its ruling in *Times Film* that the "requirement of prior submission [of motion pictures] to a censor" is permissible, since "films differ from other forms of expression."

In order to pass muster under *Freedman*, a statute or ordinance providing for administrative approval of films prior to their exhibition must:

- place on the censorship body the burden of proving that a particular film is obscene and thus not entitled to constitutional protection;
- require that the censor, within a very brief time frame, either issue a license for exhibition of the film or seek a court order to prohibit its being shown; and
- assure a prompt final judicial decision on the question of whether the film is obscene, thus minimizing the possibility that a constitutionally protected film will be banned for a lengthy period of time.

The Maryland statute at issue in *Freedman* was subsequently amended to include these safeguards and then upheld by the courts as constitutional. The statute was repealed altogether in 1981.

A statute or ordinance that enables a censorship board to assign "ratings" to films in advance of their exhibition must also meet these procedural safeguards. In addition, the standards to be employed in rating a film must be detailed and precise, for otherwise the officials charged with assigning the ratings would have wide-ranging discretion and the persons seeking to exhibit films would have only a vague idea of the criteria to be utilized. The Supreme Court struck down a "ratings" ordinance on these grounds in *Interstate Circuit, Inc. v. City of Dallas* (1968), a decision that prompted the Motion Picture Industry Association of America to impose on its members the now-familiar rating system that classifies movies from "G" (general audiences) to "X" (no one under seventeen admitted). A city may supplant this scheme with one of its own but must meet the specifity standards set out in the *Interstate Circuit* case.

Children and Obscenity. Our society has long been troubled by the exposure of children to sexually explicit material, whether or not it is legally obscene. Another matter of concern, of apparently more recent vintage, is the use of children in the production of pornographic films, books, and magazines, a practice that has been widely condemned as a form of child abuse. These related problems present similar but distinct legal issues. In the first situation, the child is a recipient of sexually oriented material, while in the second he or she is a participant in the process by which that material is created. Fortunately, and in marked contrast to obscenity law in general, the legal principles applicable in both situations are rather clear.

In *Ginsberg v. New York* (1968), the Supreme Court ruled that a state may prohibit the sale of sexually oriented material to minors even though it is not legally obscene and would thus be available to adults. There the defendant was convicted of selling "girlie" magazines to a sixteen-year-old boy in violation of a New York statute that prohibited the sale to anyone under seventeen "any picture . . . which depicts nudity . . . and which is harmful to minors" and "any magazine . . . which contains [such pictures] and which, taken as a whole, is harmful to minors." Material was "harmful" under the statute if it had "that quality of . . . representation . . . of nudity [which] predominantly appeals to the prurient, shameful or morbid interest of minors, and . . . is patently offensive to prevailing standards in the adult community . . . with respect to what is suitable material for minors and . . . is utterly without redeeming social importance for minors."

In affirming the defendant's conviction under the statute, the Supreme Court recognized the power of the legislature to "employ variable concepts of obscenity" in restricting the sale of sexual material. The New York statute, Justice Brennan wrote for the Court, "simply adjusts the definition of obscenity to social realities by permitting the appeal of this type of material to be assessed in terms of the sexual interests of minors." Because the state has a legitimate interest in "protect[ing] the welfare of children," it can take steps to ensure that they are not exposed to harmful material. Although studies at the time did not establish with certainty that children are adversely affected by sexual publications of the type at issue in this case, the Court concluded that it was "not irrational for the legislature to find that exposure to material condemned by the statute is harmful to minors."

At the time of the *Ginsberg* decision in 1968, what is now known as "child pornography"—works that visually depict sexual conduct by children—was virtually unknown. In 1970, for example, the Presidential Commission on Obscenity and Pornography only briefly alluded to child pornography, pointing out that "the taboo against pedophilia . . . has remained almost inviolate" even in extremely hard-core pornographic materials. Sixteen years later, however, the Attorney General's Commission on Pornography devoted much of its time and energy to studying what it called "the special horror of child pornography." According to a 1977 Senate report, "[c]hild pornography and child prostitution have become highly organized, multi-million dollar industries that operate on a nationwide scale. . . ."

Statutes in all fifty states and at the federal level have been enacted to deal with the problem. Unlike laws aimed at publications or films, these statutes are designed to protect children who are induced to engage in sexual activity and then photographed or filmed. This sort of exploitation, the Attorney General's Commission on Pornography observed, is "inextricably linked" to the sexual abuse of children.

Accordingly, the various state and federal statutes define "child pornography" not in terms of what is legally obscene, but rather in terms of any portrayal of sexual conduct by a child. The production, exhibition, sale, or distribution of any photographic depiction of a child engaged in sexual activity is unlawful, regardless of whether the photograph, magazine, or film is obscene under the test outlined in *Miller v. California* and subsequent cases.

Such statutes are plainly constitutional. The leading case is *New York v. Ferber* (1982), in which the Supreme Court upheld a New York statute prohibiting persons from knowingly promoting "a sexual performance by a child" under the age of sixteen by producing, manufacturing, or distributing material depicting such a performance. The term "sexual performance" was defined as any visual representation of children involved in a variety of sexual activity, including actual or simulated sexual intercourse, oral sex, bestiality, masturbation, sadomasochistic abuse, or lewd exhibition of the genitals. Paul Ferber, the proprietor of a New York City bookstore, was arrested and convicted under the statute after he sold two films involving young boys to an undercover police officer.

Relying in part on the *Ginsberg* case, the Supreme Court ruled that the statute did not violate the first amendment and established a special rule for child pornography apart from the obscenity standard established in *Miller*. In short, the Court recognized that the government has "greater leeway in the regulation of pornographic depictions of children" because of the compelling interest in protecting the "physical and psychological well-being" of children. "The prevention of sexual exploitation and abuse of children constitutes a government objective of surpassing importance," Justice White wrote for the Court. In contrast, the "value of permitting live performances and photographic reproductions of children engaged in lewd sexual conduct is exceedingly modest. . . ." Because child pornography "bears so heavily and pervasively on the welfare of the children engaged in its production," the Court concluded that "it is permissible to consider these materials as without the protection of the First Amendment."

Thus, child pornography can be banned even though the material is not legally obscene under the *Miller* test. Specifically, the material need not appeal to the prurient interest of the average person, need not portray sexual conduct in a "patently offensive" manner, and neet not be evaluated "as a whole." Rather, it is enough that the material "visually depict sexual conduct by children below a specified age" and that the category of prohibited sexual conduct be specifically described in the statute. The Court held in *Ferber* that the New York statute satisfied these requirements and was therefore constitutional. The states have toughened their child pornography laws in the aftermath of the *Ferber* decision, and in 1984 the Congress passed a more comprehensive federal statute directed at child pornography in interstate commerce. This statute was strengthened in 1988 with the addition of provisions barring the use of computer networks to exchange information about child pornography, requiring publishers and producers of sexually explicit material to keep records showing the name and age of each performer, and prohibiting the buying and selling of children, through transfers of legal custody, for pornography purposes.

"Dial-a-Porn" Services. As early as 1928, callers could pick up their telephones and obtain the correct time of day. Later, telephone companies offered weather information, sports scores, and other recorded messages. In the early 1980s, how-

ever, the Federal Communications Commission ruled that telephone companies could not provide such information themselves. The result was the "dial-it" service by which long-distance and local telephone lines are leased to companies that furnish callers with information ranging from soap-opera updates to stock quotations. The phone companies and the information providers have profited handsomely, with revenues for 1988 estimated at $450 million.

About a third of these revenues are generated by so-called "dial-a-porn" services available locally in major cities and via long-distance from just about anywhere. The services are heavily advertised in sexually explicit magazines. A dial-a-porn customer may either speak with a paid performer, who will talk in terms as explicit as the caller desires, or listen to a pre-recorded message in which sex acts are described in graphic detail. In 1984–85 Pacific Bell earned an estimated $12 million from these calls, while during approximately the same period a major dial-a-porn company earned more than $3.5 million.

Responding to a concern that children were being exposed to offensive and damaging messages via dial-a-porn services, Congress in 1983 passed a statute making the interstate transmission of obscene or indecent telephone calls to persons under the age of eighteen or to nonconsenting adults a federal offense. The statute further provided that dial-a-porn companies could avoid a conviction by showing that they had restricted access by children in accordance with procedures that were to be adopted by the Federal Communications Commission. After its initial set of regulations under the statute were declared unconstitutional, the FCC adopted rules requiring dial-a-porn companies to limit access through use of credit cards, access codes, and "scrambling" technology. These requirements were upheld by the U.S. Court of Appeals for the Second Circuit in *Carlin Communications, Inc. v. Federal Communications Commission* (1988). Shortly thereafter, the FCC imposed civil fines of $600,000 each on two dial-a-porn companies for violating the statute and accompanying regulations. Some states have passed similar statutes governing intrastate "dial-it" services.

In 1988, Congress twice amended the dial-a-porn statute. The first revision, which came in a bill signed into law in April, prohibited *all* telephone transmissions of obscene and indecent material for commercial purposes, even to consenting adults. The amendment also eliminated the FCC's rulemaking role under the statute, since there was no longer any need for regulations prescribing devices that could be used to limit children's access to dial-a-porn services. Court challenges to the statute quickly followed, and in two cases—*Sable Communications v. Federal Communications Commission* (1988) and *Roe v. Meese* (1988)—federal district courts in California and New York, respectively, ruled unconstitutional the ban on "indecent" messages that are not legally obscene. The prohibition against obscene messages was upheld, however.

When Congress subsequently amended the statute in November, it retained the prohibition against both indecent and obscene messages but provided harsher penalties for the latter. The transmission of obscene messages by telephone for commercial purposes is a felony punishable by imprisonment for not more than to two years, a fine of up to $250,000 for individuals and $500,000 for organizations, or both. Moreover, a heavier fine can be imposed on the basis of the defendant's gross profits from the illegal venture. In contrast, a person who transmits indecent messages is guilty of a misdemeanor and subject to a jail term of not more than six months, a maximum fine of $50,000, or both. At the same time, however, the amendment eliminated a provision allowing the FCC to assess a civil penalty in an administrative proceeding or to ask a court to impose such a penalty. It was under this provision that the FCC had levied the $600,000 fines mentioned above.

In June 1989, the Supreme Court affirmed the *Sable Communications* case, agreeing with the district court that a total ban on indecent but nonobscene telephone messages is unconstitutional. Because sexual expression that is not legally obscene enjoys first amendment protection, the Court said, the government may regulate it only "to promote a compelling interest if it chooses the least restrictive means to further the articulated interest." As noted previously, the Court held in *Ginsberg v. New York* that there is such a compelling interest in shielding minors from material that is not obscene by adult standards. The dial-a-porn statute, however, did not address this legitimate concern in the least restrictive manner. By imposing a total ban on indecent telephone messages, it had the impermissible effect of denying adults access to constitutionally protected speech.

An obvious alternative to a total ban is the short-lived "restricted access" approach adopted by the FCC under the 1983 version of the statute. Although the government claimed in *Sable* that the complete prohibition was justified because "nothing less" could prevent children from gaining access to indecent messages, the Supreme Court labeled that argument "quite unpersuasive" and found no evidence to support it. "For all we know from this record, the FCC's technological approach to restricting dial-a-porn messages to adults who seek them would be extremely effective," the Court said, "and only a few of the most enterprising and disobedient young people will manage to secure access to such messages." Indeed, the Court noted, the FCC had previously determined , after lengthy proceedings, that its credit card, access code, and scrambling requirements "were a satisfactory solution to the problem of keeping indecent dial-a-porn messages out of the reach of minors."

Given the existence of a less restrictive alternative that had not been "tested over time," the Court was compelled to declare the total ban unconstitutional. This ruling obviously applies to the November 1988 statute, which contains the identical prohibition as the April version that was actually before the Court. Two questions remain unresolved after the *Sable* decision, however. First, the Court's opinion seems to leave open the possibility that a total ban could be upheld if there proves to be no "fail-safe method" of ensuring that minors will not be able to access the dial-a-porn system. Second, the Court did not directly address the constitutionality of the FCC's prior rules designed to prevent access by children, though the opinion leaves one with the impression that the regulations would pass muster.

Pornography as a Civil Rights Issue. Feminists have argued for some time that pornography degrades and humiliates women by portraying them as mere outlets for male sexual desires and fantasies. More recently, some feminist writers have taken the argument a step further, contending that pornography incites violence against women. According to author Susan Brownmiller, pornography is "virulent propaganda against women" that "promotes a climate in which the ideology of rape is not only tolerated but encouraged." The Attorney General's Commission on Pornography concluded that social science evidence supports this view, at least as far as pornography that depicts sexual violence is concerned. These studies, the Commission said, indicate that "substantial exposure to sexually violent materials . . . bears a causal relationship to antisocial acts of sexual violence. . . ."

The feminist approach has led to a new legal theory on which to base regulation of pornographic materials: defining pornography as a practice that violates the civil rights of women. In 1984, the Indianapolis City Council adopted an ordinance of this type based on the work of author Andrea Dworkin and law professor Catharine MacKinnon. Though it was subsequently declared unconstitutional, the ordinance could serve as a model for future efforts along similar lines. At its center were provisions that prohibited the production, sale, exhibition, and distribution of pornography, the coercion of persons into performing for pornographic works, and the "forcing" of pornography on individuals in the home, at school or work, and in any public place. Rather than establish criminal penalties, the ordinance created various civil remedies, including an administrative proceeding by which a woman could file a complaint with the city's office of equal opportunity. Further, anyone physically injured by a person who had seen or read pornography was permitted to bring an action for damages against the seller, exhibitor, or distributor.

Most important, at least for constitutional purposes, was the ordinance's definition of pornography:

> [T]he graphic sexually explicit subordination of women, whether in pictures or in words, that also includes one or more of the following: (1) Women are presented as sexual objects who enjoy pain or humiliation; or (2) Women are presented as sexual objects who experience sexual pleasure in being raped; or (3) Women are presented as sexual objects tied up or cut up or mutilated or bruised or physically hurt, or as dismembered or truncated or fragmented or severed into body parts; or (4) Women are presented being penetrated by objects or animals; or (5) Women are presented in scenarios of degradation, injury, abasement, torture, shown as filthy or inferior, bleeding, bruised, or hurt in a context that makes these conditions sexual; or (6) Women are presented as sexual objects for domination, conquest, violation, exploitation, possession, or use, or through postures or positions of servility or submission or display.

A variety of businesses, organizations, and individuals challenged the ordinance in federal court. In *American Booksellers Association v. Hudnut* (1985), the U.S. Court of Appeals for the Seventh Circuit ruled that the ordinance violated the first amendment, and the Supreme Court summarily affirmed that decision without issuing an opinion. According to the Seventh Circuit, the definition of pornography found in the ordinance did not meet the standards set forth in *Miller v. California*, since it did not require that the offending work be "taken as a whole" and did not refer to the prurient interest, patent offensiveness, community standards, and "serious" value. Put another way, the ordinance provided penalties for expression that, while pornographic, was not legally obscene. Because the expression restricted by the ordinance enjoyed constitutional protection, it could not be regulated on the basis of content, no matter how pernicious the message might be. The court said:

> Under the ordinance graphic sexually explicit speech is "pornography" or not depending on the perspective the author adopts. Speech that "subordinates" women and also, for example, presents women as enjoying pain, humiliation, or rape, or even simply presents women in "positions of servility or submission or display" is forbidden, no matter how great the literary political value of the work taken as a whole. Speech that portrays women in positions of equality is lawful, no matter how graphic the sexual content. This is thought control. It establishes an "approved" view of women, of how they may react to sexual encounters, of how the sexes may relate to each other. Those who espouse the approved view may use sexual images; those who do not, may not.

The Supreme Court's affirmance, without opinion, of the Seventh Circuit's decision means that the ruling is binding on all lower courts. But the reluctance of the Supreme Court to write an opinion suggests that the issues presented in *Hudnut* have not been definitively resolved. Central to the Seventh Circuit's opinion is the notion that speech is entitled to full first amendment protection if it is not legally obscene under the *Miller* test. As Judge Jones' dissent in the *Herceg* case makes clear, however, that proposition is now under attack, the argument being that pornographic speech that is not technically obscene does not deserve the same constitutional treatment as political speech and other expression that lies at the "core" of the first amendment. This view is worth examining in more detail.

Pornography as Unprotected Speech. In the *American Mini Theatres* case discussed previously in connection with zoning ordinances, Justice Stevens suggested that pornographic expression that does not qualify as legally obscene under the *Miller* test is not worthy of the full constitutional protection accorded other forms of speech. In concluding that the Detroit ordinance did not impermissibily discriminate against theaters that showed sexually explicit but nonobscene films, he wrote:

> The question whether speech is, or is not, protected by the first amendment often depends on the content of the speech. * * * [E]ven though we recognize that the First Amendment will not tolerate the total suppression of erotic materials that have some arguably artistic value, it is manifest that society's interest in this type of expression is of a wholly different, and lesser, magnitude than the interest in untrammeled political debate. . . . Whether political oratory or philosophical discussion moves us to applaud or to despise what is said, every schoolchild can understand why our duty to defend the right to speak remains the same. But few of us would march our sons and daughters off to war to preserve the citizen's right to see "Specified Sexual Activities" exhibited in the theaters of our choice. Even though the First Amendment protects communication in this area from total suppression, we hold that the State may legitimately use the content of these materials as the basis for placing them in a different classification from other motion pictures.

This portion of the opinion received the support of only three other Justices, meaning that it does not stand as a controlling statement of constitutional law that binds the lower courts. Indeed, Justice Lewis Powell, while agreeing that the zoning ordinance was constitutional, wrote that he was "not inclined to agree with [Justice Stevens' conclusion] that nonobscene, erotic materials may be treated differently under First Amendment principles from other forms of protected speech." The four dissenters, led by Justice Stewart, were adamant on this point: "The fact that the 'offensive' speech at issue here may not address 'important' topics—'ideas of social and political significance,' in the Court's terminology—does not mean that it is less worthy of constitutional protection." This has long been the prevailing view. For example, in the *Schad* case discussed previously, the Court ruled that nonobscene nude dancing is within the first amendment, observing that "[e]ntertainment, as well as political and ideological speech, is [constitutionally] protected. . . ." The *Sable Communications* case holding "indecent" dial-a-porn messages to be protected by the first amendment is consistent with this traditional approach.

The debate reflected in *American Mini Theatres* is not new. Recall from Chapter 1 that Alexander Meiklejohn initially took the position that the first amendment protected only "political" speech, though he subsequently concluded that broader protection was necessary even if that meant affording some protection to obscene materials. One writer who apparently clings to Meiklejohn's original theory is Robert Bork, the former federal appeals court judge whose appointment to the Supreme Court was blocked by the Senate. In an influential law journal article, Bork wrote that only speech devoted to "the discovery and spread of political truth" is entitled of first amendment protection, and that "all other forms of speech raise only issues of human gratification." Nonpolitical speech—including sexually explicit materials that may not be legally obscene under the *Miller* standard—are in Bork's view fully subject to government regulation.

Although the Bork approach has not been adopted by the Supreme Court, the Justices have in some cases suggested that the content of particular speech makes it less worthy of full first amendment protection. As Judge Jones noted in her *Herceg* dissent, for example, the Court has distinguished between "public" and "private" speech in the defamation context, ruling in *Dun & Bradstreet, Inc. v. Greenmoss Builders, Inc.* that the latter does not merit as much constitutional protection as the former. And, as discussed at some length in Chapter 11, the Court has ruled that commercial speech that merely proposes an economic transaction may be restricted in ways that would be impermissible with respect to other forms of expresssion. Building on cases such as these, one can certainly argue that sexually explicit but nonobscene materials should receive far less protection under the first amendment than publications or films focusing on political matters.

A somewhat different approach is reflected in the report of the Attorney General's Commission on Pornography, which argues that sexually explicit materials should not be considered "speech" at all for first amendment purposes. This theory apparently has its origins in a 1967 law journal article by John Finnis, who argued that pornography is not worthy of first amendment protection "because it pertains, not to the realm of ideas, but to the realm of passion, desires, cravings and titillation. . . ." A proponent of this view, University of Michigan law professor Frederick Schauer, was a member of the Commission and the principal draftsman of its report. According to the Commission, "[t]he special power of the First Amendment ought . . . to be reserved for the conveying of arguments and information in a way that surpasses some admittedly low threshold of cognitive appeal. . . . " Pornography does not meet this threshold, since it is not "remotely related to an exchange of views in the marketplace of ideas, to an attempt to articulate a point of view, to attempt to persaude, or to attempt seriously to convey through literary or artistic means a different vision of humanity or of the world." Instead, pornography is little more than a "masturbatory aid."

Either theory could be employed to create a new category of "pornographic speech" somewhere in between obscene expression, which is not protected at all, and "political" speech, which, as everyone agrees, is fully protected. Although sexually explicit materials falling within this new classification would be entitled to partial first amendment protection, they could be regulated much more easily than other forms of expression. For example, one could argue that the Indianapolis statute discussed above would pass constitutional muster under this approach, as would prohibitions against "indecent" messages transmitted by dial-a-porn services. In addition, pornographic materials that are implicated in cases involving physical harm could lead to liability for the maker or distributor of those materials. Recall, for example, that the Indianapolis statute provided that a person physically harmed by someone who had been exposed to pornographic materials could seek damages in a civil suit against the seller, exhibitor, or distributor of such materials. Judge

Jones took a similar approach in her *Herceg* dissent, and it is to the problems presented by that case that we now turn.

COMMUNICATIONS THAT LEAD TO PHYSICAL HARM

The *Herceg* case is one of a series litigated on the theory that publishers and broadcasters can be held liable for injuries that can be traced, in some fashion, to a publication or broadcast. The ruling in *Herceg* reflects the prevailing view that the first amendment precludes recovery against the media absent a showing that the publication or broadcast "incited" the behavior that led to the injury. The minority position is that, at least in some situations, a plaintiff may recover upon a showing that the media defendant was negligent in publishing or broadcasting the material that led to the physical injury, much as such a defendant may be held liable for a negligently published statement that harms the reputation of a private individual.

The cases decided to date can be placed in one of three broad categories:

- those in which a person attempts to emulate conduct described in a publication or broadcast and, in the process, accidentally injures himself;
- those in which a person is said to have been induced to harm himself in an intentional manner; and
- those in which a person is physically harmed by someone who was apparently induced by a publication or broadcast to carry out the act.

These categories can be further subdivided on the basis of the age of the person who is the recipient of the communication (i.e., whether that individual is a child or an adult) and the nature of the communication itself (i.e., whether it is an entertainment show, an informational program, a commercial message, or a pornographic film or magazine). Generally speaking, however, the courts have reached the same result no matter which of these variations is involved.

Accidental Injury to the Recipient

Prior to the ruling in *Herceg*, the leading case with respect to the first category was probably *Walt Disney Productions, Inc. v. Shannon* (1981). There an eleven-year-old boy named Craig Shannon was partially blinded when he tried to create a sound effect after having seen the technique demonstrated on the "Mickey Mouse Club" show. One segment of the program featured "the magic you can create with sound effects." Demonstrating how to reproduce the sound of a tire coming off an automobile, one of the cast members placed a BB pellet in a large, round balloon, filled it with air, and rotated the BB inside. Craig attempted to duplicate the feat, using a large, skinny balloon and a piece of lead almost twice the size of a BB. The balloon burst and impelled the lead into Craig's eye. He then brought suit against Walt Disney Productions, the show's producer, as well the local station that had broadcast the program and the syndication company that had marketed it.

A Georgia trial court granted the defendants' motion for summary judgment, and the state supreme court affirmed. The court first pointed out that the plaintiff's was seeking to hold the defendants liable "on the ground that they invited him to do something posing a foreseeable risk of injury" and that tort law does support recovery under such a theory. By way of illustration, the court mentioned so-called "pied piper" cases in which there is an express or implied invitation extended to a child to act in a manner that is likely to cause him harm. For example, because one can easily anticipate that children will run into the street without looking, an ice cream vendor who sells his wares from a truck can be held liable for failing to protect children against traffic. However, the court concluded that the first amendment precludes application of this theory in cases against media defendants absent a showing that the express or implied invitation involved conduct that presented a "clear and present danger" that injury would result. "[I]t cannot be said that the statements uttered during the course of this television program gave rise to a clear and present danger of personal injury to the plaintiff," the court said. "To hold otherwise would . . . have a seriously chilling effect on the flow of protected speech throughout society's mediums of communications."

In at least one respect, the *Shannon* case presents a stronger argument for the imposition of liability than does *Herceg*, for the producers of the "Mickey Mouse Club" program obviously intended that young viewers try the sound-effect trick themselves. In contrast, *Hustler* magazine expressly warned readers of the dangers of autoerotic asphyxiation and thus attempted to discourage emulation. That was also the case in *DeFlippo v. NBC* (1982), in which the Rhode Island Supreme Court afffirmed a summary judgment for the network in a suit brought by the parents of a thirteen-year-old boy who had accidentally hanged himself in trying to duplicate a stunt demonstrated by a professional stunt man on the Johnny Carson show. The stunt man made clear that the activity was dangerous and warned that "it's not something you want to go and try." Using analysis similar to that employed in *Herceg*, the court ruled that the first amendment barred recovery unless the defendant had "incited" the conduct. In light of the stunt man's express warning, it could hardly be said that the requisite incitement was present.

Intentional Injury to the Recipient

The second category is similar to the first in that the communication is said to have induced certain conduct on the part of one who has received the message. It differs, however, in that the recipient's injury cannot be described as accidental, as were the deaths in *Herceg* and *DeFlippo* and the eye injury in *Shannon*. The central legal issue, however, is the same: was the defendant's expression an "incitement" and thus not protected by the first amendment? A recent California case stemming from a teenager's suicide is illustrative.

In *McCollum v. CBS, Inc.* (1988), the plaintiffs alleged that the music of rock star Ozzy Osbourne incited their nineteen-year-old son to commit suicide. The boy, who had serious emotional problems and a history of alcohol abuse, shot himself in the head one night while listening to one of Osbourne's albums. When he was found the next morning, he was still wearing stereo headphones and the album was revolving on a nearby turntable. Earlier that evening, he had been listening to different Osbourne albums on the family stereo system in another room. One of those records included a song entitled "Suicide Solution," which, according to the plaintiffs, "preaches that 'suicide is the only way out' for a person who is involved in excessive drinking." This message, the plaintiffs alleged, was consistent with the overall theme of Osbourne's music "that life is filled with nothing but despair and hopelessness and that suicide is not only acceptable, but desirable." Moreover, they claimed that Osbourne specifically sought to appeal to troubled adolescents, a target audience that was "extremely susceptible to the external influence and directions from a cult figure such as Osbourne who had become a role model and leader for many of them." Named as defendants were Osbourne and his record company, CBS.

The trial court dismissed the case, and the California Court of Appeal affirmed. Relying on the "incitement" concept discussed in *Herceg*, the court ruled that the plaintiffs could not demonstrate that Osbourne's music was "directed or intended toward the goal of bringing about the imminent suicide of listeners and . . . that it was likely to produce such a result." Nothing in the music could be characterized as a "command to an immediate suicidal act," the court said, adding that the song "Suicide Solution" could easily be interpreted as warning that alcohol, a liquid solution, is deadly. But, even if the message was "that suicide is an acceptable alternative to a life that has become unendurable," it did not constitute a direct incitement:

> [M]usical lyrics and poetry cannot be construed to contain the requisite "call to action" for the elementary reason that they simply are not intended to be and should not be read literally on their face, nor judged by a standard of prose oratory. Reasonable persons understand musical lyrics and poetic conventions as the figurative expressions which they are. No rational person would or could believe otherwise nor would they mistake musical lyrics and poetry for literal commands or directives to immediate action.

The Recipient Injures Another Person

In the third category, the media message is said to have prompted a recipient to inflict physical harm on someone else. As in the second category, the recipient acts intentionally, but his target is a third person rather than himself. The leading case of this type is *Olivia N. v. NBC*, decided by a California appellate court in 1981. Several years earlier, NBC had broadcast a prime-time television movie, "Born Innocent," which dealt with the harmful effect of a state-run home upon a teenage girl who had become a ward of the state. One particularly powerful scene in the film showed the girl being raped by four other girls with a "plumber's helper." The court described the scene as follows:

> [T]he young girl enters the community bathroom of the facility to take a shower. She is then shown taking off her clothes and stepping into the shower, where she bathes for a few moments. Suddenly, the water stops and a look of fear comes across her face. Four adolescent girls are standing across from her in the shower room. One of the girls is carrying a "plumber's helper," waving it suggestively by her side. The four girls violently attack the younger girl, wrestling her to the floor. The young girl is shown naked from the waist up, struggling as the older girls force her legs apart. Then, the television film shows the girl with the plumber's helper making intense thrusting motions with the handle of the plunger until one of the four says, "That's enough." The young girl is left sobbing and naked on the floor.

Four days later, Olivia N., a nine-year-old California girl, was attacked and raped with a bottle by older children who had seen and discussed the rape scene in "Born Innocent." The injured girl brought suit against NBC and its San Francisco affiliate, arguing that the defendants should have known that that susceptible persons might imitate the crime depicted in the movie but nonetheless broadcast it, without a warning, during prime time in an attempt to attract the largest possible audience.

The California Court of Appeal upheld the trial judge's dismissal of the plaintiff's suit. "The deterrent effect of subjecting the television networks to negligence liability because of their programming choices would lead to self-censorship which would dampen the vigor and limit the variety of public debate," the court said, adding that such liability could not logically be limited to entertainment programming. "If a negligence theory is recognized, a television network or local station could be liable when a child imitates activites portrayed in a news program or documentary." Because protected speech was involved, the court said, the plaintiff could recover only upon a showing that the movie created a "clear and present danger" by actually inciting violent behavior. There was no such incitement here, the court said, pointing out that even the plaintiff's attorneys conceded that the movie in no way encouraged or advocated violence.

Other Variables: Audience and Content

Most of the cases discussed above involved communications received by children, who are considered more susceptible than adults to "suggestive" messages and thus more likely to imitate or be influenced by what they see or read. The courts, however, have employed the same "incitement" analysis no matter whether the recipients are children or adults. Some commentators have challenged this approach, arguing that the first amendment should not operate as a bar to suits in which children have received the message and harmed themselves or others. At the center of this argument is the Supreme Court's "variable" approach to obscenity reflected in *Ginsberg v. New York*.

In *Ginsberg*, the Court ruled that society's legitimate interest in the protection of children permits regulation of speech that would not be obscene with respect to adults. As as result, a state may conclude that mere nudity is harmful to children and, consistent with the first amendment, may prohibit the sale of material containing nudity to them, even though that material is not legally obscene. If such a restriction is constitutionally permissible, the argument goes, a reduced level of first amendment protection is warranted in cases such as *Olivia N.*, for the state surely has a legitimate interest in protecting children from physical harm and in discouraging the dissemination of information that might prompt children to act violently toward others. Pointing to several studies identifying a link between violence on television and violent behavior in children, advocates of this approach contend that children are more likely to be influenced by what they see and read than adults and are thus more likely to imitate the depicted behavior.

Another variable that enters the analytical picture is the content of the particular speech. For example, one can argue that liability is more appropriate in *Herceg* than in either *Shannon* or *DeFlippo* because pornographic speech—unlike entertainment and informational material—is not entitled to full first amendment protection. Judge Jones took this position in her dissenting opinion in *Herceg*, focusing upon the content of *Hustler* magazine and the limited social value of pornographic expression. As the majority opinion in *Herceg* and our prior discussion of obscenity make plain, however, the courts have not been willing to water down the first amendment in cases involving pornographic speech that is not legally obscene. Nonetheless, Judge Jones' approach has been employed in cases involving advertisements, for commercial speech has been accorded less constitutional protection than other types of expression.

The plaintiffs in *Norwood v. Soldier of Fortune Magazine, Inc.* (1987) and *Eimann v. Soldier of Fortune Magazine, Inc.* (1988) alleged that they were injured by "hit men" whose services had been arranged through "personal services" classified ads placed in the magazine. The *Norwood* case was settled prior to trial, but in *Eimann* a Houston jury awarded the plaintiff $9.4 million. The federal courts in both cases ruled that the first amendment did not bar the lawsuits, reasoning that commercial speech does not enjoy full constitutional protection. Although the *Eimann* case was subsequently reversed on appeal, the appellate court based its ruling on tort law rather than the first amendment. The relevent tort principles are discussed below, and we shall return to these cases in Chapter 11 in connection with advertising and the commercial speech doctrine. Another case of this type is *Weirum v. RKO General, Inc.*, a 1975 California case discussed by the majority in *Herceg*. There the court held a radio station liable for the death of a motorist killed by two speeding teenagers participating in a station give-away contest. Because a promotional activity was involved, the speech was commercial in nature and thus entitled to only limited first amendment protection.

Liability for News Stories?

If the first amendment precludes recovery in a case such as *Olivia N.*, which involved an entertainment program, it seems unlikely that recovery would be permissible on the basis of a news story which somehow led to physical harm. Some courts have not ruled out that possibility, however. For example, in *Hyde v. City of Columbia* (1982), the police provided two local newspapers with the name and address of a woman who had escaped from an unknown man after he had abducted her. The newspapers printed the information in stories dealing with the incident, and the assailant—who was still at large—subsequently began to harass the woman, whose identity and address he did not know prior to publication of the news accounts. She then brought suit against the city for releasing the information and against the newspapers for publishing it.

The Missouri Court of Appeals concluded that the woman could proceed against the newspapers, as well as the city, on a negligence theory. Rejecting the newspapers' first amendment defense, the court relied heavily on *Gertz v. Robert Welch, Inc.*, which permits private persons to recover damages for injury to reputation upon a showing of negligence on the part of the news media. Because *Gertz* permits "private redress against a newspaper for a negligent publication of information" in the defamation setting, the court reasoned, there is no first amendment barrier to a suit for personal injuries. The court added:

> We [conclude] that the name and address of an abduction [victim] who can identify an assailant still at large before arrest is a matter of such trivial public concern compared with the high probability of risk to the victim by their publication, that a news medium owes a duty in such circumstances to use reasonable care not to give likely occasion for [the assailant] to do injury to the [victim]. * * * To delete the name and address of the abduction victim from the news medium publication would impair no significant news function nor public interest in the reportage of crime and apprehension of criminals. To report that information when the assailant can be identified [by the victim] . . . encourages not only a likelihood of injury but of additional crime.

The U.S. Supreme Court declined to review the *Hyde* case, which was eventually settled out of court when the plaintiff agreed to accept a payment of $6,000 from the city and nothing from the newspapers. The decision is plainly contrary to the cases discussed above, and its rationale has not been followed by other courts (although Judge Jones mentioned it with approval in a portion of her *Herceg* dissent not reproduced in the text). If the "chilling effect" of permitting a negligence action on the basis of a made-for-television movie is "obvious," as the California Court of Appeal observed in *Olivia N.*, it is equally obvious in a case such as *Hyde*. Accordingly, most courts will probably evaluate cases involving news stories under the "incitement" test described previously, thus affording almost complete protection to the press.

Tort Law Issues

To this point, our discussion has focused on the constitutional issues presented by the personal injury cases. It should also be noted that these cases pose difficult tort law problems; in fact, some courts have dismissed suits of this type on the ground that they are not permitted under traditional tort law concepts, thereby avoiding the first amendment question.

Under settled principles of tort law, there can be no recovery for negligence unless the defendant owed the plaintiff a "duty"—that is, an obligation recognized by law requiring the defendant to conform to a certain standard of conduct for the protection of the plaintiff, and others, against unreasonable risks of harm. For example, we all have a duty to drive carefully, and our breach of that duty (running a red light, for example) can give rise to liability if someone is injured. In some situations, however, the law does not recognize a duty. For instance, in most states a landowner need not post signs warning trespassers about dangerous conditions on his property, since trespassers have no right to be there in the first place.

In determining whether a duty exists, the courts usually examine several factors, including the foreseeability of harm to the plaintiff, the closeness of the connection between the defendant's conduct and the injury suffered by the plaintiff, the "moral blame" attached to the defendant's conduct, the policy of preventing future harm, and the extent of the burden to the defendant and the societal consequences of imposing a duty under the circumstances. Three of these factors are of particular importance for present purposes: foreseeability, the burden of a duty upon a defendant, and the impact on society.

Foreseeability refers to the ability of the defendant to anticipate harm as a result of his actions. No person can be expected to guard against harm from events which are not reasonably likely to occur; on the other hand, if the likelihood of an occurrence is great, a reasonable person would take some precaution against the harm that it could cause, particularly if the potential injury is serious. The probability and gravity of the risk must be balanced against other factors, including the burden on the defendant in taking precautions against the risk and the social utility of the defendant's conduct. As the late Dean William Prosser put it, the question is simply whether "the game is worth the candle." Suppose, for example, that freezing temperatures caused pipes to burst in Houston, Texas, resulting in water damage to the belongings of a person living in an apartment complex. Did the apartment owner have a duty to protect against such a freeze? Although it has been known to freeze in Houston, temperatures cold enough to burst pipes are not common. Moreover, measures to protect pipes can be expensive, especially if owners are required to renovate existing buildings. Surely the owners would pass that cost on to the tenants via increased rent. Are these consequences "worth the candle" if hard feezes occur only rarely?

Based on the cases we have examined in this section, there seems to be some risk of physical harm stemming from material that is broadcast or published. For example, children sometimes imitate what they see on television and criminals sometimes "get ideas" from reading magazines or newspapers. But how great is the likelihood of personal injury as a result of such a publication or broadcast? As great as a hard freeze in south Texas? Greater? How do we decide?

Even if we assume that there is a substantial risk of serious harm, we must balance that risk against the burden on the defendant and the possible cost to society if a duty is recognized. Publishers and broadcasters would face almost unlimited liability from negligence actions, and, in order to limit this financial exposure would be required to evaluate in careful fashion the material they disseminate. Consider the impact of such a screening process on a large daily newspaper or a network news department. Apart from the expense involved, it seems clear that many stories would never be aired or printed. The impact on society would be obvious, for the net result would be a diminished flow of information to the public.

Applying a similar balancing analysis, the U.S. Court of Appeals for the Fifth Circuit reversed the jury's verdict against *Soldier of Fortune* magazine in the *Eimann* case mentioned above. The court first determined that although the magazine's classified ads for "personal services" were ambiguous in that they did not expressly mention illegal activitites, they presented "more than a remote risk" of harm, since some had been linked to such crimes as murder and extortion. On the other side of the scale, the court placed "the pervasiveness of advertising in our society and the important role it plays." The court also pointed out that most publications are heavily dependent on advertising revenue, the loss of which would have an adverse effect on editorial content. In striking the balance, the court concluded that these considerations outweighed the risk of harm stemming from the ads. Consequently, *Soldier of Fortune* "owed no duty to refrain from publishing a facially innocuous classified advertisement when the ad's context—at most—made its message ambiguous."

PROBLEMS

1. Under the test for obscenity announced in *Miller v. California*, the challenged material must be evaluated "as a whole." Does this mean that magazines such as *Playboy* and *Penthouse*, which contain fiction and articles on "serious" subjects as well as photographs of nude women and other sexually oriented material, can never be legally obscene? Could a single issue be found obscene if, for example, it did not include fiction and news articles? *See Penthouse International, Ltd. v. McAuliffe*, 610 F.2d 1353 (5th Cir.), *cert. dism'd*, 447 U.S. 931 (1980); *Penthouse International, Ltd. v. Webb*, 594 F. Supp. 1186 (N.D. Ga. 1984); *State v. Walden Book Co.*, 386 So.2d 342 (La. 1980).

2. In the course of gathering information for its 1986 report, the Attorney General's Commission on Pornography held public hearings around the country. At one of these hearings, the executive director of the National Federation of Decency testified that certain

corporations were engaged in the sale of pornography, which, in his view, included *Penthouse* and *Playboy* magazines. He also submitted a written statement setting forth his opinions. The Commission sent a letter to these corporations (bookstore chains, convenience stores, and the like) advising them of the charges and offering them an opportunity to respond "prior to drafting its final report . . . on identified distributors" of pornographic materials. As a result of the letter, many stores pulled *Playboy* and other magazines—including *Cosmopolitan* and *American Photographer*—from their shelves. Did the Commission's action violate the first amendment? *See Playboy Enterprises, Inc. v. Meese*, 639 F. Supp. 581 (D.D.C. 1986).

3. In 1989 the Missouri legislature passed a statute making it a crime to sell or rent videotapes of violent movies to anyone under seventeen. Aimed at blood-drenched "slasher" films, the statute applies to any videotape that depicts violence in a "patently offensive" manner, tends to "appeal to [a] morbid interest in violence" on the part of persons under seventeen, and "lacks serious literary, artistic, political, or scientific value" for such persons. *See* H.B. 225, Mo. Legis. Service 241 (July 1989). Is the statute constitutional? Does the rationale of *Ginsberg v. New York* apply here? How does a video store owner decide what level of violence is permissible?

4. Is *Hyde v. City of Columbia* consistent with the Supreme Court's decisions in *Cox Broadcasting Corp. v. Cohn* and *Florida Star v. B. J. F.,* both of which are discussed in Chapter 3? If the plaintiff in *Hyde* could not prevail in a suit for invasion of privacy on the basis of admittedly truthful information obtained from official sources, why should she be permitted to recover for personal injuries?

5. Two boys were conducting a chemistry experiment described in a book designed specifically for children. Though they followed the instructions to the letter, an explosion occurred, injuring them both. The book contained erroneous information about the order in which the chemicals were to be mixed. Can the boys recover from the publisher of the book? The author? Would your answer be any different if the injured parties were adults who had been using a "how to" book? *See Lewin v. McCreight*, 655 F. Supp. 282 (E.D. Mich. 1987); *Alm v. Van Nostrand Reinhold Co.*, 480 N.E.2d 1263 (Ill. App. 1985); *Walter v. Bauer*, 439 N.Y.S.2d 821 (Sup. Ct. 1981), *aff'd*, 451 N.Y.S.2d 533 (App. Div. 1982).

6. In a span of seventy-two hours, beginning on September 29, 1982, seven people in the Chicago area died from ingesting Tylenol capsules laced with a lethal dose of cyanide. The story was front-page news across the country, and the television networks devoted considerable air time to the tragedy. Suppose that a man read of the killings in his home town newspaper and inserted poison into another brand of over-the-counter painkiller sold in capsule form. Two people died as a result of his action. When apprehended by police, he told them that he "got the idea" to poison the drugs from news accounts of the Tylenol case in the local newspaper. Can the families of the victims recover against the newspaper? Does it matter that the press had a legitimate reason to report the Tylenol story, that is, to warn people that taking the medicine might kill them? Is it relevant that such "copycat" crimes are not uncommon? *See* Floyd Abrams, "Negligent Programming? Some First Amendment Ramifications," *Communications Lawyer* (Winter 1983), p. 1.

7. Ronnie Zamora, a fifteen-year-old Florida boy, was charged with the murder of his eighty-three-year-old neighbor. As part of his defense, he claimed that he had become desensitized to violent behavior and had developed a sociopathic personality as a result of violent programs on television. He was convicted and sentenced to prison. Subse-

quently, he sued the three television networks for damages, arguing that he had become involuntarily addicted to violent programming and that the networks had "stimulated, incited and instigated" him to commit the murder. What result? Is this case any different from *Olivia N.*? The Tylenol hypothetical? *See Zamora v. CBS*, 480 F. Supp. 199 (S.D. Fla. 1979).

8. Under a Massachusetts statute, it is a crime to knowingly permit a child under eighteen years of age "to pose or be exhibited in a state of nudity . . . for purposes of visual representation in any book, magazine, pamphlet, motion picture film, photograph, or picture." Mass. Gen. Laws ch. 272, §29A. Is this statute, obviously aimed at child pornography, constitutional? Suppose that a man was charged with a violation after photographing his fifteen-year-old stepdaughter nude from the waist up. Does it matter that the statute, read literally, makes it a crime for parents to take a frontal photo of their one-year-old romping naked in a wading pool? *See Massachusetts v. Oakes*, 109 S.Ct. 2633 (1989). Several states make the possession of child pornography a crime, wholly apart from its sale, distribution, or manufacture. Are such statutes constitutionally valid in light of *Stanley v. Georgia*, in which the Supreme Court struck down statutes punishing the possession of obscene materials? Of what relevance is the *Ferber* decision to this inquiry? *See People v. Geever*, 522 N.E.2d 1200 (Ill.), *appeal dism'd*, 109 S.Ct. 299 (1988); *State v. Young*, 525 N.E.2d 1363 (Ohio 1988), *prob. juris. noted*, 109 S.Ct. 3212 (1989); Josephine R. Potuto, *"Stanley + Ferber =* The Constitutional Crime of At-Home Child Pornography Possession," 76 *Kentucky Law Journal* 15 (1987–88).

9. In addition to child pornography laws, state statute books contain numerous provisions dealing in one way or another with lewd or sexually oriented materials. For example, a California criminal statute prohibits procurement of persons "for the purpose of prostitution," which is defined in another statute as "any lewd act between persons for money. . . . " Cal. Penal Code §§266i, 647(b). Can these statutes constitutionally be used to prosecute a movie producer who had hired five actresses to perform in a sexually explicit film? Does it matter whether the film has been found to be legally obscene? *See People v. Freeman*, 758 P.2d 1128 (Cal. 1988), *cert. denied*, 109 S.Ct. 1133 (1989). Under a Georgia statute, a person who knowingly owns or operates a motor vehicle with a "sticker, decal, emblem, or other device containing profane or lewd words describing sexual acts, excretory functions, or parts of the human body" is guilty of a misdemeanor and subject to a maximum fine of $100. Ga. Code Ann. §40-1-4. Would the common bumper sticker bearing the phrase "shit happens" violate this statute? Is the statute constitutional? *See Cohen v. California*, 403 U.S. 15 (1971), discussed in Chapter 10.

10. After a study of the effects of sexually oriented businesses on the community, the Dallas City Council adopted a detailed ordinance that imposed licensing and zoning restrictions upon such businesses. Under the ordinance, bookstores, theaters, video stores, arcades, and other businesses featuring "adult" materials must be located at least 1,000 feet from another sexually oriented business or a church, school, residential area, or park. These enterprises must also obtain a license issued by the chief of police and permit inspection of their premises when open or occupied. The chief may deny a license for failure to comply with city health, fire, and building codes and may revoke a license if the licensee gave "false or misleading information" in the application or has knowingly permitted illegal conduct on the premises. A license is not available to persons formerly convicted of specified crimes, such as obscenity, public lewdness, sexual assault, and promotion of prostitution. Is the ordinance constitutional? *See FW/PBS, Inc. v. City of Dallas*, 837 F.2d 1298 (5th Cir. 1988), *cert. granted*, 109 S.Ct. 1309 (1989).

CHAPTER
10
THE ELECTRONIC MEDIA

Century Communications Corp. v. Federal Communications Commission, 835 F.2d 292 (D.C. Cir. 1987), cert. denied, 108 S.Ct. 2014 (1988).

Before WALD, Chief Judge, and MIKVA, Circuit Judge, and McGOWAN, Senior Circuit Judge.

WALD, Chief Judge:

Two years ago, in *Quincy Cable TV, Inc. v. Federal Communications Commission* (1985), we struck down as violative of the first amendment the FCC's "must-carry" rules. Those rules required cable television operators, upon request and within the limits of their channel capacity, to transmit to their subscribers every over-the-air television signal that was "significantly viewed in the community" or otherwise considered "local" under the Commission's rules. Today, we revisit this distinctive corner of first amendment jurisprudence to evaluate the constitutional va-

lidity of the scaled-down must-carry rules adopted by the FCC following our decision in *Quincy Cable TV.* Although the FCC has eliminated the more extreme demands of its initial set of regulations, its arguments in this case leave us unconvinced that the new must-carry rules are necessary to advance any substantial governmental interests, so as to justify an incidental infringement of speech under the test set forth in *United States v. O'Brien* (1968).[1] Accordingly, we invalidate as incompatible with the first amendment this latest incarnation of the FCC's must-carry rules.

I. Facts

Since the mid-1960s, when the nascent cable television industry began to loom as a threat to ordinary broadcast television, the

---

[¹This case is discussed in Chapter 1.]

Federal Communications Commission has labored to protect the local broadcast media through regulation of the cable industry. The Commission's objective in these endeavors.

was not merely to protect an established industry from the encroachment of an upstart young competitor, although such a result was clearly the by-product of the regulatory posture that developed. Rather, the Commission took the position that without the power to regulate cable it could not discharge its statutory obligation to provide for "fair, efficient, and equitable" distribution of [broadcast] service among "the several States and communities." If permitted to grow unfettered, the Commission feared, cable might well supplant ordinary broadcast television. A necessary consequence of such displacement would be to undermine the FCC's mandate to allocate the broadcast spectrum in a manner that best served the public interest. In particular, if an unregulated, unlicensed cable industry were to threaten the economic viability of broadcast television, the Commission would be powerless to effect what it saw . . . as one of its cardinal objectives: the development of a "system of [free] local broadcasting stations, such that 'all communities of appreciable size [will] have at least one television station as an outlet for local self-expression.' "

Must-carry rules in various forms have been major tools in this campaign to protect local broadcasting from cable. The FCC first introduced such rules in 1962, when it sought to impose a must-carry requirement as a condition for granting an application to construct a microwave system to transmit distant signals to a rural cable system. In time, the FCC developed a broader must-carry regime, generally requiring cable operators, "upon request, to carry any broadcast signal considered local under the Commission's complex formula." The philosophy behind these rules was

to assure that the advent of cable technology not undermine the financial viability of free, community oriented television. If cable were to "drive out television broadcasting service . . . the public as a whole would lose far more—in free service, in ser-

vice to outlying areas, and in local service with local control and selection of programs—than it would gain." The must-carry rules, together with a comprehensive body of related regulations, would channel the development of the nascent cable industry to limit the risks it might pose to conventional broadcasting, "society's chosen instrument for the provision of video services."

In 1985, this [court] faced for the first time the question whether the broad must-carry rules which had been in existence for nearly two decades were in harmony with the first amendment. Judge Wright's opinion for a unanimous panel in *Quincy Cable TV* held that they were not. As a threshold matter, we observed that our first amendment review of regulations burdening cable television was not governed by those cases, such as *Red Lion Broadcasting Co. v. FCC* (1969) and *FCC v. League of Women Voters of California* (1984), upholding regulations on broadcast television. In reaching that conclusion, we noted "the Supreme Court's oft-repeated suggestion that the First Amendment tolerates far more intrusive regulation of broadcasters than of other media precisely because of the inescapable physical limitations on the number of voices that can simultaneously be carried over the electromagnetic spectrum." Wire-carried media like cable, of course, have no such limitations, and thus we found the "scarcity rationale" that the Supreme Court has used to justify broadcast television regulations to offer no succor to those seeking to establish the constitutional validity of cable television regulations.

Quincy Cable TV did not, however, establish the precise degree of first amendment protection enjoyed by cable operators. Although our opinion noted that some parallels existed between the must-carry regulations and regulations impinging on editorial discretion that had been invalidated in the past, it pointedly declined to "definitively decide" whether cable operators enjoy the heightened protection accruing to newspapers or whether the must-carry regulations were more appropriately evaluated under the test set forth in *United*

States v. O'Brien. Rather, we concluded that the must-carry rules would fail even the *O'Brien* test's requirement of a substantial governmental interest furthered by means no greater than are essential to the furtherance of that interest.

The reasons for our invalidation of the 1985 must-carry rules under the *O'Brien* test were twofold. First, we concluded that the Commission had not adequately substantiated its assertion that a substantial governmental interest existed. In *Quincy Cable TV* we stated that, even accepting the view that the preservation of free local television was an important regulatory goal, our review of the FCC's reports and regulations suggested that the problem the sweeping must-carry rules purported to prevent—the destruction of free, local television—was merely a "fanciful threat," unsubstantiated by the record or by two decades of experience with cable TV. In general, we noted, "the mere abstract assertion of a substantial governmental interest, standing alone, is insufficient to justify the subordination of First Amendment freedoms." Second, even if the interest had been deemed substantial, the broadly-drafted must-carry rules represented a fatally overinclusive response to the problem. We observed in this vein that the rules indiscriminately protected every local broadcaster, regardless of whether it was in fact threatened, and regardless of the quantity of local service available in the community and the degree to which the cable operator in question already carried local outlets. We did, however, note that our decision in no way foreclosed the Commission from adopting new must-carry rules consonant with the *O'Brien* test.

In the aftermath of *Quincy Cable TV*, the FCC immediately suspended enforcement of the must-carry rules. Four months later, it announced its intention to undertake rulemaking proceedings, and eventually, in November 1986, the agency released a new, more limited set of must-carry rules designed to accommodate *Quincy Cable TV*'s concerns. In the decision to promulgate the new rules, the Commission took note of the many comments, submitted primarily but not exclusively by broadcasting interests, arguing that some form of FCC intervention remained necessary to protect local broadcasting.

The most salient feature of the new rules was that the Commission substantially altered its stated justification for imposing must-carry rules at all. No longer did the Commission argue, as it had prior to the *Quincy Cable TV* decision, that the rules were needed for the indefinite future to ensure viewer access to local broadcast stations. Rather, the Commission now argued that must-carry rules were needed to guarantee such access during a shorter-term transition period during which viewers could become accustomed to an existing and inexpensive but largely unknown piece of equipment known as the "input-selector device."

Such devices, if hooked up to a television, allow viewers at any given time to select, simply by flicking a switch, between shows offered by their cable system and broadcast television shows offered off-the-air. These devices, the most common of which is known in the cable industry as an "A/B switch," are about the size of a standard light switch and work by being hooked up to a roof-top, attic, or television-top antenna. According to a study cited by the Commission in its report explaining the new must-carry rules, the cost of buying such a switch is approximately $7.50, and the cost of buying an outdoor antenna to go with it is approximately $50. Outdoor antennas are generally the more expensive of the three types of antennas.

The Commission estimated that it would take approximately five years for the public to become acclimated to the existence of these switches, and, accordingly, its interim rules should be in place for that same [period]. At that point, the need for ongoing must-carry rules to ensure viewer access to local broadcast stations would be obviated. [As the Commission observed,] "once cable subscribers become accustomed to using off-the-air reception on an equal basis with cable service, the cable systems no longer will have an artificial ability to limit their subscribers' access to over-the-air broadcast signals." * * *

Because the Commission envisioned these switches as guaranteeing effective viewer choice bewteeen local and cable shows, it ultimately added to the new must-carry regime the requirement that cable systems offer subscribers, for pay, input-selector devices that could be hooked up to their TVs. It did so over the reservations of some broadcasting concerns, who viewed the input-selector devices as less protective than must-carry rules. The Commission, observing that relatively few consumers knew about the switch-and-antenna mechanism and noting that the long history of must-carry rules had created a public "misperception" that "broadcast signals will always be available as part of their basic cable service," also promised to require cable operators to educate the viewing public about the availability of the switch-and-antenna mechanism.

In addition to thus offering a new and more limited justification for must-carry rules, the Commission also substantially limited the sweep of the new rules in a number of respects. It set forth limits on how many channels a cable [operator] must devote to must-carry: [operators] with 20 channels or less wcrc not required to carry any [local] stations; [operators] with between 21 and 26 channels could be required to carry up to 7 channels of must-carry signals; and [operators] with 27 or more channels could be required to devote up to 25% of their system to must-carry signals. It also limited the pool of potential must-carry [stations] to those satisfying a "viewing standard" generally demonstrating a minimum viewership of the [station] in question. * * * The Commission also authorized cable operators to refuse to carry more than one station affiliated with the same commercial network. Finally, the Commission limited the number of noncommercial stations required to be carried, stating that when the cable system had fewer than 54 channels and an eligible noncommercial station . . . existed, the cable operator must devote at least one channel to a noncommercial station; and that when the cable system had 54 or more [channels], it must devote two must-carry channels to such endeavors.

Constitutional and statutory challenges to these new must-carry rules were lodged shortly after their promulgation by an array of cable operators and public interest groups. Petitioner Century Communications Corp., joined by 13 other cable operators . . . , protests the must-carry rules as violative of the first amendment of the Constitution, as a taking of property without just compensation in violation of the fifth amendment, and as a measure not authorized by the FCC's statutory jurisdiction and hence *ultra vires*. * * * We, however, need look no further than petitioners' first amendment claims to decide this case. Because we invalidate the entire new must-carry regime as unjustified and unduly sweeping, we do not reach—and therefore express no opinion on—the [other issues].

II. Opinion

A. The Appropriate Level of First Amendment Scrutiny

A threshold question for our first amendment analysis is what standard of review to apply. * * * Petitioners characterize the must-carry rules as posing more than an incidental burden on speech, likening the rules to the newspaper right-of-reply statute invalidated in *Miami Herald Publishing Co. v. Tornillo* (1974), where the Supreme Court held that the enactment impermissibly interfered with the newspaper's constitutionally protected "editorial discretion." Toward this end, petitioners also offer the recent case of *City of Los Angeles v. Preferred Communications, Inc.*, (1986), where the Court noted that the selection and organization of programs on cable television does involve some degree of editorial discretion.

The FCC counters by characterizing the must-carry rules as a commercial regulation that burdens speech in a far more attenuated fashion. Accordingly, the FCC argues, the must-carry rules are more appropriately analyzed under the standards set forth in *United States v. O'Brien*, where the Supreme Court stated that to be valid, a regulation incidentally burdening speech and not aimed at the suppression of free expression must advance a substantial governmental interest and must be no more restrictive than necessary to accomplish that end.

The precise level of first amendment protection due a cable television operator is clearly an issue of much moment to the industry and ultimately to viewers. However, having closely analyzed the rationale for and workings of the new must-carry rules, we conclude that we again need not resolve this vexing question. Like the original must-carry regime invalidated in *Quincy Cable TV*, the new, scaled-back edition fails to satisfy even the less-demanding first amendment test of *United States v. O'Brien*, whose use here is advocated by the FCC. We now proceed to offer our application of that test.

B. An O'Brien-Test Analysis of the New Regulations

In *United States v. O'Brien*, the Supreme Court stated:

[W]e think it clear that a government regulation is sufficiently justified if it is within the constitutional power of the Government; if it furthers an important or substantial governmental interest; if the governmental interest is unrelated to the suppression of free expression; and if the incidental restriction on alleged First Amendment freedoms is no greater than is essential to the furtherance of that interest.

Typically, analysis under *United States v. O'Brien* begins with an appraisal of whether the interest said to be served by a governmental measure is substantial. If it is, we proceed to the more delicate fact-bound issue of whether the means chosen are congruent with the desired end, or whether they are too broadly tailored to pass muster. * * *

1. The Substantiality of the Governmental Interest.

It may well be that upon a suitable record showing, the justification offered by the FCC, that interim regulations are needed to keep local broadcasts accessible to viewers while the new switch-and-antenna technology takes hold, would satisfy the *O'Brien* standard. *See, e.g., FCC v. WNCN Listeners Guild* (1981)(deeming "the policy of promoting the widest possible dissemination of information from diverse sources to be consistent with both the [Commission's] public interest standard and the First Amendment"). * * * The difficulty is that here, as in *Quincy Cable TV*, the FCC's judgment that transitional rules are needed is predicated not upon substantial evidence but rather upon several highly dubious assertions of the FCC, from which we conclude that the need for a new saga of must-carry rules is more speculative than real. * * * Such speculative fears alone have never been held sufficient to justify trenching on first amendment liberties.

The agency's first questionable contention is that consumers are not now aware and cannot be expected to become aware that installation of an A/B switch could preserve their choice of programs[.] * * * The FCC, however, adduces scant evidence for its judgment of a widespread "misperception" among cable subscribers that the only means of access to off-the-air signals is through cable service. It puts forth no attitudinal surveys, or polls, suggesting the likely pace of consumer adaptation to the A/B switch technology. Nor does it offer analogies illustrating how swiftly consumers have incorporated previous electronic innovations. Such evidence might have shown what the FCC simply assumes here: that upon the disappearance of must-carry regulations, consumers would collectively fail to install with any dispatch the switches and antennas necessary to gain access to local broadcast stations, conceivably imperiling the survival of these stations and thereby depriving viewers of diverse broadcasting offerings.

The lone item of "hard" record evidence on which the FCC relies in support of its need for a five-year interim must-carry period is a study entitled "Outdoor Antennas, Reception of Local Television Signals and Cable Television," prepared . . . for the National Association of Broadcasters ("NAB"). NAB's members have long benefited from the existence of must-carry rules, and the organization, during rulemaking, strongly criticized alternative proposed regulations that it perceived as inadequately protective of broadcasters, such as reliance on the A/B switch. * * *

[The court then determined that the NAB study did not support the FCC's conclusions. Although the study showed that most cable subscribers do not have an A/B switch and an appropriate antenna to receive off-air programs, it did not demonstrate that the cause of the problem was difficulty in installing the equipment or the lack of information as to availability. A more likely cause, the court said, is the FCC's own must-carry doctrine, since consumers are unlikely to buy the necessary equipment when the government mandates carriage of local broadcast stations by cable systems. Moreover, the court said, the study did not support in any fashion the FCC's conclusion that a five-year transition period was necessary.]

In appraising the FCC's argument that the indelibility of consumer ignorance justifies the reimposition of must-carry rules, we are thus left to ask whether the FCC's contention is so obvious or commonsensical that it needs no empirical support to stand up. We conclude that it is not. For one thing, the FCC's own report elsewhere belies the agency's fears of viewer lethargy. The Commission notes:

There is evidence that video consumers are now becoming accustomed to switching between alternate program input sources. We observe that many cable systems now offer services through dual cables in order to provide greater channel capacity. Such systems employ switching devices to select between the two cables and often mark the switch positions with "A" and "B" designations. Cable subscribers apparently have accepted this switching arrangement and do not find it inconvenient.

More generally, we simply cannot accept, without evidence to the contrary, the sluggish profile of the American consumer that the Commission's argument presupposes. In a culture in which even costly items like the video-cassette recorder, the cordless telephone, the compact disc-player and the home computer have spread like wildfire, it begs incredulity to simply assume that consumers are so unresponsive that within the span of five

years they would not manage to purchase an inexpensive hardware-store switch upon learning that it could provide access to a considerable storehouse of new television stations and shows.

Even were we to accept, however, the Commission's view that consumer ignorance cannot be readily eradicated, we have a second fundamental problem with the Commission's judgment that its interim must-carry rules are needed to advance a substantial governmental interest sufficient to support burdening cable operators' first amendment rights. The Commission relies heavily on its assumption that in the absence of must-carry rules, cable companies would drop local broadcasts. Experience belies that assertion. As cable operators reported to the Commission during rulemaking proceedings, during the 16 months between *Quincy Cable TV* and the reimposition of the modified must-carry rules, cable companies generally did not drop the local broadcast signals that they had been carrying prior to *Quincy Cable TV.* * * * Also undercutting the FCC's fearful assumption is the fact that both the Federal Trade Commission and the Department of Justice have concluded, in separate reports, that the absence of must-carry [rules] would not harm local broadcasting. * * *

For these reasons, we conclude that the FCC has not demonstrated that the new must-carry rules further a substantial governmental interest, as the rules must to outweigh the incidental burden on first amendment interests. . . . As we stated in *Quincy Cable TV*, "[a]t least in those instances in which both the existence of the problem and the beneficial effects of the agency's response to that problem are concededly susceptible of some empirical demonstration, the agency must do something more than merely posit the existence of the disease sought to be cured." The FCC error in this case was its failure to go that extra step here.

2. The Congruence Between Means and Ends. The second prong of the *O'Brien* test focuses on the congruence between the means chosen by the agency and the end it seeks to achieve. In this case, even were we convinced that the interest in whose name the FCC purports to act was more than a "fanciful threat," the new must-carry regulations, because of their lengthy duration, are too broad to pass muster even under the *O'Brien* test.

If any interim period of must-carry rules is, in fact, necessary, the FCC adduces literally no evidence that this period must last for fully five years. Such a period is strikingly long in an industry that the FCC itself characterizes as "rapidly evolving." In the absence of any empirical support for the new must-carry rules, the FCC falls back on what it terms a "sound predictive judgment" that it will take about five years for consumers to learn about the switch-and-antenna mechanism, and thus that a five-year transition period is needed during which the agency will provide consumer education.

We are, however, unpersuaded. In large part our reluctance to countenance reimposing must-carry rules for five years based on a "sound predictive judgment" that is never explained reflects our perceptions about consumer aptitude stated earlier. Such a guess about consumer instincts hardly presents the sort of issue where, "if complete factual support . . . for the Commission's judgment or prediction is not possible," we should defer to the Commission's expert judgment. It is wholly unclear to us why it should take five years to inform consumers that with the installation of a $7.50 switch and a television antenna they can view more local channels. The FCC report does nothing to shed light on this matter.

Additionally, we are skeptical—and the FCC's report says nothing to relieve this skepticism—that any consumer education campaign will have much impact so long as viewers can continue to rely on must-carry to get their fix of local broadcasts. It is entirely likely that not until the waning few months of the five-year must-carry regime would the FCC's admonitions about the need for switches and antennas begin to sink in, much as the existence of switches and antennas has largely gone unnoticed in a consumer population already accessed to local television as a result of must-carry in recent years. Opting for a five-year interim period therefore merely delays the inevitable, but almost certainly brief, period during which TV owners will learn of, purchase, and install the requisite equipment. We therefore find it difficult to defer blindly to the Commission's unproven belief that half a decade is necessary.

III. Conclusion

Our decision today is a narrow one. We hold simply that, in the absence of record evidence in support of its policy, the FCC's reimposition of must-carry rules on a five-year basis neither clearly furthers a substantial governmental interest nor is of brief enough duration to be considered narrowly tailored so as to satisfy the *O'Brien* test for incidental restrictions on speech. We do not suggest that must-carry rules are *per se* unconstitutional, and we certainly do not mean to intimate that the FCC may not regulate the cable industry so as to advance substantial governmental interests. But when trenching on first amendment interests, even incidentally, the government must be able to adduce either empirical support or at least sound reasoning on behalf of its measures. As in *Quincy Cable TV,* we reluctantly conclude that the FCC has not done so in this case. . . . Accordingly, we have no choice but to strike down this latest embodiment of must-carry.

So ordered.

INTRODUCTION

The central issue in the *Century Communications* case is the power of the government to regulate the programming provided by cable operators. In adopting the "must-carry" regulations that required a cable system to transmit the signals of local broadcast stations, the Federal Communications Commission intruded into the process by which cable operators select programming and forced them to make decisions that they might not otherwise have made. Few would argue that similar restrictions on the discretion of newspaper editors are constitutionally permissible, and in *Century Communications* the cable operators claimed that they enjoy the same first amendment rights as publishers. The court, however, expressly declined to decide this question, though it ultimately ruled in favor of the cable companies. Broadcasters, whose economic self-interest led them to support the must-carry rules aimed at cable systems, have long felt the impact of government regulations affecting the content of their own programs. Unlike the must-carry rules struck down in *Century Communications*, however, FCC restrictions on broadcasters have consistently been upheld by the courts against first amendment challenges.

What accounts for this disparate treatment? Why are broadcasters considered second-class citizens for first amendment purposes? Why are cable operators viewed in a different light than broadcasters? If cable is not to be considered on the same level as television and radio in the constitutional hierarchy, why are the courts reluctant to accord it the same status as newspapers and other print media? These questions will be explored in this chapter, which focuses on government regulations that affect the content of material transmitted by the electronic media. Though we will also examine the basic regulatory schemes now in place for broadcasting, cable, and other electronic means of information delivery, our principal concern is the government's ability to control content.

BROADCAST REGULATION: AN OVERVIEW

Suppose that the federal government established an administrative agency, headed by five persons appointed by the President and confirmed by the Senate, to license the publishers of newspapers and magazines and to adopt rules governing the content of those publications. Such a regulatory scheme would plainly be unconstitutional; although there has been considerable debate as to the meaning of the first amendment, there is no doubt that it was intended to prohibit the abhorred system of licensing that had evolved in England. Nonetheless, the U.S. Supreme Court has ruled that the statutory authority of the Federal Communications Commission to license radio and television stations and to place some restrictions on the material they broadcast is consistent with the first amendment. The Court's rationale is based primarily on the physical limitations of the electromagnetic spectrum through which broadcast signals travel.

The Notion of "Spectrum Scarcity"

Radio waves make up a portion of the electromagnetic spectrum, which also includes x-rays, visible light, and infrared rays. Produced by the acceleration or oscillation of an electric charge, these waves are labelled in terms of "frequency," which refers to the particular position they occupy on the spectrum, and "wavelength," which describes a range of frequencies with particular physical characteristics. Because the wavelengths possess different characteristics, not all are suitable for radio and television broadcasting. Indeed, less than one-fifth of one percent of the radio spectrum is assigned to broadcast stations in this country, with the remainder used primarily for so-called "point-to-point" communications by police and fire departments, the military, aircraft, private business, and amateur radio operators, as well as for atmospheric and geologic exploration.

For our purposes, the key point is that space on the spectrum is finite; simply put, there is room for only so many broadcast stations to operate without interfering with each other. Since the early 1920s, the demand for broadcast frequencies has exceeded the available supply, and, prior to passage of the first comprehensive federal broadcasting statute in 1927, there was not an adequate mechanism for their allocation. Consequently, the airwaves were jammed. As Justice Felix Frankfurter described the situation in *National Broadcasting Co. v. United States* (1943):

> From July, 1926, to February 23, 1927, when Congress enacted the Radio Act . . . , almost 200 new stations went on the air. These new stations used any frequencies they desired, regardless of the interference thereby caused to others. Existing stations changed to other frequencies and increased their power and hours of operation at will. The result was confusion and chaos. With everybody on the air, nobody could be heard.

This state of affairs led Congress to conclude that someone must decide who is to be permitted to use the limited space on the radio spectrum, for otherwise this potentially valuable public resource would be worthless. Since the Radio Act of 1927, that "someone" has been a federal administrative agency, now known as the Federal Communications Commission. Under the Communications Act of 1934, the successor to the Radio Act, the FCC has broad powers to regulate broadcasting "as [the] public interest, convenience, or necessity requires. . . ." The act, which remains the statutory basis for the federal government's regulation of broadcasting, takes the position that broadcast frequencies are a publicly-owned resource allocated to licensees on a temporary basis. In return for the privilege to exploit this resource financially, a licensee must operate his station in a manner consistent with the "public interest." The FCC has the task of determining where the public interest lies, but the Communications Act expressly provides that the Commission is not to serve as a censor or to "interfere with the right of free speech by means of [broadcast] communication."

One reading of this statutory scheme is that the FCC simply acts as a "traffic cop of the airwaves" by assigning frequencies and making certain that one broadcaster does not interfere with another. For better or worse, however, the Supreme Court has employed the scarcity theory to justify not only the FCC's authority to direct broadcast traffic, but also the agency's power to regulate content in a manner that would run afoul of the first amendment if applied to the print media. As Justice Frankfurter wrote in the *National Broadcasting Co.* case, the Communications Act "does not limit the Commission merely to the supervision of the traffic" but instead "puts upon the Commission the burden of determining the composition of that traffic." In other words, the "right of free speech" mentioned in the Communications Act is not synonymous with the first amendment rights of the print media. "[O]f all forms of communication," the Supreme Court has recently pointed out, "it is broadcasting that has received the most limited First Amendment protection."

The Court's reasoning is rather straightforward. In order to make the broadcast spectrum usable for expressive activities, the government must allocate the limited number of frequencies, a process that is obviously unnecessary with respect to such "traditional" forms of communication as printing and speaking. Accordingly, there is no first amendment right to obtain a broadcast license comparable to the first amendment right to publish a newspaper or mount a soap box in a public forum. Because there is no constitutional right to broadcast, a person granted a license to do so may be subjected to government regulations that require him to share that license with others or to air material that he might not choose to carry in the exercise of his independent judgment. In short, the broadcast spectrum is a resource that belongs to the public at large, and licensees represent those of us who are excluded from the airwaves because of the finite number of frequencies.

Justice William Brennan neatly summarized the prevailing constitutional doctrine in *Federal Communications Commission v. League of Women Voters of California* (1984):

> First, we have long recognized that Congress, acting pursuant to the Commerce Clause, has power to regulate the use of this scarce and valuable national resource. The distinctive feature of Congress' efforts in this area has been to ensure through the regulatory oversight of the FCC that only those who satisfy the "public interest, convenience and necessity" are granted a license to use radio and television broadcast frequencies.

> Second, Congress may, in the exercise of this power, seek to assure that the public receives through this medium a balanced presentation of information on issues of public importance that otherwise might not be addressed if control of the medium were left entirely in the hands of those who own and operate broadcasting stations. Although such governmental regulation has never been allowed with respect to the print media, we have recognized that "differences in the characteristics of new media justify differences in the First Amendment standards applied to them." The fundamental distinguishing characteristic of the new medium of broadcasting that, in our view, has required some adjustment in First Amendment analysis is that "[b]roadcasting frequencies are a scarce resource [that] must be apportioned among applicants." Thus, our cases have taught that, given spectrum scarcity, those who are granted a license to broadcast must serve in a sense as fiduciaries for the public by presenting "those views and voices which are representative of his community and which would otherwise, by necessity, be barred from the airwaves." * * *

> Finally, although the government's interest in ensuring balanced coverage of public issues is plainly both important and substantial, we have, at the same time, made clear that broadcasters are engaged in a vital and independent form of communicative activity. As a result, the First Amendment must inform and give shape to the manner in which Congress exercises its regulatory power in this area. Unlike common carriers, broadcasters are "entitled under the First Amendment to exercise the 'widest journalistic freedom consistent with their public [duties].' " Indeed, if the public's interest in receiving a balanced presentation of views is to be fully served, we must necessarily rely in large part upon the editorial initiative and judgment of the broadcasters who bear the public trust.

An alternative theory, which, like spectrum scarcity, is based on the physical characteristics of the broadcast media, has also emerged. For present purposes, it is sufficient to note that this rationale hinges on the "uniquely pervasive presence" of the broadcast media and their accessibility to children. However, spectrum scarcity remains the primary constitutional justification for the FCC's statutory authority to select those who shall receive radio and television licenses and to regulate the content of material that is broadcast, although this rationale has come under sharp attack in recent years. Simply stated, the argument is that the development of cable television, satellite technology, and other communications delivery systems has made the scarcity concept obsolete. We shall return to the "pervasiveness" rationale and the challenge to the scarcity theory later in the chapter.

The Scarcity Theory in Action: Access to the Media

The impact of the spectrum scarcity rationale upon the first amendment rights of broadcasters is brought into sharp focus by two U.S. Supreme Court decisions, *Red Lion Broadcasting Co. v. Federal Communications Commission* (1969) and *Miami Herald Publishing Co. v. Tornillo* (1974). In both cases, the issue was whether the government, consistent with the first amendment, can require a media entity to afford persons who have been criticized in print or on the air an opportunity to respond. The answer, as we shall see, is "yes and no," depending upon the type of medium involved.[2]

The *Red Lion* case had its origins in the 1964 presidential campaign between Democratic incumbent Lyndon B. Johnson and Republican challenger Barry Goldwater. As part of its political strategy, the Democratic National Committee agreed to purchase 50,000 copies of a proposed book about Senator Goldwater by a former newspaper reporter, Fred J. Cook. The book, entitled *Goldwater: Extremist on the Right*, was a partisan—and highly critical—biography of the Republican candidate, and it might not have attracted a publisher without the backing of the Democrats. On November 27, 1964, radio station WGCB in Red Lion, Pennsylvania, carried a fifteen-minute broadcast during which the Reverend Billy James Hargis attacked the book and its author. Hargis, an Oklahoma evangelist whose right-wing "Christian Crusade" program was carried on stations in several states, apparently believed that the book was part of a leftist media conspiracy that had contributed to President Johnson's landslide victory.

Among other things, Hargis charged on the broadcast that Cook had been fired by the *New York World-Telegram* for making false charges against city officials; that he had defended Alger Hiss in a magazine article; that he had worked for a publication affiliated with the Communist party; and that he had attacked FBI Director J. Edgar Hoover and the Central Intelligence Agency. "Now this is the man who wrote the book to smear and destroy Barry Goldwater," Hargis said. Ironically, Hargis did not refer to a Cook article that had appeared in *The Nation* magazine prior to publication of the Goldwater book. Entitled "Radio Right: Hate Clubs of the Air," the article criticized the practices of the Hargis organization and similar groups that sponsored syndicated religious programs with a right-wing political slant.

Upon learning that he had been attacked by Hargis, Cook wrote letters requesting free rebuttal time to about 200 stations that regularly carried the "Christian Crusade" program. Cook's demand was based on the FCC's "personal attack" rule, a regulation which grew out of the general obligation of broadcasters under the "fairness doctrine" to devote a reasonable amount of air time to the discussion of controversial issues and to afford reasonable opportunity for the presentation of opposing views. In its present form the personal attack rule requires broadcast licensees to offer a person whose honesty, character, integrity, or similar qualities had been attacked during the presentation of views on a controversial issue of public importance

---

[2]The account of the circumstances leading to the decisions in these cases is taken largely from Fred Friendly, *The Good Guys, The Bad Guys, and The First Amendment* (1976).

a reasonable opportunity to respond. Specifically, the licensee must, within a week of the attack, provide the person attacked with the date and time of the broadcast, a script or tape of the program, and an offer of free time to respond. A somewhat simpler version of this requirement, adopted in 1962, was in effect at the time of the Hargis broadcast.

A few stations apparently notified Cook of the attack, but he was able to obtain help from the Democratic National Committee in identifying stations that routinely carried the Hargis program. Fewer than fifty stations ultimately offered reply time, and Cook responded with a three-minute tape. While some stations simply failed to answer the letter, most either flatly rejected the demand for air time or told Cook that he could purchase time at the prevailing commercial rate. Among those stations advising Cook that he could buy rebuttal time was WGCB, licensed to the Red Lion Broadcasting Company. After some additional correspondence with WGCB, Cook filed a complaint with the FCC, which subsequently concluded that the Hargis broadcast constituted a personal attack and that the station had failed to meet its obligations under the personal attack rule. The U.S. Court of Appeals upheld the FCC, prompting WGCB to seek review by the Supreme Court. Meanwhile, the U.S. Court of Appeals for the Seventh Circuit struck down the personal attack rule in a separate case brought by the Radio and Television News Directors Association.

The Supreme Court consolidated the two cases and, in a unanimous decision, ruled that the personal attack rule did did not offend the first amendment and that the FCC had ample authority under the "public interest" provision of the Communications Act to adopt it. Speaking for the Court, Justice Byron White relied heavily on the scarcity rationale in rejecting the broadcasters' argument that the first amendment "protects their desire to use their allotted frequencies continuously to broadcast whatever they choose, and to exclude whomever they choose from ever using that frequency." He wrote:

> Because of the scarcity of radio frequencies, the Government is permitted to put restraints on licensees in favor of others whose views should be expressed on this unique medium. But the people as a whole retain their interest in free speech by radio and their collective right to have the medium function consistently with the ends and purposes of the First Amendment. It is the right of the viewers and listeners, not the right of the broadcasters, which is paramount. It is the purpose of the First Amendment to preserve an uninhibited marketplace of ideas in which truth will ultimately prevail, rather than to countenance monopolization of that market, whether it be by the Government itself or a private licensee. * * * It is the right of the public to receive suitable access to social, political, esthetic, moral, and other ideas and experiences which is crucial here.

Five years later, in the *Tornillo* case, the Court was confronted with a fifty-year-old Florida statute remarkably similar to the FCC's personal attack rule, though it was limited to political candidates. Under the statute, a newspaper that assailed the "personal character" of any candidate or attacked his official record was required, upon request, to publish without charge the candidate's reply. The reply had to appear in as conspicuous a place and in the same kind of type as the article containing the attack, although the newspaper was not required to provide any more space for the reply than that occupied by the initial article. Violation of the statute was a misdemeanor.

Shortly before the primary elections in 1972, the *Miami Herald* published two editorials criticizing Patrick Tornillo, Jr., the executive director of a teachers' union who was running for the state legislature. Noting Tornillo's leadership role in a recent teachers' strike, the editorial argued that a vote for him would be "inexcusable" and seemed to imply that he had acted illegally in connection with the strike. Tornillo drafted a reply stating that he had done nothing illegal and, citing the statute, demanded that the newspaper publish it. After losing the primary, Tornillo brought suit against the *Herald,* asking for damages and an injunction. The trial judge denied relief on the ground that the right-to-reply statute violated the first amendment, but the Florida Supreme Court reversed. In the court's view, the statute actually enhanced first amendment values by furthering the "broad societal interest in the free flow of information to the public." The court also ruled that damages were available under the statute, although it spoke only in terms of criminal penalties.

The case attracted national attention, in part because Tornillo was represented by Jerome A. Barron, a law professor at George Washington University who had for several years urged judicial recognition of a first amendment "right of access" to the print media. In essence, Professor Barron argued that the marketplace of ideas is a romantic myth in light of the decline in the total number of daily newspapers, the absence of competing newspapers in all but the largest of our cities, and the domination of the newspaper industry by media conglomerates or "chains." Just as broadcasting is plagued by spectrum scarcity, he claimed, the newspaper business faces scarcity of a different sort brought on by economic conditions. Indeed, he noted that radio stations greatly outnumber daily newspapers in this country (the ratio is five to one today) and that cities with only one newspaper are typically served by three or more television stations. If a limited number of available outlets and the "paramount" rights of citizens to receive information justify the FCC's "personal attack" rule, those same considerations suggest that similar requirements for the print media are permissible under the first amendment. In fact, Professor Barron went one step further and argued that such a right of access exists by virtue of the first amendment itself, thus eliminating the need for an access statute.

In *Tornillo*, the Supreme Court considered but firmly rejected Professor Barron's arguments. Writing for the Court, Chief Justice Warren Burger said:

> However much validity may be found in these arguments, at each point the implementation of a remedy such as an enforceable right of access necessarily calls for some mechanism, either governmental or consensual. If it is governmental, this at once brings about a confrontation with the express provisions of the First Amendment and the judicial gloss on that Amendment developed over the years.
>
> * * * [T]he Court has expressed sensitivity as to whether a restriction or requirement constituted the compulsion exerted by government on a newspaper to print that which it would not otherwise print. The clear implication has been that any such compulsion to publish that which "reason tells them not should be published" is unconstitutional. A responsible press is an undoubtedly desirable goal, but press responsibility is not mandated by the Constitution and like many other virtues it cannot be legislated.

According to the Chief Justice, the Florida statute infringed on first amendment rights in two ways. First, it "exact[ed] a penalty on the basis of the content of a newspaper" by requiring publication of a reply that might "tak[e] up space that could be devoted to other material the newspaper may have preferred to print." In order to add a statutorily mandated reply, the newspaper would either have to expand the size of the paper—and thus incur increased publishing costs—or delete stories that it would have otherwise published. In order to avoid this choice, "editors might well conclude that the safe course is to avoid controversy" by steering clear of stories that would trigger the right-of-reply statute. A government-enforced right of access thus "inescapably dampens the vigor and limits the variety of public debate."

Second, even if a newspaper would face no additional costs to comply with a compulsory access law and would not be forced to forego publication of news or opinion by the inclusion of a reply, the Court concluded that the Florida statute impermissibly intruded into the function of editors. "The choice of material to go into a newspaper, and the decisions made as to limitations on the size and content of the paper, and treatment of public issues and public officials—whether fair or unfair—constitute the exercise of editorial control and judgment," the Chief Justice wrote. "It has yet to be demonstrated how governmental regulation of this crucial process can be exercised consistent with First Amendment guarantees of a free press as they have evolved to this time."

The vote was unanimous in *Tornillo*, although Justice White wrote a brief concurring opinion. But neither the Chief Justice nor Justice White cited the *Red Lion* case, and one can hardly view this omission as a simple oversight. Some commentators have suggested that the Court did not bother to discuss the *Red Lion* ruling in *Tornillo* because it recognized that the two decisions are inherently contradictory and cannot satisfactorily be reconciled. That may well be true. As Fred Friendly, the former president of CBS News, once wrote:

> If the people's right to know is the primary goal of a free press, and if government regulation of the crucial editorial process threatens the flow of information to the citizenry, does it matter how the [medium] of communication acquired its power, even its monopoly?

> Since most Americans today receive most of their news from broadcast sources, . . . it follows that the protections of the First Amendment now apply to the media which serve a minority of the population. * * * [I]s the threat [from the monopoly power of newspapers] any less dangerous than that of a television or radio station, or network, even if the electronic monopoly is an accident of technology and the result of government license?

Lyle Denniston, a journalist who regularly covers the Supreme Court, put the matter somewhat differently. "Courts may now find it quite easy to justify a *full* measure of first amendment protection for the print media because, really, nobody cares," he wrote. "What risk is there? Do we not pay vastly less attention to what we read than to what we see and hear?"

Nonetheless, the *Red Lion* and *Tornillo* decisions make one point crystal clear: the Supreme Court considers broadcasting to be "different" for first amendment purposes. Simply put, the print media qualify for "full" constitutional protection, and the broadcast media do not, even though the rationale for such disparate treatment may not be wholly satisfactory. However, the Court has intimated that it might be prepared to rethink the scarcity theory that underlies *Red Lion*. In the *League of Women Voters* case mentioned previously and discussed in more detail below in connection with noncommercial broadcasting, the Court noted:

> The prevailing rationale for broadcast regulation based on spectrum scarcity has come under increasing criticism in recent years. Critics . . . charge that with the advent of cable and satellite technology, communities now have access to such a wide variety of stations that the scarcity doctrine is obsolete. We are not prepared, however, to reconsider our longstanding approach without some signal from Congress or the FCC that technological developments have advanced so far that some revision of the system of broadcast regulation may be required.

We will return to this question in consideration of the fairness doctrine, one of many FCC regulations that affect the content of material aired by broadcasters. Before turning to these rules, however, we shall briefly examine the process by which the Commission issues and renews broadcast licenses.

Licensing

The FCC is an independent federal regulatory agency whose five commissioners are appointed by the President with the advice and consent of the Senate. The President also designates the chairman. Commissioners serve staggered five-year terms, and no more than three can be members of the same political party. The FCC staff is organized into bureaus that carry out the agency's day-to-day responsibilities. For our purposes, the most important of these is the Mass Media Bureau, which oversees broadcasting and cable television.

Like virtually all administrative agencies, the FCC engages in both quasi-legislative and quasi-judicial activities. The former, known as rulemaking, involves the adoption of regulations that have the force of statutes, while the latter, called adjudication, consists of judicial-type hearings in which factual and legal issues are decided on a case-by-case basis. Licensing is largely adjudicative in nature, though formal hearings are not required in all cases. The FCC's rulemaking function is also important, for it is through this process that the agency typically establishes the ground rules that govern the issuance and renewal of broadcast licenses. Rulemaking also plays a central role in the allocation of broadcast frequencies, a necessary prerequisite to the issuance of licenses.

Allocation of Frequencies. As noted previously, the FCC has divided the electromagnetic spectrum into various frequencies that may be used by broadcasters. More specifically, the Commission has set aside blocks of frequencies, or "bands," for particular broadcast services. Television stations, for example, operate on either the very-high or ultra-high frequency bands, commonly known as VHF and UHF. FM radio stations also use a portion of the VHF band, while AM stations occupy space on the medium frequency band. Within each band, a given number of channels are available: twelve for VHF television, seventy for UHF television, 100 for FM radio, and 107 for AM radio. The FCC has distributed these channels geographically across the country, taking into account interference problems created when stations on the same or adjacent channels operate too close to one another. Today, there are approximately 1,300 television stations and 10,000 radio stations in operation across the country. The numbers are about equally divided between VHF and UHF for television and AM and FM for radio.

The Commission has employed two quite different procedures in allocating broadcast stations to particular communities. With respect to television, the FCC has adopted a "table of assignments" that specifies the VHF and UHF channels available in a given city. This table, which also reserves some channels for noncommercial stations, was the product of the FCC's rulemaking process, and it can be changed only by formal amendment of the Commission's rules. Low-power television stations whose signals reach only a small area (ten to fifteen miles) are not covered by the table; in effect, these stations can be operated anywhere, so long as they do not cause interference with full-power stations.

A similar "table of assignments" exists for FM radio, with particular channels being allocated to particular cities. As is the case with television, some channels are set aside for noncommercial use. However, the table recognizes various classes of FM channels based on the power with which stations on those channels may operate. For example, channels for low-power stations are generally assigned to small communities, while channels for high-power stations are assigned to urban centers. There is no table of assignments for AM radio, the oldest of the broadcast services. Since the earliest days of its existence, the Commission has allocated AM stations on a case-by-case basis: an applicant may seek a license to serve any city if he meets FCC engineering requirements designed to prevent interference with existing stations. Today, the engineering guidelines are so stringent that it is almost impossible to squeeze another AM station into most communities. As is the case with FM radio, there are various classes of AM stations defined by signal strength and geographic coverage.

A curious physical phenomenon has posed interesting problems for the FCC with respect to AM radio. Simply put, AM signals "bounce" off the earth's ionosphere and thus travel greater distances than FM and television signals, which tend to follow the earth's surface. Taking this "skywave" effect into account, the Commission designated a special class of high-power AM stations insulated from interference by other stations. The signals of these so-called "clear channel" stations could travel more than 500 miles at night, when no other stations were permitted to operate on these frequencies. One consequence of this policy was a reduction in the overall number of possible AM stations, and in 1980 the Commission relaxed the protection given the clear channel stations. By allowing low power stations to operate on frequencies previously reserved for the clear channel stations, the FCC created space for 125 new full-time AM stations.

As noted above, an applicant for a new AM radio license must accompany that application with the required engineering studies showing that there would be no objectionable interference to stations already serving the community. In contrast, persons seeking FM or television license for unoccupied frequencies simply file an application, since the table of assignments indicates that a given frequency has been allocated to a particular community and that there are no interference problems. But what if all frequencies assigned to a particular community have been licensed? In that situation, an applicant for a new station must first convince the FCC to modify the table of assignments by adding a frequency in the community for a new station.

For example, the FCC might decide to shift a particular FM frequency from City A to City B if population trends in the area indicate that the public would be better served by an additional station in the latter community. Such a change requires a formal amendment to the table of assignments and may be made only through the quasi-legislative rulemaking process mentioned previously. Once the necessary change is made in the table of assignments, the applicant may then seek a license. At this point other applicants for the license may also emerge, and the fact that they did not participate in the rulemaking process by which the table of assignments was changed is immaterial.

The latest controversy over frequency allocation involves high-definition television ("HDTV"), a broadcast system that delivers a much sharper picture than conventional television but also takes up more room on the electromagnetic spectrum. While American television equipment now uses 525 scanning lines to produce an image, proposed HDTV systems would have from 1,050 to 1,250. To deliver this additional information, which results in a high-resolution picture proportioned like a movie screen, HDTV signals require larger portions of the spectrum than the six megahertz now allotted for broadcast television. HDTV systems now under consideration would require nine or twelve megahertz.

In late 1988, the FCC tentatively decided to allocate the extra spectrum space needed for HDTV only from the existing UHF and VHF bands rather than to borrow from frequencies now devoted to other purposes. One problem, however, is that there will not be enough spectrum space to permit each existing station in the top twenty television markets to broadcast HDTV signals. Although the FCC has not settled on standards for HDTV, it has decided that any HDTV system must be compatible with existing television sets, at least during a transition period. As a result, viewers with old sets could receive HDTV broadcasts, but a set with the increased number of scanning lines would be necessary for a high-definition picture.

Initial Licensing. The first step in the licensing process is the filing of an application for a construction permit—that is, for FCC permission to build a broadcast facility designed to operate on a particular frequency. Upon completion of construction, the applicant then seeks a license to "cover" the permit. Because the license follows the construction permit almost automatically, we will use the term "license" to include the construction permit as well.

The application is filed with the FCC's Mass Media Bureau, which, in routine cases, is authorized to grant the license without a hearing and without formal review by the Commission. Generally, cases are considered routine when there is only a single applicant for a particular license and there is no doubt that the applicant is qualified to hold a broadcast license under the standards set forth in the Communications Act and the FCC's rules. Otherwise, an administrative hearing is necessary. Held before an administrative law judge assigned to the FCC, the hearing resembles a trial, though there is no jury and various procedures are somewhat more relaxed. The particpants in the hearing are the applicant or applicants for the license and, in many cases, a representative of the Mass Media Bureau. In some situations, an existing licensee in the community also takes part, usually to argue that the new station would cause technical inteference. Listeners and citizens groups also have an opportunity to participate, although they more typically become involved in license renewal proceedings. After evaluating the evidence and the various legal arguments, the administrative law judge makes an initial decision in the case, either granting or denying the license. That ruling is appealable within the FCC—to either an intermediate "review board" composed of agency staff or to the Commission itself—and ultimately to the federal courts. Most of these cases are heard by the U.S. Court of Appeals for the District of Columbia Circuit.

Minimum Qualifications. At the threshold of every licensing case is the question of whether the applicant meets the basic requirements established by the Communications Act and the FCC's regulations. These qualifications can be divided into four categories: legal, technical, financial, and character.

Legal qualifications are those that restrict the class of persons who may hold broadcast licenses. For example, the Communications Act expressly provides that a license may not be granted to a non-citizen, a foreign government, a foreign corporation, any corporation in which any officer or director is an alien, or any corporation in which more than twenty percent of the stock is owned by non-citizens. It was this provision that forced Australian media baron Rupert Murdoch to become a naturalized American citizen in order to acquire the television stations that serve as the cornerstone for his new Fox Network.

Similar ownership restrictions are found in the Commission's regulations. For instance, the so-called "multiple ownership rules" limit the number of television and radio stations that a single entity can own and prohibit the common ownership of stations in the same community. Moreover, the Commission's "cross-ownership" rules bar ownership of a broadcast station by a newspaper that serves the community. These restrictions on ownership are considered in Chapter 12.

The FCC has also adopted a series of technical standards that all applicants must meet. These include the engineering requirements for AM radio stations discussed above, as well as regulations concerning antenna height, transmitting power, broadcasting equipment, signal quality, studio location, and interference with other stations. Because in many cases the FCC may simply refuse to accept applications that do not demonstrate compliance with technical requirements, careful attention to detail is essential. With respect to financial qualifications, an applicant must demonstrate that it has sufficient financial resources to construct and operate the proposed station. The standard adopted by the Commission is whether an applicant has the financial ability to build the station and operate it for three months, even assuming that the station generates no revenue during that period.

The Communications Act requires the FCC to determine whether an applicant possesses the requisite "character" to operate a broadcast station in the public interest. Although the act does not define the term, the FCC has over the years fleshed out its meaning. In a 1986 policy statement, the Commission announced that it would focus primarily on "bad" character traits that would raise questions as to the applicant's honesty, its willingness to adhere to FCC rules, and its potential performance as a broadcaster. For example, an applicant that misrepresents a fact to the Commission is in danger of having its application denied, even though the misrepresentation may have been relatively minor. Because the Commission lacks the staff and budget to independently check information furnished by applicants and licensed, it is heavily dependent upon that information and will not tolerate knowing misrepresentations.

Criminal law violations can also result in disqualification on character grounds, particularly if an applicant has been convicted of fraud or a similar crime involving moral turpitude. Generally, however, a criminal conviction will cause problems only if there is a substantial relationship between the criminal conduct and the applicant's proclivity to be truthful or comply with FCC regulations. Thus, an applicant's conviction of violating the federal antitrust laws might serve as the basis for denial of a broadcast license.

The "Public Interest" Standard. Suppose that there is only one applicant for an available frequency and that the applicant meets the minimum qualifications set forth above. Must the Commission grant the license? The answer is "no." Under Section 307(a) of the Communications Act, the FCC "shall grant" a broadcast license "if [the] public convenience, interest, or necessity will be served thereby. . . ." At the heart of this "public interest" requirement is the notion that a broadcaster must serve the community to which the station is licensed. If the Commission is not convinced that the applicant will operate his station in this fashion, it may refuse to grant the license.

Prior to the deregulation mania that swept the federal government during the Reagan Administration, the FCC had developed a detailed procedure by which license applicants, as well as licensees seeking renewal, were required to demonstrate how they planned to serve their communities. Under this so-called "ascertainment" process, an applicant had to identify the needs and problems of the community and propose programming responsive to those concerns. In 1981, however, the Commission jettisoned the ascertainment requirement for radio, and three years later dropped the procedure for television as well. Although the applicant now may use any method he sees fit in identifying important issues facing the community, he still must demonstrate that he will provide responsive programming. However, the applicant may take into account programming offered by other stations, and there is no requirement that he promise to deliver a certain percentage of news, public affairs, and similiar programming.

Comparative Proceedings. If there are multiple applicants for a single frequency who meet the minimum requirements, the Commission must obviously select the one that it thinks will best serve the public interest. This process, which requires a hearing at which the applicants are compared, is at best an inexact science, but over the years the Commission has adopted various criteria that it will use in making the decision. The most important of these are: diversification of media ownership, full-time participation by owners in station management, and past record in broadcasting. Interestingly, the FCC will not ordinarily explore the programming proposed by the various applicants.

The ownership criteria is by far the most significant. If the applicants are about "equal" with regard to the other factors, the Commission will almost always select the applicant who does not have an ownership interest in other media operations, broadcast as well as nonbroadcast. This policy is designed to foster diversity within the media and to prevent the concentration of ownership in the hands of a relative few. Put somewhat differently, the Commission seeks to keep the channels of communication open to as large a number of owners as possible, thus increasing the number of "editorial voices." As a result of this policy, an applicant with a significant ownership interest in other media is at a considerable disadvantage.

Because the Commission believes that it is desirable for owners to participate fully in the day-to-day management of broadcast stations, the second criteria is also of substantial importance. Accordingly, an applicant who plans to run the station himself will be preferred over an applicant who will simply turn the station over to the staff. By the same token, the FCC favors a local applicant over one from outside the area, on the theory that a local owner is more likely to be familiar with the needs of the community than an "absentee landlord" residing elsewhere.

In addition, the Commission has, over the years, developed a "preference" for female applicants and those from various racial minority groups. If, for example, one applicant is a partnership controlled by blacks and other is a corporation owned exclusively by whites, the former is given an advantage in the comparative proceeding. The notion here is that minority involvement in broadcasting helps provide broader community representation and increases programming diversity. The result of this policy has been that minority and female applicants have almost always prevailed in close cases.

In 1985, however, the U.S. Court of Appeals for the District of Columbia Circuit ruled in *Steele v. Federal Communications Commission* that the FCC lacked authority under the Communications Act to grant preferences to female applicants. Upon motion for reconsideration, the court granted the Commission's request that the agency be allowed to rexamine its preference policy with respect to both race and gender. Although the FCC instituted such an inquiry, it subsequently terminated the proceeding pursuant to a congressional directive contained in an appropriations bill for fiscal year 1988. The legislation also required the Commission to continue applying the race and gender preferences. Identical provisions were included in an appropriations bill for fiscal year 1989.

The U.S. Court of Appeals for the District of Columbia Circuit upheld the minority preference policy in *Winter Park Communications, Inc. v. Federal Communications Commission* (1989) but did not address the corresponding preference for women. In that case, the FCC awarded a television license to a company owned primarily by hispanics. Because none of the three applicants enjoyed a clear advantage with respect to the comparative licensing criteria, the policy favoring minority ownership proved dispositive. The unsuccessful applicants challenged the Commission's decision on the ground that giving a preference to minorities unconstitutionally discriminates against nonminorities. Rejecting that argument, the court emphasized that "minority ownership is simply one factor among several that the Commission takes into account in the award of broadcast licenses" and that there are no "quotas or fixed targets" of the sort found unconstitutional in other cases. Moreover, the court noted that Congress, which has broad powers under the fourteenth amendment to ensure equal opportunities for minorities, had expressly approved the FCC policy in passing the bills mentioned above.

Another decision by a different panel of the same court offers an interesting contrast to the *Winter Park* case. In *Shurberg Broadcasting of Hartford, Inc. v. Federal Communications Commission* (1989), the court held unconstitutional the FCC's "distress sale" policy designed to increase ownership of broadcast stations by members of minority groups. Under the policy, a broadcaster facing a hearing on the revocation or nonrenewal of its license was permitted to sell the station at a below-market price to a minority-owned company. In holding the policy invalid, the court focused on the fact that it had the effect of freezing out nonminority applicants who would otherwise have been able to compete for the license upon revocation or in a comparative renewal proceeding. Awarding preferences in the initial licensing context does not have that effect, however. As the court pointed out in *Winter Park*, race is only one of several factors taken into account in evaluating the competing applicants.

An applicant's past record in broadcasting is relevant only if it is "unusually good or unusually poor," since that type of past performance is likely to signal similar performance in the future. On the other hand, the Commission has made clear that it is not "interested in the fact of past ownership per se" and that an applicant will not have an advantage simply because it "has owned stations in the past and another has not." Thus, a prior record of "average" performance will be disregarded.

Oddly enough, proposed programming ordinarily does not play a role in comparative proceedings. Thus, the fact that one applicant for an FM radio license proposes a "rock and roll" format while another plans to play country-western music is simply irrelevant. The Commission is of the view that the evaluation of proposed programming is a subjective task for which it is unsuited. Consistent with its deregulation philosophy, the FCC prefers to let the marketplace shape programming decisions. Programming plans will be considered only when there are "substantial differences" among the applicants, as might be the case when one applicant proposes foreign language programming aimed at a substantial segment of the community that would be served by the station. If the Commission determines that the proposed programming reflects "a superior devotion to public service," it may award an advantage in the comparative proceeding to the applicant making the proposal.

License Renewal.   The term of a radio license, either AM or FM, is seven years, while a television license is issued for a five-year period. Technically, the standard for renewing a license is precisely the same as for granting one in the first place; however, the Commission has declined to renew licenses only in the most egregious circumstances. During the 1970s, for example, the FCC refused renewal of only a dozen licenses. The most common grounds for nonrenewal are making misrepresentations to the Commission and repeatedly violating FCC rules. Generally speaking, a broadcaster does not run the risk of nonrenewal because of the programs he broadcasts, although the Commission has refused to renew licenses because of racially discriminatory programming practices and because licensees violated FCC rules prohibiting the broadcasting of obscene and indecent material.

For the most part, licenses are renewed routinely; in fact, under rules adopted as part of the Commission's effort at deregulation, most licensees simply send to the FCC a completed five-question form. Because there are few unoccupied radio and television frequencies, however, an incumbent licensee may find himself facing opposition from a challenger who wants to operate on that frequency or from a citizens' group dissatisfied with the incumbent's past performance. It is in such contested proceedings that the so-called "renewal expectancy" becomes extremely important. In essence, the question is whether the licensee will be given an advantage over other applicants for the license simply because it is an incumbent.

The Commission has for several years wrestled with problems caused by a certain tension inherent in the renewal process. If licenses are to be automatically renewed as a matter of course, the incumbent is effectively immune from a challenger seeking to offer better broadcast service on the particular frequency. Such a result is contrary to the notion, reflected in the Communications Act, that a broadcast license is a privilege granted for a term of years, not in perpetuity. In addition, a licensee assured of renewal arguably has little incentive to operate his station in the public interest. If, on the other hand, a broadcaster can easily lose his license to a newcomer who promises to outperform the incumbent, there is little incentive for the broadcaster to make the capital investment necessary to build, maintain, and operate the station at a high level. A reasonable businessman would not sink large sums of money into a broadcast operation if, in five or seven years, he faced considerable uncertainty as to whether his license would be renewed. Moreover, stability in the broadcast industry might well be threatened if incumbents routinely lost their licenses and stations regularly passed to new owners.

The Commission has attempted to balance these competing concerns by creating a reasonable expectation that a license will be renewed if the incumbent has provided "substantial" broadcast service. In such a situation, the incumbent will be given a preference vis-à-vis a challenger seeking the license, and in most cases that preference will be decisive. This is so even though the challenger has other advantages under the comparative criteria discussed previously and would have received the license if the applicants had been seeking an unoccupied frequency. If, on the other hand, the incumbent's past performance is only "minimal," he is not entitled to a renewal expectancy and may well find himself ranked behind a challenger on the basis of the comparative criteria.

Cases in which the incumbent's past performance is characterized as "minimal" are relatively unusual, but they do exist. For example, in *Geller v. Federal Communications Commission* (1984), the licensee, Simon Geller, had for more than twenty years single-handedly operated a small FM station with a classical music format when, in 1981, the Grandebanke Corporation filed a competing application for the frequency. Over ninety-nine percent of the station's programming was classical music, and Geller broadcast no news, editorials, or locally produced programs. Under these circumstances, the FCC concluded that Geller's past performance was "minimal" and that he was not entitled to a renewal expectancy. Turning to the other comparative criteria, the Commission then awarded the license to Grandebanke, the challenger. The U.S. Court of Appeals for the District of Columbia Circuit reversed. Although it agreed with the Commission that the incumbent did not deserve a renewal expectancy, the court concluded that the FCC misapplied the comparative criteria by failing to accord substantial weight to Geller's advantages with respect to diversification of media ownership and full-time participation in station management. Upon reconsideration, the FCC renewed Geller's license.

In mid-1988, the Commission announced an inquiry into the renewal expectancy issue and suggested different approaches that would not be based primarily upon past programming. Under one proposal, for example, the Commission would grant a renewal application provided that the incumbent had broadcast material responsive to matters of concern to the residents of its service area and had not committed serious violations of the Communications Act or FCC regulations. This approach would eliminate the need for the Commission to place subject labels—such as "substantial" or "minimal"—on an incumbent's programming. Instead, the question under the first prong of the test would be whether the licensee had acted reasonably in meeting its basic obligation, discussed later in this chapter, to provide issue-responsive programming. Another proposal would require even less by way of programming review by focusing on an incumbent's overall record of compliance with the Communications Act and FCC rules. This evaluation could include a look at issue-responsive programming, but such review would not automatically take place in every comparative renewal proceeding.

Other aspects of the comparative renewal process have also attracted the Commission's attention. In early 1989, for example, the FCC adopted new rules designed to "curtail the exploitation of the [system] for private gain." According to some critics, competing license applications have in the past been filed not in hopes of prevailing on the merits, but with an eye toward receiving a cash settlement from the incumbent licensee in exchange for dropping out of the renewal proceeding. This potential for abuse also existed in connection with petitions asking the Commission to deny renewal of a particular broadcast license. Such petitions are typically filed by citizens' groups dissatisfied with the licensee's programming or other policies concerning operation of the station.

To deal with these problems, the FCC banned all settlement payments to competing applicants who withdraw an application prior to the initial decision stage of a comparative license renewal proceeding. After that point, such payments are restricted to the "legitimate and prudent expenses" of the withdrawing applicant. Similarly, the Commission limited settlement payments in connection with the withdrawal of a petition to deny a license renewal application to the legitimate and prudent expenses of the petitioner. Recognizing that these petitions serve an important monitoring function regarding licensee performance, the FCC declined to prohibit settlement payments altogether in that context. In the Commission's view, it would be inappropriate to ask a citizens' group to incur considerable out-of-pocket expenses, without the possibility of reimbursement, in order to alert the agency to licensee deficiencies.

The new FCC policies also affect nonfinancial settlements (commonly known as "citizens' agreements") resulting in the withdrawal of petitions to deny. First, any promise by a broadcaster to provide certain programming is unenforceable. The Commission's decision with respect to such representations, which were once common in citizens' agreements, is consistent with its deregulatory initiatives in the programming area. Second, the FCC will review all citizens' agreements on a case-by-case basis to make sure that their terms are consistent with the public interest. There is a rebuttable presumption that certain provisions, such as promises by the broadcaster to pay the citizens' group for performing various tasks related to programming or employment matters, are contrary to the public interest. These arrangements, the Commission said, sometimes amount to "disguised payoffs" for withdrawing a petition to deny.

Transfer of Licenses. A broadcast licensee does not acquire a property interest in his assigned frequency and thus cannot "sell" it to a third party. However, the licensee can profit handsomely from the sale of the station itself, including not only its studio and equipment, but also its profit potential and "good will." In 1985, for example, Rupert Murdoch paid nearly $2 billion for seven independent television stations in major markets, later using them as the foundation for his fledgling Fox Television Network. Obviously, acquiring a station is an empty gesture unless one also obtains a license to operate it, and here is where the FCC enters the picture. Under the Communications Act, the Commission must approve all license transfers and assure that they are in the "public interest." Such transfers are routinely granted.

In the event of a proposed transfer, the only question is whether the proposed buyer will operate the station in the public interest. The Communications Act expressly provides that the Commission is not to consider whether the public might be better served if someone besides the would-be purchaser operated the station. In other words, the transfer approval process is not comparative, and it immaterial that the buyer does not match up to an applicant who had earlier sought the license—

unsuccessfully—during the initial licensing process or in a comparative renewal proceeding.

The foregoing presumes a situation in which there is a willing buyer and a willing seller. Potential transfer problems also occur in connection with hostile corporate takeovers, a business phenomenon of the 1980s. In that situation, too, the FCC must approve the transfer of control of a target company's broadcast licenses to the person or company engineering the takeover.

The FCC and the Networks

As the preceding discussion indicates, the Commission's major regulatory "hook" is the licensing process for individual broadcast stations. Although the three major networks—ABC, CBS, and NBC—are licensed to operate television and radio stations (usually located in the nation's major markets) and are thus treated as any other licensee, they are not as networks directly subject to FCC regulation under the Communications Act. Since the early 1940s, however, the FCC has asserted indirect control over network operations by adopting rules prohibiting individual broadcast licensees from entering into network contracts that contain provisions deemed contrary to the public interest. In 1943 the U.S. Supreme Court upheld the Commission's authority to so regulate the networks in *National Broadcasting Co. v. United States*.

At issue in that case were a series of FCC rules promulgated in response to the increasing dominance of the radio networks in the late 1930s. By that time, CBS, NBC, and Mutual Broadcasting together controlled about fifty percent of the radio industry, with NBC operating two separate networks (one of which later became ABC). After extensive public hearings on the subject, the Commission adopted its so-called "chain broadcasting rules" aimed at correcting a variety of perceived abuses in the industry. For example, the rules prohibited network exclusivity contracts under which stations affilated with a network were barred from carrying the programs of other networks. In the FCC's view, the effect of these arrangements was to thwart the growth of new networks and to prevent licensees from exercising their statutory obligation to program their stations in a manner to best serve the needs of the communities in which they operated. Other rules outlawed "territorial exclusivity" arrangements whereby the networks promised not to provide a program to any other stations in the same community as an affiliate, even if the affiliate declined to air the program; "optional time clauses" that required affiliates, upon demand from the network, to carry a commercial program during specified time periods; and provisions that limited the discretion of affiliates to reject network programs.

Not surprisingly, the networks brought suit to enjoin the Commission from enforcing its new rules. Among other things, the networks argued that the Communications Act did not empower the FCC to so restrict their activities. The Supreme Court gave this argument short shrift. Justice Frankfurter wrote:

> True enough, the [Communications] Act does not explicitly say that the Commission shall have power to deal with network practices found inimical to the public interest. But Congress was acting in a field of regulation which was both new and dynamic. Congress moved under the spur of a widespread fear that in the absence of governmental control the public interest might be subordinated to monopolistic domination in the

broadcasting field. In the context of the developing problems to which it was directed, the Act gave the Commission not niggardly but expansive powers. It was given a comprehensive mandate to "encourage the larger and more effective use of radio in the public interest," if need be, by making "special regulations applicable to radio stations engaged in chain broadcasting."

The chain broadcasting rules remain in effect for television, but radio has been largely deregulated. In addition to the provisions summarized above, the television rules prohibit any arrangement by which a network has control of advertising rates charged by an affiliate and prevent an organization from simultaneously operating dual networks. However, the FCC has recently eliminated a rule forbidding network affiliation contracts that run for more than two years and has proposed repealing a portion of the territorial exclusivity rule that limits the exclusivity a television station may acquire for the exhibition of network programming vis-à-vis stations licensed to other communities. In 1977, the Commission repealed virtually all of the chain broadcasting rules governing AM and FM radio, concluding that they were no longer necessary given the number of radio stations and the degree of competition between them. The only remaining regulation is a modified version of the territorial exclusivity rule.

REGULATIONS AFFECTING PROGRAM CONTENT

The "personal attack" rule at issue in *Red Lion* is one of several Commission regulations that have an impact, directly or indirectly, on the content of programs aired by broadcasters. In this section, we shall examine the fairness doctrine, of which the FCC's personal attack and political endorsement rules are also a part; two provisions of the Communications Act dealing with political candidates and campaigns, along with FCC rules dealing with such political broadcasting; prohibitions against obscene and indecent programming; and several miscellaneous regulations that affect content, such as the "prime time access rule" designed to encourage local television programming.

The Fairness Doctrine

By far the most controversial of the FCC's rules bearing on program content is the fairness doctrine, which, prior to its repeal by the Commission in 1987, required broadcasters to air discussions of controversial issues important to the community and to provide fair coverage of all reasonable points of view with respect to those issues. Since the FCC's decision to abolish the doctrine, its future has been in the hands of the Congress, the President, and the courts, and the last word on the matter has yet to be written. Shortly after the Commission's ruling, Congress passed a bill adopting the doctrine in statutory form, but President Reagan vetoed it. New legislation to so codify the doctrine was introduced in early 1989. Subsequently, the U.S. Court of Appeals for the District of Columbia Circuit upheld the FCC but managed to duck the question of whether the agency's ruling was compelled by the first amendment. Because the fairness doctrine is in such an obvious state of flux, we will examine it here in some detail, drawing on principles developed before its administrative demise.

Background. In 1941, as the nation vigorously debated the question of whether to enter World War II, the FCC ruled in *In re Mayflower Broadcasting Corp.* that broadcast licensees could not use their stations to express their own views on issues of public importance. While adopting this ban on editorializing, however, the Commission also made clear that broadcasters have an affirmative duty to cover issues of public importance: "[O]ne licensed to operate in a public domain . . . has assumed the obligation of presenting all sides of important public questions, fairly, objectively, and without bias." Four years later, in *In re United Broadcasting Co.*, the Commission attempted to clarify the scope of this obligation by ruling that a station could not adopt a general policy of refusing to sell time for the discussion of controversial issues. Though noting that broadcasters are not common carriers under the Communications Act, the FCC stressed that they have "a duty to be sensitive to the problems of public concern in the community" and, therefore, must "make sufficient time available, on a nondiscriminatory basis, for full discussion thereof."

These decisions marked the beginning of the fairness doctrine, but it was not until 1949 that the Commission issued a major policy statement with respect to the requirement. In its *Report on Editorializing by Broadcast Licensees*, which has served as the basis for all subsequent fairness doctrine rulings, the FCC explicitly recognized a two-part duty on the part of broadcasters:

- to devote a reasonable percentage of time to the coverage of controversial issues of public importance; and
- to provide a reasonable opportunity for the presentation of contrasting viewpoints on the issues.

The Commission also lifted the ban on editorializing announced in *Mayflower*, explaining that "a station's willingness to stand up and be counted" would likely contribute toward "a climate of fairness and equal opportunity for the expression of contrary views."

In language strikingly similar to that subsequently employed by the Supreme Court in the 1969 *Red Lion* decision upholding the constitutionality of the "personal attack" rule that emerged from the general fairness doctrine, the Commission explained the rationale for the concept in terms of the Communications Act's command that licensees serve the public interest: "It is the right of the public to be informed, rather than any right on the part of the Government, any broadcast licensee or any individual member of the public to broadcast his own particular views on any matter, which is the foundation of the American system of broadcasting." Accordingly, the Commission concluded that "the public interest requires that the licensee must operate on a basis of overall fairness, making his facilities available for the expression of contrasting views of all responsible elements in the community on the various issues which arise."

The Commission began to flesh out the fairness doctrine in a series of rulings in individual cases arising from complaints that particular stations had fallen short of their fairness obligations. In two important reports on the doctrine, issued in 1964 and 1974, the FCC attempted to summarize its decisions in these cases to provide more meaningful guidance to broadcasters. The 1974 *Fairness Report* remained the FCC's basic "primer" on the doctrine's application until 1987, when the Commission abolished the doctrine altogether. Thus, the 1974 report forms the basis for much of the discussion of the fairness doctrine that appears here.

As noted previously, the FCC established the fairness doctrine under its general authority, granted by the Communications Act, to regulate broadcasting in the "public interest." It was thought for some time, however, that Congress had elevated the doctrine to statutory status via a 1959 amendment to Section 315(a) of the Communications Act, which embodies the so-called "equal opportunities" rule regarding political broadcasting. Designed to exempt bona fide news programs from the equal opportunity rule discussed at length in the next section, the amendment also stated that it was not meant to "reliev[e] broadcasters . . . from the obligation imposed on them under this Act to operate in the public interest and to afford reasonable opportunity for the discussion of conflicting views on issues of public importance." Arguably, this language meant that the fairness doctrine had become part of the Communications Act itself and, consequently, that the Commission was not free to eliminate the requirement without the assent of the Congress.

In *Telecommunications Research and Action Center v. Federal Communications Commission* (1986), however, the U.S. Court of Appeals for the District of Columbia Circuit ruled that the 1959 amendment did not have this effect. Because the fairness doctrine is simply a creature of the FCC, the court said, the agency may modify or abolish it as it sees fit. This ruling cleared the way for the Commission's 1987 decision in *In re Syracuse Peace Council* eliminating the doctrine, a course of action that the agency had suggested in a special 1985 report on the fairness requirement. In *Syracuse Peace Council* the Commission concluded that the fairness doctrine is contrary to the public interest and unconstitutional, reasoning that the scarcity rationale relied upon by the Supreme Court in *Red Lion* no longer can justify a restriction on the editorial judgment of broadcasters. We shall return to this issue after examining the fairness doctrine in operation.

Covering Controversial Issues. The "first prong" of the fairness doctrine requires broadcast licensees to devote a reasonable amount of air time to the coverage of "controversial issues of public importance." Then, under the doctrine's "second prong," the licensee must afford a reasonable opportunity for the presentation of opposing viewpoints with respect to such issues. Our concern here is the broadcaster's affirmative obligation under the first prong to address controversial issues of public importance. Obviously, this requirement is central to the application of the fairness doctrine, for a broadcaster who shirks this duty never need worry about his obligation under the second prong to cover an issue "fairly." Despite the significance of the first prong, however, the FCC has been incredibly lax in enforcing it. In fact, the Commission has handed down only one decision finding that a station had ignored a controversial issue of public importance.

Moreover, the FCC has offered relatively little guidance with respect to the broadcaster's affirmative duty under the first prong, though the 1974 *Fairness Report* sheds some light on the matter. According to the Commission, an issue must be both "important" to the public and "controversial." The former involves a "subjective evaluation of the impact that the issue is likely to have on the community at large." In making this determination, a broadcaster should ask himself whether resolution of the issue will have "a significant impact on society or its institutions." A particular issue is not "important" merely because it has received attention from government officials, community leaders, or the news media, though these factors should be taken into account. However, the extent to which members of these groups have become involved with respect to an issue is "highly relevant" in determining whether the issue is "controversial." This inquiry is somewhat more objective than the determination of importance, and the licensee "should be able to tell, with a reasonable degree of objectivity, whether an issue is the subject of vigorous debate with substantial elements of the community in opposition to one another."

The Commission elaborated on these points in *In re Representative Patsy Mink* (1976), which remains the only major ruling in which the FCC has enforced the fairness doctrine's first prong. The case arose when several radio stations in West Virginia broadcast a program prepared by the U.S. Chamber of Commerce that supported strip mining. Congresswoman Mink prepared an eleven-minute tape taking the opposing view and sent it to the stations, one of which refused to air it because it had not broadcast the Chamber of Commerce program. In fact, apart from including some Associated Press wire reports in its local newscasts, the station had not covered the strip mining controversy at all, despite its obvious impact on people of West Virginia and on the state's environment and economy. Legislation on the subject was also pending before Congress, and newspapers across the state had devoted considerable space to the strip mining debate. Under these circumstances, the FCC concluded that the station had not met its obligation to broadcast programs dealing with controversial issues of public importance. The fact that it had not aired the Chamber of Commerce program did not excuse its refusal to air the congresswoman's tape, since "it is the station's obligation to make an affirmative effort to program on issues of concern to its community." The station's use of the AP news reports did not satisfy this requirement, the FCC said, for it was unclear which wire service stories had actually been aired.

By and large, however, the Commission gives licensees broad discretion in determining whether a particular issue must be covered under the first prong of the fairness doctrine. As the FCC stated in the 1974 *Fairness Report*, "we have no intention of becoming involved in the selection of issues to be discussed, nor do we expect a broadcaster to cover each and every important issue which may arise in his community." The *Mink* case, then, is the exception rather than the rule. More typical of the FCC's attitude is its decision in *In re Public Communication, Inc.* (1974), which grew out of the failure of television stations in the Los Angeles area to devote air time to legislation pending in Congress that would have made it easier for broadcasters to obtain renewal of their licenses. The stations had not covered congressional consideration of the bill on their regular news programs and had not broadcast other reports dealing with the legislation. In concluding that the stations had no obligation to cover the issue, the Commission accepted their judgment that the matter was not as important as others in the community that were being examined by the stations.

Triggering the Obligation to be "Fair." More typically, the question of whether an issue is important and controversial arises in the context of the fairness doctrine's second prong. That is, the question is not whether a broadcaster has ignored such issues, but whether he has fulfilled his responsibility to present them in a "fair" or "balanced" manner. This second inquiry is necessary only if an issue addressed by the broadcaster in a particular program is both "controversial" and "important."

For example, in *In re Avery D. Post* (1984), the leaders of several mainstream American churches filed a fairness complaint based on a "60 Minutes" segment dealing with church support of "international communism" through aid to various overseas organizations. The Commission concluded that the issue was not "controversial" and, therefore, did not trigger the obligation to afford a reasonable opportunity for the presentation of opposing views on the issue. In reaching this conclusion, the FCC found that even though membership of the churches totalled forty million, there was no indication that "any substantial number of them were 'vigorously debating' the subject issue."

The Commission also made clear in the *Post* case that licensees are given broad discretion in determining whether coverage of a particular issue calls the second prong of the fairness doctrine into play. As the FCC pointed out in its ruling, it "will review a broadcaster's decision . . . only to determine whether the broadcaster has acted reasonably under all the facts and circumstances presented, not to determine whether the Commission would have resolved this matter differently." In other words, the FCC will not second-guess the broadcaster's conclusion that an issue is not "controversial" or of "public importance," but will simply ask whether that conclusion is "reasonable." As a result, the vast majority of fairness complaints are resolved in favor of the broadcaster.

In addition to problems associated with determining whether an issue is sufficiently important and controversial, difficulties abound in deciding just what issue has been raised by a particular program. The Commission has taken the position that a program or series of programs must raise a specific, well-defined issue in order to implicate the fairness doctrine. Perhaps the leading case on the point is *American Security Council Educational Foundation v. Federal Communications Commission* (1979), in which a conservative organization monitored CBS News' coverage of "national security issues" for an entire year. The foundation then categorized the news stories as consistent with one of three viewpoints: that the threat to U.S. security is more serious than perceived by the government and that our national security efforts should be increased; that the government's perception of the national security threat and its response thereto is correct; and that the threat is less serious than perceived and that national security efforts should thus be decreased. Concluding that the news stories overwhelmingly reflected the third viewpoint and almost completely ignored the first, the foundation filed a fairness doctrine complaint with the FCC and asked that CBS be ordered to provide a reasonable opportunity for the presentation of the view that the nation should increase its national security efforts.

The FCC dismissed the complaint, ruling that the foundation had failed to identify "the particular issue of a controversial nature" addressed by the CBS programming. That decision was affirmed by the U.S. Court of Appeals for the District of Columbia Circuit. In the court's view, the foundation's "national security" label was simply too broad and amorphous, since it could reach variety of topics, some only marginally related to one another. In addition, the court concluded that use of such broad issues for fairness doctrine purposes would "unduly burden" broadcasters. Here, the court said, "[i]t would have been virtually impossible [for CBS] to know which broadcasts should be included as relevant to national security, or how views discussed . . . should be tallied to measure 'balance' under the fairness doctrine."

At the other extreme is *In re NBC*, handed down by the FCC in 1970. The case stemmed from a three-part NBC News story on air traffic safety. One of the segments contained an interview with a private pilot who had circled Shea Stadium in New York City during a World Series game. Also included in that segment was an interview with a commercial airline pilot, who stated that the greatest danger in commercial aviation came from private pilots. In addition, the reporter stated that private aviation posed a serious problem in the crowded air space around major airports. The Aircraft Owners and Pilots Association, an organization representing private pilots, filed a fairness doctrine complaint with the Commission, arguing that NBC had "presented only one side of a controversial issue of public importance, i.e., that private pilots and general aviation are a principal cause of midair collisions as compared to commercial pilots. . . ."

The FCC, however, ruled that the issue identified by the pilots was only a "sub-issue" that did not trigger the fairness doctrine. According to the Commission, the issue addressed by the NBC series was "congestion over airports and the hazards raised by such congestion," and the network gave spokesmen for both commercial and private aviation interests a reasonable opportunity to state their views on the subject. Nothing in the fairness doctrine requires balance "as to every statement or assertion made in discussing a controversial issue," the FCC said. "If every statement, or inference from statements or presentations, could be made the subject of a separate and distinct fairness requirement, the doctrine would be unworkable." Because NBC satisfied its fairness obligations with respect to the controversial issue of airport congestion and safety, it had no duty to be "fair" with respect to the sub-issue of the competence of private pilots. Thus, while the "national security" issue in the *American Security Council* case was too broad, the issue defined by the private pilots was too narrow.

Presenting Opposing Viewpoints. The second prong of the fairness doctrine requires the broadcaster to provide a reasonable opportunity for the presentation of opposing viewpoints with respect to the controversial issue of public importance. This requirement does not mean, however, that the broadcaster must afford "equal time" to persons with contrasting views, allow anyone with an opinion the chance to state his position, or include all viewpoints on an issue in a single program or series of programs. Rather, the broadcaster's responsibility is to ensure that the various sides of an issue are covered in a balanced fashion when his overall programming is taken into account. Moreover, the broadcaster has considerable discretion in deciding how to meet his fairness obligations, and the FCC will generally not intrude upon the exercise of that discretion.

In the 1974 *Fairness Report*, the Commission emphasized that there is no mathematical formula to be used in determining whether there has been an imbalance in the time that a broadcaster has allocated to contrasting viewpoints. Rather, the FCC identified three factors that must be considered:

- the total amount of time afforded to each viewpoint;
- the frequency with which each viewpoint is presented; and
- the size of the listening audience during the various broadcasts.

Thus, the fact that a station devotes fifty percent more air time to Viewpoint A than to Viewpoint B is not dispositive, since rigid "equality" is not required. Conversely, absolute equality in terms of the amount of time will not necessarily constitute "fairness." For example, a broadcaster might run into difficulty if one viewpoint were aired more frequently than another, even though the total time devoted to each were the same. By the same token, a station that devoted two programs of precisely the same length on two opposing viewpoints would fail to satisfy its fairness obligations if one program were aired in prime time and another at 3 A.M., since the viewing audience would be much smaller at the latter time period.

Two cases illustrate the application of these principles. In its initial ruling in *In re Syracuse Peace Council*—the case in which it subsequently abolished the fairness doctrine—the Commission found that a television station in Syracuse, New York, had not adequately presented opposing viewpoints concerning the proposed construction of a nuclear power plant. After the station had aired a series of paid advertisements by a pro-nuclear power organization and had presented this view on its newscasts, a group opposed to the power plant filed a fairness complaint alleging that the station had failed to provide a reasonable opportunity for opposing views. The FCC agreed. First, the Commission pointed out that the station had devoted approximately nine times as much air time to the pro-nuclear power position than to the opposing view; specifically, the station had allotted just over three hours to the former, almost all of which was paid advertising, but only twenty-two minutes to the latter. Second, the Commission noted that, in terms of frequency, the pro-nuclear viewpoint was broadcast 260 times, while the opposing position appeared only twenty times. Finally, the FCC observed that the pro-nuclear advertisements were broadcast throughout the day, with a substantial number appearing in prime time. In contrast, the anti-nuclear power viewpoints appeared only in segments on the station's local newscasts.

The Commission reached a different result in a dispute involving partisan politics, and that ruling was upheld on appeal in *Democratic National Committee v. Federal Communications Commission* (1983). The case arose in late 1981, when CBS and NBC broadcast a series of paid thirty-second advertisements, sponsored by the Republican National Committee, supporting President Reagan's economic policies. The Democratic National Committee (DNC) filed a complaint with the FCC, arguing that the advertisements addressed a controversial issue of public importance and that the networks had failed to offer opposing views. The DNC also claimed that the networks' news reports were weighted in favor of the President's policies by approximately a two-to-one margin. When the advertisements were considered along with the news reports, the DNC said, that ratio increased to about four-to-one. The FCC rejected the complaint, emphasizing that the four-to-one ratio was within the range that the Commission had previously found acceptable. In affirming this ruling, the U.S. Court of Appeals for the District of Columbia Circuit pointed out that the fairness doctrine requires "reasonableness" rather than "rigorous equality." In addition, the court noted that the DNC had failed to present evidence suggesting that the Republican position was aired more frequently than the opposing view or that the viewing audiences during the relevant broadcasts were not comparable in size.

The *Democratic National Committee* case also makes clear that broadcasters have considerable discretion in determining *how* opposing viewpoints are to be presented. The DNC had argued that the Republican-sponsored advertisements supporting President Reagan's economic policies could not be adequately "balanced" by news programs that addressed the opposing view. In effect, the DNC sought a ruling that it was entitled to free advertising "spots" to rebut the Republican messages. The court firmly rejected this argument:

> [The Commission and the courts] have emphasized, time and again, the wide discretion available to licensees in determining how to fulfill their fairness doctrine obligations, including the option of offsetting the messages of advertisements by public service messages or other modes of presentation in a licensee's overall programming.

In addition to choosing the format or manner in which opposing views are to be aired, the broadcaster may select the spokesmen to appear on the program. Thus, contrary to a popular misconception, a particular group or individual does not have the right to demand an appearance on a program dealing with a controversial issue. As the Commission observed in the 1974 *Fairness Report*, the fairness doctrine does not "dictate the selection of a particular spokesman" and "the public is best served by a system which allows individual broadcasters considerable discretion in selecting . . . the appropriate spokesmen. . . ." However, the Commission also noted that a station should make reasonable efforts to include as spokesmen "genuine partisans who actually believe in what they are saying." Thus, a broadcaster cannot adopt a "policy of excluding partisan voices and always itself presenting views in a bland, inoffensive manner. . . ."

There is one important limitation on the broadcaster's discretion regarding the presentation of opposing views. The FCC ruled in *In re Cullman Broadcasting Co.* (1963) that a broadcaster has an affirmative obligation to seek out persons to present contrasting viewpoints and may not simply wait for such spokesmen to appear on its doorstep. Moreover, if a station does not intend to present contrasting viewpoints through its own programming (e.g., news reports), it cannot refuse to broadcast those views simply because it cannot obtain paid sponsorship for the presentation. As the Commission has noted, "[t]he *Cullman* doctrine is, in reality, no more than a statement that the fairness doctrine must be complied with regardless of the availability of paying program sponsors. . . ."

This problem frequently arises with respect to paid advertisements of the type at issue in *Syracuse Peace Council* and *Democratic National Committee*. If the paid advertisements deal with a controversial issue of public importance, then the broadcaster must afford a reasonable opportunity for the presentation of opposing views. As the *Democratic National Committee* case indicates, the broadcaster may satisfy its fairness obligation by covering the opposing view in regular news reports, documentaries, or other programs produced by the station. Alternatively, the broadcaster may choose to air counter-advertisements paid for by persons taking the opposing view or may use some combination of news coverage and paid advertising. If it does neither, however, the station may not, consistent with the *Cullman* doctrine, refuse to broadcast a program or advertisement prepared by proponents of the contrasting view merely because they cannot afford to purchase air time.

Programming Covered by the Fairness Doctrine. The cases considered to this point make plain that two types of programming routinely trigger obligations under the fairness doctrine: news coverage, whether in the form of regularly scheduled reports or documentaries, and so-called "editorial" advertisements that state a point of view with respect to a particular issue. It is also possible that controversial issues of public importance can be raised in "institutional" advertisements and in entertainment programs. However, "product" advertising is beyond the reach of the fairness doctrine.

While the Commission has never found a fairness violation based on entertainment programming, there is no doubt that programs of this nature can give rise to fairness doctrine problems. For example, in *In re Committee for the Scientific Investigation of Claims of the Paranormal* (1979), a group complained of a prime time NBC program, "Exploring the Unknown," that dealt with various psychic phenomena. The network plainly considered the program to be entertainment rather than news, having labeled it as such in a introductory disclaimer advising viewers that it presented "an entertaining look" at the subject. Although the FCC dismissed the complaint, it emphasized that its decision did not turn on the entertainment nature of the program. Instead, the Commission considered the complaint under the general fairness doctrine principles discussed previously and concluded that the program had not addressed a controversial issue of public importance.

The Commission has also made clear that entertainment programs must deal directly with controversial issues in order to implicate the fairness doctrine and that the incidental treatment of such matters will not suffice. For example, in *In re NBC (WRC-TV)* (1975), the FCC rejected a fairness complaint based on entertainment programming said to depict women in a sterotypical manner. Such programs bore only a "tenuous relationship, at best, to the issue of the role of women in society," the Commission said. Because it was unclear whether the portrayal of characters on such programs "transmits any clear or singular message demonstrably linked to a controversial issue of public importance," the FCC was "unable to accord these alleged implicit messages much, if any, weight on the fairness doctrine scale."

Similarly, in *In re Thomas E. Mitchell* (1975), the FCC staff dismissed a complaint that various ABC entertainment programs, including "The Streets of San Francisco," treated the issue of handgun control in one-sided manner. "There are currently a large number of police and detective dramas on television and most portray the commission of a crime involving the use of a handgun," the staff said in its ruling. "However, it does not automatically follow that these programs present a point of view on handgun control."

The FCC's treatment of product advertising under the fairness doctrine has been marked by inconsistency and vacillation. In 1967 the Commission ruled that cigarette advertisements raised a controversial issue of public importance and required stations to present the opposing view that smoking is dangerous. In order to meet this obligation, broadcasters began to air, without charge, public service spots prepared by the National Cancer Society and other organizations about the health risks associated with smoking. Fearing that the anti-smoking advertisements were having an adverse effect on cigarette sales, the tobacco companies successfully pushed for federal legislation that banned cigarette commercials from the airwaves and thus eliminated the broadcasters' duty to carry the anti-smoking messages.

After the Commission's ruling was affirmed on appeal in *Banzhaf v. Federal Communications Commission* (1968), the agency sought to limit its reach to cigarette advertising, thereby excluding from the fairness doctrine commercials for other products. The courts rejected this attempt as arbitrary; for example, in *Friends of the Earth v. Federal Communications Commission* (1971), the U.S. Court of Appeals for the District of Columbia Circuit ruled that the FCC acted impermissibly in concluding that the fairness doctrine did not apply to advertisements for high-powered cars and premium gasoline. If cigarette ads addressed the obviously controversial issue of whether smoking is desirable, the court said, ads for cars and gasoline dealt with an equally controversial matter, the dangers of air pollution.

In its 1974 *Fairness Report*, the Commission did an about-face on the advertising question, ruling that mere "product" advertising does not trigger the fairness doctrine. Such ads, the FCC reasoned, do not make a "meaningful contribution toward informing the public on any side of any issue" but merely seek to sell products. However, the Commission determined that paid "editorial" advertising that "obviously addresses, and advocates a point of view on, a controversial issue of public importance" is covered by the fairness doctrine. Ads of this sort, which are readily recognizable, were at issue in the *Syracuse Peace Council* and *Democratic National Committee* cases discussed above. In addition, the Commission ruled that the fairness doctrine may apply to so-called "institutional" advertisements that seek to create a particular public image for a company without directly pushing its products. The critical question is whether the ad is clearly linked to a controversial issue of public importance. For example, the FCC has found the fairness doctrine applicable to an ad picturing an oil company as concerned about the environment.

Even though editorial and institutional advertisements may give rise to fairness doctrine obligations, there is no requirement that broadcasters accept such advertising in the first place. In other words, the "first prong" of the fairness doctrine means only that broadcasters must devote a reasonable amount of air time to controversial issues of public importance, not that they must carry paid advertisements dealing with such matters. The first prong may be satisfied by broadcasting news reports, documentaries, or interview programs, and a broadcaster may decline to air any and all advertisements of an editorial nature if it so chooses. Consequently, there is no right on the part of the public to purchase air time in order to address a controversial issue in an "editorial" advertisement.

The leading case on this point is *CBS, Inc. v. Democratic National Committee,* decided by the U.S. Supreme Court in 1973. There the DNC, which had encountered broadcaster resistance to its partisan fund-raising advertisements, had unsuccessfully petitioned the FCC for a ruling that no licensee could refuse to carry editorial ads taking a position on controversial public issues. In a companion case, consolidated with the DNC's challenge to the Commission's decision for purposes of appeal, a group called the Business Executive's Move for Vietnam Peace filed a fairness doctrine complaint against a Washington radio station that had rejected the organization's editorial advertisements opposing the Vietnam War. The FCC found no violation, concluding that the broadcasters had no duty to accept the ads.

On appeal, the U.S. Supreme Court agreed with the Commission. First, the Court ruled that the FCC had acted reasonably in refusing to expand the fairness doctrine to require carriage of editorial advertisements. Such a rule would not only enable "the affluent [to] determine in large part the issues to be discussed," the Court said, but also would jeopardize "the effective operation of the [fairness] doctrine" by forcing broadcasters to air advertisements dealing with issues that had already been fairly addressed by the station. The result would be a "further erosion of the journalistic discretion of broadcasters in the coverage of public issues, and a transfer of control over the treatment of public issues from the licensees who are accountable for broadcaster performance to private individuals who are not."

Second, the Court held rejected the argument that a right to purchase air time was compelled by the first amendment. "The question here is not whether there is to be discussion of controversial issues of public importance on the broadcast media, but rather who shall determine what issues are to be discussed by whom, and when," Chief Justice Burger wrote. The first amendment, he added, generally leaves decisions of this type to broadcasters: "For better or worse, editing is what editors are for; and editing is selection and choice of material." Moreover, recognition of a right of access would require the FCC to "oversee far more of the day-to-day operations" of broadcast stations, thus increasing "the risk of an enlargement of Government control over the content of broadcast discussion of public issues. . . ."

Enforcing Broadcast "Fairness." As the foregoing discussion suggests, the Commission enforces the fairness doctrine in the context of specific complaints filed against broadcast licensees. In addition, the issue of a broadcaster's compliance with the doctrine can arise at license renewal time, typically in the context of a "petition to deny" the license filed by a citizens' group that believes renewal is unwarranted. Regardless of which technique is used to obtain an FCC ruling on an alleged fairness doctrine violation, a complainant must overcome several procedural hurdles in order to prevail. These obstacles are so substantial that the success rate for complainants is only about one-tenth of one percent; in 1980, for example, just over 10,000 fairness complaints were lodged with the FCC, and only six resulted in rulings adverse to broadcasters.

The first requirement is that the complainant make a *prima facie* showing that a fairness violation has occurred; that is, he must support his allegation with sufficient facts establishing that the broadcaster has failed to provide balanced coverage of a controversial issue of public importance. As a practical matter, this means that the complainant must monitor the station's programming over a period of time in order to collect evidence that opposing viewpoints have not been aired. If the complainant carries this heavy burden, the Commission requires the broadcaster to file a response demonstrating compliance with the fairness doctrine. In more than ninety-nine percent of fairness cases, however, the complainant fails to make the requisite showing, and, consequently, the FCC's inquiry comes to a halt without the broadcaster even having to defend itself.

In the rather unlikely event that the broadcaster is called upon to respond to the complaint, the Commission considers the facts presented by both parties in deciding whether a violation has occurred. As indicated previously, however, the FCC gives the broadcaster broad discretion in determining whether a controversial issue of public importance has been raised and whether that issue has received balanced treatment within the context of the broadcaster's overall programming. Generally speaking, the question is whether the broadcaster has acted reasonably and with good faith in making these determinations, and, for the most part, the Commission is unwilling to second-guess the broadcaster's judgment.

In the rare case that the FCC finds that the fairness doctrine has been violated, the agency will typically ask the broadcaster how it intends to fulfill its obligations with respect to the particular issue. Though the Commission has other enforcement tools at its disposal, such as imposing a fine on the violator, refusing to renew a license, or renewing a license for a shorter time period than normal, these penalties are employed only in egregious cases. For example, the harshest of the possible sanctions—loss of license—has been imposed against just two stations in the forty-year history of the fairness doctrine.

This is not to say, however, that the doctrine has had little effect on broadcasters. No licensee really wants to deal with the FCC, for lawyers are expensive and the agency is one of the most hopelessly tangled bureaucracies in Washington. Thus, broadcasters faced with fairness complaints, as well as the complainants themselves, have a strong incentive to settle their disputes informally without the Commission's involvement. Consequently, the key to success for a person or group with a fairness complaint is not FCC enforcement of the doctrine, but rather vigorous organizational efforts and the unflagging presentation of demands to broadcasters for air time. A complainant's best hope is that a broadcaster will capitulate to such demands instead of running the risk of an FCC fairness inquiry and the substantial legal expenses likely to result from that investigation.

Abolition of the Fairness Doctrine. In a 1985 report, *Inquiry into the General Fairness Doctrine Obligations of Broadcast Licensees*, the FCC expressed its doubts as to the continuing validity of the requirement and suggested that its days were numbered. The Commission roundly condemned the doctrine as a regulatory mechanism of dubious constitutionality that "inhibits the presentation of issues of public importance. . . , impedes the public's access to the marketplace of ideas, and poses an unwarranted intrusion upon the journalistic freedom of broadcasters." While declining to make a constitutional ruling, the FCC concluded that the doctrine was no longer sound "as a matter of policy" and thus inconsistent with the "public interest" standard embodied in the Communications Act. However, the agency stopped short of abolishing the doctrine, primarily because of Congress' 1959 amendment to Section 315 of the Communications Act that seemed to make it a part of the statute and thus immune from FCC tinkering. After the U.S. Court of Appeals for the District of Columbia Circuit ruled in the *Telecommunications Research* case that the 1959 amendment did not so codify the fairness doctrine, the stage was set for FCC action.

Still, the Commission was somewhat reluctant to deal with the question. As noted previously, the FCC ruled in the *Syracuse Peace Council* case that a New York television station had violated the fairness doctrine but refused to rule on the broadcaster's argument that the doctrine was unconstitutional. On appeal, however, the U.S. Court of Appeals for the District of Columbia Circuit sent the case back to the Commission and ordered that it consider the station's constitutional arguments, unless it decided that enforcement of the doctrine no longer served the public interest. In response to that order, the FCC abolished the doctrine, primarily on the ground that it offended the first amendment.

The Commission's constitutional rationale in *Syracuse Peace Council* was twofold. First, the agency reasoned that the doctrine "thwarts the purpose that it is designed to promote." Instead of enhancing the discussion of controversial issues of public importance, the FCC said, the fairness doctrine is a "powerful incentive" for broadcasters not to tackle such issues beyond the point necessary to satisfy the "minimal" requirements under the first prong of the doctrine. The Commission wrote:

> Each time a broadcaster presents what may be construed as a controversial issue of public importance, it runs the risk of a complaint being filed, resulting in litigation and penalties, including loss of license. This risk still exists even if a broadcaster has met its obligations by airing the contrasting viewpoints, because the process necessarily involves a vague standard, the application and meaning of which is hard to predict. Therefore, by limiting the amount of controversial issue programming to that required by the first prong (i.e., its obligation to cover controversial issues of vital importance to the community), a licensee is able to lessen the substantial burdens associated with the second prong of the doctrine (i.e., its obligation to present contrasting viewpoints) while conforming to the strict letter of its regulatory obligations.

As a result, the FCC said, the doctrine "inhibits broadcasters . . . from covering controversial issues of public importance," thus "lessen[ing] the flow of diverse viewpoints to the public" and "reduc[ing] rather than enhanc[ing] the public's access to viewpoint diversity."

Second, the Commission took issue with the scarcity rationale employed by the Supreme Court in the *Red Lion* decision. Citing its 1985 report, the FCC observed that the media marketplace has changed radically since 1969, when *Red Lion* was decided. That period saw an increase of more than fifty percent in the number of radio and television stations on the air, the explosive growth of cable television, and the development of new technologies such as low power television, videocassette recorders, and satellite programming services. Given the public's access to "a plethora of information outlets," the Commission concluded that the scarcity rationale no longer "justifies differential First Amendment treatment of the print and broadcast media."

In the alternative, the FCC reasoned that the scaricity theory simply has no place in first amendment analysis, since all goods are "scarce" in one way or another. Just as the number of broadcast stations is limited by the electromagnetic spectrum, the Commission said, the number of newspapers is restricted by market considerations. In fact, economic reality has limited the number of daily newspapers in this country to about 1,650, of which only 125 head-to-head competition from other dailies. By way of comparison, the FCC noted, there are about 1,300 television stations and 10,000 radio stations, and competition is intense. For example, the Commission pointed out that ninety-six percent of the public has access to five or more television stations.

Consequently, the FCC concluded that constitutional analysis should not focus on spectrum scarcity, but rather "on the functional similarities between [print and electronic] media and upon the underlying values and goals of the First Amendment." Because "the function of the electronic press in a free society is identical to that of the printed press," the Commission said, "the constitutional analysis of government control of content should be no different." Under the rationale of *Miami Herald Publishing Co. v. Tornillo*, the fairness doctrine would be unconstitutional if applied to the print media, and the FCC concluded that the same result should follow with respect to broadcast media. "[W]e believe that under the First Amendment the right of viewers and listeners to receive diverse viewpoints is achieved by guaranteeing them the right to receive speech unencumbered by government intervention," the Commission said.

The FCC's decision was affirmed on appeal in *Syracuse Peace Council v. Federal Communications Commission* (1989), but the U.S. Court of Appeals for the District of Columbia Circuit did not reach the question of the fairness doctrine's constitutionality. Instead, the court held that the Commission did not act arbitrarily in deciding that the doctrine was no longer sound as a matter of policy and thus properly abolished it under the "public interest" standard of the Communications Act. Although the FCC's decision in *Syracuse Peace Council* was based largely on first amendment grounds, the court noted that the agency had also reaffirmed in that ruling its 1985 conclusion that the fairness doctrine "disserves the public interest." Because the Commission's decision was not couched "in exclusively constitutional terms," the court said, there was no need to decide the first amendment issue if the agency's "public interest" determination proved reasonable.

Turning to that question, the court emphasized that the FCC had relied on its expertise in broadcast matters in concluding that the fairness doctrine no longer served the public interest. Because a policy judgment of this type involves a "prediction" or "forecast" regarding the impact of a particular regulation, the court said, it need not be supported by hard factual evidence and is entitled to considerable deference on appeal. Applying these principles, the court had little difficulty upholding the FCC's findings that the fairness doctrine "often operated to chill broadcaster speech on controversial issues" and that "recent increases in broadcasting outlets undercut the need for the doctrine." Accordingly, the court said, the Commission's rejection of the fairness doctrine "as a matter of policy . . . seems to us by no means arbitrary or capricious. . . ."

A somewhat more troublesome problem for the court was the argument that while the Commission may have been justified in eliminating the requirement that broadcasters provide a reasonable opportunity for the presentation of opposing viewpoints concerning controversial issues, it acted unreasonably in jettisoning the fairness doctrine's "first prong" that calls upon broadcasters to devote a reasonable amount of air time to such issues. The court's affirmance of the Commission on this point prompted a dissenting opinion by Chief Judge Patricia Wald, who argued that the FCC had "failed to identify *any* deleterious effects whatsoever of continued first prong enforcement." The majority, however, said the FCC reasonably determined that, upon elimination of the "opposing viewpoints" requirement, "coverage of controversial issues will be forthcoming naturally, without the need for continued enforcement of the first prong."

As noted previously, the FCC's decision in *Syracuse Peace Council* led to congressional passage of a bill to make the fairness doctrine part of the Communications Act. President Reagan, however, vetoed the legislation. "This type of content-based regulation by the Federal Government is, in my judgment, antagonistic to the freedom of expression guaranteed by the First Amendment," he said in his veto message. "History has shown that the dangers of an overly timid or biased press cannot be averted through bureaucratic regulation, but only through the freedom and competition that the First Amendment sought to guarantee."

Congress saw things quite differently, stating in one section of the bill that the fairness doctrine "strikes a reasonable balance among the First Amendment rights of the public, broadcast licensees, and speakers other than owners of broadcast facilities." Congress also specifically rejected the FCC's conclusion that the scarcity rationale is no longer valid: "[D]espite technological advances, the electromagnetic spectrum remains a scarce and valuable public resource; * * * even when and where new video and audio services are available, they do not provide meaningful alternatives to broadcast stations for the dissemination of news and public affairs." Although no attempt was made to override the Reagan veto, a similar bill was introduced in early 1989, shortly before President Bush took office.

The Personal Attack Rule

As we saw in the *Red Lion* case, the personal attack rule developed as a corollary of sorts to the "general" fairness doctrine. Oddly enough, however, the Commission did not abolish the personal attack rule when it eliminated the fairness doctrine in the *Syracuse Peace Council* case. "[W]e need not—and do not—decide here what effect today's ruling will have on every conceivable application of the fairness doctrine," the FCC said in a footnote. Responding to a petition for reconsideration of that decision, the Commission expressly declined to address the personal attack rule and two other branches of the fairness doctrine, the "political endorsement" rule and the *Zapple* doctrine, discussed below in connection with political broadcasting. However, as FCC Chairman Dennis Patrick subsequently observed, a licensee charged with violating one of these rules would be free to argue that *Syracuse Peace Council* supports the conclusion that these corollaries, like the fairness doctrine itself, are unconstitutional.

The personal attack rule provides:

> When, during the presentation of views on a controversial issue of public importance, an attack is made upon the honesty, character, integrity or like personal qualities of an identified person or group, the licensee shall, within a reasonable time and in no event later than one week after the attack, transmit to the persons or group attacked:
>
> (1) notification of the date, time and identification of the broadcast;
>
> (2) A script or tape (or an accurate summary if a script or tape is not available) of the attack; and
>
> (3) An offer of a reasonable opportunity to respond over the licensee's facilities.

These requirements do not apply, however, to certain types of personal attacks, including those on foreign groups or foreign public figures and those made by political candidates and their spokesmen during political campaigns. In addition, the rule is inapplicable to attacks made during newscasts, news interviews, and on-the-spot coverage of news events, including commentary or analysis segments of such programs. News documentaries are not exempt from the rule, however, nor are broadcast editorials reflecting the views of the licensee.

Two important limitations on the rule's scope should be mentioned. First, the rule does not come into play unless a program addresses a controversial issue of public importance. The same analysis used under the general fairness doctrine for determining whether a particular issue so qualifies is also employed for purposes of the personal attack rule. If a program does not involve such an issue, the broadcaster has no duty to offer response time even if a blistering personal attack is made.

Second, the rule applies only if there is an attack on "honesty, character, integrity or like personal qualities" of an identified person or group. Criticism falling outside these categories does not "count," and the broadcaster has no obligations under the rule. For example, the Commission has determined that calling a congressman a "coward" and labeling a professional as "incompetent" did not amount to personal attacks within the meaning of the rule. In contrast, the radio program that led to the *Red Lion* case painted journalist Fred Cook as a subversive who had manufactured false charges against public officials and written a book to "smear" Barry Goldwater. The FCC concluded that these comments impugned Cook's honesty, character, and integrity.

In the event that a program triggers the personal attack rule, the licensee must offer the target of the attack a reasonable opportunity to respond, without charge, over the station's facilities. Unlike the fairness doctrine, which allows broadcasters considerable discretion in determining how to "balance" their coverage of a controversial public issue, this requirement gives licensees relatively little leeway with respect to response time. For example, the Commission has indicated that the amount of time set aside for such a reply should approximate that of the attack, though rigid equality is not required. Thus, a four-to-one ratio acceptable under the general fairness doctrine will not suffice with respect to the personal attack rule. Moreover, the person who has been attacked has an absolute right to appear on the station to offer his reply, and the broadcaster cannot satisfy its obligation by providing time to others who support that person and are willing to defend him. Finally, the station must afford the subject of the attack an opportunity to respond in an uninterrupted fashion and may not insist that he appear on a question-and-answer program or in an interview format.

Political Broadcasting

While the fairness doctrine and the personal attack rule are creatures of the FCC acting under its statutory authority to regulate broadcasting in the "public interest," the most important of the rules governing broadcast stations and political candidates are found in the Communications Act itself. Under the "equal opportunities" rule set out in Section 315 of the Act, a broadcaster who provides air time for one candidate must also offer time to his opponents. A related provision, Section 312(a)(7), requires stations to provide reasonable amounts of broadcast time to candidates for federal elective office. In addition to these statutory requirements, the Commission has adopted several regulations that affect political broadcasting, some of which are adjuncts to the fairness doctrine. Taken together, these statutes and FCC rules have a significant impact on the political process at the national, state, and local levels.

The Equal Opportunities Rule. Section 315 of the Communications Act reflects the notion that broadcast stations should not discriminate between qualified candidates seeking the same political office. Subsection (a) of Section 315 states, in part:

> If any licensee shall permit any person who is a legally qualified candidate for any public office to use a broadcasting station, he shall afford equal opportunities to all other such candidates for that office in the use of such broadcasting station. . . . No obligation is imposed under this subsection upon any licensee to allow the use of its station by any such candidate.

This statute gives a "legally qualified candidate" the right to "equal opportunities" in the "use" of any broadcast station which has permitted an "opposing candidate" who is also legally qualified to use that same station. Each of the quoted terms has a special legal meaning with respect to a broadcaster's obligations under the statute.

Legally Qualified Candidate. Acting under its statutory authority to implement Section 315, the FCC has adopted regulations that define the term "legally qualified candidate." There are three basic requirements that apply to persons seeking both nomination and election to office. First, the person must publicly announce that he is a candidate for a federal, state, or local office. Filing papers to qualify for a place on the ballot is considered equivalent to a public announcement of candidacy. However, the fact that a person is "expected" to run or that his supporters have taken steps to advance his candidacy will not suffice. Few questions arise about this requirement, since a candidate's formal announcement is typically a public event that attracts substantial media coverage.

Second, the person must meet the qualifications prescribed by applicable laws to hold the office. For example, the U.S. Constitution provides that the President must be at least thirty-five years of age and must have been born in the United States. Consequently, someone who is only thirty-one years old or who is a naturalized citizen would not be considered a legally qualified candidate for purposes of Section 315.

Third, the person must have qualified for a place on the ballot based on the laws of the state in which the election will take place or must have publicly determined to seek election by the write-in method, be eligible under applicable law, and have made a "substantial showing" that he is a bona fide candidate. This requirement is the most complex, and its application depends on whether the person is a candidate in a general election or is seeking his party's nomination to be such a candidate and, if the latter, whether the nominating process involves a primary election or a party convention or caucus. In addition, special rules apply to candidates for President and Vice President of the United States.

To be legally qualified for purposes of a general election, a person must either obtain a place on the ballot or be a viable write-in candidate. With respect to the former, there is no difficulty if a candidate has emerged from the nominating process of one of the two major political parties. However, most states also provide a mechanism by which candidates who do not represent the two major parties can secure a spot on the ballot. Typically, such a candidate must gather a specified number of signatures of registered voters on a "nominating petition." The number of signatures required is often tied to the number of votes cast in the last general election. Alternatively, a candidate who belongs to a "minor" political party can usually qualify for a ballot position if the party's candidate in the last election received a certain number of votes.

Write-in candidates must make a "substantial showing" that they are serious candidates for election. Whether such a showing has been made will be determined by the facts of each particular case, but the Commission has emphasized that there must be "some evidence that the candidate has engaged to a substantial degree in activities commonly associated with political campaigning." Such activities include making campaign speeches, distributing campaign literature, issuing press releases, and maintaining a campaign office. However, a mere announcement that one is running as a write-in candidate is not sufficient.

Candidates for President and Vice President—whether the Democratic and Republican nominees, minor party contenders, or write-in candidates—must comply with the foregoing rules, just like candidates for other offices. Because they are running on a national basis, however, an additional requirement is imposed. In order to be considered a legally qualified candidate for President or Vice President in all states for purposes of the general election, a candidate must be legally qualified under the rules summarized above in at least ten states. If a candidate is legally qualified in fewer than ten states, he will be treated as a legally qualified candidate only in those states and not on a nationwide basis.

With respect to the nominating process by which candidates for the general election are chosen, there is little difficulty if a primary election is employed. In that situation, the same rules apply as for candidates in the general election. If, however, candidates are chosen through caucuses or party conventions, a person seeking such a nomination must make a "substantial showing" that he is a serious candidate. The same factors considered in determining whether a write-in candidate is legally qualified are also used in this context. Moreover, no one will be considered a candidate more than ninety days before the caucus or convention is to be held.

Different rules apply to persons seeking nomination for the Presidency and Vice Presidency. Such persons are considered legally qualified candidates for nomination in those states in which they have obtained a place on the primary or Presidential preference ballot, as well as in states where they have made a "substantial showing" of being serious candidates for nomination. They will be treated as legally qualified only in those states in which they have met these requirements, unless they qualify in ten or more states. In that situation, they will be deemed qualified in all states.

Three other points should be made. First, a station may not deny a candidate "equal opportunities" under Section 315 simply because it believes that he has no chance of being nominated or elected. The question is not whether a candidate is likely to win, but whether he is "legally qualified" under the principles discussed above. Second, because the qualification issue often turns an often complex body of state law, the FCC relies heavily on rulings of state courts and state election officials in determining whether a candidate is legally qualified. Finally, it is up to the candidate to prove that he is legally qualified in order to obtain the rights granted by Section 315.

Opposing Candidate. Section 315(a) provides that a station providing air time to one legally qualified candidate must allow equal opportunites to all other legally qualified candidates "for that office." The FCC and the courts have ruled that this requirement applies only to candidates who are directly opposing each other, whether it be in a primary or general election. As the U.S. Court of Appeals for the District of Columbia Circuit observed in *Kay v. Federal Communications Commission* (1970), "Congress intended by the language it did employ to . . . restrict the benefits of 'equal opportunities' to candidates of the same class or character as the candidate or candidates who may have been permitted to use a broadcasting station in the first place."

For example, during the campaign preceding the primary election, a candidate for the Democratic Party nomination for county sheriff and a candidate for the Republican nomination are not opponents for purposes of Section 315, even if each candidate is unopposed in his own party primary. However, once each party has chosen its nominee in the primary, those individuals are opposing candidates with respect to the general election. By the same token, a candidate seeking to represent District 10 in the state legislature is not opposing a candidate running in District 11 and may not demand equal opportunities based on the latter candidate's appearances on a broadcast station.

"Use" of a Broadcast Station. As a general rule, any broadcast that contains an identifiable voice or image of a legally qualified candidate constitutes a "use" of the station for purposes of Section 315(a), unless one of the "news program" exemptions discussed below applies. Such a "use" of the station by one legally qualified candidate triggers "equal opportunities" for all opposing candidates to "use" that station in similar fashion. The most common type of "use" is a paid political advertisement featuring the candidate, but other appearances can also qualify. For example, when Ronald Reagan, a former Hollywood star, ran for President in 1976, 1980, and 1984, a station that aired one of his movies incurred obligations under Section 315, for Mr. Reagan's appearance in the film was a "use" of the station.

It does not matter how brief or perfunctory the candidate's appearance on the station happens to be, so long as he is identifiable. If, for example, an incumbent mayor appeared on screen for less than a minute to kick off a local telethon to raise funds for various charities, that appearance would constitute a "use" if the mayor were a legally qualified candidate for reelection. Similarly, a television campaign spot that highlighted a candidate's qualifications with graphics and a voice-over and then showed a photograph of the candidate is a use, even though the candidate did not appear on tape and the photo was used only briefly at the end of the commercial.

As the movie and telethon examples mentioned above make clear, the fact that the program on which the candidate appears does not address political or campaign issues is irrelevant. In the FCC's view, the broadcaster should not be required to make the often subjective determination of whether a particular "use" is political or nonpolitical. Rather, the question is simply whether a candidate has appeared on the station in an identifiable manner. For example, the FCC has ruled that a congressman's weekly televised report to his constituents is a "use" of the station that broadcasts it, even though the program is informative rather than overtly political in nature. Similarly, a commercial for a local car dealer is a "use" if the dealer is also a candidate for office, despite the fact that the advertisement had to do with cars rather than campaign issues or the candidate's qualifications. The same is true for a religious program featuring a minister who is running for office.

On the other side of the coin, an appearance by a candidate's supporters and a paid advertisement that does not include the candidate's voice or image are not considered "uses." This is because Section 315(a) is limited by its own terms to uses by "any person who is a legally qualified candidate." However, in *Letter to Nicholas Zapple* (1970), the FCC recognized a "quasi-equal opportunities" requirement as a corollary to the fairness doctrine. When the FCC abolished the fairness doctrine in 1987, it did not address the continuing vitality of this so-called "*Zapple* doctrine." Applicable only during campaign periods, this rule requires a broadcaster who provides time to a candidate's supporters or spokesmen to afford equal opportunities to supporters or spokesmen for opposing candidates. In contast to Section 315's requirement that time be provided to all opposing candidates, the *Zapple* doctrine allows the broadcaster discretion to deny air time to minor political parties and the supporters of "fringe" candidates. The same exemptions applicable to Section 315 also apply under the *Zapple* doctrine, as does the basic concept of "equal opportunities."

The "News" Exemptions. In 1959, shortly after the FCC ruled that Section 315(a) applied to appearances by candidates on regularly scheduled newscasts, Congress amended the statute to exempt most news programs from the definition of "use." Section 315(a) now provides an appearance by a candidate on any of the following news programs "shall not be deemed a use" of the broadcast station:

- bona fide newscasts;
- bona fide news interviews;
- bona fide news documentaries (if the appearance of the candidate is incidental to the presentation of the subject or subjects covered by the documentary); and
- on-the-spot coverage of bona fide news events (including but not limited to political conventions and activities incidental thereto).

By employing the term "bona fide" in connection with each of these categories, Congress meant to limit the exemptions to programs reflecting legitimate journalistic judgment based on newsworthiness, thereby excluding programs aired with the primary objective of advancing a candidate's campaign.

The newscast exemption covers regularly scheduled programs that emphasize news, such as the "NBC Nightly News," "60 Minutes," and the "Today Show." The local counterparts to programs of this type are also included within the exemption. Accordingly, a station that runs a story about a mayoral candidate on its 6 P.M. "Eyewitness News" program need not provide equal opportunities to the mayor's opponents. In addition, this exemption applies to specialized newscasts such as "Entertainment Tonight," which focuses on show business news. Portions of programs that are not exclusively devoted to newscasts can also qualify. For example, in *In re Oliver Productions, Inc.* (1988), the Commission's staff approved an exemption for news segments of "The John McLaughlin Group," a syndicated program on which brief news reports set the stage for panel discussions on current events.

The exemption for news interview shows was meant to reach such programs as "Meet the Press" and "Face the Nation," which regularly use an interview format. The FCC has said that this exemption applies if the program is regularly scheduled, has been broadcast over a substantial period of time, and the broadcaster produces and controls the program and selects interviewees on the basis of newsworthiness. Using these criteria, the FCC has ruled that the "Donahue" and "Geraldo" shows are exempt, even though they are not limited to the interview format. However, neither regular programs that occasionally include political guests, such as the "Tonight Show," nor one-time "specials" containing interview segments are within the exemption.

A candidate's appearance on a news documentary is exempt only if his participation is incidental to the subject matter of the program. On the other hand, a documentary devoted to a candidate or a particular race is not exempt and thus triggers a broadcaster's obligation to afford "equal opportunities." For example, in *In re Richard B. Kay* (1970), the Commission ruled that a network documentary entitled "Television and Politics" was exempt because the topic of the program was the use of television by candidates rather than the campaign itself. Accordingly, the appearance on the program of two candidates for the U.S. Senate did not constitute a "use" requiring stations to make time available to a third candidate who was not included in the documentary.

The spot news exemption includes coverage of such events as political conventions, Presidential reports on international crises, parades or awards ceremonies in which candidates participate, and a candidate's public announcement of his intent to run for office. The key factor in determining whether the exemption applies is the broadcaster's good faith judgment that the event is of legitimate news value. Because the exemption is couched in terms of "on-the-spot" news events, it contemplates "live" coverage or taped reports aired shortly after the event has taken place. Thus, the longer the time period between the event and the broadcast, the greater the risk that the program will not be considered exempt as spot news coverage. However, such delay poses no problems if the event is taped and covered as part of a regularly scheduled newscast.

Broadcast coverage of candidate press conferences and debates have given the FCC enormous headaches in applying the spot news exemption. Until 1975, the Commission took the position that these events did not qualify as spot news, but since that time has increasingly liberalized its interpretation of the exemption. Under present FCC guidelines, coverage of a candidate's press conferences is exempt if:

- the broadcaster determines in good faith that the event is newsworthy; and
- the broadcaster does not intend to provide one candidate with an advantage over another.

For example, in *Kennedy for President Committee v. Federal Communications Commission* (1980), the U.S. Court of Appeals for the District of Columbia Circuit upheld an FCC ruling that live network coverage of a press conference held by

President Jimmy Carter was exempt, even though he had spent several minutes criticizing his opponent for the Democratic presidential nomination, Senator Edward Kennedy of Massachusetts. The Commission concluded, and the court agreed, that broadcasters have broad discretion in determining whether a candidate's press conference has legitimate news value.

With respect to debates, the Commission has come a long way since 1962, when it ruled that live broadcasts of debates among candidates did not qualify as spot news and thus entitled candidates who did not participate to equal opportunities. In 1975, the Commission took the first step in bringing debates within the spot news exemption, concluding that they qualified as bona fide news events so long as they were sponsored by an organization other than the broadcaster, held outside the studio, and broadcast live in their entirety. This ruling permitted network coverage of presidential debates sponsored by the League of Women Voters in 1980 and 1984.

Under current FCC policy, the identity of the sponsor is immaterial, and the sole question is whether the debate is newsworthy. Thus, a broadcaster or network may sponsor a debate, as may the candidates themselves, without triggering equal opportunities for uninvited candiates or candidates choosing not to participate. For example, in *In re Lenora B. Fulani* (1988), the Commission rejected a Section 315 challenge to a television debate between Democrat Michael Dukakis and Republican George Bush held under the auspices of the Commission on Presidential Debates, an organization established by the two political parties. Moreover, a broadcaster need not carry the debate live but may air it on a tape-delayed basis within a reasonable period.

Providing Equal Opportunities. If one candidate obtains time on a broadcast station, his opponents are entitled to equal opportunities on that station. "Equal opportunities" means not only equal time, but also a right to a time slot likely to attract approximately the same size audience. Obviously, a thirty-minute program at 6 A.M. Sunday is not equivalent to a thirty-minute program on Thursday night during prime time. Moreover, the opponents are entitled to the same rate charged the first candidate and must be given free time if the first candidate did not pay for his appearance. In short, the "equal opportunities" requirement is meant to ensure that broadcasters do not discriminate among opposing candidates.

This anti-discrimination rule applies broadly to all station practices or policies with respect to candidates. For example, a broadcaster who lets one candidate "preview" an opponent's message before it is broadcast and before the candidate records his own statement is impermissible. Similarly, it is a violation to compel one candidate but not his opponent to submit the text of his proposed message in advance of its broadcast. In addition, a broadcaster must treat all candidates the same in terms of production assistance. If, for example, a station makes available background scenery and multiple cameras to one candidate, it must also make these materials and equipment available to all opposing candidates. Of course, if one candidate pays extra for facilities and equipment, his opponents must also pay for them.

Nonetheless, a broadcaster does have some discretion in meeting its obligations under Section 315. For instance, a candidate seeking equal opportunities cannot demand that his program or political advertisement be aired in a particular time slot. In providing a candidate with a time period that will reach approximately the same number of viewers as the message of an opponent, a station is not required to make available precisely the same time slot on the same day of the week or air a political advertisement on the same program on which the opponent's ad appeared.

Moreover, a broadcaster can reject a candidate's demand for six five-minute spots in response to a thirty-minute program aired by his opponent.

It is also settled that a station need not limit the time for one candidate because an opponent cannot afford to buy the same amount of time. However, FCC rules prohibit a broadcaster from allowing one candidate to purchase virtually all available commercial time, thereby denying an opponent the opportunity to get on the air. Accordingly, when one candidate seeks to buy large amounts of time, a station must take steps to ensure that it will be able to make equal opportunities available to opponents who subsequently request time under Section 315.

A broadcaster is not required to notify opponents of a candidate's "use" of the station. Rather, it is the candidate's responsibility to monitor the station's programming or review its records in order to learn of "uses" by an opponent that would trigger Section 315. (If, however, a broadcaster chooses to notify one candidate of an opponent's purchase of time or other use of the station, it must also notify all other opposing candidates.) The candidate must make a request for equal opportunities within seven days of an opponent's use of the station. For example, if Candidate A has been running paid announcements on the station for five weeks and Candidate B requests equal opportunities at the end of the fifth week, Candidate B is entitled only to buy time in the amount that Candidate A used during the fifth week.

This "seven-day rule" has an interesting twist when there are more than two candidates for the same position. In that situation, the rule applies only to the "first prior use" by a candidate. Suppose, for instance, that Candidates A, B, and C are opponents in the same race. Candidate A makes a broadcast on February 1. On February 5, Candidate B requests equal opportunities and makes his broadcast on February 15. Candidate C does not submit his request until February 16. In this case, Candidate C is not entitled to equal opportunities, even though he can argue that his request was made within seven days of Candidate B's use. He was required to make the request within seven days of Candidate A's use, which was the "first prior use" by a candidate. This requirement ensures that each political "use" creates a single right to equal opportunities that must be secured by a timely request. In other words, a single use does not give rise to an endless string of "equal opportunities" demands that the broadcaster must honor.

When a legally qualified candidate makes a "use" of a station, the broadcaster is prohibited from censoring or editing any part of the program. Section 315(a) expressly states that a licensee "shall have no power of censorship over the material broadcast under the provisions of this section." In light of this prohibition, the U.S. Supreme Court ruled in *Farmers Educational & Cooperative Union v. WDAY, Inc.* (1959) that a station cannot be held liable for defamatory statements made by a candidate, since a station cannot keep such statements off the air. All legal responsibility for the content of the program thus falls upon the candidate, who may be sued on the basis of remarks made during a "use" of the station.

A broadcaster can run afoul of the anti-censorship provision in several ways. For example, the Commission has ruled that a station may not refuse time to a candidate who wishes to discuss subjects other than his candidacy, may not require a candidate to limit his remarks to particular issues, and may not deny a candidate the choice of appearing live or on tape. In addition, a candidate cannot be required to submit a script or tape in advance so that the broadcaster may review its contents. However, a station may reject a candidate's taped program if it does not comply with FCC technical standards, provided that it has a general policy of refusing to accept ads from commercial advertisers that do not meet those standards.

The "no-censorship" rule has led to controversial political advertisements that viewers and listeners have found offensive or in bad taste. During Georgia's 1972 Democratic primary, for example, a candidate seeking the party's nomination for U.S. Senator broadcast a commercial in which he labeled himself as a "white racist" who opposed civil rights for "niggers." Arguing that this political spot had created serious racial tension, various organizations complained to the FCC and asked for a ruling that broadcasters have the responsibility to reject a candidate's announcement that poses an "imminent and immediate threat to the safety and security of the public it serves." In *Letter to Lonnie King* (1972), the FCC declined to adopt this requirement, taking the position that it would "amount to an advance approval by the Commission of licensee censhorship of a candidate's remarks" contrary to Section 315.

A broadcaster is required, however, to ensure that a paid political program identifies its sponsor. Under Section 317 of the Communications Act, a licensee who is paid to broadcast anything must announce that the broadcast is paid for and clearly disclose who paid for it. This provision applies to all sponsored programs and spots, including paid political broadcasts. In addition, the Federal Election Campaign Act and regulations adopted by the Federal Election Commission require disclosure of whether a candidate or his campaign committee has authorized a political ad paid for by someone else. Although a station may not require an advance script or tape to preview candidate programs with an eye toward content, such screening is permissible to check the adequacy of the sponsorship identification. Similarly, a station may preview a candidate's tape recording to ensure that it meets FCC technical standards.

Rates that a Station May Charge Candidates. Section 315(b) of the Communications Act sets limits on the rates that a broadcaster may charge legally qualified candidates for "uses" of the station. Generally speaking, a broadcaster may not charge a political candidate more for programs or spots that it would charge a regular commercial advertiser. In addition, during specified pre-election periods, candidates must be given the benefit of the "lowest unit rate" made available to the station's most favored advertisers, even though the candidates would not qualify for such rates under the terms of the agreement between the station and those advertisers. These restrictions on rates apply only to programs or spots in which the candidate appears and which are made in connection with the campaign.

For the most part, a station is permitted to charge a political candidate as much as it charges others for "comparable use" of the station. "Comparable use" means the same amount and class of time in the same time period. (The term "class of time" refers to the rates for particular types of spots or programs that broadcasters have established, such as fixed-position spots, run-of-schedule spots, preemptible spots, and special discount packages.) For example, if a station's lowest rate to commercial advertisers for a thirty-second spot at 8 P.M. on Thursday is $100, or $75 if the advertiser buys ten spots, a political candidate must be offered the same rate. Thus, a candidate would be charged $100 for a single spot and would be entitled to the discount if he purchased ten spots. In other words, the candidate can be treated no differently than a commercial advertiser.

The rules change, however, in the periods that begin forty-five days prior to a primary election and sixty days before a general election. During these pre-election periods, political candidates may be charged at a rate no higher than the station's "lowest unit rate" made available to its most favored commercial advertiser. The lowest unit rate for each class and amount of time will appear on the station's regular "rate card" for advertisers. If, however, a broadcaster has contracted to carry a particular advertiser's spots at a special "off-card" rate or has in effect a long-term contract with an at an old, lower rate, political candidates would be entitled to the same rates. Moreover, any bulk discount for volume purchases, promotional rebates or incentives, or special advertising packages must be made available to political candidates, despite the fact that the candidate does not purchase a sufficient number of spots to qualify for such treatment. In short, political candidates get the advantage of the lowest possible rate offered by the station for a given amount and class of time in a particular time period.

For example, a political candidate who purchases a single spot during either of the pre-election periods is entitled to the same rate offered to a commercial advertiser who has agreed to buy a number of spots. Consider the illustration offered above with regard to time purchased outside the pre-election periods. If the same situation were to arise during those periods, the political candidate could buy a single spot at $75, even though the commercial advertiser had to purchase ten such spots to get that special rate. Moreover, if the station offered an even lower rate— say, $45 per spot—to commercial advertisers who agreed to buy 100 spots, the candidate could be charged only $45 for a single thirty-second spot.

"Reasonable Access" for Candidates. Section 315(a) provides that "[n]o obligation is imposed under this subsection upon any licensee to allow the use of its station by any [legally qualified] candidate." Viewed in isolation, this language would enable a broadcaster to avoid any "equal opportunities" problems by simply refusing to permit a candidate to appear on the station in any fashion that would constitute a "use" triggering the obligation to provide "equal opportunities" to the candidate's opponents. However, another provision of the Communications Act, Section 312(a)(7), expressly requires that legally qualified candidates for federal elective office either be given "reasonable access" to or be allowed to purchase "reasonable amounts of time" on broadcast stations. In addition, broadcasters must also make time available to candidates for significant state and local offices under the "public interest" standard of the Communications Act.

Federal Races. Under Section 312(a)(7), a broadcaster must either give federal candidates "reasonable access" to the station's facilities or sell them "reasonable amounts" of air time. The Commission may revoke a broadcaster's license for "willful or repeated failure" to comply with this requirement, which must be considered in conjunction with the "equal opportunities" rule of Section 315(a). When a broadcaster makes available air time—free or paid—to a federal candidate under Section 312(a)(7), the candidate's appearance constitutes a "use" of the station entitling his opponents to "equal opportunities" under Section 315(a).

The FCC has stated that it will generally rely on the "reasonable, good faith judgments of licensees" as to what constitutes reasonable access for purposes of Section 312(a)(7). However, the Commission has also established specific guidelines that limit broadcaster discretion in this area. For example, a station cannot refuse to make program time available for federal candidates during prime time on television or "drive time" on radio, the periods during which the audience is at its peak. Moreover, a station may not reject a request by a federal candidate for the type, length, and class of time normally sold to commercial advertisers. On the other hand, a broadcaster who does not, as a matter of policy, sell five-minute blocks of time to commercial advertisers may reject a federal candidate's request for a five-minute program. In addition, a candidate may not demand that he be provided a particular time slot (e.g., within or adjacent to the most popular program on the station).

Reasonable access must be provided during the forty-five days before a primary election and sixty days before a general election. The question of whether access must be afforded federal candidates outside these time periods will be resolved by the Commission on a case-by-case basis. In 1979, for example, the FCC ruled that the three major television networks had improperly rejected President Jimmy Carter's request for a thirty-minute, prime time program in December 1979 to coincide with his formal announcement that he would seek reelection. In refusing access, the networks argued that it was too early in the political season to provide air time, since the presidential primaries did not begin until March 1980, and that demands by opponents for equal opportunities would disrupt their programming schedules. The FCC disagreed, ruling that the campaign was already underway and that the blanket refusal to provide access was impermissible. The U.S. Supreme Court upheld the Commission in *CBS, Inc. v. Federal Communications Commission* (1981), pointing out that by December 1979 a dozen candidates had formally announced their plans to run for President, campaign organizations were in place, and the national print media had been covering the candidates for several months.

In that case, the Court also approved the general guidelines developed by the Commission regarding a broadcaster's obligation to provide reasonable access prior to the forty-five and sixty day periods. Although broadcasters are free to reject requests for air time prior to the commencement of a campaign, they must give reasonable and good faith attention to access requests once a campaign has begun. Such requests must be considered on an individual basis, and a broadcaster may take into account the needs of the candidate, the amount of time previously sold the candidate, the timing of the request, the disruptive impact on regularly scheduled programming, and the likelihood of requests for time by rival candidates under Section 315(a). These considerations may not be invoked as a pretext to deny access, and a broadcaster must explain fully the reasons for refusing access or making a counteroffer that would allow the candidate more limited air time. The broadcaster's decision is subject to review by the Commission, which will also determine, on the basis of objective evidence, whether the campaign has actually begun. As a rule of thumb, once there is at least one legally qualified candidate for a federal office, the campaign is considered underway and all candidates for that office have "reasonable access" rights.

Also at issue in the *CBS* case was the constitutionality of Section 312(a)(7), with the networks claiming that the statute circumscribed their editorial discretion in violation of the first amendment. As one might expect in light of the *Red Lion* decision, the Supreme Court gave short shrift to this argument. Writing for the majority, Chief Justice Burger stressed that Section 312(a)(7) implicates "[t]he First Amendment interests of candidates and voters, as well as broadcasters" and makes "a significant contribution to freedom of expression by enhancing the ability of candidates to present, and the public to receive, information necessary for the effective operation of the democratic process." By providing a limited right of access for federal candidates, he added, the statute "properly balances the First Amendment rights of federal candidates, the public, and broadcasters."

Other Elections. As noted previously, Section 312(a)(7) applies only to legally qualified candidates for federal elective office and thus does not require stations to provide reasonable access to candidates running at the state and local levels. However, the FCC has interpreted the Communications Act's "public interest" standard to require that stations allocate reasonable amounts of time to non-federal political races, based on the broadcaster's assessment of the importance of the races and the public's interest in them. In its move toward deregulation in the 1980s, however, the FCC has not vigorously enforced this requirement.

In any event, a broadcaster has considerably more discretion under the "public interest" standard than under Section 312(a)(7). For example, a station can limit the sale of time to candidates in certain races, using its judgment as to which are the most important to the community. In addition, a station need not sell time at all if it provides news coverage of candidates in major races. If it sells time, a station is not required to accept the particular length of paid announcement that a candidate wishes to use and is not required to make specific time slots available.

Enforcement. The FCC encourages private negotiations between candidates and broadcasters to resolve disputes arising under Sections 312(a)(7) and 315. In the Commission's view, such negotiations may result in a timely resolution of the problem without the agency's involvement and the attendant expenses. If a complaint is filed, it must contain all of the essential facts on which a decision may be based. The person filing the complaint must also send a copy to the broadcaster. In the period immediately prior to an election, complaints may be made by telephone, and the FCC will attempt to resolve matters and, if necessary, take remedial action on an expedited basis.

Upon finding a violation, the Commission will typically ask the station how it intends to satisfy its obligations or ask that it provide a candidate with air time. In addition, four types of sanctions are available:

- letters of admonishment, which may range from basically informative letters to harshly worded rebukes;
- short-term license renewals, whereby a station's license is renewed for a shorter period than usual;
- so-called "forfeitures" in which a monetary fine is assessed against the licensee; and
- license revocation or nonrenewal, a penalty that is reserved for egregious situations.

The Commission's decision in a case involving an alleged violation of these sections may be appealed to either the U.S. Court of Appeals for the District of Columbia Circuit or the federal appellate court for the geographic area in which the complainant or the licensee resides.

Political Endorsements. Another corollary to the fairness doctrine comes into play when a licensee endorses or opposes a legally qualified candidate in a broadcast editorial. Like the personal attack rule and the *Zapple* doctrine, this requirement was left intact despite the Commission's decision in the *Syracuse Peace Council* case abolishing the general fairness doctrine. The FCC rule on endorsements provides:

> Where a licensee, in an editorial, (1) endorses or (2) opposes a legally qualified candidate or candidates, the licensee shall, within 24 hours after the editorial, transmit to, respectively, (i) the other qualified candidate or candidates for the same office or (ii) the candidate opposed in the editorial, (a) notification of the date and time of the editorial, (b) a script or tape of the editorial, and (c) an offer of a reasonable opportunity for the candidate or a spokesman of the candidate to respond over the licensee's facilities. Where such editorials are broadcast on the day of the election or within 72 hours prior to the day of the election, the licensee shall comply with the provisions of this [rule] sufficiently far in advance of the broadcast to enable the candidate or candidates to have a reasonable opportunity to prepare a response and to present it in a timely fashion.

For purposes of this rule, an editorial is a statement representing the view of the licensee of the station. It may be delivered by the owner or by an employee—such as the station manager—authorized to speak for the station. The fact that the statement is not labeled as an editorial is immaterial. For example, in *In re Richard A. Karr* (1971), the president and controlling stockholder of a station endorsed several candidates during an interview broadcast on the station. Subsequently, he claimed that his statements represented only his personal feelings about the candidates and did not reflect the view of the station. The Commission disagreed, concluding that the president's endorsements were "indistinguishable from a station editorial" and were thus covered by the political endorsement rule. Similarly, a news report stating that the station's owner had endorsed a particular candidate would bring the rule into play. On the other hand, a statement by a station employee—such as a commentator who appears regularly on the evening news program—is not considered an editorial on behalf of the station unless it is represented as such.

It is not always easy to determine whether an editorial endorses or opposes a candidate. There is no problem, of course, if an editorial simply urges the election or defeat of a certain candidate. But suppose a station broadcasts an editorial critical of the city council and, without mentioning any candidate by name, tells voters that "it's time for a change." The FCC has ruled that although the incumbent officeholders seeking reelection were not named, the editorial was in effect a statement of the station's opposition to their candidacies and thus covered by the rule. By way of comparison, suppose that the station had praised the council for creating a special committee to study drug problems in the community but had not discussed the upcoming election. In a similar situation, the FCC concluded that there had been no endorsement, even though the favorable commentary on the council's action could be taken as support for the incumbent members of the council up for reelection. The Commission reasoned that application of the political endorsement rule in this context would inhibit stations from addressing important issues facing the community.

A station that broadcasts an editorial falling within the rule is not required to let a candidate respond in person but is specifically given discretion to allow a spokesman for the candidate deliver the response. However, the choice of a spokesman is left to the candidate, and a station cannot demand that a particular spokesman participate. If a broadcaster permits the candidate to appear, any legally qualified opponent would then be entitled to equal opportunities under Section 315. Because a station must provide free air time to candidate it has opposed or to the opponents of a candidate it has endorsed, free time would have to be made available to those candidates who subsequently requested equal opportunities.

Whether a station has offered a "reasonable opportunity to respond" to an editorial endorsing or opposing a candidate is determined on the facts of each case. Generally speaking, a broadcaster must afford the candidate the same amount of time in a comparable time slot, but sometimes such equality will not be sufficient. For example, if a station's thirty-second editorial on the city council race stated that "the following candidates are, in our view, best qualified to serve" and then named ten persons, a candidate not on the list would obviously need more than a fraction of thirty seconds in order to present a meaningful response.

Obscene and Indecent Programming

Section 1464 of Title 18 of the U.S. Code is a criminal statute that forbids the use of "any obscene, indecent, or profane language by means of radio communications." A broadcaster who violates this provision can be fined as much as $10,000 and jailed for up to two years. Moreover, the Communications Act authorizes the FCC to order a station to "cease and desist" programming contrary to Section 1464, impose a fine of up to $2,000, and revoke its license. The U.S. Supreme Court has upheld the constitutionality of Section 1464, and the FCC has recently stepped up its enforcement of the statute. Nonetheless, some first amendment problems remain unresolved.

The George Carlin Case. As we saw in Chapter 9, obscenity is not considered protected speech for purposes of the first amendment; consequently, punitive measures directed at broadcasters who air obscene material are undoubtedly constitutional. However, "indecent" or "profane" speech that is not legally obscene enjoys first amendment protection. For example, in *Cohen v. California* (1971), the U.S. Supreme Court overturned the criminal conviction of a man who had been prosecuted for wearing a jacket with the slogan "fuck the draft." Moreover, it is settled that mere nudity, though perhaps "indecent" in the eyes of some, is not obscene. Thus, a newspaper or magazine could not, consistent with the first amendment, be punished for simply printing the word "fuck" or a nude photograph. Section 1464 and the Communications Act, however, permit sanctions against stations that broadcast such material. The Supreme Court rejected a first amendment challenge to these provisions in *Federal Communications Commission v. Pacifica Foundation* (1978).

The *Pacifica* case arose when WBAI-FM in New York City played a monologue recorded by commedian George Carlin, a well-known satiric humorist, before a live audience. Entitled "Filthy Words," the twelve-minute comedy routine focused on "the words that you couldn't say on the public airwaves," which Carlin identified as shit, piss, fuck, cunt, cocksucker, motherfucker, and tits.[3] Broadcast at about 2

---

[3] The following excerpt from the monologue is illustrative:

Now the word shit is okay for the man. At work you can say it like crazy. Mostly figuratively. Get that shit out of here, will ya? I don't want to see that shit anymore. I can't cut that shit, buddy. I've had that shit up to here. I think you're full of shit myself.*** Hot shit, holy shit, tough shit, eat shit. Shit-eating grin. Uh, whoever thought of that was ill.

P.M. one afternoon as part of a discussion of society's attitude toward language, the monologue was heard by a man while driving with his young son. The man, who had apparently not heard the station's disclaimer that the program included "sensitive language which might be offensive to some," wrote a letter to the FCC complaining about the broadcast. Pacifica, licensee of WBAI-FM, said that it was not aware of any other listener complaints.

The FCC concluded that the Carlin monologue was indecent within the meaning of Section 1464 and that Pacifica was subject to sanctions. Rather than take formal action against the licensee, however, the Commission decided to place a copy of its ruling in the station's license file for possible action in the event that subsequent complaints were received. In addressing the indecency issue, the FCC said:

> [T]he concept of "indecent" is intimately connected with the exposure of children to language that describes, in terms patently offensive as measured by contemporary community standards for the brodcast medium, sexual or excretory activities and organs at times of the day when there is a reasonable risk that children may be in the audience.

The U.S. Court of Appeals for the District of Columbia Circuit reversed, but the Supreme Court upheld the FCC. After finding "no basis for disagreeing with the Commission's conclusion that indecent language was used in this broadcast," the Court turned to the question of "whether the First Amendment denies government any power to restrict the public broadcast of indecent language in any circumstances."

The Court, in an opinion by Justice John Paul Stevens, answered that question in the negative. Although he cited the *Red Lion* and *Tornillo* cases, Justice Stevens did not rely on the traditional "spectrum scarcity" rationale to support his basic premise that "of all the forms of communication, it is broadcasting that has received the most limited First Amendment protection." Instead, he stressed that broadcasting is a "uniquely pervasive" medium that is "uniquely accessible to children." In light of these factors, Justice Stevens said, the Commission's application of Section 1464 passed constitutional muster. He wrote:

> First, the broadcast media have established a uniquely pervasive presence in the lives of all Americans. Patently offensive, indecent material presented over the airwaves confronts the citizen, not only in public, but also in the privacy of the home, where the individual's right to be left alone plainly outweighs the First Amendment rights of an intruder. Because the broadcast audience is constantly tuning in and out, prior warnings cannot completely protect the listener or viewer from unexpected program content. To say that one may avoid further offense by turning off the radio when he hears indecent language is like saying that the remedy for an assault is to run away after the first blow. One may hang up on an indecent phone call, but that option does not give the caller a constitutional immunity or avoid a harm that has already taken place.
>
> Second, broadcasting is uniquely accessible to children, even those too young to read. Although [the] written message [in *Cohen v. California*] might have been incomprehensible to a first grader, Pacifica's broadcast could have enlarged a child's vocabulary in an instant. Other forms of offensive expression may be withheld from the young without restricting the expression at its source. Bookstores and motion picture theaters, for example, may be prohibited from making indecent material available to children. * * * The ease with which children may obtain access to broadcast material . . . amply justif[ies] special treatment of indecent broadcasting.

At the same time, however, Justice Stevens emphasized the narrow nature of the Court's decision. "We have not decided that an occasional expletive . . . would justify any sanction or, indeed, that this broadcast would justifty a criminal prosecution," he said. Rather, the key question is the context of the broadcast, a determination that should take into account the time of day, the content of the program in which the language was used, the composition of the audience, and the differences between radio, television, and closed-circuit transmissions.

Subsequent Developments. Shortly after the Court's decision, the Commission stated that it intended "to observe the narrowness of the *Pacifica* holding." In *In re WGBH Educational Foundation* (1978), the FCC had received complaints that a noncommercial television station had broadcast certain programs—including "Monty Python's Flying Circus" and "Masterpiece Theatre"—that allegedly contained indecent language and nudity and dealt with "adult" themes. In a decision approving renewal of the station's license, the Commission emphasized that the Carlin monologue at issue in *Pacifica* involved the "repetitive" use of indecent language. "It was certainly not our intent . . . to inhibit coverage of diverse and controversial subjects by licensees, whether in news and public affairs or in dramatic and other programming contexts," the FCC said.

As a result of this and similar rulings, it became clear to broadcasters that the isolated use of profanity or scenes including nudity would not be enough to support sanctions against a broadcaster, particularly if the program were aired after 10 P.M., when children were not likely to be in the audience. In fact, after its ruling in *Pacifica* that the station was subject to sanctions for airing the Carlin monologue, the Commission did not find a broadcaster in violation of the "indecency" provision of Section 1464 for more than a decade.

In April 1987, however, the FCC abruptly shifted direction, apparently in response to pressure from anti-pornography groups, and issued warnings to three broadcast stations and one amateur radio operator. In the latter case, *In re David Hildebrand*, the Commission made clear that amateur operators are governed by Section 1464, reasoning that children are actively encouraged to become amateur licensees and are thus likely to be in the audience. The other cases involved FM radio stations. In *In re Pacifica Foundation*, the Commission found indecent—and possibly obscene—sexually explicit excerpts from "Jerker," a play in which two homosexual men discuss their sexual fantasies. A student-run, noncommercial station received a warning in *In re Regents of the University of California* for playing "Makin' Bacon," a song with several clearly discernible references to sex organs and various sexual activities. In these cases the offending programs were broadcast after 10 P.M.

In the most highly publicized case, *In re Infinity Broadcasting Corp.*, the FCC launched an attack on the "raunch radio" format featuring so-called "shock jocks" who specialize in sexual innuendo. At issue was "The Howard Stern Show," which Infinity carried on its FM station in Philadelphia in the 6 to 10 A.M. time slot. According to the Commission, the Stern show did not merely include "an occasional off-color reference or explicit" but rather "dwell[ed] on matters sexual and excretory in a pandering and titillating fashion." To illustrate the nature of the programming, the FCC cited excerpts from Stern shows that made reference to testicles, penis size, erections, "vibrating rubber products," and sex with animals.

In these cases, the Commission announced new guidelines for enforcement of Section 1464. First, the FCC rejected its prior rulings that had in effect limited the

term "indecent" to reptitive use of the seven words in the George Carlin monologue. Instead, the Commission said that it would apply the "generic" definition
of broadcast indecency employed in the initial *Pacifica* case: "language or material
that depicts or describes, in terms patently offensive as measured by contemporary
community standards for the broadcast medium, sexual or excretory activities or
organs."

Second, the Commission noted that, contrary to prior assumptions, recent evidence suggested a "reasonable risk" that children would be in the broadcast audience after 10 P.M. Accordingly, the Commission said that it would address the risk
that the audience would include children "during the time frame and with regard
to the market before it in each case." Third, the FCC emphasized that indecent
broadcasts must be preceded by a "warning" about program content, even though
there is not a reasonable risk that children would be watching or listening.

In response to petitions for reconsideration and clarification filed in the *Infinity*,
Pacifica, and *Regents* cases, the Commission retreated slightly from these guidelines, announcing that it would presume that children are not part of the broadcast
audience between midnight and 6 A.M. By taking this approach, the FCC created
a "safe harbor" during which broadcasters could air nonobscene, adult-oriented
material. If such programming were aired at any other time, however, the risk that
the broadcast audience included children would be assessed on a case-by-case basis.
The Commission reaffirmed its definition of indecency over objections from broadcasters that the standard was too vague.

As might be expected, a judicial challenge followed. In *Action for Children's
Television v. Federal Communications Commission* (1988), the U.S. Court of Appeals for the District of Columbia Circuit upheld the constitutionality of the indecency definition but ordered the FCC to reconsider the portion of its policy dealing
with the time periods during which indecent material may be aired. The court concluded that there was insufficient evidence to support the Commission's conclusion
in the *Pacifica* and *Regents* cases that substantial numbers of unsupervised children
were likely to be in the audience after 10 P.M. but before the onset of the "safe
harbor" period at midnight. "[I]n view of the curtailment of broadcaster freedom
and adult listener choice that [the policy] entails, the Commission failed to consider
fairly and fully what time lines should be drawn," the court said. Accordingly, the
court sent the *Pacifica* and *Regents* cases back to the FCC for further proceedings.
However, the court affirmed the Commission's ruling in *Infinity*, pointing out that
the Stern program, like the Carlin monologue in the original *Pacifica* case, was aired
during the daytime.

Despite this decision that the FCC's "safe harbor" approach was too restrictive
in light of the first amendment interests involved, the Congress subsequently passed
a bill requring the FCC to adopt regulations to enforce the indecency statute
"on a 24-hour per day basis." Republican Senator Jesse Helms of North Carolina
was successful in attaching the measure to an appropriations bill that easily passed
the House and Senate as the 100th Congress was drawing to a close. President Reagan signed the bill on October 1, 1988. The FCC subsequently amended its rules in
accordance with the legislation, emphasizing that "[t]he directive . . . affords us no
discretion" and "mandates implementation of a twenty-four hour indecency ban."
However, as Commissioner Patricia Diaz Dennis pointed out in a separate opinion
accompanying the FCC's order, the ban is constitutionally suspect in light of the
Supreme Court's decision in *Pacifica* and the court of appeals' ruling in *Action for
Children's Television*. The regulation has been stayed pending appeal.

A subsequent case, *Sable Communications v. Federal Communications Commission* (1989), also casts doubt on the twenty-four hour prohibition. In that decision, discussed more fully in Chapter 9, the Supreme Court held that a total ban on "dial-a-porn" telephone messages offended the first amendment. In attempting to defend the statute, the government relied heavily on *Pacifica,* but the Court found that case "readily distinguishable . . . because it did not involve a total ban on broadcasting indecent material." At the same time, however, the Court stressed that *Pacifica* turned on "unique attributes" of broadcasting not present in connection with telephone communications. "Placing a telephone call is not the same as turning on a radio and being taken by surprise by an indecent message," the Court said. This emphasis on the pervasive nature of broadcasting suggests that the *Sable* decision is not dispositive in the broadcast setting.

Shortly before the *Action for Children's Television* case was decided, the Commission imposed its first sanctions under its revised indecency guidelines, though it subsequently vacated its decision in light of the court's ruling. In *In re Kansas City Television, Ltd.* (1988), the FCC fined the licensee of KZKC-TV $2,000—the maximum permissible under Section 503(b) of the Communications Act—for airing the movie "Private Lessons" during prime time. The film, which contained scenes with frontal nudity, told the story of a fifteen-year-old boy who was seduced by a housekeeper. "[W]hen material such as explicit nudity and fondling is depicted as here in the context of a movie whose predominant theme emphasizes sexual activity and does so in a pandering and titillating fashion, that material would be considered patently offensive . . . with respect to what is suitable for children," the Commission said. "The story line . . . [and] explicit nudity would have commanded the attention of children, and the sexual references would have been readily understood by children who tuned into the program."

Other Content-Related Regulations

In the not-too-distant past, the FCC had in place a number of policies that directly or indirectly affected program content. During the 1980s, however, the Commission eliminated many of these restrictions as part of its general move toward deregulation of broadcasting. This policy shift was encouraged by a 1981 Supreme Court case, *Federal Communications Commission v. WNCN Listeners Guild*, upholding the FCC's decision not to regulate the programming "formats" of radio stations. A station's decision to use a particular format (e.g., rock-and-roll, classical, all news) is best shaped by market forces, the Commission said, not by government intervention. During the deregulation-minded Reagan Administration, the FCC expanded this approach under the leadership of former Chairman Mark Fowler, who believed that "the perception of broadcasters as community trustees should be replaced by a view of broadcasters as marketplace participants."

Among the casualties were FCC policies affecting public affairs programming, children's programming, and commercials. Because these decisions have proved controversial and may well be reversed by Congress, we shall examine them here, along with Commission rules on prime time programming and the "staging" of news that have survived the deregulation hatchet.

Public Affairs Programming. The Commission has never required broadcasters to devote a specified amount of air time to news or public affairs programs. In fact, it consistently refused to adopt such a requirement, reasoning that the imposition of minimum programming standards would be contrary to the first amendment and to Section 326 of the Communications Act, which denies the FCC the power to censor licensees. Nonetheless, the Commission developed guidelines for "nonentertainment programming," including coverage of news and public affairs,[4] that came into play at renewal time. The system worked this way. If a broadcaster had met or exceeded the percentages set forth in the guidelines (six percent for FM radio, eight percent for AM radio, and ten percent for television), its application for renewal would be processed "routinely" by the Commission's staff, acting under delegated authority. On the other hand, a deficiency meant that the renewal application could not be handled by the staff and would instead be sent to the Commission itself. In short, there was an unspoken presumption that a broadcaster whose nonentertainment programming satisfied the guidelines was operating in the public interest.

Because broadcasters naturally wanted the renewal process to go as smoothly as possible, most took pains to ensure that, at a minimum, their nonentertainment programming was consistent with the guidelines. Moreover, applicants for new licenses were careful to fashion their programming proposals with the applicable percentage in mind, since a deviation from the norm would be a red flag that could only invite trouble. Consequently, guidelines that technically dealt only with the administrative processing of renewal applications became quotas that licensees felt compelled to meet.

In 1981, however, the Commission abandoned the nonentertainment programming guidelines for AM and FM radio stations and three years later dropped them for television stations as well. The basic premise underlying these decisions was the FCC's belief that competitive conditions in the broadcast marketplace will ensure the continued availability of public affairs programming. Despite its abolition of the guidelines, the Commission stopped short of adopting a policy that would rely solely on market forces. In place of the guidelines, the FCC placed upon broadcasters a more general obligation: to provide programming responsive to issues confronting the communities they serve. Licensees have considerable discretion in determining how to meet this requirement; for example, a station may take into account the interests of its own listeners or viewers and the programs offered by competing stations in deciding what type of nonentertainment programming to provide.

This change in attitude toward programming, along with the elimination of a prohibition against program-length commercials, opened the door for the "home shopping" format employed by some television stations. The FCC approved the format in *In re Family Media, Inc.* (1987), describing it as "an example of licensee experimentation" and rejecting arguments that the use of a broadcasting facility for such a purpose was contrary to the public interest. In approving the transfer of station licenses in Baltimore and Cleveland to a subsidiary of the Home Shopping Network, the Commission emphasized that market forces would determine the success or failure of the format and that broadcasters have wide discretion in meeting their obligation to provide "issue-responsive programs suitable to the community."

When it eliminated the programming guidelines, the FCC also modified station recordkeeping requirements. Under the old rules, stations were obligated to main-

---

[4]In addition, the "nonentertainment programming" category included children's programs, religious programs, educational programs, licensee editorials, political broadcasts, agricultural programs, weather and market reports, sports programs, and programs of interest to minority groups. As we shall see below, children's programming has emerged as a separate issue.

tain comprehensive programming logs that would enable the Commission or the public to determine what types of programs had been aired. Now, a broadcaster must maintain quarterly lists of its issue-oriented programming. These lists must include those programs that the licensee believes contain its most significant treatment of public issues facing the community. Moreover, as noted previously in connection with licensing, the Commission has eliminated the formal "ascertainment" procedures by which broadcasters were required to identify important public issues. Although stations must still seek out such questions, they are free use any manner they choose in doing so.

Commercials. As was the case with nonentertainment programming, the Commission once had in place processing guidelines setting forth the maximum number of minutes per hour that could be devoted to commecials. If a station exceeded that figure, its renewal application could not be processed by the FCC staff but required the Commission's attention. In general, the guidelines set an upper limit of eighteen minutes of commercials per hour for radio stations and sixteen minutes for television stations. The FCC abolished these guidelines along with the programming standards, reasoning that market forces can do a job better job than government in determining appropriate commercial levels and will serve to deter overcommercialization.

At the same time, the Commission announced that it would not consider complaints of overcommercialization in connection with a petition to deny renewal of a broadcast license. Also eliminated was a rule banning "program-length commercials" in which the subject matter of the program was "so interwoven with . . . the sponsor's advertising" that the program constituted "a single, commercial promotion for the sponsor's products or services." In related proceedings, the Commission repealed policies that discouraged advertisements for alcoholic beverages in "dry" areas and restricted advertisements for horse racing.

Some restraints on broadcast advertising are imposed by statutes rather than Commission regulation. For example, advertisements for cigarettes, little cigars, and "smokeless tobacco" are prohibited on television and radio. In addition, Section 1304 of the federal criminal code prohibits the broadcasting of "any advertisement of or information concerning any lottery." For purposes of the statute, a lottery is defined as anything that involves chance, consideration (such as an entry fee to participate), and a prize. A companion statute exempts from Section 1304 advertisements for and information about lotteries that are legal within the state in which they are conducted. This exemption, as expanded in 1988, applies not only to state-operated lotteries, but also to lotteries conducted by nonprofit or governmental organizations or held as ancillary "promotional activities" by commercial enterprises, so long as the game of chance is not illegal under state law. With respect to state-run lotteries, the exemption applies only to broadcast stations licensed to a community in a state that operates a lottery. Section 1304 is also inapplicable to advertisements for lotteries conducted by Indian tribes pursuant to the Indian Gaming Regulatory Act.

Moreover, as discussed briefly in connection with political advertising, the Communications Act requires broadcasters to identify the sponsor of any programs, including commercials, that they are paid to air. This provision, found in Section 317 of the Act, was passed in response to the "payola" scandals of the late 1950s, when radio disc jockeys and program directors were often paid to play particular records on the air. Payola problems have resurfaced periodically in commercial radio despite the statute.

Children's Programming. One of the most controversial issues that the Commission has faced in recent years has been television programming and advertising aimed at children. In 1974, the FCC issued a policy statement addressing two particular concerns: the relative dearth of programming, particularly of the nonentertainment variety, specifically designed for children, and the torrent of broadcast advertising to which children are exposed. With respect to the first problem, the Commission concluded that television licensees "have a special obligation to serve children" and "to provide diversified programming designed to meet the varied needs and interests of the child audience." Accordingly, the FCC said that it expected broadcasters to "make a meaningful effort" to increase both the total amount of programming for children and the amount of such programming designed to educate and inform rather than simply entertain. In addition, the agency said that children's programming should take into account specific age groups (e.g., pre-school) and should be aired throughout the week.

Turning to the advertising question, the FCC concluded that children, because of their youth and inexperience, are "far more trusting of and vulnerable to commercial 'pitches' than are adults" and that very young children are not able to "distinguish conceptually between programming and advertising." While rejecting a proposal to ban all advertising from children's programs, the Commission announced commercial guidelines for children's advertising similar to those discussed previously for all types of commercials. Compliance with limitations voluntarily adopted by the National Association of Broadcasters—nine and a half minutes per hour on weekends, twelve minutes per hour during the week—would be considered "sufficient to resolve in favor of the stations any questions as to whether its commercial practices serve the public interest."

In addition, the FCC directed licensees to take "special measures" to ensure that an adequate separation is maintained "between programming and advertising on programs designed for children." By way of illustration, the Commission suggested the broadcasting of an announcement to clarify when a program is interrupted for commercial message and when the program is resumed after the break. The FCC specifically prohibited so-called "host selling" whereby the host of a program or a character appearing on it endorses an advertiser's product and cautioned broadcasters against "engaging in practices in the body of the program itself which promote products in such a way that they may constitute advertising."

Five years later, the Commission returned to these issues and found that while broadcasters had generally complied with the advertising guidelines, little had changed with respect to programming. The FCC noted that the amount of such programming on a per-station basis had increased less than one hour a week, from 10.5 hours to 11.3. Moreover, this slight rise had resulted solely from new programming by independent stations, for network affiliates had not increased their children's programming at all. The Commission also pointed out that there had been no significant change in educational or informational programming, in programming for specific age groups, or in programming presented outside the traditional weekend time slots. Given this state of affairs, the agency initiated an administrative proceeding to consider regulatory options ranging from a hands-off approach to mandatory programming rules.

The Commission's inquiry stalled, however, when Mark Fowler was appointed chairman, and the agency took no action on children's programming until forced to do so by the courts. In early 1984, the FCC issued an order terminating the administrative proceeding and, consistent with its deregulation philosophy during Mr. Fowler's tenure, announcing that market forces—not the Commission—would determine the amount of children's programming on television. "[S]election of programming is a matter that should be decided by station licensees and by the audience through its viewing pattern voting," the Commission said. Although recognizing that television licensees have a "continuing duty . . . to examine the program needs of the child part of the audience and be ready to demonstrate at renewal time its attention to those needs," the FCC indicated that a station "may consider what other children's program service is available in its market [including nonbroadcast sources such as cable] in executing its response to those needs." The U.S. Court of Appeals for the District of Columbia Circuit upheld the FCC's decision in *Action for Children's Television v. Federal Communications Commmission* (1985).

Subsequently, the Commission abandoned its advertising guidelines for children's programs, though it left intact the prohibition against "host selling" and the requirement that programs be adequately separated from commercials. In a 1986 report, the FCC concluded that deletion of the advertising guidelines was compelled by its previous decision to eliminate similiar rules for commercials in general and stressed the "importance of advertising as a support mechanism for the presentation of children's programming." On appeal, however, the U.S. Court of Appeals for the District of Columbia Circuit found these explanations insufficient in *Action for Children's Television v. Federal Communications Commission* (1987) and sent the matter back to the FCC for further consideration. Although elimination of the commercial guidelines for children's programs may be consistent with the elimination of such quantitative guidelines in general, the court said, that explanation was inadequate in light of the Commission's conclusion in 1974 that advertising in programs aimed at children presents a special situation. Similarly, the fact that commercials help support children's programming did not justify elimination of the guidelines, since those limitations hardly amounted to a total ban on commercials. "As the [Commission] has seen it, kids are different," the court said. "[It] cannot now cavalierly revoke its special policy for youngsters without reexamining its earlier conclusions."

When the FCC began to drag its feet on this matter, the Congress passed the "Children's Television Act of 1988" requiring the Commission to limit the amount of advertising on children's programs to ten and a half minutes per hour on weekends and twelve minutes per hour on weekdays. These limitations could be modified by the Commission after 1992. In addition, the act provided that the FCC must take into account compliance with the advertising standards at renewal time, along with the question of "whether the licensee has served the educational and informational needs of children in its overall programming." President Reagan pocket vetoed the bill, however, claiming that it "simply cannot be reconciled with the freedom of expression secured by our Constitution."

The legislation was reintroduced in early 1989, with its supporters arguing that market forces alone are not sufficient to keep down the amount of children's advertising. According to testimony at a hearing held by the telecommunications subcommittee of the House Committee on Energy and Commerce, the number of commercials aired during children's shows has risen substantially, from nine and a half minutes per hour under the former FCC guidelines to as high as fourteen minutes in the deregulated environment. During adult programming, however, commercials typically do not exceed eight minutes per hour. Subcommittee Chairman Edward Markey observed at the hearing that it is no coincidence that children are being exposed to more commercials than adults. "Advertisers perceive [children as] a particularly vulnerable audience," he said. "We have a duty to see to it that this . . . audience is protected from wave after wave of exploitative commercials."

The Prime Time Access Rule. In the mid-1960s, the Commission became concerned about network control over the production and distribution of television programs. During that period, the number of independently produced programs had dropped dramatically; most new programs were developed—and owned, at least in part—by the three major networks. After those programs had run their course on the networks, they were "syndicated" on a station-by-station basis and earned the networks healthy profits. Programs of this type dominated the syndication market, thus frustrating the efforts of independent producers to develop new, non-network "first-run" shows. Moreover, few stations produced their own local programs.

The FCC responded in 1970 by adopting two related regulations. The "network financial interest and syndication rule" was designed to limit the networks' involvement in the production and syndication of programs. More important for our purposes is the "prime time access rule," which in its initial form prohibited television stations in the fifty largest markets owned by or affiliated with a network from broadcasting more than three hours of network programming during the four-hour prime time period each evening. Exemptions were established to permit political broadcasts by candidates and coverage of fast-breaking news events. Though the rule has twice been modified, its purpose remains the same: to encourage the production of programs by local stations and independent producers by freeing up air time on network affiliates that had previously been occupied by network programs. Because the networks had traditionally offered only three and a half hours of prime time fare, the rule made available an additional half hour of "access time" for non-network programs.

The present version of the rule, in effect since 1975, has as its centerpiece the three-hour limitation described in the preceding paragraph.[5] However, the following network programs do not "count" for purposes of the rule and may thus be shown in the access period:

- except on Saturday nights, network public affairs programs, documentaries, and children's programs;
- special news programs dealing with fast-breaking news events, on-the-spot news coverage, and political broadcasts;
- regular half-hour network news programs, so long as they are adjacent to a full hour of local news or public affairs programs;
- "runovers" of live network coverage of sports events; and
- network broadcasts of special events, such as the Olympics, that occupy the entire prime time period.

---

[5]Though it technically applies only to stations in the largest fifty markets (which together account for about two-thirds of the nation's viewing audience), the rule has a spillover effect on stations in smaller communities, since the networks are unwilling to provide special programs for their affiliates in these other markets.

In addition, the rule prohibits network affiliates in the top fifty markets from using syndicated programs that have previously aired on the networks during the access period. This means that popular shows originally on the networks—such as "M*A*S*H"—can be aired during this period only by independent stations in these markets.

The courts have consistently upheld the rule's constitutionality. In *Mt. Mansfield Television, Inc. v. Federal Communications Commission* (1971), the U.S. Court of Appeals for the Second Circuit stressed the rule's impact on program diversity in rejecting a first amendment challenge. Relying on *Red Lion*, the court said:

> [T]he prime time access rule, far from violating the First Amendment, appears to be a reasonable step toward fulfillment of its fundamental precepts, for it is the stated purpose of that rule to encourage the "[d]iversity of programs and the development of diverse and antagonistic sources of program service" and to correct a situation where "[o]nly three organizations control access to the crucial prime time evening schedule." * * * To argue that the freedom of the networks to distribute and licensees to select programming is limited by the prime time access rule, and that the First Amendment is thereby violated, is to reverse the mandated priorities which subordinate these interests to the public's right of access [to information]. The licensee is in many ways a "trustee" for the public in the operation of his channel. . . .

The various exemptions in the current version of the rule formed the basis for a subsequent judicial challenge. However, the Second Circuit again found it consistent with the first amendment. By establishing the exemptions, the FCC "is not ordering any program or even any type of program to be broadcast in access time," the court said. "It has simply lifted a restriction on network programs if the licensee chooses to avail himself of such network programs in specified categories of programming. . . ."

Critics of the rule have charged that it has not served one of its intended purposes, that is, to encourage locally produced prime time programming. In fact, the FCC staff concluded in a 1980 report that many stations were simply running cheaply produced game shows during the thirty-minute access period. Two years later, the Commission proposed to scrap the rule, along with the corresponding regulation on network financial interest and syndication. Opposition immediately surfaced in the Congress, which quickly passed a bill prohibiting the FCC from expending funds to repeal or change the rules for a specified period. Moreover, President Reagan, who had longstanding ties with Hollywood producers who benefit from the rules, announced that he supported their retention. Shortly thereafter, the FCC dropped its proposal.

Distortion and Staging the News. Although the Commission does not sit in review of a broadcaster's "news judgment," it has adopted a policy against the deliberate distortion of the news and the staging of events for the purpose of media coverage. Developed in a series of cases during the late 1960s, the policy stems from the broad "public interest" standard of the Communications Act. "Rigging or slanting the news is a most heinous act against the public interest," the FCC has observed. "[I]ndeed, there is no act more harmful to the public's ability to handle its affairs." At the same time, however, the Commission has been extremely sensitive to the first amendment implications of such a policy and, accordingly, has distinguished between deliberate distortion on the one hand and mere inaccuracy or difference of opinion on the other. Only the former is a violation.

A broadcaster who engages in deliberate distortion can, in extreme cases, lose his license, though the FCC will typically admonish the offending station about the practice and require the adoption of safeguards to protect against reoccurrence. A person complaining of distortion must clear two substantial hurdles before the FCC will take action of any sort. First, he must support his claim with "extrinsic evidence" of improper conduct by the licensee. That is, the complainant must provide evidence—other than the program itself—that the broadcaster deliberately distorted the material. According to the Commission, such evidence might include written or oral instructions from station management, "outtakes" not included in the program as aired, or evidence of bribery. Obviously, a complainant will ordinarily have difficult time uncovering evidence of this type. Second, even if he offers sufficient evidence, the complainant must demonstrate that the distortion involved a significant event and not simply a minor or incidental aspect of the news report. Thus, embellishment of a story or "window dressing" will be tolerated so long as the essential facts are accurate.

The line between "distortion" and "inaccuracy" was at issue in one of the leading FCC decisions in this area, *In re "Hunger in America"* (1969). The case grew out of a CBS documentary that opened with footage of an infant receiving treatment in a hospital pediatrics ward. "Hunger is easy to recognize when it looks like this," a narrator said. "This baby is dying of starvation. He was an American. Now he is dead." The baby, however, was suffering from various other ailments, not malnutrition. In rejecting a claim that the network had deliberately distorted the facts, the Commission noted that hospital personnel had told the CBS producer that most babies in the ward were malnourished and that there was a high incidence of premature births due to maternal malnutrition. While CBS may have been guilty of sloppy journalism in not making certain that the child that it filmed was, in fact, suffering from malnutrition, the FCC said, the evidence was not sufficient to establish deliberate distortion.

Broadcasters are more likely to be found to have distorted material if they "stage" or "act out" news events and interviews. For example, the U.S. Court of Appeals for the District of Columbia Circuit ruled in *Galloway v. Federal Communications Commission* (1985) that CBS had improperly staged an interview in a "60 Minutes" segment about insurance fraud. The broadcast included a tape CBS purportedly made of an investigator interviewing an insurance claimant, who initially said that she had been involved in an accident. At this point, the reporter stated in a voice-over that the investigator "thinks [the claimant] is lying" and that the claimant, "after some hard questioning," changed her story. The claimant then admitted on film that she had filed a fraudulent claim "[b]ecause somebody told me that if I did it that I would get paid a certain amount of money." As it turned out, the investigator actually "interrogated" the claimant at least three times for CBS' cameras. The court agreed with the complainant that the interview, represented to viewers as spontaneous, had actually been staged. "The interrogation was clearly an 'event' which did not in fact occur but [was] 'acted out' at the behest of news personnel," the court said.

Although staging of this type is almost always considered distortion, the court ruled in *Galloway* that the network's conduct did not affect the "basic accuracy" of the report and was thus insignificant. The claimant actually did admit to participating in the fraud, albeit not precisely in the manner portrayed by CBS. Even though the claimant may not have confessed in response to "hard questioning" in a spontaneous interview, any misrepresentation went to a minor or incidental part of the report, not its essential facts. "[T]he real criterion with respect to staging is whether the public is deceived about a matter of significance," the court said, quoting a Commission policy statement. "Whatever we may think of [CBS'] playacting as a journalistic practice, it does not violate FCC rules as currently applied."

In this era of the "media event," it should be obvious that many events are "staged" by the participants for the benefit of television coverage. Press conferences and the appearances of political candidates, for example, are carefully orchestrated affairs. Moreover, persons involved in mass demonstrations, such as the antiwar activists of the late 1960s and the Iranian revolutionaries ten years later, have learned to "turn up the heat" when television cameras appear on the scene. The Commission, however, is concerned with staging by broadcast journalists, not by the participants. With respect to the latter, reporters must simply use their own journalistic judgment in determining the nature and amount of coverage the event warrants.

NONCOMMERCIAL BROADCASTING

In general, noncommercial radio and television stations are subject to the rules and policies applicable to their commercial counterparts. For example, they are required to comply with the "access" rule for federal candidates and the "equal opportunities" requirement, though the latter will operate in somewhat different fashion because noncommercial stations may not carry advertisements. They are also subject to restrictions on indecent programming and were governed by the fairness doctrine prior to its demise. There are, however, a few additional FCC and statutory guidelines aimed specifically at noncommercial stations.

First, Commission rules provide that noncommercial stations may be licensed only to nonprofit educational organizations, both public and private. Frequencies for FM radio and for television have been reserved for noncommercial use. Typically, noncommercial stations are licensed to public schools, state colleges and universities, governmental agencies, private educational institutions, and nonprofit citizens' groups. If a private organization's primary purpose is religious, however, it is not eligible for a license on a frequency reserved for noncommercial broadcasting but may apply to operate a noncommercial station on a channel that has not been reserved for that purpose.

Second, FCC regulations require that the stations operate in a nonprofit and noncommercial manner. This means no advertising. Under Commission rules, "[n]o promotional announcements on behalf of for profit entities shall be broadcast at any time in exchange for the receipt . . . of consideration to the licensee." However, "acknowledgments of contributions can be made." This exception, of course, enables noncommercial stations to make the now-familiar underwriting announcements that link contributors to particular programs. In recent years, the FCC has liberalized its interpretation of the exception by permitting underwriting announcements that include product brand names, company slogans, and logos.

Finally, noncommercial licensees may not endorse or oppose political candidates for political office. Section 399 of the Public Broadcasting Act provides that "[n]o noncommercial educational broadcasting station may support or oppose any candidate for public office.'' A similar prohibition on editorializing, also found in Section 399, was declared unconstitutional by the Supreme Court in a 1984 case, *Federal Communications Commission v. League of Women Voters of California*, but the Court did not pass on the validity of the no-endorsement provision.

The portion of Section 399 at issue in *League of Women Voters* stated that any noncommercial station receiving funds from the Corporation for Public Broadcasting (CPB) could not ''engage in editorializing.'' The CPB is a nonprofit corporation authorized to disburse federal funds to noncommercial television and radio stations.[6] In adopting the prohibition against editorials, Congress apparently sought to protect noncommercial stations from government influence exercised by the CPB's disbursement of federal funds and to prevent these stations from becoming vehicles for private licensees to express their own partisan views. The Supreme Court found these governmental interests inadequate to justify the statute's obvious restriction on speech.

Writing for a narrow 5 to 4 majority, Justice Brennan pointed out that the Public Broadcasting Act, which created the CPB, contains ample safeguards shielding noncommercial stations from undesirable influence by the federal government. For example, the CPB is governed by a bipartisan board of directors and is required to operate so as to ''assure the maximum freedom [of local stations] from interference with or control of program content or other activities.'' Even if these provisions were thought insufficient, he added, the ban on editorializing would not necessarily provide the necessary protection, particularly since a station is ''free to broadcast controversial views so long as [those] views are not labelled as its own.'' Moreover, the ban swept much more broadly than necessary to serve its asserted purpose, since it prohibited not only editorials that might threaten federal funding, but also those on purely local issues of no concern to the federal government.

With respect to the other proferred justification, Justice Brennan observed that the ban did not prevent ''the use of noncommercial stations for the presentation of partisan views on controverial matters,'' but merely barred a station from ''specifically communicating such views on its own behalf. . . .'' Even if the asserted governmental interests were considered substantial, he concluded, the statute was not ''crafted with sufficient precision'' to withstand scrutiny under the first amendment. Moreover, the effect the statute—''to diminish rather than augment the volume and quality of coverage of controversial issues''—ran afoul of the public's ''paramount right'' under *Red Lion* to be informed on matters of public importance.

A somewhat different problem has arisen in light of the fact that many noncommercial stations are licensed to state and local governmental entities funded, at least in part, by tax dollars. What effect, if any, does government ownership have on the ability of the licensee to control its programming? The short answer is ''none.'' State or local governments holding noncommercial broadcast licenses have the same sort of editorial discretion as private licensees when it comes to programming.

The leading case on this issue is *Muir v. Alabama Educational Television Commission*, decided by the U.S. Court of Appeals for the Fifth Circuit in 1982. The court was faced with two separate lawsuits challenging the decisions of state-owned noncommercial stations in Alabama and Texas to cancel a previously scheduled drama, ''Death of a Princess,'' about a Saudi Arabian woman who had been exe-

---

[6]The third link in noncommercial television chain is the Public Broadcasting Service (PBS), which distributes programs to its member stations via common carrier facilities. National Public Radio (NPR) provides a similar service for noncommercial radio stations.

cuted for committing adultery. The Saudi government objected strongly to the program, which was based on an actual incident that had occurred in 1977. Trial proceedings yielded different results. In the Texas case, a federal judge issued an injunction requiring a noncommercial station licensed to a state university to air the program, but the court in Alabama refused to enter such an order against the licensee, the Alabama Educational Television Commission.

On appeal, the Fifth Circuit affirmed the Alabama ruling and reversed the Texas case, rejecting the plaintiffs' argument that the first amendment rights of viewers imposed limits on the programming discretion of noncommercial television stations licensed to governmental entities. First, the court ruled that such stations are not "public forums" to which members of the general public have a right of access. To hold otherwise, the court said, would be inconsistent with the Communications Act, which places control over programming in the hands of the licensee. The right of the public "is not to schedule programs, but to watch or decline to watch what is offered," the court noted.

Second, the court concluded that cancellation of a program that had already been scheduled did not amount to government censorship, for state employees in charge of the stations were simply exercising their statutorily mandated discretion to make programming choices. "The states have not sought to forbid or curtail the right of any person to show or view the film," the court said. "There is a clear distinction between a state's exercise of editorial discretion over its own expression and a state's prohibition or suppression of the speech of another."

CABLE TELEVISION

As the *Century Communications* case reproduced at the beginning of this chapter makes clear, the relationship between broadcasters and cable television operators has changed dramatically in recent years. Once considered an adjunct to broadcasting, cable has emerged as a major competitor in the delivery of video programming. As more homes have become "wired," cable viewership has steadily increased, while the networks' share of the audience has declined substantially. Approximately 80 percent of the nation's households are now able to receive cable television service, and 55 percent actually subscribe. In this section, we shall examine the first amendment rights of cable operators, the manner in which the industry is regulated, and restrictions on program content. First, however, these matters should be placed in their historical context.

Background

Cable television was born of necessity in the late 1940s when broadcasting was in its infancy. Because the first television stations were located in major metropolitan areas, many rural communities found themselves beyond the reach of broadcast signals. Other areas, though perhaps within range of the stations, could not receive suitable signals because of mountainous terrain. Entrepreneurs soon discovered, however, that they could deliver quality signals by constructing a large antenna to which homes throughout the area were linked via wire or coaxial cable. These operations were known as "community antenna television" systems, or CATV. The term "cable" did not become widely used until the late 1960s, but we will employ it throughout this discussion for the sake of convenience.

Broadcasters were at first pleased with the development of cable, since it made their programs available to a wider audience. Within a decade or so, however, they learned that cable could also bring increased competition. For example, a cable system located in a city served by two or three broadcast stations could import the signals of stations in other communities. And, thanks to microwave relay facilities, the cable operator could gain access to the signals of television stations hundreds of miles away. Because none of these "distant" signals could not be picked up by viewers with conventional rooftop antennae, the cable system could make available programming to compete with that offered by the local television stations. Moreover, some cable systems refused to include the signals of local stations in the service package they offered to subscribers.

The FCC initially declined to assert jurisdiction over cable, but in 1962 took its first step in that direction by restricting the ability of common carriers to deliver broadcast signals via microwave to a cable systems if their importation would cause economic injury to a local station. Under increasing pressure from broadcasters, the Commission in 1965 claimed direct authority to regulate cable. By that time, the cable industry had grown dramatically. In 1952, for example, there were only seventy cable systems serving 14,000 subscribers. Seven years later, 560 systems reached 550,000 subscribers, and by 1965 the numbers had increased to 1,325 and 1.5 million. In a landmark 1968 case, *United States v. Southwestern Cable Co.*, the U.S. Supreme Court upheld FCC authority over cable, so long as the regulations were "reasonably ancillary" to the Commission's statutory duty to oversee television broadcasting.

At the outset, the Commission's policies toward cable were clearly designed to protect broadcast television, particularly UHF stations whose picture quality, for technical reasons, did not measure up to that of cable. In 1966, for example, the Commission adopted its first "must-carry" rule requiring cable systems to retransmit the signals of all television stations whose signals could be picked up over-the-air in the community. In the same proceeding, the FCC drastically limited the ability of cable operators to import distant signals in the nation's top 100 television markets, thus effectively shutting cable out of the largest cities. Even in the smaller markets where distant signals were permitted, cable operators could not carry any programs duplicating those offered on the same day by local stations.

These rules were gradually refined and new regulations adopted. For instance, the FCC required cable systems that were eligible to import distant signals to choose among television stations in the city closest to that in which the cable system was located. This "anti-leapfrogging" rule restricted the choices available to cable operators and in many cases insulated local broadcasters from competition from stations in large cities. Another regulation designed to protect local broadcasters prevented cable systems from carrying syndicated programs from distant stations to which a local station had purchased exclusive rights. The notion underlying this "syndicated exclusivity" rule was that a local station that had paid for the exclusive right to broadcast a popular program in its market would not be getting what it paid for if the same program were available on cable from a station in another city. Cable operators were also required to originate their own programs rather than simply retransmit the signals of broadcast stations.

Two other problems clouded the regulatory picture. First, broadcasters complained that retransmission of their signals via cable violated the copyright laws, since cable operators paid neither the broadcasters nor the program producers for the privilege of carrying the signals. The Supreme Court ruled in *Fortnightly Corp.*

v. United Artists Television, Inc. (1968) that the 1909 Copyright Act did not apply because the retransmission was not a "performance" within the meaning of the statute. In the Court's view, the cable system functioned just like a viewer's antenna by enabling him to receive the broadcast signals. The Court reaffirmed that ruling six years later in *Teleprompter Corp. v. Columbia Broadcasting System*, holding that a cable system's use of microwave facilities to bring in signals that a viewer could not receive with his own antenna made no difference for copyright purposes.

These decisions meant that broadcasters could not benefit financially from the fact that programs they had either bought the rights to or produced themselves were being retransmitted for profit by cable systems in other communities. As we saw in Chapter 4, Congress addressed this problem in the Copyright Act of 1976 by requiring cable systems to pay a compulsory license fee based on their carriage of nonlocal broadcast signals.

Second, municipal governments gradually became more active in the business of cable regulation, primarily by requiring that cable systems obtain a "franchise" in order to operate. In granting such franchises, cities typically imposed various requirements—programming rules, provisions for the regulation of rates, the assessment of a franchise fee—upon the cable system. Moreover, some state agencies also got into the business of regulating the industry, thereby creating another tier of governmental control. The FCC confronted this problem in 1972 by adopting rules under which state and local governments were given the task of granting individual franchises and regulating the construction and physical operation of cable systems, while the Commission assumed jurisdiction over programming matters and technical standards. This dual system of regulation remains in effect today, though Congress has significantly restricted the role played by state and local governments.

In the mid-1970s, the FCC changed its attitude toward cable and began the process of eliminating several of its "protectionist" regulations that had benefited broadcasters and thwarted the development of the cable industry. For example, abolition of the "anti-leapfrogging" rule in 1976 paved the way for "superstations" such as WTBS in Atlanta, since cable systems that could import distant signals were not limited to those of stations in nearby communities. A year later, the Commission dramatically modified the rule governing distant signals, ruling that the importation of such signals into major television markets would be presumed to have no impact on local stations and that broadcasters would have the burden of proving otherwise. This decision spurred the growth of cable into the nation's largest cities. In 1980, the Commission eliminated the restrictions on distant signals altogether, along with the "syndicated exclusivity" rule.

This deregulatory push, along with the resolution of the copyright question in 1976, set the stage for passage of the Cable Communications Policy Act of 1984, the first federal statute dealing with cable. We will examine the act's key provisions below, along with various FCC regulations, after consideration of an unsettled issue that underlies all of cable regulation: the first amendment rights of cable operators.

Cable and the First Amendment

Cable operators have long argued that government restrictions on their discretion to carry—or to refuse to carry—particular programming violates the first amendment. The industry position, as well as that of some scholars, is that the spectrum scarcity rationale employed to justify greater government control over broadcasting does not apply in the cable context and, accordingly, that cable operators enjoy the same first amendment rights as the print media. On the other hand, a number of commentators have argued that cable is sufficiently like broadcasting to warrant similar government regulation. Other possibilities also exist; for example, cable could be considered a wholly different form of communication for which new first amendment principles must be developed. Although the U.S. Supreme Court has ruled that cable is entitled to some first amendment protection, the Justices have not established the constitutional principles that govern cable regulation.

The status of cable under the first amendment reached the Court in *City of Los Angeles v. Preferred Communications, Inc.* (1986). The case arose when Los Angeles refused to permit Preferred Communications to operate a cable system in the south central portion of the city because it had failed to participate in the franchising process by which the city had selected a single company to serve the area. Preferred argued that more than one company could provide cable services, since there was room on utility poles and in underground utility facilities for several cable operators to string their cable. The city did not deny that such excess physical capacity existed but argued that limiting the franchise to one company was justified by the need to "minimiz[e] the demand that cable systems make for the use of public property." Among other things, the city claimed that cable companies create a "permanent visual blight" by stringing miles of cable and cause traffic hazards and delays when installing and repairing their facilities.

Finding no first amendment violation, the trial court dismissed Preferred's suit. However, the U.S. Court of Appeals for the Ninth Circuit reversed and ordered a trial at which Preferred would have the opportunity to prove that there was space for more than one cable company to operate. According to the court of appeals, the first amendment prevents a city from allowing one cable company to serve the community while excluding all others, so long as there is sufficient "room" on utility poles and public rights-of-way for additional companies to construct cable facilities.

The Supreme Court affirmed the Ninth Circuit's decision that a trial was necessary but did not adopt the lower court's ruling on the first amendment question. In an opinion by Justice William Rehnquist, the Court expressly declined to clarify the first amendment standards applicable to cable. Instead, the Court simply stated that the activities of a cable operater include the exercise of editorial discretion in the selection of programming and therefore "plainly implicate First Amendment interests." In a brief concurring opinion, Justice Harry Blackmun, joined by Justices Thurgood Marshall and Sandra Day O'Connor, suggested that cable might require a "new analysis" rather than application of the standards developed for the print and broadcast media. Like Justice Rehnquist, however, the concurring Justices did not adopt a set of first amendment ground rules for cable.

Following the Supreme Court's lead in this area, the lower courts have generally managed to avoid deciding the scope of the first amendment in the cable setting. The *Century Communications* case is illustrative, for there the court was able to declare the FCC's latest "must-carry" rules unconstitutional without resolving the "vexing question" of whether cable operators are to be treated like broadcasters or like the print media. Other courts, however, have addressed at least part of this question by deciding that the difference between broadcasting and cable is such that the degree of regulation permissible for the former will not be tolerated with respect to the latter.

For example, the federal appellate courts have struck down city ordinances and state statutes forbidding cable systems from carrying indecent programs that are not legally obscene. In *Cruz v. Ferre* (1985), the first case of this type to reach the appellate level, the U.S. Court of Appeals for the Eleventh Circuit found the rationale underlying the *Pacifica* case inapplicable with respect to cable. First, the court found the "pervasiveness" justification absent, since a cable subscriber must "affirmatively elect to have cable service come into his home." Unlike television and radio, cable "does not 'intrude' into the home." Second, the court rejected the argument that cable, like broadcasting, is "uniquely accessible" to children. "Parental manageability of cable television greatly exceeds the ability to manage the broadcast media," the court said. For example, parents must decide whether to subscribe to cable and whether to select particular program services, such Home Box Office or an adult channel. Program guides for cable services are widely available, the court added, and parents may obtain "lockboxes" to prevent children from watching certain cable channels.

In a later case, *Jones v. Wilkinson* (1986), the U.S. Court of Appeals for the Tenth Circuit upheld a trial court decision invalidating the Utah "Cable Television Programming Decency Act," which banned indecent as well as obscene programs. The trial judge's opinion, which was specifically approved by the appellate court, relied on the *Cruz* case in holding that *Pacifica* did not apply in the cable context. In addition, the judge pointed out that cable does not have the "spectrum scarcity" problem that pervades broadcasting and provides justification for heightened government regulation of that medium. Because the "number of [cable] channels is subject to extensive expansion," the judge said, "there is no danger of interference between channels" and the government "need not 'control traffic' by rationing channels." The U.S. Supreme Court subsequently affirmed this decision but did not issue a written opinion.

However, several courts and commentators have suggested a number of reasons why cable operators should not be afforded the same first amendment protection enjoyed by the print media. First, cable systems must make use of streets and other public property, as well as private property dedicated to the benefit of the public, such as easements. As the U.S. Court of Appeals for the Tenth Circuit pointed out in *Community Communications, Inc. v. City of Boulder* (1981):

> To disseminate information, a newspaper need not use public property in the same way that a cable operator does. A newspaper may reach its audience simply through the public streets or mails, with no more disruption to the public domain than would be caused by the typical pedestrian, motorist or user of the mail. But a cable operator must lay the means of his medium underground or string it across poles in order to deliver his message. Obviously, this manner of using the public domain entails significant disruption, especially to streets, alleys, and other public ways.

This use of the public right-of-way by cable operators is important for several reasons in terms of first amendment analysis. Obviously, as the Tenth Circuit noted in *Boulder,* "[a] city needs control over the number of times its citizens must bear the inconvenience of having its streets dug up. . . ." This governmental interest can be likened to the necessity of preventing objectionable interference between broadcast stations, and one can argue that the use of the public right-of-way by cable operators is comparable to the use of the airwaves by broadcasters. Moreover, while there may be no "scarcity" problem in terms of the number of cable channels, there are limits on the number of cables that can be accommodated along the public right-of-way. Thus, the number of cable systems that can serve a city is finite.

Second, as a federal district court observed in *Erie Telecommunications, Inc. v. City of Erie* (1987), "the ease with which [cable] operators are able to create a natural monopoly . . . [has] provided justification for government regulation." Direct competition among cable companies—"overbuilding" in industry jargon—is extremely rare, and most communities are served only by a single cable operator. Although the Supreme Court ruled in the *Tornillo* case that "economic" as opposed to "physical" scarcity is not enough to justify diminished first amendment protection, the fact that city-granted franchises often shield cable operators from competition sets cable apart from newspapers and other unlicensed print media. Even nonexclusive cable franchises have terms that tend to discourage potential competitors from entering the market, and the Cable Communications Policy Act makes franchise renewal almost automatic.

The U.S. Court of Appeals for the Seventh Circuit employed this "economic scarcity" rationale in rejecting a first amendment challenge to a franchise provision that required the cable operator to originate a small amount of local programming. "Unlike the traditional forms of print media, a cable [system] enjoys a virtual monopoly over its area, without the threat of an alternative provider," the court said in *Chicago Cable Communications v. Chicago Cable Commission* (1989). "[I]t is within the City's rights . . . to proffer some requirements guaranteeing that the cable customers are, to the extent possible, accorded a range of programming from the franchisee, since the cable viewing public has no other channel to which to turn."

Third, as the Tenth Circuit observed in the *Boulder* case, the cable industry "has always been regulated in many respects" and "[t]here is no tradition of nearly absolute freedom from government control." In contrast, the court added, the print media are "protected by a long-standing and powerful tradition [of] keeping [the] government's hands off. . . ." Finally, it can be argued that cable is more like broadcasting in the sense that there is no opportunity, as there is with newspapers, for alternative low-cost communication in the same format. A person who cannot afford to start his own newspaper is at least able to distribute leaflets expressing his views, but he cannot disseminate those views via the medium of television, either broadcast or cable, without some form of access to the medium itself.

The Cable Communications Policy Act

As the foregoing discussion suggests, first amendment issues arise in connection with the process by which cable franchises are granted and the manner in which government attempts to regulate program content. In this section, we shall examine the role of cities, states, and the federal government in the franchising process, as well as restrictions on programming imposed or authorized by the act, city franchising ordinances, and FCC regulations. Of necessity, our framework for discussion is the Cable Communications Policy Act, a complex statute passed in 1984 after extensive negotiations between the cable industry and the National League of Cities.

In general, the act—an amendment to the Communications Act of 1934—preserves the dual system of cable regulation that has long prevailed in the cable industry. First, it specifically gives the FCC direct authority over cable television. As a result, the Commission's jurisdiction no longer depends on whether its rules affecting cable are "reasonably ancillary" to its regulation of broadcasting. Second, the act leaves cable franchising in the hands of state and local governments, though it places important limitations on their authority. For example, cities cannot as a general matter regulate rates charged or program services offered by cable operators or require payment of franchise fees in excess of the ceiling set forth in the act. Moreover, the act contemplates that franchises will be routinely renewed and thus permits a city to deny renewal only if certain specified conditions are met.

The Franchising Process. Though virtually every state has on the books one or more state statutes relating to cable television, most deal with narrow issues and leave to municipal governments the task of granting franchises and directly overseeing cable systems within their jurisdictions. However, about a dozen states have placed such regulatory authority, including the power to award franchises, in the hands of state administrative agencies. Both of these schemes are permissible under the Cable Act, though neither a state statute nor a local ordinance is valid if it conflicts with the act or FCC regulations. For example, in *City of New York v. Federal Communications Commission* (1988), the U.S. Supreme Court ruled that cities cannot establish technical standards for cable signal quality more stringent than those adopted by the FCC.

A cable operator may not provide service in an area without first obtaining a franchise from the appropriate governmental body. The Cable Act gives a city or other franchising authority discretion to "award . . . one or more cable franchises within its jurisdiction." Although this language obviously contemplates the possibility that a single cable company could be granted an exclusive franchise, the first amendment may preclude such arrangements so long as it is physically possible for more than one company to operate in the city. As discussed previously, this issue remains unsettled.

Under the act, a city has the discretion to impose a variety of requirements on the cable operator. For example, a city may establish the duration of the franchise (a term of fifteen years has been typical), specify the number of channels and type of facilities and equipment that must be provided, set a timetable for the construction of the cable system, establish financial and insurance requirements that the cable operator must meet, place restrictions on the sale or transfer of the cable system, set standards for customer service, and adopt consumer protection safeguards. The act also permits a city to impose a tax, generally known as a "franchise fee," of up to five percent of the cable operator's annual gross revenues.

In addition to these optional provisions, there are certain matters that must be addressed in the franchise. With respect to requirements for facilities and equipment, for instance, the franchise must permit the cable operator to request modification of the terms in the event that compliance is commercially impracticable. It must also assure that cable service is not denied to any group of residential subscribers because of the income level of the area in which the group resides.

Other key provisions of the act expressly limit the powers of cities in the franchising process. As discussed more fully below, a city may not demand that the cable operator offer particular programming services, although it can require the company to set aside channels for public access, educational, and governmental purposes. Moreover, a city may not ordinarily regulate the rates charged by the cable operator. (The FCC is also precluded from rate regulation, as are state governments.) As a result, the two major concerns of cable subscribers—the programming services available to them on the system and the rates they must pay for those services—cannot be addressed by a city or other franchising authority. According to a recent study, the Cable Act has led to a sharp increase in cable rates: an average of thirty-two percent nationally in the four years following its passage. For the twelve months ending in October 1988, rates jumped thirteen percent, though the consumer price index rose only four percent during that period. Critics have complained that rate deregulation is inappropriate in the cable industry, since only about thirty of the nation's 8,000-plus cable systems face head-to-head competition from other cable operators.

There is one exception to the prohibition against municipal rate regulation. The act provides that the FCC "shall prescribe . . . regulations which authorize a franchising authority to regulate rates for the provision of basic cable service in circumstances in which a cable system is not subject to effective competition." Under a Commission rule adopted pursuant to this provision, a cable system is deemed subject to "effective competition" when 100 percent of the city where the cable system is located receives at least three off-air television signals. For purposes of this rule, a television station is considered available in the community if its signal is of a specified strength, as determined by engineering maps. As a result, the test is one of theoretical rather than actual availability of the signals from three television stations. If, however, a city is able to conduct engineering studies showing that the requisite number of signals cannot be received over-the-air in the community because of mountainous terrain or other factors, it may obtain a waiver from the FCC permitting rate regulation.

If a city qualifies under the "effective competition" exception or secures a waiver, it may regulate rates only for "basic" cable service, which is defined in the Cable Act as "any service tier which includes the retransmission of local television broadcast signals." This provision recognizes the fact that many cable operators use a marketing device known as "tiering" in which multiple levels of service are available to the consumer. Suppose, for instance, that a cable system offers a basic package of twenty channels, including at least one local television station, for $12.95 per month; a second tier of ten channels, all of which are satellite-delivered services such as ESPN and Cable News Network, for an additional $5.95 per month; and a third tier of "premium" channels such as Home Box Office and the Disney Channel for $8.95 each. Only the rates for the twenty-channel basic service may be regulated by the city, because only that tier includes local television stations. Charges for installation, disconnection, and equipment are not subject to regulation.

In addition to the limitations on rate regulation, the Cable Act restricts significantly the discretion of cities to refuse to renew cable franchises upon their expiration. Indeed, one of the express purposes of the statute was to "establish an orderly process for franchise renewal which protects cable operators against unfair denials of renewal where the operator's past performance and proposal for future performance meet the standards by [the act]." In effect, Congress had created for cable operators a "renewal expectancy" similar to that developed by the FCC with respect to broadcast licensees. As the U.S. Court of Appeals for the Third Circuit observed in *Eastern Telecom Corp. v. Borough of East Conemaugh* (1989), "[t]he Cable Act establishes a significant federal law property expectation in the renewal of a franchise." While renewal is not automatic by any means, the act plainly contemplates that a cable operator's franchise will ordinarily be renewed.

The act sets forth a rather complex procedure that a city must follow in deciding whether to renew a cable operator's franchise, although it also provides that a mutually acceptable renewal agreement may be reached outside this formal process via negotiations. If the parties are unable to agree upon the terms of a new franchise, the city must initiate renewal proceedings, the first step of which is a preliminary assessment of the cable operator's past performance and identification of the community's future cable-related needs. At this point the city can decide to stiffen various franchise requirements, subject to the limitations discussed previously. The cable operator will then make a specific proposal for renewal. If the city decides to renew the franchise, the matter comes to an end; if not, the city advises the cable operator of its preliminary decision not to renew, thus triggering a formal administrative hearing on the renewal question. If this trial-type process results in a negative decision, the cable operator may appeal to the appropriate state or federal court.

This "formal" renewal process does not involve a comparison between the incumbent cable operator and potential competitors who might wish to serve the community. Rather, the only questions are whether the cable operator has:

- substantially complied with the material terms of the franchise;
- provided cable service responsive to the needs of the community;
- offered a renewal proposal designed to meet the future cable-related needs of the community; and
- demonstrated the financial and technical ability to deliver on the promises made in that proposal.

In evaluating these issues, the city may not take into account the programming services offered on the cable system or the rates charged. Moreover, a refusal to renew can be based on the operator's failure to comply with the franchise only if the city has given the operator notice and an opportunity to correct the deficiencies.

Programming Restrictions. In general, the Cable Act affects program content in four ways. First, it allows a city to require that certain types of "access" channels be set aside for use by the public, governmental agencies, and educational institutions. Similarly, the act by its own terms requires that cable operators make available, for a fee, "leased access" channels that can be used by persons unaffiliated with the cable system. Second, the act permits a city to prohibit obscene programming and makes the transmission of obscene material over a cable system a federal offense. Third, it permits a city to enforce a cable operator's promise to provide "broad categories" of program services. Finally, although the act prohibits the FCC from adopting new rules that affect cable programming, it "grandfathers" several such regulations that were in place at the time of the act's passage.

Access Channels. Beginning in 1972, the FCC attempted to force cable systems to designate a certain number of channels for use by members of the general public. The Supreme Court, however, ruled in *Federal Communications Commission v. Midwest Video Corp.* (1979) that these provisions were not "reasonably ancillary" to the agency's power to regulate broadcasting and thus invalid. Though the Cable Act gave the FCC express regulatory authority over cable, it left the "public access" issue to the cities, which are permitted to adopt franchise provisions requiring cable operators to set aside channels for "public, education, or governmental use."

The act does not define these terms, but so-called "PEG" access includes "electronic soapbox" channels on which any member of the general public may appear, channels reserved for the "cablecasting" of city council meetings, and channels for educational programs prepared by the local public schools or colleges. In addition to mandating the reservation of channels for these purposes, a city may demand that the cable operator provide production facilities, video cameras, and other equipment for PEG use.

Any franchise that calls for PEG channels must also contain rules and procedures setting forth the circumstances under which a cable operator may use channel capacity which is designated for PEG purposes but not actually being used. If a channel is being utilized by PEG group, the cable operator may not exercise any editorial control over the channel. This prohibition ensures that persons unrelated to the cable operator are responsible for programming of these channels and, consequently, that the public will receive information from a diversity of sources. Because the cable system has no control over what appears on these channels, the act immunizes it from liability for libel, invasion of privacy, obscenity, and similar claims arising out of any programming on PEG channels.

Typically, educational and governmental channels are designated for use by particular entities, such as government boards, colleges, or public schools. Channels set aside for public access are usually run by either the cable operator, the city, or a private, nonprofit corporation. If the cable operator manages an access channel, it is barred under the provision mentioned in the preceding paragraph from exerting editorial control over programming. Similarly, a city or other governmental entity in charge of a PEG channel will be probably be prohibited by the first amendment from controlling program content, since an access channel seems to be a "public forum" that the government has opened to expressive activity by the public. The editorial control question becomes more difficult if a nonprofit corporation administers the access channel, and it is arguable that the private entity is free to establish restrictions on use of the access channel. On the other hand, the corporation could be subject to the same first amendment restrictions as the city in terms of editorial control, since the private entity is managing a public facility created by government for public use.

In another effort to stimulate program diversity, the Cable Act by its own terms requires cable operators to make available a certain number "leased access" channels. Persons not affiliated with the cable operator may lease these channels, for a fee set by the cable operator subject to certain restrictions, to provide programming. The number of leased access channels that must be provided varies with the size of the cable system. On a system with fewer than thirty-six channels, no leased access channels are necessary. Systems with between thirty-six and fifty-four channels must generally make ten percent of them available for leasing, while those with more than fifty-five channels must dedicate fifteen percent. As is the case with PEG channels, a cable operator may use the designated leased access channels for other purposes if there is no demand for them. Moreover, a cable operator may not exert editorial control over programming on the leased channels but is permitted to consider program content in establishing the rental fee.

As might be expected, the cable industry is not fond of PEG and leased access, since channels used for these purposes cannot be used to deliver other programming services that cable operators might find preferable—and more profitable. Having successfully challenged similar FCC requirements on nonconstitutional grounds in the *Midwest Video* case, they are now mounting first amendment attacks on the franchises that require access in light of the Supreme Court's decision in *Preferred Communications*. Only a handful of lower courts have considered the issue, and the results to this point have been mixed.

For example, in the *Erie Telecommunications* case discussed previously, a federal district court in Pennsylvania upheld franchise provisions that required the cable operator to dedicate certain channels for public access and to provide production equipment and training for persons wishing to use them. Like the court in the *Century Communications* case reproduced at the beginning of this chapter, the court analyzed the first amendment question in terms of *United States v. O'Brien*. "[G]overnmental entities clearly possess a substantial interest in affording full first amendment protection to the viewers (and listeners) of telecommunication broadcasts," the court said, adding that the access channels were available on a nondiscriminatory basis to any member of the public who wished to communicate a message. Moreover, the requirements "produce[d] only a minimal intrusion on [the cable operator's] exercise of first amendment rights," since seventy-one of the system's eighty-four channels remained under the cable operator's exclusive control. The U.S. Court of Appeals for the Third Circuit affirmed the district court's decision without considering the first amendment question.

A federal district court in California reached the opposite result in *Group W Cable, Inc. v. City of Santa Cruz* (1987). There the court struck down a franchise provision that required the cable operator to devote separate access channels to public, governmental, and institutional users. Relying heavily on the *Tornillo* case, the court likened the first amendment rights of cable operators to those of newspaper publishers rather than to those of broadcasters. "The physical scarcity rationale that may justify the imposition of narrowly drawn access requirements on broadcasters does not apply to this case," the court said, "nor does [the city] assert any rational nexus between its legitimate interest in minimizing cable's disruption of the public domain and its attempt to regulate public access to cable television." Moreover, the court was troubled by the fact that the city had "reserved to itself broad powers" with respect to the access channels.

Obscene and Indecent Programming. In general, the Cable Act prohibits cities from regulating program services provided by cable systems. However, cities may enact and enforce local ordinances prohibiting or regulating obscene programs, and the Cable Act itself makes the transmission of such material on a cable system a federal crime punishable by a fine of up to $10,000, a maximum jail term of two years, or both. These provisions apply only to programming that is legally obscene under the constitutional standards discussed in Chapter 9 and thus unprotected by the first amendment.

As noted previously, attempts by cities and states to prohibit or restrict cable programming that is indecent but not legally obscene have been ruled unconstitutional. As a result, one of the two provisions in the Cable Act dealing with indecent programming is probably invalid. Under the portion of the statute governing leased access channels, a city can prohibit programming not only obscene programming, but also that which, in its judgment, is "lewd, lascivious, filthy, or indecent." The other indecency provision in the act is likely to withstand a first amendment challenge. It simply requires cable operators to provide "lockboxes" or similar devices for a fee to subscribers who desire them. As stated in the act, the purpose of this requirement is to enable a subscriber "to restrict the viewing of programming which is obscene or indecent" by prohibiting access to "a particular cable service during periods selected by that subscriber." Unlike a ban on indecent programming, the lockbox requirement permits subscribers to be protected without infringing the rights of cable operators and those subscribers who wish to view such programming.

"Broad Categories" of Programming. A city may not, as a condition of granting or renewing a franchise, require that a cable operator provide particular video or other information services. If, however, a cable operator offers to provide "broad categories of video programming or other services," that promise is enforceable if it is embodied in the franchise agreement. As a congressional report accompanying the Cable Act points out, "[t]his ability to enforce provisions related to program service assures the franchising authority that commitments made in an arms-length [franchise negotiation] will be met, yet also protects the cable operator from being forced to provide specific programming."

To be enforceable, a franchise agreement with respect to programming must be couched in broad terms. Examples of appropriate categories include children's programming, sports programming, news and public affairs programming, and programming in a foreign language or of interest to a particular minority group. However, a franchise cannot specify that a cable operator must provide a particular service falling within one of these categories, such as the Disney Channel, ESPN, or Cable News Network. Accordingly, a cable operator who voluntarily agrees to provide certain broad categories of programming has wide discretion in determining how to fulfill that promise.

FCC Regulations. Except as expressly provided in the Cable Act, no federal agency may "impose requirements regarding the provision or content of cable services." The act further states, however, that federal regulations governing program content that were on the books when the act was passed may be enforced. Moreover, these rules may be amended, if necessary, so long as the change does not conflict with the act. The principal effect of this provision is to "grandfather" several content-related FCC regulations, the most important of which are the must-carry rule, various rules governing political broadcasting, the fairness doctrine, the sports blackout rule, and the network nonduplication rule. In addition, the Commission recently readopted the syndicated exclusivity rule that it had abolished in 1980.

The must-carry rule in effect when the act was passed was declared unconstitutional in the *Quincy Cable* case, and its successor was similarly voided in the *Century Communications* decision.[7] As a result, cable operators are free to decide which broadcast stations to carry and may devote their channel space to programming services that they think will be most profitable. For example, a cable operator may decide to replace a local television station with a satellite-delivered service such as Cable News Network or a so-called "superstation." To date, however, most operators have been reluctant to drop local stations from their lineups, even though some of the programs broadcast by those stations duplicate those on other stations. According to a 1988 study by the National Cable Television Association, the industry's chief trade group, ninety-eight percent of all broadcast stations that would have qualified under the FCC's must-carry rules were being carried by cable systems.

Despite the rulings in *Quincy Cable* and *Century Communications*, the debate over the must-carry question is very much alive. As the court of appeals observed

---

[7]The *Century Communications* case did not invalidate that portion of the must-carry rule requiring cable operators to inform subscribers about the use of A/B switches to receive broadcast signals not carried by the cable system. Cable operators must also make the switches available to subscribers but are not required to provide them free of charge.

in the latter case, these decisions do not mean that any form of must-carry requirement will fail to pass muster under the first amendment. Though the FCC has apparently given up trying to fashion a must-carry rule that will survive a constitutional challenge, the scene has now shifted to Congress, where legislation has been introduced to link the must-carry requirement with the compulsory license system under the Copyright Act. Under a bill introduced in early 1989, cable companies would be ineligible for the compulsory license discussed in Chapter 4 unless they carried a certain number of local broadcast stations. A cable system with more than twenty-six channels would be required to allocate twenty-five percent of its channels to must-carry signals, while a system with twenty-one to twenty-six channels would have to provide seven channels. If a cable system has twenty or fewer channels, the must-carry provision would not apply.

The "equal opportunities" provision found in Section 315 of the Communications Act applies to cable operators who offer time on their systems to legally qualified candidates for public office. Under FCC rules, this requirement applies only to channels over which the cable operator exerts exclusive control and thus does not apply to channels occupied by broadcast stations or to "access" channels operated by persons not affiliated with the cable operator. Unlike broadcast stations, however, cable systems are not covered by the "reasonable access" requirement of Section 312(a)(7). The statute as initially enacted included cable systems within its definition of broadcasters, but Congress deleted this provision in 1974.

Although the FCC announced in the *Syracuse Peace Council* case that it would no longer enforce the fairness doctrine against broadcasters, the agency did not mention cable operators in the decision. It appears, therefore, that cable systems remain obligated to afford reasonable opportunity for the discussion of conflicting views on controversial issues of public importance on the nonbroadcast channels over which they have exclusive control. However, if the fairness doctrine is indeed unconstitutional with respect to broadcasters, it would also be invalid as to cable operators, whose first amendment rights are apparently "greater" than those of broadcast licensees. Irrespective of the status of the "general" fairness doctrine, its various corollaries—such as the political editorializing and personal attack rules—continue to apply to cable operators as well as to broadcasters.

The sports blackout rule permits an owner of the television rights to a sports event to distribute the program on a regional or national basis but maintain control over its availability on cable in the market where the event takes place, so long as the event is not carried on a local television station. The rule is based on the fear that sports teams would not permit any broadcasting of their games if cable systems could import the signals of distant stations carrying telecasts of those games that had been "blacked out" on local stations. In order to obtain a cable blackout under this rule, the owner of the television rights must give the cable operator notice of the event to be protected. For regularly scheduled games, that notice must be provided no later than the Monday preceding the calendar week during which the blackout is sought. For nonregularly scheduled events, twenty-four hour notice is necessary. There is an exception for National Football League games, however, in light of NFL rules prohibiting local telecasts of games not sold out seventy-two hours in advance. Because information as to a game's status is publicly available, no notice to the cable operator is required.

Under the nonduplication rule, a local television station affiliated with a network may request that a cable operator delete duplicated network programming from a nonlocal network affiliate carried on the system. If a local station makes such a request, the cable operator must delete the duplicated programming from the nonlocal station. Rather than leave the channel "blank," the cable operator is permitted to substitute other programming, usually that of the local station whose programs are duplicated. The rationale for this rule is that the duplicated network fare provides little by way of program diversity and could cause substantial harm to the advertising revenues of the local network affiliates, whose cable audience may watch the same program on another channel. "There is evidence that the importation of duplicating network signals can have severe adverse effects on a station's audience," the FCC has observed. "Loss of audience by affiliates undermines the value of network programming both to the affiliate and to the network."

Enforcement of the nonduplication rule rests with the local broadcast stations, which need not be carried on a cable system in order to invoke its protection. Under a 1988 amendment to the rule, effective January 1, 1990, the extent of nonduplication protection depends on the contractual arrangements between the networks and their affiliates with respect to program exclusivity. As a result, nonduplication is not necessarily limited to the simultaneous broadcasts of network programs by local and nonlocal stations, as was the case under the original rule. If, for example, the contract between a network and its affiliated stations provides for "same day" exclusivity, a cable operator is required, upon receiving a proper request from a local station, to delete the network programs of a nonlocal station, including those aired by the latter at a different time on the same day.

At the same time that it amended the nonduplication rule, the FCC reinstated—in somewhat different form—its syndicated exclusivity rule, which had been dropped in 1980. In reversing its position, the Commission concluded that it had failed in 1980 to appreciate "the role that cable would come to play as a full competitor in the video marketplace" and the adverse impact that the lack of syndicated exclusivity protection would have on the revenues of broadcasters and program suppliers. As a result, the FCC said, the absence of such a rule "work[ed] against the public interest by preventing television viewers from getting the best possible mix of programs across different types of video outlets." Reimposition of the rule would, in the Commission's view, "lead to the development of new [syndicated] programs to take the place of those for which broadcasters [secure] exclusivity."

Effective on January 1, 1990, the new syndicated exclusivity rule operates much like the nonduplication rule discussed above, the principal difference being that it applies to syndicated rather than network programming. All types of syndicated programs are covered, from "M*A*S*H" and "I Love Lucy" reruns to game shows such as "Wheel of Fortune." The nature of the protection depends on the terms of the contract between the local broadcast station and the program supplier, and the broadcaster is required to give the cable operator notice of the contract. If a local broadcast station holds the exclusive rights in that market to a syndicated program, the rule requires the cable operator, on receipt of the appropriate notice, to delete that program broadcast by a nonlocal station whose signal is carried on on the cable system. The operator is allowed to substitute a program from any other television broadcast station for the syndicated program that must be deleted.

THE "NEW TECHNOLOGY"

As mentioned briefly in Chapter 1, the technology that has led to new information delivery systems has also created difficulties with respect to application of the first amendment. Indeed, the *Preferred Communications* decision and subsequent cable cases make plain that resolution of the constitutional questions posed by various forms of media is not an easy task. Our concern here is a somewhat different legal problem, the manner in which some of the new electronic media are to be regulated. The central issue is whether these media that make use of the electromagnetic spectrum—subscription television, multipoint distribution service, direct broadcast satellites, and teletext—are to be considered "broadcasting" and thus subject to the programming restrictions and other rules that govern radio and television licensees. In addition, we will examine different regulatory issues pertaining to two other methods of delivering video programming, home satellite "dishes" and satellite master antenna systems.

Is It Broadcasting, or Isn't It?

Before turning to their status under the Communications Act, it is necessary to determine how the various systems operate. Subscription television (STV) is perhaps the most straightforward, since it involves the use of conventional broadcast frequencies. An STV operator, either a television licensee or a company that leases time from such a licensee, transmits a "scrambled" signal to subscribers who view it via a decoding device attached to their television sets. STV has not proved successful, primarily because only one programming service—such as Home Box Office—can be provided. Moreover, the cost has typically exceeded that of cable systems, which usually offer between twenty and thirty channels as "basic" service. The growth of the cable industry has cut significantly into the STV market, and only a handful of stations remain in operation.

Multipoint distribution service (MDS) works in a fashion similar to STV but uses microwave rather than broadcasting frequencies. MDS operators deliver a signal via microwave to customers who have a special antenna and a device that converts the signal to a normal broadcast frequency for viewing on a unoccupied VHF television channel. Though the range of an MDS transmission is only about twenty-five miles, the service has been used to distribute Home Box Office and similar video programming to hotels, apartment buildings, and single-family homes in areas not served by cable. In some cities, multichannel multipoint distribution service (MMDS) enables subscribers to receive several channels, usually "superstations" and cable networks such as ESPN and CNN, in this manner.

Perhaps the most promising new delivery system is the direct broadcast satellite (DBS). From geostationary orbit several thousand miles above the earth, these high-powered satellites can transmit television signals directly to individual homes equipped with small, inexpensive receivers. While a conventional television station can reach only a small area with its signal, a station using DBS technology could blanket the entire continental United States. Thus far, the unavailability of satellites with sufficient power has hampered the development of DBS, and in late 1988 the FCC extended until December 1992 the deadline for two companies holding DBS permits to complete construction of their systems and begin operations. DBS differs from home satellite dishes (HSD) used to receive programming delivered by satellite to cable systems and to television stations affiliated with the networks. Regulations affecting HSD are discussed in the following section.

Teletext, as its name implies, is information in textual form transmitted via a portion of a broadcast signal known as a "vertical blanking interval," which is ordinarily invisible. Because the broadcasting of a television picture does not require use of the VBI, this "blank space" can be devoted to the transmission of additional information without interfering with regular programming. A viewer wishing to receive teletext must secure a decoder and a device that enables him to select "pages" of information for display on the television screen. Teletext can also be sent by other video delivery systems, such as DBS, MDS, or cable. A related service, known as videotext, is a two-way "interactive" system that allows a subscriber to send as well as receive information. Videotext requires use of telephone lines or cable.

Obviously, none of these systems was in existence in 1934 when the Communications Act was passed, and the FCC has been left with the task of fitting each into the statutory framework. In general, the Act distinguishes between entities engaged in broadcasting and those providing common carrier services. (Unlike broadcasters, common carriers do not send their own messages but simply transmit those of others in a nondiscriminatory manner without exercising any control over content.) If a delivery system does not fall into one category or the other, the FCC's regulatory authority is limited. Recall, for example, that prior to the enactment of the Cable Communications Policy Act the Commission's authority over cable hinged on its power to regulate matters "reasonably ancillary" to broadcasting. Because cable could not be labeled either a broadcast or common carrier service, a new statute was necessary to clarify the extent of the FCC's jurisdiction over the medium. Unfortunately, no statutory changes have been made with respect to the four new media discussed above. As a result, it has fallen to the FCC and the courts to determine how each is to be treated under the Communications Act.

One of the delivery systems, MDS, has posed few problems in this regard. As a "point-to-point" microwave service, it has long been regulated by the FCC as a common carrier and is thus not subject to the various regulations that apply to broadcasters. Trouble arose, however, when MDS operators began offering video programming in much the same manner as STV systems. Because STV was considered a form of broadcasting, it was subject to the various programming rules applicable to broadcast stations, while MDS was not. The Commission remedied this anamolous situation in *In re Subscription Video* (1987) by reclassifying STV as a nonbroadcast service. Under the FCC's new approach, the question is whether a particular service is meant to be received by the general public or by individual subscribers. Only the former is considered broadcasting for regulatory purposes. Consequently, STV is not a broadcast service, since it is not receivable without special antennae and decoding equipment supplied by the STV operator as part of the subscription agreement.

The U.S. Court of Appeals for the District of Columbia Circuit upheld this ruling, which also classified subscription DBS as a nonbroadcast service, in *National Association for Better Broadcasting v. Federal Communications Commission* (1988). Though the court noted that the Communications Act is ambiguous as to the definition of "broadcasting," it concluded that the FCC's interpretation was reasonable. Chief Judge Patricia Wald dissented, finding "no basis for the Commission's wholesale reclassification of [STV and DBS] as nonbroadcasting." Quoting former FCC Commissioner Henry Rivera, she argued that a new service that "looks like broadcasting, smells like broadcasting, tastes like broadcasting, [and] has all the benefits of broadcasting" should be regulated like broadcasting, even though it did not exist when the Communications Act was passed.

The FCC did not specifically consider teletext in *Subscription Video*, but the definitional approach adopted in that case presumably means that teletext delivered by television stations on a subscription basis would not be regulated as a broadcasting service. With respect to non-subscription teletext, the Commission had previously determined in *In re Transmission of Teletext* (1983) that the service would be exempt from content restrictions such as the fairness doctrine, the equal opportunities requirement of Section 315, and the "reasonable access" rule for federal candidates established by Section 312(a)(7). In the 1986 *Telecommunications Research and Action Center* case discussed previously, the U.S. Court of Appeals for the District of Columbia Circuit affirmed this decision as to the fairness doctrine and Section 312(a)(7) but ruled that Section 315 was applicable.

Other Regulatory Issues

Particularly in rural areas beyond the reach of cable service, receive-only satellite earth stations have become increasingly common since 1979, when the FCC dropped a requirement that they be licensed. With such a home satellite dish (HSD), a viewer has access to hundreds of signals being distributed by communications satellites in geostationary orbit above the earth. Among those signals are programming services delivered to cable systems, such as Home Box Office and the "superstations," network "feeds" of programs to their affiliate stations, and foreign programming.

Two recent federal statutes come into play with respect to HSD. First, under a provision added to the Communications Act in 1984, an HSD owner can lawfully receive unscrambled "satellite cable programming" for private viewing if a marketing system has not been established for the particular programming service. For purposes of the statute, "satellite cable programming" is defined as video programming delivered by satellite to cable operators for retransmission to cable subscribers. If a marketing system has been established, the HSD owner must obtain authorization for private viewing under that system. However, at this point none of the programming services that do not scramble their signals have such marketing plans in place.

Because the statute makes lawful only the reception of unscrambled signals, many satellite signals are now scrambled.[8] To receive these signals, an HSD owner must purchase a decoding device and pay a monthly fee for each service. Because one type of decoder has emerged as the industry standard, an HSD owner need only purchase one such device to receive the various satellite-delivered services. According to a 1988 FCC report, rates for program packages are comparable to or below cable subscriber rates for the same services. An HSD owner who circumvents the scrambling process—by using a black market decoder and not paying the fees, for example—is in violation of the prohibition against unauthorized reception. As amended in 1988, the statute provides for criminal penalties ranging from a $2,000 fine and six months in jail if no commercial benefit is involved to a $50,000 fine and two years imprisonment if the unauthorized reception is for purposes of financial gain or commercial advantage. A person harmed by the violation may also recover civil damages.

Second, the Satellite Home Viewer Act of 1988 deals with HSD receipt of so-called "superstations," that is, television stations whose signals have been "uplinked" by an independent common carrier and retransmitted via satellite. Initially, superstations were independent television stations such as WTBS in Atlanta and WGN in Chicago, but recently the signals of network affiliates have also been

---

[8]Under a 1988 amendment to the Communications Act, PBS programs delivered by satellite to member stations cannot be scrambled if they are "intended for public viewing by retransmission by television broadcast stations. . . ."

available via satellite. Under 1988 legislation, the signals of independent superstations such as WTBS and WGN can be distributed to any dish owner, but signals of network affiliates can be delivered only to households in "white areas" where viewers cannot pick up network signals with a conventional antenna. The FCC has estimated that there are from 800,000 to one million households in such areas. As discussed in Chapter 4, the act also establishes a compulsory licensing scheme by which the carriers that distribute the signals of television stations pay copyright royalties based on the number of persons who receive those signals.

The FCC has generally taken a "hands-off" attitude with respect to satellite programming. For example, the Commission has decided that the transmission of such programming is not "broadcasting" for regulatory purposes; consequently, the various rules governing broadcasters are inapplicable. In addition, the agency has declined to set standards for the "scrambling" of satellite signals or to regulate rates for programming delivered in this manner. Under the Satellite Home Viewer Act, however, the FCC is required to examine the question of whether a uniform scrambling standard is necessary and to consider adopting a syndicated exclusivity rule, similar to that applicable in the cable context, to govern syndicated programs on television stations whose signals are delivered via satellite to HSD owners.

A satellite master antenna system (SMATV) works much like cable but serves only a single building, such as a hotel, or a multiple-unit dwelling under common ownership, such as an apartment complex. The SMATV operator simply sets up one or more satellite "dishes" on top of the building and connects them by wire or cable to each individual unit. No local franchise is required, since the operator does not make use of the public right-of-way. In fact, the courts have upheld an FCC ruling that state and local governments have no authority to regulate SMATV systems. Moreover, under the Cable Communications Policy Act, these systems are also exempt from federal cable regulations, including those that affect programming.

PROBLEMS

1. Section 309 of the Communications Act authorizes the FCC to use lotteries in connection with broadcast licensing, and the Commission has done so with respect to low-power television. *See* 47 C.F.R. §§1.1601-1.1623 (1988). Moreover, the FCC has proposed a lottery system for awarding new licenses for full-power television stations and AM and FM radio stations. *See Selection from Among Competing Applicants for New AM, FM, and Television Stations by Random Selection,* 4 F.C.C. Rcd. 2256 (1989). Is this a wise idea? Is a lottery preferable to the "comparative" licensing process described in the text? How should the lottery method be administered? For example, should all applicants who meet certain minimum qualifications (financial, technical, etc.) be placed in a pool, with the one whose name is drawn being granted the license? Or should the lottery be used as a "tie-breaking" device when it appears that two or more applicants are on equal footing in terms of comparative licensing criteria? Should the lottery be weighted to take into account particular matters now considered in the comparative licensing process, such as policies favoring minority ownership of broadcast stations and diversification of media ownership?

2. Under the present licensing scheme, broadcast licensees pay nothing for the privilege of using the airwaves. Is this sound policy? With respect to other public resources, the federal government simply sells the right to exploit those resources to the highest bidder. For example, oil companies that want to drill on land owned by the federal government participate in an auction process, with the highest bidder obtaining the exploration rights.

Why not establish such an auction for broadcast licenses, with the proceeds going to support public broadcasting? *See* Kenneth Robinson, "Some Thoughts on Broadcasting Reform," 7 *Regulation* 17 (May/June 1983); Milton Mueller, "Spectrum Fees vs. Spectrum Liberation," 7 *Regulation* 21 (May/June 1983).

3. To what extent should the conduct of a parent company be attributed to its broadcasting subsidiary in terms of applying the "character" requirement for licensees? If, for instance, the parent company has been convicted of violating the antitrust laws, is the subsidiary tainted to the extent that it is no longer fit to hold a license? *See RKO General, Inc. v. Federal Communications Commission*, 670 F.2d 215 (D.C. Cir. 1981), *cert. denied*, 457 U.S. 1119 (1982).

4. Consider whether the following would give rise to the obligation to present opposing viewpoints under the fairness doctrine:
   a. A character in a network situation comedy becomes pregnant and ponders whether to have an abortion. "We women finally have the right to decide what we can do with our own bodies," she tells her husband. "And it's as simple as going to the dentist." The couple agrees that they are "too old" to have a baby and agree that an abortion is the "right thing." *See In re Diocesan Union of Holy Name Societies*, 41 F.C.C.2d 297 (1973).
   b. Several ethnic jokes are told by participants in a comedy skit on an entertainment program. Would your answer change if a person being interviewed on a newscast or talk show told jokes of this type? *See Polish American Congress v. Federal Communications Commission*, 520 F.2d 1248 (7th Cir. 1975), *cert. denied*, 424 U.S. 927 (1976); *In re William Hughes*, 69 F.C.C.2d 952 (1978).
   c. A documentary, "In Search of Noah's Ark," not only examines an explorer's efforts to locate the vessel, but also states as fact that the ark actually exists and appears to misstate the views of historians and archaeologists on the issue. *See In re Religion & Ethics Institute, Inc.*, 42 P&F Radio Reg.2d 1657 (1978).
   d. A San Francisco television station carries various "PTL Club" programs advocating the defeat of legislation designed to protect homosexuals from discrimination with regard to housing and employment. Is it significant that San Francisco has a substantial homosexual population? Does it matter that the legislation discussed on the program was pending in other states? *See In re Council on Religion and the Homosexual*, 68 F.C.C.2d 1500 (1978).

5. In September 1984, ABC reported allegations on its evening news program that the Central Intelligence Agency had been involved in a plot to kill an American citizen. Two months later, the network reported that efforts to prove the charges had failed and that there was "no reason to doubt" the agency's denial. The CIA filed a fairness doctrine complaint with the FCC, as did a private group, the American Legal Foundation. What is the "controversial issue of public importance" here? Should government agencies such as the CIA be permitted to file fairness doctrine complaints? Would such a practice have a chilling effect on broadcast journalism? *See In re Central Intelligence Agency*, 58 P&F Radio Reg.2d 1544 (1985), *appeal dismissed*, *American Legal Foundation v. Federal Communications Commission*, 808 F.2d 84 (D.C. Cir. 1987).

6. Is it possible to reconcile the FCC's abolition of the fairness doctrine with its stepped-up enforcement of the indecency statute? If, as the Commission contends, the fairness doctrine violates the first amendment because it imposes on the broadcast media content-based restrictions that cannot be imposed on the print media, why doesn't the same reasoning lead to the conclusion that the indecency statute is unconstitutional? Consider carefully Justice Stevens' opinion in the *Pacifica* case in connection with this question.

7. In light of the 1988 Presidential campaign, which some commentators called the most negative and least enlightening in recent memory, Congress is likely to be presented with proposed legislation addressing the problem. Suppose that one such bill, the "Clean Campaign Act," requires political candidates who attack their opponents in radio or television commercials to appear personally in such advertisements. A broadcaster who violates this provision (e.g., by running an ad in which supporters or political action committees attack a candidate) must provide—at no cost—an equal amount of air time in a similar time slot to the particular opponent who was the target of the attack. Section 315 would continue to apply if the candidate personally delivered the attack. In addition, a candidate would be entitled to free response time if his opponent were endorsed by a political action committee. Would this bill be constitutional? What about a bill that would prohibit paid political advertisements and require broadcasters to provide free time in specified amounts to all candidates during the period immediately preceding the election? Would your analysis change if either of these bills were made applicable to cable operators in addition to broadcasters?

8. Another controversy that has surfaced with respect to presidential elections is the insistence of network news departments to "project" the outcome and report that projection before the polls close in western states. Suppose that Congress passed a statute prohibiting any broadcast news organization from estimating the result of a federal election prior to the closing of the polls. If, for example, a statewide race for the U.S. Senate were involved, a station could not announce its projection until the polls had closed across the state. In a presidential election, the networks would have to wait until the polls had closed in all states. Would such a statute be constitutional? What about a statute mandating a uniform national poll closing time in presidential elections?

9. Prior to the Republican National Convention in 1988 but after he had cinched his party's presidential nomination, Vice President George Bush threw out the "first ball" at major league baseball's all-star game. The ceremonial pitch was telecast live as part of network coverage of the game. Did this appearance by Mr. Bush, who played college baseball at Yale, have any implications under Section 315(a)? See In re NBC, 37 F.C.C.2d 678 (1972).

10. A television station planned three programs featuring the 1988 Republican and Democratic presidential candidates. All would be taped in the studio for later broadcast, and the candidates would not appear together. The first was a one-hour program in which the two candidates would be alloted thirty minutes each to set forth their positions. In the second program, a journalist would conduct separate interviews with the candidates. The third program, structured in the same manner as the first, would provide the candidates an opportunity for rebuttal. Seeking a ruling from the FCC that Section 315 did not apply, the station argued that the first and third programs were no different from debates and thus fell within the "spot news" exemption, while the second program was covered by the "news interview" exemption. What result? Why? See King Broadcasting Co. v. Federal Communications Commission, 860 F.2d 465 (D.C. Cir. 1988).

11. Suppose that a comedian who appeared regularly on a weekly television program desired to run for political office. Would his appearances on the show trigger Section 315? If so, the network would probably not permit him to perform, thereby forcing him to give up his means of earning a living in order to run for public office. Should Section 315 be interpreted to produce such a harsh result? What if a general assignments reporter for a television station decided to seek office? Is the journalist's situation any different from that of the comedian? Can it be argued that any broadcast on which the reporter appeared falls within one of the "news" exemptions to Section 315? See Paulsen v. Federal

Communications Commission, 491 F.2d 887 (9th Cir. 1974); *Branch v. Federal Communications Commission,* 824 F.2d 37 (D.C. Cir. 1987), *cert. denied,* 108 S.Ct. 1220 (1988).

12. The publisher of a concededly pornographic magazine announced plans to run for President and revealed a campaign strategy that included television commercials featuring sexually explicit scenes from X-rated movies. Assuming that the publisher became a "legally qualified" candidate, would television stations be required to broadcast the commercials under Section 315, even though they are indecent or perhaps even legally obscene? Suppose that the commercials did not include sexually explicit footage but instead featured the publisher criticizing his opponents as a "crazy bunch of cocksuckers" who are "all full of shit"? *Cf. In re Julian Bond,* 69 F.C.C.2d 943 (1978).

13. Reconsider, in light of this chapter, the questions posed in Problem 3 of Chapter 1. In terms of the FCC's authority to deal with radio airplay of "offensive" records, must the lyrics be sexual in nature? Or may the FCC take action against stations that play records that glorify drugs or violence? What sort of action might the FCC take? *See Yale Broadcasting Co. v. Federal Communications Commission,* 478 F.2d 594 (D.C. Cir.), *cert. denied,* 414 U.S. 914 (1973).

14. In late 1988, an NBC miniseries entitled "Favorite Son" featured a female character who managed to sleep with almost everyone else in the film, and the steamy sex scenes left little to the imagination. For example, the actress was once shown, in bra and panties, seducing a young FBI agent with promises of bondage. In another revealing scene, she disrobed behind see-through curtains that hardly concealed her nudity. "Favorite Son" was not an isolated case of titillating programming. *See generally* "Where Are the Censors?" *Time* (December 12, 1988), p. 95. Does the current FCC indecency policy reach programs of this type?

15. Another recent development in television programming has been the trashy talk show. The "Oprah Winfrey Show," for example, has examined such topics as subservient women, infidelity, sexual "threesomes," and paternity fights. The "Geraldo" program, featuring former ABC newsman Geraldo Rivera, has dealt with transsexuals and their families, teen prostitutes, mud-wrestling women, male strippers, and Charles Manson. Mr. Rivera made the cover of *Newsweek* after his nose was broken during a brawl that erupted during the taping of a program about "hatemongers." Is it mere coincidence that shows of this type have emerged since the FCC largely deregulated television and radio in favor of a "marketplace" approach? Do these programs, as some critics charge, take away air time that could be devoted to issues of public importance? *See* Tom Shales, "Where Talk Is Cheap and the Bucks Are Big," *Washington Post Weekly Edition* (November 28, 1988), p. 11.

16. Which of the following, if any, would be considered "distortion" that could result in FCC sanctions?

    a. The owner of a television station has a financial interest in a business venture being investigated by a federal regulatory agency. Taken as a whole, the station's news coverage of the investigation is critical of the agency and suggests that the whole matter is politically motivated. There is no mention of the fact that the station owner is an investor in the business. Would your answer be any different if editorials rather than news stories were involved? *See In re Gross Telecasting, Inc.,* 14 F.C.C.2d 239 (1968); *In re NBC,* 14 F.C.C.2d 713 (1968); *In re Clifford H. Wilmath,* 43 F.C.C.2d 1266 (1973).

    b. The owner of a radio station tells his news staff to give extensive—and favorable—coverage to one candidate for the U.S. Senate and to air only negative stories about his opponent. Suppose that he also advises the staff on a regular basis of potentially newsworthy activities of local businesses that regularly purchase advertising time on the station. *See In re Tri-State Broadcasting Co.,* 59 F.C.C.2d 1240 (1976); *In re Star Stations of Indiana, Inc.,* 51 F.C.C.2d 95 (1975).

c. To illustrate wire service reports about the day's developments in the presidential campaign and the war in the Middle East, a television station uses videotape several days old without indicating to viewers that the events depicted had taken place earlier. *See In re WPIX, Inc.,* 68 F.C.C.2d 381 (1978).

d. A television reporter induces several students at a nearby university to hold a "marijuana party" so that he can film the affair for use in connection with a story about drugs. *See In re WBBM-TV,* 18 F.C.C.2d 124 (1969).

e. In editing an interview for a news program, a television journalist splices the videotape so that his subject's answer to one question appears as a response to a different question. *See In re "The Selling of the Pentagon,"* 30 F.C.C.2d 150 (1971).

17. Although the Cable Communications Policy Act of 1984 settled many important questions concerning the regulation of cable television, other issues remain unresolved. Consider the following:

a. The Act permits cities to own and operate cable systems, though management authority must be placed in the hands of an independent board or commission. Suppose that a city, dissatisfied with the service provided by the incumbent cable operator, decides to offer a competing cable service. Would such action violate the first amendment rights of the incumbent? *See Warner Cable Communications, Inc. v. City of Niceville,* No. PCA 85-4414-RV (N.D. Fla. 1988); *City of Issaquah v. Teleprompter Corp.,* 611 P.2d 741 (Wash. 1980). *Cf. PAM News Corp. v. Butz,* 514 F.2d 272 (D.C. Cir. 1975).

b. Does the Act's prohibition on rate regulation mean that a cable operator's voluntary agreement to "freeze" rates for a given period of time (e.g., the first two years of the franchise) is unenforceable? *See Nashoba Communications Limited Partnership v. Town of Danvers,* 703 F. Supp. 161 (D. Mass. 1988); *City of Burlington v. Mountain Cable Co.,* 559 A.2d 153 (Vt. 1988).

c. Despite the fact that the Act expressly permits municipalities to impose franchise fees on cable systems, is this portion of the statute constitutional in light of the taxation cases discussed in Chapter 12? *See Erie Telecommunications, Inc. v. City of Erie,* 659 F. Supp. 580 (W.D. Pa. 1987), *aff'd,* 853 F.2d 1084 (3d Cir. 1988); *Century Federal, Inc. v. City of Palo Alto,* 710 F. Supp. 1559 (N.D. Cal. 1988); Henry Geller, Alan Ciamporcero, and Donna Lampert, "The Cable Franchise Fee and the First Amendment, 39 *Federal Communications Law Journal* 1 (1987).

18. A multi-part series entitled "Race and Reason" has been shown on the public access channels of about two dozen cable systems around the country. Produced by the California-based White Aryan Resistance, the program sparked protests in several cities, including Cincinnati, Ohio, and Pocatello, Idaho. When a Ku Klux Klan group sought to cablecast the program over a public access channel in Kansas City, Missouri, the city council voted to eliminate the access channel altogether. Is the council's action constitutional? Could the city or the group charged with operating the channel have denied access to the Klan while permitting others to use the it? *See Missouri Knights of the Ku Klux Klan v. Kansas City,* 1989 U.S. Dist. Lexis 7029 (W.D. Mo. 1989); David A. Kaplan, "Is the Klan Entitled to Public Access?" *New York Times* (July 31, 1988), p. 24A.

19. Part of the controversy surrounding television programs and advertisements aimed at children has been the practice of basing cartoon shows on popular toys. For example, a program entitled "He-Man and the Masters of the Universe" was built around a line of fantasy-action figures created and manufactured by Mattel, Inc. Should shows of this

type, which are arguably little more than lengthy toy commercials, be prohibited or restricted by the FCC? Do these shows fall within existing the prohibition against children's programs that do not adequately separate program content from commercial material? Does it matter whether the toy or the program was developed first? A related question concerns "high tech" toys that interact with specific children's programs. Such toys include "action figures" that can be turned on by an inaudible signal in a show's sound track. Should this product tie-in be prohibited? Is it any more "commercial" than the practice described above? To what extent would FCC regulations of this type be affected by the commercial speech doctrine discussed in Chapter 11? *See Revision of Programming and Commercialization Policies*, 2 F.C.C. Rcd. 6822 (1987); *In re Action for Children's Television*, 58 P&F Radio Reg.2d 61 (1985); *Children's Television Report & Policy Statement*, 50 F.C.C.2d 1 (1974).

20. As the use of home satellite dishes became more widespread, many cities adopted zoning ordinances to regulate their placement. Under FCC rules, however, these ordinances are permissible only if they "[h]ave a reasonable and clearly defined health, safety or aesthetic objective" and "[d]o not operate to impose unreasonable limitations on or prevent reception of satellite delivered signals. . . ." 47 C.F.R. § 25.104. In light of this rule, can a city ban all satellite dishes from rooftops and limit them to back yards? Require that they be screened from the view of neighbors? Does it matter that a homeowner who complies with these requirements would be able to receive signals from some but not all of the various satellites? *See Van Meter v. Township of Maplewood*, 696 F. Supp. 1024 (D.N.J. 1988); *Preemption of Local Zoning and Other Regulation of Receive-Only Satellite Earth Stations*, 51 *Federal Register* 5519 (February 14, 1986).

21. Most television stations regularly carry religious broadcasts, and some are devoted almost exclusively to religious programming. "Televangelists" like Jerry Falwell, Pat Robertson, and Jimmy Swaggert have become household names, and the financial stakes are high. In 1984, for example, Jimmy Swaggert had an operating budget of $75 million and received more than $1 million in contributions each week. To what extent can—or should—the FCC regulate religious broadcasting? For example, could the agency revoke a license held by a religious organization because of questionable on-the-air fundraising practices? Because the station's religious programs featured faith healing? Does the first amendment protection for the "free exercise" of religion place limits on the broad authority granted the Commission by the Communications Act? *See In re Faith Center, Inc.*, 82 F.C.C.2d 1 (1980), *aff'd without opinion*, 679 F.2d 261 (D.C. Cir. 1982), *cert. denied*, 459 U.S. 1203 (1983); *In re PTL of Heritage Village Church & Missionary Fellowship, Inc.*, 71 F.C.C.2d 324 (1979); *In re KCOP Television, Inc.*, 59 F.C.C.2d 1321 (1976). *See generally* Ashton R. Hardy and Lawrence W. Secrest III, "Religious Freedom and the Federal Communications Commission," 16 *Valparaiso University Law Review* 57 (1981); Comment, "Televangelism and the Federal Communications Commission: To Regulate or Retreat," 91 *Dickinson Law Review* 553 (1986).

22. Since 1952, Congress has held nearly two dozen hearings exploring the harmful effect of television violence on children. Considerable legislative support emerged in 1989 for a bill that would grant broadcasters, cable operators, and program producers a three-year exemption from the antitrust laws to enable them to consider voluntary programming guidelines. Does this approach raise first amendment problems? Can it be argued, for example, that the bill is a thinly veiled threat rather than a measure aimed at facilitating a voluntary solution? *Cf. Writers Guild of America, West, Inc. v. Federal Communications Commission*, 423 F. Supp. 1064 (C.D. Cal. 1976), *vacated*, 609 F.2d 355 (9th Cir. 1979), *cert. denied*, 449 U.S. 824 (1980).

CHAPTER
11
ADVERTISING AND COMMERCIAL SPEECH

Posadas de Puerto Rico Associates v. Tourism Co. of Puerto Rico, 478 U.S. 328 (1986).

JUSTICE REHNQUIST delivered the opinion of the Court.

In this case we address the facial constitutionality of a Puerto Rico statute and regulations restricting advertising of casino gambling aimed at the residents of Puerto Rico. * * * In 1948, the Puerto Rico Legislature legalized certain forms of casino gambling. The Games of Chance Act of 1948 . . . authorized the playing of roulette, dice, and card games in licensed "gambling rooms." Bingo and slot machines were later added to the list of authorized games. The legislature's intent was . . . "to contribute to the development of tourism. . . ." The Act also provided that "[n]o gambling room shall be permitted to advertise or otherwise offer their facilities to the public of Puerto Rico."

The Act authorized the Economic Develop-

ment Administration of Puerto Rico to issue and enforce regulations implementing the various provisions of the Act. Appellee Tourism Company of Puerto Rico, a public corporation, assumed the regulatory powers of the Economic Development Administration under the Act in 1970. The two regulations at issue in this case were originally issued in 1957 for the purpose of implementing the advertising restrictions contained in . . . the Act. Regulation 76-218 basically reiterates the language of [the Act]. Regulation 76a.-1(7), as amended in 1971, provides in pertinent part:

"No concessionaire, nor his agent or employee is authorized to advertise the gambling parlors to the public in Puerto Rico. The advertising of our games of chance is hereby authorized through newspapers, magazines, radio, television and other publicity media outside Puerto Rico subject to the prior editing and approval by the Tourism Development Company of the advertisement to be submitted in draft to the Company."

In 1975, appellant Posadas de Puerto Rico Associates . . . obtained a franchise to operate a gambling casino and began doing business under the name Condado Holiday Inn Hotel and Sands Casino. In 1978, appellant was twice fined by the Tourism Company for violating the advertising restrictions in the Act and implementing regulations. Appellant protested the fines in a series of letters to the Tourism Company. On February 16, 1979, the Tourism Company issued to all casino franchise holders a memorandum setting forth the following interpretation of the advertising restrictions:

"This prohibition includes the use of the word 'casino' in matchbooks, lighters, envelopes, inter-office and/or external correspondence, invoices, napkins, brochures, menus, elevators, glasses, plates, lobbies, banners, flyers, paper holders, pencils, telephone books, directories, bulletin boards or in any hotel dependency or object which may be accessible to the public in Puerto Rico."

Pursuant to this administrative interpretation, the Tourism Company assessed additional fines against appellant. The Tourism Company ordered appellant to pay the outstanding total of $1,500 in fines by March 18, 1979, or its gambling franchise would not be renewed. Appellant continued to protest the fines, but ultimately paid them without seeking judicial review of the decision of the Tourism Company. In July 1981, appellant was again fined for violating the advertising restrictions. Faced with another threatened nonrenewal of its gambling franchise, appellant paid the $500 fine under protest.

Appellant then filed a declaratory judgment action against the Tourism Company in the Superior Court of Puerto Rico, San Juan Section, seeking a declaration that the Act and implementing regulations, both facially and as applied by the Tourism Company, violated appellant's commercial speech rights under the United States Constitution. The Puerto Rico Secretary of Justice appeared for the purpose of defending the constitutionality of the statute and regulations. After a trial, the Superior Court held that "[t]he administrative

interpretation and application has been capricious, arbitrary, erroneous and unreasonable, and has produced absurd results which are contrary to law." The court therefore determined that it must "override the regulatory deficiency to save the constitutionality of the statute." The court reviewed the history of casino gambling in Puerto Rico and concluded:

"We assume that the legislator was worried about the participation of the residents of Puerto Rico on what on that date constituted an experiment. . . . Therefore, he prohibited the gaming rooms from announcing themselves or offering themselves to the public—which we reasonably infer are the *bona fide* residents of Puerto Rico. . . . [W]hat the legislator foresaw and prohibited was the invitation to play at the casinos through publicity campaigns or advertising in Puerto Rico addressed to the resident of Puerto Rico. He wanted to protect him."

Based on this view of the legislature's intent, the court issued a narrowing construction of the statute, declaring that "the only advertisement prohibited by law originally is that which is contracted with an advertising agency, for consideration, to attract the resident to bet at the dice, card, roulette and bingo tables." The court also issued the following narrowing construction of Regulation 76a-1(7):

"Advertisements of the casinos in Puerto Rico are prohibited in the local publicity media addressed to inviting the residents of Puerto Rico to visit the casinos. * * * We hereby allow, within the jurisdiction of Puerto Rico, advertising by the casinos addressed to tourists, provided they do not invite the residents of Puerto Rico to visit the casino, even though said announcements may incidentally reach the hands of a resident. Within the ads of casinos allowed by this regulation figure, for illustrative purposes only, advertising distributed or placed in landed airplanes or cruise ships in jurisdictional waters and in restricted areas to travelers only in the international airport and the docks where tourist cruise ships arrive since the principal objective of said announcements is to make the tourist in transit through Puerto Rico aware of the availability of the games of chance as a tourist amenity; the ads of casinos in magazines for distribution primarily in Puerto Rico to the tourist, including the official guide of the Tourism Company 'Que Pasa in Puerto Rico' and any other tourist facility guide in Puerto Rico, even though said magazines may be available to the residents and in movies, television, radio, newspapers and trade magazines which may be published, taped, or filmed in the exterior for tourism promotion in the exterior even though they may be exposed or incidentally circulated in Puerto Rico. For example: an advertisement in the *New York Times*, an advertisement in CBS which reaches us through Cable TV, whose main objective is to reach the potential tourist.

"We hereby authorize advertising in the mass communication media of the country, where the trade name of the hotel is used even though it may contain a reference to the casino provided that the word casino is never used alone nor specified. Among the announcements allowed, by way of illustration, are the use of the trade name with which the hotel is identified for the promotion of special vacation packages and activities at the hotel, in invitations, 'billboards,' bulletins and programs or activities sponsored by the hotel. The use of the trade name, including the reference to the casino, is also allowed in the hotel's facade, provided the word 'casino' does not exceed in proportion the size of the rest of the name, and the utilization of lights and colors will be allowed if the rest of the laws regarding this application are complied with; and in the menus, napkins, glasses, tableware, glassware and other items used within the hotel, as well as in calling cards, envelopes and letterheads of the hotel and any other use which constitutes a means of identification.

"The direct promotion of the casinos within the premises of the hotels is allowed. In-house guests and clients may receive any type of information and promotion regarding the location of the casino, its schedule and the procedure of the games as well as magazines, souvenirs, stirrers, matchboxes, cards, dice, chips, T-shirts, hats, photographs, postcards and similar items used by the tourism centers of the world.

"Since a *clausus* enumeration of this regulation is unforeseeable, any other situation or incident relating to the legal restriction must be measured in light of the public policy of promoting tourism. If the object of the advertisement is the tourist, it passes legal scrutiny."

The court entered judgment declaring that appellant's constitutional rights had been violated by the Tourism Company's past applica-

tion of the advertising restrictions, but that the restrictions were not facially unconstitutional and could be sustained, as "modified by the guidelines issued by this Court on this date."

The Supreme Court of Puerto Rico dismissed appellant's appeal of the Superior Court's decision on the ground that it "d[id] not present a substantial constitutional question." * * * One judge dissented. * * * The Supreme Court's dismissal of appellant's appeal . . . constituted a decision on the merits in favor of the validity of the challenged statute and regulations. * * *

Because this case involves the restriction of pure commercial speech which does "no more than propose a commercial transaction," *Virginia State Board of Pharmacy v. Virginia Citizens Consumer Council, Inc.* (1976),[1] our First Amendment analysis is guided by the general principles identified in *Central Hudson Gas & Electric Corp. v. Public Service Comm'n* (1980). Under *Central Hudson*, commercial speech receives a limited form of First Amendment protection so long as it concerns a lawful activity and is not misleading or fraudulent. Once it is determined that the First Amendment applies to the issue, then the speech may be restricted only if the government's interst in doing so is substantial, the restrictions directly advance the government's asserted interest, and the restrictions are no more extensive than necessary to serve that interest.

The particular kind of commercial speech at issue here, namely, advertising of casino gambling aimed at the residents of Puerto Rico, concerns a lawful activity and is not misleading or fraudulent, at least in the abstract. We must therefore proceed to the three remaining steps of the *Central Hudson* analysis in order to determine whether Puerto Ri-

---

[1]The narrowing construction of the statute and regulations announced by the Superior Court effectively ensure that the advertising restrictions cannot be used to inhibit either the freedom of the press in Puerto Rico to report on any aspect of casino gambling, or the freedom of anyone, including casino owners, to comment publicly on such matters as legislation relating to casino gambling. * * *

co's advertising restrictions run afoul of the First Amendment. The first of these three steps involves an assessment of the strength of the government's interest in restricting the speech. The interest at stake in this case, as determined by the Superior Court, is the reduction of demand for casino gambling by the residents of Puerto Rico. * * * The Tourism Company's brief before this Court explains the legislature's belief that "[e]xcessive casino gambling among local residents . . . would produce serious harmful effects on the health, safety and welfare of the Puerto Rican citizens, such as the disruption of moral and cultural patterns, the increase in local crime, the fostering of prostitution, the development of corruption, and the infiltration of organized crime." These are some of the very same concerns, of course, that have motivated the vast majority of the 50 States to prohibit casino gambling. We have no difficulty in concluding that the Puerto Rico Legislature's interest in the health, safety, and welfare of its citizens constitutes a "substantial" governmental interest.

The last two steps of the *Central Hudson* analysis basically involve a consideration of the "fit" between the legislature's ends and the means chosen to accomplish those ends. Step three asks the question whether the challenged restrictions on commercial speech "directly advance" the government's asserted interest. In the instant case, the answer to this question is clearly "yes." The Puerto Rico Legislature obviously believed . . . that advertising of casino gambling aimed at the residents of Puerto Rico would serve to increase the demand for the product advertised. We think the legislature's belief is a reasonable one, and the fact that appellant has chosen to litigate this case all the way to this Court indicates that appellant shares the legislature's views. * * *

Appellant argues, however, that the challenged advertising restrictions are underinclusive because other kinds of gambling such as horse racing, cockfighting, and the lottery may be advertised to the residents of Puerto Rico. Appellant's argument is misplaced for two reasons. First, whether other kinds of gambling are advertised in Puerto Rico or not, the restrictions on advertising of casino gambling "directly advance" the legislature's interest in reducing demand for games of chance. * * * Second, the legislature's interest, as previously identified, is not necessarily to reduce demand for all games of chance, but to reduce demand for casino gambling. According to the Superior Court, horse racing, cockfighting, "picas," or small games of chance at fiestas, and the lottery "have been traditionally part of the Puerto Rican's roots," so that "the legislator could have been more flexible than in authorizing more sophisticated games which are not so widely sponsored by the people." In other words, the legislature felt that for Puerto Ricans the risks associated with casino gambling were significantly greater than those associated with the more traditional kinds of gambling in Puerto Rico. In our view, the legislature's separate classification of casino gambling, for purposes of the advertising ban, satisfies the third step of the *Central Hudson* analysis.

We also think it clear beyond peradventure that the challenged statute and regulations satisfy the fourth and last step of the *Central Hudson* analysis, namely, whether the restrictions on commercial speech are no more extensive than necessary to serve the government's interest. The narrowing constructions of the advertising restrictions announced by the Superior Court ensure that the restrictions will not affect advertising of casino gambling aimed at tourists, but will apply only to such advertising when aimed at the residents of Puerto Rico. Appellant contends, however, that the First Amendment requires the Puerto Rico Legislature to reduce demand for casino gambling among the residents of Puerto Rico not by suppressing commercial speech that might *encourage* such gambling, but by promulgating additional speech designed to *discourage* it. We reject this contention. We think it is up to the legislature to decide whether or not such a "counterspeech" policy would be as effective in reducing the demand for casino gambling as a restriction on advertising. The legislature could conclude, as it apparently did here, that residents of Puerto

Rico are already aware of the risks of casino gambling, yet would nevertheless be induced by widespread advertising to engage in such potentially harmful conduct. * * *

In short, we conclude that the statute and regulations at issue in this case, as construed by the Superior Court, pass muster under each prong of the *Central Hudson* test. We therefore hold that the Supreme Court of Puerto Rico properly rejected appellant's First Amendment claim.

Appellant argues, however, that the challenged advertising restrictions are constitutionally defective under our decisions in *Carey v. Population Services Int'l* (1977) and *Bigelow v. Virginia* (1975). In *Carey*, this Court struck down a ban on any "advertisement or display" of contraceptives, and in *Bigelow*, we reversed a criminal conviction based on the advertisement of an abortion clinic. We think appellant's argument ignores a crucial distinction between the *Carey* and *Bigelow* decisions and the instant case. In *Carey* and *Bigelow*, the underlying conduct that was the subject of the advertising restrictions was constitutionally protected and could not have been prohibited by the State. Here, on the other hand, the Puerto Rico Legislature surely could have prohibited casino gambling by the residents of Puerto Rico altogether. In our view, the greater power to completely ban casino gambling necessarily includes the lesser power to ban advertising of casino gambling, and *Carey* and *Bigelow* are inapposite.

Appellant also makes the related argument that, having chosen to legalize casino gambling for residents of Puerto Rico, the legislature is prohibited by the First Amendment from using restrictions on advertising to accomplish its goal of reducing demand for such gambling. We disagree. In our view, appellant has the argument backwards. As we noted in the preceding paragraph, it is precisely *because* the government could have enacted a wholesale prohibition of the underlying conduct that it is permissible for the government to take the less intrusive step of allowing the conduct, but reducing the demand through restrictions on advertising. It would surely be a Pyrrhic victory for casino owners such as appellant to gain recognition of a First Amendment right to advertise their casinos to the residents of Puerto Rico, only to thereby force the legislature into banning casino gambling by residents altogether. It would just as surely be a strange constitutional doctrine which would concede to the legislature the authority to totally ban a product or activity, but deny to the legislature the authority to forbid the stimulation of demand for the product or activity through advertising on behalf of those who would profit from such increased demand. Legislative regulation of products or activities deemed harmful, such as cigarettes, alcoholic beverages, and prostitution, has varied from outright prohibition on the one hand . . . to legalization of the product or activity with restrictions on stimulation of its demand on the other hand. * * * To rule out the latter, intermediate kind of response would require more than we find in the First Amendment.

Appellant's final argument in opposition to the advertising restrictions is that they are unconstitutionally vague. In particular, appellant argues that the statutory language, "to advertise or otherwise offer their facilities," and "the public of Puerto Rico," are not sufficiently defined to satisfy the requirements of due process. Appellant also claims that the term "anunciarse," which appears in the controlling Spanish version of the statute, is actually broader than the English term "to advertise," and could be construed to mean simply "to make known." Even assuming that appellant's argument has merit with respect to the bare statutory language, however, we . . . are bound by the Superior Court's narrowing construction of the statute. Viewed in light of that construction, and particularly with the interpretive assistance of the implementing regulations as modified by the Superior Court, we do not find the statute unconstitutionally vague. * * *

JUSTICE BRENNAN, with whom JUSTICE MARSHALL and JUSTICE BLACKMUN join, dissenting.

* * * It is well settled that the First Amendment protects commercial speech from unwarranted governmental regulation. "Commer-

cial expression not only serves the economic interest of the speaker, but also assists consumers and furthers the societal interest in the fullest possible dissemination of information." Our decisions have recognized, however, "the 'common-sense' distinction between speech proposing a commercial transaction, which occurs in an area traditionally subject to government regulation, and other varieties of speech." We have therefore held that the Constitution "accords less protection to commercial speech than to other constitutionally safeguarded forms of expression." Thus, while the First Amendment ordinarily prohibits regulation of speech based on the content of the communicated message, the government may regulate the content of commercial speech in order to prevent the dissemination of information that is false, deceptive, or misleading, or that proposes an illegal transaction. We have, however, consistently invalidated restrictions designed to deprive consumers of accurate information about products and services legally offered for sale.

I see no reason why commercial speech should be afforded less protection than other types of speech where, as here, the government seeks to suppress commercial speech in order to deprive consumers of accurate information concerning lawful activity. * * * I believe that where the government seeks to suppress the dissemination of nonmisleading commercial speech relating to legal activities, for fear that recipients will act on the information provided, such regulation should be subject to strict judicial scrutiny. * * * The Court, rather than applying strict scrutiny, evaluates Puerto Rico's advertising ban under the relaxed standards normally used to test government regulation of commercial speech. Even under these standards, however, I do not believe that Puerto Rico constitutionally may suppress all casino advertising directed to its residents. * * *

The Court asserts that the Commonwealth has a legitimate and substantial interest in discouraging its residents from engaging in casino gambling. * * * Neither the statute on its face nor the legislative history indicates that the Puerto Rico Legislature thought that serious harm would result if residents were allowed to engage in casino gambling; indeed, the available evidence suggests exactly the opposite. Puerto Rico has legalized gambling casinos, and permits its residents to patronize them. * * * Residents . . . are also permitted to engage in a variety of other gambling activities—including horse racing, "picas," cockfighting, and the Puerto Rico lottery—all of which are allowed to advertise freely to residents. * * * [I]n light of the legislature's determination that serious harm will *not* result if residents are permitted and *encouraged* to gamble, I do not see how Puerto Rico's interest in discouraging its residents from engaging in casino gambling can be characterized as "substantial," even if the legislature had actually asserted such an interest which, of course, it has not. * * *

Even assuming that . . . the challenged restrictions are supported by a substantial governmental interest, . . . [Puerto Rico] must still demonstrate that the challenged advertising ban directly advances [its] interest in controlling the harmful effects allegedly associated with casino gambling. * * * [E]ven assuming that an advertising ban would effectively reduce residents' patronage of gambling casinos, it is not clear how it would directly advance Puerto Rico's interest in controlling the "serious harmful effects" the Court associates with casino gambling. In particular, it is unclear whether banning casino advertising aimed at residents would affect local crime, prostitution, the development of corruption, or the infiltration of organized crime. Because Puerto Rico actively promotes its casinos to tourists, these problems are likely to persist whether or not residents are also encouraged to gamble. * * *

Finally, [Puerto Rico has] failed to show that [its] interest in controlling the harmful effects allegedly associated with casino gambling "cannot be promoted adequately by more limited regulation of appellant's commercial expression." Rather than suppressing constitutionally protected expression, Puerto Rico could seek directly to address the specific harms thought to be associated with casino gambling. [For example], Puerto Rico could continue carefully to monitor casino operations to guard against "the development of corruption and the infiltration of organized crime." * * * Such measures would directly address the problems [Puerto Rico] associates with casino gambling, while avoiding the First Amendment problems raised where the government seeks to ban constitutionally protected speech. * * *

The Court believes that Puerto Rico constitutionally may prevent its residents from obtaining truthful commercial speech concerning otherwise lawful activity because of the effect it fears this information will have. However, "[i]t is precisely this kind of choice between the dangers of suppressing information, and the dangers of its misuse if it is freely available, that the First Amendment makes for us." * * * The First Amendment presupposes that "people will perceive their own best interests if only they are well enough informed, and . . . the best means to that end is to open the channels of communication rather than to close them." * * * Accordingly, I would hold that Puerto Rico may not suppress the dissemination of truthful activity about entirely lawful activity merely to keep its residents ignorant. The Court, however, would allow Puerto Rico to do just that, thus dramatically shrinking the scope of First Amendment protection available to commercial speech, and giving government officials unprecedented authority to eviscerate constitutionally protected expression. I respectfully dissent.

JUSTICE STEVENS, with whom JUSTICE MARSHALL and JUSTICE BLACKMUN join, dissenting.

The Court concludes that "the greater power to completely ban casino gambling necessarily includes the lesser power to ban advertising of casino gambling." Whether a State may ban all advertising of an activity that it permits but could prohibit—such as gambling, prostitution, or the consumption of marijuana or liquor—is an elegant question of constitutional law. It is not, however, appropriate to address that question in this case because Puerto Rico's rather bizarre restraints

on speech are so plainly forbidden by the First Amendment.

Puerto Rico does not simply "ban advertising of casino gambling." Rather, Puerto Rico blatantly discriminates in its punishment of speech depending on the publication, audience, and words employed. Moreover, the prohibitions, as now construed by the Puerto Rico courts, establish a regime of prior restraint and articulate a standard that is hopelessly vague and unpredictable.

With respect to the publisher, in stark, unabashed language, the Superior Court's construction favors certain identifiable publications and disfavors others. If the publication (or medium) is from outside Puerto Rico, it is very favored indeed. * * * If the publication is native to Puerto Rico, however—the *San Juan Star*, for instance—it is subject to a far more rigid system of restraints and controls regarding the manner in which a certain form of speech (casino ads) may be carried in its pages. * * * I do not understand why [the Court] is willing to uphold a Puerto Rico regulation that applies one standard to the *New York Times* and another to the *San Juan Star.*

With respect to audience, the newly construed regulations plainly discriminate in terms of the intended listener or reader. Casino advertising must be "addressed to tourists." It must not "invite the residents of Puerto Rico to visit the casino." * * * I cannot imagine that this Court would uphold an Illinois regulation that forbade advertising "addressed" to Illinois residents while allowing the same advertiser to communicate his message to visitors and commuters[.] * * *

With respect to the message, the regulations now take one word of the English language—"casino"—and give it a special opprobrium. Use of that suspicious six-letter word is permitted only "where the trade name of the hotel is used even though it may contain a reference to the casino." The regulations explicitly include an important provision—"that the word casino is never used alone nor specified." * * * Singling out the use of a particular word for official sanctions raises grave First Amendment concerns[.] * * *

With respect to prior restraint, the Superior Court's opinion establishes a regime of censorship. In a section of the opinion that the majority fails to include, the court explained:

"We hereby authorize the publicity of the casinos in newspapers, magazines, radio, television or any other publicity media, of our games of chance in the exterior *with the previous approval of the Tourism Company* regarding the text of said ad, which must be submitted in draft to the Company. Provided, however, that no photographs, or pictures may be approval of the Company."

A more obvious form of prior restraint is difficult to imagine.

With respect to vagueness, the Superior Court's construction yields no certain or predictable standards for Puerto Rico's suppression of particular kinds of speech. Part of the problem lies in the delineation of permitted speech in terms of the audience to which it is addressed. * * * At oral argument, Puerto Rico's counsel stated that a casino advertisement in a publication with 95% local circulation—perhaps the *San Juan Star*—might actually be permissible, so long as the advertisement "is addressed to tourists and not to residents." Then again, maybe not. Maybe such an ad would not be permissible, and maybe there would be considerable uncertainty about the nature of the required "address." * * *

The general proposition advanced by the majority today—that a State may prohibit the advertising of permitted conduct if it may prohibit the conduct altogether—bears little resemblance to the grotesquely flawed regulation of speech advanced by Puerto Rico in this case. The First Amendment surely does not permit Puerto Rico's frank discrimination among publications, audiences, and words. Nor should sanctions for speech be as unpredictable and haphazardous as the roll of dice in a casino.

I respectfully dissent.

INTRODUCTION

Advertising is a $100 billion-a-year industry in the United States, and the efforts of businesses to promote their products and services produce enormous revenues for the news media and advertising agencies. Not surprisingly, government attempts to place restrictions on advertising practices have spawned controversy. For example, the deregulation mania of the 1980s has caused some to question the Federal Trade Commission's powers to punish false and deceptive advertising, and the tobacco industry, arm in arm with the nation's newspapers and magazines, are fighting proposed federal legislation that would ban tobacco advertising altogether. As the *Posadas* case indicates, advertising enjoys some degree of first amendment protection, and the development of this "commercial speech doctrine" has given the debate over government regulation a constitutional dimension.

Government regulation of advertising grew out of the excesses of the nineteenth century, when manufacturers of patent medicines claimed that these products would cure almost any ailment known to man. At the same time, monopoly power was the name of the game in the American business community, with the "trusts" holding unprecedented economic power. As a result, the federal government's *laissez faire* attitude gave way to a philosophy of intervention in the free-for-all economy, and the desirability of such government regulation has been a matter of controversy ever since.

With respect to advertising, the crux of the dispute is the effect of marketing campaigns on the consumer and on the economy as a whole. Under one view, advertising artificially creates demand by changing consumer preferences—that is, by persuading consumers that they really need a particular product or service, whether they do or not. At the same time, sellers use advertising to achieve economic power that enables them to suppress competition and thus raise prices. Proponents of this theory thus advocate strict controls on advertising.

Other economists have argued, however, that advertising provides purchasers with information that they use in deciding what to buy. According to this view, the commercial message is a signal to consumers about product quality and performance and a mechanism by which sellers can identify consumer preferences. Further, advertising is said to intensify competition by making it easier for new companies to enter the market and get across their messages to prospective customers. The end result, advocates of this theory contend, is increased competition and lower prices. A substantial body of empirical data supports this conclusion. For example, a 1972 study found that consumers in states that banned advertising for eyeglasses paid more than twice as much as those buying glasses in states where advertising was allowed.

Embracing the second of these theories, the law has recognized that advertising is worthy of some protection. Under the federal Lanham Act, for example, an advertiser can prevent a competitor from using his trademark or brand name, since product identification is at the heart of advertising. At the same time, however, the law has sought to discourage false and deceptive advertising, for such messages run counter to the notion that advertising is meant to inform consumers about product choices rather than simply whip them into a buying frenzy by manufacturing demand. Put another way, false advertising distorts the operation of the marketplace by placing inaccurate information in the hands of would-be purchasers. This distortion also works to the disadvantage of competitors who do not stoop to such tactics, for they may find themselves losing customers as a result of the false advertising. With respect to the latter problem, the common law provided a remedy: the tort of unfair competition, which protects against this wrongful diversion of business. It was not until the 1930s, however, that the law began to take consumer protection seriously.

When the Federal Trade Commission was established in 1914, its primary job was to enforce the antitrust statutes passed just before the turn of the century. Though the Commission also had authority to prevent "unfair methods of competition," a series of court decisions interpreted the agency's power rather narrowly. For example, the FTC could not declare an advertisement illegal unless there had been an injury to competitors or competition; harm to the consumer was not enough. Consequently, protecting consumers from false and deceptive advertising was not among the FTC's top priorities, and the agency instead focused on advertisements that disparaged a competitor's product or unlawfully used trade names. In 1938, however, Congress expanded the statutory mandate of the Commission to include "unfair and deceptive acts or practices." The clear intent of this legislative change was to extend FTC jurisdiction to acts and practices that were deceptive and unfair to consumers irrespective of their impact on competitors or competition.

The role of the Federal Trade Commission in regulating advertising practices will be the focus of this chapter. We will also examine remedies available to businesses harmed by the false advertising of competitors (unfair competition, trade libel, trademark infringement), the right of the media to reject advertising, and the liability of advertisers and publishers for injury caused by advertising. First, however, we will explore in more detail the first amendment issues discussed in the *Posadas* decision.

THE COMMERCIAL SPEECH DOCTRINE

As we saw in Chapter 2, the landmark libel case of *New York Times Co. v. Sullivan* (1964) involved a newspaper advertisement urging support for the civil rights movement in the South. Before dealing with the defamation issues presented in that case, the U.S. Supreme Court quickly brushed aside the argument that the first amendment was inapplicable because the speech in question appeared in an advertisement. "[W]e hold that if the allegedly libelous statements would otherwise be constitutionally protected. . . , they do not forfeit that protection because they were published in the form of a paid advertisement." A contrary result, the Court said, "would discourage newspapers from carrying 'editorial advertisements' of this type, and so might shut off an important outlet for . . . persons who do not themselves have access to publishing facilities. . . ." At the same time, however, the Court reaffirmed its earler ruling in *Valentine v. Chrestensen* (1942) that a purely *commercial* advertisement is not covered by the first amendment. It was not until the mid-1970s that the Court accorded such speech some degree of constitutional protection.

Historical Development

The *Chrestensen* decision was not one of the Supreme Court's brighter moments, though, in fairness, the facts of the case may have led the Justices to treat the first amendment issues in a casual, almost off-hand manner. F.J. Chrestensen, the owner of a surplus Navy submarine, docked the vessel in New York City and printed a handbill advertising tours for a fee. When he began handing out the flyers, the police advised him that this activity violated a provision of the city's Sanitary Code prohibiting the distribution of commercial and business advertising matter in the streets. Leaflets devoted solely to "information or a public protest" were just fine, he was told. Armed with this information, Chrestensen prepared a handbill with his original message on one side, without the reference to the admission fee, and a statement critical of his treatment by city dock officials on the other. The police again stopped his distribution efforts, and a lawsuit ensued.

Ruling in Chrestensen's favor, a federal district judge in New York enjoined the city from enforcing the Sanitary Code provision, and the U.S. Court of Appeals for the Second Circuit affirmed. The Supreme Court, however, unanimously reversed. In an opinion joined by first amendment stalwarts Hugo Black and William O. Douglas, Justice Owen Roberts disposed of the first amendment issue in two short paragraphs. Although the govermnment may not "unduly burden or proscribe" the dissemination of information and opinion in the public streets, "the Constitution imposes no such restraint on government as respects purely commercial advertising." Further, Justice Roberts said, Chrestensen could not seriously argue that he was engaged in a noncommercial activity, for "the affixing of the protest against official conduct to the advertising circular was with the intent . . . of evading the prohibition of the ordinance."

The erosion of *Chrestensen* began in 1973 with the Supreme Court's decision in *Pittsburgh Press Co. v. Human Relations Comission*, which arose from a city ordinance that prohibited discriminatory employment practices. Acting under this ordinance, a city commission ordered that a newspaper stop publishing help-wanted advertisements in columns labeled "Jobs—Male Interest" and "Jobs—Female Interest." In upholding the order, the Court emphasized that discrimination in employment was illegal under the city ordinance. "We have no doubt that a newspaper could be forbidden to publish a want ad proposing a sale of narcotics or soliciting prostitutes,'' Justice Lewis Powell wrote in the majority opinion. ''Any First Amendment interest which might be served by advertising an ordinary commercial proposal . . . is altogether absent when the commercial activity itself is illegal and the restriction on advertising is incidental to a valid limitation on economic activity.'' Thus, the Court suggested, contrary to *Chrestensen*, that the advertisements would have received some degree of first amendment protection had the underlying commercial activity been legal.

The next major development came two years later in *Bigelow v. Virginia*, a case briefly discussed in the *Posadas* opinion. Jeffrey Bigelow, the managing editor of a weekly newspaper in Charlottesville, Virginia, was convicted of violating a state statute making it a misdemeanor to encourage abortion by ''publication, lecture, advertisement, or by the sale or circulation of any publication. . . .'' Abortions were then illegal in Virginia. Bigelow's newspaper, the *Virginia Weekly*, had printed an advertisement for an abortion referral service in New York City, where abortions were permitted. The Virgnia Supreme Court affirmed Bigelow's conviction, relying heavily on *Chrestensen*, but the U.S. Supreme Court reversed. Writing for the majority, Justice Harry Blackmun emphasized that the *Chrestensen* ruling was quite narrow: ''the ordinance [in that case] was upheld as a reasonable regulation of the manner in which commercial advertising could be distributed,'' and the fact that it ''had the effect of banning a particular handbill does not mean . . . that all statutes regulating commercial advertising are immune from constitutional challenge.''

Justice Blackmun also stressed that the advertisement published by the *Virginia Weekly* ''did more than simply propose a commercial transaction.'' Rather, it contained factual material concerning the availability of abortions, a matter of potential interest to readers who might need the services or who merely had a ''general curiosity'' about the subject matter. Also, the advertisement ''pertained to constitutional interests,'' a reference to the Court's controversial ruling in *Roe v. Wade* (1973) that the right to privacy prevents the states from outlawing abortions during the first trimester of pregnancy. The Virginia courts had thus erred in assuming ''that advertising was entitled to no First Amendment protection and that . . . Bigelow had no First Amendment interest.''

Justice Blackmun then employed the familiar balancing process utilized in first amendment cases and concluded that the State of Virginia did not have a compelling interest in restricting the speech. Though Virginia claimed a legitimate interest in protecting the quality of health care within its borders, the Court pointed out that the advertisement in question did not in any way affect medical services in the state. In effect, Virginia was ''asserting an interest in regulating what Virginians may hear or read about the New York services'' and in ''shielding its citizens from information about activities . . . that Virginia's police powers do not reach.'' This interest was not sufficient to permit the state to punish Bigelow for publishing the advertisement.

In striking down the Virginia statute, however, the Court made plain that it was not deciding ''the extent to which constitutional protection is afforded commercial advertising under all circumstances and in the face of all kinds of regulation.'' Because the advertisement in *Bigelow* touched on a matter of public concern, the question remained as to whether ''purely commercial'' advertising was covered by the first amendment. That issue arose in *Virginia State Board of Pharmacy v. Virginia Citizens Consumer Council, Inc.* (1976), which involved a Virginia statute prohibiting pharmacists from publishing or advertising ''any amount, price, fee, premium, discount, rebate or credit terms . . . for any drugs which may be dispensed only by prescription.'' Declaring the statute unconstitutional, the Supreme Court for the first time ruled that even advertising that conveys nothing more than the price of goods and services is covered by the first amendment.

Again speaking for the Court, Justice Blackmun first made plain that the speech at issue was purely commercial: ''Our pharmacist does not wish to editorialize on any subject . . . [or] to report any particularly newsworthy fact, or to make generalized observations even about commercial matters,'' he wrote. ''The 'idea' he wishes to communicate is simply this: 'I will sell you the X prescription drug at the Y price.''' The economic motive of the advertiser does not make the speech unworthy of first amendment protection, however, for one must also take into account the interests of the consumer in receiving such information. Turning to this issue, Justice Blackmun stressed that the Virginia statute hit hardest at the poor, the sick, and the elderly, who may have a greater interest in the free flow of commercial information than in the ''day's most urgent political debate.'' Similarly, society as a whole has an interest in the widespread dissemination of commercial messages. ''So long as we preserve a predominantly free enterprise economy, the allocation of our resources in large measure will be made through numerous private economic decisions,'' he wrote. ''It is a matter of public interest that those decisions, in the aggregate, be intelligent and well informed.''

Having concluded that the speech was protected by the first amendment, the Court then considered the state's justification in the advertising ban. Virginia had advanced several arguments: advertising the price of prescription drugs would result in lower-quality professional services, since pharmacists would have to cut corners to compete effectively; the price of drugs might increase, since the cost of advertising inflates the cost of doing business and the prices that must be charged for drugs; the pharmacist-customer relationship would be impaired as consumers go from one pharmacy to another in search of the lowest price; and advertising would reduce the status of the pharmacist as a professional to that of a mere retailer. Justice Blackmun dismissed these concerns as unwarranted. After pointing out that the problem of substandard professional practices could be handled by the state agency that licensed and regulated pharmacists, he rejected the other proffered justifications as inconsistent with the basic premise of the first amendment:

> It is precisely this kind of choice, between the dangers of suppressing information and the dangers of its misuse if it is freely available, that the First Amendment makes for us. Virginia is free to require whatever professional standards it wishes of its pharmacists; it may subsidize them or protect them from competition in other ways. But it may not do so by keeping the public in ignorance of the entirely lawful terms that competing pharmacists are offering. In this sense, the justifications Virginia has offered for suppressing the flow of prescription drug price information, far from persuading us that the flow is not protected by the First Amendment, have reinforced our view that it is.

Justice Blackmun was careful to emphasize, however, that commercial speech could be regulated under certain circumstances. In particular, he noted that the Court's holding in *Virginia Pharmacy* is no obstacle to regulations aimed at false or misleading advertising. ''The First Amendment . . . does not prohibit the State from insuring that the stream of commercial information flows cleanly as well as freely.'' He also indicated that there is no constitutional impediment to restrictions on advertisements for illegal activities. Finally, in a lengthy footnote, Justice Blackmun explained that commercial speech is not entitled to the same degree of protection under the first amendment as other speech:

> In concluding that commercial speech enjoys First Amendment protection, we have not held that it is wholly undifferentiable from other forms. There are commonsense differences between speech that does "no more than propose a commercial transaction" and other varieties. * * * The truth of commercial speech, for example, may be more easily verifiable by its disseminator than, let us say, news reporting or political commentary, in that ordinarily the advertiser seeks to disseminate information about a specific product or service that he himself provides and presumably knows more about than anyone else. Also, commercial speech may be more durable than other kinds. Since advertising is the *sine qua non* of commercial profits, there is little likelihood of its being chilled by proper regulation and foregone entirely.
>
> Attributes such as these, the greater objectivity and hardiness of commercial speech, may make it less necessary to tolerate inaccurate statements for fear of silencing the speaker. They may also make it appropriate to require that a commercial message appear in such a form, or include such additional information, warnings and disclaimers, as are necessary to prevent its being deceptive.

Although *Virginia Phamarcy* makes clear that commercial speech is something of a second-class citizen as far as the first amendment is concerned, it provides neither a comprehensive definition of the term nor an analytical framework with which to evaluate claims that government restrictions on such speech offend the first amendment. We now turn to these issues, which the Supreme Court addressed in subsequent decisions.

Defining Commercial Speech

There was no doubt in *Virginia Pharmacy* that the speech in question was commercial in nature; as Justice Blackmun observed, the case involved price advertising that did nothing more than "propose a commercial transaction." But what if an advertisement also did something more, such as provide information on a matter of some importance? Is such an ad closer to the one at issue in *New York Times Co. v. Sullivan* and thus fully protected under the first amendment, or to the ad involved in *Virginia Pharmacy* and therefore entitled to lesser protection by virtue of its commercial nature? In other words, how do we draw the line between commercial and noncommercial speech?

This question reached the Supreme Court in *Bolger v. Youngs Drugs Products Corp.* (1983). There a condom manufacturer challenged a federal statute prohibiting the mailing of unsolicited advertisements for contraceptives. When the company proposed to mail to the public pamphlets promoting its products and discussing venereal disease and family planning, the Postal Service concluded that the material fell within the statutory prohibition. A lawsuit ensued, and a federal court ruled that the statute offended the first amendment. The Supreme Court agreed.

The threshold issue was whether the advertisements constituted commercial or noncommercial speech. Three types of advertisements were involved: multi-page flyers promoting a large variety of the company's products sold at drugstores, including condoms; flyers exclusively or substantially devoted to promoting the company's condoms; and informational pamphlets (e.g., "Condoms and Human Sexuality" and "Plain Talk about Venereal Disease") discussing the desirability and availability of condoms in general and the company's condoms in particular. The Supreme Court had no trouble concluding that the first and second types did "no more than propose a commercial transaction," since they consisted primarily of price and quantity information.

Although the Court said that the informational pamphlets could not "be characterized merely as proposals to engage in commercial transactions," it determined that they also fell into the commercial speech category. In reaching this conclusion, the Court identified three relevant factors:

- the information was in the form of an advertisement;
- specific references were made to the company's products; and
- the company had an economic motive for mailing the pamphlets.

The combination of these three characteristics "provided strong support" for the conclusion that the pamphlets constituted commercial speech, even though each factor, standing alone, might not compel that result.

The fact that the pamphlets contained discussions of important public issues such as venereal disease and family planning was immaterial. "[A]dvertising which links a product to a current public debate is not thereby entitled to the constitutional protection afforded noncommercial speech," Justice Thurgood Marshall wrote for the Court. "A company has the full panoply of [first amendment] protections available to its direct comments on public issues, so there is no reason for providing similar constitutional protection when such statements are made in the context of commercial transactions." To hold otherwise, he said, would be to immunize false or misleading product information from government regulation, for advertisers could secure full first amendment protection by simply including references to public issues in their ads.

In addition to identifying the three factors—advertising form, product references, and economic motive—as relevant to the commercial speech inquiry, the Court was careful to note that it did "not mean to suggest that each of the characteristics . . . must necessarily be present in order for speech to be commercial." For example, the Court specifically left open the possibility that corporate "image" advertisements could be considered commercial speech even though they do not specifically mention particular products or services.

The Court returned to the definitional issue in *Board of Trustees v. Fox* (1989), a case involving a first amendment attack on a state university regulation that prohibited attack on a state university regulation that prohibited private commercial activity in dormitories. As a result of this regulation, a company that sold housewares was prevented from holding what is popularly known as a "Tupperware party" in a dorm room. The company argued that the commercial speech doctrine was inapplicable because its representatives also touched on noncommercial subjects, such as how to be financially responsible and how to run an efficient home, at the gatherings. Relying on *Bolger,* the Court rejected that argument and held that the speech was commercial in nature.

"Nothing in the [regulation] prevents the speaker from conveying, or the audience from hearing, these noncommercial messages, and nothing in the nature of things requires them to be combined with commercial messages," Justice Antonin

Scalia wrote for the Court. "Including these home economics elements no more converted [the company's] presentations into educational speech than opening sales presentations with a prayer or a Pledge of Allegiance would convert them into religious or political speech."

Evaluating Restrictions on Commercial
Speech: The Four-Part Test

As the *Posadas* case indicates, the Supreme Court has developed a four-part test to be employed in determining whether government regulations on commercial speech conflict with its limited first amendment protection. Announced in a 1980 case, *Central Hudson Gas & Electric Corp. v. Public Service Commission*, the test is considerably easier to state than to apply.

The *Central Hudson* case arose when the New York Public Service Commission, responding to the 1973 Arab oil embargo, entered an order prohibiting the electric companies that it regulated from advertising to promote the use of electricity. Because most electrical power in the state was generated by burning fuel oil, the Commission feared that the oil shortages would not enable the electric companies to meet consumer demand. After the immediate crisis passed, the Commission decided in 1977 to keep the advertising ban in effect, reasoning that promotional advertising designed to increase the use of electricity was contrary to the national policy of energy conservation. The Central Hudson Gas & Electric Corporation unsuccessfully challenged the order in the state courts, which rejected the utility's argument that the advertising ban was an impermissible restriction on commercial speech.

By the time the dispute reached the U.S. Supreme Court in 1980, the Justices had decided a handful of other cases elaborating on the principles announced in *Virginia Pharmacy*. For example, in *Linmark Associates, Inc. v. Township of Willingboro* (1977), the Court struck down a city ordinance forbidding the display of "for sale" signs in front of houses. Similarly, in *Carey v. Population Services International* (1977), the Court declared invalid a statute that prohibited the advertising of contraceptives. And, in a series of cases beginning with *Bates v. State Bar of Arizona* (1977), the Court ruled that state restrictions on advertising by lawyers are unconstitutional. Building on these decisions, the Court in *Central Hudson* announced a four-step analysis for determining whether a particular regulation impermissibly infringes on the first amendment right of commercial speech. Writing for the Court, Justice Powell explained:

> At the outset, we must determine whether the expression is protected by the First Amendment. For commercial speech to come within that provision, it at least must concern lawful activity and not be misleading. Next, we ask whether the asserted governmental interest is substantial. If both inquiries yield positive answers, we must determine whether the regulation directly advances the governmental interest asserted, and whether it is not more extensive than is necessary to serve that interest.

It is important to understand how this test differs from that employed when noncommercial speech is at stake, for that comparison should give us some idea of the lesser degree of protection afforded commercial speech. With respect to the first step, there is no requirement under traditional first amendment analysis that the underlying activity be lawful or that the speech not be false or misleading. As we saw in Chapter 1, speech that calls for the violent overthrow of the United States government—an obviously illegal activity—is protected under most circumstances by virtue of the "clear and present danger" doctrine. The same is not true with respect to commercial speech; in *Pittsburgh Press*, for example, the Court upheld a prohibition on advertising for jobs that discriminated on the basis of sex. Moreover, as Chapter 2 indicates, speech that is false and defamatory warrants first amendment protection. According to *New York Times Co. v. Sullivan*, such erroneous speech is tolerated in order to give "breathing space" to those who comment on the activities of public officials and public figures. Obviously, there is no such room for error when commercial speech is involved, since false and misleading statements of a commercial variety are not entitled to any first amendment protection.

Another significant difference between conventional first amendment analysis and the *Central Hudson* test lies in the second step, which asks whether there is a "substantial" governmental interest that will justify the restriction on commercial speech. If noncommercial speech is at issue, however, the governmental interest must be "compelling"—that is, there is a strong presumption in favor of first amendment rights, and any restriction on freedom of expression carries a heavy burden of justification. Because the countervailing interest need only be "substantial" when commercial speech is involved, the government's burden in justifying a restriction on such expression is considerably lighter. The *Posadas* case is illustrative, for there is no doubt that the statute and regulation at issue in that case would have been unconstitutional had it been directed at news stories about casino gambling rather than at advertising. Justice Rehnquist said as much in a footnote, pointing out that the ban on advertising did not inhibit the freedom of the Puerto Rican press to report on casino operations.

Finally, the requirement that the regulation must be no more extensive than necessary to serve the asserted governmental interest is easier to satisify than the "least restrictive alternative" test imposed in cases that do not involve commercial speech. The *Posadas* case suggests this distinction, for there the Court deferred to the legislative judgment that a flat ban on casino advertising would be more effective in discouraging gambling than a method less restrictive of commercial expression, such as counteradvertising by the government. However, the matter was not definitively resolved until 1989, when the Court announced in *Board of Trustees v. Fox* that a regulation restricting commercial speech need only be a "reasonable" means of accomplishing the governmental objective. To apply a more rigid standard, the Court said, would be inconsistent with the "subordinate position" of commercial speech on the scale of first amendment values.

As noted previously, the *Fox* case involved a regulation prohibiting commercial activities in dormitories at a state university. In defending the regulation, the university claimed that the regulation was designed to promote an educational rather than commercial atmosphere on campus, prevent the commercial exploitation of students, and preserve residential tranquility. The Supreme Court held that these interests were substantial but sent the case back to the lower courts for a determination of whether the regulation was a reasonable means of furthering those interests.

After determining in *Central Hudson* that the speech in question was commercial (a conclusion that foreshadowed the subsequent ruling in *Bolger*), the Court then applied the four-part test and found the New York regulation invalid. Because the speech in question did not involve an illegal activity and was neither false nor misleading, the first major question was whether the government's interest in prohibiting promotional advertising was substantial. The Public Service Commission offered two justifications for the ban: conserving energy and preventing higher electric rates. Both interests qualified as substantial, the Court said. The question then became whether state's regulation directly advanced the government's interests—that is, whether the advertising ban actually "does the job." With respect to conservation, the link between the restriction on advertising and the policy of energy conservation was clear. "There is an immediate connection between advertising and demand for electricy," Justice Powell wrote. "Central Hudson would not contest the advertising ban unless it believed that promotion would increase its sales." The impact of the advertising ban on electric rates, however, was dismissed as "highly speculative."

The Court then turned to the final part of the test: whether the advertising ban "is no more extensive than necessary" to further the state's interest in energy conservation. Here the Commission's regulation ran into trouble, since it prohibited all promotional advertising, even that which had no impact on energy use. By way of example, Justice Powell pointed out the Central Hudson could not advertise the energy-efficient "heat pump" or suggest that its customers use electric heat as a backup to solar and other heat sources. In addition, the Commission had failed to demonstrate that its interest in energy conservation could not be protected by a more narrowly tailored regulation. For example, the Commission could "attempt to restrict the format and content of Central Hudson's advertising" by requiring that the advertisements "include information about the relative efficiency and expense of the offered service, both under current conditions and the foreseeable future."

Subsequent cases demonstrate that the four-part test is a malleable standard that can yield apparently contradictory results. If, under *Posadas*, a state can prohibit advertising that encourages its citizens to gamble, why should it be denied the power to prohibit advertising that encourages its citizens to waste energy? Two other decisions are worth mentioning in this regard. Recall that in the 1983 *Bolger* case discussed previously, the Court ruled that a Postal Service regulation prohibiting the mailing of unsolicited advertisements for contraceptives violated the first amendment. There the Court rejected the argument that the regulation was justified by a substantial government interest in shielding people from offensive material. However, in *City Council v. Taxpayers for Vincent* (1984), the Court upheld a city ordinance that outlawed the posting of signs on public property, concluding that there was a direct link between the ban and the city's substantial interest in limiting "visual clutter and blight." If the government may protect its citizens from "visual clutter and blight," why can't it protect them from offensive materials sent through the mail into their own homes?

REGULATION OF ADVERTISING

As the *Virginia Pharmacy* case and its progeny make plain, commercial speech that is false or misleading is not protected at all by the first amendment and may thus be prohibited by the government. Justice Blackmun, author of the *Virginia Pharmacy* opinion, elaborated on this point in *Bates v. State Bar of Arizona*, the lawyer advertising case:

> Advertising that is false, deceptive, or misleading of course is subject to restraint. . . . Since the advertiser knows his product and has a commercial interest in its dissemination, we have little worry that regulation to assure truthfulness will discourage protected speech. . . . And any concern that strict requirements for truthfulness will unde-

sirably inhibit spontaneity seems inapplicable because commercial speech generally is calculated. Indeed, the public and private benefits from commercial speech derive from confidence in its accuracy and reliability. Thus, the leeway for untruthful or misleading expression that has been allowed in other contexts has little force in the commercial arena.

Even though it is now settled that prohibitions against false or deceptive advertising are constitutionally permissible, there has long been considerable disagreement as to how to best combat the problem. At least six approaches have emerged:

- let the marketplace take care of advertising excesses;
- encourage advertisers to police themselves through a system of voluntary self-regulation;
- provide legal remedies for businesses harmed by the advertising practices of their competitors;
- provide legal remedies for consumers who are victimized by false or deceptive advertising claims;
- place regulatory powers in the hands of state governments; and
- assign primary enforcement responsibilities to federal administrative agencies.

These mechanisms obviously can—and do—exist side-by-side, but the task of protecting the public from false and deceptive advertising has largely fallen to the federal government, particularly the Federal Trade Commission. Accordingly, the FTC is our focus here, but the other mechanisms warrant a brief glimpse.

Those who favor a "free market" approach contend that the rigors of competition make government regulation of advertising unnecessary. This argument can be summarized as follows. First, improved education has made consumers more knowledgeable and thus less susceptible to false advertising. As a result, sellers are more likely to gear their advertising to this more informed audience. Second, most sellers cannot afford to develop a reputation for dishonesty, for disgruntled customers will take their business elsewhere. Third, a seller who makes a false claim runs the risk of being exposed by a competitor. Because the competitor stands to lose business as a result of the seller's false advertising, he has every incentive to go on the offensive.

Experience has shown, however, that the marketplace is not perfect. Though consumers may be better educated, they often lack sufficient information to make a sensible choice among competing products or to decide whether to buy the product at all. Real competition does not exist in many sectors of the economy, and even where it does, there is no guarantee that sellers will provide their potential customers with accurate information about products and services. And, rather than attack a seller's false claims with his own ads, a competitor may just as easily decide to "fight fire with fire" by engaging in false advertising himself.

Efforts at self-regulation date to the early part of this century when newspapers and magazines began to review—and reject—advertisements containing outrageous claims by makers of patent medicines. Advertising acceptability guidelines also emerged; in 1910, for example, publisher Cyrus H.K. Curtis produced the "Curtis Advertising Code," which was designed "to protect both our advertisers and our readers from all copy that is fraudulent or deceptive." The following year, George Rowell, founder of *Printer's Ink* magazine (and, ironically, owner of a patent medicine company) proposed a model statute to deal with deceptive advertising practices. So-called "Printer's Ink" statutes making deceptive advertising a misdemeanor were subsequently enacted in most states.

Today, organizations representing the three participants in advertising—the media, advertising agencies, and the advertisers themselves—have adopted ethical codes and advertising acceptability standards. Examples include guidelines established by each of the three major television networks, the Advertising Code of American Business developed by the American Advertising Federation, and the Standards of Practice established by the American Association of Advertising Agencies. Moreover, in 1971 the Council of Better Business Bureaus set up a National Advertising Review Board to hear complaints based on false or deceptive advertising.

Although competitors and consumers harmed by false advertising claims may bring damage suits against the wrongdoer, these remedies have, on the whole, proved ineffective. In an action for unfair competition, for example, a competitor must usually demonstrate not only that the advertisement was false and that the defendant knew it, but also that the offending message diverted specific customers and caused measurable economic loss. Because these stringent requirements are seldom met, some states have by statute eliminated the need to prove knowledge and particularized damages, while others have made it easier to obtain an injunction against deceptive advertising. A competitor has more potent remedies at his disposal if an advertisement uses his brand name or other product identification to create confusion among consumers or makes false and disparaging remarks about his product. These remedies, notably the federal Lanham Act and the common law of trade libel, are discussed below.

An individual consumer injured by a false or deceptive advertisement may be able to sue the advertiser for misrepresentation or breach of contract. In addition to these remedies, most states have enacted specific consumer protection statutes that typically relax the common law requirements for recovery and provide that a successful plaintiff may recover his attorney's fees and other litigation costs from the defendant. The problem here is not the adequacy of the remedies, but rather the fact that most consumer cases based on deceptive advertising involve relatively small amounts of money. In states where the recovery of attorney's fees is not permitted, the cost of the litigation might well exceed the amount of recovery. And, even if these costs may be shifted to the defendant, the sheer hassle of litigation deters many potential plaintiffs who have only minimal damages. One possible solution to these problems is to allow several consumers to pool their claims against a single defendant, thereby increasing the amount of money at stake and making the lawsuit viable. However, there are substantial legal obstacles to the use of this technique,[2] and today its utility in the consumer setting is rather limited.

Finally, it should be noted that almost all states have enacted statutes that prohibit deceptive advertising and other unfair trade practices. For example, the "Printer's Ink" statutes mentioned previously are still on the books in many states. They

---

[2]In most states, for example, a judge has wide discretion to decide whether to allow such a lawsuit, known as a "class action," to proceed or to instead require that separate lawsuits be brought by each injured person. Moreover, some jurisdictions impose certain conditions on class action cases, such as the typical requirement that the legal and factual issues common to the members of the class dominate any individual issues. In the federal courts, class actions based on state law (as are most consumer suits) are not permissible unless the claim of each class member exceeds $50,000.

have not been particularly effective, primarily because they make deceptive advertising a misdemeanor and place enforcement in the hands of prosecuting attorneys and other law enforcement officials who face far more pressing matters. The consumerism movement of the 1960s and 1970s led to the strengthening of some state laws, and when the Federal Trade Commission began to take a rather lax approach toward deceptive advertising during the Reagan Administration, state officials used their own statutes—which generally parallel federal law—to fill the regulatory gap. However, these efforts are restricted to activities occurring within the state, and many state consumer protection agencies lack sufficient staff and funds to adequately police advertising practices.

The Federal Trade Commission

Although the Federal Trade Commission is only one of several federal administrative agencies with regulatory and enforcement responsibilities relating to advertising, its jurisdiction is broader than the other agencies and its influence more pervasive. Generally speaking, any authority over advertising not assigned to a particular agency belongs to the FTC.[3] Of particular note in this regard is the division of labor between the FTC and the Federal Communications Commission. As discussed in Chapter 10 and later in this chapter, various FCC policies affect broadcast advertising, and the agency's broad mandate to regulate broadcasting "in the public interest" would seem to reach advertising carried by its licensees. The FCC, however, has left control of false and deceptive broadcast advertising to the FTC, though the FCC handles complaints about station self-promotion.

The Federal Trade Commission is an independent federal agency whose five members are appointed by the President with approval of the Senate. The commissioners serve staggered seven-year terms and may be removed from office by the President only in limited circumstances. One commissioner is designated by the President as chairman and serves in that capacity at the President's pleasure. The length of the terms and the safeguard against arbitrary dismissal help insulate the FTC from political pressures, as does a requirement that no more than three commissioners can belong to the same political party. Nonetheless, a President may use his power of appointment to alter the FTC's regulatory philosophy, as President Reagan did during his two terms in office. The FTC's work is carried on by 1600 employees organized into three principal divisions, called "bureaus": the Bureau of Competition, which enforces the antitrust laws; the Bureau of Economics, which prepares financial statistics and economic analyses; and the Bureau of Consumer Protection, which deals with false and deceptive advertising and other unfair trade practices. The Bureau of Consumer Protection has several divisions, including an "advertising practices" section, and has eleven regional offices scattered across the country.

The cornerstone of the FTC's authority, for our purposes, is Section 5 of the

---

[3]A number of federal agencies have such powers within narrowly defined areas. The U.S. Postal Service, for instance, may exclude deceptive advertising from the mails, while the Food and Drug Administration is primarily concerned with the labeling of food, drugs, and cosmetics. Similarly, the Securities and Exchange Commission has authority over promotional materials issued in connection with the sale of stocks and bonds, and the Alcohol and Tobacco Tax Division of the Internal Revenue Service has adopted regulations governing liquor advertising. In dealing with false and deceptive advertising, these agencies generally follow principles established by the FTC.

Federal Trade Commission Act, which declares unlawful "unfair methods of competition" and "unfair or deceptive acts or practices" in or affecting interstate commerce. The requirement that the offending practices involve interstate commerce is grounded in Article I, Section 8 of the Constitution, which gives Congress power to "regulate Commerce with foreign Nations, and among the several states. . . ." This power has been expansively interpreted by the courts. As Justice Robert Jackson once observed, "[i]f it is interstate commerce that feels the pinch, it does not matter how local the operation which applies the squeeze." Under this broad approach, the FTC's jurisdiction is not limited to what one might think of as "national" advertising. There is, however, a very important limitation on the Commission's powers: its budget, which is approximately $70 million per year. Of that amount, only a tiny fraction—about $3 million—is directed toward to false and deceptive advertising. That is a drop in the bucket compared to the $100 *billion* spent annually on advertising in the United States.

Even with this limited budget, the FTC has stirred considerable controversy with its efforts at consumer protection. The Commission was particularly aggressive during the 1970s, when the consumerism movement was at its zenith, but it cut back its enforcement activities during the Reagan Administration. Nonetheless, the basic principles governing deception in advertising have remained essentially the same, as have the remedies at the FTC's disposal. We now turn to these matters.

What is Deceptive Advertising? For purposes of FTC jurisdiction, the courts have defined the term "advertising" to include any action intended to draw the public's attention to a product, service, person, or organization. This broad definition reaches not only what one might call "traditional" advertising such as newspaper ads, television commercials, billboards, and direct mail, but also product labels, trading stamps, lotteries and similar games of chance, and the use of premiums and give-away promotions to lure customers. In enforcing the Federal Trade Commission Act, the FTC has considerable discretion to determine whether advertising is deceptive. That authority is so broad that critics of the Commission have complained that almost any advertisement can be found deceptive. Responding to such criticism, the FTC announced a more conservative enforcement policy in late 1983. To be deceptive under these guidelines, which were formally adopted in *In re Cliffdale Associates, Inc.* (1984), an advertisement must involve a representation or omission that is likely to mislead a consumer acting reasonably under the circumstances and is "material" in that it is likely to affect a consumer's purchasing decision.

Representation or Omission. Obviously, a false statement—that is, an outright misrepresentation of fact—can mislead a consumer and therefore qualify as deceptive. Advertisers are usually more subtle, and ads that convey a false impression while stopping short of overt falsehood are also impermissible. Even an advertisement that is literally true can be deceptive if it buries critical information or omits material which, if disclosed, would paint a different picture for the consumer. "Advertisements as a whole may be completely misleading although every sentence separately considered is literally true," Justice Black wrote in *Donaldson v. Read Magazine, Inc.* (1948). "This may be because things are omitted that should be said, or because advertisements are composed or purposefully printed in such a way as to mislead."

A blatant falsehood is almost always deceptive. For example, a furniture dealer may not call his wares "antiques" when they are reproductions and may not describe them as "new" when they are, to borrow a term favored by auto dealers, "previously owned." Similarly, a seller of arts and crafts may not tout his goods as "handmade" when they are not, a cereal manufacturer may not state that the package is an "economy size" when it is more expensive than the "regular" size on a per-ounce basis, and a jeweler may not claim that his watches are "shockproof" and "waterproof" when they are merely resistant to shock and water.

One of the most famous decisions of this type involved the word "free." In *Federal Trade Commission v. Mary Carter Paint Co.* (1965), a paint company advertised that every purchaser of a can of paint for $6.98 would receive another can "free." The problem, however, was that the company had not previously sold single cans of paint for $6.98. In light of this prior marketing history, the FTC concluded that the company in effect allocated the price of two cans to one can, thus misleading consumers. The U.S. Supreme Court affirmed the Commission's decision.

False claims that a product is "unique" or has certain performance characteristics also cause problems. For example, in *Porter & Dietsch, Inc. v. Federal Trade Commission* (1979), the U.S. Court of Appeals for the Seventh Circuit upheld an FTC determination that advertising for "X-11" diet pills was deceptive. Among other things, the company that produced the pills had stated that they had a "unique" formula, when in fact the active ingredient was the same as that found in other appetite suppression pills sold over the counter. Along the same lines is the Ninth Circuit's decision in *Sears, Roebuck & Co. v. Federal Trade Commission* (1982). In that case, Sears had boasted that a dishwasher "cleans dishes so well that they do not have to be pre-rinsed." Unfortunately, this advertising pitch was not true; in fact, the owner's manual for the dishwasher indicated that pre-rinsing was necessary.

Reported decisions involving explicit falsehoods are legion, but the number seems to have dwindled in recent years as advertising has become more sophisticated. More typical is an implied misrepresentation. For example, in *Firestone Tire & Rubber Co. v. Federal Trade Commission* (1973), the FTC moved against Firestone on the basis of an advertising campaign stressing the safety of its tires. Headlined "The Safe Tire: Firestone," the ads emphasized that "[w]hen you buy a Firestone tire— no matter how much or how little you pay—you get a safe tire." Though the ad made no explicit claim that all Firestone tires are free from defects and safe under all conditions, the FTC concluded that it did so implicitly, and the U.S. Court of Appeals for the Sixth Circuit agreed. Of course, no tire is absolutely safe, and Firestone admitted that, despite state-of-the-art manufacturing technology and rigorous quality control, defective tires can and do reach consumers.

In determining whether an advertisement is implicitly false, the FTC and the courts will consider the advertisement as a whole, not simply isolated passages. The test is the overall impression created by the advertisement and its effect on the reader or viewer, and literal truth is not a defense. An illustrative case is *Bristol-Myers Co. v. Federal Trade Commission* (1984), in which the U.S. Court of Appeals for the Second Circuit upheld a Commission ruling that a Bufferin television advertisement was deceptive. The video portion of the ad stated without qualification that "doctors specify Bufferin most," while a voice-over added a reference to a survey comparing Bufferin to "all leading brands of pain reliever." That survey showed that doctors did recommend Bufferin more often than the "leading brands," but that they also recommended other products—including generic aspirin—more frequently than Bufferin. Though the ad may have been literally true, the FTC and the court concluded that, taken as a whole, it gave the false impression that physicians suggested Bufferin more often than *any* other over-the-counter analgesic, not just the "leading brands."

Sometimes the sin is one of omission. For example, in *National Bakers Services, Inc. v. Federal Trade Commission* (1964), a company that licensed bakers to produce "Hollywood Bread" produced a series of print advertisements picturing beautiful women and a loaf of the company's bread. The text of one such ad read: "When a woman's panther slim, she's vital as well as slender. A good figure is more than luck when a lady watches her weight the famous Hollywood way. Hollywood Bread is high in protein, vitamins and minerals, yet has only 46 calories per 18 gram slice." While the caloric content of the bread was indeed as advertised, the company failed to mention that both Hollywood Bread and "regular" white bread contained 276 calories per one-pound loaf. The only reason that Hollywood Bread contained fewer calories per slice than its competitors was that it was sliced more thinly. Because the typical consumer had no conception of the weight or caloric content of a slice of bread, the FTC concluded that the ad conveyed the erroneous message that the bread was lower in calories than "regular" bread and thus could be beneficial to dieters and other weight-conscious persons. The U.S. Court of Appeals for the Seventh Circuit upheld the Commission's decision, pointing out that "[d]eception may be by innuendo rather than outright false statements."

False impressions can be created in other ways as well. For example, in what has come to be known as the "sandpaper shave" case, the FTC ruled that the use of a mock-up in the filming of a television commercial resulted in a deceptive message about the attributes of shaving cream. The advertisement at issue in *Federal Trade Commission v. Colgate-Palmolive Co.* (1965) was built around the "super-moisturizing power" of Rapid Shave, which could enable a man to shave a beard as tough as sandpaper. To make the point, the ad showed Rapid Shave being applied to what appeared to be a piece of sandpaper and then shaved right off with a single stroke of a razor. But the advertising agency that produced the ad did not actually use a piece of sandpaper; instead, it covered a piece of plexiglass with sand to create what appeared to be sandpaper. This mock-up was necessary for two reasons. First, although Rapid Shave was capable of moistening a piece of sandpaper to the point that it could be shaved, more than an hour's "soaking time" was necessary. Second, a real piece of sandpaper did not photograph particularly well and would have appeared to viewers as plain, colored paper.

According to the FTC, the ad was deceptive in two ways. Because Rapid Shave could not sufficiently moisten sandpaper within the time depicted by the commercial, the product's moistening power had been misrepresented. Moreover, the ad conveyed to viewers the false impression that they were seeing an actual demonstration of the capabilities of Rapid Shave, when in fact they were not because of the undisclosed use of the plexiglass mock-up. Only the second rationale was at issue on appeal to the Supreme Court. In an opinion by Chief Justice Earl Warren, the Court upheld the Commission, concluding that the undisclosed use of the plexiglass was deceptive, wholly apart from the misrepresentation as to the time required to moisten the sandpaper. Rejecting the argument that it would be impractical to inform viewers that they were not witnessing an actual demonstration or experiment, the Chief Justice said:

> [W]e think it inconceivable that the ingenious advertising world will be unable, if it so desires, to conform to the Commission's insistence that the public be not misinformed. If, however, it becomes impossible or impractical to show simulated demonstrations

on television in a truthful manner, this indicates that television is not a medium that lends itself to this type of commercial, not that the commercial must survive at all costs. Similarly unpersuasive is [the] objection that the Commission's decision discriminates against sellers whose product claims cannot be "verified" on television without the use of simulations. All methods of advertising do not equally favor every seller. If the inherent limitations of a method do not permit its use in the way a seller desires, the seller cannot by material misrepresentation compensate for those limitations.

Another technique that has caused difficulties is the use of endorsements and testimonials by consumers and celebrities. The FTC has responded with rather detailed guidelines dealing with this popular tactic. Suppose, for example, that a television advertisement portrays a crowded restaurant in which the advertiser's coffee is being served. A spokesman for the advertiser then interviews various persons in the restaurant, asking for their spontaneous, honest opinions on the coffee. What is the overall impression created? Most viewers would probably think that these were actual interviews with actual patrons of the restaurant. If the advertiser had staged the interviews, using actors, without disclosing that fact, the ad would be deceptive.

Or, suppose that the president of a janitorial service stated in an ad that his company used a particular brand of cleanser. The company must in fact use the cleanser; otherwise, the statement would simply be false. Assume that the company does use the product, but only because the advertiser supplies it at a huge discount. That arrangement must be disclosed, for otherwise the implication is that the company had independently chosen the cleanser after comparing a number of brands. In contrast, the fact that a film star or athlete had been paid to endorse a soft drink would not have to be disclosed, since consumers are generally aware that such celebrities receive compensation for such promotional activities. However, any comments made about the taste of the soft drink or its other qualities must reflect the actual opinions of the person making the endorsement.

Likely to Mislead a Reasonable Consumer. An advertisement need not actually mislead anyone in order to be found deceptive by the FTC, and the fact that the advertiser did not intend to deceive anyone is quite beside the point. Accordingly, there is no need for evidence showing that that some consumers had interpreted an advertisement in a certain fashion or had otherwise been deceived, or that an advertiser had acted in good faith without malicious intent. Instead, the test is whether an advertisement is likely to deceive a consumer acting reasonably under the circumstances. The courts typically defer to the FTC's expert judgment as to whether such a likelihood exists.

Prior to the 1983 FTC policy statement, the Commission had for many years found advertising to be deceptive if it had a "tendency to deceive" even the most naive, foolish, or gullible consumer. This position is illustrated by the famous case of *Charles of the Ritz Distributing Corp. v. Federal Trade Commission*, decided by the U.S. Court of Appeals for the Second Circuit in 1944. At issue was "Rejuvenescence Cream" sold by Charles of the Ritz, a major cosmetics company. According to advertisements, the product brought to the user's skin "the petal-like quality and texture of youth," restored "natural moisture necessary for a live, healthy skin," and kept skin "clear, radiant, and young looking." The FTC's theory was that the advertising campaign, plus the very name of the cream, created the false impression that the product actually rejuvenated aging skin. Charles of the Ritz claimed that there was no deception because "no straight-thinking person" could possibly believe that the cream would make old skin young. Judge Charles Clark rejected that argument:

> Such a view results from a grave misconception of the purposes of the Federal Trade Commission Act. That law was not "made for the protection of experts, but for the public—that vast multitude which includes the ignorant, the unthinking, and the credulous," and the "fact that a false statement may be obviously false to those who are trained and experienced does not change its character nor take away its power to deceive others less experienced." * * * [W]hile the wise and the worldly may well realize the falsity of any representations that the present product can roll back the years, there remains "that vast multitude" of others who, like Ponce de Leon, still seek a perpetual fountain of youth.

Under this approach, the Commission could find almost any advertising claim to be deceptive, so long as only one simple-minded person could possibly have been misled. As one member of the FTC observed, an ad for "Danish pastry" would be deceptive if "a few misguided souls believe . . . that all [such pastry] is made in Denmark." Not surprisingly, the FTC shifted gears and ruled that an advertisement is deceptive only if it has the tendency or capacity to deceive the average person in the audience that it can be expected to reach.

The 1983 FTC policy statement goes even further. First, there must be a likelihood of deception, rather than a mere tendency to deceive. Put another way, deception must be probable, not simply possible. Second, that probability is to be measured from the perspective of the "reasonable consumer," even if unsophisticated or uneducated consumers might be misled. By adopting what appears to be an objective standard similar to the "reasonable person" test used in negligence law, the FTC is apparently willing to rule that the response of an average or typical consumer to an advertisement may be unreasonable under certain circumstances.

However, the FTC will take into account the special characteristics of the target audience as a whole. If, for example, advertising is aimed at children, the issue will be the effect of the message on a reasonable child. Obviously, an advertisement that would not mislead a reasonable adult could easily deceive a reasonable child, since children typically lack the maturity and experience to appreciate the possibility that representations may be exaggerated or untrue. By the same token, the elderly and the terminally ill may be particularly susceptible to misleading advertising, and the FTC policy takes this into account. Even ads directed at overweight persons will be more carefully scrutinized. As the Commission has observed:

> It is obvious that dieting is the conventional method of losing weight. But it is equally obvious that many people who need or want to lose weight regard dieting as bitter medicine. To these corpulent consumers the promises of weight loss without dieting are the Siren's call, and advertising that heralds unrestrained consumption while muting the inevitable need for temperance, if not abstinence, simply does not pass muster.

On the other hand, an advertisement directed to a well-educated group—such as a prescription drug ad in a medical journal—will be evaluated in light of the knowledge and sophistication of the members of that group.

The Commission is also willing to assume that some advertising practices are unlikely to mislead reasonable consumers. Subjective claims based on taste, feel, appearance, or smell fall into this category, as do statements of honestly held opinion that cannot be reasonably interpreted as factual representations. Opinions of persons portrayed as experts are generally treated as statements of fact, however, and, as noted previously, the opinions of celebrities or other persons endorsing a product must be their own.

In addition, the Commission will permit some degree of "puffing," that is, exaggerated "sales talk" that ordinary consumers do not take seriously. Terms like "best" and "exceptional" are usually considered to be puffing, and salesmen who describe a used car as "a really good deal" or as being in "perfect shape" are engaging in this time-honored tactic. Though one commentator has described the puffing doctrine as simply a license to "lie one's head off," the FTC takes something of a "no harm, no foul" position. If, however, a claim is not so outrageous or exaggerated as to be unbelievable, the doctrine is inapplicable. In a 1978 case, for instance, the manufacturer of a television antenna had described the product as an "electronic miracle." Despite the hyperbole, the Commission rejected the "puffing" defense, reasoning that the claim gave "added credence to the overall suggestion that this device is superior to other types of antennae."

Materiality. Even if an advertisement is likely to deceive a reasonable consumer, it is not illegal under the FTC Act unless the representation or omission is "material," that is, likely to affect a consumer's decision to purchase the advertised product or service. In other words, the representation or omission must involve important information on which consumers could be expected to rely. If inaccurate or omitted information is material, injury to the consumer is assumed. There is no requirement that actual injury be shown.

The FTC considers certain categories of information presumptively material: all express claims about a product or service; implied claims as to durability, performance, quality, safety, effectiveness, cost, warranties, or guarantees; and omitted information that the advertiser knew or should have known would affect the ability of an ordinary consumer to evaluate the product or service. In effect, the Commission takes the position that the advertiser is in the best position to assess the impact of his ad, and that he would not make express or implied claims or omit key information unless he believed that the resulting advertisement would influence consumers. If the claim does not fall within these categories, the Commission may require evidence that the representation or omission is likely to be considered important by consumers. This evidence might include expert testimony, surveys of consumers, and advertisements for competing products or services.

Two interesting cases illustrate the FTC's materiality analysis. In *In re American Home Products Corp.* (1981), a series of advertisements for Anacin pain reliever attempted to differentiate that product from mere aspirin. One ad, for example, proclaimed that "Anacin isn't just like an ordinary aspirin tablet" and that it "has more of the drug doctors themselves most choose to relieve pain." Another ad said that Anacin "contains the pain reliever most recommended by doctors plus an extra active ingredient not found in leading buffered aspirin." That extra ingredient is a small amount of caffeine, and the drug that doctors "recommend most" is—surprise—aspirin. Because the ads did not inform consumers that the analgesic in Anacin is in fact aspirin, the FTC found that they "foster[ed] the impression that Anacin contains something other than aspirin." The Commission also concluded that the omission of this information was material: "The very fact that [American Home Products] sought to distinguish its products from aspirin strongly implies that knowledge of the true ingredients of those products would be material to purchasers." The FTC also pointed out that "the actual identity of the ingredient takes on particular significance due to the potentially serious consequences which may result from aspirin consumption" by some persons.

The *Cliffdale Associates* case mentioned previously involved advertisements for the "Ball-Matic," a device designed to allow additional air to enter an automobile's engine in order to improve gasoline mileage. Among other things, the ads claimed that the device would significantly increase fuel economy in the typical car and cited scientific tests showing increases of up to twenty percent. The FTC found that the representation as to improved gasoline mileage was false and that the test results did not support the fuel economy claims. Both claims were also held material. "Claims about enhanced fuel efficiency resulting from the use of the Ball-Matic are clearly material to consumers," the Commission said. "While consumers will not necessarily expect to achieve the specific fuel economy level represented in a particular advertisement, the claimed performance . . . should be representative of consumers' expected savings from the Ball-Matic." Moreover, because consumers are not able to easily evaluate for themselves the performance capability of a device such as this, the FTC observed, they "will tend to rely more heavily on the scientific support claims. . . ."

FTC Enforcement Techniques. Deceptive advertising cases usually start with a complaint filed with the FTC by a consumer or a competitor. If the Bureau of Consumer Protection determines that the matter is worth pursuing, it contacts the advertiser and commences an investigation. Sometimes that is all it takes to convince an advertiser to withdraw or modify his ads, for he may determine that adverse publicity from the FTC proceedings and the legal fees necessary to fight the charges are simply not worth it. Should the Bureau's staff conclude that no further action is warranted, it will drop the case if the advertiser provides a letter of "voluntary compliance" promising to eliminate the deceptive features from the advertisements and to refrain from such advertising in the future. Such a letter does not constitute an admission on the part of the advertiser that the material was deceptive.

In other situations, such a prompt settlement is not possible. The advertiser may want to contest the matter, or the Bureau's staff may decide that a letter of compliance is not appropriate in light of the severity of the alleged deception, the fact that the advertiser is a repeat offender, or other considerations. At this point, a formal administrative proceeding is intiated, with the Bureau's staff acting as prosecutor. The case is assigned to an administrative law judge, who, after a trial-type hearing, renders an initial decision that is final unless appealed to the full Commission. If the administrative law judge or, ultimately, the Commission determines that the advertising is deceptive, a "cease and desist" order is entered directing the advertiser to stop the deceptive practices. The order may, under appropriate circumstances, apply to all of the company's products, not simply those advertised in a deceptive fashion. Violation of such an order can lead to penalties of up to $10,000 per offense per day. Because the advertiser may appeal the Commission's decision to a federal appellate court, the enforcement process can take years; for example, litigation over advertising claims for Geritol and Carter's Little Liver Pills dragged on for twelve and sixteen years, respectively.

Most deceptive advertising cases are resolved short of a full-blown administrative hearing, however. Just as the parties in a civil case often settle their differences short of a trial, the Bureau's staff and the advertiser may agree to a "consent order" to dispose of the dispute. Although a consent order is similar to a letter of compliance in that the advertiser agrees to discontinue the ads and does not admit any wrong-doing, there is an important difference. As its name implies, a consent order is an order of the Commission. As such, it carries the same weight as a cease and desist order entered after a hearing before the administrative law judge and an appeal to the Commission. Thus, an advertiser who violates the terms of a consent order faces the same penalties described above.

In some cases, a cease and desist order or a consent order embodying such a directive is not sufficient to cure the harm caused by the deceptive advertising. Accordingly, the Commission has developed other remedies that can be used in either a consent agreement or an order entered after an administrative hearing. Unlike a negative order that prohibits a certain practice, these remedies—forced disclosure of information and so-called "corrective" advertising—are affirmative in nature and require the advertiser to take certain steps to eliminate the deceptive impact of his ads.

Forced Disclosure. As we have seen, advertisements may be found deceptive because they omit important information; for example, the Anacin advertisements in the *American Home Products* case neglected to mention that the pain reliever's principal ingredient is aspirin. Similarly, in the celebrated case of *J.B. Williams Co. v. Federal Trade Commission* (1967), the makers of Geritol advertised that the product, which was supposedly good for "iron-poor blood," could reduce tiredness and fatigue. The ads were found to be deceptive because they did not indicate that in most cases those problems are caused by factors other than a lack of the vitamins and iron contained in the medicine. Employing similar reasoning, the FTC has concluded that advertisements promoting cures for baldness were deceptive because they did not disclose that most baldness results from heredity and cannot be treated and that claims touting the powers of a diet pill to produce significant weight loss were misleading absent a disclosure that actual dieting—that is, limiting one's calorie intake—is also required.

In cases such as these, the Commission may order the advertiser to supply the missing information in future advertisements making the claims. For example, in the *J.B. Williams* case, the FTC ordered that Geritol advertisements mentioning tiredness and fatigue disclose the fact that a great majority of persons who suffer these symptoms do not experience them because of a vitamin or iron deficiency. This order was upheld by the U.S. Court of Appeals for the Sixth Circuit. In later cases, advertisers have challenged such orders on first amendment grounds, but these arguments have been uniformly rejected. Because deceptive advertising is not entitled to protection under the commercial speech doctrine, the courts have reasoned that an affirmative disclosure order designed to prevent such deception is constitutionally permissible.[4]

Corrective Advertising. Suppose that Geritol simply decided to drop references to fatigue and tiredness in its advertisements. Would it then be required to make the affirmative disclosure ordered by the FTC? The answer is "no," since the Commis-

---

[4]The Commission also uses other types of affirmative orders. For example, if an advertiser sets up a contest or other promotional game but fails to award the promised prizes, the FTC will order the company to follow through with its commitment.

sion's order applied only to ads that mentioned those symptoms. As a result, other Geritol advertisements would be unaffected. In response to this possible loophole, the FTC devised a remedy known as "corrective advertising." Under this approach, an advertiser found to have engaged in deceptive advertising is required to "correct" the misimpressions created by his past practices even if he discontinues them. Accordingly, Geritol could be ordered to atone for its sins by stating in all future advertisements that tiredness and fatigue are not usually caused by vitamin and iron deficiencies even though the ads in question make no reference to the symptoms.

This potentially potent remedy was employed in *Warner-Lambert Co. v. Federal Trade Commission* (1977). The case involved Listerine Mouthwash, which for a hundred years had been touted as being effective against the common cold. This claim, of course, was false. Although Listerine could "kill germs by the million on contact," it had no effect on the viruses that cause colds. The FTC ordered the Warner-Lambert Company, the maker of Listerine, to cease and desist from advertising that the mouthwash prevents, cures, or alleviates the common cold. Further, the Commission directed the company to include the following statement in all future advertising: "Contrary to prior advertising, Listerine will not help prevent colds or sore throats or lessen their severity." Warner-Lambert was to make this disclosure in all Listerine ads until it had spent an amount equal to its average annual advertising expenditures for the ten-year period from April 1962 to March 1972—that is, about $10 million. The U.S. Court of Appeals for the District of Columbia Circuit upheld the FTC, though it allowed Warner-Lambert to drop the phrase "contrary to prior advertising" from the required disclosure.

The Commission's theory in requiring corrective advertising in this case was simple: several decades of false advertising about the effectiveness of Listerine against colds had built up a large reservoir of erroneous consumer belief which would persist, unless corrected, long after Warner-Lambert stopped making the claims. The Court of Appeals aggreed. Writing for the court, Judge J. Skelly Wright said:

> We think this [approach] is entirely reasonable. It dictates two factual inquiries: (1) did Listerine's advertisements play a substantial role in creating or reinforcing in the public's mind a false belief about the product? and (2) would this belief linger on after the false advertising ceases? It strikes us that if the answer to both questions is not yes, companies everywhere may be wasting their massive advertising budgets. Indeed, it is more than a little peculiar to hear [Warner-Lambert] assert that its commercials really had no effect on consumer belief.

The court also rejected the company's argument that the corrective advertising order was unconstitutional by virtue of the commercial speech doctrine. Relying heavily on the *Virginia Pharmacy* case, which had been only recently decided, Judge Wright pointed out that deceptive and misleading commercial speech is not protected by the first amendment. The FTC order did not regulate truthful speech, but was "merely requiring certain statements which, if not present in current and future advertisements, would render those advertisements themselves part of a continuing deception of the public." He added:

> Admittedly, corrective advertising orders . . . may give rise to concern as to their chilling effect on protected truthful speech. The potential advertiser must consider not only the possibility that he will be forced, at some future date, to abandon his advertising campaign, but also that he may be required to include specific disclaimers. But this

danger seems more theoretical than real. As the Supreme Court pointed out in [*Virginia Pharmacy*], not only is the truth of commercial speech "more easily verifiable by its disseminator" than other forms of speech, but "[s]ince advertising is the *sine qua non* of commercial profits, there is little likelihood of its being chilled by proper regulation and foregone entirely."

Moreover, whatever incremental chill is caused by a corrective advertising order beyond that which would result from a cease and desist order may well be necessary if the interest of consumers in truthful information is to be served at all. Otherwise, advertisers remain free to misrepresent their products to the public through false and deceptive claims, knowing full well that even if the FTC chooses to prosecute they will be required only to cease an advertising campaign which by that point will, in all likelihood, have served its purpose be deceiving the public and already been replaced.

A more serious First Amendment problem which may be raised by corrective advertising orders involves the burden thereby imposed upon the constitutional right . . . to advertise truthfully: the party subject to a corrective advertising order may be precluded from exercising his right to advertise unless he also includes specified statements undermining his prior deceptive claims. On the facts of this case, no burden is imposed upon truthful, protected advertising since, as the Commission makes clear, Listerine's current advertising, if not accompanied by a corrective message, would itself continue to mislead the public.

The court then turned to the specifics of the FTC's order, which was quite detailed. Warner-Lambert was required to include the disclosure statement in every future Listerine advertisement until it spent about $10 million, which, given the company's advertising budget for the product, would take a year or so. "We cannot say that is an unreasonably long time in which to correct a hundred years of cold claims," the court said.

With respect to print advertisements, the order required that the disclosure appear in type at least as large as that used for the principal portion of the text, but separate from the text so that it could be readily noticed. In television commercials, the disclosure had to be presented simultaneously by audio and video. No other sound, such as background music, was to be used on television and radio spots when the disclosure was being made. These requirements, the court said, "are well calculated to assure that the disclosure will reach the public." As noted above, the court made only one change in the FTC's order, directing that the phrase "contrary to prior advertising" be deleted. This "confessional preamble" was unnecessary in light of the other safeguards to call attention to the disclosure, the court said, and would serve to only "humiliate" the company.

Other Tools. In the early 1970s, the Commission began requiring advertisers to substantiate the claims made for their products. At one point, the FTC was requiring major companies in certain industries—the manufacturers of automobiles, air conditioners, electric shavers, and television sets, for example—to submit to the agency all tests, studies, and other data that supported their advertising claims with respect to product quality, efficacy, performance, and safety. Although this program proved ineffective (in part because companies swamped the FTC with useless data) and has been discontinued, the Commission uses lack of substantiation as a basis for ruling that an advertisement is deceptive.

A 1986 case, *Thompson Medical Co. v. Federal Trade Commission*, is illustrative. At issue were advertisements for Aspercreme, an over-the-counter pain reliever advertised as being effective against minor aches and pains caused by arthritis. A television ad for the product included the following monologue:

> When you suffer from arthritis, imagine putting the strong relief of aspirin right where you hurt. Aspercreme is an odorless rub which concentrates the relief of aspirin. When you take regular aspirin, it goes throughout your body like this. But, in seconds, Aspercreme starts concentrating all the temporary relief of two aspirin directly at the point of minor arthritis pain. . . . Aspercreme. The strong relief of aspirin right where you hurt.

The FTC found the ad to be deceptive for two reasons. First, the ad suggested that Aspercreme contained aspirin when in fact it did not. Second, the ad represented to consumers that Aspercreme was more effective than aspirin while there was no scientific proof for that claim. To deal with the first problem, the FTC ordered that Thompson Medical Co., the manufacturer, cease and desist from using the name "Aspercreme" unless its advertising and packaging made clear that the product does not contain aspirin. With respect to the substantiation issue, the Commission directed the company to refrain from making any statement as to the product's efficacy until it developed at least two "well-controlled, double-blinded clinical studies" to support the claim. The U.S. Court of Appeals for the District of Columbia Circuit upheld this order.

The substantiation requirement was initially developed in FTC decisions under the so-called "unfairness doctrine." Recall that the FTC Act proscribes "unfair" as well as "deceptive" trade practices. As a result, advertising that is not necessarily deceptive can be prohibited if it is "unfair." In the leading substantiation case, *In re Pfizer, Inc.* (1972), the Commission took the position that advertisements for a sunburn remedy were unfair because claims for the product's effectiveness lacked scientific support, even though the ads were not deceptive.

Although the FTC today typically handles substantiation cases under a deception theory, the "unfairness doctrine" can come into play with respect to other kinds of advertisements. For example, ads showing children riding bicycles in violation of proper highway safety rules and cooking on a gas stove without adult supervision have been deemed unfair, although they were in no sense deceptive. Generally speaking, however, the unfairness doctrine is employed against particular business practices—such as high-pressure sales tactics—rather than against advertising. This is due in part to first amendment considerations, for commercial speech that is not deceptive enjoys some degree of constitutional protection. Thus, restrictions on advertising that is merely "unfair" must be evaluated under the *Central Hudson* criteria.

In addition to proceeding administratively against advertisers who use deceptive or unfair techniques, the FTC has the authority to ask a federal district court to enjoin the advertisement. By employing this remedy, the FTC can avoid problems with delay that often plague the administrative process. Most administrative proceedings take several months or even years to resolve, and all the while the advertiser can continue using the disputed advertisements. If it concludes that an advertisement is particularly egregious, the FTC will seek an injunction that stops the ads until the matter is resolved administratively. This course of action is particularly appropriate if the advertisements concern products that could pose an immediate health threat to consumers. For example, in *Federal Trade Commission v. Pharm-*

tech Research, Inc. (1983), the Commission obtained a preliminary injunction prohibiting the maker of a dietary supplement from representing in its advertising that the product reduced the risk of cancer.

The tools discussed thus far enable the FTC to deal with deceptive advertising on a case-by-case basis, using a quasi-judicial process that can be rather cumbersome. Alternatively, the agency may use the quasi-legislative device known as rulemaking to address deceptive advertising problems on a broader, industrywide basis. In adopting these so-called "trade regulations," the FTC attempts decide in advance that certain advertising practices are deceptive or unfair. The regulations that emerge from this process have the same force and effect as statutes enacted by the Congress, and advertisers that violate them are subject to fines of up to $10,000 per day. Unfortunately, the rulemaking process can be quite lengthy. The FTC must publish in the *Federal Register* a "notice of proposed rulemaking" that outlines the thrust of the proposed regulations and the rationale behind them. Obviously, the agency's staff must devote considerable effort to a proposal before it reaches this stage. Interested parties, usually advertisers who would be affected by the regulation, are then given an opportunity to comment on the proposal, both in writing and at a hearing. After the agency digests the comments, it issues the final version of the regulations, which may then be challenged in the courts.

Trade regulations can be quite controversial. For example, the FTC dropped proposed rules governing over-the-counter drugs when the industry vigorously resisted them. Even more controversial was an FTC proposal to restrict advertising aimed at children. Congress responded by passing legislation that expressly precluded the agency from taking any steps in that direction. The Commission has managed to put some trade regulations into place, including rules governing used cars, funerals, mail-order merchandise, car batteries, home insulation, motor oil, and eyeglasses. By and large, however, the FTC's experience with trade regulations has not been particularly pleasant or successful, and the Commission cut back on its efforts in this area during the deregulation-minded Reagan Administration.

In addition to regulations of this type, the FTC has promulgated several "industry guides" with respect to certain advertising practices. Though these guides lack the binding force of regulations, they give the advertiser some idea of the what the FTC regards as lawful and unlawful. The guides cover such topics as fuel economy data for new cars, use of endorsements and testimonials, deceptive pricing, "bait and switch" advertising, use of the word "free," and advertising in connection with products ranging from dog food and household furniture to wrist watches and tires.

Competitor Remedies

False and deceptive advertising practices can have an adverse impact on competitors as well as consumers. For example, a company that attempts to "pass off" its product as that of a more widely known rival with a better reputation may confuse consumers and divert profits from its competitor. Similarly, a company that makes misleading claims about its own product may attract more customers than a competitor who refrains from making such representations. And, a business that uses so-called "comparative advertising" to measure its product to that of a competitor may make false statements in the course of the comparison or disparage the competitor's product. Unlike consumers, who, as a practical matter, cannot sue an advertiser and must instead complain to the Federal Trade Commission or another federal or state agency, a competitor has additional remedies at his disposal that permit a lawsuit directly against the advertiser. The most important of these are unfair competition, trade libel, and trademark infringement.

Unfair Competition. As noted in the introduction to this chapter, the common law has long recognized the tort of unfair competition. Initially developed as a remedy for the "passing off" technique, the tort gradually expanded to cover other objectionable trade practices. For present purposes, we are concerned with the branch of unfair competition that involves false or deceptive advertising. On this score, the common law remedy was relatively ineffective, for it required that the plaintiff demonstrate actual injury, such a drop in sales or loss of customers, as a result of the advertisement. This burden of proof was quite difficult to carry, and plaintiffs were rarely successful.

In 1946, however, Congress passed the Lanham Act, which deals with a variety of unfair trade practices, including "passing off" and trademark infringement. As initially enacted, Section 43(a) of the act prohibited any "false representation or description" of a product, thus reaching false and deceptive advertising. The federal courts broadly interpreted this provision, which in effect became a federal unfair competition statute that was considerably more effective than the common law. For example, a plaintiff seeking an injunction against the dissemination of false and deceptive advertising was not required to show actual losses, but only that he was likely to suffer injury as a result of the defendant's action. Proof of actual harm was not required unless the plaintiff also sought an award of monetary damages. Following enactment of the Lanham Act, several states also passed legislation liberalizing the common law.

Congress amended Section 43(a) when it overhauled the Lanham Act in 1988, but the revision was generally meant to reflect rather than alter the judicial interpretations that had emerged over four decades. Section 43(a) now provides:

> Any person who, on or in connection with any goods or services, or in any container for goods, uses in [interstate] commerce any word, term, name, or device, or any combination thereof, or any false designation of origin, false or misleading description of fact, or false or misleading representation of fact, which—
>
> (1) is likely to cause confusion, or to cause mistake, or to deceive as to the affiliation, connection, or association of such person with another person, or as to the origin, sponsorship, or approval of his or her goods, services, or commercial activities by another person, or
> (2) in commercial advertising or promotion, misrepresents the nature, characteristics, qualities, or geographic origin of his or her or another person's goods, services, or commercial activities,
>
> shall be liable in a civil action by any person who believes that he or she is or is likely to be damaged by such act.

The first paragraph is designed to prevent an advertiser from using a person's name or likeness without permission, as in the Woody Allen "look-alike" case discussed in Chapter 3 with regard to commercial appropriation. The *Allen* case arose under the 1946 version of Section 43(a), but the result would be the same under the more specific 1988 amendment.

Our concern here is the second paragraph, which deals with false and deceptive advertising. It applies when an advertiser misrepresents the characteristics of its own product or service, draws false comparisons between its product or service and that of a competitor, or misrepresents the characteristics of someone else's product or service. Although the first two situations were covered by the 1946 statute as interpreted by the courts, the third was not. In the leading case on the question, *Bernard Food Industries v. Dietene Co.* (1969), the U.S. Court of Appeals for the Seventh Circuit ruled that the original version of Section 43(a) did not apply to misrepresentations about a competitor's products or services. Thus, the 1988 amendment represents a significant expansion of the statute's scope.

The first situation is illustrated by *Coca-Cola Co. v. Tropicana Products, Inc.* (1982), a case that involved a television commercial featuring Olympic gold medalist Bruce Jenner. The thirty-second spot for Tropicana orange juice showed Jenner squeezing an orange while saying, "It's pure, pasteurized juice as it comes from the orange." Jenner then was shown pouring the freshly squeezed juice into a Tropicana carton. Coca-Cola, maker of Minute Maid orange juice, brought suit under Section 43(a) of the Lanham Act and sought a preliminary injunction barring Tropicana's use of the advertisement. A federal district judge in New York denied relief, but the U.S. Court of Appeals for the Second Circuit reversed and ordered the preliminary injunction. The appellate court concluded that the ad falsely implied that Tropicana contained unprocessed, freshly squeezed orange juice when in fact the juice was heated to about 200 degrees during pasteurization and sometimes frozen prior to packaging.

The second situation arises in the course of so-called "comparative advertising," a relatively recent technique by which one product is compared to another by name in an attempt to demonstrate its superiority. Prior to 1971, two of the three television networks and a number of prominent newspapers and magazines refused to accept advertising that specifically mentioned another product, although comparisons to "Brand X" or "other leading brands" were permitted. In 1971, however, the Federal Trade Commission endorsed brand comparisons and prevailed upon the media to change their policies in this area. The FTC reasoned that such advertising would provide consumers with more information on which to make purchasing decisions, lead to product improvement and innovation, and result in decreased prices. Because the FTC supports comparative advertising, it has been reluctant to intervene in cases of alleged abuse, particularly when the victim of a misleading ad is able to present "the other side of the story" in an ad of its own. Accordingly, the principal remedy for false and misleading advertising of this nature has been Section 43(a) of the Lanham Act.[5]

One of the most famous comparative advertising cases is *American Home Products Corp. v. Johnson & Johnson* (1978), which grew out of an advertising battle between the makers of Anacin and Tylenol. The case had its origins in two Anacin advertisements deployed shortly after Tylenol had displaced Anacin as the best-

---

[5]Many media organizations have developed their own guidelines for comparative advertising. NBC's guidelines, for example, provide that: (1) the products identified in the ad must actually be in competition with one another; (2) competitors must be fairly and properly identified; (3) advertisers must not discredit, disparage, or unfairly attack competitors and their products; (4) the identification must be for comparison purposes and not simply to "upgrade" one's product by association; (5) the advertising must compare related or similar properties or ingredients of the product, using a side-by-side comparison whenever possible; (6) the properties being compared must be significant in terms of value or usefulness of the product to consumers; and (7) the difference in properties must be measurable and significant.

selling over-the-counter pain reliever. One ad, a thirty-second television spot aired on NBC and CBS, stated that "your body knows the difference between these pain relievers [showing Tylenol and other products] and Adult Strength Anacin." The ad asserted that Anacin "reduces the inflammation that often comes with pain," while Tylenol and the others did not, and that Anacin worked faster than the other products. The second ad, which appeared in national magazines, took the same approach: "Anacin can reduce inflammation that comes with most pain. Tylenol cannot." McNeil Laboratories, the maker of Tylenol, complained to the two networks, the magazines, and the National Advertising Division of the Better Business Bureau that the ads were deceptive and misleading. These protests, which had little impact, prompted American Home Products Corp., manufacturer of Anacin, to bring suit against McNeil and its parent company, Johnson & Johnson, for interfering with dissemination of the advertisements. McNeil retailiated by charging that the Anacin ads were deceptive under Section 43(a) of the Lanham Act.

After examining consumer reaction surveys, a federal district judge in New York determined that the advertisements represented Anacin to be a "superior analgesic generally" that also did a better job of reducing inflammation. The judge then reviewed the medical evidence and found that both claims were false. Accordingly, he entered an injunction prohibiting American Home Products from making such representations. The U.S. Court of Appeals for the Second Circuit affirmed, concluding that a reader or listener "could reasonably infer that Anacin is superior to Tylenol in reducing pain generally . . . and in reducing certain kinds of pain. . . ." Because the medical literature did not support those claims, the court said, the advertisements falsely represented Anacin in violation of the Lanham Act.

The third situation—misrepresentation of someone else's product or service—also can arise in the comparative advertising context. As noted previously, a misrepresentation of this type was not considered within the reach of the original version of Section 43(a). In the *Bernard Food* case, for example, the U.S. Court of Appeals for the Seventh Circuit denied recovery because the defendant's alleged misrepresentation in a product comparison involved the plaintiff's instant custard mix, not the defendant's own competing brand. Designed to change this result, the 1988 amendment expressly provides for liability if an advertiser misrepresents the characteristics or qualities of *"another person's* goods, services, or commercial activities." Suppose, for instance, that the ads at issue *American Home Products* case had not misrepresented Anacin's pain-relieving qualities but had only claimed, inaccurately, that Tylenol could not reduce inflammation. Although such advertisements would not have violated Section 43(a) prior to the 1988 change in the law, they would run afoul of the amended version of the statute.

This expansion of Section 43(a) could have a significant impact on comparative advertising, since advertisers may well become quite cautious in commenting upon the products or services of competitors. As noted trademark attorney Jerome Gilson has written:

> [The amended statute] now adds an enormously important weapon to the legal arsenal of the business community and a significant deterrent to unfair competitors. The change makes actionable material false representations concerning the plaintiff's products or services, and effectively creates a federal cause of action for product or trade disparagement. A competitor cannot state falsely in advertising that the plaintiff's product causes cancer, does not effectively cut the grass, or causes headaches without violating [Section 43(a)].

Though injunctive relief is the most common remedy sought and achieved in Section 43(a) cases, monetary damages are also available. For example, in *U-Haul International, Inc. v. Jartran, Inc.* (1986), the U.S. Court of Appeals for the Ninth Circuit upheld a $40 million damage award on the basis of false and deceptive comparative advertisements. The case stemmed from an aggressive advertising campaign that Jartran waged against U-Haul, the leader in the "self-move" rental industry. The $6 million campaign, which won a prestigious "Gold Effie" award from the American Marketing Association, apparently worked, for Jartran's gross revenues jumped from $7 million in 1979 to $95 million in 1981, while U-Haul's revenues fell for the first time in its history. Among other things, the ads claimed that Jartran's rates were lower and that its rental trucks were superior. However, Jartran quoted its own promotional rates rather than its customary charges and calculated U-Haul's rates in a fashion that artificially inflated them. Jartran also used photographs of U-Haul trucks that made them appear smaller and less attractive than its own vehicles.

After entering a preliminary injunction against these and other practices, a federal judge in Arizona made that order permanent and awarded U-Haul $40 million in damages. In arriving at that figure, the trial judge took into account $13.6 million that U-Haul spent on advertising to counteract the Jartran ads, plus approximately $6 million in financial benefits that Jartran received as a result of the deceptive advertising. Although Jartran did not actually make a profit during the period in question, the judge assumed that the company's financial benefit from the ads was at least as much as their cost. The total, $20 million, was then doubled under a provision of the Lanham Act that permits such enhancement.

Although amended Section 43(a) provides potent remedies for companies whose competitors engage in false and deceptive advertising, its utility for consumers is unclear. The House version of the 1988 bill revising the Lanham Act contained a provision making plain that consumers may sue under Section 43(a), but this language does not appear in the legislation as ultimately enacted. It is arguable, however, that the provision was not necessary to give consumers the right to sue, for Section 43(a) specifically states that "any person who believes that he or she is or is likely to be damaged" may bring suit. This interpretation is supported by statements in congressional reports accompanying the 1988 legislation.

Trade Libel. As noted previously, the original version of Section 43(a) of the Lanham Act did not apply to advertising that falsely misrepresented another's product or service. The common law of torts, however, has long provided a remedy, known variously as trade libel, commercial disparagement, or injurious falsehood. While the 1988 amendment expands the reach of Section 43(a) in this regard, the common law remedy remains available and should not be overlooked, particularly in cases where the link with interstate commerce required by the federal statute is not present.

Obviously, trade libel bears some resemblance to defamation, but a distinction between the two is traditionally recognized. While defamation affords a basis of recovery when the plaintiff's entrepreneurial reputation is harmed, trade libel is the proper remedy if the quality of the plaintiff's goods or products is impugned. The line between the two may blur on occassion, for an attack on a product might be well be construed as an attack upon its maker or seller. However, the courts have permitted defamation suits in such situations only when the statement fairly implies that the plaintiff is dishonest or lacks integrity.

Two cases involving sales tactics of competing chemical companies illustrate this distinction. In *Blens Chemicals, Inc. v. Wyandotte Chemical Corp.* (1950), the plaintiff manufactured a chemical compound called "Spur," which it sold to laundries. The defendant, a competitor, provided its salesmen with a letter stating that a "major change had been made in the formulation" of Spur, rendering it inferior to the defendant's product. The salesmen showed the letter to various customers, and the plaintiff filed suit. A New York court concluded that the remedy was trade libel rather than defamation, because the letter "neither directly nor by inference in any way impugns the character, integrity or business practices of the plaintiff."

In contrast is *Lehigh Chemical Co v. Celanese Corp.* (1968). There the plaintiff furnished aircraft engine oil to a federal agency pursuant to a contract. The agency canceled contract after it learned from one of the defendant's salesmen that the plaintiff had been supplying used oil. The plaintiff subsequently sued the defendant on both disparagement and defamation theories. Though a Maryland federal court dismissed the case on other grounds, it indicated that the salesman's statement not only brought into question the quality of the oil, but also implied that the plaintiff was guilty of fraud. Under those circumstances, a defamation suit would be proper.

The distinction between trade libel and "ordinary" defamation was important at common law because the plaintiff's burden in a trade libel action was much heavier than in a defamation suit. However, the constitutionalization of the law of defamation in the wake of *New York Times Co. v. Sullivan* makes these differences less significant today. At common law, a plaintiff seeking damages for trade libel was typically required to prove that the disparaging statement was false, that it was made with intent to injure or with knowledge of its falsity, and that he suffered actual economic loss as a result of the statement. As we saw in Chapter 2, the common law of defamation left to the defendant the burden of proving truth, did not require any proof of malicious intent or fault, and presumed that the plaintiff suffered damages. These rules have all changed as a result of *New York Times* and subsequent cases, and the plaintiff's burden in a defamation action—at least one involving a matter of public concern—is now much the same as in a trade libel case at common law.

It is unclear whether all of the constitutional safeguards developed in *New York Times* and its progeny apply in trade libel cases. The U.S. Supreme Court left open this question in *Bose Corp. v. Consumers Union of United States* (1984), in which the manufacturer of stereo speakers alleged that it lost sales because of a false, derogatory review of its product in *Consumer Reports* magazine. Several lower courts have employed constitutional defamation principles in disparagement cases, and this approach seems reasonable in cases such as *Bose*, where the speaker is a not a competitor and the speech noncommercial. Different considerations come into play, however, if the disparaging speech is commercial in nature, as is the case when a company launchs an advertising attack on a rival's product. As discussed previously in this chapter, only truthful, nonmisleading commercial speech is protected under the first amendment. Because the tort of disparagement limits recovery to damage caused by false speech, commercial speech shown to be disparaging is by definition false and therefore without first amendment protection. In that situation, the *New York Times* line of cases should be inapplicable.

The Congress confronted these problems in debating the 1988 legislation amending the Lanham Act, and its solution was to limit to "commercial advertising" the portion of Section 43(a) dealing with misrepresentation. According to a House report accompanying the bill, the revised version of Section 43(a) is "narrowly drafted to encompass only clearly false and misleading commercial speech." The amended statute "should not be read in any way to limit political speech, consumer or editorial comment, parodies, satires, or other constitutionally protected material." It is therefore clear that Section 43(a) does not allow recovery based on a disparaging product "review" of the type at issue in *Bose*. The common law of trade libel might provide a remedy in that situation, but, as noted above, the constitutional safeguards of *New York Times* probably apply because of the noncommercial nature of the speech.

Trademark Infringement. As mentioned briefly in Chapter 4, the original function of a trademark was to identify a product as the work of a particular medieval craftsman or his guild. Today, a trademark functions on three different levels:

- as an indication of origin or ownership;
- as a guarantee of the quality or other characteristics of a product or service; and
- as a medium of advertising.

With respect to the advertising function, the law recognizes and protects the "goodwill" that a seller has developed with its customers over a period of time. To those who are familiar with the product, the trademark is a symbol of quality and reliability. For potential customers, the trademark fosters name recognition, sets the product apart from competing brands, and helps create a favorable impression of the product.

Before going any further, some definitions are in order. According to the federal trademark statute, the Lanham Act, a trademark is any word, name, symbol, or device adopted and used by a manufacturer or merchant to identify his goods and distinguish them from those manufactured or sold by others. Examples are legion: "Levi's" jeans, "Ford" trucks, "Rolex" watches. While trademarks are used in connection with tangible goods, service marks are used to identify services, a term that includes everything from plumbing ("Roto-Rooter") to retail stores ("Sears") to entertainment ("The Beach Boys"). For the sake of convenience, the following discussion will for the most part use only the term "trademark."[6]

Trademark protection is based on a curious blend of state and federal law. In contrast to the federal patent and copyright laws, which create specific rights, the Lanham Act simply provides a framework for the enforcement, at the federal level, of the common law affecting trademarks. The reason for this different approach can be found in the Constitution, which directly empowers Congress to deal with patent and copyright matters but which says nothing about trademarks. When Congress attempted to federalize trademark law in the 1870s, the Supreme Court declared the statutes unconstitutional. Subsequently, Congress enacted statutes ad-

---

[6]Two other types of marks warrant brief mention. As its name implies, a certification mark certifies product characteristics and is used on products that are not owned or sold by the mark's owner. For example, the "Union Label" on clothing certifies that it was made by members of the garment worker's union. A collective mark is a trademark or service mark used to indicate membership in a cooperative, association, or other collective group. Thus, the 4H Club symbol, which resembles a four-leaf clover, is used to reflect membership in that organization.

dressing only the interstate use of trademarks, relying on the interstate commerce clause of the Constitution. The most recent of these statutes is the Lanham Act, passed in 1946 and amended significantly by the Trademark Law Revision Act of 1988. It provides a system by which companies can "register" with the federal government trademarks used in interstate commerce and bring suits in federal court against infringers. Each state also has an administrative system to register marks used within that state.

Under the initial version of the Lanham Act, federal registration was good for a period of twenty years, with renewal for an additional twenty years available upon a showing of continued use of the mark. The 1988 amendments shorten both periods to ten years, though the term of a registration or renewal in effect at the time of the statutory revision is not affected. The primary reason for the change was to help eliminate "deadwood," that is, trademarks that have been properly registered but are no longer in actual use. So long as these marks remain on the register without being formally abandoned, they prevent the registration of similar marks. There are approximately 600,000 federally registered marks, with about 50,000 new marks and 5,000 renewals each year. Absent registration, a trademark is protected under the common law only within the geographic area in which it is used.

Either actual use of a mark or a representation of one's intent to use it is necessary for federal registration. The Lanham Act initially required actual use, and the alternative "intent-to-use" system was one of the key features of the Trademark Law Revision Act of 1988. When actual use is the basis for registration, the difference between trademarks and service marks is important. With respect to products, the trademark must be applied to the product itself or used in connection with it. For example, the trademark can be stamped on the product, affixed to a container or label, or used with a display at the point of sale. Advertising, however, is not sufficient to establish usage for a trademark. On the other hand, advertising is critical to prove usage of a service mark, since services are intangible. Of course, the advertised service must also actually be offered to the public. For purposes of federal registration, the use must also affect interstate commerce; if the business is truly local in nature, only state registration is available.

Under the "intent-to-use" system, a person may file an application for registration with the Patent and Trademark Office stating simply that he intends to use a proposed mark. As is the case with applications based on actual use, the application will be reviewed for conflicts with registered marks. If it has no objection to the proposed mark, the Patent and Trademark Office will "publish" the mark, thus giving notice to persons to object to the mark's registration. Opposition typically triggers an administrative proceeding to determine whether the mark is to be registered, and that decision is subject to review by the courts. If an application based on actual use is unopposed, the mark will be registered following the notice, but an additional step is necessary under the intent-to-use system. In the event that such an application is not opposed, the Patent and Trademark Office will "allow" the mark, and within six months the applicant must file an affidavit stating that he has in fact used it. At that point, the mark will be registered. The Patent and Trademark Office may extend the allowance period for an additional six months upon at the request of the applicant and for two more years upon a showing of "good cause."

The "allowance" procedure, along with the time necessary for the Patent and Trademark Office to review an application, in effect creates a potentially lengthy period during which a person may "reserve" a trademark and prevent anyone else from adopting it. Because the application review process typically takes from eight to twelve months, a mark can be reserved for up to eighteen months—or as long as four years, if the maximum extension of the "allowance" is granted—before it must actually be used. Although this "reservation" feature has been the criticized because it arguably may encourage applications simply to keep others from using particular marks, Congress believed that the "intent-to-use" system was necessary to bring federal registration practices in line with those in other developed nations. Moreover, the new system removes some of the financial risk accompanying the actual use requirement, under which a company might spend substantial sums to develop and use a mark only to encounter an objection from the owner of a similar mark.

The principal advantage of federal registration is that it offers nationwide protection and prevents others from using the mark or similar marks that may confuse consumers. State registration offers similar protection, but only with respect to use of the mark within the state. If a federal registration has been secured, the letter "R" in a circle should appear as a superscript adjacent to the mark to ensure full protection. This symbol may not be used if only state registration has been obtained, however. In that situation, it is customary for companies to use the superscripts "TM" and "SM" for trademarks and service marks, respectively. Federal registration also entitles the trademark owner to bring suit in federal court for infringement. Otherwise, he must proceed in state court.

Registration does not mean that the trademark is automatically valid; however, it does create a presumption of validity in the event of litigation. The principal characteristic of a trademark is "distinctiveness," that is, the capacity of a mark to distinguish a particular product or service from its competitors. Accordingly, the generic name of a product can never serve as a trademark, since it does not indicate the source of the product. "Baby oil," for example, is a generic term, as is "shredded wheat."

Similarly, a term that merely describes a product or service usually cannot serve as a trademark. While a generic term to some degree describes a product or service, a descriptive term identifies specific qualities or characteristics, such as color, size, function, ingredients, or other attributes. For instance, "micro-wheel" connotes size, and "five-second glue" describes a characteristic. By the same token, "auto market" is descriptive with respect to a business that sells automobiles and accessories, and the title "Daytime TV" summarizes the subject matter of a magazine.

At some point, however, a descriptive mark (but not one that is generic) may take on a "secondary meaning" and thus be registered and protected under trademark law. By being associated over a long period of time with a particular product, a term may come to be known by the public as identifying that product. Notable examples include "Book-of-the-Month Club," "Radio Shack," and "TV Guide." Similarly, although geographic names and names of individuals may not ordinarily be registered, they may over time acquire a secondary meaning. Some famous trademarks incorporate the names of people, such as "L.L. Bean" and "Hilton Hotels," while others, such as "Columbia Broadcasting System" and "American Airlines," utilize geographic references. However, geographic terms rarely acquire secondary meaning standing alone.

Two other categories of trademarks are considered more distinctive and thus easier to register and protect: "suggestive" marks, which suggest to the consumer—but do not actually describe—the characteristics of the product or service, and "fanciful" marks coined solely for the purpose of serving as trademarks. No secondary meaning is necessary with respect to either. Suggestive marks include "Coppertone" suntan lotion, "Orange Crush" soft drink, "Playboy" magazine, and "Sani-

Flush" toilet bowl cleaner. Some famous trademarks are purely fanciful, such as "Clorox" bleach, "Kodak" photographic supplies, and "Exxon" gasoline. Closely related to these fanciful marks are arbitrary terms that bear no relationship to the products or services with which they are connected. "Cannon" towels and "Apple" computers fall into this category.

Keep in mind that trademark protection is not limited to words. Pictures, symbols, logos, numerals, and letters may also be registered under certain circumstances, though their descriptive qualities may require proof of a secondary meaning. Examples of valid trademarks of this type include a symbol showing meshed gears, "V-8" vegetable juice, "A&P" food stores, and "LA" low alcohol beer. Slogans pose similar problems. For example, "scientific dentistry at moderate prices" is obviously descriptive. On the other hand, the famous Clairol slogan "haircoloring so natural, only her hairdresser knows for sure" has been held sufficiently distinctive to qualify for trademark protection.

No matter how distinctive a particular trademark, the danger exists that it will, through popular usage, become accepted as the common or generic term for a type of product or service. Several words that are now part of our common vocabulary were once protected trademarks, including aspirin, cellophane, escalator, and thermos. As Judge Learned Hand once observed, the "very success [of a trademark] may prove its failure." Advertising that makes heavy use of the mark can contributes to the problem; with respect to cellophane, for example, the trademark's owner consistently used the word generically in advertisements and direct mailings. Accordingly, owners of trademarks—and their advertising agencies—must be quite careful in their use of trademarks for advertising purposes.

In a 1986 article in *The Business Lawyer*, Boston attorney David A. Westenberg identified several steps that can be taken to preserve the distinctiveness of a trademark:

> (i) The trademark or service mark should only be used as a proper adjective in conjunction with the generic name of the goods or services. . . . For example, if microcomputers were sold under the trademark GOLIATH, proper use would be "the GOLIATH microcomputer." The mark should never be used in the possessive form (GOLIATH's), as a verb (to GOLIATH), as a noun (the GOLIATH), or in the plural form (GOLIATHs). The mark should not be modified with prefixes, suffixes, deletions, or additions.

> (ii) The trademark or service mark should appear in a distinctive form so that the public will identify it as a mark. Possibilities include presenting the mark with an initial capital letter . . . , in all capital letters, in quotation marks, in italics, in logo form, or in some other distinctive style or typeface.

> (iii) The trademark or service mark always should be used in the same form or in a small number of closely similar forms. The size of a logo mark may change, but its proportions and relative location of elements should be constant. If color is a feature of the mark, it is preferable always to use the same color or color combination.

> (iv) To give notice to the public and enhance its recognition as a trademark or service mark, the legal status of the mark should be indicated [by using the appropriate symbol, such as the "R" in a circle for federally registered trademarks].

> (v) The public's awareness of the trademark or service mark as a badge of origin can be expanded by extending use of the mark to a family of related goods. * * *

(vi) The owner's correct use of the mark on goods or in the advertising of services, if extensive and continuous, can bolster a weak mark . . . and establish its distinctive nature. The owner should extend its correct trademark or service mark usage to all facets of its advertising and business, such as catalogs, business correspondence, annual reports, press releases, brochures, and publications.

(vii) The owner should instruct its employees, dealers, suppliers, agents, and licensees as to proper use of trademarks and service marks. If a trademark or service mark owner is aware of misuse of its mark by the public, it should use advertising to educate and persuade the public to use the mark properly. [Xerox Corporation, for example, has run ads advising that a person cannot "xerox something" but can "make copies on a Xerox copier."]

A trademark owner should also take action against other companies that improperly use the trademark or use a very similar mark. The failure to "police" the mark in this fashion can result in a judicial determination that it has been abandoned. There are obviously other reasons why a trademark owner would proceed with legal action: a competitor who uses the trademark could "pass off" his product as that of the trademark owner and thus divert business; the competitor's use of the mark could tarnish the owner's reputation, as would be the case when the competitor's goods are inferior; and a competitor's use of the mark on goods related to but different from those of the owner might make it more difficult for owner to expand into that product line.

In an action for trademark infringment, the plaintiff must first show that the mark is protectable under the basic principles described above and that he used or "reserved" the mark before the defendant. The question then becomes whether there is a "likelihood of confusion" between the two marks. In dealing with this issue, the courts have identified several relevant factors: the nature of the plaintiff's mark (suggestive, fanciful, etc.); the degree of similarity between the marks; the degree of similarity between the products involved; whether the products are sold through the same stores and aimed at the same group of purchasers; whether the same advertising media are utilized; the existence of similar marks on similar goods; the length of time that the marks have been used; intent of the defendant; and evidence of actual confusion among consumers. If the plaintiff prevails, the court may award actual and punitive damages, permanently enjoin the defendant from use of the mark, and order that the infringing materials be destroyed.

As the factors listed above suggest, the "likelihood of confusion" question hinges on the peculiar facts and circumstances of each case. Trademarks that look or sound alike, for example, may well create confusion when used in connection with identical products but cause little difficulty when used with those that are dissimilar or unrelated. Even if the products are the same, however, the fact that they are particularly expensive or are marketed for a sophisticated audience reduces the likelihood of confusion. For instance, similar trademarks used on "big-ticket" consumer items such as air conditioners may not be confusing, since purchasers are typically more thoughtful in buying items with large price tags. The same cannot be said for goods that are often bought on impulse, such as candy at a supermarket. By the same token, there is less likely to be confusion where the products are sold to professionals, such as physicians or engineers, who are not likely to be confused by trademark similarity.

The use of a competitor's trademark in the course of comparative advertising—a fairly common practice—generally does not constitute infringement, although there are arguments against this technique. Suppose, for example, that the manufacturer of a pain reliever advertises that its brand "contains the same ingredient as Tylenol," thus using the trademark of a well-known rival. It could be argued that this use of the trademark enables one seller to capitalize upon the advertising device of another and thus get something of a "free ride." Moreover, a competitor's ability to freely use a famous mark might help contribute to that mark's becoming generic. The courts, however, have taken the position that disallowing use of the trademark in this situation would prevent the competitor from informing the public about the availability of a substitute at a lower price. In effect, the courts have created a "fair use" doctrine similar to that found in copright law.

For example, in *Calvin Klein Cosmetics Corp. v. Lenox Laboratories, Inc.* (1987), the defendant produced a line of perfumes called "The Great Pretenders" that included "Crystal Rose," an imitation of a perfume marketed by the plaintiff under the registered trademark "Obsession." The defendant used the trademark "Obsession" and pictures of the perfume's distinctive oval-shaped bottle in its packaging and store displays, along with a statement disclaiming any connection with the plaintiff. A federal judge in Minnesota granted a preliminary injunction barring this practice, but the U.S. Court of Appeals for the Eighth Circuit reversed. "A trademark is not a monopoly on the use of a name or a phrase," the court said. "An imitator may use in a truthful way an originator's trademark when advertising that the imitator's product is a copy so long as that use is not likely to create confusion in the consumer's mind as to the source of the product being sold." Noting that "Crystal Rose" was priced at less than $10 per quarter ounce and that "Obsession" carried a $55 price tag, the court added that there is a "strong public interest in lowest possible prices . . . and in encouraging, not stifling, competition."

Liability of Advertising Agencies and the Media

Thus far, we have operated under the premise that the advertiser is liable for false and deceptive avertising, unfair competition, trademark infringement, and the like. This liability is based on the simple notion that an advertiser is ultimately responsible for the tactics employed in marketing his goods or services. But the advertiser is only one player in the advertising game, and the roles of advertising agencies in preparing ads and media organizations in disseminating them can hardly be overlooked. Under the principles discussed in Chapters 2 and 3, an ad agency or a media outlet can obviously be held liable for defamation or invasion of privacy on the basis of an advertisement; by the same token, either can be held liable for other wrongs stemming from ads, but for the most part this latter liability is more theoretical than real, particularly with respect to the media.

Let us first consider deceptive advertising cases initiated by the Federal Trade Commission. Advertising agencies are frequently targets of FTC orders with respect to deceptive advertising. Their liability for violations of the FTC Act is governed by two general principles. First, the agency must have been an active participant in the preparation of the offending advertisements. Second, the agency must have known or have had reason to know that the advertisements were false or deceptive. Moreover, the degree of care that an agency must exercise in this regard increases in direct relation to the agency's participation in the project. The degree of participation is measured by a number of factors, including the agency's role in writing and editing the text of the ad, its work in creating and designing the graphics or audio-visual material, its research and analysis of public opinion, and its selection of the appropriate audience for the advertisement.

For example, in *Standard Oil Co. of California v. Federal Trade Commission* (1978), the U.S. Court of Appeals for the Ninth Circuit upheld the FTC's cease and desist order against Standard Oil and its advertising agency, Batten, Barton, Durstine & Osborn (BBD&O). The case involved three television commercials promoting a gasoline additive that was supposed to reduce air pollution. One of the ads showed a metering device that measured the level of hydrocarbon emissions. The gauge revealed, accurately, a drop from 100 units to twenty units based on use of the fuel additive but did not provide explain what the numbers meant. Moreover, the ad failed to indicate that the device did not measure other types of emission pollutants which were unaffected by the additive. The FTC found the ad deceptive because it falsely implied that the use of the additive would reduce all exhaust emissions by as much as eighty percent, when in fact the device measured only a fifty percent reduction in hydrocarbon emissions. In holding both Standard Oil and BBD&O responsible, the FTC stressed that ad agency representatives were involved in the development of the campaign from the earliest stages. Moreover, they reviewed test results, played a major role in meetings during which alternative advertising approaches were evaluated, and actively participated in the filming of the ads, the drafting of the texts, the preparation of layouts, and the promotion and distribution of the advertisements.

The court of appeals, in an opinion by Judge Anthony M. Kennedy (now a U.S. Supreme Court Justice), affirmed the Commission's decision. With respect to the responsibility of BBD&O, the court rejected the ad agency's argument that it was entitled to rely on various independent laboratory tests and the review of the ad campaign by Standard Oil's engineers, attorneys, and high-level management. "[W]hile the technical accuracy of the tests was fully investigated, the review procedures did not have a specific focus on the accuracy of the implicit representations the ads conveyed to the viewing public," the court said. "No specialized engineer was needed to put BBD&O on notice that a gauge which drops from a reading of 100 ("dirty") to 20 ("clean") implies a sweeping representation with reference to the change in level of pollution discharge." In light of the agency's active participation in developing the ads, the court said, "it was BBD&O's responsibility to assure itself not only that the gauge was not rigged, but also that use of the gauge did not convey a distorted impression."

Advertising agencies have also been sued by competitors of a client and by consumers of the client's products. For example, in *Eastern Airlines, Inc. v. New York Air, Inc.* (1983), Eastern brought a deceptive advertising claim under Section 43(a) of the Lanham Act, arguing that New York Air's ads for its "air shuttle" between New York City and Washington, D.C., erroneously suggested that the service was identical to that offered by Eastern. New York Air was held liable and enjoined from using the deceptive ads, but the claim against the ad agency was moot because it no longer worked for the airline. Subsequently, Eastern sued New York Air and its new ad agency for violating the injunction, and a federal judge in New York ordered both the airline and the agency to stop the ads.

Suits of this type have also been brought by consumers pursuant to state law. In *Committee on Children's Television v. General Foods Corp.* (1983), several consumer groups alleged that a cereal manufacturer, two advertising agencies, and a supermarket chain had "engaged in a sophisticated advertising and marketing program . . . designed to capitalize on the unique susceptibilities of children and preschoolers in order to induce them to consume products which, although promoted and labelled as 'cereals,' are in fact more accurately described as sugar products or candies." The trial court dismissed the suit, but the California Supreme Court reversed, ruling that the plaintiffs could proceed against all of the defendants under the state's deceptive trade practices statute.

Newspapers, magazines, broadcast stations, and other media that carry advertising found to be deceptive are rarely targets of FTC action or lawsuits by competitors and consumers. First amendment concerns obviously enter into the picture, and, in contrast to ad agencies, the media usually do not take an active role in preparing the advertisements but simply serve as a conduit through which the message reaches the public. For these reasons, the FTC has been disinclined to proceed against media organizations, though a newspaper or television station that actually prepares an advertisement would presumably stand in the same shoes as an ad agencies and thus face sanctions under the standards set forth in *Standard Oil*. Similarly, the Congress has exempted the media from liability for damages under the Lanham Act if they have "innocently" disseminated false advertising that falls within Section 43(a) or published advertisements that infringe on trademarks, although injunctive relief is available in limited situations.

The common law has also taken the position that the media are not liable to competitors or consumers for false and deceptive advertisements, absent a showing that the particular medium either knew the advertisement was false or undertook to guarantee or endorse the advertised product or service. Some states have gone even further by enacting statutes that completely exempt the media from liability for false or deceptive advertisements.

A 1987 case involving the *Wall Street Journal* reflects the traditional common law view. In *Pittman v. Dow Jones & Co.*, the plaintiffs lost $50,000 they had deposited in a Texas financial institution that went bankrupt. The institution had advertised its "jumbo" interest rates in the *Journal*, falsely stating that all deposits were backed by the U.S. government. When the plaintiffs were unable to recover any of their losses from the institution, they filed suit against the *Journal*, alleging that it had negligently published the false advertisement. A Lousiana federal court granted summary judgment for the newspaper. After pointing out that losses by depositors totaled $17 million, the court said:

> Courts seem to be sensitive to the [potential for] devastating liability . . . since to ignore such arguments could have the effect of discouraging the publication of ads dealing with valuable public information to enable people to make informed choices. Quite simply, courts have placed more value on the societal benefits of information availability than on the rights of private persons who claim to have been harmed. * * *
>
> To impose the burden of investigating the accuracy of every ad would, under ordinary circumstances, be too onerous. In weighing private and public considerations, . . . the public policy of not subjecting newspapers to the chilling prospect of hordes of suits by disgruntled readers of inaccurate ads dominates.

Accordingly, the court concluded that there is no obligation "for a newspaper publisher to investigate its advertisers for the correctness of the ads placed in the publication, even though the *Journal* is arguably one held in high esteem whose very stature lends credibility to the advertisements themselves." The U.S. Court of Appeals for the Fifth Circuit affirmed.

Under this reasoning, the news media need not screen advertisements prior to publication to ensure that they are not false or deceptive. Most major media organizations, however, have adopted such screening procedures, as well as advertising acceptability standards.[7] The fact that a false or deceptive ad slips through this process and finds its way into print or on the air is of no consequence, since there is no duty to investigate in the first place. In other words, a plaintiff cannot argue that the medium was negligent because its screening system did not detect the presence of a false or deceptive claim in an advertisement. Indeed, in the *Pittman* case the court noted that the *Wall Street Journal* had made some effort to investigate the ad in question before accepting it for publication, though that effort obviously proved unsuccessful. But a claim of mere negligence on the part of a publisher or broadcaster in publishing an advertisement is not enough; instead, there must be proof that the defendant either knew that the ad was false but published it anyway or acted negligently in guaranteeing or endorsing a product or service.

Cases of the first type are rare indeed, for it is difficult for a plaintiff to prove such knowledge. And, should he be successful on that score, the plaintiff must also point to specific pecuniary damages that he suffered as a result of the offending ad, another difficult task. With respect to the second category, few publishers and broadcasters purport to guarantee what they advertise or even go so far as to endorse particular products or services. If they do so, however, the media are potentially liable not only for economic harm stemming from false or misleading statements in the ads, but also for physical injuries sustained by consumers who have purchased the product.

The most famous case arising from such an endorsement is *Hanberry v. Hearst Publishing Corp.*, a 1969 California appellate decision involving *Good Housekeeping* magazine. There the plaintiff slipped and fell while wearing a pair of shoes that carried "Good Housekeeping's Consumer Guaranty Seal." The seal stated: "We satisfy ourselves that products advertised in Good Housekeeping are good ones and that the advertising claims made for them in our magazine are truthful." The plaintiff alleged that the shoes were defective in that they were unsuitable for vinyl floor coverings and similar surfaces. Pointing to the seal, the court ruled that the plaintiff could proceed with her suit and attempt to prove that the magazine had negligently misrepresented the product. The court also observed that in using its seal to sell products, *Good Housekeeping* "in effect loaned its reputation to promote and induce the sale of a given product." In doing so, the magazine "placed itself in the position where public policy imposes on it the duty to use ordinary care in the issuance of its seal and certification of quality so that members of the consuming public who rely on its endorsement are not unreasonably exposed to the risk of harm."

---

[7]These screening procedures can be quite important with respect to defamation and invasion of privacy. Although the media do not have a duty to investigate claims made in ads, they must take reasonable steps to ensure that ads are neither defamatory nor invasive of one's privacy. For example, in *Triangle Publications, Inc. v. Chumley* (1984), the Georgia Supreme Court ruled that it was for the jury to decide whether the *Atlanta Constitution* and *TV Guide* magazine had been negligent in printing an ad that allegedly defamed the plaintiff and invaded her privacy. The newspaper apparently had a screening procedure (which was ineffective in this case), while the magazine did not. The court left to the jury the questions of whether the newspaper used reasonable care in screening the ad and whether the magazine's reliance on the advertiser was reasonable under the circumstances.

As *Hanberry* suggests, a plaintiff who suffers personal injuries will not be able to recover against a media entity on the basis of an advertisement unless there is some sort of guarantee or endorsement. Another California case makes the point. In *Walters v. Seventeen Magazine* (1987), the plaintiff became violently ill with toxic shock syndrome after using a particular brand of tampon she had seen advertised in the magazine. She then brought suit against against *Seventeen* on the basis of the advertisement. In affirming the trial judge's dismissal of the case, the appellate court found *Hanberry* inapposite because *Seventeen* did not in any way sponsor or endorse products advertised in its pages. The court added:

> [W]e are loathe to create a new tort of negligently failing to investigate the safety of an advertised product. Such a tort would require publications to maintain huge staffs scrutinizing and testing each product offered. The enormous cost of such groups, along with skyrocketing insurance rates, would deter many magazines from accepting advertising, hastening their demise from lack of revenue. Others would comply, but raise their prices beyond the reach of the average reader. Still others would be wiped out by tort judgments, never to revive. Soon the total number of publications in circulation would drop dramatically.

The court also ruled, without extended discussion, that the commercial speech doctrine precluded recovery, observing that the consequences of imposing liability in cases such as this one may have prompted the U.S. Supreme Court to be "so vigilant about linking commercial speech to the First Amendment."

As noted in Chapter 9, however, two recent cases involving *Soldier of Fortune* magazine reflect the willingness of some courts to adopt the negligence theory that the court in *Walters* rejected. Both cases stemmed from classified advertisements in the "personal services" section of the magazine. The first, *Norwood v. Soldier of Fortune Magazine, Inc.* (1987), arose from the attempted murder of a law student in a plot traced to a "gun for hire" ad describing the qualifications of a "professional mercenary" who would consider "all jobs." Responding to the ad, the ex-husband of the student's wife arranged to have him murdered. Though the attempt was unsuccessful, the student was shot and wounded on one occasion at his home, and a bomb was placed in his car. The case was settled prior to trial after a federal district court in Arkansas denied the magazine's motion for summary judgment. Because the speech was commercial in nature, the court said, it was entitled to only limited first amendment protection that did not preclude an award of damages if the jury were to find that the ad "had a substantial probability of ultimately causing harm to some individual."

The second case, *Eimann v. Soldier of Fortune Magazine, Inc.* (1988), resulted in a $9.4 million jury verdict against the publication that was subsequently overturned on appeal. In *Eimann,* a former Marine who had bought a classified ad in *Soldier of Fortune* was subsequently hired to kill the plaintiff's daughter. The ad said:

> EX-MARINE—'67–'69 'Nam vet—ex-DI—weapons specialist—jungle warfare, pilot, M.E., high risk assignments U.S. or overseas.

A Texas federal court ruled that the commercial speech doctrine did not bar the plaintiff's suit for the wrongful death of her daughter and that it was for the jury to decide whether the magazine was negligent in failing to investigate the ad.

In dealing with the first amendment issue, the court built on the analysis employed in *Norwood*. Apparently because the ad did not expressly propose an illegal transaction, the court determined that it fell within the commercial speech doctrine. However, the court then concluded that this limited first amendment protection had to yield to the superior interests of the plaintiff, reasoning that the first amendment "does not sanction the infliction of physical injury merely because [it is] achieved by word, rather than act." With respect to the negligence question, the court emphasized that its ruling was a narrow one not intended to require all publishers to investigate all ads. "[P]ublication, without investigation, of the advertisement that is the subject of this suit in a city newspaper of general circulation in all likelihood would not be unreasonable," the court said. However, the failure of *Soldier of Fortune* to investigate prior to publication might be unreasonable "given the nature of the magazine and its readership and given the fact that many advertisements submitted for publication expressly offered criminal services."

In 1989 the U.S. Court of Appeals for the Fifth Circuit reversed the jury's award and ruled that *Soldier of Fortune* could not be held liable. As discussed in Chapter 9, the court's opinion was grounded in tort law rather than the first amendment. The magazine argued on appeal that the trial judge's ruling impermissibly required it to guard against criminal solicitation by investigating advertisers and their ads. The Fifth Circuit said the burden imposed by the lower court was even more onerous than that because it "required publishers to recognize ads that reasonably could be interpreted as an offer to engage in illegal activity based on their words or context and refrain from printing them." Citing the same policy considerations mentioned in *Walters* and *Pittman,* the court of appeals held that *Soldier of Fortune* "owed no duty to refrain from publishing a facially innocuous classified advertisement when the ad's context—at most—made its message ambiguous."

THE RIGHT TO REFUSE ADVERTISING

We saw in Chapter 10 that the Supreme Court has rejected a first amendment "right of access" to the print and broadcast media, though recognizing that, in some cases, a statute requiring that broadcasters grant such access is not unconstitutional. In *Miami Herald Publishing Co. v. Tornillo* (1974), Chief Justice Warren Burger observed:

> A newspaper is more than a passive receptacle or conduit for news, comment, and advertising. The choice of material to go into a newspaper, and the decisions made as to limitations on the size and content of the paper, and treatment of public issues and public officials—whether fair or unfair—constitute the exercise of editorial control and judgment. It has yet to be demonstrated how governmental regulation of this crucial process can be exercised consistent with First Amendment guarantees of a free press. . . .

He made the same point a bit more succinctly in *CBS, Inc. v. Democratic National Committee* (1973): "For better or worse, editing is what editors are for; and editing is selection and choice of material."

Even before these decisions, the lower courts had used similar reasoning in concluding that newspapers may accept or refuse advertising as they see fit. As early as 1933, the Supreme Court of Iowa ruled in *Schuck v. Carroll Daily Herald* that newspaper publishers "have a right to publish whatever advertisements they desire and to refuse to publish whatever advertisements they do not desire to publish." In so holding, the court rejected the advertiser's argument that newspapers are common carriers which, like telegraph companies, must serve all who wish to make use of their services. The newspaper business, the court said, is "as private as that of the banker, grocer, or milkman, all of whom perform a service on which, to a greater or lesser extent, the communities depend, but which bears no relation to the public as to warrant its inclusion in the category of businesses charged with a public use."

Though the *Schuck* case involved a purely commercial advertisement for a dry cleaning business, the courts have reached the same result with respect to so-called "cause" advertising that takes a stance on a public issue. Several major companies, notably Mobil Oil, have used these "advertorials" to comment upon issues ranging from foreign policy to media coverage of business. Other organizations, such as the AFL-CIO, the American Jewish Committee, and the National Rifle Association, have also bought newspaper and magazine ads to express their views. But the fact that these advertisements are not purely commercial messages does not change the fact that a newspaper or magazine can reject all or some of them, for any reason or no reason.

The leading case of this type is *Chicago Joint Board, Amalgamated Clothing Workers of America v. Chicago Tribune Co.*, decided by the U.S. Court of Appeals for the Seventh Circuit in 1970. There the plaintiff labor union was conducting a campaign to limit the importation of foreign-made clothing into the United States on the ground that these imports reduced the number of jobs available to union members. As part of this campaign, the union picketed Marshall Field & Co., a large Chicago department store that carried imported clothing. In addition, the union sought to purchase full-page advertisements in the four daily newspapers that then served Chicago, all of which carried advertising by Marshall Field. The purpose of the ads was to explain why the union was picketing the department store and to set forth the union's reasons for opposing the sale of foreign-made clothing. When all four newspapers refused to publish the ads, the union asked a federal judge to order that they do so. The judge entered summary judgment for the newspapers, and the Seventh Circuit affirmed.

First, the court of appeals rejected the union's argument that the newspapers' refusal to print the ads was governmental action triggering the first amendment. As discussed in Chapter 1, the activities of private parties that restrain speech do not violate the first amendment, which protects only against the government's infringement of freedom of speech and press. The union, however, contended that the newspapers should be considered quasi-governmental entities in light of the special benefits that they enjoyed, including certain tax exemptions, the right to sell their product on city streets and sidewalks, a source of income from state statutes that required newspaper publication of various legal notices, and free working space for reporters at various public buildings, such as city hall and the state capitol. Though recognizing that, in some cases, a very close relationship between a private entity and the government can result in a finding of governmental action, the court held that no such relationship existed here. There was no government involvement "in the operation of defendants' newspapers, or in the formulation or application of defendants' policies with respect to the acceptance or rejection of editorial advertising," the court said, adding that "the function of the press from the days the Constitution was written to the present time has never been conceived as anything but a private enterprise, free and independent of government control. . . ."

Second, the court gave short shrift to an argument similar to that advanced a few years later in *Tornillo*: a newspaper has a ''reciprocal obligation'' under the first amendment to serve as a ''public forum'' and publish all editorial advertising submitted to it. ''We do not understand this to be the concept of freedom of the press recognized in the First Amendment,'' the court said. ''The Union's right to free speech does not give it the right to make use of the defendants' printing presses and distribution systems without defendants' consent.''

Three years later, the U.S. Supreme Court employed similar reasoning in *CBS, Inc. v. Democratic National Committee*, a decision considered in Chapter 10 in connection with broadcasting. There the Court made plain that a broadcaster's refusal to accept editorial advertising is not governmental action for purposes of the first amendment, even though broadcast stations, unlike newspapers, are licensed and regulated by the federal government. Moreover, the Court ruled that neither the fairness doctrine nor the ''public interest'' standard of the Communications Act requires broadcasters to air editorial advertisements. Thus, radio and television stations are free to reject editorial advertising if they so choose, just as they may refuse to broadcast commercial advertisements. Keep in mind, however, that Section 312(a)(7) of the Communications Act requires broadcasters to sell or provide air time to candidates for federal elective office. The Supreme Court upheld this provision against a first amendment challenge in *CBS, Inc. v. Federal Communications Commission* (1981).

Apart from this special ''political advertising'' statute that applies only to broadcasters, there may be other restrictions on the media's right to refuse advertising. First, a media organization may find itself obligated as a matter of contract law to publish an advertisement. If, for example, an advertiser's payment for an ad is accepted by a newspaper's advertising department, a valid and enforceable contract may be formed at that point. Should the newspaper later change its mind and decide that the ad is unacceptable, the advertiser may be able to sue for breach of contract and obtain a court order directing the newspaper to honor the agreement by publishing the ad. This problem can be eliminated by making clear to prospective advertisers that the publisher or broadcaster reserves the right to reject an advertisement and that a refund will be made if the ad is ultimately considered unacceptable.

Second, the right to refuse advertising is limited to some extent by the federal antitrust laws. As discussed in Chapter 12, however, the media are unlikely to encounter antitrust problems so long as they act unilaterally in making the decision to reject advertising. Difficulties in this area generally arise only when a media organization allows outsiders to become involved in the decision making process. If, for example, a newspaper bows to pressure from one department store—a major advertiser—and rejects all advertising from a rival store, the newspaper may well find itself the target of an antitrust suit.

Finally, special problems exist with respect to government-owned media, for here there is no doubt that governmental action is present. Moreover, the ''public forum'' doctrine discussed in Chapter 1 arguably applies to such media. Accordingly, it would seem that a government-owned medium, unlike its counterparts in the private sector, does not have unbridled authority to refuse advertising. The U.S. Supreme Court has not spoken directly to this question, and decisions of the lower courts are woefully inconsistent.

The general rule, however, seems to be this: if a government-owned medium is considered a public forum and has made the decision to accept advertising, it may not arbitrarily reject advertisements that a privately-owned medium would be free to refuse. For example, in *Radical Lawyers Caucus v. Pool* (1970), a federal court ruled that the official journal of the Texas State Bar, a government agency, could not reject a "political" ad submitted by a lawyers' group when it accepted commercial advertising and published articles on political topics. In contrast, the U.S. Supreme Court concluded in *Lehman v. City of Shaker Heights* (1974) that a city bus was not a public forum and that the city transit authority could limit signs in the buses to commercial advertising and reject paid political messages.

Cases involving newspapers at public schools have been particularly troublesome. The only Supreme Court decision touching on the issue, *Hazelwood School District v. Kuhlmeier* (1988), did not deal with advertising. There the Court held that a high school newspaper published as part of a journalism class was not a public forum. In cases involving college newspapers, the lower courts have divided on the question of whether such publications may freely reject advertising. For example, in *Mississippi Gay Alliance v. Goudelock* (1976), the U.S. Court of Appeals for the Fifth Circuit ruled that a student newspaper at a state university acted permissibly in refusing to publish an ad submitted by an organization for homosexual students. In contrast, the U.S. Court of Appeals for the Seventh Circuit held in *Lee v. Board of Regents* (1971) that a state-supported college newspaper that accepted commercial advertising could not refuse paid editorial ads.

PROBLEMS

1. According to a 1988 *Sports Illustrated* article, Anheuser-Busch Brewing Co., which has captured forty percent of the American beer market, spends approximately two-thirds of its $344 million annual advertising budget in sports-related areas, including nearly $110 million for advertising on the three major networks' sports telecasts. The same article quoted physicians and other experts critical of the advertising connection between alcohol and sports, cited studies finding a link between beer advertising and drunken driving and other "macho" behavior, and pointed out that between the ages of two and eighteen, American children see 100,000 television commercials for beer. William O. Johnson, "Sports and Suds," *Sports Illustrated* (August 8, 1988), p. 68. Can Congress constitutionally pass a statute banning beer commercials from sports events on television and radio? Forbidding beer companies from sponsoring sports events? Prohibiting beer and liquor advertising altogether, regardless of the medium? Requiring broadcast stations and the print media to carry public service announcements regarding alcohol consumption and abuse? *See Dunagin v. City of Oxford*, 718 F.2d 738 (5th Cir. 1983), *cert. denied*, 467 U.S. 1259 (1984); Comment, "Alcoholic Beverage Advertising on the Airwaves: Alternatives to a Ban or Counteradvertising," 34 *U.C.L.A. Law Review* 1139 (1987).

2. Reconsider the questions posed in Problem 2 at the end of Chapter 1 with respect to tobacco advertising. Are there constitutionally acceptable alternatives to a total ban on such advertising? For example, would mandatory counteradvertising of the type suggested above in connection with liquor advertising pass muster under the first amendment? What about a statute restricting tobacco advertising to displays bereft of colorful images, beautiful models, and catchy slogans? *See* Note, "*Posadas de Puerto Rico Associates v. Tourism Co. of Puerto Rico*: Promising Precedent for Proponents of Tobacco Advertising Prohibition?" 40 *Arkansas Law Review* 877 (1987); "Should Tobacco Advertising Be Banned?" 72 *American Bar Association Journal* 38 (1986).

3. For years, Avis Rent-a-Car has billed itself as "Number 2" in the car rental business, while the Hertz Corporation has claimed the top spot. A magazine ad for Hertz sought to emphasize the "gap" between first and second place, proclaiming that "Hertz has more new cars than Avis has cars." The ad, which was published in the *Wall Street Journal, Golf Magazine*, and American Airlines' in-flight magazine, advised readers to "rent from Hertz" if they would "like to drive some of the newest cars on the road." An accompanying photo showed mechanics shepherding a truckload of new cars into an airport parking lot. Avis promptly filed suit under Section 43(a) of the Lanham Act, arguing that Hertz' claim to have more new cars than Avis had cars was false. According to the evidence produced at trial, the statement was false if one compared the total cars owned by the two companies—that is, those leased to corporations and other businesses as well as those available for rental to the public. If, however, one counted only the cars in the companies' rental fleets, the statement was true. How should the ad be interpreted? Does it matter that the ad was aimed at travelers who would be renting cars at airports rather than at companies who would be leasing them on a long-term basis? *See Avis Rent-a-Car System, Inc. v. Hertz Corp.*, 782 F.2d 381 (2d Cir. 1986).

4. The use of celebrities to endorse products has become commonplace, resulting in financial bonanzas for entertainers and professional athletes. For example, products are promoted by such well-known figures as actors James Garner and Cybill Shephard, football-baseball star Bo Jackson, and broadcaster John Madden, a former NFL coach. To what extent, if at all, should an endorser be held liable for a false and deceptive advertisement in which he or she appears? Should the endorser be required to investigate the claims made about the product? *See Ramson v. Layne*, 668 F. Supp. 1162 (N.D. Ill. 1987); *In re Cooper*, 94 F.T.C. 674 (1979); *In re Cooga Mooga, Inc.*, 92 F.T.C. 310 (1978).

5. In 1980, Bristol-Myers Co. began an aggressive advertising campaign for its new shampoo, "Body on Tap." A television ad featured fashion model Cristina Ferrare, apparently fresh from shampooing her hair, holding a bottle of Body on Tap. She said: "In shampoo tests with over nine hundred women like me, Body on Tap got higher ratings than Prell for body. Higher than Flex for conditioning. Higher than Sassoon for strong, healthy looking hair." Prell, Flex, and Sassoon are shampoo competitors of Body on Tap. The shampoo tests mentioned in the ad were conducted for Bristol-Myers by an independent market research firm. Though more than 900 women (about one-third of whom were teenagers) were actually involved in the tests, no woman tried more than one shampoo and made a product-to-product comparison. Rather, groups of about 200 women each tested one unidentified shampoo and rated it on a scale from "poor" to "excellent" with respect to twenty-seven attributes such as body and conditioning. Using these ratings, the research firm determined that thirty-six percent of the women who tested Body on Tap found in "outstanding or excellent" as to "strong or healthy looking hair," while only twenty-four percent of the separate group of women who tested Sassoon gave it such ratings. Does the ad accurately reflect the results of the tests? If not, does that make the ad deceptive? Did the ad falsely describe the qualities of the shampoo? *See Vidal Sassoon, Inc. v. Bristol-Myers Co.*, 661 F.2d 272 (2d Cir. 1981).

6. Recall the "Hollywood Bread" case discussed previously in this chapter. Suppose that the FTC had ordered corrective advertising in that case to clear up the misimpression that the bread was lower in calories than "regular" bread, when in fact it had the same number of calories but was simply sliced thinner. Suppose further that the company had responded with the following television advertisement:

> Hi, I'm [Hollywood actress], for "Hollywood Bread." Like all of you, I'm concerned about nutrition and balanced meals. So, I'd like to clear up any misunderstanding you

may have about "Hollywood Bread." Does "Hollywood Bread" have fewer calories than other breads? No. It has about the same per ounce as other breads, but it has seven fewer calories per slice. That's because it's sliced thinner. But eating "Hollywood Bread" will not cause you to lose weight. A reduction of seven calories is insignificant. It's total calories and balanced nutrition that count. And "Hollywood Bread" can help you achieve a balanced meal because it provides protein and B vitamins as well as other nutrients. How do I feel about "Hollywood Bread"? I think it's great, and, like many of my friends here in Hollywood, I prefer it to any other bread.

Do you think this "correction" is satisfactory? Would the FTC be likely to approve it?

7. Because of the heat from television lights, the producers of a commercial for ice cream used mashed potatoes as a substitute when filming the ad. Is this practice deceptive? What about the use of a substitute for a given beverage—coffee or orange juice, for example—on the ground that photographs made the liquid appear lighter than its actual color? Would your answer change if the voice-over or ad copy emphasized the "richness" of the ice cream or the coffee? Is it deceptive to place marbles at the bottom of a bowl of vegetable soup so that the vegetables could be seen when the soup was photographed? *See Federal Trade Commission v. Colgate-Palmolive Co.*, 380 U.S. 374 (1965); *Libbey-Owens-Ford Glass Co. v. Federal Trade Commission*, 352 F.2d 415 (6th Cir. 1965); *Carter Products, Inc. v. Federal Trade Commission*, 323 F.2d 523 (5th Cir. 1963); *In re Campbell Soup Co.*, 77 F.T.C. 664 (1970).

8. Suppose that radio station KBRQ-FM operates on 102.1 mHz in Austin, Texas. Given its position on the dial and the "Q" in its call letters, the station refers to itself as "Q102" on the air and in advertising and other promotional materials. When KBRQ began using "Q102," it was unaware that a station in Cleveland, Ohio, had registered the alphanumerical term as a service mark. The Cleveland station, WCCQ-FM, threatened KBRQ with a lawsuit after the Texas station referred to itself as "Q102" in a national trade journal. Is "Q102" a valid service mark? Or, is it merely "descriptive" in that it says something about the station's call letters and the frequency on which the station operates? Does it matter that this practice of combining a station's call letters and frequency is quite common in the radio industry? That the two stations are in cities hundreds of miles apart? *See KSH Plastics, Inc. v. Carolite, Inc.*, 408 F.2d 54 (9th Cir.), *cert. denied*, 396 U.S. 825 (1969); *Nature's Bounty, Inc. v. Basic Organics*, 432 F. Supp. 546 (E.D.N.Y. 1977); *Snelling & Snelling, Inc. v. Snelling & Snelling, Inc.*, 331 F. Supp. 750 (D.P.R. 1970); *Bamberger Broadcasting Service, Inc. v. Orloff*, 44 F. Supp. 904 (S.D.N.Y. 1942).

9. You are the new general manager of Channel 7, a television station in a medium-sized market. Though your station is not ranked first in the market in any category measured by the ratings services, it has for some time referred to itself in advertising as "number one in sports" and "number one in news." Are these advertisements false and deceptive, or are they merely examples of "puffing?" What if the ads said only that the station has the "best" sports and news or simply that "Seven's Best?" *See Audience Ratings— Distortion*, 58 F.C.C.2d 513 (1976); *In re Key Broadcasting Corp.*, 60 F.C.C.2d 575 (1976); *In re Peacock Buick, Inc.*, 86 F.T.C. 1532 (1975).

10. North American Precis Syndicate, Inc., a firm specializing in the distribution of press releases to the news media, placed an advertisement about its services in the *Public Relations Journal*. The ad contained a quotation from a corporate official explaining that his company had terminated its relationship with Christopher Lisa Matthew Policano (another public relations firm) and had decided to do business with North American. The quote read, in part: "Instead of doing three or four things in a scattered way, we wanted to do one or two things really well." Under what legal theories could the Christopher firm proceed against North Ameri-

can? What is the likely outcome of such a suit? Is the *Journal* potentially liable as well? *See Christopher Lisa Matthew Policano, Inc. v. North American Precis Syndicate,* 514 N.Y.S.2d 239 (App. Div. 1987).

11. *High Society,* a sexually oriented magazine, published a parody of the L.L. Bean catalogue in its October 1984 issue. The parody, titled "L.L. Beam's Back-to-School Sex Catalog," featured photos of nude models in sexually explicit positions using outdoor equipment and sporting goods as props. L.L. Bean brought suit on several grounds, including trademark infringement, and sought an injunction against further publication or distribution of the article. Would such an injunction violate the first amendment? How important is the fact that the magazine did not use L.L. Bean's mark to identify or promote goods to consumers? That the article was plainly a parody? *See L.L. Bean, Inc. v. Drake Publishers, Inc.,* 811 F.2d 26 (1st Cir.), *cert. denied,* 483 U.S. 1013 (1987). *See also Mutual of Omaha Ins. Co. v. Novak,* 836 F.2d 397 (8th Cir. 1987), *cert. denied,* 109 S.Ct. 326 (1988); *Cliff's Notes, Inc. v. Bantam Doubleday Dell Publishing Group, Inc.,* 16 Media L. Rptr. 2025 (S.D.N.Y. 1989); Comment, "Trademark Parodies and Free Speech," 73 *Iowa Law Review* 961 (1988).

12. Just how effective is the Federal Trade Commission's fight against deceptive advertising? Is Section 43(a) of the Lanham Act a more potent remedy? For a fascinating account of the FTC's attempt to police the advertising of over-the-counter analgesics and the Lanham Act litigation among the major manufacturers of pain relievers, see Charles C. Mann and Mark L. Plummer, "The Big Headache," *The Atlantic* (October 1988), p. 39. Ask yourself whether the following Anacin advertisement, which is described in the article, is deceptive. Aired on network television, the ad opens with man who appears to be a journalist standing in front of a newspaper printing press. "I've been writing a lot of stories about aspirin lately," he says. "But if you think you've heard it all, think again." He then displays a newspaper with a bold headline proclaiming "A Better Aspirin Formula." A graph then shows that the "pain relief level" of regular-strength aspirin compares rather poorly to that of Anacin. A voice-over adds, "Anacin. A better aspirin formula." What the ad does not say is that Anacin's "aspirin formula" is simply aspirin plus caffeine. It also does not mention that the Food and Drug Administration has refused to confirm that caffeine enhances the power of aspirin. Moreover, the graph showing "pain relief levels" does not indicate that each Anacin has twenty-three percent more aspirin that a regular-strength aspirin tablet.

13. The 1988 presidential campaign was widely criticized as one of the most negative in recent times, and some of the candidates' advertisements played fast and loose with the facts. *See, e.g.,* Michael Oreskes, "Final Pitches to an Electorate Grown Cold," *New York Times* (October 23, 1988), sec. 4, p. 1; Walter Goodman, "Take 2 Candidates and Call Me in the Morning," *id.,* sec. 2, p. 27. Is there any legal remedy for deceptive political advertising of this nature? Since candidates today are packaged much like commercial products, should their ads be held up to the same scrutiny as other forms of advertising? Does the nature of the speech as "political" rather than "commercial" make any difference? *See generally* Comment, "Misrepresentation in Political Advertising: The Role of Legal Sanctions," 36 *Emory Law Journal* 853 (1987).

14. A county ordinance makes it a criminal misdemeanor to publish, in any publication distributed primarily in the county, an advertisement relating to contracting services unless the advertisement includes the contractor's state or county certification number or the publisher obtains an affidavit from the contractor stating that such a number is not required. The ordinance, a consumer protection measure, was designed to supplement a state statute prohibiting uncertified contractors from advertising or otherwise holding

themselves out as contractors. Two newspapers challenged the ordinance as unconstitutional. What result? Why? *See News & Sun-Sentinel Co. v. Board of County Commissioners*, 693 F. Supp. 1066 (S.D. Fla. 1987). Is this ordinance any different from a state statute requiring newspaper liquor advertisements placed by out-of-state retailers to carry a forty-word warning that transporting alcoholic beverages into the state without a permit is illegal? *See Memphis Publishing Co. v. Leech*, 539 F. Supp. 405 (W.D. Tenn. 1982). From a state statute providing that all advertisements, print and broadcast, for opticians must include a disclaimer stating that "this firm is not licensed to make eye examinations"? *See* Ark. Code Ann. § 17–88–406. *Cf. Friedman v. Rogers,* 440 U.S. 1 (1979).

15. As discussed briefly in Chapter 10, federal statutes prohibit, with various exceptions, the broadcasting of lottery advertisements. Companion statutes deal with the mailing of newspaper advertisements for lotteries and establish parallel exemptions. Under 18 U.S.C. § 1302, it is a crime to deliver by mail a "publication of any kind containing any advertisement of any lottery, gift enterprise, or scheme of any kind offering prizes dependent in whole or in part upon lot or chance. . . ." Another statute, 18 U.S.C. § 1307, exempts advertisements for a state-run lottery "contained in a publication published in that State or in a State which conducts such a lottery." The statute also exempts advertisements for lotteries by nonprofit or governmental organizations or by commercial enterprises for promotional purposes, so long as the lottery is not illegal under the law of the state in which it is conducted. Yet another statute, 25 U.S.C. § 2720, exempts advertisements for certain "gaming activities" of Indian tribes. Evaluate these statutes under the commercial speech doctrine. Are the various exemptions constitutionally required? Do they go far enough? *See Minnesota Newspaper Association v. Postmaster General,* 677 F. Supp. 1400 (D. Minn. 1987), *vacated as moot,* 109 S.Ct. 1734 (1989).

CHAPTER
12

THE MEDIA INDUSTRY

***Arkansas Writers' Project, Inc. v.
Ragland,*** **481 U.S. 221 (1987).**

JUSTICE MARSHALL delivered the opinion
of the Court.

The question presented in this case is
whether a state sales tax scheme that taxes
general interest magazines, but exempts newspapers and religious, professional, trade, and
sports journals violates the First Amendment's guarantee of freedom of the press.

I

Since 1935, Arkansas has imposed a tax on receipts from sales of tangible personal property. The rate of tax is currently four percent
of gross receipts. Numerous items are exempt
from the state sales tax, however. These include "[g]ross receipts or gross proceeds derived from the sale of newspapers," and "reli-

gious journals, professional trade and sports
journals and/or publications printed and published within this State . . . when sold through
regular subscriptions."

Appellant Arkansas Writers' Project, Inc.
publishes Arkansas Times, a general interest
monthly magazine with a circulation of approximately 28,000. The magazine includes
articles on a variety of subjects, including religion and sports. It is printed and published in
Arkansas, and is sold through mail subscriptions, coin-operated stands, and over-the-
counter sales. In 1980, following an audit, appellee Commissioner of Revenue assessed tax
on sales of Arkansas Times. Appellant initially contested the assessment, but eventually
reached a settlement with the State and agreed
to pay the tax beginning in 1982. However,
appellant reserved the right to renew its challenge if there were a change in the tax law or
a court ruling drawing into question the validity of Arkansas' exemption structure.

532

Subsequently, in *Minneapolis Star & Tribune Co. v. Minnesota Comm'r of Revenue* (1983), this Court held unconstitutional a Minnesota tax on paper and ink used in the production of newspapers. In January 1984, relying on this authority, appellant sought a refund of sales tax paid since October 1982, asserting that the magazine exemption must be construed to include Arkansas Times. It maintained that subjecting Arkansas Times to the sales tax, while sales of newspapers and other magazines were exempt, violated the First and Fourteenth Amendments. The Commissioner denied appellant's claim for refund.

Having exhausted available administrative remedies, appellant filed a complaint in the Chancery Court for Pulaski County, Arkansas, seeking review of the Commissioner's decision. * * * The parties stipulated that Arkansas Times is not a "newspaper" or "religious, professional, trade or sports journal" and that, during the relevant time period, appellant had paid $15,838.22 in sales tax. The Chancery Court granted appellant summary judgment, construing [the statute] to create two categories of tax-exempt magazines sold through subscriptions, one for religious, professional, trade, and sports journals, and one for publications published and printed within the State of Arkansas. Because Arkansas Times came within the second category, the court held that the magazine was exempt from sales tax and appellant was entitled to a refund. The court determined that resolution of the dispute on statutory grounds made it unnecessary to address the constitutional issues raised in appellant's . . . claim.

The Arkansas Supreme Court reversed the decision of the Chancery Court. It construed [the statute] as creating a single exemption and held that, in order to qualify for this exemption, a magazine had to be a "religious, professional, trade, or sports periodical." * * * As to appellant's First Amendment objections, the court noted that this Court has held that "the owners of newspapers are not immune from any of the 'ordinary forms of taxation' for support of the government." In contrast to *Minneapolis Star, supra,* and

[*Grosjean v. American Press Co.* (1936)] . . . the Arkansas Supreme Court concluded that the Arkansas sales tax was a permissible "ordinary form of taxation." * * * [W]e now reverse.

II

[The Court concluded that the appellant was a proper party to challenge the statute, even though a ruling in its favor—that the statute was unconstitutional—would not entitle it to an exemption but would rather invalidate the exemptions accorded other publications.]

III

A

Our cases clearly establish that a discriminatory tax on the press burdens rights protected by the First Amendment. In *Minneapolis Star*, the discrimination took two distinct forms. First, in contrast to generally applicable economic regulations to which the press can legitimately be subject, the Minnesota use tax treated the press differently from other enterprises. * * * Second, the tax targeted a small group of newspapers. This was due to the fact that the first $100,000 of paper and ink were exempt from the tax; thus, "only a handful of publishers pay any tax at all, and even fewer pay any significant amount of tax."

Both types of discrimination can be established even where, as here, there is no evidence of an improper censorial motive. * * * This is because selective taxation of the press—either singling out the press as a whole or targeting individual members of the press—poses a particular danger of abuse by the State.

"A power to tax differentially, as opposed to a power to tax generally, gives a government a powerful weapon against the taxpayer selected. When the State imposes a generally applicable tax, there is little cause for concern. We need not fear that a government will destroy a selected group of taxpayers by burdensome taxation if it must impose the same burden on the rest of its constituency." [Quoting *Minneapolis Star.*]

Addressing only the first type of discrimination, the Commissioner defends the Arkansas sales tax as a generally applicable economic regulation. He acknowledges the numerous statutory exemptions to the sales tax, including those exempting newspapers and religious, trade, professional, and sports magazines. Nonetheless, apparently because the tax is nominally imposed on receipts from sales of *all* tangible personal property, he insists that the tax should be upheld.

On the facts of this case, the fundamental question is not whether the tax singles out the press as a whole, but whether it targets a small group within the press. While we indicated in *Minneapolis Star* that a genuinely nondiscriminatory tax on the receipts of newspapers would be constitutionally permissible, the Arkansas sales tax cannot be characterized as nondiscriminatory, because it is not evenly applied to all magazines. To the contrary, the magazine exemption means that only a few Arkansas magazines pay any sales tax;[1] in that respect, it operates in much the same way as did the $100,000 exemption to the Minnesota use tax. Because the Arkansas sales tax scheme treats some magazines less favorably than others, it suffers from the second type of discrimination identified in *Minneapolis Star*.

Indeed, this case involves a more disturbing use of selective taxation than *Minneapolis Star*, because the basis on which Arkansas differentiates between magazines is particularly repugnant to First Amendment principles: a magazine's tax status depends entirely on its *content*. "[A]bove all else, the First Amendment means that government has no power to restrict expression because of its message, its ideas, its subject matter, or its content." *Po-*

lice Dept. of Chicago v. Mosley* (1972). See also *Carey v. Brown* (1980). "Regulations which permit the Government to discriminate on the basis of the content of the message cannot be tolerated under the First Amendment." *Regan v. Time, Inc.* (1984).

If articles in Arkansas Times were uniformly devoted to religion or sports, the magazine would be exempt from the sales tax. . . . However, because the articles deal with a variety of subjects (sometimes including religion and sports), the Commissioner has determined that the magazine's sales may be taxed. In order to determine whether a magazine is subject to sales tax, Arkansas' "enforcement authorities must necessarily examine the content of the message that is conveyed. . . .'" *FCC v. League of Women Voters of California* (1984). Such official scrutiny of the content of publications as the basis for imposing a tax is entirely incompatible with the First Amendment's guarantee of freedom of the press.

Arkansas' system of selective taxation does not evade the strictures of the First Amendment merely because it does not burden the expression of particular *views* by specific magazines. We rejected a similar distinction between content and viewpoint restrictions in *Consolidated Edison Co. v. Public Service Comm'n of New York* (1980). As we stated in that case, "[t]he First Amendment's hostility to content-based regulation extends not only to restrictions on particular viewpoints, but also to prohibition of public discussion of an entire topic."

Nor are the requirements of the First Amendment avoided by the fact that Arkansas grants an exemption to other members of the media that might publish discussions of the various subjects contained in Arkansas Times. For example, exempting *newspapers* from the tax does not change the fact that the State discriminates in determining the tax status of *magazines* published in Arkansas. "It hardly answers one person's objection to a restriction on his speech that another person, outside his control, may speak for him." *Regan v. Taxation With Representation of Washington* (1983) (BLACKMUN, J., con-

---

[1]Appellant maintains that Arkansas Times is the *only* Arkansas publication that pays sales tax. The Commissioner contends that there are two periodicals, in addition to Arkansas Times, that pay tax. Whether there are three Arkansas magazines paying tax or only one, the burden of the tax clearly falls on a limited group of publishers.

curring). See also *Virginia State Board of Pharmacy v. Virginia Citizens Consumer Council, Inc.* (1976) ("We are aware of no general principle that freedom of speech may be abridged when the speaker's listeners could come by his message by some other means").

B

Arkansas faces a heavy burden in attempting to defend its content-based approach to taxation of magazines. In order to justify such differential taxation, the State must show that its regulation is necessary to serve a compelling state interest and is narrowly drawn to achieve that end.

The Commissioner has advanced several state interests. First, he asserts the State's general interest in raising revenue. While we have recognized that this interest is an important one, it does not explain selective imposition of the sales tax on some magazines and not others, based solely on their content. In *Minneapolis Star*, this interest was invoked in support of differential treatment of the press in relation to other businesses. In that context, we noted that an interest in raising revenue,

"[s]tanding alone, . . . cannot justify the special treatment of the press, for an alternative means of achieving the same interest without raising concerns under the First Amendment is clearly available: the State could raise the revenue by taxing businesses generally, avoiding the censorial threat implicit in a tax that singles out the press."

The same is true of a tax that differentiates between members of the press.

The Commissioner also suggests that the exemption of religious, professional, trade, and sports journals was intended to encourage "fledgling" publishers, who have only limited audiences and therefore do not have access to the same volume of advertising revenues as general interest magazines such as the Arkansas Times. Even assuming that an interest in encouraging fledgling publications might be a compelling one, we do not find the exemption . . . of religious, professional, trade, and sports journals narrowly tailored to achieve

that end. To the contrary, the exemption is both overinclusive and underinclusive. The types of magazines enumerated . . . are exempt, regardless of whether they are "fledgling"; even the most lucrative and well-established religious, professional, trade, and sports journals do not pay sales tax. By contrast, struggling general interest magazines and struggling specialty magazines on subjects other than those specified in [the statute] are ineligible for favorable tax treatment.

Finally, the Commissioner asserted for the first time at oral argument a need to "foster communication" in the State. While this state interest might support a blanket exemption of the press from the sales tax, it cannot justify selective taxation of certain publishers. The Arkansas tax scheme only fosters communication on religion, sports, and professional and trade matters. It therefore does not serve its alleged purpose in any significant way.

C

Appellant argues that the Arkansas tax scheme violates the First Amendment because it exempts all newspapers from the tax, but only some magazines. Appellant contends that, under applicable state regulations, the critical distinction between newspapers and magazines is not format, but rather content: newspapers are distinguished from magazines because they contain reports of current events and articles of general interest. Just as content-based distinctions between magazines are impermissible under prior decisions of this Court, appellant claims that content-based distinctions between different members of the media are also impermissible, absent a compelling justification.

Because we hold today that the State's selective application of its sales tax to magazines is unconstitutional and therefore invalid, our ruling eliminates the differential treatment of newspapers and magazines. Accordingly, we need not decide whether a distinction between different types of periodicals presents an additional basis for invalidating the sales tax, as applied to the press.

IV

[Having prevailed on its first amendment claim, the appellant argued that it was entitled to an award of attorney's fees under a federal statute. The Court ruled that this issue should first be addressed by the state courts. Because the appellant had won in the trial court on nonconstitutional grounds and lost in the Arkansas Supreme Court, there had been no occasion for those courts to consider a fee award.]

V

We stated in *Minneapolis Star* that "[a] tax that singles out the press, or that targets individual publications within the press, places a heavy burden on the State to justify its action." In this case, Arkansas has failed to meet this heavy burden. It has advanced no compelling justification for selective, content-based taxation of certain magazines, and the tax is therefore invalid under the First Amendment. Accordingly, we reverse the judgment of the Arkansas Supreme Court and remand for proceedings not inconsistent with this opinion.

It is so ordered.

JUSTICE SCALIA, with whom THE CHIEF JUSTICE joins, dissenting.

All government displays an enduring tendency to silence, or to facilitate silencing, those voices that it disapproves. In the case of the Judicial Branch of Government, the principal restraint upon that tendency, as upon other judicial error, is the requirement that judges write opinions providing logical reasons for treating one situation differently from another. I dissent from today's decision because it provides no rational basis for distinguishing the subsidy scheme here under challenge from many others that are common and unquestionably lawful. It thereby introduces into First Amendment law an element of arbitrariness that ultimately erodes rather than fosters the important freedoms at issue.

The Court's opinion does not dispute, and I think it is evident, that the tax exemption in this case has a rational basis sufficient to sustain the tax scheme against ordinary [constitutional] attack. Though assuredly not "narrowly tailored," it is reasonably related to the legitimate goals of encouraging small publishers with limited audiences and advertising revenues (a category which in the State's judgment includes most publishers of religious, professional, trade, and sports magazines) and of avoiding the collection of taxes where administrative cost exceeds tax proceeds. The exemption is found invalid, however, because it does not pass the "strict scrutiny" test applicable to discriminatory restriction or prohibition of speech, namely, that it be "necessary to serve a compelling state interest and . . . narrowly drawn to achieve that end."

Here, as in the Court's earlier decision in *Minneapolis Star & Tribune Co. v. Minnesota Comm'r of Revenue* (1983), application of the "strict scrutiny" test rests upon the premise that for First Amendment purposes denial of exemption from taxation is equivalent to regulation. That premise is demonstrably erroneous and cannot be consistently applied. Our opinions have long recognized—in First Amendment contexts as elsewhere—the reality that tax exemptions, credits, and deductions are "a form of subsidy that is administered through the tax system," and the general rule that "a legislature's decision not to subsidize the exercise of a fundamental right does not infringe the right, and thus is not subject to strict scrutiny." *Regan v. Taxation With Representation of Washington* (1983)(upholding denial of tax exemption for organization engaged in lobbying even though veterans' organizations received exemption regardless of lobbying activities). * * *

The reason that denial of participation in a tax exemption or other subsidy scheme does not necessarily "infringe" a fundamental right is that—unlike direct restriction or prohibition—such a denial does not, as a general rule, have any significant coercive effect. It may, of course, be manipulated so as to do so, in which case the courts will be available to provide relief. But that is not remotely the case here. It is implausible that the 4% sales tax, generally applicable to all sales in the state with the few enumerated exceptions, was meant to inhibit, or had the effect of inhibiting, this appellant's publication.

Perhaps a more stringent, prophylactic rule is appropriate, and can consistently be applied, when the subsidy pertains to the expression of a particular viewpoint on a matter of political concern—a tax exemption, for example, that is expressly available only to publications that take a particular point of view on a controversial issue of foreign policy. Political speech has been accorded special protection [in other contexts]. * * * There is no need, however, and it is realistically quite impossible, to extend to all speech the same degree of protection against exclusion from a subsidy that one might think appropriate for opposing shades of political expression.

By seeking to do so, the majority casts doubt upon a wide variety of tax preferences and subsidies that draw distinctions based upon subject matter. The United States Postal Service, for example, grants a special bulk rate to written material disseminated by certain nonprofit organizations—religious, educational, scientific, philanthropic, agricultural, labor, veterans', and fraternal organizations. Must this preference be justified by a "compel-

ling governmental need" because a nonprofit organization devoted to some other purpose—dissemination of information about boxing, for example—does not receive the special rate? The Kennedy Center, which is subsidized by the Federal Government in the amount of up to $23 million per year, is authorized by statute to "present classical and contemporary music, opera, drama, dance, and poetry." Is this subsidy subject to strict scrutiny because other kinds of expressive activity, such as learned lectures and political speeches, are excluded? Are government research grant programs or the funding activities of the Corporation for Public Broadcasting subject to strict scrutiny because they provide money for the study or exposition of some subjects but not others?

Because there is no principled basis to distinguish the subsidization of speech in these areas—which we would surely uphold—from the subsidization that we strike down here, our decision today places the granting or denial of protection within our own idiosyncratic discretion. In my view, that threatens First Amendment rights infinitely more than the tax exemption at issue. I dissent.

[The concurring opinion of Justice Stevens is omitted.]

INTRODUCTION

Although some journalists may not like to equate "the media" with "business," there is no doubt that news organizations are part of a communications industry in which billions of dollars are at stake. In 1989, for example, Time, Inc. and Warner Communications, Inc. merged to become the world's largest information and entertainment company with a market value of $18 billion and annual revenues of $10 billion from magazines, books, cable systems, programming for television and cable, movies, and records. The deal was not easily consummated, for Time first had to fight off a $12 billion hostile takeover attempt by another media conglomerate, Paramount Communications, Inc. A few months earlier, international media baron Rupert Murdoch, who in 1985 spent nearly $2 billion to acquire seven independent television stations as part of his Fox Network venture, paid $2.85 billion for Triangle Publications, Inc., publisher of *TV Guide* and *Seventeen* magazines. Since January 1985 the three major television networks have changed hands in the marketplace. In one such deal, General Electric bought RCA, parent company of NBC, for $6.3 billion.

These prices may seem high, but the profit potential is enormous. In 1988 Time had a net income of $289 million from magazines, books, cable programming services, and cable systems; Paramount earned $385 million from movies, television programming, books, and various nonmedia ventures; and Warner netted $423 million from records, movies, television programming, and cable systems. Among the television networks, NBC posted profits of $200 million in 1988, while Ted Turner's Cable News Network had an estimated operating profit of $80 million. The largest newspaper chain in the country, the Gannett Co., generated $3.1 billion in revenues and $319.4 million in profits in 1987, while the second largest chain, Knight-Ridder, Inc., had 1987 profits of $155.2 million on revenues of $2.07 billion.

Like all businesses, media companies are subject to a wide range of statutes and administrative regulations that govern their conduct in the economic marketplace. Thus, they must pay taxes, refrain from anticompetitive business practices, and comply with laws prohibiting unfair labor practices and employment discrimination. And, generally speaking, they are not entitled to special treatment by virtue of the first amendment. This principle was clearly stated in *Associated Press v. National Labor Relations Board* (1937), a case that arose when the NLRB ordered the AP to reinstate an editor who had been fired for his activities in connection with the Newspaper Guild. The federal labor statutes prohibit employers from terminating or otherwise punishing employees simply because they join or support unions. Nonetheless, the AP argued that it had absolute freedom under the first amendment "to employ and discharge those who . . . edit the news." Rejecting this argument, the U.S. Supreme Court upheld the NLRB. "The business of the Associated Press is not immune from regulation because it is an agency of the press," the Court said. "The publisher of a newspaper has no special immunity from the application of general laws."

The *Arkansas Writers' Project* case makes clear, however, that first amendment considerations can come into play with respect to government regulation of the media industry, particularly when content is affected in some manner. As we examine areas of the law ranging from antitrust to taxation, keep in mind the potential impact of the first amendment on the regulatory scheme.

TAXATION

During the early 1930s, the Louisiana legislature passed a statute requiring newspapers with circulations exceeding 20,000 copies per week to pay a license tax. Of the 124 newspapers in the state, only thirteen were subject to the statute, which imposed a tax on two percent of the papers' gross receipts from the sale of advertising. All but one of the thirteen had "ganged up" on U.S. Senator Huey Long, the former governor who was later shot to death in the state capitol. According to a circular that Long had distributed to each member of the legislature in support of what he called a "tax on lying," the newspapers had conducted a "vicious campaign" against him and his supporters.

In *Grosjean v. American Press Co.* (1936), the U.S. Supreme Court unanimously ruled the tax unconstitutional, pointing out that it curtailed the flow of information by encouraging newspapers to reduce their press runs. Though the Court did not discuss the events leading to the passage of the statute, the Justices labeled it "a deliberate and calculated device in the guise of a tax to limit the circulation of information." This statement indicates that the Court's ruling hinged on the improper motive of the legislature in attempting to censor a selected group of newspapers, albeit indirectly.

The Court was careful to emphasize, however, that it was not "suggest[ing] that the owners of newspapers are immune from any of the ordinary forms of taxation for support of the government." That message was driven home the following year when the Court dismissed an appeal in an Arizona tax case "for want of a substantial federal question," a technique employed to avoid full review of a lower court's ruling on a point of constitutional law considered to have been resolved by prior Supreme Court decisions. At issue in *Giragi v. Moore* (1937) was a general tax statute which, in the words of the Arizona Supreme Court, "direct[ed] the State Tax Commission to collect a tax on the sales or gross income of practically every person or concern engaged in selling merchancise or services in the state." Distinguishing *Grosjean*, the Arizona court noted that the tax statute was a general revenue measure necessitated by the Great Depression. "No hostility is shown the press," the court said, "nor is any purpose or design to restrain the press apparent." In short, the press was taxed in the same manner as all other businesses.

It was not until 1983 that another first amendment challenge to a tax statute reached the U.S. Supreme Court. In *Minneapolis Star & Tribune Co. v. Minnesota Commissioner of Revenue*, a case discussed at some length in the *Arkansas Writers' Project* opinion, the Court struck down a Minnesota statute that imposed a "use tax" on the cost of paper and ink products consumed in the production of periodicals. The first $100,000 worth of paper and ink was exempt from the tax, and periodicals continued to be exempt from the state sales tax. This special use tax was apparently unique under Minnesota law. Although the state also had a generally applicable use tax statute on the books, that provision taxed only the retail sale to consumers rather than intermediate transactions involving component products. In contrast, publishers were taxed under the special statute on their purchase of ink and paper, even though they eventually sold their publications at retail.

The Supreme Court, in an opinion by Justice Sandra Day O'Connor, first observed that "the States and the Federal Government can subject newspapers to generally applicable economic regulations without creating constitutional problems." Here, however, Minnesota did not apply its general sales and use taxes to newspapers, but instead adopted "a special tax that applies only to certain publications protected by the First Amendment." This scheme was objectionable, she said, for two reasons.

First, it singled out the press for special tax treatment, thereby "giv[ing] the government a powerful weapon against the taxpayer selected." Although, in contrast to the situation in *Grosjean*, there was no evidence of any improper legislative motive in enacting the tax on publishers, the Court concluded that the mere threat of burdensome taxes "can operate as effectively as a censor to check critical comment by the press. . . ."[2]

---

[2]Interestingly, the use tax on ink and paper was apparently less burdensome on the Minneapolis Star & Tribune Co. than the state's four percent sales tax would have been. According to calculations made by Justice William Rehnquist in his dissenting opinion, the publisher paid about $600,000 per year in use taxes but would have paid $1.8 million in sales taxes absent the provision exempting newspapers from the sales tax. Because the use tax actually benefited the newspaper, Justice Rehnquist, along with Justice Byron White, argued that there was no first amendment violation. The majority, however, concluded that the mere threat of more burdensome tax treatment was itself contrary to the first amendment. In addition, the majority was unwilling to undertake the task of evaluating the "relative burdens of various methods of taxation," pointing out that courts as institutions are "poorly equipped" for the job.

Second, the $100,000 exemption meant that only a handful of publishers—the largest newspapers in the state—would pay any tax at all. "[W]e think that recognizing a power in the State not only to single out the press but also to tailor the tax so that it singles out a few members of the press presents such a potential for abuse that no interest suggested by Minnesota can justify the scheme," Justice O'Connor wrote.

After handing down its decision in *Arkansas Writers' Project*, the Court in 1988 dismissed an appeal in a controversial California case for want of a substantial federal question. At issue in *Times Mirror Co. v. City of Los Angeles* was a municipal ordinance requiring payment of a "business tax" as a prerequisite for engaging in certain businesses or occupations within the city. The ordinance covered a variety of businesses and established different methods of calculating the tax, including flat fees, daily charges, percentages of payroll, and percentages of gross receipts.

Newspapers, magazines, and other periodicals were classified as "goods, wares, and merchandise" and, like other businesses falling in that category, were taxed on the basis of their gross receipts. Radio and television stations were taxed in the same manner and at the same rate. The motion picture industry, however, was treated differently; movie producers, for example, paid a tax based on gross production costs, distributors paid according to their gross receipts, and theater operators paid on the basis of retail sales.

As a result of the classification scheme and the varying methods for calculating the tax due, some businesses obviously paid more taxes than others. For instance, a newspaper, magazine, or broadcast station with $50 million in gross receipts would owe the city $62,500, but a movie producer with $50 million in production costs would pay only $10,250. Other businesses, such as junk dealers, operators of amusement rides, and trucking companies, would pay a flat fee as little as $125 per year, regardless of their gross receipts.

The publisher of the *Los Angeles Times*, which paid $1.4 million in city taxes each year, joined with other newspaper companies in challenging the ordinance, but a California appeals court upheld the provision. First, the tax was "generally applicable to all those engaged in wholesale or retail business activities" and was not "a penalty directed at only a few publications." Second, the press—newspapers, magazines, and broadcast stations—were not singled out for special treatment, "since the tax rates . . . apply to all manufacturers and sellers alike, including publishers." All businesses classified as sellers of "goods, wares, or merchandise" were taxed in precisely the same manner.

Finally, the the fact that other businesses, including those associated with the movie industry, were not placed in that particular category and were thus taxed differently was immaterial, for a taxing authority has broad powers in defining various classes for purposes of taxation. "No constitutional rights are violated if the burden of the . . . tax falls equally upon all members of a class, though other classes have lighter burdens or are wholly exempt, provided that the classification is reasonable. . . ." Because there is an "inherent difference" between periodicals and the broadcast media on the one hand and the motion picture industry on the other, the city may tailor its tax system to reflect those differences. The movie industry is "highly fragmented," and the ordinance separately classified each of those "fragments" (i.e., production, distribution, exhibition) as different business activities. Similarly, the city reasonably placed other businesses—junk dealers, for example—in a separate category for tax purposes.

LABOR LAW

In light of the *Associated Press* case discussed in the introduction to this chapter, the media obviously cannot claim a first amendment exemption from the application of the nation's labor laws. Therefore, publishers and the owners of broadcast stations must comply with a variety of statutes that govern employer-employee relations, though there are some situations in which first amendment concerns require a departure from labor law principles. Moreover, the operation of the labor laws may from time to time have an impact upon newsgathering activities.

The centerpiece of the federal labor statutes is the National Labor Relations Act (NLRA), passed in 1935 after two decades of labor-management strife. Among other things, the NLRA guarantees the right of workers to join unions and bargain collectively with employers, prohibits employers from interfering with union activities and discriminating against union members, defines other "unfair labor practices," and creates a federal administrative agency, the National Labor Relations Board, to enforce the act. Congress has significantly amended the NLRA on two occasions. The Taft-Hartley Act of 1947 prohibits certain union activities, notably secondary boycotts, while the Landrum-Griffin Act of 1959 restricts the right of unions to picket under certain circumstances.

Under the NLRA, employees are free to select a union as their exclusive representative in bargaining with management over wages, hours, and other terms and conditions of employment. If they do so, management must bargain with the union in good faith. A threshold question is whether the employees are an appropriate "bargaining unit"—that is, whether they share a community of interest. This determination is based on several factors, including similarity of work, training, skills, pay and other benefits, and hours worked.

A recurring problem is whether certain employees should be considered part of "management" and thus ineligible for inclusion in the bargaining unit. For example, in *Wichita Eagle & Beacon Publishing Co. v. National Labor Relations Board* (1973), the newspaper argued that two editorial writers should be excluded from a bargaining unit for reporters, since they participated directly in stating the views of the publisher in the editorial columns. The NLRB disagreed and placed them in the bargaining unit, but the U.S. Court of Appeals for the Tenth Circuit reversed. Pointing out that the editorial writers were "closely aligned with the newspaper's management" in the formulation of editorial policy, the court concluded that placing them on the other side of the fence from management would compromise "the newspaper's freedom to determine the content of its editorial voice in an atmosphere of free discussion and exchange of ideas."

Once a bargaining unit is determined and a union is chosen as its representative, the collective bargaining process begins. Under the NLRA, management must negotiate with the union over so-called "mandatory subjects of bargaining," including pay levels, hours, and working conditions. An employer may not unilaterally adopt policies dealing with these issues but must instead bargain with the union.

In the media setting, the first amendment has influenced the classification of matters as "mandatory." For example, in *Newspaper Guild v. National Labor Relations Board* (1980), the *Pottstown Mercury* announced that reporters and editors would be required to comply with a "code of ethics" which prohibited such "freebies" as sports tickets, trips, and gifts. The union complained that implementation of the code without collective bargaining violated the NLRA, since the "freebie" provision affected the "terms and conditions" of employment. Agreeing in part with the union, the NLRB concluded that bargaining was required, but only with respect to the penalties that could be imposed for violating the code. The U.S. Court of Appeals for the District of Columbia Circuit reversed.

Because the code's rules would be meaningless without the penalties established for their violation, the court held that the two must be considered together. "Both are either mandatorily bargainable or they are not," the court said. Turning to that issue, the court recognized that "matters lying at the heart of a newspaper's independence" are protected by the first amendment and thus not subject to the mandatory bargaining requirement. The court said:

> At least with respect to most news publications, credibility is central to their ultimate product and to the conduct of the enterprise. Moreover, . . . editorial control and the ability to shield that control from outside influences are within the First Amendment's zone of protection and therefore entitled to special consideration. In order to preserve these qualities, a news publication must be free to establish, without interference, reasonable rules designed to prevent its employees from engaging in activities which may directly compromise their standing as responsible journalists and that of the publication for which they work as a medium of integrity.

Nonetheless, the court was not convinced that all of the code's provisions qualified under this test. For example, it perceived a "significant difference" between a gift from a news source designed to influence news coverage and free tickets to a sporting event handed out rather indiscriminately. The former, in the court's view, would "appear to be related to the core concerns of a newspaper's management without vitally affecting the interests of the employees," while the latter would not. The court sent the case back to the NLRB, which ultimately ordered that the entire code be rescinded because it went well beyond matters critical to the newspaper's credibility. However, the NLRB was careful to point out that the *Mercury* was free to establish a more narrowly drawn code of ethics without collective bargaining.

Another federal statute, the Equal Employment Opportunity Act, also affects employer-employee relations. Enacted as part of the Civil Rights Act of 1964, this statute prohibits employers from discriminating against any individual because of his "race, color, religion, sex, or national origin" with respect to hiring, firing, compensation, and all other terms and conditions of employment. Victims of such discrimination may bring suit against the employer, and a federal agency—the Equal Employment Opportunity Commission—also plays an enforcement role. In addition, the Federal Communications Commission helps ensure that women and minorities are afforded equal employment opportunities in broadcasting. Radio and television licensees are required to take affirmative action in recruiting and training women and members of minority groups. Stations must also file annual reports reflecting the composition of their work force with the FCC, which takes employment practices into account when broadcasters seek license renewal.

Employment discrimination problems can arise in a variety of contexts. For example, in *Equal Employment Opportunity Commission v. New York Times Broadcasting Service* (1976), a television station was charged with discrimination after it refused to hire a woman for a vacant reporter's position. According to the unsuccessful applicant, the station manager told her in an interview that he "already had a woman reporter and did not expect to hire another." The U.S. Court of Appeals for the Sixth Circuit concluded that this statement, viewed in connection with statistical evidence showing that the station had only a single female reporter and no female anchors, supported the inference of a pattern of discrimination.

Similarly, in *Lowery v. WMC-TV* (1987), a federal district court in Tennessee ruled that a black weekend anchorman was denied a promotion to anchor position on the weeknight news program because of his race. Despite several years experience as a weekend anchor, high ratings, and award-winning work as a reporter, the plaintiff was twice passed over for promotion in favor of two white men without prior experience as anchors. After the court's ruling, a settlement was reached and the lawsuit dismissed.

In a lawsuit alleging race or sex discrimination in employment, an employer may defend the charges by establishing that there was a legitimate, nondiscriminatory reason for its action. Thus, the mere fact that a woman or a member of a racial minority is not hired or promoted does not mean that there has been unlawful discrimination. For example, a newspaper that plans to shift a general assignments reporter to a prominent "beat" may select a male journalist over a female on the basis of prior experience and qualifications, so long as the articulated reason is not a mere pretext for discrimination. If religious discrimination is alleged, an employer has a somewhat different defense, for the law requires him only to "reasonably accommodate" an employee's religious beliefs without "undue hardship" on the conduct of the business.

The "accommodation" issue arose in *Reid v. Memphis Publishing Co.* (1975), a case involving a Seventh Day Adventist who had applied for a copy editor's job with a daily newspaper. The position required Saturday work, contrary to the plaintiff's religious beliefs, and his unavailability for that time slot was the basis for the newspaper's refusal to hire him. Rejecting the plaintiff's claim of unlawful discrimination, the U.S. Court of Appeals for the Sixth Circuit ruled that accommodating his religion would cause the newspaper undue hardship. The court pointed out that the paper employed only a limited number of copy editors and that one of these editors, who would have had seniority over the plaintiff, would have to be involuntarily assigned to the Saturday shift in order to accommodate the plaintiff's religious views. This arrangement, the court said, would cause morale problems and result in overtime expenses that would otherwise not be incurred. The only other alternative—hiring the plaintiff plus another new copy editor who could work Saturdays—was also deemed unreasonable, since the paper needed only one additional editor.

The most celebrated employment discrimination case in media circles is undoubtedly *Craft v. Metromedia, Inc.*, decided by the U.S. Court of Appeals for the Eighth Circuit in 1985. The plaintiff, Christine Craft, was reassigned from anchor to reporter at KMBC-TV in Kansas City after a survey indicated that she was having an adverse impact on viewers. She then brought suit in federal court, alleging that she had been discriminated against on the basis of her sex. Her contention was that the station's appearance standards for on-air female personnel were more strict and more strictly enforced than the standards for their male counterparts.

The trial judge, sitting without a jury, disagreed. He found that KMBC required both male and female on-air personnel to maintain professional, businesslike appearances "consistent with community standards" and that the station enforced that requirement in a nondiscriminatory manner. The judge also determined that station had reasonably relied on the viewer survey as the basis for the personnel change. In so ruling, the judge rejected Ms. Craft's argument that she had been reassigned because she was "too old, too unattractive, and not deferential enough to men."

In affirming the trial judge's decision in favor of the station, the court of appeals emphasized that the case turned largely on witness credibility. In short, the trial judge believed the testimony of witnesses for KMBC-TV to the effect that Ms. Craft was relieved of her anchor duties for a legitimate reason (i.e., the viewer survey) and not because of her sex. Moreover, the judge concluded that the survey was properly conducted and was not merely a pretext for demoting Ms. Craft. These factual matters, the court of appeals said, are within the province of the trial judge, who in a non-jury trial will be upheld unless clearly wrong. Here, the evidence was deemed sufficient to support the trial judge's conclusions. The appellate court also observed:

> Courts have recognized that the appearance of a company's employees may contribute greatly to the company's image and success with the public and thus that a reasonable dress or grooming code is a proper management prerogative. Evidence showed a particular concern with appearance in television; the district court stated that reasonable appearance requirements were "obviously critical" to KMBC's economic well-being; and even Craft admitted she recognized that television was a visual medium and that on-air personnel would need to wear appropriate clothes and makeup. * * * While we believe the record shows an overemphasis by KMBC on appearance, we are not the proper forum in which to debate the relationship between newsgathering and dissemination and considerations of appearance and presentation—i.e., questions of substance versus image—in television journalism.[3]

Labor law disputes can also have a direct impact upon newsgathering activities, particularly in the heavily unionized broadcasting industry. For example, in *National Labor Relations Board v. National Association of Broadcast Employees* (1980), a union representing electronic technicians in ABC's Washington, D.C., bureau called for a strike and planned to picket news events covered by the network in Washington on May 16, 1977. Among the sites chosen was a downtown hotel where Vice President Walter Mondale was to give a speech. Union members picketed and handed out leaflets at the hotel's main entrance, and, as a result, CBS employees present to cover the Mondale speech would not enter the hotel. The National Labor Relations Board concluded that the union's picketing was an illegal "secondary boycott," and the U.S. Court of Appeals for the District of Columbia Circuit agreed.

Generally speaking, "primary" union activity aimed at an employer with whom the union has a labor dispute is protected by the labor laws. Thus, if a union pickets the premises of such an employer, this activity is lawful even if it adversely affects the employer and companies with whom the employer does business. On the other hand, "secondary" activity aimed at other employers is usually illegal. If, for example, picketing extends beyond the premises of the employer embroiled in a labor dispute and disrupts the operations of a "neutral" employer, the union has committed an unfair labor practice. In the *Broadcast Employees* case, the court was required to apply these basic principles in the newsgathering context.

At the outset, the court rejected the union's argument that the hotel should be

---

[3]Ms. Craft also claimed that the station had fraudulently induced her to accept the anchor job by misrepresenting that it was satisfied with her appearance. This portion of the case was tried before a jury, which returned a verdict in Ms. Craft's favor and awarded her $325,000 in damages. The court of appeals reversed, concluding that the evidence was insufficient to support the jury's decision.

considered part of ABC's "premises" because network employees who cover news events must necessarily travel away from the company's main office. In the union's view, the network's "primary business" was conducted at sites other than the office, and the union was thus free to picket those locations. The court found this argument unpersuasive, pointing out that there was no indication that Congress, in passing the labor laws, had meant to treat broadcasters any differently than other employers. "Once the news reporters and technicians are away from the news station," the court said, "they are away from their employer's primary situs."

Because the union's picketing and handbilling did not take place at ABC's main office, the court was required to determine if illegal secondary activity had occurred. The fact that the union had picketed the hotel—a neutral employer—was not, standing alone, enough to make that action illegal. Instead, the court said, the key question was whether the union activity had been aimed at ABC or had also been intended to pressure neutral employers. In examining the union's motive, the court first observed that the union activity at the hotel was limited to the time that ABC was covering the speech as part of its normal newsgathering operations. This suggested that the union's intent was to call attention to its dispute with ABC. However, the court also pointed out that the union had urged persons not to enter the hotel without ever addressing the event being picketed. By encouraging individuals other than ABC employees—potential patrons and the CBS workers, for instance—to stay away from the hotel, the union impermissibly affected the operations of neutral employers. Had the union confined its activities to special entrances at the hotel set up for ABC employees, there would have been no violation, since picketing at that location would have been linked specifically to the labor dispute with ABC and the news event that the network had planned to cover.

SECURITIES REGULATION

In the aftermath of the stock market crash of 1929, the Congress passed several statutes designed to regulate practices concerning the issuance and sale of corporate stock and other securities, such as bonds, debentures, and similar investment vehicles. These statutes reach activities that affect interstate commerce, and the states have enacted similar laws governing intrastate securities transactions. Although the various statutes are quite complex, their purpose is simple: to protect the integrity of markets in which securities are bought and sold, to safeguard the investing public, and to prevent the abuses that contributed to the 1929 crash and the depression that followed. Because the markets have been particularly susceptible to deceptive practices, the securities laws contain so-called "anti-fraud" provisions designed to reach such activities as the manipulation of prices, "insider trading" by which persons with access to non-public information about particular companies seek to reap huge profits on the basis of that knowledge, and the dissemination of misleading sales materials to potential investors.

At the federal level, the principal regulatory agency overseeing the securities industry is the Securities and Exchange Commission (SEC), established in 1934. Among other statutes, the SEC administers and enforces the Securities Act of 1933, which regulates the sale of newly issued securities; the Securities and Exchange Act of 1934, which governs the trading of securities that have already been issued and the activities of brokers and dealers who participate in these transactions; the Investment Company Act of 1940, which establishes regulatory controls over companies engaged primarily in the business of investing and trading in securities; and the Investment Advisers Act of 1940, which allows the SEC to regulate individuals and firms offering investment advice to the general public.

It has been estimated that as many as 5,000 firms are engaged in activities that fall under the watchful eye of the SEC and the various state securities agencies. These range from major brokerage houses such as Merrill Lynch to one-person firms that provide investment advice and other financial services on the local level. To service the information demands of the industry, there has emerged a diverse "financial press" that includes not only the *Wall Street Journal* and *Forbes* magazine, but also a variety of highly specialized journals and newsletters. From time to time, persons involved with these publications have run afoul of the securities laws.

The most notorious of the recent cases is *Carpenter v. United States* (1987), in which the U.S. Supreme Court upheld the criminal conviction of a *Wall Street Journal* reporter for violating the anti-fraud provisions of the Securities and Exchange Act of 1934 as well as other federal laws. The journalist, R. Foster Winans, was one of two writers of the *Journal*'s influential "Heard on the Street" column that regularly reviewed selected stocks and discussed their investment potential. Because of the column's perceived quality and integrity, it had the potential of affecting the price of the stocks that it discussed. The official policy and practice at the *Journal* was that the information learned by reporters in the course of their newsgathering activities belonged to the newspaper and was to be kept confidential prior to publication.

Despite this policy, Winans provided two stockbrokers, Kenneth Felis and Peter Brant, with advance information as to the timing and contents of the column. Winans' roommate, a former *Journal* employee named David Carpenter, participated in the scheme by serving as a messenger. Armed with this information, the stockbrokers bought and sold stock on the basis of the anticipated impact of the column on the stock market. Over a four-month period in late 1983 and early 1984, the stockbrokers obtained prepublication information from more than two dozen "Heard on the Street" columns and made trades that netted $690,000 in profits. Winans did not write the column or alter its contents with the scheme in mind, since the success of the venture was dependent in large part on the perceived quality and integrity of the reports. An SEC investigation led to the filing of criminal charges in a New York federal court, where Winans and Felis were ultimately convicted of securities fraud, mail and wire fraud, and conspiracy. Carpenter was convicted of aiding and abetting the commission of securities fraud and mail and wire fraud, while Brant was the prosecution's principal witness in the case. The U.S. Court of Appeals for the Second Circuit affirmed the convictions, as did the Supreme Court.

On appeal, the major question was whether the scheme violated Section 10(b) of the Securities and Exchange Act of 1934, which prohibits the use "in connection with the purchase or sale of any security . . . [of] any manipulative or deceptive device or contrivance in contravention of such rules and regulations as the [SEC] may prescribe. . . ." Under the corresponding SEC regulation, it is unlawful for any person to "employ any device, scheme, or artifice to defraud" and to "engage in any act, practice, or course of business which operates or would operate as a fraud or deceit upon any person, in connection with the purchase or sale of any security." The defendants argued that this regulation could not be stretched to reach their conduct. Specifically, they claimed that they had not misappropriated "inside" information available only to the management of the companies whose stock was traded, but had used information that Winans had legitimately acquired as a reporter. That information was theoretically available to anyone who had done the necessary legwork, and no "inside" information had been used to manipulate the stock market or harm investors. The only injured party was the *Journal*, they argued, and that injury, which stemmed from the newspaper's internal confidentiality policy, did not rise to the level of a federal securities law violation.

The U.S. Court of Appeals rejected this argument, emphasizing that the SEC regulation was intended to be broad in scope and to serve as a "catchall . . . to prevent fraudulent practices." The issue was not whether the information in question came from inside or outside a particular corporation, the court said, but whether the defendants had sought to gain an advantage in the securities marketplace not through skill, but through an unfair practice. Here the unfair practice was the misappropriation of information in breach of the newspaper's confidentiality requirement. "It was the advance knowledge of the timing and content of [the columns], upon which [the defendants], acting secretively, reasonably expected to and did realize profits in securities transactions," the court said. "[B]ecause of his duty of confidentiality to the *Journal*, defendant Winans—and Felis and Carpenter, who knowingly participated with him—had a corollary duty . . . under Section 10(b) to abstain from trading securities on the basis of the misappropriated information or to do so only upon making adequate disclosure to those with whom they traded."

The court also rejected a first amendment argument raised by several journalism organizations in a friend-of-the-court brief:

> [W]e cannot see how the convictions will chill free speech. If Winans had respected his employer's reasonable confidentiality policy, he would have had nothing to fear by publishing his . . . columns. * * * The First Amendment generally empowers a journalist with no "special privilege" merely for the exercise of his craft, and the securities law require of him, no less than of others, compliance therewith in the pursuit of his financial interests. In short, having failed to sustain their burden of persuasion that application of the securities laws infringed First Amendment rights, . . . [defendants] remain subject to Section 10(b) as a rule of general applicability.

The U.S. Supreme Court affirmed the convictions, albeit in a somewhat unusual fashion. Because the case was decided prior to the confirmation of Justice Anthony M. Kennedy, only eight Justices participated, dividing four to four on the securities law question. In that situation the decision of the lower court is affirmed, although the ruling does not carry the weight of a Supreme Court determination. However, the Court unanimously upheld the convictions of the defendants under the federal mail and wire fraud statutes, which prohibit the use of the mail and wire communications in connection with a scheme to defraud. On this point, the Court concluded that the *Journal* had a property right in keeping confidential and making exclusive use, prior to publication, of the schedule and contents of the "Heard on the Street" columns. That right is protected by the statutes, the Court said, and the defendants' activities constituted an illegal scheme to defraud the newspaper.

Prior to *Carpenter*, the most important securities law case involving the media to reach the Supreme Court was *Lowe v. Securities & Exchange Commission* (1985). Christopher Lowe was president and principal shareholder of Lowe Management Corporation, which was registered with the SEC as an investment adviser under the Investment Advisers Act of 1940. The SEC revoked the company's registration in 1981, after Lowe was convicted of misappropriating funds of an investment client, stealing from a bank, and various other offenses. In addition, the SEC ordered Lowe not to associate with any other investment adviser. About a year later, the SEC brought suit in federal court, alleging that Lowe was violating the order by publishing, for paid subscribers, semi-monthly newsletters containing investment advice and commentary. The SEC asked for an injunction ordering Lowe to stop publishing the newsletters, but the trial judge concluded that such an order would violate the first amendment.

The U.S. Court of Appeals for the Second Circuit reversed, reasoning that the case involved "the kind of regulation of commercial activity permissible under the First Amendment." In addition, the court found that Lowe's prior criminal conduct while acting as an investment adviser justified the characterization of his publications as "potentially deceptive commercial speech" not entitled to first amendment protection.

The U.S. Supreme Court agreed to review the case in order to decide whether an injunction against the publication and distribution of the newsletters would offend the first amendment. Lowe argued that the injunction was a licensing scheme and thus invalid as a prior restraint on publication, but the Court ultimately decided the case without reaching the constitutional question. In the Court's view, the Investment Advisers Act reflected Congress' intent to regulate the business of rendering personalized investment advice rather than nonpersonalized publishing activities.

Sensitive to first amendment concerns, Congress specifically exempted from the statute "the publisher of any bona fide newspaper, news magazine or business or financial publication of general and regular circulation." The Court concluded that Lowe's newsletters qualified for this exemption, pointing out that they contained "disinterested commentary" rather than promotional material and that they were "offered to the general public on a regular schedule." Moreover, Lowe's unsavory past did not mean that the newsletters were not "bona fide" within the meaning of the exemption. Because Lowe's publishing activity fell outside the scope of the statute, there was no basis for an injunction restraining the publication of future newsletters.

The Court's reasoning leaves open the possibility that an injunction against publication of an investment newsletter would be possible if the publisher has a financial stake in the investments he recommends or the publication is an irregularly published "bulletin" that touts particular stocks. In these situations, the statutory exemption for which Lowe's newsletters qualified would be unavailable, and the courts would be required to address the first amendment issue. Of course, if such nonexempt publications are considered "commercial speech," the first amendment restrictions on government regulation are somewhat relaxed, as we saw in Chapter 11, and a court order enjoining publication might well be constitutional.

In a concurring opinion in *Lowe*, however, three Justices expressed doubt that a prior restraint would be permissible in this context. Justice Byron White, joined by Chief Justice Warren Burger and Justice William Rehnquist, disagreed with the majority's interpretation of the statute but concurred in the result on the ground that an injunction would violate the first amendment. Even in the commercial speech setting, Justice White wrote, such a restraint is "too blunt an instrument to survive even the reduced level of scrutiny called for by restrictions on commercial speech." In any event, it seems clear that an injunction would be valid if the information is shown to be deceptive or misleading, since this type of commercial speech enjoys no constitutional protection whatsoever.

The issues raised but not resolved in *Lowe* resurfaced in *Securities & Exchange Commission v. Wall Street Publishing Institute, Inc.,* a 1988 decision of the U.S. Court of Appeals for the District of Columbia Circuit. The case involved an "anti-touting" provision of the Securities Act of 1933 making it unlawful to publish an article (or other communication) describing a company's stock if the company paid for the article, unless the payment is fully disclosed. The SEC sought to enforce this provision against the publisher of *Stock Market Magazine*, which regularly published glowing articles about particular companies.

According to the SEC, the articles were written by employees of the featured companies or by public relations firms acting on behalf of those companies. On occasion, the magazine's editors would write the articles on a freelance basis, receiving fees from the companies. In addition, the featured companies regularly purchased reprints of the articles and purchased advertising in the magazine. None of this was disclosed to the magazine's readers. The SEC alleged that these practices constituted a *quid pro quo* arrangement by which the magazine provided free space for the laudatory articles in return for the freelance writing fees and the companies' agreements to buy reprints and advertising. Because the magazine failed to disclose these financial arrangements, the SEC charged its publisher with violating the anti-touting provision and asked for an injunction requiring that appropriate disclosures be made.

A federal district judge in Washington, D.C., denied relief and granted summary judgment for the magazine, ruling that such an injunction would violate the first amendment. However, the court of appeals reversed and sent the case back for further proceedings. Distinguishing *Lowe*, the court pointed out that the order requested by the SEC would not forbid publication but would only require a disclosure statement. Moreover, the court observed that *Lowe* did not involve any allegation that the publication at issue was false or misleading, while in this case the magazine's "presentation of articles as objective reporting, if in fact the articles are paid for by the company featured, would be inherently misleading." Although the court declined to label the articles in question as commercial speech, it nonetheless concluded that "regulation of the exchange of information regarding securities is subject only to limited First Amendment scrutiny" because of the "federal government's broad power to regulate the securities industry." Thus, the magazine's "failure to disclose [payments] received in return for publication is, in principle, constitutionally proscribable."

The court emphasized, however, that "permissibility of the disclosure requirement must necessarily turn solely on whether [the payments were made] to the magazine for publication of the article—and not on the content of the publication." Accordingly, an order mandating disclosure would be constitutional if the SEC were able to prove that the magazine printed a favorable article in exhange for a company's commitment to buy reprints or purchase advertising, since the disclosure requirement "would not interfere with either editorial judgments concerning the content of the feature article or newsgathering practices."

On the other hand, a disclosure order based on the magazine's alleged practice of publishing articles in substantially the same form as provided by the companies or their publicists would be invalid. In that situation, the court said, the trial judge would be forced to examine a particular article and determine whether and to what extent it was the product of a company or its public relations firm. "If, for example, the editor of the magazine were to add several paragraphs to the article and edit the rest,'' the court asked, ''would that have to be disclosed?'' Such a determination would result in government interference with ''the crucial process of editorial control'' and thus run afoul of the first amendment.

ANTITRUST

The American economic system is grounded on the theory that competition will lead to the availability, at the lowest possible price, of goods and services that consumers want. As Dean Ernest Gellhorn has written:

> [I]n economic terms, competition maximizes consumer welfare by increasing both allocative efficiency (making what consumers want as shown by their willingness to pay) and productive efficiency (producing goods or services at the lowest cost thus using the fewest resources), and by encouraging progressiveness (rewarding invention).

Unfortunately, the system does not always work that way, and the antitrust laws reflect legislative recognition that breakdowns can and do occur. For example, competitors may decide among themselves to set prices at a level above that established by the marketplace, thus depriving consumers of goods at the lowest possible price. Or, a company facing competition from two or three rivals may sell its product at an artificially low price, hoping that the competitors will lose so much money trying to match it that they will be forced out of business. The antitrust laws are designed to eliminate these scenarios and thus preserve a truly competitive economy. How well they work is a matter of sharp debate.

At the federal level, the principal antitrust statutes are the Sherman Act of 1890, the Clayton Act of 1914, the Federal Trade Commission Act of 1914, and the Robinson-Patman Act of 1936. Enforcement lies in the hands of two federal agencies, the Department of Justice and the Federal Trade Commission, though civil suits for injunctive relief and treble damages may also be brought by persons injured as a result of statutory violations. Because the Constitution gives Congress regulatory powers only over interstate and foreign commerce, the federal antitrust statutes are necessarily limited to anticompetitive practices that affect these types of commerce.

As a practical matter, however, even activities that seem quite local in nature can have the requisite impact on interstate or foreign commerce. For example, in a 1980 case the U.S. Supreme Court ruled that the federal antitrust statutes applied to real estate brokerage in New Orleans, reasoning that activites of real estate agents had an appreciable effect on interstate commerce in residential financing and title insurance. Even if a particular trade practice is truly local, almost all states have enacted statutes that mirror the federal antitrust statutes but apply only to intrastate activities. In addition to these federal and state statutes, the media are affected by regulations of the Federal Communications Commission governing the ownership of broadcast stations and cable television systems.

At the outset, it should be emphasized that the first amendment does not exempt the media from the operation of the antitrust laws. The Supreme Court made this point quite clearly more than forty years ago in *Associated Press v. United States* (1945), a case stemming from an AP policy that effectively prevented more than one newspaper in a given city from becoming a member of the wire service. The U.S. Department of Justice filed suit against the AP, claiming that the policy violated the Sherman Act by impermissibly restraining the flow of news in interstate commerce and by fostering a monopoly. The case was heard by one of the most respected federal judges in the nation's history, Judge Learned Hand, who rejected the AP's argument that application of the Sherman Act would violate the first amendment. The Supreme Court affirmed in an opinion by Justice Hugo Black, one of the most vigorous defenders of the first amendment ever to serve on that body.

In Justice Black's view, the antitrust laws complemented rather than contradicted the first amendment:

> Member publishers of the AP are engaged in business for profit exactly as are other businessmen who sell food, steel, aluminum, or anything else people need or want. . . . All are alike covered by the Sherman Act. The fact that the publisher handles news while others handle goods does not . . . afford the publisher a peculiar constitutional sanctuary in which he can with impunity violate laws regulating his business practices. * * * The First Amendment, far from providing an argument against application of the Sherman Act, here provides powerful reasons to the contrary. That Amendment rests on the assumption that the widest possible dissemination of information from diverse and antagonistic sources is essential to the welfare of the public, that a free press is a condition of a free society. * * * Freedom to publish means freedom for all and not for some. Freedom to publish is guaranteed by the Constitution, but freedom to combine to keep others from publishing is not.

In the pages that follow, we shall consider a variety of antitrust problems, including what is generally known as "media concentration"—that is, the domination of the industry by a comparative handful of companies that own broadcast stations, newspapers, magazines, and other media properties. We shall also explore antitrust issues that are common to certain types of media organizations. Newspapers, for example, have been accused of selling advertising at artifically low rates in order to thwart competition from "shoppers," while cable companies have run into antitrust difficulties in connection with the municipal franchising process.

Media Concentration

The media business is big business, and, as in other American industries, the modern trend is toward concentration of ownership, with large conglomerates emerging to dominate the field. For example, more than two-thirds of the nation's 1,650 daily newspapers are owned by "chains" that together control about three-fourths of daily circulation. Moreover, media conglomerates are involved in a variety of ventures, including newspapers, magazines, broadcast stations, direct mail operations, billboard companies, and cable television systems. When Gannett merged with Combined Communications in 1979, for instance, the result was a company that owned seventy-nine daily newspapers, seven television stations, and twelve radio stations.

The new Time-Warner corporation not only publishes two dozen magazines (including *Time, Sports Illustrated,* and *People*), but also owns book publishers (Little, Brown & Co. and Warner Books) and the Book-of-the-Month Club. In addition to these publishing ventures, the media giant owns Warner Brothers, a Hollywood studio that produces movies and television programming; Home Box Office and Cinemax, the satellite-delivered movie services; two of the nation's largest cable television operators; and three major record companies. The News Corp., Ltd., Rupert Murdoch's company, now owns more than 150 media properties on four continents, and his holdings in the United States include two daily newspapers, over twenty magazines, a movie studio (Twentieth Century Fox), Harper & Row publishers, and seven television stations that serve as the foundation for his fledgling Fox Television Network.

Developments such as these have alarmed several commentators, who fear the domination of the communications media by a handful of powerful corporations and the concomitant loss of independent editorial voices. As presently written, however, the antitrust laws offer little solace to those who oppose media concentration. The reason is that the media outlets owned by a given communications company do not compete with each other in the same geographic market. Under Section 7 of the Clayton Act, only mergers or acquisitions that may tend to create a monopoloy or lessen competition in a particular market are impermissible.

With respect to newspapers, for example, the relevant market is considered local in nature, and a company with a newspaper in one city will not be allowed to purchase another paper in that area. In *United States v. Times Mirror Corp.* (1967), the U.S. Department of Justice obtained a court order to stop the publisher of the *Los Angeles Times* from acquiring the nearby *San Bernadino Sun*, a suburban daily that competed directly with the *Times* in the greater Los Angeles area. However, there is no barrier to the publishing company's acquisition of a newspaper in a distant city or state, for such a purchase would have no effect on the Los Angeles market.

Even if one assumes that the appropriate market is national rather than local, existing levels of concentration are not sufficiently high to raise antitrust concerns. For example, the twenty largest newspaper chains account for about fifty percent of the nation's daily circulation, a pattern similar to that in magazine and book publishing, and the largest chain—Gannett—controls less than ten percent of that circulation. At some point, however, concentration at the national level may pose antitrust problems. Writing in the *American Bar Journal* a decade ago, a Justice Department attorney observed that "[c]ontrol of all daily newspapers by five chains, for example, would cause me as an American citizen far greater concern that would control of a similarly sized manufacturing industry by five business entities."

For the moment, however, the major check on media concentration is the Federal Communications Commission, which has adopted rules that restrict ownership not only of radio and television stations but newspapers as well. These rules forbid multiple ownership of broadcast stations in the same community, limit the number of stations that a single entity may own, and prohibit the "cross-ownership" of newspapers and television stations in the same community. Similarly, the Cable Communications Policy Act of 1984 prevents cross-ownership of television stations and cable systems in certain situations.

Multiple Ownership of Broadcast Stations. At the local level, a single entity may not own more than one particular type of broadcast station in the same community or in a nearby community if there would be a significant overlap in their signals. Known as the "duopoly rule," this FCC regulation prevents a single company from owning two television stations, two AM radio stations, or two FM radio stations in the same viewing or listening area. The purpose of the rule is to stimulate competition—and thus provide different programming and editorial viewpoints—through diversification of ownership. In applying the duopoly rule, as well as the other ownership rules discussed in this and the following section, the FCC will as a general matter consider anyone with an interest of at least five percent in the media company as an "owner." For investment companies, banks, and other passive investors, the minimum ownership interest necessary to trigger the rules is ten percent.

Complementing the duopoly rule is the "one-to-a-market" rule under which an entity may not own a television station and an AM or FM radio station in the same community, or in nearby communities if their signals significantly overlap. Ownership of one AM and one FM radio station in a community is permissible, and some TV-radio combinations exist pursuant to a "grandfather" clause covering stations under common ownership in 1970 when the rule was adopted. Until recently, the FCC had on a case-by-case basis waived the rule to permit ownership of a UHF television station and a radio station in the same market as part of its long-standing policy of encouraging the growth of UHF stations. In late 1988, the Commission adopted a more liberal waiver policy not limited to UHF stations.

Under the new guidelines, the FCC will "look favorably" on waiver applications if the proposed TV-radio combination is in one of the twenty-five largest television markets and there would be at least thirty separately owned broadcast "voices" in the market if the waiver were granted, or if the proposed combination involves a "failed" station that has that has not been operating for a substantial period of time or is in bankruptcy. If a proposed combination does not satisfy either of these two standards, the Commission may still grant a waiver if such action would serve the public interest. In this situation, the FCC will conduct a "more rigorous" review of the application and consider such factors as the types of stations involved, the potential benefits of the proposed combination, the nature of the market, and the number of stations already owned by the applicant.

The Commission applied its liberalized policy in July 1989 to grant waivers for Capital Cities/ABC's television-radio combinations in four of the nation's top five television markets: New York City, Chicago, Los Angeles, and San Francisco. In each city except San Francisco, where it has a television station and an AM radio station, the company operates a TV-AM-FM combination. In granting the waiver, the FCC pointed out that there are ninety-four broadcast owners in New York City, 105 in Chicago, seventy-nine in Los Angeles, and fifty-seven in San Francisco.

Another regulation restricts the total number of television stations and radio stations a single company may own, irrespective of their location. This regulation, popularly known as the "12-12-12" rule, is obviously designed to foster diversity of ownership at the national level. Under the rule, a single entity cannot own more than twelve television stations, twelve AM radio stations, and twelve FM radio stations.

With respect to television stations, an additional restriction applies: a single company may not own stations that reach more than twenty-five percent of the national television audience. Thus, a company whose stations exceed this "audience cap" will not be permitted to purchase additional stations, even though it does not own its "full complement" of twelve. For purposes of this provision, owners of UHF stations will be attributed with only fifty percent of the actual audience in a given television market. In New York City, for example, the television audience comprises 7.72 percent of the nation's total. Though this figure would be used in calculating the audience of a New York VHF television station in determining whether its owner's total audience exceeds the twenty-five percent "cap," half of that figure—3.86 percent—would be used for a UHF station. This is another example of the FCC's effort to help the development of UHF stations.

The "12-12-12" rule also has special provisions designed to encourage ownership of broadcast stations by members of minority groups. Owners of multiple television and radio stations may add two additional stations in each of the three categories provided that at least two of the stations in which they hold ownership interests are controlled by members of minority groups. Similarly, an owner having an interest in minority controlled television stations is allowed to reach a maximum of thirty percent of the national audience, provided that at least five percent of the aggregate reach of its stations is contributed by minority controlled stations. These provisions are consistent with a variety of FCC policies adopted over the years to promote minority ownership in broadcasting.

Cross-Ownership Restrictions. In 1975, the FCC adopted a regulation that prohibits newspaper-broadcast combinations in the same geographic area. Specifically, the rule provides that the owner of a daily newspaper cannot hold a license for a television station, AM radio station, or FM radio station whose signal reaches the community in which the newspaper is located. Combinations of this type in existence at the time of the rule's adoption were almost all "grandfathered," although the properties could not be resold as a unit to new buyers. However, the FCC ordered divestiture of either the newspaper or broadcast station in sixteen "egregious cases" where there was common ownership of the only daily newspaper in the community and the only radio or television station that provided the entire community with a clear signal.

The rule was quickly challenged in the federal courts. The American Newspaper Publishers Association, the National Association of Broadcasters, and owners of newspaper-broadcast combinations argued that the rule exceeded the FCC's authority under the Communications Act of 1934 and violated the first amendment rights of the newspaper owners. At the same time, a citizens' group argued that the FCC had acted arbitrarily in "grandfathering" almost all of the existing newspaper-broadcast combinations and that the agency should have ordered across-the-board divestiture. The U.S. Supreme Court upheld the FCC's action in *Federal Communications Commission v. National Citizens Committee for Broadcasting* (1978).

Writing for a unanimous Court, Justice Thurgood Marshall first pointed out that the FCC has broad authority to regulate the broadcast industry under the "public interest" standard of the Communications Act. "It was not inconsistent with [the Act] . . . for the Commission to conclude that the maximum benefit to the 'public interest' would follow from the allocation of broadcast licenses so as to promote diversification of the mass media as a whole," Justice Marshall said. The FCC was entitled to rely on its judgment, based on experience, that "it is unrealistic to expect true diversity from a commonly owned station-newspaper combination." Moreover, he said, the FCC did not act arbitrarily in declining to order complete divestiture, since the agency rationally concluded that the "potential gains that would follow from increasing diversification of ownership" were outweighed by a variety of other factors. A sweeping divestiture order, the FCC had reasoned, would disregard the meritorious service of broadcast stations owned by newspapers, cause serious disruption during the transition period, and likely result in a decline of local ownership of broadcast stations.

Turning to the constitutional issue, Justice Marshall made two major points: the regulation governed ownership of the broadcast media, which are treated differently than the print media under the first amendment; and the purpose of the regulation was to achieve "the widest possible dissemination of information from diverse and antagonistic sources," a goal fully compatible with the first amendment.

The argument that the rule violated the first amendment rights of newspaper owners, he said, "ignores the fundamental proposition that there is no unabridgeable First Amendment right to broadcast comparable to the right of every individual to speak, write, or publish."

Quoting from the *Red Lion* decision, Justice Marshall observed that "to deny a station license because the public interest requires it is not a denial of free speech." In this case, the public interest was in diversification of ownership in the media industry. "[F]ar from seeking to limit the flow of information, the Commission has acted . . . to enhance the diversity of information heard by the public. . . ." Further, he pointed out that the regulation was similar to the prohibitions imposed by the antitrust laws. "This Court has held that application of the antitrust laws to newspapers is not only consistent with, but is actually supportive of, the values underlying the First Amendment."

The Commission adopted a similar rule forbidding cross-ownership of a television station and cable system in the same community. Congress incorporated this prohibition into the Cable Communications Policy Act of 1984, which prevents the licensee of a local television station, directly or indirectly, from owning a cable system in an area served by the station's signal. By enacting the FCC rule as part of the statute, Congress took away the agency's ability to consider changes in the rule—or its elimination—at some point in the future. Unlike the FCC rule on which it was modeled, the statutory provision does not contain a "grandfather" provision. After the statute went into effect, the FCC ordered divestiture of the remaining cable-broadcast combinations. Although the Cable Act does not specifically restrict ownership of cable systems by the television networks, FCC rules prevent ABC, CBS, and NBC from owning cable systems. However, the Commission has proposed eliminating this prohibition, which arguably thwarts competition in the cable industry. Neither the statute nor FCC regulations bar newspaper ownership of cable systems.

Of considerable controversy is the question of whether telephone companies should be able to offer cable television services. The Cable Act codified the FCC's longstanding ban on cable ownership by telephone companies in the areas where they provide telephone service, with an exception for rural areas that cable operators are unwilling to serve. In 1988 the FCC commenced an inquiry to consider whether this ban should be lifted. Obviously, the FCC cannot act unilaterally in this area, but can only recommend to Congress that telephone companies be permitted to offer cable services. Such a change in the law would likely provide head-to-head competition for cable operators, who, as noted in Chapter 10, typically enjoy monopoly status in the communities they serve.

Newspaper Antitrust Problems

The antitrust laws affect newspapers in a variety of ways. With respect to circulation, for example, any attempt by a publisher to set the price at which its independent distributors must sell the newspaper—either to local carriers or to subscribers—is a violation of the Sherman Act. In terms of editorial content, a publisher's contract for the exclusive use of syndicated feature material such as political columns and comic strips is illegal if it unreasonably restrains competition. Thus, a metropolitan daily that has exclusive rights to "Doonsbury" within a large geographic area might well face antitrust difficulties, particularly if the newspaper's circulation would not be adversely affected if small dailies or weeklies within the region were to carry the popular strip. Because space does not permit treatment of the multitude of antitrust issues in the newspaper business, our focus will be on two problem areas: advertising and joint operating agreements.

Advertising. As noted in Chapter 11, a newspaper may, as a general rule, refuse to accept advertising for any reason or no reason. This discretion, however, is limited by the antitrust laws. For example, in *Lorain Journal Co. v. United States* (1951), a newspaper publisher refused to accept advertising from local merchants who also advertised on an upstart radio station that was the newspaper's only competitor for advertising in the geographic area. The U.S. Justice Department sought a court order to stop this practice on the ground that the newspaper was violating Section 2 of the Sherman Act, which prohibits monopolization and any "attempt to monopolize" a particular market. A federal judge agreed and issued an injunction that prohibited the newspaper from discriminating against persons or businesses who advertised in other media. The Supreme Court unanimously affirmed, ruling that the refusal to accept advertising "is a purposeful means of monopolizing interstate commerce prohibited by the Sherman Act."

At the same time, however, the Court made plain that the critical element is an intent to monopolize. "In the absence of any purpose to create or maintain a monopoly, the [Sherman Act] does not restrict the long recognized right of trader or manufacturer . . . to exercise his own independent discretion as to parties with whom he will deal." In this case, the Court had little difficulty in concluding that the requisite intent was present, describing the newspaper's conduct as "bold, relentless, and predatory commercial behavior." The newspaper, which reached virtually all homes in the community, had enjoyed a monopoly prior to the licensing of the radio station and had unsuccessfully sought to obtain the broadcast license itself. Faced with this new competitor, the newspaper adopted its advertising policy in an obvious attempt to drive the radio station out of business. The policy plainly discouraged businesses from purchasing air time on the radio station, since they could not afford to be shut out of a newspaper that blanketed the community.

A refusal to accept advertising can have other antitrust consequences as well. In *Home Placement Service, Inc. v. Providence Journal Co.* (1982), a company that offered a "finder's service" for persons seeking to rent homes and apartments brought an antitrust action after the *Providence Journal* refused to accept its classified ads unless the company agreed not to charge its clients a fee for properties that had been advertised in the newspaper. The trial court denied relief, but the U.S. Court of Appeals for the First Circuit reversed and ordered further proceedings. In the appellate court's view, the newspaper's refusal to accept the advertising violated both Sections 1 and 2 of the Sherman Act. The trial court ultimately enjoined the newspaper from continuing the practice but found that the plaintiff was entitled only to nominal damages.

Section 1 of the Sherman Act declares unlawful "[e]very contract, combination . . . , or conspiracy in restraint of trade. . . ." Obviously, a unilateral business decision by a newspaper not to accept advertising would not violate this provision, which prohibits concerted activity involving at least two participants. In other words, it takes two to tango. Thus, if a newspaper agreed with a major advertiser not to accept ads from the advertiser's principal competitor, an impermissible combination would exist. On the other hand, there would be no Section 1 violation had the newspaper unilaterally decided not to publish the ads.

In the *Home Placement* case, the court observed that the newspaper would not have run afoul of the statute had it simply told the plaintiff that it would not accept any advertising for rental properties for which a finder's fee would be charged. The newspaper went further, however, in agreeing to print the ads if the plaintiff would not charge a fee in connection with properties advertised in the *Journal*. This agreement constituted illegal concerted action, the court concluded, since "a plaintiff can claim an unlawful combination between defendant and itself as of the day it unwillingly agreed to comply with defendant's restriction."

The court also found a violation of Section 2 of the act, reasoning that the *Journal* was attempting to monopolize the "housing vacancy information market" in which it competed with the plaintiff. As in the *Lorain Journal* case, the newspaper was seeking to protect its dominant position as the vehicle used by advertisers to reach prospective customers. Here, the advertisers were landlords who wanted to make known the availability of their rental properties to potential tenants. If the plaintiff company were successful in convincing landlords to utilize its services, the court noted, "it could siphon off [the newspaper's] advertisers and essentially redefine the market for the listing of rental information, thereby perhaps forcing [the newspaper] to lower its advertising prices." Because of its "monopoly power over rental listings" in the geographic area, the court concluded, "the *Journal*'s refusal to run [plaintiff's] ads where a fee was charged put plaintiff out of the rental referral business."

An earlier decision by the same court is an interesting counterpoint to the *Home Placement* case. In *Homefinder's of America, Inc. v. Providence Journal Co.* (1980), another company that listed rental properties sued the *Journal* for antitrust violations after the newspaper had refused to accept its ads. Here, however, the *Journal* based its decision on the objectionable sales tactics used by the company. Specifically, the firm would advertise an individual rental with a brief description, followed by its office phone number. When a prospective tenant called about the property, he would be told that the advertised property was no longer available but that other listings were available at the office for a fee of $20. This was nothing more than a "bait and switch" scheme, the court said, since the purpose of the ad was not to rent the advertised property (which may not even have existed) but to sell the would-be renter a list of other properties. As a result of the company's advertisements, the *Journal* decided to reject such ads after receiving a "torrent" of complaints from its readers. Even though the *Journal* may have had a monopolistic position, the court ruled, it was justified in refusing the advertising because of its deceptive nature. No such independent basis for the refusal existed in the *Home Placement* case, however.

Policies that require advertisers to purchase ads in two newspapers owned by the same publisher (or in other media under common ownership) can also give rise to antitrust difficulties. Such "forced combination advertising" is a form of what is known in antitrust jargon as "tying." Suppose, for example, that a company selling photocopiers and supplies refuses to permit a buyer to purchase a copier unless he agrees to buy the supplies as well. Conditioning the sale of the copier (the "tying" product) on an agreement to purchase supplies (the "tied" product) amounts to a package deal that the purchaser may not want.

Whether such an arrangement violates the antitrust laws[4] depends on several factors, but as the Supreme Court observed in *Jefferson Parish Hospital District*

---

[4]Tying is potentially illegal under both the Sherman Act and Section 3 of the Clayton Act. The latter statute applies only with respect to the sale or lease of commodities, while the former is not so limited.

v. Hyde (1984), the key issue is whether "the seller possesses some special ability—usually called 'market power'—to force a purchaser to do something that he would not do in a competitive market." The legal analysis focuses on the impact of the arrangement on the market for the tied product (supplies in the above example), with the concern being that the scheme could harm existing competitors in that market or discourage other companies from entering it.

The "tying" problem arose in the advertising context in *Times-Picayune Publishing Co. v. United States* (1953). There the U.S. Department of Justice brought a civil action against the publisher two newspapers in New Orleans, the morning *Times-Picayune* and the afternoon *States*. Under the publisher's "unit plan," advertisers were required to purchase space in both papers and could not simply choose one or the other. According to the Justice Department, this requirement harmed the city's other afternoon newspaper, the *Item*. Because advertisers could not buy an ad in the *Times-Picayune* without also purchasing space in the *States*, there was arguably little incentive for them to duplicate their afternoon advertising in the *Item*. A federal district judge ruled in favor of the government and issued an injunction prohibiting the continued use of the "unit plan," but the U.S. Supreme Court reversed.

In the Court's view, the alleged tying arrangement did not link two distinct services that were distinguishable in the eyes of buyers. Writing for the Court, Justice Tom Clark observed:

> Although advertising space in the *Times-Picayune*, as the sole morning daily, was doubtless essential to blanket coverage of the local newspaper readership, nothing in the record suggests that advertisers viewed the city's newspaper readers, morning or evening, as other than fungible customer potential. We must assume, therefore, that the readership "bought" by advertisers was the selfsame "product" sold by the *States* and, for that matter, the *Item*.

This decision does not mean that forced combination rates are permissible; rather, the Court simply concluded that the Justice Department had not proved that there were two separate advertising markets in New Orleans at that time. The outcome might well have been different had the evidence established that the morning *Times-Picayune* was the dominant newspaper in the city and that the afternoon newspapers were less desirable for advertisers.

Indeed, shortly after the *Times-Picayune* decision, the Justice Department was successful in a criminal prosecution based in part on a tying theory. In *Kansas City Star Co. v. United States* (1957), the U.S. Court of Appeals for the Eighth Circuit upheld a jury's finding that the publisher of two Kansas City newspapers, the morning *Times* and the afternoon *Star*, employed forced combination advertising with the intent and effect of excluding competition in the market. Central to this issue was the jury's determination that the two newspapers were separate advertising vehicles. Relying on the *Times-Picayune* decision, the publisher argued on appeal that it produced only a single newspaper with morning and afternoon editions. The court rejected the argument: "The *Times-Picayune* case was, in the last analysis, determined on the basis of a failure of proof." Here, however, the evidence was sufficient to support the jury's conclusion that the *Times* and the *Star* "were separate newspapers with distinct and separate uses for advertisers."

Another potential antitrust problem in the advertising area stems from what is known as "predatory pricing" or "sales below cost." Simply put, this practice involves the sale of a product or service below its actual cost of production, with the hope that competitors will go out of business trying to meet the price. A company that prices its products or services in this fashion is engaging in an economic war of attrition; that is, it is willing to lose money in the short term in exchange for a lucrative monopoly position in the long term. Deliberate below-cost pricing is generally considered a severely anticompetitive practice. Although it may not be illegal in itself, such pricing can provide evidence of intent to monopolize in violation of Section 2 of the Sherman Act.

Antitrust suits of this type have arisen when daily newspapers, fearing competition from upstart "shoppers," responded with what is known in the trade as "total market coverage" or "TMC." Typically, a daily newspaper publisher hoping to keep advertisers from being attracted to a free-circulation shopper would begin its own shopper, which would be delivered at no cost to persons who were not subscribing to the newspaper. The publisher could then assure an advertiser that his ad was reaching the entire community. In addition, the newspaper would sell advertising in its shopper at a cut rate, offering special deals to advertisers who also bought space in the daily. Thus, a business that wanted to advertise in a daily paper and in a shopper would obviously have an incentive to choose the newspaper's own shopper rather than one published by a competitor, since he could take advantage of a lower ad rate. Publishers of independent shoppers have fought this tactic in the courts, arguing, among other things, that these cut-rate pricing policies are predatory.

A 1974 case, *Greenville Publishing Co. v. Daily Reflector, Inc.*, is illustrative. There the defendants published the *Daily Reflector*, a newspaper in Greenville, North Carolina. After the plaintiff began publishing a weekly "shopper" known as the *Advocate*, the defendants countered with a new publication, the *Shoppers Guide*, that was delivered to all households that did not subscribe to the *Reflector*. In addition, the defendants offered a special advertising rate that permitted advertisers buying space in the *Reflector* to reprint the same ad in the *Shoppers Guide* for half-price. Faced with mounting operating losses, the plaintiff then brought an antitrust action on the theory that the defendants had deliberately set advertising rates for the *Shoppers Guide* below cost in an attempt to drive the *Advocate* out of business. The plaintiff claimed that the defendants had lost money on the *Shoppers Guide*, since it did not generate sufficient advertising revenue to cover its production costs. The defendants, however, argued that the *Shoppers Guide* turned a slight profit in its second year and that first-year losses were to be expected in any new venture.

A federal district judge granted summary judgment for the defendants, ruling that publication of the *Shoppers Guide* was "based on competitive business considerations" and that any losses suffered by the defendant were attributable "to the beginning of a new enterprise." In addition, the court pointed out that although the *Shoppers Guide* had lost money during its first year of publication, it had turned a profit of about $300 the following year. The U.S. Court of Appeals for the Fourth Circuit reversed and sent the case back for trial, ruling that disputed factual issues precluded summary judgment. "It is not at all clear that defendants set the *Shoppers Guide* rates at a level that could reasonably be expected to generate a profit," the court said. Specifically, there was strong disagreement between plaintiff and defendants as to the proper accounting techniques to be employed in determining whether the *Shoppers Guide* was in fact profitable. The court said:

Plaintiff contends that defendants' method of cost accounting does not give an accurate picture of the expense of producing the *Shoppers Guide*, and that defendants' profit figures would be wiped out if the balance sheet reflected all publishing costs that are fairly atributable to the shopper. Defendants admit that their method of cost accounting does not charge the *Shoppers Guide* with any portion of the company's fixed expenses or personnel costs. They claim, however, that their accounting methods give a fair picture of the shopper's profitability because publishing the *Shoppers Guide* does not increase the fixed costs or personnel costs of the enterprise as a whole.

As this passsage indicates, it is often difficult to determine whether advertising is sold "below cost." In this case, the plaintiff's position was that the defendants were in effect subsidizing the money-losing *Shoppers Guide* with ad revenue generated by the *Daily Reflector*. The defendants, on the other hand, argued that their additional costs for publishing the shopper—paper, ink, personnel, overhead, and so forth—were minimal, since most of those costs would be incurred in publishing only the daily newspaper.

Another difficulty present in cases of this type is defining the relevant market in which the parties compete. Here, the plaintiff contended that the appropriate market was print advertising in the Greenville area. While agreeing with the geographic boundaries, the defendants claimed that all other forms advertising—including radio, television, billboards, circulars, and the Yellow Pages—should also be included. If the market were defined in broad rather than narrow terms, it would be difficult, if not impossible, for the plaintiff to prove that the defendants possessed the economic power necessary to monopolize the market. The court of appeals declined to decide the question in the *Greenville* case, pointing to a lack of evidence in the record. Despite these problems, antitrust suits based on predatory pricing have been relatively common, but for the most part the defendants have prevailed.

A different antitrust statute, the Robinson-Patman Act, potentially comes into play with respect to advertising rates. Passed during the Great Depression, the statute seeks to limit the purchasing power of "chain stores"—particularly supermarkets—by curtailing price discounts often afforded high-volume buyers. Generally speaking, the statute prohibits sellers from discriminating among buyers in terms of price if injury to competition results. However, the act applies only to the sale of "commodities," thus raising the question of its applicability to the common practice of newspapers and other media in offering "volume discounts" to merchants who purchase large quantities of advertising. Although the courts have unanimously concluded that broadcast advertising is an intangible service rather than a commodity and thus outside the scope of the act, there has been some disagreement as to the nature of newspaper advertising.

It is possible to distinguish broadcast and newspaper advertising in the sense that the former involves only a fleeting auditory or visual image while the latter is in tangible form. While a handful of courts have embraced this distinction in ruling that newspaper advertising is subject to the statute, the majority view is that such advertising is an "intangible service" by which a business may send commercial messages to the newspaper's readers. To be sure, newspaper advertising does have tangible characteristics (i.e., newsprint and ink) that broadcast advertising may lack. However, the courts have generally recognized that the printed page is simply the tangible vehicle by which the service is provided. As a federal district court observed in *National Tire Wholesale, Inc. v. Washington Post Co.* (1977), newspaper advertising is "in the nature of a service," and its tangible features are "only incidental to the dominant intangible nature of the transaction." Accordingly, all advertising, whether print or broadcast, should be considered beyond the reach of the Robinson-Patman Act.

Joint Operating Agreements. As noted previously, Section 7 of the Clayton Act prohibits mergers that tend to create a monopoly or lessen competition within a particular market. The courts, however, have fashioned an exception to this rule. Under the "failing company doctrine," a merger between two competitors that would otherwise be unlawful is permissible when one is on the verge of financial collapse and no other prospective purchaser is in sight. After the U.S. Supreme Court found the doctrine inapplicable in a 1969 case involving a joint operating agreement (JOA) between two Tucson newspapers, the Congress passed a special statute—the Newspaper Preservation Act of 1970—that allows the partial merger of competing newspapers under circumstances that would not trigger the failing company doctrine. This statute has proved to be controversial.

The Tucson case, *Citizen Publishing Co. v. United States* (1969), arose from a 1940 joint operating agreement under which the only two daily newspapers in that city merged their business operations but maintained separate news and editorial departments. As a result of this arrangement, there was no longer any competition in the market with respect to advertising rates or subscription prices. A single business entity formed by the two publishers controlled printing, advertising, and circulation, with the publishers sharing the profits. The U.S. Department of Justice challenged the JOA on a variety of antitrust grounds, including violation of Section 7 of the Clayton Act. The district court found the agreement illegal and the Supreme Court affirmed, rejecting the newspapers' argument that the failing company doctrine applied. At the time the papers entered into the agreement, the Court said, there was no serious probability that the weaker of the two was on the verge of failure, as required by the failing company doctrine. Moreover, there was no indication that the stronger publisher was the only potential purchaser.

Because the *Citizen Publishing* decision cast serious doubts on the vaildity of twenty-two other joint operating agreements then in effect, the Congress quickly passed the Newspaper Preservation Act to clarify the law. Under the act's key provisions, the existing joint operating agreements were "grandfathered" and the failing company doctrine was modified to permit future JOA's even though a financially troubled newspaper was not on its economic deathbed. The Congress believed that this liberalization of the failing company doctrine was necessary in light of market forces that had led to the elimination of competition among daily newspapers in all but the largest of the nation's cities. In short, the Congress believed that a joint operating agreement that preserves two independent editorial voices under a single economic umbrella is preferable to a "one-newspaper town." This premise has not been universally accepted, and opponents of the act have taken their fight to the courts.

The first round of court challenges involved the grandfathering of the twenty-two JOA's in place when the act was passed, most of which remain in effect today. In *Bay Guardian Co. v. Chronicle Publishing Co.* (1972), the publisher of a monthly newspaper in San Francisco argued that the act violated the first amendment by effectively barring him from the market. Under a 1965 agreement, two newspapers—the morning *Chronicle* and the evening *Examiner*—operated jointly but with separate editorial and news staffs. As part of the deal, the publisher of the *Examiner* had shifted that paper from morning to evening publication and had folded its morning paper. Not surprisingly, advertising rates rose significantly under the JOA, and the two dailies offered a special rate to advertisers who bought space in both papers. The plaintiff, who had planned to mount a competitive effort against the dailies, claimed that this arrangement prevented him from doing so, thereby infringing on his first amendment rights. He was joined in the suit by advertisers who faced steep rate increases as a result of the JOA.

A federal district court in San Francisco gave short shrift to the first amendment argument. In upholding the act's constitutionality, the court said:

> The simple answer to the plaintiffs' contention is that the Act does not authorize any conduct. It is a narrow exception to the antitrust laws for newspapers in danger of failing. * * * Much of plaintiffs' argument seems directed at a phantom Act which conveys a government license to monopolize to certain newspapers at the expense of others. Whatever might be the constitutional status of such an Act, it is not the one now before us. The Act pertinent to this case does not confer any license to monopolize and indeed has a specific provision prohibiting "predatory practices." * * * [T]he Act was designed to preserve independent editorial voices. Regardless of the economic or social wisdom of such a course, it does not violate the freedom of the press. Rather, it is merely a selective repeal of the antitrust laws. It merely looses the same shady market forces which existed before the passage of the . . . antitrust laws.

The court was obviously convinced that the act enhanced rather than restrained press freedom, since it helped ensure "independent editorial voices" in the marketplace of ideas. But this ruling did not end the litigation, for the plaintiffs also contended that the JOA was impermissible because neither the *Chronicle* nor the *Examiner* was in any danger of failing. Prior to trial, however, the parties settled the case, with the plaintiffs receiving $1.35 million.

Subsequent lawsuits have focused on the provisions in the act governing the formation of new joint operating agreements. In this regard, the act permits JOA's that receive the prior approval of the Attorney General of the United States. In order to grant such approval, the Attorney General must determine that one of the newspapers is "in probable danger of financial failure" and that the JOA would "effectuate the policy and purpose" of the act. Under implementing regulations adopted by the Department of Justice, an administrative hearing is held on a JOA application, after which an administrative law judge makes a recommended decision. The Attorney General need not follow the recommendation but must base his ruling on the facts developed at the hearing. Although the Attorney General's approval or disapproval of the application may be challenged in the courts, his decision is generally accorded considerable deference on appeal.

Of the five joint operating agreements approved by the Attorney General under this portion of the act, two have spawned major judicial battles. The first case, *Committee for an Independent P-I v. Hearst Corp.* (1983), arose in 1981 when the publishers of Seattle's two daily newspapers, the *Times* and *Post-Intelligencer*, sought approval of a JOA from Attorney General William French Smith, arguing that the latter was in a state of "probable financial failure." After administrative proceedings of the type described above, the Attorney General approved the joint operating agreement. He concluded that the *Post-Intelligencer* was caught in a "downward spiral" in which declining circulation and falling advertising revenue feed off one another, creating irreversible financial difficulties. The Attorney General also determined that a sale of the paper to a third party was improbable. A group of advertisers, newspaper employees, and publishers of smaller newspapers challenged the Attorney General's decision in federal court, arguing, among other things, that approval was not permissible under the Newspaper Preservation Act because the Hearst Corporation, publisher of the *Post-Intelligencer*, had not made a good faith effort to sell the newspaper. In fact, they claimed, Hearst had not pursued inquiries from companies that had expressed some interest in purchasing the troubled paper. The district court agreed with the plaintiffs, but the U.S. Court of Appeals for the Ninth Circuit upheld the Attorney General.

The Ninth Circuit's decision turned on interpretation of the statute, with the central question being whether the owner of a financially troubled newspaper is required to search for an available purchaser before resorting to a JOA. Although such an effort is necessary under the failing company doctrine, the court concluded that Congress, in passing the Newspaper Preservation Act, intended to eliminate this requirement. However, the court ruled that the possibility of a sale to a third party is relevant to the question of whether the newspaper is in "probable danger of financial failure" within the meaning of the act. As the court observed:

> The [presence] of interested purchasers . . . may require a JOA applicant to prove that the "new ownership and management could not convert the [paper] into a profitable enterprise without resort to a joint operating arrangement." * * * This interpretation of the Act . . . prevent[s] newspapers from allowing or encouraging financial difficulties in the hope of reaping long-term financial gains through a JOA. A JOA applicant should not be allowed to engage in poor business practices or maintain inept personnel in anticipation that it may later qualify for an antitrust exemption. . . . In this respect, "alternatives" to a JOA are relevant to both the causes of a newspaper's financial decline and its future prospects.

Therefore, the "critical question" was whether the *Post-Intelligencer*'s financial condition was such that a new owner operating the paper in competition with the *Times* "might be successful in reversing [its] financial difficulties." With respect to this issue, the court found sufficient evidence in the record to support the Attorney General's negative answer. The evidence developed during the administrative proceedings showed that the *Post-Intelligencer* had lost over $14 million since 1969 and that the newspaper's management had acted competently and reasonably in attempting to reverse the trend, though those efforts had not been successful. Further, the evidence did not establish that a new owner would be able to succeed where Hearst had failed. Accordingly, the newspaper's failure to seek another purchaser or to explore inquiries from companies that expressed some interest in buying the paper was immaterial. "When the proponents of the JOA established, as they did here, that the paper was managed reasonably and its trend toward failure is irreversible under any management," the court said, "we have no difficulty concluding that [their] burden of proof [under the Newspaper Preservation Act] has been met."

The plaintiffs also contended that the act requires a determination that a newspaper would be closed if the JOA application were disapproved. The district court rejected this argument, as did the Ninth Circuit. It was sufficient, the appellate court said, that the Attorney General concluded that without the ownership of Hearst the *Post-Intelligencer* would probably be closed. In so ruling, the court made clear that a financially troubled newspaper is to be evaluated as a free-standing entity, disregarding the fact that it may be owned by a newspaper chain which, on the whole, is financially successful.

Here the court relied on a provision in the act defining a newspaper as "failing" if it is in "probable danger" of financial collapse "regardless of its ownership or affilations." This language, the court said, supported the Attorney General's conclusion that "the financial strength of Hearst need not be considered in determining whether the [*Post-Intelligencer*] is failing." In addition, the court stressed that the Congress intended to repudiate the requirement, established under the failing company doctrine, that a newspaper actually be "on the brink of collapse." Instead, there must simply be a "probability that the paper would be closed and an editorial voice lost." Examining the evidence, the court agreed with the Attorney General that the *Post-Intelligencer* was "in dire financial trouble and, without the backing of Hearst, it would probably close."

The court also rejected the plaintiffs' argument that the Attorney General's approval of the JOA should be set aside because it did not "effectuate the policy and purpose of the Act." Specifically, the plaintiffs claimed that the Attorney General failed to consider the potential injury to other newspapers in the market, a condition that the plaintiffs considered to be implicit in the act. The court, however, concluded that reading such a requirement into the statute would be contrary to the intent of Congress. "[T]he Act itself is a policy determination that the preservation of editorial diversity through joint operating agreements outweighs any potentially anticompetitive effects [that] this antitrust exemption might cause," the court noted. "Congress struck the balance in favor of [JOA's] notwithstanding opposition that decried the potential harm to smaller, usually suburban, newspapers competing in the market area. * * * This was a national policy choice Congress was free to make." The court also pointed out that the act itself contains an "important safeguard" that prevents the parties to a JOA from engaging in any conduct which, if carried out by a single newspaper, would violate the antitrust laws. This provision, the court said, was designed "to protect the competitive position of newspapers which share the market with a joint operating arrangement."

Finally, the court concluded that, contrary to the plaintiffs' argument, the Newspaper Preservation Act does not violate the first amendment by making economic life more difficult for smaller newspapers that must compete with the participants in a JOA. The act's limited antitrust exemption "will not affect the content of speech of these smaller newspapers," the court reasoned. "At most, [it] may affect the number of readers that a newspaper has." So viewed, the act is merely an "economic regulation" to which the press is subject, and such regulatory efforts do not contravene the first amendment.

When the U.S. Supreme Court declined to review the case, it seemed that some major issues concerning the act had been put to rest. Questions about the statute soon reemerged, however, in connection with a JOA application filed by two Detroit newspapers in 1987. The application caused considerable controversy because it was made by the nation's two largest newspaper chains: Gannett, publisher of the *Detroit News*, and Knight-Ridder, publisher of the *Detroit Free Press*. Disregarding the recommendation of a Justice Department administrative law judge that the application be denied, Attorney General Edwin Meese III approved the JOA in August 1988, shortly before leaving office. A coalition of Detroit citizens, advertisers, and newspaper employees promptly filed suit to block the agreement, but a federal judge in Washington, D.C., upheld the Attorney General's decision. The U.S. Court of Appeals for the District of Columbia Circuit affirmed.

This case, *Michigan Citizens for an Independent Press v. Thornburgh* (1989), grew out of a battle between the Detroit dailies in what has been dubbed the "Great

American Newspaper War." In an effort to achieve market domination, each paper cut subscription prices, discounted advertising rates, and made significant capital investments. Consequently, the papers were the least expensive dailies in the nation, both for subscribers and advertisers, and Detroit had the highest per capita newspaper readership rate of any major metropolitan center in the country. And, with the exception of New York City, Detroit was the only urban area supporting two general interest daily newspapers with circulations in excess of 650,000 each. Neither newspaper, however, was able to win a clear-cut victory in the war, and the result was what the Attorney General described as a "competitive stalemate." Both publications began suffering huge operating losses in the 1980's, with the *Free Press*—the weaker of the two—losing more than $10 million per year.

In approving the JOA, the Attorney General concluded that the *Free Press* was in "probable danger of financial failure," as required by the Newspaper Preservation Act. This was so, he said, because of its persistent operating losses and its inability to reverse the trend unilaterally. In his view, the *Free Press* could survive only if it raised its advertising and circulation rates, an unlikely prospect in light of the ongoing "war" and a pledge by the *News* to keep its rates low. The *Free Press* "has no realistic prospect of outlasting the *News* given the latter's substantial and persistent advertising and circulation lead," the Attorney General concluded, while the *News* "undoubtedly has the ability . . . to outlast the *Free Press*."

On appeal, the group challenging the JOA first argued that the Attorney General had misinterpreted the "probable danger of financial failure" standard. In its opinion, a newspaper must have actually entered a "downward spiral" of circulation and advertising revenue in order to take advantage of the Newspaper Preservation Act. Rejecting this argument, the court of appeals said that the Attorney General correctly relied on the test fashioned in the Seattle case: whether one newspaper is "suffering losses which more than likely cannot be reversed." Under this standard, the court said, it is sufficient that a newspaper "be poised on the brink of the [downward] spiral, its future depend[ing] on the competitive behavior of [its rival]."

Taking a different tack, the challengers then argued that the Attorney General had in any event misapplied this test to the facts. Pointing to evidence that the *Free Press* trailed the *News* only slightly in circulation (fifty-one percent to forty-nine percent), the group claimed that the *Free Press* was "within striking distance" of its competitor, not on the brink of a downward spiral. Moreover, the group described the *News'* lead as "vulnerable" and argued that both papers could survive financially if they raised their circulation and advertising rates.

The court, however, found that the Attorney General's view of the facts was not unreasonable. For example, even though the *News* had only a slight circulation edge over the *Free Press*, it enjoyed a wide advantage in advertising lineage (sixty percent to forty percent). Further, there was ample evidence suggesting that the *Free Press* could not unilaterally attain profitability, since it could not be expected to raise advertising and subscription prices on its own if the *News* kept its rates low. Though the challengers claimed that the *News* would probably be forced to raise its rates in light of its own deepening losses, thus permitting the *Free Press* to do the same, the court said that the evidence was sufficient to support the Attorney General's contrary conclusion.

First, the court noted that *News* officials had stated their intention not raise rates if the JOA were disapproved. This business strategy was not unreasonable, considering that a rate hike would put at risk the *News'* narrow circulation advantage, which in turn could jeopardize its position as the financially healthier paper. Second, the

Attorney General's "judgment of the *News'* future behavior was premised on his [reasonable] determination . . . that the *News* had the competitive strength to out-last the *Free Press*," the court said.

A potentially more difficult question was presented by the challengers' argument that the losses suffered by the *Free Press* were in part the result of a conscious strategy of forcing prices so low that it would either drive the *News* out of business or cause losses that would permit a JOA. The challengers claimed that both newspapers felt free to adopt "bold strategies of price-cutting" in an attempt to dominate the market because they were "secure in the belief" that failure would lead to a JOA. Although the court of appeals shared the concern that newspapers might "compete recklessly because of a recognition that the loser will be assured a soft landing" under the Newspaper Preservation Act, it upheld the Attorney General's determination that the *News* and *Free Press* were motivated by competitive aims, not a JOA, in their business strategies. "[Y]ears of fierce competition and consequent losses to both papers led the Attorney General reasonably to conclude that both papers were principally pursuing market domination and that their strategies had been followed before any mutual discussion of a JOA," the court said.

The U.S. Supreme Court subsequently agreed to review the *Michigan Citizens* case, and its ruling is expected to clarify the act's requirement that a newspaper be "in probable danger of financial failure." Other questions, however, may remain unresolved. For example, some observers are troubled by the notion that the act could permit a large chain to pour its resources into a newspaper war knowing full well that the worst case scenario would be a profitable JOA. It is one thing to permit a JOA when the market will not support two newspapers but quite another to allow such an agreement when one newspaper has taken affirmative steps to create a failing rival by employing anticompetitive practices. The court of appeals found no evidence of such improper conduct in *Michigan Citizens*. Moreover, one must wonder whether Congress made a sound decision in excluding the profits of a newspaper's corporate parent from the JOA process. Critics have argued that a newspaper should not be considered in danger of failing if the chain that owns it is financially healthy.

The Electronic Media

The newspaper industry does not have a monopoly on antitrust problems. For example, the advertising practices of television stations, the broadcasting of college football games, and the cable franchising process have been significantly affected by antitrust suits. Three key cases provide some idea of the legal issues involved.

In *United States v. National Association of Broadcasters* (1982), the U.S. Department of Justice attacked advertising standards adopted by the NAB for the networks and local television stations. In 1952, the NAB—a trade association whose membership includes the three major networks and over five hundred television stations—adopted a "television code" containing various guidelines for broadcasters. By the late 1970s, about two-thirds of all commercial television stations subscribed to the code and were thus entitled to display the "NAB Television Seal of Good Practice." A subscriber found guilty of violating the code's provisions lost the right to display the seal. The Justice Department claimed that three of the code's advertising standards violated the antitrust laws:

- a limit on the amount of time that could be devoted to advertisements in a given hour;
- a maximum limit on the number of commercial interruptions per program and the number of consecutive announcements per interruption; and
- a prohibition against the advertising of two or more products or services in a single commercial less than sixty seconds in duration.

Both parties moved for summary judgment. With respect to the first and second standards, the court ruled that summary judgment was not appropriate and that a trial would be necessary. However, the court concluded that the "multiple product" restriction violated Section 1 of the Sherman Act and granted summary judgment for the government on that issue. Because the restriction prevented an advertiser from purchasing one thirty-second spot to advertise two products, the court said, it forced him to buy a sixty-second spot for that purpose—twice as much time as he may actually want or need. On a highly-rated network program, the difference in cost between the two could easily exceed $100,000. "In thus artificially increasing the demand for commercial time," the court said, "the [multiple product] standard raises both the price of time and the revenues of the broadcasters, to the detriment of the users of the broadcast medium and the consumers of their product." The case was eventually settled, with the NAB agreeing to stop enforcing all three of the code provisions in question. Subsequently, the NAB abandoned the advertising standards altogether.

A similar problem arose in *NCAA v. Board of Regents of University of Oklahoma*, a case that reached the U.S. Supreme Court in 1984. At issue was a plan adopted by the National Collegiate Athletic Association that governed the televising of football games played by its member colleges and universities. In brief, the NCAA granted to ABC and CBS the right to televise college football games, with limits on the number of times a given team could appear on television and a ceiling on the total number of games that could be broadcast. Moreover, the networks were required to televise the games of a specified number of different teams over a two-season period. Member schools were not permitted to make any arrangements for the television rights to their games except in accordance with the NCAA plan.

Dissatisfied with this arrangement, a number of colleges with big-time football programs formed their own organization—the College Football Association—which entered into a separate television agreement with NBC. This contract would have allowed a greater number of television appearances by each team and would have increased the television revenues for those schools. In response, the NCAA announced that it would take disciplinary action against any school that complied with the CFA-NBC contract.

The University of Oklahoma and the University of Georgia then filed suit against the NCAA in an Oklahoma federal court, arguing that the organization's television plan violated the antitrust laws. After a trial, the court ruled that the plan was illegal under Section 1 of the Sherman Act, a decision subsequently affirmed by the U.S. Court of Appeals for the Tenth Circuit. The Supreme Court agreed. "Because it places a ceiling on the number of games member institutions may televise, the . . . agreement places an artificial limit on the quantity of televised football that is available to broadcasters and consumers," Justice John Paul Stevens wrote for the Court.

This limitation had the effect of raising the price that the networks paid for television rights, since it ensured that the ABC and CBS broadcasts would not be forced to compete with games carried by NBC, local stations, or cable. Absent such an agreement, neither ABC nor CBS would have been willing to pay so large a fee—$132 million over four years—for NCAA television rights. "The anticompetitive consequences of this arrangement are apparent," Justice Stevens wrote. "Price is higher and [the number of televised games] lower than they would otherwise be, and both are unresponsive to consumer preferences."

The process by which cities award cable television franchises has long been fraught with antitrust difficulties, though recent congressional action has eliminated some of the problems. The landmark case is this area of the law is *Community Communications Co. v. City of Boulder* (1982), which arose when the city council of Boulder, Colorado, passed an ordinance prohibiting a cable company that served part of the city from expanding its operations. In passing the ordinance, the council apparently feared that without such a "freeze" the incumbent, Community Communications, would obtain a natural monopoly before the council could evaluate the proposal of another cable company that had expressed an interest in serving the city. Faced with an obstacle to its expansion plans, Community Communications filed suit alleging that the city and Boulder Communications Co., the potential competitor, had engaged in an antitrust conspiracy in violation of Section 1 of the Sherman Act.

The primary question in the case was whether an exemption from the antitrust laws enjoyed by states also applied to cities. In arguing that it was entitled to the exemption, the City of Boulder relied on the Colorado "home rule" statute which, it claimed, conveyed to the city all regulatory powers of the state with respect to matters of local concern. Since the powers of the state flowed to the city via the statute, the city said, so did the exemption from the antitrust laws. In affirming the trial court's decision rejecting this argument, the U.S. Supreme Court held that a city is entitled to immunity only if a state statute clearly authorizes the anticompetitive conduct and that the Colorado "home rule" statute was not sufficiently specific.

Though the Court did not rule on the merits of the antitrust claim, the *Boulder* ruling opened the door to antitrust suits against cities in connection with the cable franchising process. Needless to say, the prospect of antitrust liability alarmed city officials, particularly after a federal court in Houston awarded $6.3 million in damages in an antitrust case against the city and five cable companies.

In response to the *Boulder* decision, some state legislatures promptly passed statutes designed to meet the Supreme Court's specificity requirement and thus insulate municipalities from antitrust lawsuits. Meanwhile, subsequent rulings by the Supreme Court and the lower federal courts in antitrust cases outside the cable context seemed to limit the scope of *Boulder* and thus give municipalities considerable protection. In addition, the Congress entered the fray in 1984 by passing two important statutes, the Cable Communications Policy Act and the Local Government Antitrust Act.

Under the Cable Act, which is discussed in more detail in Chapter 10, Congress gave cities the right to grant one or more cable franchises and prohibited operation of a cable system without a franchise. Because a city is expressly permitted to select among applicants, it seems that the exercise of this franchising authority cannot ordinarily serve as the basis for an antitrust suit, though there might well be liability if a city "rigs" the franchising process or otherwise departs from normal procedures. By the same token, a city that complies with the statute's detailed provisions for renewal of a franchise is not likely to encounter antitrust problems.

The Local Government Antitrust Act prohibits an award of monetary damages in an antitrust suit against a local government or its employees for actions in their official capacities. Moreover, damages may not be assessed against a private person or entity (e.g., another cable company) if the suit is based on "any official action directed by a local government" or its employees. Thus, both cities and successful cable franchise applicants are protected against damages—which are trebled under the antitrust statutes—in suits stemming from the franchising process. However, the statute does not prevent a court from issuing an injunction that overturns a cable franchise granted or renewed in violation of the antitrust laws.

MISCELLANEOUS REGULATORY ISSUES

Two other matters involving economic regulation of the print media are worthy of brief mention: postal rates and restraints on distribution. With respect to the former, the U.S. Postal Service has adopted regulations that permit certain publishers to qualify for lower second-class mailing rates. With regard to the latter, many cities have passed ordinances that restrict the use of "newsracks" or otherwise limit the manner in which newspapers and other publications may be sold.

Postal Regulations

Prior to passage of the Postal Reorganization Act of 1970, mailing rates were subject to control by Congress, which also set up various "classes" of mail to which different rates applied. Under the act, these matters are determined in administrative proceedings by the Board of Governors of the U.S. Postal Service, an independent federal agency, and a five-member Postal Rate Commission. As was the case before 1970, newspapers, magazines, and other periodicals are eligible for reduced "second class" rates, though these rates, along with postal rates in general, have increased steadily over the past several years. The ratemaking process is subject to review in the courts, and Postal Service rate increases have typically been followed by lawsuits.

For example, in *National Association of Greeting Card Publishers v. U.S. Postal Service* (1983), the U.S. Supreme Court was asked to resolve a dispute among the lower courts as to the proper methodology to be employed by the Postal Rate Commission in recommending rates to the Board of Governors. Other cases, such as *Direct Marketing Association v. U.S. Postal Service* (1985), have involved the reasonableness of particular rates. There U.S. Court of Appeals for the Second Circuit upheld new rates that went into effect in 1985, including those for third-class rates for bulk mail attacked by the "direct mail" industry as too high and by newspaper publishers as too low. Of course, both groups compete for advertising dollars, and the newspaper publishers obviously believed that higher third-class rates would discourage advertisers from using direct mail and encourage them to buy newspaper advertising.

Various regulations affecting the different classes of mail have also been the subject of litigation. For example, in *Combined Communications Corp. v. U.S. Postal Service* (1988), newspaper publishers successfully challenged a Postal Service regulation that made newspaper "plus" issues ineligible for second-class rates. The regulation treated a "plus" issue—a weekly shopper-like publication mailed to persons who do not subscribe to the newspaper—as separate from the newspaper itself. As a result, "plus" issues had to be mailed at the higher third-class rate, since second-class rates are not available to publications that do not have paid subscribers. A federal district court in Tennessee held that the regulation was invalid because it was adopted without the participation of the Postal Rate Commission, as required by the Postal Service Reorganization Act.

The second-class classification scheme has also spawned a first amendment challenge. In *The Enterprise, Inc. v. United States* (1987), the publisher of a free-circulation weekly newspaper challenged the constitutionality of the "paid subscriber" requirement. Under this regulation, a publication is eligible for second-class rates only if it has a "legitimate list of persons who have subscribed by paying or promising to pay at a rate above nominal for copies to be received during a stated time. . . ." The purpose of this rule, which was embodied for nearly 100 years in a statute that predated the Postal Reorganization Act of 1970, is to distinguish between publications issued in response to reader demand and those primarily designed for advertising purposes. The former are entitled to the lower second-class rate, while the latter must be sent third class.

In attacking the paid subscriber rule, the publisher of the *Enterprise* claimed that it discriminated against his free-circulation newspaper by granting more favorable mailing rates to publications available for a fee via subscription. The U.S. Court of Appeals for the Sixth Circuit disagreed, pointing out that the courts have long sustained the "broad authority" of the government "to establish content-neutral standards for favorable second-class mailing rates." The paid subscriber rule is content neutral, the court said, because it focuses on "the desires of the public, as expressed by their willingness to either subscribe and pay or formally 'request' a publication" rather than on "the subjective newsworthy qualities of a publication or other equally subjective methods of assessing the amount of pure editorial/educative material as opposed to commercial/advertising material. . . ."

In addition, the court noted that the first amendment was not violated merely because the regulation raised the cost of free-circulation papers while granting a subsidy to more "desirable" publications. The court relied heavily on *Regan v. Taxation With Representation of Washington*, a 1983 U.S. Supreme Court decision upholding a provision of the Internal Revenue Code that denies tax-exempt status to organizations involved in substantial lobbying activities. "Congress has not infringed on any First Amendment rights or regulated any First Amendment activity," the Supreme Court said in that case. "Congress has simply chosen not to pay for [the plaintiff's] lobbying." The Sixth Circuit found the paid subscriber rule to be analogous, since the denial of the second-class mail subsidy to the *Enterprise* did not place an affirmative burden on the publisher's exercise of his first amendment rights. The court also emphasized that the regulation was reasonably related to two important governmental objectives: helping ensure "an educated public" by subsidizing the mailing of informational material, and preventing abuse of subsidized mailing privileges by publications "having little or no demonstrable value to their recipients. . . ."

Restrictions on Distribution

One of the most frequently litigated issues in recent years has been the power of municipalities and other governmental bodies to restrict the use of newspaper vending machines, commonly called "newsracks," on public property. The question is of considerable economic importance to newspaper publishers, many of whom rely heavily on vending machine sales. According to testimony in a 1974 case, for example, newsrack sales accounted for fifteen percent of the daily circulation of the *Philadelphia Inquirer* and the *Philadelphia Daily News*. Moreover, *USA Today* is sold almost exclusively from vending machines. The Gannett chain, publisher of *USA Today*, has explained the importance of newsracks this way:

> Newsracks are an especially important means . . . to distribute *USA Today* because they make the newspaper available around the clock, when newsstands and stores selling papers are closed. Newsracks are economically justified by the sale of a comparatively small number of papers, and enable publishers to distribute newspapers in locations where other means of distribution [such as carrier delivery] are not feasible.

In *City of Lakewood v. Plain Dealer Publishing Co.* (1988), the U.S. Supreme Court struck down a city ordinance governing newsracks on city sidewalks because it vested too much discretion in city officials. However, the Court left open the the broader question of whether an ordinance completely prohibiting this form of newspaper distribution on public property is constitutionally acceptable. In a dissenting opinion, three Justices argued that such an outright prohibition is consistent with the first amendment, a position contrary to that taken by most lower courts.

The case arose when the City of Lakewood, Ohio, a suburb of Cleveland, denied the *Plain Dealer*'s application to place its newsracks on city sidewalks. City officials based this action on an ordinance that prohibited the private placement of any structure on public property. The newspaper then brought suit attacking the ordinance on first amendment grounds, and a federal district judge in Ohio ruled that the absolute prohibition was unconstitutional.

Rather than appeal this decision, the city amended its ordinance to give the mayor authority to grant or deny applications for annual newsrack permits. If the mayor approved such an application, the permit would be conditioned on approval of the newsrack's design by a city architectural board and the newspaper's agreement to indemnify the city against any liability arising from the newsrack, guaranteed by a $100,000 insurance policy to that effect. Dissatisfied with the new ordinance, the *Plain Dealer* chose not to seek a permit and instead returned to federal court, where the district judge upheld the revised requirements. The U.S. Court of Appeals for the Sixth Circuit reversed, finding the ordinance unconstitutional for three reasons:

- it gave the mayor unbridled discretion to grant or deny a permit;
- it gave similar discretion to the architectural board, since no design standards or guidelines were specified; and
- it required an indemnity agreement and insurance policy for newsrack opera-

tors but not for others who might seek to place private structures on public property.

The U.S. Supreme Court affirmed the Sixth Circuit, but only with respect to the first rationale. Moreover, the Court split 4 to 3 in the case, with two Justices not participating. Writing for the four-member majority, Justice William Brennan indicated that a city "may require periodic licensing and may even have special licensing procedures for conduct commonly associated with expression." In other words, expressive activity in a "public forum" such as a city sidewalk is subject to reasonable "time, place, and manner" restrictions. However, the first amendment requires that a city "establish neutral criteria to insure that the licensing decision is not based on the content or viewpoint of the speech being considered." The Lakewood ordinance was invalid because it lacked such safeguards, Justice Brennan said. The ordinance "contains no explicit limits on the Mayor's discretion" but rather gives him "unfettered discretion to deny a permit application. . . ." In a footnote, Justice Brennan expressly stated that the Court was not passing on the power of a city to completely prohibit newsracks on public property.

Speaking for the dissenters, Justice White took the position that "there is no constitutional right to place newsracks on city sidewalks over the objections of the city." Because an absolute ban is constitutional, he argued, the Lakewood ordinance was not on its face violative of the first amendment. Accordingly, the *Plain Dealer* should not be allowed to challenge the ordinance without having first sought a permit from the city. In addressing the validity of an absolute ban on newsracks, Justice White wrote:

> [The *Plain Dealer*] has a right to distribute its newspapers on the City's streets, as others have a right to leaflet, solicit, speak, or proselytize in this same public forum area. But this does not mean that it can . . . distribute its newspapers where, when, and how it chooses. More specifically, the *Plain Dealer*'s right to distribute its papers does not encompass the right to take city property—a part of the *public* forum, as [the newspaper] so vigorously argues—and appropriate it for its own exclusive use, on a semi-permanent basis, by means of the erection of a newsbox. The publisher of a newspaper . . . has no special privilege to invade the rights and liberties of others; these protected "rights of others" have always included the public-at-large's right to use the public forum for its chosen activities, including free passage of the streets. * * * Just as there is no First Amendment right to operate a bookstore or locate a movie theater however or wherever one chooses notwithstanding local laws to the contrary, the First Amendment does not create a right of newspaper publishers to take city streets to erect structures to sell their papers.

Justice White also emphasized that although a city street is a public forum, a municipal government has compelling reasons to prohibit newsracks. First, he noted that the Court has recognized a legitimate governmental interest in protecting the safety of citizens. In this case, trial testimony reflected numerous incidents where objects located on city sidewalks (e.g., signposts, signal poles, and newsracks) were hit by cars, bicycles, and pedestrians. The testimony also showed that drivers stop in traffic so that they may purchase newspapers, thus creating obvious safety hazards, and that newsracks can block ramps for the handicapped or restrict access to fire hydrants.

Second, Justice White pointed to prior decisions making plain that aesthetic considerations are sufficient to justify restrictions on speech. Because the city's "interest in attempting to preserve the quality of urban life is one that must be accorded high respect," a ban on newsracks as being "discordant with the surrounding area" does not offend the first amendment. Moreover, he noted that newspaper publishers have "ample alternative channels" for distribution, citing trial testimony that no person in the City of Lakewood lived more than one-fourth of a mile from either a convenience store open twenty-four hours a day or a newsrack located on private property. "The First Amendment does not require Lakewood to make its property available to the Plain Dealer so that it may undertake the most effective possible means of selling newspapers," Justice White wrote.

Because only seven of the nine Justices participated in the *Plain Dealer* decision, it is certainly possible that Justice White's view will one day become that of a majority of the Court. Moreover, although the Lakewood ordinance was declared invalid, Justice Brennan's opinion makes plain that reasonable restrictions on newsracks will pass muster under the first amendment. In that case, the ordinance simply placed too much disrection in the hands of city officials, thus giving them the ability to make decisions based on such impermissible factors as the content of a publication.

An ordinance with procedural safeguards to protect against such arbitrary administration is apparently permissible, as are carefully drafted restrictions on newsrack placement. For example, in *Gannett Satellite Information Network, Inc. v. Township of Pennsauken* (1989), a federal district court in New Jersey upheld an ordinance prohibiting newsracks on the city's main street and on side streets within thirty feet of any intersection with the thoroughfare. The ordinance, which had been adopted for safety and aesthetic reasons, did not completely ban newsracks from the business district but simply restricted them to particular areas. By the same token, a governmental authority may apparently establish a permit system that conditions the use of public property upon payment of a reasonable fee. In *Gannett Satellite Information Network, Inc. v. Metropolitan Transportation Authority* (1984), the U.S. Court of Appeals for the Second Circuit upheld a plan to charge fees for newsracks placed in subway stations owned by a government agency.

PROBLEMS

1. Under a "union shop" agreement with the American Federation of Television and Radio Artists, a television network agreed not to hire any performers or commentators unless they either joined the union or paid the equivalent dues to the union. William F. Buckley, Jr., the political commentator, challenged the requirement on first amendment grounds. What result? Why? *See Buckley v. American Federation of Television and Radio Artists*, 496 F.2d 305 (2d Cir.), *cert. denied*, 419 U.S. 1093 (1974).

2. A newspaper published a regular financial column by one of its business writers. In one of the columns, the writer discussed in somewhat laudatory terms the management, products, and fiscal condition of a particular company. However, he did not mention that he had recently invested in the company's stock. After the column appeared, the value of the stock jumped dramatically, and the writer took advantage of the increase by selling his shares and realizing a profit. Did the columnist violate Section 10(b) of the Securities and Exchange Act of 1934, the anti-fraud provision at issue in the *Carpenter* case? Could the

newspaper be held responsible? Could the court, consistent with the first amendment, order the columnist to disclose to his readers any financial stake in the subject matter of his columns? *See Zweig v. Hearst Corp.*, 521 F.2d 1129 (9th Cir.), *cert. denied*, 423 U.S. 1025 (1975); *Securities & Exchange Commission v. Blavin*, 760 F.2d 706 (6th Cir. 1985).

3. Suppose that a daily newspaper owns a radio station in the same community, having been "grandfathered" under the FCC's cross-ownership rules. Suppose further that the newspaper requires businesses wishing to place ads in the paper to purchase air time on its radio station as well. Does this policy constitute an impermissible "tying" arrangement? What other facts do you need in order to evaluate the newspaper's policy? Would it matter, for example, if the newspaper were the only daily paper in the community? If there were four intensely competitive radio stations?

4. On December 22, 1987, Congress passed and President Reagan signed a 471-page continuing resolution appropriating all of the funds for the federal government for fiscal year 1988. Buried in the resolution was a paragraph that prohibited the Federal Communications Commission from expending any of the funds appropriated to it to repeal or reexamine its cross-ownership rules or "to extend the time period of current grants of temporary waivers to achieve compliance with such rules. . . ." At that time, the only holder of a temporary waiver from the rules was Rupert Murdoch's News America Publishing, Inc., which then owned the *New York Post* and the *Boston Herald*. Another Murdoch-controlled company, Fox Television, Inc., owned WNYW-TV in New York City and WXNE-TV in Boston. News America subsequently asked the FCC to extend the waivers, but the Commission denied that request on the basis of the continuing resolution.

   Though News America then sold the *Post*, it challenged the constitutionality of the "no extension" provision as it applied to the *Herald* and WXNE-TV. What result? Why? Does it matter that the provision was aimed specifically at Mr. Murdoch? That it was apparently added to the resolution without debate and without the knowledge of most members of Congress? That one of the provision's proponents, Senator Edward M. Kennedy of Massachusetts, had clashed with the *Herald* in the past? *See News America Publishing, Inc. v. Federal Communications Commission*, 844 F.2d 800 (D.C. Cir. 1988). Subsequently, Congress included in an appropriations act for fiscal year 1989 a provision simply preventing the FCC from using the appropriated funds "to repeal, to retroactively apply changes in, or to begin or continue a reexamination of" the cross-ownership rules. Public Law No. 100–459, 102 Stat. 2186, 2217 (October 1, 1988).

5. The City of Wheaton, Illinois, passed an ordinance banning newsracks in residential areas of the city. The stated purposes of the ordinance were to promote "motor vehicle and pedestrian safety" and to maintain the "residential character" of the city's neighborhoods. Is the ordinance constitutional? Does it matter that the city has not completely prohibited newsracks in non-residential areas but instead placed restrictions on their location (e.g., not within fifteen feet of a fire hydrant or five feet of a marked crosswalk)? That the city has not taken other steps to protect the "character" of residential areas, such as requiring that power lines and other utilities be placed underground? How important is the fact that some neighborhoods affected by the ban are located up to three miles away from a newsrack or a store at which newspapers can be purchased? *See Chicago Newspaper Publishers Association v. City of Wheaton*, 697 F. Supp. 1464 (N.D. Ill. 1988). *See also Chicago Tribune Co. v. City of Chicago*, 705 F. Supp. 1345 (N.D. Ill. 1989) (restrictions on newsracks in passenger concourse area at public airport).

6. Newsracks are not the only form of distribution scheme targeted by city ordinances. For example, the township of Doylestown, Pennsylvania, passed an ordinance prohibiting the distribution of advertising materials at residences and other property without the prior

consent of the owner. The ostensible purpose of the ordinance was to cut down on burglaries, on the theory that the presence of "shoppers" and other free-circulation materials in front of a residence indicated that it was then unoccupied. The ordinance was also justified on the grounds that it preserved the privacy of persons who did not want to receive the materials and helped prevent unsightliness caused by this manner of distribution. Is the ordinance valid? *See Ad World, Inc. v. Township of Doylestown*, 672 F.2d 1136 (3d Cir.), *cert. denied*, 456 U.S. 975 (1982). What about a Houston, Texas, ordinance that prohibited "hawkers" from selling or offering to sell newspapers to any occupant of a motor vehicle on a public street? The "hawkers"—typically children or elderly men—worked busy intersections, peddling their papers to motorists stopped at traffic lights. *See Houston Chronicle Publishing Co. v. City of Houston*, 620 S.W.2d 833 (Tex. App. 1981). *See also Washington Post Co. v. Turner,* 708 F. Supp. 405 (D.D.C. 1989) (regulation banning "hawkers" from Washington, D.C., subway stations).

7. Consider the constitutionality of these state taxation schemes:
   (a) A Texas statute exempts from the state sales and use tax periodicals that are "published or distributed by a religious faith and that consist wholly of writings promulgating the teaching of the faith" and books that "consist wholly of writings sacred to a religious faith." A general interest magazine would not fall within the exemption and would thus be subject to the tax. Is this statute distinguishable from the one at issue in the *Arkansas Writers' Project* case? *See Texas Monthly, Inc. v. Bullock*, 109 S.Ct. 890 (1989).
   (b) Under a California statute, the gross receipts of any newspaper or periodical issued at regular intervals not exceeding three months is exempt from the state sales and use tax. By administrative regulation, "shoppers" and other publications that contain more than ninety percent advertising are not considered newspapers or periodicals and thus cannot take advantage of the exemption. Does the commercial speech doctrine come into play here? *See Redwood Empire Publishing Co. v. State Board of Equalization*, 255 Cal. Rptr. 514 (Ct. App. 1989).

8. The Fair Labor Standards Act, 29 U.S.C. §§207 *et seq.*, generally requires that employers pay overtime to employees who work more than forty hours per week. However, professional, administrative, and executive employees are exempt from this provision and thus not entitled to overtime compensation. Relying on the exemption, KDFW-TV in Dallas did not pay overtime to general assignment reporters, sportscasters, weathercasters, assignment editors, newscast producers, and directors. Employees who held these positions filed suit in federal court, arguing that their jobs did not fall within the exemption and seeking an award of back pay for the overtime compensation that they had been denied. What result? Does it matter that reporters typically have college degrees in journalism or communications, and that some weathercasters are meteorologists? That editors, directors, and producers perform some tasks that could be described as administrative? *See Dalheim v. KDFW-TV*, 706 F. Supp. 493 (N.D. Tex. 1988). *See also Sherwood v. Washington Post Co.,* 871 F. 2d 1144 (D.C. Cir. 1989) (newspaper reporters and editors).

THE AMERICAN LEGAL SYSTEM

"Law alone saves society from being rent by internecine strife or ruled by mere brute power however disguised," Justice Felix Frankfurter once wrote. "Civilization involves subjugation of force to reason, and the agency of this subjugation is law." His point, of course, is that law is a civilizing mechanism that establishes the general rules by which members of a society live, work, and interact. These rules serve a variety of functions; for example, they maintain order, provide a framework for commercial and social transactions, and protect people against excessive power wielded by government or by private bodies. In this section, we shall briefly examine the sources of these legal rules and the structure of our judicial system, which plays a key role in their creation and enforcement. A brief description of the procedure employed in civil and criminal cases is also included.

SOURCES OF LAW

At the risk of oversimplification, one can say that law in the United States stems from four basic sources: constitutions, statutes, administrative agencies, and the courts. Constitutional law is the cornerstone of our system of government. The U.S. Constitution, for example, establishes the structure of the federal government and defines the powers of the legislative, executive, and judicial branches. At the same time, however, it places important limits on those powers by guaranteeing to all citizens certain rights. This book deals extensively with one of those limitations, the first amendment. Each state also has its own constitution, reflecting the fact that ours is a system of dual sovereignty in which the states retain substantial powers. These state constitutions may not conflict with the U.S. Constitution, which, by virtue of its so-called "supremacy clause," is the supreme law of the land.

Statutory law emanates from the legislative branches of federal, state, and local governments. The statutes passed by Congress and state legislatures and the ordinances adopted by city councils are the work product of elected representatives and, at least in theory, reflect the will of the majority. As might be expected, statutes cover a wide range of topics. Some establish criminal penalties for wrongdoing, while others deal with civil matters such as contractual relationships between buyers and sellers or the manner in which marriages are to be dissolved. Statutes also create benefits—such as social security and welfare—for citizens and establish administrative agencies to carry out government programs. Whatever their purpose, statutes must conform to the applicable constitution. For example, a state statute is invalid if at odds with either the U.S. Constitution or the constitution of that state.

As noted above, administrative agencies are creatures of legislative bodies. As government has grown increasingly complex at all levels, legislatures have found it necessary to delegate various tasks to specialized agencies that can oversee particular programs or regulate the activities of certain businesses. Among federal agencies, the Veterans' Administration is an example of the former, while the Federal Communications Commission is an example of the latter. Administrative agencies "make law" in two ways, by adjudication and rulemaking. The adjudicative process is quasi-judicial in nature; that is, the agency announces a legal principle in the course of resolving a specific dispute before it. This principle then becomes applicable in subsequent cases of the same type. In contrast, the rulemaking process is quasi-legislative in that the agency, after opportunity for public comment, adopts a regulation of general application that has the same legal effect as a statute.

The courts play a major role with respect to constitutional, statutory, and administrative law. Under what is commonly known as "judicial review," the courts are routinely asked to ascertain the meaning of a constitutional provision, a statute, or an administrative regulation; to decide whether a statute conflicts with the governing constitution; to determine if a regulation of an administrative agency is within that body's statutory authority; or to decide whether an agency has acted arbitrarily in adjudicating a particular dispute within its jurisdiction. Of these, the first is by far the most controversial, since a court decision construing a constitution is definitive unless the constitution is subsequently amended to overturn the judicial interpretation. Amending a constitution is not a simple task, particularly at the federal level. In contrast, a judicial decision interpreting a statute can be "corrected" relatively easily by the legislature, which can simply pass a new statute on the subject.

As discussed briefly in Chapter 1, the role of the U.S. Supreme Court in constitutional interpretation has been the subject of considerable debate, some of it rather heated. There is little doubt, however, that the Justices do more than simply "interpret" the Constitution. Because the document is by design vague and imprecise in some places, the Court is left with the task of filling in the gaps. In the process, it necessarily "makes law." A notable example is the constitutional right to privacy mentioned in Chapter 3. Although the term "privacy" does not appear in the Constitution, the Court has ruled in a series of cases that various constitutional provisions, taken together, implicitly recognize such a right to be "let alone." These decisions—which include *Roe v. Wade* (1973) and other cases involving abortion—have been extremely controversial, in part because the Constitution does not in so many words deal with the privacy issue. Nonetheless, it is clear that the Constitution must be interpreted and applied if it is to have meaning in an ever-changing society, and in our system of government that task has fallen to the Supreme Court. As Justice Robert Jackson once observed about the Court's role in this regard, "we are not final [arbiters of the Constitution] because we are infallible, but we are infallible only because we are final."

In a sense, the Supreme Court's role in interpreting the Constitution is merely an outgrowth of a type of judicial lawmaking that has long been accepted in Anglo-American jurisprudence. In deciding cases brought to them, courts in early England had little guidance other than their own sense of justice, since statutes were few and far between. The legal principles developed in the resolution of a particular case, the courts reasoned, should be applied in subsequent cases of the same type. This notion that "like cases should be decided alike" was at the heart of what is known the "common law." This judge-made law, found in court opinions rather than statute books, was imported to this country and has had a tremendous impact on American law. For example, the law of defamation discussed in Chapter 2 is in large part based on legal principles developed at early common law by the English courts.

In the United States, common law is largely the province of the state courts, for the U.S. Supreme Court has ruled that the federal courts do not have broad authority to fashion common law. The state courts are not so constrained and have developed an enormous body of common law that covers such matters contracts, real and personal property, unfair competition, defamation, invasion of privacy, personal injuries, products liability, and medical malpractice. At the center of the process by which this development has taken place is the doctrine of *stare decisis*, a Latin term that means "let the decision stand." Once an appellate court establishes a legal principle in the course of deciding a case, that decision is "precedent" that binds the courts of that jurisdiction in later cases involving the same legal issues. *Stare decisis* does not mean that decisions are cast in stone for all time; rather, courts may—and do—depart from precedent to mold the law to the needs of a changing society. The flexible nature of the common law is one of its hallmarks.

THE JUDICIAL SYSTEM

The United States has a dual system of courts with overlapping jurisdiction. The federal courts, for example, hear civil cases that arise under the laws, treaties, and constitution of the United States, as well as so-called "diversity" cases that involve state law disputes between citizens from different states. While it is obvious that cases of the latter type may also be decided by state courts, suits involving federal law may be also be brought there unless Congress has by statute provided that those cases can only be heard by a federal court. Thus, federal courts are not limited to cases dealing with federal law, and state courts are not restricted to cases that raise questions of state law. In many situations, the plaintiff may file his suit in either federal or state court, and his choice is often based on tactical considerations.

Most states and the federal government employ a three-level judicial system. The first level consists of trial courts, which take the raw material of litigation—testimony of witnesses, physical evidence, and arguments of counsel—and reach a decision based on the applicable legal principles, often with the assistance of a jury. At the second level are intermediate appellate courts that hear appeals from the trial courts. In general, appellate courts have limited power to review factual determinations made by trial judges and juries. Their principal function is to ensure that the trial court did not make erroneous legal rulings with respect to both the merits of the case and the manner in which it was tried. Appellate cases are decided on the basis of the record developed at trial, briefs filed by attorneys for both sides, and, in many cases, oral argument before the court by opposing counsel. The third level consists of an appellate court of last resort, usually known as the jurisdiction's "supreme court." Although a losing litigant typically has the right to have his case heard by the intermediate appellate court, he is not automatically entitled to a further appeal of an adverse decision. Rather, the supreme court has discretion as to which appeals it will hear and typically limits its review to cases that pose important legal questions.

For the most part, the state and federal court systems are independent of one another. However, because state courts can decide questions of federal law, the U.S. Supreme Court may hear appeals from state court rulings on such issues. For example, in the case of *Cox Broadcasting Corp. v. Cohn* (1975) discussed in Chapter 3, the U.S. Supreme Court reversed a Georgia Supreme Court decision upholding a state statute challenged as unconstitutional under the first amendment. Interestingly, the Court's jurisdiction in cases of this type is not limited to decisions handed down by state supreme courts; rather, the ruling must be one of the highest state court in which the case could be heard. For example, the Court once reviewed a decision of the Louisville, Kentucky, police court, where the fines imposed were so small that they could not be appealed under Kentucky law to any other court in the state.

The Federal Courts

Article III of the U.S. Constitution states that the "judicial power" of the federal government "shall be vested in one supreme Court, and in such inferior Courts as the Congress may from time to time ordain and establish." Although this provision requires only one federal court—the Supreme Court—Congress quickly moved to set up a three-tiered court system of the type described previously. Federal trial courts are known as "district courts," the intermediate appellate courts are "courts of appeals," and the Supreme Court is the court of last resort.

District Courts. The trial level of the federal system is composed of ninety-four U.S. District Courts, ninety of which are distributed throughout the fifty states and the District of Columbia, with at least one court in each. In addition, Puerto Rico, Guam, the Virgin Islands, and the Northern Mariana Islands have one district court each. Congress has authorized approximately 550 judgeships for these courts, with the number of judges ranging from one in the smaller districts to twenty-seven in the Southern District of New York, which includes Manhattan. With only one minor exception, the districts do not extend across state lines, ensuring that there will be at least one district per state. Some small states have only one judicial district, while larger states may contain as many as four.

Like all federal judges, district judges are appointed by the President with the advice and consent of the Senate and hold office during good behavior. Each judge, with the exception of those in the District of Columbia, must reside in the district for which he is appointed. In each district having more than one judge, the judge with seniority in terms of length of service is generally the chief judge of the district and is responsible for assigning cases to the various judges and assuring observance of the rules and orders of the court. In addition to the judges, the district courts have judicial personnel who handle specialized matters as adjuncts to the court. Bankruptcy judges, appointed by the chief judge of the appellate court in which the district court is located, hear matters arising under the federal bankruptcy statutes. Decisions of the bankruptcy judge may be appealed to the district court and then to the court of appeals. Federal magistrates also work to help ease the caseload crunch in the district courts. These officials, selected by the judges of each district court, perform a variety of tasks ranging from trying minor criminal cases and hearing applications for search warrants to presiding over criminal arraignments and conducting pretrial discovery proceedings in civil cases.

Courts of Appeals. The courts of appeals, representing the intermediate appellate level of the federal judiciary, are properly identified as the "U.S. Court of Appeals for the _____ Circuit." There are eleven numbered circuits, one circuit solely for the District of Columbia, and a specialized "Federal Circuit," making a total of thirteen. Congress has authorized about 170 judgeships for these courts. Although the number of judges varies from circuit to circuit, appeals are normally decided by a panel of three judges; exceptional cases are heard by the entire court sitting "en banc." The courts of appeals not only review decisions of the district courts, but also hear appeals from orders or decisions of federal administrative agencies, such as the Federal Communications Commission and the National Labor Relations Board.

Apart from the Federal Circuit, which hears certain appeals involving patents, trademarks, customs, and international trade, the circuits are organized geographically. With the exception of the District of Columbia Circuit, each contains at least three states. For example, Texas, Louisiana, and Mississippi comprise the Fifth Circuit, while Arkansas, Iowa, Minnesota, Missouri, Nebraska, North Dakota, and South Dakota make up the Eighth Circuit. Decisions of the courts of appeals are binding only on the federal district courts within the particular circuit. Thus, a federal district court in Texas is not required to follow a decision of the U.S. Court of Appeals for the Eighth Circuit. In terms of media law, the most important of courts of appeals are the Second Circuit, which includes New York; the Ninth Circuit, which includes California; and the District of Columbia Circuit, which reviews most decisions of the FCC.

The Supreme Court. The U.S. Supreme Court consists of nine members, one chief justice and eight associate justices. The number has remained at nine for more than a century, and because of the furor caused by President Franklin D. Roosevelt's famous "court-packing" plan, that number is not likely to change. However, the number of justices is not specified in the Constitution and is within the control of the Congress. The first Court had only six justices, and there have been as many as ten. Under present practice, six justices constitute a quorum, and all justices participate in each decision of the court unless one disqualifies himself from a particular case. The Court begins its annual term on the first Monday in October and usually recesses for the summer in early July.

Quotations frequently appear in news stories from litigants who claim that they will "take this case all the way to the Supreme Court." They may well carry the case there, but the Court is not required to hear it. Unlike the courts of appeals, the Supreme Court's appellate jurisdiction is discretionary. The Court is asked to hear approximately 4,500 cases each term, and it issues full opinions in only about 175 of them. Most are simply not accepted for review. The procedural device for invoking the Court's appellate jurisdiction is the petition for *certiorari*, a Latin term that literally means "to be informed of" the lower court's ruling. When the Supreme Court decides not to review a case, it "denies *certiorari*" and the ruling of the lower court stands. However, the Court's refusal to hear a case does not constitute affirmance of the lower court's decision and does not set a precedent with respect to the legal issue involved.

Copies of the *certiorari* petitions go to all of the justices, some of whom read virtually all of them. Other justices read selectively, assigning some cases to law clerks for summary memoranda. If at least one justice so desires, a case is discussed at the Court's day-long Friday conference of the justices. The vast majority of cases never even get to this stage, which is itself a considerable hurdle. If four justices agree to hear a case, the petition for *certiorari* is granted and the case is scheduled for argument some months later. During the interim, lawyers file briefs on behalf of their clients' positions, and it is not unusual for the Court to authorize briefs by *amici curiae*—"friends of the court"—who elaborate on the legal questions presented by the case.

Oral argument generally lasts an hour, with thirty minutes allotted for each side. The attorneys make their arguments and are flooded with questions from the justices, who focus upon the underlying policy considerations as well as the relevant law. One observer has described oral argument as "verbal fencing," and the interchange is an intellectually challenging experience for attorneys and justices alike. Some commentators have doubted its utility, and many lawyers believe that cases are won and lost on the quality of the briefs rather than on the debating skills of counsel. After oral argument, the case returns to the Friday conference, this time to be decided tentatively. The chief justice voices his views, followed by each justice in order of seniority. After discussion, which can grow quite heated, the justices vote, with the junior member of the Court going first. If the chief justice is in the majority, he assigns a justice to write the opinion; if he is in the minority, the assignment is made by the senior justice in the majority. The dissenters usually agree among themselves who will write a dissent, or each of the justices in the minority may draft his own opinion.

This decision is tentative; according to tradition, any justice can change his mind up to the moment when an opinion is publicly announced. Thus, the majority arranged at the conference can quickly fall apart. Moreover, the opinion writing process is long and involved, creating many opportunities for changes in position. Once the justice assigned an opinion completes it to his satisfaction (normally after working with his law clerks), he circulates the draft among the other justices. The draft may win over justices who originally planned to dissent, or it may cause a majority to evaporate. The justices usually respond to the opinion writer by memorandum, requesting certain additions, deletions, or changes in language. "To write an opinion you have to sew a big enough umbrella for five justices to get under," one commentator has noted. "That can require some pretty fancy sewing." Indeed, an opinion may go through more than twenty drafts before it wins approval of a majority of the court, and it is obviously more difficult to write a unanimous opinion. The process is lengthy, and most opinions are handed down several months after oral argument.

Jurisdiction. It is often said that federal courts have "limited" jurisdiction. This means that they may hear only the types of cases authorized by the Constitution and by Congress. The federal courts may hear two basic types of cases: civil and criminal cases that arise under federal law, and civil cases in which the litigants are from different states (or one is from a foreign country) and the amount of money at stake exceeds $50,000. The former are known as "federal question" cases, while the latter are called "diversity" cases, a shorthand term for "diversity of citizenship."

In a federal question case, of course, the court will apply federal law. This jurisdictional category includes a wide variety of cases, both civil and criminal. Typical civil cases include antitrust, tax, securities regulation, land condemnation, civil rights, employment discrimination, labor law, environmental disputes, copyright, trademark, bankruptcy, admiralty, consumer credit, school desegregation, and cases involving the action of federal administrative agencies. Generally, these cases are based on specific federal statutes—such as the Copyright Act and the National Labor Relations Act—but some arise directly from provisions in the Constitution or from treaties with foreign countries.

On the criminal side, federal courts hear cases that fall into two broad categories: those involving criminal conduct in federally owned or controlled territory outside the jurisdiction of the states, and those involving conduct taking place within the borders of states but also within the territory of the United States. In the first category, where the federal government must shoulder the entire burden of criminal law enforcement without help from the states, there exists a broad federal police power to regulate conduct. This category includes federal land areas not located within the states, such as the District of Columbia and Puerto Rico; federal enclaves—"islands" of federal territory within the states—such as military bases and national parks; and ships and aircraft of American nationality when outside the jurisdiction of the states, such as on the high seas.

In the second category, however, there is no such broad police power, and the federal government must share power with the various states. The federal government can exercise only those powers granted to it by the Constitution. This power can be either express or implied. For example, Article I, Section 8 of the Constitution specifically gives Congress the power to punish counterfeiting and piracy. The so-called "necessary and proper" clause, which gives the federal government the power to do what is necessary to carry out the various express powers, is the source of implied federal authority. Because Congress is given the power to regulate interstate commerce, establish post offices, and tax, for example, the necessary and proper clause allows criminal regulation in these areas as well.

Federal courts regularly hear criminal cases involving drug law violations, illegal immigration, auto theft, forgery, counterfeiting, homicide, weapons and firearms violations, bank robbery, tax evasion, mail fraud, and racketeering. In many situations, federal and state law enforcement officials have concurrent jurisdiction. For instance, a state has jurisdiction over bank robbery, as does the federal government if the robbery is of a federally insured institution. Similarly, a state has jurisdiction over auto theft, while the federal government prosecutes cases of interstate transportation of stolen vehicles. A criminal defendant may find himself accused of violating both state and federal statutes, and prosecution by both state and federal authorities is not precluded by the constitutional prohibition against double jeopardy, since separate offenses are involved. Often, however, state and federal officials will cooperate in deciding which statutes a defendant will be charged with violating.

In a civil case falling within the diversity jurisdiction, a federal court will apply state law, usually that of the state in which the court sits. The notion here is that the outcome of these cases, which are heard in federal court merely because the litigants are from different states, should be the same as in similar cases brought in the courts of the state where the federal court is located. If a federal court could apply legal principles different from those that would govern cases brought in the state court down the street, litigants would be encouraged to select the court that would follow the legal doctrine most favorable to their positions. Moreover, in that situation the federal courts would be intruding upon the power of the state courts to fashion their own common law.

Although a federal court in a diversity case must apply state law, the controlling legal principles are not always easily ascertained. Of course, if the state legislature has enacted an applicable statute or the state supreme court has announced a rule of law, the federal court in a diversity case is bound thereby. But what if there is no state statute or court decision addressing the issue? In some states, for example, the tort of invasion of privacy is not particularly well developed. Faced with a privacy law question neither governed by state statute nor decided by the state's highest court, the federal court must make a prediction as to how the state supreme court would rule on the legal issue.

State Courts

There are enormous variations among the court systems of the fifty states, though most employ the three-tiered structure discussed above. Moreover, there are three important differences between most state court systems and the federal courts:

- the existence of more than one type of trial court;
- jurisdiction that is general rather than limited; and
- the election of judges by popular vote.

The state counterpart to the federal district court goes by several names: circuit court, district court, superior court, and, in New York, supreme court. Unlike the federal system, however, most states have another rung of "inferior" trial courts that handle minor matters such as traffic cases, misdemeanor criminal cases, and civil cases involving small sums. An unsuccessful litigant in one of these courts—which carry such labels as municipal court, county court, and justice court—can usually appeal the decision to the principal trial court. However, that court will generally hold a new trial in the case rather than review the decision in the manner of an appellate court.

Unlike the federal district courts, the major trial courts in most states have general jurisdiction. This means that they may hear any type of case that has not been specifically assigned to another of the state's courts. For example, a trial court might routinely hear cases involving personal injuries, breach of contract, will contests, landlord-tenant disputes, divorces and child custody, and property matters. If, however, the state has created a specialized family law court, the trial court would no longer have jurisdiction over divorce cases and related matters such as child custody.

Separate family law courts are fairly common, as are courts to handle juvenile cases and probate matters. Still another variation is found in three states—Arkansas, Mississippi, and Tennessee—that retain the dual trial court system of England. In these states, "law courts" and "chancery courts" share the major trial duties, with their jurisdiction in civil cases turning largely on the type of relief that the plaintiff seeks. Suits for damages are brought in the law court, while those for injunctions are heard by the chancery court. Criminal cases in these states are handled by the law courts.

While appellate court structure also varies considerably, most states have a court of last resort and at least one intermediate appellate court. Large states have several such intermediate courts. California, for example, has six (three of which have multiple divisions), while Texas has fourteen. The Texas court system is unusual in that it also has two courts of last resort: the Texas Supreme Court, which handles civil cases, and the Texas Court of Criminal Appeals, which hears appeals in criminal matters. As noted previously, in most states an unsuccessful litigant may appeal as a matter of right to the intermediate appellate court and, if still dissatisfied, ask the court of last resort to review the case in the exercise of its discretion. In many states, however, some cases may be appealed directly from the trial court to the court of last resort.

State court judges are typically elected by popular vote. In some states, judicial races are nonpartisan, while in others the judges run as Democrats or Republicans. There are other methods of judicial selection, however. In Virginia, for example, the legislature appoints state court judges to terms ranging from six to twelve years, with the governor making interim appointments if vacancies occur between legislative sessions. Under the so-called "Missouri Plan" used by several states, a special commission selects a panel of three lawyers from which the governor chooses one for appointment to a judgeship. At the first general election held after the judge has served at least one year, the judge runs for retention. There is no opponent, and the only issue submitted to the voters is whether the judge will continue to hold office.

PROCEDURE IN CIVIL CASES

A civil suit is commenced when the plaintiff files a complaint against the defendant in the proper court. This document, called a petition in some states, sets forth in general terms the facts giving rise to the litigation and the legal theories on which the plaintiff bases his claim. It also specifies the type of relief that the plaintiff seeks, such as money damages or an injunction that orders the defendant to cease certain conduct.

The defendant responds with an answer, a document that agrees to or takes issue with the facts as alleged in the complaint, attacks the legal theories on which the plaintiff has relied, and, if appropriate, raises procedural objections to the manner in which the suit was brought. With respect to the latter, for example, the defendant might argue that the court lacks jurisdiction over the case or that the plaintiff's complaint is improperly drafted. The answer may also contain one or more affirmative defenses that point to a legal reason that the defendant should prevail even if the plaintiff's allegations are correct. Should the defendant wish to seek relief from the plaintiff without filing a separate lawsuit, he may include in his answer a counterclaim, which contains the same type of information found in a complaint.

Prior to filing an answer, the defendant usually has the option of asserting some of his objections to the suit in what is known as a pre-answer motion. A motion is simply an application to the court for an order of a particular kind. If, for instance, the plaintiff has brought a diversity action in federal court but has claimed damages of only $25,000, the defendant would file a motion to dismiss the case for lack of jurisdiction, since there must be more than $50,000 at stake in cases of this type. In this situation, the court would grant the motion and enter an order dismissing the case, and there would obviously be no need for the defendant to file an answer.

Should the plaintiff's complaint survive such early attacks, the parties engage in a pretrial factfinding process called discovery. At this stage of the case, the litigants seek to learn as much as possible about the pertinent facts from their opponents and from other persons who might have relevant information. There are several procedures available for discovery. One of the most common is the oral deposition, in which an attorney questions the opposing party or a witness in the presence of a court reporter, who stenographically records the questions and answers. If the person sought to be deposed is not a party to the lawsuit, he must often be commanded by court order—a subpoena—to appear for that purpose. Depositions usually take place in a private setting, such as a lawyer's office. Another discovery device, written interrogatories, consists of a series of written questions directed at an opposing party, who must respond to them in writing within a specified time. Because discovery is an investigative process, it may well turn up information that will not be admissible into evidence at trial.

If the facts developed through discovery indicate that a litigant is likely to prevail, he will file a motion for summary judgment. The court's granting of such a motion, which is typically made by a defendant, disposes of the case without a trial and results in a favorable judgment for the moving party. Generally, a motion for summary judgment is granted in one of two situations. In the first, the legal principles governing the lawsuit are well established and only the facts are in dispute. Normally, it is for the jury—or the trial judge sitting without a jury—to hear the evidence and resolve this factual dispute. If, however, the facts developed prior to trial are such that a reasonable jury would reach only one conclusion if the evidence were presented at a trial, summary judgment is proper and a trial unnecessary. In the second situation, the litigants agree about the facts but disagree as to the legal principles that govern the case. Here there is no need for a full-blown trial, since rulings on the applicable law are made by the trial judge rather than by a jury.

Should a trial be required, an important preliminary question is whether the case must be tried before a jury. This issue generally hinges on the type of relief that is sought by the plaintiff. For example, if the complaint seeks an injunction (that is, an order that the defendant cease certain conduct), neither party has the right to a jury trial and the case is decided by the judge. On the other hand, a complaint that demands money damages entitles either party to a trial by jury, provided that a timely request is made. If a jury is to be employed, jurors are chosen during a pretrial process called *voir dire*, a French term that literally means "to speak the truth." Potential jurors selected at random from the community are questioned by the judge and counsel for both parties in an effort to determine whether they are biased or would otherwise be unable to render a decision based solely on the evidence presented at trial. Such jurors are disqualified from service. In addition, the plaintiff and the defendant are each given a certain number of preemptory challenges that can be used to strike particular persons from the jury for virtually any reason. For example, the plaintiff's attorney might decide to strike a prospective juror who seemed to be tight with money and thus not inclined to award a large sum of damages.

As noted previously, there is a division of labor between judge and jury. Simply put, the judge presides over the trial and decides questions of law, while the jury resolves disputed questions of fact. For example, the judge might be required to interpret the meaning of a particular statute that is potentially relevant to the case. In addition, he decides whether the evidence offered by the parties is admissible and thus appropriate for the jury's consideration and instructs the jury as to the legal principles that it must apply to the facts in reaching a verdict. In a defamation case, for instance, the judge would instruct the jury as to the applicable fault standard, either negligence or recklessness. It would then be up to the jury to determine whether the defendant published the defamatory statement with the requisite degree of fault. In making that determination, the jury might well have to decide whether to believe the testimony of particular witnesses or decide whose evidence was most convincing. Here the burden of proof is often critical. Generally, it is the plaintiff's job to persuade the jury, by a preponderance of the evidence, that his version of the facts is the most plausible. If he fails to carry this burden, the jury will return a verdict for the defendant.

During the course of the trial, either party (but usually the defendant) may make a motion for a directed verdict. This device, which works like a delayed motion for summary judgment, enables the judge to decide that the party with the burden of proof has not introduced sufficient evidence to warrant a jury verdict in his favor. The granting of such a motion means that the case is not submitted to the jury and that judgment is entered for the moving party. A similar motion, called a motion for judgment notwithstanding the verdict, can be made after the jury has reached its decision. In addition, the losing party may move for a new trial on the ground that the jury's verdict is against the weight of the evidence, that the amount of damages awarded was excessive, or that various legal errors were made during the trial. The posttrial motions, while common, are not required to preserve the right to take an appeal. If the motions are made, no appeal is possible until the trial court has ruled on them. If the judge denies the motions, the jury's decision stands and an appeal may then be taken.

PROCEDURE IN CRIMINAL CASES

A criminal case usually begins with the arrest of a person suspected of a criminal offense, usually by a law enforcement officer. An arrest may be made with or without an arrest warrant issued by a court. Such a warrant is based on a showing of probable cause that the person has committed a crime, violated the conditions of a pretrial release bond, or violated the conditions of parole or probation. An arrest without a warrant may be made if a crime, either a felony or misdemeanor, is committed in the presence of a law enforcement officer. In addition, a law enforcement officer may make an arrest without a warrant if he has probable cause to believe a person has committed a felony, even though it was not committed in the officer's presence.

After an arrest, the accused appears before a judge, who advises him of the crime charged, his right to an attorney, and the right to remain silent. The judge also sets the amount of bail, if any. The purpose of bail is to ensure that the defendant will appear in court for subsequent proceedings. In determining the amount of bail, the judge will consider the crime charged, the defendant's prior record, the permanence of his residence, and similar factors. This initial appearance is followed by a preliminary hearing, at which the court determines whether there is probable cause to believe that a crime has been committed and that the defendant committed it. The prosecuting attorney presents evidence on behalf of the government, and the defendant has the right to cross-examine the government's witnesses and to offer his own evidence.

If the court concludes that there is no probable cause, the case is dismissed and the defendant discharged. Upon a finding of probable cause, the judge will "bind the case over" for further proceedings by either information or indictment. An information is filed by the prosecutor, while an indictment is handed down by a grand jury after reviewing the government's evidence. In many states, only the information is employed, while in others both procedures are available. The information or indictment is analogous to the complaint in civil cases and must contain a statement of the specific criminal statute that the defendant is charged with having violated and the government's allegations of the facts constituting the offense. After the information or indictment is filed, the defendant again appears before a judge at an arraignment, where he is again advised of the charges against him and required to enter a plea of guilty or not guilty. Of course, a guilty plea at this stage terminates the proceeding, except for the setting of the sentence. If the defendant pleads not guilty, the pretrial process begins.

As is the case in civil litigation, both sides conduct pretrial discovery, though the procedures differ considerably from those employed in civil cases. Generally speaking, the prevailing philosophy is to require both the prosecution and the defense to reveal the evidence they plan to use at trial. For example, each side must reveal the names and addresses of witnesses, statements taken from witnesses, and reports made by experts, including the results of physical and mental examinations and scientific tests or experiments. Such disclosure is made when the prosecuting attorney or defense counsel files a written motion requesting the information from the opposing party.

Criminal litigation is characterized by the liberal use of pretrial motions. For example, the prosecutor might file motions to require the defendant to appear in a line-up or give voice, handwriting, or blood samples. Among the most common defense motions are those asking that the court preclude the government from using particular evidence at trial. A defense lawyer filing such a motion—commonly called a "motion to suppress"—might argue that physical evidence should be excluded because it was obtained illegally (e.g., without a search warrant when one was required) or that a confession should not be admissible at trial because it was secured through force or without adequate warnings to the defendant as to his constitutional rights. These defense motions are often dispositive of the case; for example, if a confession or critical physical evidence is deemed inadmissible, the government might be forced to drop its case. By the same token, the court's denial of a motion to suppress often means that the defendant will accept a plea bargain rather than face an almost certain conviction at trial.

The plea bargaining process is an important part of the criminal justice system; in fact, over ninety percent of criminal cases are resolved through plea bargaining rather than by trial. Rather than run the risk of being convicted of the crime with which he has been charged, a defendant will often plead guilty to a lesser offense that carries a lighter sentence. The negotiation process between the prosecuting attorney and defense counsel takes place in secret, but the plea bargain must be disclosed in open court and approved by the judge. If the arrangement is approved, the judge is bound to accept the defendant's guilty plea and enter the agreed-upon punishment. The judge is free to reject the plea bargain and to suggest alternative arrangements, though he does not participate in the negotiations.

In most criminal cases, the defendant has a right to a trial by jury, though he may waive this right and have the case tried by the judge. The jury selection process works the same way as in civil cases, with the number of preemptory challenges for the defense increasing along with the severity of the crime charged. The defendant is presumed innocent until found guilty, and the government has the burden of proving its case "beyond a reasonable doubt." There is never a burden on the defendant to prove his innocence. The defendant also is entitled to face his accusers and cross-examine witnesses against him, though he is not required to testify.

After the prosecution has presented its case, the defendant's attorney may move for a verdict of acquittal on the ground that the government has not carried its burden of proof. This motion is analogous to the motion for a directed verdict in a civil case. If the jury returns a "not guilty" verdict, the government is barred by the principle of double jeopardy from retrying the defendant on that charge. In the event of a guilty verdict, the defendant is then sentenced in accordance with the punishment options specified by statute. The sentencing decision is made by the jury in some jurisdictions and by the trial judge in others. A defendant who has been found guilty may file posttrial motions for a new trial or for acquittal notwithstanding the jury's verdict. In many jurisdictions, these motions are not optional—as is the case in civil litigation—but are necessary to protect the right to appeal. Generally, only a defendant may file an appeal, though in some jurisdictions the prosecution may seek appellate review of certain trial court rulings.

Even if a defendant's conviction is affirmed on appeal, another important remedy is available: the writ of *habeas corpus*, a Latin term meaning "you have the body." In an action of this type, which is civil rather than criminal in nature, a person who has been convicted of a crime attacks that conviction as unconstitutional. A defendant might argue, for instance, that his lawyer performed so ineffectively at trial that he was denied adequate legal representation or that intense media coverage made a fair trial impossible. By using the writ of *habeas corpus*, a defendant may obtain further review of his case, perhaps in a different court system. For example, a person convicted in a state court is able to bring a *habeas corpus* action in federal court if he has exhausted all possible avenues of appeal in the state courts.

B

GLOSSARY OF LEGAL TERMS

Acquit. To find a criminal defendant not guilty.

Action. A lawsuit.

Actionable. Conduct that provides grounds for a lawsuit.

Adjudication. The process by which a court or administrative agency reaches a decision in a particular case.

Adversary system. The system of legal practice in the United States by which all participants in a lawsuit have the full opportunity to present arguments, through counsel if they desire, to the court.

Affirm. To uphold a lower court's decision or ruling.

Allegation. The assertion, declaration, or statement of a litigant, made in a pleading, that sets out what he expects to prove in the case.

Amend. To modify.

Amicus curiae. "Friend of the court." Used to describe legal briefs submitted to a court by persons or groups not directly involved in the case but who have an interest in its outcome.

Answer. A pleading in which the defendant responds to the complaint filed by the plaintiff.

Appellant. The litigant who, after losing in a lower court, appeals the decision to a higher court.

Appellate court. A court having jurisdiction to review the decisions of trial courts, and, in many instances, those of administrative agencies.

Appellee. The successful litigant in a lower court proceeding who opposes an appeal by seeking to have the court's ruling affirmed by the appellate court.

Bail bond. An obligation signed by a person accused of a crime, with or without sureties, to secure his later appearance in court.

Brief. A persuasive document prepared by an attorney setting forth the facts and law in support of his client's position.

Burden of proof. The obligation imposed on one litigant or the other to prove a disputed fact. Should the litigant fail to carry that burden, he loses the case.

Certiorari. "To be informed of." The principal method of obtaining appellate review of a case by the U.S. Supreme Court. Such review is discretionary, not mandatory.

Change of venue. The transfer of a case filed in a county or district to another geographic area for trial.

Civil action. A lawsuit brought to enforce a right or redress a wrong.

Class action. A civil action in which the plaintiffs represent the interests of persons who have suffered similar injuries but who are not parties to the suit.

Code. A collection of statutes or ordinances adopted by legislative bodies.

Common law. Judge-made law. Also called "case law."

Compensatory damages. Money awarded in a civil action as compensation for harm to one's person, property, or rights; also called "actual damages."

Complaint. A pleading, filed by the plaintiff to commence a civil action, alleging that he has been injured by the defendant and seeking relief for that injury.

Contempt of court. Any act that obstructs a court in the administration of justice or that lessens its authority or dignity. Direct contempts are those committed in the presence of the court, while indirect contempts occur outside the courtroom, as when a person refuses to obey a judicial order.

Continuance. A court order delaying a trial or other proceeding.

Counterclaim. A legal action asserted by the defendant against the plaintiff.

Cross-examination. The questioning of a witness who has been called to testify by an opposing party.

Damages. See compensatory damages; punitive damages.

Declaratory judgment. A ruling that declares the rights of the litigants or expresses the opinion of the court on a question of law, without ordering that anything be done.

Decree. A decision or order of a court.

Defendant. In civil cases, a person against whom the plaintiff has filed a complaint; in criminal cases, a person accused of a crime by the government.

Deposition. The testimony of a witness during the pretrial discovery process.

Dictum. A statement in an appellate court opinion that is not necessary to the decision in the case and therefore is not binding precedent.

Directed verdict. A determination by the trial judge that reasonable jurors could not differ as to the proper result in a case. The effect of such a ruling is that the case is taken out of the jury's hands.

Discovery. The exchange of information by parties to a civil or criminal action prior to trial.

Dismissal. A court's termination of a lawsuit. If the dismissal is "with prejudice," the action may not be brought again.

Diversity action. A civil case within the jurisdiction of the federal courts because the parties are citizens of different states or one party is a citizen of a foreign country.

Due process. A guarantee, expressed in the fifth and fourteenth amendments to the U.S. Constitution, that litigants in civil and criminal cases will receive a fair trial. In addition, the due process clause of the fourteenth amendment prevents the states from interfering with substantive constitutional rights, such as freedom of expression.

En banc. "On the bench." Typically used in connection with a case decided by all of a court's judges.

Enjoin. To require a person, by injunction issued by a court, to perform certain acts or refrain from certain conduct.

Entrapment. Action by law enforcement officers to induce suspects to commit crimes.

Equal protection. A guarantee of equal treatment secured by the fourteenth amendment to the U.S. Constitution.

Equitable action. A lawsuit seeking injunctive relief or other remedies rather than damages.

Ex parte. A legal proceeding by which only one party to a lawsuit seeks judicial action without notice to the opposing party, usually in emergency situations.

Felony. A serious criminal offense, in contrast to a misdemeanor; usually punishable by imprisonment for more than one year, a fine, or both.

Finding. The result reached by a court or a jury.

Fraud. An intentional perversion of truth; deceitful practice or device resorted to with intent to deprive another of property or other right, or in some manner to inflict injury.

Grand jury. A jury whose responsibility it is to determine whether probable cause exists to warrant the trial of a person accused of a crime.

Habeas corpus. "You have the body." A legal action by which a person convicted of a crime can challenge the constitutionality of his conviction after appeals have been unsuccessful.

Holding. The controlling principle of law announced in a court decision; in contrast to *dictum*, a court's holding has precedential effect.

In camera. In the judge's chambers.

Indictment. A grand jury's formal accusation that a person committed a crime.

Information. A document filed by a prosecuting attorney formally charging a person with a crime.

Injunction. A court order directing that a person perform or refrain from a particular act; an equitable remedy.

Interrogatories. Written questions propounded by a litigant to his opponent, who must provide written answers; a discovery device for obtaining information prior to trial.

Instructions. An outline of applicable legal principles that a court provides the jury.

Judgment. The formal document entered by a trial court that reflects the final decision in a case. In a case tried before a jury, the judgment embodies the jury's verdict.

Judgment notwithstanding the verdict. A ruling by the trial judge, handed down after the jury verdict, that in effect sets aside the jury's decision in favor of one party and results in a judgment for the opposing party; also called "judgment *non obstante verdicto*" or "judgment NOV." The technical basis for such a ruling is the same as that for a directed verdict.

Jurisdiction. The power of the court. Subject matter jurisdiction refers to the type of cases that a court may hear, while personal jurisdiction describes the authority of a court enter an order binding a particular person.

Jury. A certain number of persons (traditionally twelve) who hear the evidence and decide the facts in civil and criminal cases; also called "petit jury" to distinguish it from a grand jury.

Liable. Legally responsible.

Litigant. A party to a lawsuit.

Long-arm statute. A state statute permitting a court in a civil case to exercise jurisdiction over a defendant who is outside the state.

Mandamus. An order issued by a court directing a lower court or a government official to perform a particular act; in appellate practice, the procedure enables a litigant to obtain review of a lower court ruling when an appeal would not be available.

Misdemeanor. A criminal offense that is less serious than a felony; usually punishable by a jail term of up to one year, a fine, or both.

Mistrial. A trial that is terminated prior to its conclusion because of a serious procedural error or because the jury cannot reach a decision.

Moot. Unsettled or undecided. A moot case is one in which the factual issues or other matters are resolved in a manner that makes it unnecessary for a court to decide a legal question.

Motion. An application to the court for an order; usually accompanied by a brief.

Movant. A litigant who makes a motion; also called "moving party."

No bill. A grand jury's determination that there was not sufficient evidence to charge a person with a crime.

Ordinance. A law enacted by the legislative body of a city, county, or similar local governmental entity.

Original jurisdiction. A court's authority to decide a case in the first instance, as opposed to reviewing it on appeal from a lower court.

Panel. A group of some but not all the judges on an appellate court who sit to hear a case. The decision of the panel, which usually consists of three judges, may be reviewed by the court sitting *en banc*.

Parties. Litigants; the participants in a lawsuit.

Per curiam. "By the court." A phrase used to distinguish an unsigned appellate court opinion issued by the whole court from one written by a single judge on behalf of the court.

Petitioner. One who petitions a court for an order or ruling. In some appellate courts, the term is used instead of "appellant."

Plaintiff. The party who initiates a civil action.

Pleadings. Documents, including the plaintiff's complaint and the defendant's answer, in which the litigants initially present their contentions to the court.

Preemption. A constitutional doctrine that permits the federal government to exercise regulatory control over an activity, to the exclusion of states and local governments.

Precedent. A judicial decision stating a legal principle that is binding on lower courts in that jurisdiction under the doctrine of *stare decisis*.

Preponderance of the evidence. The standard of proof that applies in most civil cases; sufficient evidence to convince the judge or jury that it is more likely than not that an incident occurred in the manner claimed by the party with the burden of proof.

Prima facie. "On its face." Usually used to describe evidence which, absent other evidence to the contrary, would support a judgment for the plaintiff in a civil action.

Probable cause. Substantial reason to believe that a person has committed a crime or other act; legal standard used by judges in issuing search warrants, police officers in making warrantless arrests, and grand juries in deciding whether to indict a person for a criminal offense.

Punitive damages. A sum awarded to a plaintiff not to compensate him but to punish the defendant and to deter egregious conduct by the defendant and by others.

Quash. To vacate or annul.

Quasi-judicial. Authority of a judicial nature vested in an administrative agency.

Quasi-legislative. Authority of a legislative nature vested in an administrative agency.

Reasonable doubt. The standard of proof applicable in criminal cases. A person accused of a crime is entitled to acquittal if the jurors cannot say they feel an "abiding conviction" as to the truth of the charge.

Record on appeal. The transcript of the trial and other documents compiled in the lower court. This material is filed with the appellate court for its use in deciding the case on appeal.

Remand. An order of a higher court sending a case back to a lower court for further proceedings in conformity with the higher court's decision.

Respondeat superior. Legal principle making an employer liable for any torts committed by its employees during the scope of their employment.

Respondent. The party opposing the grant of a petition. In some appellate courts, the term is used instead of "appellee."

Restatement of Torts. A publication of the American Law Institute which states in comprehensive fashion the principles of tort law as recognized in a majority of the states.

Reverse. To overturn a lower court's decision or ruling. A reversal may result in an outright victory for the appellant or a remand to the lower court.

Rulemaking. The quasi-legislative process by which an administrative agency adopts regulations of general application.

Scienter. Guilty knowledge; a state of mind that the prosecution must prove in order to obtain a conviction for certain criminal offenses. Must also be shown in some tort actions, such as fraud.

Search warrant. An order issued by a judge upon a showing of probable cause that authorizes law enforcement officers to search specified premises in an effort to discover contraband or evidence of a crime.

Sentence. The judgment in a criminal action, following a verdict or plea of guilty, stating the punishment assessed.

Sequester. To "lock up" or isolate jurors during a trial.

Specific performance. An order directing a person to perform specifically what that person has promised in a contract to do. Like other equitable remedies, this relief is available only when an award of damages would not be adequate to compensate the injured party.

Stare decisis. "Let the decision stand." A doctrine based on the notion that a legal principle applicable in one case should be applied in factually similar cases.

Statute of limitations. The time period in which a civil or criminal action must be brought. The period, set by statute, usually begins to run upon the occurrence of the event or conduct giving rise to the action.

Stay. A judicial act stopping a court proceeding or delaying the effect of an order or judgment.

Subpoena. A court order that a witness appear to give testimony at a trial or deposition. A subpoena *duces tecum* requires the witness to bring specified documents with him.

Summary judgment. A pretrial device to dispose of a case without a trial where there is no dispute as to the facts and only legal issues are to be decided.

Summons. A notice to the defendant that a civil action has been filed against him. The summons is accompanied by a copy of the plaintiff's complaint and advises the defendant of his obligation to respond.

Supra. A reference to a case or other material that has previously been cited; often used in briefs, court opinions, and law journals.

Temporary restraining order. A court order that maintains the *status quo* between the parties in a lawsuit, thus enabling the court to fully consider the issues. Typically issued in an emergency situation on an *ex parte* basis.

Tort. A civil wrong not based on contract. Examples include battery, defamation, invasion of privacy, medical malpractice, and trespass.

Tortfeasor. One who commits a tort; a wrongdoer.

Trespass. Unlawful entry on to the property of another.

Venire. Prospective jurors who have been summoned for jury duty.

Venue. The county, district, or other geographic area in which a civil or criminal action may be filed, tried, and decided.

Verdict. The formal decision or finding made by a jury.

Voir dire. "Speak the truth." The questioning of prospective jurors by the trial judge and attorneys to determine whether they are qualified to serve on a jury in a particular case.

C

CONSTITUTIONAL AND STATUTORY PROVISIONS

1. CONSTITUTION OF THE UNITED STATES

Amendment I [1791]

Congress shall make no law respecting an establishment of religion, or prohibiting the free exercise thereof; or abridging the freedom of speech, or of the press; or the right of the people peaceably to assemble, and to petition the Government for a redress of grievances.

Amendment VI [1791]

In all criminal prosecutions, the accused shall enjoy the right to a speedy and public trial, by an impartial jury of the State and district wherein the crime shall have been committed, which district shall have been previously ascertained by law, and to be informed of the nature and cause of the accusation; to be confronted with the witnesses against him; to have compulsory process for obtaining Witnesses in his favor, and to have the Assistance of Counsel for his defence.

Amendment XIV [1868]

SECTION 1. All persons born or naturalized in the United States and subject to the jurisdiction thereof, are citizens of the United States and of the State wherein they reside. No State shall make or enforce any law which shall abridge the privileges or immunities of citizens of the United States; nor shall any State deprive any person of life, liberty, or property, without due process of law; nor deny to any person within its jurisdiction the equal protection of the laws.

* * *

SECTION 5. The Congress shall have power to enforce, by appropriate legislation, the provisions of this article.

2.   COMMUNICATIONS ACT OF 1934. TITLE 47, U.S. CODE.

Section 223(b)

(1) Whoever knowingly—

(A) in the District of Columbia or in interstate or foreign communication, by means of telephone, makes (directly or by recording device) any obscene communication for commercial purposes to any person, regardless of whether the maker of such communication placed the call; or

(B) permits any telephone facility under such person's control to be used for an activity prohibited by clause (i),

shall be fined in accordance with Title 18, or imprisoned not more than two years, or both.

(2) Whoever knowingly—

(A) in the District of Columbia or in interstate or foreign communication, by means of telephone, makes (directly or by recording device) any indecent communication for commercial purposes to any person, regardless of whether the maker of such communication placed the call; or

(B) permits any telephone facility under such person's control to be used for an activity prohibited by clause (i),

shall be fined not more than $50,000, or imprisoned not more than six months, or both.

Section 301

It is the purpose of this chapter . . . to maintain the control of the United States over all the channels of radio transmission; and to provide for the use of such channels, but not the ownership thereof, by persons for limited periods of time, under licenses granted by Federal authority, and no such license shall be construed to create any right, beyond the terms, conditions, and periods of the license. No person shall use or operate any apparatus for the transmission of energy or communications or signals by radio . . . except under and in accordance with this chapter and with a license in that behalf granted under the provisions of this chapter.

Section 303

Except as otherwise provided in this chapter, the [Federal Communications] Commission from time to time, as public convenience, interest, or necessity requires, shall—

(a) Classify radio stations;

(b) Prescribe the nature of the service to be rendered by each class of licensed stations and each station within any class;

(c) Assign bands of frequencies to the various classes of stations, and assign frequencies for each individual station and determine the power which each station shall use and the time during which it may operate;

(d) Determine the location of classes of stations or individual stations;

(e) Regulate the kind of apparatus to be used with respect to its external effects and the purity and sharpness of the emissions from each station and from the apparatus therein;

(f) Make such regulations not inconsistent with law as it may deem necessary to prevent interference between stations and to carry out the provisions of this chapter: *Provided, however,* That changes in the frequencies, authorized power, or in the times of operation of any station, shall not be made without the consent of the station licensee unless, after a public hearing, the Commission shall determine that such changes will promote public convenience or interest or will serve public necessity, or the provisions of this chapter will be more fully complied with;

(g) Study new uses for radio, provide for experimental uses of frequencies, and generally encourage the larger and more effective use of radio in the public interest;

(h) Have authority to establish areas or zones to be served by any station;

(i) Have authority to make special regulations applicable to radio stations engaged in chain broadcasting;

(j) Have authority to make general rules and regulations requiring stations to keep such records of programs, transmissions of energy, communications, or signals as it may deem desirable;
* * *

(m)(1) Have authority to suspend the license of any operator upon proof sufficient to satisfy the Commission that the licensee—

(A) has violated, or caused, aided, or abetted the violation of, any provision of any Act, treaty, or convention binding on the United States, which the Commission is authorized to administer, or any regulation made by the Commission under any such Act, treaty, or convention; or * * *

(D) has transmitted superfluous radio communications or signals or communications containing profane or obscene words, language, or meaning . . . or

(E) has willfully or maliciously interfered with any other radio communications or signals; * * *

(o) Have authority to designate call letters of all stations; * * *

(r) Make such rules and regulations and prescribe such restrictions and conditions, not inconsistent with law, as may be necessary to carry out the provisions of this chapter, or any international radio or wire communications treaty or convention, or regulations annexed thereto, including any treaty or convention insofar as it relates to the use of radio, to which the United States is or may hereafter become a party;

(s) Have authority to require that apparatus designed to receive television pictures broadcast simultaneously with sound be capable of adequately receiving all frequencies allocated by the Commission to television broadcasting when such apparatus is shipped in interstate commerce, or is imported from any foreign country . . . for sale or resale to the public.
* * *

Section 307

(a) The Commission, if public convenience, interest, or necessity will be served thereby, subject to the limitations of this chapter, shall grant to any applicant therefore a station license provided for by this chapter.

(b) In considering applications for licenses, and modifications and renewals thereof, . . . the Commission shall make such distribution of licenses, frequencies, hours of operation, and of power among the several States and communities as to provide a fair, efficient, and equitable distribution of radio service to each of the same.

(c) No license granted for the operation of a television broadcasting station shall be for a longer term than five years . . . , and any license granted may be revoked as hereinafter provided. Each license granted for the operation of a radio broadcasting station shall be for a term of not to exceed seven years. * * * Upon the expiration of any license, upon application therefor, a renewal of such license may be granted from time to time for a term of not to exceed five years in the case of television broadcasting licenses, [and] for a term of not to exceed seven years in the case of radio broadcasting station licenses . . . if the Commission finds that public interest, convenience, and necessity would be served thereby. * * *

Section 308

(a) The Commission may grant construction permits and station licenses, or modifications or renewals thereof, only upon written application therefore received by it. . . .

(b) All applications for station licenses, or modifications or renewals thereof, shall set forth such facts as the Commission by regulation may prescribe as to the citizenship, character, and financial, technical, and other qualifications of the applicant to operate the station; the ownership and location of the proposed station . . . ; the frequencies and the power desired to be used; the hours of the day or other periods of time during which it is proposed to operate the station; the purposes for which the station is to be used; and such other information as it may require.* * *

Section 309

(a) Subject to the provisions of this section, the Commission shall determine, in the cases of each application filed with it to which section 308 of this title applies, whether the public interest, convenience, and necessity will be served by the granting of such application, and, if the Commission, upon examination of such application and upon consideration of such other matters as the Commission may officially notice, shall find that public interest, convenience, and necessity would be served by the granting thereof, it shall grant such application.
* * *

(d)(1) Any party in interest may file with the Commission a petition to deny any application . . . .

(2) If the Commission finds on the basis of the application, the pleadings filed, or other matters which it may officially notice that there are no substantial and material questions of fact and that a grant of the application would be consistent

with subsection (a) of this section, it shall make the grant, deny the petition, and issue a concise statement of the reasons for denying the petition. . . . If a substantial and material question of fact is presented or if the Commission for any reason is unable to find that grant of the application would be consistent with subsection (a) of this section, it shall proceed as provided in subsection (e) of this section.

(e) If, in the case of any application to which subsection (a) of this section applies, a substantial and material question of fact is presented or the Commission for any reason is unable to make the finding specified in such subsection, it shall formally designate the application for hearing . . . and shall forthwith notify the applicant and all other known parties in interest of such action and the grounds and reasons therefor, specifying with particularity the matters and things in issue. . . . Any hearing subsequently held upon such application shall be a full hearing in which the applicant and all other parties in interest shall be permitted to participate. The burden of proceeding with the introduction of evidence and the burden of proof shall be upon the applicant, except that with respect to any issue presented by a petition to deny or a petition to enlarge the issues, such burdens shall be as determined by the Commission.

* * *

Section 310

(a) The station license required under this chapter shall not be granted to or held by any foreign government or the representative thereof.

(b) No broadcast or common carrier or aeronautical en route or aeronautical fixed radio station license shall be granted to or held by—

(1) any alien or the representative of any alien;

(2) any corporation organized under the law of any foreign government;

(3) any corporation of which any officer or director is an alien or of which more than one-fifth of the capital stock is owned of record or voted by aliens or their representatives or by a foreign government or representative thereof or by any corporation organized under the laws of a foreign country;

(4) any corporation directly or indirectly controlled by any other corporation of which any officer or more than one-fourth of the directors are aliens, or of which more than one-fourth of the capital stock is owned of record or voted by aliens, their representatives, or by a foreign government or representative thereof, or by any corporation organized under the laws of a foreign country, if the Commission finds that the public interest will be served by the refusal or revocation of such license.

* * *

(d) No construction permit or station license, or any rights thereunder, shall be transferred, assigned, or disposed of in any manner, voluntarily or involuntarily, directly or indirectly, or by transfer of control of any corporation holding such permit or license, to any person except upon application to the Commission and upon finding by the Commission that the public interest, convenience, and necessity will be served thereby. Any such application shall be disposed of as if the proposed transferee or assignee were making application under section 308 of this title for the permit or license in question; but in acting thereon the Commission may not consider whether the public interest, convenience, and necessity might be served by the transfer, assignment, or disposal of the permit or license to a person other than the proposed transferee or assignee.

* * *

Section 312

(a) The Commission may revoke any station license or construction permit—

(1) for false statements knowingly made either in the application or in any statement of fact which may be required pursuant to section 308 of this title;

(2) because of conditions coming to the attention of the Commission which would warrant it in refusing to grant a license or permit on an original application;

(3) for willful or repeated failure to operate substantially as set forth in the license;

(4) for willful or repeated violation of, or willful or repeated failure to observe any provision of this chapter or any rule or regulation of the Commission authorized by this chapter or by a treaty ratified by the United States;

(5) for violation of or failure to observe any final cease and desist order issued by the Commission under this section;

(6) for violation of section 1304, 1343, or 1464 of Title 18; or

(7) for willful or repeated failure to allow reasonable access to or to permit purchase of reasonable amounts of time for the use of a broadcasting station by a legally qualified candidate for Federal elective office on behalf of his candidacy.

(b) Where any person (1) has failed to operate substantially as set forth in a license, (2) has violated or failed to observe any of the provisions of this chapter, or section 1304, 1343, or 1464 of Title 18, or (3) has violated or failed to observe any rule or regulation of the Commission authorized by this chapter or by a treaty ratified by the United States, the Commission may order such person to cease and desist from such action.

(c) Before revoking a license or permit pursuant to subsection (a) of this section, or issuing a cease and desist order pursuant to subsection (b) of this section, the Commission shall serve upon the licensee, permittee, or person involved an order to show cause why an order of revocation or a cease and desist order should not be issued. * * * If after hearing, or a wavier thereof, the Commission determines that an order of revocation or a cease and desist order should issue, it shall issue such order, which shall include a statement of the findings of the Commission and the grounds and reasons therefor and specify the effective date of the order, and shall cause the same to be served on said licensee, permittee, or person.

(d) In any case where a hearing is conducted pursuant to the provisions of this section, both the burden of proceeding with the introduction of evidence and the burden of proof shall be upon the Commission.

* * *

Section 315

(a) If any licensee shall permit any person who is a legally qualified candidate for any public office to use a broadcasting station, he shall afford equal opportunities to all other such candidates for that office in the use of such broadcasting station: *Provided*, That such licensee shall have no power of censorship over the material broadcast under the provisions of this section. No obligation is imposed under this subsection upon any licensee to allow the use of its station by any such candidate. Appearance by a legally qualified candidate on any—

    (1) bona fide newscast,

    (2) bona fide news interview,

    (3) bona fide news documentary (if the appearance of the candidate is incidental to the presentation of the subject or subjects covered by the news documentary), or

    (4) on-the-spot coverage of bona fide news events (including but not limited to political conventions and activities incidental thereto),

shall not be deemed to be a use of a broadcasting station within the meaning of this subsection. Nothing in the foregoing sentence shall be construed as relieving broadcasters, in connection with the presentation of newscasts, news interviews, news documentaries, and on-the-spot coverage of news events, from the obligation imposed upon them under this chapter to operate in the public interest and to afford reasonable opportunity for the discussion of conflicting views on issues of public importance.

    (b) The charges made for the use of any broadcasting station by any person who is a legally qualified candidate for any public office in connection with his campaign for nomination for election, or election to such office shall not exceed—

    (1) during the forty-five days preceding the date of a primary or primary runoff election and during the sixty days preceding the date of a general or special election in which such person is a candidate, the lowest unit charge of the station for the same class and amount of time for the same period; and

    (2) at any other time, the charges made for comparable use of such stations by other users thereof.

    (c) For purpose of this section—

    (1) the term "broadcasting station" includes a community antenna television system; and

    (2) the terms "licensee" and "station license" when used with respect to a community antenna television system mean the operator of such system.

Section 317

    (a)(1) All matter broadcast by any radio station for which any money, service or other valuable consideration is directly or indirectly paid, or promised to or charged or accepted by, the station so broadcasting, from any person, shall, at the time the same is so broadcast, be announced as paid for or furnished, as the case may be, by such person: *Provided,* That "service or other valuable consideration" shall not include any service or property furnished without charge or at a nominal charge for use on, or in connection with, a broadcast unless it is so furnished in consideration for an identification in a broadcast of any person, product, service, trademark, or brand name beyond an identification which is reasonably related to the use of such service or property on the broadcast.

    * * *

    (c) The licensee of each radio station shall exercise reasonable diligence to obtain from its employees, and from other persons with whom it deals directly in connection with any program or program matter for broadcast, information to enable such licensee to make the announcement required by this section.

    * * *

Section 326

Nothing in this chapter shall be understood or construed to give the Commission the power of censorship over the radio communications or signals transmitted by any radio station, and no regulation or condition shall be promulgated or fixed by the Commission which shall interfere with the right of free speech by means of radio communication.

Section 503(b)

(1) Any person who is determined by the Commission [after notice and an opportunity to respond] to have—

(A) willfully or repeatedly failed to comply substantially with the terms and conditions of any license, permit, certificate, or other instrument or authorization issued by the Commission;

(B) willfully or repeatedly failed to comply with any of the provisions of this chapter or of any rule, regulation, or order issued by the Commission under this chapter or under any treaty, convention, or other agreement to which the United States is a party and which is binding upon the United States;

(C) violated any provision of section 317(c) or 509(a) of this title;

(D) violated any provision of section 1304, 1343, or 1464 of Title 18;

shall be liable to the United States for a forfeiture penalty. A forfeiture penalty under this subsection shall be in addition to any other penalty provided for by this chapter; except that this subsection shall not apply to any conduct which is subject to forfeiture under . . . section 507 of this title.

(2) The amount of any forfeiture penalty determined under this subsection shall not exceed $2,000 for each violation. Each day of a continuing violation shall constitute a separate offense, but the total forfeiture penalty which may be imposed under this subsection, for acts or omissions described in paragraph (1) of this subsection and set forth in the notice of apparent liability issued under this subsection shall not exceed—

(A) $20,000, if the violator is (i) a common carrier subject to the provisions of this chapter, (ii) a broadcast station licensee or permittee, or (iii) a cable television operator; or

(B) $5,000, in any case not covered by subparagraph (A).

The amount of the forfeiture penalty shall be assessed by the Commission, or its designee, by written notice. In determining the amount of such a forfeiture, the Commission or its designee shall take into account the nature, circumstances, extent, and gravity of the prohibited acts committed and, with respect to the violator, the degree of culpability, any history of prior offenses, ability to pay, and such other matters as justice may require.

    * * *

Section 509

(a) It shall be unlawful for any person, with intent to deceive the listening or viewing public—

(1) To supply to any contestant in a purportedly bona fide contest of intellectual knowledge or intellectual skill any special and secret assistance whereby

the outcome of such contest will be in whole or in part prearranged or predetermined.

(2) By means of persuasion, bribery, intimidation, or otherwise, to induce or cause any contestant in a purportedly bona fide contest of intellectual knowledge or intellectual skill to refrain in any manner from using or displaying his knowledge or skill in such contest, whereby the outcome thereof will be in whole or in part prearranged or predetermined.

(3) To engage in any artifice or scheme for the purpose of prearranging or predetermining in whole or in part the outcome of a purportedly bona fide contest of intellectual knowledge, intellectual skill, or chance.

(4) To produce or participate in the production for broadcasting of, to broadcast or participate in the broadcasting of, to offer to a licensee for broadcasting, or to sponsor, any radio program, knowing or having reasonable ground for believing that, in connection with a purportedly bona fide contest of intellectual knowledge, intellectual skill, or chance constituting any part of such program, any person has done or is going to do any act or thing referred to in paragraph (1), (2), or (3) of this subsection.

(5) To conspire with any other person or persons to do any act or thing prohibited by paragraph (1), (2), (3), or (4) of this subsection, if one or more of such persons do any act to effect the object of such conspiracy.
* * *

(c) Whoever violates subsection (a) of this section shall be fined not more than $10,000 or imprisoned not more than one year, or both.

Section 605

(a) * * * No person not being authorized by the sender shall intercept any radio communication and divulge or publish the existence, contents, substance, purport, effect, or meaning of such intercepted communication to any person. No person not being entitled thereto shall receive or assist in receiving any interstate or foreign communication by radio and use such communication (or any information therein contained) for his own benefit or for the benefit of another not entitled thereto. No person having received any intercepted radio communication or having become acquainted with the contents, substance, purport, effect, or meaning of such communication (or any part thereof) knowing that such communication was intercepted, shall divulge or publish the existence, contents, substance, purport, effect, or meaning of such communication (or any part thereof) or use such communication (or any information therein contained) for his own benefit or for the benefit of another not entitled thereto. This section shall not apply to the receiving, divulging, publishing, or utilizing the contents of any radio communication which is transmitted by any station for the use of the general public, which relates to ships, aircraft, vehicles, or persons in distress, or which is transmitted by an amateur radio station operator or by a citizens band radio operator.

(b) The provisions of subsection (a) of this section shall not apply to the interception or receipt by any individual, or the assisting (including the manufacture or sale) of such interception or receipt, of any satellite cable programming for private viewing if—

(1) the programming involved is not encrypted; and

(2)(A) a marketing system is not established under which—

(i) an agent or agents have been lawfully designated for the purpose of authorizing private viewing by individuals, and

(ii) such authorization is available to the individual involved from the appropriate agent or agents; or

(B) a marketing system described in subparagraph (A) is established and the individuals receiving such programming have obtained authorization for private viewing under that system.

(c) No person shall encrypt or continue to encrypt satellite delivered programs included in the National Program Service of the Public Broadcasting Service and intended for public viewing by retransmission by television broadcast stations; except that as long as at least one unencrypted satellite transmission of any program subject to this subsection is provided, this subsection shall not prohibit additional encrypted satellite transmissions of the same program.

(d) For purposes of this section—

(1) the term "satellite cable programming" means video programming which is transmitted via satellite and which is primarily intended for the direct receipt by cable operators for their retransmission to cable subscribers;

* * *

(3) the term "encrypt," when used with respect to satellite cable programming, means to transmit such programming in a form whereby the aural and visual characteristics (or both) are modified or altered for the purpose of preventing the unauthorized receipt of such programming by persons without authorized equipment which is designed to eliminate the effects of such modification or alteration;

(4) the term "private viewing" means the viewing for private use in any individual's dwelling unit by means of equipment, owned or operated by such individual, capable of receiving satellite cable programming directly from a satellite;

(5) the term "private financial gain" shall not include the gain resulting to any individual for the private use in such individual's dwelling unit of any programming for which the individual has not obtained authorization for that use; and

(6) the term "any person aggrieved" shall include any person with proprietary rights in the intercepted communication by wire or radio, including wholesale or retail distributors of satellite cable programming, and, in the case of a violation of paragraph (4) of subsection (e) of this section, shall also include any person engaged in the lawful manufacture, distribution, or sale of equipment necessary to authorize or receive satellite cable programming.

(e)(1) Any person who willfully violates subsection (a) of this section shall be fined not more than $2,000 or imprisoned for not more than 6 months, or both.

(2) Any person who violates subsection (a) of this section willfully and for purposes of direct or indirect commercial advantage or private financial gain shall be fined not more than $50,000 or imprisoned for not more than 2 years, or both, for the first such conviction and shall be fined not more than $100,000 or imprisoned for not more than 5 years, or both, for any subsequent conviction.

(3)(A) Any person aggrieved by any violation of subsection (a) of this section or paragraph (4) of subsection (e) of this section may bring a civil action in a United States district court or in any other court of competent jurisdiction.

(B) The court—

(i) may grant temporary and final injunctions on such terms as it may deem reasonable to prevent or restrain violations of subsection (a) of this section;

(ii) may award damages as described in subparagraph (C);

(iii) shall direct the recovery of full costs, including awarding reasonable attorneys' fees to an aggrieved party who prevails.

(C)(i) Damages awarded by any court under this section shall be computed, at the election of the aggrieved party, in accordance with either of the following subclauses:

(I) the party aggrieved may recover the actual damages suffered by him as a result of the violation and any profits of the violator that are attributable to the violation which are not taken into account in computing the actual damages . . . ; or

(II) the party aggrieved may recover an award of statutory damages for each violation of subsection (a) involved in the action in a sum of not less than $1,000 or more than $10,000, as the court considers just, and for each violation of paragraph (4) of this subsection involved in the action an aggrieved party may recover statutory damages in a sum not less than $10,000 or more than $100,000, as the court considers just.

(ii) In any case in which the court finds that the violation was committed willfully and for purposes of direct or indirect commercial advantage or private financial gain, the court in its discretion may increase the award of damages, whether actual or statutory, by an amount of not more than $100,000 for each violation of subsection (a) of this section.

(iii) In any case where the court finds that the violator was not aware and had no reason to believe that his acts constituted a violation of this section, the court in its discretion may reduce the award of damages to a sum of not less than $250.

(4) Any person who manufactures, assembles, modifies, imports, exports, sells, or distributes any electronic, mechanical, or other device or equipment, knowing or having reason to know that the device or equipment is primarily of assistance in the unauthorized decryption of satellite cable programming, or is intended for any other activity prohibited by subsection (a) of this section, shall be fined not more than $500,000 for each violation, or imprisoned for not more than 5 years for each violation, or both. For purposes of all penalties and remedies established for violations of this paragraph, the prohibited activity established herein as it applies to each such device shall be deemed a separate violation.

(5) The penalties under this subsection shall be in addition to those prescribed under any other provision of this subchapter.

(6) Nothing in this subsection shall prevent any State, or political subdivision thereof, from enacting or enforcing any laws with respect to the importation, sale, manufacture, or distribution of equipment by any person with the intent of its use to assist in the interception or receipt of radio communications prohibited by subsection (a) of this section.

(f) Nothing in this section shall affect any right, obligation, or liability under [the Copyright Act], any rule, regulation, or order thereunder, or any other applicable Federal, State, or local law.

* * *

3. CABLE COMMUNICATIONS POLICY ACT OF 1984. TITLE 47, U.S. CODE.

Section 521

The purposes of this subchapter are to—

(1) establish a national policy concerning cable communications;

(2) establish franchise procedures and standards which encourage the growth and development of cable systems and which assure that cable systems are responsive to the needs and interests of the local community;

(3) establish guidelines for the exercise of Federal, State, and local authority with respect to the regulation of cable systems;

(4) assure that cable communications provide and are encouraged to provide the widest possible diversity of information sources and services to the public;

(5) establish an orderly process for franchise renewal which protects cable operators against unfair denials of renewal where the operator's past performance and proposal for future performance meet the standards established by this subchapter; and

(6) promote competition in cable communications and minimize unnecessary regulation that would impose an undue economic burden on cable systems.

Section 531

(a) A franchising authority may establish requirements in a franchise with respect to the designation or use of channel capacity for public, educational, or governmental use only to the extent provided in this section.

(b) A franchising authority may in its request for proposals require as part of a franchise, and may require as part of a cable operator's proposal for a franchise renewal subject to section 546 of this title, that channel capacity be designated for public, educational, or governmental use . . . and may require rules and procedures for the use of the channel capacity designated pursuant to this section.

(c) A franchising authority may enforce any requirement in any franchise regarding the providing or use of such channel capacity. Such enforcement authority includes the authority to enforce any provisions of the franchise for services, facilities, or equipment proposed by the cable operator which relate to public, educational, or governmental use of channel capacity. . . .

* * *

(e) Subject to section 544(d) of this title, a cable operator shall not exercise any editorial control over any public, educational, or governmental use of channel capacity provided pursuant to this section.

* * *

Section 532

(a) The purpose of this section is to assure that the widest possible diversity of information sources are made available to the public from cable systems in a manner consistent with growth and development of cable systems.

(b)(1) A cable operator shall designate channel capacity for commercial use by persons unaffiliated with the operator in accordance with the following requirements:

(A) An operator of any cable system with 36 or more (but not more than 54) activated channels shall designate 10 percent of such channels which are not otherwise required for use (or the use of which is not prohibited) by Federal law or regulation.

(B) An operator of any cable system with 55 or more (but not more than 100) activated channels shall designate 15 percent of such channels which are not otherwise required for use (or the use of which is not prohibited) by Federal law or regulation.

(C) An operator of any cable system with more than 100 activated channels shall designate 15 percent of all such channels.

(D) An operator of any cable system with fewer than 36 activated channels shall not be required to designate channel capacity for commercial use by persons unaffiliated with the operator, unless the cable system is required to provide such channel capacity under the terms of a franchise in effect on October 30, 1984.

* * *

(c)(1) If a person unaffiliated with the cable operator seeks to use channel capacity designated pursuant to subsection (b) of this section for commercial use, the cable operator shall establish, consistent with the purpose of this section, the price, terms, and conditions of such use which are at least sufficient to assure that such use will not adversely affect the operation, financial condition, or market development of the cable system.

(2) A cable operator shall not exercise any editorial control over any video programming provided pursuant to this section, or in any other way consider the content of such programming, except that an operator may consider such content to the minimum extent necessary to establish a reasonable price for the commercial use of designated channel capacity by an unaffiliated person.

* * *

(d) Any person aggrieved by the failure or refusal of a cable operator to make channel capacity available for use pursuant to this section may bring an action in the district court of the United States for the judicial district in which the cable system is located to compel that such capacity be made available. If the court finds that the channel capacity sought by such person has not been made available in accordance with this section, or finds that the price, terms, or conditions established by the cable operator are unreasonable, the court may order such system to make available to such person the channel capacity sought, and further determine the appropriate price, terms, or conditions for such use consistent with subsection (c) of this section, and may award actual damages if it deems such relief appropriate. In any such action, the court shall not consider any price, term, or condition established between an operator and an affiliate for comparable services.

(e)(1) Any person aggrieved by the failure or refusal of a cable operator to make channel capacity available pursuant to this section may petition the Commission for relief under this subsection upon a showing of prior adjudicated violations of this section. * * * If the Commission finds that the channel capacity sought by such person has not been made available in accordance with this section, or that the price, terms, or conditions established by such system are unreasonable under subsection (c) of this section, the Commission shall, by rule or order, require such operator to make available such channel capacity under price, terms, and conditions consistent with subsection (c) of this section.

* * *

(h) Any cable service offered pursuant to this section shall not be provided, or shall be provided subject to conditions, if such cable service in the judgment of the franchising authority is obscene, or is in conflict with community standards in that it is lewd, lascivious, filthy, or indecent or is otherwise unprotected by the Constitution of the United States.

Section 533

(a) It shall be unlawful for any person to be a cable operator if such person, directly or through 1 or more affiliates, owns or controls the licensee of a television broadcast station and the predicted Grade B contour of such station covers any portion of the community served by such operator's cable system.

(b)(1) It shall be unlawful for any common carrier, subject in whole or in part to subchapter II of this chapter, to provide video programming directly to subscribers in its telephone service area, either directly or indirectly through an affiliate owned by, operated by, controlled by, or under common control with the common carrier.
 * * *

(d) Any State or franchising authority may not prohibit the ownership or control of a cable system by any person because of such person's ownership or control of any media of mass communications or other media interests.

(e)(1) Subject to paragraph (2), a State or franchising authority may hold any ownership interest in any cable system.

(2) Any State or franchising authority shall not exercise any editorial control regarding the content of any cable service on a cable system in which such governmental entity holds ownership interest (other than programming on any channel designated for educational or governmental use), unless such control is exercised through an entity separate from the franchising authority.
 * * *

Section 541

(a)(1) A franchising authority may award, in accordance with the provisions of this subchapter, 1 or more franchises within its jurisdiction.

(2) Any franchise shall be construed to authorize the construction of a cable system over public rights-of-way, and through easements, which are within the area to be served by the cable system and which have been dedicated for compatible uses.
. . .

(3) In awarding a franchise or franchises, a franchising authority shall assure that access to cable service is not denied to any group of potential residential cable subscribers because of the income of the residents of the local area in which such group resides.

(b)(1) Except to the extent provided in paragraph (2), a cable operator may not provide cable service without a franchise.

(2) Paragraph (1) shall not require any person lawfully providing cable service without a franchise on July 1, 1984, to obtain a franchise unless the franchisinɼ authority so requires.

(c) Any cable system shall not be subject to regulation as a common carrier or utility by reason of providing any cable service.
 * * *

(e) Nothing in this subchapter shall be construed to affect the authority of any State to license or otherwise regulate any facility or combination of facilities which serves only subscribers in one or more multiple unit dwellings under common ownership, control, or management and which does not use any public right-of-way.

Section 542

(a) Subject to the limitation of subsection (b) of this section, any cable operator may be required under the terms of any franchise to pay a franchise fee.

(b) For any twelve-month period, the franchise fees paid by a cable operator with respect to any cable system shall not exceed 5 percent of such cable operator's gross revenues derived in such period from the operation of the cable system. * * *

(c) A cable operator may pass through to subscribers the amount of any increase in a franchise fee, unless the franchising authority demonstrates that the rate structure specified in the franchise reflects all costs of franchise fees and so notifies the cable operator in writing.

* * *

(e) Any cable operator shall pass through to subscribers the amount of any decrease in a franchise fee.

(f) A cable operator may designate that portion of a subscriber's bill attributable to the franchise fee as a separate item on the bill.

* * *

Section 543

(a) Any Federal agency or State may not regulate the rates for the provision of cable service except to the extent provided under this section. Any franchising authority may regulate the rates for the provision of cable service . . . but only as to the extent provided under this section.

(b)(1) Within 180 days after October 30, 1984, the Commission shall prescribe and make effective regulations which authorized a franchising authority to regulate rates for the provision of basic cable service in circumstances in which a cable system is not subject to effective competition. * * *

(2) For purpose of rate regulation under this subsection, such regulations shall—

(A) define the circumstances in which a cable system is not subject to effective competition; and

(B) establish standards for such rate regulation.

(3) The Commission shall periodically review such regulations, taking into account developments in technology, and may amend such regulations, consistent with paragraphs (1) and (2), to the extent the Commission determines necessary.

* * *

(h) Not later than 6 years after October 30, 1984, the Commission shall prepare and submit to the Congress a report regarding rate regulation of cable services, including such legislative recommendations as the Commission considers appropriate. Such report and recommendations shall be based on a study of such regulation which the Commission shall conduct regarding the effect of competition in the marketplace.

Section 544

(a) Any franchising authority may not regulate the services, facilities, and equipment provided by a cable operator except to the extent consistent with this subchapter.

(b) In the case of any franchise granted after the effective date of this subchapter, the franchising authority, to the extent related to the establishment or operation of a cable system—

> (1) in its request for proposals for a franchise (including requests for renewal proposals, subject to section 546 of this title), may establish requirements for facilities and equipment, but may not establish requirements for video programming or other information services; and

> (2) subject to [the statutory provision dealing with franchise modification], may enforce any requirements contained within the franchise—

>> (A) for facilities and equipment; and

>> (B) for broad categories of programming or other services.

* * *

(d)(1) Nothing in this subchapter shall be construed as prohibiting a franchising authority and a cable operator from specifying, in a franchise or renewal thereof, that certain cable services shall not be provided or shall be provided subject to conditions, if such cable services are obscene or are otherwise unprotected by the Constitution of the United States.

(2)(A) In order to restrict the viewing of programming which is obscene or indecent, upon the request of a subscriber, a cable operator shall provide (by sale or lease) a device by which the subscriber can prohibit viewing of a particular cable service during periods selected by that subscriber.

* * *

(e) The Commission may establish technical standards relating to the facilities and equipment of cable systems which a franchising authority may require in the franchise.

* * *

Section 546

(a) During the 6-month period which begins with the 36th month before the franchise expiration, the franchising authority may, on its own initiative, and shall at the request of the cable operator, commence proceedings which afford the public in the franchise area appropriate notice and participation for the purpose of—

> (1) identifying the future cable-related community needs and interests; and

> (2) reviewing the performance of the cable operator under the franchise during the then current franchise term.

(b)(1) Upon completion of a proceeding under subsection (a) of this section, a cable operator seeking renewal of a franchise may, on its own initiative or at the request of a franchising authority, submit a proposal for renewal.

(2) Subject to section 544 of this title, any such proposal shall contain such material as the franchising authority may require, including proposals for an upgrade of the cable system.

(3) The franchising authority may establish a date by which such proposal shall be submitted.

(c)(1) Upon submittal by a cable operator of a proposal to the franchising authority for the renewal of a franchise, the franchising authority shall provide prompt public notice of such proposal and, during the 4-month period which begins on the completion of any proceedings under subsection (a) of this section, renew the franchise or issue a preliminary assessment that the franchise should not be renewed and, at the request of the operator or on its own initiative, commence an administrative proceeding, after providing prompt public notice of such proceeding . . . to consider whether—

(A) the cable operator has substantially complied with the material terms of the existing franchise and with applicable law;

(B) the quality of the operator's service, including signal quality, response to consumer complaints, and billing practices, but without regard to the mix, quality, or level of cable services or other services provided over the system, has been reasonable in light of community needs;

(C) the operator has the financial, legal, and technical ability to provide the services, facilities, and equipment as set forth in the operator's proposal; and

(D) the operator's proposal is reasonable to meet the future cable-related community needs and interests, taking into account the cost of meeting such needs and interests.

(2) In any proceeding under paragraph (1), the cable operator shall be afforded adequate notice and the cable operator and the franchising authority, or its designee, shall be afforded fair opportunity for full participation, including the right to introduce evidence . . . , to require the production of evidence, and to question witnesses. A transcript shall be made of any such proceeding.

(3) At the completion of a proceeding under this subsection, the franchising authority shall issue a written decision granting or denying the proposal for renewal based upon the record of such proceeding, and transmit a copy of such decision to the cable operator. Such decision shall state the reasons therefor.

(d) Any denial of a proposal for renewal shall be based on one or more adverse findings made with respect to the factors described in subparagraphs (A) through (D) of subsection (c)(1) of this section. . . . A franchising authority may not base a denial of renewal on a failure to substantially comply with material terms of the franchise under subsection (c)(1)(A) of this section or on events considered under subsection (c)(1)(B) of this section in any case in which a violation of the franchise or the events considered under subsection (c)(1)(B) of this section occur after the effective date of this subchapter unless the franchising authority has provided the operator with notice and the opportunity to cure, or in any case in which it is documented that the franchising authority has waived its right to object, or has effectively acquiesced.

(e)(1) Any cable operator whose proposal for renewal has been denied by a final decision of a franchising authority made pursuant to this section, or has been adversely affected by a failure of the franchising authority to act in accordance with the procedural requirements of this section, may appeal such final decision pursuant to the provisions of section 555 of this title.

* * *

(h) Notwithstanding the provisions of subsections (a) through (g) of this section, a cable operator may submit a proposal for the renewal of a franchise pursuant to this subsection at any time, and a franchising authority may, after affording the public adequate notice and opportunity for comment, grant or deny such proposal at any time (including after proceedings pursuant to this section have commenced).

The provisions of subsections (a) through (g) of this section shall not apply to a decision to grant or deny a proposal under this subsection. The denial of a renewal pursuant to this subsection shall not affect action on a renewal proposal that is submitted in accordance with subsections (a) through (g) of this section.

Section 555

(a) Any cable operator adversely affected by any final determination made by a franchising authority under section 545 or 546 of this title may commence an action within 120 days after receiving notice of such determination, which may be brought in—

(1) the district court of the United States for any judicial district in which the cable system is located; or

(2) in any State court of general jurisdiction having jurisdiction over the parties.

(b) The court may award any appropriate relief consistent with the provisions of the relevant section described in subsection (a) of this section.

Section 558

Nothing in this subchapter shall be deemed to affect the criminal or civil liability of cable programmers or cable operators pursuant to the Federal, State, or local law of libel, slander, obscenity, incitement, invasion of privacy, false or misleading advertising, or other similar laws, except that cable operators shall not incur any such liability for any program carried on any channel designated for public, educational, or governmental use or on any other channel obtained under section 532 of this title or under similar arrangements.

Section 559

Whoever transmits over any cable system any matter which is obscene or otherwise unprotected by the Constitution of the United States shall be fined not more than $10,000 or imprisoned not more 2 years, or both.

4. FEDERAL CRIMINAL STATUTES. TITLE 18, U.S. CODE.

Section 1302

Whoever knowingly deposits in the mail, or sends or delivers by mail:

* * *

Any newspaper, circular, pamphlet, or publication of any kind containing any advertisement of any lottery, gift enterprise, or scheme of any kind offering prizes dependent in whole or in part upon lot or chance, or containing any list of the prizes drawn or awarded by means of any such lottery, gift enterprise, or scheme, whether said list contains any part or all of such prizes;

* * *

Shall be fined not more than $1,000 or imprisoned not more than two years, or both; and for any subsequent offense shall be imprisoned not more than five years.

Section 1304

Whoever broadcasts by means of any radio or television station for which a license is required by any law of the United States, or whoever, operating any such station, knowingly permits the broadcasting of, any advertisement of or information concerning any lottery, gift enterprise, or similar scheme, offering prizes dependent in whole or in part upon lot or chance, or any list of the prizes drawn or awarded by means of any such lottery, gift enterprise, or scheme, whether said list contains any part or all of such prizes, shall be fined not more than $1,000 or imprisoned not more than one year, or both.

Each day's broadcasting shall constitute a separate offense.

Section 1307

(a) The provisions of sections 1301, 1302, 1303, and 1304 shall not apply to—
    (1) an advertisement, list of prizes, or other information concerning a lottery conducted by a State acting under the authority of State law which is—
        (A) contained in a publication published in that State or in a State which conducts such a lottery; or
        (B) broadcast by a radio or television station licensed to a location in that State or a State which conducts such a lottery; or
    (2) an advertisement, list of prizes, or other information concerning a lottery, gift enterprise, or similar scheme, other than one described in paragraph (1), that is authorized or not otherwise prohibited by the State in which it is conducted and which is—
        (A) conducted by a not-for-profit organization or a governmental organization; or
        (B) conducted as a promotional activity by a commercial organization and is clearly occasional and ancillary to the primary business of that organization.
    * * *

Section 1343

Whoever, having devised or intending to devise any scheme or artifice to defraud, or for obtaining money or property by means of false or fraudulent pretenses, representations, or promises, transmits or causes to be transmitted by means of wire, radio, or television communication in interstate or foreign commerce, any writings, signs, signals, pictures, or sounds for the purpose of executing such scheme or artifice, shall be fined not more than $1,000 or imprisoned not more than five years, or both.

Section 1461

Every obscene, lewd, lascivious, indecent, filthy or vile article, matter, thing, device, or substance . . . [i]s declared to be nonmailable matter and shall not be conveyed in the mails or delivered from any post office or by any letter carrier.

Whoever knowingly uses the mails for the mailing, carriage in the mails or delivery of anything declared by this section . . . to be nonmailable, or knowingly causes to be delivered by mail according to the direction thereon, or at the place at which it is directed to be delivered by the person to whom it is addressed, or knowingly takes any such thing from the mails for the purpose of circulating or disposing thereof, or of aiding in the circulation or disposition thereof, shall be fined not more than $5,000 or imprisoned not more than five years, or both, for the first such offense, and shall be fined not more than $10,000 or imprisoned not more than ten years, or both, for each such offense thereafter. * * *

Section 1462

Whoever brings into the United States, or any place subject to the jurisdiction thereof, or knowingly uses any express company or other common carrier, for carriage in interstate or foreign commerce—

(a) any obscene, lewd, lascivious, or filthy book, pamphlet , picture, motion-picture film, paper, letter, writing, print, or other matter of indecent character; or

(b) any obscene, lewd, lascivious, or filthy phonograph recording, electrical transcription, or other article or thing capable of producing sound; * * *

Shall be fined not more than $5,000 or imprisoned not more than five years, or both, for the first such offense and shall be fined not more than $10,000 or imprisoned not more than ten years, or both, for each such offense thereafter.

Section 1464

Whoever utters any obscene, indecent, or profane language by means of radio communication shall be fined not more than $10,000 or imprisoned not more than two years, or both.

Section 1465

Whoever knowingly transports in interstate or foreign commerce for the purpose of sale or distribution, or knowingly travels in interstate commerce, or uses a facility or means of interstate commerce for the purpose of transporting obscene material in interstate or foreign commerce, any obscene, lewd, lascivious, or filthy book, pamphlet, picture, film, paper, letter, writing, print, silhouette, drawing, figure, image, cast, phonograph recording, electrical transcription, or other article capable of producing sound or any other matter of indecent or immoral character, shall be fined not more than $5,000 or imprisoned not more than five years, or both.
* * *

Section 1466

(a) Whoever is engaged in the business of selling or transferring obscene matter, who knowingly receives or possesses with intent to distribute any obscene book, magazine, picture, paper, film, videotape, or phonograph or other audio recording which has been shipped or transported in interstate or foreign commerce, shall be punished by imprisonment for not more than 5 years or by a fine under this title, or both.
* * *

Section 1467

(a) A person who is convicted of an offense involving obscene material under this chapter shall forfeit to the United States such person's interest in—
    (1) any obscene material produced, transported, mailed, shipped, or received in violation of this chapter;
    (2) any property, real or personal, constituting or traceable to gross profits or other proceeds obtained from such offense; and
    (3) any property, real or personal, used or intended to be used to commit or to promote the commission of such offense, if the court in its discretion so determines, taking into consideration the nature, scope, and proportionality of the use of the property in the offense.
        * * *
(e) The court shall order forfeiture of property referred to in subsection (a) if—
    (1) the trier of fact determines, beyond a reasonable doubt, that such property is subject to forfeiture; and
    (2) with respect to property referred to in subsection (a)(3), if the court exercises the court's discretion under that subsection.
        * * *

Section 1468

(a) Whoever knowingly utters any obscene language or distributes any obscene matter by means of cable television or subscription services on television, shall be punished by imprisonment for not more than 2 years or by a fine in accordance with this title, or both.

(b) As used in this section, the term ''distribute'' means to send, transmit, retransmit, telecast, broadcast, or cablecast, including by wire, microwave, or satellite, or to produce or provide material for such distribution.

(c) Nothing in this chapter, or the Cable Communications Policy Act of 1984, or any other provision of Federal law, is intended to interfere with or preempt the power of the States, including political subdivisions thereof, to regulate the uttering of language that is obscene or otherwise unprotected by the Constitution or the distribution of matter that is obscene or otherwise unprotected by the Constitution, of any sort, by means of cable television or subscription services on television.

5. ILLUSTRATIVE "SHIELD" LAWS

California Constitution
Article I, Section 2

* * *

(b) A publisher, editor, reporter, or other person connected with or employed upon a newspaper, magazine, or other periodical publication, or by a press association or wire service, or any person who has been so connected or employed, shall not be adjudged in contempt by a judicial, legislative, or administrative body, or any other body having the power to issues subpoenas, for refusing to disclose the source of any information procured while so connected or employed for publication in a newspaper, magazine or other periodical publication, or for refusing to disclose any unpublished information obtained or prepared in gathering, receiving or processing of information for communication to the public.

Nor shall a radio or television news reporter or other person connected with or employed by a radio or television station, or any person who has been so connected or employed, be so adjudged in contempt for refusing to disclose the source of any information procured while so connected or employed for news or news commentary purposes on radio or television, or for refusing to disclose any unpublished information obtained or prepared in gathering, receiving or processing of information for communication to the public.

As used in this subdivision, "unpublished information" includes information not disseminated to the public by the person from whom disclosure is sought, whether or not related information has been disseminated, and includes, but is not limited to, all notes, outtakes, photographs, tapes or other data of whatever sort not itself disseminated to the public through a medium of communication, whether or not published information based upon or related to such material has been disseminated.

Minnesota Statutes Annotated
Section 595.022. Public policy

In order to protect the public interest and the free flow of information, the news media should have the benefit of a substantial privilege not to reveal sources of information or to disclose unpublished information. To this end, the freedom of the press requires protection of the confidential relationship between the news gatherer and the source of information. The purpose of [this act] is to insure and perpetuate, consistent with the public interest, the confidential relationship between the news media and its sources.

Section 595.023. Disclosure prohibited

No person who is or has been directly engaged in the gathering, procuring, compiling, editing, or publishing of information for the purpose of transmission, dissemination or publication to the public shall be required by any court, grand jury, agency, department or branch of the state, or any of its political subdivisions or other public body, or by either house of the legislature or any committee, officer, member, or employee thereof, to disclose in any proceeding the person or means from or through which information was obtained, or to disclose any unpublished information procured by the person in the course of work or any of the person's notes, memoranda, recording tapes, film or other reportorial data which would tend to identify the person or means through which the information was obtained.

Section 595.024. Exception and procedure

Subdivision 1. A person seeking disclosure may apply to the district court of the county where the person employed by or associated with a news media resides, has a principal place of business or where the proceeding in which the information sought is pending.

Subd. 2. The application shall be granted only if the court determines after hearing the parties that the person making application, by clear and convincing evidence, has met all three of the following conditions:

(1) that there is probable cause to believe that the source has information clearly relevant to a specific violation of the law other than a misdemeanor,

(2) that the information cannot be obtained by any alternative means or remedy less destructive of first amendment rights, and

(3) that there is a compelling and overriding interest requiring the disclosure of the information where the disclosure is necessary to prevent injustice.

Subd. 3. Determination; appeal. The district court shall consider the nature of the proceedings, the merits of the claims and defenses, the adequacies of alternative remedies, the relevancy of the information sought, and the possibility of establishing by other means that which the source is expected or may tend to prove. The court shall make its appropriate order after making findings of fact. The order may be appealed directly to the court of appeals according to the rules of appellate procedure. The order is stayed and nondisclosure shall remain in full force and effect during the pendency of the appeal.

Section 595.025. Defamation

Subdivision 1. The prohibition of disclosure provided in section 595.023 shall not apply in any defamation action where the person seeking disclosure can demonstrate that the identity of the source will lead to relevant evidence on the issue of actual malice.

Subd. 2. Notwithstanding the provisions of subdivision 1, the identity of the source of information shall not be ordered disclosed unless the following conditions are met:

(a) that there is probable cause to believe that the source has information clearly relevant to the issue of defamation;

(b) that the information cannot be obtained by any alternative means or remedy less destructive of first amendment rights.

Subd. 3. Determination; appeal. The court shall make its order on the issue of disclosure after making findings of fact, which order may be appealed to the court of appeals according to the rules of appellate procedure. During the appeal the order is stayed and nondisclosure shall remain in full force and effect.

BIBLIOGRAPHY

CHAPTER 1

ABRAMS, FLOYD, "The Press *is* Different: Reflections on Justice Stewart and the Autonomous Press," 7 *Hofstra Law Review* 563 (1979).

ANDERSON, DAVID A., "The Origins of the Press Clause," 30 *U.C.L.A. Law Review* 455 (1983).

BARNETT, STEPHEN R., "The Puzzle of Prior Restraint," 29 *Stanford Law Review* 539 (1977).

BLACKSTONE, WILLIAM, *Commentaries on the Laws of England,* Book IV, pp. *151–152 (Philadelphia: Rees Welsh & Co., 1898).

BLASI, VINCE, "The Checking Value in First Amendment Theory," 1977 *American Bar Foundation Research Journal* 521.

BOLLINGER, LEE C., *The Tolerant Society: Freedom of Speech and Extremist Speech in America* (New York: Oxford University Press, 1986).

CAHN, EDMOND, "Justice Black and First Amendment Absolutes—A Public Interview," 37 *New York University Law Review* 549 (1962).

CHAFEE, ZECHARIAH, "Book Review," 62 *Harvard Law Review* 891 (1949).

CHAFEE, ZECHARIAH, *Free Speech in the United States* (Cambridge: Harvard University Press, 1941).

EMERSON, THOMAS I., *The System of Freedom of Expression* (New York: Random House, 1970).

FREUND, PAUL, "The Great Disorder of Speech," 44 *American Scholar* 541 (1975).

GREENAWALT, KENT, "Free Speech Justifications," 89 *Columbia Law Review* 119 (1989).

LABUNSKI, RICHARD, "The 'Collateral Bar' Rule and the First Amendment: The Constitutionality of Enforcing Unconstitutional Orders," 37 *American University Law Review* 323 (1988).

LEVY, LEONARD W., *Emergence of a Free Press* (New York: Oxford University Press, 1985).

MADISON, JAMES, *Letters and Other Writings of James Madison,* Vol. III (Philadelphia: J.B. Lippincott & Co., 1865).

MARCUSE, HERBERT, "Repressive Tolerance," in Wolff, Robert, et al., *A Critique of Pure Tolerance* (Boston: Beacon Press, 1965).

MEIKLEJOHN, ALEXANDER, *Free Speech and Its Relation to Self-Government* (New York: Harper & Brothers, 1948).

MEIKLEJOHN, ALEXANDER, "The First Amendment is an Absolute," 1961 *Supreme Court Review* 245.

MILL, JOHN STUART, *On Liberty* (New York: Bobbs-Merrill Co., 1956) (Currin V. Shields, ed.).

MILTON, JOHN, "Areopagitica," in *The Works of John Milton,* Vol. IV (New York: Columbia University Press, 1931).

NIMMER, MELVILLE B., *Freedom of Speech* (New York: Matthew Bender & Co., 1984).

OFFICE OF TECHNOLOGY ASSESSMENT, U.S. CONGRESS, *Science, Technology and the First Amendment* (Washington: U.S. Government Printing Office, 1988).

POOL, ITHIEL DE SOLA, *Technologies of Freedom* (Cambridge, Mass.: Belknap Press, 1983).

STEWART, POTTER, "Or of the Press," 26 *Hastings Law Journal* 631 (1975).

STRONG, FRANK R., "Fifty Years of 'Clear and Present Danger': From *Schenck* to *Brandenburg*—and Beyond," 1969 *Supreme Court Review* 41.

TRIBE, LAURENCE H., *American Constitutional Law* (Mineola, N.Y.: Foundation Press, Second ed. 1988).

CHAPTER 2

AMERICAN LAW INSTITUTE, *Restatement of the Law of Torts* (St. Paul: American Law Institute Publishers, Second ed. 1977).

ANDERSON, DAVID A., "Libel and Press Self-Censorship," 53 *Texas Law Review* 422 (1975).

ANDERSON, DAVID A., "Reputation, Compensation, and Proof," 25 *William & Mary Law Review* 747 (1984).

BEZANSON, RANDALL P., GILBERT CRANBERG, AND JOHN SOLOSKI, "Libel Law and the Press: Setting the Record Straight," 71 *Iowa Law Review* 215 (1985).

EATON, JOEL, "The American Law of Defamation Through *Gertz v. Robert Welch Inc.* and Beyond: An Analytical Primer," 61 *Virginia Law Review* 1349 (1975).

FRANKLIN, MARC A., "Suing the Media for Libel: A Litigation Study," 1981 *American Bar Foundation Research Journal* 795.

FRANKLIN, MARC A., "What Does Negligence Mean in Defamation Cases?" 6 *Comm/Ent Law Journal* 259 (1984).

GOODALE, JAMES, "Survey of Recent Media Verdicts, Their Disposition on Appeal, and

Media Defense Costs," in *Media Insurance and Risk Management* (New York: Practising Law Institute, 1985).

KEETON, W. PAGE, et al., *Prosser and Keeton on Torts* (St. Paul: West Publishing Co., Fifth ed. 1984).

LEWIS, ANTHONY, "*New York Times v. Sullivan* Reconsidered: Time to Return to 'The Central Meaning of the First Amendment,' " 83 *Columbia Law Review* 603 (1983).

NOTE, "The Fact-Opinion Determination in Defamation," 88 *Columbia Law Review* 809 (1988).

PIERCE, SAMUEL R., JR., "Anatomy of an Historic Decision: *New York Times Co. v. Sullivan*," 43 *North Carolina Law Review* 315 (1965).

ROBERTSON, DAVID, "Defamation and the First Amendment: In Praise of *Gertz v. Robert Welch, Inc.*," 54 *Texas Law Review* 199 (1976).

SACK, ROBERT D., *Libel, Slander, and Related Problems* (New York: Practising Law Institute, 1980).

SANFORD, BRUCE W., *Libel and Privacy: The Prevention and Defense of Litigation* (Clifton, N.J.: Prentice Hall Law & Business, 1987).

SMOLLA, RODNEY A., "Emotional Distress and the First Amendment: An Analysis of *Hustler v. Falwell*," 20 *Arizona State Law Journal* 369 (1988).

SMOLLA, RODNEY A., *Law of Defamation* (New York: Clark Boardman Co., 1986).

SMOLLA, RODNEY A., *Suing the Press* (New York: Oxford University Press, 1986).

SOWLE, KATHRYN, "Defamation and the First Amendment: The Case for a Constitutional Privilege of Fair Report," 54 *New York University Law Review* 469 (1979).

WATKINS, JOHN J., AND CHARLES W. SCHWARTZ, "*Gertz* and the Common Law of Defamation: Of Fault, Nonmedia Defendants, and Conditional Privileges," 15 *Texas Tech Law Review* 823 (1984).

CHAPTER 3

AMERICAN LAW INSTITUTE, *Restatement of the Law of Torts* (St. Paul: American Law Institute Publishers, Second ed. 1977).

FLETCHER, PETER L., AND EDWARD L. RUBIN, "Privacy, Publicity, and the Portrayal of Real People by the Media," 88 *Yale Law Journal* 1577 (1979).

KARLEN, PETER H., "Descendible Publicity Rights: California's Grateful Dead," 8 *Comm/Ent Law Journal* 111 (1986).

KEETON, W. PAGE, et al., *Prosser and Keeton on Torts* (St. Paul: West Publishing Co., Fifth ed. 1984).

MCCARTHY, J. THOMAS, *The Rights of Publicity and Privacy* (New York: Clark Boardman Co., 1987).

MIDDLETON, KENT R., "Journalists, Trespass, and Officials: Closing the Door on *Florida Publishing Co. v. Fletcher*," 16 *Pepperdine Law Review* 259 (1989).

NIMMER, MELVILLE B., "The Right to Publicity," 19 *Law & Contemporary Problems* 203 (1954).

NOTE, "Human Cannonballs and the First Amendment: *Zacchini v. Scripps-Howard Broadcasting Co.*," 30 *Stanford Law Review* 1185 (1978).

NOTE, "The Ambush Interview: A False Light Invasion of Privacy?" 34 *Case Western Reserve Law Review* 72 (1983).

PEMBER, DON R., *Privacy and the Press* (Seattle: University of Washington Press, 1972).

PROSSER, WILLIAM L., "Privacy," 48 *California Law Review* 383 (1960).

ROPSKI, GARY P., "The Right of Publicity and the Celebrity Look-Alike: Now Section 43(a) Proscribes Faces that Deceive," 77 *Trademark Reporter* 31 (1987).

RUBENFELD, JED, "The Right of Privacy," 102 *Harvard Law Review* 737 (1989).

SANFORD, BRUCE W., *Libel and Privacy: The Prevention and Defense of Litigation* (Clifton, N.J.: Prentice Hall Law & Business, 1987).

SMOLLA, RODNEY A., *Law of Defamation* (New York: Clark Boardman Co., 1986).

TREECE, JAMES M., "Commercial Exploitation of Names, Likenesses, and Personal Histories," 51 *Texas Law Review* 637 (1973).

WALDEN, RUTH, AND EMILE NETZHAMMER, "False Light Invasion of Privacy: Untangling the Web of Uncertainty," 9 *Comm/Ent Law Journal* 347 (1987).

WARREN, SAMUEL D., AND LOUIS D. BRANDEIS, "The Right to Privacy," 4 *Harvard Law Review* 193 (1890).

WATKINS, JOHN J., "Private Property vs. Reporter Rights—A Problem in Newsgathering," 54 *Journalism Quarterly* 690 (1977).

ZIMMERMAN, DIANE L., "Requiem for a Heavyweight: A Farewell to Warren and Brandeis's Privacy Tort," 68 *Cornell Law Review* 291 (1983).

CHAPTER 4

ABRAMSON, ELLIOTT M., "How Much Copying Under Copyright? Contradictions, Paradoxes, Inconsistencies," 61 *Temple Law Review* 133 (1988).

FISHER, WILLIAM W. III, "Reconstructing the Fair Use Doctrine," 101 *Harvard Law Review* 1659 (1988).

FRANCIONE, GARY L., "Facing *The Nation*: The Standards for Copyright, Infringement, and Fair Use of Factual Works," 134 *University of Pennsylvania Law Review* 519 (1986).

HAZARD, JOHN W., *Copyright Law in Business and Practice* (Larchmont, N.Y.: Prentice Hall, Rosenfeld Launer Publications, 1989).

LATMAN, ALAN, *The Copyright Law* (Washington: Bureau of National Affairs, Fifth ed. 1979).

LLOYD, FRANK W., AND DANIEL M. MAYEDA, "Copyright Fair Use, The First Amendment, and New Communications Technologies: The Impact of Betamax," 38 *Federal Communications Law Journal* 59 (1986).

NIMMER, MELVILLE B., *Nimmer on Copyright* (New York: Matthew Bender & Co., 1988).

NOTE, "Fair Use of Copyrighted Work Under *Harper & Row Publishers, Inc. v. Nation Enterprises*," 61 *Tulane Law Review* 415 (1986).

NOTE, "The Chilling Effect of Overprotecting Factual Narrative Works," 11 *Comm/Ent Law Journal* 75 (1988).

NOTE, "The 'Works Made for Hire' Doctrine and the Employee/ Independent Contractor Dichotomy: The Need for Congressional Clarification," 10 *Comm/Ent Law Journal* 591 (1988).

NOTE, "When 'Fair is Foul': A Narrow Reading of the Fair Use Doctrine in *Harper & Row Publishers, Inc. v. Nation Enterprises*," 72 *Cornell Law Review* 218 (1986).

SHIPLEY, DAVID E., "Three Strikes and They're Out at the Old Ball Game: Preemption of Performers' Rights of Publicity Under the Copyright Act of 1976," 20 *Arizona State Law Journal* 369 (1988).

CHAPTER 5

BERG, RICHARD, AND STEPHEN KLITZMAN, *An Interpretive Guide to the Government in the Sunshine Act* (Washington: Administrative Conference of the United States, 1978).

BRAVERMAN, BURT, AND FRANCES CHETWYND, *Information Law* (New York: Practising Law Institute, 1985).

CROSS, HAROLD, *The People's Right to Know* (New York: Columbia University Press, 1953).

DAUGHERTY, REBECCA (ED.), *How to Use the Federal FOI Act* (Washington: FOI Service Center, Sixth ed. 1987).

"Freedom of Information Act," in *Federal Administrative Procedure Sourcebook* (Washington: Administrative Conference of the United States, 1985).

"Government in the Sunshine Act," in *Federal Administrative Procedure Sourcebook* (Washington: Administrative Conference of the United States, 1985).

LEWIS, ANTHONY, "A Public Right to Know About Public Institutions: The First Amendment as Sword," 1980 *Supreme Court Review* 1.

MIDDLETON, KENT R., "Journalists' Interference with Police: The First Amendment, Access to News, and Official Discretion," 5 *Comm/Ent Law Journal* 443 (1983).

NOTE, "Facilitating Government Decision Making: Distinguishing Between Meetings and Nonmeetings Under the Federal Sunshine Act," 66 *Texas Law Review* 1195 (1988).

NOTE, "National Security Information Disclosure under the FOIA: The Need for Effective Judicial Enforcement," 25 *Boston College Law Review* 614 (1984).

NOTE, "Stone Got Caught Between a Rock and a Hard Place: Grand Juries' Power to Subpoena Outtakes That Reveal Confidential News Sources," 10 *Comm/Ent Law Journal* 623 (1988).

NOTE, "What Ever Happened to the 'Right to Know'?: Access to Government Controlled Information since *Richmond Newspapers*," 73 *Virginia Law Review* 1111 (1987).

O'REILLY, JAMES T., *Federal Information Disclosure* (Colorado Springs: McGraw-Hill, 1988).

PARKS, WALLACE, "The Open Government Principle: Applying the Right to Know Under the Constitution," 26 *George Washington Law Review* 1 (1957).

STEWART, POTTER, "Or of the Press," 26 *Hastings Law Journal* 631 (1975).

SYMPOSIUM, "Government Information and the Rights of Citizens," 73 *Michigan Law Review* 971 (1975).

SYMPOSIUM, "Your Business, Your Trade Secrets, and Your Government," 34 *Administrative Law Review* 107 (1982).

WATKINS, JOHN J., "Access to Public Records under the Arkansas Freedom of Information Act," 37 *Arkansas Law Review* 741 (1984).

WATKINS, JOHN J., "Newsgathering and the First Amendment," 53 *Journalism Quarterly* 406 (1976).

WATKINS, JOHN J., "Open Meetings under the Arkansas Freedom of Information Act," 38 *Arkansas Law Review* 268 (1984).

CHAPTER 6

AMERICAN BAR ASSOCIATION PROJECT ON MINIMUM STANDARDS FOR CRIMINAL JUSTICE, *Standards Relating to Fair Trial and Free Press* (New York: American Bar Association, 1966).

BABCOCK, BARBARA ALLEN, "Voir Dire: Preserving Its Wonderful Power,'" 27 *Stanford Law Review* 545 (1975).

COHEN, SUSAN B., "Reconciling Media Access with Confidentiality for the Individual in Juvenile Court," 20 *Santa Clara Law Review* 405 (1980).

COMMENT, "Common Law or First Amendment Right of Access to Sealed Settlement Agreements," 54 *Journal of Air Law and Commerce* 577 (1988).

COMMENT, "First Amendment Right of Access to Pretrial Proceedings in Criminal Cases," 32 *Emory Law Journal* 619 (1983).

COMMENT, "The First Amendment Right of Access to Civil Trials After *Globe Newspaper Co. v. Superior Court*," 51 *University of Chicago Law Review* 286 (1984).

COMMENT, "Sequestration: A Possible Solution to the Free Press-Fair Trial Dilemma," 23 *American University Law Review* 923 (1974).

COMMENT, "The First Amendment and Pretrial Discovery Hearings: When Should the Public and Press Have Access?" 36 *U.C.L.A. Law Review* 609 (1989).

DYER, CAROLYN, AND NANCY HAUSERMAN, "Electronic Coverage of the Courts: Exceptions to Exposure," 75 *Georgetown Law Journal* 1633 (1987).

FRANK, RICHARD H., "Cameras in the Courtroom: A First Amendment Right of Access," 9 *Comm/Ent Law Journal* 749 (1987).

FRASCA, RALPH, "Estimating the Occurrence of Trials Prejudiced by Press Coverage," 72 *Judicature* 162 (1988).

LEWIS, ANTHONY, "A Public Right to Know About Public Institutions: The First Amendment as Sword," 1980 *Supreme Court Review* 1.

LINDE, HANS A., "Fair Trials and Press Freedom—Two Rights Against the State," 13 *Willamette Law Journal* 211 (1977).

NOTE, "An Assessment of the Use of Cameras in State and Federal Courts," 18 *Georgia Law Review* 389 (1984).

NOTE, "The Common Law Right of Access to Taped Evidence," 50 *George Washington Law Review* 465 (1982).

NOTE, "The Constitutionality of Statutorily Restricting Public Access to Judicial Proceedings: The Case of the Rape Shield Mandatory Closure Provision," 66 *Boston University Law Review* 271 (1986).

NOTE, "The Free Press-Fair Trial Controversy: A New Standard for Closure Motions in Criminal Proceedings," 38 *Arkansas Law Review* 403 (1984).

SYMPOSIUM, "*Nebraska Press Association v. Stuart*," 29 *Stanford Law Review* 383 (1977).

CHAPTER 7

COMMENT, "The Newsman's Privilege After *Branzburg*: The Case for a Federal Shield Law," 24 *U.C.L.A. Law Review* 160 (1976).

D'ALEMBERTE, TALBOT, "Journalists Under the Axe: Protection of Confidential Sources of Information," 6 *Harvard Journal on Legislation* 307 (1969).

"FBI, Police Invade Newsrooms," *The News Media and the Law* (Fall 1988), p. 4.

GOODALE, JAMES C., "Branzburg v. Hayes and the Developing Qualified Privilege for Newsmen," 26 *Hastings Law Journal* 709 (1975).

LANGLEY, MONICA, AND LEE LEVINE, "*Branzburg* Revisited: Confidential Sources and First Amendment Values," 57 *George Washington Law Review* 13 (1988).

MARCUS, PAUL, "The Reporter's Privilege: An Analysis of the Common Law, *Branzburg v. Hayes*, and Recent Statutory Developments," 25 *Arizona Law Review* 816 (1983).

MURASKY, DONNA M., "The Journalist's Privilege: *Branzburg* and its Aftermath," 52 *Texas Law Review* 829 (1974).

"Seek Help Immediately to Block Search," *The News Media and the Law* (Fall 1988), p. 6.

WATKINS, JOHN J., "The Journalist's Privilege in Arkansas," 7 *U.A.L.R. Law Journal* 473 (1984).

WATKINS, JOHN J., "The Status of Confidential Privilege for Newsmen in Civil Libel Actions," 52 *Journalism Quarterly* 505 (1975).

WHALEN, CHARLES W., *Your Right to Know* (New York: Vintage Books, 1973).

CHAPTER 8

ABRAMS, FLOYD, HENRY M. HOLZER, DON OBERDORFER, AND RICHARD K. WILLARD, "The First Amendment and National Security," 43 *University of Miami Law Review* 61 (1988).

AMERICAN BAR ASSOCIATION STANDING COMMITTEE ON LAW AND NATIONAL SECURITY, *National Security and the First Amendment* (Washington: American Bar Association, 1984).

"Battle Coverage Restrictions Debated," *The News Media and the Law* (Summer 1986), p. 23.

CASSELL, PAUL G., "Restrictions on Press Coverage of Military Operations: The Right of Access, Grenada, and 'Off-the-Record Wars,' " 73 *Georgetown Law Journal* 931 (1985).

EDGAR, HAROLD, AND BENNO C. SCHMIDT, "*Curtiss-Wright* Comes Home: Executive Power and National Security Secrecy," 21 *Harvard Civil Rights-Civil Liberties Law Review* 349 (1986).

EDGAR, HAROLD, AND BENNO C. SCHMIDT, "The Espionage Statutes and Publication of Defense Information," 73 *Columbia Law Review* 929 (1973).

HENKIN, LOUIS, "The Right to Know and the Duty to Withhold: The Case of the Pentagon Papers," 120 *University of Pennsylvania Law Review* 271 (1971).

NIMMER, MELVILLE B., "National Security Secrets v. Free Speech: The Issues Left Undecided in the Ellsberg Case," 26 *Stanford Law Review* 311 (1974).

NOTE, "The Constitutionality of Section 793 of the Espionage Act and its Application to Press Leaks," 33 *Wayne Law Review* 205 (1986).

NOTE, "The Constitutionality of the Intelligence Identities Protection Act," 83 *Columbia Law Review* 727 (1983).

PETERZELL, JAY, "The Government Shuts Up," *Columbia Journalism Review* (July-August 1982), pp. 31–37.

"Pool Stories Delayed, Censored," *The News Media and the Law* (Fall 1987), p. 3.

PINCUS, ROGER W., "Press Access to Military Operations: Grenada and the Need for a New Analytical Framework," 135 *University of Pennsylvania Law Review* 813 (1987).

"Troops To Take Media Into Battle," *The News Media and the Law* (November/December 1984), p. 43.

UNGAR, SANFORD J., *The Papers and The Papers* (New York: E.P. Dutton & Co., 1972).

CHAPTER 9

BORK, ROBERT, "Neutral Principles and Some First Amendment Problems," 47 *Indiana Law Journal* 1 (1971).

COMMENT, "Telephones, Sex, and the First Amendment," 33 *U.C.L.A. Law Review* 1221 (1986).

Final Report of the Attorney General's Commission on Pornography (Nashville, Tenn.: Rutledge Hill Press, 1986).

DIAMOND, JOHN L., AND JAMES L. PRIMM, "Rediscovering Traditional Tort Typologies to Determine Media Liability for Physical Injuries: From the *Mickey Mouse Club* to *Hustler Magazine*," 10 *Comm/Ent Law Journal* 969 (1988).

EGGENBERGER, TOD R., "RICO vs. Dealers in Obscene Matter: The First Amendment Battle," 22 *Columbia Journal of Law & Social Problems* 71 (1988).

GEY, STEVEN G., "The Apologetics of Suppression: The Regulation of Pornography as Act and Idea," 86 *Michigan Law Review* 1564 (1988).

KENDRICK, WALTER, *The Secret Museum* (New York: Viking Penguin, Inc., 1987).

LINDER, DOUGLAS, "When Names Are Not News, They're Negligence: Media Liability for Personal Injuries Resulting from the Publication of Accurate Information," 52 *U.M.K.C. Law Review* 421 (1984).

LOCKHART, WILLIAM B., "Escape from the Chill of Uncertainty: Explicit Sex and the First Amendment," 9 *Georgia Law Review* 533 (1975).

LYNN, BARRY W., " 'Civil Rights' Ordinances and the Attorney General's Commission: New Developments in Pornography Regulation," 21 *Harvard Civil Rights-Civil Liberties Law Review* 27 (1986).

MACKINNON, CATHERINE, "Not a Moral Issue," 2 *Yale Law & Policy Review* 321 (1983).

MACKINNON, CATHERINE, "Pornography, Civil Rights, and Speech," 20 *Harvard Civil Rights-Civil Liberties Law Review* 1 (1985).

NOTE, "Enjoining Obscenity as a Public Nuisance and the Prior Restraint Doctrine," 84 *Columbia Law Review* 1616 (1984).

NOTE, "Media Liability for Physical Injury Resulting from the Negligent Use of Words," 72 *Minnesota Law Review* 1193 (1988).

NOTE, "Pornography, Padlocks, and Prior Restraints: The Constitutional Limits of the Nuisance Power," 58 *New York University Law Review* 1478 (1983).

NOTE, "Publisher Liability for Material that Invites Reliance," 66 *Texas Law Review* 1155 (1988).

PRETTYMAN, E. BARRETT, JR., AND LISA A. HOOK, "The Control of Media-Related Imitative Violence," 38 *Federal Communications Law Journal* 317 (1987).

SCHAUER, FREDERICK, "Speech and 'Speech'—Obscenity and 'Obscenity': An Exercise in the Interpretation of Constitutional Language," 67 *Georgetown Law Journal* 899 (1979).

"Symposium on the Attorney General's Commission on Pornography," 1987 *American Bar Foundation Research Journal* 641.

WOODWARD, BOB, AND SCOTT ARMSTRONG, *The Brethren* (New York: Simon & Schuster, 1979).

CHAPTER 10

BARRON, JEROME A., "Access to the Press—A New First Amendment Right," 80 *Harvard Law Review* 1641 (1967).

BRENNER, DANIEL L., "Cable Franchising and the First Amendment: *Preferred* Problems, Undesirable Solutions," 10 *Comm/Ent Law Journal* 999 (1988).

BRENNER, DANIEL L., and MONROE PRICE, *Cable Television and Other Nonbroadcast Video: Law and Policy* (New York: Clark Boardman Co., 1989).

CARTER, T. BARTON, MARC A. FRANKLIN, AND JAY B. WRIGHT, *The First Amendment and the Fifth Estate* (Westbury, N.Y.: Foundation Press, Second ed. 1989).

COMMENT, "Protecting Wireless Communications: A Detailed Look at Section 605 of the Communications Act," 38 *Federal Communications Law Journal* 411 (1987).

FERRIS, CHARLES D., FRANK W. LLOYD, AND THOMAS J. CASEY, *Cable Television Law: A Video Communications Practice Guide* (New York: Matthew Bender & Co., 1988).

FRIENDLY, FRED, *The Good Guys, The Bad Guys, and The First Amendment* (New York: Random House, 1976).

GARRETT, ROBERT A., AND PHILIP R. HOCHBERG, "Sports Broadcasting and the Law," 59 *Indiana Law Journal* 156 (1984).

GELLER, HENRY, "The FCC Under Mark Fowler: A Mixed Bag," 10 *Comm/Ent Law Journal* 521 (1988).

GINSBURG, DOUGLAS H., *Regulation of Broadcasting* (St. Paul: West Publishing Co., 1979).

HAMBURG, MORTON I., *All About Cable* (New York: Law Journal Seminars-Press, 1982).

KRATTENMAKER, THOMAS G., AND L.A. POWE, JR., "The Fairness Doctrine Today: A Constitutional Curiosity and an Impossible Dream," 1985 *Duke Law Journal* 151.

LABUNSKI, RICHARD, "May It Rest in Peace: Public Interest and Public Access in the Post-Fairness Doctrine Era," 11 *Comm/Ent Law Journal* 219 (1989).

NADEL, MARK S., "Editorial Freedom: Editors, Retailers, and Access to the Mass Media," 9 *Comm/Ent Law Journal* 213 (1987).

NOTE, "Alternatives to the Fairness Doctrine: Structural Limits Should Replace Content Controls," 11 *Comm/Ent Law Journal* 291 (1989).

NOTE, "Rock is a Four-Letter Word: The Potential for FCC Regulation of (Un)Popular Music," 9 *Comm/Ent Law Journal* 423 (1987).

NOTE, "The Cable Communications Policy Act of 1984 and Content Regulation of Cable Television," 20 *New England Law Review* 779 (1986).

POLS, CYNTHIA M., NORMAN M. SINEL, AND PAUL S. RYERSON (EDS.), *Cable Franchising & Regulation: A Local Government Guide to the New Law* (Washington: National League of Cities, 1985).

POWE, L.A., JR., *American Broadcasting and the First Amendment* (Berkeley: University of California Press, 1987).

POWE, L.A., JR., "Tornillo," 1987 *Supreme Court Review* 345.

SPITZER, MATTHEW, *Seven Dirty Words and Six Other Stories: Controlling the Content of Print and Broadcast* (New Haven: Yale University Press, 1986).

VAN EATON, JOSEPH, "Old Franchises Never Die? Denying Renewal Under the First Amendment and the Cable Act," 6 *Cardozo Arts & Entertainment Law Journal* 37 (1987).

CHAPTER 11

CALLMAN, RUDOLF, AND LOUIS ALTMAN, *The Law of Unfair Competition, Trademarks, and Monopolies* (Wilmette, Ill.: Callaghan & Co., Fourth ed. 1983 & Supp. 1988).

CRASWELL, RICHARD, "Interpreting Deceptive Advertising," 65 *Boston University Law Review* 657 (1985)."Developments in the Law: Competitive Torts," 77 *Harvard Law Review* 888 (1964).

"Developments in the Law: Competitive Torts," 77 *Harvard Law Review* 888 (1964).

DEVORE, P. CAMERON, "*Posadas de Puerto Rico v. Tourism Company of Puerto Rico*: The End of the Beginning," 10 *Comm/Ent Law Journal* 579 (1988).

EVANS, LAWRENCE E., "A Primer on Trademarks and Service Marks," 18 *St. Mary's Law Journal* 137 (1986).

GILSON, JEROME, *Trademark Law and Practice* (New York: Matthew, Bender & Co., 1988).

NOTE, "Corporate Defamation and Product Disparagement: Narrowing the Analogy to Personal Defamation," 75 *Columbia Law Review* 963 (1975).

NOTE, "The Tort of Disparagement and the Developing First Amendment," 1987 *Duke Law Journal* 727.

NOTE, "To Tell the Truth: Comparative Advertising and Lanham Act Section 43(a)," 36 *Catholic University Law Review* 565 (1987).

NOTE, "Trademark Parody: A Fair Use and First Amendment Analysis," 72 *Virginia Law Review* 1079 (1986).

RECENT DEVELOPMENT, "Trends in First Amendment Protection of Commercial Speech," 41 *Vanderbilt Law Review* 173 (1988).

ROBINSON, GLEN O., ERNEST GELLHORN, AND HAROLD H. BRUFF, *The Administrative Process* (St. Paul: West Publishing Co., Third ed. 1986).

ROSDEN, ERIC, AND PETER ROSDEN, *The Law of Advertising* (New York: Matthew Bender & Co., 1988).

WESTENBERG, DAVID A., "What's in a Name? Establishing and Maintaining Trademark and Service Mark Rights," 42 *Business Lawyer* 65 (1986).

CHAPTER 12

BAGDIKIAN, BEN H., *The Media Monopoly* (Boston: Beacon Press, 1983).

BALL, PETER, "Extra! Extra! Read All About It: First Amendment Problems in the Regulation of Coin-Operated Newspaper Vending Machines," 19 *Columbia Journal of Law & Social Problems* 183 (1985).

BORK, ROBERT, *The Antitrust Paradox* (New York: Basic Books, Inc., 1978).

COMMENT, "Media Cross-Ownership, Effective Enforcement of the Antitrust Laws, and the FCC," 32 *Federal Communications Law Journal* 105 (1980).

COMMENT, "Minneapolis Star & Tribune Co. v. Minnesota Commissioner of Review: Differential Taxation of the Press Violates the First Amendment," 69 *Iowa Law Review* 1103 (1984).

GELLHORN, ERNEST, *Antitrust Law & Economics* (St. Paul: West Publishing Co., 3d ed. 1986).

GETMAN, JULIUS, AND BERTRAND POGREBIN, *Labor Relations: The Basic Processes, Law and Practice* (Westbury, N.Y.: Foundation Press, 1988).

HOWARD, HERBERT H., "A Critique of the Fowler FCC's 1984–85 Multiple Ownership Rules," 10 *Comm/Ent Law Journal* 555 (1988).

LEE, WILLIAM E., "Antitrust Enforcement, Freedom of the Press, and the 'Open Market': The Supreme Court on the Structure and Conduct of Mass Media," 32 *Vanderbilt Law Review* 1249 (1979).

MCINTOSH, TOBY J., "Why the Government Can't Stop Press Mergers," *Columbia Journalism Review* (December 1980), pp. 48–50.

NOTE, "A Tale of Two Standards: Antitrust, the Public Interest, and the Television Industry," 6 *Comm/Ent Law Journal* 887 (1984).

NOTE, "Media Conglomerates, Antitrust Law, and the Marketplace of Ideas," 9 *Memphis State University Law Review* 257 (1979).

NOTE, "Newspaper Preservation Act: A Critique," 46 *Indiana Law Journal* 392 (1971).

NOTE, "Sex Discrimination in Newscasting," 84 *Michigan Law Review* 443 (1985).

NOTE, "Title VII Limits on Discrimination Against Television Anchorwomen on the Basis of Age-Related Appearance," 85 *Columbia Law Review* 190 (1985).

PRICE, MONROE E., AND MARK S. NADEL, "Antitrust Issues in the New Video Media," 3 *Cardozo Arts & Entertainment Law Journal* 27 (1984).

SHENEFIELD, JOHN H., "Ownership Concentration in Newspapers," 65 *American Bar Association Journal* 1332 (1979).

SHUMADINE, CONRAD M., MICHAEL S. IVES, AND WALTER D. KELLEY, JR., "Antitrust and the Media," in *Communications Law 1984* (New York: Practising Law Institute, 1984).

SULLIVAN, CHARLES A., MICHAEL J. ZIMMER, AND RICHARD F. RICHARDS, *Employment Discrimination* (Boston: Little, Brown & Co., Second ed. 1988).

SYMPOSIUM, "The First Amendment and Federal Securities Regulation," 20 *Connecticut Law Review* 261 (Winter 1988).

CASES AND STATUTES

Cases

631

Statutes

INDEX

284 FSupp 925